·GOOD· HOUSEKEEPING COOKBOOK

1,200 TRIPLE-TESTED RECIPES

·GOOD· HOUSEKEEPING COOKBOOK

1,200 TRIPLE-TESTED RECIPES

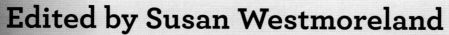

Edited by Susan Westmoreland

Culinary Director, *Good Housekeeping*

HEARST
books

contents

Foreword

Welcome!

The *Good Housekeeping Cookbook* that you have in your hands right now is the *ultimate* collection of our best-ever recipes. There are more than 1,200 fresh and satisfying meal ideas for every occasion, from on-the-go breakfasts and fast and easy dinners to pull-out-all-the-stops holiday feasts sure to delight the entire family.

Every single recipe in this collector's edition has been tested 'til perfect by our team in the iconic Good Housekeeping Test Kitchen. So when you whip up one of our classics in your own home, we guarantee the steps will be easy to follow and your results will always be simply delicious.

We also thought a lot about how you are going to use this book. Flavor always comes first, but we know that our lives dictate different choices for a weeknight dinner than for a weekend meal. That's why, whether you have 20 minutes or 2 hours, you'll find endless options, from super-healthy to downright indulgent, using some of everyone's most loved tools: the multicooker, slow cooker, sheet pan, and skillet! Plus the ingredients are all supermarket-shoppable with seasonal veggies, fresh herbs, fun pasta shapes, and yummy sauces and condiments.

And all the recipes include nutritional info so you will know how many calories and carbs are in them, as well as the amount of fat (total and saturated), fiber, sodium, and protein.

Since the first issue in 1885, *Good Housekeeping* has been "food-forward," and this book is no exception. We all want to make the most of our time with family and friends and to dig in to the tastiest dishes, all while balancing our diets with easy meal ideas. To that end, we've included many of *Good Housekeeping*'s all-time favorites as well as chapters on Breakfast & Brunch, Vegetarian & Grains, and Grilling. In the Breakfast & Brunch chapter you can find new ideas for your morning smoothie, Overnight French Toast (page 545), or how to poach eggs for a crowd (yes, our famous Eggs Benedict recipe (page 538) is here!). And if you're trying to get more healthful, plant-based dishes into your meal rotation, we've got you covered! Vegetarian & Grains, as well as our Vegetables chapter, will help move veggies to the center of the plate with crave-worthy main dishes and easy sides. Grilling has become a wildly popular way to get dinner on the table all year round, so in that chapter you'll also find genius tips on how to get the best from your grill and grill pan, plus new recipes for meats, fish, vegetables, and pizza!

And because many of us did not grow up cooking by our mom's or grandma's side, the experts in the Good Housekeeping Test Kitchen and Culinary Innovation Lab also have some really great advice to guide you through everything, from what pots and pans you really need to how to perfectly roast and carve a rib roast. Whether you're a beginner or have been cooking for years, you'll find essential information on cooking techniques, safe food handling, and healthy eating right here!

This *Good Housekeeping Cookbook*, a brand-new edition in our line of books that began in 1903, was created by Susan Westmoreland, culinary director at the Good Housekeeping Institute. Susan first learned to love cooking in her Italian mom's kitchen. A trained chef who studied at culinary schools in the US and abroad, Susan has been overseeing recipe and food-content development at *Good Housekeeping* for over 20 years. She cooks and bakes in her home life, too, often testing upcoming *Good Housekeeping* recipes with her own family.

So from our family to yours: Happy cooking—we hope you enjoy every bite!

Jane Francisco
Editor in Chief

CHAPTER

1

GETTING
started

Since you've picked up this book, we'll assume you want to cook. This chapter will give you advice on everything from what equipment you'll need to how to set up your kitchen to how to set a table. But before we start, think about how comfortable you feel in your kitchen. Imagine yourself as the pilot and the counters, cabinets, and drawers as your flight deck. Are the things you use most often within easy reach? Are they laid out in a way that makes sense to you? Whatever the configuration of your kitchen appliances, organize the tools and storage around them to your comfort. Outfit your kitchen with good basic equipment. Do this thoughtfully and you'll make your cooking life easier—and your kitchen a place where you'll want to hang out.

The Set Up

You don't need a lot of equipment. With a few sharp knives, several well-chosen pans, and some useful tools, you can prep and cook delicious meals.

Pots & Pans

Consider these basic pots and pans when outfitting your kitchen:

STOVETOP STARS

DUTCH OVEN This is ideal for braising roasts and stews on the stovetop as well as in the oven. A 6- to 7-quart Dutch oven is the most useful.

SAUCEPAN Choose two or three saucepans with lids, ranging from 1 to 4 quarts. Look for ones that are 4 to 5 inches deep, so you can stir without spilling.

SAUCEPOT This wide-bottomed, deep pot can be used for steaming veggies or making soups. A 4- or 5-quart size with a tight-fitting lid is versatile.

SKILLETS Opt for a small (7- to 8-inch) one for omelets and other single items and a large (12-inch) one as your weeknight workhorse.

STOCKPOT A tall, narrow 6- to 8-quart stockpot for pasta, soups, stocks, lobster, and corn on the cob (and, in a pinch, a large mixing vessel!) is essential.

GOOD TO KNOW

HOW TO MEASURE A PAN

Measure across the top of the dish from inside edge to inside edge. Measure the depth on the inside of the dish from the bottom to the rim. To measure volume of a pan or casserole, pour water by cupfuls (4 cups equals 1 quart) into the pan, right up to the top.

NICE BUT NOT NECESSARY

DOUBLE BOILER This is a saucepan topped with another covered saucepan; water simmering in the bottom pan gently cooks food in the top pan.

GRIDDLE This flat metal pan is perfect for pancakes, French toast, cheese sandwiches, and bacon. Electric models (some with nonstick surfaces) are also available.

GRILL PAN If you don't have an outdoor grill, this pan is the next best thing for quick-grilled items. Check out a flat two-burner-style pan.

OVENWARE

Some of the most popular materials for oven cooking are the same as those noted on page 12, with the addition of heat-resistant glass (a good inexpensive choice) and glass-ceramic (which can go from oven to freezer). Earthenware and stoneware are good choices for long, slow baking, like stews or beans.

Look for: Aluminum with a dull finish for most baked goods

Avoid: Shiny metals, such as stainless steel, which reflect the heat

Good to Know: Dark metal pans, which absorb heat quickly, are great for roasting and yeast breads but will likely overbrown your cakes and bar cookies.

PAN SMARTS

For cooking success, you need a variety of pans made of different materials. For quick weeknight sautés, a large nonstick skillet is great. For braising, enamel-coated cast iron is the hands-down favorite. For searing and getting a good crust on meat, cast iron or stainless steel is the go-to. High-quality equipment made from durable materials last longer, so buy the best you can afford.

BAKING PAN Ideal for runny cake batters or savory hot dishes, look for an 8- or 9-inch square and a 13 x 9-inch pan.

BAKING SHEETS These are great for cooking sweet bites or a quick and easy weeknight meal. Choose shiny (or nonstick), heavy, metal baking sheets with one or two slightly raised sides. For roasting vegetables, we suggest a rimmed baking sheet. If your oven heats unevenly, consider double-thick insulated pans. We recommend using 18 x 13-inch baking sheets, which are the standard for a half sheet.

BREAD/LOAF PANS Standard sizes are 9 x 5 inches (8 cups) and 8½ x 4½ inches (6 cups). Always read through the recipes before beginning to make sure you have the right size.

TESTING NOTE When reading a recipe, word choice is important. If the method calls for a *dish*, it cues glass or ceramic, compared to a *pan*, which implies metal.

Aluminum
Pros: Excellent heat conductor; inexpensive

Cons: Reacts to acidic ingredients; can discolor food

Look for: Anodized aluminum, which is nonreactive and nonstick

Cast Iron
Pros: Excellent heat conductor; inexpensive

Cons: Heavy; reacts to acidic ingredients; requires care to prevent rusting

Look for: Preseasoned skillets; enamel-coated pots and Dutch ovens

Copper
Pros: Beautiful; an excellent conductor of heat

Cons: Pots must be polished; may be lined with tin, which reacts to acidic ingredients; expensive; heavy

Look for: Stainless steel–lined pots

Nonstick
Pros: Food releases easily from surface; easier cleanup

Cons: Surface scratches can reduce nonstick property; classic nonstick coatings should not be used on high heat (over 500°F)

Look for: Ceramic coating or multiple layers of traditional nonstick coating

Stainless Steel
Pros: Sophisticated look; not too heavy; nonreactive to acidic ingredients

Cons: Difficult to clean after using to brown meat on high heat—you'll need Bar Keepers Friend® and a lot of elbow grease

Look for: Stainless that's bonded (or clad) with aluminum or copper to improve its heat-conducting properties

What is the difference between a reactive and nonreactive pan?

A: A reactive pan is one that contains metals that might interact with certain foods. Aluminum, cast iron, and unlined copper pans are all reactive—they all conduct heat well, too. Nonactive metals include stainless steel, tin, and tin-lined copper. You can use these for all types of cooking, but you might not get the same heat conductivity.

CAKE PANS Look for 8- or 9-inch round pans and get a few—recipes tend to call for two or three.

CASSEROLE OR BAKING DISH Oval or rectangular dishes with sides about 2 inches high; 10 x 15 inches (4 quarts), 13 x 9 inches (3½ quarts), 11 x 7 inches (6 cups), and 8 inches square (1½ quarts) are the most common.

CUSTARD CUPS Glass cups or ceramic ramekins with a 6-ounce capacity will do the trick.

HALF SHEET & JELLY-ROLL PAN A half sheet pan is 12 x 18 inches and perfect for baking large batches of cookies and roasting vegetables. Use a standard aluminum 15½ x 10½-inch pan for jelly-roll cakes.

MUFFIN TINS Opt for a 12-muffin capacity in aluminum or nonstick standard 2½ x 1¼-inch muffin-pan cups; 1¾ x 1-inch mini muffin-pan cups are another option.

PIE PLATE The standard size is 9 x 1 inch; deep-dish pie plates are 9½ x 1½ inches or 9½ x 2 inches. Glass, dark metal, and aluminum pans yield crisp, nicely browned piecrusts.

ROASTING PAN This large, deep, rectangular pan is typically made of enameled steel, aluminum, or stainless steel. A roasting rack is useful to keep the bottom of the roast from steaming in its own juices.

SPRINGFORM PAN 9 x 3 inches is the most common size and is perfect for cheesecakes and other dishes with delicate crusts.

TART PAN A shallow metal pan with fluted sides and a removable bottom; 9 x 1-inch and 11 x 1-inch round pans are the most common.

TUBE, BUNDT® & DECORATIVE PANS A 10-inch (12 cups) size is good for most needs.

TART PAN

DUTCH OVEN

GOOD TO KNOW

SOS FOR A BURNED POT

When a pot boils dry, all is not lost. Depending on when you catch it, you may be able to save some of the food—and, of course, the pot.

1 Taste the food; if it tastes burnt, ditch it. Otherwise use a serving spoon to transfer food to another pot. Scoop across, not down. When you hit resistance or burnt-looking food, stop.

2 Fill the scorched pot with hot water and a couple generous squirts of dishwashing liquid. Return the pot to the stove and simmer for 15 to 30 minutes. Carefully loosen the burned bits with a spatula as they soften. When done, empty the pot and scrub clean.

MUFFIN TIN

Knives 101

A good-quality knife will enable you to slice and dice through jobs with ease; a dull or poorly made one will make it feel like a chore.

It is important to take good care of your knives. Wash and dry them by hand; store them in a knife block, on a magnetic strip, or in sleeves in a drawer; sharpen them regularly—and they'll last a lifetime.

THREE MUST-HAVE KNIVES

CHEF'S KNIFE You'll use it for slicing, chopping, and mincing. Choose an 8- or 10-inch blade, depending on your comfort level and your hand size.

PARING KNIFE You'll use this for fruits, vegetables, and other small items.

LONG SERRATED KNIFE This slices breads, cakes, tomatoes, and other soft fruits and vegetables.

NICE BUT NOT NECESSARY

These are nice to have if you cook a lot of meat:

CARVING KNIFE for slicing meats; often comes in a set with a carving fork

THIN-BLADED BONING KNIFE for trimming fat and cutting poultry and meat

HEAVY CLEAVER for cutting up poultry

HOW TO SHOP FOR A CHEF'S KNIFE

SHOP IN PERSON IF YOU CAN

- **HOLD THE KNIFE.** If there's no demo surface, do a few air chops to get the feel.

- **CONSIDER THE GRIP.** Do you like a contoured handle or rubberized grip?

- **NOTICE THE HEFT.** A heavy knife is great for tasks like cutting through bones or root vegetables, but it may tire your hand out after repetitive cutting.

LOOK AT HOW THE KNIFE IS MADE

- **KNIVES ARE EITHER STAMPED OR FORGED.** Stamped blades are punched out from a sheet of metal and are completely flat. Forged blades are heated and formed from a single piece of steel and feel sturdier in your hand. They often have a bolster (a thick piece of metal between the handle and the blade), which offers extra weight, helps balance the knife, and provides an easy place to grip. They are also noticeably thicker at the top edge of the knife than at the blade edge.

- **TIP:** For best control, look for knives with a full tang (a blade made of a single piece of metal that runs from the blade tip to the end of the handle).

CONSIDER THE SHAPE OF THE BLADE

- **A CURVED BLADE**, which is easy to rock back and forth on a cutting board, will help with finer tasks like mincing or slicing.

- **NOTE:** Knives that are touted to "never need sharpening" have two drawbacks: The blades are finely serrated, so their ridges can tear food instead of cutting it. Also, when the knives eventually *do* need sharpening, it won't be possible.

OUR TOP PICK →

High-carbon stainless steel, an alloy that contains a large proportion of carbon, makes excellent knives that sharpen well. Some chefs prefer carbon-steel knives because they hold a very sharp edge. Note that they are reactive to acidic ingredients, so they stain and corrode easily.

CUTTING BASICS

Use a chef's knife and sharpen it on a steel before each use. To prevent the cutting board from slipping, place a damp towel underneath. Hold the knife handle in your preferred hand, near the blade. Your thumb should be on one side of the handle and your fingers close together and wrapped around the other side of the handle. In this book, we coarsely chop, slice, cube, cut into matchstick strips, finely chop, and mince. Here's how:

CHOP To cut small, irregular pieces about the size of peas: Coarsely cut up the food, then move the knife through the food until you have the desired size.

COARSELY CHOP To cut food into ½- to ¾-inch irregular pieces: When chopping, keep the tip of the knife on the cutting board; raise and lower the knife handle in a rocking motion while the knife is moved from left to right. If necessary, tuck under the fingers of your opposite hand and carefully push the food toward the blade.

FINELY CHOP To cut very small (less than ¼ inch) irregular pieces

CUBE To cut into ½-inch blocks: First cut the food lengthwise into ½-inch-thick slices. Stack the slices and cut them into ½-inch-wide sticks, then cut crosswise into ½-inch cubes.

MATCHSTICK To cut into thin ⅛ inch by ⅛ inch by 1–2 inch strips: First, cut the food into slices 2 inches long and ⅛ inch thick. Stack the slices, and cut them lengthwise into ⅛-inch-wide sticks.

MINCE To cut tiny (less than ⅛ inch) irregular pieces.

CHOP

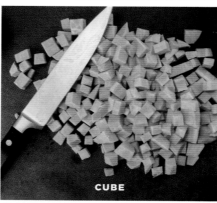

CUBE

MATCHSTICK

MINCE

Utensil Central

Having the correct tools for the task makes prepping easier and yields better results.

INDISPENSABLE KITCHEN TOOLS

COLANDER Choose a large colander with a stable footed base; the more holes it has, the more quickly liquid can drain.

COOLING RACKS If you bake a lot of cookies, use large rectangular wire racks. For cakes, two or three round racks are best for inverting layers.

CORKSCREW Invest in a good-quality waiters' corkscrew or a winged or lever-style one.

CUTTING BOARDS Plastic boards are lightweight and dishwasher safe. Hardwood and bamboo boards are extremely durable and, in GH testing, did not attract or retain any more bacteria than plastic ones. They do need to be hand-washed.

GRATER This flat, wand, or box-shaped tool can grate (small holes), shred (large holes), or slice (large slots). We love a rasp for citrus and hard cheeses.

ICE CREAM / COOKIE SCOOPS Great for portioning everything from cookies to muffin batter to burgers and ice cream. We like the trigger-handled ones.

MEASURING CUPS To measure dry ingredients accurately, use metal or plastic cups that come in nested sets. For liquids, use clear glass or plastic cups with pouring spouts.

MEASURING SPOONS These also come in nesting sets; stainless steel spoons are the most durable.

CORKSCREW

BOX GRATER

VEGETABLE PEELER

ICE CREAM SCOOP

MEASURE INGREDIENTS ACCURATELY FOR BEST RESULTS

- **FOR LIQUIDS**, use a clear measuring cup with a spout. Place it on a flat surface and add the desired amount of liquid. Bend down to check the accuracy; don't measure in midair.

- **FOR DRY INGREDIENTS**, spoon and sweep the ingredient into flat-topped measuring cups. When measuring flour, stir it with a fork or whisk to aerate it before spooning (it tends to settle and pack down during storage). Overfill the cup slightly, and use a straightedge or metal spatula to level it off. Don't scoop the cup directly into flour; you'll pack it down, and the result will be a drier baked good or thicker sauce than desired.

- **BROWN SUGAR, BUTTER, AND SHORTENING**—unlike flour—should be firmly packed into the cup.

- **WHEN MEASURING STICKY INGREDIENTS** like molasses, honey, or maple syrup, lightly grease the cup with vegetable oil or cooking spray first. The ingredient will slide out, leaving none behind.

MIXING BOWLS Glass or ceramic bowls work well and are microwave safe. Stainless-steel bowls are great when you need to quick-chill something, as they react quickly to temperature changes. Plus, they're lightweight.

ROLLING PINS The classic American rolling pin spins between two handles. Some bakers prefer a longer dowel-style pin. This straight cylinder style is sometimes called a Shaker pin; one with tapered ends is called a French pin. A heavy hardwood pin is our Test Kitchen favorite. Even though a nonstick pin sounds like a good idea, our testing proved otherwise.

SIEVES/STRAINERS A wire 7- to 8-inch mesh sieve is good for sifting ingredients and straining liquids. You may want a tea strainer for smaller jobs, like sprinkling sugar.

SPATULAS Heatproof silicone spatulas are the favorite for baking and sauce-making. Use heatproof or metal spatulas (pancake turner) to turn food. A long, narrow metal offset spatula is a must for frosting cakes.

THERMOMETERS Meat thermometers are vital when roasting meats and poultry. Instant-read thermometers, which register up to 220°F, are very accurate. Probe-type thermometers give a digital reading on a unit that is placed outside the oven. Candy thermometers register temperatures up to 400°F and can be used for candy making and deep-frying.

TONGS Spring-action tongs are the best for picking up foods and for turning meats without piercing them.

VEGETABLE PEELERS Swivel-blade peelers come in several configurations and styles, including traditional and Y-handled (a Test Kitchen favorite), with plain, serrated, or julienne blades.

WIRE WHISKS Use a medium-size whisk for sauces, vinaigrettes, and batters. No mixer? Large balloon-shaped whisks are ideal for whipping air into heavy cream or egg whites.

MORTAR & PESTLE

CITRUS JUICER

MELON BALLER

PASTRY BRUSH

ADJUSTABLE-BLADE SLICER OR MANDOLINE Many models slice, cut matchstick strips, and waffle-cut in varying thicknesses.

APPLE CORER This cylindrical tool neatly cores whole apples as well as pears.

ICE-CREAM MAKER Available in manual and electric models, some have insulated liners that must be frozen overnight.

CITRUS JUICER This simple ridged cone easily juices citrus fruits. Small electric versions are great for a large quantity of juice.

KITCHEN SCISSORS Use these for cutting kitchen string, snipping fresh herbs, and trimming artichoke leaves. Shears, which are larger and spring-loaded, make cutting up poultry simple. Buy sturdy stainless steel.

MELON BALLER Besides scooping perfect globes of melon (and potatoes), this tool neatly cores halved apples and pears if you do not have an apple corer.

MORTAR & PESTLE You crush with the pestle (the bat-like tool) in the mortar (the bowl). Use for grinding whole spices and herbs.

MULTICOOKER / SLOW COOKER For slow set-it-and-forget-it cooking or last-minute pressure cooking, these appliances have redefined weeknight cooking. Look for a 6- to 8-quart capacity.

PASTRY BAG Disposable plastic pastry bags don't retain odors and flavors as plastic-lined canvas bags can.

PASTRY BLENDER This tool's metal wires easily cut cold fat into flour for tart dough, pastry dough, biscuits, and scones. (They're also great for mashing avocados for guacamole.)

PASTRY BRUSH Use this to brush dough with melted butter or beaten egg and to apply glazes; it's also great for dusting excess flour from dough. When buying, look for 1- to 1½-inch-wide brushes with well-anchored natural or silicone bristles.

POTATO MASHER This tool is perfect for mashing potatoes and other root vegetables and for turning cooked beans into a chunky puree.

RULER Keep a stainless-steel or plastic model for measuring pans, pastry shapes, and more.

SALAD SPINNER We love using centrifugal force to dry greens, herbs, and other tender veggies.

SKEWERS Always soak wooden and bamboo skewers in water for 30 minutes before use to prevent them from burning over a flame.

STEAMER The collapsible metal style easily fits into various sizes of pots and pans. It can also be a saucepot with a metal, perforated, bowl-like insert that allows steam to penetrate.

ZESTER This removes the flavorful outer layer of citrus in either fine shreds or strips, leaving the bitter pith behind. We love the wand style from Microplane®.

GOOD TO KNOW

READY, SET, COOK!

To set yourself up for cooking success, do a bit of organizing before you start.

- Read through the entire recipe.
- Clean and clear the counter where you'll be prepping. Wash your hands.
- Rinse and dry any fruits and veggies.
- Gather all the ingredients, pans, and utensils called for in the recipe.
- Measure out ingredients so you can roll from start to finish.

Food Safety & Storage

Keeping food safe has become a major concern at every link in the food chain. For most of us, it starts when we shop. At the store, read labels for expiration dates, check meat for packed-on and use-by dates, and choose the freshest lively-not-limp vegetables and fruits. Shop perishables like meat, fish, dairy, and frozen items last. At home, refrigerate those perishables immediately. Follow the simple rules here to keep your food safe.

REFRIGERATOR KNOW-HOW →

- **Use the Readout** in your fridge or a refrigerator thermometer to maintain a temperature between 33°F and 39°F.

- **Store Meat, Fish, and Poultry** on a plate to catch drips; if you're not cooking them within two days, freeze them.

- **Don't Store** eggs in the refrigerator door; it's too warm. Keep them in their container to prevent them from absorbing the odors of other foods.

- **Store Dairy Products** tightly closed in their packaging or wrapped airtight to prevent them from absorbing flavors of other foods. Avoid keeping them in the refrigerator door.

FIVE RULES OF FOOD SAFETY

At Home

1 Keep It Clean

Always wash and dry your hands before handling food. Wash kitchen towels, dishcloths, and sponges frequently. Rinse fruits and vegetables thoroughly before eating. Sterilize plastic cutting boards by running them through the dishwasher after use, or sterilize them once a week in a solution of 1 tablespoon bleach per 1 gallon water.

2 Avoid Cross-Contamination

Don't put cooked food on a plate that has been in contact with raw meat, poultry, or fish. Keep several cutting boards: one for raw meats, poultry, and fish; one for vegetables and cheese; and a third for fruits and nuts.

3 Cook It Right

The United States Department of Agriculture recommends cooking raw eggs, fish, poultry, and meat to at least 160°F to kill harmful bacteria. (See specific chapters for more information). An instant-read thermometer is the most accurate way to check for doneness.

4 Keep Food at Safe Temps

The safe zones for storing food are below 40°F and above 140°F. Don't leave food at room temperature for longer than two hours. In hot weather, food should not be left out of the refrigerator for more than one hour.

5 Respect your Leftovers

Refrigerate leftovers as soon as possible. Divide large amounts among smaller containers for quicker cooling. Label and date containers. When in doubt about a food's freshness, throw it out.

On the Road

1 Chill

A cooler cannot make foods colder than they already are, so chill foods completely before placing them in the cooler. Juice packs can be frozen and used as extra "ice." Pack about a half pound of ice per quart capacity of your cooler.

2 Separate the perishables

Pack a separate cooler for snacks, fruit, and drinks. That way, every time the cooler's opened, meat and salads won't be exposed to hot air.

3 Double-wrap

Seal meat and poultry in airtight, resealable plastic bags so the juices don't leak out and contaminate other food. Pack perishable items, like meat, next to the ice packs.

4 Food First

Fill your cooler with food, then place the ice packs on the top and sides. If you're packing several layers of food, add a layer of ice packs in the middle, too.

5 Keep the Sun Away

At a picnic site, keep the cooler under a tree or in a shaded spot where it's out of direct sunlight.

Eating Well

The message is simple: Eat well to stay well. You can find plenty of information to overcomplicate this message, but eating a wide variety across the major food groups described below will help keep your diet balanced. Whether you're a vegan, an omnivore, or something in between, the advice holds true. To make eating well even easier, all the recipes in this book have complete nutritional profiles.

Dietary Guidelines for Americans

Consume a range of nutrient-dense foods and beverages within the basic food groups. Choose foods that limit your intake of saturated and trans fats, added sugars, salt, and alcohol.

THE US GOVERNMENT'S KEY RECOMMENDATIONS FOR HEALTHY EATING

- A variety of vegetables from all the subgroups—dark green, red and orange, legumes (beans and peas), starchy, and other
- Fruits, especially whole fruits
- Grains, at least half of which are whole grains
- Fat-free or low-fat dairy, including milk, yogurt, cheese, and/or fortified soy beverages

- A variety of protein foods, including seafood, lean meats and poultry, eggs, legumes (beans and peas), and nuts, seeds, and soy products
- Plant-based oils, such as canola and olive

REMEMBER THESE LIMITS FOR HEALTHY EATING

- Consume less than 10 percent of calories per day from added sugars
- Consume less than 10 percent of calories per day from saturated fats
- Consume less than 2,300 milligrams (mg) per day of sodium
- If alcohol is consumed, it should be consumed in moderation— up to one drink per day for women and up to two drinks per day for men

Using the Nutritional Values in This Book

At the bottom of each recipe, you'll find nutritional information. Our nutritional calculations do not include any optional ingredients or garnishes. When alternative ingredients are given, our calculations are based on the first item listed.

GOOD TO KNOW

READING THE NUTRITION LABEL

The FDA requires that all commercially packaged food have a nutrition label, which they've updated (see right). Use it to help make informed choices about the foods (and how much of them!) to include in your diet.

The Percent Daily Values reflect the recommended daily amount of a nutrient in each serving (based on 2,000 calories daily). Budget your intake of nutrients by adding up these percentages.

Food labels are required to list ingredients in descending order according to their weight, so you can easily see which products contain larger amounts of ingredients that are healthful, or not.

Five Things to Check Out on

THE NEW LABEL

1

Larger print on the calories per serving number

2

No calories from fat listed (if you want to do the math, 1g fat has 9 calories)

4

Total sugar now has a breakout of added sugars

Nutrition Facts

8 servings per container

Serving size   **1 cup (68g)**

Amount per serving

Calories   370

	% Daily Value*
Total Fat 5g	**7%**
Saturated Fat 1g	**5%**
Trans Fat 0g	
Cholesterol 0mg	**0%**
Sodium 150mg	**6%**
Total Carbohydrate 48g	**15%**
Dietary Fiber 5g	**14%**
Total Sugars 13g	
Includes 10g Added Sugars	**20%**
Protein 12g	
Vitamin A 10mcg	20%
Vitamin C 1mg	100%
Vitamin D 1mcg	50%
Vitamin E 2mcg	100%
Riboflavin 5mcg	75%
Folic Acid 200mcg	60%
Thiamin 2mcg	35%
Vitamin B12 5mcg	100%
Zinc 7mg	50%
Biotin 300mcg	100%
Calcium 50mcg	25%
Phosphorus 90mcg	90%
Magnesium 400mcg	100%
Chromium 75mcg	80%
Potassium 5g	100%

* The % Daily Value (DV) tells you how much a nutrient in a serving of food contributes to a daily diet. 2,000 calories a day is used for general nutrition advice.

3

More realistic serving sizes, in most cases larger

5

Values for vitamin D (many of us are deficient in this) and potassium (which can counterbalance sodium, so it's prevalent in processed foods) are added, along with calcium and iron from the former label

Entertaining

What makes a successful party? One where guests feel welcomed, the food is delicious, beverages are plentiful, and there's a festive buzz in the air. The best hosts make all of this look effortless. How? Planning, planning, planning! Think about the style of your event. Do you want to keep it more formal and have everything done beforehand? Or is this an it-takes-a-village party, where you're happy to have a few friends cooking in your kitchen with you? Or is it a potluck? Some people like to theme their potlucks, and others love the random nature of "bring a dish."

Hosting 101

You've got this! Ready to make your event look effortless? With your party style in mind, follow these simple strategies so you'll be in control and ready to mingle with your guests.

PLAN AHEAD

MAKE LISTS. You need a guest list, a menu, a shopping list, and a day-by-day and detailed day-of menu-prep timetable. Keep them visible and check things off as they are done.

INVITE GUESTS. Send invites two to four weeks ahead. Unless it's a formal occasion, a phone call or an e-vite is fine.

BALANCE THE MENU. Think flavor, color, texture, and richness, and plot a variety of each. Avoid repeating ingredients.

KEEP IT SIMPLE. Plan some dishes like soups, stews, casseroles, sides, and desserts that can be made a day or two ahead or that freeze well. Try not to have more than two dishes that require your last-minute attention. Make dishes you've cooked before.

INDULGE IN TIME-SAVERS. For example, purchase cleaned shrimp if making a shrimp dish.

COOK SEASONALLY. Use in-season fruits and vegetables when possible. They will be at their peak of flavor—and more reasonably priced.

STOCK THE BAR. Buy wine, beer, spirits, and plenty of nonalcoholic mixers in advance. Have more ice on hand than you need.

AVOID MUSICAL CHAIRS. A week or two before the party, check your supply of chairs and servingware. For an open house, consider the space needed for guests to circulate easily, and shift or remove furniture if necessary.

THE FORMAL TABLE

Have you ever looked at an elaborately set table and thought, *uh-oh*? Yes, there is an order to setting a table. And it's pretty logical.

- To begin, set a dinner plate at each place, about 2 inches from the table's edge. Top each with a salad plate.

- If needed, place the soup bowls on top of the salad plates.

- Set the bread plates to the left of the dinner plates (above forks).

- Napkins go either to the left of the forks or in the center of the dinner plates.

- Flatware is arranged in the order used, beginning farthest from the plate. Forks are placed on the left, while knives (cutting edge facing the plate) and spoons are on the right. If needed, the soup spoons are placed to the right of the knives, and salad forks are set to the left of the dinner forks. Butter knives can go right on the butter plates.

Five Tips to
KEEP A BUFFET MOVING

1

Avoid traffic jams. Place the table in a central location so guests can serve themselves from both sides. Provide two serving utensils for each platter.

2

Plot one or two main dishes for a hot buffet, and pair them with simple sides. Or create a menu of all room-temperature dishes.

3

Make it easy for guests. Unless you have table seats for everyone, avoid dishes that require knives. Bundle forks and napkins together, and place them at the far end of the buffet to grab last.

4

Practice food safety. Don't leave food out at room temperature for longer than two hours. Replenish the table with fresh platters you've prepared in advance. Don't mix the new food with what's been sitting.

5

Keep desserts simple. Opt for cakes, tarts, and cookies that can be easily cut and eaten out of hand.

- If you have enough flatware (and room on the table), the dessert forks and spoons can be placed above the dinner plates. Otherwise, set out the dessert and coffee flatware with the dessert.

- If serving only one wine, place the wineglasses slightly above the dinner knives and set the water glasses to their left. If serving wine to accompany the first course, place those glasses to the right of the main wineglasses.

THE KEEP-IT-SIMPLE TABLE

Forks to the left of the plate, knife close right, spoon to the right of the knife, water and wine to the right of the plate. If the meal uses two forks, place whichever one will be used first to the farthest left of the plate. Napkin to the left of the fork or on the plate.

HOW TO

QUICK-CHILL WINE

To quick-chill white or sparkling wine, submerge the bottle in a bucket or pot filled with half ice and half water. Or wrap the bottle in several thicknesses of wet paper towels and place it in the freezer for 20 to 30 minutes, or until chilled. (Check after 20 minutes to make sure the wine doesn't freeze.)

Wine Notes

There really aren't any strict rules when it comes to pairing wine with food.

CHOOSING WINE

TRY TO MATCH THE WINE with the intensity of flavor in the dish. For example, serve a light wine with a delicate entrée and a robust wine with a full-flavored dish. A crisp, dry Muscadet is lovely with oysters, and a fruity off-dry Gewürztraminer is a good match for gingery Asian dishes, while full-bodied Zinfandel can stand up to grilled foods and the spicy flavors of Mexican food.

PAIR WINE with food from the same region or country as the flavors of the recipe you are preparing. For example, a paella pairs nicely with a Spanish wine such as a young Rioja or an Albarino; pasta with tomato sauce is ideally matched with an Italian red wine.

RED WINES go well with meats, roast chicken, salmon, tomato-based pasta dishes, and hard cheeses (like Parmesan).

WHITE WINES are a good match for delicately flavored fish; skillet poultry dishes; vegetable dishes; cheese-based pasta dishes; and soft, semisoft, and blue cheeses. Wines like Riesling and Gewürztraminer that have a touch of sweetness pair well with spicy foods like Indian and Thai.

DON'T BE AFRAID OF BUBBLES. Dry (brut) sparkling wines pair well with rich appetizers and can stand up to fatty foods. Try them with everything from french fries to a creamy chicken dish to a velvety soup.

SERVING WINE

Serving wine at the proper temperature helps to bring out all its flavor.

White, rosé, and sparkling wines should be served well chilled but not so cold that their flavors are hidden.

Red wine should be served at cool room temperature (about 68°F). If it's too warm, place it in a bucket of ice water for five minutes. Some young and fruity reds, such as Beaujolais, are tasty when slightly chilled.

WINEGLASSES

Wine is traditionally served in stemmed glasses. But if you serve it in hand-blown stemmed glasses or juice glasses, don't fill the glass more than half full to leave enough room for the wine to breathe and to swirl comfortably.

The large flat base of a stemmed glass allows you to swirl the wine, which helps release its aroma and flavor. When drinking wine, hold the glass by the stem. This is especially important with chilled wines; it prevents the heat of your hand from warming the wine.

How does a wine breathe?

A: Exposing wine to air lets it "breathe" and release its flavor, but simply uncorking the bottle doesn't do much—the wine needs to be poured. If you wish, pour it into a decanter before serving. (If decanting an aged wine, leave any sediment in the bottle.)

The Five S's of
TASTING WINE

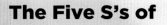

(OR HOW TO IMPRESS YOUR FRIENDS)

1
SEE

Note the bottle, the country, and the area, and then pour the wine. Observe the color, clarity, and opacity of the wine. This is best done against a white surface.

2
SWIRL

Either on the table or in your hand, swirl the glass in a circular motion. Are there long drips that stay a while? These are "legs" and inform you of the wine's viscosity.

3
SNIFF

Stick your nose into the glass and take a whiff. Evaluate the bouquet. You might smell fruit or flowers. You also might pick up on the wood from the barrel or other flavors. Close your eyes and have fun with it. Your vocabulary is your only limit!

4
SIP

Take a small mouthful, hold it in your mouth for three to five seconds, and let it rest so that your tongue is enveloped. With pursed lips, take in a little air and move the wine around. Oxygen will release more flavor notes.

5
SAVOR

Take in the wine. What is the mouthfeel? Heavy or light? Are you getting sweet, sour, bitter, fruity, or mellow notes? Is there a pleasant balance or a bitter finish or aftertaste? Or is it gone in a matter of seconds? Most importantly, do you like it?

WHIP

DRIZZLE

PIPE

BLIND BAKE

Glossary of Cooking Terms

AL DENTE Italian for "to the tooth," this describes perfectly cooked pasta: just tender and with a slight resistance.

BASTE To spoon or brush a liquid over food to keep it moist during cooking; the liquid can be a sauce, marinade, broth, melted butter, or pan juices.

BEAT To briskly mix or stir a mixture with a spoon, whisk, fork, or electric mixer

BLANCH Typically, to cook fruits or vegetables briefly in boiling water, then plunge into ice water to stop the cooking (shock); it locks in the color, texture, and flavor. Blanch tomatoes and peaches for 10 to 15 seconds for easy peeling.

BLIND BAKE To line an empty piecrust with foil and weights (to help it hold its shape) and bake before it's filled (see Cakes, Pies & Other Desserts, page 621).

BOIL To heat a liquid until bubbles break vigorously on the surface; water boils at 212°F. It also means to cook food, such as pasta or potatoes, in a boiling liquid.

BRAISE To cook food by first browning it in fat, then covering it in a small amount of liquid on the stove top or in the oven; this slow method tenderizes tough cuts of meat by breaking down their fibers.

BUTTERFLY To split food, such as shrimp or boneless meat, horizontally, cutting almost all the way through, then opening it up (like a book) to form a butterfly shape; it exposes a more uniform surface area so food cooks more evenly and quickly.

CARAMELIZE To heat sugar until it becomes syrupy and golden to deep amber in color; sugar-topped desserts like crème brûlée are caramelized under the broiler or with a propane torch. Onions become caramelized when slowly cooked until golden brown and very tender.

CORE To remove the seeds or tough woody centers from fruits such as apples, pears, and pineapple and from vegetables such as cabbage and fennel

CREAM To beat butter or another fat until it's creamy looking or with sugar until it's fluffy and light; this incorporates air, creating light-textured baked goods.

CRIMP To decoratively pinch or press the edges of a piecrust

CUT IN To work a solid fat, such as butter, into dry ingredients using a pastry blender or two knives, scissor-fashion

DEGLAZE To scrape up the flavorful browned (meat or poultry) bits from the bottom of a skillet or roasting pan by adding water, wine, or broth and stirring while heating

DEVEIN To remove the dark intestinal vein of shrimp; insert scissors blades at the wide, rounded end of the shrimp; cut through the shell and top of shrimp flesh, peel, and use the scissors or tip of a paring knife to remove the vein.

DOLLOP To spoon soft food, such as yogurt, whipped cream, or pesto, atop a dish

DOT To scatter bits of butter or margarine over a pie filling, casserole, or other dish before baking

DREDGE To lightly coat with flour, cornmeal, or bread crumbs; meats and fish are dredged before cooking to create a crisp, browned exterior.

DRIPPINGS The melted fat and juices that collect in a pan when meat or poultry is cooked; drippings form the base for gravies and pan sauces.

DRIZZLE To pour melted butter, syrup, melted chocolate, or another liquid back and forth over food in a fine stream

DUST To coat lightly with flour (e.g., greased baking pans) or with confectioners' sugar or cocoa (e.g., cakes and pastries)

EMULSIFY To bind liquids that usually can't blend easily, such as

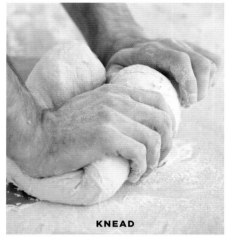

KNEAD

SHAVE

GLAZE

oil and vinegar; the trick is to slowly add one liquid, usually the oil, to the other while mixing vigorously. Natural emulsifiers, such as egg yolks or mustard, are often added to vinaigrettes or sauces to emulsify them for a longer period.

FLOUR As a verb, to coat food, a surface, or a baking pan with flour

FOLD To combine a light mixture (such as beaten egg whites, whipped cream, or sifted flour) with a heavier mixture (such as a cake batter or the base of a soufflé) without deflating either; a silicone spatula is the best tool to use for folding.

FORK-TENDER A degree of doneness for cooked vegetables and meats; when the food is pierced with a fork, there is only a very slight resistance.

GLAZE To coat food by brushing with melted jam or barbecue sauce, or to brush piecrust with milk or beaten egg before baking

JULIENNE To cut food into thin matchstick strips about 2 inches long

KNEAD To work dough until it's smooth by pressing and folding it with the heel of the hand

PANFRY To cook food in a small amount of fat in a skillet until browned and cooked through

PARE To cut away the skin or rind of a fruit or vegetable with a vegetable peeler or paring knife

PASTEURIZE To kill the bacteria in milk, fruit juice, or another liquid by heating to a moderately high temperature, then rapidly cooling it

PINCH The amount of salt, pepper, or a spice you can hold between your thumb and forefinger (about 1/16 teaspoon)

PIPE To force a food, such as frosting, whipped cream, or mashed potatoes, through a pastry bag fitted with a pastry tip in a decorative manner, or to shape meringues or éclairs; you can also use a plastic bag with a corner snipped off.

POACH To cook food in a gently simmering (barely moving) liquid; the amount and type of liquid will depend on the food being poached.

POUND To flatten to a uniform thickness using a meat mallet, meat pounder, or rolling pin to ensure even cooking; pounding also tenderizes tough meats by breaking up connective tissue.

PUREE To mash or grind food until completely smooth, usually in a food processor, blender, sieve, or food mill

REDUCE To rapidly boil a sauce, wine, or stock, until it has reduced in volume in order to concentrate the flavor

RENDER To slowly cook animal fat or skin until the fat separates from its connective tissue; it is strained before being used. The crisp brown bits left in the pan are called cracklings.

ROAST To cook in an uncovered pan in the oven by dry heat; roasted food develops a well-browned exterior. Many vegetables and tender cuts of meat, poultry, and fish are suitable for roasting.

ROLLING BOIL A full, constant boil that cannot be stirred down

SAUTÉ To cook food quickly in a small amount of hot fat in a skillet; the term derives from the French word *sauter* ("to jump").

SCALD To heat a liquid, such as cream or milk, just until tiny bubbles appear around the edge of the pan

SCORE To make shallow cuts (usually parallel or crisscross) in the surface of food before cooking; this is done to help flavor absorption in marinating meats, chicken, and fish, and for decorative purposes on hams.

SEAR To brown meat, fish, or poultry quickly by placing it in a pan over very high heat.

SHAVE To cut wide, paper-thin slices of food, such as Parmesan cheese or chocolate

SHUCK To remove the shells of oysters or clams or to remove the husks and silks from ears of corn

SIFT To press ingredients, such as flour or confectioners' sugar, through a sifter or sieve. Sifting incorporates air and removes lumps, which helps ingredients combine more easily.

SIMMER To cook food in a liquid over low heat (at about 185°F); a few small bubbles should be visible on the surface.

SKIM To remove fat or froth from the surface of a liquid, such as broth, boiling jelly, or soup; a skimmer—a long-handled metal utensil with a flat mesh disk or perforated bowl at one end—is the ideal tool for the job.

SOFT PEAKS When cream or egg whites are beaten until they stand in peaks that bend over at the top when the beaters are lifted

STEAM To cook food, covered, over a small amount of boiling water; the food is usually set on a rack. Since it's not immersed in water, the food retains more of its nutrients, color, and flavor than it would with other cooking methods.

STIFF PEAKS When cream or egg whites are beaten until they stand in firm peaks that hold their shape when the beaters are lifted

STIR-FRY To cook pieces of food quickly in a small amount of oil over high heat, stirring and tossing almost constantly; stir-frying is used in Asian cooking; a wok is the traditional pan, although a large skillet will work well.

TEMPER To warm food gently before adding it to a hot mixture so it doesn't separate or curdle

TENDER-CRISP The ideal degree of doneness for many fresh vegetables; they're tender but still retain some of their crunch.

TOAST To brown bread, croutons, whole spices, or nuts in a dry skillet or in the oven; toasting enhances flavor.

WHIP To beat an ingredient (especially heavy cream) or mixture rapidly to incorporate air and increase volume; you can use a whisk or electric mixer.

WHISK To beat ingredients (such as heavy cream, eggs, salad dressings, or sauces) with a fork or whisk to blend or incorporate air

ZEST To remove the flavorful colored part of citrus skin, avoiding the bitter white pith underneath; use the fine holes of a grater, a zester, or a vegetable peeler.

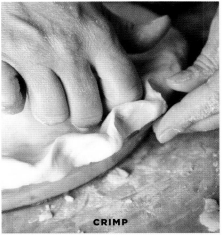

CRIMP

SOFT PEAKS

ZEST

whole NUTMEG | FENNEL seeds | whole CORIANDER | OREGANO | THYME | BAY LEAF

CHILE powder | CUMIN | CORIANDER | CAYENNE | CURRY powder | PAPRIKA

VANILLA extract | DAVIS OK BAKING POWDER NET WT 8.1 OZ (230g) | ground GINGER | CINNAMON sticks | ground CLOVES | ALLSPICE

pantry
& BASICS

Cooking, like most things in life, is easier if you're prepared. In the kitchen, it starts with the pantry. For our purposes, the pantry includes the standard shelf-stable items like canned goods, grains, beans, herbs, spices, and condiments. But we go a bit further. When you want to make meals from pantry items, you'll probably look to your fridge and freezer as well, so we'll outline staples that store well there, too.

Our pantry also includes a collection of back-pocket recipes that you can make and store, as well as everyday recipes using basic pantry items.

Pantry Essentials

Here's everything you should stockpile for those time-is-tight nights.

Dry Goods

Stocking your pantry with canned staples gives you the basis for everything from soups to sauces to salads. Pay attention to expiration dates, and rotate your cans with oldest dates first when you stock up!

BEANS Mainstays include cannellini, pinto, and black beans along with chickpeas. Dried beans are less costly than canned. Rinse well and soak overnight before using.

CHICKEN BROTH A superstar staple that boosts the flavor of sauces, stews, and sautés; low-sodium varieties are the heart-healthiest. See page 139.

CHIPOTLE CHILES Packed in adobo sauce, a tangy-hot tomato puree, these spicy, smoky peppers add zip to dishes with just a teaspoon.

COCONUT MILK A staple of Thai and Indian cuisine, its mildness cuts heat. Light versions are best—creamy but with half the fat.

LEGUMES Learn to love lentils—they're inexpensive and don't need presoaking. Try earthy black and green varieties in pilafs, soups, and salads.

GOOD TO KNOW

DIFFERENCES BETWEEN KOSHER, SEA & TABLE SALT

Crystal size is the key difference here: Table salt is the finest, kosher salt's grains are larger, and sea salt can be fine or the coarsest of all. When cooked, the taste variations are undetectable; at the table, there are distinctions. Sea salt, harvested from evaporated seawater, has a high mineral content, which adds flavor. Both sea and kosher salt are preservative-free; table salt has calcium silicate (to prevent clumping), which some people find bitter. Our advice: Cook with kosher or table salt, and save the sea salt for seasoning.

MARINARA SAUCE This Italian gravy goes beyond pairing with pasta. Use to make a pan sauce for pork or turkey cutlets, to poach eggs, or to make minestrone.

OLIVES Instantly improve salads, sauces, pizzas, and pastas. Choose a global assortment, from Italian to Greek to French.

ONIONS, GARLIC, SHALLOTS Store in a cool, dry spot, and they'll last a month. It's handy to have red, yellow, and sweet onions.

POTATOES, SWEET POTATOES Forever the family favorite. Scrub them well and you can skip the peeling step for most recipes.

ROASTED PEPPERS An adaptable add-in; toss these with garlic and capers for an insta-bruschetta, or sauté with sherry, chicken, and capers.

SALSA Amazingly versatile; it can sub for butter on baked potatoes and for ketchup on a burger. Or spoon it over fish or other proteins, then broil.

TOMATOES Fire-roasted tomatoes will jump-start Tex-Mex meals; peeled whole tomatoes are a shortcut to sauces as fresh as summer.

TUNA Water-packed, of course, but keep a couple of cans of oil-packed white albacore, too; it's stellar in sauces and Nicoise salad.

Spices come from the bark, buds, fruit, roots, seeds, or stems of plants and trees, unlike herbs, which come from the leafy parts of plants. Spices have always been used for flavoring food and drinks, as well as for medicinal and ceremonial purposes. The most common spices are allspice, anise, caraway, celery seed, chili powder, cinnamon, coriander, cumin, fennel, juniper, mustard, and black pepper.

COOK RICE

Rice can be finicky, but with the right amount of water and heat, you can master it. If you're cooking a long grain rice, like basmati, where you want the grains to be separate, rinse the rice in a strainer under cool running water until the liquid is no longer milky and water runs clear.

Use **1¾ cups water** to **1 cup white rice**. Bring the water to a boil in a 2- to 3-quart saucepan (this will help keeps grains separate and fluffy), then add the rice and **¼ teaspoon salt**. Reduce the heat to low; cover and cook 15 minutes for white rice and 45 minutes for brown rice. Don't stir it—seriously! (Stirring releases starch and makes rice gummy.) Next, turn off the heat and let the rice steam 10 minutes without lifting the lid—releasing steam prevents the cooking from finishing.

Grains

With any of these as your base, you can turn out easy weeknight dinners in no time. For more grain options, see the Grains Glossary on page 309 in the Vegetarian & Grains chapter.

BULGUR Quicker than rice, this mild, nutty side is best with pork or salmon.

COUSCOUS Precooked, so it's weeknight-speedy; serve with stews or as a simple side.

GRITS For a fast Southern supper, all you need to add to this is shrimp. Cheese delivers oomph.

OATS Use this to stretch meatballs and meat loaf, or to coat oven-fried chicken.

PASTA Stock a range of shapes and sizes. Whole wheat varieties are healthiest.

POLENTA Ready in three minutes, it's tasty with marinara and cheese or with sausage.

QUINOA Add this fiber-rich protein to pilafs, risottos, salads, and even rolls or biscuits.

RICE Buy in bulk, then pop in the freezer—it will keep for up to a year.

TESTING NOTE Cooked grains last up to a week in the fridge, so make a double batch for later in the week.

Herbs, Spices & Condiments

This is your go-to flavor bank; organize it well. To maximize space, group herbs and spices in a two-tiered Lazy Susan or in graduated shelf racks. Use one area for pepper, seeds, and whole spices, another for ground spices, and one for dried herbs. Alphabetize or group things that you use often together. Be sure the labels are facing outward.

LIQUID CONDIMENTS Olive oils, vegetable oils, balsamic vinegar, soy sauce, red wine vinegar, Worcestershire sauce, and hot sauce can lend great flavor to your recipes.

SPICES & SEEDS Thyme, oregano, dill, tarragon, rosemary, chili powder, cumin, coriander, curry, cinnamon, red pepper, fennel seeds, salt, and pepper should be on a well-stocked spice rack.

SOY SAUCE

One of the oldest condiments known, soy sauce originated in China over 2,500 years ago. But it wasn't until the sixth century, when Buddhism and its meatless principles were embraced, that it began to be used in Japanese cuisine. The strict vegetarian diet meant giving up traditional meat- and fish-based seasonings. Luckily, a Japanese priest who had studied in China began making a seasoning from fermented soybeans or soy sauce in Japan. After some time, wheat was added to give the sauce a more balanced flavor. Today, supermarkets carry several types of soy sauce for consumers.

REGULAR SOY SAUCE

Brewed from wheat, soybeans, water, and salt and aged for several months to develop its flavor

REDUCED-SODIUM SOY SAUCE

Brewed the same way as regular soy sauce but contains about 40 percent less sodium

TAMARI/GLUTEN-FREE SOY SAUCE

Richer and a bit less salty than traditional soy sauce; it is brewed with little or no wheat. There are several brands on the market that are gluten-free. Reduced sodium is also available.

INGREDIENT SPOTLIGHT

Peppercorns have been used to flavor foods for hundreds of years. Peppercorn berries grow in clusters on a plant that is native to India and Indonesia. Whether peppercorns end up being black, white, or green depends upon how they are processed. Black peppercorns are picked when the berries are not quite ripe, then dried until shriveled and brownish black. White peppercorns are picked ripe, then skinned and dried. They are smaller and milder than black peppercorns. Green peppercorns are soft, underripe berries and are usually processed in brine. They have a fresh, mild flavor. Whole black, white, and green peppercorns can be stored in a cool, dark place for up to a year. Green peppercorns in brine should be used within a month after opening the jar.

Ingredient Ideas

creole seasoning

An all-purpose spice blend, you can purchase this Cajun seasoning premixed. Here are some of our favorite uses.

WING DING

Toss **2 tablespoons Creole seasoning** with **2 pounds chicken wings** before frying or oven-roasting.

NEW ORLEANS SCRAMBLE

Beat **1 tablespoon Creole seasoning** into **8 large eggs** along with **1 cup shredded Cheddar cheese**, then scramble.

BLOODY MARIE

Pour **3 tablespoons Creole seasoning** into a shallow dish to coat the rims of **Bloody Mary glasses**.

CREOLE SCAMPI

Sauté **1 tablespoon Creole seasoning** with **3 cloves garlic**, chopped, and **1 pound shrimp** in **½ cup each butter and olive oil**. Serve with **pasta**.

Ingredient Ideas
coconut milk

FRAGRANT PILAF

Use **1 can (15 ounces) coconut milk** and **1¼ cups water** to cook **2 cups jasmine rice**.

ASIAN-STYLE SLAW

Whisk **½ cup coconut milk** with **2 tablespoons fish sauce**, **1 tablespoon rice vinegar**, and **2 chopped green onions**. Use to dress **6 cups slaw**.

PORK MARINADE

Blend **½ cup coconut milk** with **1 chopped shallot** and **½ cup mint** for **1 pound pork**.

Ingredient Ideas
just a spoonful of mustard

DIJON MUSTARD FOR FISH TOPPING

Mix **1 tablespoon Dijon mustard**, **2 tablespoons mayonnaise**, and **1 tablespoon chopped dill**; spread on **6 flounder or cod fillets**. Broil 3 minutes. **Serves 4.**

BROWN MUSTARD FOR BASTING GRILLED PORK CHOPS

Mix **2 tablespoons brown mustard**, **2 tablespoons brown sugar**, and **1 tablespoon bourbon**. **Serves 4.**

GRAINY MUSTARD FOR SALAD DRESSING

Combine **3 tablespoons olive oil**, **1½ tablespoons white balsamic vinegar**, **1 tablespoon grainy mustard**, and **½ teaspoon grated orange zest**; toss with **salad mix** and **orange segments**. **Serves 4.**

Ingredient Ideas
pink beans

CORN & BEAN BURGERS

In a food processor, pulse **1 can (15 ounces) pink beans**, rinsed and drained well; **½ cup bread crumbs**; and **¼ teaspoon each salt and ground black pepper** until ground. Add **1 cup corn kernels** and **½ cup shredded sharp Cheddar cheese**; pulse to just combine. Form into four 4-inch round patties. Coat a 12-inch nonstick skillet with **cooking spray**. Add patties; coat with spray. Cook on medium 15 minutes or until browned, turning once. Serve on **buns with lettuce and tomatoes**. **Serves 4.**

SPICED RICE & BEANS

In 4-quart saucepan, heat **2 tablespoons oil** and **3 cloves garlic**, minced, on medium until golden. Add **1 cup basmati rice**, **½ teaspoon ground cumin**, and **¼ teaspoon salt**; cook 2 minutes, stirring. Add **1 can (15 ounces) pink beans**, rinsed and drained well, and **2 cups water**. Heat to boiling. Cover; reduce heat to low. Simmer 20 minutes, or until the water is absorbed and the rice is just tender. Fluff with fork. **Serves 4.**

CREAMY FAT-FREE DIP

In a food processor, puree **1 can (15 ounces) pink beans**, **¼ cup roasted red pepper**, **1 tablespoon fresh lime juice**, **½ teaspoon ground cumin**, and **⅛ teaspoon salt**. Top with **chopped cilantro**. **Makes 1½ cups.**

HUEVOS RANCHEROS

From one **1 can (15 ounces) pink beans**, rinsed and drained well, reserve **¼ cup beans**. Mash the remaining beans with **¼ cup chopped cilantro** and **2 tablespoons salsa**. Coat a 12-inch nonstick skillet with cooking spray. Crack **4 large eggs** into the skillet. Cover and cook over medium heat 4 minutes, or until the whites set. Spread the bean mixture on **4 warm corn tortillas**; top each with **1 egg**, **2 tablespoons salsa**, 1 tablespoon reserved beans, and **1 teaspoon chopped cilantro**. **Serves 4.**

HEARTY HAM SALAD

In a large bowl, toss one **1 can (15 ounces) pink beans**, rinsed and drained well; **2 hearts romaine lettuce**, chopped; **2 stalks celery**, sliced; **½ cup diced ham**; and **¼ cup Italian dressing**. **Serves 4.**

EXTRA VIRGIN OLIVE OIL

When you're buying olive oil, the most important thing
to remember is that you're buying a juice that doesn't stay fresh forever.
Would you keep orange juice for two years and still use it for cooking?
Olive oil isn't like wine, which improves with age.
Here's what to keep in mind the next time you need to
restock on the cooking staple.

LOOK FOR A "HARVEST DATE" OR "CROP DATE" ON THE BOTTLE

The "Harvest Date" tells you exactly when the olives were picked. Olive oil is best if it's used within 18 to 24 months of harvesting. If more time has passed, the oil is still edible, but it's probably better for cooking than drizzling. Many olive oil brands have a "best if used by" date, but this doesn't tell you how long the olives were sitting before being pressed. Plus, different companies have different views on how long olive oil is good. A small taste or a good sniff will tell you if the oil has gone rancid.

THE MOST EXPENSIVE OLIVE OIL ISN'T NECESSARILY WORTH THE SPLURGE

Excellent olive oil comes from all over the world, including California, Spain, Italy, Greece, and, increasingly, Australia and South America. The soil and other environmental factors influence the growth, but taste quality is also heavily dependent upon the olive variety, crop management, picking, ripeness, and the condition of olives when pressed. Take advantage of tastings in your market to learn which varieties you like or buy a proprietor's or miller's blend.

LOOK FOR CERTIFYING SEALS

If you're set on buying olive oil from a specific region, look for certifying seals that authenticate that the olive oil is grown and pressed in one location. These seals help prevent olive oil fraud, including lying about an olive oil's origin or the ingredients in the product. The Toscano seal certifies that the olives are grown, pressed, and packaged in Toscano, Italy. DOP (*Denominazione di Origine Protetta*, literally "Protected Designation of Origin") and IGP (*Indicazione Geografica Protetta*, or "Indication of Geographic Protection") are other seals that guarantee the production and processing of the olive oil was done in a specific geographical area.

Baking Pantry

You'll never fear last-minute bake sales with these basics.

CHOCOLATE Stock unsweetened cocoa, unsweetened chocolate squares, and semisweet chocolate chips.

CORNSTARCH For in-a-pinch cake flour, swap 2 tablespoons of cornstarch for every cup of all-purpose flour.

CUPCAKE LINERS Pleated greaseproof liners come in every size and style.

FLOURS Store all-purpose, whole wheat, and cake flours in airtight containers.

LEAVENERS After opening, baking powder keeps for six to twelve months, and baking soda for two years.

SUGARS Pack granulated, confectioners', and light and dark brown sugars in airtight containers.

VANILLA EXTRACT Though pricey, the all-natural extracts beat artificial for flavor.

TESTING NOTE Prevent brown sugar from hardening by adding an apple slice to the container. Make sure to change it monthly.

FLAVORED BUTTERS

Flavored butters are ideal for dressing up panfried or grilled steak or fish when unexpected company drops by. Here are a few favorites.

For strong-flavored ingredients like horseradish or capers, start with about 2 tablespoons per ½ cup of butter. You can add up to ¼ cup of ingredients total; just be sure to drain any wet items well. Prepare ahead—these take just 10 minutes—and freeze to eliminate last-minute fussing.

In a medium bowl, beat ½ **cup butter**, softened, with a wooden spoon until creamy. Beat in your choice of flavor ingredients (below); blend well. Transfer the flavored butter to waxed paper and shape it into a log about 6 inches long; wrap, twisting the ends of the waxed paper to seal. Overwrap the log in plastic or foil before chilling or freezing. Flavored butters can be refrigerated up to 2 days or frozen up to 1 month. To serve, cut into ½-inch-thick slices. **Makes 12 servings each.**

MAÎTRE D' HÔTEL BUTTER	Very versatile, use this on beef, veal, chicken, pork, and fish. 2 tablespoons chopped fresh parsley ¼ teaspoon freshly grated lemon zest 1 tablespoon fresh lemon juice
OLIVE BUTTER	Best on fish and chicken ⅓ cup Kalamata olives, pitted and finely chopped 1 tablespoon chopped fresh parsley
GINGER-CILANTRO BUTTER	Good on chicken and fish 2 tablespoons finely chopped fresh cilantro 2 teaspoons fresh lime juice ½ teaspoon grated, peeled fresh ginger
CAPER BUTTER	Good on beef, veal, pork, fish, and chicken 2 tablespoons capers, drained and chopped 1 tablespoon chopped fresh parsley ½ teaspoon freshly grated lemon zest

The Fridge & Freezer

Store items in the right place for maximum freshness and convenience.

Fridge Door

Store the treasured condiments that can turn ordinary dinner into a wow here. Along with those listed, consider: curry paste, harissa, pomegranate molasses, sesame oil, and tahini.

CAPERS Their salty sharpness perks up fish, pasta, or chicken dishes.

HOISIN SAUCE Try its chile-spiced sweetness in Asian dishes and dipping sauces.

MANGO CHUTNEY, APRICOT JAM, MARMALADE The sugars in the fruits caramelize during cooking, so these are great as fuss-free glazes. Slather them straight from the jar onto pork or poultry before grilling or broiling.

MUSTARD This can-do condiment, whether it's a grainy Dijon, a full-bodied brown, or a more mellow yellow, enlivens everything from cream sauces to vinaigrettes.

PICKLES Chop cornichons into tuna salad or sweet pickles into potato salad.

REDUCED-FAT MAYONNAISE For a go-to glaze for broiled fish, mix with mustard or horseradish.

TUBE OF TOMATO PASTE If a recipe calls for a few spoonfuls, using this easy-squeeze container is less wasteful than opening a whole can. It's double-concentrated, with an intense tomato-ness.

Fridge Shelves

Use your fridge wisely and you can keep a pantry of root veggies, dairy, and citrus for weeks. Keep fridge temperature between 35°F and 38°F. Keep fruit and veggies in the crisper drawer, which holds in humidity to keeps items crisp.

CANTALOUPES, APPLES Segregate these ethylene emitters from produce sensitive to the gas, such as lettuces and parsley.

CHEESE DRAWER Semihard and hard cheese will last for 1 to 3 months—just trim one inch around moldy spots and rewrap tightly.

EGGS Avoid putting egg trays in the door, where temperatures are too warm. Leave eggs in the carton and place them on a back shelf, where it's consistently colder.

LEMONS, LIMES, ORANGES Unbeatable for brightening up dishes, citrus fruit can be stored for up to two weeks with zero falloff in flavor.

MILK, YOGURT, SOUR CREAM Group dairy items together on the middle shelves or at eye level.

VEGETABLES Don't wash these before putting them in the fridge. Leave them in the supermarket's plastic produce bags and keep them in the crisper. The only exception: celery. Wrap it in foil and the stalks will stay colorful and crunchy for several weeks.

FREEZE BERRIES

Berries freeze with ease,
so stock up in the summer
for year-round eating.
Here are three steps for
perfect chilling.

1 Wash berries and gently pat
dry with paper towels. Discard
any that are bruised or spoiled.
Hull and chop strawberries.

2 Arrange berries in a single
layer on a rimmed baking
sheet lined with parchment
paper. Pop in the freezer for
at least three hours.

3 Transfer frozen berries into
resealable plastic bags—the
quart size is great for single-
serving portions. Lay flat
and freeze up to a year.

Foolproof Your Fridge

Temps and humidity levels in your fridge vary from spot to spot. Stash items in the proper section and they'll last longer. We've food-mapped it for you.

APPLES & ORANGES Set bin controls to the low-humidity or open position.

CONDIMENTS & SOFT DRINKS It's safe to keep these nonperishable items in door compartments.

EGGS Store these in their original carton on a shelf, not in the door.

LEAFY GREENS Always keep crisper controls closed for high humidity.

MEATS & COLD CUTS Most fridges have temperature-controlled drawers. Use the lowest setting to keep meats fresher.

WARM LEFTOVERS OR HOT SOUP When food hasn't cooled down yet, transfer it to small containers and store on the top shelf, since heat rises. Keep it away from milk.

YOGURT & MILK Stash on an interior shelf—not in a door bin, where temps are highest.

#SavetheFood

storing ginger & miso

If you don't use ginger or miso often, don't worry—they will keep. Both can be stored for about two months (ginger in the freezer, miso in the fridge).

GOOD TO KNOW

FREEZE EXTRAS IN ICE CUBE TRAYS

Is the fridge packed with jars and bags of extra ingredients? Ease the overcrowding by freezing those bits of batter and extra broth. Freeze everything from coconut milk to ripe bananas in two-tablespoon portions in ice cube trays, then pop them out and use them to add extra flavor to cooked dishes and smoothies.

Freezer

This should be your fallback—not a food cemetery. Make large batches of sauces, soups, and stews for nights when you're pressed for time. Wrap items well, then date and label them (see page 47).

BACON Stays freezer-friendly for three months.

BREAD Slices should go straight from the freezer to the toaster—no need to thaw in between.

NUTS Freezing stops their oils from going rancid. When they go on sale, squirrel away walnuts, almonds, pistachios, pecans, and cashews. Nuts can be kept in the freezer for up to a year.

SHRIMP Since most shellfish in the grocer's seafood case has been previously frozen and thawed, stow a bag from the frozen foods aisle in your own home. Streamline prep time by choosing shelled, deveined shrimp.

VEGETABLES, FRUITS Picked at their peak and flash-frozen, they're often more nutritious than fresh. Buy packages of peas, spinach, corn, strawberries, raspberries, cranberries, blueberries, and peaches to have on-hand all year round.

Tip Freeze cookie dough, then heat a couple of cubes in the toaster oven for a freshly baked (and portion-controlled!) treat.

HOW LONG WILL IT KEEP?

Foods frozen for longer than the recommended times aren't harmful—
they just won't be at their peak flavor and texture.

FOOD	TIME IN FREEZER (0°F)	FOOD	TIME IN FREEZER (0°F)
Milk	3 months	Casseroles, cooked, meat	2 to 3 months
Butter	6 to 9 months	Soups and stews	2 to 3 months
Cheese, hard (Cheddar, Swiss)	6 months	Fish, lean (cod, flounder, haddock)	6 months
Cheese, soft (Brie, Bel Paese)	6 months	Fish, fatty (bluefish, mackerel, salmon)	2 to 3 months
Cream, half-and-half	4 months	Fish, cooked	4 to 6 months
Sour cream	don't freeze	Fish, smoked	2 months in vacuum pack
Eggs (raw yolks, whites)	1 year	Shrimp, scallops, squid, shucked clams, mussels, oysters	3 to 6 months
Frankfurters (opened or unopened packages)	1 to 2 months	Pizza	1 to 2 months
Luncheon meats (opened or unopened packages)	1 to 2 months	Breads and rolls, yeast	3 to 6 month
Bacon	1 month	Breads, quick	2 to 3 months
Sausage, raw, links, or patties	1 to 2 months	Cakes, unfrosted	3 months
Ham, fully cooked (whole, half, slices)	1 to 2 months	Cheesecakes	2 to 3 months
Ground or stew meat	3 to 4 months	Cookies, baked	3 months
Steaks	6 to 12 months	Cookie dough, raw	2 to 3 months
Chops	3 to 6 months	Pies, fruit, unbaked	8 months
Roasts	4 to 12 months	Pies, custard or meringue-topped	don't freeze
Chicken or turkey, whole	1 year	Piecrust, raw	2 to 3 months
Chicken or turkey, pieces	9 months	Nuts, salted	6 to 8 months
Casseroles, cooked, poultry	4 to 6 months	Nuts, unsalted	9 to 12 months

homemade mayo

PREP: 5 MIN / TOTAL: 5 MIN / MAKES ABOUT 1 CUP

- 1 large egg yolk
- 2 teaspoons white wine vinegar
- 1 teaspoon Dijon mustard
- ¼ teaspoon salt
- 1 cup vegetable oil
- 2 teaspoons lemon juice

In a medium bowl and using a hand mixer on medium speed, beat the egg yolk with the vinegar, Dijon, and salt until smooth. With the mixer running, slowly drizzle in the oil drop by drop, stopping and scraping occasionally. Stir in the lemon juice. Refrigerate up to 1 week.

Each tablespoon About 130 calories, 0g protein, 0g carbohydrate, 14g fat (1g saturated), 0g fiber, 44mg sodium.

VARIATIONS

Spicy Mayo

Stir in **1 tablespoon sriracha** and **½ teaspoon soy sauce**.

Curry Mayo

Stir in **2 teaspoons grated, peeled fresh ginger**; **½ teaspoon curry powder**; **¼ teaspoon ground cumin**; and a **pinch of sugar**.

easy eggless mayo

PREP: 8 MIN / TOTAL: 8 MIN / MAKES 1¼ CUPS

- ¼ cup chickpea brine (from a 15-ounce can of chickpeas)
- 2 teaspoons fresh lemon juice
- 1 teaspoon distilled white vinegar
- 1 teaspoon sugar
- 1 teaspoon dry mustard
- ¾ teaspoon salt
- 1 cup vegetable oil

In a food processor or 2-cup measuring cup, combine the chickpea brine, lemon juice, vinegar, sugar, dry mustard, and salt. Process or blend with an immersion blender until combined. With the processor or blender running, slowly drizzle in the oil in a thin, steady stream. Process 4 to 5 minutes. Cover and refrigerate up to 2 weeks.

Each tablespoon About 100 calories, 0g protein, 0g carbohydrate, 11g fat (1g saturated), 0g fiber, 180mg sodium.

GOOD TO KNOW

UP YOUR MAYO GAME

Just a few ingredients can turn your sandwich spread or tuna salad from simple to crave-worthy. Mix these flavoring into the homemade mayo (left) or into store-bought versions.

ROASTED RED PEPPER MAYONNAISE
½ cup mayonnaise, ¼ cup finely chopped roasted red pepper, and 1 tablespoon chopped fresh parsley

LEMON MAYONNAISE
½ cup mayonnaise, 1½ teaspoons fresh lemon juice, 1 teaspoon freshly grated lemon zest, and a pinch of ground black pepper

GINGER-SESAME MAYONNAISE
½ cup mayonnaise; 2 small green onions, finely chopped; 1 tablespoon chopped fresh cilantro; 1 teaspoon minced, peeled fresh ginger; and ¼ teaspoon Asian sesame oil

CHUTNEY MAYONNAISE
½ cup mayonnaise; ¼ cup mango chutney, finely chopped; and 1 tablespoon chopped fresh cilantro

BASIL MAYONNAISE
½ cup mayonnaise, ¼ cup chopped fresh basil, and ⅛ teaspoon ground black pepper

CHIPOTLE MAYONNAISE
½ cup mayonnaise, 1 finely chopped chipotle chile in adobo, 1 teaspoon adobo sauce, and ¼ teaspoon ground cumin

PESTO MAYONNAISE
½ cup mayonnaise and 4 teaspoons pesto

HORSERADISH MAYONNAISE
½ cup mayonnaise, 1 tablespoon bottled white horseradish, and 1 teaspoon fresh lemon juice

PICKLED JALAPEÑO MAYONNAISE
½ cup mayonnaise, ¼ cup chopped fresh cilantro, and 1 to 2 pickled jalapeño chiles, finely chopped

easy aioli

PREP: 5 MIN / TOTAL: 25 MIN, PLUS COOLING / MAKES
ABOUT ¾ CUP

4 cups water
Salt
1 head garlic, separated into cloves
½ cup mayonnaise
2 teaspoons fresh lemon juice
½ teaspoon Dijon mustard
⅛ teaspoon cayenne pepper
¼ cup extra-virgin olive oil

1. In a 2-quart saucepan, combine the water and 1 teaspoon salt; heat to boiling over high heat. Add the garlic and boil until the garlic has softened, about 20 minutes. Drain. When cool enough to handle, squeeze the soft garlic from each clove into a small bowl.

2. In a blender, puree the garlic, mayonnaise, lemon juice, mustard, ⅛ teaspoon salt, and cayenne until smooth. With the blender running, through the hole in the cover, add the oil in a slow, steady stream until the mixture is thickened. Transfer to a bowl; cover and refrigerate up to 4 hours.

Each tablespoon About 110 calories, 0g protein, 2g carbohydrate, 12g fat (2g saturated), 0g fiber, 275mg sodium.

VARIATION

Smoky Aioli

Prepare as directed above, but replace the mustard and cayenne with **½ teaspoon each lemon zest and smoked paprika.**

GLOSSARY →

Aioli (ay-OH-lee), a garlic mayonnaise from Provence, is the classic condiment for bouillabaisse (page 156). It's also wonderful as a dip for vegetables and as a sauce for fish or lamb.

white sauce (béchamel)

PREP: 5 MIN / TOTAL: 20 MIN / MAKES 1 CUP

2 tablespoons butter
2 tablespoons all-purpose flour
1 cup milk, warmed
½ teaspoon salt
Pinch of ground nutmeg

In a heavy 1-quart saucepan, melt the butter over low heat. Add the flour and cook, stirring, 1 minute. With a wire whisk, gradually whisk in the warm milk. Cook over medium heat, stirring constantly with a wooden spoon, until the sauce has thickened and boils. Reduce the heat and simmer, stirring frequently, 5 minutes. Remove from the heat and stir in the salt and nutmeg.

Each tablespoon About 25 calories, 1g protein, 1g carbohydrate, 2g fat (1g saturated), 0g fiber, 95mg sodium.

VARIATIONS

Cheese Sauce

Prepare sauce as directed above. Remove the saucepan from the heat. Add **4 ounces sharp Cheddar cheese**, shredded (1 cup); stir until the cheese has melted and the sauce is smooth. Makes about 1¼ cups.

Mornay Sauce

Prepare sauce as directed above. Remove the saucepan from the heat. Add **2 ounces Gruyère cheese**, shredded (½ cup); stir until the cheese has melted and the sauce is smooth. Makes about 1 cup.

hollandaise sauce

PREP: 5 MIN / TOTAL: 15 MIN / MAKES 1 CUP

3 large egg yolks

¼ cup water

2 tablespoons fresh lemon juice

½ cup cold butter, cut into 8 pieces

¼ teaspoon salt

1. In a heavy, 1-quart saucepan and using a wire whisk, mix the egg yolks, water, and lemon juice until well blended. Cook over medium-low heat, stirring constantly with a wooden spoon or heat-safe rubber spatula, until the egg yolk mixture just begins to bubble at edge, 6 to 8 minutes.

2. Reduce the heat to low. With a wire whisk, whisk in the butter, one piece at a time, until each addition is incorporated and the sauce has thickened. Remove from the heat and stir in the salt. Strain through a sieve to remove the chalaza and any bits of cooked egg, if you like.

Each tablespoon About 60 calories, 1g protein, 0g carbohydrate, 7g fat (4g saturated), 0g fiber, 95mg sodium.

VARIATIONS

Caper Sauce

Prepare as directed above, but stir **1 tablespoon drained chopped capers** into the sauce. Serve with fish or chicken.

Maltese Sauce

Prepare as directed above, but substitute **orange juice** for the lemon juice and add 1½ **teaspoons orange zest** to the sauce after straining. Pair this with asparagus.

TESTING NOTE The chalaza is the ropey strands of egg white which anchor the yolk in place in the center of the thick white. Chalazae are neither imperfections nor beginning embryos. The more prominent the chalaza the fresher the egg. Chalazae don't interfere with the cooking or beating of the white and you don't need to remove them, although some cooks like to strain them from stirred custard.

béarnaise sauce

PREP: 5 MIN / TOTAL: 35 MIN / MAKES 1 CUP

½ cup tarragon vinegar

⅓ cup dry white wine

2 shallots, finely chopped

3 large egg yolks

¼ cup water

Pinch of ground black pepper

½ cup cold butter, cut into 8 pieces

1 tablespoon chopped fresh tarragon

¼ teaspoon salt

1. In a 1-quart saucepan, combine the vinegar, wine, and shallots; heat to boiling over high heat. Boil until the liquid has reduced to ¼ cup, about 7 minutes. With the back of a spoon, press the mixture through a fine sieve into a medium bowl or the top of a double boiler.

2. With a wire whisk, beat the egg yolks, water, and pepper into the vinegar mixture. Set the bowl over a saucepan of simmering water. Cook, whisking constantly, until the egg yolk mixture bubbles around the edge and has thickened, about 10 minutes.

3. Reduce the heat to very low. With a wire whisk, whisk in the butter, one piece at a time, until each addition is incorporated and the sauce has thickened. Remove from the heat and stir in the tarragon and salt.

Each tablespoon About 70 calories, 1g protein, 1g carbohydrate, 7g fat (4g saturated), 0g fiber, 60mg sodium.

 Tip If you don't have tarragon vinegar, use white wine vinegar and toss in an extra teaspoon of fresh tarragon.

homemade ketchup

PREP: 5 MIN / TOTAL: 1 HR 15 MIN, PLUS COOLING / MAKES ABOUT 2½ CUPS

- 1 can (28 ounces) whole peeled tomatoes
- 2 teaspoons canola oil
- 1 small onion, chopped
- ⅛ teaspoon ground clove
- ¼ teaspoon ground black pepper
- ⅓ cup brown sugar, packed
- ⅓ cup cider vinegar
- 3 tablespoons tomato paste
- 1 tablespoon soy sauce

1. In a blender, puree the tomatoes until smooth.

2. In a medium saucepan, heat the oil over medium heat. Add the onion and cook 6 minutes, or until browned. Add the ground clove and pepper; cook 1 minute.

3. Add the brown sugar, cider vinegar, tomato paste, soy sauce, and pureed tomatoes. Heat to boiling over high heat. Reduce the heat to medium-low; simmer 50 minutes, or until thickened, stirring occasionally.

4. Cool slightly. In a blender, puree until smooth. Refrigerate until cold; keeps for 3 weeks in the fridge.

Each tablespoon About 15 calories, 0g protein, 3g carbohydrate, 0g fat (0g saturated), 0g fiber, 66mg sodium.

 Tip No soy sauce? Worcestershire adds a similar savory boost that amps up the tomato flavor.

VARIATIONS

Pineapple-Chipotle
In step 2, cook **1 cup pineapple chunks** with the onion for 10 minutes. In step 3, add **1 chipotle chile in adobo** along with pureed tomatoes.

Cilantro-Ginger
In step 2, cook **2 tablespoons finely chopped, peeled fresh ginger** and **½ teaspoon ground cumin** with the onion. In step 4, stir in **¼ cup chopped cilantro** after pureeing.

Cocktail
In step 2, cook **2 cloves garlic**, chopped, with the onion. In step 4, stir in **¼ cup bottled horseradish** and **2 tablespoons fresh lemon juice** after pureeing.

Ingredient Ideas
homemade ketchup

CAMPFIRE BAKED BEANS

In a 12-inch oven-safe skillet, cook **6 slices bacon** over medium heat until the fat is rendered. Transfer to a plate; coarsely crumble. To the skillet, add **1 onion**, chopped; **1 green bell pepper**, chopped; and **¼ teaspoon salt**. Cook 8 minutes. Off the heat, stir in the bacon; **3 cans (15 ounces each) navy beans**, drained; **1¼ cups Ketchup**; **¼ cup molasses**; **4 teaspoons dry mustard**; and **½ teaspoon ground black pepper**. Bake, covered, in a preheated 325°F oven 1 hour. **Serves 8.**

MEXICAN GRILLED CHEESE

Spread **3 tablespoons Pineapple-Chipotle Ketchup** on one side of each of **2 slices of bread**. Top with **3 tablespoons each shredded Cheddar and Gruyère cheese** and **¼ teaspoon chili powder**, then make a sandwich. In a nonstick skillet over medium heat, melt **1 tablespoon butter**. Cook the sandwich, covered, until the cheese melts, turning once. **Serves 1.**

GINGERY GLAZED SALMON

Brush **¼ cup Cilantro-Ginger Ketchup** over **4 fillets of skin-on salmon**; sprinkle with **¼ teaspoon salt**. Place skin side down on a grill over medium heat. Cover; cook 12 minutes, without turning. Serve with additional ketchup. **Serves 4.**

MACARONI CHOPPED SALAD

Whisk **½ cup each Cocktail Ketchup and mayonnaise**, **2 tablespoons each cider vinegar and Dijon mustard**, and **½ teaspoon each salt and ground black pepper**; toss with **1 pound pasta shells**, cooked; **4 hard-cooked eggs**, chopped; **2 stalks celery**, chopped; and **¼ cup each chopped parsley and red onion**. **Serves 8.**

tomato salsa

PREP: 20 MIN / TOTAL: 20 MIN, PLUS CHILLING / MAKES ABOUT 3 CUPS

- 1 large lime
- 1½ pounds ripe tomatoes (3 large), chopped
- ½ small red onion, finely chopped
- 1 small jalapeño chile, seeded and minced
- 2 tablespoons chopped fresh cilantro
- ¾ teaspoon salt
- ¼ teaspoon coarsely ground black pepper

From the lime, grate 1½ teaspoons zest and squeeze 2 tablespoons juice. In a medium bowl, gently stir the lime zest and juice, tomatoes, onion, jalapeño, cilantro, salt, and pepper until well mixed. Cover and refrigerate at least 1 hour or up to 2 days.

Each ¼ cup About 15 calories, 1g protein, 3g carbohydrate, 0g fat (0g saturated), 1g fiber, 150mg sodium.

tomatillo salsa

PREP: 25 MIN / TOTAL: 25 MIN, PLUS CHILLING / MAKES ABOUT 2 CUPS

- 1 pound fresh tomatillos (about 10 medium), husked, washed well, and cut into quarters
- ¾ cup loosely packed fresh cilantro leaves, chopped
- ¼ cup finely chopped onion
- 1 or 2 serrano or jalapeño chiles, seeded and minced
- 1 clove garlic, minced
- 1 tablespoon olive oil
- 1 teaspoon sugar
- ½ teaspoon salt

1. In a food processor with the knife blade attached, coarsely chop the tomatillos.

2. In a medium bowl, gently stir the chopped tomatillos, cilantro, onion, chiles, garlic, oil, sugar, and salt until well mixed. Cover and refrigerate at least 1 hour to blend flavors or up to 3 days.

Each ¼ cup About 35 calories, 1g protein, 3g carbohydrate, 2g fat (0g saturated), 1g fiber, 145mg sodium.

HOMEMADE KETCHUP 52

TOMATO SALSA 53

asian peanut sauce

PREP: 10 MIN / TOTAL: 10 MIN / MAKES 1½ CUPS

½ cup creamy peanut butter

½ cup water

¼ cup soy sauce

1 tablespoon grated, peeled fresh ginger

2 tablespoons distilled white vinegar

2 tablespoons Asian sesame oil

1 tablespoon packed brown sugar

¼ teaspoon hot sauce

In a blender or food processor with the knife blade attached, combine the peanut butter, water, soy sauce, ginger, vinegar, sesame oil, brown sugar, and hot sauce; puree until smooth. Serve immediately or cover and refrigerate up to 1 day.

Each tablespoon About 50 calories, 2g protein, 2g carbohydrate, 4g fat (1g saturated), 0g fiber, 190mg sodium.

GOOD TO KNOW

GARLIC

There are hundreds of varieties of garlic but two main types: softneck and hardneck.

SOFTNECK This type of garlic has several layers of cloves that get smaller at the center of the bulb.

HARDNECK This type has a stem in the center of the bulb.

GARLIC SCAPES The scape is the extension of the garlic stalk; they are cut to help the garlic to bulb. Scapes have a mild garlic flavor and are delicious raw or cooked.

ELEPHANT Not a true garlic but a member of the leek family, it has a mild garlic flavor.

BLACK GARLIC Low and slow fermentation and dehydration makes the sugars in the garlic caramelize and turn black. This has a soft sticky texture and molasses-like sweetness. Use it like roasted garlic.

Ingredient Ideas
peanut butter

CURRIED SHRIMP

Melt **2 tablespoons each creamy peanut butter and butter** with **1 teaspoon curry powder** and **1 tablespoon fresh lemon juice**; use to baste **1 pound shrimp**.

STEAK MARINADE

Mix **2 tablespoons peanut butter** with **2 tablespoons fresh lime juice** and **2 cloves garlic** for **1 pound steak**.

SPICY NOODLES

Blend **1 tablespoon peanut butter** with **½ cup each rice vinegar and chicken broth** and **1 tablespoon sriracha**. Toss with **8 ounces cooked noodles**.

NUTTY HOT WINGS

Blend **1 tablespoon peanut butter** with **¼ cup hot sauce**, **2 tablespoons soy sauce**, and **2 tablespoons cilantro**. Toss with **1 pound broiled chicken wings**.

GARLICKY BEANS

Toss **2 tablespoons peanut butter** with **2 cloves sautéed garlic** and **1 pound cooked green beans**.

Ingredient Ideas
miso paste

CHICKEN MARINADE

Blend **2 tablespoons miso paste** with **2 tablespoons maple syrup** and **½ cup orange juice**. Toss with **1½ pounds boneless chicken breasts and thighs**.

GLAZE FOR SALMON

Whisk **2 tablespoons miso paste** with **1 tablespoon brown sugar** and **1 tablespoon balsamic vinegar**; brush on **1¼ pounds salmon** before roasting.

DYNAMITE DRESSING

Mix **1 tablespoon miso paste** with **2 tablespoons sherry vinegar**, **1 tablespoon chopped cilantro**, and **¼ cup olive oil**.

italian green sauce (salsa verde)

PREP: 20 MIN / TOTAL: 20 MIN / MAKES 1 CUP

- 1 large clove garlic, minced
- ¼ teaspoon salt
- 2 cups tightly packed fresh flat-leaf parsley leaves
- 8 anchovy fillets, drained and finely chopped (optional)
- 3 tablespoons capers, drained
- 1 teaspoon Dijon mustard
- ⅛ teaspoon ground black pepper
- ½ cup olive oil
- 3 tablespoons fresh lemon juice

1. With the side of a chef's knife, mash the garlic and salt to a smooth paste on a cutting board.

2. In a blender or food processor with the knife blade attached, puree the parsley; anchovies, if using; capers; mustard; pepper; oil; lemon juice; and garlic mixture until almost smooth. Serve immediately or cover and refrigerate up to 4 hours.

Each tablespoon About 70 calories, 1g protein, 2g carbohydrate, 7g fat (1g saturated), 0g fiber, 125mg sodium.

tartar sauce

PREP: 15 MIN / TOTAL: 15 MIN / MAKES ABOUT ¾ CUP

- ½ cup mayonnaise
- ¼ cup finely chopped dill pickle
- 1 tablespoon chopped fresh parsley
- 2 teaspoons milk
- 2 teaspoons distilled white vinegar
- ½ teaspoon finely chopped onion
- ½ teaspoon Dijon mustard

In a small bowl, combine the mayonnaise, pickle, parsley, milk, vinegar, onion, and mustard until well blended. Serve immediately or cover and refrigerate up to 2 days.

Each tablespoon About 70 calories, 0g protein, 0g carbohydrate, 7g fat (1g saturated), 0g fiber, 125mg sodium.

salmoriglio sauce

PREP: 10 MIN / TOTAL: 10 MIN, PLUS STANDING / MAKES SCANT ⅔ CUP

- ¼ cup fresh lemon juice
- 1 clove garlic, crushed with side of chef's knife
- 1 teaspoon dried oregano, crumbled
- ¼ teaspoon salt
- ¼ teaspoon coarsely ground black pepper
- ⅓ cup extra-virgin olive oil

1. In a medium bowl, combine the lemon juice, garlic, oregano, salt, and pepper. Let stand 10 minutes.

2. With a wire whisk, in a thin, steady stream, whisk in the oil until blended. Serve, or let stand up to 4 hours at room temperature. Whisk just before serving.

Each tablespoon About 65 calories, 0g protein, 1g carbohydrate, 7g fat (1g saturated), 0g fiber, 57mg sodium.

 Tip Do as they do in Sicily and add a mashed anchovy fillet to the lemon mixture for extra tang. Serve on grilled fish, chicken, or steamed vegetables.

chimichurri

PREP: 20 MIN / TOTAL: 20 MIN / MAKES 1 CUP

- 1 large clove garlic, minced
- ½ teaspoon salt
- 1½ cups loosely packed fresh parsley leaves, chopped
- 1 cup loosely packed fresh cilantro leaves, chopped
- ¾ cup olive oil
- 2 tablespoons red wine vinegar
- ½ teaspoon crushed red pepper

1. With the side of a chef's knife, mash the garlic and salt to a smooth paste on a cutting board.

2. In a small bowl, combine the garlic mixture, parsley, cilantro, oil, vinegar, and crushed red pepper until well blended. Serve immediately or cover and refrigerate up to 4 hours.

Each tablespoon About 95 calories, 0g protein, 1g carbohydrate, 10g fat (1g saturated), 0g fiber, 75mg sodium.

classic dill pickles

PREP: 10 MIN / TOTAL: 20 MIN, PLUS PICKLING / MAKES 16 SERVINGS

- 1¼ distilled white vinegar
- 1 cup water
- 4 cloves garlic, crushed and peeled
- 3 tablespoons sugar
- 2 tablespoons kosher salt
- 1 pound Kirby or pickling cucumbers, quartered lengthwise
- 3 sprigs fresh dill

1. In a small saucepan, combine the vinegar, water, garlic, sugar, and kosher salt. Heat over medium until sugar dissolves, stirring.

2. Arrange the cucumbers and dill in a 32-ounce jar; pour the warm brine over the cucumbers to cover. (This can be made in 2 or more smaller jars as long as there's enough brine to cover.) Let cool slightly.

3. Replace the lid and refrigerate at least 4 hours or up to 2 weeks.

Each serving About 10 calories, 0g protein, 2g carbohydrate, 0g fat (0g saturated), 0g fiber, 241mg sodium.

VARIATIONS

Spicy Beans

In step 1, replace the distilled white vinegar with **cider vinegar**. In step 2, replace the cucumbers with **12 ounces green beans**; replace the dill with **2 teaspoons crushed red pepper**. In step 3, refrigerate at least 1 day.

Giardiniera

In step 2, replace the cucumbers with **3 cups total sliced carrots, small cauliflower florets, and chopped red bell peppers**; replace the dill with **2 sprigs rosemary**. In step 3, refrigerate at least 1 day.

Quick Sauerkraut

In step 1, replace the distilled white vinegar with **unseasoned rice vinegar**. In step 2, replace the cucumbers with **2 cups packed thinly sliced cabbage** and **1 small onion**, thinly sliced; replace the dill with **4 star anise** and **2 teaspoons mustard seeds**.

Ingredient Ideas

homemade pickles

CHEESEBURGER TOSTADAS

Arrange **4 medium flour tortillas** on 2 baking sheets sprayed with **nonstick cooking spray**. Top with **8 ounces cooked ground beef, 1 cup shredded Cheddar cheese**, and **¼ teaspoon salt**. Bake in a preheated 475°F oven 12 minutes. Top with shredded lettuce, chopped tomatoes, and chopped Classic Dill Pickles. Drizzle with ketchup, if desired. *Serves 4.*

ITALIAN-PICKLED VEGGIE DIP

In a food processor, pulse **4 ounces cream cheese**, softened; **½ cup plain Greek yogurt; ½ cup chopped Giardiniera; 2 green onions**, chopped; and **¼ teaspoon each salt and ground black pepper** just until combined, scraping the bowl occasionally. Serve with crackers or crudités. *Serves 8.*

SPICY TUNA SANDWICHES

Combine **two 5-ounce cans tuna**, drained; **½ cup mayonnaise; ⅔ cup chopped Spicy Beans; 2 stalks celery**, finely chopped; **2 tablespoons Spicy Bean brine**; and **1 tablespoon snipped fresh chives**. Serve on soft white bread. *Serves 4.*

PORK & SAUERKRAUT STIR-FRY

In a 12-inch skillet, heat **1 tablespoon toasted sesame oil** over medium-high heat. Add **1 pound ground pork** and **½ teaspoon salt**; cook 5 minutes, breaking up the meat with the side of a spoon. Add **1½ cups Quick Sauerkraut** and **8 ounces shiitake mushrooms**, stemmed and sliced. Cook 3 minutes, stirring. Serve with rice. *Serves 4.*

GLOSSARY →

Giardiniera pronounced "jahr-dee-NYAY-rah," is an Italian mix of pickled veggies (typically carrots, cauliflower, and bell peppers). Look for it next to the pickled peppers on store shelves.

QUICK SAUERKRAUT 56

CLASSIC
DILL PICKLES 56

SPICY BEANS 56

QUICK SAUERKRAUT 56

RE-USABLE

GIARDINIERA 56

carrot top pesto

PREP: 10 MIN / TOTAL: 10 MIN / MAKES 1 SCANT CUP

- **2 cups rinsed carrot tops (tough stems removed)**
- **½ cup packed fresh basil leaves**
- **½ cup grated Parmesan cheese**
- **⅓ cup toasted almonds**
- **1 small clove garlic**
- **½ teaspoon salt**
- **¼ teaspoon ground black pepper**
- **¾ cup extra-virgin olive oil**

1. In a food processor, combine the carrot tops, basil, Parmesan, almonds, garlic, salt, and pepper.

2. Pulse to finely chop. Drizzle in the olive oil; pulse to combine. Serve over cooked pasta or as a tasty dip.

Each tablespoon About 135 calories, 1g protein, 1g carbohydrate, 14g fat (2g saturated), 0g fiber, 128mg sodium.

 Tip Don't toss carrot tops, radish leaves, or beet greens! Instead, add to smoothies, stir-fries, soups, or make pesto.

#SavetheFood

citrus hack

Save your lemon, orange, and lime peels! They're great for flavoring vinegar and vodka or giving zing to dressings and marinades. Plus they're super-deodorizers: Toss a few slivers into the garbage disposal to de-stink, or add sliced peels to a bowl of water and nuke 5 minutes to refresh the microwave.

Ingredient Ideas

leftover parsley

COUSCOUS SALAD

Cook **1 cup couscous** as the label directs. From **1 lemon**, grate 1 teaspoon zest and squeeze 3 tablespoons juice. Transfer the cooked couscous to a bowl; cool slightly. Add **3 cups parsley**, finely chopped; **2 plum tomatoes**, seeded and chopped; **2 tablespoons extra-virgin olive oil**; the lemon zest and juice; and **¼ teaspoon each salt and ground black pepper**. **Serves 4.**

LENTIL STEW

In a 6-quart saucepot, heat **4 cups chicken broth** to boiling over high heat. Stir in **1 cup lentils**, picked over, and **1 large all-purpose potato**, peeled and cut into ½-inch cubes. Reduce the heat to maintain a simmer. Cover; simmer 25 minutes, or until the lentils are almost tender, stirring occasionally. With a potato masher, gently mash the mixture to break up the potato. Add **10 ounces sliced mushrooms**. Cook, covered, 10 to 15 minutes, or until the lentils are tender. Stir in **2 cups parsley**, finely chopped, and **⅛ teaspoon ground black pepper**. **Serves 4.**

GREEN ONION RICE

Thinly slice **4 green onions**; separate the green parts from the white. In a 4-quart saucepot, heat **1 tablespoon vegetable oil** over medium heat. Add the white parts of the green onion; cook 2 minutes, or until golden, stirring. Add **1 cup long-grain white rice**. Cook 1 minute, stirring. Add **1½ cups chicken broth** and **⅛ teaspoon salt**. Heat to boiling over high heat. Reduce the heat to maintain a simmer. Cover; simmer 25 minutes. Remove from the heat. Let stand 5 minutes. Stir in **2 cups parsley**, finely chopped, and remaining green onions. **Serves 4.**

PISTACHIO PESTO

In a food processor, pulse **2 cups parsley**; **1 cup roasted**, **salted pistachios**, shelled; **¼ cup grated Pecorino cheese**; **1 clove garlic**; **¼ teaspoon salt**; and **⅛ teaspoon ground black pepper** until combined. With the processor running, add **⅔ cup extra-virgin olive oil** until smooth. Serve with **grilled shrimp** or **1 pound cooked pasta**. **Makes ¾ cup.**

classic preserved lemons

(See photo on page 60.)

PREP: 20 MIN / TOTAL: 20 MIN, PLUS STANDING / MAKES 1 QUART

- 4 or 5 small lemons, ends trimmed
- 5 to 6 tablespoon kosher or sea salt
- 1½ cups fresh lemon juice

1. Heat a covered 6-quart saucepot of water to boiling over high heat. With tongs, place a 1-quart widemouthed glass canning jar and metal lid into the boiling water. Boil 2 minutes, turning occasionally. Remove and invert it onto a clean kitchen towel to dry.

2. Scrub the lemons; cut each one lengthwise into quarters, leaving ¼ inch of the bottom (not the stem end) intact. For each lemon, rub 1 tablespoon kosher or sea salt between the quarters; place in the jar. Add enough lemon juice to cover the lemons completely. Cover with the lid. Let stand at least 4 weeks in a cool spot. Refrigerate after opening for up to 6 months.

Each tablespoon About 5 calories, 0g protein, 1g carbohydrate, 0g fat (0g saturated), 1g fiber, 145mg sodium.

VARIATIONS

Spicy Cinnamon Preserved Lemons
After the lemons have stood for 1 week, remove the lid, firmly press down on the lemons, and add: **1 cinnamon stick**, broken up; **2 whole cloves**; and **½ teaspoon crushed red pepper**.

Fennel-Anise Preserved Lemons
After the lemons have stood for 1 week, remove the lid, firmly press down on the lemons, and add: **4 star anise, 2 tablespoons fennel seeds, and 1 tablespoon black peppercorns.**

Garlicky Herb Preserved Lemons
After the lemons have stood for 1 week, remove the lid, firmly press down on the lemons, and add: **3 bay leaves, 1 sprig (5 inches) fresh rosemary,** and **1 clove garlic**, peeled.

Ingredient Ideas

preserved lemons

TUNISIAN SKILLET CHICKEN
In a large skillet, heat **2 tablespoons olive oil** over medium-high heat. Cook **2 pounds chicken legs and thighs**, sprinkled with ½ **teaspoon salt**, 4 minutes per side. Set aside. Add **1 large onion**, sliced, and **1 cup pitted green olives**. Cook 4 minutes. Add **1 Spicy Cinnamon Preserved Lemon**, sliced; **1 cup chicken broth**; and the **chicken**. Cover; cook on medium 15 minutes, until chicken is cooked. Top with chopped fresh parsley and pepper. **Serves 4.**

PARTY DIP
In a food processor, pulse the **rind from ¼ Classic Preserved Lemon**, chopped; **1 green onion**, chopped; **¼ cup fresh cilantro**; **¼ cup Greek yogurt**; **1 teaspoon hot sauce**; and **¼ teaspoon salt** until finely chopped. Pulse in **1 ripe avocado** until almost smooth. Serve with chips. **Serves 6.**

POTATO SALAD
Stir together ¾ **cup mayonnaise**; ¼ **cup fresh parsley**, chopped; **rind from ½ Garlicky Herb Preserved Lemon**, finely chopped; **1 tablespoons fresh dill**, chopped; **1 clove garlic**, crushed with a garlic press; a **pinch of salt**; and ¼ **teaspoon ground black pepper**. Toss with 1¾ **pounds chopped red potatoes**, cooked. **Serves 4.**

YOGURT SAUCE
Stir together ½ **cup Greek yogurt**, ¼ **cup olive oil**, ¼ **cup chopped fresh mint**, **2 tablespoons chopped Fennel-Anise Preserved Lemon**, **1 teaspoon honey**, and ¼ **teaspoon salt**. Serve with lamb, pork, or steak. **Serves 4.**

CLASSIC HUMMUS 61

CHERRY TOMATO CONFIT 64

HOMEMADE RICOTTA CHEESE 63

CLASSIC PRESERVED LEMONS 59

classic hummus

PREP: 15 MIN / TOTAL: 1 HR 15 MIN, PLUS STANDING / MAKES
3½ CUPS

1 cup dried chickpeas

1 teaspoon baking soda

4 cloves garlic

6 tablespoons fresh
lemon juice

¾ teaspoon ground
cumin

¾ teaspoon salt

¾ cup tahini

⅓ cup water

1. In a 4-quart saucepan, place the chickpeas and baking soda;
add enough cold water to cover by 2 inches. Let stand at room
temperature overnight; drain (do not rinse) and return the chickpeas to the saucepan along with enough cold water to cover by
2 inches. Heat to boiling over high heat. Reduce the heat to
medium; simmer 1 hour or until the chickpeas are soft and their
skins have loosened.

2. In a food processor or blender, pulse the garlic, lemon juice,
cumin, and salt until chopped. Add the tahini and water; pulse until
smooth. Drain the cooked chickpeas, discarding any loose skins,
and add them to the tahini mixture; process until smooth, stopping and stirring occasionally. Store in an airtight container in the
refrigerator up to 2 weeks.

Each tablespoon About 30 calories, 1g protein, 3g carbohydrate, 2g fat
(0g saturated), 1g fiber, 33mg sodium.

 Tip For a quick version, use 2 cans (15 ounces each) chickpeas.
Rinse well and drain; discard any loose skins. Proceed with
step 2 of the recipe.

VARIATIONS

Cardamom-Ginger Hummus
Stir in **1 tablespoon grated, peeled fresh ginger** and **½ teaspoon
ground cardamom.**

Roasted Pepper & Mint Hummus
Finely chop **¾ cup each packed fresh mint and roasted red peppers** with **2 tablespoons capers**; stir into hummus.

Spicy Cilantro Hummus
Stir in **1 cup packed fresh cilantro**, finely chopped, and **¼ cup
sriracha sauce.**

Ingredient Ideas

homemade hummus

FLATBREAD WEDGES
Spread **¼ cup Classic Hummus** on **1 pita**. Top with
2 thin slices red onion, separated; **2 tablespoons
crumbled feta cheese**; and a **pinch of ground black
pepper**. Drizzle with **1 teaspoon olive oil**. Toast until
crisp around edges. Top with **fresh basil leaves**.
Serves 1.

GINGERY CHICKEN
Arrange **4 small skinless, boneless chicken breasts**
(1¼ pounds) on a foil-lined baking sheet; sprinkle with
½ teaspoon salt and spread with **¾ cup Cardamom-
Ginger Hummus**. Bake in a preheated 375°F oven
40 minutes, or until cooked (165°F). Garnish with
chopped fresh parsley. Serve with cooked rice pilaf.
Serves 4.

LOADED VEGGIE 'WICH
Spread **⅓ cup Roasted Pepper & Mint Hummus** on
2 slices lightly toasted whole-grain bread. Top 1 piece
of bread with **2 slices sharp Cheddar cheese**, then
sliced **cucumbers** and **tomatos**, **shredded carrots**, and
sprouts. Top with the second piece of bread. Serves 1.

SOBA SALAD
Whisk together **½ cup Spicy Cilantro Hummus**,
¼ cup seasoned rice vinegar, **2 tablespoons canola
oil**, **1 tablespoon soy sauce**, and **¼ teaspoon salt**.
Toss with **8 ounces soba noodles**, cooked; **1 cup
frozen shelled edamame**, thawed; **1 cup shredded
red cabbage**; and **½ cup roasted cashews**, chopped.
Top with **sesame seeds**. Serves 4.

Ingredient Ideas

store-bought ricotta cheese

This fresh, creamy cheese isn't just for lasagna. Take these three fast dishes, with savory and sweet options. They're made with part-skim ricotta—which has 41 percent less fat but no less flavor than the whole-milk variety— and all call for a 15- to 16-ounce tub.

ORANGE-RICOTTA PANCAKES

From **1 navel orange**, grate 2 teaspoons zest. Cut off and discard the remaining peel and white pith; cut the fruit into segments and reserve. In a bowl, whisk together the **ricotta**, **4 large eggs**, and the reserved orange zest. Whisk in ½ cup **all-purpose flour** and ½ **teaspoon baking powder**. Spray a 12-inch nonstick skillet with **nonstick cooking spray**; heat over medium heat 1 minute. Drop the batter by ¼ cupful into the skillet, making 4 or 5 pancakes at a time. Cook 5 minutes on one side and then flip and repeat until golden on both sides. Serve with the reserved orange segments and **maple syrup**. Serves 4.

PUFFY BACON-CHIVE CASSEROLE

Preheat the oven to 350°F. Brown **3 slices bacon**; drain. Crumble when cool. Separate **5 large eggs**, placing the yolks in a large bowl and the whites in a medium bowl. Whisk the yolks with the bacon, **ricotta**, ¼ cup grated **Parmesan cheese**, **2 tablespoons snipped fresh chives**, and ¼ **teaspoon each salt and ground black pepper**. Add **2 more egg whites** to the whites in the bowl and, using an electric mixer, beat on high to stiff peaks. Fold the whites into the ricotta mixture, one-third at a time, just until blended. Bake in a greased shallow 2½-quart baking dish 30 to 35 minutes. Serves 6.

EASY CASSATA PARFAITS

Slightly thaw **1 package (10 ounces) frozen cherries**. Meanwhile, cut **4 ounces pound cake** into 1-inch cubes (2 cups). In a bowl, whisk the **ricotta** with ⅓ cup **confectioners' sugar**. Using 4 wine goblets or parfait glasses, layer half of each with the ricotta mixture, cake, and cherries, and sprinkle on **1 tablespoon mini chocolate chips**. Repeat the layering. Serves 4.

GOOD TO KNOW

WHAT IS CRÈME FRAÎCHE?

IT'S CREAM—WITH CULTURE. Crème fraîche is simply heavy cream that's been transformed by the addition of healthy bacteria, which enhances its flavor and thickens it. This process—the same one used to make dairy products ranging from yogurt to sour cream to cheese—has existed for millennia. Crème fraîche is often used for finishing sauces; chefs love it for its slightly tangy flavor and because of its versatility: With 28 percent fat, it is richer and thicker than sour cream (which can be substituted in a pinch but is made with light cream and curdles when boiled). It's delicious to add to a skillet sauce or to dollop on anything from asparagus to summer fruits and chocolate tarts. With a day's notice, crème fraîche is a cinch to make at home and will last in your fridge for a couple of weeks.

MAKE YOUR OWN Pour **1 cup heavy cream** into a clean glass jar with a tight-fitting lid. Stir in **3 tablespoons buttermilk** until well blended. Cover the jar and let stand at room temperature for at least 12 hours and up to 24 hours, until the cream has thickened. Store in the refrigerator up to 2 weeks.

#SavetheFood

whey

Use the liquid that's strained out of the cheesecloth! That's the whey. Splash some into smoothies for extra protein or into marinades to tenderize meat. It'll keep in the fridge for up to a week.

homemade ricotta cheese

(See photo on page 60.)

PREP: 15 MIN / TOTAL: 1 HR / MAKES 2 CUPS

8 cups whole milk
1 teaspoon salt
3 tablespoons distilled
    white vinegar

2 tablespoons fresh
    lemon juice

1. In a 4-quart saucepot, combine the whole milk and salt. Heat over medium heat until the temperature of the milk reaches 185°F to 190°F on a candy thermometer, about 20 minutes, stirring occasionally. Remove from the heat. Stir in the vinegar and lemon juice. Let stand 20 minutes.

2. Line a colander with 2 layers of cheesecloth and set it over a large bowl. Ladle the curds into the colander. Let drain 5 minutes. Use the ricotta immediately or refrigerate in a covered container up to 1 week.

Each tablespoon About 25 calories, 2g protein, 0g carbohydrate, 2g fat (1g saturated), 0g fiber, 31mg sodium.

VARIATIONS

Hot 'n' Smoky Ricotta Cheese

Stir together 1 cup Homemade Ricotta, 2 teaspoons crushed red pepper, and 1 teaspoon smoked paprika.

Spiced Citrus Ricotta Cheese

Stir together 1 cup Homemade Ricotta, 2 tablespoons honey, and ½ teaspoon each orange zest and ground cinnamon.

Savory Herb Ricotta Cheese

Stir together 1 cup Homemade Ricotta; 3 slices bacon, cooked and crumbled; 1 tablespoon chopped fresh basil; 1 clove garlic, crushed with a garlic press; and ¼ teaspoon ground black pepper.

Ingredient Ideas

homemade ricotta

JALAPEÑO POPPERS

Stir together 1 cup Homemade Ricotta; ½ cup shredded sharp Cheddar cheese; 1 green onion, finely chopped; and ¼ teaspoon salt. Spoon into 6 jalapeño chiles, halved lengthwise and seeded; place in prepared baking dish and top with ½ cup finely crushed potato chips. Bake in a preheated 375°F oven 20 minutes, or until chiles are tender and cheese melts. Serves 6.

CROSTINI SPREAD

Stir together 1 cup Savory Herb Ricotta and 1 large egg; transfer to a ramekin or small baking dish. Top with 2 tablespoons grated Parmesan cheese and 1 tablespoon olive oil. Bake in a preheated 400°F oven 15 minutes. Serve with toasted baguette slices. Serves 6.

BERRY BREAD PUDDING

Arrange 8 cups toasted cubes of brioche in a greased 2-quart baking dish. Whisk 2 cups frozen mixed berries and 1½ cups milk with 3 large eggs; pour over the bread, pressing it down to soak. Dollop 1 cup Spiced Citrus Ricotta over the top. Bake in a preheated 375°F oven 40 minutes, or until set. Serves 6.

MARGHERITA PASTA

In a large skillet, heat ¼ cup olive oil over medium-high heat. Add 1 large onion, thinly sliced, and ½ teaspoon salt; cook 10 minutes, stirring. Add 1 can (28 ounces) diced tomatoes, drained. Cook 2 minutes. Toss with 1 pound cooked linguine or fettuccine. Top with 1 cup Hot 'n' Smoky Ricotta and ¼ cup grated Parmesan cheese. Garnish with fresh basil leaves. Serves 4.

cherry tomato confit

(See photo on page 60.)

PREP: 10 MIN / TOTAL: 1 HR / MAKES 4 CUPS

- 4 pints cherry tomatoes
- 6 cloves garlic, smashed and peeled
- 6 sprigs fresh thyme
- ¼ cup olive oil
- ¼ teaspoon salt
- ¼ teaspoon ground black pepper

1. Preheat the oven to 350°F.

2. On a large rimmed baking sheet, toss the tomatoes, garlic, and thyme with the oil, salt, and pepper. Bake until the tomatoes are wrinkled and fragrant, 45 to 50 minutes, shaking the pan halfway through. Let cool.

3. Use the confit on bruschetta, in salads, or over pasta, grilled meat, or fish. To store, transfer the confit to a jar, top with olive oil, and refrigerate up to 1 week.

Each ¼ cup About 45 calories, 1g protein, 3g carbohydrate, 4g fat (1g saturated), 1g fiber, 35mg sodium.

GOOD TO KNOW

DIFFERENCES BETWEEN REGULAR & GREEK YOGURT

Greek yogurt is classic yogurt with the whey strained; what's left is thicker and creamier. Compared to classic yogurt, in a 6-ounce nonfat serving, calories increase from 80 to 100. The straining alters key nutrients, too: Protein more than doubles, from 8 or 9 grams to 18 or 20, and some calcium is lost—classic delivers 30 percent of the daily value, and Greek only delivers 20 percent. Dieters beware: Full-fat Greek yogurt may contain up to 70 more calories per serving.

---

sicilian pesto

PREP: 10 MIN / TOTAL: 10 MIN / MAKES 1½ CUPS

- 1 cup sun-dried tomatoes packed in oil, drained
- ½ cup olive oil
- ¼ cup packed fresh parsley
- 2 tablespoons fresh lemon juice
- 1 tablespoon capers, drained
- 1 teaspoon grated lemon zest
- 1 clove garlic

In a food processor, blend the sun-dried tomatoes, oil, parsley, lemon juice, capers, lemon zest, and garlic until mostly smooth. Scoop into a covered container and refrigerate up to 3 days or freeze up to 3 months.

Each tablespoon About 50 calories, 0g protein, 1g carbohydrate, 5g fat (1g saturated), 0g fiber, 21mg sodium.

 Tip Toss with pasta and shredded chicken or use on grilled-veggie sandwiches.

#SavetheFood
freeze the cheese

For harder types, like Parmesan and Cheddar, wrap and freeze extras. To use, defrost 1 hour—or grate frozen for almost-instant thawing. Never behold mold again! Can be frozen for up to six weeks.

---

homemade pesto

(See photo on page 67.)

PREP: 15 MIN / TOTAL: 15 MIN / MAKES ¾ CUP

- 3 cups loosely packed fresh basil leaves
- 1 large clove garlic, crushed with a garlic press
- ½ cup olive oil
- ¼ cup grated Parmesan cheese
- ¼ cup toasted pine nuts
- 2 teaspoons fresh lemon juice
- ¼ teaspoon ground black pepper

In a food processor or blender, pulse the basil, garlic, oil, Parmesan, pine nuts, lemon juice, and pepper until smooth. Scoop into a covered container and refrigerate up to 3 days or freeze up to 3 months.

Each tablespoon About 110 calories, 1g protein, 1g carbohydrate, 11g fat (2g saturated), 0g fiber, 31mg sodium.

VARIATIONS

Smoky Almond Pesto

Replace the basil with **parsley**, the pine nuts with **blanched almonds**, and the Parmesan with **grated Manchego**. Add ½ **cup roasted red peppers** and **1 teaspoon smoked paprika**.

Spicy Cilantro Pesto

Omit the cheese and lemon juice. Replace half of the basil with **cilantro** and replace the pine nuts with **roasted unsalted peanuts**. Add **1 tablespoon fresh lime juice; 1 teaspoon sesame oil; 1 teaspoon grated, peeled ginger; 1 small serrano chile** (seeded and chopped); and ½ **teaspoon salt**.

Hazelnut-Arugula Pesto

Replace the basil with **2 ½ cups arugula** and ½ **cup fresh parsley**, and replace the pine nuts with **hazelnuts**. Add a **pinch of nutmeg**.

Ingredient Ideas

homemade pesto

BBQ-HERBED DRUMSTICKS

Pat **2 pounds chicken drumsticks** dry with paper towels and place them in a gallon-size resealable bag with ½ **cup Homemade Pesto**. Shake to coat, then refrigerate at least 1 hour or overnight. Remove the chicken and wipe off any excess pesto. Season all over with ¼ **teaspoon salt**. Grill over medium heat until golden and crisped, 15 minutes, turning occasionally. Brush with additional pesto and serve. **Serves 4.**

CRISPY SPANISH POTATOES

Spray a foil-lined baking sheet with **nonstick cooking spray**. Slice 1½ **pounds fingerling potatoes** lengthwise in half. Toss with ⅓ **cup Smoky Almond Pesto** and ½ **teaspoon salt**. Roast in a preheated 425°F oven until golden, 30 minutes. Garnish with **chopped fresh parsley**. Serve with additional pesto for dipping. Serves 4.

CHILE-LIME-GRILLED CORN

Brush **4 ears corn** (husked) with **1 tablespoon olive oil**. Grill over high heat until slightly charred, 8 to 10 minutes, turning occasionally. Brush with ½ **cup Spicy Cilantro Pesto**. Sprinkle with **grated Pecorino cheese**. Serves 4.

CREAMY RICOTTA & PROSCIUTTO CROSTINI

Fold together **1 cup ricotta**, ½ **cup Greek yogurt**, and ¼ **teaspoon salt** until just combined. Transfer to a small serving bowl. Swirl in ¼ **cup Hazelnut-Arugula Pesto**. Serve with toasted baguette slices and sliced prosciutto. **Makes 1¾ cups spread.**

pistachio-mint pesto

PREP: 15 MIN / TOTAL: 15 MIN / MAKES ABOUT ¾ CUP

½ cup packed fresh mint leaves

½ cup olive oil

⅓ cup shelled pistachios

Grated zest of 1 medium orange (about 1½ teaspoons)

¼ cup packed finely grated Pecorino cheese (about 1 ounce)

¼ teaspoon salt

In a food processor, blend the mint, oil, pistachios, orange zest, Pecorino, and salt until mostly smooth. Use on steamed halibut or cod or with roasted green beans.

Each tablespoon About 110 calories, 1g protein, 1g carbohydrate, 11g fat (2g saturated), 1g fiber, 63mg sodium.

spicy thai pesto

PREP: 15 MIN / TOTAL: 15 MIN / MAKES ABOUT ¾ CUP

1 medium sweet long red pepper, seeded and chopped

½ cup vegetable oil

1 stalk lemongrass, outer layer discarded, thinly sliced

2 thin slices peeled fresh ginger

2 Thai chiles or serrano chiles, seeded

2 tablespoons fish sauce

1 clove garlic

½ teaspoon coriander seeds

In a food processor, blend the pepper, oil, lemongrass, ginger, chiles, fish sauce, garlic, and coriander seeds until smooth. Scoop into a covered container and refrigerate up to 3 days or freeze up to 3 months.

Each tablespoon About 90 calories, 0g protein, 1g carbohydrate, 9g fat (1g saturated), 0g fiber, 199mg sodium.

 Tip Use on grilled shrimp or roasted chicken.

pepita pesto

PREP: 15 MIN / TOTAL: 15 MIN / MAKES ¾ CUP

1 cup packed fresh cilantro leaves

½ cup olive oil

⅓ cup pepitas (pumpkin seeds)

2 tablespoons fresh lime juice

1 clove garlic

¼ teaspoon cayenne pepper

½ teaspoon salt

In a food processor, blend the cilantro, oil, pepitas, lime juice, garlic, cayenne, and salt until mostly smooth. Scoop into a covered container and refrigerate up to 3 days or freeze up to 3 months.

Each tablespoon About 100 calories, 1g protein, 1g carbohydrate, 11g fat (2g saturated), 0g fiber, 99mg sodium.

 Tip Use on grilled steak or chicken tacos.

GOOD TO KNOW

PEPITAS OR PUMPKIN SEEDS

If you've ever scooped the seeds from a pumpkin and toasted them, you know that they are hard to open and not green inside. So how are prepackaged pretty green ones so perfect? Most pumpkin seeds/pepitas you get from the store come from the hull-less oilseed type of pumpkins that have seeds without shells.

roasted garlic

PREP: 10 MIN / TOTAL: 1 HR 10 MIN, PLUS COOLING / MAKES
ABOUT 1¼ CUPS

- 4 heads garlic
- 2 tablespoons extra-virgin olive oil
- ⅛ teaspoon salt
- ⅛ teaspoon coarsely ground black pepper
- 4 thyme sprigs

1. Preheat the oven to 350°F. Remove any loose papery skin from the garlic, leaving the heads intact. Place the garlic on a sheet of heavy-duty foil; drizzle with the oil and sprinkle with salt and pepper. Place 1 thyme sprig on top of each head.

2. Loosely wrap the foil around the garlic, folding the foil edges securely to keep in the oil. Roast until the garlic has softened, about 1 hour. Transfer the packet to a plate. Open carefully and discard the foil and thyme sprigs.

3. When cool enough to handle, separate the garlic into cloves. Squeeze the soft garlic from each clove into a small bowl and stir until smooth.

Each tablespoon About 25 calories, 1g protein, 3g carbohydrate, 1g fat (0g saturated), 0g fiber, 15mg sodium.

Ingredient Ideas
roasted garlic

BREAD SPREAD Mash roasted garlic with softened butter. Pack into a small crock and serve as a spread for bread.

PAN SAUCE Whisk roasted garlic into the pan juices after roasting a chicken or sautéing meat. Add a squeeze of fresh lemon juice for a fabulous sauce.

SOUP SEASONING Whisk some roasted garlic into homemade or canned minestrone soup for rich flavor.

PIZZA TOPPER Dot a homemade pizza or focaccia with bits of roasted garlic for extra flavor.

VEGETABLE SAUTÉ After steaming green beans, heat oil in a skillet and sauté some halved cherry tomatoes and roasted garlic. Add the beans, season with salt and pepper, and toss until heated through.

Ingredient Ideas
cream cheese

BLACK-BOTTOM BROWNIES

Beat one **8-ounce package cream cheese**, softened, **1 large egg**, and **1½ cup sugar** with a mixer until smooth. Pour over one **18-ounce box prepared brownie mix** in a square baking pan. Bake in a preheated 350°F oven 45 minutes, or until a toothpick comes out almost clean. **Serves 8.**

HOLIDAY CHEESE BALL

Beat one **8-ounce package cream cheese**, softened, **2 cups shredded extra-sharp Cheddar cheese**, and **⅓ cup sour cream** with a mixer until smooth. Roll into a ball, then roll in **¼ cup each chopped pistachios and dried cranberries**. Chill 1 hour. **Serves 8.**

CREAMY BACON-WALNUT PASTA

Cook **1 pound spaghetti** as the label directs; reserve ¾ cup cooking water. Toss the pasta, reserved water, and one **8-ounce package cream cheese**, softened; add **½ cup grated Parmesan cheese**, then **⅓ cup each crumbled bacon and walnut pieces** and toss. **Serves 4.**

CHEESY CHIVE OMELET

Whisk **2 eggs**, **1 tablespoon water**, and **⅛ teaspoon salt**; cook in a small nonstick skillet with **2 teaspoons melted butter**, pushing the eggs toward the center, until almost set. Top with **1 ounce cream cheese** and **2 teaspoons snipped chives**; fold over. **Serves 1.**

SPICY CRAB DIP

Beat one **8-ounce package cream cheese**, softened; **¼ cup milk**; **2 teaspoons hot sauce**; and **1 teaspoon fresh lemon juice** with a mixer until smooth. Fold in **1 cup crabmeat**. Serve with crudités. **Serves 8.**

HOW TO

MAKE FLAVORED VINEGARS

A splash of flavored vinegar can perk up anything from dressings to marinades to fruit plates. They are simple to prep and add zero calories! And they make pretty hostess gifts!

1. Start with a clean wide-mouth quart jar with a tight-fitting lid.

2. Rinse and dry your herbs and other flavorings (below). Add flavorings to the jar.

3. In a medium saucepan, heat 1 quart distilled, white wine or apple cider vinegar to boiling. Pour into the jar, leaving ½ inch headspace. Cover and let stand in a cool dark place for 2 to 4 weeks.

4. Strain vinegar through a fine sieve into a clean 4-cup measure; discard solids.

5. Use a funnel to pour flavored vinegar into decorative bottle(s). Add clean, dry herbs or other flavorings to bottle, if desired. Cover and store at room temperature up to 6 months.

LEMON THYME VINEGAR Peel 1 lemon with a vegetable peeler. Place the peel and 6 sprigs of fresh thyme in the jar.

CHILE CILANTRO VINEGAR Add 2 to 4 halved jalapeño or serrano chiles and 8 sprigs of cilantro to the jar.

STRAWBERRY-MINT Add 1½ cups chopped strawberries and 6 sprigs of mint to the jar.

STAR ANISE AND ORANGE VINEGAR Peel 3 (3-inch) strips of peel from an orange with a vegetable peeler. Add to the jar with 6 star anise.

fennel-roasted olives

PREP: 15 MIN / TOTAL: 45 MIN / MAKES ABOUT 5 CUPS

6 cups assorted olives (not pitted)	2 tablespoons plus ½ cup extra-virgin olive oil
4 cloves garlic, peeled	½ teaspoon ground black pepper
4 strips (3 inches long) lemon zest	¼ cup fennel seeds
4 strips (3 inches long) orange zest	½ cup sherry vinegar

1. Preheat the oven to 425°F. On a large rimmed baking sheet, toss the olives, garlic, zests, 2 tablespoons olive oil, and pepper. Spread in a single layer. Roast 30 minutes, shaking the pan once.

2. Divide the olives, garlic, and zest among 4 (1-pint) jars. Add 1 tablespoon fennel seeds to each. Pour the sherry vinegar and ½ cup extra-virgin olive oil over the olives to cover. Store in the refrigerator up to 1 month.

Each tablespoon About 30 calories, 0g protein, 1g carbohydrate, 3g fat (0g saturated), 0g fiber, 170mg sodium.

 Tip Create an antipasto platter with breadsticks, prosciutto, and marinated vegetables.

spicy citrus vodka

PREP: 15 MIN / TOTAL: 15 MIN, PLUS STANDING / MAKES 3½ CUPS

1 bottle (750 milliliters) vodka	2 jalapeños, seeded and sliced
5 strips (3 inches long) grapefruit peel	

In a bottle, combine the vodka with the grapefruit peel and jalapeños. Cover and let stand 1 day. Strain, pour into bottles, and keep for up to 2 months.

Each tablespoon About 30 calories, 0g protein, 0g carbohydrate, 0g fat (0g saturated), 0g fiber, 0mg sodium.

Serving Suggestion Combine with simple syrup and seltzer for a fierce take on a Greyhound; serve with pineapple juice and ginger ale for a tropical getaway in a glass; add a splash and some chopped fruit to white wine for a spicy sangria.

chai vodka

PREP: 15 MIN / TOTAL: 15 MIN, PLUS STANDING / MAKES 3½ CUPS

- 1 bottle (750 milliliters) vodka
- 3 cinnamon sticks
- 2 tablespoons chopped candied ginger
- 12 black peppercorns
- 10 whole cloves
- 10 cardamom pods, lightly crushed

In a bottle, combine the vodka with the cinnamon sticks, candied ginger, peppercorns, cloves, and cardamom. Cover and let stand at least 1 day or up to 3 days. Strain, pour into bottles, and keep for up to 2 months.

Each tablespoon About 30 calories, 0g protein, 0g carbohydrate, 0g fat (0g saturated), 0g fiber, 0mg sodium.

Serving Suggestion Combine with tea and honey for a twist on a hot toddy; mix with lemonade; use instead of vermouth for a spiced Manhattan.

cucumber tarragon vodka

PREP: 10 MIN / TOTAL: 10 MIN, PLUS STANDING / MAKES 3½ CUPS

- 1 bottle (750 milliliters) vodka
- 1 medium cucumber, thinly sliced
- 4 large sprigs fresh tarragon

In a bottle, combine the vodka with the cucumber and tarragon. Cover and let stand at least 1 day or up to 2 days. Strain, pour into bottles, and keep for up to 2 months.

Each tablespoon About 30 calories, 0g protein, 0g carbohydrate, 0g fat (0g saturated), 0g fiber, 0mg sodium.

Serving Suggestion Combine with lemon juice, Pimm's, and seltzer for an easy Pimm's cup; serve with tonic and lime wedges for a next-level vodka tonic; add to your favorite lemon-lime soda for an insta-cocktail whenever.

FENNEL-ROASTED OLIVES 70

SPICY CITRUS VODKA 70, CHAI VODKA 71, CUCUMBER TARRAGON VODKA 71

Ingredient Ideas
bacon

BAR NUTS

In a 12-inch skillet, cook **6 slices bacon**, chopped, over medium heat 8 minutes, or until browned. Discard the fat. To the bacon in the pan, stir in **2 cups roasted, salted peanuts**; **1 teaspoon sugar**; and **⅛ teaspoon cayenne pepper**. Cook 2 minutes, or until the nuts brown lightly, stirring constantly. **Makes 2½ cups.**

SAVORY SCONES

Preheat the oven to 450°F. In a 12-inch skillet, cook **6 slices bacon** over medium heat until browned. Drain on paper towels; crumble. Transfer bacon and ¼ cup bacon fat to a large bowl. Mix in **2 cups all-purpose flour, 1 tablespoon baking powder, ¼ cup finely chopped green onions**, and **¼ teaspoon each salt and ground black pepper**. Stir in ¾ **cup milk**. Drop the batter by heaping tablespoons onto a baking sheet. Bake 12 minutes, or until golden brown. **Makes 20 scones.**

WILTED KALE SALAD

In a 12-inch skillet over medium heat, cook **6 slices bacon**, chopped, for 8 minutes. Stir in **1 cup chopped onion**; cook 8 minutes, or until tender. In a large bowl, toss **7 cups thinly sliced kale leaves** with **2 tablespoons red wine vinegar, ½ teaspoon salt**, and ¼ **teaspoon ground black pepper**, and then add the bacon mixture.

EASY CARBONARA

Cook **1 pound spaghetti** in boiling salted water 2 minutes less than the label directs. Add **2 cups frozen peas**; cook 2 minutes. Reserve ½ cup cooking water; drain the pasta and peas. Meanwhile, in a 12-inch skillet, cook **6 slices bacon**, chopped, over medium heat 8 minutes, or until browned; reserve the fat. In a large bowl, beat **4 large eggs**, ½ **cup finely grated Pecorino Romano cheese**, 2 tablespoons reserved fat, the reserved cooking water, and ½ **teaspoon each salt and ground black pepper**. Toss in the pasta mixture and bacon. **Serves 6.**

caramelized onion & bacon jam

(See photo on page 75.)

PREP: 20 MIN / TOTAL: 1 HR 50 MIN, PLUS CHILLING / MAKES ABOUT 3 CUPS

1½ pounds bacon, finely chopped	½ cup balsamic vinegar
3 large onions, finely chopped	½ cup packed brown sugar
1 medium leek, finely chopped	½ teaspoon dried oregano
2 cloves garlic, finely chopped	¼ teaspoon ground nutmeg
½ teaspoon salt	½ teaspoon coarsely ground black pepper

1. In a deep 12-inch skillet, cook the bacon over medium heat 30 minutes or until crisp and the fat has rendered, stirring occasionally. With a slotted spoon, transfer the bacon to a paper-towel-lined plate. Remove and discard all but 2 tablespoons bacon fat from the skillet.

2. To the fat in the skillet, add the onions, leek, garlic, and salt. Cook over medium heat 50 minutes, or until caramelized and soft, stirring occasionally. Add the vinegar, brown sugar, oregano, nutmeg, pepper, and bacon. Cook 15 minutes, or until the onions are very soft.

3. Transfer the mixture to a food processor; pulse until finely chopped. Transfer to four 8-ounce jars; refrigerate until cold. Jam may be refrigerated up to 2 weeks.

Each tablespoon About 45 calories, 2g protein, 4g carbohydrate, 3g fat (1g saturated), 0g fiber, 95mg sodium.

Serving Suggestion Spread on baguette slices with goat cheese for hors d'oeuvres; use in a grilled cheese with apples; spread on pizza dough instead of tomato sauce; mix with egg yolks for deviled eggs; use to top baked potatoes or burgers; or stir into barbecued beans.

10-minute jam

(See photo on page 75.)

PREP: 5 MIN / TOTAL: 10 MIN, PLUS COOLING / MAKES ¾ CUP

2 cups berries   **⅓ cup granulated sugar**

In a large microwave-safe bowl, mash the berries and sugar. Microwave, uncovered, on High 10 minutes, stirring once. Cool completely.

Each tablespoon About 30 calories, 0g protein, 8g carbohydrate, 0g fat (0g saturated), 1g fiber, 0mg sodium.

apple butter

PREP: 30 MIN / TOTAL: 2 HR / MAKES 4 CUPS

5 pounds assorted apples, peeled, cored, and each cut into 8 wedges

1½ cups apple cider

5 strips lemon peel

3 tablespoons fresh lemon juice

1 cinnamon stick

1 cup packed brown sugar

1. In a 6-quart Dutch oven, combine all ingredients except the sugar; heat to boiling. Reduce heat and simmer on medium, partially covered, 20 minutes or until the apples are soft, stirring occasionally.

2. Stir in the sugar; heat to boiling on high. Reduce heat to medium-low; cook, partially covered, 45 to 55 minutes or until very thick, stirring often and breaking up the apples. Increase heat to medium-high; cook, stirring, until a spatula run along the bottom of the pan leaves a clean trail, 10 to 15 minutes.

3. Discard the cinnamon stick. Transfer to a food processor; puree until smooth. Refrigerate, in an airtight container, up to 3 weeks, or freeze up to 6 months.

Each tablespoon About 30 calories, 0g protein, 8g carbohydrate, 0g fat (0g saturated), 0g fiber, 2mg sodium.

Ingredient Ideas
homemade jams

PROSCIUTTO-MELON PANINI

On a split **ciabatta roll**, spread **2 tablespoons Cantaloupe Jam** (page 74); layer the bottom with **4 thin slices of mozzarella cheese**, **4 slices prosciutto**, and a **handful of arugula**. Replace the top. Bake in a preheated 425°F oven until the cheese melts. **Serves 1.**

PEACH SHORTCAKES

Split **8 homemade or store-bought biscuits**. Fill each with **3 tablespoons whipped cream**; top with **1 tablespoon Peach & Honey Jam** (page 74). **Serves 8.**

BERRY-STUFFED CUPCAKES

With a paring knife held at an angle, cut the centers from the tops of **2 dozen vanilla cupcakes**. Fill each hole with **1 teaspoon Mixed Berry Jam** (page 74). Into **2½ cups vanilla frosting**, stir **1 tablespoon Mixed Berry Jam**. Spoon the frosting into a piping bag fitted with a pastry tip; pipe onto the cupcakes. **Serves 24.**

PEPPERY AVOCADO TOAST

Mash **½ small ripe avocado** with **½ teaspoon fresh lime juice** and **⅛ teaspoon salt**; spread on **1 large slice whole wheat sourdough bread**, toasted. Top with **1 tablespoon Tomato–Black Pepper Jam** (page 74). **Serves 1.**

INGREDIENT SPOTLIGHT

Pectin is a natural, fruit-based ingredient used to thicken jams and jellies. For best results, Ball® RealFruit™ Low or No-Sugar Flex Batch Needed Pectin was tops in our recipes. If you use Sure-Jell® Premium Fruit Pectin (for less- or no-sugar-needed recipes), increase the amount of pectin by 50 percent and omit the water.

cranberry sauce

PREP: 5 MIN / TOTAL: 15 MIN / MAKES ABOUT 2 CUPS

1 bag (12 ounces) cranberries

½ cup sugar
¼ cup water

In a 2-quart saucepan, heat the cranberries, sugar, and water to boiling over high heat, stirring occasionally. Reduce the heat; simmer 5 to 10 minutes, or until the cranberries pop and the sauce thickens. Transfer to a container and refrigerate until chilled, 1 hour or up to 3 days.

Each tablespoon About 15 calories, 0g protein, 4g carbohydrate, 0g fat (0g saturated), 0g fiber, 0mg sodium.

VARIATIONS

Warm Spiced Cranberry Sauce

Add **2 whole star anise** and **2 cinnamon sticks**. Instead of water, use ¼ **cup orange juice**.

Sweet Heat Cranberry Sauce

Add **1 pickled jalapeño chile**, chopped, and **2 tablespoons honey**. Instead of water, use ¼ **cup cider vinegar**.

Gingery Citrus Cranberry Sauce

Add **1 tablespoon grated, peeled fresh ginger** and **1 teaspoon grated lemon zest**. Instead of water, use ¼ **cup apple cider**.

cranberry orange relish

PREP: 15 MIN / TOTAL: 15 MIN, PLUS CHILLING / MAKES 3 CUPS

1 bag (12 ounces) cranberries, picked over and rinsed

1 medium orange, cut into pieces, seeds discarded
⅔ cup sugar

In a food processor with the knife blade attached, combine the cranberries, orange, and sugar; pulse until coarsely chopped. Transfer to a bowl. Cover and refrigerate until well-chilled, about 2 hours or up to 2 days.

Each ¼ cup About 60 calories, 0g protein, 17g carbohydrate, 0g fat (0g saturated), 1g fiber, 0mg sodium.

peach & honey jam

PREP: 15 MIN / TOTAL: 30 MIN / MAKES ABOUT 2½ CUPS

3 cups coarsely chopped peeled ripe peaches (about 5 medium)
⅔ cup water
3 tablespoons lemon juice

1 tablespoon powdered no- or low-sugar pectin
½ cup sugar
⅓ cup honey

1. In a food processor, pulse the peaches until finely chopped, stopping and stirring occasionally.

2. In a 4-quart saucepan, combine the peaches, water, and lemon juice; stir in the pectin. Stirring frequently, heat over high heat to a vigorous boil that cannot be stirred down. Stir in the sugar and honey. Return to a vigorous boil that cannot be stirred down, stirring constantly. Boil 1 minute. Remove from the heat.

3. Transfer the mixture to heatproof jars or a container. Let cool at room temperature. Cover and refrigerate overnight or until set. Keeps, refrigerated, for 1 month.

Each tablespoon About 25 calories, 0g protein, 6g carbohydrate, 0g fat (0g saturated), 0g fiber, 1mg sodium.

VARIATIONS

Tomato–Black Pepper Jam

In step 1, replace the peaches with **4 cups coarsely chopped ripe tomatoes** (about 5 medium). In step 2, use ⅓ **cup water** and **2 tablespoons fresh lemon juice**. In step 3, stir in ¼ **teaspoon salt** and ½ **teaspoon ground black pepper** before transferring the mixture to jars. Makes 4 cups.

Cantaloupe Jam

In step 1, replace the peaches with **3 cups coarsely chopped ripe cantaloupe**. In step 2, use **2 tablespoons pectin**. Boil 3 minutes instead of 1 minute. Makes 3 cups.

Mixed Berry Jam

In step 1, replace the peaches with **3 cups mixed fresh raspberries, blueberries, and blackberries**. Makes about 2½ cups.

10-MINUTE JAM 73

CRANBERRY SAUCE 74

CARAMELIZED ONION & BACON JAM 72

TOMATO–BLACK PEPPER JAM, MIXED BERRY JAM,
CANTALOUPE JAM, AND PEACH & HONEY JAM 74

HOMEMADE CARAMEL SAUCE 76

CHOCO-NUT SPREAD 77

homemade caramel sauce

PREP: 20 MIN / TOTAL: 20 MIN / MAKES ABOUT 2⅓ CUPS

2 cups sugar

½ cup water

2 tablespoons light corn syrup

1 cup heavy cream, warmed

4 tablespoons salted butter, softened

1 teaspoon vanilla extract

½ teaspoon salt

1. In a 4-quart saucepan, stir together the sugar, water, and corn syrup. With a pastry brush dipped in water, brush any sugar crystals off the side of the pan. Heat to boiling over medium-high heat without stirring, about 3 minutes. Boil until dark amber (320°F to 345°F on a candy thermometer, if using), about 9 minutes.

2. Working quickly, remove the pan from the heat and add the heavy cream and butter, stirring until smooth (the caramel will steam and bubble up).

3. Let the caramel cool slightly. Stir in the vanilla extract and salt. Let cool completely. Store at room temperature up to 1 month or in the refrigerator up to 2 months. Reheat in the microwave 1 minute before serving.

Each tablespoon About 80 calories, 0g protein, 12g carbohydrate, 4g fat (2g saturated), 0g fiber, 44mg sodium.

Ingredient Ideas

homemade caramel sauce

TOFFEE "PUDDING" TRIFLE

In a small serving bowl, layer a handful of bite-size **angel food cake** pieces, **2 tablespoons whipped cream**, **1 tablespoon Homemade Caramel Sauce**, and **1 tablespoon chopped candied walnuts or pecans**. Repeat the layering once. Serves 1.

CAFÉ AU RUM

Spoon **1 to 2 tablespoons Homemade Caramel Sauce** into the bottom of a coffee cup. Add a **shot of dark rum** and stir to blend. Pour on **hot coffee** and top with **whipped cream** if desired. Serves 1.

sublime chocolate sauce

PREP: 5 MIN / TOTAL: 15 MIN / MAKES 1¾ CUPS

- 4 squares (4 ounces) unsweetened chocolate, chopped
- 1 cup heavy or whipped cream
- ¾ cup sugar
- 2 tablespoons light corn syrup
- 2 tablespoons butter
- 2 teaspoons vanilla extract

1. In a heavy 2-quart saucepan, combine the chopped chocolate, cream, sugar, and corn syrup; heat to boiling over high heat, stirring constantly. Reduce the heat to medium. Cook at a gentle boil, stirring constantly, until the sauce has thickened slightly, about 5 minutes.

2. Remove from the heat; stir in the butter and vanilla until smooth and glossy. Serve hot, or cool completely, then cover and refrigerate up to 1 week. Gently reheat before using.

Each tablespoon About 85 calories, 1g protein, 8g carbohydrate, 6g fat (4g saturated), 1g fiber, 15mg sodium.

Tip Coconut Milk Whipped Cream: Chill a 15-ounce can of unsweetened coconut milk overnight, scoop out the cream that rises to the top, and beat until soft peaks form—easy and dairy-free!

choco-nut spread

PREP: 30 MIN / TOTAL: 40 MIN, PLUS COOLING / MAKES ABOUT 2 CUPS

- 1 cup hazelnuts
- ½ teaspoon salt
- 3½ ounces dark chocolate, chopped
- 1 cup sweetened condensed milk
- 2 tablespoons light corn syrup

1. Preheat the oven to 375°F. Roast the hazelnuts on a rimmed baking sheet 10 minutes, shaking the baking sheet once or twice. Wrap the hot hazelnuts in a kitchen towel and roll vigorously to remove most peels; cool completely.

2. In a food processor, process the peeled hazelnuts and salt until mostly smooth and runny, about 8 minutes, stopping and scraping the side of the bowl occasionally.

3. In a microwave-safe bowl, melt the chocolate in 20-second intervals; stir in the condensed milk and corn syrup. Add the chocolate mixture to the pureed hazelnuts; pulse until just combined. Store in an airtight container at room temperature up to 2 weeks.

Each tablespoon About 80 calories, 2g protein, 8g carbohydrate, 5g fat (1g saturated), 1g fiber, 50mg sodium.

VARIATIONS

Mixed-Nut Spread
Skip step 1. In step 2, replace the hazelnuts with ¾ cup pecans and ¼ cup unsalted cashews.

Mocha Spread
In step 3, add 2 tablespoons espresso powder to the melted chocolate.

Vanilla-Bourbon Spread
In step 2, add 2 tablespoons bourbon and ½ teaspoon vanilla extract to the nuts before processing.

Ingredient Ideas
choco-nut spread

NO-BAKE MOCHA CHEESECAKE

With an electric mixer on high speed, beat 8 ounces softened cream cheese, ¾ cup Mocha Spread, and ¼ cup confectioners' sugar until smooth. Fold in 1 cup whipped cream. Transfer to a prepared graham cracker crust; refrigerate at least 4 hours or up to 1 day. Dollop additional whipped cream on top of the pie. Garnish with shaved chocolate. Serves 6.

NUTTY BANANA PANINI

Spread four ½-inch slices of pound cake with 2 tablespoons Choco-Nut Spread each; top 2 cake slices with ½ banana, sliced, then the remaining cake slices. Melt 1 tablespoon butter in an 8-inch nonstick skillet over medium heat. Place the sandwiches in the pan and gently press down with another small pot or skillet. Cook 4 to 5 minutes to brown the bottoms, turning over halfway through. Serves 2.

CHOCOLATE-BOURBON MILKSHAKE

Blend ½ cup Vanilla-Bourbon Spread with 1 large scoop vanilla ice cream, ¼ cup milk, and ¼ cup Irish cream liqueur until smooth. Serves 1.

APPETIZERS &
drinks

A platter of sticky chicken wings, a rainbow of veggies with a savory dip, a basket of warm cheesy *gougère* ... there's something come-hither about finger foods. Whether you call them appetizers, nibbles, snacks, or hors d'oeuvres, they set the tone for your event. For a dinner party, choose one or two light options. Cocktail parties showcase hors d'oeuvres as the meal, so plot a variety of textures, colors, and flavors. Be sure to include a selection of vegetable-, bread-, meat-, and fish-based options.

Some of our favorite appetizers like Chickpea Nuts (page 100) and Cauliflower "Popcorn" (page 89) are perfect for snacks any day of the week. Consider a signature cocktail for your party. It will add a festive touch and be easy on your budget. Choose a pitcher of Sangria (page 111) or one of our party ices; there are nonalcoholic versions, too.

BERRY & CITRUS SPRITZER 107

FRICO CUPS WITH GRAPE TOMATO, OLIVE & FETA SALAD 86

TOMATO & MOZZARELLA BITES 87

HOMEMADE IRISH CREAM 113

Back-Pocket Appetizers To Make Ahead

CRUDITÉS All vegetables can be prepared up to one day ahead. Asparagus, broccoli, green beans, and cauliflower benefit from quick cooking in boiling water for 1 minute. Drain, rinse under cold water until cool, and pat dry. Wrap all cut-up vegetables in damp paper towels and refrigerate separately in plastic bags.

DIPS AND SPREADS (except guacamole) can be made up to several days ahead and refrigerated.

PÂTÉS AND RILLETTES taste best if made one to two days ahead. They can be frozen for up to two months. Defrost overnight in the refrigerator.

PASTRY APPETIZERS can be frozen, raw or baked, for up to one month. Layer them in baking pans, separating the layers with waxed paper, then double wrap in foil. Arrange baked pastries on cookie sheets and reheat at 350°F for about 10 minutes. Bake frozen raw pastries as the recipe directs, allowing extra time.

TEA SANDWICHES can be assembled up to four hours ahead. Arrange in baking sheets. Separate the layers with damp paper towels, wrap with plastic wrap, and refrigerate.

Make Appetizers More Appetizing

THINK BEYOND THE PLATTER Arrange cut-up vegetables on a tray or in a large basket lined with plastic wrap and covered with leafy greens. Stand cheese straws and breadsticks in jars or glasses.

BE CREATIVE Serve dips and spreads in hollowed-out loaves of bread or vegetables. Serve saucy one bite items in Chinese spoons.

HEIGHTEN THE DRAMA Place platters on inverted baking dishes or pedestals covered with brightly colored napkins.

5 PLANNING TIPS FROM THE PROS

1
Appetizers should: be easy to handle, not be messy, need no utensils, and be enjoyable in a couple of bites.

2
Serve only one or two appetizers that require last-minute prep.

3
Plan on only one or two hot appetizers unless you have more than one oven.

4
Figure about ten to twelve appetizers per person if no meal follows. Otherwise, allow five or six pieces.

5
Remove cold appetizers from the fridge a half hour before serving.

PUFF PASTRY MINIS (PAGE 83) WITH BUTTERY SAUTÉED MUSHROOMS (PAGE 83), ROASTED RED PEPPER & ARUGULA

ROOT-VEGGIE LATKES (PAGE 83) WITH SMOKED SALMON SPREAD (PAGE 84), RED ONION & LEMON ZEST

PUFF PASTRY MINIS (PAGE 83) WITH CHICKEN LIVER MOUSSE, CARMELIZED ONIONS (PAGE 84), PISTACHIOS & APPLE

PUFF PASTRY MINIS (PAGE 83) WITH LEMONY WHIPPED RICOTTA (PAGE 84), SALMON CAVIAR, CHIVES & BLACK PEPPER

BASES

puff pastry minis

PREP: 10 MIN / TOTAL: 30 MIN / MAKES 50 PIECES

1 sheet frozen puff pastry, thawed

1. Preheat the oven to 400°F. Unfold the puff pastry onto parchment-lined large baking sheet; roll into a 10-inch square. With a sharp chef's knife, cut the pastry into 2 × 1-inch rectangles. Separate and lay the pieces on the parchment, spacing them 1 inch apart; prick with fork.

2. Cover the pastry with another sheet of parchment and another baking sheet. Bake 15 minutes. Remove the top baking sheet and parchment. Bake 5 minutes longer, or until the pastry is brown on the bottom. Cool completely. Pieces can be stored in an airtight container at room temperature up to 2 days.

Each piece About 20 calories, 0g protein, 2g carbohydrate, 1g fat (0g saturated), 0g fiber, 24mg sodium.

root-veggie latkes

PREP: 15 MIN / TOTAL: 45 MIN / MAKES ABOUT 24

1 medium russet potato
1 small peeled sweet potato, grated
1 small peeled carrot, grated
1 large egg, beaten
½ teaspoon salt
½ teaspoon ground black pepper
Nonstick cooking spray

1. Preheat the oven to 425°F. Onto a clean kitchen towel, grate the russet potato. Squeeze it very dry. In a large bowl, combine the potato with the sweet potato, carrot, egg, salt, and pepper.

2. Spray 1 large baking sheet with nonstick cooking spray. Scoop the mixture by heaping tablespoons onto the prepared sheet, 1 inch apart. Flatten to form even disks; spray the tops generously with cooking spray. Bake 30 minutes, or until browned and crisp, turning over once with a stiff, thin spatula. Serve immediately or store at room temperature up to 3 hours. Reheat in a preheated 375°F oven for 7 minutes.

Each latke About 15 calories, 1g protein, 2g carbohydrate, 0g fat (0g saturated), 0g fiber, 55mg sodium.

TOPPINGS

buttery sautéed mushrooms

PREP: 15 MIN / TOTAL: 35 MIN / MAKES 3 CUPS

1 small leek, chopped
Salt
3 tablespoons olive oil
1½ pounds mixed mushrooms, thinly sliced
½ teaspoon ground black pepper
¼ cup dry white wine
2 tablespoons cream
1 tablespoon butter

1. In a deep 12-inch skillet over medium heat, cook the leek and a pinch of salt in the olive oil 5 minutes, stirring. Add the mushrooms, ½ teaspoon salt, and pepper. Cook 12 minutes, or until tender, stirring. Add the white wine; cook 1 minute, scraping the pan.

2. Off the heat, stir in the cream and butter. Refrigerate, covered, up to 3 days.

Each tablespoon About 10 calories, 0g protein, 1g carbohydrate, 1g fat (0g saturated), 0g fiber, 31mg sodium.

HOW TO

DIY CANAPES

Set out a variety of bases: Puff Pastry Minis, Root-Veggie Latkes, sliced cucumbers, water crackers, etc. Arrange several toppings and garnishes in small bowls and let guests customize their Instagram® moment.

caramelized onions

(See photo on page 82.)

PREP: 10 MIN / TOTAL: 35 MIN / MAKES 1 CUP

- 3 large onions, peeled and thinly sliced
- 3 tablespoons olive oil
- 2 cloves garlic, chopped
- 1 teaspoon fresh thyme
- ¼ teaspoon salt
- 2 tablespoons balsamic vinegar

In a 12-inch skillet over medium heat, cook the onions, olive oil, garlic, thyme, and salt 25 minutes, or until dark brown, stirring. Remove from the heat. Stir in the balsamic vinegar. Refrigerate, covered, up to 3 days.

Each tablespoon About 35 calories, 0g protein, 3g carbohydrate, 3g fat (0g saturated), 0g fiber, 38mg sodium.

smoked salmon spread

(See photo on page 82.)

PREP: 10 MIN / TOTAL: 10 MIN / MAKES 1½ CUPS

- 2 ounces cream cheese, softened
- ¼ cup sour cream
- 4 ounces smoked salmon, finely chopped
- 1 hard-cooked egg, coarsely grated
- 1 tablespoon capers, chopped
- 1 tablespoon fresh lemon juice
- 1 teaspoon snipped fresh chives
- ¼ teaspoon ground black pepper

In a medium bowl, stir the cream cheese with the sour cream until smooth. Fold in the smoked salmon, egg, capers, lemon juice, chives, and pepper. Refrigerate, covered, up to 3 days.

Each tablespoon About 20 calories, 2g protein, 0g carbohydrate, 2g fat (1g saturated), 0g fiber, 65mg sodium.

lemony whipped ricotta

(See photo on page 82.)

PREP: 10 MIN / TOTAL: 10 MIN / MAKES 2¼ CUPS

- 4 ounces cream cheese, softened
- 1½ cups ricotta cheese
- ¼ cup grated Pecorino cheese
- 3 tablespoons milk
- ¼ teaspoon salt
- ¼ teaspoon ground black pepper
- ½ teaspoon grated lemon zest

With an electric mixer on medium speed, beat the cream cheese until fluffy. Mix in the ricotta, Pecorino, milk, salt, and pepper until smooth. Fold in the lemon zest. Refrigerate, covered, up to 3 days.

Each tablespoon About 35 calories, 2g protein, 1g carbohydrate, 3g fat (2g saturated), 0g fiber, 50mg sodium.

beet tapenade

PREP: 10 MIN / TOTAL: 10 MIN / MAKES 1¼ CUPS

- 1 orange
- ⅔ cup pitted green olives
- ¼ cup packed fresh basil leaves
- 1 clove garlic
- 4 ounces cooked beets, blotted dry and chopped
- ¼ cup olive oil
- ⅛ teaspoon salt
- ¼ teaspoon ground black pepper

1. From the orange, grate ¼ teaspoon zest and squeeze 2 tablespoons juice.

2. In a food processor, pulse the olives, basil, garlic, orange zest, and orange juice until chopped, scraping the processor as needed. Add the cooked beets, olive oil, salt, and pepper. Pulse until just chopped, scraping. Refrigerate, covered, up to 1 day.

Each tablespoon About 30 calories, 0g protein, 1g carbohydrate, 3g fat (0g saturated), 0g fiber, 79mg sodium.

prosciutto crisps

PREP: 5 MIN / TOTAL: 20 MIN / SERVES 8

4 ounces thinly sliced prosciutto

Preheat the oven to 375°F. On a parchment-lined rimmed baking sheet, arrange the prosciutto in a single layer. Bake 15 minutes. Transfer to paper towels; cool. Store at room temperature up to 2 days.

Each serving About 30 calories, 4g protein, 0g carbohydrate, 2g fat (0g saturated), 0g fiber, 330mg sodium.

itty-bitty taco cups

(See photo on page 88.)

PREP: 15 MIN / TOTAL: 30 MIN / MAKES 24

Nonstick cooking spray
24 wonton wrappers, each cut horizontally in half
1 tablespoon vegetable oil
8 ounces ground beef
1 tablespoon taco seasoning
1½ cups shredded Cheddar cheese
½ cup pico de gallo
¼ cup sour cream
Chopped fresh cilantro and hot sauce, for garnish (optional)

1. Preheat the oven to 375°F. Spray 24 mini muffin cups with non-stick cooking spray.

2. Place 2 wonton halves in each cup, overlapping them to form an X. Bake 6 to 8 minutes, or until golden and crisp.

3. In a 10-inch skillet, heat the oil over medium-high heat and brown the beef until cooked through. Add the taco seasoning and simmer 1 to 2 minutes, or until thickened, stirring.

4. In each wonton cup, layer a scant 1 tablespoon meat mixture and 1 tablespoon cheese. Return to the oven and bake 5 minutes, or until the edges are golden brown.

5. Top the cups with pico de gallo and sour cream; garnish with cilantro and hot sauce, if desired.

Each cup About 85 calories, 4g protein, 5g carbohydrate, 5g fat (2g saturated), 0g fiber, 120mg sodium.

caponata

PREP: 30 MIN / TOTAL: 1 HR 25 MIN, PLUS COOLING / MAKES ABOUT 5 CUPS

2 small eggplants (1 pound each), ends trimmed, cut into ¾-inch pieces
½ cup extra-virgin olive oil
¼ teaspoon salt
3 small red onions, peeled and thinly sliced
1½ pounds ripe tomatoes (4 medium), peeled and seeded, chopped
1 cup olives, such as Gaeta, green Sicilian, or Kalamata, pitted and chopped
3 tablespoons capers, drained
3 tablespoons golden raisins
¼ teaspoon coarsely ground black pepper
4 stalks celery with leaves, thinly sliced
⅓ cup red wine vinegar
2 teaspoons sugar
¼ cup chopped fresh flat-leaf parsley

1. Preheat the oven to 450°F. In 2 rimmed baking sheets, place the eggplant, dividing evenly. Drizzle with ¼ cup oil and sprinkle with salt; toss to coat. Roast the eggplant 10 minutes; stir, then roast until browned, about 10 minutes longer.

2. Meanwhile, in a 12-inch nonstick skillet, heat the remaining ¼ cup oil over medium heat. Add the onions and cook, stirring, until tender and golden, about 10 minutes. Add the tomatoes, olives, capers, raisins, and pepper. Reduce the heat; cover and simmer 15 minutes.

3. Add the eggplant and celery to the skillet and cook, uncovered, over medium heat, stirring frequently, until the celery is just tender, 8 to 10 minutes. Stir in the vinegar and sugar and cook 1 minute longer. Cool to room temperature, or cover and refrigerate up to overnight. To serve, sprinkle with parsley.

Each ¼ cup About 105 calories, 1g protein, 9g carbohydrate, 8g fat (1g saturated), 2g fiber, 335mg sodium.

frico cups

(See photo on page 80.)

PREP: 20 MIN / TOTAL: 40 MIN / MAKES 24

> **6 ounces Parmesan cheese, coarsely grated (1½ cups)**

1. Preheat the oven to 375°F. Line a large baking sheet with a silicone bakeware liner. Drop 3 level tablespoons Parmesan cheese 3 inches apart onto the baking sheet; spread it out to form rounds.

2. Bake until the edges just begin to color, 6 to 7 minutes. Use a thin metal spatula to quickly transfer each round to a muffin pan, pressing lightly in the centers. Cool before filling.

Each crisp About 30 calories, 3g protein, 0g carbohydrate, 2g fat (1g saturated), 0g fiber, 115mg sodium.

VARIATIONS

Parmesan Crisps

Arrange by 1 tablespoonfuls on a silicone bakeware liner. Bake 6 minutes per batch. Transfer the crisps, still on a bakeware liner, to a wire rack; cool 2 minutes. Transfer to paper towels to drain. Repeat with the remaining Parmesan.

Cheddar Crisps

Prepare as directed above but substitute **6 ounces sharp Cheddar cheese**, coarsely shredded (1½ cups) for the Parmesan. Bake until bubbling but not browned, 6 to 7 minutes per batch.

 **GLOSSARY** → **Frico** (pronounced "FREE-koh") is what Italians call the wafer-like crisp that forms when you bake or fry shredded cheese.

grape tomato, olive & feta salad

(See photo on page 80.)

PREP: 15 MIN / TOTAL: 15 MIN / SERVES 4

> **4 cups grape tomatoes, halved**
>
> **¼ cup sliced pitted green olives**
>
> **⅓ cups crumbled feta cheese**
>
> **1 tablespoon sherry vinegar**
>
> **1 tablespoon olive oil**
>
> **Salt and ground black pepper**
>
> **Fresh basil, for garnish**

In a medium bowl, combine the grape tomatoes, olives, feta, sherry vinegar, and olive oil. Season to taste with salt and pepper. Garnish with basil. Serve in Frico Cups or as desired.

Each serving About 100 calories, 3g protein, 7g carbohydrate, 8g fat (3g saturated), 2g fiber, 240mg sodium.

sesame, cucumber & radish salad

PREP: 10 MIN / TOTAL: 10 MIN / SERVES 4

> **1 English (seedless) cucumber**
>
> **3 large radishes**
>
> **1 tablespoon fresh lime juice**
>
> **2 teaspoons toasted sesame oil**
>
> **2 tablespoons black and white sesame seeds**
>
> **Salt and ground black pepper**

Finely chop the cucumber and slice the radishes. Toss with lime juice, toasted sesame oil, and sesame seeds. Season to taste with salt and pepper. Serve in Frico Cups or as desired.

Each serving About 55 calories, 2g protein, 3g carbohydrate, 5g fat (1g saturated), 2g fiber, 295mg sodium.

farro, corn & green onion salad

PREP: 15 MIN / TOTAL: 40 MIN / SERVES 4

- 4 ears corn, husked
- 2 cups cooked farro
- 2 thinly sliced green onions
- 3 tablespoons fresh lemon juice
- 1½ tablespoons olive oil
- Salt and ground black pepper

Preheat an outdoor grill for direct grilling over medium-high heat. Grill the corn 10 minutes, turning occasionally. Remove from grill; let cool. Cut the kernels into a large bowl; toss with the cooked farro, green onions, lemon juice, and olive oil. Season to taste with salt and pepper. Serve in Frico Cups or as desired.

Each serving About 305 calories, 10g protein, 55g carbohydrate, 8g fat (1g saturated), 7g fiber, 310mg sodium.

tomato & mozzarella bites

(See photo on page 80.)

PREP: 15 MIN / TOTAL: 15 MIN / MAKES 20 SKEWERS

- 2 tablespoons olive oil
- 2 tablespoons white balsamic vinegar
- ¼ teaspoon dried oregano
- ¼ teaspoon salt
- ¼ teaspoon ground black pepper
- 20 mini fresh mozzarella balls (ciliegini)
- 20 grape tomatoes
- 40 basil leaves

In a large bowl, whisk the olive oil, vinegar, oregano, salt, and pepper. Add the mozzarella balls, tossing to coat. Thread the mozzarella onto skewers, alternating with grape tomatoes and basil leaves.

Each skewer About 95 calories, 5g protein, 1g carbohydrate, 8g fat (4g saturated), 0g fiber, 45mg sodium.

mozzarella in carrozza

PREP: 20 MIN / TOTAL: 25 MIN / SERVES 8

- 8 ounces part-skim mozzarella cheese
- 8 slices firm white bread, crusts removed
- 2 large eggs, well beaten
- ¼ cup milk
- ¼ cup all-purpose flour
- ½ teaspoon salt
- ¼ teaspoon ground black pepper
- ½ cup plain dried bread crumbs
- 3 tablespoons vegetable oil
- 4 tablespoons butter
- 8 anchovy fillets, drained
- 1 tablespoon chopped fresh parsley
- 1 teaspoon capers, drained
- 1 teaspoon fresh lemon juice

1. Stand the mozzarella on its side and cut it lengthwise into 4 equal slices. Place 1 slice cheese between 2 slices bread to form a sandwich. Repeat with the remaining cheese and bread.

2. Preheat the oven to 200°F.

3. In a pie plate and using a wire whisk, beat the eggs and milk. On waxed paper, combine the flour, salt, and pepper; spread the bread crumbs out on a separate sheet of waxed paper. Dip the sandwiches, one at a time, in the flour mixture, shaking off the excess, then in the egg mixture, and finally in the bread crumbs, shaking off the excess.

4. In a 12-inch nonstick skillet, heat the oil over medium heat until hot. Add the sandwiches; cook until golden brown, about 1½ minutes per side. Cut each sandwich on the diagonal in half. Arrange the sandwiches on a platter in a single layer. Keep warm in the oven.

5. In the same skillet, melt the butter; add the anchovies and cook, stirring constantly, 1 minute. Add the parsley, capers, and lemon juice; cook 30 seconds longer. Transfer the sauce to a small bowl. Serve the sauce with sandwiches.

Each serving About 310 calories, 13g protein, 22g carbohydrate, 19g fat (8g saturated), 1g fiber, 715mg sodium.

GLOSSARY → This Italian dish translates to **"mozzarella in a carriage"** and is usually deep-fried.

VEGGIE ROLLS 89

CAULIFLOWER "POPCORN" 89

ITTY-BITTY TACO CUPS 85

CAULIFLOWER TAPENADE 90

veggie rolls

PREP: 40 MIN / TOTAL: 40 MIN / MAKES 20 ROLLS

- 4 zucchini or yellow squash
- 8 ounces cream cheese, softened
- ⅛ teaspoon salt
- Flavorings, veggies, and/or fruits (below)

1. With a vegetable peeler, peel the squash into wide ribbons.

2. Mix the cream cheese and salt with flavorings.

3. Cut vegetables and fruits into 2-inch-long matchsticks. Spread 1 tablespoon flavored cream cheese on one end of veggie ribbon. Add veggie/fruit sticks and roll each tightly into a bundle. Make up to 1 hour ahead; let stand at room temperature.

RED PEPPER–BASIL Mix ½ **cup roasted red peppers**, finely chopped, into the cream cheese. Serve with basil, bell peppers, and green apples.

ASIAN GARDEN Mix **1 tablespoon soy sauce** and **2 teaspoons fresh lime juice** into the cream cheese. Roll with radishes, green onions, and carrots.

VEGGIE CHILI Mix ½ **cup shredded Cheddar cheese** and **1 teaspoon chili powder** into the cream cheese. Roll with cilantro, cucumber, and jicama.

ZIPPY PEAR Mix **1½ tablespoons bottled horseradish** and **1 tablespoon snipped fresh chives** into the cream cheese. Roll with parsley, pears, and celery.

RED PEPPER–BASIL Each roll About 65 calories, 1g protein, 4g carbohydrate, 5g fat (3g saturated), 1g fiber, 80mg sodium.
ASIAN GARDEN Each roll About 55 calories, 1g protein, 3g carbohydrate, 5g fat (3g saturated), 1g fiber, 131mg sodium.
VEGGIE CHILI Each roll About 75 calories, 2g protein, 3g carbohydrate, 6g fat (4g saturated), 1g fiber, 93mg sodium.
ZIPPY PEAR Each roll About 60 calories, 1g protein, 4g carbohydrate, 5g fat (3g saturated), 1g fiber, 78mg sodium.

cauliflower "popcorn"

PREP: 10 MIN / TOTAL: 40 MIN / SERVES 6

- 8 cups small cauliflower florets (about 1¼ pounds), stems trimmed
- 3 tablespoons olive oil
- ¼ cup grated Parmesan cheese
- 1 teaspoon garlic powder
- ½ teaspoon ground turmeric
- ½ teaspoon salt

1. Preheat the oven to 475°F.

2. On a large rimmed baking sheet, toss the cauliflower florets with olive oil, grated Parmesan, garlic powder, turmeric, and salt. Roast 25 to 30 minutes, or until browned and tender. Serve immediately.

Each serving About 110 calories, 4g protein, 8g carbohydrate, 8g fat (2g saturated), 3g fiber, 267mg sodium.

VARIATIONS

Truffle

Omit the Parmesan, garlic powder, and turmeric. Toss the roasted cauliflower with **2 tablespoons truffle butter** and ½ **teaspoon pepper** before serving.

Chili Lime

Substitute **1 teaspoon chili powder** for the Parmesan and turmeric. Grate the **zest of 1 lime** over roasted cauliflower before serving.

#SavetheFood
leftover stems?

Peel and slice cauliflower stems for a crunchy snack with hummus or use them to make quick pickles.

cauliflower tapenade

(See photo on page 88.)

PREP: 20 MIN / TOTAL: 25 MIN, PLUS CHILLING / SERVES 8

3 cups cauliflower florets (about 12 ounces)
2 tablespoons water
1 cup olive oil
1 cup pitted green olives
2 green onions, sliced
2 tablespoons fresh lemon juice
½ teaspoon salt
Baguette slices or crudités, for serving

1. In a microwave-safe bowl, combine the cauliflower and water. Cover; microwave on High 7 minutes, or until very soft. Let cool.

2. In a blender, combine the oil, olives, green onions, and lemon juice; blend until mostly smooth. Add the cauliflower and salt; blend until smooth, stopping and stirring occasionally. Refrigerate until cool. Serve with baguette slices or crudités.

Each serving About 275 calories, 1g protein, 3g carbohydrate, 29g fat (4g saturated), 1g fiber, 390mg sodium.

artichoke dip

PREP: 10 MIN / TOTAL: 10 MIN / MAKES ABOUT 1¼ CUPS

1 lemon
1 can (13¾ ounces) artichoke hearts, drained
¼ cup light mayonnaise
¼ cup freshly grated Parmesan cheese
2 tablespoons olive oil

1. From the lemon, grate ½ teaspoon zest and squeeze 2 teaspoons juice.

2. In a food processor with the knife blade attached, puree the lemon zest and juice, artichoke hearts, Parmesan, and oil until smooth. Transfer to serving bowl. If you're not serving right away, cover and refrigerate up to 3 days.

Each tablespoon About 30 calories, 1g protein, 1g carbohydrate, 3g fat (1g saturated), 1g fiber, 70mg sodium.

 Tip Need a dip for your crudité platter? Consider making Classic Hummus (page 61) or one of its variations for your next dinner party.

turkey sliders

PREP: 40 MIN / TOTAL: 50 MIN / SERVES 12

2 medium stalks celery, chopped
1 medium carrot, chopped
1 medium onion, chopped
1 tablespoon fresh thyme leaves
5 large fresh sage leaves, torn
1 tablespoon olive oil
Salt
¼ teaspoon ground black pepper
Nonstick cooking spray
2½ cups all-purpose flour
1 tablespoon sugar
1 tablespoon baking powder
½ teaspoon baking soda
4 tablespoons cold butter, cut into pieces
1¼ cups buttermilk
1½ pounds ground turkey (93% lean)
½ cup mayonnaise
¼ cup cranberry preserves or sauce

1. In a food processor, pulse the celery, carrot, onion, thyme, and sage until finely chopped. In a 12-inch skillet, heat the oil over medium heat. Add the vegetable mixture, ¼ teaspoon salt, and pepper; cook 15 minutes or until tender, stirring occasionally. Transfer to a medium bowl; cool completely.

2. Preheat the oven to 450°F. Spray two 12-cup muffin pans with nonstick cooking spray. Line a large rimmed baking sheet with parchment paper.

3. In a clean food-processor bowl, pulse the flour, sugar, baking powder, baking soda, and ¾ teaspoon salt until blended. Add the butter. Pulse just until coarse crumbs form. Transfer the mixture to a large bowl. Stir in the buttermilk, then one-third of cooked vegetable mixture until just blended. Evenly divide the batter among the cups of the prepared muffin pans (about 3 tablespoons each). Bake 15 minutes, or until golden brown. Transfer the biscuits to wire racks; let cool slightly.

4. Meanwhile, in a medium bowl, combine the turkey, the remaining cooked vegetable mixture, and ¼ teaspoon salt until just combined. Form into 24 patties (2 inches wide); place on the prepared baking sheet. Bake at 165°F 15 minutes or until cooked through.

5. When the biscuits are cool enough to handle, slice them in half. Add the turkey patties and dollops of mayo and cranberry preserves.

Each serving About 330 calories, 15g protein, 27g carbohydrate, 18g fat (5g saturated), 1g fiber, 600mg sodium.

roasted eggplant dip
with herbs

PREP: 15 MIN / TOTAL: 1 HR 15 MIN, PLUS COOLING AND DRAINING / MAKES ABOUT 2 CUPS

- 2 small eggplants (1 pound each)
- 2 cloves garlic, thinly sliced
- 2 tablespoons olive oil
- 4 teaspoons fresh lemon juice
- 1 teaspoon salt
- ¼ teaspoon ground black pepper
- 2 tablespoons chopped fresh parsley
- 2 tablespoons chopped fresh mint
- Toasted pita bread wedges, for serving

1. Preheat the oven to 400°F. With a knife, cut slits all over the eggplants; insert garlic slices in the slits. Place the eggplants in a rimmed baking sheet and roast until collapsed and tender, about 1 hour.

2. When cool enough to handle, cut the eggplants in half. Scoop out the flesh and place it in a colander set over a bowl; discard the skin. Let drain 10 minutes.

3. Transfer the eggplant to a food processor with the knife blade attached. Add the oil, lemon juice, salt, and pepper; pulse to coarsely chop. Add the parsley and mint, pulsing to combine. Spoon the mixture into a bowl; cover and refrigerate up to 4 hours. Serve with toasted pita bread wedges.

Each tablespoon About 15 calories, 0g protein, 2g carbohydrate, 1g fat (0g saturated), 1g fiber, 75mg sodium.

VARIATION

Baba Ghanoush
Prepare as directed above. Omit the parsley and mint. Stir in ½ teaspoon ground cumin, ¼ cup tahini (sesame seed paste), and ½ cup low-fat plain yogurt.

roasted red pepper dip

PREP: 45 MIN / TOTAL: 45 MIN / MAKES ABOUT 2 CUPS

- 4 red bell peppers, roasted (page 446)
- ½ teaspoon ground cumin
- ½ cup walnuts, toasted
- 2 slices firm white bread, torn into pieces
- 2 tablespoons raspberry or balsamic vinegar
- 1 tablespoon olive oil
- ½ teaspoon salt
- ⅛ teaspoon cayenne pepper
- Toasted pita bread wedges, for serving

1. Cut the roasted peppers into large pieces. In a small skillet, toast the cumin over low heat, stirring constantly, until very fragrant, 1 to 2 minutes.

2. In a food processor with the knife blade attached, process the walnuts until ground. Add the roasted bell peppers, cumin, bread, vinegar, oil, salt, and cayenne; puree until smooth. Transfer to a bowl. If you're not serving right away, cover and refrigerate up to 4 hours. Serve with toasted pita bread wedges.

Each tablespoon About 25 calories, 0g protein, 2g carbohydrate, 2g fat (0g saturated), 0g fiber, 45mg sodium.

INGREDIENT SPOTLIGHT

This red pepper dip is based on **muhammara** (which translates from Arabic as "red"), a red-pepper-and-walnut spread that is popular in Lebanon, Syria, and Turkey. The original version uses pomegranate molasses. If you can find it, use it instead of the raspberry vinegar. Serve the dip with warm pita bread or use it to top grilled chicken or fish.

perfect guacamole

PREP: 15 MIN / TOTAL: 15 MIN / MAKES ABOUT 1¾ CUPS

- 1 jalapeño chile, seeded and finely chopped
- ⅓ cup loosely packed fresh cilantro leaves, chopped
- ¼ cup finely chopped sweet onion, such as Vidalia or Maui
- ½ teaspoon salt
- 2 ripe avocados
- 1 plum tomato
- Plain tortilla chips, for serving

1. In a mortar, combine the jalapeño, cilantro, onion, and salt; with the pestle, grind the mixture until it becomes juicy and thick (the onion can still be slightly chunky).

2. Cut each avocado lengthwise in half around seed. Twist the halves in opposite directions to separate them. Slip a spoon between the pit and the fruit and work the pit out. With a spoon, scoop the fruit from peel onto a cutting board.

3. Cut the tomato crosswise in half. Squeeze the halves to remove the seeds and juice. Coarsely chop the tomato.

4. If the mortar is large enough, add the avocado and chopped tomato to the mixture in the mortar. (If the mortar is small, combine the avocado, tomato, and onion mixture in a bowl.) Mash slightly with the pestle or a spoon until the mixture is blended but still somewhat chunky.

5. Guacamole is best when served as soon as it's made. If you're not serving right away, press plastic wrap directly onto the surface of the guacamole to prevent discoloration and refrigerate up to 1 hour. Serve with chips.

Each tablespoon About 25 calories, 0g protein, 1g carbohydrate, 2g fat (0g saturated), 1g fiber, 45mg sodium.

 Tip If you don't have a mortar and pestle, combine the ingredients in a bowl and use a fork or metal pastry blender to mash them as directed.

warm layered bean dip

PREP: 35 MIN / TOTAL: 50 MIN / MAKES ABOUT 5½ CUPS

- 2 cups plus 1 tablespoon water
- 2 cloves garlic, peeled
- 1 can (15 to 19 ounces) pinto beans, rinsed and drained
- 2 green onions, finely chopped
- 1 tablespoon tomato paste
- 4 ounces Monterey Jack cheese, shredded (1 cup)
- 1 cup mild to medium salsa
- 2 avocados, each cut in half, pitted, and peeled
- ¼ cup chopped fresh cilantro
- 3 tablespoons finely chopped red onion
- 2 tablespoons fresh lime juice
- ½ teaspoon salt
- 1 cup sour cream
- Tortilla chips, for serving

1. Preheat the oven to 350°F. In a 1-quart saucepan, heat 2 cups water to boiling over high heat. Add the garlic and cook 3 minutes to blanch; drain. With the flat side of a chef's knife, mash the garlic; transfer to a medium bowl and add the beans, half of the green onions, tomato paste, and 1 tablespoon water. Mash until well combined but still slightly chunky. Spread in the bottom of 9-inch glass pie plate.

2. Sprinkle the cheese over the bean mixture, then spread the salsa on top. Bake until piping hot, about 12 minutes.

3. Meanwhile, in a medium bowl, mash the avocados until just slightly chunky. Stir in the cilantro, red onion, lime juice, and salt. Spoon the avocado mixture over the hot mixture and spread sour cream on top. Sprinkle with the remaining green onions. Serve with tortilla chips.

Each tablespoon About 20 calories, 1g protein, 1g carbohydrate, 2g fat (1g saturated), 1g fiber, 60mg sodium.

 Tip The pinto bean, Jack cheese, and salsa layers can be assembled several hours in advance, then baked just before serving.

tzatziki

PREP: 20 MIN / TOTAL: 20 MIN, PLUS DRAINING AND CHILLING
/ MAKES ABOUT 1¼ CUPS

2 cups plain low-fat
yogurt (16 ounces)

½ English (seedless)
cucumber, unpeeled,
seeded, and finely
chopped, plus a few
very thin slices

Salt

1 to 2 cloves garlic,
chopped

1 tablespoon chopped
fresh mint or dill, plus
additional sprigs

1 tablespoon extra-virgin
olive oil

½ teaspoon red wine
vinegar

¼ teaspoon ground
black pepper

1. Spoon the yogurt into a sieve lined with cheesecloth or a coffee filter set over a bowl; cover and refrigerate overnight. Transfer the drained yogurt to a medium bowl and discard the liquid.

2. Meanwhile, in a colander set over a bowl, toss the chopped cucumber with 1 teaspoon salt. Let drain at least 1 hour at room temperature, or cover and refrigerate up to 8 hours. In batches, wrap the chopped cucumber in a kitchen towel and squeeze to remove as much liquid as possible. Pat dry with paper towels, then add to the bowl with the yogurt.

3. With the flat side of a chef's knife, mash the garlic to a paste with ½ teaspoon salt. Add the garlic, chopped mint, oil, vinegar, and pepper to the yogurt and stir to combine. Cover and refrigerate at least 2 or up to 4 hours. Serve chilled or at room temperature, topped with cucumber slices and mint sprigs.

Each tablespoon About 20 calories, 1g protein, 1g carbohydrate, 1g fat (0g saturated), 0g fiber, 180mg sodium.

VARIATION

Herbed Yogurt-Cheese Dip

Prepare yogurt as in step 1. Stir in **1 clove garlic**, crushed with a garlic press; **¾ cup chopped fresh basil**; **1 tablespoon olive oil**; and **½ teaspoon salt**. Serve with crackers or cut-up vegetables. Makes about 1 cup.

Ingredient Ideas
english cucumbers

If you've never tried one of these lo-o-o-ong, sweet, thin-skinned cukes, you're in for a treat. There's no need to peel 'em, since they're not waxed, and no need to seed, as they're virtually seedless. Our recipes call for one-half to two 13- to 14-ounce cucumbers.

CUCUMBER CANAPÉS

Cut **½ English cucumber** into 24 thin slices. Arrange them on a work surface and top each slice with **¼ teaspoon pesto**. Crumble **1 ounce goat cheese** and sprinkle on top of canapés. **Makes 24.**

MELON 'N' CUKE SALSA

In large bowl, combine **1 cucumber**, peeled and cut into ¼-inch pieces; **2 cups ripe melon chunks**, cut into ¼-inch pieces; **1 jalapeño chile**, seeded and finely chopped; **3 tablespoons fresh lime juice**; **2 tablespoons chopped fresh basil leaves**; and **¼ teaspoon salt**. **Makes 4½ cups.**

COOL-AS-A-CUKE BUTTERMILK SOUP

In a blender, puree until smooth **2 peeled, chopped English cucumbers**, **1 cup buttermilk**, **½ cup loosely packed fresh mint leaves**, **½ teaspoon salt**, and **⅛ teaspoon ground black pepper**. Stir in **1 cup buttermilk**. Serve the soup chilled; garnish with **snipped fresh chives** and **chopped mint leaves**. **Makes 4¼ cups.**

MEDITERRANEAN TUNA

In a large bowl, combine **1 English cucumber** cut into ¾-inch chunks; **2 cans (5 ounces each) drained and flaked chunk light tuna in water**; **⅓ cup pitted Kalamata olives**, chopped; **2 small tomatoes**, chopped; and **3 tablespoons olive oil vinaigrette**. Stir until blended. Serve over greens or on a toasted baguette. **Makes 5 cups.**

SCANDINAVIAN SHRIMP SALAD

In a large bowl, combine **1 very thinly sliced English cucumber**; **1 pound cooked, shelled large shrimp**; **½ cup reduced-fat sour cream**; **¼ teaspoon freshly grated lemon zest**; **2 tablespoons fresh lemon juice**; **2 tablespoons chopped fresh dill**; **¼ teaspoon salt**; and **⅛ teaspoon ground black pepper**. Serve on rye toast. **Makes 4 cups.**

pimiento-cheese deviled eggs

PREP: 25 MIN / TOTAL: 45 MIN / SERVES 12

12 large eggs

⅓ cup mayonnaise

2 teaspoons hot sauce

¼ teaspoon salt

½ cup shredded Cheddar cheese

1 jar (4 ounces) pimientos, drained well and finely chopped

1 green onion, finely chopped

Paprika, for garnish

1. In a 4-quart saucepan, combine the eggs and enough cold water to cover. Heat to boiling over high heat. Remove from the heat. Cover the saucepan and let stand 14 minutes. Rinse the eggs with cold water until cool, then peel.

2. Cut the eggs in half lengthwise. Transfer the yolks to a medium bowl and mash with the mayonnaise, hot sauce, and salt until almost smooth. Fold in the cheese, pimientos, and green onion. Scoop or pipe the filling into the whites and garnish the filled eggs with paprika.

Each serving About 140 calories, 8g protein, 1g carbohydrate, 11g fat (3g saturated), 0g fiber, 195mg sodium.

VARIATIONS

Classic
Mash 12 hard-cooked yolks with ½ cup mayonnaise, 1 tablespoon Dijon or spicy brown mustard, and ½ teaspoon hot sauce. Garnish the filled eggs with paprika.

Guacamole
Mash 12 hard-cooked yolks with 1 small ripe avocado; ¼ cup mayonnaise; ¼ cup fresh cilantro, finely chopped; 1 very small shallot, finely chopped; 2 tablespoons fresh lime juice; and ½ teaspoon salt. Garnish the filled eggs with broken tortilla chips and thinly sliced serrano chiles.

Caesar
Mash 12 hard-cooked yolks with ½ cup mayonnaise; ¼ cup grated Parmesan cheese; 2 tablespoons fresh lemon juice; 2 teaspoons Dijon mustard; and 1 small clove garlic, crushed with a garlic press. Garnish the filled eggs with broken Parmesan crisps, ground black pepper, and fresh basil.

Miso-Ginger
Mash 12 hard-cooked yolks with ½ cup mayonnaise; 2 tablespoons white or yellow miso; 1 teaspoon grated, peeled fresh ginger; ½ teaspoon ground black pepper; and ¼ teaspoon sugar. Garnish the filled eggs with snipped fresh chives and finely julienned fresh ginger.

Ham & Cheese
Mash 12 hard-cooked yolks with ½ cup mayonnaise; ½ cup finely grated sharp Cheddar cheese; 3 tablespoons sweet relish, drained; 2 slices deli ham, finely chopped; 1 tablespoon spicy brown mustard; and ¼ teaspoon salt.

Crunchy Curry
Mash 12 hard-cooked yolks with ½ cup mayonnaise, 2 teaspoons curry powder, 2 teaspoons fresh lemon juice, and ¼ teaspoon salt. Spoon into the whites; garnish with sliced almonds and snipped fresh chives.

Pesto-Bacon
Mash 12 hard-cooked yolks with ½ cup mayonnaise, ¼ cup pesto, and 2 tablespoons fresh lemon juice. Spoon into the whites; garnish with crumbled cooked bacon.

Smoky Chipotle
Mash 12 hard-cooked yolks with ½ cup mayonnaise, 2 tablespoons chopped chipotles in adobo, 1 teaspoon white vinegar, and ¼ teaspoon salt. Spoon into the whites; garnish with chili powder and fresh cilantro.

BEET-DYED EGGS

ADD A SPLASH OF COLOR TO YOUR STUFFED EGG "SHELLS"

In a medium 2-quart saucepan, heat 8 cups water; 4 medium beets, peeled and thinly sliced; 2 cups distilled white vinegar; and 1 tablespoon salt to boiling over high heat. Reduce the heat to a simmer; cook 20 minutes. Cool the liquid completely. Remove and reserve the beets for another use. Transfer the pickling liquid to a gallon-size resealable bag set in a large bowl; add 12 peeled hard-cooked eggs. Squeeze the air out of the bag and seal, making sure the eggs are submerged. Refrigerate 1 hour. Remove the eggs from the liquid and blot completely dry with paper towels before using for Classic Deviled Eggs.

PIMIENTO-CHEESE DEVILED EGGS 94

sweet & spicy nuts

PREP: 15 MIN / TOTAL: 40 MIN, PLUS COOLING / MAKES ABOUT 8 CUPS

1 cup sugar

2 teaspoons salt

1 teaspoon ground cumin

1 teaspoon ground cinnamon

1 teaspoon coarsely ground black pepper

½ teaspoon cayenne pepper

1 large egg white

6 cups raw unsalted nuts, such as walnuts, pecans, natural almonds, and/or cashews

1. Preheat the oven to 325°F. Grease two 15½ × 10½-inch rimmed baking sheets.

2. In a small bowl, combine the sugar, salt, cumin, cinnamon, black pepper, and cayenne; stir until blended. In a large bowl and using a wire whisk, beat the egg white until foamy. Add the nuts to the egg white; stir to coat evenly. Add the sugar mixture; toss until the nuts are thoroughly coated.

3. Divide the nut mixture between the prepared rimmed baking sheets, spreading it evenly. Bake, stirring twice during baking, until golden brown and dry, 25 to 27 minutes. With a slotted spoon, transfer the nuts to waxed paper; spread them in a single layer. Cool. Store in airtight container at room temperature up to 1 month.

Each ¼ cup About 165 calories, 4g protein, 11g carbohydrate, 12g fat (2g saturated), 1g fiber, 150mg sodium.

shrimp rillettes

PREP: 15 MIN / TOTAL: 20 MIN, PLUS CHILLING / MAKES 1¾ CUPS OR THREE 6-OUNCE JARS OF 6 SERVINGS EACH

6 tablespoons butter, softened

1 pound shelled and deveined shrimp

2 tablespoons brandy or dry sherry

¼ teaspoon cayenne pepper

2 tablespoons fresh lemon juice

¼ teaspoon salt

1. In a 10-inch skillet, melt 2 tablespoons butter over medium-high heat. Add the shrimp and cook 2 minutes, or until the shrimp turn opaque throughout, stirring frequently. Add the brandy and cook 30 seconds. Transfer the shrimp mixture to a food processor with the knife blade attached; pulse until finely chopped.

2. To the shrimp mixture in the processor, add the cayenne, lemon juice, remaining 4 tablespoons butter, and salt; pulse until evenly blended.

3. Transfer the shrimp mixture into 3 small jars and cover with plastic wrap, pressing the wrap directly onto the surface of the shrimp mixture. Refrigerate at least 8 hours or up to 3 days to blend flavors. Let stand 30 minutes at room temperature before serving.

Each serving About 75 calories, 6g protein, 0g carbohydrate, 5g fat (3g saturated), 0g fiber, 125mg sodium.

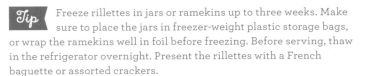 *Tip* Freeze rillettes in jars or ramekins up to three weeks. Make sure to place the jars in freezer-weight plastic storage bags, or wrap the ramekins well in foil before freezing. Before serving, thaw in the refrigerator overnight. Present the rillettes with a French baguette or assorted crackers.

marinated mixed olives

PREP: 10 MIN / TOTAL: 15 MIN, PLUS STANDING AND MARINATING / MAKES ABOUT 6 CUPS

¼ cup extra-virgin olive oil

2 teaspoons fennel seeds, crushed

4 small bay leaves

2 pounds assorted Mediterranean olives,

such as Nicoise, picholine, or Kalamata

6 strips (3 × 1 inch each) lemon peel

4 cloves garlic, crushed with the side of a chef's knife

1. In a 1-quart saucepan, heat the oil, fennel seeds, and bay leaves over medium heat until hot but not smoking. Remove the saucepan from the heat; let stand 10 minutes.

2. In a large bowl, combine the olives, lemon peel, garlic, and oil mixture. Cover and refrigerate, stirring occasionally, at least 24 hours or up to several days to blend the flavors. Store in the refrigerator up to 1 month. Drain to serve.

Each ¼ cup About 110 calories, 1g protein, 3g carbohydrate, 10g fat (1g saturated), 1g fiber, 680mg sodium.

salmon pâté

PREP: 10 MIN / TOTAL: 12 MIN, PLUS CHILLING / MAKES ABOUT 2 CUPS

1 lemon

8 ounce salmon fillet, skin removed

¼ teaspoon salt

⅛ teaspoon ground black pepper

2 tablespoons water

8 ounces smoked salmon

3 tablespoons butter, softened

2 tablespoons reduced-fat cream cheese

2 tablespoons chopped fresh chives

Toast rounds or unsalted crackers, for serving

1. From the lemon, grate 1 teaspoon zest. Cut the lemon in half. From 1 lemon half, squeeze 1 tablespoon juice; cut the other lemon half into 3 slices. Set the zest and juice aside.

2. Sprinkle the salmon fillet with the salt and pepper to season both sides. Place it in a microwave-safe shallow bowl or glass pie plate. Top the salmon with the lemon slices and water. Cook, covered, in microwave oven on High 2 minutes. Let stand, covered, 2 minutes longer. Remove the salmon from the liquid and place it in a medium bowl; flake with a fork and set aside to cool.

3. Meanwhile, in a food processor with the knife blade attached, pulse the smoked salmon, butter, cream cheese, and lemon zest and juice just until smooth (do not over-process). Gently stir the smoked salmon mixture and 1 tablespoon chives into the flaked salmon just until combined. Wrap the remaining chives in plastic wrap and refrigerate for garnishing later. Spoon the salmon pâté into a serving bowl or crock; cover and refrigerate for at least 2 hours or overnight.

4. To serve, let the pâté stand at room temperature 30 minutes or until soft enough to spread. Garnish the pâté with the remaining chives. Serve with toast rounds or crackers.

Each tablespoon About 30 calories, 3g protein, 0g carbohydrate, 2g fat (1g saturated), 0g fiber, 180mg sodium.

chicken liver pâté

PREP: 25 MIN / TOTAL: 45 MIN, PLUS CHILLING / MAKES ABOUT 1½ CUPS

2 tablespoons butter

1 small onion, finely chopped

1 clove garlic, finely chopped

1 pound chicken livers, trimmed

2 tablespoons brandy

½ cup heavy or whipping cream

½ teaspoon salt

¼ teaspoon dried thyme

¼ teaspoon ground black pepper

Assorted crackers, toast, and/or thinly sliced apples for serving

1. In a 10-inch skillet, melt the butter over medium-high heat. Add the onion and cook, stirring frequently, until tender and golden, about 10 minutes. Stir in the garlic and chicken livers and cook until the livers are lightly browned but still pink inside, about 5 minutes. Stir in the brandy; cook 5 minutes.

2. In a blender or food processor with the knife blade attached, puree the chicken-liver mixture, the cream, salt, thyme, and pepper until smooth, stopping the blender occasionally and scraping down the sides with a rubber spatula.

3. Spoon the mixture into a small bowl; cover and refrigerate at least 3 hours or up to overnight. Let stand 30 minutes at room temperature before serving. Serve with crackers, toast, and/or apples.

Each tablespoon About 55 calories, 4g protein, 1g carbohydrate, 4g fat (2g saturated), 0g fiber, 75mg sodium.

GOOD TO KNOW

CREAM CHEESE TO THE RESCUE

Unexpected guests? For an almost-instant spread, place an **8-ounce block of cream cheese** on a serving platter and generously spread **hot pepper jelly**, **mango chutney, olive paste (olivada)**, or **salsa** over the top. Or, in a food processor with the knife blade attached, puree cream cheese with marinated dried tomatoes, roasted peppers, pickled jalapeño chiles, bottled horseradish, or grated onion; season with coarsely ground black pepper. (If you wish, thin the spread with milk to make a dip.) No crackers? Toast some bread and cut it into triangles.

potato halves

with salmon & dill

PREP: 20 MIN / TOTAL: 30 MIN / SERVES 12

- 18 baby red potatoes (1½ pounds), halved
- 1 tablespoon olive oil
- ½ teaspoon salt
- ¼ teaspoon coarsely ground black pepper
- ¼ cup reduced-fat sour cream
- 4 ounces sliced smoked salmon, cut into 36 pieces
- 1 tablespoon snipped fresh dill

1. In a microwave-safe large bowl, place the potatoes and 2 tablespoons water. Cover the bowl with vented plastic wrap and microwave on High 5 to 6 minutes, or until the potatoes are just fork-tender.

2. Meanwhile, prepare an outdoor grill for direct grilling over medium heat.

3. Transfer the potatoes to a rimmed baking sheet. Brush the potatoes all over with the olive oil and sprinkle with the salt and pepper. Place the potatoes on the hot grill grate; cook 5 to 6 minutes, or until lightly charred on both sides, turning once.

4. Arrange the potato halves, rounded sides down, on a serving plate. Top each with about ¼ teaspoon sour cream, 1 piece salmon, and some dill.

Each serving About 75 calories, 3g protein, 12g carbohydrate, 2g fat (1g saturated), 1g fiber, 290mg sodium.

 Tip For ease of arranging and serving, cut a thin slice from the rounded side of each potato half before steaming so it will sit flat on the serving platter.

smoked trout pâté

PREP: 25 MIN / TOTAL: 25 MIN / MAKES ABOUT 3 CUPS

- 3 whole smoked trout (1¼ pounds total)
- 1 container (8 ounces) whipped cream cheese
- ¼ cup low-fat mayonnaise dressing
- 3 tablespoons fresh lemon juice
- ⅛ teaspoon ground black pepper
- 1 tablespoon finely chopped fresh chives or green onion
- Cucumber slices and assorted crackers, for serving

1. Cut the head and tail from each trout; discard along with the skin and bones. In a food processor with the knife blade attached, puree the trout, cream cheese, mayonnaise dressing, lemon juice, and pepper until smooth.

2. Spoon the trout mixture into a medium bowl; stir in the chives. Cover and refrigerate up to overnight, if not serving right away. Before serving, let stand 15 minutes at room temperature to soften. Serve with cucumber slices and crackers.

Each tablespoon About 30 calories, 2g protein, 1g carbohydrate, 2g fat (1g saturated), 0g fiber, 101mg sodium.

poker (pita) chips

PREP: 10 MIN / TOTAL: 20 MIN / MAKES 8 DOZEN CHIPS

- ½ cup olive oil
- 1 tablespoon freshly grated Parmesan or Pecorino Romano cheese
- 1 tablespoon chili powder
- 1 teaspoon ground cumin
- 12 ounces white or whole-wheat pitas

1. Preheat the oven to 425°F. In a cup and using a fork, mix the oil, Parmesan, chili powder, and cumin.

2. With a knife, carefully split open each pita. Brush the insides of the pita halves lightly with the oil mixture. Cut each half into 8 wedges.

3. Transfer the pita wedges to 2 ungreased baking sheets (wedges can overlap). Place the baking sheets on 2 oven racks and bake the pita chips until the edges are golden, 8 to 10 minutes. Watch carefully, as they can burn quickly.

4. Transfer the baking sheets to wire racks and cool completely. Store the chips in an airtight container up to 1 week.

Each chip About 20 calories, 0g protein, 2g carbohydrate, 1g fat (0g saturated), 0g fiber, 20mg sodium.

bruschetta

PREP: 25 MIN / TOTAL: 25 MIN / MAKES 16 BRUSCHETTA

- 1 loaf (8 ounces) Italian bread, cut on the diagonal into ½-inch-thick slices
- 8 cloves garlic, each cut in half
- 1 pound ripe plum tomatoes (6 medium), seeded and cut into ½-inch pieces
- 1 tablespoon finely chopped red onion
- 1 tablespoon chopped fresh basil
- 4 ounces ricotta salata, feta, or goat cheese, cut into ½-inch pieces
- 2 tablespoons extra-virgin olive oil
- 2 teaspoons balsamic vinegar
- ¼ teaspoon salt
- ¼ teaspoon coarsely ground black pepper

1. Preheat the oven to 400°F. Place the bread slices on a baking sheet and bake until lightly toasted, about 5 minutes. Rub one side of each toast slice with the cut side of the garlic.

2. Meanwhile, in a bowl, gently toss the tomatoes, onion, basil, cheese, oil, vinegar, salt, and pepper until combined.

3. To serve, spoon the tomato mixture on the garlic-rubbed side of the toast slices.

Each bruschetta About 80 calories, 2g protein, 9g carbohydrate, 4g fat (1g saturated), 1g fiber, 235mg sodium.

VARIATION

Tuscan White-Bean Bruschetta

Prepare toast as directed, but prepare the topping as follows: In a bowl and using a fork, lightly mash **1 can (15½ to 19 ounces) white kidney beans** (cannellini), rinsed and drained, with **1 tablespoon fresh lemon juice**. Stir in **1 tablespoon olive oil, 2 teaspoons chopped fresh parsley, 1 teaspoon minced fresh sage, ¼ teaspoon salt**, and **⅛ teaspoon coarsely ground black pepper**. Just before serving, spoon the mixture over the garlic-rubbed side of the toast slices. Sprinkle with 1 teaspoon chopped fresh parsley.

GLOSSARY →

Bruschetta is toasted Italian bread that is rubbed with garlic and drizzled with olive oil. It's often topped with savory ingredients to make a simple appetizer.

easy spicy cheese straws

PREP: 30 MIN / TOTAL: 1 HR 10 MIN / MAKES ABOUT 48 CHEESE STRAWS

- 1 tablespoon paprika
- ½ teaspoon dried thyme
- ¼ to ½ teaspoon cayenne pepper
- ¼ teaspoon salt
- 1 package (17¼ ounces) frozen puff pastry sheets, thawed
- 1 large egg white, lightly beaten
- 8 ounces sharp Cheddar cheese, shredded (2 cups)

1. Preheat the oven to 375°F. Grease 2 large baking sheets. In a small bowl, combine the paprika, thyme, cayenne, and salt.

2. Unfold 1 puff pastry sheet. On a lightly floured surface and using a floured rolling pin, roll the pastry into a 14-inch square. Lightly brush it with the egg white. Sprinkle half the paprika mixture on the pastry. Sprinkle half the Cheddar on half the pastry. Fold the pastry over to cover the cheese, forming a rectangle. With the rolling pin, lightly roll over the pastry to seal the layers together. With a pizza wheel or knife, cut the pastry crosswise into ½-inch-wide strips.

3. Place the strips ½ inch apart on the prepared baking sheets, twisting each strip twice to form a spiral and pressing the ends against the baking sheet to prevent the strips from uncurling. Bake until golden, 20 to 22 minutes. With a spatula, carefully transfer the cheese straws to wire racks to cool.

4. Repeat with the remaining puff pastry sheet, egg white, paprika mixture, and cheese. Store in an airtight container up to 1 week.

Each straw About 80 calories, 2g protein, 5g carbohydrate, 5g fat (2g saturated), 0g fiber, 68mg sodium.

CHICKPEA "NUTS" 100

chickpea "nuts"

PREP: 10 MIN / TOTAL: 40 MIN / MAKES ABOUT 2 CUPS

2 cans (15 ounces each) chickpeas

2 tablespoons olive oil

¼ teaspoon salt

¼ teaspoon ground black pepper

Seasonings (below; optional)

1. Preheat the oven to 425°F.

2. Rinse and drain the chickpeas; pat very dry with paper towels, discarding any loose skins.

3. On a large rimmed baking sheet, toss the chickpeas with olive oil, salt, and pepper. Roast 30 minutes, or until crisp, shaking the baking sheet occasionally. Remove from the oven and transfer to a bowl; toss with seasonings, if desired. The chickpeas will continue to crisp as they cool.

Each ¼ cup About 120 calories, 5g protein, 15g carbohydrate, 5g fat (1g saturated), 4g fiber, 214mg sodium.

Tip If you're not eating these immediately, recrisp the chickpeas in a preheated 425°F oven 8 to 10 minutes to extend their shelf life to 1 week. Cool completely and store in an airtight container.

VARIATIONS

Honey-Sesame

Toss roasted chickpeas in **2 tablespoons honey; 1 tablespoon each sesame oil, sesame seeds,** and **sugar;** and **½ teaspoon each garlic powder** and **five-spice powder.** Return to the oven until caramelized and crisp, 5 minutes.

BBQ

Toss roasted chickpeas in **1 teaspoon dark brown sugar** and **½ teaspoon each ground cumin, smoked paprika, garlic powder,** and **chili powder.**

Masala

Toss roasted chickpeas in **½ teaspoon each garam masala, ground cumin,** and **ground ginger,** and **¼ teaspoon cayenne pepper.** Return to the oven until dry and crisp, 5 minutes.

PRETZEL BITES 101

Spicy Buffalo

Toss roasted chickpeas in ¼ **cup cayenne pepper hot sauce**. Return to the oven until dry and crisp, 5 minutes.

Maple-Cinnamon

Toss roasted chickpeas in **2 tablespoons maple syrup, 2 teaspoons sugar, 1 teaspoon ground cinnamon**, and ¼ **teaspoon ground nutmeg**. Return to oven until caramelized and crisp, 5 minutes.

Parmesan-Herb

Toss roasted chickpeas in ¼ **cup finely grated Parmesan** and **1 teaspoon each garlic powder, finely chopped fresh rosemary**, and **loosely packed lemon zest**.

pretzel bites

PREP: 20 MIN / TOTAL: 40 MIN / MAKES 36 BITES

1¼ **pounds pizza dough**
⅓ **cup baking soda**
5 **cups boiling water**

1 **egg, beaten**
Coarse sea salt
Green onions and grainy mustard, for serving

1. Tear the pizza dough into cherry-size pieces (about ½ ounce each) and roll into balls. Bring a saucepan with 5 cups water and baking soda to a boil over medium heat; add the dough balls and cook 1 minute, or until slightly puffed.

2. Preheat the oven to 450°F.

3. With a slotted spoon, remove the balls and drain them on paper towels. Transfer to parchment-lined baking sheet, spaced ½ inch apart. Brush the dough with the egg; sprinkle with sea salt. Bake at 12 to 15 minutes, or until golden. Serve with green onions and grainy mustard.

Each bite About 35 calories, 1g protein, 6g carbohydrate, 0g fat (0g saturated), 0g fiber, 507mg sodium.

 Tip SWEET SWAP: Skip the sea salt and coat the dough balls with cinnamon sugar before baking.

mini gougères

PREP: 20 MIN / TOTAL: 50 MIN / MAKES ABOUT 48 PUFFS

6 **ounces Gruyère or Swiss cheese**
1 **cup water**
6 **tablespoons butter, cut up**
1½ **teaspoons Dijon mustard**

½ **teaspoon hot sauce**
¼ **teaspoon salt**
1 **cup all-purpose flour**
4 **large eggs**

1. Preheat the oven to 400°F. Grease and flour 2 large baking sheets. Shred the cheese to equal 1 cup; finely dice the remaining cheese.

2. In a 3-quart saucepan, heat the water, butter, mustard, hot sauce, and salt to boiling. Remove the saucepan from the heat. With a wooden spoon, vigorously stir in the flour all at once until the mixture forms into a ball and leaves the sides of the pan.

3. Add the eggs, one at a time, beating well after each addition, until the batter is smooth and satin-like. Stir in the shredded and diced cheese. Drop batter by rounded teaspoons, about 2 inches apart, onto the prepared baking sheets.

4. Bake 30 to 35 minutes, rotating the sheets between the upper and lower racks halfway through baking, until deep golden. Transfer the puffs to wire racks to cool. Serve warm or at room temperature.

Each puff About 60 calories, 3g protein, 3g carbohydrate, 4g fat (2g saturated), 0g fiber, 65mg sodium.

VARIATION

Cheddar-Curry Puffs

Prepare gougères as directed above, but use **Cheddar cheese** in place of Gruyère cheese. Add **2 teaspoons curry powder**, ½ **teaspoon ground coriander**, and ½ **teaspoon ground cumin** to the water mixture in step 2.

tortilla chips

These crisps aren't just for dipping! Here are clever ways to turn even the broken bits into your new secret ingredient. (Our recipes call for baked chips, which have 20 fewer calories per ounce, as well as less fat—but use traditional chips if you prefer.)

CHILES RELLENOS PIE

Preheat the oven to 350°F. Drain **2 cans (4 to 4½ ounces each) whole green chiles**. Slit each chile on 1 side; open it flat and pat dry. Grease a 9½-inch deep-dish pie plate; use the chiles to line the bottom. In a bowl, whisk **5 large eggs** with **1½ cups reduced-fat (2%) milk** and **½ cup finely chopped fully cooked chorizo** (2 ounces); pour this over the chiles. Top with **2 cups coarsely crushed tortilla chips**. Bake 40 minutes, or until set in the center. Serves 6.

MEXICAN COCKTAIL MEATBALLS

Preheat the oven to 425°F. From **1 jar (16 ounces) picante sauce**, measure out ⅓ cup and place it in a medium bowl. Mix in **1 pound ground beef**, **½ cup crushed tortilla chips**, **¼ cup chopped fresh cilantro**, **2 tablespoons water**, and **1 large egg**. Scoop the mixture into 1-inch balls; place them on a foil-lined baking sheet. Bake 20 minutes. Microwave the remaining picante sauce on High 2 minutes. Place the meatballs in a serving bowl; top with sauce; provide cocktail picks for serving. Serves 8.

TOMATO & CORN SOUP

In a saucepan, heat **1 tablespoon olive oil** over medium heat. Add **1 chopped small onion** and cook 8 minutes, or until lightly browned and tender, stirring often. Add **2 cans (14 to 14½ ounces each) reduced-sodium chicken broth**, **1 can (14½ ounces) diced tomatoes with chiles**, and **1 package (10 ounces) frozen corn kernels**; heat to boiling. Spoon into 4 bowls. Divide **1 cup coarsely crushed tortilla chips** among the bowls to top the soup. Serves 4.

PIZZA BITES

Preheat the oven to 425°F. Arrange **40 bite-size tortilla chip cups** on 1 or 2 baking sheets. In a bowl, stir **1 cup shredded Italian cheese blend** with **2 tablespoons pesto**; spoon onto the chips. Slice **10 grape tomatoes** into 4 pieces each; place 1 on each pizza bite. Bake 6 minutes to melt the cheese. Serves 8.

quick quesadillas

PREP: 10 MIN / TOTAL: 15 MIN / MAKES 32 WEDGES

- 8 (7- to 8-inch) flour tortillas
- 1 jar (7 ounces) roasted red peppers, drained and thinly sliced
- 2 small green onions, thinly sliced
- 4 ounces pepper Jack cheese, shredded (1 cup)
- ¾ cup loosely packed fresh cilantro leaves

1. Preheat the oven to 400°F. Place 4 tortillas on a large baking sheet. Sprinkle one-fourth of the roasted peppers, green onions, cheese, and cilantro on each tortilla; top with the remaining tortillas to make 4 quesadillas.

2. Bake the quesadillas until heated through and cheese melts, about 5 minutes. Cut each quesadilla into 8 wedges. Serve warm.

Each wedge About 45 calories, 2g protein, 5g carbohydrate, 2g fat (1g saturated), 0g fiber, 74mg sodium.

cubano quesadillas

PREP: 20 MIN / TOTAL: 20 MIN / SERVES 8

- 8 (6-inch) low-fat tortillas
- ¼ cup yellow mustard
- 4 ounces thinly sliced Black Forest ham
- 8 sandwich-cut dill pickle slices
- 4 ounces thinly sliced roast pork from deli
- 4 ounces thinly sliced part-skim Swiss cheese

1. Prepare an outdoor grill for direct grilling over medium heat.

2. Brush 1 side of each tortilla with mustard. Evenly divide the ham, pickles, pork, and cheese between 4 tortillas, placing them on top of the mustard. Top with the remaining tortillas, mustard-side down, pressing firmly.

3. With a large metal spatula, place the quesadillas on the hot grill grate and cook 2 to 3 minutes, or until the tortillas are browned on both sides and the Swiss cheese melts, carefully turning the quesadillas once. Transfer the quesadillas to a large cutting board; let stand 1 minute. Cut each quesadilla into 4 wedges to serve.

Each serving (2 wedges) About 190 calories, 15g protein, 18g carbohydrate, 6g fat (2g saturated), 1g fiber, 640mg sodium.

chorizo & black bean nachos

PREP: 20 MIN / TOTAL: 30 MIN / MAKES 36 NACHOS

- 36 unbroken large tortilla chips
- 3 large ripe plum tomatoes, cut into ¼-inch pieces
- ⅓ cup chopped fresh cilantro
- ¼ teaspoon salt
- 1 tablespoon vegetable oil
- 1 fully cooked chorizo sausage (3 ounces), finely chopped, or ¾ cup finely chopped pepperoni (3 ounces)
- 1 medium onion, finely chopped
- 1 clove garlic, finely chopped
- ½ teaspoon ground cumin
- 1 can (15 to 19 ounces) black beans, rinsed and drained
- 4 ounces Monterey Jack cheese, shredded (1 cup)
- 2 pickled jalapeño chiles, very thinly sliced

1. Preheat the oven to 400°F. Arrange as many tortilla chips as will fit in a single layer on 2 ungreased large baking sheets. In a small bowl, combine the tomatoes, cilantro, and salt.

2. In a 10-inch skillet, heat the oil over medium heat. Add the chorizo, onion, garlic, and cumin; cook, stirring, until the onion is tender, about 5 minutes. Stir in the beans and heat through.

3. Place 1 tablespoon bean mixture on each tortilla chip. Sprinkle the cheese over the beans and top each nacho with 1 jalapeño slice. Bake until the cheese begins to melt, about 5 minutes.

4. Spoon about 1 teaspoon tomato mixture on each nacho. Transfer the nachos to a serving platter.

Each nacho About 50 calories, 2g protein, 4g carbohydrate, 3g fat (1g saturated), 1g fiber, 112mg sodium.

buffalo wings

PREP: 15 MIN / TOTAL: 35 MIN / SERVES 18

- 4 ounces blue cheese, crumbled (1 cup)
- ½ cup sour cream
- ¼ cup mayonnaise
- ¼ cup milk
- ¼ cup chopped fresh parsley
- 1 tablespoon fresh lemon juice
- Salt
- 3 pounds chicken wings (18 wings), tips discarded, if desired
- 3 tablespoons butter
- ¼ cup hot sauce
- 1 medium bunch celery, cut into sticks

1. Preheat the broiler. In a medium bowl, combine the blue cheese, sour cream, mayonnaise, milk, parsley, lemon juice, and ¼ teaspoon salt. Cover and refrigerate.

2. Arrange the chicken wings on a rack in a broiling pan; sprinkle with ¼ teaspoon salt. Broil 5 inches from the heat source for 10 minutes. Turn the wings and broil until golden, 10 to 15 minutes longer.

3. Meanwhile, in a small saucepan, melt the butter with the hot sauce over low heat, stirring occasionally; keep hot.

4. In a large bowl, toss the wings with the seasoned butter to coat all sides. Arrange the chicken wings and celery on a platter along with the blue-cheese sauce and serve.

Each serving (without wing tip) About 170 calories, 10g protein, 3g carbohydrate, 13g fat (5g saturated), 1g fiber, 350mg sodium.

GOOD TO KNOW

BUFFALO SLIDERS? YES!

Replace the wings with 8 boneless chicken thighs, halved. Proceed with recipe as directed except thinly slice or chop 4 ribs celery. Toss celery with half the dressing. Spread each of 16 slider rolls with some dressing, top with chicken and celery slaw. Serve with additional hot sauce.

mini remoulade crab cakes

PREP: 25 MIN / TOTAL: 45 MIN / MAKES ABOUT 50 MINI CRAB CAKES

2 tablespoons butter

1 small onion, finely chopped

½ red bell pepper, finely chopped

1 stalk celery, finely chopped

¼ cup light mayonnaise

1 tablespoon sour cream

2 teaspoons grainy Dijon mustard

½ teaspoon freshly grated lemon zest

¼ teaspoon salt

⅛ teaspoon cayenne pepper

1 pound lump crabmeat, picked over

1 cup fresh bread crumbs (from about 2 slices bread)

Lemon Sauce (below)

1. In a 10-inch skillet, melt the butter over medium heat. Add the onion, bell pepper, and celery. Cook, stirring frequently, until the vegetables are tender, about 10 minutes. Let cool.

2. In a large bowl, stir the mayonnaise, sour cream, mustard, lemon zest, salt, and cayenne until blended; stir in the crabmeat and bread crumbs just until mixed. Cover and refrigerate 30 minutes.

3. Meanwhile, prepare the Lemon Sauce.

4. Preheat the oven to 400°F. Lightly grease 2 baking sheets. Drop level tablespoons of the crab mixture, pressing lightly, onto the prepared baking sheets. Bake until golden brown, about 15 minutes. Top each crab cake with about ½ teaspoon Lemon Sauce. Serve hot.

LEMON SAUCE In small bowl, stir together ¼ cup light mayonnaise, ¼ cup sour cream, 1 teaspoon freshly grated lemon zest, 1 tablespoon fresh lemon juice, a pinch of salt, and a pinch of cayenne until blended. **Makes about ½ cup.**

Each crab cake (with sauce) About 30 calories, 2g protein, 1g carbohydrate, 2g fat (1g saturated), 0g fiber, 70mg sodium.

VARIATION

Main-Dish Crab Cakes

Prepare the crab cakes (above) but divide the crab mixture into 8 portions, about ½ cup each, and shape each into a 3-inch cake. Place on a greased baking sheet. Bake until golden brown, about 20 minutes, gently turning each cake over with a spatula halfway through baking. Serve with Lemon Sauce (above), if desired.

shrimp cocktail

PREP: 25 MIN / TOTAL: 45 MIN, PLUS CHILLING / SERVES 8

1 lemon, thinly sliced

4 bay leaves

20 whole black peppercorns

10 whole allspice berries

2 teaspoons salt

24 extra-large shrimp (1 pound), shelled and deveined (see page 297)

Southwestern-Style Cocktail Sauce (below)

Mustard Dipping Sauce (below)

12 small romaine lettuce leaves

1. In a 5-quart Dutch oven, combine 2 quarts water, the lemon, bay leaves, peppercorns, allspice berries, and salt; heat to boiling. Cover and boil 15 minutes.

2. Add the shrimp and cook just until they are opaque throughout, 1 to 2 minutes. Drain and rinse with cold running water to stop further cooking. Cover and refrigerate the shrimp up to 24 hours.

3. Prepare the Southwestern-Style Cocktail Sauce and/or Mustard Dipping Sauce.

4. Just before serving, place bowls of the sauces in the center of a platter; arrange romaine leaves around the bowls, leaf tips facing out. Thread each shrimp on a bamboo skewer and arrange the skewers on the romaine leaves.

SOUTHWESTERN-STYLE COCKTAIL SAUCE In a bowl, stir **1 cup bottled cocktail sauce, 2 tablespoons chopped fresh cilantro, 2 teaspoons minced jalapeño chile,** and **2 teaspoons fresh lime juice** until well combined. Cover and refrigerate up to 24 hours. **Makes about 1 cup.**

MUSTARD DIPPING SAUCE In a small serving bowl, stir **1 cup reduced-fat sour cream, 3 tablespoons grainy Dijon mustard, 3 tablespoons chopped fresh parsley, ¼ teaspoon freshly grated lemon zest, ¼ teaspoon salt,** and **⅛ teaspoon coarsely ground black pepper** until well combined. Cover and refrigerate up to 24 hours. **Makes about 1 cup.**

SHRIMP COCKTAIL Each serving (without sauce) About 50 calories, 10g protein, 1g carbohydrate, 1g fat (0g saturated), 0g fiber, 140mg sodium.

SOUTHWESTERN-STYLE COCKTAIL SAUCE Each tablespoon About 20 calories, 0g protein, 4g carbohydrate, 0g fat (0g saturated), 0g fiber, 190mg sodium.

MUSTARD DIPPING SAUCE Each tablespoon About 30 calories, 1g protein, 1g carbohydrate, 2g fat (1g saturated), 0g fiber, 110mg sodium.

prosciutto-wrapped asparagus

PREP: 25 MIN / TOTAL: 35 MIN / SERVES 24

24 thick asparagus spears, trimmed and peeled

12 thin slices prosciutto (5 ounces)

½ cup freshly grated Parmesan cheese

¼ teaspoon coarsely ground black pepper

1. In a 5-quart Dutch oven, heat 3 quarts water to boiling over high heat. Add the asparagus; cook 3 minutes to blanch. Drain; rinse with cold running water. Pat dry with paper towels.

2. Preheat the oven to 450°F. Working in batches, spread out the prosciutto slices on a cutting board; cut each slice lengthwise in half and separate it slightly. Evenly sprinkle 1 teaspoon Parmesan on each prosciutto strip. Place 1 asparagus spear at end of 1 strip; wrap the prosciutto in a spiral along the length of the asparagus (don't cover the asparagus tip). Transfer to a rimmed baking sheet. Repeat with the remaining prosciutto, Parmesan, and asparagus. Sprinkle with pepper. If not serving right away, cover and refrigerate up to 6 hours.

3. Bake the prosciutto-wrapped asparagus 10 minutes. Transfer to paper towels to drain. Arrange on platter and serve warm.

Each serving About 30 calories, 3g protein, 1g carbohydrate, 2g fat (1g saturated), 0g fiber, 150mg sodium.

TESTING NOTE Asparagus pairs with many flavors. To add a bit of Spanish flair, replace the prosciutto with serrano ham and use aged manchego cheese instead of Parmesan. For French style, use Bayonne ham and aged gruyere.

chinese dumplings & sauce

PREP: 45 MIN / TOTAL: 55 MIN / MAKES 36 DUMPLINGS

2 cups packed sliced Napa cabbage (Chinese cabbage)

8 ounces ground pork

1 green onion, finely chopped

1½ teaspoons minced, peeled fresh ginger

2 tablespoons soy sauce

1 tablespoon dry sherry

2 teaspoons cornstarch

36 wonton wrappers

1 large egg white, beaten

Soy Dipping Sauce (below)

1. In a 2-quart saucepan, heat 1 inch water to boiling over high heat. Add the cabbage and boil 1 minute; drain. Immediately rinse the cabbage with cold running water to stop further cooking. With your hands, squeeze out as much water from the cabbage as possible. Finely chop the cabbage. Squeeze out any remaining water from the cabbage; place it in a medium bowl. Stir in the pork, green onion, ginger, soy sauce, sherry, and cornstarch until well blended.

2. Arrange half of the wonton wrappers on waxed paper. With a pastry brush, brush each wrapper lightly with egg white. Spoon 1 rounded teaspoon of filling into the center of each wrapper. Bring two opposite corners of each wonton wrapper together over the filling; pinch and pleat the edges together to seal in the filling. Repeat with remaining wrappers, egg white, and filling.

3. In a deep 12-inch nonstick skillet, heat ½ inch water to boiling over high heat. Place all dumplings, pleated edges up, in one layer in the skillet. With a spatula, move the dumplings gently to prevent them from sticking to the bottom of skillet; heat the water to boiling. Reduce the heat; cover and simmer until the dumplings are cooked through, about 5 minutes.

4. Meanwhile, prepare Soy Dipping Sauce.

5. With a slotted spoon, transfer the dumplings to a platter. Serve with dipping sauce.

SOY DIPPING SAUCE In a small serving bowl, stir ¼ **cup soy sauce,** ¼ **cup seasoned rice vinegar or white wine vinegar,** and **2 tablespoons peeled fresh ginger,** cut into very thin slivers, until blended. Makes about ½ cup.

Each dumpling (with sauce) About 45 calories, 2g protein, 6g carbohydrate, 1g fat (1g saturated), 0g fiber, 325mg sodium.

LEMON JULEP 107

STRAWBERRY ICED TEA 107

CITRUS SPRITZER 107

strawberry iced tea

PREP: 10 MIN / TOTAL: 30 MIN / MAKES ABOUT 10 CUPS

1 pound strawberries, hulled and sliced

¾ cup sugar

¼ cup water

8 cups unsweetened iced tea

1. In a large pitcher, stir together strawberries, sugar and water. Let stand 20 minutes.

2. Add the iced tea, stirring to combine. Refrigerate until cold. Serve over ice.

Each serving About 75 calories, 1g protein, 18g carbohydrate, 0g fat (0g saturated), 1g fiber, 6mg sodium.

lemon julep

PREP: 15 MIN / TOTAL: 15 MIN / MAKES ABOUT 9 CUPS

2 cups fresh mint leaves, plus more for garnish

2 lemons, sliced

6 cups lemonade

1 cup bourbon (optional)

In a large pitcher, combine the mint leaves and lemons. With the handle end of a wooden spoon, mash the mint and lemons. Stir in the lemonade and bourbon, if desired. Serve over crushed ice and garnish with mint.

Each serving About 90 calories, 0g protein, 22g carbohydrate, 0g fat (0g saturated), 1g fiber, 14mg sodium.

citrus spritzer

PREP: 10 MIN / TOTAL: 40 MIN / MAKES ABOUT 10 CUPS

4 cups orange juice

4 cups lemon-lime seltzer

2 oranges, sliced

2 limes, sliced

In a large pitcher, stir together the orange juice, seltzer, oranges, and limes. Refrigerate at least 30 minutes. Serve over ice.

Each serving About 60 calories, 1g protein, 15g carbohydrate, 0g fat (0g saturated), 1g fiber, 12mg sodium.

berry & citrus spritzer

(See photo on page 80.)

PREP: 15 MIN / TOTAL: 15 MIN, PLUS CHILLING / SERVES 6

1 bottle (750 milliliters) dry rosé wine

8 ounces strawberries, hulled and sliced

1 medium orange, cut into quarters and sliced

6 ounces mixed berries

1 lime, sliced

¼ cup orange liqueur

¼ cup sugar

Seltzer or lemon-lime soda

In a large pitcher, stir together the wine, strawberries, orange, berries, lime, orange liqueur, and sugar. Refrigerate until cold, at least 2 and up to 6 hours. To serve, pour into glasses and top with some seltzer.

Each serving About 205 calories, 1g protein, 25g carbohydrate, 0g fat, 3g fiber, 10mg sodium.

berry bellini party ice

(See photo on page 110.)

PREP: 15 MIN / TOTAL: 15 MIN, PLUS FREEZING / SERVES 6

½ cup pureed
strawberries
(7 to 8 large berries)

¼ cup lemonade
Prosecco

Combine the strawberries and lemonade; use to fill each cup of an ice cube tray half full. Freeze until solid. Repeat with Prosecco to form a second layer. Serve in glasses of more Prosecco.

Each serving About 30 calories, 0g protein, 3g carbohydrate, 0g fat (0g saturated), 0g fiber, 3mg sodium.

pineapple-mango-orange party ice

(See photo on page 110.)

PREP: 20 MIN / TOTAL: 20 MIN, PLUS FREEZING / SERVES 6

½ cup pineapple juice
½ cup mango juice

½ cup orange juice
Rum, for serving

Fill an ice tray one-third full with pineapple juice; freeze until solid. Repeat with mango juice, then orange juice to form 2 more layers. Serve in glasses of rum.

Each serving About 30 calories, 0g protein, 7g carbohydrate, 0g fat (0g saturated), 0g fiber, 3mg sodium.

piña colada party ice

PREP: 15 MIN / TOTAL: 15 MIN, PLUS FREEZING / SERVES 6

1 cup pineapple juice
½ cup coconut milk

Coconut rum,
for serving

Fill an ice tray one-third full with pineapple juice; freeze until solid. Repeat with the coconut milk, then more pineapple juice to form 2 more layers. Serve in glasses of coconut rum.

Each serving About 60 calories, 1g protein, 6g carbohydrate, 4g fat (4g saturated), 0g fiber, 4mg sodium.

strawberry-kiwi lemonade party ice

(See photo on page 110.)

PREP: 15 MIN / TOTAL: 15 MIN, PLUS FREEZING / SERVES 6

1 cup pureed kiwifruit
(4 to 5 kiwis)
¼ cup lemonade

4 strawberries, sliced
Lemonade, for serving

Combine the kiwi with the lemonade; pour into each cup of an ice tray. Top each cube with 1 strawberry slice. Freeze until solid. Serve in lemonade.

Each serving About 45 calories, 1g protein, 10g carbohydrate, 0g fat (0g saturated), 2g fiber, 2mg sodium.

razzie spritzers

PREP: 10 MIN / TOTAL: 15 MIN / MAKES ¾ CUP

6 ounces raspberries

¼ cup sugar

¼ cup water

1 tablespoon lemon juice

Prosecco, Champagne, or sparkling water

1. In a small saucepan, combine the raspberries, sugar, and water to boiling over medium-high heat. Cook, mashing the berries, 3 minutes. Strain through a fine sieve and stir in the lemon juice.

2. Spoon 1 or 2 tablespoons into each glass and top with Prosecco.

Each tablespoon of syrup About 25 calories, 0g protein, 5g carbohydrate, 0g fat (0g saturated), 0g fiber, 0mg sodium.

TESTING NOTE Forgot to put the bubbly in the fridge? Cool any wine in 20 minutes or less: Add a handful of salt to a bucket of ice and water. Salt allows the water to drop to a temp below freezing without turning into ice.

GOOD TO KNOW

ICED TEA & LEMONADE FOR A CROWD

For iced tea, use 1 tea bag for every 8 ounces of water. The best method is to measure your water and chill half of it. Boil the remaining water, pour it into a heatproof pitcher over the tea bags, and steep for 5 minutes. (You can add mint leaves, lemon peel, or other flavorings to the hot liquid.) Remove the tea bags and flavorings and add the chilled water. For lemonade, use a 1-to-1-to-1 ratio: Make a syrup with equal amounts of water and sugar, then add an equal amount of lemon juice. Mix 1 part of this very concentrated base with 1 part water, then serve over ice.

mojito party ice

PREP: 15 MIN / TOTAL: 15 MIN, PLUS FREEZING / SERVES 6

1¼ cups limeade

¼ cup lime juice

Lime zest

Chopped mint

Rum, for serving

Combine the limeade and lime juice; pour into an ice tray. Add a pinch each of lime zest and chopped mint to each cube. Freeze until solid; serve in glasses of rum.

Each serving About 30 calories, 0g protein, 7g carbohydrate, 0g fat (0g saturated), 0g fiber, 4mg sodium.

homemade raspberry & ginger cocktail syrup

(See photo on page 110.)

PREP: 20 MIN / TOTAL: 20 MIN, PLUS CHILLING / MAKES ABOUT 2 CUPS

6 cups raspberries (about 1½ pounds)

2 cups sugar

2 tablespoons grated, peeled fresh ginger

Pinch of salt

¼ cup cider vinegar

Mash the raspberries, sugar, ginger, and salt until mostly smooth. Refrigerate 1 to 2 days. Strain the mixture into a medium bowl. Discard the solids. Stir in the cider vinegar. Syrup can be refrigerated up to 6 months.

Each tablespoon About 60 calories, 0g protein, 14g carbohydrate, 0g fat (0g saturated), 0g fiber, 5mg sodium.

TROPICAL FAUX-GRIA AND ROSÉ–WHITE PEACH SANGRIA 111

MELON RUM PUNCH 111

HOMEMADE RASPBERRY & GINGER COCKTAIL SYRUP 109

BERRY BELLINI PARTY ICE, PINEAPPLE-MANGO-ORANGE PARTY ICE, AND STRAWBERRY-KIWI LEMONADE PARTY ICE 108

sangria

PREP: 15 MIN / TOTAL: 15 MIN / SERVES 14

- 2 oranges
- 2 lemons
- 1 bottle (750 milliliters) dry red wine, chilled
- ¼ cup brandy
- ¼ cup orange-flavored liqueur
- ⅓ cup sugar
- 3 cups plain seltzer or club soda, chilled
- Ice cubes (optional)

1. With a vegetable peeler, remove the peel from 1 orange and 2 lemons. (Refrigerate the lemons for another use.) Squeeze the juice from both oranges.

2. In a 2½-quart pitcher, combine the wine, orange juice, brandy, liqueur, and sugar; stir until the sugar completely dissolves.

3. Stir in the orange and lemon peels and seltzer. To serve, fill wine glasses halfway with ice, if desired, and pour sangria over.

Each serving About 80 calories, 0g protein, 7g carbohydrate, 0g fat (0g saturated), 0g fiber, 15mg sodium.

VARIATIONS

White Sangria

Prepare as directed, but substitute **1 bottle (750 milliliters) dry white wine** for red wine and add **1 ripe peach**, peeled, pitted, and cut into thin wedges, or **1 cup sliced unsweetened frozen peaches** with the citrus peel in step 3.

Cucumber-Melon Sangria

(See photo on page 78.)
In a large pitcher, mix **1 bottle (750 milliliters) dry white wine**; **½ cup each gin and packed mint leaves**; **½ English cucumber**, sliced; **½ honeydew melon**, cubed; and **3 tablespoons superfine sugar**. Chill at least 1 hour or up to 1 day; to serve, top with **1 cup seltzer**.

Restaurant-Style Red Sangria

(See photo on page 78.)
On a tray, freeze **2 cup grapes** and **12 ounces blackberries and raspberries**. In a large pitcher, mix **1 bottle (750 millileters) dry red wine**, **1 cup orange juice**, **½ cup tequila**, **¼ cup orange-flavored liqueur**, **3 tablespoons superfine sugar**, and **1 orange**, sliced. Chill 1 hour or up to 1 day; to serve, add fruit.

Tropical Faux-Gria

In a large pitcher, mix **4 cups pineapple juice**; **2 cups each orange juice, cream soda, and pineapple chunks**; **1 medium orange**, sliced; and **½ green apple**, thinly sliced. Chill at least 1 hour or up to 1 day.

Rosé–White Peach Sangria

In a large pitcher, mix **1 bottle (750 milliliters) dry rosé wine**, **½ cup elderflower liqueur**, **¼ cup brandy**, **1 cup raspberries**, and **2 medium white peaches**, sliced. Chill at least 1 hour or up to 1 day.

melon rum punch

PREP: 15 MIN / TOTAL: 15 MIN / SERVES 12

- 6 cups watermelon, seedless
- 1 cup lemon sorbet
- 2 tablespoons lemon juice
- 1 cup light rum
- Pinch of salt

Puree the watermelon, sorbet, lemon juice, rum, and salt. Strain and pour into a watermelon keg or punch bowl. Serve over ice.

Each serving About 85 calories, 0g protein, 12g carbohydrate, 0g fat (0g saturated), 1g fiber, 14mg sodium.

TESTING NOTE To create a watermelon keg: Take a thin slice off the bottom of a watermelon, cut off the top, and scoop out the insides. Carve a hole, and attach a spigot.

wassail

PREP: 10 MIN / TOTAL: 35 MIN / SERVES 16

- ½ gallon apple cider or juice
- 1 lemon, thinly sliced
- 2 tablespoons packed brown sugar
- 2 cinnamon sticks (3 inches each)
- 12 whole allspice berries
- 12 whole cloves
- 6 lady apples, or 1 Golden Delicious apple
- 1 cup applejack or apple brandy

1. In a 5-quart nonreactive Dutch oven, combine the cider, lemon slices, brown sugar, cinnamon sticks, and allspice berries; heat to boiling over medium-high heat. Reduce the heat and simmer 10 minutes.

2. Insert 2 cloves into each lady apple or all the cloves into the Golden Delicious apple. Add the apples and applejack to the cider and cook until heated through, about 2 minutes. Serve hot.

Each serving About 110 calories, 0g protein, 18g carbohydrate, 0g fat (0g saturated), 0g fiber, 5mg sodium.

hot mulled wine

PREP: 10 MIN / TOTAL: 30 MIN / SERVES 16

- 2 cups sugar
- 1 cup water
- 1 small orange, thinly sliced
- 1 small lemon, thinly sliced
- 3 cinnamon sticks (3 inches each)
- 8 whole cloves
- 1 bottle (750 milliliters) dry red wine

1. In a 4-quart nonreactive saucepan, combine the sugar, water, orange, lemon, cinnamon sticks, and cloves; heat to boiling over high heat, stirring until the sugar dissolves. Reduce the heat to medium and cook 3 minutes.

2. Add the wine to the saucepan and heat, stirring, until hot (but do not boil). Serve hot.

Each serving About 170 calories, 0g protein, 28g carbohydrate, 0g fat (0g saturated), 0g fiber, 5mg sodium.

holiday champagne punch & ice ring

PREP: 20 MIN / TOTAL: 20 MIN, PLUS FREEZING / SERVES 20

- 1 pint strawberries
- 1 pound seedless green grapes, stemmed
- 2 cups orange juice
- ¼ cup orange-flavored liqueur
- 1 bottle (1 liter) ginger ale, chilled
- 1 bottle (750 milliliters) Champagne
- 1 bunch fresh mint

1. Prepare the ice ring: Fill a 5-cup ring mold with ¼ inch cold water; freeze until hard, about 45 minutes. Reserve 8 strawberries; slice the remaining strawberries. On top of the ice in the ring mold, decoratively arrange half of the sliced strawberries and ½ cup grapes. Add just enough water to cover but little enough to prevent fruit from floating. Freeze until hard, about 45 minutes. Repeat with the remaining strawberry slices, another ½ cup grapes, and enough water to cover the fruit; freeze until hard, about 45 minutes.

2. With kitchen shears, cut the remaining grapes into small bunches; arrange the grape bunches and reserved whole strawberries alternately in the ring mold. Add enough water to come up to rim of mold, allowing some fruit to be exposed above the water; freeze until hard, about 45 minutes or up to 6 hours.

3. About 15 minutes before serving, and in a 5-quart punch bowl or bowl large enough to hold the ice ring, combine the orange juice and liqueur. Stir in the ginger ale and Champagne.

4. Unmold the ice ring and turn it fruit side up. Tuck small mint sprigs between the grapes and strawberries. Add the ice ring to the punch bowl.

Each serving About 85 calories, 0g protein, 14g carbohydrate, 0g fat (0g saturated), 1g fiber, 10mg sodium.

Tip This is a perfect time to use budget bubbles. Look for Prosecco or Spanish Cava to get the best bang for your buck. For an alcohol-free version, skip the bubbly, add a bottle of sparkling lemonade or double the ginger ale, and add ¼ cup fresh lemon juice.

irish coffee

PREP: 5 MIN / TOTAL: 5 MIN / SERVES 1

- **5 ounces strong freshly brewed coffee**
- **1 jigger (3 tablespoons) Irish whiskey**
- **2 to 3 teaspoons sugar**
- **¼ cup whipped cream**

In a heatproof stemmed glass or mug, stir the coffee, whiskey, and sugar until the sugar dissolves. Top with whipped cream. Serve hot.

Each serving About 255 calories, 1g protein, 12g carbohydrate, 11g fat (7g saturated), 0g fiber, 15mg sodium.

homemade irish cream

(See photo on page 80.)

PREP: 10 MIN / TOTAL: 15 MIN / SERVES 14

- **1 can (14 ounces) sweetened condensed milk**
- **1 cup heavy cream**
- **1 cup Irish whiskey (or milk for a nonalcoholic version)**
- **2 tablespoons chocolate syrup**
- **1½ teaspoons instant coffee or espresso granules**
- **1 teaspoon vanilla extract**
- **½ teaspoon almond extract**
- **Coffee or ice cream, for serving (optional)**

In a blender, blend the sweetened condensed milk, heavy cream, Irish whiskey, chocolate syrup, instant coffee granules, and extracts until smooth. If desired, add a splash to coffee or pour it over ice cream, or sip it on the rocks. Pour into a glass bottle or jar and refrigerate up to 1 month.

Each serving 195 calories, 3g protein, 18g carbohydrate, 9g fat (5g saturated), 0g fiber, 43mg sodium.

peach melba slushie

PREP: 10 MIN / TOTAL: 10 MIN / SERVES 6

- **3 cups ice**
- **2 cups peeled and sliced peaches (fresh or frozen)**
- **1 container (6 ounces) raspberries, lightly mashed**
- **¼ cup agave nectar**
- **2 tablespoons sugar**
- **1 tablespoon fresh lemon juice**
- **1 teaspoon vanilla extract**
- **1 cup vodka (optional)**

In a blender, blend the ice, peaches, raspberries, agave, sugar, lemon juice, vanilla, and vodka until smooth.

Each serving About 95 calories, 1g protein, 23g carbohydrate, 0g fat (0g saturated), 3g fiber, 0mg sodium.

frozen margarita

PREP: 10 MIN / TOTAL: 10 MIN / SERVES 4

- **4 cups ice**
- **½ cup tequila**
- **½ cup orange-flavored liqueur**
- **¼ cup fresh lime juice (from 2 to 3 limes)**

In a blender, blend the ice, tequila, liqueur, and lime juice until smooth.

Each serving About 150 calories, 0g protein, 11g carbohydrate, 0g fat (0g saturated), 0g fiber, 1mg sodium.

mango margarita

PREP: 15 MIN / TOTAL: 15 MIN / SERVES 8

- 6 cups ice
- 3 ripe mangoes, peeled and chopped
- 3 tablespoons orange juice
- 2 tablespoons honey
- 2 tablespoons lime juice
- 1 teaspoon grated orange peel
- 1 cup white tequila (optional)

In a blender, blend the ice, mangoes, orange juice, honey, lime juice, orange peel, and tequila, if desired, until smooth.

Each serving About 95 calories, 1g protein, 24g carbohydrate, 0g fat (0g saturated), 2g fiber, 2mg sodium.

pineapple coconut slushie

PREP: 10 MIN / TOTAL: 10 MIN / SERVES 8

- 6 cups ice
- 3 cups fresh pineapple chunks
- 1 can (15 ounces) cream of coconut
- 1 cup pineapple juice
- 1 teaspoon grated orange peel
- 1½ cups dark rum (optional)

In a blender, blend the ice, pineapple, cream of coconut, pineapple juice, orange peel, and dark rum, if desired, until smooth.

Each serving About 295 calories, 0g protein, 52g carbohydrate, 10g fat (9g saturated), 1g fiber, 30mg sodium.

kiwi slushie

PREP: 10 MIN / TOTAL: 10 MIN / SERVES 6

- 4 cups ice
- 6 kiwis, peeled and sliced
- 6 tablespoons agave nectar
- ⅓ cup packed fresh mint
- 2 teaspoons fresh lime juice
- 1 cup light rum (optional)

In a blender, blend the ice, kiwis, agave, mint, lime juice, and rum, if desired, until smooth.

Each serving About 105 calories, 1g protein, 27g carbohydrate, 0g fat (0g saturated), 2g fiber, 4mg sodium.

bourbon peach sweet tea

PREP: 5 MIN / TOTAL: 15 MIN, PLUS CHILLING / SERVES 12

- 8⅔ cups water
- 8 bags peach-flavored tea
- 2 bags black or English breakfast tea
- 20 thin slices peeled fresh ginger, chopped
- ⅔ cup sugar
- 1 cup bourbon
- ¼ cup fresh lemon juice
- Mint, for garnish

1. In a small saucepan, heat 4 cups water to simmering over high heat. Remove the saucepan from the heat. Add the peach-flavored tea bags; steep 5 minutes. Add the black tea bags; steep 5 minutes. Remove all tea bags, pressing to squeeze out any tea. Discard the bags. Transfer the tea to a medium pitcher. Add 4 cups cold water; refrigerate until cold, about 4 hours.

2. Meanwhile, in the same saucepan, combine the ginger, sugar, and ⅔ cup water; heat to simmering over medium heat. Reduce the heat to maintain a simmer; simmer 15 minutes. Strain out and discard the ginger. Refrigerate the syrup until cold.

3. Stir the cold ginger syrup into the tea along with the bourbon and lemon juice. Serve over ice; garnish with mint.

Each serving About 130 calories, 0g protein, 18g carbohydrate, 0g fat (0g saturated), 0g fiber, 5mg sodium.

BOURBON PEACH SWEET TEA 114

one pot

Soup, stew, chili, and chowder. The recipes in this chapter run the gamut from elegant first courses to hearty dinners in a bowl. Whether you simmer them on your stovetop or in a slow-cooker or multicooker, the wafting aroma of Chili-Braised Beef (page 140) or Classic Chicken Noodle Soup (page 160) will have the whole family standing by for dinner. Pair soups with a salad (see chapter 12, page 467) and some bread to make a complete meal. Partner chili with warmed tortillas or cornbread, and stews with a crispy baguette or biscuits. How easy is that?

Many of these recipes yield a large batch. Make one! They taste even better a day or two later, and most freeze beautifully. Pack up extras in single- or double-portion containers and freeze for those "I don't feel like cooking" nights.

TACO NIGHT CARNITAS 124

SPRING MINESTRONE 149

WINTER SQUASH & LENTIL STEW 133

QUICKER COQ AU
VIN BLANC 136

Stew

Stew is a mélange of meat, vegetables, liquid, and seasonings cooked slowly to tenderize the meat and meld the flavors of all the ingredients. One can be made with chicken, pork, beef, veal, fish, or root vegetables cut into small pieces or hearty chunks. Some stews are chock-full of a variety of vegetables; others contain only one or two for flavoring. The liquid can be water, broth, tomato juice, wine, or a combination. Just about every culture has stews in its repertoire, and you'll find many in this chapter. For a soul-satisfying dinner, serve stew in large shallow bowls with hunks of bread for sopping up all the flavorful juices.

Chili

Just who cooked up the first chili is in dispute, but many "chili heads" believe credit goes to the Texas trail cooks who fed the cowboys while "winning the West." In fact, by 1880, eating a "bowl of red" was commonplace in cities like San Antonio. We've collected a tasty variety of all-American chilis. Some are made with chunks of beef or pork, others with ground beef. Beans? Tomato? What's verboten in Texas is de rigueur in Cincinnati, and the New Mexican Green Chili (page 168)—a bold pot of pork, onions, jalapeños, cumin, fresh tomatillos, and poblanos—is the best of the Southwest.

Soup

A soup can be a crystal-clear golden liquid; a silky smooth and creamy puree; or thick with vegetables, noodles, and a protein, such as chicken or beef. Whether you serve soup as a light and elegant first course, a substantial rib-sticking meal-in-a-pot, or a refreshing cooler on a summer's day, there is a soup to suit your menu. Some soups are always served cold, like gazpacho, and some are always served hot, such as split pea soup. And others are so versatile that they are just as delicious hot, cold, or at room temperature.

Chowder

Somewhere between soup and stew, chowder uses flour, potatoes, or crumbled crackers as a thickener. The term comes from the French *chaudière*, the pot in which chowder was originally cooked. A Dutch oven or stockpot is all you need to make one. Clam chowder, either New England with a cream base or Manhattan with a tomato base, is the most famous, but corn, fish, and all manner of vegetables are all foods for chowder.

SOY-BRAISED BEEF &
TOMATO-MINT SALAD 125

10 Tips for the
SLOW COOKER

1 **Less tender cuts** of meat and poultry—such as pork and lamb shoulder, chuck roast, beef brisket, and poultry legs—are best suited for slow cooking. Skim and discard fat from the cooking liquid when done.

2 **Fish and other seafood** are not a good fit unless they are added during the last hour of cooking.

3 **Avoid using ground meat;** long, slow cooking compromises its texture, giving it a mealy, sandy quality. If you do, cook on Low for no more than 4 hours.

4 **Slow cooking** tends to intensify flavorful spices and seasonings such as chili powder and garlic, so use them conservatively. Dried herbs may lose flavor, so adjust the seasonings at the end of cooking. If you're using fresh herbs, save some to toss in at the last minute for best flavor.

5 **For richer flavor** in stews, sprinkle the meat and poultry with flour and brown it in a skillet before slow cooking. Scrape up any browned bits in the skillet and add them to the slow cooker to help thicken the sauce and enhance flavor.

6 **To make cleanup easier,** use slow-cooker liners, or spritz the slow cooker with vegetable cooking spray.

7 **For even cooking,** fill the slow cooker at least halfway—but never to the brim. For soups and stews, leave about 2 inches of space between food and lid.

8 **Don't peek!** Keep the lid on until near the end of cooking time. Even a quick look will release heat and increase cooking time. Resist stirring the pot, because meat and vegetables may break up.

9 **If your recipe produces more liquid** than you want, remove the solids with a slotted spoon to a serving dish and keep them warm. Turn the slow cooker temperature to High; cook the remaining liquid, uncovered, to reduce it to the desired thickness.

10 **Most recipes can be prepped the night before**—all you have to do in the morning is toss in the ingredients and flip the switch on the slow cooker! Premeasure ingredients, precut vegetables, trim meats, and mix liquids and seasonings. Refrigerate components separately in bowls or resealable plastic bags.

GOOD TO KNOW

PRESSURE COOKING TIPS

READ THE MANUAL. A stove-top cooker will work differently from an electric one, and they can vary from model to model.

RAISE THE PRESSURE. Use high heat to crank up the pressure inside the cooker, then reduce the temp to maintain pressure.

SPEED THINGS UP EVEN MORE. Use the quick pressure release setting. If your cooker doesn't have one, run cold water all over its outside (avoiding the vents) until the pressure on the indicator drops.

short ribs
with root vegetables

PREP: 35 MIN / TOTAL: 8 HR 30 MIN ON LOW / SERVES 6

- 3 pounds bone-in beef chuck short ribs
- Salt
- Ground black pepper
- 2 large parsnips (about 4 ounces each), peeled and cut into 1-inch chunks
- 1 medium turnip (about 8 ounces), peeled and cut into 1-inch chunks
- 1 bag (16 ounces) peeled baby carrots
- 1 jumbo onion coarsely chopped
- 4 large cloves garlic, thinly sliced
- 1 teaspoon dried thyme
- 2 cups dry red wine
- ¼ cup tomato paste

1. Heat a 12-inch skillet over medium-high heat until hot. Add the ribs to the skillet and sprinkle with ½ teaspoon salt and ¼ teaspoon pepper. Cook the ribs about 10 minutes, or until well browned on all sides, turning occasionally.

2. Meanwhile, in a 5- to 6-quart slow cooker, place the parsnips, turnip, and carrots.

3. Transfer the ribs to the slow cooker on top of vegetables. Discard any drippings in the skillet. Reduce the heat to medium; add the onion to the skillet and cook about 8 minutes, or until browned, stirring frequently. Stir in the garlic and thyme and cook 1 minute, stirring constantly. Add the wine and heat to boiling over high heat, stirring to loosen any browned bits from the bottom of the skillet. Remove the skillet from heat and stir in the tomato paste, ½ teaspoon salt, and ¼ teaspoon pepper.

4. Pour the wine mixture over the ribs in the slow cooker. Cover the slow cooker with the lid and cook as the manufacturer directs on the Low setting 8 to 10 hours (or on the High setting 4 to 5 hours), or until the meat is fork-tender and falling off the bones.

5. With the tongs, transfer the ribs to a deep platter; discard bones, if you like. With a spoon, skim and discard fat from the sauce in the slow cooker. Spoon the vegetables and sauce over the ribs.

Each serving About 655 calories, 27g protein, 24g carbohydrate, 50g fat (21g saturated), 5g fiber, 535mg sodium.

slow-cooker tex-mex chicken soup

PREP: 20 MIN / TOTAL: 4 HR 20 MIN / SERVES 6

- 2½ pounds bone-in, skin-on chicken thighs, skin removed (about 6 thighs)
- 4 cups lower-sodium chicken broth
- 3 large stalks celery, sliced
- 3 medium carrots, sliced
- 2 poblano peppers, seeded and chopped
- 1 medium onion, chopped
- 3 cloves garlic, chopped
- 1 tablespoon ground cumin
- 1 tablespoon ground coriander
- 2 cans (15 ounces each) white (cannellini) beans, drained
- Salt
- 8 ounces Monterey Jack cheese, shredded
- 2 tablespoons fresh lime juice
- Chopped avocado, cilantro leaves, sour cream, and Baked Tortilla Strips (optional; below), for garnish

1. To a 6- to 7-quart slow cooker, add the chicken, broth, celery, carrots, peppers, onion, garlic, cumin, coriander, beans, and ½ teaspoon salt. Cover and cook on Low 4 to 5 hours, or until the carrots are tender.

2. Remove and discard the bones from the chicken; shred the chicken and return it to the slow cooker.

3. Add the cheese, lime juice, and ¼ teaspoon salt to the slow-cooker bowl, stirring until the cheese melts. Serve topped with avocado, cilantro, sour cream, and Baked Tortilla Strips, if desired.

BAKED TORTILLA STRIPS Preheat the oven to 425°F. Stack **4 small (4-inch) corn tortillas**; thinly slice them into ⅛-inch-wide strips. Arrange the strips in a single layer on a large baking sheet. Spray all over with **nonstick cooking spray**. Bake 4 to 5 minutes, or until deep golden brown. Let cool completely.

Each serving (soup only) About 445 calories, 40g protein, 34g carbohydrate, 16g fat (7g saturated), 14g fiber, 1,070 mg sodium.

Tip Make tortilla strips in your air fryer! Preheat air fryer to 350°F. Spray 4 small corn tortillas with oil and stack. Cut stack into pieces. Place in air fryer basket. Air-fry 6 minutes or until deep golden brown, stirring twice. Let cool completely.

SLOW-COOKER TEX-MEX CHICKEN SOUP 122

taco night carnitas

(See photo on page 118.)

PREP: 20 MIN / TOTAL: 7 HR 30 MIN / SERVES 8

- 1 tablespoon canola oil
- 4 pounds boneless pork shoulder, trimmed, cut into 3 pieces
- 2 tablespoons ground cumin
- 1 teaspoon salt
- 1 large white onion, chopped
- 3 poblano chiles, seeded and chopped
- 2 serrano chiles, sliced
- 4 cloves garlic, crushed with a garlic press
- ½ cup chicken broth or water
- ¼ cup fresh lime juice
- 24 small (4-inch) tortillas, warmed
- Cilantro leaves, sliced green onions, sliced radishes, salsa, and lime wedges, for serving

1. In a 12-inch skillet, heat the oil over medium-high heat until hot. Season the pork all over with the cumin and salt. Cook 5 minutes, or until browned on both sides, turning over once halfway through. Transfer the pork to the slow cooker.

2. To the skillet, add the onion, chiles, and garlic; cook 2 minutes, stirring often. Transfer to the slow-cooker bowl along with the broth and lime juice. Cover and cook on Low 7 hours, or until very tender.

3. Transfer the pork to a cutting board; with 2 forks, pull the meat into bite-size shreds, discarding any fat. Serve with tortillas and fixings.

Each serving About 430 calories, 36g protein, 38g carbohydrate, 14g fat (4g saturated), 4g fiber, 430 mg sodium.

Tip Use a dry nonstick skillet over medium heat to toast the tortillas on both sides until brown in spots; wrap first in a damp paper towel, then in foil. Pressed for time? You can also microwave them, wrapped in damp paper towels!

tangy chicken cacciatore

(See photo on page 126.)

PREP: 15 MIN / TOTAL: 5 HR 15 MIN / SERVES 4

- 1 cup chicken broth
- 1 can (6 ounces) tomato paste
- 2½ pounds bone-in, skin-on chicken thighs, skin removed and discarded
- ½ teaspoon salt
- ½ teaspoon ground black pepper
- 2 medium red bell peppers, seeded and sliced
- 12 ounces cremini (baby bella) mushrooms, trimmed and cut into halves
- 1 medium onion, chopped
- 2 pickled cherry peppers, stemmed and cut into halves
- 2 cloves garlic, crushed with a garlic press
- 2 small sprigs fresh rosemary
- Cooked polenta, for serving
- 2 tablespoons capers, drained and finely chopped, for garnish

1. In the bowl of a 7- to 8-quart slow cooker, whisk together the broth and tomato paste.

2. Sprinkle the chicken with salt and black pepper; transfer the chicken to the slow cooker along with the bell peppers, mushrooms, onion, cherry peppers, garlic, and rosemary. Cover and cook on Low 5 hours, or until the chicken is cooked through (165°F).

3. To serve, spoon the chicken over polenta. Garnish with capers.

Each serving (without polenta) About 300 calories, 38g protein, 20g carbohydrate, 8g fat (2g saturated), 4g fiber, 990 mg sodium.

latin-style beef (ropa vieja)

PREP: 20 MIN / TOTAL: 9 HR 20 MIN ON LOW / SERVES 8

- 1 can (14½ ounces) diced tomatoes
- 1 tablespoon capers, drained
- 1 tablespoon ground cumin
- ½ teaspoon ground cinnamon
- 1 teaspoon salt
- 3 cloves garlic, sliced
- 2 large red, yellow, and/ or green bell peppers, sliced
- 2 large pickled jalapeño chiles, sliced
- 1 medium onion, sliced
- 1 fresh beef brisket (about 3 pounds)
- Warm flour or corn tortillas and/or cooked white rice with parsley (optional)

1. In a 4½- to 6-quart slow cooker, combine the tomatoes with their juice, the capers, cumin, cinnamon, and salt. Add the garlic, bell peppers, jalapeños, onion, and brisket; stir to coat the brisket and vegetables with the tomato mixture. Cover and cook on the Low setting 9 to 10 hours (or on High 6 to 6½ hours).

2. With a slotted spoon, transfer the brisket and vegetables to a large bowl. With 2 forks, shred the brisket along the grain into fine strips. Skim and discard the fat from the cooking liquid. Stir the cooking liquid into the brisket mixture. Serve the brisket mixture with tortillas and/or rice, if you like.

Each serving About 400 calories, 35g protein, 7g carbohydrate, 25g fat (9g saturated), 2g fiber, 690mg sodium.

easiest-ever spinach lasagna

(See photo on page 126.)

PREP: 20 MIN / TOTAL: 4 HR 20 MIN / SERVES 8

- 1 pound part-skim ricotta cheese
- 10 ounces frozen chopped spinach, thawed and squeezed dry
- 2 cups shredded mozzarella cheese
- 1 large egg
- Salt
- 1 jar (32 ounces) marinara sauce
- 1 box (9 ounces) no-boil lasagna noodles

1. In a medium bowl, stir together the ricotta, spinach, all but 1 cup mozzarella, the egg, and ¼ teaspoon salt.

2. In a slow cooker, layer the marinara, noodles, and ricotta mixture, starting and ending with marinara and breaking the noodles to fit. Top with the remaining 1 cup shredded mozzarella. Cover and cook on Low 4 hours, or until the noodles are tender.

Each serving About 355 calories, 20g protein, 37g carbohydrate, 14g fat (7g saturated), 4g fiber, 815 mg sodium.

soy-braised beef & tomato-mint salad

(See photo on page 120.)

PREP: 10 MIN / TOTAL: 6 HR / SERVES 6

- 3 pounds beef brisket, trimmed of excess fat and cut into 1-inch chunks
- 5 cloves garlic, chopped
- ¼ cup packed brown sugar
- ¼ cup rice vinegar
- ¼ cup soy sauce
- 3 tablespoons fish sauce
- ½ teaspoon ground black pepper
- 1 pint grape tomatoes, cut into halves
- 1 small red onion, thinly sliced
- ½ cup fresh mint leaves
- jasmine rice, for serving

In a 7- to 8-quart slow cooker, combine the brisket, garlic, brown sugar, rice vinegar, soy sauce, fish sauce, and pepper. Cook on Low 6 to 8 hours, or until tender; toss with the tomatoes, red onion, and mint leaves. Serve with steamed jasmine rice.

Each serving About 290 cals, 42g protein, 9g carbohydrate, 10g fat (4g saturated), 2g fiber, 510mg sodium.

SLOW-BRAISED BEEF RAGÙ 127

TANGY CHICKEN CACCIATORE 124

BIG-BATCH TOMATO SAUCE 127

EASIEST-EVER SPINACH LASAGNA 125

big-batch tomato sauce

PREP: 20 MIN / TOTAL: 8 HR 20 MIN ON LOW / MAKES 12 CUPS

8 ounces thick-cut pancetta or bacon, chopped

2 medium red onions, thinly sliced

2 cloves garlic, crushed with a garlic press

½ teaspoon dried oregano

½ teaspoon crushed red pepper

Salt

Ground black pepper

4 cans (28 ounces each) whole peeled tomatoes

¼ cup tomato paste

Cooked pasta, chicken, or pork, for serving

Grated Pecorino Romano cheese, for serving

1. In a 12-inch skillet, cook the pancetta over medium-high heat 8 minutes or until crisp, stirring occasionally; with a slotted spoon, transfer the pancetta to a bowl. To the same skillet, add the onions, garlic, oregano, crushed red pepper, and ½ teaspoon each salt and black pepper. Reduce the heat to medium. Cook 4 minutes, or until the onions begin to soften, stirring often.

2. Drain 2 cans of tomatoes. In a 7- to 8-quart slow cooker, combine the drained tomatoes with the undrained tomatoes; crush with your hands. Add the tomato paste, pancetta, onion mixture, and 1 teaspoon salt. Replace the lid; cook on High 4 hours or on Low 8 hours.

3. Serve over cooked pasta, chicken, or pork. Garnish with Pecorino Romano cheese. Sauce can be frozen in airtight containers up to 1 month.

Each cup About 115 calories, 5g protein, 12g carbohydrate, 5g fat (2g saturated), 2g fiber, 925 mg sodium.

VARIATION

Vegetarian Big-Batch Tomato Sauce

Replace the pancetta with ¼ **cup olive oil.** Heat over medium heat and add **2 carrots,** peeled and chopped, and **2 ribs celery,** chopped, along with the onions and seasonings. Proceed as directed.

slow-braised beef ragù

PREP: 15 MIN / TOTAL: 10 HR 15 MIN / SERVES 8

3 stalks celery, cut into large chunks

1 medium carrot, cut into large chunks

1 medium onion, cut into large chunks

4 cloves garlic, peeled

1 tablespoon olive oil

1 beef chuck roast (3 to 4 pounds), trimmed and cut into quarters

Salt

½ teaspoon ground black pepper

¼ cup tomato paste

1 can (14 ounces) diced tomatoes, drained

1 cup dry red wine

2 sprigs fresh rosemary

1 pound pappardelle or curly egg noodles, cooked as the label directs

Finely chopped fresh parsley and grated Parmesan cheese, for garnish

1. In a food processor, pulse the celery, carrot, onion, and garlic until finely chopped, scraping down the sides of the bowl occasionally.

2. In a large skillet, heat the oil over medium-high heat until hot. Sprinkle the beef all over with ½ teaspoon salt and the pepper. Add the beef to the skillet; cook 6 to 8 minutes, or until browned on all sides, turning occasionally. Transfer the beef to a 6- to 7-quart slow cooker.

3. To the same skillet, add the vegetable mixture and ¼ teaspoon salt. Reduce the heat to medium. Cook 5 minutes, stirring occasionally. Add the tomato paste; cook 1 minute, stirring. Stir in the diced tomatoes and wine. Cook 2 minutes, stirring and scraping up the browned bits. Pour the mixture over the beef. Add the rosemary. Cover and cook on Low 10 hours, or until very tender.

4. Transfer the beef to a cutting board. Skim and discard the fat from the cooking liquid. Remove and discard any chunks of fat from the beef. Shred the beef into bite-size chunks and return it to the cooking liquid.

5. Serve the beef tossed with pappardelle; garnish with parsley and Parmesan, if desired.

Each serving About 510 calories, 48g protein, 49g carbohydrate, 12g fat (3g saturated), 4g fiber, 400 mg sodium.

african sweet potato & peanut stew

PREP: 25 MIN / TOTAL: 8 HR 25 MIN ON LOW / SERVES 6

- 3 cloves garlic, peeled
- 2 cups loosely packed fresh cilantro leaves and stems
- 1 can (28 ounces) diced tomatoes
- ½ cup creamy or chunky peanut butter
- 2 teaspoons ground cumin
- ½ teaspoon ground cinnamon
- ¼ teaspoon cayenne pepper
- ¾ teaspoon salt
- 1 cup water
- 3 pounds sweet potatoes (4 medium), peeled and cut into 2-inch chunks
- 1 can (15 to 19 ounces) chickpeas, rinsed and drained
- 1 package (16 ounces) frozen whole or cut green beans

1. In a blender or food processor with the knife blade attached, blend the garlic, cilantro, tomatoes with their juice, peanut butter, cumin, cinnamon, cayenne, and salt until pureed.

2. Into a 4½- to 6-quart slow cooker, pour the peanut butter mixture; stir in the water. Add the sweet potatoes and chickpeas; stir to combine. Cover and cook on Low 8 to 10 hours (or on High 4 to 5 hours), or until the potatoes are very tender.

3. About 10 minutes before the sweet potato mixture is done, cook the green beans as the label directs. Gently stir the green beans into the stew.

Each serving About 495 calories, 16g protein, 83g carbohydrate, 13g fat (3g saturated), 12g fiber, 1,105mg sodium.

red-cooked turkey thighs
with leeks

PREP: 20 MIN / TOTAL: 8 HR 20 MIN ON LOW / SERVES 6

- 4 large leeks
- ½ cup dry sherry
- ⅓ cup soy sauce
- ¼ cup packed brown sugar
- 2 tablespoons minced, peeled fresh ginger
- 1 teaspoon Chinese five-spice powder
- 3 small turkey thighs (about 1 pound each), skin removed
- 3 cloves garlic, crushed with a garlic press
- 2 cups (about half a 16-ounce bag) peeled baby carrots

1. Cut off the roots and dark-green tops from the leeks. Discard the tough outer leaves. Cut each leek lengthwise in half, then crosswise in half. Rinse the leeks in a large bowl of cold water, swishing to remove any sand. Transfer the leeks to a colander. Repeat several times, until no sand remains. Drain well.

2. In a 4½- to 6-quart slow cooker, combine the sherry, soy sauce, brown sugar, ginger, and five-spice powder. Add the leeks, turkey, garlic, and carrots, and toss to coat with the soy mixture. Cover and cook on Low 8 to 10 hours (or on High 4 to 5 hours).

3. Transfer the turkey and vegetables to a deep platter, removing and discarding the turkey bones. Skim and discard any fat from the cooking liquid. Spoon the cooking liquid over the turkey and vegetables.

Each serving About 355 calories, 41g protein, 24g carbohydrate, 10g fat (3g saturated), 2g fiber, 1,005mg sodium.

tomatillo pork

PREP: 10 MIN / TOTAL: 8 HR 10 MIN ON LOW / SERVES 8

- 1 large bunch fresh cilantro
- 3 cloves garlic, sliced
- 2 pounds small red potatoes (about 8), cut into quarters
- 1 bone-in pork-shoulder roast (about 3 pounds), well trimmed
- 1 jar (16 to 18 ounces) salsa verde (green salsa)

1. From the bunch of cilantro, remove and set aside 15 large sprigs. Remove enough leaves from the remaining cilantro to equal ½ cup, loosely packed. Refrigerate the leaves to sprinkle over the pork after cooking.

2. In a 4½- to 6-quart slow cooker, combine the cilantro sprigs, garlic, and potatoes. Place the pork on top of the potato mixture. Pour the salsa over and around the pork. Cover and cook on Low 8 to 10 hours (or on High 5 to 5½ hours).

3. Transfer the pork to a cutting board and slice against the grain. Transfer the pork and potatoes to a deep platter; keep warm. Skim and discard the fat and cilantro from the cooking liquid. Spoon the cooking liquid over the pork and potatoes. Sprinkle the reserved cilantro leaves over the pork.

Each serving About 300 calories, 25g protein, 27g carbohydrate, 9g fat (3g saturated), 2g fiber, 295mg sodium.

GLOSSARY

Mexican **salsa verde** can be cooked or raw and is usually a mix of tomatillos, onion, serrano chiles, cilantro, and garlic. To make your own, heat 2 tablespoons vegetable oil over medium heat. Add 2 chopped medium onions and cook until translucent. Stir in 1 teaspoon ground cumin and 3 cloves garlic, crushed with a garlic press; cook 1 minute. Add 4 poblano chiles, roasted and peeled; ½ cup chopped cilantro; 2 pounds chopped tomatillos; and ½ cup water. Cover and heat to boiling; reduce heat and simmer 15 minutes, or until tomatillos are soft and easy to mash.

chicken tagine

PREP: 20 MIN / TOTAL: 8 HR 20 MIN ON LOW / SERVES 6

- 1 medium butternut squash (1½ pounds), peeled and cut into 2-inch chunks
- 2 medium tomatoes, coarsely chopped
- 1 medium onion, chopped
- 2 cloves garlic, crushed with a garlic press
- 1 can (15 to 19 ounces) chickpeas, rinsed and drained
- 1 cup chicken broth
- ⅓ cup raisins
- 2 teaspoons ground coriander
- 2 teaspoons ground cumin
- ½ teaspoon ground cinnamon
- ½ teaspoon salt
- ¼ teaspoon ground black pepper
- 3 pounds bone-in skinless chicken thighs (about 8 thighs)
- 1 box (10 ounces) plain couscous
- ½ cup pitted green olives

1. In a 6-quart slow cooker, combine the squash, tomatoes, onion, garlic, chickpeas, broth, and raisins. In a cup, combine the coriander, cumin, cinnamon, salt, and pepper. Rub the spice mixture all over the chicken thighs; place the chicken on top of the vegetable mixture. Cover and cook on Low 8 hours (or on High 4 hours).

2. About 10 minutes before serving, prepare the couscous as the label directs.

3. To serve, fluff the couscous with a fork. Stir the olives into the chicken mixture. Serve the chicken mixture over couscous.

Each serving About 545 calories, 39g protein, 80g carbohydrate, 9g fat (2g saturated), 10g fiber, 855mg sodium.

crock-star chicken

with walnut-herb sauce

PREP: 40 MIN / TOTAL: 4 HR 40 MIN / SERVES 6

- 1 medium onion, cut into ½-inch slices
- 2 tablespoons olive oil
- 1 tablespoon ground coriander
- ¼ teaspoon ground cinnamon
- ½ teaspoon ground black pepper
- 1 whole chicken (about 4 pounds)
- Salt
- ⅔ cup walnuts, toasted
- ½ cup packed fresh mint leaves, plus more for garnish
- ¼ cup packed fresh basil leaves
- 1 tablespoon fresh lemon juice
- 6 flatbreads, toasted
- Cabbage-Kohlrabi Slaw (below)

1. Arrange the onion in a single layer toward the center of the bottom of a 6- to 8-quart slow cooker. Combine the oil, coriander, cinnamon, and pepper; rub all over and inside chicken. With butcher's twine, tie the drumsticks together. Sprinkle ¾ teaspoon salt all over the chicken. Place the chicken on the onion in the slow cooker.

2. Cover and cook on High 4 hours. Transfer the chicken to a cutting board.

3. In a blender, puree 1 cup liquid from the slow cooker with the onion, walnuts, mint, basil, lemon juice, and ¼ teaspoon salt until smooth. Serve the chicken with the Walnut-Herb Sauce, flatbreads, and Cabbage-Kohlrabi Slaw.

CABBAGE-KOHLRABI SLAW Toss together **4 cups thinly sliced red cabbage; 2 small bulbs kohlrabi** (or 1 large bulb jicama), peeled and cut into matchsticks; **1 English (seedless) cucumber**, center removed, cut into matchsticks; **½ cup loosely packed fresh parsley; 2 green onions**, thinly sliced on an angle; **¼ cup fresh lemon juice;** and **¼ teaspoon salt.**

Each serving About 785 calories, 45g protein, 54g carbohydrate, 44g fat (11g saturated), 7g fiber, 1,005 mg sodium.

smoky vegan black bean chili

PREP: 20 MIN / TOTAL: 6 HR 30 MIN ON LOW / SERVES 6

- 2 tablespoons olive oil
- 2 medium carrots, chopped
- 2 stalks celery, sliced
- 1 medium onion, finely chopped
- ¼ cup tomato paste
- 3 cloves garlic, crushed with a garlic press
- 1½ teaspoon ground cumin
- 3 cups lower-sodium vegetable broth
- 3 cans (15 ounces each) lower-sodium black beans, undrained
- 1 cup frozen corn
- Avocado chunks and cilantro leaves, for serving

1. In a 12-inch skillet, heat the oil over medium-high heat. Add the carrots, celery, and onion. Cook 6 to 8 minutes, or until it starts to brown, stirring occasionally. Add the tomato paste, garlic, and cumin. Cook, stirring, 1 to 2 minutes, or until the garlic is golden and the tomato paste has browned. Stir in ½ cup broth, scraping up any browned bits.

2. Transfer the contents of the skillet to a 6- to 8-quart slow cooker along with the beans, corn, and remaining broth. Cover and cook on High 4 hours or on Low 6 hours. Serve with avocado and cilantro.

Each serving About 325 calories, 14g protein, 51g carbohydrate, 11g fat (1g saturated), 19g fiber, 535 mg sodium.

 Tip Don't sub dried beans for canned. Acidic ingredients, like the tomatoes, make the beans stay tough and take longer to cook.

INGREDIENT SPOTLIGHT

↓

Kohlrabi may resemble a white beet, but this odd-looking veggie is actually a cousin of cabbage and broccoli and tastes a bit similar to the latter. Like other members of the Brassicaeae (mustard) family, it's full of cancer-fighting phytonutrients. After peeling off the tough, fibrous skin, slice it thin and add it raw to salads and slaws. Be sure to keep the leaves to sauté (as you would kale).

CROCK-STAR CHICKEN WITH WALNUT-HERB SAUCE 130

FRENCH DIP BRISKET REUBENS 132

POT ROAST WITH RED WINE SAUCE 136

SMOKY VEGAN BLACK BEAN CHILI 130

french dip brisket reubens

(See photo on page 131.)

PREP: 10 MIN / TOTAL: 7 HR / SERVES 6

- 1 small beef brisket (about 2½ pounds), trimmed and cut into 3 pieces
- 2 medium onions, sliced
- 4 cloves garlic, crushed
- 1¾ cups beef broth
- 3 tablespoons soy sauce
- 6 sandwich rolls, split
- ¾ cup drained sauerkraut
- 6 slices Swiss cheese

1. In a 6- to 8-quart slow cooker, place the brisket, onions, garlic, beef broth, and soy sauce. Cook on Low 7 to 8 hours, or until very tender.

2. Pull the meat apart with 2 forks; place on rolls, and top each sandwich with 2 tablespoons sauerkraut and 1 slice Swiss cheese.

3. Broil just until the cheese melts. Replace the tops of each roll. Serve with cooking liquid for dipping, if desired.

Each serving About 450 calories, 47g protein, 27g carbohydrate, 17g fat (7g saturated), 2g fiber, 600mg sodium.

#SavetheFood
sauerkraut

What else can you do with sauerkraut? Use it in a sandwich instead of pickles. Sauté it with apples and onions and serve with pork chops or kielbasa, or use it in a stir-fry.

cajun surf 'n' turf stew

PREP: 30 MIN / TOTAL: 6 HR 30 MIN ON LOW / SERVES 8

- ¼ cup vegetable oil
- ¼ cup all-purpose flour
- 2 medium green bell peppers, chopped
- 1 large red bell pepper, chopped
- 3 medium stalks celery, sliced
- 1 large onion, chopped
- Salt
- 2 pounds skinless, boneless chicken thighs, cut into 1-inch chunks
- 12 ounces fresh or frozen (thawed) okra, sliced
- 6 ounces andouille sausage, sliced
- 1½ cups chicken broth
- ½ teaspoon cayenne pepper
- ¼ teaspoon dried thyme
- ½ teaspoon ground black pepper
- 12 ounces medium (16 to 20 count) shelled, deveined shrimp
- Cooked white rice, for serving

1. In a 6-quart saucepot, heat the oil over medium heat. Sprinkle in the flour, whisking to combine. Reduce the heat to medium-low. Cook 10 to 15 minutes, or until the flour is brown, whisking constantly.

2. To the same pot, add the bell peppers, celery, onion, and ¼ teaspoon salt. Increase the heat to medium. Cook 4 minutes, stirring. Transfer to a 7- to 8-quart slow cooker; stir in the chicken, okra, sausage, broth, cayenne, thyme, 1 teaspoon salt, and black pepper. Replace the lid and cook on High 4 hours or on Low 6 hours, or until the chicken is cooked through (165°F).

3. Once the chicken is cooked, add the shrimp to the slow cooker. If cooking on Low, increase to High. Cook, covered, another 5 minutes, or until the shrimp are cooked through. Serve with rice.

Each serving About 325 calories, 34g protein, 13g carbohydrate, 16g fat (3g saturated), 3g fiber, 1,065mg sodium.

winter squash & lentil stew

(See photo on page 118.)

PREP: 15 MIN / TOTAL: 35 MIN / SERVES 6

- 2 medium shallots, thinly sliced
- 1 tablespoon finely chopped, peeled fresh ginger
- 1 tablespoon vegetable oil
- 1 teaspoon ground coriander
- ½ teaspoon ground cardamom
- 1 small butternut squash, peeled, seeded and cut into 1½-inch chunks
- 1 pound green lentils, picked over
- 6 cups chicken or vegetable broth
- Salt
- 5 cups packed baby spinach
- 1 tablespoon cider vinegar
- Ground black pepper

1. In a pressure-cooker pot over medium heat, cook the shallots and ginger in oil 5 minutes, or until the shallots are golden, stirring occasionally. Add the coriander and cardamom; cook 1 minute, stirring. Add the squash, lentils, broth, and ¼ teaspoon salt.

2. Cover, lock, and bring up to pressure over high heat. Reduce the heat to medium-low. Cook 12 minutes. Release pressure by using the quick-release function.

3. Stir in the spinach, vinegar, and ½ teaspoon each salt and pepper.

Each serving About 325 calories, 19g protein, 57g carbohydrate, 4g fat (0g saturated), 15g fiber, 705mg sodium.

 Tip Green, black, or brown lentils work nicely in this—but avoid red varieties, which tend to fall apart.

chipotle lentil chili

(See photo on page 134.)

PREP: 10 MIN / TOTAL: 30 MIN / SERVES 6

- 2 chipotles in adobo
- 2 cloves garlic
- ½ cup sun-dried tomatoes
- 1 can (28 ounces) whole peeled tomatoes
- 1 tablespoon olive oil
- 1 medium onion, chopped
- 1 medium green bell pepper, chopped
- 1 tablespoon chili powder
- 4 cups lower-sodium chicken or vegetable broth
- 2 cup brown lentils
- ½ teaspoon salt
- Chopped avocado, shredded Cheddar cheese, chopped fresh cilantro leaves, and tortilla chips, for serving

1. In a food processor, puree the chipotles in adobo, garlic, and sun-dried tomatoes; pulse in the whole tomatoes until chopped.

2. In the pressure cooker, heat the oil over medium heat, cook the onion, bell pepper, and chili powder 2 minutes. Add the tomato mixture, broth, lentils, and salt. Lock the lid; cook under high pressure 12 minutes. Release pressure. Serve with chopped avocado, shredded Cheddar, fresh cilantro, and tortilla chips.

Each serving About 310 calories, 19g protein, 52g carbohydrate, 4g fat (0g saturated), 18g fiber, 870mg sodium.

CHIPOTLE LENTIL CHILI 133

WEEKNIGHT TUSCAN RAGÙ 134

weeknight tuscan ragù

PREP: 15 MIN / TOTAL: 1 HR 10 MIN / SERVES 8

- 8 ounces sweet Italian sausage, casings removed
- 2 teaspoons olive oil
- 2½ pounds boneless pork shoulder, trimmed, cut into 1-inch chunks
- Salt
- Ground black pepper
- 2 medium carrots, finely chopped
- 1 medium onion, finely chopped
- 3 cloves garlic, chopped
- 1 cup dry red wine
- 1 can (28 ounces) crushed tomatoes
- ½ cup whole milk
- 3 bay leaves
- ½ cup packed fresh basil leaves, torn
- 1 pound pappardelle pasta, cooked as the label directs
- Grated Parmesan cheese, for serving

1. In a pressure-cooker pot over medium-high heat, cook the sausage in oil 5 minutes, or until the fat has rendered, breaking up meat as it cooks. With a slotted spoon, transfer the sausage to a large bowl.

2. Season the pork all over with ½ teaspoon each salt and pepper. In batches, add the pork to the pot; cook 4 minutes, or until browned on both sides, turning once halfway through. Transfer the pork to the bowl with the sausage. To the pot, add the carrots, onion, and garlic; cook 8 minutes, stirring often. Add the wine; cook 3 minutes.

3. Return the meat to the pot and add the tomatoes, milk, bay leaves, and ¼ teaspoon salt. Cover and bring up to pressure over high heat. Reduce the heat to medium-low, maintaining pressure. Cook 20 minutes. Remove from the heat; let the pressure release naturally.

4. Uncover the cooker, discard bay leaves, and stir in the basil. Serve tossed with pasta and topped with Parmesan.

Each serving About 550 calories, 37g protein, 54g carbohydrate, 19g fat (6g saturated), 5g fiber, 500mg sodium.

no-time chicken tikka masala

PREP: 15 MIN / TOTAL: 35 MIN / SERVES 4

- 1 tablespoon vegetable oil
- 1 medium onion, finely chopped
- 1 tablespoon grated, peeled fresh ginger
- 3 cloves garlic, crushed with a garlic press
- 1 tablespoon curry powder
- 1 teaspoon paprika
- 1½ pounds boneless, skinless chicken thighs, cut into 1½-inch chunks
- 1 cup canned crushed tomatoes
- ½ cup chicken broth
- 2 teaspoons sugar
- ¾ teaspoon salt
- ½ cup half-and-half
- 1½ teaspoons cornstarch
- ¼ cup cilantro leaves, chopped
- Cooked rice, for serving

1. In a multicooker, using sauté function, heat oil. Add onion and cook, uncovered, for 4 minutes, or until golden, stirring occasionally. Add ginger and garlic; cook 1 minute, stirring. Add curry powder and paprika; cook 30 seconds, stirring. Stir in chicken, tomatoes, broth, sugar, and salt. Hit cancel to turn off sauté function.

2. Cover and lock lid. Select Manual/Pressure Cook and cook at high pressure for 12 minutes. Once cooking is complete, release pressure by using the quick-release function.

3. In cup, mix half-and-half and cornstarch. Set pot to sauté function and bring chicken to a simmer. Stir in half-and-half mixture. Simmer 2 minutes, or until thickened, stirring occasionally. Stir in cilantro. Serve with rice.

Each serving (without rice) About 335 calories, 37g protein, 14g carbohydrate, 14g fat (4g saturated), 3g fiber, 738mg sodium.

chicken cacciatore

PREP: 10 MIN / TOTAL: 35 MIN / SERVES 4

- 1 package (8 ounces) sliced cremini mushrooms
- 1 tablespoon olive oil
- 1 medium onion, thinly sliced
- 3 cloves garlic, thinly sliced
- 2 tablespoons all-purpose flour
- 1 can (28 ounces) diced tomatoes
- 1¼ teaspoons dried oregano
- ¼ teaspoon salt
- ¼ teaspoon crushed red pepper flakes
- 4 bone-in, skinless chicken thighs (about 8 ounces each)
- 1 medium yellow or green bell pepper, thinly sliced
- 3 tablespoons chopped fresh basil or parsley
- 1 teaspoon balsamic vinegar
- Freshly grated Parmesan cheese, for serving

1. In a multicooker, select sauté function and adjust heat to More. Cook mushrooms in oil, uncovered, for 4 minutes. Stir in onion and garlic; cook 4 minutes, or until onions soften. Sprinkle on flour and stir. Add tomatoes, oregano, salt, and pepper flakes. Stir and scrape up any browned bits on pan bottom.

2. Add chicken thighs, pressing into sauce. Cover and lock lid. Select Manual/Pressure Cook and cook at high pressure for 9 minutes. Once cooking is complete, release pressure by using the quick-release function. Transfer chicken to plate. Stir and scrape any bits off bottom of pan if needed.

3. Choose sauté function and adjust heat to More. Stir in bell pepper and cook 4 minutes, or until peppers are just tender. Stir in basil and balsamic vinegar. Serve with grated Parmesan.

Each serving About 295 calories, 31g protein, 21g carbohydrate, 9g fat (2g saturated), 3g fiber, 724mg sodium.

quicker coq au vin blanc

(See photo on page 118.)

PREP: 10 MIN / TOTAL: 35 MIN / SERVES 4

- 4 ounces pancetta, chopped
- 2 teaspoons olive oil
- 3 pounds assorted chicken pieces
- ½ teaspoon dried thyme
- Salt
- Ground black pepper
- 1 medium leek, thinly sliced and well rinsed
- 1½ cups dry white wine
- 1 pound golden potatoes, cut into 1-inch chunks
- 12 ounces cremini mushrooms, quartered
- Chopped fresh parsley, for garnish

1. In multicooker, using sauté function, cook pancetta in oil, uncovered, for 5 to 7 minutes, or until fat has rendered. Transfer pancetta to plate.

2. Meanwhile, pat chicken dry with paper towels; season all over with thyme and ½ teaspoon each salt and pepper.

3. In batches, add chicken, skin side down, to pot; cook 6 minutes or until browned on two sides, turning once halfway through. Transfer chicken to large plate.

4. To pot, add leek and ¼ teaspoon salt; cook 3 minutes, stirring. Add wine. Hit cancel, reselect sauté function, and adjust heat to More; heat to boiling. Hit cancel again, then reselect sauté function (this returns heat to Normal); simmer 5 minutes. Hit cancel to turn off sauté function.

5. Add potatoes, mushrooms, and chicken to pot. Cover and lock lid. Select Manual/Pressure Cook and cook at high pressure for 8 minutes. Once cooking is complete, release pressure by using the quick-release function.

6. Serve chicken and vegetables with some cooking liquid. Garnish with parsley.

Each serving About 725 calories, 52g protein, 29g carbohydrate, 43g fat (13g saturated), 2g fiber, 785mg sodium.

pot roast

with red wine sauce

(See photo on page 131.)

PREP: 25 MIN / TOTAL: 2 HR 30 MIN / SERVES 8

- 1 boneless beef chuck roast (3 to 3½ pounds)
- Salt
- Ground black pepper
- 1 tablespoon vegetable oil
- 1 stalk celery, chopped
- ¾ cup dry red wine
- 1 can (14½ ounces) diced tomatoes
- 4 cloves garlic, smashed with side of chef's knife
- ½ teaspoon dried thyme
- 1 bay leaf
- 1 pound carrots, peeled and cut into 2-inch chunks
- 1 package (1 pound) frozen pearl onions
- 1 tablespoon cornstarch dissolved in 2 tablespoons water

1. Pat beef dry with paper towels; season on all sides with ¼ teaspoon each salt and pepper. In multicooker, select sauté function and adjust heat to More. Cook beef in oil for 6 minutes, until browned, turning once. Set on plate. Add celery and wine; cook 2 minutes. Stir in tomatoes, garlic, thyme, and bay leaf. Hit cancel to turn off sauté function.

2. Place beef on top and press into sauce. Cover and lock lid. Select Manual/Pressure Cook and cook at high pressure for 1 hour 15 minutes. Once cooking is complete, release pressure by using the natural-release function. Transfer beef to cutting board. Discard bay leaf.

3. Skim off any excess fat from surface of cooking liquid. Choose sauté function and adjust heat to More. Cook 18 minutes, or until reduced by about half (2½ cups). Hit cancel to turn off sauté function.

4. Add carrots and onions. Cover and lock lid. Select Manual/Pressure Cook and cook at high pressure for 4 minutes. Once cooking is complete, release pressure by using a quick release. Using sauté function, keep at a simmer. Gradually stir in cornstarch mixture and cook 1 minute. Season with salt and pepper to taste.

5. Slice meat across the grain and serve with vegetables and sauce.

Each serving About 525 calories, 45g protein, 15g carbohydrate, 30g fat (11g saturated), 3g fiber, 318mg sodium.

korean pork lettuce wraps

PREP: 10 MIN / TOTAL: 1 HR 10 MIN / SERVES 8

- ¼ cup miso
- ¼ cup lower-sodium soy sauce
- ¼ cup water
- 3 tablespoons gochujang (Korean red pepper paste) or Sriracha sauce, plus more for serving
- 1 tablespoon toasted sesame oil
- 1 teaspoon ground black pepper
- 1 boneless pork shoulder (about 4 pounds), trimmed of excess fat and quartered
- Lettuce leaves, for serving
- Thinly sliced radishes, cucumber, and green onions, for serving

1. In small bowl, whisk together miso, soy sauce, water, gochujang, sesame oil, and black pepper until smooth.

2. Pour half of sauce into multicooker. Add pork and pour remaining sauce over top. Cover and lock lid. Select Manual/Pressure Cook and cook at high pressure for 1 hour. Once cooking is complete, release pressure by using the quick-release function.

3. Shred pork and serve in lettuce leaves with radishes, cucumbers, green onions, and additional gochujang or Sriracha.

Each serving (pork only) About 450 calories, 53g protein, 6g carbohydrate, 21g fat (7g saturated), 1g fiber, 784mg sodium.

lemon-dill chicken meatball soup

(See photo on page 141.)

PREP: 20 MIN / TOTAL: 35 MIN / SERVES 4

- 2 tablespoons olive oil
- 2 carrots, sliced
- 2 stalks celery, sliced
- 1 small onion, chopped
- 5 cups lower-sodium chicken broth
- 3 cups water
- 1¾ cups bulgur
- 12 ounces ground chicken breast
- ¼ cup finely chopped fresh dill
- 1 teaspoon grated lemon zest
- Salt
- ¼ teaspoon ground black pepper

1. Heat the oil in a 6- to 7-quart saucepot over medium heat. Add the carrots, celery, and onion; cook 10 minutes, stirring occasionally.

2. Add the chicken broth and water; heat to boiling over high heat. Stir in the bulgur. Reduce the heat; simmer 8 to 10 minutes, or until the bulgur is almost tender.

3. Meanwhile, combine the ground chicken, dill, lemon zest, and ¼ teaspoon salt and the pepper. Form the chicken mixture into 1-inch balls; add to the simmering soup along with ¼ teaspoon salt. Cook 6 minutes, or until the meatballs are cooked through.

Each serving About 435 calories, 22g protein, 53g carbohydrate, 16g fat (1g saturated), 9g fiber, 925mg sodium.

STORING SOUPS & STOCK

Soup and stock should be quickly cooled before storing in the refrigerator or freezer. To cool down a pot of soup or stock, place the pot in a sink filled with ice water and let stand, stirring until tepid. Or pour the soup into small containers. Cool for 30 minutes and then refrigerate.

- Stocks and most soups freeze well in airtight containers for up to three months. Be sure to leave at least ½ inch of headspace to allow for expansion. Freezing may diminish some of a soup's flavor, so be sure to taste the soup and adjust the seasoning before serving.

- Soup enriched with cream, yogurt, or eggs cannot be frozen because it will curdle when reheated; the soup base can be frozen, however. Prepare the soup just to the point of adding the cream, yogurt, or eggs. Freeze like any other soup, then thaw and reheat, adding the enrichment at the last minute— just long enough to heat through. Do not allow the soup to boil.

vegetable broth

PREP: 25 MIN / TOTAL: 2 HR 25 MIN / MAKES 6 CUPS

4 large leeks
2 to 4 cloves garlic, unpeeled
13 cups water
Salt
1 large all-purpose potato, peeled, cut lengthwise in half, and thinly sliced
1 small fennel bulb, trimmed and chopped (optional)
3 parsnips, peeled and thinly sliced (optional)

2 large carrots, peeled and thinly sliced
3 stalks celery with leaves, thinly sliced
4 ounces mushrooms, trimmed and thinly sliced
10 fresh sprigs parsley
4 sprigs thyme
2 bay leaves
1 teaspoon whole black peppercorns
Ground black pepper

1. Cut off the roots and trim the dark-green tops from the leeks; thinly slice the leeks. Rinse the leeks in a large bowl of cold water, swishing to remove any sand; transfer to a colander to drain, discarding the sand in bottom of bowl.

2. In a 6-quart saucepot, combine the drained leeks, garlic, 1 cup water, and a pinch of salt; heat to boiling over high heat. Reduce the heat to medium; cover and cook until the leeks are tender, about 15 minutes.

3. Add the potato; fennel, if using; parsnips, if using; carrots; celery; mushrooms; parsley; thyme; bay leaves; peppercorns; and the remaining 12 cups water. Heat to boiling; reduce the heat and simmer, uncovered, at least 1 hour 30 minutes.

4. Taste and continue cooking if the flavor is not concentrated enough. Season with salt and pepper to taste. Strain the broth through a fine-mesh sieve into containers, pressing on the solids with the back of a wooden spoon to extract as much liquid and flavor as possible; cool. Cover and refrigerate to use within 3 days, or freeze up to 4 months.

Each cup About 20 calories, 1g protein, 4g carbohydrate, 0g fat (0g saturated), 0g fiber, 10mg sodium.

 Tip We recommend making a large batch of the broth and freezing it to have on hand for use in recipes throughout this book.

chicken broth

PREP: 10 MIN / TOTAL: 4 HR 40 MIN / MAKES 5 CUPS

- 1 chicken (3 to 3½ pounds), including neck (giblets reserved for another use)
- 2 carrots, peeled and cut into 2-inch pieces
- 1 stalk celery, cut into 2-inch pieces
- 1 medium onion, peeled and cut into quarters
- 5 fresh sprigs parsley
- 1 clove garlic
- ½ teaspoon dried thyme
- ½ bay leaf

1. In a 6-quart saucepot, combine the chicken, chicken neck, carrots, celery, onion, parsley, garlic, thyme, bay leaf, and 3 quarts water or enough water to cover; heat to boiling over high heat. Skim any foam from the surface. Reduce the heat and simmer 1 hour, turning the chicken once and skimming as needed.

2. Remove from the heat; transfer the chicken to a large bowl. When cool enough to handle, remove the skin and bones from the chicken. (Reserve the chicken for another use.) Return the skin and bones to the saucepot and heat to boiling. Skim the foam; reduce heat and simmer 3 hours.

3. Strain the broth through a colander into a large bowl; discard the solids. Strain again through a sieve into containers; cool. Cover and refrigerate to use within 3 days, or freeze up to 4 months.

4. To use, skim and discard the fat from the surface of the broth.

Each cup About 35 calories, 3g protein, 4g carbohydrate, 1g fat (1g saturated), 0g fiber, 90mg sodium.

VARIATION

Pressure Cooker Chicken Broth

In a 6-quart pressure cooker, place all the ingredients for Chicken Broth (above) but use only **4 cups water**. Following the manufacturer's directions, cover the pressure cooker and bring it up to high pressure (15 pounds). Cook 15 minutes. Remove the cooker from the heat and allow the pressure to drop for 5 minutes, then follow the manufacturer's directions for quick release of pressure. Strain the broth through a colander into a large bowl; discard the solids. Strain again through a sieve into containers; cool. Meanwhile, remove the skin and bones from the chicken; discard. (Reserve the chicken for another use.) Cover the broth and refrigerate to use within 3 days, or freeze up to 4 months. To use, skim and discard the fat from the surface of the broth. **Makes about 5½ cups or 6 first-course servings.**

 You can use our homemade version instead of store-bought whenever chicken broth is called for in this book.

brown beef stock

PREP: 5 MIN / TOTAL: 7 HR 35 MIN / MAKES 5 CUPS

- 5 pounds beef bones, cut into 3-inch pieces
- 2 medium onions, each cut in half
- 3 carrots, peeled and each cut in half
- 2 stalks celery, each cut in half
- 13 cups water
- 1 small bunch parsley
- 1 bay leaf
- ½ teaspoon dried thyme

1. Preheat the oven to 450°F. Spread the beef bones, onions, carrots, and celery in a large roasting pan (17½ × 11½ inches). Roast, stirring every 15 minutes, until well browned, about 1 hour.

2. With tongs, transfer the browned bones and vegetables to a 6-quart saucepot. Carefully pour off the fat from the roasting pan. Add 1 cup water to the roasting pan and heat to boiling, stirring until the browned bits are loosened from the bottom of the pan; add to the pot. Add the remaining 12 cups water, the parsley, bay leaf, and thyme to the pot. Heat to boiling over high heat, skimming the foam from the surface. Reduce the heat and simmer, skimming the foam occasionally, 6 hours.

3. Strain the broth through colander into a large bowl; discard the solids. Strain again through a fine-mesh sieve into containers. Cool. Cover and refrigerate to use within 3 days, or freeze up to 4 months.

4. To use, skim and discard the fat from the surface of the stock.

Each cup About 40 calories, 5g protein, 5g carbohydrate, 0g fat (0g saturated), 0g fiber, 75mg sodium.

 Flavor pasta sauce, cook rice or other grains, and poach chicken with stock.

savory pumpkin & sage soup

PREP: 25 MIN / TOTAL: 1 HR 30 MIN / SERVES 8

¼ cup olive oil

3 large sweet onions, sliced

Salt

3 cloves garlic, chopped

2 large fresh sage leaves, chopped

2 teaspoons grated, peeled fresh ginger

¼ teaspoon ground nutmeg

2 quarts lower-sodium vegetable or chicken broth

3 cans (15 ounces each) pure pumpkin

1 tablespoon fresh lemon juice

¼ teaspoon ground black pepper

Sage & Shiitake Garnish (below)

1. In a 5-quart saucepot, heat the oil over medium heat. Add the onions and ¼ teaspoon salt. Cook 40 minutes, or until deep golden brown, stirring occasionally. Add the garlic, sage, ginger, and nutmeg. Cook 5 minutes, or until the garlic is golden, stirring occasionally. Add the broth and pumpkin. Heat to simmering over high heat, scraping up the browned bits from the bottom of the pot. Reduce the heat to maintain a simmer; cook 20 minutes, stirring occasionally.

2. With an immersion blender or in batches in a blender, puree the soup until smooth. Stir in the lemon juice, 1 teaspoon salt, and pepper. Soup can be refrigerated up to 2 days in advance; reheat over medium heat. (If the soup is too thick, add water or broth for the desired consistency. Season to taste and add garnish. Makes 10 cups.

SAGE & SHIITAKE GARNISH In a 2-quart saucepan, heat 1 inch of **oil** over high heat until hot but not smoking. Add **24 small fresh sage leaves** to the oil. Fry 1 to 2 minutes, or until the leaves are browned, stirring occasionally. With a slotted spoon, transfer the sage to a large paper-towel-lined plate; sprinkle with a **pinch of salt**. In batches, add **7 ounces shiitake mushrooms**, stemmed and very thinly sliced, to the hot oil. Fry 2 minutes, or until deep golden brown, stirring occasionally. Transfer the mushrooms to the same plate as the sage; sprinkle with **a pinch of salt**. Cool completely. Garnish can be made up to 3 hours ahead. Let stand at room temperature.

Each serving About 215 calories, 5g protein, 32g carbohydrate, 10g fat (1g saturated), 9g fiber, 750mg sodium.

chile-braised beef
with noodles

PREP: 20 MIN / TOTAL: 2 HR 30 MIN / SERVES 8

2 tablespoons vegetable oil

2½ pounds beef chuck roast, trimmed and cut into 2-inch chunks

Salt

Ground black pepper

1 large onion, chopped

4 cloves garlic, chopped

1 tablespoon ancho chile powder

1 tablespoon chipotle chile powder

2 teaspoons smoked paprika

½ teaspoon ground cinnamon

1 can (6 ounces) tomato paste

3 cups beef broth

1 tablespoon molasses

1 pound egg noodles, cooked as the label directs

2 cups baby spinach

Fresh parsley leaves and thinly sliced green onions, for garnish

1. Preheat the oven to 325°F. In a 7- to 8-quart heavy-bottomed saucepot or Dutch oven, heat the oil over medium-high heat until hot. Season the beef with ½ teaspoon each salt and pepper. Add to the pot; cook 10 minutes, or until browned on both sides, turning occasionally. Transfer the beef to cutting board. Reduce the heat to medium.

2. To the pot, add the onion, garlic, chile powders, paprika, and cinnamon. Cook 2 minutes, stirring occasionally. Add the tomato paste. Cook 1 minute, stirring. Add the broth, scraping up the browned bits with a wooden spoon. Return the beef to the pot. Heat to simmering over high heat. Cover and bake 2 to 2½ hours, or until the beef is pull-apart tender, stirring twice.

3. Remove the pot from the oven. Transfer the beef to a medium bowl; remove and discard any solid fat. With 2 forks, shred the meat and return it to the pot with the sauce, along with molasses and ½ teaspoon salt.

4. To serve, toss the noodles with baby spinach; spoon the meat over the noodles. Garnish with parsley and green onions.

Each serving About 595 calories, 41g protein, 48g carbohydrate, 26g fat (9g saturated), 5g fiber, 720mg sodium.

SAVORY PUMPKIN & SAGE SOUP 140

LEMON-DILL CHICKEN MEATBALL SOUP 137

SUPERGREEN MUSHROOM & ORZO SOUP 142

CHILE-BRAISED BEEF WITH NOODLES 140

BUILD YOUR OWN SOUP

Soup can be made from almost any combo of vegetables and broth. And it's a perfect way to rescue less than pristine vegetables. Check your pantry and fridge for a world of possibilities. Use one or more from each category below. See recipe at right for instructions.

AROMATICS

2 cups total: chopped onions, chopped carrots, chopped celery, chopped leeks, chopped shallots, and/or up to **5 cloves garlic**, minced

BROTH

8 cups **chicken**, **vegetable**, or **beef**

HEARTY VEGGIES

3 cups total: chopped **broccoli**, **cauliflower**, **potatoes**, **turnips**, **celery root**, **butternut squash**, and/or **carrots**

TENDER VEGGIES

4 cups total: sliced or whole **leafy greens** (including kale, collards, chard, spinach), **Brussels sprouts**, **mushrooms**, **cabbage**, **sugar snap peas**, **green beans**, **peas**, **corn** and/or **canned beans**

STARCH

1 cup total: uncooked **angel hair**, broken-up; **orzo**; **egg noodles**; **ditalini**; or 2 cups cooked **rice**

FLAVOR BOOSTER

To taste add: **pesto** (basil or sun-dried tomato), **fresh lemon juice**, **fresh lime juice**, **soft herbs** (including basil, parsley, cilantro), **Parmesan cheese**, **toasted sesame oil**, **salt** and/or **pepper**

supergreen mushroom & orzo soup

(See photo on page 141.)

PREP: 20 MIN / TOTAL: 40 MIN / SERVES 6

2 tablespoon extra-virgin olive oil

¼ teaspoon Kosher salt

AROMATICS

1¼ cups celery, sliced

½ cup chopped shallots

¼ cup garlic, minced

BROTH

8 cups vegetable or chicken broth

HEARTY VEGGIE

3 cups broccoli, chopped

TENDER VEGGIES

3 cups sliced spinach

1 cup sliced mushrooms

STARCH

1 cup orzo, uncooked

FLAVOR BOOST

Basil pesto, for serving

1. In an 8-quart saucepot, heat olive oil over medium heat. Add ¼ teaspoon salt and AROMATICS. Cook 8 minutes, or until golden, stirring.

2. Add 8 cups BROTH and HEARTY VEGGIES. Heat to simmering over high heat. Reduce the heat to medium-low; simmer 15 minutes, stirring occasionally.

3. Add TENDER VEGGIES and a STARCH. Simmer 8 to 10 minutes, or until the starch and veggies are softened.

4. Remove from heat. Stir in a FLAVOR BOOSTER to taste.

Each serving About 230 calories, 7g protein, 34g carbohydrate, 8g fat (1g saturated), 5g fiber, 360mg sodium.

chicken & bacon chowder

PREP: 15 MIN / TOTAL: 45 MIN / SERVES 6

- 4 slices thick-cut bacon, chopped
- 3 stalks celery, finely chopped
- 2 medium shallots, finely chopped
- ¼ teaspoon cayenne pepper
- Salt
- ½ cup all-purpose flour
- 1 quart lower-sodium chicken broth
- 1 pound skinless, boneless chicken thighs (about 4 thighs)
- 1 pound red potatoes, cut into ½-inch chunks
- 2 cups whole milk
- 2 cups fresh or frozen corn
- Thinly sliced fresh basil, for garnish
- Oyster crackers, for serving (optional)

1. In a 6-quart saucepot, cook the bacon over medium heat until crispy and browned, stirring occasionally. With a slotted spoon, transfer the bacon to a paper-towel-lined plate; set aside.

2. To the same pot, add the celery, shallots, cayenne, and ¼ teaspoon salt. Cook 7 to 10 minutes, or until the vegetables are almost tender, stirring occasionally. Sprinkle the flour over the vegetables. Cook 1 minute, stirring constantly.

3. Slowly stir in the broth. Heat to simmering over high heat. Add the chicken and potatoes. Reduce the heat to medium. Cook 12 to 15 minutes, or until the chicken is cooked and the potatoes are tender, stirring occasionally. With tongs, transfer the chicken to a bowl and shred it using 2 forks. Return the chicken to the pot. Stir in the milk, corn, and ½ teaspoon salt. Cook 3 minutes, or until the corn is hot. Garnish with basil and reserved bacon. Serve with oyster crackers, if desired.

Each serving About 400 calories, 25g protein, 35g carbohydrate, 18g fat (9g saturated), 3g fiber, 895mg sodium.

spicy gazpacho
with serrano ham

(See photo on page 144.)

PREP: 20 MIN / TOTAL: 35 MIN, PLUS CHILLING / SERVES 4

- 3 cups torn or cubed stale crustless country-style white bread
- 3 pounds ripe tomatoes, cored and coarsely chopped
- 4 serrano chiles, sliced
- 3 cloves garlic, coarsely chopped
- ¾ cup extra-virgin olive oil, plus more (optional) for garnish
- 5 teaspoons sherry vinegar
- 1 teaspoon salt
- 2 ounces serrano ham, thinly sliced into strips, for garnish
- Chopped fresh parsley, for garnish

1. In a medium bowl, cover the bread with enough cold water to soak. Let stand 15 minutes. Drain well and squeeze out the excess water.

2. In a food processor, blend half of the tomatoes, chiles, garlic, oil, and soaked bread until smooth, stopping and scraping down occasionally. Transfer to an 8-cup measuring cup or other large container. Repeat blending with the remaining tomatoes, chiles, garlic, bread, and oil; add to the measuring cup with the first batch of soup. Stir in the vinegar and salt. Cover with plastic wrap and refrigerate until cold, about 3 hours or up to 1 day. Divide the cold soup among serving bowls. Drizzle with additional oil, if desired. Garnish with ham and parsley.

Each serving About 545 calories, 9g protein, 28g carbohydrate, 45g fat (7g saturated), 5g fiber, 990mg sodium.

VARIATIONS

Turn It Up
Drizzle the soup with **chile oil**.

Cool It Down
Replace the serrano chiles with **1 cubanelle pepper**.

SPICY GAZPACHO WITH SERRANO HAM 143

TOMATO SOUP WITH CUPID CROUTONS 144

tomato soup
with cupid croutons

PREP: 15 MIN / TOTAL: 45 MIN / SERVES 4

2 tablespoons olive oil

1 medium onion, chopped

2 cloves garlic, chopped

3 cups lower-sodium vegetable or chicken broth

1 can (28 ounces) whole peeled tomatoes

2 bay leaves

½ teaspoon salt

4 slices white bread

1 tablespoons butter

½ teaspoon sugar

¼ teaspoon ground black pepper

1. In a 5- to 6-quart saucepot, heat the oil over medium heat. Add the onion and garlic; cook 10 minutes, stirring. Add the broth, tomatoes, bay leaves, and salt. Heat to boiling over high heat. Reduce the heat; simmer 20 minutes, stirring occasionally.

2. Meanwhile, trim the crusts from the bread. With a heart-shaped cookie cutter, cut 4 hearts from the bread slices; toast the hearts. Stir the bread scraps into the soup, if desired.

3. Remove and discard the bay leaves from the soup. Stir in the butter and sugar. In batches in the blender or with an immersion blender, blend the soup until smooth. Stir in the black pepper. Serve topped with heart croutons.

Each serving About 220 calories, 4g protein, 27g carbohydrate, 11g fat (3g saturated), 3g fiber, 928mg sodium.

GOOD TO KNOW

GARNISHING SOUP

As delicious as soup is, almost any bowl of soup will be enhanced by an added splash of color or a bit of extra flavor. Chopped fresh herbs are the simplest of all garnishes. Choose an herb that complements the soup's flavor and color. For the best results, chop or snip fresh herbs just before using. Pureed soups can accommodate other kinds of garnishes. The smooth texture of a pureed bean or tomato soup calls out for a sprinkling of grated Parmesan cheese or crumbled bacon. Pureed vegetable soups are often topped with a drizzle of heavy cream.

cream of asparagus

PREP: 5 MIN / TOTAL: 35 MIN / SERVES 4

2 tablespoons butter
or margarine

1 medium onion,
chopped

12 ounces asparagus,
trimmed and cut into
1-inch pieces (3 cups)

3 tablespoons all-
purpose flour

¼ teaspoon salt

⅛ teaspoon ground
black pepper

1¾ cups chicken or
vegetable broth

1 cup half-and-half
or light cream

1. In a 3-quart saucepan, melt the butter over medium heat; add the onion and cook, stirring frequently, until tender and golden, about 10 minutes. Add the asparagus; cook 1 minute.

2. Stir in the flour, salt, and pepper until blended. Gradually stir in the broth; heat to boiling, stirring constantly. Reduce the heat; cover and simmer until the asparagus is tender, 5 to 10 minutes.

3. Spoon half of the mixture into a blender; cover, with the center part of the lid removed to let the steam escape, and puree until smooth. Pour into a bowl. Repeat with the remaining mixture.

4. Return the puree to the saucepan; stir in the half-and-half. Heat through (do not boil). Serve the soup hot, or cover it and refrigerate to serve chilled later. If the chilled soup is too thick, stir in some milk.

Each serving About 195 calories, 6g protein, 14g carbohydrate, 14g fat (8g saturated), 2g fiber, 657mg sodium.

VARIATIONS

Cream of Cauliflower or Broccoli Soup

Prepare as directed above, but substitute **3 cups small cauliflower or broccoli florets** for the asparagus. Use **1¼ cups half-and-half or light cream** and add a **dash of cayenne pepper**. If desired, stir in **4 ounces (1 cup) sharp Cheddar cheese**, shredded and **½ teaspoon Dijon mustard** when heating it through.

Cream of Mushroom Soup

Prepare as directed above, but substitute **1 pound mushrooms**, trimmed and sliced, for the asparagus.

butternut-apple soup

PREP: 15 MIN / TOTAL: 50 MIN / SERVES 8

2 tablespoons vegetable
oil

1 small onion, chopped

2 medium butternut
squash (1¾ pounds
each), peeled, seeded,
and cut into ¾-inch
pieces

¾ pound Golden
Delicious apples
(2 medium), peeled,
cored, and coarsely
chopped

1¾ cups vegetable broth

1½ cups water

1 teaspoon freshly
chopped fresh thyme,
or ¼ teaspoon dried

1 teaspoon salt

⅛ teaspoon coarsely
ground black pepper

1 cup half-and-half or
light cream

1. In a 4-quart saucepan, heat the oil over medium heat. Add the onion and cook until tender and golden, about 10 minutes. Stir in the squash, apples, broth, water, thyme, salt, and pepper; heat to boiling over high heat. Reduce the heat to low; cover and simmer, stirring often, until the squash is very tender, 20 to 25 minutes.

2. Spoon one-third of the squash mixture into a blender; cover, with the center part of the lid removed to let the steam escape, and puree until smooth. Pour the puree into a bowl. Repeat with the remaining mixture.

3. Return the puree to the saucepan; stir in the half-and-half. Heat through over medium heat, stirring occasionally (do not boil).

Each serving About 175 calories, 3g protein, 28g carbohydrate, 7g fat (3g saturated), 4g fiber, 525mg sodium.

VARIATION

Spicy Curried Carrot Soup

Prepare as directed above, but substitute **2 pounds carrots**, peeled and cut into 2-inch pieces, for the squash. Increase the broth to 3½ cups. In step 1, omit the thyme and add **2 teaspoons curry powder** and **2 teaspoons grated, peeled fresh ginger**. Omit the half-and-half.

french onion soup

PREP: 10 MIN / TOTAL: 2 HR 10 MIN / SERVES 4

4 tablespoons butter or margarine

6 medium onions, thinly sliced

¼ teaspoon salt

4 cups water

1¾ cups beef broth

¼ teaspoon dried thyme

4 diagonal slices (½-inch thick) French bread

4 ounces Gruyère or Swiss cheese, shredded (1 cup)

1. In a 12-inch nonstick skillet, melt the butter over medium-low heat. Add the onions and salt and cook, stirring occasionally, until the onions are very tender and begin to caramelize, about 45 minutes. Reduce the heat to low and cook, stirring frequently, until onions are deep golden brown, about 15 minutes longer.

2. Transfer the onions to a 5-quart Dutch oven. Add ½ cup water to the same skillet and heat to boiling, stirring until the browned bits are loosened from the bottom of the skillet. Add this to the onions in the Dutch oven. Add the remaining 3½ cups water, the broth, and the thyme to the onions and heat to boiling over high heat. Reduce the heat and simmer 30 minutes.

3. Preheat the oven to 450°F. Arrange the bread slices on a baking sheet and bake until lightly toasted, about 5 minutes. Place 4 oven-proof bowls in a jelly-roll pan for easier handling. Spoon the soup evenly into the bowls and top with the toasted bread, slightly pressing the bread into the soup. Sprinkle the cheese evenly on top. Bake until the cheese has melted and begins to brown, 12 to 15 minutes.

Each serving About 400 calories, 15g protein, 37g carbohydrate, 22g fat (13g saturated), 3g fiber, 890mg sodium.

 Tip This recipe is easily doubled; simply cook the onions in 2 skillets.

quick cream of broccoli soup

PREP: 5 MIN / TOTAL: 25 MIN / SERVES 4

1 tablespoon butter or margarine

1 medium onion, chopped

1 package (10 ounces) frozen chopped broccoli

1¾ cups chicken broth

¼ teaspoon dried thyme

⅛ teaspoon salt

⅛ teaspoon ground black pepper

Pinch of ground nutmeg

Pinch of cayenne pepper (optional)

1½ cups milk

2 teaspoons fresh lemon juice

1. In a 3-quart saucepan, melt the butter over medium heat. Add the onion and cook, stirring occasionally, until tender, about 5 minutes. Add the frozen broccoli, broth, thyme, salt, black pepper, nutmeg, and cayenne, if using; heat to boiling over high heat. Reduce the heat and simmer 10 minutes.

2. Spoon half of the mixture into a blender; cover, with the center part of the lid removed to let the steam escape, and puree until smooth. Pour into a bowl. Repeat with the remaining mixture.

3. Return the puree to the saucepan; stir in the milk. Heat through, stirring often (do not boil). Remove from the heat and stir in the lemon juice.

Each serving About 130 calories, 6g protein, 12g carbohydrate, 7g fat (4g saturated), 3g fiber, 595mg sodium.

VARIATIONS

Cream of Corn Soup

Prepare as directed above, but substitute **1 package (10 ounces) frozen whole-kernel corn** for the broccoli; if you like, add ¾ **teaspoon chili powder** after cooking the onion, and cook 30 seconds before adding the broth.

Cream of Pea Soup

Prepare as directed above, but substitute **1 package (10 ounces) frozen peas** for the broccoli; if you like, add ¼ **teaspoon dried mint leaves** with the broth.

Cream of Asparagus Soup

Prepare as directed above, but substitute **1 package (10 ounces) frozen asparagus** for the broccoli; if you like, add ¼ **teaspoon dried tarragon** with the broth.

apple & parsnip soup

PREP: 15 MIN / TOTAL: 30 MIN / SERVES 6

- 1 package (32 ounces) chicken broth
- 2 cups water
- 1 tablespoon olive oil
- 2 large shallots, finely chopped (½ cup)
- 1 stalk celery, finely chopped
- 2 pounds McIntosh or Braeburn apples (4 to 6 medium), peeled, cored, and chopped
- 1 pound parsnips, peeled and chopped
- ¼ teaspoon dried thyme
- ½ teaspoon salt
- ¼ teaspoon ground black pepper
- Roasted, hulled pepitas (pumpkin seeds), for garnish

1. In a covered 2-quart saucepan, heat the chicken broth and water to boiling over high heat.

2. Meanwhile, in a 5- to 6-quart saucepot, heat the oil over medium heat. Add the shallots and celery; cook about 5 minutes, or until softened and lightly browned. Add the apples, parsnips, thyme, salt, and pepper; cook 1 minute.

3. Add the hot broth mixture to the saucepot; cover and heat to boiling over high heat. Reduce the heat to low and simmer, covered, 6 to 7 minutes, or until the parsnips are very tender.

4. Spoon one-third of the apple mixture into a blender; cover, removing the center part of the lid to let the steam escape. Lay a paper towel over the top and puree until smooth. Pour the puree into a bowl. Repeat with the remaining mixture. Return to saucepot to reheat. Garnish with pumpkin seeds and serve.

Each serving About 160 calories, 3g protein, 34g carbohydrate, 3g fat (0g saturated), 6g fiber, 600mg sodium.

 Tip If you have an immersion blender, use it to puree the soup right in the pot.

cool cucumber soup

PREP: 25 MIN / TOTAL: 30 MIN / SERVES 4

- 2 English (seedless) cucumbers (about 12 ounces each), peeled
- 1 small clove garlic, crushed with a garlic press
- 2 cups (16 ounces) plain low-fat yogurt
- ½ cup low-fat (1%) milk
- 1 tablespoon fresh lemon juice
- 1¼ teaspoons salt
- 2 tablespoons olive oil
- ½ teaspoon curry powder
- ½ teaspoon ground cumin
- ¼ teaspoon crushed red pepper
- 1 small tomato, chopped
- 1 tablespoon sliced fresh mint leaves

1. Cut enough cucumber into ¼-inch pieces to equal ½ cup; reserve for garnish. Cut the remaining cucumbers into 2-inch pieces. In a food processor with the knife blade attached or in a blender, puree the large cucumber pieces, garlic, yogurt, milk, lemon juice, and salt until almost smooth. Pour the mixture into a medium bowl; cover and refrigerate until cold, at least 2 hours.

2. Meanwhile, prepare the curry oil. In a small saucepan, heat the oil over low heat. Stir in the curry powder, cumin, and crushed red pepper; cook until fragrant and the oil is hot, about 3 minutes. Remove the saucepan from the heat; strain the curry oil through a sieve into a cup. Set aside.

3. In a small bowl, combine the tomato and reserved cucumber.

4. To serve, stir the soup and ladle it into bowls. Garnish each bowl with a spoonful of the cucumber mixture; sprinkle with mint and drizzle with curry oil.

Each serving About 170 calories, 8g protein, 15g carbohydrate, 9g fat (2g saturated), 1g fiber, 830mg sodium.

spring pea soup

PREP: 15 MIN / TOTAL: 40 MIN / SERVES 10

- 2 tablespoons butter
- 2 large shallots, thinly sliced (¾ cup)
- 1 carton (32 ounces) reduced-sodium chicken broth
- 2 cups water
- 2 bags (16 ounces each) frozen peas, thawed
- 1 large all-purpose potato (8 ounces), peeled and cut into 1-inch chunks
- ½ cup loosely packed fresh mint leaves, chopped
- ¾ teaspoon salt
- ¼ teaspoon ground black pepper
- 3 tablespoons fresh lemon juice
- 10 nasturtium flowers for garnish (optional)

1. In a 4-quart saucepan, melt the butter over medium-low heat. Add the shallots and cook 10 to 12 minutes, or until very tender.

2. Add the broth, water, peas, potato, half the chopped mint, the salt, and the pepper; heat to boiling over high heat. Reduce the heat to medium; simmer 10 minutes, stirring occasionally.

3. Spoon half of the mixture into a blender; cover, removing the center part of the lid to let the steam escape. Lay a paper towel over the top and puree until smooth. Pour the puree into a medium bowl. Repeat with the remaining mixture. Return the soup to the saucepan, and reheat over medium heat if necessary. Stir in the lemon juice and remaining mint.

4. To serve, spoon the soup into serving bowls; garnish with nasturtiums, if using.

Each serving About 120 calories, 6g protein, 19g carbohydrate, 3g fat (1g saturated), 5g fiber, 475mg sodium.

 Tip Nasturtiums and other edible flowers can be found in the produce section of specialty supermarkets and at farmers' markets.

split pea soup
with ham

PREP: 10 MIN / TOTAL: 1 HR 25 MIN / SERVES 6

- 2 tablespoons vegetable oil
- 2 white turnips (6 ounces each), peeled and chopped (optional)
- 2 carrots, peeled and finely chopped
- 2 stalks celery, finely chopped
- 1 medium onion, finely chopped
- 1 package (16 ounces) dry split peas, rinsed and picked over
- 2 smoked ham hocks (1½ pounds)
- 8 cups water
- 1 bay leaf
- 1 teaspoon salt
- ¼ teaspoon ground allspice

1. In a 5-quart Dutch oven, heat the oil over medium-high heat. Add the turnips, if using, along with the carrots, celery, and onion; cook, stirring frequently, until the carrots are tender-crisp, about 10 minutes. Add the split peas, ham hocks, water, bay leaf, salt, and allspice; heat to boiling over high heat. Reduce the heat; cover and simmer 45 minutes.

2. Discard the bay leaf. Transfer the ham hocks to a cutting board; discard the skin and bones. Finely chop the meat and return it to the soup. Heat through.

Each serving About 345 calories, 21g protein, 52g carbohydrate, 7g fat (1g saturated), 17g fiber, 1,175mg sodium.

VARIATION

German Lentil Soup

Prepare as directed above, but omit the turnips. Substitute **1 pound lentils**, rinsed and picked over, for the peas, and substitute ½ **teaspoon dried thyme** for the allspice.

#SavetheFood
make stock from scraps

Instead of tossing herb stems, veggie peels, or Parmesan rinds, use them to add flavor to homemade stock (see pages 138–139). It's super simple and tastes better than canned stock, plus it can be frozen for four to six months.

spring minestrone

(See photo on page 118.)

PREP: 20 MIN / TOTAL: 50 MIN / SERVES 4

2 tablespoons olive oil

2 medium carrots, chopped

1 medium leek, well rinsed and thinly sliced

8 sprigs fresh thyme, tied together

Salt

3 large red potatoes, peeled and chopped

2 quarts lower-sodium vegetable or chicken broth

1 bunch asparagus, sliced

1 can (15 ounces) navy beans, rinsed and drained (optional)

2 tablespoons chopped fresh dill

½ teaspoon ground black pepper

1. In an 8-quart saucepot, heat the oil over medium heat. Add the carrots, leek, thyme, and ¼ teaspoon salt. Cook 8 minutes, stirring.

2. Add the potatoes and broth. Partially cover and heat to boiling over high heat; reduce to a simmer. Cook 25 minutes, or until the potatoes are tender.

3. Add the asparagus; simmer 3 minutes, or until tender. Discard the thyme. Stir in the beans, dill, ¼ teaspoon salt, and pepper, and serve.

Each serving About 330 calories, 7g protein, 62g carbohydrate, 7g fat (1g saturated), 7g fiber, 1,030mg sodium.

 Tip Slice asparagus in seconds: Leave stalks rubber-banded together, trim the ends, and cut through the bunch with just a few strokes.

spicy black bean soup

PREP: 10 MIN / TOTAL: 40 MIN / SERVES 6

1 tablespoon vegetable oil

1 medium onion, chopped

2 cloves garlic, finely chopped

2 teaspoons chili powder

1 teaspoon ground cumin

¼ teaspoon crushed red pepper

2 cans (15 to 19 ounces each) black beans, rinsed and drained

2 cups water

1¾ cups chicken broth

¼ cup coarsely chopped fresh cilantro

Lime wedges, for serving

1. In a 3-quart saucepan, heat the oil over medium heat. Add the onion and cook, stirring occasionally, until tender, 5 to 8 minutes. Stir in the garlic, chili powder, cumin, and crushed red pepper; cook 30 seconds. Stir in the beans, water, and broth; heat to boiling over high heat. Reduce the heat and simmer 15 minutes.

2. Spoon one-third of the mixture into a blender; cover, with the center part of the lid removed to let the steam escape, and puree until smooth. Pour the puree into a bowl. Repeat with the remaining mixture. Sprinkle with chopped cilantro and serve with lime wedges.

Each serving About 140 calories, 7g protein, 19g carbohydrate, 4g fat (0g saturated), 10g fiber, 565mg sodium.

curried lentil soup

PREP: 30 MIN / TOTAL: 1 HR 30 MIN / SERVES 5

2 tablespoons olive oil

4 large carrots, peeled and finely chopped

2 large stalks celery, finely chopped

1 large onion, finely chopped

1 medium Granny Smith apple, peeled, cored, and finely chopped

1 tablespoon grated, peeled fresh ginger

1 large clove garlic, crushed with a garlic press

2 teaspoons curry powder

¾ teaspoon ground cumin

¾ teaspoon ground coriander

1 package (16 ounces) lentils, rinsed and picked over

5 cups water

3½ cups vegetable or chicken broth

¼ cup chopped fresh cilantro

½ teaspoon salt

Plain low-fat yogurt, for serving

1. In a 5-quart Dutch oven, heat the oil over medium-high heat. Add the carrots, celery, onion, and apple; cook, stirring occasionally, until lightly browned, 10 to 15 minutes.

2. Add the ginger, garlic, curry powder, cumin, and coriander; cook, stirring, 1 minute.

3. Add the lentils, water, and broth; heat to boiling over high heat. Reduce the heat; cover and simmer, stirring occasionally, until the lentils are tender, 45 to 55 minutes. Stir in the cilantro and salt. To serve, top the soup with dollops of yogurt.

Each serving (without yogurt) About 435 calories, 27g protein, 69g carbohydrate, 7g fat (1g saturated), 25g fiber, 965mg sodium.

fresh melon soup

with crispy pancetta

PREP: 20 MIN / TOTAL: 25 MIN, PLUS CHILLING / SERVES 4

- 2 small ripe cantaloupes, peeled, seeded and chopped
- ¼ cup fresh lemon juice
- 1¼ cups water
- 1 teaspoon salt
- ¼ cup packed fresh basil leaves
- ½ cup olive oil
- 1 tablespoons snipped fresh chives, plus more for garnish
- 8 thin slices pancetta
- Ground black pepper

1. In a blender, combine the cantaloupe, lemon juice, water, and salt. Blend until smooth. Cover and refrigerate until cold, about 2 hours.

2. Heat a 2-quart saucepan of water to boiling over high heat. Fill a bowl with ice water. Add the basil to the boiling water; boil 30 seconds, or until bright green. With a slotted spoon, transfer the basil to the ice water. Let stand 5 minutes; drain thoroughly. Pat the basil dry. To a blender, add basil, oil, and chives. Blend until smooth; set aside or refrigerate up to 2 days.

3. Preheat the oven to 400°F. Line a rimmed baking sheet with foil. Arrange the pancetta in a single layer. Bake 14 to 16 minutes, or until golden brown. Transfer to a paper towel to drain.

4. To serve, divide the cold soup among serving bowls. Top each with herb oil, a pinch of black pepper, chives, and pancetta.

Each serving About 335 calories, 3g protein, 19g carbohydrate, 29g fat (4g saturated), 2g fiber, 680mg sodium.

squash gazpacho

PREP: 20 MIN / TOTAL: 40 MIN, PLUS CHILLING / SERVES 4

- 2 tablespoons olive oil
- 1½ pounds yellow squash, seeded and sliced
- 1 large yellow bell pepper, seeded and sliced
- 2 cloves garlic, chopped
- 1 teaspoon ground cumin
- 1 teaspoon salt
- 2 cups lower-sodium vegetable or chicken broth
- 1 tablespoon fresh lemon juice
- 4 ounces soft goat cheese
- 8 slices baguette, toasted
- Smoked paprika, for garnish

1. In a 5-quart saucepot, heat oil on medium. Add squash, bell pepper, garlic, cumin, and salt. Cook 10 minutes, or until the vegetables are almost soft, stirring occasionally. Add the broth. Heat to simmering over high heat. Reduce the heat to medium; simmer 15 minutes, or until the vegetables are very soft. Pour into a blender; blend until smooth. Stir in the lemon juice. Refrigerate until cold, about 8 hours.

2. When ready to serve, spread the goat cheese on toasted baguette slices. Serve the soup with goat cheese toasts and garnish with a pinch of smoked paprika.

Each serving About 255 calories, 11g protein, 26g carbohydrate, 13g fat (5g saturated), 4g fiber, 945mg sodium.

sweet beet soup

PREP: 15 MIN / TOTAL: 25 MIN, PLUS CHILLING / SERVES 4

- 1 tablespoons olive oil
- 1 medium onion, thinly sliced
- Salt
- 1 pound cooked beets
- 1 Granny Smith apple, peeled, cored, chopped
- 2 cups lower-sodium vegetable or chicken broth
- Sour cream and dill, for garnish

1. In a 10-inch skillet, heat the oil over medium-high heat. Add the onion and a pinch of salt. Cook 5 minutes, or until browned and starting to soften, stirring frequently. Let cool.

2. To a blender, add the beets, apple, broth, onion, and ½ teaspoon salt. Blend until smooth. Refrigerate until cold, about 3 hours.

3. To serve, garnish with sour cream and dill.

Each serving About 120 calories, 2g protein, 21g carbohydrate, 4g fat (1g saturated), 3g fiber, 580mg sodium.

SQUASH GAZPACHO 150

FRESH MELON SOUP WITH CRISPY PANCETTA 150

SWEET BEET SOUP 150

caldo verde

PREP: 15 MIN / TOTAL: 1 HR / SERVES 5

- 2 tablespoons olive oil
- 1 large onion, chopped
- 3 cloves garlic, finely chopped
- 2½ pounds all-purpose potatoes (8 medium), peeled and cut into 2-inch pieces
- 3½ cups chicken broth
- 3 cups water
- 1 teaspoon salt
- ¼ teaspoon coarsely ground black pepper
- 1 pound kale, tough stems and veins trimmed and leaves very thinly sliced

1. In a 5-quart Dutch oven, heat the oil over medium heat. Add the onion and garlic; cook until the onion is golden, about 10 minutes. Add the potatoes, broth, water, salt, and pepper; heat to boiling over high heat. Reduce the heat; cover and simmer until the potatoes are tender, about 20 minutes.

2. Mash the potatoes in the broth, keeping the potatoes lumpy. Stir in the kale; simmer, uncovered, until kale is tender, 5 to 8 minutes.

Each serving About 250 calories, 7g protein, 41g carbohydrate, 7g fat (1g saturated), 6g fiber, 1,190mg sodium.

chilled tuscan tomato soup

PREP: 15 MIN / TOTAL: 20 MIN, PLUS CHILLING / SERVES 4

- 1 teaspoon olive oil
- 1 clove garlic, minced
- 3 ounces country-style bread, cut into 1-inch cubes (2 cups)
- 3 pounds ripe tomatoes (9 medium), quartered
- ¼ cup loosely packed fresh basil leaves, chopped, plus additional leaves for garnish
- 1 teaspoon sugar
- ½ teaspoon salt

1. In a small skillet, heat the oil over medium heat until hot. Add the garlic and cook 1 minute, stirring. Remove the skillet from the heat.

2. In a food processor with the knife blade attached, pulse the bread until coarsely chopped. Add the tomatoes and garlic; pulse until the soup is almost pureed. Pour the soup into a bowl; stir in the chopped basil, sugar, and salt. Cover and refrigerate until well chilled, at least 2 hours or overnight. Garnish each serving with basil leaves.

Each serving About 145 calories, 5g protein, 28g carbohydrate, 3g fat (1g saturated), 4g fiber, 445mg sodium.

GOOD TO KNOW

SOUP SAVVY

Here are some of the most popular types of soup.

BISQUE	A classic French soup with a rich, creamy texture. It is usually made from shellfish and thickened with rice.
BROTH	A flavorful liquid made from simmered meat, fish, or poultry and/or vegetables
CONSOMMÉ	Broth that has been clarified into a crystal-clear liquid
GUMBO	A signature Cajun thick soup that can contain chicken, duck, seafood, or ham and the holy trinity of vegetables such as onion, bell peppers, and celery. It is thickened with a roux (a browned butter and flour mixture), okra, and is served over white rice.
STOCK	Similar to broth but made from bones, often roasted, that are simmered with water and/or vegetables

minestrone
with pesto

PREP: 20 MIN / TOTAL: 1 HR 20 MIN, PLUS SOAKING / SERVES 6

- 8 ounces dry great northern beans (1⅓ cups), soaked and drained
- 2 tablespoons olive oil
- 3 carrots, peeled and cut into ¼-inch-thick slices
- 2 stalks celery, cut into ¼-inch-thick slices
- 1 large onion, finely chopped
- 2 ounces pancetta or bacon, finely chopped
- 1 pound all-purpose potatoes (3 medium), peeled and chopped
- 2 medium zucchini (8 ounces each), each cut lengthwise
- into quarters, then crosswise into ¼-inch-thick slices
- ½ medium head savoy cabbage, thinly sliced
- 1 large clove garlic, crushed with a garlic press
- 1 can (14½ ounces) diced tomatoes
- 3½ cups chicken broth
- 1 cup water
- Quick Pesto (top right), or ½ cup store-bought pesto
- ½ teaspoon salt

1. In a 4-quart saucepan, combine the beans and enough water to cover by 2 inches; heat to boiling over high heat. Reduce the heat; cover and simmer, stirring occasionally, until the beans are tender, 40 minutes to 1 hour. Drain the beans.

2. Meanwhile, in a nonreactive 5-quart Dutch oven, heat the oil over medium-high heat. Add the carrots, celery, onion, and pancetta; cook, stirring occasionally, until the onions begin to brown, about 10 minutes. Add the potatoes, zucchini, cabbage, and garlic; cook, stirring constantly, until the cabbage has wilted. Add the tomatoes with their juice, the broth, and the water; heat to boiling over high heat. Reduce the heat; cover and simmer until the vegetables are tender, about 30 minutes.

3. Meanwhile, prepare the Quick Pesto.

4. In a blender or a food processor with the knife blade attached, puree ½ cup beans with 1 cup soup mixture until smooth. Stir the puree, remaining beans, and salt into the soup; heat to boiling. Reduce the heat; cover and simmer 10 minutes. Dollop each bowl with a tablespoon of pesto.

QUICK PESTO In a blender, puree ⅔ cup packed fresh basil leaves, ¼ cup freshly grated Parmesan cheese, ¼ cup olive oil, 1 tablespoon water, and ¼ teaspoon salt until smooth.

Each serving (with 1 tablespoon pesto) About 445 calories, 18g protein, 53g carbohydrate, 20g fat (4g saturated), 13g fiber, 1,205mg sodium.

VARIATION

Quick Minestrone

Prepare as recipe directs, omitting step 1. Use **2 cans (15 to 19 ounces each) great northern beans**, rinsed and drained, for the soaked beans; add the beans with the tomatoes.

hearty mushroom-barley soup

PREP: 20 MIN / TOTAL: 1 HR 20 MIN / SERVES 10

- ¾ cup pearl barley
- 8 cups water
- 2 tablespoons olive oil
- 3 stalks celery, cut into ¼-inch-thick slices
- 1 large onion, chopped
- 1½ pounds mushrooms, trimmed and sliced
- 2 tablespoons tomato paste
- 5 carrots, each peeled and cut lengthwise in half, then crosswise into ¼-inch-thick slices
- 3½ cups beef broth
- ¼ cup dry sherry
- 1½ teaspoons salt

1. In a 3-quart saucepan, combine the barley and 4 cups water; heat to boiling over high heat. Reduce the heat; cover and simmer 30 minutes. Drain. Set aside

2. Meanwhile, in a 5-quart Dutch oven, heat the oil over medium-high heat. Add the celery and onion; cook, stirring, until golden, about 10 minutes. Increase the heat to high; add the mushrooms and cook, stirring occasionally, until the liquid has evaporated and mushrooms are lightly browned, 10 to 12 minutes.

3. Reduce the heat to medium-high; add the tomato paste and cook, stirring, 2 minutes. Add the barley, carrots, broth, sherry, salt, and remaining 4 cups water; heat to boiling. Reduce the heat; cover and simmer until the carrots and barley are tender, 20 to 25 minutes.

Each serving About 135 calories, 5g protein, 21g carbohydrate, 4g fat (1g saturated), 5g fiber, 685mg sodium.

pasta fagioli
with sausage

PREP: 15 MIN / TOTAL: 1 HR 15 MIN / SERVES 8

- 1 pound sweet Italian sausage links, casings removed
- 1 tablespoon olive oil
- 2 medium onions, chopped
- 2 cloves garlic, crushed with a garlic press
- 1 can (28 ounces) plum tomatoes
- 3½ cups chicken broth
- 2 cups water
- 3 cans (15 to 19 ounces) great northern or white kidney (cannellini) beans, rinsed and drained
- 6 ounces ditalini or tubetti pasta (1 rounded cup)
- 5 ounces spinach, washed and dried very well, tough stems trimmed, and leaves cut into 1-inch-wide strips
- Freshly grated Parmesan cheese (optional)

1. Heat a 5-quart nonreactive Dutch oven over medium-high heat until very hot. Add the sausage and cook until well browned, breaking up the sausage with the side of a spoon. Transfer the sausage to a bowl.

2. Reduce the heat to medium; add the oil to the Dutch oven. Add the onions and cook until tender and golden, about 10 minutes. Add the garlic; cook 1 minute. Add the tomatoes with their juice, breaking them up with the side of a spoon.

3. Add the broth and water; heat to boiling over high heat. Reduce the heat; cover and simmer 15 minutes. Add the beans and heat to boiling; cover and simmer 15 minutes longer. Add the sausage and heat through.

4. Meanwhile, in a 4-quart saucepan, cook pasta as the label directs, but do not add salt to the cooking water; drain.

5. Just before serving, stir the spinach and cooked pasta into the soup. Serve with Parmesan, if you like.

Each serving About 560 calories, 28g protein, 65g carbohydrate, 22g fat (7g saturated), 12g fiber, 1,430mg sodium.

turkey soup

PREP: 15 MIN / TOTAL: 5 HR 15 MIN, PLUS CHILLING / SERVES 12

- 6 carrots, peeled
- 3 stalks celery
- Roasted turkey carcass, plus 2 cups cooked turkey meat, finely chopped
- 2 medium onions, peeled and cut into quarters
- 5 fresh sprigs parsley
- 1 clove garlic, peeled
- ¼ teaspoon dried thyme
- ½ bay leaf
- 1¼ teaspoons salt
- 1 cup regular long-grain rice, cooked as the label directs
- 2 tablespoons fresh lemon juice, or 1 tablespoon dry sherry

1. Cut 2 carrots and 1 stalk celery into 2-inch pieces. In a 12-quart stockpot, combine the turkey carcass, carrot and celery pieces, onions, parsley sprigs, garlic, thyme, bay leaf, and 6 quarts water or enough water to cover; heat to boiling over high heat. Skim the foam from the surface. Reduce the heat and simmer, skimming occasionally, 4 hours.

2. Strain the broth through a colander set over a large bowl; discard the solids. Strain again through the sieve into several containers; cool. Cover and refrigerate overnight.

3. Remove and discard the fat from the surface of the broth; measure the broth and pour it into a 5-quart saucepot. If necessary, boil the broth over high heat until reduced to 10 cups to concentrate the flavor.

4. Cut the remaining 4 carrots and 2 stalks celery into ½-inch pieces; add to the broth with the salt. Heat the soup to boiling. Reduce the heat and simmer until the vegetables are tender, about 15 minutes. Stir in the cooked rice and remaining 2 cups turkey; heat through, about 5 minutes. Remove from the heat and stir in the lemon juice.

Each serving About 115 calories, 10g protein, 12g carbohydrate, 2g fat (1g saturated), 1g fiber, 355mg sodium.

beef vegetable soup

PREP: 30 MIN / TOTAL: 2 HR 15 MIN, PLUS SOAKING / SERVES 8

- 1 tablespoon vegetable oil
- 2 pounds bone-in beef shank cross cuts, each 2 inches thick
- 2 medium onions, chopped
- 3 cloves garlic, finely chopped
- ⅛ teaspoon ground cloves
- 4 large carrots, peeled and chopped
- 2 stalks celery, chopped
- ½ small head green cabbage (8 ounces), cored and chopped (5 cups)
- 4 cups water
- 1¾ cups beef broth
- 2 teaspoons salt
- ½ teaspoon dried thyme
- ½ teaspoon ground black pepper
- 8 ounces dry large lima beans (1¼ cups), soaked and drained
- 1 pound all-purpose potatoes, peeled and cut into 1-inch pieces
- 1 can (14 to 16 ounces) diced tomatoes, chopped
- 1 cup frozen whole-kernel corn
- 1 cup frozen peas
- ¼ cup chopped fresh parsley

1. In an 8-quart nonreactive saucepot, heat the oil over medium-high heat until very hot. Add the beef, in batches, and cook until well browned, transferring the meat to a bowl as it is browned. Reduce the heat to medium; add the onions and cook, stirring, until tender, about 5 minutes. Stir in the garlic and cloves and cook 30 seconds. Return the beef to the saucepot; add the carrots, celery, cabbage, water, broth, salt, thyme, and pepper; heat to boiling. Reduce the heat; cover and simmer until the beef is tender, about 1 hour.

2. Meanwhile, in a 4-quart saucepan, combine the beans and enough water to cover by 2 inches; heat to boiling over high heat. Reduce the heat; cover and simmer until the beans are just tender, about 30 minutes; drain.

3. Add the potatoes and beans to the saucepot; heat to boiling. Reduce heat, cover and simmer 5 minutes. Stir in the tomatoes with their juices; cover and simmer until the potatoes are tender, about 10 minutes longer.

4. With a slotted spoon, transfer the beef to cutting board. Cut the beef into ½-inch pieces, discarding the bones and gristle. Return the beef to the saucepot and add the frozen corn and peas; heat through. Spoon into bowls and sprinkle with parsley.

Each serving About 280 calories, 24g protein, 35g carbohydrate, 6g fat (1g saturated), 10g fiber, 955mg sodium.

tomato quinoa soup

(See photo on page 156.)

PREP: 15 MIN / TOTAL: 30 MIN / SERVES 6

- 1 cup red or white quinoa, rinsed
- 3 tablespoons butter
- 1 tablespoon olive oil
- 2 medium shallots, chopped
- 2 cloves garlic, chopped
- 1 tablespoon fennel seeds
- 2 cans (28 ounces each) whole peeled tomatoes
- 2 cups lower-sodium chicken or vegetable broth
- ¼ cup roasted, salted pepitas (pumpkin seeds)
- 1 tablespoon snipped fresh chives
- ½ teaspoon crushed red pepper

1. Cook the quinoa as the label directs.

2. In a 4-quart saucepan, heat the butter and oil over medium heat until the butter melts. Add the shallots, garlic, and fennel seeds. Cook 4 to 6 minutes, or until the vegetables begin to soften, stirring occasionally. Add the tomatoes and broth; heat to simmering over high heat. Simmer 15 minutes, stirring occasionally. With an immersion or regular blender, puree the mixture until smooth. Reheat the soup if necessary.

3. In a medium bowl, combine the cooked quinoa, pepitas, chives, and crushed red pepper. Serve the soup topped with the quinoa mixture.

Each serving About 275 calories, 9g protein, 34g carbohydrate, 13g fat (5g saturated), 7g fiber, 875 mg sodium.

#SavetheFood

soup-er-size it

There's nothing like a hot bowl to keep you cozy. And if you've got produce on the verge of going bad, there's no better way to use it than in a big batch of soup—when the veggies are cooked, you won't notice that they were past their prime.

TOMATO QUINOA SOUP 155

SAUCY SHRIMP CREOLE 157

bouillabaisse

PREP: 1 HR / TOTAL: 2 HR / SERVES 6

3 leeks

2 tablespoons olive oil

1 large fennel bulb (1½ pounds), trimmed and thinly sliced

1 medium onion, chopped

2 cloves garlic, finely chopped

Pinch of cayenne pepper

1 cup dry white wine

2 bottles (8 ounces each) clam juice

1 can (14 to 16 ounces) whole tomatoes

1 cup water

3 strips (3 × 1 inch each) orange peel

½ bay leaf

¾ teaspoon salt

¼ teaspoon dried thyme

⅛ teaspoon ground black pepper

1 pound monkfish, dark membrane removed, cut into 1-inch pieces

1 dozen medium mussels, scrubbed and debearded (see page 298)

1 pound cod fillet, cut into 1-inch pieces

1 pound medium (26 to 30 count) shrimp, shelled and deveined (see page 297)

2 tablespoons chopped fresh parsley

Easy Aioli (page 50)

1 loaf French bread, thinly sliced and lightly toasted

1. Cut off the roots and trim the dark-green tops from the leeks; cut each leek lengthwise in half, then crosswise into thin slices. Rinse the leeks in a large bowl of cold water, swishing to remove any sand; transfer to a colander to drain, discarding the sand in the bottom of the bowl.

2. In a 5-quart nonreactive Dutch oven, heat the oil over medium heat. Stir in the leeks, fennel, and onion; cook, stirring occasionally, until the vegetables are tender, about 15 minutes. Add the garlic and cayenne and cook 30 seconds.

3. Add the wine and heat to boiling; boil 1 minute. Stir in the clam juice, tomatoes with their juices, water, orange peel, bay leaf, salt, thyme, and pepper, breaking up the tomatoes with the side of a spoon; heat to boiling. Reduce the heat and simmer 20 minutes. Discard the bay leaf.

4. Increase the heat to medium-high. Stir in the monkfish; cover and cook 3 minutes. Stir in the mussels; cover and cook 1 minute. Stir in the cod and shrimp; cover and cook until the mussels open and the fish and shrimp are just opaque throughout, 2 to 3 minutes longer. Discard any mussels that do not open.

5. To serve, ladle the bouillabaisse into large shallow soup bowls; sprinkle with chopped parsley. Spoon the Easy Aioli onto toasted French bread and float it in the bouillabaisse.

Each serving (without toast or Easy Aioli) About 310 calories, 42g protein, 17g carbohydrate, 8g fat (1g saturated), 4g fiber, 835mg sodium.

saucy shrimp creole

PREP: 20 MIN / TOTAL: 35 MIN / SERVES 6

- 4 tablespoons butter
- 2 stalks celery, finely chopped
- 1 large green bell pepper, finely chopped
- 1 medium onion, finely chopped
- 1 teaspoon salt-free Creole seasoning
- ¼ cup all-purpose flour
- 2 medium tomatoes, chopped
- 8 ounces clam juice
- 1½ pounds peeled, deveined (see page 297) jumbo (16 to 20 count) shrimp
- 1 tablespoon Worcestershire sauce
- 1 tablespoon Louisiana-style hot sauce, plus more (optional) for serving
- 1½ cups white rice, cooked as the label directs

1. In a 5-quart saucepot, melt the butter over medium heat. Add the celery, bell pepper, onion, and Creole seasoning. Cook 15 minutes, or until the vegetables are tender, stirring occasionally.

2. Sprinkle the flour over the vegetables. Cook 2 minutes, stirring. Add the tomatoes; cook 2 minutes, or until the tomatoes are very soft, scraping up the browned bits. Stir in the clam juice. Heat to simmering over high heat.

3. Add the shrimp, Worcestershire sauce, and hot sauce. Simmer 5 minutes, or until the shrimp are just cooked through, stirring occasionally. Serve over rice with additional hot sauce, if desired.

Each serving About 380 calories, 21g protein, 51g carbohydrate, 9g fat (5g saturated), 2g fiber, 915mg sodium.

manhattan clam chowder

PREP: 30 MIN / COOK 1 HR 10 MIN, PLUS COOLING / SERVES 12

- 5 cups water
- 3 dozen chowder or cherrystone clams, scrubbed (see page 299)
- 5 slices bacon, finely chopped
- 1 large onion, finely chopped
- 2 large carrots, peeled and finely chopped
- 2 stalks celery, finely chopped
- 1 pound all-purpose potatoes, peeled and finely chopped
- ½ bay leaf
- 1¼ teaspoons dried thyme
- ¼ teaspoon ground black pepper
- 1 can (28 ounces) plum tomatoes
- 2 tablespoons chopped fresh parsley
- Salt

1. In an 8-quart nonreactive saucepot, heat 1 cup water to boiling over high heat. Add the clams; heat to boiling. Reduce the heat; cover and simmer until the clams open, 5 to 10 minutes, transferring the clams to a bowl as they open. Discard any clams that do not open. Reserve the clam broth. Rinse and wipe out the pot.

2. When cool enough to handle, remove the clams from their shells and coarsely chop them. Strain the clam broth through a sieve lined with paper towels into a bowl.

3. In same clean saucepot, cook the bacon over medium heat until browned; add the onion and cook until tender, 5 minutes. Add the carrots and celery; cook 5 minutes.

4. Add the clam broth to the bacon mixture in the saucepot. Add the potatoes, the remaining 4 cups water, the bay leaf, thyme, and pepper; heat to boiling. Reduce the heat; cover and simmer 10 minutes. Add the tomatoes with their liquid, breaking them up with the side of a spoon, and simmer 10 minutes longer.

5. Stir in the chopped clams and heat through. Discard the bay leaf and sprinkle the chowder with parsley. Taste for seasoning; add salt as needed.

Each serving About 120 calories, 5g protein, 12g carbohydrate, 6g fat (2g saturated), 2g fiber, 345mg sodium.

healthy new england clam chowder

PREP: 20 MIN / TOTAL: 55 MIN / SERVES 6

1½ cups water, plus more for broth

12 large cherrystone or chowder clams, scrubbed (see page 299)

2 slices bacon, chopped

1 medium onion, chopped

1 medium carrot, chopped

1 stalk celery, chopped

2 tablespoons all-purpose flour

1 large potato (12 ounces), peeled and cut into ½-inch chunks

2 cups reduced-fat (2%) milk

⅛ teaspoon ground black pepper

1 tablespoon finely chopped fresh chives

1. In a 4-quart saucepan, heat 1½ cups water to boiling over high heat. Add the clams; return to boiling. Reduce the heat to medium-low; cover and simmer 10 minutes or until the clams open, transferring the clams to a bowl as they open. Discard any unopened clams.

2. Into a 4-cup liquid measuring cup, strain the clam broth through a sieve lined with a paper towel. Add water to the broth to equal 2½ cups total.

3. Rinse out the saucepan to remove any grit. In the same sauce-pan, cook the bacon over medium heat until browned. With a slot-ted spoon, transfer the bacon to paper towels to drain, leaving the bacon fat in the pan. Add the onion, carrot, and celery to the saucepan and cook 9 to 10 minutes, or until tender, stirring occa-sionally. Meanwhile, remove the clams from the shells and coarsely chop them.

4. Stir the flour into the vegetable mixture; cook 1 minute, stirring. Gradually stir in the clam broth. Add the potato; heat to boiling. Cover; simmer over low heat 12 minutes, or until the potato is ten-der, stirring occasionally. Stir in the milk, clams, pepper, and bacon; heat through (do not boil). Sprinkle with chives to serve.

Each serving About 180 calories, 8g protein, 20g carbohydrate, 9g fat (4g saturated), 2g fiber, 155mg sodium.

new england clam chowder

PREP: 25 MIN / TOTAL: 1 HR 10 MIN, PLUS COOLING / MAKES 6 CUPS

1½ dozen large littleneck clams (about 4 pounds), scrubbed (see page 299)

3 slices bacon, chopped

1 medium onion, finely chopped

1 tablespoon all-purpose flour

¼ teaspoon ground black pepper

1 pound all-purpose potatoes (3 medium), peeled and chopped

2 cups half-and-half

1 cup milk

Salt

1. In a 5- to 6-quart saucepot, heat 1 cup water to boiling over high heat. Add the clams; heat to boiling. Reduce the heat slightly; cover and simmer until the clams open, 5 to 10 minutes. Transfer the clams to a bowl as they open. Discard any clams that do not open. Reserve the clam broth. Rinse and wipe out the pot.

2. When cool enough to handle, remove the clams from their shells and coarsely chop them. Discard the shells. Strain the clam broth through a sieve lined with paper towels into a measuring cup; if necessary, add enough water to equal 2 cups.

3. In the same clean saucepot, cook the bacon over medium heat until lightly browned. With a slotted spoon, remove the bacon to paper towels. Add the onion to the drippings in the pot; cook, stirring occasionally, until tender, about 5 minutes. Stir in the flour and pepper until blended; cook 1 minute. Gradually stir in the clam broth until smooth. Add the potatoes; heat to boiling. Reduce the heat; cover and simmer until the potatoes are tender, about 15 minutes.

4. Stir in the half-and-half, milk, and chopped clams; heat through (do not boil). Stir in the bacon. Taste for seasoning; add salt as needed.

Each cup About 370g calories, 18g protein, 24g carbohydrate, 22g fat (11g saturated), 2g fiber, 535mg sodium.

Yankee Cod Chowder

Prepare as directed, omitting the water and clams in steps 1 and 2. Follow step 3 through stirring in the flour and pepper and cooking for 1 minute. Then stir in **3 bottles (8 ounces each) of clam juice** until smooth. Add potatoes and cook as directed. Add **1 pound cod fillet**, cut into 1½-inch pieces, to the pot. Cover and simmer until the fish is just opaque throughout, 2 to 5 minutes. Stir in the half-and-half; omit the milk. Heat through (do not boil). Stir in the bacon. Taste for seasoning; add salt as needed. **Makes about 8½ cups.**

GOOD TO KNOW

———

A BRIEF HISTORY OF CHOWDER

In the 16th and 17th centuries, fish chowder was enjoyed by the French as well as by the Native Americans. In America, by 1751, recipes for fish chowder began to appear in newspapers. Many were prepared by "layering chowder ingredients." Each ingredient was placed in a pot in a layer of uniform thickness, then slowly cooked. By the mid-18th century, chowder was a mainstay throughout the Northeast. Clams and other shellfish were added to chowders largely because of their great availability, as all one had to do was dig them up along the shore. When the 1896 edition of the *Boston Cooking School Cookbook* contained three recipes for chowder, it was clear that chowder was here to stay.

andouille shrimp gumbo

PREP: 30 MIN / TOTAL: 1 HR 40 MIN / SERVES 6

⅓ cup plus 1 tablespoon vegetable oil

½ cup all-purpose flour

2 stalks celery, chopped

2 cloves garlic, minced

1 medium green bell pepper, chopped

1 medium onion, chopped

3½ cups chicken broth

1 can (14½ ounces) stewed tomatoes

1 pound skinless, boneless chicken thighs, cut into thin strips (about 4 thighs)

½ pound andouille or chorizo sausage, cut into ¼-inch-thick slices

6 ounces okra, cut into ½-inch-thick slices

1 cup loosely packed fresh parsley leaves, chopped

1 tablespoon minced fresh thyme leaves

1 tablespoon minced fresh sage leaves

¾ teaspoon salt

½ teaspoon coarsely ground black pepper

4 cups water

1 pound medium (36 to 40 count) shrimp, shelled and deveined (see page 297), with tail part of shell left on

1 cup long-grain white rice, cooked as the label directs

1. In a 6-quart saucepot, heat ⅓ cup oil over medium-low heat until hot. Gradually stir in the flour until blended and cook, stirring, until the mixture is dark brown, about 15 minutes.

2. Meanwhile, in a 12-inch nonstick skillet, heat the remaining 1 tablespoon oil over medium heat until hot. Add the celery, garlic, bell pepper, and onion and cook, stirring occasionally, until the vegetables are tender.

3. When the flour mixture is ready, gradually stir in the broth until blended and smooth. Add the stewed tomatoes, chicken, andouille, okra, parsley, thyme, sage, salt, pepper, cooked vegetables, and water; heat to boiling over high heat. Reduce the heat to low; simmer, uncovered, 40 minutes.

4. Skim off the fat and discard. Add the shrimp and cook, uncovered, until the shrimp turn opaque throughout, about 5 minutes longer.

5. Ladle the gumbo into large bowls. Top with a scoop of hot rice.

Each serving About 525 calories, 40g protein, 46g carbohydrate, 19g fat (6g saturated), 3g fiber, 1,515mg sodium.

san francisco–style seafood stew

PREP: 20 MIN / TOTAL: 50 MIN / SERVES 4

1 (25-inch) sourdough baguette

2 tablespoons olive oil

¼ teaspoon coarsely ground black pepper

1 medium onion, chopped

1 medium red bell pepper, chopped

2 cloves garlic, crushed with a garlic press

½ cup dry white wine

1 can (28 ounces) whole tomatoes in juice

1 cup water

⅛ teaspoon crushed red pepper

½ cup loosely packed fresh parsley leaves, chopped

1 pound large mussels, scrubbed and beards removed (see page 298)

¾ pound striped bass fillet, skin removed, cut into 1½-inch pieces

½ pound large (26 to 30 count) shrimp, shelled and deveined (see page 297)

¼ cup loosely packed fresh basil leaves, chopped

1. Preheat the oven to 400°F. Cut enough bread on the diagonal to make eight ½-inch-thick slices. Wrap the remaining bread; reserve for another use. Place the bread slices on a baking sheet. Brush with 1 tablespoon oil and sprinkle with pepper. Toast the bread in the oven 8 to 10 minutes, or until golden.

2. Meanwhile, in a 5- to 6-quart Dutch oven, heat the remaining 1 tablespoon oil over medium-high heat until hot. Add the onion, bell pepper, and garlic; cook 6 to 8 minutes, or until very tender and browned, stirring frequently. Add the wine; heat to boiling. Boil 1 to 2 minutes, or until the wine reduces by half. While the vegetables are cooking, pour the tomatoes with their juices into a medium bowl; with kitchen shears, chop the tomatoes.

3. Stir the tomatoes with their juices, the water, and the crushed red pepper into the Dutch oven; cover and heat to boiling. Add the parsley, mussels, striped bass, and shrimp; heat to boiling. Reduce the heat to medium-low and simmer, covered, 8 to 10 minutes, or until the striped bass and shrimp are opaque and the mussels open, stirring occasionally.

4. Remove the Dutch oven from the heat. Discard any mussels that have not opened. Stir the basil into the stew. Serve with sourdough toasts.

Each serving About 425 calories, 37g protein, 41g carbohydrate, 13g fat (2g saturated), 5g fiber, 850mg sodium.

chicken soup, five ways

PREP: 10 MIN / TOTAL: 20 MIN / SERVES 4

Start with **6 cups simmering chicken broth**. Add **spices** and **veggies** and simmer until tender; stir in **2 cups cooked, shredded chicken**; **precooked items**; and **flavorings**. Pick your favorite variation below and complete the recipe:

VARIATIONS

Classic Chicken Noodle

2 stalks celery, chopped; **1 medium carrot**, chopped; **2 tablespoons chopped dill**; and **2 cups cooked noodles**

Tex-Mex

2 tablespoons lime juice; **1 teaspoon ground cumin**; chopped **fresh cilantro**; **1 can (14 ounces) black beans**, rinsed and drained; and **1 cup crushed tortilla chips**

Tortellini en Brodo

4 cups baby spinach; **2 tablespoons grated Parmesan cheese**; and **1 package (9 ounces) fresh cheese tortellini**, cooked as the label directs

Coconut-Lime

1 can (14 ounces) coconut milk; **8 ounces sliced cremini mushrooms**; **¼ cup cilantro leaves**; **¼ cup Asian fish sauce**; and **¼ cup fresh lime juice**

Lemony Greek

¼ cup fresh lemon juice; **2 large eggs**, beaten; **1 green onion**, thinly sliced; and **4 ounces orzo pasta**, cooked as the label directs (to yield 1¼ cups)

TEX-MEX 160

CLASSIC CHICKEN NOODLE 160

TORTELLINI EN BRODO 160

COCONUT-LIME 160

LEMONY GREEK 160

boeuf bourguignon

PREP: 30 MIN / TOTAL: 3 HR 15 MIN / SERVES 6

2 slices bacon, chopped

2 pounds lean boneless beef chuck, trimmed and cut into 1½-inch pieces

2 teaspoons vegetable oil

1 large onion, chopped

2 carrots, peeled and chopped

2 cloves garlic, finely chopped

2 tablespoons all-purpose flour

2 teaspoons tomato paste

2 cups dry red wine, such as Pinot Noir

½ bay leaf

1 teaspoon plus a pinch of salt

¼ teaspoon plus a pinch of ground black pepper

1 pound small white onions, peeled

3 tablespoons butter or margarine

1 teaspoon sugar

1 cup water

1 pound mushrooms, trimmed and cut into quarters if large

1. In a 5-quart nonreactive Dutch oven, cook the bacon over medium heat until it just begins to brown. With a slotted spoon, transfer the bacon to a medium bowl.

2. Pat the beef dry with paper towels. Add 1 teaspoon oil to the Dutch oven and increase the heat to medium-high. Add the beef, in batches, to the bacon drippings and cook until well browned, using a slotted spoon to transfer the beef as it is browned to the bowl with the bacon. Add the remaining 1 teaspoon oil if necessary.

3. Reduce the heat to medium. Add the chopped onion, carrots, and garlic to the Dutch oven; cook until the onion and carrots are tender, about 8 minutes. Stir in the flour; cook 1 minute. Stir in the tomato paste; cook 1 minute. Add the wine, bay leaf, 1 teaspoon salt, and ¼ teaspoon pepper, stirring until the browned bits are loosened from the bottom of the pot.

4. Return the beef and bacon to the Dutch oven; heat to boiling. Reduce the heat; cover and simmer until the beef is very tender, about 1 hour 30 minutes. Remove the bay leaf. Skim and discard the fat.

5. Meanwhile, in a 10-inch skillet, combine the small white onions, 1 tablespoon butter, the sugar, and water; heat to boiling. Reduce the heat; cover and simmer until the onions are just tender, about 10 minutes. Remove the cover and cook over medium-high heat, swirling the pan occasionally, until the water has evaporated and the onions are golden. Transfer to a bowl; keep warm.

6. In the same skillet, melt the remaining 2 tablespoons butter over medium-high heat. Add the mushrooms and the remaining pinch each of salt and pepper; cook, stirring, until the mushrooms are tender and the liquid has evaporated. Stir the onions and mushrooms into stew.

Each serving About 415 calories, 33g protein, 20g carbohydrate, 23g fat (9g saturated), 3g fiber, 260mg sodium.

moroccan vegetable stew

PREP: 15 MIN / TOTAL: 55 MIN / SERVES 4

1 tablespoon olive oil

1 medium butternut squash (about 2 pounds), peeled, seeded, and cut into 1-inch pieces

2 carrots, peeled and cut into ¼-inch-thick slices

1 medium onion, chopped

1 can (15 to 19 ounces) chickpeas, rinsed and drained

1 can (14½ ounces) stewed tomatoes

½ cup pitted prunes, chopped

½ teaspoon ground cinnamon

½ teaspoon salt

⅛ to ¼ teaspoon crushed red pepper

1½ cups water

1 cup couscous (Moroccan pasta)

1¼ cups vegetable or chicken broth

2 tablespoons chopped fresh cilantro or parsley

1. In a 12-inch nonstick skillet, heat the oil over medium-high heat. Add the squash, carrots, and onion and cook, stirring frequently, until the onion is tender and golden, about 10 minutes.

2. Stir in the chickpeas, tomatoes, prunes, cinnamon, salt, crushed red pepper, and water; heat to boiling. Reduce the heat; cover and simmer until all the vegetables are tender, about 30 minutes.

3. Meanwhile, prepare the couscous as the label directs, but use the broth in place of water.

4. To serve, stir the cilantro into stew and spoon it over the couscous.

Each serving About 475 calories, 14g protein, 95g carbohydrate, 6g fat (1g saturated), 15g fiber, 1,020mg sodium.

chicken bouillabaisse

PREP: 1 HR / TOTAL: 1 HR 30 MIN / SERVES 4

- 1 tablespoon olive oil
- 8 large bone-in chicken thighs (2½ pounds), skin and fat removed
- 2 large carrots, peeled and finely chopped
- 1 medium onion, finely chopped
- 1 large fennel bulb (1½ pounds), cut into ¼-inch-thick slices
- ½ cup water
- 3 cloves garlic, finely chopped
- 1 can (14½ ounces) diced tomatoes
- 1¾ cups chicken broth
- ½ cup dry white wine
- 2 tablespoons anisette (anise-flavored liqueur; optional)
- ¼ teaspoon dried thyme
- ¼ teaspoon salt
- ⅛ teaspoon cayenne pepper
- 1 bay leaf
- Pinch of saffron threads

1. In a 5-quart Dutch oven, heat the oil over medium-high heat until very hot. Add the chicken, in batches, and cook until golden brown, about 5 minutes per side, using a slotted spoon to transfer the chicken pieces to a bowl as they are browned.

2. Add the carrots and onion to the Dutch oven and cook over medium heat, stirring occasionally, until tender and golden, about 10 minutes. Transfer the mixture to the bowl with the chicken.

3. Preheat the oven to 350°F. Add the fennel and water to the Dutch oven, stirring until the browned bits are loosened from the bottom of the pot. Cook over medium heat, stirring occasionally, until the fennel is tender and browned, about 7 minutes. Add the garlic and cook 3 minutes.

4. Return the chicken and carrot mixture to the Dutch oven. Add the tomatoes with their juices; broth; wine; anisette, if using, thyme; salt; cayenne; bay leaf; and saffron; heat to boiling. Cover and bake until the juices run clear when the thickest part of the chicken is pierced with the tip of a knife, about 30 minutes. Discard the bay leaf.

Each serving About 320 calories, 36g protein, 18g carbohydrate, 11g fat (2g saturated), 7g fiber, 1,035mg sodium.

lamb navarin

PREP: 20 MIN / TOTAL: 2 HR 20 MIN / SERVES 8

- 3 pounds boneless lamb shoulder, trimmed and cut into 1-inch pieces
- 2 tablespoons butter or margarine
- 2 small onions, each cut into quarters, then crosswise into slices
- 1½ cups dry white wine
- 1½ cups chicken broth
- 1 cup water
- 6 sprigs plus 2 tablespoons chopped fresh parsley
- 2 sprigs fresh thyme, or ¼ teaspoon dried thyme
- 2 bay leaves
- 4 cloves garlic, finely chopped
- ½ teaspoon salt
- ¼ teaspoon ground black pepper
- 8 ounces peeled baby carrots (1⅓ cups)
- 2 small turnips (4 ounces each), peeled and cut into ¾-inch pieces
- 8 ounces pearl onions, peeled (1 cup)
- 1½ pounds asparagus, trimmed and cut into 2-inch lengths
- 2 teaspoons sugar

1. Pat the lamb dry with paper towels. In a 5-quart nonreactive Dutch oven, melt the butter over medium heat. Cook the lamb, in batches, until well browned, using a slotted spoon to transfer the meat to a bowl as it is browned. Add the onions to the Dutch oven and cook, stirring, until tender, about 5 minutes. Add the wine, broth, water, parsley sprigs, thyme, bay leaves, and lamb to the pot; heat to boiling over high heat. Reduce the heat; cover and simmer 15 minutes. Add the garlic, salt, and pepper and simmer 30 minutes longer.

2. Add the carrots, turnips, and pearl onions to the Dutch oven; partially cover and cook until the lamb is tender, about 30 minutes longer. Stir in the asparagus and cook until the vegetables are tender, 5 to 10 minutes longer.

3. With a slotted spoon, transfer the meat and vegetables to a deep dish and keep warm. Boil the stew liquid over medium-high heat until it has reduced and thickened, about 10 minutes.

4. Discard the parsley and thyme sprigs and bay leaves. Stir in the sugar. Taste for seasoning; add salt as needed. Spoon the stew liquid over the meat and vegetables and sprinkle with the chopped parsley.

Each serving About 310 calories, 39g protein, 14g carbohydrate, 11g fat (5g saturated), 3g fiber, 500mg sodium.

country borscht stew

PREP: 1 HR 15 MIN / TOTAL: 3 HR 15 MIN / SERVES 12

2 bunches beets (1¾ pounds without tops)

1 medium head red cabbage (about 2¾ pounds)

5 pounds beef chuck short ribs

1 pound carrots, peeled and each cut lengthwise in half, then crosswise into 1-inch-thick pieces

1 pound parsnips, peeled and each cut lengthwise in half, then crosswise into 1-inch-thick pieces

1 large onion, peeled and cut into 1-inch pieces

2 teaspoons salt

1 teaspoon caraway seeds, crushed

¼ teaspoon ground cloves

1 quart chicken broth

2 bay leaves

½ cup loosely packed sprigs fresh dill, chopped

Sour cream (optional)

1. Trim the tops, if any, from the beets. Peel and shred the beets (you should have about 6½ cups shredded beets). Cut the cabbage into quarters; remove and discard the core. Cut the cabbage into ½-inch slices.

2. Heat an 8-quart Dutch oven over medium-high heat until hot. Pat the beef ribs dry with paper towels. Add the beef in batches and cook until well browned on all sides, 5 to 6 minutes per batch, using tongs to transfer the meat to a medium bowl as it is browned. (You may need to reduce the heat to medium if the fat in the Dutch oven begins to smoke.) Preheat the oven to 325°F.

3. Reduce the heat to medium. Discard all but ¼ cup drippings in the Dutch oven. Add the carrots, parsnips, onion, salt, caraway seeds, and cloves; cook, stirring occasionally, until the vegetables are golden, about 10 minutes. Add the cabbage and cook, stirring frequently, until wilted, about 10 minutes.

4. Return the meat with its juices to the Dutch oven; stir in the broth, bay leaves, and beets. Heat to boiling over high heat, stirring until the browned bits are loosened from the bottom of the Dutch oven. Cover and bake until the meat is fork-tender, 2 hours to 2 hours 15 minutes.

5. Remove the stew from the oven. With tongs, transfer the short-rib meat and bones to a large bowl to cool slightly. Discard the bay leaves. Skim and discard the fat. When the short ribs are cool enough to handle, cut the meat into 1-inch pieces; discard the bones and fat.

6. Return the meat to the Dutch oven. Heat over medium heat until hot. Stir in the dill. To serve, ladle the borscht into shallow soup bowls and top with sour cream, if you like.

Each serving About 525 calories, 22g protein, 22g carbohydrate, 39g fat (16g saturated), 6g fiber, 830mg sodium.

GOOD TO KNOW

STEW SAVVY

A few simple steps are the keys to success when making stew.

- Always use a heavy pot, such as a Dutch oven, which promotes even cooking.

- When browning meat or vegetables, first pat them dry. Always add meat to the hot oil without crowding the pan, so that it browns rather than steams. Give meat or vegetables a chance to brown before turning, which will create browned bits on the bottom of the pan. Adding liquid will deglaze the pans, and these bits will add rich flavor.

- Add enough liquid to cover or almost cover the ingredients.

- Cook stews slowly on top of the stove over low heat to tenderize the meat.

- Quicker-cooking ingredients, such as potatoes and peas, are usually added near the end of the cooking time, so they don't get overcooked.

provençal beef stew (daube)

PREP: 15 MIN / TOTAL: 2 HR 45 MIN / SERVES 6

- **2 pounds lean boneless beef chuck, trimmed and cut into 2-inch pieces**
- **4 teaspoons olive oil**
- **1 large onion, chopped**
- **2 carrots, peeled and chopped**
- **2 cloves garlic, finely chopped**
- **1 can (14 to 16 ounces) tomatoes**
- **2 cups dry red wine**
- **4 strips (3 × ¾ inch each) orange peel**
- **3 whole cloves**
- **1 teaspoon salt**
- **¼ teaspoon ground black pepper**
- **¼ teaspoon dried thyme**
- **1 bay leaf**
- **2 tablespoons chopped fresh parsley**

1. Pat the beef dry with paper towels. In a 5-quart nonreactive Dutch oven, heat 2 teaspoons oil over medium-high heat until very hot. Add half the beef and cook until well browned, using a slotted spoon to transfer the meat to a bowl as it is browned. Repeat with the remaining 2 teaspoons oil and remaining beef.

2. Reduce the heat to medium. Add the onion and carrots to the Dutch oven and cook, stirring occasionally, until tender, about 5 minutes. Stir in the garlic and cook until very fragrant, about 30 seconds. Stir in the tomatoes with their juices, breaking them up with the side of a spoon. Add the wine, orange peel, cloves, salt, pepper, thyme, bay leaf, and beef; heat to boiling over high heat.

3. Reduce the heat; cover and simmer 2 hours to 2 hours 30 minutes, until the meat is very tender. With a slotted spoon, transfer the meat to a serving bowl and keep warm. Skim and discard the fat from the stew liquid.

4. Increase the heat to medium-high and boil the liquid 10 minutes to concentrate flavors. Discard the bay leaf and spoon the liquid over the meat. Sprinkle with parsley.

Each serving About 290 calories, 30g protein, 11g carbohydrate, 14g fat (4g saturated), 2g fiber, 600mg sodium.

GOOD TO KNOW

STEW SPEAK

Meat stews are enjoyed around the world. Here are some of the most famous.

BEEF BOURGUIGNON	This French beef stew is flavored with onions, mushrooms, and bacon.
BEEF CARBONNADE	A Belgian stew that contains dark beer and caramelized onions.
BLANQUETTE DE VEAU	A rich, creamy veal stew, so named because the meat is not browned.
DAUBE	In France, daubes, or Provençal braised stew, are often baked in a pot known as a *daubière*.
GOULASH	Called *gulyás* in its native Hungary, this stew is flavored with paprika.
NAVARIN	A French stew made with lamb and usually onions, potatoes, turnips, and herbs.
STIFADO	A Greek stew prepared with lamb or beef, flavored with tomatoes and oregano, and baked in a casserole.

creamy veal stew

PREP: 35 MIN / TOTAL: 1 HR 50 MIN / SERVES 6

2 pounds boneless veal shoulder, cut into 1½-inch pieces

¼ cup all-purpose flour

1 teaspoon salt

¼ teaspoon ground black pepper

2 tablespoons plus 2 teaspoons vegetable oil

1 cup dry white wine

2 medium onions, chopped

1 cup chicken broth

1 bay leaf

¼ teaspoon dried thyme

¼ cup heavy or whipping cream

1. Preheat the oven to 350°F. Pat the veal dry with paper towels. On waxed paper, combine the flour, salt, and pepper. Coat the veal with the seasoned flour, shaking off any excess.

2. In a 12-inch nonstick skillet, heat 1 tablespoon oil over medium-high heat until very hot. Add half the veal and cook until browned, using a slotted spoon to transfer the meat to a bowl as it is browned. Repeat with 1 tablespoon oil and the remaining veal. Add the wine to the skillet and heat to boiling, stirring until the browned bits are loosened from the bottom of the skillet; remove from the heat.

3. In a 5-quart nonreactive Dutch oven, heat the remaining 2 teaspoons oil over medium heat. Add the onions and cook until tender, about 5 minutes. Stir in the veal, broth, bay leaf, thyme, and pan-juice mixture from the skillet. Heat to boiling; cover and bake until the veal is tender, about 1 hour 15 minutes. Discard the bay leaf; stir in the heavy cream.

Each serving About 285 calories, 31g protein, 10g carbohydrate, 13g fat (4g saturated), 1g fiber, 695mg sodium.

 Tip See Veal 101 on page 196 to learn more about veal.

pork & peppers ragù

PREP: 45 MIN / TOTAL: 2 HR 30 MIN / SERVES 10

3 tablespoons olive oil

1 boneless pork shoulder (about 3½ pounds), trimmed well and cut into 4-inch chunks

Salt

Ground black pepper

1 large red bell pepper, seeded and sliced

1 large green bell pepper, seeded and sliced

1 large onion, chopped

3 cloves garlic, chopped

3 tablespoons tomato paste

¾ cup dry red wine

1 can (28 ounces) crushed tomatoes

2 bay leaves

1. Preheat the oven to 325°F. In a 6- to 8-quart Dutch oven or heavy saucepot, heat the oil over medium-high heat until hot but not smoking. Season the pork all over with ¾ teaspoon salt and ½ teaspoon pepper; add to the pot. Cook 10 to 12 minutes, or until browned on both sides; transfer to a large plate.

2. To the same pot, add the bell peppers, onion, garlic, and ½ teaspoon salt. Cook 5 minutes, or until the vegetables are beginning to soften, stirring occasionally. Add the tomato paste; cook 1 minute, stirring. Add the wine. Heat to boiling over high heat; boil 2 minutes, or until reduced slightly. Add the tomatoes and bay leaves; return the pork to the pot. Heat to boiling. Cover and cook 1½ to 2 hours, or until the pork is very tender.

3. Transfer the pork to a cutting board; with 2 forks, pull the pork into bite-size pieces. Discard the bay leaves. Return the pork and any juices to the pot with tomato sauce, stirring to coat.

Each serving About 260 calories, 25g protein, 11g carbohydrate, 13g fat (4g saturated), 3g fiber, 535 mg sodium.

Serving Suggestion Serve the ragu with polenta (page 328) or cooked egg noodles. Polenta, made from corn, is a staple in Italy and makes a delicious centerpiece (and conversation starter) for a dinner party. Pour hot polenta onto a large board or into a casserole. Surround with the ragù, a couple of sautéed vegetables, maybe mushrooms and broccoli, some cheese, pesto, or other condiments.

mole chili con carne

PREP: 1 HR 10 MIN / TOTAL: 2 HR 55 MIN / SERVES 10

- 2 pounds boneless pork shoulder, trimmed and cut into 1-inch pieces
- 2 pounds boneless beef chuck, trimmed and cut into 1-inch pieces
- 2 teaspoons vegetable oil
- 6 cloves garlic, crushed with a garlic press
- 2 medium onions, chopped
- 1 tablespoon ground coriander
- 1 tablespoon ground cumin
- 1 tablespoon paprika
- 1½ teaspoons chipotle chile powder
- ½ teaspoon ground cinnamon
- 3 cans (15 to 19 ounces each) pink beans, red kidney beans, or a mix
- 1 can (28 ounces) diced tomatoes
- 1 cup water
- 2 squares (2 ounces) unsweetened chocolate, chopped
- 1½ teaspoons salt
- Warm corn tortillas, for serving (optional)

1. Pat the pork and beef dry with paper towels. In a 6- to 8-quart Dutch oven, heat the oil over medium-high heat until very hot. Add the meat in batches and cook until well browned, 5 to 6 minutes, adding more oil if necessary and using a slotted spoon to transfer the meat to a medium bowl as it is browned. (You may need to reduce the heat to medium if the oil in the Dutch oven begins to smoke.) Preheat the oven to 325°F.

2. Reduce the heat to medium. Add the garlic, onions, coriander, cumin, paprika, chipotle chile powder, and cinnamon to the drippings in the Dutch oven and cook, stirring frequently, until the onion is tender, about 5 minutes.

3. Return the meat with its juices to the Dutch oven. Stir in the beans with their liquid, the tomatoes with their juices, the water, chocolate, and salt; heat to boiling over high heat, stirring until the browned bits are loosened from the bottom of the Dutch oven.

4. Cover and bake until the meat is fork-tender, 1 hour and 45 minutes to 2 hours. Skim and discard any fat. Spoon the chili into bowls and serve with tortillas, if you like.

Each serving About 525 calories, 55g protein, 34g carbohydrate, 19g fat (7g saturated), 10g fiber, 1,335mg sodium.

new mexican green chili

PREP: 30 MIN / TOTAL: 3 HR / SERVES 6

- 1 bunch cilantro
- 3 cloves garlic, finely chopped
- 1½ teaspoons salt
- 2 pounds boneless pork shoulder, trimmed and cut into ¾-inch pieces
- 2 medium onions, chopped
- 3 serrano or jalapeño chiles, seeded and finely chopped
- 1 teaspoon ground cumin
- ¼ teaspoon cayenne pepper
- 2 pounds tomatillos, husked, rinsed, and cut into quarters
- 4 poblano chiles, or 2 green peppers, roasted (see page 446), seeded, and cut into 1-inch pieces
- 1 can (15¼ to 16 ounces) whole-kernel corn, drained
- Sour cream and warm flour tortillas, for serving (optional)

1. Preheat the oven to 325°F. Chop enough cilantro leaves and stems to equal ¼ cup; chop and reserve another ¼ cup cilantro leaves for garnish. With the side of a chef's knife, mash the garlic and salt to a paste; transfer to a 5-quart Dutch oven. Add the pork, onions, serranos, cilantro leaves and stems, cumin, and cayenne; toss to combine. Cover and bake 1 hour.

2. Stir in the tomatillos and roasted poblanos. Cover and bake until the pork is very tender, 1 hour 30 minutes to 2 hours longer.

3. Skim and discard the fat. Stir in the corn and heat through. Sprinkle with the reserved cilantro and serve with sour cream and tortillas, if you like.

Each serving About 380 calories, 34g protein, 27g carbohydrate, 16g fat (5g saturated), 5g fiber, 800mg sodium.

five-spice braised pork & cabbage

PREP: 1 HR / TOTAL: 2 HR 30 MIN / SERVES 8

- 4 pounds boneless pork shoulder, trimmed and cut into 2-inch pieces
- 2 tablespoons brown sugar
- 1 tablespoon Chinese five-spice powder
- 1 tablespoon vegetable oil
- 1 teaspoon fresh orange zest
- ¾ teaspoon salt
- 1 medium head green cabbage (about 2½ pounds)
- 1 large onion, cut in half, then sliced crosswise
- 1 piece (3 inches) peeled fresh ginger, cut into slivers
- 1¾ cups chicken broth
- ¼ cup soy sauce
- 2 tablespoons seasoned rice vinegar or cider vinegar
- Long-grain white rice (optional)
- ¼ cup cornstarch
- 3 tablespoons water

1. Pat the pork dry with paper towels. In a large bowl, toss the pork with the brown sugar, five-spice powder, oil, orange zest, and salt until evenly coated. Set aside.

2. Remove the tough outer leaves from the cabbage. Cut the cabbage into 4 wedges; remove and discard the core. Cut the cabbage into 2-inch pieces. Set aside.

3. Heat a 6- to 8-quart Dutch oven over medium-high heat until hot. Add the pork, in batches, and cook until well browned, 4 to 7 minutes, adding more oil if necessary and transferring the pork with a slotted spoon to a medium bowl as it is browned. (You may need to reduce the heat to medium if the oil begins to smoke.) Preheat the oven to 325°F.

4. Reduce the heat to medium. To the fat remaining in the Dutch oven, add onion and ginger and cook, stirring frequently, until tender, about 5 minutes. Add the cabbage and cook, stirring frequently, until the cabbage wilts, 6 to 8 minutes. Add the broth, soy sauce, and vinegar and stir until the browned bits are loosened from the bottom of the Dutch oven. Return the pork with its juices to the Dutch oven; heat to boiling.

5. Cover and bake until the meat is fork-tender, about 1 hour 30 minutes.

6. About 30 minutes before serving, prepare the rice as the label directs, if you like.

7. Skim and discard the fat from the stew. In a cup, combine the cornstarch and water. Heat the stew to boiling over medium heat. Stir in the cornstarch mixture; heat to boiling. Boil until the stew thickens slightly, about 1 minute. Serve with rice, if using.

Each serving About 455 calories, 49g protein, 19g carbohydrate, 20g fat (6g saturated), 4g fiber, 1,210mg sodium.

hoppin' john

PREP: 15 MIN / TOTAL: 1 HR 15 MIN / SERVES 18

- 1 tablespoon vegetable oil
- 2 stalks celery, chopped
- 1 large onion, chopped
- 1 red bell pepper, chopped
- 2 cloves garlic, finely chopped
- 1 package (16 ounces) dry black-eyed peas, rinsed and picked over
- 1 large smoked ham hock (12 ounces)
- 4 cups water
- 3½ cups chicken broth
- 2 teaspoons salt
- ¼ teaspoon crushed red pepper
- 1 bay leaf
- 2 cups regular long-grain rice

1. In a 4-quart saucepan, heat the oil over medium heat; add the celery, onion, and chopped bell pepper. Cook, stirring frequently, until the onion is golden, about 10 minutes. Add the garlic; cook 2 minutes longer.

2. Add the black-eyed peas, ham hock, water, broth, 1 teaspoon salt, crushed red pepper, and bay leaf to the celery mixture; heat to boiling over high heat. Reduce the heat; cover and simmer, stirring occasionally, until the black-eyed peas are tender, about 40 minutes. Discard the bay leaf.

3. Prepare the rice as the label directs, adding the remaining 1 teaspoon salt. (Do not add butter or margarine.)

4. In a large bowl, combine the black-eyed pea mixture and rice.

Each serving About 190 calories, 9g protein, 33g carbohydrate, 2g fat (0g saturated), 5g fiber, 550mg sodium.

cincinnati chili

PREP: 25 MIN / TOTAL: 3 HR 25 MIN / SERVES 8

- 2 teaspoons vegetable oil
- 2 medium onions, chopped
- 2 teaspoons finely chopped garlic
- 2 pounds ground beef chuck
- 2 tablespoons chili powder
- 1 tablespoon ground cumin
- 1 teaspoon ground cinnamon
- 1 teaspoon salt
- ½ teaspoon dried oregano
- ½ teaspoon cayenne pepper
- 2 cans (16 ounces each) tomatoes
- 1¾ cups beef broth
- 1½ cups water
- ½ square (½ ounce) unsweetened chocolate, chopped
- 1 package (16 ounces) spaghetti or linguine

1. In a 5-quart nonreactive Dutch oven, heat the oil over medium heat. Add the onions and cook, stirring occasionally, until tender, about 5 minutes. Transfer to a small bowl; set aside. Add the garlic to the Dutch oven; cook 1 minute longer. Transfer to the bowl with the onions.

2. In the same Dutch oven, cook the ground beef over high heat, breaking up the meat with the side of a spoon, until the meat is browned. Discard the fat. Stir in the chili powder, cumin, cinnamon, salt, oregano, and cayenne; cook 1 minute longer.

3. Add the tomatoes with their juices to the Dutch oven, breaking them up with the side of a spoon. Stir in the broth, water, chocolate, browned beef, and onion-garlic mixture; heat to boiling. Reduce the heat; cover and simmer 2 hours 30 minutes. Remove the cover and simmer until thickened, about 30 minutes longer.

4. Meanwhile, cook the pasta as the label directs. Drain. Serve the chili over pasta.

Each serving (without spaghetti) About 270 calories, 26g protein, 12g carbohydrate, 14g fat (5g saturated), 3g fiber, 755mg sodium.

hungarian pork goulash

PREP: 20 MIN / TOTAL: 1 HR 50 MIN / SERVES 6

- 2 tablespoons vegetable oil
- 2 large onions (12 ounces each), chopped
- 1 clove garlic, finely chopped
- ¼ cup paprika, preferably sweet Hungarian
- 2 pounds boneless pork shoulder blade roast (fresh pork butt), trimmed and cut into 1½-inch pieces
- 1 bag (16 ounces) sauerkraut, rinsed and drained
- 1 can (14½ ounces) diced tomatoes
- 1¾ cups beef broth
- ½ teaspoon salt
- ¼ teaspoon ground black pepper
- 1 container (8 ounces) sour cream

1. Preheat the oven to 325°F. In a 5-quart nonreactive Dutch oven, heat the oil over medium heat. Add the onions and cook, stirring frequently, 10 minutes. Stir in the garlic; cook until the onions are very tender, about 5 minutes longer.

2. Add the paprika to the onions, stirring well; cook 1 minute. Add the pork, sauerkraut, tomatoes with their juices, broth, salt, and pepper; heat to boiling over high heat. Cover and bake until the pork is tender, about 1 hour 30 minutes.

3. Remove the stew from the oven. Stir in the sour cream. Heat through over medium heat (do not boil).

Each serving About 450 calories, 33g protein, 17g carbohydrate, 28g fat (11g saturated), 6g fiber, 1,135mg sodium.

paella

PREP: 30 MIN / TOTAL: 1 HR 30 MIN / SERVES 8

- 1 tablespoon olive oil
- 1½ pounds skinless, boneless chicken thighs, cut into 2-inch pieces (about 6 thighs)
- 2 fully cooked chorizo sausages (3 ounces each)
- 1 medium onion, finely chopped
- 1 red bell pepper, finely chopped
- 2 cloves garlic, finely chopped
- ¼ teaspoon cayenne pepper
- ½ cup canned tomatoes in puree
- ½ cup dry white wine
- 2 cups medium- or short-grain rice
- 4 ounces green beans, cut into 1-inch pieces
- 2½ cups water
- 1¾ cups chicken broth
- 1½ teaspoons salt
- ¼ teaspoon loosely packed saffron threads, crumbled
- ⅛ teaspoon dried thyme
- ½ bay leaf
- 1 pound mussels, scrubbed and debearded (see page 298)
- 12 ounces medium (26 to 30 count) shrimp, shelled and deveined (see page 297)
- ¼ cup chopped fresh parsley
- Lemon wedges, for serving

1. In a deep, 12-inch nonreactive skillet, heat the oil over medium-high heat until very hot. Add the chicken and chorizo; cook until browned, about 10 minutes. With a slotted spoon, transfer the chicken and chorizo to a bowl.

2. Reduce the heat to medium. Add the onion and pepper to the skillet; cook, stirring frequently, until the onion is tender, about 5 minutes. Stir in the garlic and cayenne; cook, stirring, 30 seconds. Add the tomatoes with their puree and the wine; cook, breaking up the tomatoes with the side of a spoon, until the liquid has evaporated.

3. Stir the rice, green beans, water, broth, salt, saffron, thyme, and bay leaf into the skillet. Thinly slice the chorizo; return it and the chicken to the skillet. Heat to boiling over high heat. Reduce the heat; cover and simmer 20 minutes.

4. Tuck the mussels into the paella; cover and cook 3 minutes. Tuck the shrimp into the paella; cover and cook just until mussels have opened and shrimp are opaque throughout, about 3 minutes longer. Remove from heat and let stand 5 minutes. Discard the bay leaf and any mussels that have not opened. Sprinkle the paella with parsley and serve with lemon wedges.

Each serving About 470 calories, 35g protein, 45g carbohydrate, 15g fat (4g saturated), 2g fiber, 1,110mg sodium.

jambalaya

PREP: 20 MIN / TOTAL: 1 HR 15 MIN, PLUS COOLING / SERVES 6

- 8 ounces hot Italian sausage links, pricked with a fork
- 1 medium onion, finely chopped
- 1 green bell pepper, chopped
- 1 stalk celery, chopped
- 1 clove garlic, finely chopped
- ⅛ teaspoon cayenne pepper
- 1½ cups regular long-grain rice
- 1¾ cups chicken broth
- 1¼ cups water
- ¼ teaspoon salt
- ⅛ teaspoon dried thyme
- 1 can (14 to 16 ounces) tomatoes, drained and chopped
- 1 pound medium (26 to 30 count) shrimp, shelled and deveined (see page 297)
- 2 green onions, thinly sliced
- Hot sauce, for serving (optional)

1. In a 5-quart nonreactive Dutch oven, cook the sausages over medium heat until browned, about 10 minutes. With a slotted spoon, transfer the sausages to paper towels to drain. When cool enough to handle, cut the sausages into ½-inch pieces.

2. To the drippings in the Dutch oven, add the onion, bell pepper, and celery; cook, stirring frequently, until tender, about 10 minutes. Stir in the garlic and cayenne and cook, stirring, 30 seconds. Add the rice and cook, stirring, 1 minute. Stir in the sausages, broth, water, salt, and thyme; heat to boiling over high heat. Reduce the heat; cover and simmer 15 minutes.

3. Stir in the tomatoes; cover and cook 5 minutes. Stir in the shrimp; cover and cook until the shrimp are opaque throughout, about 5 minutes longer. Transfer to serving bowl and sprinkle with green onions. Serve with hot sauce, if you like.

Each serving About 405 calories, 23g protein, 45g carbohydrate, 14g fat (5g saturated), 2g fiber, 875mg sodium.

meat

As American icons go, steak, burgers, and chops are right up there with apple pie—and we eat a lot more meat than pie! These days we're exploring new ways to cook meat. The multicooker (recipes on pages 135–137) has given meat a new license for weeknight cooking. And the sheet pan has become the week-night darling for roasting small cuts of meat and veggies for an all-in-one meal. A beautifully cooked roast is the jewel in the crown of the entertaining table, so when we do one, we want perfection. Use our roasting charts and an instant-read ther-mometer to gauge doneness. In this chapter and in Grilling (page 367), we unlock the secrets to choosing and storing meat as well as provide dozens of tempting recipes for meat as the star of the plate or as a delicious supporting player.

BALSAMIC-GLAZED PORK CHOPS WITH SPINACH MASH 209

PORK CHOPS WITH ROSEMARY-TRUFFLE BUTTER 210

CHILI PIE WITH CORN-BREAD CRUST 193

MINI COTTAGE PIES 220

Decoding Meat Labels

→

Label lingo can be confusing. Here we've broken it down so it's easy to understand.

USDA INSPECTED All meat in the United States is inspected by the United States Department of Agriculture (USDA) to ensure that it is safe to eat and free of disease. That said, some diseases, such as E. coli and salmonella, cannot be detected by the naked eye.

GRADING Once meat has passed inspection, processors may request this as voluntary USDA procedure. It is based on the meat's age (older meat is tougher) and level of fat marbling (streaks of fat within the flesh)—not on safety. The meat available to consumers is graded Prime, Choice, or Select. Beef and lamb are often graded; veal is only occasionally. Pork is rarely graded because only the highest grade is sold to consumers. About 50 percent of all graded meat is Choice.

ORGANIC USDA Regulations require that animals be raised in living conditions accommodating their natural behaviors (like the ability to graze on pasture), fed 100 percent organic feed and forage, and not administered any antibiotics or hormones.

GRASSFED This label is not regulated by the USDA. According to the American Grassfed Association, these animals are raised on family farms, are fed only grass and forage, are pasture raised without confinement to feedlots, and are not administered any antibiotics or hormones.

Safety Savvy

→

DON'T CROSS CONTAMINATE. Keep meat separate from other ingredients until ready to cook.

DON'T ALLOW RAW MEAT TO STAY AT ROOM TEMPERATURE FOR MORE THAN 1 HOUR. We use refrigerator-temperature meat for all our recipe timings unless noted.

WASH CUTTING BOARDS, PLATES, AND UTENSILS that have touched raw meat before using for other ingredients or for cooked food.

Cook It Right

→

There is only one way to know that your meat is cooked to the desired/safe temperature: Use a meat thermometer (see page 18). The USDA recommends that all meat be cooked until well-done (160°F) to kill any bacteria that could cause illness. This is especially important with ground meats as bacteria may be introduced during the grinding/handling process. For whole cuts, such as steaks and roasts, we recommend cooking to lower temperatures for optimum flavor and texture, as noted in the Roasting Times charts (pages 176, 198, and 203).

Carving

EASY AS 1-2-3

1 **Set Up** Place a damp paper towel under your cutting board to keep it from sliding. Transfer the meat to the cutting board and tent loosely with foil to keep warm.

2 **Rest** Let steaks and roasts stand before carving so the internal juices can redistribute, making the meat juicy and firming it for easier carving. Allow five minutes for steak, up to 20 for a standing rib or other large roast.

3 **Carve** Use a thin sharp knife and a two-tined carving fork for easy handling. Slice across the grain, not parallel to the fibers, for the most tender results. Transfer meat to a warm platter and serve.

GOOD TO KNOW

ROASTING TIMES FOR BEEF

This roasting chart gives guidelines for cooking a variety of cuts from medium-rare to well-done when cooking without a recipe. Start with meat at refrigerator temperature. Remove a roast from the oven when it reaches 5°F to 10°F below desired doneness; the temperature will continue to rise as it stands.

CUT	WEIGHT	TEMP	MINUTES PER POUND		
			MEDIUM-RARE	MEDIUM	WELL-DONE
			CUT TEMPERATURE WEIGHT		
			(135°F to 140°F)	(145°F to 155°F)	(OVER 160°F)
RIB ROAST (CHINE BONE REMOVED)	4 to 6 pounds 6 to 8 pounds	325°F	24 to 30 minutes 15 to 20 minutes	30 to 36 minutes 22 to 26 minutes	34 to 38 minutes 22 to 26 minutes
RIB EYE ROAST	4 to 6 pounds	350°F	15 to 20 minutes	18 to 22 minutes	20 to 24 minutes
WHOLE TENDERLOIN	4 to 5 pounds	450°F	40 to 60 minutes (total time)		
HALF TENDERLOIN	2 to 3 pounds	450°F	35 to 50 minutes (total time)		
ROUND TIP ROAST	3 to 4 pounds 6 to 8 pounds	325°F	25 to 30 minutes 22 to 25 minutes	30 to 35 minutes 26 to 32 minutes	35 to 38 minutes 30 to 35 minutes
EYE ROUND ROAST	2 to 3 pounds	325°F	20 to 25 minutes	25 to 30 minutes	30 to 35 minutes

CUBAN-STLYE PULLED PORK WITH OLIVES 206

5 Tips for
STORING AND FREEZING MEAT

1

Place the meat on a plate or tray (to catch any drips) in the coldest part of the refrigerator (usually the bottom shelf), away from cooked and ready-to-eat foods.

2

Refrigerate uncooked ground meat for up to two days, other meat for up to three days.

3

Freeze ground meat for up to three months, other meat up to six months. To prevent freezer burn, seal meat in freezer-weight plastic storage bags or rewrap the meat in freezer wrap or heavy-duty foil, pressing out all the air. Stack steaks, chops, and patties between sheets of freezer paper before wrapping.

4

Label each package with the name of the cut, the number of servings, and the date.

5

Thaw frozen meat on a plate (to catch any drips) overnight in the refrigerator—not at room temperature. Do not refreeze uncooked meat or the texture will suffer.

country pot roast

PREP: 25 MIN / TOTAL: 3 HR 25 MIN / SERVES 8

- 1 tablespoon vegetable oil
- 1 boneless beef chuck cross-rib pot roast or boneless chuck eye roast, trimmed
- 1 large onion, coarsely chopped
- 1 carrot, peeled and coarsely chopped
- 1 stalk celery, coarsely chopped
- 2 cloves garlic, finely chopped
- 1 can (15 ounces) crushed tomatoes
- ½ cup chicken broth
- 1 teaspoon salt
- ½ teaspoon dried thyme, crumbled
- ¼ teaspoon ground black pepper
- 1 bay leaf

1. Preheat the oven to 350°F. In a 5-quart nonreactive Dutch oven, heat the oil over high heat until very hot. Add the roast and cook until browned. Transfer the roast to a plate.

2. Add the onion, carrot, and celery to the Dutch oven and cook over medium-high heat until lightly browned. Add the garlic; cook, stirring constantly, until fragrant, about 20 seconds.

3. Return the roast to the Dutch oven; add the tomatoes, broth, salt, thyme, pepper, and bay leaf; heat to boiling. Cover and place in the oven. Bake, turning the roast once, until the roast is tender, about 3 hours.

4. When the roast is done, transfer it to a large platter and keep warm. Discard the bay leaf. Skim and discard the fat from the liquid in the Dutch oven. Transfer half of the vegetables and liquid to a blender; cover, with the center part of the lid removed to let the steam escape, and puree until smooth. Pour the pureed mixture into the Dutch oven and stir until combined; heat to boiling. Cut the meat into thin slices and serve with vegetables and sauce.

Each serving About 305 calories, 35g protein, 6g carbohydrate, 15g fat (5g saturated), 2g fiber, 573mg sodium.

TESTING NOTE To give this home-style sauce a bit more body and flavor, we pureed half the vegetables.

ropa vieja

PREP: 45 MIN / TOTAL: 4 HR 25 MIN / SERVES 6

- 1 beef flank steak (1¾ pounds)
- 1 medium onion, coarsely chopped
- 1 carrot, peeled and coarsely chopped
- 1 bay leaf
- 2 teaspoons salt
- 5 cups water
- 4 teaspoons olive oil
- 1 large onion, sliced
- 1 red bell pepper, cut into ½-inch-wide strips
- 1 yellow bell pepper, cut into ½-inch-wide strips
- 1 green bell pepper, cut into ½-inch-wide strips
- 3 cloves garlic, crushed with a garlic press
- 3 serrano or jalapeño chiles, seeded and finely chopped
- ¼ teaspoon ground cinnamon
- 1 can (14 to 16 ounces) tomatoes
- Capers, for serving

1. Cut the flank steak crosswise into thirds. In a 5-quart nonreactive Dutch oven, combine the flank steak, chopped onion, carrot, bay leaf, 1 teaspoon salt, and water; heat to boiling over high heat. Reduce the heat; cover and simmer until the meat is very tender, 2 hours 30 minutes to 3 hours. Remove the Dutch oven from the heat. Remove the cover and let the flank steak stand 30 minutes.

2. In a 12-inch skillet, heat the oil over medium-high heat. Add the sliced onion, bell peppers, and remaining 1 teaspoon salt; cook, stirring often, until the vegetables are tender, about 15 minutes. Stir in the garlic, serrano chiles, and cinnamon; cook 30 seconds. Stir in the tomatoes with their juices, breaking them up with the side of a spoon, and cook 5 minutes.

3. With a slotted spoon, transfer the beef to a large bowl; strain the broth. Set aside 2 cups broth (reserve the remaining broth for another use). Using 2 forks, shred the beef into fine strips.

4. Stir 2 cups broth and the shredded meat into the bell pepper mixture and simmer, stirring occasionally, 10 minutes. Sprinkle with capers to serve.

Each serving About 245 calories, 25g protein, 10g carbohydrate, 12g fat (4g saturated), 3g fiber, 779mg sodium.

GLOSSARY → In Spanish, **ropa vieja** means "old clothes." The stew is simmered for such a long time that the meat can be shredded into thin strips, resembling tattered fabric.

new orleans grillades

PREP: 15 MIN / TOTAL: 1 HR 15 MIN / SERVES 4

- 4 beef minute steaks (6 ounces each)
- ½ teaspoon salt
- ¼ teaspoon ground black pepper
- 3 teaspoons vegetable oil
- 1 medium onion, chopped
- 1 green bell pepper, chopped
- 1 stalk celery, chopped
- 2 cloves garlic, finely chopped
- 1 can (14 to 16 ounces) tomatoes in puree
- 1 cup beef broth
- 1 teaspoon Worcestershire sauce
- 2 bay leaves
- 1 tablespoon red wine vinegar

1. Sprinkle the beef with salt and pepper. In a 12-inch nonstick skillet, heat 1 teaspoon oil over medium-high heat until very hot. Add the steaks and cook until browned, about 2 minutes per side, transferring the steaks to a plate as they are browned.

2. Add the remaining 2 teaspoons oil to the skillet; reduce the heat to medium. Add the onion and cook, stirring, 5 minutes. Add the bell pepper, celery, and garlic; cook, stirring, 3 minutes longer. Add the tomatoes with their puree, breaking them up with the side of a spoon. Stir in the broth, Worcestershire, and bay leaves. Increase the heat to high; heat to boiling.

3. Return the steaks to the skillet and reduce the heat. Cover and simmer 40 minutes. Transfer the steaks to a platter; keep warm. Increase the heat to high; stir in the vinegar and heat to boiling. Boil until the sauce has thickened, about 5 minutes. Discard the bay leaves. To serve, spoon the sauce over the steaks.

Each serving About 435 calories, 37g protein, 13g carbohydrate, 26g fat (9g saturated), 2g fiber, 772mg sodium.

flank steak
with red onion marmalade

PREP: 10 MIN / TOTAL: 45 MIN / SERVES 6

- 3 tablespoons butter or margarine
- 2 medium red onions (1 pound), peeled and thinly sliced
- 3 tablespoons distilled white vinegar
- 3 tablespoons sugar
- 1 teaspoon salt
- 1 beef flank steak (1½ pounds)
- ¼ teaspoon coarsely ground pepper

1. In a 12-inch nonstick skillet, melt 2 tablespoons butter over medium heat. Add the onions and cook, stirring occasionally, until tender, about 15 minutes. Stir in the vinegar, sugar, and ½ teaspoon salt. Reduce the heat and simmer 5 minutes. Spoon the red onion marmalade into a small bowl; keep warm.

2. Wash the skillet and wipe it dry. Sprinkle the steak with the pepper and remaining ½ teaspoon salt. In the skillet, melt the remaining 1 tablespoon butter over medium-high heat. Add the steak and cook 6 to 8 minutes per side for medium-rare or to the desired doneness.

3. Slice the steak and serve with red onion marmalade.

Each serving About 280 calories, 24g protein, 14g carbohydrate, 14g fat (7g saturated), 1g fiber, 150mg sodium.

HOW TO

ROAST SMALL CUTS OF MEAT

AVOID OVERCROWDING. Space food out or it will steam vs. brown. Use a large rimmed baking sheet or two smaller ones, switching between racks halfway through.

GREASE THE SHEET. It's the only way to limit sticking.

TURN UP THE HEAT. The magic temp to cook small cuts quickly and maximize browning is 450°F.

roasted beef tenderloin

PREP: 5 MIN / TOTAL: 55 MIN / SERVES 12

2 tablespoons butter or margarine, melted

2 teaspoons Worcestershire sauce

1 teaspoon salt

1 teaspoon coarsely ground black pepper

1 whole beef tenderloin (5 pounds), trimmed and tied

1. Preheat the oven to 450°F. In a small bowl, combine the butter, Worcestershire, salt, and pepper. Brush mixture on the tenderloin.

2. Place tenderloin in a large rimmed baking sheet and roast until a meat thermometer inserted in the center of the meat reaches 140°F, about 50 minutes. Internal temperature of meat will rise to 145°F (medium) upon standing. Or roast to the desired doneness.

3. Transfer the tenderloin to a warm platter and let stand 15 minutes to set the juices for easier slicing.

Each serving About 250 calories, 29g protein, 0g carbohydrate, 14g fat (6g saturated), 0g fiber, 276mg sodium.

SWEET PEPPER SAUCE In a food processor, pulse 1½ **cups roasted red peppers**; **2 tablespoons tomato paste**; ⅓ **cup blanched sliced almonds**; ½ **cup canola or vegetable oil**; **2 tablespoons sherry vinegar**; **1 clove garlic**, and ½ **teaspoon salt** until smooth. *Makes 2 cups.*

Each 2-tablespoon serving About 85 calories, 0g protein, 3g carbohydrate, 8g fat (0g saturated), 1g fiber, 120mg sodium.

SAUCES FOR BEEF TENDERLOIN

Béarnaise Sauce (page 51) or **Sweet Pepper Sauce** (left) is perfect with Roasted Beef Tenderloin.
Chimichurri (page 55) is a good choice for the Asian-Flavored Tenderloin. For the Southwestern-Flavored variation, try either **Chimichurri**, **Italian Green Sauce** (page 55), or **Tomato Salsa** (page 53).

VARIATIONS

Southwestern-Flavored Tenderloin

In a small bowl, combine **1 tablespoon vegetable oil**, **1 teaspoon honey**, **1 tablespoon chili powder**, **2 teaspoons ground cumin**, **1 teaspoon salt**, and ¼ **teaspoon dried oregano**, crumbled. Brush the mixture on tenderloin instead of the butter mixture; roast as directed.

Asian-Flavored Tenderloin

In a small bowl, combine **2 teaspoons soy sauce**, **2 teaspoons Asian sesame oil**, **1 teaspoon honey**, **1 teaspoon Chinese five-spice powder**, ¼ **teaspoon ground ginger**, and ⅛ **teaspoon cayenne pepper**. Brush the mixture on the tenderloin instead of the butter mixture; roast as directed.

Coffee-Rubbed Tenderloin

(See photo on page 185.)
In a small bowl, combine **1 tablespoon vegetable oil**, ¼ **cup packed brown sugar**, **3 tablespoons ground coffee**, ½ **teaspoon cayenne pepper**, **2 teaspoons smoked paprika**, **2 teaspoons garlic powder**, 2½ **teaspoons salt**, and **1 teaspoon ground black pepper**. Brush the mixture on the tenderloin instead of the butter mixture; roast as directed. Pair with the Sweet Pepper Sauce (left).

GOOD TO KNOW

BEST COOKING METHODS FOR CUTS

To cook a tender piece of beef, it's best to match the cut of meat to the right cooking technique.

BROILING, GRILLING, & PANFRYING	Choose porterhouse steak, T-bone steak, London broil (top round), top loin, rib eye, sirloin steak, tenderloin, flank steak, skirt steak, cube steak, minute steak, and ground beef.
BRAISING & STEWING	Choose chuck roast, brisket, short ribs, shin (shank cross cuts), and oxtails. Cubes for stew are usually cut from boneless chuck or bottom round, but chuck gives the moistest results. Bone-in cuts add flavor and body to stews.
ROASTING	Choose standing rib roast, tenderloin, rib eye, eye round, and tri-tip.

new england boiled dinner

PREP: 15 MIN / TOTAL: 3 HR 45 MIN / SERVES 8

- 1 corned beef brisket (4 to 4½ pounds)
- 1 medium onion studded with 4 whole cloves
- 8 cups water
- 8 medium all-purpose potatoes (2½ pounds), peeled and each cut in half
- 8 carrots, peeled and each cut in half
- 1 small rutabaga (2 pounds), peeled and cut in half, each half cut into 8 wedges
- 1 small green cabbage (2 pounds), cut into 8 wedges
- 2 tablespoons chopped fresh parsley
- Dijon mustard and bottled white horseradish, for serving

1. In an 8-quart Dutch oven, place the brisket, clove-studded onion, and water and heat to boiling over high heat. With a slotted spoon, skim and discard the foam from the surface. Reduce the heat; cover and simmer until the brisket is tender, 2 hours 30 minutes to 3 hours.

2. Add the potatoes, carrots, and rutabaga to the Dutch oven; heat to boiling over high heat. Reduce the heat; cover and simmer until the vegetables are tender, about 30 minutes.

3. With a slotted spoon, transfer the brisket and vegetables to a deep, large platter; keep warm.

4. Heat the liquid remaining in the Dutch oven to boiling over high heat. Add the cabbage; heat to boiling. Cover and boil until cabbage is tender, about 5 minutes.

5. Slice the brisket very thinly across the grain. Transfer the sliced meat to the platter with the vegetables. Place the cabbage wedges on the platter, sprinkle parsley on the vegetables, and serve mustard and horseradish alongside.

Each serving About 590 calories, 35g protein, 43g carbohydrate, 31g fat (10g saturated), 9g fiber, 1,887mg sodium.

#SavetheFood

corned beef hash

Add a few additional potatoes to our New England Boiled Dinner (above) so you can make Corned Beef Hash (right) with the tasty leftovers!

corned beef hash

PREP: 15 MIN / TOTAL: 40 MIN / SERVES 4

- 3 tablespoons butter or margarine
- 1 large onion, chopped
- 2 cups chopped lean cooked corned beef
- 2 cups chopped cooked all-purpose potatoes
- ¼ teaspoon coarsely ground pepper
- 1 tablespoon chopped fresh parsley

1. In a 10-inch skillet, melt the butter over medium heat. Add the onion and cook, stirring often, until tender, about 5 minutes.

2. Stir in the corned beef, potatoes, and pepper until well combined. Cook, pressing the hash down firmly with the spatula, until the bottom of the hash has browned, about 15 minutes.

3. With the spatula, turn the hash over, one small section at a time. Press down with the spatula and cook until the second side has browned, 5 to 10 minutes longer. Sprinkle with parsley.

Each serving About 340 calories, 23g protein, 21g carbohydrate, 18g fat (9g saturated), 3g fiber, 947mg sodium.

VARIATION

Red Flannel Hash

Prepare as directed, adding **1 cup finely chopped cooked beets** with the onion, corned beef, potatoes, and pepper.

GOOD TO KNOW

HOW DO I KNOW IT'S DONE?

Use this quick test to ensure your meat is cooked to your preference.

The easiest way to check a steak for doneness is to cut into its center. It's not the most attractive, though. To test for doneness without cutting the meat, compare it to the pad of skin on your palm below your thumb. Here's how: A rare steak feels soft and spongy and offers little resistance, like a relaxed hand. A medium-rare steak is springy to the touch, as on a loosely fisted hand. A medium steak feels firm with minimal give like a tight fist.

filet mignon
with shallot butter

PREP: 15 MIN / TOTAL: 25 MIN / SERVES 2

- 2 teaspoons plus 1 tablespoon vegetable oil
- 1 small shallot, finely chopped
- ⅛ teaspoon dried rosemary
- ¼ cup dry red wine
- 2 tablespoons butter, softened
- 1 tablespoon fresh parsley leaves, chopped
- 2 beef tenderloin (filet mignon) steaks, 1 inch thick (6 ounces each)
- ⅛ teaspoon salt
- ⅛ teaspoon ground black pepper

1. In a 10-inch skillet, heat 2 teaspoons oil over medium heat. Add the shallot and rosemary; cook 2 minutes, or until the shallot is golden, stirring. Add the wine. Cook 2 to 3 minutes, or until most of wine has evaporated, stirring occasionally. Cool slightly. In a small bowl, combine the butter and shallot mixture. Stir in the parsley. Cover and refrigerate.

2. Wipe out the skillet; add the remaining 1 tablespoon oil. Heat over medium-high heat until very hot. Season the steaks with ⅛ teaspoon each salt and pepper. Place the steaks in the skillet. Cook 3 minutes, or until browned. Turn over; cook 3 minutes, or to the desired doneness (145°F for medium-rare). Transfer to a plate; let stand 5 minutes.

3. To serve, top the steaks with red wine–shallot butter.

Each serving About 410 calories, 33g protein, 2g carbohydrate, 29g fat (12g saturated), 0g fiber, 320mg sodium.

Serving Suggestion Serve this with Oven Fries (page 451) and Creamed Spinach (page 461).

filet mignon
with mustard caper sauce

PREP: 5 MIN / TOTAL: 25 MIN / SERVES 4

- 4 beef tenderloin steaks (filet mignon), 1½ inches thick (6 ounces each)
- ½ teaspoon salt
- ¼ teaspoon coarsely ground black pepper
- 1 tablespoon olive oil
- 3 tablespoons finely chopped shallots
- ⅓ cup dry white wine
- ⅓ cup beef broth
- ⅓ cup heavy or whipping cream
- 3 tablespoons capers, drained
- 1 tablespoon Dijon mustard
- ¼ cup chopped watercress leaves, plus additional leaves for garnish

1. Sprinkle the steaks with the salt and pepper. In a 12-inch nonstick skillet, heat the oil over high heat until very hot. Add the steaks and cook, without turning, until browned, about 7 minutes. Turn the steaks and cook 7 minutes longer for medium-rare, or to the desired doneness. Transfer to plates; keep warm.

2. Add the shallots to the drippings in the skillet; cook 30 seconds. Stir in the wine; cook, stirring, until the browned bits are loosened from the bottom of the skillet. Stir in the broth and boil 1 minute. Stir in the cream; boil 1 minute longer. Stir in the capers, mustard, and chopped watercress.

3. To serve, spoon the sauce over the meat and garnish with watercress.

Each serving About 335 calories, 27g protein, 3g carbohydrate, 22g fat (9g saturated), 0g fiber, 799mg sodium.

VARIATION

Steak au Poivre

Prepare as directed, but in step 1 use **2 tablespoons crushed black peppercorns**. In step 2 omit the shallots, broth, capers, and mustard; stir in the wine and **2 tablespoons brandy**, stirring until the browned bits are loosened. Stir in the cream and boil until thickened. Replace the watercress with **1 tablespoon chopped fresh parsley**.

steak

with red wine sauce

PREP: 5 MIN / TOTAL: 25 MIN / SERVES 4

- 2 teaspoons vegetable oil
- 4 boneless beef strip (shell) steaks, 1 inch thick (8 ounces each)
- ½ teaspoon salt
- ¼ teaspoon ground black pepper
- ¼ cup finely chopped shallots
- 1 cup dry red wine
- Pinch of dried thyme, crumbled
- 2 tablespoons butter, cut into pieces
- 2 teaspoons chopped fresh tarragon or flat-leaf parsley

1. In a 12-inch skillet, heat the oil over medium-high heat until very hot. Sprinkle the steaks with the salt and pepper. Cook 5 to 6 minutes per side for medium-rare, or to the desired doneness. Transfer the steaks to a warm platter.

2. Discard the drippings from the skillet. Add the shallots to the pan and cook, stirring, until tender, about 1 minute. Add the wine and thyme; heat to boiling over high heat. Boil until the sauce has reduced to ⅓ cup, about 5 minutes. Remove the pan from the heat; add the butter, stirring just until incorporated.

3. Cut the steaks into thin slices. Transfer to a warm platter; pour the sauce on top, and sprinkle with tarragon.

Each serving About 435 calories, 49g protein, 3g carbohydrate, 24g fat (10g saturated), 0g fiber, 179mg sodium.

TESTING NOTE Be sure to cook this steak over a high heat. A well-browned exterior (accomplished by searing) is the key to maximum flavor for beef.

COFFEE-RUBBED TENDERLOIN 180

FILET MIGNON WITH SHALLOT BUTTER 182

tangerine beef stir-fry

PREP: 25 MIN / TOTAL: 45 MIN / SERVES 4

- 2 or 3 tangerines
- ¼ cup dry sherry
- 1 tablespoon grated, peeled fresh ginger
- 1 teaspoon Asian sesame oil
- 1 teaspoon plus 1 tablespoon cornstarch
- 2 tablespoons low-sodium soy sauce
- 1 beef flank steak (about 1 pound), cut crosswise into ⅛-inch-thick slices
- 4 teaspoons vegetable oil
- 1 large red bell pepper, thinly sliced
- 6 ounces snow peas, strings removed
- 3 green onions, cut into 1-inch pieces
- ¼ cup water

1. With a vegetable peeler, remove the peel in strips from the tangerines. Using a small knife, remove any white pith from the peel; set the peel aside. Cut the remaining pith from the tangerines. Working with 1 tangerine at a time and holding it over a 2-cup liquid measuring cup to catch the juice, cut on either side of the membranes to remove each segment, allowing the fruit and juice to drop into the cup. Into the same measuring cup, squeeze the juice from the remaining membranes until the fruit and juice mixture equals ½ cup. Discard the seeds, if any. Stir in the sherry, ginger, sesame oil, and 1 teaspoon cornstarch; set aside. In a medium bowl, mix the soy sauce and the remaining 1 tablespoon cornstarch. Add the beef and toss to coat; set aside.

2. In a 12-inch skillet, heat 2 teaspoons vegetable oil over medium-high heat until hot. Add the tangerine peel and cook 2 to 3 minutes, or until lightly browned. Transfer the peel to a large bowl.

3. To the same skillet, add the bell pepper, peas, and green onions and toss to coat with oil; cook 1 minute. Add the water and cook about 2 minutes longer, or until vegetables are tender-crisp, stirring frequently. Drain the vegetables and transfer them to the large bowl with the peel.

4. To the same skillet, add 1 teaspoon vegetable oil and heat until very hot. Add half the beef mixture and cook 2 minutes, or until the beef is lightly browned, stirring frequently. Transfer to the bowl with the vegetables. Repeat with the remaining 1 teaspoon vegetable oil and beef mixture.

5. Add the juice mixture to the skillet and heat to boiling; boil 1 minute. Return the beef mixture to the skillet; heat through.

Each serving About 330 calories, 25g protein, 17g carbohydrate, 18g fat (6g saturated), 4g fiber, 385mg sodium.

stuffed tomatoes
with ground beef

PREP: 25 MIN / TOTAL: 1 HR / SERVES 6

- ½ cup quick-cooking (10-minute) brown rice
- 1 tablespoon olive oil
- 1 medium onion, chopped
- 1¼ pounds lean (90%) ground beef
- ⅓ cup loosely packed fresh mint leaves, chopped, plus mint sprigs for garnish
- ½ teaspoon ground cinnamon
- ¼ teaspoon salt
- ¼ teaspoon ground black pepper
- 6 large tomatoes (10 ounces each)
- ½ cup crumbled feta cheese (2 ounces)
- ¼ cup panko (Japanese-style bread crumbs)

1. Preheat the oven to 425°F. In a 3-quart saucepan, cook the rice as the label directs.

2. Meanwhile, in a 12-inch nonstick skillet, heat the oil over medium heat 1 minute. Add the onion and cook 10 to 12 minutes, or until lightly browned and tender. Stir in the ground beef, half the chopped mint, the cinnamon, salt, and pepper. Cook 5 to 6 minutes, or until the beef loses its pink color throughout, breaking up the meat with a spatula and stirring occasionally. Stir in the remaining chopped mint.

3. While the ground beef cooks, cut each tomato horizontally in half. With a melon baller or spoon, scoop out the tomato pulp; place it in a large bowl. Remove 1 cup tomato pulp from the bowl and chop it; discard the remaining pulp or save it for another use. Return the chopped pulp to the bowl. Add the rice, feta cheese, and beef mixture; stir until well blended.

4. In a 15½ × 10½-inch rimmed baking sheet, arrange the hollowed-out tomato halves, cut sides up. Mound a scant ½ cup beef filling in each tomato half; sprinkle with panko. Bake the tomatoes 25 to 30 minutes, or until the panko is browned and the filling is heated through. Garnish with mint sprigs.

Each serving About 270 calories, 26 protein, 21g carbohydrate, 10g fat (3g saturated), 4g fiber, 285mg sodium.

beef rib roast
with creamy horseradish sauce

PREP: 25 MIN / TOTAL: 3 HR 25 MIN / SERVES 10

**1 (4-rib) beef rib roast
from small end
(7 pounds), trimmed,
chine bone removed**

**3 tablespoons whole
tricolor peppercorns
(red, green, and black)**

**1 teaspoon salt
Creamy Horseradish
Sauce (below)**

1. Preheat the oven to 325°F. On a rack in a medium roasting pan (14 × 10 inches), place the rib roast, fat side up. In mortar and using a pestle, crush the peppercorns with the salt. Use this to rub on the fat side of the roast.

2. Roast the beef until a meat thermometer inserted in the thickest part of the meat (not touching bone) reaches 140°F, about 3 hours. Internal temperature of the meat will rise to 145°F (medium) upon standing. Or roast to the desired doneness.

3. When the roast is done, transfer it to a warm, large platter and let stand 15 minutes to set the juices for easier carving. Meanwhile, prepare the Creamy Horseradish Sauce.

CREAMY HORSERADISH SAUCE In a small bowl, combine **1 jar (6 ounces) white prepared horseradish**, drained; **½ cup mayonnaise**; **1 teaspoon sugar**; and **½ teaspoon salt**. Whip **½ cup heavy or whipping cream**; fold this into the horseradish mixture. Makes about 1⅔ cups.

YORKSHIRE PUDDING Preheat the oven to 450°F. In a medium bowl and using a wire whisk, combine **1½ cups all-purpose flour** and **¾ teaspoon salt**. Add **1½ cups milk** and **3 large eggs**, beaten. Beat until smooth. Pour **3 tablespoons drippings** from the roast beef pan into a 13 x 9–inch metal baking pan; bake 2 minutes. Remove the pan from the oven and pour the batter over the drippings. Bake until puffed and lightly browned, about 25 minutes. Cut into squares. Serves 8.

BEEF RIB ROAST (WITHOUT SAUCE) Each serving About 315 calories, 39g protein, 1g carbohydrate, 16g fat (7g saturated), 1g fiber, 322mg sodium.

CREAMY HORSERADISH SAUCE Each tablespoon About 50 calories, 0g protein, 1g carbohydrate, 5g fat (2g saturated), 0g fiber, 74mg sodium.

YORKSHIRE PUDDING Each serving About 185 calories, 6g protein, 20g carbohydrate, 8g fat (4g saturated), 1g fiber, 246mg sodium.

#SavetheFood

au jus

Reserve the fat from the pan drippings when making Beef Rib Roast to make Yorkshire Pudding (left), then prepare an au jus sauce. Add 2 cups of homemade Brown Beef Stock (page 139) to the pan drippings and bring to a boil, scraping up all the flavorful browned bits.

HOW TO

CARVE A RIB ROAST

Ask your butcher to remove the chine bone so you can carve the roast between the rib bones. Carving will be easier and the meat will be juicier if the roast stands at least 15 minutes after you have removed it from the oven.

Place the roast, rib side down, on a cutting board. With a carving knife, make a vertical cut toward the ribs, cutting a slice about ¼ inch thick.

Release the slice by cutting horizontally along the top of the rib bone. Transfer the slice to a warm platter.

Repeat to cut more slices. As each rib bone is exposed, cut it away from the roast and add to the platter. This will make it easier to carve the remaining meat.

fajitas

PREP: 15 MIN / TOTAL: 35 MIN, PLUS MARINATING / SERVES 6

- 3 tablespoons fresh lime juice
- 3 tablespoons fresh orange juice
- Salt
- ½ teaspoon dried oregano, crumbled
- 1 beef skirt steak (1¾ pounds)
- 1 tablespoon olive oil
- 2 medium onions, thinly sliced
- 2 cloves garlic, thinly sliced
- 3 large red bell peppers, cut into ½-inch-thick strips
- 1 large green bell pepper, cut into ½-inch-thick strips
- 2 teaspoons finely chopped pickled jalapeño chile
- 12 (6-inch) flour tortillas

1. In a cup, combine the lime and orange juices, ½ teaspoon salt, and oregano. Transfer to a resealable plastic bag; add the meat, turning to coat. Seal the bag, pressing out as much air as possible. Refrigerate the beef 1 hour to marinate, turning the bag once.

2. Preheat the broiler. Meanwhile, in a 12-inch skillet, heat the oil over medium heat. Add the onions and garlic and cook, stirring frequently, until the onions are tender, about 5 minutes. Add the bell peppers, jalapeño, and ¼ teaspoon salt; cook, stirring frequently, until the peppers are tender, about 7 minutes.

3. Place the meat on a rack in a broiling pan. Broil the steak 6 inches from the heat source 3 to 4 minutes per side for medium-rare, or to the desired doneness. Cut the meat into thin slices across the grain and serve with tortillas and the pepper mixture.

Each serving About 420 calories, 30g protein, 34g carbohydrate, 17g fat (6g saturated), 5g fiber, 531mg sodium.

Serving Suggestion Pair these with homemade Tomato Salsa (page 53) and guacamole (page 92) for an instant party! Don't forget a big batch of Frozen Margaritas (page 113).

italian meatballs

(See photo on page 189.)

PREP: 20 MIN / TOTAL: 1 HR 20 MIN / SERVES 6

- 3½ cups Marinara Sauce (page 338) or bottled marinara
- 1½ pounds ground meat for meat loaf (beef, pork, and veal) or ground beef chuck (85% lean)
- 1 cup fresh bread crumbs (from about 2 slices bread)
- 1 large egg
- ¼ cup freshly grated Pecorino Romano or Parmesan cheese
- ¼ cup chopped fresh parsley
- 1 clove garlic, crushed with a garlic press
- 1 teaspoon salt
- ¼ teaspoon ground black pepper
- 2 teaspoons olive oil
- Spaghetti, for serving

1. Prepare Marinara Sauce, if using homemade.

2. Meanwhile, prepare the meatballs: In a large bowl, combine the ground meat, bread crumbs, egg, cheese, parsley, garlic, salt, and pepper just until blended but not overmixed. Shape into twelve meatballs, handling the meat as little as possible.

3. In a 10-inch nonstick skillet, heat the oil over medium heat until hot. Add the meatballs and cook, gently turning, until browned and just cooked through, about 20 minutes. Add the sauce to the meatballs and heat to boiling, stirring to loosen the browned bits from the bottom of the skillet. Reduce the heat and simmer while you cook the pasta.

4. In large saucepot, cook the pasta as the label directs. Drain. In a warm serving bowl, gently toss the pasta with meatballs and sauce.

Each serving About 690 calories, 34g protein, 69g carbohydrate, 30g fat (10g saturated), 3g fiber, 1,077mg sodium.

 *Serving Suggestion* Use leftover meatballs on top of a pizza. For a homemade dough recipe see page 569.

TESTING NOTE These large meatballs are all cooked at the same time in one skillet. If you prefer smaller meatballs, you'll need to cook them in two skillets or in batches. Or consider baking them in a rimmed baking sheet at 450°F for 20 minutes.

danish meatballs

PREP: 25 MIN / TOTAL: 40 MIN / SERVES 6

1½ pounds ground beef chuck or ground meat for meat loaf (beef, pork, and veal) (85% lean)

½ cup plain dried bread crumbs

1 large egg

¼ cup chopped fresh flat-leaf parsley

2 tablespoons chopped fresh dill

1 tablespoon grated onion

1 teaspoon salt

¼ teaspoon ground black pepper

⅛ teaspoon ground nutmeg

2 tablespoons butter or margarine

2 tablespoons all-purpose flour

1½ cups milk

1 cup low-sodium chicken broth

Lingonberry preserves and cooked egg noodles, for serving (optional)

1. In a large bowl, combine the ground beef, bread crumbs, egg, parsley, dill, onion, salt, pepper, and nutmeg just until well blended but not overmixed. Shape the mixture into 24 meatballs, handling the meat as little as possible.

2. In a 12-inch skillet, melt the butter over medium-high heat. Add the meatballs and cook until browned, using a slotted spoon to transfer the meatballs to clean, large bowl as they are browned. Discard all but 2 tablespoons drippings from the skillet.

3. Stir the flour into the drippings in the skillet; cook over medium heat, stirring, 1 minute. Gradually add the milk and broth; cook, stirring constantly, until the mixture has thickened and comes to a boil.

4. Add the meatballs to the skillet; heat to boiling. Reduce the heat; cover and simmer 10 minutes. Serve with lingonberry preserves and egg noodles, if desired.

Each serving About 330 calories, 28g protein, 12g carbohydrate, 19g fat (9g saturated), 1g fiber, 991mg sodium.

HANDLE GROUND MEAT

BUYING & STORING

The label on ground beef often denotes the percentage of lean meat to fat, but sometimes the cut of meat is also listed. You can buy ground chuck, which is about 80 percent lean; ground sirloin, which is 90 to 95 percent lean; and ground round, which at 85 percent lean is juicy, flavorful, and the most popular cut. If the meat is labeled "ground beef," it comes from a combination of cuts and is only 70 percent lean. Keep in mind that the amount of fat in ground beef affects the moistness and texture of the cooked dish, so you will get different results when using ground chuck, ground round, or ground sirloin.

Ground beef should be cherry red. Don't worry if the meat in the center looks darker than the meat on the exterior. The darker color comes from a lack of oxygen. When exposed to the air, this darker meat will become redder.

E.coli, a strain of potentially deadly bacteria, has been found in mass-produced meat patties. To guard against this bacteria, always purchase ground beef from a reliable source and shape your own burgers.

COOKING GROUND BEEF SAFELY

Disease-causing bacteria like E. coli contaminate only the surface of food. The bacteria is killed when the outside of the food is exposed to high temperatures—when grilling and roasting, for example. When beef is ground, any outer surface contamination gets mixed throughout the meat. The bacteria on the surface of a grilled burger may be killed, but unless the interior of the meat is cooked to 160°F, dangerous bacteria can still be present. To eliminate this danger, always cook ground beef until well-done. When pressed in the center, a burger or patty should feel firm and spring back.

mexican meatballs

PREP: 30 MIN / TOTAL: 1 HR 15 MIN / SERVES 6

1½ pounds ground beef chuck (85% lean)

¾ cup plain dried bread crumbs

1 large egg

3 cloves garlic, finely chopped

1 teaspoon salt

½ teaspoon ground black pepper

¼ cup water

1 can (28 ounces) tomatoes

1 chipotle chile in adobo

2 teaspoons vegetable oil

1 small onion, finely chopped

1 teaspoon ground cumin

1 cup chicken broth

¼ cup chopped fresh cilantro

1. In a large bowl, combine the ground beef, bread crumbs, egg, one-third of the garlic, the salt, pepper, and water just until well blended but not overmixed. Shape the mixture into 1-inch meatballs, handling the meat as little as possible.

2. In a blender, puree the tomatoes with their juices and the chipotle chile until smooth.

3. In a 5-quart nonreactive Dutch oven, heat the oil over medium heat. Add the onion and cook, stirring often, until tender, about 5 minutes. Stir in the cumin and the remaining garlic; cook 30 seconds. Stir in the tomato mixture and broth; heat to boiling over high heat.

4. Add the meatballs; heat to boiling. Reduce the heat and simmer 30 minutes. To serve, sprinkle with cilantro.

Each serving About 320 calories, 28g protein, 18g carbohydrate, 15g fat (5g saturated), 2g fiber, 1,001mg sodium.

TESTING NOTE If chipotle chiles are hard to find, substitute 1 seeded and minced jalapeño chile and ¼ teaspoon liquid smoke.

greek meatballs

PREP: 20 MIN / TOTAL: 40 MIN / SERVES 8

1 pound ground beef chuck (85% lean)

1 pound lean ground lamb

1 cup fresh bread crumbs (from about 2 slices bread)

2 large eggs

4 ounces feta cheese, finely crumbled (1 cup)

3 bunches green onions, finely chopped (1 cup)

¼ cup chopped fresh flat-leaf parsley

2 cloves garlic, finely chopped

1 tablespoon dried mint, crumbled

2 tablespoons olive oil

1 tablespoon red wine vinegar

½ teaspoon salt

¼ teaspoon ground black pepper

1. Preheat the oven to 425°F. In a large bowl, combine the ground beef, ground lamb, bread crumbs, eggs, feta, green onions, parsley, garlic, mint, oil, vinegar, salt, and pepper just until well blended but not overmixed.

2. Shape the mixture into scant ¼-cup meatballs, handling the meat as little as possible. Place the meatballs 1 inch apart on 2 rimmed baking sheets. Bake until cooked through, 20 to 25 minutes.

Each serving About 365 calories, 26g protein, 5g carbohydrate, 27g fat (11g saturated), 1g fiber, 425mg sodium.

GOOD TO KNOW

SHAPING MEATBALLS & LOAVES

Be gentle when shaping meatballs and burgers. Pressing or tightly packing the meat makes it tough and dry.

SAUTÉED BEEF & PEPPER SKILLET 190

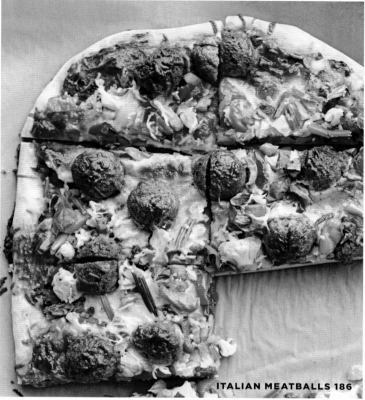

ITALIAN MEATBALLS 186

FETA & MINT
MINI MEATLOAVES 191

MUSTARD-CRUSTED MINI
MEATLOAVES WITH
ROASTED APPLES 190

sautéed beef & pepper skillet

(See photo on page 189.)

PREP: 20 MIN / TOTAL: 50 MIN / SERVES 4

1 pound beef sirloin, trimmed and thinly sliced into bite-size pieces	12 ounces frozen french fries
3 tablespoons soy sauce	3 tablespoons vegetable oil
2 tablespoons cider vinegar	1 large yellow bell pepper, seeded and thinly sliced
3 cloves garlic, crushed with a garlic press	1 small red onion, thinly sliced
1 tablespoon grated, peeled fresh ginger	2 plum tomatoes, halved and thinly sliced
1 teaspoon ground cumin	Chopped fresh parsley, for garnish

1. In a large resealable plastic bag, combine the beef, soy sauce, vinegar, garlic, ginger, and cumin. Seal the bag and let stand in the refrigerator for 20 minutes or up to overnight. Cook the french fries as the label directs.

2. In a 12-inch skillet, heat the oil over medium-high heat until hot. Drain the beef, discarding the marinade; add the beef to the skillet (the oil may spatter). Cook 3 minutes, or until browned, stirring twice. Transfer the beef to a plate.

3. To the same skillet, add the bell pepper and onion. Cook 5 minutes, or until almost tender, stirring occasionally. Add the tomatoes and beef. Cook 2 minutes. Remove from the heat. Fold in the fries and garnish with parsley. Serve immediately.

Each serving About 390 calories, 26g protein, 28g carbohydrate, 19g fat (3g saturated), 3g fiber, 605mg sodium.

GLOSSARY →

Our Sautéed Beef & Pepper Skillet takes its inspiration from **Lomo Saltado**, a Peruvian comfort favorite that Chinese immigrants to Peru made combining local ingredients and the stir-fry technique. Delicious in any language.

susan's meat loaf

PREP: 15 MIN / TOTAL: 1 HR 15 MIN / SERVES 8

2 pounds ground beef chuck (85% lean)	1 medium onion, finely chopped
2 large eggs	¾ cup ketchup
2 cups fresh bread crumbs (from about 4 slices bread)	¼ cup milk
2 green onions, finely chopped	2 tablespoons bottled white horseradish
	1½ teaspoons salt
	1 teaspoon dry mustard

1. Preheat the oven to 400°F. In a large bowl, combine the ground beef, eggs, bread crumbs, green onions, onion, ¼ cup ketchup, the milk, horseradish, salt, and dry mustard just until well blended but not overmixed.

2. Spoon the mixture into a 9 × 5-inch metal loaf pan, pressing firmly. Spread the remaining ½ cup ketchup on top of the loaf. Bake 1 hour. Let stand 10 minutes to set the juices for easier slicing.

Each serving About 285 calories, 27g protein, 15g carbohydrate, 13g fat (5g saturated), 1g fiber, 845mg sodium.

mustard-crusted mini meat loaves
with roasted apples

(See photo on page 189.)

PREP: 10 MIN / TOTAL: 40 MIN / SERVES 4

1¼ pounds ground meat (beef or dark-meat turkey)	3 small Gala or Empire apples, cored and cut into 8 wedges
1 small zucchini, grated	1 teaspoon fresh rosemary, chopped
⅓ cup seasoned dried bread crumbs	¼ teaspoon cayenne pepper
Salt	1 tablespoon olive oil
Ground black pepper	Snipped fresh chives, for garnish
2 tablespoons Dijon mustard	

1. Preheat the oven to 425°F. In a large bowl, combine the ground meat, zucchini, bread crumbs, and ½ teaspoon each salt and pepper. Form the mixture into 4 meat loaves and place them on the prepared baking sheet; brush with Dijon mustard.

2. In another bowl, toss the apples with the rosemary, cayenne, olive oil, and a pinch of salt; arrange them around the meat loaves. Bake 30 minutes, or until loaves are cooked (165°F). Garnish with snipped chives.

Each serving About 420 calories, 32g protein, 24g carbohydrate, 20g fat (7g saturated), 4g fiber, 665mg sodium.

feta & mint mini meat loaves

(See photo on page 189.)

PREP: 10 MIN / TOTAL: 30 MIN / SERVES 4

1¼ pounds ground beef chuck (85% lean)

½ cup crumbled feta cheese

½ cup fresh mint, finely chopped

Salt

1 large leek, well rinsed and sliced

3 medium yellow squash, chopped

1 cup pitted green olives

1 tablespoons olive oil

1. Preheat the oven to 450°F.

2. Combine the ground beef, feta, mint, and ¼ teaspoon salt. Form into 4 mini loaves on a baking sheet. Toss the leek, squash, and olives with the olive oil and ⅛ teaspoon salt; arrange the mixture around the loaves on the baking sheet. Roast 15 to 20 minutes, or until the meat loaves are cooked (165°F).

Each serving About 415 calories, 30g protein, 12g carbohydrate, 28g fat (10g saturated), 4g fiber, 935mg sodium.

TESTING NOTE Dark-colored pans hold more heat and brown foods more quickly. If you're baking cookies, go light—even if you choose a baking sheet with a nonstick finish. If you're roasting meat or veggies, the darker finish helps your roasting!

cajun meat loaf

PREP: 20 MIN / TOTAL: 1 HR 35 MIN / SERVES 8

2 tablespoons butter

2 carrots, peeled and finely chopped

1 large onion, chopped

1 large stalk celery, chopped

1 small green bell pepper, finely chopped

2 cloves garlic, crushed with a garlic press

2 pounds ground meat for meat loaf (beef, pork, and veal)

2 large eggs

1 cup fresh bread crumbs (from about 2 slices bread)

½ cup plus 2 tablespoons ketchup

¼ cup milk

1 tablespoon Worcestershire sauce

2 teaspoons salt

1 teaspoon ground cumin

½ teaspoon dried thyme

½ teaspoon ground nutmeg

½ teaspoon cayenne pepper

½ teaspoon coarsely ground black pepper

1. In a 12-inch nonstick skillet, melt the butter over medium heat. Add the carrots, onion, celery, and bell pepper and cook, stirring occasionally, until the vegetables are tender, about 15 minutes. Add the garlic and cook 1 minute longer. Set aside to cool slightly.

2. Preheat the oven to 375°F. In a large bowl, combine the ground meat, eggs, bread crumbs, ½ cup ketchup, milk, Worcestershire, salt, cumin, thyme, nutmeg, cayenne, pepper, and the cooked vegetable mixture just until well blended but not overmixed.

3. In a 13 × 9-inch baking pan, shape the meat mixture into a 10 × 5-inch loaf, pressing it firmly. Brush the remaining 2 tablespoons ketchup on top of the loaf. Bake 1 hour 15 minutes. Let stand 10 minutes to set the juices for easier slicing.

Each serving About 365 calories, 24g protein, 14g carbohydrate, 23g fat (10g saturated), 2g fiber, 961mg sodium.

GOCHUJANG-GLAZED MEAT LOAF 193

gochujang-glazed meat loaf
with green beans

PREP: 10 MIN / TOTAL: 1 HR 5 MIN / SERVES 8

- 1 pound ground beef (85% lean)
- 1 pound ground pork
- 1 small onion, grated
- 6 saltines, finely crushed
- ½ cup packed fresh mint, chopped
- 5 tablespoons gochujang (Korean chile paste)
- 1 large egg
- ½ teaspoon salt
- ¼ cup ketchup
- Green Beans (below), for serving

1. Preheat the oven to 425°F. Line a baking sheet with foil.

2. Mix the ground beef, ground pork, onion, saltines, mint, 3 tablespoons gochujang, egg, and ½ teaspoon salt. Mold into a loaf shape on the prepared baking sheet; bake 25 minutes.

3. Stir together the ketchup and the remaining 2 tablespoons gochujang; brush over the meat loaf. Bake another 30 minutes, or until cooked through (160°F). Serve with Green Beans.

GREEN BEANS In a medium bowl, whisk **4 tablespoons olive oil** with **4 tablespoons gochujang, 2 teaspoons coriander,** and **1 teaspoon salt.** Add **2 pounds trimmed green beans** and toss to coat. Evenly distribute on a rimmed baking sheet and roast in the oven for 25 minutes. While roasting, toss green beans twice.

Each serving (with Green Beans) About 395 calories, 25g protein, 24g carbohydrate, 23g fat (7g saturated), 5g fiber, 1,001mg sodium.

INGREDIENT SPOTLIGHT
↓

Korean Chile Sauce It's called *gochujang* (pronounced "GO-choo-jong"), and we think it's the ideal blend of sweet, savory, and sour. Unlike the other hot-hot sauce—sriracha—it won't burn your mouth, so it's a no-brainer for spice rookies. We bet you'll want to use it to douse everything from grilled meats to stir-fries. Did we mention it makes a killer meat-loaf glaze?

chili pie
with corn-bread crust

(See photo on page 174.)

PREP: 15 MIN / TOTAL: 55 MIN / SERVES 6

- 4 tablespoons vegetable oil
- 1 pound ground beef chuck (85% lean)
- 1 large onion, finely chopped
- 2 medium bell peppers, seeded, chopped
- 2 cloves garlic, chopped
- 1 tablespoons chili powder
- ¼ teaspoon ground chipotle chile
- 1 can (14 ounces) fire-roasted diced tomatoes
- 1 can (14 ounces) kidney beans, rinsed and drained
- 1 can (14 ounces) fat-free refried beans
- Salt
- ⅔ cup fine- to medium-ground cornmeal
- ⅔ cup all-purpose flour
- 1 teaspoon baking powder
- 1 large egg
- ⅔ cup milk
- 2 serrano chiles, thinly sliced
- Fresh cilantro, for garnish

1. Preheat the oven to 400°F.

2. In a 12-inch oven-safe skillet, heat 1 tablespoon oil over medium heat. Add the beef; cook 3 minutes, or until browned, breaking up the meat to crumble. With a slotted spoon, transfer the beef to a bowl; discard the excess fat. To the same skillet, add the onion and bell peppers; cook 7 minutes, stirring. Add the garlic, chili powder, and ground chipotle. Cook 2 minutes, stirring. Return the beef to the skillet. Stir in the tomatoes, beans, and ½ teaspoon salt. Cook 3 minutes, or until the mixture is hot. Remove from the heat.

3. Meanwhile, whisk the cornmeal, flour, baking powder, and ¼ teaspoon salt. In a separate bowl, whisk the egg, milk, and the remaining 3 tablespoons oil; add to the cornmeal, stirring to combine. Fold half the serrano chiles into the batter. Pour over the beef mixture, spreading it to cover. Dot the top with the remaining serranos.

4. Transfer the skillet to the oven. Bake 25 minutes, or until a toothpick inserted into the topping comes out clean. Let stand 10 minutes. Garnish with cilantro.

Each serving About 485 calories, 26g protein, 50g carbohydrate, 20g fat (5g saturated), 11g fiber, 930mg sodium.

thai basil stir-fry

PREP: 5 MIN / TOTAL: 20 MIN / SERVES 4

- 1 medium onion, finely chopped
- 4 cloves garlic, chopped
- 2 tablespoons canola oil
- 1 pound ground beef chuck (85% lean) or ground pork
- 3 tablespoons fish sauce
- ½ cup packed fresh basil leaves, plus more for serving
- 2 tablespoons fresh lime juice
- Steamed rice and 1 cup shredded carrots, for serving

1. In a 12-inch skillet over medium heat, cook the onion and garlic in the oil 6 minutes, or until the garlic is golden, stirring occasionally.

2. Add the ground beef and increase the heat to medium-high. Cook 5 minutes, or until browned, stirring occasionally. Add the fish sauce; cook 1 minute. Remove from the heat; stir in the basil and lime juice.

3. Serve over steamed rice, topped with carrots and additional basil.

Each serving About 460 calories, 26g protein, 33g carbohydrate, 24g fat (7g saturated), 1g fiber, 980mg sodium.

 GLOSSARY →

Mise en place: Slice, prep, and arrange your ingredients ahead of time for a perfect stir-fry.

picadillo

PREP: 10 MIN / TOTAL: 35 MIN / SERVES 6

- 4 teaspoons olive oil
- 1 medium onion, finely chopped
- 4 cloves garlic, finely chopped
- 2 pounds ground beef chuck (85% lean)
- 1 can (15 ounces) crushed tomatoes
- ½ cup pimiento-stuffed olives (salad olives), coarsely chopped
- ⅓ cup dark seedless raisins
- 3 tablespoons tomato paste
- 1 tablespoon red wine vinegar
- 1 teaspoon unsweetened cocoa
- 1 teaspoon ground cumin
- ½ teaspoon salt
- ¼ cup slivered almonds, toasted

1. In a 12-inch skillet, heat the oil over medium heat. Add the onion and garlic and cook, stirring frequently, until the onion is tender, about 5 minutes. Stir in the ground beef and cook, breaking up the meat with the side of a spoon, until the meat is no longer pink, about 5 minutes.

2. Add the tomatoes, olives, raisins, tomato paste, vinegar, cocoa, cumin, and salt; stir to combine and heat to boiling. Reduce the heat and simmer until slightly thickened, about 5 minutes. Stir in the almonds and serve.

Each serving About 400 calories, 34g protein, 17g carbohydrate, 23g fat (7g saturated), 3g fiber, 743mg sodium.

#SavetheFood
ground meat

Turn this meat mixture into a filling for empanadas or turnovers by cooking it longer, until almost all of the liquid has been evaporated.

THAI BASIL STIR-FRY 194

VEAL 101

To cook a piece
of veal, it's best to match
the cut of meat to the
right cooking technique.
Follow these instructions
when preparing veal.

BUYING VEAL

MILK-FED VEAL is the finest and most expensive veal. The milk is either their mother's milk or a special milk formula. Milk-fed veal is rarely labeled as such but can be recognized by its pale-pink, almost-white, color.

GRAIN-FED VEAL comes from older calves that were raised on grain or grass. It has a deep, rosy-pink color and a slightly stronger flavor than milk-fed veal. This veal is sometimes labeled "calf," but more often it is just labeled "veal."

LET YOUR EYE BE YOUR GUIDE. Look for meat that is fine-textured and pale. While marbling in beef is desirable, veal should have very little marbling, and what fat there is should be firm and very white. The bones of milk-fed veal have reddish marrow. Prime veal is usually milk-fed, whereas grain-fed veal is usually graded choice. Veal marketed under brand names is rarely graded.

VEAL CUTLETS are ideally cut from a single muscle, usually the top or bottom round. If they are cut from two or three muscles, they will curl when cooked.

STORING VEAL

Because veal is a moist meat, it is fairly perishable. Large cuts and stew meat will only keep for two days, tightly wrapped, in the refrigerator. Be sure to cook veal cutlets the day of purchase.

COOKING VEAL

BROILING, GRILLING, & PANFRYING	For broiling or grilling, choose thick chops and steaks so they won't dry out. Veal cutlets, which are thin, are usually panfried. **Best Bets:** shoulder or blade steaks, loin or rib chops, ground veal, and cutlets
BRAISING & STEWING	Bone-in pieces are especially suited to braising and stewing. Veal stew meat, cut from the neck or shoulder, is readily available and delicious. **Best Bets:** shanks, shank cross cuts (osso buco), arm (shoulder) or blade steak, breast, and shoulder
ROASTING VEAL	Roasts are generally very lean, so you'll get juicier results by cooking them to only 155°F, since the temperature will rise as it stands. Veal breast and shoulder roasts should be cooked until well done and tender. **Best Bets:** rib roast, loin roast, round, shoulder roast, and breast

stuffed veal breast

PREP: 25 MIN / TOTAL: 2 HR 50 MIN, PLUS COOLING / SERVES 6

1 tablespoon olive oil
1 small onion, chopped
3 cloves garlic, finely chopped
2 packages (10 ounces each) frozen chopped spinach, thawed and squeezed dry

1 lemon
⅓ cup golden raisins
Salt
1 bone-in veal breast (4 pounds), with pocket for stuffing
1 cup chicken broth

1. Preheat the oven to 425°F. In a 12-inch skillet, heat the oil over medium-low heat. Add the onion and garlic and cook, stirring frequently, until the onion is tender, about 5 minutes. Add the spinach and cook, stirring frequently, until the liquid has evaporated, about 2 minutes. Remove from the heat.

2. From the lemon, grate ¾ teaspoon zest and squeeze 2 tablespoons juice; set juice aside. Add the raisins, ½ teaspoon salt, and lemon zest to the spinach. Cool to room temperature. Spoon the mixture into the pocket of the veal.

3. Place the breast, meat side up, on a rack in a medium roasting pan (14 × 10 inches). Sprinkle ¼ teaspoon salt on the meat side (not the rib side) of the veal and roast 1 hour. Turn the veal, rib side up, and pour the broth and lemon juice into the bottom of the roasting pan. Cover the veal with a loose tent of foil and bake until tender, about 1 hour 15 minutes longer.

4. Transfer the veal, rib side down, to a cutting board and let stand 10 minutes to set the juices for easier carving. Skim and discard the fat from the drippings in the pan. Carve the veal by slicing down along one rib bone. Cut away the rib bone and discard, then continue carving. Transfer the slices to a warm platter and serve with pan juices.

Each serving About 425 calories, 51g protein, 13g carbohydrate, 18g fat (6g saturated), 3g fiber, 637mg sodium.

VARIATION

Bacon & Collard Greens Stuffing

Substitute ¼ cup minced shallots for the onion and cook with the garlic as directed. Stir in 2 packages (10 ounces each) of frozen chopped collard greens, thawed and squeezed dry, instead of the spinach. Omit the lemon zest and raisins and stir 4 slices of crisp-cooked and chopped bacon into the greens mixture. Proceed as directed.

braised veal chops

with tomatoes & peas

PREP: 10 MIN / TOTAL: 1 HR 25 MIN / SERVES 4

1 slice bacon, chopped
2 veal shoulder blade chops, 1 inch thick (1 pound each)
¼ teaspoon salt
⅛ teaspoon ground black pepper
1 medium onion, chopped

2 cloves garlic, finely chopped
1 can (14½ ounces) tomatoes in puree
1 cup chicken broth
½ cup dry white wine
¼ teaspoon dried sage, crumbled
1 cup frozen peas

1. In a 12-inch skillet, cook the bacon over medium-high heat until browned. With a slotted spoon, transfer the bacon to paper towels to drain; reserve.

2. Pat the veal dry with paper towels. Sprinkle the chops with salt and pepper. Cook the chops in the drippings in the skillet over medium-high heat until browned, about 5 minutes per side. Transfer the veal to a plate.

3. Reduce the heat to medium. Add the onion to the skillet and cook, stirring occasionally, until lightly browned, about 5 minutes. Stir in the garlic and cook 1 minute longer. Stir in the tomatoes with their puree, the broth, wine, and sage and heat to boiling, breaking up the tomatoes with the side of a spoon.

4. Return the chops to the skillet; cover and simmer over medium-low heat until the veal is tender, about 45 minutes. Transfer the veal to a platter; keep warm. Add the peas to the skillet and cook 5 minutes. To serve, cut the veal into serving portions, spoon sauce over the veal, and sprinkle bacon on top.

Each serving About 290 calories, 35g protein, 16g carbohydrate, 9g fat (3g saturated), 3g fiber, 782mg sodium.

osso buco
with gremolata

PREP: 40 MIN / TOTAL: 2 HR 40 MIN / SERVES 4

4 meaty veal shank cross cuts (osso buco), each about 2 inches thick (1 pound each)

½ teaspoon salt

¼ teaspoon ground black pepper

1 tablespoon olive oil

2 medium onions, chopped

3 carrots, peeled and chopped

2 stalks celery, chopped

4 cloves garlic, finely chopped

1 can (14½ to 16 ounces) tomatoes in puree

1 cup dry white wine

1 cup chicken broth

1 bay leaf

2 tablespoons chopped fresh parsley

½ teaspoon freshly grated lemon zest

1. Preheat the oven to 350°F. Sprinkle the shanks with salt and pepper. In a 5-quart nonreactive Dutch oven, heat the oil over medium-high heat until very hot. Add the shanks and cook until browned, about 10 minutes, transferring the shanks to a plate as they are browned.

2. Add the onions to the Dutch oven and cook over medium heat, stirring occasionally, until slightly browned, about 5 minutes. Add the carrots, celery, and three-fourths of the garlic; cook 2 minutes longer.

3. Return the veal to the Dutch oven. Stir in the tomatoes with their puree, the wine, broth, and bay leaf; heat to boiling over high heat. Cover and place in the oven. Bake until the veal is tender when pierced with fork, about 2 hours.

4. Meanwhile, prepare the gremolata: In a small bowl, mix the parsley, lemon zest, and remaining garlic. Cover and refrigerate until ready to serve.

5. Transfer the veal to a platter. Heat the sauce in the Dutch oven to boiling over high heat; boil until it has reduced to 4 cups, about 10 minutes. Pour the sauce over the veal and sprinkle with gremolata.

Each serving About 375 calories, 53g protein, 20g carbohydrate, 8g fat (2g saturated), 4g fiber, 874mg sodium.

Serving Suggestion This aromatic recipe from northern Italy is especially wonderful with Creamy Stove-Top Polenta (page 328).

(page 328)

VARIATION

Veal Stew with Gremolata

Use **2½ pounds boneless veal shoulder**, cut into 1½-inch pieces. Proceed as in step 1 but brown the veal in batches, transferring the meat to a bowl as it is browned. Continue as directed but bake only 1 hour 30 minutes. **Makes 6 main-dish servings.**

GOOD TO KNOW

ROASTING TIMES FOR VEAL

Start with meat at refrigerator temperature. Preheat oven to 325°F. When oven reaches 325°F place meat in oven to cook. Remove roast from oven when it reaches 5°F below desired doneness; temperature will continue to rise as roast stands.

CUT	TEMP	TIME
BONELESS SHOULDER ROAST	160°F	35 to 40 minutes
LEG RUMP OR ROUND ROAST (BONELESS)	160°F	35 to 40 minutes
BONELESS LEG ROAST	160°F	25 to 30 minutes
RIB ROAST	160°F	30 to 35 minutes

veal scaloppine marsala

PREP: 10 MIN / TOTAL: 25 MIN / SERVES 6

- 1 pound veal cutlets
- ¼ cup all-purpose flour
- ¼ teaspoon salt
- ⅛ teaspoon coarsely ground pepper
- 3 tablespoons butter or margarine
- ½ cup dry Marsala wine
- ½ cup chicken broth
- 1 tablespoon chopped fresh parsley

1. Place the cutlets between 2 sheets of plastic wrap or waxed paper. With a meat mallet or rolling pin, pound the cutlets to an ⅛-inch thickness. Cut the cutlets into 3 × 3-inch pieces. On waxed paper, combine the flour, salt, and pepper; coat both sides of the veal with the seasoned flour, shaking off the excess.

2. In a 10-inch skillet, melt the butter over medium-high heat. Cook the veal, in batches, until lightly browned, 45 to 60 seconds per side, using tongs to transfer the pieces to a warm platter as they are browned; keep warm.

3. Add the Marsala and broth to the veal drippings in the pan and cook, stirring until the browned bits are loosened from the bottom of the skillet, until syrupy, 4 to 5 minutes. Pour the sauce over the veal and sprinkle with parsley.

Each serving About 180 calories, 17g protein, 5g carbohydrate, 7g fat (4g saturated), 0g fiber, 288mg sodium.

wiener schnitzel

PREP: 15 MIN / TOTAL: 35 MIN / SERVES 6

- 6 veal cutlets (1½ pounds)
- 2 large eggs
- 1⅓ cups all-purpose flour
- 1 teaspoon salt
- ½ teaspoon coarsely ground black pepper
- 1½ cups plain dried bread crumbs
- 4 tablespoons butter or margarine
- 6 anchovy fillets (optional)
- 2 tablespoons capers, drained
- 2 tablespoons chopped fresh parsley
- 2 lemons, each cut into 6 wedges, for garnish

1. Place the cutlets between 2 sheets of plastic wrap or waxed paper. With a meat mallet or rolling pin, pound the cutlets to an ⅛-inch thickness.

2. In a pie plate, beat the eggs; on waxed paper, combine the flour, salt, and pepper. Place the bread crumbs on a separate sheet of waxed paper. Coat the cutlets in the seasoned flour, dip in the eggs, and then coat them evenly with the bread crumbs.

3. In a 12-inch skillet, melt 2 tablespoons butter over medium-high heat. Add the cutlets, a few at a time, and cook until browned, 3 to 4 minutes per side, adding the remaining 2 tablespoons butter as needed. Using tongs, transfer the cutlets to a warm platter as they are browned.

4. To serve, top the cutlets with anchovies, if using, and capers; sprinkle with parsley and garnish with lemon wedges.

Each serving About 350 calories, 30g protein, 25g carbohydrate, 13g fat (6g saturated), 2g fiber, 920mg sodium.

VARIATIONS

Schnitzel à La Holstein

Prepare Wiener Schnitzel as directed, but serve each cutlet topped with **1 fried egg.**

Veal Cutlets with Tomato & Arugula Salad

In a medium bowl, toss **2 large tomatoes**, coarsely chopped; **¼ cup thinly sliced red onion**; and **1 cup basil leaves** with **4 teaspoons lemon juice, 3 tablespoons olive oil, ½ teaspoon salt,** and **¼ teaspoon ground black pepper.** Prepare Wiener Schnitzel as directed through step 3. To serve, add **5 ounces baby arugula** to the tomatoes in the bowl; toss. Serve atop cutlets.

veal parmigiana

PREP: 30 MIN / TOTAL: 55 MIN / SERVES 6

2 cups Marinara Sauce (page 336) or bottled marinara sauce

1 cup plain dried bread crumbs

½ teaspoon salt

⅛ teaspoon ground black pepper

1 large egg

2 tablespoons water

6 veal cutlets (1½ pounds)

3 tablespoons butter or margarine

¼ cup freshly grated Parmesan cheese

4 ounces part-skim mozzarella cheese, shredded (1 cup)

1. Prepare Marinara Sauce, if using. On waxed paper, combine the bread crumbs, salt, and pepper. In a pie plate, beat the egg and water. Dip the cutlets in the egg mixture, then in bread crumbs; repeat to coat each cutlet twice.

2. In a 12-inch skillet, melt the butter over medium heat. Add the cutlets, a few at a time, and cook until browned, about 5 minutes per side, using tongs to transfer the cutlets to a platter as they are browned.

3. Return the cutlets to the skillet. Spoon the marinara sauce evenly over the cutlets. Sprinkle with Parmesan and top with mozzarella. Reduce heat to low; cover and cook just until cheese melts, about 5 minutes.

Each serving About 370 calories, 35g protein, 19g carbohydrate, 17g fat (8g saturated), 2g fiber, 913mg sodium.

VARIATION

Chicken Parmigiana

Substitute 1½ pounds skinless, boneless chicken breast halves for the veal and prepare as directed above.

panfried calf's liver & bacon

PREP: 10 MIN / TOTAL: 20 MIN / SERVES 4

4 slices bacon

3 tablespoons all-purpose flour

4 slices calf's liver, ½-inch thick (1 pound)

¼ teaspoon salt

Chopped fresh parsley

1 small lemon, cut into 4 wedges, for serving

1. In a 12-inch skillet, cook the bacon over medium-high heat until browned. With a slotted spoon, transfer the bacon to paper towels to drain; keep warm. Discard all but 1 tablespoon bacon drippings from skillet.

2. Place the flour on waxed paper. Coat the liver with flour, shaking off the excess.

3. Add the liver slices to the hot drippings in the skillet and cook over medium-high heat until crisp and browned but slightly pink inside, 1½ to 2 minutes per side. (Don't overcook liver or it will be tough.) Sprinkle with salt.

4. Place the liver and bacon on a warm platter; sprinkle with parsley and serve with lemon wedges.

Each serving About 235 calories, 23g protein, 10g carbohydrate, 11g fat (4g saturated), 0g fiber, 331mg sodium.

GOOD TO KNOW

MEAT BARGAINS

You don't have to deplete your savings to incorporate quality meat into a meal. While less-expensive cuts often require more time to cook or marinate to keep them tender, the end result will be rich and flavorful. Here are some tips to help stretch your dinner dollar:

- **BUY LARGER CUTS OF MEAT.** They're often sold at a lower price per pound than smaller ones. Ask the butcher to cut the pork shoulder arm picnic, beef chuck shoulder, beef rump, or bottom round roast into smaller pieces, or purchase family packs of meat in bulk from a club store. Label and freeze any portions you're not going to use right away.

- **LOOK FOR THE BONE-IN CHOICES.** For less tender meats, they tend to cost less, and the bone adds a depth of flavor to stews and soups. Look for chuck blade steaks, shoulder lamb chops, veal breast, and lamb shanks.

- **DON'T SHY AWAY FROM FAT.** The leaner the cut, the more expensive it'll be. Fresh ham, beef chuck, and cross-rib pot roast are tender and juicy after a long braise, and the fat can easily be skimmed off after cooking.

veal piccata

PREP: 10 MIN / TOTAL: 25 MIN / SERVES 4

1 pound veal cutlets

¼ cup all-purpose flour

½ teaspoon salt

¼ teaspoon ground black pepper

4 teaspoons olive or vegetable oil

⅓ cup dry white wine

1 cup chicken broth

2 tablespoons fresh lemon juice

1 tablespoon butter

1 tablespoon chopped fresh flat-leaf parsley

1. Place the cutlets between 2 sheets of plastic wrap or waxed paper. With a meat mallet or rolling pin, pound the cutlets to a ¼-inch thickness. On waxed paper, combine the flour, salt, and pepper. Coat the cutlets with the seasoned flour, shaking off the excess.

2. In a 12-inch skillet, heat 2 teaspoons oil over medium-high heat until very hot. Add half the cutlets and cook until browned, about 2 minutes. Turn the cutlets and cook 1 minute longer. Using tongs, transfer the cutlets to a platter; keep warm. Repeat with the remaining 2 teaspoons oil and the remaining veal.

3. Increase the heat to high and add the wine to the skillet, stirring until the browned bits are loosened from the bottom of the skillet. Add the broth and heat to boiling; boil until the sauce has reduced to ½ cup, 4 to 6 minutes. Stir in the lemon juice, butter, and parsley. When the butter has melted, pour the sauce over the veal.

Each serving About 225 calories, 26g protein, 7g carbohydrate, 10g fat (3g saturated), 0g fiber, 643mg sodium.

TESTING NOTE Don't substitute margarine. This piquant dish depends on real dairy butter for its success. (The sauce will not thicken properly without it!)

vitello tonnato

PREP: 20 MIN / TOTAL 2 HR 30 MIN, PLUS COOLING AND CHILLING / SERVES 8

1 rolled boneless veal shoulder roast (about 3 pounds), trimmed and tied

10 anchovy fillets

2 cloves garlic, thinly sliced

3 cups water

1¾ cups chicken broth

1 cup dry white wine

1 medium onion, thinly sliced

2 carrots, peeled and thinly sliced

1 can (5 ounces) tuna packed in oil, undrained

½ cup mayonnaise

½ cup heavy or whipping cream

1 tablespoon fresh lemon juice

½ teaspoon salt

2 tablespoons chopped fresh parsley, for serving

1. With a sharp knife, make slits all over the veal. Coarsely chop 2 anchovies; insert chopped anchovies and garlic into slits.

2. In a nonreactive 5-quart Dutch oven, combine water, broth, wine, onion, and carrots and heat to boiling over medium heat. Add roast to Dutch oven. Reduce heat; cover and simmer until veal is tender, about 1 hour and 45 minutes.

3. Remove from heat; cool veal in broth 1 hour, then transfer veal to plate and refrigerate to cool completely. Strain broth, reserving ¾ cup; discard remaining broth. Transfer reserved broth to food processor fitted with knife blade. Add tuna, mayonnaise, cream, lemon juice, salt, and remaining 8 anchovies; puree until smooth.

4. Cut veal into thin slices; transfer to deep platter large enough to hold veal in one or two layers. Pour sauce over veal; cover and refrigerate at least 1 hour or up to 24 hours. Serve chilled or at room temperature, sprinkled with parsley.

Each serving About 400 calories, 37g protein, 3g carbohydrate, 26g fat (7g saturated), 1g fiber, 801mg sodium.

pork roast
with fennel & garlic

PREP: 10 MIN / TOTAL: 1 HR 40 MIN / SERVES 8

4 cloves garlic, finely chopped

2½ teaspoons fennel seeds, crushed

1 teaspoon salt

½ teaspoon ground black pepper

2 teaspoons olive oil

1 bone-in pork loin roast (4 pounds), trimmed

⅓ cup dry white wine

⅔ cup chicken broth

1. Preheat the oven to 450°F. In a cup, combine the garlic, fennel seeds, salt, pepper, and oil to make a paste.

2. Place the roast in a small roasting pan (13 × 9 inches) and rub the fennel paste on the outside of the pork and between the bones. Roast the pork 45 minutes. Turn the oven control to 350°F, cover the meat loosely with a tent of foil, and roast until the meat thermometer inserted in the thickest part of the roast (not touching bone) reaches 155°F, about 45 minutes longer. Internal temperature of the meat will rise to 160°F upon standing. When the roast is done, transfer it to a warm platter and let stand 15 minutes to set the juices for easier carving.

3. Meanwhile, add the wine to the roasting pan and heat to boiling over high heat, stirring until the browned bits are loosened from the bottom of the pan. Add the broth and heat to boiling. Remove from the heat; skim and discard the fat. Serve the sauce with the roast.

Each serving About 270 calories, 35g protein, 1g carbohydrate, 13g fat (4g saturated), 0g fiber, 440mg sodium.

VARIATION

Pork Roast with Fresh Sage

Prepare as above, but substitute ¼ cup fresh parsley, 2 tablespoons chopped fresh sage, and ½ teaspoon dried thyme for the fennel seeds.

GOOD TO KNOW

PORK 101

BUYING PORK

Look for fresh pork that's pinkish white to grayish pink. (The leg and shoulder cuts tend to be darker than the loin cuts). The flesh should be firm to the touch. The amount of marbled fat should be minimal, and any external fat should be firm and white. Cured and smoked pork products, however, are darker in color due to the curing process.

STORING PORK

Fresh pork can be refrigerated, tightly wrapped, for up to two days. Cured and smoked products, if unsliced and sealed in their original packaging, will last for two weeks or longer but only one week after being opened. Do not store according to the "purchase by" date on the package, as supermarket refrigerators are colder than those at home.

COOKING PORK SAFELY

Like other meats, today's pork is much leaner than in the past. Recipes used to require pork to be cooked to 170°F to prevent any possible infection from trichinosis, a disease that could be passed to humans through undercooked pork. Not only has trichinosis now been eradicated from pork products, but the parasite that carries the disease is killed at 137°F. So for tender, juicy pork, do not cook it above 160°F. The exceptions are large cuts like fresh ham, which should be cooked to 170°F. When carved, they will have just a hint of pink at the center (with a deeper pink color near the bone), but the juices will run clear. Cook ground pork just until no trace of pink remains in the center. And to keep pork chops juicy, cook just until the meat is opaque at the bone.

cider-glazed pork & apples

(See photo on page 204.)

PREP: 20 MIN / TOTAL: 1 HR 40 MIN / SERVES 8

1 tablespoons ground fennel

1 teaspoon crushed red pepper

Salt

Ground black pepper

1 boneless pork loin (about 3 pounds), butterflied (see page 207)

2 tablespoons vegetable oil

3 medium Gala or Fuji apples, cored and cut into 6 wedges

2 large onions, cut into thin wedges

2 tablespoons butter, cut into pieces

1½ cups apple cider

¼ cup cider vinegar

2 sticks cinnamon

3 whole star anise

5 thin slices peeled fresh ginger

Parsley leaves, for garnish

1. Preheat the oven to 375°F. In a small bowl, combine the fennel, crushed red pepper, and 1 teaspoon each salt and pepper. Rub the mixture all over the inside of the pork loin. Roll the pork loin up and tie it tightly with 5 or 6 pieces of kitchen twine. Rub the outside with ¼ teaspoon salt.

2. In a 7- to 8-quart Dutch oven or heavy-bottomed pot, heat the oil over medium-high heat. Add the pork to the pot; brown the pork on all sides. Transfer to a cutting board. To the pot, add the apples, onions, and butter. Cook 2 minutes, stirring. Nestle the pork on top of the apple mixture. Place in the oven; cook, uncovered, 20 minutes.

3. Meanwhile, in a small saucepan, combine the cider, vinegar, cinnamon, star anise, and ginger. Heat to boiling over high heat. Boil 15 minutes, or until reduced by half, stirring occasionally. Brush the pork all over with some of the cider mixture, discarding the solids.

4. Roast the pork another 45 minutes, or until cooked through (145°F), brushing with the cider mixture every 15 minutes. Remove the pork from the oven; loosely tent it with a large sheet of foil. Let rest 20 minutes before slicing. Serve the pork with the apple mixture. Garnish with parsley.

Each serving About 490 calories, 35g protein, 18g carbohydrate, 31g fat (10g saturated), 3g fiber, 465mg sodium.

GOOD TO KNOW

ROASTING TIMES FOR PORK

Start with meat from the refrigerator. Roast at 350°F. Remove roast from oven when it reaches 5°F below desired doneness. Temperature will continue to rise 5° to 10° as roast stands.

CUT	WEIGHT	TEMP	MINUTES PER POUND
FRESH PORK (WITH BONE)			
CROWN ROAST	6 to 10 pounds	145 to 160°F	15 to 20 minutes
CENTER LOIN ROAST	3 to 5 pounds	160°F	25 to 30 minutes
BONELESS TOP LOIN ROAST	2 to 4 pounds	145°F	8 to 11 minutes
WHOLE LEG (FRESH HAM)	10 to 14 pounds	160°F	25 to 30 minutes
LEG HALF, SHANK OR BUTT PORTIO	3 to 5 pounds	160°F	30 minutes
BOSTON BUTT	3 to 6 pounds	160°F	35 minutes
TENDERLOIN	½ to 1½ pounds	roast at 425°F to 450°F	20 to 25 minutes total
SMOKED, COOK BEFORE EATING (HEAT AT 325°F)			
WHOLE HAM	14 to 16 pounds	160°F	15 to 18 minutes
SMOKED, FULLY COOKED PORK			
WHOLE HAM	14 to 16 pounds	140°F	1 to 1¾ hours total
HALF HAM	6 to 8 pounds	140°F	1 hour total

PORK TENDERLOIN WITH MELON SALSA 205

CUBAN-STYLE PULLED PORK WITH OLIVES 206

SLOW-COOKED TERIYAKI RIBS 207

CIDER-GLAZED PORK & APPLES 203

pork loin

with lemon & coriander

PREP: 20 MIN / TOTAL: 1 HR 20 MIN, PLUS BRINING / SERVES 16

3 lemons

½ cup kosher salt

½ cup sugar

3 tablespoons coriander seeds

3 tablespoons cracked black peppercorns

3 cloves garlic, crushed with the side of a chef's knife

3 cups water

4 cups ice cubes

1 boneless pork loin roast (5 pounds), trimmed of fat

Cilantro sprigs, for garnish

1. Prepare the brine: From 2 lemons and using a vegetable peeler, remove the peel in ¾-inch-wide strips. In a 4-quart saucepan, heat the lemon peel, salt, sugar, coriander, peppercorns, garlic, and 2 cups water to boiling over high heat. Reduce the heat to medium-low and simmer 3 minutes, stirring to make sure the salt and sugar dissolve. Remove the saucepan from the heat, add the ice cubes, and stir until the ice cubes almost melt; stir in the remaining 1 cup water.

2. Place the pork in very large (2- to 2½-gallon) resealable plastic bag with the brine and seal it, pressing out the excess air. (If necessary, cut the pork loin crosswise in half and use one or two 1-gallon bags.) Place the bag in a large bowl, making sure that the pork is completely covered with brine, and refrigerate the pork at least 18 or up to 48 hours.

3. When ready to cook the pork, preheat the oven to 400°F. Remove the pork from the brine and place it, fat side up, on a rack in large roasting pan (17 × 11½ inches). Drain the brine through a sieve, discarding the liquid. Press the spices from the sieve on top of the pork; discard the lemon peel and garlic.

4. Roast the pork 55 to 65 minutes, or until an instant-read thermometer inserted in the thickest part of the meat registers 150°F (the internal temperature will rise 5°F to 10°F upon standing). (Pork loins vary in length and thickness, which can affect cooking time, so begin to check the pork's internal temperature at 50 minutes.) Transfer the pork to a large platter; cover and set aside at least 10 minutes to allow the juices to set for easier slicing. Cut the remaining lemon into wedges; use them to garnish the platter along with cilantro sprigs.

Each serving About 200 calories, 27g protein, 2g carbohydrate, 9g fat (3g saturated), 1g fiber, 425mg sodium.

TESTING NOTE Brining the pork loin allows you a lot of leeway in how far ahead you start your recipe—anywhere from 18 to 48 hours. For the best flavor and texture, do not leave the meat in the brine any longer.

VARIATION

Spice-Brined Pork Loin

Add **2 tablespoons each fennel seeds and cumin seeds** to the saucepan in step 1.

pork tenderloin

with melon salsa

PREP: 10 MIN / TOTAL: 25 MIN / SERVES 4

1 pork tenderloin (1¼ pounds)

1 tablespoon butter, melted

Salt

2 cups finely chopped cantaloupe

¼ cup packed fresh cilantro, finely chopped

¼ cup chopped orange segments

2 tablespoons lime juice

½ teaspoon chili powder

Mixed greens, for serving

1. Preheat the oven to 450°F. On a baking sheet, brush the pork tenderloin with melted butter; season with ¼ teaspoon salt. Roast 20 minutes, or until cooked (145°F).

2. Combine the cantaloupe, cilantro, orange, lime juice, chili powder, and ¼ teaspoon salt. Slice the pork and serve it over mixed greens; top with melon salsa.

Each serving About 215 calories, 28g protein, 10g carbohydrate, 7g fat (3g saturated), 1g fiber, 410mg sodium.

cuban-style pulled pork
with olives

(See photo on page 204.)

PREP: 20 MIN / TOTAL: 3 HR 30 MIN / SERVES 8

- 2 tablespoons vegetable oil
- 2 medium green bell peppers, seeded and sliced
- 1 medium onion, sliced
- 3 cloves garlic, chopped
- Salt
- 2 teaspoons ground cumin
- 2 teaspoons dried oregano
- 2 cups lower-sodium beef broth
- 1 can (6 ounces) tomato paste
- 1 boneless pork shoulder (about 4 pounds), trimmed of excess fat and cut into quarters
- 1 cup pimiento-stuffed olives, sliced
- 1 tablespoons distilled white vinegar
- 8 cups cooked yellow rice, for serving
- Cilantro leaves, for garnish

1. Preheat the oven to 350°F. In a 6- to 7-quart oven-safe sauce-pot, heat the oil over medium heat. Add the bell peppers, onion, garlic, and ¼ teaspoon salt. Cook 10 minutes, stirring occasionally. Add the cumin and oregano; cook 1 minute, stirring.

2. In a bowl, whisk the broth and tomato paste; add to the pot along with the pork. Heat to simmering over medium heat. Cover the pot and place it in the oven; cook 2½ to 3 hours, or until the pork is very tender.

3. Transfer the pork to a large bowl. Remove and discard any solid fat. Transfer the vegetable mixture to a large fat separator; remove and discard the fat. With 2 forks, shred the pork and return it to the pot along with the vegetable mixture. Stir in the olives and vinegar. Reserve 3 cups pork mixture for Quick 'n' Easy Empanadas (right). Serve the remaining pork with yellow rice and cilantro.

Each serving About 345 calories, 19g protein, 38g carbohydrate, 12g fat (4g saturated), 2g fiber, 1,065mg sodium.

#SavetheFood

quick 'n' easy empanadas

PREP: 30 MIN / TOTAL: 50 MIN / SERVES 4

- 1 package (17.3 ounces) frozen puff pastry sheets, thawed
- 3 cups leftover Cuban-Style Pulled Pork with Olives (left)
- 1 large egg, beaten
- 1 cup salsa verde or Italian Green Sauce (page 55)

1. Preheat the oven to 400°F. Line a large baking sheet with parchment paper.

2. On a lightly floured surface and using a lightly floured rolling pin, roll 1 sheet puff pastry into a 12-inch square. Cut it lengthwise and crosswise in half to make 4 squares. Trim the corners off each square to form a rough 6-inch round. Scoop ⅓ cup pork mixture into the center of each round. Wet the edges of the round with water. Fold each round in half to form half-moons, pressing to flatten them slightly and pinching and rolling the dough to seal the edges. Transfer the empanadas to prepared cookie sheet. Repeat with the remaining pastry sheet and pork.

3. Brush the empanadas with the beaten egg. Bake 25 minutes, or until golden brown. Serve with salsa verde.

Each serving About 540 calories, 25g protein, 32g carbohydrate, 33g fat (10g saturated), 3g fiber, 1,095mg sodium.

slow-cooked teriyaki ribs

(See photo on page 204.)

PREP: 15 MIN / TOTAL: 7 HR 15 MIN ON LOW / SERVES 4

- 1 large rack baby back ribs (2½ pounds), cut into pairs
- ½ teaspoon ground black pepper
- ⅔ cup teriyaki sauce
- 1 tablespoon balsamic vinegar
- 2 cloves garlic, crushed with a garlic press
- Slaw, for serving
- Sesame seeds, for garnish (optional)

1. Sprinkle the baby back ribs with pepper; place them in a slow-cooker bowl with ⅓ cup teriyaki sauce. Cover; cook on High 4 hours or Low 7 hours, until tender. Cut ribs apart.

2. In a small saucepan, simmer the remaining ⅓ cup teriyaki sauce, the balsamic vinegar, and garlic over medium-high heat 5 minutes; brush onto the cooked ribs. Serve with slaw. Garnish with sesame seeds, if desired.

Each serving (with slaw) About 495 calories, 30g protein, 20g carbohydrate, 32g fat (11g saturated), 1g fiber, 1,100mg sodium.

 Tip DIY Teriyaki: Simmer ½ cup lower-sodium soy sauce, 2 tablespoons rice wine vinegar, ¼ cup packed brown sugar, and 1 teaspoon grated fresh ginger for 2 minutes.

VARIATION

Slow-Cooked BBQ Ribs

Replace teriyaki with your favorite **barbecue sauce**, adding ⅔ cup to the cooker at the beginning. Omit the balsamic and garlic in step 2 and reduce juices from cooker until syrupy. Brush on ribs.

HOW TO

BUTTERFLY PORK LOIN

With a sharp chef's knife, cut the pork loin almost all the way in half lengthwise; open the halves like a book. Cut 1 slit lengthwise in the center of each half. After seasoning the inside, roll the pork back up and then tie.

quatre épices pork roast

PREP: 5 MIN / TOTAL: 1 HR 5 MIN / SERVES 6

- 1 boneless pork loin roast (2 pounds), trimmed
- 1 teaspoon salt
- ¾ teaspoon dried thyme
- ½ teaspoon ground cinnamon
- ½ teaspoon ground black pepper
- ⅛ teaspoon ground nutmeg
- ⅛ teaspoon ground cloves
- ⅓ cup dry white wine
- ⅔ cup chicken broth
- Applesauce, for serving

1. Preheat the oven to 350°F. Pat the pork dry with paper towels.

2. In a cup, combine the salt, thyme, cinnamon, pepper, nutmeg, and cloves. Use this to rub on the pork.

3. Place the roast on a rack in a small roasting pan (13 × 9 inches). Roast the pork until a meat thermometer inserted in the center of the roast reaches 155°F, about 1 hour. Internal temperature of the meat will rise to 160°F upon standing.

4. When the roast is done, transfer it to a warm platter and let stand 15 minutes to set the juices for easier slicing.

5. Meanwhile, add the wine to the roasting pan and heat to boiling over high heat, stirring until the browned bits are loosened from the bottom of the pan. Add the broth and heat to boiling; boil 2 minutes. Remove from the heat; skim and discard the fat. Serve the pan juices and applesauce with pork.

Each serving About 255 calories, 33g protein, 1g carbohydrate, 11g fat (4g saturated), 0g fiber, 561mg sodium.

GLOSSARY →

Quatre Epices means "four spices" in French. It is a classic French combination of warm spices. We've taken the liberty of adding some thyme in our recipe for a savory note. Once the pork begins roasting, the savory aroma will fill your kitchen.

breaded pork tenderloin

PREP: 20 MIN / TOTAL: 30 MIN / SERVES 4

1 pork tenderloin (12 ounces), trimmed

1 large egg

2 tablespoons water

½ teaspoon salt

¼ teaspoon dried rosemary, crumbled (optional)

¾ cup plain dried bread crumbs

3 tablespoons vegetable oil

1. Using a sharp knife, cut the tenderloin lengthwise almost in half, being careful not to cut all the way through. Open and spread it flat like a book. Place pork the between 2 sheets of plastic wrap or waxed paper. With a meat mallet or rolling pin, pound the pork to a ¼-inch thickness; cut crosswise into 4 equal pieces.

2. In a pie plate and using a fork, lightly beat the egg, water, salt, and rosemary, if using. Place the bread crumbs on a sheet of waxed paper. Using tongs, dip the pork in the egg mixture, then in the bread crumbs. Repeat to coat each piece of pork twice.

3. In a 12-inch skillet, heat the oil over medium-high heat until very hot. Add the pork and cook until browned and cooked through, about 5 minutes per side.

Each serving About 290 calories, 22g protein, 15g carbohydrate, 15g fat (3g saturated), 1g fiber, 522mg sodium.

orange glazed pork rolls

PREP: 5 MIN / TOTAL: 1 HR 55 MIN / SERVES 12

2 smoked pork shoulder rolls (3 pounds each)

¼ teaspoon whole black peppercorns

1 bay leaf

1 jar (10 to 12 ounces) orange marmalade

2 tablespoons bottled white horseradish

1. Remove the stockinette casing (if any) from the pork rolls, if directed on the label. In an 8-quart saucepot, place the shoulder rolls, peppercorns, bay leaf, and enough water to cover the meat; heat to boiling over high heat. Reduce the heat; cover and simmer until the pork rolls are tender, about 1 hour 30 minutes.

2. Preheat the oven to 350°F. In a small bowl, combine the orange marmalade and horseradish.

3. When the shoulder rolls are done, arrange them in a 13 × 9-inch baking pan; bake, brushing them occasionally with the marmalade mixture, 20 minutes.

4. To serve, cut the rolls into slices and arrange them on a warm platter.

Each serving About 605 calories, 33g protein, 18g carbohydrate, 44g fat (16g saturated), 0g fiber, 1,847mg sodium.

HOW TO

COOK PORK

Since pork is usually tender, many cuts are perfectly suitable for several of these cooking methods.

BROILING, GRILLING, PANFRYING & STIR-FRYING	Many lean cuts lend themselves to these methods. **Best Bets:** Tenderloin, loin, rib and loin chops, sirloin chops and cutlets, blade chops, and sausages; spareribs are good broiled or grilled if they're first precooked.
BRAISING & STEWING	Many cuts of pork stand up well to long, slow cooking in liquid. **Best Bets:** sirloin chops, blade chops, shoulder, spareribs and pork cubes for stew
ROASTING	Use tender cuts from the loin. **Best Bets:** rib crown roast, shoulder arm roast, arm picnic roast, fresh ham, whole boneless tenderloin

balsamic-glazed pork chops
with spinach mash

(See photo on page 174.)

PREP: 10 MIN / TOTAL: 30 MIN / SERVES 4

- 1 pound Yukon Gold potatoes, scrubbed and chopped
- Salt
- 1 package (5 ounces) baby spinach
- 4 tablespoons butter, melted
- 2 tablespoons brown sugar
- 1 tablespoon balsamic vinegar
- ½ teaspoon ground black pepper
- 4 bone-in pork chops, about 1 inch thick
- Snipped fresh chives, for garnish

1. In a large pot, cover the potatoes with water. Add 1 tablespoon salt and cover; heat to boiling over high heat. Boil 15 minutes, or until very tender, then stir in the baby spinach. Drain, then mash the potatoes with the butter.

2. Preheat the broiler.

3. In a small bowl, combine the brown sugar, balsamic vinegar, pepper and ½ teaspoon salt; brush all over the pork chops. Broil 4 minutes per side, or until cooked (145°F). Serve with the spinach mash. Garnish with chives.

Each serving About 500 calories, 36g protein, 29g carbohydrate, 26g fat (12g saturated), 2g fiber, 540mg sodium.

TESTING NOTE We're big fans of bone-in chops. They tend to come out juicier and are harder to overcook than boneless cuts.

rye-crusted pork chops

(See photo on page 213.)

PREP: 10 MIN / TOTAL: 25 MIN / SERVES 6

- 1 tablespoon olive oil
- 3 slices rye bread, torn into pieces
- 6 bone-in pork chops, 1 inch thick
- Salt
- ½ teaspoon ground black pepper
- 2 tablespoons Dijon mustard
- 2 tablespoons butter
- ½ head red cabbage, thinly sliced
- 1 Granny smith apple, peeled, cored, and thinly sliced
- ¼ cup water
- ¼ cup red wine vinegar

1. Preheat the oven to 425°F. Grease a rimmed baking sheet.

2. In a food processor, pulse the olive oil and bread into fine crumbs. Season the pork chops with ½ teaspoon salt and the pepper; arrange them on the prepared baking sheet. Top each chop with 1 teaspoon Dijon mustard; press on rye crumbs. Roast 14 to 16 minutes, or until cooked through (145°F).

3. Meanwhile, in a large skillet, heat the butter over medium-high heat until melted. Add the cabbage, apple, water, red wine vinegar, and ¼ teaspoon salt. Heat to simmering. Cook 10 minutes, covered, or until the cabbage is wilted and soft. Serve with the chops.

Each serving About 355 calories, 26g protein, 16g carbohydrate, 20g fat (8g saturated), 3g fiber, 605mg sodium.

pork chops

with rosemary-truffle butter

(See photo on page 174.)

PREP: 15 MIN / TOTAL: 30 MIN / SERVES 4

- 2 tablespoons olive oil
- 4 bone-in pork chops, each about 1 inch thick
- Salt
- ½ teaspoon ground black pepper
- 3 medium shallots, chopped
- 12 ounces cremini mushrooms, trimmed and thinly sliced
- ½ teaspoon chopped fresh rosemary
- ⅔ cup half-and-half
- 2 tablespoons truffle butter

1. In a 12-inch skillet, heat the oil over medium-high heat until hot but not smoking. Season the pork chops all over with ½ teaspoon salt and the pepper. Cook the pork chops 6 minutes, or until browned on both sides, turning over once; transfer to a large plate. Reduce the heat to medium and pour off the excess fat from the skillet. To the skillet, add the shallots, mushrooms, rosemary, and ⅛ teaspoon salt. Cook 5 minutes, stirring.

2. Stir in the half-and-half and truffle butter. Nestle the pork in the sauce. Simmer 4 to 6 minutes, or until pork is cooked through (145°F).

Each serving About 400 calories, 33g protein, 9g carbohydrate, 25g fat (10g saturated), 1g fiber, 400mg sodium.

pepper bacon

PREP: 10 MIN / TOTAL: 35 MIN / SERVES 12

- 1½ pounds sliced lean bacon
- 2½ teaspoons coarsely ground black pepper

1. Preheat the oven to 400°F. Arrange the bacon slices on 2 rimmed baking sheets or roasting pans, overlapping the lean edge of each bacon slice with the fat edge of the next one. Sprinkle the pepper evenly over the bacon. Bake until the bacon is golden brown and crisp, about 25 minutes, rotating the baking pans between the upper and lower oven racks halfway through baking.

2. Transfer the bacon to paper towels. Keep warm until ready to serve.

Each serving About 95 calories, 5g protein, 0g carbohydrate, 8g fat (3g saturated), 0g fiber, 254mg sodium.

chorizo-stuffed acorn squash

(See photo on page 213.)

PREP: 15 MIN / TOTAL: 35 MIN / SERVES 4

- 2 medium acorn squash, halved and seeded
- 2 teaspoons oil
- 1½ cups cooked quinoa
- 1 cup grated Manchego cheese
- 4 ounces dried chorizo, finely chopped
- ¼ cup mild pickled peppers, drained and finely chopped

1. Preheat the oven to 425°F.

2. Brush the cut sides of the acorn squash with oil. On a large rimmed baking sheet, place the squash cut side down and bake for 20 minutes. Combine the quinoa, Manchego, chorizo, and pickled peppers.

3. Turn the squash over on the baking sheet; fill each with the quinoa mixture. Bake 15 minutes, or until the squash is tender.

Each serving About 430 calories, 18g protein, 39g carbohydrate, 24g fat (11g saturated), 5g fiber, 680mg sodium.

#SavetheFood

4 more ideas for chorizo

SAUSAGE FRIED RICE: Stir-fry chorizo with cooked rice, onions and peas.

PARMESAN OMELETS: Chop and put into omelets with bell peppers and Parmesan.

CHORIZO TACOS: Cook with chopped tomatoes, then spoon into tortillas.

SPICY QUESADILLAS: Sandwich thin slices with spinach and pepper Jack between tortillas; panfry.

italian sausage & broccoli rabe

PREP: 5 MIN / TOTAL: 35 MIN / SERVES 4

1 bunch broccoli rabe (1 pound), tough ends trimmed

2 teaspoons salt

1 pound sweet Italian sausage links, pricked with a fork

¼ cup water

1 tablespoon olive oil

1 large clove garlic, finely chopped

⅛ teaspoon crushed red pepper

1. In a 5-quart saucepot, heat 4 quarts water to boiling. Add the broccoli rabe and salt. Cook just until the stems are tender, about 5 minutes; drain. When cool enough to handle, coarsely chop the broccoli rabe.

2. Meanwhile, in a 10-inch skillet, heat the sausage links and water to boiling over medium heat. Cover and cook 5 minutes. Remove the cover and cook, turning the sausages frequently, until the water has evaporated and the sausages are well browned, about 20 minutes longer. Using tongs, transfer the sausages to paper towels to drain; cut each sausage diagonally in half.

3. Discard the fat from the skillet but do not wipe it clean. To the drippings in skillet, add the oil, garlic, and crushed red pepper. Cook, stirring, until very fragrant, about 15 seconds. Add the broccoli rabe and cook, stirring, until well coated and heated through, about 2 minutes. Stir in the sausages, remove from the heat, and serve.

Each serving About 325 calories, 19g protein, 6g carbohydrate, 25g fat (8g saturated), 2g fiber, 1,079mg sodium.

Serving Suggestion If you're a fan of the bitter greens, double 'em in this recipe.

sausage-stuffed zucchini boats

(See photo on page 213.)

PREP: 10 MIN / TOTAL: 55 MIN / SERVES 4

4 small zucchini

2 teaspoons olive oil

1 small onion, chopped

2 links sweet Italian sausage, casings removed

Salt

1¼ cups Marinara Sauce (page 336) or bottled marinara sauce

1 cup shredded mozzarella cheese

Chopped fresh parsley, for garnish

Cooked pasta, for serving

1. Preheat the oven to 450°F.

2. Cut the zucchini lengthwise in half; scrape out and chop the flesh, leaving a ¼-inch shell.

3. In a 10-inch skillet, heat the olive oil over medium-high heat. Add the chopped zucchini flesh, the onion, sausage, and ¼ teaspoon salt. Cook 8 minutes, breaking up the sausage with the back of a spoon.

4. In a 3-quart baking dish, spread the marinara sauce on the bottom; arrange the zucchini shells on top, cut sides up. Spoon the sausage mixture into the shells. Top with mozzarella. Cover with foil; bake 30 minutes. Uncover; bake 5 minutes longer. Garnish with parsley. Serve with pasta.

Each serving (without pasta) About 325 calories, 16g protein, 15g carbohydrate, 23g fat (9g saturated), 3g fiber, 925mg sodium.

mexican-style spareribs

PREP: 15 MIN / TOTAL: 2 HR 10 MIN / SERVES 4

1 cup firmly packed fresh cilantro leaves & stems

½ small onion, thinly sliced

4 cloves garlic, crushed

1 pickled jalapeño chile

½ cup fresh lime juice

¼ cup fresh orange juice

¼ cup tequila

1 tablespoon olive oil

2 tablespoons sugar

½ teaspoon dried oregano

3 pounds pork spareribs

1. Preheat the oven to 350°F.

2. In a blender, combine the cilantro, onion, garlic, jalapeño, lime and orange juices, tequila, oil, sugar, and oregano and puree until smooth.

3. Place the spareribs in a nonreactive roasting pan just large enough to hold them in a single layer. Pour the cilantro mixture over the ribs, turning to coat well. Roast, turning the ribs twice, 1 hour 30 minutes. Turn the oven control to 450°F and roast the ribs until very tender and richly colored, about 20 minutes longer.

4. Transfer the ribs to a warm platter. Skim and discard the fat from the sauce remaining in the pan and spoon the sauce over the ribs.

Each serving About 610 calories, 40g protein, 13g carbohydrate, 44g fat (15g saturated), 1g fiber, 183mg sodium.

crispy sesame pork

PREP: 10 MIN / TOTAL: 20 MIN / SERVES 4

3 tablespoons lower-sodium soy sauce

2 tablespoons brown sugar

⅓ cup panko (Japanese-style bread crumbs)

2 tablespoons sesame seeds

1 large egg

4 thin boneless pork chops (about 1 pound)

3 tablespoons canola oil

5 ounces salad greens

1 cup grape tomatoes, halved

1 cup shredded carrots

1. In a small saucepan, whisk together the soy sauce and brown sugar. Heat to simmering over medium heat. Simmer 2 minutes; cool.

2. On medium plate, combine the panko and sesame seeds. In a shallow bowl, beat the egg. Dip the pork chops first in the egg, then coat in the panko mixture.

3. In a 12-inch skillet, heat the canola oil over medium-high heat until hot. Fry the chops 3 minutes per side, or until cooked (145°F). Drain on paper towels; cut into cubes.

4. In a large bowl, toss the salad greens, grape tomatoes, shredded carrots, and pork with the soy reduction.

Each serving About 375 calories, 24g protein, 19g carbohydrate, 22g fat (4g saturated), 2g fiber, 520mg sodium.

 Tip For perfectly crisp meat, test the oil temp before frying: Drop in a bread crumb; if it sizzles, it's hot enough.

choucroute garni

PREP: 20 MIN / TOTAL: 1 HR 10 MIN / SERVES 6

4 slices bacon, cut into 1-inch pieces

¼ cup water

1 large onion, thinly sliced

2 McIntosh apples, peeled, cut into quarters, and thinly sliced

2 bags (16 ounces each) sauerkraut, rinsed and drained

1½ cups fruity white wine, such as Riesling

6 juniper berries, crushed

1 bay leaf

6 smoked pork chops, ½ inch thick (4 ounces each)

1 pound kielbasa (smoked Polish sausage), cut into 1½-inch pieces

1. In a 5-quart nonreactive Dutch oven, combine the bacon and water; cook over medium-low heat until the bacon is lightly crisped, about 4 minutes. Add the onion and cook, stirring frequently, until the onion is tender and golden, about 7 minutes.

2. Add the apples and cook until tender, about 3 minutes. Stir in the sauerkraut, wine, juniper berries, and bay leaf and heat to boiling. Reduce the heat; cover and simmer 15 minutes.

3. Nestle the pork chops and kielbasa into the cabbage mixture; cover and cook until the pork is heated through and the sauerkraut is tender, about 20 minutes. Discard the bay leaf and serve.

Each serving About 525 calories, 27g protein, 19g carbohydrate, 37g fat (13g saturated), 4g fiber, 3,151mg sodium.

RYE-CRUSTED PORK CHOPS 209

CRISPY SESAME PORK 212

SAUSAGE-STUFFED ZUCCHINI BOATS 211

CHORIZO-STUFFED ACORN SQUASH 210

fresh ham
with spiced glaze

PREP: 15 MIN / TOTAL: 5 HR 15 MIN / SERVES 24

- 1 whole pork leg (fresh ham; 15 pounds), trimmed
- 2 teaspoons dried thyme
- 2 teaspoons ground cinnamon
- 2 teaspoons salt
- 1 teaspoon coarsely ground black pepper
- ½ teaspoon ground nutmeg
- ½ teaspoon ground cloves
- 1 jar (10 ounces) apple jelly
- ¼ cup balsamic vinegar

1. Preheat the oven to 350°F. With a knife, remove the skin and trim excess fat from the pork leg, leaving only a thin layer of fat.

2. In a cup, combine the thyme, cinnamon, salt, pepper, nutmeg, and cloves. Use to rub on the pork. Place the pork, fat side up, on a rack in large roasting pan (17 × 11½ inches). Roast the pork 3 hours. Cover the pork loosely with a tent of foil. Continue roasting until a meat thermometer inserted into the thickest part of the pork (not touching bone) registers 150°F, about 1 hour.

3. Meanwhile, in a 1-quart saucepan, heat the apple jelly and vinegar to boiling over high heat; boil 2 minutes. Set aside.

4. When the pork has reached 150°F, remove the foil and brush the pork with the glaze. Continue roasting the pork, brushing occasionally with remaining glaze, until the meat thermometer registers 165°F. (Meat near bone will be slightly pink.) Internal temperature of pork will rise to 170°F upon standing.

5. When the roast is done, transfer to a warm large platter; let stand 20 minutes to set the juices for easier carving.

Each serving About 300 calories, 38g protein, 6g carbohydrate, 12g fat (4g saturated), 0g fiber, 232mg sodium.

TYPES OF HAM

Smoked hams are what most of us think when we say ham. Check out the variations and other styles of ham.

- **SMOKED HAM** comes from the hind leg of pork, whereas **PICNIC HAM** comes from the shoulder. These hams are labeled either "partially cooked" or "fully cooked." In either case, be sure to follow the label's cooking instructions.

- **PARTIALLY COOKED HAM** must be cooked to 155°F before eating.

- **FULLY COOKED HAM** is ready to serve, but its flavor is much improved by heating it to an internal temperature of 130° to 140°F. It is available in several forms:
  - **bone-in:** whole, shank, or butt portions
  - **semiboneless:** the aitch- and shank bones have been removed; only the leg bone remains
  - **boneless:** rolled and shaped or formed

- **SPIRAL-SLICED HAM** is ham that has been cut in one long, continuous slice. It's ideal buffet food.

- **CANNED HAM** is cured but not always smoked.

- **BONELESS SMOKED PORK SHOULDER** (also called boneless pork butt), rolled and wrapped in a mesh stockinette that is removed before serving. It is much smaller than ham, making it a great option when serving pork to a small number of people.

- **COUNTRY HAMS,** such as Smithfield and Virginia, are heavily salted and smoked. They should be soaked in cold water for 24 to 36 hours to remove the excess salt, then thoroughly cooked.

- **PROSCIUTTO, PROSCIUTTO DE PARMA, AND JAMON SERRANO** are cured, air-dried hams that have not been smoked. Imported and domestic versions can be purchased in specialty food stores and in many supermarkets.

- **FRESH HAM** is an uncured leg of pork. It should be roasted like other cuts of fresh pork.

slow-cooked fresh ham

PREP: 15 MIN / TOTAL: 3 HR 30 MIN, PLUS STANDING / SERVES 12

3 tablespoons coriander seeds

2 tablespoons fennel seeds

2 teaspoons salt

4 cloves garlic, crushed with a garlic press

1 tablespoon olive oil

2 teaspoons coarsely ground black pepper

1 shank or butt-half pork leg (fresh ham), about 9 pounds

1¾ cup reduced-sodium chicken broth

½ cup water

1. Preheat the oven to 350°F. In a mortar and using a pestle, crush the coriander seeds and fennel seeds with the salt (or place the seeds and salt in a heavyweight reasealable plastic bag and crush the seeds with a rolling pin or heavy saucepan). In a small bowl, combine the seed mixture, garlic, oil, and pepper.

2. With a knife, trim any skin and excess fat on the pork leg to ¼ inch. Place the pork leg, fat side up, on a rack in a medium roasting pan (15½ × 10½ inches). With your hands, rub the spice mixture over the pork. Insert a meat thermometer into the center of the thickest part of the pork, being careful that the pointed end of the thermometer does not touch bone. Roast 3 hours, or until the thermometer registers 155°F. Internal temperature of the meat will rise 5°F to 10°F upon standing. (Meat near the bone will be slightly pink.)

3. When the pork is done, transfer it to a warm, large platter. Let stand 15 minutes to set the juices for easier carving; keep warm.

4. Meanwhile, skim and discard any fat from the drippings in the roasting pan. Add the chicken broth, water, and any meat juice from the platter to the drippings in the roasting pan; heat to boiling over medium heat, stirring to loosen brown bits from bottom of pan. Makes about 2¼ cups. Serve the pan juices with the pork.

Each serving About 435 calories, 37g protein, 2g carbohydrate, 30g fat (11g saturated), 1g fiber, 475mg sodium.

#SavetheFood

fresh ideas for ham

They say that the definition of eternity is two people and a ham. Here are some ideas for using your extra meat.

ZESTY SANDWICH SPREAD

In a food processor, grind enough **ham** to equal 2 cups. Transfer to a medium bowl and stir in ½ **cup sweet pickle relish**, ½ **cup finely chopped celery**, and **1 package (3 ounces) cream cheese**. Serve as sandwich spread or with unsalted crackers.

EGGS BENEDICT

For Sunday brunch, serve **thinly sliced ham** on a toasted **English muffin**, topped with a **poached egg** and **Hollandaise Sauce (page 51)**.

HEARTY SOUPS

Use a **ham bone** in **Split Pea Soup (page 148)**, **bean soup**, or **lentil soup**.

OPEN-FACED GRILLED CHEESE SANDWICHES

Brown **slices of ham** and **pineapple** in **butter or margarine**. Place on a toasted **kaiser roll** halves, top with **Cheddar cheese**, and broil until the cheese melts.

FLAVORFUL SAUCE

Add some **minced ham** to **White Sauce (Béchamel, page 50)** and serve over **chicken or vegetables**.

MAIN-DISH SALADS

Toss some **chopped ham** into **macaroni, potato, or rice salad** for a tasty main dish. Or add ½ **cup chopped ham** to **Creamy Potato Salad (page 482)**.

HAM & MELON

Arrange **thinly sliced ham** on **thinly sliced melon wedges or other fruit** to serve for breakfast, lunch, or as a first course.

HAM BISCUITS

Make **biscuits (page 558)**. Split, spread with **butter**, and top with **thinly sliced ham**.

pineapple-glazed ham

PREP: 15 MIN / TOTAL: 2 HR 25 MIN / SERVES 20

- 1 fully cooked smoked bone-in ham (14 pounds)
- 1 can (20 ounces) crushed pineapple, drained
- 1 cup packed dark brown sugar
- 1 tablespoon Dijon mustard

1. Preheat the oven to 325°F. With a sharp knife, remove the skin and trim the fat from the ham, leaving about ¼-inch-thick layer of fat. Place the ham on a rack in a large roasting pan (17 × 11½ inches). Bake the ham 1 hour 45 minutes.

2. Meanwhile, prepare the pineapple glaze: In a medium bowl, combine the pineapple, brown sugar, and mustard until blended. Remove the ham from the oven. Brush the pineapple mixture on the ham. Bake until a meat thermometer inserted in the thickest part of the ham (not touching bone) reaches 135°F, 25 to 30 minutes longer. Internal temperature of the ham will rise to 140°F upon standing. Transfer the ham to a warm platter and let stand 15 minutes to set the juices for easier slicing.

Each serving About 195 calories, 21g protein, 15g carbohydrate, 5g fat (2g saturated), 0g fiber, 1,150mg sodium.

VARIATIONS

Melba-Glazed Ham

Prepare the ham as directed, but in step 2, in a small saucepan, heat ⅔ cup peach preserves and ½ cup red raspberry jelly or jam until melted and smooth. During the last 30 minutes of roasting time, brush the glaze over the ham two or three times. Makes about 1 cup glaze.

Tomato & Onion Glazed Ham

Prepare the ham as directed, but in step 2, in small a saucepan, melt 1 tablespoon butter or margarine over medium heat. Add 2 tablespoons finely chopped onion and cook until tender. Stir in 1 can (8 ounces) tomato sauce, 2 tablespoons brown sugar, and 1 teaspoon Worcestershire sauce; heat to boiling. Reduce the heat; simmer until the glaze thickens, about 5 minutes. During the last 30 minutes of roasting time, brush the glaze over the ham two or three times. Makes about 1 cup glaze.

apricot-mustard ham

PREP: 10 MIN / TOTAL: 3 HR 10 MIN / SERVES 12

- 1 (8- to 10-pound) fully cooked bone-in smoked half ham (not spiral-sliced)
- 1 cup packed brown sugar
- 1 cup apricot jam
- ½ cup spicy brown mustard
- 2 teaspoons ground black pepper

1. Preheat the oven to 300°F. Place the ham in a large roasting pan (17 × 11½ inches), cut side down. With the tip of a sharp knife, make long cuts from the top of the ham to the bottom, cutting through the tough skin and fat. Cover with foil. Bake 1½ hours.

2. In a medium bowl, whisk together the brown sugar, jam, mustard, and pepper. Transfer 1 cup glaze to a separate bowl; cover and refrigerate. Remove the foil from the ham. Brush the remaining glaze all over the ham. Bake, uncovered, another 1 to 1½ hours, or until the glaze is dark brown and the internal temperature of ham has reached 140°F. Allow the ham to rest 20 minutes before carving. Serve with the reserved glaze.

Each serving About 310 calories, 23g protein, 37g carbohydrate, 6g fat (2g saturated), 1g fiber, 1,360mg sodium.

 *Serving Suggestion* Serve with Herb-Roasted Root Vegetables (page 432).

roast rack of lamb

PREP: 10 MIN / TOTAL: 35 MIN / SERVES 4

- 2 teaspoons dried rosemary, crumbled
- 2 teaspoons olive oil
- ½ teaspoon dried thyme
- 1 large clove garlic, minced
- ½ teaspoon salt
- ¼ teaspoon ground black pepper
- 2 lamb rib roasts (racks of lamb), 8 ribs each (1¼ pounds each), trimmed

1. Preheat the oven to 450°F. In a small cup, combine the rosemary, oil, thyme, garlic, salt, and pepper to form a paste. Rub the paste on the top (fat side) of the racks. Place the racks, rub side up, in a large, shallow roasting pan.

2. Roast the lamb until a meat thermometer inserted in the center of the lamb (not touching bone) reaches 135°F to 140°F for medium-rare, 20 to 25 minutes. Transfer to a cutting board and let stand 10 minutes to set the juices for easier carving. Cut between the ribs to serve.

Each serving About 675 calories, 31g protein, 1g carbohydrate, 60g fat (25g saturated), 0g fiber, 379mg sodium.

VARIATION

Crumb-Topped Roast Rack of Lamb

In a small bowl, combine **1 cup fresh bread crumbs** (from 2 slices of firm white bread), **1 teaspoon olive oil**, and ⅛ **teaspoon each salt and ground black pepper**. Follow recipe as directed, rubbing the racks with the paste. After roasting the lamb for 10 minutes, remove it from the oven. Spread **2 tablespoons Dijon mustard** over the top of the racks. Press the bread crumb mixture over the mustard and pat it to stick. Roast the lamb in a preheated 450°F oven until it reaches 135°F to 140°F for medium-rare, 10 to 15 minutes longer.

TESTING NOTE Ask the butcher to loosen the backbone from the ribs for easy carving.

rosemary leg of lamb

PREP: 5 MIN / ROAST: 1 HR 45 MIN / SERVES 10

- 1 whole bone-in lamb leg (7½ pounds), trimmed
- ½ teaspoon dried rosemary, crumbled
- ½ teaspoon dried thyme, crumbled
- ½ teaspoon salt
- ¼ teaspoon ground black pepper

1. Preheat the oven to 450°F. Place the lamb in a large roasting pan (17 × 11½ inches). In a cup, combine the rosemary, thyme, salt, and pepper. Rub the mixture on the lamb.

2. Roast the lamb 15 minutes. Turn the oven control to 350°F and roast, basting every 15 minutes with the pan juices, until a meat thermometer inserted in the thickest part of the lamb (not touching bone) reaches 140°F, 1 hour 30 to 45 minutes longer. The internal temperature of the meat will rise to 145°F (medium) upon standing. Alternatively, roast to the desired doneness.

3. When the lamb is done, transfer it to a cutting board and let it stand 15 minutes to set the juices for easier carving.

4. Carve the lamb into slices and arrange it on a warm platter.

Each serving About 310 calories, 46g protein, 0g carbohydrate, 13g fat (5g saturated), 0g fiber, 227mg sodium.

TESTING NOTE Lamb has a small flap of fat and meat that covers the top of the loin. If the rack you want still has the flap, ask the butcher to cut it off for picture-perfect chops.

LAMB 101

The unique, relatively mild flavor of lamb calls for bold seasonings, like garlic, rosemary, and wine, or intriguing combinations of assertive, exotic spices and sweet fruits.

BUYING LAMB

Most supermarket lamb is from animals six to twelve months old. **MILK-FED LAMB** is less than two months old and has a delicate flavor and pale-pink color.

Even though it is raised year-round, so-called **SPRING OR EASTER LAMB** comes from slightly older sheep up to five months old. Both of these younger lambs are specialty items that are most easily found during the holiday season. Look for lamb from Australia and New Zealand in supermarkets and in butcher shops. The cuts are smaller but still tender and more flavorful than those of American lamb, since they come from smaller—not younger—animals.

LOOK FOR MEAT THAT IS PINKISH-RED. Darker meat indicates an older animal, and it will have a stronger flavor. The fat should look white, firm, and waxy. The bones should be porous and unsplintered, with a reddish tinge at the cut end. If you buy a large cut of lamb, be sure the fell (the thin membrane covering the fat) has been removed. If necessary, peel it off with the help of a sharp knife. In any case, the fat should be trimmed away so only a thin covering remains.

STORING LAMB

Chops, stew meat, and roasts can be stored for up to two days in the refrigerator. Ground lamb is perishable, so it should be used within one day of purchase.

COOKING LAMB

Start with the meat from the refrigerator. Preheat the oven to 350°F. When oven reaches 350°F, cook meat according to recipe instructions. Remove the roast from the oven when it reaches 5°F below desired doneness (135°F for pink); the internal temperature will continue to rise as it stands.

lamb steak
with red pepper relish

PREP: 30 MIN / TOTAL: 40 MIN / SERVES 4

- ⅓ cup cider vinegar
- ¼ cup sugar
- 1¼ teaspoons salt
- Pinch of dried thyme, crumbled
- Pinch of fennel seeds, crushed
- 2 small red bell peppers, chopped
- 1 medium Golden Delicious apple, peeled, cored, and chopped
- 2 jalapeño chiles, seeded and finely chopped
- 1 center-cut lamb steak, 1 inch thick (1½ pounds), or 8 lamb loin chops, 1 inch thick (4 ounces each)

1. In a 2-quart saucepan, combine the vinegar, sugar, 1 teaspoon salt, the thyme, and fennel seeds; heat to boiling over high heat. Add the bell peppers, apple, and jalapeños; heat to boiling. Reduce the heat and simmer, stirring occasionally, until the liquid has evaporated, 15 to 20 minutes. Keep warm.

2. Meanwhile, preheat the broiler. Sprinkle the lamb with the remaining ¼ teaspoon salt. Place the lamb on a rack in a broiling pan. Place the pan at the closest position to the heat source and broil the lamb 5 minutes. Turn the lamb and broil 5 minutes longer for medium-rare, or to the desired doneness. Serve the lamb with the warm red pepper relish.

Each serving About 265 calories, 26g protein, 21g carbohydrate, 9g fat (3g saturated), 2g fiber, 799mg sodium.

lamb shanks

with white beans & roasted endive

PREP: 1 HR 30 MIN / TOTAL: 3 HR 30 MIN / SERVES 8

LAMB SHANKS WITH WHITE BEANS

- 1 package (16 ounces) dry great northern beans
- 8 small lamb shanks (about 1 pound each)
- 2½ teaspoons salt
- 1 teaspoon coarsely ground pepper
- 2 tablespoons vegetable oil
- 6 medium cloves garlic, crushed with the side of a chef's knife
- 4 carrots, peeled and cut into 1-inch pieces
- 1 large onion, coarsely chopped
- ¼ cup all-purpose flour
- 2 tablespoons tomato paste
- 2 cups dry white wine
- 1¾ cups chicken broth
- 1 cup water
- 2 sprigs fresh rosemary, plus 8 sprigs for garnish

ROASTED ENDIVE

- 1 tablespoon olive oil
- ½ teaspoon salt
- ¼ teaspoon coarsely ground pepper
- 8 medium heads Belgian endive (about 1½ pounds)

1. Prepare the white beans: In a 4-quart saucepan, combine the beans and enough water to cover by 2 inches; heat to boiling over high heat. Cook 3 minutes; remove from the heat. Cover and set aside until the beans are softened, about 1 hour. Drain and rinse the beans. (Or, if you prefer, soak the beans overnight in cold water. Drain and rinse.)

2. Meanwhile, prepare the lamb shanks: Pat the shanks dry with paper towels; sprinkle with 1 teaspoon salt and ½ teaspoon pepper. In an 8-quart Dutch oven, heat the oil over medium-high heat until very hot but not smoking. Add the shanks in batches and cook until browned, 12 to 15 minutes, using tongs to transfer the shanks to a large bowl as they are browned. If necessary, reduce the heat to medium before adding the second batch of shanks to prevent overbrowning.

3. Preheat the oven to 375°F. Add the garlic, carrots, and onion to the Dutch oven; cook, stirring frequently, until browned and tender, about 10 minutes. Add the flour, tomato paste, and the remaining 1½ teaspoons salt and ½ teaspoon pepper; cook, stirring constantly, 2 minutes. Add the wine and heat to boiling, stirring until the browned bits are loosened from the bottom of the Dutch oven; boil 5 minutes. Add the broth and water; heat to boiling. Stir in the beans and 2 sprigs rosemary. Return the shanks to the Dutch oven; heat to boiling. Cover the Dutch oven and bake 1 hour.

4. Meanwhile, prepare the roasted endive: In a large bowl and using a fork, mix the oil, salt, and pepper. Trim the root ends of the endive and cut each lengthwise in half. Add the endive to the oil mixture and toss until evenly coated. Arrange the endive, cut sides down, in a 15½ × 10½-inch rimmed baking sheet.

5. After 1 hour, turn the shanks and replace the cover. Place the endive in the same oven. Bake the shanks and endive until the meat is fork-tender and easily separates from the bone and until the endive is very tender and the bottoms begin to brown, about 1 hour.

6. When the shanks are done, transfer them to a large bowl. Skim and discard the fat from the liquid in the Dutch oven. Remove and discard the rosemary. To serve, spoon some beans and cooking liquid onto each of 8 large dinner plates. Top each with 1 lamb shank and 2 endive halves. Garnish with a rosemary sprig.

LAMB AND BEANS Each serving About 725 calories, 67g protein, 46g carbohydrate, 28g fat (11g saturated), 14g fiber, 1,110mg sodium. **ENDIVE** Each serving About 30 calories, 1g protein, 3g carbohydrate, 2g fat (0g saturated), 2g fiber, 145mg sodium.

HOW TO

CARVE A LEG OF LAMB

1 Cut a slice from the thin side of the leg so it can lie flat for easier carving; turn the leg cut side down. Holding the meat steady with a carving fork, make a vertical cut to the bone 1 inch from the shank. Holding the knife horizontally, cut along the top of the bone about halfway down its length.

2 Holding the leg steady by grasping the bone or by inserting a carving fork into the lamb, slice the meat that has been released from the bone. Make a second horizontal cut almost to the end of the leg, then slice the remaining lamb.

3 Turn the leg over. With the knife blade almost flat and working away from you, cut long slices following the line of the bone.

slow-roasted lamb
with pistachio gremolata

PREP: 20 MIN / TOTAL: 2 HR / SERVES 6

3 cloves garlic, finely chopped

2 teaspoons ground coriander

Salt

1 teaspoon ground black pepper

1 boneless leg of lamb (about 4 pounds), trimmed of excess fat

1 pound thin carrots, quartered lengthwise

1 pound parsnips, quartered lengthwise

2 medium leeks, sliced

2 tablespoons olive oil

½ cup salted roasted pistachios, shelled

½ cup packed fresh mint leaves

½ cup packed fresh parsley leaves

2 teaspoons lemon zest

1. Preheat the oven to 325°F. In a small bowl, combine the garlic, coriander, 2 teaspoons salt, and pepper; rub the mixture all over the lamb. Roll the lamb into a cylinder. With butcher's twine, tie the lamb in 2-inch intervals to hold its shape. Place on a rack fitted into a foil-lined rimmed baking sheet. Roast 1 hour.

2. Increase the oven temperature to 475°F. On another large rimmed baking sheet, toss the carrots, parsnips, and leeks with the oil and ¼ teaspoon salt. Roast the vegetables and lamb 30 minutes, or until the vegetables are tender and the lamb is cooked to the desired doneness (145°F for medium), stirring the vegetables once.

3. Meanwhile, on a cutting board, combine the pistachios, mint, parsley, and lemon zest; chop finely. Reserve one-fourth of the vegetables, one-fourth of the lamb and 2 tablespoons pistachio gremolata for Mini Cottage Pies (right). Slice the remaining lamb and serve with the vegetables; sprinkle with the remaining gremolata.

Each serving About 380 calories, 37g protein, 22g carbohydrate, 16g fat (5g saturated), 6g fiber, 715mg sodium.

#SavetheFood
mini cottage pies
(See photo on page 174.)

PREP: 25 MIN / TOTAL: 1 HR / SERVES 4

1 pound Yukon Gold potatoes, peeled and chopped

Salt

1 cup beef broth

2 tablespoons tomato paste

2 tablespoons cornstarch

Leftover roasted vegetables (left), chopped

Leftover Slow-Roasted Lamb (left), chopped

1 cup frozen peas

4 tablespoons butter, melted

½ cup shredded Gruyère or Swiss cheese

2 tablespoons leftover Pistachio Gremolata (left)

1. Place the potatoes in a 4-quart saucepot; cover with cold water and 2 tablespoons salt. Cover partially and heat to boiling over high heat. Reduce the heat to maintain a simmer. Simmer 10 minutes, or until tender. Drain. Preheat the oven to 425°F.

2. Meanwhile, in a large bowl, whisk the broth, tomato paste, and cornstarch until smooth. Add the vegetables, lamb, and peas; fold to combine. Divide the mixture among 4 individual oven-safe baking dishes.

3. In a medium bowl, mash the cooked potatoes; stir in the butter. Divide among the baking dishes, spreading and smoothing the top. Top with cheese. Bake 20 to 25 minutes, or until the cheese is golden brown. Garnish with the reserved pistachio gremolata.

Each serving About 530 calories, 29g protein, 50g carbohydrate, 24g fat (12g saturated), 6g fiber, 900mg sodium.

 Tip Pulse leftover roast lamb or beef in a food processor and add along with the tomato paste in step 2.

shepherd's pie

PREP: 40 MIN / TOTAL: 1 HR / SERVES 4

- 2 pounds all-purpose potatoes, peeled and cut into quarters
- ½ cup milk
- 3 tablespoons butter or margarine
- ¼ cup plus 1 tablespoon freshly grated Parmesan cheese
- Salt
- Ground black pepper
- 1 medium onion, chopped
- 2 carrots, peeled and chopped
- 1 pound ground lamb
- 2 tablespoons tomato paste
- 2 tablespoons all-purpose flour
- ¼ cup dry red wine
- 1 cup chicken broth
- ¼ teaspoon dried thyme
- 1 cup frozen peas

1. Preheat the oven to 425°F. In a 4-quart saucepan, combine the potatoes and enough water to cover; heat to boiling. Boil until the potatoes are tender, about 20 minutes; drain and return them to the saucepan. With a potato masher, mash the potatoes with milk and 2 tablespoons butter. Stir in ¼ cup Parmesan, ½ teaspoon salt, and ¼ teaspoon pepper; set aside.

2. Meanwhile, in a 10-inch nonstick skillet, melt the remaining 1 tablespoon butter over medium heat. Add the onion and carrots; cook until the vegetables are tender, about 5 minutes. Add the ground lamb and cook over medium-high heat, stirring and breaking up the meat with a spoon, until the lamb is no longer pink, about 5 minutes. Skim and discard the fat. Add the tomato paste and cook, stirring, 1 minute. Add the flour and cook, stirring, 1 minute longer. Stir in the wine and cook until the wine has evaporated. Add the broth, thyme, ½ teaspoon salt, and ⅛ teaspoon pepper, stirring until the browned bits are loosened from the bottom of the skillet. Heat to boiling; stir in the peas.

3. Transfer the lamb mixture to a 9-inch deep-dish pie plate. Spoon the mashed potatoes evenly on top and sprinkle with the remaining 1 tablespoon Parmesan. Place it on a foil-lined baking sheet and bake until slightly browned, about 20 minutes.

Each serving About 600 calories, 31g protein, 50g carbohydrate, 31g fat (15g saturated), 7g fiber, 1,272mg sodium.

glazed rosemary lamb chops

PREP: 10 MIN / TOTAL: 20 MIN / SERVES 4

- 8 lamb loin chops, 1 inch thick (4 ounces each)
- 1 large clove garlic, cut in half
- 2 teaspoons chopped fresh rosemary, or ½ teaspoon dried rosemary, crumbled
- ¼ teaspoon salt
- ¼ teaspoon coarsely ground black pepper
- ¼ cup apple jelly
- 1 tablespoon balsamic vinegar

1. Preheat the broiler. Rub both sides of the chops with the cut side of garlic; sprinkle with rosemary, salt, and pepper. In a cup, combine the apple jelly and vinegar.

2. Place the chops on a rack in a broiling pan. Place the pan in the broiler at the closest position to the heat source; broil the chops 4 minutes. Brush the chops with half of the apple-jelly mixture; broil 1 minute. Turn the chops and broil 4 minutes longer. Brush the chops with the remaining jelly mixture and broil 1 minute longer for medium-rare, or to the desired doneness.

3. Transfer the lamb to a warm platter. Skim and discard the fat from the drippings in the pan. Serve the chops with the pan juices, or drizzle them with additional balsamic vinegar.

Each serving About 240 calories, 26g protein, 14g carbohydrate, 8g fat (3g saturated), 0g fiber, 223mg sodium.

CHAPTER

6

poultry

Like many cooks, you're probably serving poultry a couple of times a week—and looking for new inspiration. You're not alone. Last year Americans consumed over 108 pounds of poultry per person, and new ideas are in demand. Luckily poultry is not just an American favorite; it has found its way into pots around the globe, and flavorful preparations abound. Whether you want to do fix-it-and-forget-it roast chicken pieces like Sweet & Sticky Chicken (page 239), a stir-fry like Fiery Kung Pao Chicken (page 250), or a last-minute skillet like Chicken Chilaquiles (page 235), we have the recipes. And many of them take less than an hour total. Welcome to your new weeknight favorites!

MAPLE-GLAZED CHICKEN 232

ROSEMARY-LEMON ROAST CHICKEN 233

HARISSA GRILLED CHICKEN KEBABS 253

SWEET & STICKY CHICKEN WITH SNOW PEAS 239

Know Your Chicken

BROILER-FRYERS Tender young birds that weigh 2½ to 5 pounds. They can be roasted, fried, sautéed, grilled, or broiled.

ROASTERS Meaty birds that usually weigh 6 to 8 pounds and are best when roasted.

CORNISH HENS Small birds that weigh up to 2 pounds each. They are tasty grilled, broiled, or roasted.

FOWL Also called stewing hens, these tough older birds weigh 4 to 6 pounds and are available especially around the holidays. They are best braised or stewed and make the tastiest chicken broth.

CAPONS These are the big boys! Neutered male chickens that weigh 8 to 10 pounds on average. They are very meaty and tender and are usually roasted.

Poultry Shopping Choices

The United States Department of Agriculture (USDA) inspection sticker on poultry guarantees that it was raised and processed according to strict government guidelines. Grade A birds, the most common variety in supermarkets, are the highest quality. And more than 90 percent of all broiler-fryers are marketed under a brand name—a further assurance of quality.

ORGANIC The term *organic* is not recognized by the USDA, so it cannot appear on labels. The term can be used in advertisements to promote a brand, however. Generally, organic poultry has been raised on organically grown, antibiotic-free feed.

FREE-RANGE These birds have been raised in an environment that provides access to open spaces but not necessarily an open farmyard. This free movement allows them to develop more muscle, which contributes to fuller-flavored meat.

ALL-NATURAL This simply means that the poultry has been minimally processed. Its feed was not necessarily organic and might have contained antibiotics.

KOSHER Birds have been processed according to kosher dietary laws under the strict supervision of a rabbi. The procedure includes salting to draw out the blood and season the meat.

HALAL If you live in an area that has a Muslim community, look for a halal butcher. These birds are not fed hormones and are processed manually while a special prayer is recited.

Buying Fresh & Frozen Poultry

FRESH Look for fresh whole birds that appear plump and have meaty breasts. Chicken sold as parts should also look plump. Poultry skin should be smooth and moist and free of bruises and pinfeathers. The color of the skin can range from creamy white to yellow, depending on the bird's feed and breed, and is not an indication of flavor or quality. In general, tenderness depends on the age of the bird.

Buy fresh poultry according to the "sell-by" date on the package. When you open the package, the chicken may have a slight odor. This is caused by oxidation and should disappear in a few minutes. If the poultry still smells, return it to the market. Be sure to avoid packages with leaks or tears.

FROZEN If you buy frozen poultry, the meat should be rock-hard and without any signs of freezer burn, and make certain that there are no ice crystals. The packaging should be tightly sealed and intact. Frozen liquid in the bottom can indicate that the bird was thawed and refrozen.

GLAZED BACON-WRAPPED TURKEY BREAST 260

Handling & Storing Poultry

Store raw poultry in its original store wrapping on a plate to catch any leaks. If wrapped in butcher paper, remove the paper and place the bird in a large plastic bag. Keep poultry in the coldest part of the refrigerator (usually the bottom shelf), away from cooked or ready-to-eat foods, and use within two days. Store uncooked giblets separately in the refrigerator and use within a day, or wrap and freeze for up to one month.

Don't rinse poultry. Pat dry with paper towels. Juices can cause cross-contamination. Be sure to wash your hands, the cutting board, and any utensils that have come in contact with raw poultry with hot, soapy water. To destroy germs, bleach your cutting board once a week or so with a solution of 1 tablespoon chlorine bleach to 1 gallon warm water.

Freeze raw poultry for up to six months. Ground poultry will keep in the refrigerator for one day or in the freezer for up to three months. Cool cooked poultry as quickly as possible, then cover and refrigerate it up to three days, or tightly wrap and freeze it for up to three months. Make sure to date all packages before placing in the freezer.

Thawing Poultry

For safety's sake, thaw poultry either in the refrigerator or by immersion in cold water—not on the kitchen counter at room temperature.

THAWING IN THE REFRIGERATOR is the preferred method. Leave the bird in its original wrapper and place it on a tray to catch any drips. As a general rule, allow about six hours per pound. For example, a 24-pound turkey will take approximately four days to thaw completely.

THAWING IN COLD WATER If there's no time to thaw the bird in the refrigerator, use this method, which takes less time but requires more attention. Place the bird (in its original wrapper or in a watertight plastic bag) in a large pan or in the sink with enough cold water to cover. (Warm water thaws poultry too quickly and can encourage bacterial growth.) Change the water every 30 minutes to maintain the temperature. Allow about 30 minutes of thawing time per pound, then add 1 hour to that total.

5 SAFE THAWING TIPS

1
Frozen poultry should be thawed completely before being cooked.

2
Remove giblets as soon as possible during thawing, then wrap and refrigerate.

3
A whole bird is thawed if the ice crystals have disappeared from the body cavity and the meat is soft.

4
Once thawed, cook the bird within 12 hours.

5
For reasons of texture—not safety—do not refreeze thawed poultry.

mahogany roast chicken

PREP: 10 MIN / TOTAL: 1 HR 25 MIN / SERVES 4

1 whole chicken
(3½ pounds)

¾ teaspoon salt

½ teaspoon coarsely
ground black pepper

2 tablespoons dark
brown sugar

2 tablespoons
balsamic vinegar

2 tablespoons dry
vermouth

¼ cup water

1. Preheat the oven to 375°F. Remove the giblets and neck from the chicken; reserve for another use. Pat dry with paper towels. Sprinkle salt and pepper on the outside of the chicken.

2. With the chicken breast side up, lift the wings up toward neck, then fold the wing tips under the back of the chicken so the wings stay in place. Tie the legs together with string. Place the chicken, breast side up, on a rack in a small roasting pan (13 × 9 inches). Roast the chicken 45 minutes.

3. Meanwhile, prepare the glaze: In a bowl, stir together the brown sugar, vinegar, and vermouth until the sugar dissolves.

4. After the chicken has roasted 45 minutes, brush it with some of the glaze. Turn the oven control to 400°F and continue to roast the chicken, glazing twice more, until the chicken is deep brown, about 30 minutes longer. The chicken is done when the temperature on a meat thermometer inserted into the thickest part of the thigh, next to the body but not touching bone, reaches 165°F and the juices run clear when the thigh is pierced with the tip of a knife.

5. Transfer the chicken to a warm platter; let stand 10 minutes to set the juices for easier carving.

6. Meanwhile, remove the rack from the roasting pan. Skim and discard the fat from the pan drippings. Add the water to the pan; heat to boiling over medium heat, stirring until the browned bits are loosened from the bottom of the pan. Serve the chicken with the pan juices.

Each serving About 445 calories, 48g protein, 7g carbohydrate, 24g fat (7g saturated), 0g fiber, 583mg sodium.

rustic smoky glazed chicken & veggie bake

PREP: 10 MIN / TOTAL: 50 MIN / SERVES 6

2 teaspoons smoked
paprika

2 teaspoons ground
cumin

½ teaspoon ground
black pepper

2 tablespoons plus 2
teaspoons olive oil

Salt

1 pound potatoes,
cut into chunks

½ pound carrots, peeled
and cut into chunks

¼ pound Brussels
sprouts, cut into
chunks

¼ pound onion, peeled
and cut into chunks

¼ pound mushrooms,
trimmed and halved

¼ pound asparagus,
trimmed and cut up

¼ pound whole green
beans

1½ pounds assorted
chicken pieces

Chopped fresh parsley
and fresh lemon
wedges, for garnish

1. Preheat the oven to 450°F. Make a rub by combining the paprika, cumin, and pepper in a small bowl.

2. On a large rimmed baking sheet, toss 2 tablespoons olive oil, one-third of the rub, and ½ teaspoon salt with the potatoes, carrots, Brussels sprouts, and onion. Spread them out in an even layer and roast 10 minutes.

3. On another large rimmed baking sheet, toss the remaining 2 teaspoons olive oil and one-third of the rub with the mushrooms, asparagus, and green beans; push them to one side of the baking sheet. On the other side, arrange the chicken and sprinkle with the remaining rub. Season the entire baking sheet with ½ teaspoon salt. Roast both pans 20 to 35 minutes, or until the chicken is cooked through and all the veggies are softened. The chicken is done when the temperature on a meat thermometer inserted in the thickest part of the thigh, but not touching bone, reaches the correct temperature and the juices run clear when the thigh is pierced with the tip of a knife. Transfer the chicken from the baking sheet to a platter if it's cooked before the veggies are tender.

4. To serve, garnish with chopped parsley and a squeeze of lemon.

Each serving About 270 calories, 18g protein, 23g carbohydrate, 13g fat (3g saturated), 5g fiber, 440mg sodium.

RUSTIC SMOKY GLAZED CH
& VEGGIE BA

apple & thyme roast chicken

PREP: 20 MIN / TOTAL: 1 HR 20 MIN / SERVES 4

1 whole chicken
(3½ pounds)

2 sprigs fresh thyme plus
1 tablespoon chopped
fresh thyme

¾ teaspoon salt

¼ teaspoon coarsely
ground black pepper

⅛ teaspoon ground
allspice

1 jumbo onion, cut into
12 wedges

¼ cup water

2 teaspoons olive oil

2 large Granny Smith
apples, each cored and
cut into quarters

2 tablespoons applejack
brandy or Calvados

½ cup chicken broth

1. Preheat the oven to 450°F. Remove the giblets and neck from the chicken; reserve for another use. Pat chicken dry with paper towels.

2. With your fingertips, gently separate the skin from the meat on the chicken breast. Place 1 thyme sprig under the skin of each breast half. With the breast side up, lift the wings up toward the neck, then fold the wing tips under the back of the chicken so the wings stay in place. Tie the legs together with string.

3. In a cup, combine the chopped thyme, salt, pepper, and allspice.

4. In a medium roasting pan (14 × 10 inches), toss the onion with the thyme mixture, water, and oil. Push the onion mixture to the sides of the pan. Place the chicken, breast side up, on a small rack in the center of the roasting pan.

5. Roast the chicken and onion mixture for 40 minutes. Add the apples to the pan; roast about 20 minutes longer. The chicken is done when the temperature on a meat thermometer inserted in the thickest part of the thigh, next to the body but not touching bone, reaches 165°F and the juices run clear when the thigh is pierced with the tip of a knife. Transfer the chicken to a warm platter; let stand 10 minutes to set the juices for easier carving.

6. Meanwhile, remove the rack from the roasting pan. With a slotted spoon, transfer the onion mixture to the platter with the chicken. Skim and discard the fat from the pan drippings. Add the applejack to the pan drippings; cook 1 minute over medium heat, stirring constantly. Add the broth; heat to boiling. Serve the pan-juice mixture with the chicken; remove the skin from the chicken before eating, if desired.

Each serving (with skin) About 590 calories, 49g protein, 22g carbohydrate, 33g fat (9g saturated), 5g fiber, 708mg sodium.
Each serving (without skin) About 440 calories, 43g protein, 22g carbohydrate, 20g fat (5g saturated), 5g fiber, 686mg sodium.

roast chicken
with 40 cloves of garlic

PREP: 15 MIN / TOTAL: 1 HR 15 MIN / SERVES 4

1 whole chicken
(3½ pounds)

6 sprigs fresh thyme

½ teaspoon salt

¼ teaspoon coarsely
ground black pepper

40 cloves garlic (from
2 heads), loose papery
skin discarded but
unpeeled

1 cup chicken broth

1. Preheat the oven to 450°F. Remove the giblets and neck from the chicken; reserve for another use. Pat the chicken dry with paper towels.

2. With your fingertips, gently separate the skin from the meat on the chicken breast. Place 2 thyme sprigs under the skin of each breast half. Place the remaining 2 sprigs inside the cavity of the chicken. Sprinkle salt and pepper on the outside of the chicken.

3. With the chicken breast side up, lift the wings up toward the neck, then fold the wing tips under the back of the chicken so the wings stay in place. Tie the legs together with string. Place the chicken, breast side up, on a rack in a small roasting pan (13 × 9 inches).

4. Roast the chicken 30 minutes. Add the garlic to the bottom of the pan around the chicken; roast about 30 minutes longer. The chicken is done when the temperature on a meat thermometer inserted in the thickest part of the thigh, next to the body but not touching bone, reaches 165°F and the juices run clear when the thigh is pierced with the tip of a knife.

5. Transfer the chicken to a warm platter; let stand 10 minutes to set the juices for easier carving.

6. Meanwhile, remove the rack from the roasting pan. With a slotted spoon, transfer the garlic cloves to a small bowl. Skim and discard the fat from the pan drippings. Remove and discard the skin from 6 garlic cloves; return the peeled garlic to the roasting pan and add broth. Heat the broth mixture to boiling over medium heat, stirring to loosen the browned bits from the bottom of the pan and mashing the garlic with the back of a spoon until well blended. Serve the chicken with pan juices and the remaining garlic cloves. Remove the skin from the chicken before eating, if desired.

Each serving (with skin) About 500 calories, 50g protein, 11g carbohydrate, 28g fat (8g saturated), 1g fiber, 688mg sodium.
Each serving (without skin) About 355 calories, 44g protein, 10g carbohydrate, 14g fat (4g saturated), 1g fiber, 667mg sodium.

 Tip Slow-roasting mellows garlic to a sweet nuttiness. Serve this dish with lots of crusty bread for spreading the extra garlic cloves.

thyme-roasted chicken & vegetables

PREP: 20 MIN / TOTAL: 1 HR 10 MIN / SERVES 4

1 chicken (3½ pounds), cut into 8 pieces, skin removed from all but the wings

1 pound all-purpose potatoes (3 medium), unpeeled, cut into 2-inch pieces

1 large fennel bulb (1½ pounds), trimmed and cut into 8 wedges

1 large red onion, peeled and cut into 8 wedges

1 tablespoon chopped fresh thyme, or 1 teaspoon dried thyme

1 teaspoon salt

½ teaspoon ground black pepper

2 tablespoons olive oil

⅓ cup water

1. Preheat the oven to 450°F. In a large roasting pan (17 × 11½ inches), arrange the chicken and place the potatoes, fennel, and onion around it. Sprinkle the chicken with the thyme, salt, and pepper. Drizzle the oil over the chicken and vegetables.

2. Roast the chicken and vegetables 20 minutes; baste with drippings in pan. Roast, basting once more, until the juices run clear when the chicken breasts are pierced with the tip of a knife, about 20 minutes longer. Transfer the chicken breasts to a platter; keep warm.

3. Continue roasting the remaining chicken pieces until the juices run clear when the thickest part of the chicken is pierced with the tip of a knife and the vegetables are fork-tender, about 10 minutes longer. Transfer the chicken and vegetables to the platter with the breasts; keep warm.

4. Skim and discard the fat from the pan drippings. To the drippings, add the water; heat to boiling over medium heat, stirring until the brown bits are loosened from the bottom. Spoon the pan juices over the chicken and vegetables.

Each serving About 400 calories, 43g protein, 28g carbohydrate, 13g fat (2g saturated), 7g fiber, 870mg sodium.

HOW TO

CUT UP A RAW CHICKEN

TO REMOVE A LEG

Cut down between the thigh and the body. Bend the leg portion back; twist to crack the hip joint. Cut through the joint. Repeat for the other leg.

TO SEPARATE THE LEG FROM THE THIGH

Place the leg skin side down and cut through the center joint. Repeat with the other leg.

TO REMOVE A WING

Pull the wing away from the body, then cut between the wing joint and the breast. Repeat with the other wing.

TO REMOVE THE BACKBONE

Using kitchen shears, cut through the rib cage along one side of the backbone, from the tail to the neck. Repeat on the other side to remove the backbone in one piece.

TO REMOVE THE BREASTBONE

Place the breast skin side down and cut it in half by placing a heavy knife lengthwise along the center of the breastbone. Press the knife to cut through the bone and meat.

herbed skillet chicken

(See photo on page 234.)

PREP: 20 MIN / TOTAL: 1 HR / SERVES 4

- 1 pound white mushrooms, halved
- 1 small red onion, peeled and cut into 8 wedges
- 2 tablespoons olive oil
- 1 teaspoon fresh thyme leaves
- 4 chicken leg quarters (about 1½ pounds)
- 1 teaspoon salt
- ½ teaspoon coarsely ground black pepper

1. Preheat the oven to 450°F.

2. In a 12-inch cast-iron skillet or another heavy skillet, toss together the mushrooms, onion, olive oil, and thyme. Place the chicken on top; sprinkle with salt and pepper.

3. Roast 35 to 40 minutes. The chicken is done when the temperature on a meat thermometer inserted in the thickest part of the thigh, but not touching bone, reaches 165°F and the juices run clear when the thigh is pierced with the tip of a knife.

Each serving About 625 calories, 66g protein, 6g carbohydrate, 37g fat (9g saturated), 3g fiber, 841mg sodium.

GOOD TO KNOW

CARVING TIPS

- Letting the bird rest after roasting results in firmer, juicer meat that is easier to carve. Poultry should stand at least 10 minutes before carving so the juices can relax back into the meat.

- When carving, use a sharp, thin-bladed knife that is long enough to slice off the breast of large birds like turkey or long-bodied birds such as duck or goose.

maple-glazed chicken

(See photo on page 224.)

PREP: 15 MIN / TOTAL: 30 MIN / SERVES 4

- 3 tablespoons pure maple syrup
- 2 tablespoons miso paste
- 2 tablespoons rice vinegar
- 1 tablespoon sugar
- 2 teaspoons lower-sodium soy sauce
- 1 teaspoon grated, peeled fresh ginger
- ¼ teaspoon ground black pepper
- 8 ounces French green beans (haricots verts) or regular green beans, trimmed
- 10 ounces frozen peas, thawed
- 1¼ pounds boneless, skinless chicken thighs (about 5 thighs)
- ⅛ teaspoon salt
- ¼ cup fresh cilantro leaves, for garnish

1. In a 1-quart saucepan, whisk together the maple syrup, miso, vinegar, sugar, soy sauce, and ginger; heat to boiling over medium-high heat. Boil 1 minute or until reduced by half, whisking constantly. Remove from the heat; stir in the pepper. Cool slightly. Transfer 2 tablespoons to a small bowl and reserve for brushing the chicken.

2. Place the beans and 3 tablespoons water in a 2-quart glass baking dish; cover with vented plastic wrap. Microwave on High 3 minutes or until tender. Stir in the peas. Cover and microwave 3 minutes longer. Drain well; toss with 1 tablespoon of the sauce. Transfer to a platter and keep warm.

3. Heat a grill pan over medium-high heat. Sprinkle the chicken with the salt. Grill the chicken 4 minutes, or until grill marks appear. Brush the chicken with the reserved 2 tablespoons sauce. Turn chicken over; grill 4 to 5 minutes longer, or until it is cooked through (165°F). Place the chicken on top of the vegetables. Garnish with cilantro and serve with the remaining sauce.

Each serving About 350 calories, 31g protein, 30g carbohydrate, 11g fat (3g saturated), 5g fiber, 635mg sodium.

rosemary-lemon roast chicken

(See photo on page 224.)

PREP: 10 MIN / TOTAL: 40 MIN / SERVES 4

- 1 pound carrots, peeled and cut into 2-inch lengths
- 1 pound fennel bulbs, trimmed and thinly sliced
- 2 tablespoons olive oil
- Salt
- 8 small chicken drumsticks and thighs, patted dry (about 2½ pounds)
- 2 lemons
- 2 tablespoons loosely packed fresh rosemary leaves
- ½ teaspoon ground black pepper

1. Preheat the oven to 475°F.

2. In a large roasting pan (17 × 11½ inches) or rimmed baking sheet, toss together the carrots, fennel, olive oil, and ¼ teaspoon salt; spread them in a single layer. Arrange the chicken pieces on top of the vegetables.

3. Grate the lemon peel all over the chicken. Sprinkle the rosemary, pepper, and ½ teaspoon salt over the chicken. Thinly slice the lemons and place them on top.

4. Roast 30 minutes, or until the vegetables are tender and the chicken is cooked through (165°F). The chicken is done when the temperature on a meat thermometer inserted in the thickest part of the thigh, but not touching bone, reaches the correct temperature and the juices run clear when the thigh is pierced with the tip of a knife.

Each serving (without skin) About 455 calories, 53g protein, 19g carbohydrate, 18g fat (4g saturated), 6g fiber, 805mg sodium.
Each serving (with skin) About 700 calories, 53g protein, 19g carbohydrate, 51g fat (13g saturated), 6g fiber, 805mg sodium.

honey mustard–glazed chicken bake

(See photo on page 234.)

PREP: 25 MIN / TOTAL: 1 HR / SERVES 4

- 1 pound parsnips, peeled and sliced on an angle
- 1 pound Yukon Gold potatoes, scrubbed and quartered
- ½ pound carrots, peeled, quartered lengthwise, and cut into 2-inch pieces
- 1 medium red onion, peeled and cut into 8 wedges
- 2 tablespoons olive oil
- 5 sprigs fresh thyme
- Salt
- 4 small chicken thighs (about 1½ pounds)
- 4 small chicken drumsticks (about 1 pound)
- ¼ teaspoon ground black pepper
- 3 tablespoons Dijon mustard
- 2 tablespoons whole-grain mustard
- 2 tablespoons honey
- 1 tablespoon brown sugar

1. Preheat the oven to 425°F. In large roasting pan, toss together the parsnips, potatoes, carrots, onion, oil, thyme, and ½ teaspoon salt. Roast for 15 minutes.

2. Place the chicken pieces in a single layer over the vegetables. Sprinkle with ½ teaspoon salt and the pepper. Roast 15 minutes or until cooked through (165°F).

3. In a medium bowl, whisk together the Dijon mustard, whole-grain mustard, honey, and brown sugar. Drizzle it over the chicken and vegetables. Roast 25 minutes, or until the chicken is cooked through (165°F) and the vegetables are tender.

Each serving About 760 calories, 42g protein, 60g carbohydrate, 38g fat (9g saturated), 8g fiber, 1,105mg sodium.

Tip The vegetables can be prepared, covered, and refrigerated up to 1 day before roasting. To prevent the cut potatoes from discoloring, place them in a bowl with enough cold water to cover plus the juice of ½ lemon; drain and pat dry before roasting. The glaze also can be made, covered, and refrigerated up to 1 day ahead.

GARLIC-HERB CORNISH HENS 235

HERBED SKILLET CHICKEN 232

CHICKEN CHILAQUILES 235

HONEY MUSTARD–GLAZED CHICKEN BAKE 233

chicken chilaquiles

PREP: 10 MIN / TOTAL: 20 MIN / SERVES 4

1 can (28 ounces) fire-roasted tomatoes

2 green onions, sliced

1 teaspoon ground cumin

¼ teaspoon salt

2 tablespoons oil

2 cups shredded cooked chicken

6 ounces tortilla chips (4 cups)

½ cup sour cream

1 tablespoon fresh lime juice

Sliced radishes, cilantro, and lime wedges, for serving

1. In a blender or food processor, puree the tomatoes, green onions, cumin, and salt until smooth.

2. In a 12-inch skillet, heat the oil over medium heat; add the tomato mixture. Partially cover and cook 8 minutes, or until slightly thickened. Stir in the shredded chicken and tortilla chips. Cook 2 minutes, uncovered.

3. In a small bowl, mix the sour cream and lime juice. Serve the chilaquiles with lime-sour cream, sliced radishes, cilantro, and lime wedges.

Each serving About 500 calories, 27g protein, 40g carbohydrate, 26g fat (6g saturated), 4g fiber, 805mg sodium.

 Tip Use extra-thick tortilla chips (we like Late July® and Garden of Eatin'®), which will stay crisp after cooking.

GLOSSARY → **Chilaquiles** is a traditional Mexican dish of fried tortillas simmered in salsa or mole and then topped with sour cream.

garlic-herb cornish hens

PREP: 40 MIN / TOTAL: 1 HR 5 MIN, PLUS MARINATING / SERVES 8

12 cloves garlic, peeled

¾ cup packed fresh mint leaves

¾ cup packed fresh basil leaves

½ cup red wine vinegar

⅓ cup soy sauce

¼ cup packed fresh tarragon leaves

2 serrano chiles, stemmed and seeded

3 tablespoons sugar

1 tablespoon ground cumin

½ cup plus 3 tablespoons olive oil

Salt

4 large Cornish hens (about 1½ pounds each)

3 pounds baby new potatoes, cut into halves

Herb Sauce (below)

1. In a food processor or blender, puree the garlic, mint, basil, vinegar, soy sauce, tarragon, chiles, sugar, cumin, ½ cup oil, and 1½ teaspoons salt until smooth to create the marinade. Place the hens in 2 gallon-size resealable plastic bags and add half the marinade to each. Seal the bags and turn them over a few times to distribute the marinade. Refrigerate at least overnight or up to 24 hours.

2. Preheat the oven to 425°F. On a large rimmed baking sheet, arrange the hens, breast side up; discard the marinade. Tuck the wings behind the hens; tie the legs together with twine. Roast 45 minutes, or until the hens reach 165°F. The hens are done when the temperature on a meat thermometer inserted in the thickest part of the thigh,next to the body but not touching bone, reaches the correct temperature and the juices run clear when the thigh is pierced with the tip of a knife. Let stand 10 minutes.

3. Meanwhile, on another large rimmed baking sheet, toss the potatoes with the remaining 3 tablespoons oil and ¾ teaspoon salt. Roast 45 minutes, or until tender and browned, stirring once.

4. Using kitchen shears, cut each hen in half. Serve with potatoes and Herb Sauce.

HERB SAUCE In a food processor, puree **1 cup sour cream; 6 tablespoons fresh -lime juice; ¼ cup extra-virgin olive oil; ½ cup fresh mint; ½ cup fresh basil; 2 tablespoons fresh tarragon; 2 cloves peeled garlic; 1 serrano chile**, stemmed and seeded; and **1 teaspoon salt** until smooth. Makes 2 cups.

Each serving (with ¼ cup sauce) About 755 calories, 41g protein, 35g carbohydrate, 49g fat (13g saturated), 3g fiber, 530mg sodium.

crispy sesame-panko chicken

PREP: 20 MIN / TOTAL: 30 MIN / SERVES 4

Nonstick cooking spray

1 large egg

½ teaspoon garlic powder

2 teaspoons dry mustard powder

1¾ teaspoons ground ginger

Ground black pepper

1 cup panko (Japanese-style bread crumbs)

3 tablespoons sesame seeds

1¼ pounds thin chicken cutlets (about 5 cutlets)

1 pound shredded cabbage

1 green onion, thinly sliced

1 teaspoon sugar

2 tablespoons plus 2 teaspoons cider vinegar

1 tablespoon plus ½ teaspoon lower-sodium soy sauce

¼ teaspoon salt

¾ cup ketchup

1 teaspoon Worcestershire sauce

⅛ teaspoon cayenne pepper

1. Preheat the oven to 450°F. Place a rack in a foil-lined 18 × 12-inch jelly-roll pan. Spray with cooking spray.

2. In a shallow dish, whisk the egg, garlic powder, 1 teaspoon dry mustard, 1 teaspoon ground ginger, and ¼ teaspoon pepper. In another dish, combine the panko and sesame seeds.

3. Dip the chicken into the egg mixture and then into the panko mix. Place on the rack. Spray the chicken with cooking spray; bake 15 to 20 minutes, or until cooked through (165°F).

4. Meanwhile, toss the cabbage with the green onion, sugar, 2 table-spoons vinegar, ½ teaspoon soy sauce, ¼ teaspoon pepper, and the salt.

5. In a bowl, mix the ketchup, Worcestershire, cayenne, 1 table-spoon soy sauce, 2 teaspoons vinegar, 1 teaspoon dry mustard, and ¾ teaspoon ground ginger. Serve the chicken with the sauce and slaw.

Each serving About 435 calories, 38g protein, 42g carbohydrate, 12g fat (1g saturated), 3g fiber, 1,070mg sodium.

pecorino chicken fingers

PREP: 20 MIN / TOTAL: 30 MIN / SERVES 4

Nonstick cooking spray

1 cup panko (Japanese-style bread crumbs)

⅓ cup freshly grated Pecorino-Romano cheese

¼ teaspoon cayenne pepper

Salt

2 large egg whites

1 clove garlic, crushed with a press

1½ pounds chicken tenders

3 medium zucchini (8 ounces), cut into ¼-inch-thick half-moons

1 tablespoon fresh lemon juice

1 cup Marinara Sauce (page 336) or prepared marinara sauce

¼ cup loosely packed fresh basil leaves, chopped, plus small whole basil leaves for garnish

1. Preheat the oven to 475°F. Place a rack in 15½ × 10½-inch jelly-roll pan; spray the pan and rack with cooking spray.

2. On a plate, combine the panko, Pecorino-Romano, cayenne, and ¼ teaspoon salt. Set aside. In a pie plate, whisk the egg whites and garlic until well mixed.

3. One at a time, dip the chicken tenders in the egg white mixture, then into the panko mixture to coat evenly; press firmly so the crumbs adhere. Arrange the chicken on the rack in the jelly-roll pan; spray the chicken lightly with cooking spray.

4. Bake the chicken 10 to 12 minutes, or until the crust is golden brown and the chicken is no longer pink throughout.

5. While the chicken cooks, in a medium microwave-safe bowl, place the zucchini and 2 tablespoons water. Cover with vented plastic wrap and cook in the microwave on High for 5 minutes, or until the zucchini is just fork-tender. Carefully remove the plastic wrap and drain the zucchini; stir in the lemon juice and ¼ teaspoon salt.

6. Meanwhile, in 1-quart saucepan, heat the marinara sauce over medium-low heat for 5 minutes, or until hot, stirring occasionally. Remove the saucepan from the heat and stir in the chopped basil. Garnish both the chicken and dipping sauce with whole basil leaves. Serve the chicken fingers with the dipping sauce and zucchini.

Each serving About 325 calories, 47g protein, 18g carbohydrate, 6g fat (2g saturated), 2g fiber, 790mg sodium.

Ingredient Ideas
wings

Pierce **2½ pounds split chicken wings** all over with the tip of a knife; pat dry. Place them on a wire rack fitted into a foil-lined 18 × 12-inch rimmed baking sheet. Sprinkle with **⅛ teaspoon salt**. Bake in a preheated 425°F oven for 35 minutes, or until cooked through (165°F), turning once. Broil 7 minutes on High, turning once. Toss with **sauce** of choice below. Makes about 25 wings.

FIERY BUFFALO

In a 1-quart saucepan, melt **2 tablespoons butter** over medium heat. Whisk in **½ cup cayenne hot pepper sauce** and **2 tablespoons distilled white vinegar**. Transfer to a bowl; toss with **cooked wings** and **¼ cup blue cheese dip**.

SESAME TERIYAKI

In a large bowl, whisk together **3 tablespoons teriyaki sauce**, **2 tablespoons rice vinegar**, **1 tablespoon dark brown sugar**, and **2 teaspoons toasted sesame oil**; toss with **cooked wings** and **2 tablespoons sesame seeds**.

BOURBON BBQ

In a 2-quart saucepan, combine **¾ cup barbecue sauce**, **¼ cup bourbon**, and **1 tablespoon yellow mustard**. Heat to simmering over medium-high heat; simmer 3 minutes, stirring. Toss with **cooked wings**.

BALLPARK

In a bowl, whisk **¼ cup Dijon mustard**, **2 tablespoons cider vinegar**, **2 tablespoons honey**, and **⅛ teaspoon cayenne pepper**; toss with **cooked wings** and **¼ cup chopped roasted, salted peanuts**.

HOT CARIBBEAN

In a 2-quart saucepan, mix **1 cup mango nectar**, **2 teaspoons habanero hot sauce**, a **pinch of ground allspice**, and **⅛ teaspoon each salt and ground black pepper**. Cook over medium-high heat for 8 minutes to reduce the mixture by half. Stir in **2 teaspoons fresh lime juice**; toss with **cooked wings** and **¼ cup chopped fresh cilantro**.

SWEET 'N' STICKY THAI

In a bowl, stir together **½ cup Thai sweet chili sauce**, the **grated peel from 1 lime**, and **1 teaspoon fish sauce**; toss with the **cooked wings** and **⅓ cup french-fried onions**.

pancetta chicken

(See photo on page 240.)

PREP: 5 MIN / TOTAL: 45 MIN / SERVES 4

1½ pounds small skinless, boneless chicken breast halves

Salt

½ pound sliced pancetta (8 to 10 slices)

Ground black pepper

1 pound green beans

2 teaspoons olive oil

Lemon wedges, for serving

1. Preheat the oven to 450°F. Line a large rimmed baking sheet with foil.

2. Sprinkle the chicken with ½ teaspoon salt; drape 2 slices pancetta over each piece, tucking the ends under. Sprinkle with pepper. Place on the prepared baking sheet.

3. On another baking sheet, toss the green beans with the olive oil; season to taste with salt and pepper. Place sheets in the oven for 30 minutes, or until the chicken is cooked through (165°F). Serve with lemon wedges.

Each serving About 265 calories, 38g protein, 10g carbohydrate, 8g fat (2g saturated), 4g fiber, 520mg sodium.

chicken potpie

(See photo on page 240.)

PREP: 15 MIN / TOTAL: 45 MIN / SERVES 4

1 sheet frozen puff pastry, thawed

1 tablespoon vegetable oil

1 large onion, chopped

1 pound Yukon Gold potatoes, chopped in ½-inch pieces

1 cup chicken broth

½ teaspoon salt

1 tablespoon cornstarch

½ cup half-and-half

2 cups shredded cooked chicken

¾ cup frozen corn

¾ cup frozen peas

¼ cup cooked bacon, for serving

1. Cut four 4-inch circles from the puff pastry; arrange them on a parchment-lined baking sheet. Bake at 400°F for 15 minutes.

2. In a large skillet, heat the oil over medium heat; add the onion and cook 5 minutes. Add the potatoes, chicken broth, and salt. Cover and cook 10 minutes. Stir the cornstarch into the half-and-half, and add to the skillet along with the chicken, corn, and peas. Simmer 3 minutes. Serve topped with pastry and cooked bacon.

Each serving About 510 calories, 24g protein, 49g carbohydrate, 28g fat (8g saturated), 4g fiber, 715mg sodium.

roman chicken sauté

with artichokes

PREP: 15 MIN / TOTAL: 30 MIN / SERVES 6

1¼ pounds chicken breast tenders, each cut crosswise in half, then cut lengthwise in half (about 4 chicken breasts)

¼ teaspoon salt

¼ teaspoon ground black pepper

3 teaspoons olive oil

2 cloves garlic, thinly sliced

1 can (13¾ to 14 ounces) artichoke hearts, drained and cut into quarters

½ cup dry white wine

½ cup chicken broth

1 pint grape tomatoes

1 teaspoon grated fresh lemon peel, plus additional for garnish

1 bag (5 to 6 ounces) baby arugula

1. Sprinkle the chicken with the salt and pepper to season all sides.

2. In a 12-inch skillet, heat 2 teaspoons oil over medium-high heat until very hot. Add the chicken and cook 8 minutes, or until browned on the outside and no longer pink inside, stirring occasionally. With a slotted spoon, transfer the chicken to a bowl.

3. To the same skillet, add the remaining 1 teaspoon oil. Reduce the heat to medium and add the garlic; cook 30 seconds, or until golden. Stir in the artichokes and cook 3 to 4 minutes, or until browned. Stir in the wine, increase the heat to medium-high, and cook 1 minute.

4. Add the chicken broth and tomatoes to the skillet; cover and cook 2 to 3 minutes, or until most tomatoes have burst. Remove the skillet from the heat. Return the chicken to the skillet, and stir in the lemon peel until combined.

5. Arrange the arugula on a platter; top with the sautéed chicken mixture. Garnish chicken with additional lemon peel and serve.

Each serving About 165 calories, 25g protein, 7g carbohydrate, 4g fat (1g saturated), 1g fiber, 330mg sodium.

picnic chicken

with three sauces

PREP: 30 MIN / TOTAL: 1 HR / SERVES 12

Olive oil nonstick cooking spray

1¾ cups walnuts (about 8 ounces)

1 cup plain dried bread crumbs

1½ teaspoons salt

¼ to ½ teaspoon cayenne pepper

2 large eggs

8 medium bone-in chicken breast halves (4 pounds), skin removed

8 medium chicken drumsticks (1¾ pounds), skin removed

Your choice of sauce (see below)

1. Preheat the oven to 425°F. Grease two 15½ × 10½-inch jelly-roll pans with cooking spray.

2. In a food processor with the knife blade attached, process the walnuts with ¼ cup bread crumbs until the walnuts are finely ground. In a medium bowl, combine the nut mixture, the salt, cayenne, and the remaining ¾ cup bread crumbs; stir until well mixed. In a pie plate, beat the eggs.

3. Cut each chicken breast half crosswise into 2 pieces. One at a time, dip the breast pieces and drumsticks in the beaten egg, then into the walnut mixture to coat evenly, pressing firmly so the mixture adheres. Arrange the chicken in the jelly-roll pans; lightly coat the chicken with cooking spray.

4. Bake the chicken 30 to 35 minutes, or until it is golden brown and the juices run clear when the thickest part of the chicken is pierced with the tip of a knife, rotating the pans between the upper and lower oven racks halfway through baking.

5. Meanwhile, prepare the sauce of your choice (below and right). Cover and refrigerate sauce if not serving right away.

6. Serve the chicken hot with a dipping sauce, or cool the chicken slightly, cover, and refrigerate to serve cold later with the sauce.

BLUE-CHEESE SAUCE In a medium bowl, combine **4 ounces blue cheese**, crumbled (1 cup); **½ cup mayonnaise**; **½ cup plain low-fat yogurt**; **½ teaspoon hot sauce**; and **¼ teaspoon coarsely ground black pepper** until blended. Makes about 1½ cups sauce.

CREAMY HONEY-MUSTARD SAUCE In a medium bowl, combine **⅔ cup Dijon mustard**, **¼ cup sour cream**, **¼ cup honey**, and **¾ teaspoon Worcestershire sauce** until well blended. Makes about 1¼ cups sauce.

APRICOT-BALSAMIC SAUCE In a medium bowl, combine **1 jar (12 ounces)** apricot preserves, **2 tablespoons** balsamic vinegar, **1 tablespoon** soy sauce, and **¼ teaspoon** freshly grated orange peel until well blended. *Makes about 1¼ cups sauce.*

PICNIC CHICKEN Each serving (without sauce) About 310 calories, 32g protein, 10g carbohydrate, 16g fat (2g saturated), 2g fiber, 468mg sodium.

BLUE-CHEESE SAUCE Each tablespoon About 55 calories, 1g protein, 1g carbohydrate, 5g fat (1g saturated), 0g fiber, 98mg sodium.

CREAMY HONEY-MUSTARD SAUCE Each tablespoon About 30 calories, 0g protein, 4g carbohydrate, 1g fat (0g saturated), 0g fiber, 197mg sodium.

APRICOT-BALSAMIC SAUCE Each tablespoon About 40 calories, 0g protein, 11g carbohydrate, 0g fat (0g saturated), 0g fiber, 58mg sodium.

sweet & sticky chicken

with snow peas

(See photo on page 224.)

PREP: 5 MIN / TOTAL: 50 MIN / ERVES 4

- **2½ pounds chicken drumsticks and thighs**
- **¼ cup hoisin sauce**
- **½ teaspoon ground black pepper**
- **Salt**
- **1 pound snow peas**
- **½ teaspoon crushed red pepper**
- **2 teaspoon toasted sesame oil**
- **Chopped cilantro, for garnish**

1. Preheat the oven to 450°F. Line a large rimmed baking sheet with foil.

2. In a large bowl, toss the chicken with the hoisin sauce, pepper, and ½ teaspoon salt. Arrange the chicken on the foil-lined baking sheet. Roast 30 minutes, or until cooked through (165°F).

3. While the chicken roasts, boil the snow peas for 5 minutes, or until tender; drain and toss with the crushed red pepper, sesame oil, and a pinch of salt. Serve chicken over snow peas, garnished with chopped cilantro.

Each serving About 370 calories, 38g protein, 16g carbohydrate, 16g fat (4g saturated), 4g fiber, 680mg sodium.

salsa verde enchiladas

PREP: 50 MIN / TOTAL: 1 HR 10 MIN / SERVES 8

- **2 cooked rotisserie chickens**
- **2 jars (16 to 17.6 ounces each) mild salsa verde**
- **6 green onions, thinly sliced**
- **¼ cup fresh lime juice (from 2 to 3 limes)**
- **½ cup loosely packed fresh cilantro leaves, chopped**
- **16 (6-inch) corn tortillas**
- **1 container (8 ounces) reduced-fat sour cream**
- **½ cup reduced-sodium chicken broth**
- **1 package (8 ounces) reduced-fat (2%) shredded Mexican cheese blend (2 cups)**

1. Remove the meat from the chickens and coarsely shred it; place it in a medium bowl (you will need 5½ cups; reserve any extra for another use). Discard the skin and bones. Stir ½ cup salsa verde into the chicken to evenly coat it.

2. Preheat the oven to 350°F. Grease two 13 × 9-inch glass or ceramic baking dishes; set aside.

3. In a 12-inch skillet, heat the remaining salsa verde, the green onions, and lime juice to boiling over medium-high heat. Boil 2 minutes, stirring occasionally. Stir in 2 tablespoons cilantro; keep warm over very low heat.

4. With tongs, dip 1 tortilla in the salsa verde mixture; heat 10 seconds. Place the tortilla on waxed paper; top with about ⅓ cup of the shredded-chicken mixture. Roll up the tortilla and place it, seam side down, in a prepared baking dish. Repeat with the remaining tortillas and chicken mixture, arranging 8 tortillas side by side in each dish.

5. Stir the sour cream and broth into the remaining salsa verde mixture in the skillet; spoon it evenly over the filled tortillas. Cover one baking dish with foil and bake 15 minutes. Remove the foil; sprinkle with 1 cup cheese and 1 tablespoon cilantro. Bake 5 minutes longer or until cheese melts. Meanwhile, sprinkle remaining cheese and cilantro over second casserole and prepare for freezing (up to 3 months). Makes 2 casseroles with 4 servings each.

Each serving About 465 calories, 39g protein, 36g carbohydrate, 18g fat (7g saturated), 3g fiber, 785mg sodium.

PANCETTA CHICKEN 237

CHICKEN POTPIE 237

CHICKEN CAPRESE 241

CILANTRO-LIME CHICKEN
WITH SPICE-ROASTED CARROTS 241

chicken caprese

PREP: 10 MIN / TOTAL: 20 MIN / SERVES 4

3 tablespoons oil

¼ cup all-purpose flour

4 chicken breast cutlets (about 1¼ pounds)

1¼ pounds grape tomatoes, halved

3 cloves garlic, sliced

½ teaspoon salt

8 ounces fresh mozzarella balls, halved

Fresh basil, for serving

Roasted broccolini, for serving

1. In a 12-inch skillet, heat the oil over medium-high heat until very hot. Lightly flour the chicken and add it to the skillet; cook for 6 minutes, or until cooked through, turning once. Transfer the cutlets to a plate.

2. To the same skillet, add the tomatoes, garlic, and salt. Cook 3 minutes, stirring and scraping. Top the chicken with the tomato mixture, mozzarella, and fresh basil. Serve with roasted broccolini.

Each serving About 475 calories, 45g protein, 12g carbohydrate, 28g fat (10g saturated), 4g fiber, 570mg sodium.

HOW TO

SEAR & DEGLAZE

- **PAT YOUR PROTEIN DRY** with a paper towel. Liquid interferes with searing.

- **SEASON IT RIGHT.** Sprinkle your meat on both sides with ¼ teaspoon each salt and pepper.

- **HEAT OIL UNTIL NICE AND HOT** over medium-high heat. It should ripple slightly before you add the meat. Once the meat is in the pan, don't move it until it releases easily.

- **CHOOSE THE RIGHT TOOL.** After adding liquid like wine or stock/broth to the pan to deglaze, use a wooden spoon to scrape up all the tasty browned bits.

cilantro-lime chicken

with spice-roasted carrots

PREP: 35 MIN / TOTAL: 1 HR 20 MIN, PLUS MARINATING / SERVES 6

1 cup packed fresh cilantro leaves

1 cup packed fresh mint leaves

¼ cup packed fresh tarragon leaves

½ cup olive oil

⅓ cup soy sauce

¼ cup fresh lime juice

3 tablespoons cider vinegar

5 cloves garlic

1 jalapeño chile, sliced

2 tablespoons chopped, peeled fresh ginger

1 teaspoon dried oregano

1 teaspoon ground cumin

1 teaspoon salt

12 assorted chicken pieces (about 3 pounds)

⅓ cup mayonnaise

Spice-Roasted Carrots (below)

1. In a food processor, puree the fresh herbs with the oil, soy sauce, lime juice, vinegar, garlic, jalapeño, ginger, oregano, cumin, and salt until smooth. Transfer ¾ cup of the marinade to a small bowl; set aside. Transfer the remaining marinade to a gallon-size resealable plastic bag; add the chicken. Seal the bag, tossing to coat, and refrigerate at least 5 hours or up to overnight.

2. Preheat the oven to 375°F. Place a wire rack on a foil-lined rimmed baking sheet. Arrange the chicken on the rack, discarding the marinade in the bag; bake 30 minutes. Increase the oven temperature to 450°F and roast until chicken is cooked (165°F), another 15 to 20 minutes. The chicken is done when the temperature on a meat thermometer inserted in the thickest part of the thigh, but not touching bone, reaches the correct temperature and the juices run clear when pierced with the tip of a knife.

3. Whisk the mayonnaise into the reserved marinade. Serve the chicken with the reserved marinade and Spice-Roasted Carrots.

SPICED-ROASTED CARROTS Quarter 1½ **pounds medium carrots** and toss with **2 tablespoons oil, 1 teaspoon ground cumin, ½ teaspoon smoked paprika,** and ½ **teaspoon each salt and pepper.** Roast on rimmed baking sheet in 450°F oven 30 minutes or until tender, stirring twice.

CILANTRO-LIME CHICKEN Each serving (with sauce)
About 500 calories, 32g protein, 4g carbohydrate, 39g fat (8g saturated), 1g fiber, 1,140mg sodium.
SPICE-ROASTED CARROTS About 85 calories, 2g protein, 11g carbohydrate, 5g fat (0g saturated), 3g fiber, 282mg sodium.

chicken breasts
with quick sauces

PREP: 5 MIN / TOTAL: 15 MIN, PLUS MAKING SAUCE / SERVES 4

1 teaspoon vegetable oil

4 small skinless, boneless chicken breast halves (1 pound)

Your choice of sauce (below)

1. In a 12-inch nonstick skillet, heat the oil over medium heat until very hot. Add the chicken and cook until it is golden brown and loses its pink color throughout, 4 to 5 minutes per side. Transfer the chicken to a platter; keep warm.

2. Prepare a sauce (below) and spoon it over the chicken.

APPLE-CURRY SAUCE After removing the chicken from the skillet, add **2 teaspoons vegetable oil** to the skillet over medium heat. Add **1 Golden Delicious apple**, peeled, cored, and chopped; and **1 small onion**, chopped. Cook, stirring, until tender. Stir in **1½ teaspoons curry powder** and ¼ **teaspoon salt**; cook, stirring, for 1 minute. Stir in ½ **cup mango chutney**, ½ **cup frozen peas**, and ½ **cup water**. Heat to boiling; boil 1 minute. Spoon over chicken.

BLACK BEAN SALSA After removing the chicken from the skillet, add **1 can (15 to 19 ounces) black beans**, rinsed and drained; **1 jar (10 ounces) thick-and-chunky salsa**; **1 can (8 ¾ ounces) whole-kernel corn**, drained; **2 tablespoons chopped fresh cilantro**; and ¼ **cup water** to the skillet. Cook over medium heat, stirring, until heated through, about 1 minute. Spoon over chicken.

CHINESE GINGER SAUCE After removing the chicken from the skillet, heat **1 teaspoon vegetable oil** over medium heat. Add **1 red bell pepper**, thinly sliced, and cook until tender-crisp. Add ½ **cup water**, **2 tablespoons soy sauce**, **2 tablespoons seasoned rice vinegar**, and **1 tablespoon grated, peeled fresh ginger**. Raise heat to high and bring to boil; boil 1 minute. Sprinkle with **2 chopped green onions**. Spoon over chicken.

PROVENÇAL SAUCE After removing the chicken from the skillet, add **1 teaspoon olive or vegetable oil** to the skillet. Add **1 medium onion**, chopped, and cook, stirring, until tender. Stir in **1 can (14½ ounces) Italian-style stewed tomatoes**; ½ **cup pitted ripe olives**, each cut in half; **1 tablespoon drained capers**; and ¼ **cup water**. Cook over medium heat, stirring, until heated through, about 1 minute. Spoon over chicken.

CREAMY MUSHROOM SAUCE After removing the chicken from the skillet, add **1 teaspoon vegetable oil** to the skillet. Add **10 ounces mushrooms**, trimmed and sliced; **1 medium onion**, thinly sliced; and ¾ **teaspoon salt**. Cook over medium heat, stirring, until vegetables are golden brown and tender. Reduce the heat to low; stir in ½ **cup light sour cream** and ¼ **cup water**; heat through—do not boil. Spoon over chicken.

DIJON SAUCE After removing the chicken from the skillet, reduce the heat to low. Add ½ **cup half-and-half or light cream**, **2 tablespoons Dijon mustard with seeds**, and ¾ **cup seedless red or green grapes**, each cut in half, to the skillet. Cook, stirring to blend flavors, until the sauce has thickened, about 1 minute. Spoon over chicken.

CUCUMBER RAITA Peel, seed, and coarsely shred **1 medium cucumber**. Squeeze out as much liquid as possible. In a small bowl, combine the shredded cucumber with **1 cup (8 ounces) plain yogurt**. Season with **salt and pepper**. Add **1 tablespoon of chopped fresh mint**, if you like.

APPLE-CURRY SAUCE Each serving (with chicken) About 350 calories, 34g protein, 38g carbohydrate, 5g fat (1g saturated), 3g fiber, 596mg sodium.

BLACK BEAN SALSA Each serving (with chicken) About 280 calories, 38g protein, 22g carbohydrate, 4g fat (1g saturated), 9g fiber, 1,086mg sodium.

CHINESE GINGER SAUCE Each serving (with chicken) About 195 calories, 34g protein, 4g carbohydrate, 4g fat (1g saturated), 1g fiber, 757mg sodium.

PROVENÇAL SAUCE Each serving (with chicken) About 255 calories, 35g protein, 11g carbohydrate, 7g fat (1g saturated), 2g fiber, 785mg sodium.

CREAMY MUSHROOM SAUCE Each serving (with chicken) About 260 calories, 37g protein, 9g carbohydrate, 8g fat (3g saturated), 1g fiber, 548mg sodium.

DIJON SAUCE Each serving (with chicken) About 235 calories, 34g protein, 7g carbohydrate, 7g fat (3g saturated), 1g fiber, 285mg sodium.

CUCUMBER RAITA Each serving (with chicken) About 175 calories, 25g protein, 4g carbohydrate, 6g fat (2g saturated), 0g fiber, 157mg sodium.

coq au vin

PREP: 45 MIN / TOTAL: 1 HR 30 MIN / SERVES 6

- 4 slices bacon, cut into ¾-inch pieces
- 4 tablespoons butter
- 1 chicken (3½ pounds), cut into 8 pieces, skin removed (except from the wings)
- ¼ teaspoon salt
- ⅛ teaspoon ground black pepper
- 1 small onion, finely chopped
- 1 carrot, peeled and finely chopped
- 18 pearl onions (generous 1 cup), peeled
- 10 ounces mushrooms, trimmed
- ⅓ cup all-purpose flour
- 2 cups dry red wine
- 1⅓ cups chicken broth
- 2 tablespoons tomato paste
- 1 stalk celery
- 12 sprigs fresh parsley plus 3 tablespoons chopped parsley
- 2 bay leaves

1. Preheat the oven to 325°F.

2. In a 5-quart Dutch oven, cook the bacon over medium-high heat until crisp. With a slotted spoon, transfer it to paper towels to drain. Reduce the heat to medium and add the butter to the drippings. Sprinkle the chicken with salt and pepper. Add the chicken to the Dutch oven, in batches if necessary, and cook until golden brown, about 5 minutes per side, using tongs to transfer chicken pieces to a bowl as they are browned.

3. Add the chopped onion and carrot to the Dutch oven and cook until lightly browned, about 5 minutes. With a slotted spoon, transfer the onion and carrots to the bowl with the chicken. Add the pearl onions to the Dutch oven and cook, stirring, until browned, about 6 minutes; transfer to the bowl. Add the mushrooms to the Dutch oven and cook, stirring, until browned, about 6 minutes; transfer to the bowl.

4. Add the flour to the Dutch oven and cook, stirring, 2 minutes. With a wire whisk, whisk in ½ cup wine until smooth. Add the remaining 1½ cups wine, the broth, and the tomato paste. Heat to boiling, whisking constantly; boil 2 minutes. Return chicken, vegetables, and three-fourths of the bacon to the Dutch oven.

5. With string, tie together the celery, parsley sprigs, and bay leaves; add them to the Dutch oven. Cover and place the pot in the oven. Bake, stirring occasionally, 45 minutes.

6. When the chicken is tender and the sauce is slightly thickened, skim the fat from the top and discard the celery bundle. Sprinkle the coq au vin with the remaining bacon and chopped parsley.

Each serving About 415 calories, 32g protein, 17g carbohydrate, 24g fat (10g saturated), 2g fiber, 645mg sodium.

coq au riesling

PREP: 30 MIN / TOTAL: 1 HR / SERVES 4

- 1 cut-up chicken (3½ pounds), skin removed (except from the wings), breasts halved crosswise
- Salt
- Ground black pepper
- 3 slices thick-cut bacon, cut crosswise into 1-inch pieces
- 4 medium leeks, light-green and white parts only
- 2 cups baby carrots
- 4 large cloves garlic, chopped
- 1 tablespoon tomato paste
- 2 cups slightly dry Riesling wine
- 2 sprigs fresh rosemary
- 1 teaspoon chopped fresh thyme
- 2 tablespoons chopped flat-leaf parsley leaves

1. Sprinkle the chicken with salt and pepper.

2. In a 6-quart Dutch oven, cook the bacon over medium heat for 6 minutes, or until crisp, stirring frequently. With a slotted spoon, transfer the bacon to a paper-towel-lined plate. Pour off and reserve the drippings.

3. Return 1 tablespoon drippings to pot; heat over medium-high heat. Add half of chicken; cook 7 to 10 minutes, turning once, to brown. Remove chicken to plate. Repeat with 2 teaspoons drippings and the remaining chicken.

4. While the chicken cooks, cut each leek lengthwise in half and then crosswise into ½-inch-wide slices. Rinse the leeks thoroughly to remove any sand, repeating as necessary. Drain well.

5. To the drippings remaining in the Dutch oven, add the leeks and carrots. Cover and cook over medium heat 3 minutes, or until the leeks begin to soften, stirring once. Add the garlic and tomato paste; cook 1 minute, stirring. Add the wine, rosemary, thyme, ¼ teaspoon salt, and ⅛ teaspoon pepper. Heat to boiling over high heat. Add the chicken with their juices, placing the breast pieces on top, bone side down. Reduce the heat to low; cover and simmer 35 to 40 minutes, or until the chicken is cooked through (165°F), stirring once. Discard the rosemary sprigs. Sprinkle with bacon and parsley.

Each serving About 425 calories, 47g protein, 23g carbohydrate, 15g fat (5g saturated), 3g fiber, 725mg sodium.

chicken curry

PREP: 15 MIN / TOTAL: 1 HR 30 MIN, PLUS COOLING / SERVES 6

- 1 chicken (3½ pounds), cut into 8 pieces
- 4 medium onions, finely chopped
- 2 carrots, peeled and finely chopped
- 2 stalks celery with leaves, finely chopped
- 8 sprigs fresh parsley
- 1 lime
- 4 tablespoons butter
- 2 Granny Smith apples, peeled, cored, and chopped
- 3 cloves garlic, finely chopped
- 1 tablespoon curry powder
- 3 tablespoons all-purpose flour
- ½ cup half-and-half or light cream
- ⅓ cup golden raisins
- 2 tablespoons mango chutney, chopped
- 2 teaspoons minced, peeled fresh ginger
- ½ teaspoon salt
- Pinch of cayenne pepper

1. In a 5-quart Dutch oven, combine the chicken, one-fourth of the onions, the carrots, celery, and parsley sprigs. Add just enough water to cover. Heat to boiling over high heat. Reduce the heat, partially cover, and simmer, turning once, until chicken loses its pink color throughout, 25 to 30 minutes. Using tongs, transfer the chicken to a bowl. When it's cool enough to handle, remove and discard the skin and bones; with your hands, shred the chicken.

2. Meanwhile, strain the broth through a sieve, discarding the vegetables. Return the broth to the Dutch oven; heat to boiling and reduce the broth to 2 cups. Skim the broth and discard any fat; reserve the broth.

3. From the lime, grate ½ teaspoon peel and squeeze 5 teaspoons juice; set aside.

4. In a 12-inch skillet, melt the butter over medium heat. Add the remaining three-fourths onions, the apples, garlic, and curry powder and cook, stirring, until the apples are tender, about 10 minutes. Sprinkle with flour, stirring to blend. Gradually add the reserved 2 cups broth, stirring constantly until the broth has thickened and comes to a boil. Stir in the lime peel and juice, the half-and-half, raisins, chutney, ginger, salt, and cayenne. Reduce the heat and simmer, stirring occasionally, for 5 minutes. Add the chicken and heat through.

Each serving About 380 calories, 30g protein, 33g carbohydrate, 14g fat (7g saturated), 4g fiber, 449mg sodium.

chicken tikka masala

PREP: 10 MIN / TOTAL: 25 MIN / SERVES 4

- 1 cup basmati rice
- 1 tablespoon vegetable oil
- 1 medium onion, chopped
- 2 teaspoons grated, peeled fresh ginger
- 1 clove garlic, crushed with a press
- 2 tablespoons Indian curry paste
- 1¼ pounds skinless, boneless chicken
- breast, cut into 1-inch chunks (about 4 breasts)
- ¼ teaspoon salt
- ¼ teaspoon ground black pepper
- 1 cup crushed tomatoes (from a 15-ounce can)
- ½ cup half-and-half or light cream
- ¼ cup loosely packed fresh cilantro leaves, chopped, plus additional for garnish

1. Prepare the rice as the label directs.

2. Meanwhile, in a 12-inch nonstick skillet, heat the oil over medium heat for 1 minute. Add the onion and cook 6 minutes, stirring frequently. Add the ginger, garlic, and curry paste; cook 3 minutes longer.

3. Add the chicken, salt, and pepper, and cook 2 minutes, or until the chicken is no longer pink on the outside, stirring occasionally. Add the tomatoes; cover and cook 3 to 4 minutes longer, or just until the chicken loses its pink color throughout.

4. Uncover and stir in the half-and-half and cilantro. Spoon the rice into 4 shallow bowls; top with chicken mixture and garnish with chopped cilantro.

Each serving About 430 calories, 39g protein, 42g carbohydrate, 13g fat (4g saturated), 6g fiber, 685mg sodium.

GLOSSARY →

Chicken Tikka Masala may have Indian origins, but this cross-cultural mash-up is thought to have been invented in mid-20th century Britain to sauce dry grilled tikka chicken. Today it is one of the most popular takeout dishes in the UK and has gained popularity here in the US.

REMOVE SKIN FROM RAW CHICKEN

TO REMOVE THE SKIN FROM A CHICKEN THIGH

Grasp the skin tightly and pull it off in one piece. If you like, grasp the skin with a piece of paper towel or dip your fingers into a little coarse salt to get a better grip.

TO REMOVE THE SKIN FROM A DRUMSTICK

Grasp the skin at the meaty end of the drumstick; pull the skin down and off the end of the drumstick. (If necessary, use a sharp knife to cut the skin off.)

TO REMOVE THE SKIN FROM A CHICKEN BREAST

Grasp the skin at the thin end of breast and pull it off. (It is difficult to remove the skin from chicken wings—don't bother.)

country captain

PREP: 30 MIN / TOTAL: 1 HR 30 MIN / SERVES 8

- 2 tablespoons plus 1 teaspoon vegetable oil
- 2 whole chickens (3½ pounds each), each cut into 8 pieces, skin removed (except from the wings)
- 2 medium onions, chopped
- 1 large Granny Smith apple, peeled, cored, and chopped
- 1 large green bell pepper, chopped
- 3 large cloves garlic, finely chopped
- 1 tablespoon grated, peeled fresh ginger
- 3 tablespoons curry powder
- ½ teaspoon coarsely ground black pepper
- ¼ teaspoon ground cumin
- 1 can (28 ounces) plum tomatoes in puree
- 1¾ cups chicken broth
- ½ cup dark seedless raisins
- 1 teaspoon salt
- ¼ cup chopped fresh parsley, for serving

1. In a nonreactive 8-quart Dutch oven, heat 2 tablespoons oil over medium-high heat until very hot. Add the chicken, in batches, and cook until golden brown, about 5 minutes per side. Using tongs, transfer the chicken pieces to a bowl as they are browned.

2. Preheat the oven to 350°F. In the same Dutch oven, heat the remaining 1 teaspoon oil over medium-high heat. Add the onions, apple, bell pepper, garlic, and ginger; cook, stirring frequently, 2 minutes. Reduce heat to medium; cover and cook 5 minutes longer.

3. Stir in the curry powder, pepper, and cumin; cook 1 minute. Add the tomatoes with their puree, the broth, raisins, salt, and chicken pieces, breaking up tomatoes with side of spoon. Heat to boiling over high heat; boil 1 minute. Cover and place in oven. Bake 1 hour. Sprinkle with parsley to serve.

Each serving About 350 calories, 43g protein, 19g carbohydrate, 11g fat (2g saturated), 4g fiber, 825mg sodium.

Serving Suggestion This dish is often served over plain white rice. The delicate, nutty flavor of basmati would be a good choice.

roasted jerk chicken

(See photo on page 222.)

PREP: 15 MIN / TOTAL: 1 HR 30 MIN / SERVES 8

- 4 green onions, sliced
- 3 cloves garlic
- 2 jalapeño chiles, sliced
- ¼ cup canola oil
- 3 tablespoons fresh lime juice
- 3 tablespoons soy sauce
- 2 tablespoons brown sugar
- ½ teaspoon ground allspice
- 1 teaspoon salt
- ½ teaspoon ground black pepper
- 2 whole chickens (about 4 pounds each)

1. Preheat the oven to 425°F. Line a large rimmed baking sheet with foil; place a rack on top of the foil.

2. In a blender, puree the green onions, garlic, jalapeños, oil, lime juice, soy sauce, sugar, allspice, salt, and pepper until smooth.

3. Arrange the chickens on the rack. Gently loosen the chicken skin from the meat. Spoon some onion mixture into the cavity of the chicken and under the skin; rub the remaining mixture all over the exterior of the chicken. Tuck the wings behind the breast and tie the legs together with butcher's twine. Roast 1 hour.

4. Reduce the oven temperature to 375°F. Roast another 15 minutes, or until the chicken is cooked through (165°F). If you like, reserve remaining chicken for Spicy Bánh Mì Sandwiches below.

Each serving About 600 calories, 60g protein, 5g carbohydrate, 36g fat (9g saturated), 0g fiber, 395mg sodium.

#SavetheFood
spicy bánh mì sandwiches

Thinly slice the meat from one chicken; discard the skin and bones. Spread **1 cup mayonnaise** on **6 toasted sandwich rolls**. Top with the **chicken, 1 thinly sliced cucumber**, **¾ cup shredded carrots**, and **½ cup fresh cilantro leaves**. Drizzle with **sriracha sauce**. Serves 6.

Each serving About 610 calories, 34g protein, 25g carbohydrate, 41g fat (7g saturated), 2g fiber, 680mg sodium.

spicy jerk drumsticks

PREP: 15 MIN / TOTAL: 55 MIN, PLUS MARINATING / SERVES 6

- ¼ cup olive oil
- ¼ cup soy sauce
- 3 tablespoons fresh lime juice
- 3 tablespoons brown sugar
- 5 thin slices peeled fresh ginger
- 3 green onions, sliced
- 2 cloves garlic
- 3 jalapeño chiles, or 1 habanero chile
- 5 sprigs fresh thyme
- ¼ teaspoon ground allspice
- ¾ teaspoon salt
- 12 chicken drumsticks (about 3¾ pounds)
- Sliced jalapeños and lime wedges, for garnish (optional)

1. In a blender, puree the oil, soy sauce, lime juice, sugar, ginger, green onions, jalapeños, chiles, thyme, allspice, and salt until smooth; transfer to a gallon-size resealable bag along with chicken. Seal the bag, removing the excess air. Toss to coat the chicken; place the bag on a large plate. Refrigerate at least 4 hours or up to overnight.

2. Preheat the oven to 425°F. Line a large rimmed baking sheet with foil; fit a rack into the baking sheet. Remove the drumsticks from the marinade (discard marinade) and gently pat them dry with paper towels; arrange the drumsticks on the rack, spacing them 1 inch apart. Roast 35 to 40 minutes, or until cooked through to 160°F. Garnish with jalapeños and lime wedges, if desired.

Each serving About 195 calories, 21g protein, 2g carbohydrate, 11g fat (3g saturated), 0g fiber, 300mg sodium.

arroz con pollo

PREP: 15 MIN / TOTAL: 55 MIN / SERVES 4

- 1 tablespoon vegetable oil
- 6 medium bone-in chicken thighs (1½ pounds), skin and fat removed
- 1 medium onion, finely chopped
- 1 red bell pepper, chopped
- 1 clove garlic, finely chopped
- ⅛ teaspoon cayenne pepper
- 1 cup regular long-grain rice
- 1¾ cups chicken broth
- ¼ cup water
- 1 strip (3 × ½ inch) lemon peel
- ¼ teaspoon dried oregano
- ¼ teaspoon salt
- 1 cup frozen peas
- ¼ cup chopped pimiento-stuffed olives (salad olives)
- ¼ cup chopped fresh cilantro
- Lemon wedges, for serving

1. In a 5-quart Dutch oven, heat the oil over medium-high heat until very hot. Add the chicken and cook until golden brown, about 5 minutes per side. With tongs, transfer the chicken pieces to a bowl as they are browned.

2. Reduce the heat to medium. Add the onion and bell pepper to the Dutch oven and cook until tender, about 5 minutes. Stir in the garlic and cayenne and cook 30 seconds. Add the rice and cook, stirring, 1 minute. Stir in the broth, water, lemon peel, oregano, salt, and chicken pieces; heat to boiling. Reduce the heat to low; cover and simmer until juices run clear when the thickest part of the chicken is pierced with tip of knife, about 20 minutes.

3. Stir in the peas; cover and heat through. Remove from the heat and let stand 5 minutes.

4. Transfer the chicken and rice to a serving bowl. Sprinkle with olives and cilantro; serve with lemon wedges.

Each serving About 390 calories, 26g protein, 48g carbohydrate, 9g fat (2g saturated), 3g fiber, 927mg sodium.

mediterranean chicken
with soft polenta

PREP: 15 MIN / TOTAL: 55 MIN / SERVES 4

- 2 tablespoons all-purpose flour
- Salt
- Ground black pepper
- 4 medium chicken leg quarters (2¼ pounds), skin and fat removed
- 1 tablespoon olive oil
- 1 small onion, cut in half and thinly sliced
- ½ cup dry white wine
- 1 can (14½ ounces) diced tomatoes
- ½ cup Kalamata olives, pitted and coarsely chopped
- 4 strips (3 × 1 inch each) fresh lemon peel
- 6 sprigs fresh thyme plus additional for garnish
- 2¼ cups whole milk
- 1¾ cups chicken broth
- 1 cup yellow cornmeal
- 2 tablespoons butter or margarine, cut into pieces

1. On waxed paper, combine the flour, ½ teaspoon salt, and ¼ teaspoon pepper. Coat the chicken legs with this mixture, shaking off the excess.

2. In a 12-inch nonstick skillet, heat the oil over medium heat until hot. Add the legs and cook, turning once, until browned, 10 to 12 minutes. With a slotted spoon, transfer the legs to a plate.

3. To the drippings in the skillet, add the onion and cook, stirring frequently, until golden brown, about 5 minutes. Add the wine; boil until reduced by half, about 2 minutes. Add the tomatoes with their juice, the olives, lemon peel, thyme sprigs, and ¼ teaspoon salt. Return the legs and any accumulated juices to the skillet, stirring to coat; bring the mixture to a boil over high heat. Reduce the heat to low; cover and simmer just until the juices run clear when the thickest part of the leg is pierced with tip of knife, about 20 minutes.

4. Meanwhile, in a 3-quart nonreactive saucepan, heat the milk and broth to boiling over high heat. Reduce the heat to low; gradually whisk in the cornmeal. Cook, stirring occasionally, until the mixture is very thick, about 10 minutes. Remove the saucepan from the heat; stir in the butter and ⅛ teaspoon pepper.

5. Remove the lemon peel and thyme sprigs from the chicken mixture. Divide the polenta among 4 dinner plates; top each with 1 chicken leg and some sauce. Garnish with additional thyme sprigs.

Each serving About 550 calories, 41g protein, 43g carbohydrate, 23g fat (6g saturated), 4g fiber, 1,685mg sodium.

spicy chicken & miso stir-fry

(See photo on page 251.)

PREP: 5 MIN / TOTAL: 20 MIN / SERVES 4

- 2 cloves garlic, chopped
- 2 serrano chiles, thinly sliced
- 1 tablespoon chopped, peeled fresh ginger
- 2 tablespoons vegetable oil
- 1¼ pound skinless, boneless chicken breasts, cut into ½-inch chunks (about 4 breasts)
- ¼ teaspoon salt
- ¼ teaspoon ground black pepper
- 2 tablespoons yellow or white miso
- 2 tablespoons water
- 4 green onions, sliced
- 3 cups cooked riced cauliflower

1. In a 12-inch skillet over medium heat, cook the garlic, serrano chiles, and ginger in the oil, stirring, for 3 minutes, or until the garlic is golden. Add the chicken, salt, and pepper. Cook 4 minutes.

2. In a small bowl, whisk the miso and water until smooth; add to the skillet along with green onions. Cook 3 minutes, or until the chicken is cooked through (165°F), stirring occasionally. Serve with riced cauliflower.

Each serving About 285 calories, 36g protein, 9g carbohydrate, 12g fat (1g saturated), 3g fiber, 595mg sodium.

HOW TO

PIT AN OLIVE

You can buy pitted olives, but we think that unpitted olives are more flavorful, and it is very easy to pit them yourself. Place the olives on a cutting board. With the bottom of a small, heavy saucepan, a rolling pin, or the flat side of a large chef's knife, press down hard on the olives, one at a time, to split them open. Lift out the pits with your fingers and discard.

creamy chicken & mushroom pie

PREP: 35 MIN / TOTAL: 50 MIN / SERVES 6

- 1 sheet frozen puff pastry, thawed
- 1 tablespoon butter
- 1½ pounds chicken tenders, cut into 1-inch chunks
- Salt
- Ground black pepper
- 2 shallots, chopped
- 1 pound assorted mushrooms, sliced
- 3 carrots, thinly sliced (8 ounces)
- ⅓ cup dry white wine
- ¼ cup all-purpose flour
- 2 cups lower-sodium chicken broth
- ¾ cup half-and-half
- 1 cup frozen peas, thawed
- 2 teaspoons chopped fresh tarragon

1. Preheat the oven to 400°F. Unfold the pastry; roll it out to the size of 2½-quart baking dish. Invert the dish over the pastry; with a knife, trim the pastry to fit. Place the pastry on a baking sheet; refrigerate.

2. In a 12-inch skillet, melt ½ tablespoon butter over medium-high heat. Add the chicken; sprinkle with ¼ teaspoon each salt and pepper. Cook 5 minutes, or until browned, stirring; transfer to a plate.

3. With a fork, prick the pastry all over. Bake 10 to 15 minutes, or until browned.

4. Meanwhile, in the same 12-inch skillet, melt the remaining ½ tablespoon butter over medium-high heat. Add the shallots; cook, stirring, 2 minutes. (If the pan is dry, add 2 tablespoons water.) Add the mushrooms and carrots; cook 6 minutes, stirring. Add the wine; boil 2 minutes, or until dry. Stir in the flour, then the broth; heat to boiling over high heat. Stir in the chicken and any accumulated juices. Simmer over medium heat 5 minutes, or until chicken is cooked (165°F). Stir in the half-and-half, peas, and tarragon; simmer 1 minute. Pour into the baking dish; top with pastry.

Each serving About 430 calories, 32g protein, 33g carbohydrate, 19g fat (6g saturated), 4g fiber, 720mg sodium.

spanish chicken & peppers

PREP: 10 MIN / TOTAL: 45 MIN / SERVES 4

- 2½ pounds assorted chicken pieces (cut breasts crosswise into halves)
- 1 pound mini sweet peppers
- 1½ tablespoon oil
- ½ teaspoon salt
- ½ teaspoon ground black pepper
- 1 clove garlic, crushed with a garlic press
- ½ cup light mayonnaise
- ½ teaspoon smoked paprika
- Baguette, for serving

1. Preheat the oven to 450°F. Toss the chicken parts and peppers with the oil, salt, and pepper. Arrange everything in a single layer on a foil-lined rimmed baking sheet, avoid overcrowding. Roast 35 minutes, or until chicken is cooked (165°F).

2. Meanwhile, combine garlic, mayonnaise, and paprika in a small bowl. Set aside.

3. Serve the chicken and peppers with garlic mayo and baguette.

Each serving About 500 calories, 38g protein, 10g carbohydrate, 34g fat (7g saturated), 2g fiber, 595mg sodium.

TESTING NOTE In our tests, dark-colored pans held too much heat and overbrowned foods. Go light—even if you choose a baking sheet with a nonstick finish.

fiery kung pao chicken

PREP: 15 MIN / TOTAL: 30 MIN, PLUS MARINATING / SERVES 6

- ¼ cup unsweetened rice wine
- ¼ cup soy sauce
- 1 tablespoon cornstarch
- 1½ pounds skinless, boneless chicken thighs, trimmed and cut into scant 1-inch chunks (about 6 thighs)
- 1 tablespoon vegetable oil
- 1 bunch green onions, thinly sliced
- 3 cloves garlic, chopped
- 2 tablespoons finely chopped, peeled fresh ginger
- ½ cup roasted unsalted peanuts
- 3 tablespoons balsamic vinegar
- 8 whole dried chiles de arbol
- Cilantro, for garnish
- Cooked rice, for serving

1. In a medium bowl, whisk the rice wine, soy sauce, and cornstarch until smooth. Add the chicken; cover and let stand 30 minutes or refrigerate up to 1 hour.

2. In a 12-inch nonstick skillet, heat the oil over medium-high heat. Add the green onions, garlic, and ginger; cook 3 minutes, or until garlic is golden brown, stirring occasionally. Add the chicken and marinade; cook 3 to 5 minutes, or until chicken is cooked through, stirring.

3. Stir in the peanuts, vinegar, and chiles; cook 2 minutes, stirring. Garnish with cilantro and serve with rice.

Each serving About 260 calories, 27g protein, 9g carbohydrate, 13g fat (2g saturated), 2g fiber, 700mg sodium.

TRIPLE-DECKER TORTILLA PIE 253

SPANISH CHICKEN & PEPPERS 250

FIERY KUNG PAO CHICKEN 250

SPICY CHICKEN & MISO STIR-FRY 249

chicken thighs provençal

PREP: 30 MIN / TOTAL: 1 HR 30 MIN / SERVES 8

- 2 pounds skinless, boneless chicken thighs, fat removed, cut into quarters (about 8 thighs)
- Salt
- 3 teaspoons olive oil
- 2 red bell peppers, cut into ¼-inch-wide strips
- 1 yellow bell pepper, cut into ¼-inch-wide strips
- 1 jumbo onion, thinly sliced
- 3 cloves garlic, crushed with a garlic press
- 1 can (28 ounces) plum tomatoes
- ¼ teaspoon dried thyme
- ¼ teaspoon fennel seeds, crushed
- 3 strips (3 × 1 inch each) orange peel
- ½ cup loosely packed fresh basil leaves, chopped

1. Sprinkle the chicken with ½ teaspoon salt. In a nonreactive 5-quart Dutch oven, heat 1 teaspoon oil over medium-high heat until very hot. Add half of the chicken and cook until golden brown, about 5 minutes per side. With tongs, transfer the chicken pieces to a bowl as they are browned. Repeat with 1 teaspoon oil and the remaining chicken.

2. Reduce the heat to medium. To the drippings in the Dutch oven, add the remaining 1 teaspoon oil, the bell peppers, the onion, and ¼ teaspoon salt. Cook, stirring frequently, until the vegetables are tender and lightly browned, about 20 minutes. Add the garlic; cook 1 minute longer.

3. Return the chicken to the Dutch oven. Add the tomatoes with their juice, the thyme, fennel seeds, and orange peel; heat to boiling over high heat, breaking up the tomatoes with the side of a spoon. Reduce the heat to medium; cover and simmer until the chicken loses its pink color throughout, about 15 minutes.

4. Transfer to a serving bowl and sprinkle with basil.

Each serving About 205 calories, 24g protein, 12g carbohydrate, 7g fat (1g saturated), 3g fiber, 480mg sodium.

chicken breasts
with lemon-caper sauce

PREP: 15 MIN / TOTAL: 30 MIN / SERVES 4

- 4 medium skinless, boneless chicken breast halves (1¼ pounds)
- 2 tablespoons plus 1½ teaspoons all-purpose flour
- ½ teaspoon salt
- 1 large egg
- 2 teaspoons olive oil
- 2 tablespoons butter
- 2 lemons, each cut in half
- 3 cloves garlic, crushed with the side of a chef's knife
- ½ cup chicken broth
- ¼ cup dry white wine
- 2 tablespoons capers, drained
- 1 tablespoon chopped fresh parsley

1. Place the chicken breast halves between 2 sheets of plastic wrap or waxed paper. With a meat mallet or rolling pin, pound them to a ½-inch thickness. On another sheet of waxed paper, combine 2 tablespoons flour and the salt. In a pie plate, beat the egg.

2. In a 12-inch skillet, heat the oil over medium-high heat until very hot. Add 1 tablespoon butter and stir until melted. One by one, dredge each chicken breast in the flour mixture, dip it in the egg, and add it to skillet; cook 5 minutes. Reduce the heat to medium, turn the chicken, and cook until it loses its pink color throughout, 8 to 10 minutes longer. Using tongs, transfer the cooked chicken breasts to a platter; keep warm.

3. From 1 lemon half, cut thin slices; from the remaining 1½ lemons, squeeze 2 tablespoons juice. Add the lemon slices and garlic to the drippings in the skillet; cook, stirring, until the garlic is golden. In a small bowl, blend the broth, wine, lemon juice, and remaining 1½ teaspoons flour until smooth; stir this into the mixture in the skillet. Heat the sauce to boiling; boil 1 minute. Stir in the capers and the remaining 1 tablespoon butter until it melts. Discard the garlic. Arrange the lemon slices over and between the chicken breasts. Pour the sauce over the chicken; sprinkle with chopped parsley.

Each serving About 285 calories, 35g protein, 7g carbohydrate, 11g fat (5g saturated), 1g fiber, 773mg sodium.

triple-decker tortilla pie

(See photo on page 251.)

PREP: 10 MIN / TOTAL: 20 MIN / SERVES

1 (2- to 2½-pound) cooked rotisserie chicken	1 cup shredded Monterey Jack cheese
1 can (12 ounces) enchilada sauce	Shredded romaine, halved cherry tomatoes, and diced avocado, for serving
3 (10-inch) flour tortillas	

1. Preheat the oven to 450°F.

2. Remove the meat from the chicken and coarsely shred it; place it in a medium bowl. Discard the skin and bones. Stir in the enchilada sauce.

3. Place 1 flour tortilla in a 10- to 12-inch skillet. Top with half of the chicken mixture and ⅓ cup shredded Monterey Jack cheese; repeat the layering, then top with the remaining tortilla. Sprinkle ⅓ cup shredded Monterey Jack cheese on top; bake 8 to 10 minutes, or until heated through and the cheese has melted.

4. To serve, top with lettuce, tomatoes, and avocado.

Each serving About 550 calories, 48g protein, 33g carbohydrate, 24g fat (9g saturated), 2g fiber, 980mg sodium.

harissa grilled chicken kebabs

(See photo on page 224.)

PREP: 10 MIN / TOTAL: 20 MIN / SERVES 4

¼ cup harissa pepper paste	1 can (15 ounces) chickpeas, rinsed and drained
2 tablespoons olive oil	1 cup quick-cooking bulgur, cooked
2 tablespoons honey	¾ cup finely chopped fresh parsley
1¼ pounds skinless, boneless chicken breasts, thinly sliced (about 4 breasts)	½ teaspoon salt

1. In a large bowl, whisk the harissa with the olive oil and honey; set half aside for serving.

2. To the remaining harissa mixture, add the chicken, tossing; thread onto 4 skewers. Grill over a medium-high heat 6 minutes, or until cooked through, turning once.

3. In a medium bowl, toss the chickpeas with the bulgur, chopped parsley, and salt. Divide the tabbouleh mixture among 4 plates. Serve the chicken over the tabbouleh with the reserved harissa sauce.

Each serving About 495 calories, 39g protein, 57g carbohydrate, 13g fat (2g saturated), 13g fiber, 560mg sodium.

spicy ginger chicken in lettuce cups

PREP: 15 MIN / TOTAL: 25 MIN / SERVES 4

3 tablespoons soy sauce	1 pound ground chicken
1 tablespoon grated, peeled fresh ginger	2 medium stalks celery, chopped
1 teaspoon sugar	½ cup sliced water chestnuts, chopped
⅛ teaspoon crushed red pepper	¼ cup dry-roasted peanuts, coarsely chopped
1 clove garlic, crushed with a garlic press	8 to 12 large Boston lettuce leaves
Nonstick cooking spray	

1. In a cup and using a fork, stir the soy sauce, ginger, sugar, crushed red pepper, and garlic; set aside.

2. Spray a 10-inch nonstick skillet with cooking spray; heat over medium heat until hot. Add the ground chicken and cook, breaking up the meat with the side of a spoon, until no longer pink, 4 to 5 minutes.

3. Add the celery to the chicken in the skillet and cook 2 minutes, stirring occasionally. Add the water chestnuts and soy-sauce mixture and cook, stirring constantly, 1 minute to blend the flavors. Stir in the peanuts.

4. Divide the chicken mixture among the lettuce leaves. Fold the leaves over the chicken mixture and eat out of hand.

Each serving About 305 calories, 24g protein, 8g carbohydrate, 20g fat (1g saturated), 2g fiber, 825mg sodium.

buttermilk fried chicken

PREP: 25 MIN / TOTAL: 1 HR, PLUS BRINING / SERVES 5

- **10 assorted pieces chicken (3 pounds)**, breasts cut into halves if large
- **5 cups room temperature water**
- **¾ cup cayenne pepper hot sauce**
- **Salt**
- **2 tablespoons sugar**
- **2 teaspoons garlic powder**
- **4 cups canola oil**
- **2 cups all-purpose flour**
- **2 cups buttermilk**
- **Corn-off-the-Cob Salad (below)**
- **Hot Sauce Honey (right)**

1. Place a 1-gallon resealable plastic bag in large bowl. Add the chicken to the bag.

2. In another bowl, whisk the water, hot sauce, 3 tablespoons salt, sugar, and garlic powder until the salt and sugar dissolves. Pour this mixture over the chicken in the bag; seal the bag. Refrigerate 3 to 5 hours.

3. Place a wire rack on a large foil-lined rimmed baking sheet. In a heavy, deep 12-inch skillet, heat the oil over medium-high heat until it registers 325°F on a deep-fry thermometer.

4. While the oil heats, place the flour in large, shallow dish and the buttermilk in a large bowl. Drain the chicken. Dredge 5 pieces first in the flour and then in the buttermilk, letting the excess drip off, then return the chicken to the flour again, shaking off any excess. Place the chicken in the hot oil. Cook 12 to 18 minutes, or until chicken is cooked (165°F) and deep golden brown, turning occasionally and adjusting the heat to maintain the proper oil temperature.

5. Transfer the cooked chicken to the wire rack; sprinkle with ¼ teaspoon salt. Repeat the breading and frying with the remaining chicken. Serve with Corn-Off-the-Cob Salad and drizzle of Hot Sauce Honey.

CORN-OFF-THE-COB SALAD Whisk together **3 tablespoons fresh lime juice, 2 tablespoons Dijon mustard, ½ teaspoon ground cumin, 3 tablespoons olive oil**, and ½ **teaspoon salt**. Cut the kernels off of **6 large ears corn**, grilled. Add the corn to the dressing along with **1 pint multicolored grape tomatoes**, halved; and ¼ **cup each chopped fresh cilantro and mint**. Stir until combined. Makes 6 cups.

HOT SAUCE HONEY Microwave ¼ **cup honey** on low 30 seconds or just until runny. Whisk in **2 tablespoons cayenne pepper hot sauce.** Makes about ⅓ cup.

BUTTERMILK FRIED CHICKEN Each serving (2 pieces) About 650 calories, 41g protein, 27g carbohydrate, 41g fat (7g saturated), 1g fiber, 650mg sodium.

CORN-OFF-THE-COB SALAD Each serving About 240 calories, 6g protein, 37g carbohydrate, 11g fat (2g saturated), 5g fiber, 375mg sodium.

HOT SAUCE HONEY Each tablespoon About 15 calories, 0g protein, 4g carbohydrate, 0g fat (0g saturated), 0g fiber, 65mg sodium.

spicy peanut chicken

PREP: 15 MIN / TOTAL: 1 HR 10 MIN / SERVES 4

- **1 teaspoon ground cumin**
- **¼ teaspoon ground cinnamon**
- **4 medium chicken leg quarters (2¼ pounds)**, skin and fat removed
- **1 tablespoon vegetable oil**
- **1 medium onion, thinly sliced**
- **1 can (28 ounces) plum tomatoes, drained and** coarsely chopped, juice reserved
- **¼ cup creamy peanut butter**
- **¼ cup packed fresh cilantro leaves, plus additional sprigs for garnish**
- **2 cloves garlic, peeled**
- **½ teaspoon salt**
- **¼ teaspoon crushed red pepper**

1. In a cup, combine the cumin and cinnamon, and rub it on the chicken.

2. In a 12-inch nonstick skillet, heat the oil over medium-high heat until very hot. Add the chicken and cook until golden brown, about 5 minutes per side. Add the onion and cook until golden, about 5 minutes.

3. Meanwhile, in a blender or in food processor with knife blade attached, puree the reserved tomato juice, the peanut butter, cilantro, garlic, salt, and crushed red pepper until smooth.

4. Pour the peanut butter mixture and chopped tomatoes over the chicken; heat to boiling. Reduce to medium heat; cover and simmer until the juices run clear when the thickest part of the chicken is pierced with the tip of a knife, about 40 minutes. Garnish with cilantro sprigs.

Each serving About 360 calories, 36g protein, 16g carbohydrate, 18g fat (3g saturated), 3g fiber, 817mg sodium.

poule au pot
with tarragon

PREP: 15 MIN / TOTAL: 1 HR / SERVES 4

- 3 medium leeks
- 1 whole chicken (3½ pounds), cut into 8 pieces
- 1 pound small red potatoes
- 1 bag (16 ounces) carrots, peeled and cut into 3-inch pieces
- 4 cups water
- 1¾ cups chicken broth
- ½ teaspoon salt
- ¼ teaspoon dried thyme
- ¼ teaspoon ground black pepper
- 1 large sprig fresh tarragon plus 1 tablespoon chopped fresh tarragon

1. Cut off the roots and trim the dark-green tops from the leeks; cut each leek lengthwise in half, then crosswise into 3-inch pieces. Place the leeks in a large bowl of cold water, swishing to remove any sand; transfer to colander to drain, leaving the sand in the bottom of the bowl.

2. In a 6- to 8-quart Dutch oven, combine the leeks, chicken, potatoes, carrots, water, broth, salt, thyme, pepper, and tarragon sprig. Heat to boiling over high heat. Reduce the heat; cover and simmer until the chicken loses its pink color throughout, about 45 minutes.

3. With a slotted spoon, transfer the chicken and vegetables to a serving bowl. Remove and discard the skin from the chicken. Skim and discard the fat from the broth. Pour 1 cup broth over the chicken (refrigerate the remaining broth for another use). To serve, sprinkle chopped tarragon on top.

Each serving About 470 calories, 47g protein, 44g carbohydrate, 11g fat (3g saturated), 6g fiber, 859mg sodium.

poached chicken breast
with sauces

PREP: 5 MIN / TOTAL: 20 MIN / SERVES 6

- 6 small skinless, boneless chicken breast halves (1 ¾ pounds)
- 1 medium onion, thinly sliced
- 3 cups water
- 1 bay leaf

1. In a 12-inch skillet, combine the chicken, onion, water, and bay leaf. Heat to boiling over high heat. Reduce the heat; cover and simmer 1 minute, turning the chicken over halfway through cooking. Remove the skillet from the heat; cover and let stand 10 minutes. Reserve cooking liquid for sauces.

2. Transfer the poached chicken to a plate; cover loosely and refrigerate until chilled. Serve with sauce (see below).

TURKISH CHICKEN IN WALNUT SAUCE In a food processor with the knife blade attached, process **1¼ cups toasted walnuts** and **3 slices firm white bread** (torn into pieces) until the walnuts are finely ground. Add **1 cup chicken broth**; **1 small clove garlic** (minced), **¾ teaspoon salt**, **½ teaspoon paprika**, and **⅓ teaspoon cayenne pepper**; process until well combined. Chop the **poached chicken breasts**, place them in a medium bowl, and stir half of the walnut sauce into the chicken until combined. Spoon the chicken onto a serving platter and pour the remaining sauce on top. Cover with plastic wrap and let stand 30 minutes or refrigerate up to 8 hours.

CHICKEN BREASTS TONNATO In a blender or food processor with knife blade attached, blend **1 can (6½ ounces) white tuna in oil**, **4 anchovy fillets**, **2 tablespoons capers** (drained), **¼ cup olive oil**, **¼ cup fresh lemon juice**, **¼ teaspoon salt**, and **¾ cup reserved poaching liquid** until smooth. Line a platter with **1 bunch of arugula** or several lettuce leaves. Dip each **cold chicken breast** half into the tuna sauce to coat; arrange on the arugula. Pour any remaining sauce over the chicken. Garnish with **lemon slices** and **2 teaspoons capers**.

TURKISH CHICKEN IN WALNUT SAUCE Each serving About 330 calories, 34g protein, 9g carbohydrate, 18g fat (2g saturated), 2g fiber, 576mg sodium.
CHICKEN BREASTS TONNATO Each serving About 340 calories, 38g protein, 1g carbohydrate, 19g fat (3g saturated), 0g fiber, 450mg sodium.

fried chicken
with spicy raspberry honey

PREP: 35 MIN / TOTAL: 40 MIN / SERVES 6

- 12 assorted chicken pieces (about 4 pounds, breasts cut crosswise in half if large)
- ¾ cup low-fat buttermilk
- 3 tablespoons sugar
- 1 tablespoon garlic powder
- 3 cups cold water
- ¼ cup plus 3 tablespoons hot sauce
- Salt
- 1 container (6 ounces) raspberries
- ¼ cup water
- ½ cup honey
- ½ teaspoon smoked paprika
- Vegetable oil, for frying
- 1 cup all-purpose flour

1. Place 2 gallon-size resealable bags in 2 medium bowls. Divide the chicken evenly between the bags. In a large bowl, whisk the buttermilk, sugar, garlic powder, cold water, ¼ cup hot sauce, and 3 tablespoons salt until the salt dissolves. Pour the liquid over the chicken in the bags. Press out the air and seal the bags. Refrigerate the bowls of chicken at least 3 hours or up to 7 hours. (If using only wings, refrigerate at least 1 hour.)

2. Meanwhile, in blender, puree the raspberries with ¼ cup water; strain through fine-mesh sieve set over a medium bowl, pushing the mixture through with rubber spatula. Discard the remains in the sieve. Into the raspberry mixture, whisk the honey, smoked paprika, ⅛ teaspoon salt, and the remaining 3 tablespoons hot sauce. Set aside.

3. In a deep, heavy 12-inch skillet, pour enough oil to reach ¾ inch up the side. Heat over medium-high heat until the oil reaches 325°F on a deep-fry thermometer.

4. Preheat the oven to 375°F. Place the flour in a 2-quart baking dish.

5. Transfer the chicken from the brine to the flour in batches, tossing to coat. Tap off the excess flour; carefully place the chicken in the hot oil, making sure not to crowd the skillet. Reduce the heat to medium. Fry the chicken 12 to 15 minutes, or until golden brown and cooked through (165°F), turning the pieces halfway through. Repeat with remaining chicken, adjusting the heat to maintain 325°F. If the pieces brown before they are cooked, transfer them to a rack fitted into an 18 × 12-inch jelly-roll pan and bake 5 to 8 minutes, or until cooked through. Serve with the spicy raspberry honey.

Each serving About 435 calories, 41g protein, 30g carbohydrate, 17g fat (5g saturated), 2g fiber, 695mg sodium.

nashville hot chicken

(See photo on page 258.)

PREP: 25 MIN / TOTAL: 1 HR, PLUS BRINING / SERVES 5

- 10 small pieces (3 pounds) skin-on, bone-in chicken parts (breasts cut into halves)
- 5 cups water
- ¾ cup cayenne pepper hot sauce
- 2 tablespoons plus 2 teaspoons sugar
- 2¾ teaspoons garlic powder
- Salt
- 6 cups peanut oil
- 2 cups all-purpose flour
- 2 cups buttermilk
- 2 to 5 tablespoons cayenne pepper, to taste
- 2 teaspoons paprika
- ½ teaspoon ground black pepper
- White bread and pickle slices, for serving

1. Place 1 gallon-size resealable plastic bag in a large bowl. Add the chicken to the bag.

2. In another bowl, whisk the water, hot sauce, 2 tablespoons sugar, 2 teaspoons garlic, and 3 tablespoons salt until the salt and sugar dissolves. Pour the mixture over the chicken; seal the bag. Refrigerate 5 to 8 hours.

3. Fit a wire rack into a foil-lined rimmed baking sheet. In a 12-inch cast-iron skillet, heat the oil over medium-high heat until it registers 325°F on a deep-fry thermometer.

4. While the oil heats, place the flour in a large dish and the buttermilk in a large bowl. Drain chicken, discarding the brine. Dredge 5 pieces of chicken in the flour, then dip them in the buttermilk, letting the excess drip off; dredge them in flour again, shaking off any excess. Carefully place each piece in the hot oil. Cook 12 to 18 minutes, or until chicken is deep golden brown and cooked (165°F), turning it and adjusting the heat to maintain the oil temperature. Transfer the cooked chicken to the rack; sprinkle with ¼ teaspoon salt. Repeat with remaining chicken.

5. In another bowl, combine the cayenne to your taste, paprika, remaining 2 teaspoons sugar, ¾ teaspoon granulated garlic, and the pepper. Ladle ⅓ cup hot oil from the skillet into the bowl with the spices. Stir well.

6. To serve, brush the chicken generously with the spice paste.

Each serving About 725 calories, 43g protein, 43g carbohydrate, 42g fat (10g saturated), 3g fiber, 740mg sodium.

NASHVILLE HOT CHICKEN 257

crispy chicken
with white wine pan sauce

PREP: 15 MIN / TOTAL: 35 MIN / SERVES 4

2 teaspoons olive oil

2½ pounds chicken thighs (about 8 thighs)

Salt

2 medium shallots, chopped

⅔ cup white wine

¼ teaspoon dried rosemary

3 tablespoons low-fat sour cream

½ cup chicken broth

Snipped fresh chives, for garnish

1. Preheat the oven to 450°F. Line a rimmed baking sheet with foil.

2. In a 12-inch skillet, heat oil over medium-high heat. Season the chicken with ½ teaspoon salt. Cook, skin side down, 6 to 8 minutes, or until browned; transfer the chicken to the foil-lined baking sheet, skin side up. Bake 15 minutes, or until the chicken is cooked through (165°F).

3. To the same skillet, sauté the shallots 2 minutes over medium heat. Add the white wine, rosemary, and ¼ teaspoon salt. Simmer 2 minutes, scraping up the browned bits. Whisk in the sour cream and chicken broth, stirring until smooth. Serve the chicken with some sauce; garnish with snipped chives.

Each serving About 465 calories, 40g protein, 4g carbohydrate, 31g fat (9g saturated), 1g fiber, 615mg sodium.

CRISPY CHICKEN WITH WHITE WINE PAN SAUCE 258

chicken livers marsala

PREP: 15 MIN / TOTAL: 30 MIN / SERVES 4

- 3 tablespoons butter
- 1 pound chicken livers, trimmed, cut in half, and patted dry
- Salt
- 1 medium onion, chopped
- 8 ounces mushrooms, trimmed and cut in half
- ¼ teaspoon ground black pepper
- ¼ cup dry Marsala wine
- 1 tablespoon chopped fresh parsley

1. In a 10-inch skillet, melt 1 tablespoon butter over medium-high heat. Add the livers, sprinkle with ½ teaspoon salt, and cook, stirring often, until the livers are browned but still pink in the center, 3 to 4 minutes. Transfer the livers to a bowl.

2. Melt the remaining 2 tablespoons butter in the skillet. Add the onion and cook until tender, about 5 minutes. Add the mushrooms, pepper, and ¼ teaspoon salt, and cook until the mushrooms are tender. Stir in the Marsala and heat to boiling. Add the livers and heat through. Sprinkle with parsley.

Each serving About 270 calories, 22g protein, 12g carbohydrate, 13g fat (7g saturated), 1g fiber, 619mg sodium.

turkey meat loaf

PREP: 15 MIN / TOTAL: 1 HR 15 MIN / SERVES 8

- 1 tablespoon olive oil
- 1 medium onion, finely chopped
- 2 cloves garlic, finely chopped
- 2 pounds ground turkey meat
- 2 large eggs
- 1 cup fresh bread crumbs (from about 2 slices firm white bread)
- ¼ cup milk
- ¼ cup mango chutney, chopped
- 2 tablespoons ketchup
- 1¼ teaspoons salt
- ½ teaspoon dried sage

1. Preheat the oven to 350°F.

2. In a 6-inch skillet, heat the oil over medium heat. Add the onion and garlic and cook, stirring frequently, until tender, about 5 minutes. Transfer to a medium bowl; cool to room temperature.

3. Add the ground turkey, eggs, bread crumbs, milk, chutney, ketchup, salt, and sage to the bowl; combine just until well blended but not overmixed. Spoon the mixture into a 9 × 5-inch metal loaf pan; press down gently. Cover with foil and bake until a meat thermometer inserted in center of the meat loaf registers 170°F, about 1 hour. Cool in the pan 10 minutes; turn out onto warm platter and slice.

Each serving About 260 calories, 23g protein, 14g carbohydrate, 12g fat (3g saturated), 1g fiber, 657mg sodium.

GOOD TO KNOW

MARSALA WINE

Marsala, Italy's most famous fortified wine, is produced by a process similar to the one used in Spain to make sherry. Marsala is made in several different styles: *secco* (dry), *semisecco* (semisweet), and *dolce* (sweet). It is also classified based on its flavor characteristics and aging. When cooking, we recommend dry or semidry styles. For desserts such as zabaglione, sweet marsala is preferred.

FINE	Usually aged less than one year
SUPERIORE	Aged at least two years
SUPERIORE RISERVA	Aged at least four years
VERGINE E/O SOLERAS	Aged at least five years
VERGINE E/O SOLERAS STRAVECCHIO OR VERGINE E/O SOLVERAS RISERVA	Aged at least 10 years

glazed bacon-wrapped turkey breast

(See photo on page 226.)

PREP: 20 MIN / TOTAL: 2 HR / SERVES 10

- 1 boneless turkey breast (4 to 5 pounds), skin removed
- Salt
- 1½ bunches green onions, sliced
- 2 cup packed fresh parsley
- ⅓ cup olive oil
- 4 cloves garlic
- 12 ounces thick-cut bacon
- 4 cups water
- ½ cup packed dark brown sugar
- ¼ cup balsamic vinegar
- ¼ cup maple syrup

1. Preheat the oven to 375°F. Line a roasting pan with foil.

2. Place the turkey breast, smooth side down, on a cutting board. On the left breast, cut along right side of tenderloin without cutting it off to separate it from the breast; fold the tenderloin back. Repeat on the right breast, cutting along the left side of the tenderloin and folding it back. Cover the surface of turkey with 3 large sheets of plastic wrap. With the flat side of a meat mallet or a heavy rolling pin, pound the turkey until it is about 1 inch thick all over. Discard the plastic wrap.

3. Sprinkle the surface of the turkey with ¾ teaspoon salt. In a food processor, pulse the green onions, parsley, oil, and garlic until finely chopped, stopping to stir occasionally. Spread the herb mixture in an even layer on the whole breast. Starting with one short side, roll the breast tightly. Place the seam side down and drape the bacon over the turkey roll, overlapping slices slightly. Tuck the ends of the bacon strips under the turkey roll. Using 16-inch pieces of kitchen string, tie the turkey tightly at 1½-inch intervals. (The turkey may be wrapped tightly in plastic and refrigerated up to overnight at this point.) Transfer the turkey roll to a rack fitted into the foil-lined roasting pan. Add water to the bottom of the pan. Roast 45 minutes.

4. Meanwhile, whisk together the sugar, vinegar, and syrup. Brush it over the turkey after it has roasted 45 minutes. Roast another 45 minutes, or until turkey is cooked to an internal temperature of 160°F, basting it with the sugar mixture every 15 minutes. Loosely cover with foil; let rest 20 minutes. Cut and discard the strings before slicing and serving.

Each serving About 450 calories, 56g protein, 19g carbohydrate, 16g fat (4g saturated), 1g fiber, 520mg sodium.

turkey thighs, osso buco–style

PREP: 20 MIN / TOTAL: 1 HR 50 MIN / SERVES 4

- ¼ teaspoon salt
- ¼ teaspoon ground black pepper
- 2 turkey thighs (1¼ pounds each), skin removed
- 2 teaspoons vegetable oil
- 2 medium onions, finely chopped
- 4 carrots, peeled and cut into ¾-inch pieces
- 2 stalks celery, cut into ½-inch pieces
- 4 cloves garlic, finely chopped
- 1 can (14½ ounces) tomatoes in puree
- ½ cup dry red wine
- 1 bay leaf
- ¼ teaspoon dried thyme

1. Preheat the oven to 350°F. Sprinkle salt and pepper on turkey.

2. In a nonreactive 5-quart Dutch oven, heat the oil over medium-high heat until very hot. Add 1 turkey thigh and cook, turning occasionally, until golden brown, about 5 minutes. With tongs, transfer the thigh to a plate; repeat with the second thigh. Discard all but 1 tablespoon fat from Dutch oven.

3. Reduce the heat to medium. Add the onions to the Dutch oven and cook, stirring occasionally, 5 minutes. Add the carrots, celery, and garlic; cook, stirring frequently, 2 minutes longer.

4. Stir in the tomatoes with the puree, the wine, bay leaf, and thyme, breaking up the tomatoes with the side of a spoon; heat to boiling. Add the browned turkey; cover the pot and place it in the oven. Bake until the turkey is tender, about 1 hour 30 minutes. Discard the bay leaf. Remove the turkey meat from the bones and cut it into bite-size pieces; return the meat to the Dutch oven and stir well.

Each serving About 325 calories, 36g protein, 24g carbohydrate, 9g fat (3g saturated), 4g fiber, 483mg sodium.

curried sweet potato shepherd's pie

PREP: 1 HR / TOTAL: 1 HR 35 MIN / SERVES 12

- 5 medium (about 12 ounces each) sweet potatoes
- 2 tablespoons vegetable oil
- 2 pounds ground turkey or chicken
- Salt
- ⅓ cup all-purpose flour
- 1 tablespoon curry powder
- 1¾ cups chicken broth
- 1½ pounds carrots, peeled and chopped
- 1½ pounds parsnips, peeled and chopped
- 1 medium onion, chopped
- 1 tablespoon grated, peeled fresh ginger
- 1 package (10 ounces) frozen peas
- 1 cup reduced-fat (2%) milk, warmed
- 2 tablespoons butter

1. Pierce the potatoes all over with a fork. Cook in the microwave oven on High for 15 to 17 minutes, or until potatoes are tender when pierced with fork, turning the potatoes over once; set aside.

2. Meanwhile, in a 12-inch skillet, heat 1 tablespoon oil over medium-high heat until hot. Add the turkey; sprinkle with ½ teaspoon salt and cook 5 to 6 minutes, or until no longer pink, stirring and breaking up the turkey with the side of a spoon.

3. Stir the flour and curry powder into the skillet; cook 1 minute, stirring. Add the broth and bring to a boil. Cook 1 minute, or until the mixture thickens slightly. Evenly divide the turkey mixture between two 2½- to 3-quart glass or ceramic baking dishes; spread it out evenly.

4. Preheat the oven to 375°F. Wipe the skillet dry and then heat the remaining 1 tablespoon oil over medium heat until hot. Add the carrots, parsnips, and onion and cook, covered, about 15 minutes, or until the vegetables are browned and tender, stirring occasionally. Stir in the ginger, frozen peas, and ½ teaspoon salt. Divide the vegetable mixture between the baking dishes, spreading it evenly over the turkey mixture.

5. When cool enough to handle, cut the potatoes in half lengthwise and scoop the flesh from the skins into a large bowl. With a potato masher, coarsely mash the potatoes. Stir in the milk, butter, and 1 teaspoon salt; mash until well blended. Spread the potatoes over the vegetables.

6. Bake one shepherd's pie, uncovered, 35 to 40 minutes, or until the top is browned. Meanwhile, prepare second casserole for freezing (up to 3 months) if not planning to serve right away. Makes 2 casseroles with 6 servings each.

Each serving About 365 calories, 19g protein, 47g carbohydrate, 12g fat (3g saturated), 9g fiber, 630mg sodium.

TESTING NOTE When microwaving sweet potatoes, it's important to use potatoes that are as uniform in size and shape as possible. Otherwise, they will not cook evenly.

turkey cutlets
with chopped salad

PREP: 15 MIN / TOTAL: 25 MIN / SERVES 4

- 1 green onion, thinly sliced
- 2 tablespoons freshly grated Parmesan cheese
- 4 tablespoons olive oil
- 1 tablespoon red wine vinegar
- ½ teaspoon Dijon mustard
- ¼ teaspoon salt
- ¼ teaspoon coarsely ground black pepper
- 1 pound turkey cutlets
- ⅓ cup seasoned dried bread crumbs
- 1 pound plum tomatoes (4 large), cut into ¾-inch pieces
- 2 small bunches arugula (6 to 8 ounces), coarsely chopped

1. Prepare the dressing: In a medium bowl and using a fork, mix the green onion, Parmesan, 2 tablespoons oil, vinegar, mustard, salt, and pepper; set aside.

2. Place the turkey cutlets between 2 sheets of plastic wrap or waxed paper. With a meat mallet or rolling pin, pound the cutlets to a ¼-inch thickness. Coat the cutlets with bread crumbs.

3. In a 12-inch skillet, heat the remaining 2 tablespoons oil over medium-high heat until very hot. Add the turkey cutlets, a few at a time, and cook until the cutlets are golden brown and lose their pink color throughout, about 2½ minutes per side. Transfer the cutlets to a warm plate as they are done.

4. Add the tomatoes and arugula to the reserved dressing; gently toss to mix well. Pile the salad on a platter and top with cutlets.

Each serving About 335 calories, 33g protein, 15g carbohydrate, 16g fat (3g saturated), 3g fiber, 559mg sodium.

turkey potpie
with cornmeal crust

PREP: 30 MIN / TOTAL: 1 HR 30 MIN / SERVES 10

- 1 tablespoon vegetable oil
- 1 medium rutabaga (1 pound), peeled and cut into ½-inch pieces
- 3 carrots, peeled and cut into ½-inch pieces
- 1 large onion, chopped
- 1 pound all-purpose potatoes (3 medium), peeled and cut into ½-inch pieces
- 2 large stalks celery, chopped
- Salt
- 1 pound cooked turkey or chicken, cut into ½-inch pieces (4 cups)
- 1 package (10 ounces) frozen peas
- 1¾ cups chicken broth
- 1 cup milk
- ¼ cup all-purpose flour
- ¼ teaspoon ground black pepper
- ⅛ teaspoon dried thyme
- Cornmeal Crust (right)
- 1 large egg, beaten

1. Prepare the potpie filling: In a 12-inch skillet, heat the oil over medium-high heat; add the rutabaga, carrots, and onion, and cook 10 minutes. Stir in potatoes, celery, and ½ teaspoon salt; cook, stirring frequently, until the rutabaga is tender-crisp, about 10 minutes longer. Spoon into a 13 × 9-inch baking dish; add the turkey and peas.

2. In a 2-quart saucepan, heat the broth to boiling. Meanwhile, in a small bowl, whisk the milk and flour until smooth. Stir the milk mixture into the broth. Add the pepper, thyme, and ¼ teaspoon salt; heat to boiling over high heat, stirring. Stir the sauce into the chicken-vegetable mixture in the baking dish.

3. Prepare the Cornmeal Crust (right). Preheat oven to 425°F. Line a rimmed baking sheet with foil.

4. On a lightly floured surface and using a floured rolling pin, roll the dough into a rectangle 2 inches longer and wider than the baking dish. Arrange the dough rectangle over the filling; trim the edge, leaving a 1-inch overhang on all sides. Fold under the overhang; flute the edge. Brush the crust with some egg. If desired, reroll the trimmings and cut them into decorative shapes to garnish the top of the pie. Brush the dough cutouts with egg. Cut several slits in the crust to allow the steam to escape during baking.

5. Place the potpie on the foil-lined baking sheet to catch any overflow. Bake the potpie until the crust is golden brown and filling is hot and bubbling, 35 to 40 minutes. During the last 10 minutes of baking, cover the edges of crust with foil to prevent overbrowning, if necessary.

CORNMEAL CRUST In a large bowl, combine 1½ **cups all-purpose flour**, ¼ **cup cornmeal**, and ¾ **teaspoon salt**. With a pastry blender or 2 knives used scissor-fashion, cut in ⅔ **cup vegetable shortening** until the mixture resembles coarse crumbs. Sprinkle **6 to 7 tablespoons cold water**, 1 tablespoon at a time, over flour the mixture, mixing it with a fork after each addition, until the dough is just moist enough to hold together.

Each serving About 415 calories, 21g protein, 42g carbohydrate, 18g fat (5g saturated), 5g fiber, 644mg sodium.

ginger-glazed duck

PREP: 10 MIN / TOTAL: 2 HR 20 MIN / SERVES 4

- 1 duck (4½ pounds), cut into quarters, fat removed
- 3 teaspoons grated, peeled fresh ginger
- ½ teaspoon salt
- ¼ teaspoon ground black pepper
- 2 tablespoons honey
- 1 tablespoon soy sauce

1. Preheat the oven to 350°F. Pat the duck dry with paper towels and, with a large two-tine fork, prick the skin in several places.

2. In a cup, combine 1 teaspoon ginger, salt, and pepper. Rub the mixture on the meat side of each duck quarter. Place the duck, skin side up, on a rack in a large 17 × 11½-inch foil-lined roasting pan. Roast 2 hours, using a spoon or bulb baster to remove fat from pan occasionally.

3. Meanwhile, in a cup, combine the honey, soy sauce, and the remaining 2 teaspoons ginger.

4. Turn the oven control to 450°F. Remove the duck from the oven and brush the ginger glaze all over. Return the duck to the oven and roast 10 minutes longer.

Each serving About 690 calories, 37g protein, 9g carbohydrate, 55g fat (19g saturated), 0g fiber, 662mg sodium.

VARIATION

Chipotle-Glazed Duck

Prepare as directed, but omit the honey, soy sauce, and ginger. While the duck roasts, press **2 tablespoons chopped canned chipotle chiles in adobo** through a sieve into a small bowl; discard the skin and seeds. Stir **2 tablespoons light (mild) molasses** into the chipotle chiles. Proceed as in step 4.

crispy roast goose
with orange

PREP: 30 MIN / TOTAL: 4 HR 55 MIN, PLUS STANDING / SERVES 10

- 1 goose (12 pounds)
- 5 navel oranges, each cut in half
- 1 bunch fresh thyme
- 4 bay leaves
- ½ teaspoon dried thyme
- Salt
- ½ teaspoon coarsely ground black pepper
- 3 tablespoons orange-flavored liqueur
- 2 tablespoons cornstarch
- ½ cup orange marmalade

1. Preheat the oven to 400°F. Remove the giblets and neck from the goose; reserve them for another use. Trim and discard the fat from the body cavity and any excess skin. Rinse the goose inside and out with cold running water and drain well; pat it dry with paper towels. With the goose breast side up, lift the wings up toward the neck, then fold the wing tips under the back of the goose so the wings stay in place. Place 6 orange halves, the thyme sprigs, and bay leaves in the body cavity. Tie the legs and tail together with string. Fold the neck skin over the back. With a large two-tine fork, prick the skin in several places to drain the fat during roasting.

2. Place the goose, breast side up, on a rack in large roasting pan (17 × 11½ inches). In a cup, combine the dried thyme, 1 teaspoon salt, and the pepper; rub the mixture over the goose. Cover the goose and roasting pan with foil. Roast 1 hour 30 minutes; turn the oven control to 325°F and roast 2 hours longer.

3. Meanwhile, in a small bowl, squeeze ¾ cup juice from the remaining 4 orange halves. Stir in 1 tablespoon liqueur, the cornstarch, and ¼ teaspoon salt; set aside. In another cup, mix the orange marmalade with the remaining 2 tablespoons liqueur.

4. With a spoon or bulb baster, remove as much fat from the roasting pan as possible. Remove the foil and roast goose 45 minutes longer. Remove the goose from the oven and increase the oven temperature to 450°F. Brush the marmalade mixture over the goose. Roast the goose until the skin is golden brown and crisp, about 10 minutes longer. Transfer the goose to a warm platter; let stand at least 15 minutes to set the juices for easier carving.

5. Prepare the sauce: Remove the rack from the roasting pan. Strain the pan drippings through a sieve into an 8-cup measuring cup or large bowl. Let stand until the fat separates from the meat juice; skim and reserve the fat for another use (there should be about 5 cups fat). Measure the meat juice; if necessary, add enough water to the meat juice to equal 1 cup. Return the meat juice to the pan and add the reserved orange juice mixture. Heat the sauce to boiling over medium heat, stirring; boil 1 minute.

6. Serve the sauce with the goose. Remove the skin before eating, if desired. (Makes about 1¾ cups sauce.)

Each serving (with skin) About 810 calories, 66g protein, 5g carbohydrate, 57g fat (18g saturated), 0g fiber, 472mg sodium.
Each serving (without skin) About 490 calories, 57g protein, 5g carbohydrate, 25g fat (9g saturated), 0g fiber, 440mg sodium.

red cooked duck

PREP: 25 MIN / TOTAL: 2 HR 25 MIN / SERVES 4

- 4 green onions
- 1 duck (4½ pounds), cut into 8 pieces, fat removed
- 1 tablespoon olive oil
- ¼ cup soy sauce
- 2 tablespoons dry sherry
- 1 tablespoon minced, peeled fresh ginger
- 3 cloves garlic, each cut in half
- 1 tablespoon brown sugar
- 2 whole star anise, or ½ teaspoon anise seeds
- ¼ teaspoon cayenne pepper
- ¾ cup water

1. Preheat the oven to 350°F. Cut the green onions on the diagonal into 1½-inch pieces. Pat the duck dry with paper towels.

2. In an 8-quart Dutch oven, heat the oil over high heat until very hot. Cook the duck, in batches, until golden brown, about 8 minutes, using tongs to transfer the duck pieces to a large bowl as they are browned. Discard all but 1 tablespoon fat from the Dutch oven. Add the green onions and cook, stirring, until lightly browned, about 5 minutes.

3. Stir in the soy sauce, sherry, ginger, garlic, brown sugar, star anise, cayenne, and water. Heat to boiling over high heat, stirring until the browned bits are loosened from the bottom of the Dutch oven.

4. Return the duck to the Dutch oven. Cover and place it in the oven. Bake 2 hours, basting the duck several times with the pan liquid.

5. With tongs, transfer the duck to a warm deep platter. Strain the sauce through a sieve; skim and discard the fat. Serve the duck topped with sauce.

Each serving About 720 calories, 38g protein, 8g carbohydrate, 59g fat (19g saturated), 0g fiber, 1,293mg sodium.

crispy duck with apricots

PREP: 20 MIN / TOTAL: 35 MIN / SERVES 2

1 large duck breast (about 1 pound)

1 pound parsnips, peeled and chopped

1 cup lower-sodium chicken broth

3 teaspoons olive oil

Salt

Ground black pepper

½ small red onion, finely chopped

½ cup dry white wine

¼ cup dried apricots, chopped

1 tablespoon apricot jam

1 tablespoon red wine vinegar

Chopped parsley, for garnish (optional)

1. Preheat the oven to 400°F. Line a small jelly-roll pan with foil.

2. Place the duck on a cutting board. Cover with plastic wrap. With the flat side of a meat mallet, pound the duck to an even 1-inch thickness. With a knife, make ¼-inch-deep cuts diagonally across the skin side of the duck breast, about ½ inch apart. Make another set of cuts perpendicular to first set to create a diamond pattern.

3. In a 4-quart saucepan, bring the parsnips and broth to a simmer over medium-high heat. Reduce the heat to medium. Partially cover and simmer the parsnips 13 to 18 minutes, or until very tender.

4. In a 10-inch skillet, heat 1 teaspoon oil over medium heat. Sprinkle the duck with ¼ teaspoon each salt and pepper to season both sides. Add the duck to the skillet, skin side down. Cook 5 minutes, or until crisp and browned. Turn over. Cook another 2 minutes, or until browned. Transfer the duck to prepared jelly-roll pan, skin side up. Roast 5 to 7 minutes, or until cooked to the desired doneness (145°F for medium). Transfer the duck to a clean cutting board and loosely tent it with foil.

5. Drain all but 1 teaspoon fat from skillet. Add the onion to the skillet. Cook on medium 2 minutes, or until browned, stirring frequently. Add the wine and apricots. Cook 2 minutes, or until the wine is reduced by about half. Stir in the jam, vinegar, and ⅛ teaspoon each salt and pepper. Cook 1 minute, or until jam is melted, stirring frequently. Remove from heat.

6. With a slotted spoon, transfer the cooked parsnips to the food processor, along with ¼ cup cooking liquid, the remaining 2 teaspoons oil, and ⅛ teaspoon salt. Pulse just until smooth.

7. Divide the parsnips between 2 serving plates. Thinly slice the duck breast; arrange the duck on top of the parsnips. Top with apricot sauce and garnish with parsley, if desired.

Each serving About 645 calories, 46g protein, 58g carbohydrate, 26g fat (6g saturated), 12g fiber, 990mg sodium.

seared duck breast

with dried cherries & port

PREP: 5 MIN / TOTAL: 30 MIN / SERVES 4

4 boneless fresh or frozen (thawed) duck-breast halves with skin (6 ounces each)

¼ teaspoon salt

⅛ teaspoon coarsely ground black pepper

1 large shallot, thinly sliced

1 clove garlic, crushed with a press

1 cup port wine

2 tablespoons balsamic vinegar

⅓ cup dried cherries

1. Pat the duck breasts dry with paper towels. With a sharp knife, cut 4 diagonal slashes, about ¼ inch deep, in the skin and fat on each breast half. On a sheet of waxed paper, evenly season the duck breasts, on both sides, with the salt and pepper.

2. In a 12-inch nonstick skillet, cook the breasts, skin side down, over medium heat for 15 minutes, or until the skin is well browned and crispy. As the breasts cook, spoon off and discard excess fat in the skillet. Turn the breasts over and cook them on the flesh side about 4 minutes for medium-rare, or to the desired doneness. Transfer the breasts to a cutting board; cover with foil to keep warm until ready to serve.

3. Discard all but 1 teaspoon duck fat remaining in skillet. Add the shallot and cook over medium heat 2 to 3 minutes, or until beginning to brown. Stir in garlic and cook 1 minute. Add port wine, balsamic vinegar, and cherries; heat to boiling over high heat. Boil 3 minutes, or until sauce is reduced to ¾ cup, stirring frequently.

4. To serve, thinly slice each breast and transfer it to a dinner plate. Spoon some port sauce over the breasts.

Each serving About 315 calories, 28g protein, 19g carbohydrate, 13g fat (4g saturated), 1g fiber, 245mg sodium.

caramelized onion & rye bread stuffing

PREP: 20 MIN / TOTAL: 1 HR 20 MIN / SERVES 10

8 cups (½-inch cubes) day-old seeded rye bread

3 tablespoons vegetable oil

3 medium onions, chopped

5 stalks celery, chopped

1 pound cremini or button mushrooms, trimmed and chopped

1 small bunch collard greens, leaves only, chopped

2 tablespoons butter

1 tablespoon fresh thyme leaves

½ teaspoon salt

1 cup chicken broth

¼ cup finely chopped fresh parsley

3 large eggs, beaten

1. Preheat the oven to 375°F. Arrange the bread on a large rimmed baking sheet. Bake 15 to 20 minutes, or until crisp and dry. Set aside.

2. In a 7- to 8-quart saucepot, heat the oil over medium heat. Add the onions and celery; cook 15 to 20 minutes, or until the onions have browned and the celery is tender, stirring occasionally.

3. To the pot, add the mushrooms, collards, butter, thyme, and salt. Cook 7 to 10 minutes, or until the collards are almost tender, stirring occasionally. Remove from the heat and add the bread, broth, and parsley. Toss until well combined; cool the mixture slightly.

4. To the pot, add eggs; stir to combine. Transfer the mixture to a 3-quart baking dish. Cover with foil; bake 35 minutes. Remove the foil; bake another 10 minutes, or until top is crispy.

Each serving About 205 calories, 4g protein, 25g carbohydrate, 9g fat (3g saturated), 5g fiber, 465mg sodium.

TESTING NOTE Make sure to read our stuffing poultry tips on page 266.

CRISPY DUCK WITH APRICOTS 264

CARAMELIZED ONION & RYE BREAD STUFFING 265

STUFF POULTRY

Tradition often dictates a stuffed bird (especially the holiday turkey), so the juices of the bird can moisten the stuffing. But some cooks prefer to roast their birds unstuffed and heat the stuffing in a separate baking dish. If you prefer your poultry stuffed, here are some pointers on how to do it safely.

- **ONE IMPORTANT RULE OF THUMB:** Remember that the stuffing is only being heated through while inside the bird and does not actually cook. Therefore, it is important that the ingredients be thoroughly cooked before being combined.

- **TO SAVE TIME,** cut up the raw stuffing ingredients the night before, then cover and refrigerate. If you wish, you can cook the vegetables and meat, then cool, cover, and refrigerate. When you're ready to put the stuffing together, reheat the cooked ingredients in a large skillet before proceeding with the recipe.

- **STUFF THE BIRD JUST BEFORE ROASTING**—never in advance—and roast immediately. Use warm, cooked ingredients and hot broth or stock for your stuffing. A warm stuffing will reach the safe temperature of 160°F more quickly. At this safe temperature, bacteria, including salmonella, are killed.

- **LIGHTLY STUFF THE BODY AND NECK CAVITIES;** do not pack. Stuffing needs room to expand during cooking. You will rarely be able to fit all of the stuffing inside the bird, so bake the extra stuffing in a greased baking dish for about 30 minutes or until heated through.

- **AFTER COOKING,** the stuffing temperature should have reached 160°F to be safe. Check the temperature with a meat thermometer inserted deep into the stuffing. If the poultry has reached the proper temperature but the stuffing hasn't, transfer the stuffing to a greased baking dish, cover, and continue baking until it reaches 160°F.

- **ANY LEFTOVER STUFFING** should be promptly removed from the bird (to avoid potential bacterial growth). Transfer the stuffing to a covered container and use within three days, or freeze up to one month.

southwest corn bread stuffing

PREP: 20 MIN / TOTAL: 2 HR 10 MIN, PLUS COOLING / MAKES ABOUT 11 CUPS

- 2 cups yellow cornmeal
- 2 teaspoons baking powder
- 1 teaspoon baking soda
- 1 teaspoon salt
- 2 cups buttermilk
- ½ cup butter, melted and cooled
- 1 can (14¾ ounces) cream-style corn
- 2 cans (4 to 4½ ounces each) chopped mild green chiles
- 8 ounces Monterey Jack cheese, shredded (2 cups)
- 4 large eggs, lightly beaten
- ½ cup chicken broth

1. Preheat the oven to 350°F. Grease a 13 × 9-inch baking pan or a deep 12-inch oven-safe skillet (if your skillet is not oven-safe, wrap the handle with a double layer of foil).

2. In a large bowl, combine the cornmeal, baking powder, baking soda, and salt. Stir in the buttermilk, butter, corn, chiles, cheese, and eggs, and stir until thoroughly blended. Pour the batter into the prepared baking pan.

3. Bake the corn bread until the top is browned and a toothpick inserted in the center comes out clean, 60 to 65 minutes. Cool in the pan on a wire rack. (The corn bread can be used after cooling to make stuffing, but it will make a firmer stuffing if it's allowed to stale slightly. If desired, cover and reserve the corn bread up to 2 days.)

4. Prepare the stuffing: Crumble the corn bread into a large bowl. Drizzle with broth; toss to mix well. Stuff a 12- to 16-pound turkey, or heat the stuffing in a baking dish and serve alongside poultry or ham: Spoon the stuffing into a greased 13 × 9-inch baking dish; cover with foil and bake in preheated 325°F oven until heated through, about 45 minutes.

Each serving (½ cup) About 160 calories, 6g protein, 15g carbohydrate, 9g fat (5g saturated), 1g fiber, 481mg sodium.

chestnut & apple stuffing

PREP: 1 HR / TOTAL: 1 HR 45 MIN / MAKES ABOUT 12 CUPS

- 2 pounds fresh chestnuts
- 1 loaf (16 ounces) day-old French bread, cut into ½-inch cubes (10 cups)
- 6 tablespoons butter
- 2 stalks celery, sliced
- 1 medium onion, coarsely chopped
- 1¾ pounds Gala or Granny Smith apples (3 large), peeled, cored, and coarsely chopped
- 2 teaspoons poultry seasoning
- 1¾ cups chicken broth
- 1 cup water
- 1 teaspoon salt

1. Preheat the oven to 400°F. With a sharp knife, slash the shell of each chestnut. Place the chestnuts in a jelly-roll pan and roast until the shells burst open, about 20 minutes. When cool enough to handle, peel the chestnuts using a paring knife. Chop the chestnut meat; place it in a large bowl. Add the bread cubes to bowl and toss to combine.

2. In a 3-quart saucepan, melt the butter over medium-high heat. Add the celery and onion and cook until golden brown and tender, about 10 minutes. Add the apples and poultry seasoning; cook, stirring occasionally, 2 minutes longer. Stir in the broth, water, and salt; heat to boiling over high heat.

3. Pour the hot vegetable mixture over the chestnut mixture; stir to combine thoroughly. Stuff a 12- to 16-pound turkey, or heat the stuffing in a baking dish and serve alongside poultry or ham: Spoon the stuffing into a greased 13 × 9-inch baking dish; cover with foil and bake in preheated 325°F oven until heated through, about 45 minutes.

Each serving (½ cup) About 160 calories, 3g protein, 28g carbohydrate, 4g fat (2g saturated), 2g fiber, 321mg sodium.

Tip For this recipe, you want an apple that has a sweet-tart flavor and will hold its shape during cooking. Fuji, Gala, and Golden Delicious are all good choices. For a tarter apple, go with Granny Smith. For information on chestnuts, see page 268.

northwest fruit stuffing

PREP: 40 MIN / TOTAL: 1 HR 25 MIN / MAKES ABOUT 12 CUPS

- ½ cup butter
- 1 large red onion, coarsely chopped
- 1 medium fennel bulb (1¼ pounds), trimmed and coarsely chopped
- 2 large pears, peeled, cored, and coarsely chopped
- 1 large Granny Smith apple, peeled, cored, and coarsely chopped
- 1½ loaves (16 ounces each) sliced firm white bread, cut into ¾-inch cubes and lightly toasted
- 1 cup chicken broth
- ⅔ cup dried tart cherries
- ½ cup golden raisins
- ⅓ cup chopped fresh parsley
- 2 teaspoons chopped fresh thyme
- 1 teaspoon chopped fresh sage
- 1 teaspoon salt
- ½ teaspoon coarsely ground black pepper

1. In a 12-inch skillet, melt the butter over medium-high heat. Add the onion and fennel and cook, stirring occasionally, until the vegetables are golden brown and tender, 10 to 12 minutes. Add the pears and apple and cook 5 minutes longer. Transfer to a large bowl.

2. Add the bread cubes, broth, cherries, raisins, parsley, thyme, sage, salt, and pepper to the bowl with the pears and apple; toss to combine thoroughly. Stuff a 12- to 16-pound turkey, or heat the stuffing in a baking dish and serve alongside poultry or ham: Spoon the stuffing into a greased 13 × 9-inch baking dish; cover with foil and bake in preheated 325°F oven until heated through, about 45 minutes.

Each serving (½ cup) About 150 calories, 3g protein, 24g carbohydrate, 5g fat (3g saturated), 2g fiber, 351mg sodium.

moist bread stuffing

PREP: 25 MIN / TOTAL: 1 HR 10 MIN / MAKES ABOUT 10 CUPS

½ cup butter

5 stalks celery, finely chopped

1 medium onion, finely chopped

2 loaves (16 ounces each) sliced firm white bread, cut into ¾-inch cubes

1¾ cups chicken broth

¼ cup chopped fresh parsley

1 teaspoon dried thyme

¾ teaspoon salt

½ teaspoon ground black pepper

½ teaspoon dried sage

1. In a 5-quart Dutch oven, melt the butter over medium heat. Add the celery and onion and cook, stirring occasionally, until tender, about 15 minutes.

2. Remove the Dutch oven from the heat. Add the bread cubes, broth, parsley, thyme, salt, pepper, and sage; toss to combine thoroughly. Stuff a 12- to 16-pound turkey, or heat the stuffing in a baking dish and serve alongside poultry or ham: Spoon the stuffing into a greased 13 × 9-inch baking dish; cover with foil and bake in a preheated 325°F oven until heated through, about 45 minutes.

Each serving (½ cup) About 170 calories, 4g protein, 24g carbohydrate, 6g fat (3g saturated), 1g fiber, 473mg sodium.

TESTING NOTE For the best results, use firm white bread. If you wish, set the bread cubes out overnight so they become stale.

herb & chestnut stuffing

PREP: 20 MIN / TOTAL: 1 HR / SERVES 12

12 cups cubed (¾-inch) good-quality white Pullman bread (from about a 1-pound loaf)

3 tablespoons vegetable oil

4 stalks celery, finely chopped

2 medium carrots, finely chopped

2 medium onions, finely chopped

10 large fresh sage leaves, finely chopped

2 tablespoons fresh thyme leaves, chopped

½ teaspoon salt

½ teaspoon ground black pepper

1 package (6 to 8 ounces) cooked chestnuts, chopped

1½ cups turkey or vegetable broth

2 large eggs, beaten

1. Preheat the oven to 375°F. Lightly grease a 3-quart baking dish. Arrange the bread in a single layer on two large rimmed baking sheets; toast 15 minutes or until dry and crunchy.

2. In a 6- to 7-quart saucepot, heat the oil over medium heat. Add the celery, carrots, onion, sage, thyme, salt, and pepper. Cook 8 to 10 minutes, or until the vegetables begin to soften, stirring occasionally. Remove from the heat.

3. To the pot, add the toasted bread, chestnuts, broth, and eggs. Toss until well combined. Transfer the mixture to the prepared baking dish. Bake 30 to 35 minutes, or until the edges and top are golden brown and crunchy.

Each serving About 210 calories, 6g protein, 32g carbohydrate, 7g fat (1g saturated), 3g fiber, 470mg sodium.

INGREDIENT SPOTLIGHT

Chestnuts are in season in the fall, in time for holiday cooking and baking. If you want to roast your own for stuffing or snacking: Preheat oven to 400°F. With sharp knife, cut an X in the flat side of each shell. Place on a sheet pan and roast until shells open, about 20 minutes. Cover the chestnuts with a clean kitchen towel. When cool enough to handle, peel with a paring knife, keeping unpeeled chestnuts warm for easier peeling.

tex-mex corn bread stuffing

PREP: 20 MIN / TOTAL: 1 HR 20 MIN / SERVES 12

Nonstick cooking spray

2 cups coarsely ground cornmeal

2 teaspoon baking powder

1 teaspoon baking soda

Salt

1½ cups reduced-fat sour cream

4 tablespoons butter, melted

¼ cup honey

2 large eggs

1 cup whole milk

2 cups fresh or frozen (thawed) corn kernels

8 ounces Cheddar cheese, shredded

½ cup finely chopped pickled jalapeño chiles

1 tablespoon snipped fresh chives, for garnish

1. Preheat the oven to 400°F. Line an 8-inch square baking pan with foil. Spray the foil with nonstick cooking spray.

2. In a large bowl, whisk the cornmeal, baking powder, baking soda, and ½ teaspoon salt. In a medium bowl, whisk the sour cream, butter, honey, and 1 egg; stir into the cornmeal mixture just until well mixed. Pour into the prepared pan. Bake 25 to 30 minutes, or until golden on top and brown around edges. Cool slightly on a wire rack.

3. Meanwhile, in a medium bowl, whisk the milk and remaining egg. Stir in the corn, cheese, jalapeños, and ½ teaspoon salt; set aside.

4. Cut the cooled cornbread into 1-inch chunks. Arrange in a single layer in a 3-quart baking dish. Pour the milk mixture over the cornbread, spreading the cheese and jalapeños in an even layer. Bake 25 to 30 minutes, or until the top is golden. Let stand at least 5 minutes before serving. Garnish with chives.

Each serving About 310 calories, 11g protein, 30g carbohydrate, 17g fat (10g saturated), 2g fiber, 655mg sodium.

sausage-fennel stuffing

PREP: 15 MIN / TOTAL: 1 HR / SERVES 12

12 cups cubed fruit-nut bread, such as raisin-pecan or cranberry-walnut (about 1½ pounds)

2 tablespoons vegetable oil

12 ounces sweet Italian sausage, casings removed

2 medium bulbs fennel, trimmed and finely chopped

2 medium onions, finely chopped

4 cloves garlic, finely chopped

¼ teaspoon salt

2 cups turkey or chicken broth

½ cup fresh flat-leaf parsley leaves, chopped

1. Preheat the oven to 375°F. Lightly grease a 3-quart baking dish. Arrange the bread on 2 large rimmed baking sheets in a single layer. Toast 15 minutes, or until dry and crunchy.

2. Meanwhile, in a 6- to 7-quart saucepot, heat the oil over medium heat. Add the sausage; cook 5 to 6 minutes, or until browned, breaking it up with the side of a spoon. With a slotted spoon, transfer the sausage to a medium bowl. To the same pot, add the fennel, onion, garlic, and salt. Cook 6 to 8 minutes, or until the vegetables soften, stirring occasionally. Remove from the heat. Add the sausage to the pot along with the toasted bread, broth, and parsley. Toss until well combined. Transfer the mixture to the prepared baking dish.

3. Cover the baking dish with foil and bake 20 minutes. Remove the foil and bake another 10 minutes, or until the top is crunchy.

Each serving About 185 calories, 10g protein, 27g carbohydrate, 6g fat (1g saturated), 5g fiber, 490mg sodium.

 Tip Add some heat and use hot Italian sausages instead.

seafood

The growing popularity of fish and shellfish is hardly a surprise. Fish cooks quickly, and this makes it perfect for our busy lives. Customer demand and improved shipping has brought everything from Norwegian salmon to Thai shrimp to Chilean sea bass to American markets. And we're cooking it all!

And fish is good for you. Seafood is a rich source of protein, vitamins, and minerals and is low in fat. And oily fish, such as salmon and tuna, are high in omega-3 fatty acids, which can lower blood cholesterol levels. So whether you're in the mood for Spicy Soy-Glazed Salmon (page 290), a bowl of Mussels with Tomatoes & White Wine (page 297), or a Saucy Shrimp Curry (page 295), you'll find recipes and tips on choosing and cooking your perfect fish.

SAUCY SHRIMP CURRY 295

CRISPY COD CAKES WITH ALMOND-PEPPER VINAIGRETTE 293

CIOPPINO 298

SKILLET SHRIMP TACOS 297

Buying Fish & Shellfish

The surface of a whole fish should glisten but not look slimy. Ask the fishmonger to show you the gills; they should be bright red with no tinge of brown. The eyes should not be sunken, but don't worry if they are clouded over, because the eyes of some fish lose their shine soon after they are caught.

FISH FILLETS AND STEAKS are often sold in plastic-wrapped trays. Look for fish that appears moist and has no gaps in the flesh, which should feel firm through the plastic. The meat of dark fish, such as tuna, should not contain any rainbow streaks.

MOLLUSKS (including clams, mussels, and oysters) must be purchased alive because their viscera deteriorate quickly once dead. Tightly closed shells indicate the mollusks are alive, but if you tap a gaping shell and it closes, it's also fine. Don't buy mollusks with broken shells. And if a clam or mussel feels especially heavy, it could be filled with mud, so discard it. Mollusks sold out of their shells, like scallops and squid, should be as sweet smelling as an ocean breeze. And the siphons of soft-shell clams should retract slightly when touched.

CRUSTACEANS, including crabs and lobsters, should be purchased alive from a store with a large turnover and appear lively. Fresh shrimp should also be subjected to the sniff test; black spots on the shells mean the shrimp are over the hill.

Storing Fish & Shellfish

- Keep fish and shellfish as cold as possible. Between the store and home, pack the seafood you purchase in ice, or place it in the same bag as your frozen food.

- Store fish in the coldest part of the refrigerator, where the temperature is between 35°F and 40°F. Or store it on ice: Fill a baking dish with ice and place the wrapped seafood on top, replenishing the ice as needed. You can also cover frozen artificial ice packets with a kitchen towel and place the wrapped fish on top.

- It is especially important to keep oily fish, such as mackerel and bluefish, as cold as possible. Their high fat content means they can go rancid quickly at less-than-ideal temperatures.

- If you must freeze seafood, be sure it is very fresh, and wrap it tightly in plastic wrap and heavy-duty foil. Freeze for up to three months.

- Shellfish should also be placed in the coldest part of the refrigerator. Store live clams, mussels, and oysters in a large bowl covered with a wet towel; use within one day. Refrigerate live crabs in a tightly closed, heavy-duty paper bag poked with a few air holes; cook within one day of purchase. Lobsters should be cooked on the day of purchase, because they don't last long once out of water. Keep them well wrapped in a wet cloth or in several layers of newspaper in the refrigerator.

- Cooked crab and lobster should be eaten within one day of purchase. Shucked oysters and crabmeat are often pasteurized, which extends their shelf life but decreases their flavor.

Cooking Success

Here's the simple secret to cooking fish successfully: Don't overcook it. Cook until the flesh is just opaque throughout; it will continue to cook after it has been removed from the heat.

Before cooking fillets, especially thick ones, run your fingers over the flesh to feel for any stray bones. Remove them with tweezers set aside for that purpose.

To check fish fillets or steaks for doneness, use the tip of a small knife to separate the flesh in the thickest part; it should be uniformly opaque. To check whole fish, make an incision at the backbone to see if the flesh is opaque, or insert an instant-read thermometer in the thickest part near the backbone; it should read 135°F to 140°F.

Before cooking clams, mussels, or oysters, scrub the shells well under cold running water to remove any surface sand and grit.

Know Your Fish

Fish is categorized two ways: by shape (round or flat) and by fat content (lean to oily). It is helpful to know the fat content, flavor, and texture of various fish so you can easily substitute one for another.

ROUND FISH have a plump, cylindrical shape and an eye on each side of the head. The backbone runs down the center of the fish, separating the two thick fillets. Round fish are generally filleted or cut into steaks but can also be cooked whole. Common round fish include salmon, red snapper, sea bass, monkfish, and catfish.

FLATFISH have wide, thin bodies with both eyes on the same side of the head. The backbone runs down the center of the fish, with two lines of bones fanning out on either side, separating the top and bottom fillets. Flatfish are usually filleted. The most common are sole, flounder, and halibut.

The fat content of a fish is a good indicator of the flavor you can expect.

LEAN FISH make up the majority of fish. They have the blandest flavor and most delicate texture.

MODERATELY OILY FISH have a slightly higher fat content, a pleasant texture, and a mild flavor. Some fish, such as tuna, can be categorized as either *moderately oily* or *oily*, depending on the species.

OILY FISH have flesh that is strong-tasting, firm, and meaty. They are high in omega-3 fatty acids.

Fish Glossary

Here is a glossary of some of the fish you are likely to find in your market.

ARCTIC CHAR Very similar to salmon; usually farm-raised. Also known as salmon trout.

BLUEFISH A dark-fleshed, strong-flavored, oily fish. The fresher it is, the milder the flavor.

CATFISH A beloved freshwater fish of the American South. Farm-raised catfish are readily available.

COD This saltwater fish, found in both Atlantic and Pacific waters, is known for its mild flavor and white, flaky flesh. Small cod are called *scrod*.

FLOUNDER A popular flatfish with white flesh, a delicate texture, and mild flavor.

GROUPER Has firm, meaty, white flesh and is sold whole or filleted.

HALIBUT A large flatfish with firm, flavorful flesh. Often sold as fillets, it's one of the few flatfish thick enough to be cut into steaks.

MACKEREL An oily fish with a pronounced fish flavor. When more than three pounds, it is called *Spanish mackerel*.

MONKFISH A favored fish in Provence, monkfish has firm flesh and a lobster-like flavor.

POMPANO On the West Coast, pompano is called *yellowtail*. It has somewhat oily flesh and a firm texture.

RED SNAPPER An excellent all-purpose fish and one of the few fillets firm enough to be grilled.

SALMON Much of the salmon in our markets is farm-raised, even when labeled "Atlantic" or "Norwegian." Wild salmon, such as *coho, king*, and *sockeye*, has superior flavor but is available in limited quantities.

SOLE A flatfish with firm white flesh and a distinctively delicate flavor.

STRIPED BASS Most striped bass in today's markets is a farm-raised hybrid of striped bass and white bass.

SWORDFISH A fish with a firm and meaty texture that is a good choice for broiling and grilling.

TROUT Rainbow trout and brook trout are about 12 ounces each and serve one person.

TUNA A huge fish with plenty of muscle and flavor. The most common varieties are *bluefin, yellowfin, albacore*, and *skipjack*. Tuna is also known as *ahi* and *bonito*.

GOOD TO KNOW

THE FISH EXCHANGE

When the market doesn't have the fish called for in your recipe, you have options.

LEAN

Cod, Scrod • Flounder • Grouper
Haddock • Halibut • Monkfish
Ocean perch • Orange roughy
Pike Pollock • Red snapper
Rockfish • Sea bass • Sole • Tilapia
Tilefish • Turbot • Whiting

MODERATE

Bluefish • Catfish • Mahi-mahi
Rainbow trout • Lake trout
Striped bass • Swordfish
Yellowfin tuna

OILY

Bluefin tuna • Butterfish • Herring
Mackerel • Pompano • Salmon
Shad • Whitefish

Know Your Shellfish

MOLLUSKS

Mollusks have soft bodies that are protected by shells consisting of one or more parts. This glossary lists the most popular shellfish.

HARD-SHELL CLAMS, the most common Atlantic Coast variety, are categorized by size. *Littlenecks* are the smallest, *cherrystones* are medium, and *chowder clams* are the largest.

SOFT-SHELL CLAMS have delicate shells that don't completely close because of the long, neck-like siphon that protrudes between the two halves of the shell. On the East Coast, they are usually called *steamers*, because they are so delicious when steamed. They are also known as *Ipswich clams*, so named for the location of one of the largest clam beds. West Coast soft-shell clams include the huge *geoduck* (GOO-ee-duck) and the long *razor* clam.

MUSSELS Most markets carry *blue mussels*, which have bluish-black shells and are harvested wild or cultivated. *New Zealand green mussels* are slightly larger and have a bright green shell.

OYSTERS Oysters are usually named for the location of their beds: *Wellfleet*, *Chincoteague*, and *Apalachicola* on the East Coast and *Westcott Bay*, *Tomales Bay*, and the tiny *Olympia* on the West Coast are examples.

SCALLOPS Sea scallops are gathered year-round and are relatively large. Small *bay scallops* are only available in the fall and winter. *Calico scallops* are very small, but they have the least flavor and the toughest texture.

SQUID Also called *calamari*, many fish markets sell it already cleaned.

CRUSTACEANS

Crustaceans have elongated bodies that are covered by jointed shells.

CRAB On the West Coast, there is *Dungeness crab*, whose season runs from October to April. *King crab*, usually from Alaska, provides the large legs that are sold fresh or frozen. Small *blue crabs* are found along the East and Gulf Coasts. The large pieces of meat from the body are sold as lump, jumbo, or backfin crabmeat.

SOFT-SHELL CRABS These are blue crabs caught during the short period after they have shed their hard shells and before their new, soft shells have hardened. They are available fresh from May to September.

STONE CRABS Popular in Florida, the claws are harvested, and the rest of the crab is tossed back into the water so new claws can regenerate.

LOBSTER There are two types: *American (Maine) lobster*, from the North Atlantic coast, and rock (*spiny*) lobster, which is harvested off the coasts of Florida, California, Australia, and New Zealand. It is usually sold as frozen lobster tail.

SHRIMP More than 95 percent of the shrimp sold has been previously frozen. *Warm-water shrimp* live in tropical waters and are usually categorized by the color of their shells: pink, white, blue, or black tiger.

SPANISH MUSSELS & PAPRIKA FRIES 298

fish 'n' chips

PREP: 15 MIN / TOTAL: 30 MIN / SERVES 4

Nonstick cooking spray

1½ pounds cod fillets, cut into strips

3 large egg whites, beaten

1 bag (6 ounces) salt-and-vinegar potato chips, finely crushed

Salt

1 pound frozen peas

3 tablespoons butter

1 tablespoon fresh lemon juice

¼ teaspoon ground black pepper

Lemon wedges and chives, for serving

1. Preheat the oven to 450°F. Line a large baking sheet with foil; spray generously with nonstick spray.

2. Dip the cod fillets into the egg whites, then the potato chips; arrange on the prepared pan. Spray the fish with nonstick spray. Bake 12 minutes. Sprinkle with ¼ teaspoon salt.

3. Microwave the peas, butter, lemon juice, pepper, and ¼ teaspoon salt on High for 5 minutes; puree in the food processor until smooth. Serve the fish with the pea puree, lemon wedges, and chives.

Each serving About 295 calories, 35g protein, 16g carbohydrate, 10g fat (6g saturated), 6g fiber, 570mg sodium.

 Tip For less mess, crush chips right in the bag. Make a small hole in the top and go to town with a rolling pin.

VARIATION

Oven-Fried Fish

Preheat the oven to 450°F. Grease a rimmed baking sheet with **2 teaspoons vegetable oil**; set aside. On waxed paper, combine ¼ **cup all-purpose flour**, ½ **teaspoon salt**, and ¼ **teaspoon cayenne pepper**. In a shallow bowl, beat **2 large egg whites** just until foamy. On a separate sheet of waxed paper, place **1 cup plain dried bread crumbs**. Cut **1 pound flounder or sole fillets** on diagonal into 1-inch-wide strips and coat with the seasoned flour, shaking off the excess. Dip the strips into the egg whites, then coat them in bread crumbs, patting the crumbs to adhere. Arrange the fish strips on the prepared baking sheet. Place the baking sheet on the lowest oven rack and bake the fish 5 minutes. With a wide spatula, turn the fish. Bake until just opaque throughout and golden, 4 to 5 minutes longer.

brandade

PREP: 20 MIN / TOTAL: 40 MIN, PLUS SOAKING / MAKES 4 CUPS

1 pound salt cod fillets

1 large baking potato (12 ounces), peeled and thinly sliced

3 cloves garlic, peeled

3 cups water

1 cup heavy or whipping cream

Pinch of ground nutmeg

2 tablespoons extra-virgin olive oil

Thinly sliced French bread, toasted

1. In a medium bowl, combine the salt cod fillets and enough cold water to cover generously. Cover and refrigerate, changing the water several times, for 24 to 36 hours. Drain and rinse well.

2. In a 3-quart saucepan, combine the potato, garlic, and water; heat to boiling over high heat. Reduce the heat and simmer until the potato is tender, 12 to 15 minutes. Drain, reserving 1 cup water. Mash the potato and garlic until almost smooth. Transfer the mixture to a medium bowl.

3. Meanwhile, in a clean 3-quart saucepan, combine the cod and enough water to cover; heat to boiling. Reduce the heat and simmer until the fish can be flaked with a fork, 5 to 10 minutes; drain. When cool enough to handle, discard any skin or bones. Transfer the cod to a food processor with the knife blade attached and pulse until flaked.

4. In a clean 3-quart saucepan, heat the cream over low heat. With a wooden spoon, stir in the cod, potato mixture, reserved potato water, and nutmeg; stir until well combined. With a wire whisk, gradually whisk in oil. Serve with toasted French bread.

Each ¼ cup (without toast) About 215 calories, 25g protein, 5g carbohydrate, 11g fat (5g saturated), 0g fiber, 0mg sodium.

GLOSSARY →

Literally meaning "to shake," this Provençal classic is sometimes called **brandade de morue** (cod). It stars salt cod that has been soaked and cooked, then whipped with olive oil, milk or cream, seasonings, and often potatoes. There are similar dishes around Europe. In Spain it is called *brandada de bacalao* and in Italy, *bacalao mantecato*.

tarragon-roasted salmon

PREP: 10 MIN / TOTAL: 50 MIN / SERVES 10

- 2 large lemons, thinly sliced
- 1 whole salmon (5½ pounds), cleaned and scaled
- 2 tablespoons olive oil
- ½ teaspoon salt
- ½ teaspoon coarsely ground black pepper
- 1 large bunch tarragon
- 1 small bunch parsley
- Caper Sauce (below)
- Lemon wedges, for serving

1. Preheat the oven to 450°F. Line a jelly-roll pan with foil. Arrange one-third of the lemon slices in a row down the center of the pan.

2. Rinse the salmon inside and out with cold running water; pat dry with paper towels. Rub the outside of the salmon with oil. Place the salmon on top of the lemon slices. Sprinkle the cavity with the salt and pepper. Place tarragon and parsley sprigs and half of the remaining lemon slices in cavity. Arrange the remaining lemon slices on top of the fish. Roast the salmon until just opaque throughout when a knife is inserted at backbone, about 40 minutes.

3. Meanwhile, prepare Caper Sauce.

4. Carefully remove the lemon slices and peel off the skin from the top of the salmon; discard. Using 2 wide spatulas, transfer the salmon to a cutting board.

5. To serve, slide a cake server under the front section of the top fillet and lift off the fillet; transfer to a warm large platter. Slide the server under backbone and lift it away from the bottom fillet; discard. Slide the cake server between the bottom fillet and the skin and transfer the fillet to the platter. Serve with lemon wedges and Caper Sauce.

CAPER SAUCE In medium bowl, mix ¾ **cup sour cream**; ½ **cup mayonnaise**; ¼ **cup milk**; 3 **tablespoons capers**, drained and chopped; 2 **tablespoons chopped fresh tarragon**; ½ **teaspoon freshly grated lemon zest**; and ⅛ **teaspoon coarsely ground black pepper** until blended. Cover and refrigerate until ready to serve, up to two days. Makes 1⅔ cups.

TARRAGON-ROASTED SALMON Each serving (without sauce) About 325 calories, 33g protein, 1g carbohydrate, 20g fat (4g saturated), 0g fiber, 213mg sodium.
CAPER SAUCE Each tablespoon About 60 calories, 0g protein, 1g carbohydrate, 6g fat (2g saturated), 0g fiber, 90mg sodium.

cold poached salmon steaks
with watercress sauce

PREP: 15 MIN / TOTAL: 25 MIN, PLUS COOLING / SERVES 4

- 1 medium lemon
- 4 salmon steaks, 1 inch thick (6 ounces each)
- ¾ teaspoon salt
- ½ teaspoon coarsely ground black pepper
- 1 medium onion, thinly sliced
- Watercress Sauce (below)

1. From the lemon, squeeze the juice; reserve for Watercress Sauce. Set the lemon shells aside. Rub the salmon steaks evenly with the salt and pepper.

2. In a 12-inch skillet, heat ½ inch water to boiling over high heat. Add the salmon, onion, and lemon shells; heat to boiling. Reduce the heat; cover and simmer until the fish is just opaque throughout, 5 to 8 minutes. With a slotted spatula, transfer the fish to a platter. Let cool 30 minutes, or cover and refrigerate to serve later.

3. Meanwhile, prepare the Watercress Sauce.

4. Remove the skin and bones from the salmon, if you like. Serve with the sauce.

WATERCRESS SAUCE In blender or in food processor with the knife blade attached, puree ½ **bunch watercress**, tough stems trimmed (1 cup), ½ **cup sour cream**, 1 **tablespoon fresh lemon juice**, 1 **teaspoon chopped fresh tarragon** or ⅛ **teaspoon dried tarragon**, 1½ **teaspoons sugar**, and 1 **teaspoon salt** until smooth. Cover and refrigerate. Makes about ½ cup.

COLD POACHED SALMON STEAKS Each serving (without sauce) About 275 calories, 30g protein, 0g carbohydrate, 16g fat (3g saturated), 0g fiber, 231mg sodium.
WATERCRESS SAUCE Each tablespoon About 35 calories, 1g protein, 2g carbohydrate, 3g fat (2g saturated), 0g fiber, 301mg sodium.

trout meunière

PREP: 10 MIN / TOTAL: 30 MIN, PLUS STANDING / SERVES 4

- **4 brook or rainbow trout (10 to 12 ounces each), cleaned and scaled**
- **1 cup milk**
- **¼ cup all-purpose flour**
- **½ teaspoon salt**
- **4 tablespoons vegetable oil**
- **¼ cup fresh lemon juice**
- **4 tablespoons butter**
- **¼ cup chopped fresh parsley**

1. Rinse the trout inside and out with cold running water; pat dry with paper towels. Soak the trout in milk 10 minutes. On waxed paper, combine the flour and salt. Remove the trout from the milk and coat it evenly with the flour mixture, shaking off the excess.

2. In a 12-inch skillet, heat 2 tablespoons oil over medium heat until very hot. Add 2 trout and cook until just opaque throughout when a knife is inserted at the backbone, 4 to 5 minutes per side. Transfer to a platter and keep warm. Repeat with the remaining 2 tablespoons oil and the remaining fish.

3. Pour off any fat remaining in the skillet and wipe it clean with paper towels. Return the skillet to the heat; add the lemon juice and cook 15 seconds. Add the butter; cook until foamy, about 2 minutes. Stir in the parsley and pour the butter sauce over the fish.

Each serving About 495 calories, 41g protein, 8g carbohydrate, 32g fat (10g saturated), 0g fiber, 468mg sodium.

VARIATIONS

Trout with Brown Butter & Sage
Prepare as directed through step 2. In step 3, substitute **2 tablespoons chopped fresh sage** for the parsley and cook until the butter is lightly browned, about 3 minutes. Add **1 teaspoon fresh lemon juice**. Pour the sauce over the fish.

Trout Amandine
Prepare as directed through step 2. In step 3, omit the parsley. Add **¼ cup sliced almonds** to the skillet with the butter and cook until the almonds are golden, 2 to 3 minutes. Add **1 teaspoon fresh lemon juice**. Pour the sauce over the fish.

Trout Grenobloise
Prepare as directed through step 2. In step 3, omit the lemon juice. From **1 lemon**, remove the peel and white pith. Cut the lemon into ¼-inch-thick slices; discard the seeds. Cut the slices into ½-inch pieces. After cooking the butter until foamy, add the lemon pieces, **4 teaspoons capers**, and **1 tablespoon chopped fresh parsley**. Spoon the sauce over the fish.

Trout with Cornmeal & Bacon
Prepare as directed through step 2, substituting ⅓ **cup cornmeal** for the flour in step 1 and **bacon drippings from 4 strips bacon** for the oil in step 2. Omit step 3. Garnish the fish with **crumbled cooked bacon**.

INGREDIENT SPOTLIGHT

Trout Rainbow trout and brook trout are marketed at just the right size for single servings: between 8 and 12 ounces. They belong to the Salmonidae (salmon) family. Rainbow trout has a green or blue back, silvery sides covered with tiny dark spots, and a thin red stripe running along each side. Brook trout, on the other hand, has a green-brown back and green sides, and its skin is mottled with yellow and red spots. Although trout is still caught in the wild, most of the trout in stores has been farmed in spring water–fed ponds. Trout is mild flavored and delicate and is best enjoyed when prepared simply as in our tasty recipes.

salt-baked fish

PREP: 5 MIN / TOTAL: 35 MIN / SERVES 2

4 cups kosher salt

1 whole red snapper, striped bass, or porgy (1½ to 2 pounds), cleaned and scaled

1 lemon

3 sprigs fresh rosemary or thyme

1. Preheat the oven to 450°F. Line 13 × 9–inch baking pan with foil; spread 2 cups salt in the bottom of the pan.

2. Rinse the snapper inside and out with cold running water; pat dry with paper towels. From the lemon, cut 3 slices. Cut the remaining lemon into wedges. Place the lemon slices and rosemary in the cavity of the fish. Place the fish on the bed of salt; cover with the remaining 2 cups salt. Bake until the fish is just opaque throughout when a knife is inserted at the backbone, about 30 minutes.

3. To serve, tap the salt crust to release it from the top of the fish; discard. Slide a cake server under the front section of the top fillet and lift off the fillet; transfer to a platter. Slide the server under the backbone and lift it away from the bottom fillet; discard. Slide the cake server between the bottom fillet and the skin and transfer the fillet to the platter. Serve with reserved lemon wedges.

Each serving About 190 calories, 37g protein, 6g carbohydrate, 3g fat (1g saturated), 0g fiber, 800mg sodium.

VARIATION

Roast Striped Bass

Prepare as directed above, substituting **1 whole striped bass** (2¼ pounds), cleaned and scaled, for the snapper and omitting the salt. Make diagonal slashes on each side of the fish at 1-inch intervals, about ¼ inch deep. Place the bass in medium roasting pan (14 × 10 inches). Proceed as above. **Makes 4 main-dish servings.**

cod veracruz

PREP: 15 MIN / TOTAL: 50 MIN / SERVES 4

4 tablespoons vegetable oil

1 yellow bell pepper, cut into thin strips

1 medium onion, thinly sliced

1 jalapeño chile, seeded and finely chopped

1 clove garlic, thinly sliced

¾ teaspoon chili powder

Salt

1 can (14½ to 16 ounces) tomatoes in puree

½ teaspoon ground coriander

¼ teaspoon ground cumin

⅛ teaspoon cayenne pepper

4 cod steaks, ¾ inch thick (4 ounces each)

1. In a 12-inch nonstick skillet, heat 2 tablespoons oil over medium heat. Add the yellow bell pepper and onion and cook, stirring, until tender and golden, 15 minutes. Add the jalapeño, garlic, ½ teaspoon chili powder, and ¼ teaspoon salt and cook, stirring, 3 minutes.

2. Add the tomatoes with their puree and cook, breaking up the tomatoes with the side of a spoon, until the mixture has slightly reduced, about 10 minutes.

3. Meanwhile, in a cup, combine the coriander, cumin, the remaining ¼ teaspoon chili powder, ¼ teaspoon salt, and the cayenne. Sprinkle both sides of the cod steaks with the spice mixture.

4. In a 10-inch skillet, heat the remaining 2 tablespoons oil over medium-high heat until hot. Add the cod and cook until the steaks are just opaque throughout and nicely browned, 3 to 4 minutes per side. To serve, arrange the fish on a platter and top with the warm tomato sauce.

Each serving About 255 calories, 19g protein, 12g carbohydrate, 14g fat (2g saturated), 2g fiber, 508mg sodium.

broiled cod steaks montauk

PREP: 5 MIN / TOTAL: 15 MIN / SERVES 4

¼ cup mayonnaise

½ teaspoon Dijon mustard

⅛ teaspoon salt

⅛ teaspoon ground black pepper

Nonstick cooking spray

4 cod steaks, ½ inch thick (6 ounces each)

1. Preheat the broiler.

2. In a small bowl, mix the mayonnaise, mustard, salt, and pepper until blended.

3. Lightly oil a broiling-pan rack. Place the cod on the rack in the broiling pan. Place the pan in the broiler, 4 inches from the heat source. Broil the cod until just opaque throughout, 5 to 7 minutes. Remove the broiling pan from the broiler. Brush the mayonnaise mixture on the fish. Return the pan to the broiler; broil until the mayonnaise mixture is lightly browned and bubbling, 1 to 2 minutes longer.

Each serving About 220 calories, 27g protein, 0g carbohydrate, 12g fat (2g saturated), 0g fiber, 247mg sodium.

VARIATIONS

Lemon Topping

Prepare as directed, but substitute ½ **teaspoon freshly grated lemon zest** for the Dijon mustard.

Horseradish Topping

Prepare as directed, but substitute **1 teaspoon bottled white horseradish** for the Dijon mustard.

Dill-Pepper Topping

Prepare as directed, but substitute **2 tablespoons chopped fresh dill** for the Dijon mustard and ¼ **teaspoon coarsely ground black pepper** for the ground black pepper.

Lime-Jalapeño Topping

Prepare as directed, but substitute ½ **teaspoon freshly grated lime zest** for the Dijon mustard and add **1 small jalapeño chile**, seeded and minced, to the mayonnaise mixture.

Parmesan Topping

Prepare as directed, but substitute **2 tablespoons freshly grated Parmesan cheese** for the Dijon mustard.

broiled swordfish steaks

with maître d'hôtel butter

PREP: 15 MIN / TOTAL: 25 MIN / SERVES 4

4 teaspoons Maître d'Hôtel Butter (below)

4 swordfish steaks, 1 inch thick (6 ounces each)

1. Prepare the Maître d'Hôtel Butter.

2. Preheat the broiler. Place the swordfish on a rack in a broiling pan. Spread ½ teaspoon Maître d'Hôtel Butter on each side of each fish steak. Place the pan in the broiler, 4 inches from the heat source. Broil the swordfish, without turning, until just opaque throughout, 8 to 10 minutes. Spoon pan juices over fish to serve.

MAÎTRE D'HÔTEL BUTTER In a medium bowl, beat ½ **cup butter** softened, with a wooden spoon until creamy. Beat in **2 tablespoon chopped fresh parsley**, ¼ **teaspoon freshly grated lemon zest**, and **1 tablespoon fresh lemon juice**; blend well. Transfer the flavored butter to waxed paper and shape it into a log about 6 inches long; wrap, twisting the ends of waxed paper to seal. Overwrap in plastic or foil before chilling or freezing. Flavored butter can be refrigerated up to two days or frozen up to one month. To serve, cut into ½-inch thick slices. **Makes 12 servings.**

Each serving About 215 calories, 30g protein, 0g carbohydrate, 10g fat (4g saturated), 0g fiber, 75mg sodium.

roasted salmon

with tarragon & capers

PREP: 10 MIN / TOTAL: 40 MIN / SERVES 6

- 3 tablespoons butter or margarine
- ⅓ cup plain dried bread crumbs
- ¼ cup loosely packed fresh parsley leaves, minced
- 3 tablespoons drained capers, minced
- 1 teaspoon dried tarragon
- 2 teaspoons freshly grated lemon zest
- ¼ teaspoon salt
- ¼ teaspoon coarsely ground black pepper
- 1 whole salmon fillet (2 to 2½ pounds)
- Lemon wedges, for serving

1. Preheat the oven to 450°F. Line a jelly-roll pan with foil; grease the foil.

2. In a 1-quart saucepan, melt the butter over low heat. Remove the saucepan from the heat; stir in the bread crumbs, parsley, capers, tarragon, lemon zest, salt, and pepper.

3. Place the salmon, skin-side down, in the prepared jelly-roll pan. Pat the crumb mixture on top. Roast until the salmon turns opaque throughout and the topping is lightly browned, about 30 minutes.

4. With 2 large spatulas, carefully transfer the salmon to a platter (it's okay if the salmon skin sticks to the foil). Serve with lemon wedges.

Each serving About 325 calories, 28g protein, 5g carbohydrate, 21g fat (4g saturated), 1g fiber, 425mg sodium.

fried catfish

PREP: 15 MIN / TOTAL: 35 MIN, PLUS STANDING / SERVES 6

- ¾ cup cornmeal
- 2 tablespoons all-purpose flour
- ½ teaspoon salt
- ¼ teaspoon ground black pepper
- ¼ cup milk
- 6 catfish fillets (6 ounces each)
- 4 tablespoons vegetable oil
- Lemon wedges, for serving

1. In a resealable plastic bag, combine the cornmeal, flour, salt, and pepper. Pour the milk into a pie plate. Dip the catfish fillets, one at a time, into the milk to coat well, then into the cornmeal mixture, shaking the bag to coat the fish. Place the coated catfish on a wire rack set over waxed paper; set aside to dry 20 minutes.

2. In a 10-inch skillet, heat 2 tablespoons oil over medium-high heat until hot. Add 3 catfish fillets to the skillet and fry until just opaque throughout and golden, 4 to 5 minutes per side. Transfer to paper towels to drain. Repeat with remaining 2 tablespoons oil and remaining catfish. Serve with lemon wedges.

Each serving About 380 calories, 28g protein, 16g carbohydrate, 22g fat (4g saturated), 1g fiber, 255mg sodium.

fennel-crusted bluefish

PREP: 5 MIN / TOTAL: 15 MIN / SERVES 4

- 2 teaspoons fennel seeds, crushed
- ½ teaspoon whole black peppercorns, crushed
- ½ teaspoon salt
- 4 pieces bluefish fillet (6 ounces each)
- 1 tablespoon butter
- 1 teaspoon olive oil

1. In a cup, combine the fennel seeds, peppercorns, and salt. Use this to rub on both sides of the bluefish fillets.

2. In a 12-inch skillet, melt the butter with the oil over medium-high heat. Add the bluefish and cook until the fish is just opaque throughout, 4 to 6 minutes per side.

Each serving About 250 calories, 34g protein, 0g carbohydrate, 11g fat (3g saturated), 0g fiber, 422mg sodium.

 Tip To turn fish fillets so they don't fall apart, use a wide slotted spatula, supporting the fillet with your fingers as you turn it.

TESTING NOTE If you prefer to use the grill, rub the bluefish with the olive oil, then with the fennel mixture. Grill over medium-high heat 4 to 5 minutes. Serve with lemon wedges.

cod, cabbage & bacon in parchment

PREP: 20 MIN / TOTAL: 40 MIN / SERVES 4

2 slices bacon, chopped

2 teaspoons vegetable oil

½ head savoy cabbage (¾ pound), thinly sliced (6 cups)

Salt

Ground black pepper

Pinch of dried thyme

4 thick pieces cod fillet (6 ounces each)

1 tablespoon butter, cut into very small pieces

1. Preheat the oven to 400°F and ready 4 squares (12 inches each) of parchment or foil.

2. In a 12-inch skillet, cook the bacon over medium-low heat until browned. With a slotted spoon, transfer it to paper towels to drain. Discard the drippings from the skillet; wipe the skillet clean.

3. In the same skillet, heat the oil over high heat. Add the cabbage, ½ teaspoon salt, ¼ teaspoon pepper, and the thyme; cook, stirring, until the cabbage is tender. Stir in the bacon.

4. With tweezers, remove any bones from the cod. Place one-fourth of the cabbage mixture on one half of each parchment square. Place the fillets on top of the cabbage. Sprinkle the fillets with ⅛ teaspoon each of salt and pepper and evenly dot with the butter.

5. Fold the unfilled half of the parchment over the cod. To seal the packets, beginning at a corner where the parchment is folded, make ½-inch-wide folds, with each new fold overlapping the previous one, until the packet is completely sealed. The packets will resemble half circles. Place the packets on a jelly-roll pan. Bake 20 minutes (packets will puff up and brown). Cut the packets open to serve.

Each serving About 230 calories, 33g protein, 7g carbohydrate, 8g fat (3g saturated), 2g fiber, 567mg sodium.

baked scrod
with fennel & potatoes

PREP: 15 MIN / TOTAL: 1 HR 10 MIN / SERVES 4

1½ pounds red potatoes (4 large), unpeeled, thinly sliced

1 medium fennel bulb (1 pound), trimmed and thinly sliced, feathery tops reserved

1 clove garlic, finely chopped

2 tablespoons olive oil

Salt

Ground black pepper

4 pieces scrod fillet (5 ounces each)

1 large ripe tomato (8 ounces), seeded and chopped

1. Preheat the oven to 425°F.

2. In a shallow 2½-quart baking dish, toss the potatoes, fennel, garlic, oil, ¾ teaspoon salt, and ¼ teaspoon pepper until well combined; spread evenly in the baking dish. Bake, stirring once, until the vegetables are tender and lightly browned, about 45 minutes.

3. With tweezers, remove any bones from the scrod. Sprinkle the scrod with ⅛ teaspoon salt and ¼ teaspoon pepper. Arrange the fish on top of the potato mixture. Bake until the fish is just opaque throughout, 10 to 15 minutes.

4. Sprinkle with tomato and garnish with the reserved fennel tops.

Each serving About 335 calories, 30g protein, 35g carbohydrate, 8g fat (1g saturated), 5g fiber, 679mg sodium.

HOW TO

REMOVE PIN BONES

Run your fingers along each fillet to check for pin bones (the sharp bones that are often in the thickest part of the fish, toward the middle). If you feel a spiky bone, use tweezers or pin-nose pliers (set aside for that purpose) to pull it out.

asian-style flounder baked in parchment

PREP: 15 MIN / TOTAL: 25 MIN / SERVES 4

2 large green onions

2 tablespoons soy sauce

2 tablespoons seasoned rice vinegar

4 flounder fillets (6 ounces each)

2 teaspoons grated, peeled fresh ginger

1. Cut the green onion tops into 2 × ¼-inch matchstick strips; reserve for garnish. Thinly slice the white part of the green onions.

2. In a small bowl, combine the soy sauce and vinegar.

3. Preheat the oven to 425°F and ready four sheets (12 × 15-inch each) of parchment or foil. Place 1 flounder fillet on one half of each parchment sheet. Sprinkle with some ginger and sliced green onions; drizzle with some soy-sauce mixture. Fold unfilled half of parchment over the fish. To seal packets, beginning at a corner where the parchment is folded, make ½-inch-wide folds, with each new fold overlapping the previous one, until the packet is completely sealed. The packets will resemble half circles. Place the packets on a jelly-roll pan. Bake 8 minutes (packets will puff up and brown).

4. Cut the packets open and garnish the fish with the reserved green onion strips.

Each serving About 170 calories, 33g protein, 3g carbohydrate, 2g fat (0g saturated), 0g fiber, 802mg sodium.

 Tip Baking in parchment packets is a simple way to seal in the juices and the flavor of delicate fish. Substitute foil for the parchment paper, if necessary.

VARIATION

Whole Flounder in Parchment

Prepare as directed, but use a **3-pound whole flounder**, cleaned and scaled, and two 24 × 12-inch pieces of parchment or foil. Preheat the oven to 400°F. Line a rimmed baking sheet with one piece of parchment paper. Follow steps 1 and 2. Place the fish on the parchment-lined baking sheet. Sprinkle with the ginger and sliced green onions; drizzle with the soy-sauce mixture. Top with the second piece of parchment. To seal the fish, beginning at one corner, make ½-inch-wide folds, with each new fold overlapping the previous one, until the packet is sealed. Roast the fish about 30 minutes or until the fish is just opaque when a knife is inserted at the backbone. Cut the parchment open and, using 2 wide slotted spatulas, transfer the fish to a large platter. Pour the juices over the fish and garnish with the reserved green onion strips. Makes 4 main-dish servings.

scrod
with lemon garlic crumbs

PREP: 20 MIN / TOTAL: 30 MIN / SERVES 4

2 tablespoons butter

1 clove garlic, finely chopped

1 cup fresh bread crumbs (from about 2 slices bread)

4 pieces scrod or cod fillet (6 ounces each)

2 tablespoons fresh lemon juice

½ teaspoon salt

1 tablespoon chopped fresh parsley

Lemon wedges

1. Preheat the oven to 450°F. In a 10-inch skillet, melt the butter over medium heat. Add the garlic; cook until golden. Add the bread crumbs and cook, stirring frequently, until lightly toasted. Remove the skillet from the heat.

2. With tweezers, remove any bones from the scrod. In a 13 × 9-inch baking dish, arrange the fillets in a single layer; sprinkle with lemon juice and salt. Press the bread-crumb mixture onto the fillets. Bake until the fish is just opaque throughout, 10 to 15 minutes.

3. Sprinkle the scrod with parsley and serve with lemon wedges.

Each serving About 230 calories, 32g protein, 8g carbohydrate, 7g fat (4g saturated), 1g fiber, 517mg sodium.

red snapper in parchment

with tomatoes & basil

PREP: 25 MIN / TOTAL: 40 MIN / SERVES 4

1 tablespoon butter

1 large clove garlic, finely chopped

1 pound ripe plum tomatoes, seeded and chopped (2 cups)

Salt

Ground black pepper

⅓ cup chopped fresh basil

4 red snapper fillets (6 ounces each), skin removed

1. Preheat the oven to 400°F and ready four squares (12 inches each) parchment or foil.

2. In a 12-inch skillet, melt the butter over medium-high heat. Add the garlic and cook 30 seconds. Add the tomatoes, ¼ teaspoon salt, and ⅛ teaspoon pepper. Cook, stirring frequently, until the liquid has almost evaporated, about 5 minutes. Remove from the heat and stir in the basil.

3. With tweezers, remove any bones from the snapper fillets. Place 1 fillet, skinned-side down, on one half of each parchment square. Sprinkle with ⅛ teaspoon each salt and pepper on each fillet; top with tomato mixture.

4. Fold the unfilled half of parchment over the fish. To seal the packets, beginning at a corner where the parchment is folded, make ½-inch-wide folds, with each new fold overlapping the previous one, until the packet is completely sealed. The packets will resemble half circles. Place the packets on a jelly-roll pan. Bake 15 minutes (packets will puff up and brown). Cut packets open to serve.

Each serving About 210 calories, 33g protein, 6g carbohydrate, 5g fat (2g saturated), 1g fiber, 359mg sodium.

portuguese-style monkfish

PREP: 25 MIN / TOTAL: 1 HR 5 MIN / SERVES 4

1 tablespoon olive oil

1 medium onion, chopped

3 cloves garlic, finely chopped

1 fully cooked chorizo sausage (3 ounces), cut lengthwise into quarters, then crosswise into thin slices

1 red bell pepper, chopped

⅔ cup chicken broth

1 can (14 to 16 ounces) tomatoes, chopped

¼ teaspoon salt

¼ teaspoon crushed red pepper

1½ pounds monkfish, dark membrane removed, cut into 1-inch pieces

¼ cup chopped fresh parsley

1. In a 10-inch nonstick skillet, heat the oil over medium-low heat. Add the onion and garlic and cook, stirring frequently, until the onion is tender, about 5 minutes.

2. Add the chorizo and bell pepper and cook, stirring frequently, until the pepper is tender, about 5 minutes. Add the broth and heat to boiling. Stir in the tomatoes with their juices, the salt, and the crushed red pepper; heat to boiling.

3. Add the monkfish to the skillet. Reduce the heat; cover and simmer until the monkfish is tender, about 10 minutes. With a slotted spoon, transfer the monkfish to a bowl. Increase the heat to high and boil the liquid until the sauce has reduced and thickened, about 5 minutes. Return the fish to the skillet and stir in the parsley.

Each serving About 310 calories, 32g protein, 11g carbohydrate, 15g fat (4g saturated), 2g fiber, 781mg sodium.

fresh salmon burgers

with capers & dill

PREP: 20 MIN / TOTAL: 30 MIN / SERVES 4

- 1 large lemon
- ¼ cup light mayonnaise
- 1 tablespoon capers, drained and coarsely chopped 1 pound salmon fillet, skin removed
- ¼ cup loosely packed fresh dill, chopped
- 2 green onions, thinly sliced
- ½ cup plain dried bread crumbs
- ¾ teaspoon salt
- Nonstick cooking spray
- 4 whole-wheat hamburger buns, split and toasted
- Green-leaf lettuce leaves

1. Prepare a grill pan or outdoor grill for direct grilling over medium heat.

2. Meanwhile, from the lemon, grate 1 teaspoon zest and squeeze 1 tablespoon juice.

3. In a small bowl, stir the lemon juice, ½ teaspoon lemon zest, mayonnaise, and capers until blended. Set the lemon-caper sauce aside. (Makes about ⅓ cup.)

4. With tweezers, remove any bones from the salmon. With a large chef's knife, finely chop the salmon; place it in a medium bowl. Add the dill, green onions, ¼ cup bread crumbs, salt, and the remaining ½ teaspoon lemon zest; gently mix with a fork until combined. Shape the salmon mixture into four 3-inch round burgers.

5. Sprinkle both sides of the burgers with the remaining bread crumbs; pat gently to adhere. Spray both sides of the burgers with nonstick cooking spray.

6. Place the burgers on the grill. Cook burgers 6 to 8 minutes for medium or to desired doneness, turning once.

7. Serve the burgers on buns with the lettuce and lemon-caper sauce.

Each serving About 380 calories, 27g protein, 34g carbohydrate, 15g fat (3g saturated), 4g fiber, 990mg sodium.

VARIATION

Salmon Teriyaki Burgers

Prepare as directed, but omit the lemon-caper sauce. In step 3, substitute ½ cup diced **water chestnuts**, ¼ cup **teriyaki sauce**, and ¼ teaspoon **crushed red pepper** for the dill, green onions, bread crumbs, salt, and lemon zest. Do not sprinkle the burgers with bread crumbs. Proceed as directed. To serve, place the burgers on buns with lettuce and spoon 1 tablespoon **hoisin sauce** over each.

baked salmon

PREP: 5 MIN / TOTAL: 20 MIN / SERVES 4

- 4 pieces salmon fillet with skin (6 ounces each)
- 1 teaspoon olive oil
- ⅛ teaspoon salt
- ⅛ teaspoon ground black pepper

1. Preheat the oven to 400°F and grease a 13 × 9-inch baking dish.

2. With tweezers, remove any bones from the salmon fillets. Arrange the fillets in the prepared baking dish; rub with the oil and sprinkle with salt and pepper. Bake until the salmon is just opaque throughout, 15 to 20 minutes.

Each serving About 330 calories, 34g protein, 0g carbohydrate, 21g fat (4g saturated), 0g fiber, 174mg sodium.

 Tip Thick center-cut pieces of salmon bake in about 20 minutes. If you're using thinner pieces cut nearer the tail, check after 15 minutes to avoid overcooking.

salmon & lentils

PREP: 10 MIN / TOTAL: 1 HR / SERVES 4

1 cup lentils, rinsed and picked over

2¼ cups water

Salt

4 pieces salmon fillet with skin (6 ounces each)

1 teaspoon plus 2 tablespoons olive oil

⅛ teaspoon plus ¼ teaspoon coarsely ground black pepper

1 lemon

1 teaspoon Dijon mustard

4 teaspoons chopped fresh tarragon

1 tablespoon butter

¼ cup finely chopped shallots

¼ cup chopped fresh parsley

1. Preheat the oven to 400°F. In a 2-quart saucepan, combine the lentils, water, and ½ teaspoon salt; heat to boiling over high heat. Reduce the heat; cover and simmer until the lentils are tender, 20 to 30 minutes. Drain.

2. Meanwhile, grease a 13 × 9-inch baking dish. With tweezers, remove any bones from the salmon. Arrange the fillets in a single layer in the prepared baking dish. Rub with 1 teaspoon oil and sprinkle with ⅛ teaspoon each salt and pepper. Bake until the fish is just opaque throughout, 15 to 20 minutes.

3. While the salmon is baking, prepare the dressing: From the lemon, grate ½ teaspoon zest and squeeze 2 tablespoons juice. In a small bowl and using a wire whisk, whisk together the lemon juice, mustard, and ¼ teaspoon salt. Gradually whisk in the remaining 2 tablespoons oil, then stir in 2 teaspoons tarragon.

4. In a 10-inch skillet, melt the butter over medium heat. Add the shallots and cook, stirring, 2 minutes. Stir in the lentils, lemon zest, and the remaining ¼ teaspoon pepper. Remove from the heat and stir in the parsley and the remaining 2 teaspoons tarragon. Spread the lentil mixture on a platter. Arrange the salmon on top of the lentils and spoon the dressing over the salmon.

Each serving About 580 calories, 48g protein, 30g carbohydrate, 30g fat (7g saturated), 12g fiber, 604mg sodium.

kedgeree

PREP: 35 MIN / TOTAL: 1 HR 5 MIN / SERVES 6

1 tablespoon butter

1 small onion, chopped

¾ teaspoon curry powder

1½ cups regular long-grain rice

3 cups water

1 teaspoon salt

¼ teaspoon coarsely ground black pepper

1 pound smoked haddock fillet (finnan haddie)

1 lemon

4 large hard-cooked eggs, coarsely chopped

¼ cup chopped fresh parsley

½ cup heavy or whipping cream

1. In a 2-quart saucepan, melt the butter over medium heat. Add the onion and cook until tender, about 5 minutes. Stir in the curry powder and rice. Add the water, salt, and pepper; heat to boiling. Reduce the heat; cover and simmer, without stirring or lifting the lid, until the rice is tender and all the liquid has been absorbed, about 20 minutes. Transfer to a large bowl.

2. Meanwhile, in a 10-inch skillet, combine the smoked haddock fillet with enough water to cover; heat to boiling. Reduce the heat and simmer just until the haddock begins to flake, 5 to 10 minutes. Drain and cool slightly.

3. Preheat the oven to 350°F. From the lemon, grate ½ teaspoon zest and squeeze 1 tablespoon juice; add the lemon zest and juice to the rice, fluffing it with a fork. Flake the haddock, discarding any skin or bones. Add the fish, eggs, and parsley to the rice, tossing gently. Transfer to a 13 × 9-inch baking dish and spread it evenly; drizzle cream over the top. Cover with foil and bake 30 minutes.

Each serving About 405 calories, 27g protein, 42g carbohydrate, 14g fat (7g saturated), 1g fiber, 0mg sodium.

GLOSSARY

Kedgeree, an Anglo-Indian favorite, has roots that go back to 14th century India, when it was *khichri*, a combination of rice, lentils, fried onions, and ginger. Along with fish, it was a staple on the Raj breakfast table, and at some point Indian chefs combined the two. The dish has as many iterations as cooks: different fish, eggs in, eggs as garnish. However you choose to embellish it, it makes a delicious brunch dish.

HOMEMADE CLASSIC GRAVLAX 291

snapper livornese

PREP: 10 MIN / TOTAL: 35 MIN / SERVES 4

- 1 tablespoon olive oil
- 1 clove garlic, finely chopped
- 1 can (14 to 16 ounces) tomatoes
- ⅛ teaspoon salt
- ⅛ teaspoon ground black pepper
- 4 red snapper fillets (6 ounces each)
- ¼ cup chopped fresh basil
- ¼ cup Kalamata or Gaeta olives, pitted and chopped
- 2 teaspoons capers, drained

1. In a 10-inch nonstick skillet, heat the oil over medium heat. Add the garlic and cook just until very fragrant, about 30 seconds. Stir in the tomatoes with their juices, salt, and pepper, breaking up the tomatoes with a spoon. Heat to boiling; reduce the heat and simmer 10 minutes.

2. With tweezers, remove any bones from the snapper fillets. Place the fillets, skin-side down, in the skillet. Cover and simmer until the fish is just opaque throughout, about 10 minutes. With a wide slotted spatula, transfer the fish to a warm platter. Stir the basil, olives, and capers into the tomato sauce and spoon it over the snapper.

Each serving About 250 calories, 36g protein, 6g carbohydrate, 8g fat (1g saturated), 1g fiber, 571mg sodium.

spicy soy-glazed salmon

PREP: 15 MIN / TOTAL: 30 MIN / SERVES 4

- 5 stalks celery, very thinly sliced
- 1 bunch green onions, thinly sliced
- 4 jalapeño chiles, seeded and thinly sliced
- 1 tablespoon oil
- Salt
- 4 (6-ounce) skinless salmon fillets
- 2 tablespoons lower-sodium soy sauce
- Bok choy, steamed, for serving
- ¼ cup unsalted peanuts, chopped, and sliced green onions, for garnish

SPICY SOY-GLAZED SALMON 290

1. Preheat the oven to 450°F. On a large rimmed baking sheet, toss the celery, green onions, jalapeños, oil, and ⅛ teaspoon salt. Roast 15 minutes, stirring twice.

2. Place the salmon in a 2-quart square baking dish and drizzle with soy sauce. Roast the salmon alongside the vegetables 12 minutes or until just opaque. Serve the salmon with the celery mixture and steamed bok choy. Garnish with peanuts and green onions.

Each serving About 335 calories, 39g protein, 11g carbohydrate, 14g fat (3g saturated), 4g fiber, 690mg sodium.

homemade classic gravlax

PREP: 15 MIN / TOTAL: 15 MIN, PLUS CHILLING / SERVES 8

3 tablespoons kosher salt	**1 cup chopped fresh dill**
2 tablespoons sugar	**1 (2-pound) piece skin-on salmon**
1 teaspoon ground black pepper	

1. Combine salt, sugar, and black pepper. On a very large sheet of plastic wrap, sprinkle ½ cup dill. Rinse the salmon with cold water; pat dry. Rub the skin of the salmon with half of the salt mixture; place it on the dill, skin-side down. Rub the remaining salt mixture on the flesh of the salmon, then pack with the remaining dill. Wrap tightly with plastic. Place in a baking dish; top with another baking dish to weight it down. Refrigerate 1 day.

2. The next day, turn the packet of salmon over; weight down and refrigerate 2 more days. Lightly rinse the salmon and pat it dry before serving. The gravlax will keep, refrigerated, up to 1 week.

Each serving About 170 calories, 25g protein, 1g carbohydrate, 7g fat (1g saturated), 0g fiber, 628mg sodium.

 Tip For silky-smooth slices, use a long, sharp knife and cut thinly at an angle.

VARIATIONS

Smoky Cumin Gravlax

To the salt mixture, add **1 teaspoon ground coriander** and **1 teaspoon ground cumin**.

Fennel-Orange Gravlax

To the salt mixture, add **2 teaspoons fennel seeds**. To the dill, add **2 teaspoons grated orange zest** and **¼ cup fresh tarragon**, chopped.

Rye 'n' Gin Gravlax

To the salt mixture, add **1 tablespoon caraway seeds**, coarsely ground or crushed. Drizzle **¼ cup gin** over the dill on top of the salmon.

Ingredient Ideas

classic gravlax

MASALA WEDGE FRIES

On a large rimmed baking sheet, toss **2 pounds russet potatoes**, peeled and cut into skinny wedges, with ¼ **cup canola oil**, **2 teaspoons garam masala**, and ½ **teaspoon salt**. Roast in a preheated 450°F oven, without stirring, 45 minutes or until crispy. Transfer the potatoes to a serving platter. Drape with **8 thin slices Smoky Cumin Gravlax**, torn; ½ **small red onion**, thinly sliced; and ¼ **cup chopped fresh cilantro**. Serves 4.

CONFETTI SALAD

Toss **1 can (15 ounces) white (cannellini) beans**, rinsed and drained; **1 cucumber, chopped**; **2 medium tomatoes**, chopped; ⅓ **cup chopped Fennel-Orange Gravlax**; **2 tablespoons fresh lemon juice**; **1 tablespoon olive oil**; ¾ **teaspoon salt**; and ½ **teaspoon pepper**. Serves 4.

SKINNY BAGEL APPS

Top each of **24 "everything" bagel chips or pretzel chips** with ½ **thin slice Rye 'n' Gin Gravlax**, a dollop of **sour cream**, and **chopped capers**, drained. Serves 8.

FANCY SCRAMBLE

Whisk together **8 large eggs**, ¼ **cup mascarpone cheese**, and ¼ **teaspoon salt**. In a 10-inch nonstick skillet, heat **1 tablespoon butter** over medium heat until melted. Add the eggs; cook 5 minutes or until mostly set, stirring frequently. Fold in **6 thin slices Classic Gravlax**, chopped. Top with **fresh chopped basil**. Serves 4.

wild salmon cakes
with quinoa salad

(See photo on page 294.)

PREP: 15 MIN / TOTAL: 20 MIN, PLUS CHILLING / SERVES 4

- 1 pound skinless wild salmon, cut into small chunks
- 2 green onions, sliced
- ½ teaspoon grated orange zest
- Salt
- 2 teaspoons plus 2 tablespoons olive oil
- ¼ cup fresh basil, chopped
- 3 tablespoons fresh orange juice
- 3 tablespoons sherry vinegar
- ¼ teaspoon ground black pepper
- 5 cups cooked quinoa
- 5 cups packed mixed greens
- Orange wedges, for serving (optional)

1. In a food processor, pulse the salmon, green onions, and orange zest until the salmon is finely chopped. Form the mixture into 8 cakes; freeze 10 minutes. Season with ¼ teaspoon salt.

2. In a 12-inch nonstick skillet, heat 2 teaspoons olive oil over medium heat. Add the salmon cakes; cook 4 minutes per side.

3. Meanwhile, in a large bowl, whisk the basil, orange juice, sherry vinegar, 2 tablespoons olive oil, pepper, and ¼ teaspoon salt. Add the cooked quinoa and mixed greens, tossing to combine. Serve with the salmon cakes and orange wedges, if desired.

Each serving About 505 calories, 33g protein, 52g carbohydrate, 18g fat (3g saturated), 7g fiber, 340mg sodium.

"bbq" salmon & brussels bake

(See photo on page 270.)

PREP: 20 MIN / TOTAL: 40 MIN / SERVES 6

- 2 tablespoons brown sugar
- 1 teaspoon garlic powder
- 1 teaspoon onion powder
- 1 teaspoon smoked paprika
- 3 tablespoons olive oil
- 1¼ pounds Brussels sprouts, trimmed and halved
- Salt
- Ground black pepper
- 1 side of salmon (about 3½ pounds)
- Snipped fresh chives, for garnish

1. Preheat the oven to 450°F. Line a large rimmed baking sheet with foil. In a small bowl, stir together the brown sugar, garlic powder, onion powder, smoked paprika, and 2 tablespoons oil.

2. On another large rimmed baking sheet, toss the Brussels sprouts with the remaining 1 tablespoon oil and ¼ teaspoon each salt and pepper. Roast the sprouts 5 minutes.

3. Meanwhile, cut the salmon into 10 fillets; arrange them, skin side down, on the foil-lined baking sheet. Brush the spice rub all over the salmon; sprinkle with 1 teaspoon salt. Roast the salmon with the Brussels sprouts 15 minutes, or until the sprouts are tender and the salmon is just cooked through, stirring the sprouts once halfway through. Reserve 4 smaller salmon fillets for Farro & Arugula Salad with Mustard Vinaigrette (below). Serve the remaining salmon with the Brussels sprouts. Garnish with chives.

Each serving About 280 calories, 35g protein, 11g carbohydrate, 11g fat (2g saturated), 3g fiber, 380mg sodium.

#SavetheFood
farro & arugula salad
with mustard vinaigrette

PREP: 10 MIN / TOTAL: 35 MIN / SERVES 4

- 12 ounces farro
- Salt
- ¼ cup fresh lemon juice
- 1 small shallot, finely chopped
- 2 tablespoons Dijon mustard
- 2 tablespoons extra-virgin olive oil
- 1 pint grape tomatoes, each cut into halves
- 4 cups arugula
- 4 leftover fillets "BBQ" Salmon, skin removed and discarded, broken up into bite-size chunks

1. In a medium saucepot, combine the farro with enough water to cover by 1 inch and 2 teaspoons salt. Partially covered, heat to boiling over high heat. Reduce the heat to maintain a simmer. Cook, partially covered, 20 to 25 minutes, or until tender, stirring occasionally; drain well.

2. Meanwhile, in a large bowl, whisk the lemon juice, shallot, mustard, oil, and ¼ teaspoon salt. Add the cooked faro and tomatoes, stirring to combine. Fold in the arugula and salmon.

Each serving About 625 calories, 44g protein, 71g carbohydrate, 18g fat (3g saturated), 11g fiber, 935mg sodium.

shrimp & potatoes in feta & tomato sauce

PREP: 20 MIN / TOTAL: 1 HR 10 MIN / SERVES 4

- 1 tablespoon olive oil
- 2 medium onions, chopped
- 1½ pounds all-purpose potatoes, peeled and cut into 1-inch pieces
- 1 large clove garlic, finely chopped
- Pinch of cayenne pepper
- ¾ cup water
- ½ teaspoon salt
- 1 can (14 to 16 ounces) tomatoes
- 1 pound medium (36 to 41 count) shrimp, shelled and deveined
- 4 ounces feta cheese, crumbled (1 cup)
- ¼ cup chopped fresh dill

1. In a 10-inch nonstick skillet, heat the oil over medium heat. Add the onions and cook, stirring frequently, until tender and golden, about 10 minutes.

2. Add the potatoes and cook, stirring, until the potatoes begin to brown, about 10 minutes. Stir in the garlic and cayenne and cook 30 seconds. Stir in the water and salt; cover and cook until the potatoes are almost tender, about 10 minutes.

3. Add the tomatoes with their juice, breaking up the tomatoes with the side of a spoon. Cook, uncovered, until the liquid has thickened slightly, about 10 minutes.

4. Stir in the shrimp and feta. Cover and cook until the shrimp are opaque throughout, 3 to 5 minutes. Remove from the heat and stir in the dill.

Each serving About 360 calories, 27g protein, 37g carbohydrate, 11g fat (5g saturated), 5g fiber, 926mg sodium.

crispy cod cakes
with almond-pepper vinaigrette

(See photo on page 272.)

PREP: 15 MIN / TOTAL: 20 MIN / SERVES 4

- 1 pound cod or haddock fillets, cut into chunks
- ⅓ cup packed fresh basil leaves
- 3 cloves garlic, crushed with a garlic press
- ½ teaspoon smoked paprika
- Salt
- ¼ teaspoon ground black pepper
- 1 large egg, beaten
- 1 cup panko (Japanese-style bread crumbs)
- 2 tablespoons vegetable oil
- ⅓ cup salted almonds
- 5 tablespoons sherry vinegar
- 5 tablespoons olive oil
- ⅓ cup roasted red peppers
- Salad greens, for serving

1. In a food processor, pulse the fillets, basil, garlic, smoked paprika, pepper, and ¼ teaspoon salt until the cod is finely chopped, stirring occasionally. Form the mixture into 8 patties; dip each first into the egg and then into the panko, patting to adhere.

2. In a 12-inch skillet, heat vegetable oil over medium heat; fry the cakes 3 minutes per side, or until deep golden brown.

3. In a blender, puree the salted almonds, sherry vinegar, olive oil, and ¼ teaspoon salt until smooth. Add the roasted red peppers; pulse until almost smooth. Serve the cod cakes with the vinaigrette and salad greens.

Each serving About 450 calories, 24g protein, 21g carbohydrate, 30g fat (4g saturated), 3g fiber, 470mg sodium.

"BBQ" SALMON & BRUSSELS BAKE 292

WILD SALMON CAKES WITH QUINOA SALAD 292

SPANISH MUSSELS & PAPRIKA FRIES 298

EASY SHRIMP & GRITS 295

easy shrimp & grits

PREP: 25 MIN / TOTAL: 30 MIN / SERVES 4

2⅓ cups whole milk

2 cups water

Salt

1 cup quick-cooking grits (not instant)

6 slices bacon, chopped

1 bunch green onions, thinly sliced, plus more (optional) for garnish

2 cloves garlic, finely chopped

Ground black pepper

1 small red bell pepper, finely chopped

1 pound frozen shelled and deveined raw large (25 to 30 count) shrimp, thawed

½ teaspoon Louisiana-style hot sauce, plus more (optional) for serving

1. In a 4-quart saucepan, heat 2 cups milk, the water, and ⅛ teaspoon salt to simmering over medium-high heat. Whisk in the grits. Cover; reduce the heat to medium-low. Cook 10 minutes, or until the liquid is absorbed and the grits are tender, stirring often. Keep warm.

2. Meanwhile, in a 12-inch skillet, cook the bacon over medium-high heat 5 to 7 minutes, or until brown and crisp, stirring occasionally. With a slotted spoon, transfer the bacon to a paper-towel-lined plate. Discard all but 2 tablespoons of fat in the pan.

3. To the same skillet, add the green onions, garlic, and ¼ teaspoon pepper. Cook 2 minutes, stirring. Add the red bell pepper; cook 2 minutes, stirring often. Stir in the shrimp and the remaining ⅓ cup milk; cook 5 to 6 minutes, or until the shrimp just turn opaque, scraping up the browned bits from the bottom of the skillet. Remove from the heat. Stir in the bacon and hot sauce.

4. To serve, spoon grits into shallow bowls; top with shrimp. Garnish with additional green onions and serve with hot sauce, if desired.

Each serving About 450 calories, 28g protein, 44g carbohydrate, 18g fat (7g saturated), 2g fiber, 1,070mg sodium.

saucy shrimp curry

(See photo on page 272.)

PREP: 15 MIN / TOTAL: 25 MIN / SERVES 4

2 tablespoons canola oil

2 medium shallots, thinly sliced

½ teaspoon curry powder

½ teaspoon ground cumin

½ teaspoon ground black pepper

3 cloves garlic, finely chopped

⅔ cup ketchup

½ teaspoon cayenne pepper

¼ teaspoon salt

1 pound medium (36 to 42 count) shelled, deveined shrimp

Cooked basmati rice or toasted naan, for serving

Fresh cilantro leaves, for garnish

1. In a 12-inch nonstick skillet, heat the oil over medium heat. Add the shallots, curry powder, cumin, and pepper. Cook 3 minutes, stirring occasionally. Add the garlic; cook 1 minute, stirring. Add the ketchup, cayenne, and salt. Cook 2 minutes, or until thickened, stirring frequently.

2. To the skillet, add the shrimp. Cook 3 minutes, or until the shrimp are just opaque, stirring occasionally. Serve with rice or naan and garnish with cilantro.

Each serving (curry only) About 205 calories, 17g protein, 17g carbohydrate, 8g fat (1g saturated), 1g fiber, 1,155mg sodium.

 Tip Add 2 teaspoons sriracha to the ketchup for some heat. Use mild curry powder and leave out the cayenne if sensative to spice.

HOW TO

BUTTERFLY SHRIMP

Remove the shell, leaving the tail segment in place. With kitchen shears or a small knife, cut the shrimp along the outer curve, about three-fourths of the way through the flesh. Spread the flesh open and remove the dark vein with the tip of the knife. Rinse the butterflied shrimp with cold running water.

shrimp risotto

PREP: 20 MIN / TOTAL: 55 MIN / SERVES 4

- 1 pound medium (26 to 30 count) shrimp
- 4 cups water
- 1¾ cups chicken broth
- 2 tablespoons butter or olive oil
- Salt
- 1 small onion, finely chopped
- 2 cups Arborio, Carnaroli rice, or medium-grain rice
- ½ cup dry white wine
- 1 cup frozen baby peas
- ¼ cup chopped fresh parsley

1. Shell and devein the shrimp (see page 297), reserving the shells.

2. In a 2-quart saucepan, heat the water, broth, and shrimp shells to boiling over high heat. Reduce the heat and simmer 15 minutes. Strain the broth through a sieve set over a bowl and measure it. If necessary, add enough water to equal 5 cups. Return the broth to a clean saucepan; heat to boiling. Reduce the heat; cover and simmer.

3. In a 4-quart saucepan, melt 1 tablespoon butter over medium-high heat. Add the shrimp and ½ teaspoon salt; cook, stirring, until the shrimp are just opaque but not fully cooked, 1½ to 2 minutes. Transfer the shrimp to a bowl.

4. Meanwhile, in a 4-quart saucepan, melt remaining butter over medium heat. Add the onion and cook, stirring occasionally, until tender, about 5 minutes. Add the rice and 1 teaspoon salt and cook, stirring frequently, until the rice grains are opaque. Add the wine; cook until the wine has been absorbed.

5. Add about ½ cup hot broth to the rice, stirring until the liquid has been absorbed. Continue cooking, adding the broth, about ½ cup at a time, and stirring until most of the liquid has been absorbed. Continue in this manner until all the broth has been absorbed and the rice is tender but still firm, about 15 minutes longer. The risotto should have a creamy consistency. Stir in peas and shrimp and cook until heated through, 1 to 2 minutes. Remove the pot from the heat; stir in ¼ cup chopped fresh parsley.

Each serving About 485 calories, 21g protein, 81g carbohydrate, 7g fat (4g saturated), 4g fiber, 1,943mg sodium.

shrimp étouffée

PREP: 30 MIN / TOTAL: 1 HR 30 MIN / SERVES 6

- 4 tablespoons butter
- ¼ cup all-purpose flour
- 1 yellow bell pepper, chopped
- 2 medium onions, chopped
- 2 stalks celery with some leaves, chopped
- 2 cloves garlic, finely chopped
- 3 cups water
- 3 tablespoons tomato paste
- 2 bay leaves
- 1½ teaspoons salt
- ¾ teaspoon chili powder
- ¼ teaspoon dried thyme
- ¼ teaspoon ground black pepper
- 1½ pounds medium (36 to 42 count) shrimp, shelled and deveined
- 1 cup chopped green onions (5 medium)
- ¼ cup plus 2 tablespoons chopped fresh parsley
- 1 cup regular long-grain rice, cooked as the label directs, for serving

1. In a 4-quart Dutch oven, melt the butter over medium heat. With a wooden spoon, gradually stir in the flour until blended and cook, stirring constantly, until the flour mixture is the color of peanut butter; do not burn. Add the bell pepper, onions, celery, and garlic. Cook, stirring frequently, until the onions are tender, about 5 minutes. Stir in the water and tomato paste and heat to boiling. Add the bay leaves, salt, chili powder, thyme, and pepper; reduce the heat and simmer 30 minutes.

2. Stir in the shrimp, green onions, and ¼ cup parsley. Return to simmer and cook 3 minutes. Remove from the heat, cover, and let stand 10 minutes. Discard the bay leaves and sprinkle the étouffée with the remaining 2 tablespoons parsley. Serve with hot rice.

Each serving (without rice) About 230 calories, 21g protein, 15g carbohydrate, 10g fat (5g saturated), 2g fiber, 882mg sodium.

VARIATION

Crawfish Étouffée

Prepare as directed, but substitute **1 pound fresh or frozen cooked crawfish tail meat** for the shrimp.

skillet shrimp tacos

(See photo on page 272.)

PREP: 15 MIN / TOTAL: 20 MIN / SERVES 4

2 limes, plus more
for serving

4 cups thinly sliced
red cabbage

12 ounces shelled,
deveined small
(61 to 70 count)

shrimp

¼ cup fresh cilantro,
finely chopped

2 tablespoons canola oil

8 small (4-inch) flour
tortillas

Sour cream and hot sauce, for serving

1. From the limes, grate 2 teaspoons zest and squeeze 2 table-spoons juice. Toss the cabbage with the lime juice. Toss the shrimp and cilantro with the grated lime peel.

2. In a 12-inch skillet, heat the oil over medium-high heat until very hot; add the shrimp in a single layer. Cook 2 minutes (do not stir); turn the shrimp over. Cook another 2 minutes, or until opaque throughout. Serve the shrimp in flour tortillas with cabbage, sour cream, hot sauce, and lime wedges.

Each serving About 385 calories, 19g protein, 45g carbohydrate, 14g fat (4g saturated), 4g fiber, 970mg sodium.

HOW TO

SHELL & DEVEIN SHRIMP

1 With kitchen shears and a small knife, cut the shrimp shell along the outer curve, just deep enough into the flesh to expose the dark vein.

2 Peel back the shell from the cut and gently separate the shell from the shrimp. Discard the shell (or use to make fish stock).

3 Remove the vein with the tip of a small knife; discard. Rinse the shrimp with cold running water. Pat dry with paper towels.

mussels
with tomatoes & white wine

PREP: 20 MIN / TOTAL: 45 MIN / SERVES 8 AS A FIRST COURSE, 4 AS A MAIN DISH

1 tablespoon olive or
vegetable oil

1 small onion, chopped

2 cloves garlic, finely
chopped

¼ teaspoon crushed red
pepper

1 can (14 to 16 ounces)
tomatoes

¾ cup dry white wine

4 pounds large
mussels, scrubbed
and debearded
(see page 298)

2 tablespoons chopped
fresh parsley

1. In a 5-quart nonreactive Dutch oven, heat the oil over medium heat. Add the onion and cook until tender and golden, 6 to 8 minutes. Add the garlic and crushed red pepper and cook 30 seconds longer. Stir in the tomatoes with their juices and wine, breaking up the tomatoes with the side of a spoon. Heat to boiling; boil 3 minutes.

2. Add the mussels; heat to boiling. Reduce the heat; cover and simmer until the mussels open, about 5 minutes, transferring the mussels to a large bowl as they open. Discard any mussels that do not open. Pour the mussel broth over the mussels and sprinkle with parsley.

Each first-course serving About 105 calories, 9g protein, 6g carbohydrate, 3g fat (1g saturated), 1g fiber, 277mg sodium.

 Tip This saucy dish should be served with plenty of good, crusty bread for dipping.

VARIATION

Moules à la Marinière

Prepare as above, substituting ⅓ **cup chopped shallots** for the onion. Omit crushed red pepper and tomatoes; use 1½ **cups dry white wine**. Proceed as directed.

spanish mussels & paprika fries

(See photo on page 277.)

PREP: 10 MIN / TOTAL: 25 MIN / SERVES 6

1 package (26 ounces) frozen french fries

1 tablespoon olive oil

1 medium onion, chopped

6 ounces dried chorizo

3 cloves garlic, crushed with a garlic press

2 cups dry white wine

4 pounds mussels, scrubbed

Fresh parsley, for garnish

½ teaspoon smoked paprika

1. Prepare the french fries as the label directs.

2. Meanwhile, in a large Dutch oven, heat the olive oil over medium-high heat. Add the onion; cook 6 minutes.

3. Remove the casing from the chorizo; roughly chop. Add the chorizo and garlic to the Dutch oven and cook, stirring, 3 minutes. Add white wine; heat to simmering and cook 3 minutes, or until reduced slightly. Add the mussels. Cover and cook 5 to 7 minutes, or until most shells open, stirring twice. Discard any unopened mussels. Garnish with parsley. Sprinkle the cooked french fries with smoked paprika and serve alongside the mussels.

Each serving About 460 calories, 24g protein, 40g carbohydrate, 22g fat (6g saturated), 3g fiber, 710mg sodium.

HOW TO

SCRUB & DEBEARD MUSSELS

Scrub mussels well under cold running water. To debeard, grasp the hairlike beard firmly with your thumb and forefinger and pull it away, or scrape it off with a knife.

NOTE: Cultivated mussels usually do not have beards.

---

cioppino

(See photo on page 272.)

PREP: 15 MIN / TOTAL: 40 MIN / SERVES 6

3 tablespoons oil

1 medium onion, finely chopped

2 cloves garlic, crushed with a garlic press

½ teaspoon salt

1 can (28 ounces) crushed tomatoes

2 bottles (8 ounces each) clam juice

2 tablespoons butter

1 pound shelled, deveined large (25 to 30 count) shrimp

2 pounds mussels, scrubbed

1 pound boneless cod fillet, cut into 3-inch chunks

Chopped fresh parsley, for garnish

Crusty bread, for serving

1. In a 7- to 8-quart saucepot, heat the oil over medium heat. Add the onion, garlic, and salt, and cook 8 minutes, stirring. Add the tomatoes, clam juice, and butter. Heat to simmering over high heat.

2. Add the shrimp, mussels, and cod. Cover; simmer 10 to 12 minutes, or until most mussels have opened. Discard any unopened mussels. Sprinkle with chopped parsley; serve in bowls with crusty bread.

Each serving About 295 calories, 31g protein, 14g carbohydrate, 13g fat (4g saturated), 3g fiber, 980mg sodium.

---

steamed soft-shell clams

PREP: 5 MIN / TOTAL: 15 MIN / SERVES 6

6 dozen steamer (soft-shell) clams

Melted butter (optional)

1. In a very large bowl or in the kitchen sink, place the clams and enough cold water to cover; drain. Repeat the rinsing and draining until sand no longer falls to the bottom of the bowl.

2. In a steamer or 8-quart saucepot fitted with a rack, heat enough water to cover the pan bottom to boiling over high heat. Place the clams on the rack in the steamer. Reduce the heat; cover and steam until clams open, 5 to 10 minutes, transferring the clams to a bowl as they open. Discard any clams that do not open.

3. Strain the clam broth through a sieve lined with paper towels and pour it into 6 soup cups or mugs.

4. To eat, with your fingers, pull the clams from their shells by the neck; peel off and discard the black sheath that covers the neck. Dip clams first into the broth to remove any sand, then into melted butter, if you like. When the sand has settled to the bottom, broth can be sipped, if desired.

Each serving (without butter) About 75 calories, 13g protein, 3g carbohydrate, 1g fat (0g saturated), 0g fiber, 57mg sodium.

chinese-style steamed clams

PREP: 10 MIN / TOTAL: 20 MIN / SERVES 4

- 1 tablespoon vegetable oil
- 2 green onions, finely chopped
- 1 tablespoon minced, peeled fresh ginger
- 1 clove garlic, finely chopped
- 2 dozen cherrystone or littleneck clams,

- scrubbed (see right), or mussels, scrubbed and debearded (see page 298)
- ½ cup water
- 3 tablespoons dry sherry
- 2 tablespoons soy sauce
- 2 tablespoons chopped fresh cilantro

In an 8-quart saucepot, heat the oil over high heat. Add the green onions, ginger, and garlic; cook until the green onions are tender, about 1 minute. Add the clams, water, sherry, and soy sauce; heat to boiling. Reduce the heat; cover and simmer 5 to 10 minutes, transferring the clams to a large platter as they open. Discard any clams that do not open. Pour the broth over the clams on the platter and sprinkle with cilantro.

Each serving About 130 calories, 14g protein, 5g carbohydrate, 4g fat (1g saturated), 0g fiber, 576mg sodium.

panfried oysters

PREP: 15 MIN / TOTAL: 25 MIN / SERVES 4

- 1 pint shucked oysters, drained
- ⅔ cup finely crushed saltine crackers
- 2 tablespoons butter

- 2 tablespoons vegetable oil
- Lemon wedges, for serving

1. Gently pat the oysters dry with paper towels. Place the cracker crumbs on waxed paper and coat the oysters with the crumbs.

2. In a 10-inch skillet, heat 1 tablespoon butter and 1 tablespoon oil over medium-high heat until hot. Add half the oysters to the skillet and cook until golden brown, 2 to 3 minutes per side. Repeat with remaining butter, oil, and oysters. Serve with lemon wedges.

Each serving About 250 calories, 10g protein, 13g carbohydrate, 17g fat (5g saturated), 0g fiber, 353mg sodium.

 Tip   Large plump oysters work best in this seaside favorite.

HOW TO

SCRUB & SHUCK CLAMS

1 Scrub the clams well with a stiff brush under cold running water to remove all the grit.

2 Protecting your hand with a folded towel, hold the clam with the "hinge" facing you; wedge the thin edge of a clam knife between the shells.

3 Slide the knife around to separate the shells.

4 Open the shell. Cut the clam meat away from the top shell; discard the top shell.

5 Slide the knife underneath the meat in the bottom shell to release it.

panfried scallops

PREP: 5 MIN / TOTAL: 10 MIN / SERVES 4

1 pound bay scallops
2 tablespoons olive oil
½ teaspoon salt

2 tablespoons chopped fresh parsley
4 lemon wedges, for serving

Pat the scallops dry with paper towels. In a 12-inch skillet, heat the oil over medium-high heat until hot. Add the scallops to the skillet and sprinkle with salt. Cook, stirring, until just opaque throughout, about 4 minutes. Add the parsley and toss. Serve with lemon wedges.

Each serving About 160 calories, 19g protein, 3g carbohydrate, 8g fat (1g saturated), 0g fiber, 473mg sodium.

 Tip Try these during the fall and winter months, when small bay scallops are in season. Otherwise, substitute sea scallops and increase the cooking time accordingly.

scalloped oysters

PREP: 40 MIN / TOTAL: 55 MIN / SERVES 8 AS A FIRST COURSE

10 slices firm white bread, torn into 1-inch pieces
4 tablespoons butter, melted
1½ pints shucked oysters with their liquid

¾ cup heavy or whipping cream
¼ teaspoon salt
⅛ teaspoon coarsely ground black pepper
2 tablespoons chopped fresh parsley

1. Preheat the oven to 400°F. Place the bread pieces in a jelly-roll pan and drizzle with melted butter, tossing to coat evenly. Toast the bread in the oven, stirring occasionally, until crisp and golden, about 25 minutes.

2. Meanwhile, drain the oysters, reserving the liquid, and refrigerate. In a 1-quart saucepan, heat the oyster liquid to boiling over high heat. Reduce the heat to medium and cook until the oyster liquid has reduced to 3 tablespoons, about 5 minutes. Add the cream, salt, and pepper; heat to boiling. Remove the saucepan from the heat.

3. In a large bowl, gently combine the toasted bread pieces, oysters, and parsley. Spoon the mixture into eight 12-ounce ramekins, dividing it evenly. Pour about 2 tablespoons cream mixture over each. Bake just until the edges of the oysters begin to curl, about 15 minutes.

Each serving About 290 calories, 10g protein, 22g carbohydrate, 18g fat (10g saturated), 1g fiber, 436mg sodium.

 Tip Bake these delectable oysters in individual ramekins, if you have them, or in a shallow 2½-quart baking dish. The baking time will depend on the depth of the dish.

scallops provençal

PREP: 20 MIN / TOTAL: 40 MIN / SERVES 4

1 large leek
2 tablespoons olive oil
2 cloves garlic, finely chopped
1 can (14 to 16 ounces) tomatoes, chopped

Salt
½ teaspoon freshly grated orange zest
Pinch of cayenne pepper
1 pound sea scallops
¼ cup all-purpose flour

1. Cut off the roots and trim the dark-green tops from the leek; cut lengthwise in half, then crosswise into thin slices. Rinse in large bowl of cold water, swishing to remove the sand; transfer to a colander to drain, discarding the sand in bottom of the bowl.

2. In a 10-inch nonstick skillet, heat 1 tablespoon oil over medium heat. Add the leek and garlic and cook, stirring frequently, until the leek is tender, about 7 minutes. Add the tomatoes with their juices, ½ teaspoon salt, orange zest, and cayenne; heat to boiling. Reduce the heat and simmer until the sauce has thickened slightly, about 5 minutes.

3. Meanwhile, pull off and discard the tough crescent-shaped muscle from each scallop. Pat the scallops dry with paper towels. If scallop is larger than 1½ inches, cut it horizontally in half.

4. In a 12-inch skillet, heat the remaining 1 tablespoon oil over medium-high heat until hot. Place the flour on waxed paper and coat the scallops with flour, shaking off the excess. Sprinkle ½ teaspoon salt on the scallops. Add the scallops to the skillet and cook, stirring, until just opaque throughout and lightly golden, about 4 minutes. Stir in the sauce and heat through.

Each serving About 225 calories, 21g protein, 17g carbohydrate, 8g fat (1g saturated), 2g fiber, 944mg sodium.

scallop & asparagus stir-fry

PREP: 20 MIN / TOTAL: 35 MIN / SERVES 4

- 1 pound sea scallops
- 2 tablespoons reduced-sodium soy sauce
- 1 tablespoon minced, peeled fresh ginger
- 2 tablespoons vegetable oil
- 2 cloves garlic, thinly sliced
- 1½ pounds asparagus, trimmed and cut into 2-inch pieces
- ¼ teaspoon crushed red pepper
- ½ cup loosely packed fresh basil leaves, chopped, plus additional leaves
- Rice, for serving

1. Pull off and discard the tough crescent-shaped muscle from each scallop. In bowl, toss the scallops with 1 tablespoon soy sauce and the ginger.

2. In a 12-inch skillet, heat 1 tablespoon oil over medium-high heat. Add the garlic and cook, stirring often, until golden. With a slotted spoon, transfer the garlic to a medium bowl.

3. Add the asparagus and crushed red pepper to the skillet and cook, stirring frequently (stir-frying), until the asparagus is tender-crisp, about 7 minutes. Transfer the asparagus to the bowl with the garlic.

4. Add the remaining 1 tablespoon oil to the skillet; add the scallop mixture and stir-fry until the scallops are just opaque throughout, 3 to 5 minutes.

5. Return the asparagus and garlic to the skillet along with remaining 1 tablespoon soy sauce; heat through. Add basil, tossing to combine. Spoon the mixture onto a warm platter, top with basil leaves, and serve with rice.

Each serving About 205 calories, 24g protein, 10g carbohydrate, 8g fat (1g saturated), 2g fiber, 487mg sodium.

panfried soft-shell crabs

PREP: 30 MIN / TOTAL: 40 MIN / SERVES 4

- ½ cup all-purpose flour
- ¾ teaspoon salt
- ½ teaspoon ground black pepper
- 8 live soft-shell crabs (6 ounces each), cleaned (see below)
- 4 tablespoons butter
- Lemon wedges, for serving

1. On waxed paper, combine the flour, salt, and pepper. Coat the crabs with the seasoned flour, shaking off the excess.

2. In a 12-inch skillet, melt 2 tablespoons butter over medium heat until hot; add 4 crabs and cook until golden, 3 to 4 minutes per side. Transfer the crabs to a platter and keep warm. Repeat with the remaining butter and crabs. Serve with lemon wedges.

Each serving About 255 calories, 19g protein, 12g carbohydrate, 15g fat (8g saturated), 0g fiber, 1,207mg sodium.

HOW TO

CLEAN SOFT-SHELL CRABS

Soft-shell crabs are sometimes available already cleaned, but it is better to do it yourself at home, because crabs begin to spoil once their viscera are removed. To clean, with kitchen shears, cut across each crab ¼ inch behind the eyes; discard the front portion. Cut off the flat pointed "apron" on the underside. Bend back the top shell on each side and snip off the spongy gills. Rinse with cold running water; pat dry with paper towels.

STORE HARD-SHELLED CRABS

It's best to cook crabs the day they are purchased, but they can be stored up to one day. Place the crabs in a large shallow bowl, then nestle the bowl in a larger bowl of ice. Cover the crabs with a damp kitchen towel. Refrigerate, replacing the ice as needed.

crab boil

PREP: 10 MIN / TOTAL: 50 MIN / SERVES 4

2 medium onions, coarsely chopped

1 carrot, peeled and coarsely chopped

1 stalk celery, coarsely chopped

1 lemon, sliced

½ cup crab boil seasoning

1 tablespoon crushed red pepper

1 tablespoon salt

1 gallon (16 cups) water

1 can or bottle (12 ounces) beer

2 dozen live hard-shell blue crabs, rinsed

1. In a 12-quart stockpot, combine the onions, carrot, celery, lemon, crab boil seasoning, crushed red pepper, salt, water, and beer. Heat to boiling over high heat; cook 15 minutes.

2. Using tongs, transfer the crabs to the stockpot. Cover and heat to boiling; boil 5 minutes; the crabs will turn red. With tongs, transfer the crabs to a colander to drain, then place them on a warm platter.

3. To eat the crab, twist off the claws and legs, then crack the shell to remove the meat. Break off the flat pointed "apron" from the underside of the crab; remove the top shell. Discard the feathery gills. With kitchen shears or your hands, break the body in half down the center. With your fingers or a lobster pick, remove the meat.

Each serving About 125 calories, 24g protein, 0g carbohydrate, 2g fat (0g saturated), 0g fiber, 1,410mg sodium.

shrimp tempura

PREP: 25 MIN / TOTAL: 40 MIN / SERVES 4

Vegetable oil, for frying

1 pound large (26–30) shrimp, shelled, deveined, and butterflied (see pages 295 & 297)

DIPPING SAUCE

⅓ cup chicken broth

3 tablespoons soy sauce

2 tablespoons water

1 tablespoon plus 1 teaspoon seasoned rice vinegar

2 teaspoons sugar

1 teaspoon minced, peeled fresh ginger

BATTER

¾ cup ice-cold water

1 cup cake flour (not self-rising)

1 teaspoon baking powder

¼ teaspoon salt

1. In a 5-quart Dutch oven, heat 2½ inches vegetable oil until the temperature reaches 400°F on a deep-fry thermometer.

2. Meanwhile, make the dipping sauce: In a small saucepan, combine the broth, soy sauce, water, vinegar, sugar, and ginger; heat to boiling over high heat. Boil 2 minutes. Strain through a sieve into a small bowl and keep warm.

3. Prepare the batter: Pour the ice-cold water into a medium bowl; sift the flour, baking powder, and salt into the water. With a fork, stir just until barely incorporated; a few lumps may remain.

4. Dip 4 shrimp at a time into the batter to coat lightly. Allowing excess batter to drip off, add the shrimp to the hot oil and fry, turning once or twice, until the coating is very pale golden, 1 to 2 minutes. With a slotted spoon, transfer the shrimp to paper towels to drain. Serve immediately with warm dipping sauce.

Each serving About 310 calories, 22g protein, 27g carbohydrate, 12g fat (2g saturated), 1g fiber, 1,355mg sodium.

VARIATION

Beer-Battered Fried Shrimp

Prepare as above, omitting step 2. In step 3, omit the baking powder and substitute **1 cup beer** for the water; proceed as directed. Serve the shrimp with **Tartar Sauce (page 55)**. Makes 6 first-course servings.

TESTING NOTE Shrimp tempura waits for no one—it gets soggy quickly. Serve as soon as the shrimp are lifted out of the pot and drained.

fried calamari fra diavolo

PREP: 10 MIN / TOTAL: 35 MIN / SERVES 4 AS A FIRST COURSE

1 tablespoon olive oil

2 cloves garlic, crushed with the side of a chef's knife

⅛ to ¼ teaspoon crushed red pepper

1 can (14 to 16 ounces) tomatoes

Salt

1 pound cleaned squid

⅔ cup all-purpose flour

1 cup water

Vegetable oil, for frying

1. In a 1-quart nonreactive saucepan, heat the olive oil over medium heat. Add the garlic and crushed red pepper; cook until the garlic is golden, about 30 seconds. Add the tomatoes with their juice and ½ teaspoon salt, breaking up the tomatoes with the side of a spoon; heat to boiling. Reduce the heat; cover and simmer 10 minutes. Keep warm.

2. Rinse the squid under cold running water and gently pat dry with paper towels. Slice the squid bodies crosswise into ¾-inch rings. Cut the tentacles into pieces if larger than 1½ inches.

3. To make the batter, in a small bowl and using a fork, mix the flour and water until smooth. In a 10-inch skillet, heat ½ inch vegetable oil over medium heat until very hot. (A small piece of bread dropped into the oil should sink, then rise to top and begin bubbling.) In small batches, drop the squid into batter. Allowing the excess batter to drip off, add the squid to the hot oil. Fry, turning to brown all sides, until golden, about 2 minutes. With a slotted spoon, transfer the squid to paper towels to drain; sprinkle with ¼ teaspoon salt. Serve with the tomato sauce for dipping.

Each serving About 325 calories, 21g protein, 25g carbohydrate, 16g fat (2g saturated), 2g fiber, 660mg sodium.

steamed lobster

PREP: 5 MIN / TOTAL: 25 MIN / SERVES 2

2 live lobsters (1¼ to 1½ pounds each)

4 tablespoons butter, melted

2 teaspoons fresh lemon juice

1. In a 12-quart stockpot, heat 1½ inches water to boiling over high heat. Plunge the lobsters, headfirst, into the boiling water. Cover and heat to boiling; steam 12 minutes. With tongs, transfer the lobsters to a colander to drain, then place them on a platter.

2. Combine melted butter and lemon juice; transfer to small cups for dipping.

3. Shell lobster (see below). Dip the lobster meat into lemon butter.

Each serving (with butter) About 340 calories, 29g protein, 2g carbohydrate, 24g fat (15g saturated), 0g fiber, 760mg sodium.

HOW TO

SHELL A LOBSTER

Twist off the claws and legs from a cooked lobster. Crack the large claws with a mallet or hammer; remove the meat, in one piece, if possible. Separate the legs at the joints; push out the meat. Twist the tail to separate it from the body. With kitchen shears, cut down along the center of the tail's underside; gently remove meat, in one piece, if possible. Remove the black vein from the center of the tail meat and discard. Lift the bony portion behind the small legs from the shell; with a lobster pick or fork, remove any small nuggets of meat. A 1½-pound lobster will give you approximately 8 ounces of meat.

VEGETARIAN &
grains

We are all vegetarians, at least some of the time. And now there's more impetus than ever to add vegetarian meals to your repertoire. The new USDA guidelines encourage us to fill three-quarters of our plates with vegetables, fruits, and grains, and to swap in beans, eggs, soy, nuts, and seeds for meat. As with all foods we eat, the bottom line is taste, so start by preparing foods your family regularly enjoys. Throughout this book you'll find vegetable-rich pastas, stir-fries, soups, and stews, and in this chapter you'll find delicious options: Risotto Puttanesca (page 322), Black Bean Cakes (page 314), Sweet & Sticky Tofu (page 323), and many more. The added benefits of eating more plant-based foods include helping to prevent obesity, diabetes, and chronic disease.

PROVENÇAL GOAT CHEESE TART 312

BUTTERNUT SQUASH RISOTTO 326

PESTO RISOTTO 325

VEGGIE TRIO ON SWEET MASH 319

Beans & Grains

For many cultures, beans and grains are the major source of protein. Although this low-fat, high-fiber dynamic duo also provides a healthful amount of minerals and vitamins, the protein in beans or grains alone is incomplete. Luckily, the amino acids missing from beans can be found in grains, and vice versa, so when served together, they create a complete protein. Beans or grains can also be served along with small amounts of meat or dairy to complete the protein. Dry beans encompass a variety of legumes, including split peas and lentils. Since tofu is made from soybeans (actually, soy milk), it is included here as well.

Beans & Other Legumes

Legumes are a class of vegetables that includes dried beans, split peas, and lentils. They are a delicious canvas for myriad flavors and prized as a protein source in many cultures. And they are high in fiber.

STORE Keep in an airtight container in a cool dry place for up to 2 years. Note that older beans take longer to cook.

SORT AND RINSE Sort through beans to remove tiny stones or debris. Rinse in a colander and transfer to a large bowl.

SOAK (Lentils do not need to be soaked) Add enough cold water to cover by 2 inches. Overnight soaking time is convenient and allows the beans to hydrate naturally. They're ready when they about double their size. In hot weather, refrigerate the beans while they soak to prevent them from fermenting.

QUICK-SOAK Combine the beans and water as above in a pot and heat to boiling; cook for three minutes. Remove from the heat, cover tightly, and set aside for one hour. Drain and rinse the beans.

CANNED BEANS are a great time-saver. Just rinse under cold water and drain before using. One can (15 ounces) yields about 1½ cups beans.

Be a Savvy Vegetarian

The Academy of Nutrition and Dietetics identifies a few nutrients to keep top-of-mind while following a vegetarian or vegan diet, as they're more often found in abundance in animal products. Be sure to include in your diet:

- **B12:** fortified cereals, soy and rice milk
- **CALCIUM:** bok choy, broccoli, kale
- **VITAMIN D:** sunlight, milk alternatives like soy and rice, breakfast cereals
- **OMEGA-3 FATTY ACIDS:** chia, flax, walnuts, canola oil, soy
- **IRON:** beet greens, kale, lentils, fermented foods (miso or tempeh)

You can increase your body's absorption of iron by consuming vitamin C, zinc (found in soy, legumes, grains, and nuts), and iodine (in soy beans, cabbage, broccoli, and sweet potatoes).

Rice Glossary

↓

LONG-GRAIN RICE

AROMATIC Some rice varieties become fragrant when cooked. The best-known is basmati, a rice valued for its nutty aroma and delicate flavor and texture. When cooked, the slender grains swell lengthwise, resulting in thin, dry grains perfect for pilafs. Similar fragrant rice varieties include *jasmine* and *popcorn*.

INSTANT Rice that has been partially or fully cooked, then dehydrated. It cooks quickly.

PARBOILED (CONVERTED) Rice that has been steamed, pressure-treated, and dehydrated; the grains remain firm and separate after cooking.

REGULAR Slender, polished, elongated white grains that cook into dry grains that separate easily.

MEDIUM-GRAIN RICE

ARBORIO The most widely available rice for Italian risotto, this plump, roundish, medium-grain rice has a high starch content and yields a moist, creamy texture. Vialone Nano and Carnaroli rice varieties (Italian and Test Kitchen favorites) are worth seeking out, as they make excellent risotto.

JAPANESE (SUSHI) Starchy medium-grain rice that clings together after cooking, making it the perfect rice for sushi.

BOMBA (ALSO CALLED VALENCIA) The preferred rice in Spanish and Latino dishes, it cooks up creamy and slightly sticky. Also look for Calasparra or Calrose, which are excellent in paellas.

SHORT-GRAIN RICE

STICKY Also called glutinous or sweet rice. An opaque, white, short-grain rice with a slightly sweet taste and a soft, sticky texture.

BROWN & BLACK RICE

BROWN The outer hull of rice has been removed, but the nutritious, high-fiber bran layer remains. Brown rice can be long-, medium-, or short-grain. Other varieties include Wehani, a new brown rice, and red rice, which has a red bran layer.

BLACK There are many varieties of this hulled rice with its black bran, including Thai black sticky rice and Chinese black rice.

WILD RICE

WILD RICE Not a true rice but the seed of a water grass. The hand-harvested variety of wild rice, called *manohmin* by Native Americans, is gathered the traditional way: in canoes. The rice grains vary in both length and color and have a slightly smoky, earthy flavor and a chewy texture. Commercially cultivated wild rice is uniform in size and color, less expensive than the true wild variety, and available in supermarkets.

COCONUT-CAULIFLOWER CURRY BOWLS 328

Grain Glossary

Whole grains are the most minimally processed version of grains. All the edible parts that were present when the grain was growing in the field—the bran, the endosperm, and the germ—are intact, though they are often ground up for use in cooking. Whole grains retain their fiber, vitamins, and minerals. Store whole grains in tightly covered containers and refrigerate them during the warmer months.

AMARANTH is a tiny grain native to Central America. It's one of the few whole grains that contain all of the essential amino acids, making it an ideal source of protein. Choose it as a hot cereal, add it to soups as a thickener, or use the flour in pancakes and quick breads.

BUCKWHEAT isn't actually a wheat but the seed from a plant in the rhubarb family. It's quick-cooking, gluten-free, and a good source of fiber and magnesium. Most familiar to Americans in the form of buckwheat pancakes, it's a grain with global popularity and is found in everything from Japanese soba noodles to Russian porridge.

BULGUR WHEAT cooks so quickly (in less than 15 minutes) because it has been boiled, dried, and cracked before reaching the market. Perfect for fast side dishes and salads—and the main ingredient in Middle Eastern tabbouleh, bulgur has a mild flavor that makes it a great starter grain for picky eaters. Cracked wheat is often confused with bulgur. Cracked wheat is raw wheat kernels that have been cracked to speed the cooking process. Both are available in fine, medium, and coarse textures.

CORNMEAL is dried corn kernels that have been ground to a fine, medium, or coarse texture. Stone-ground cornmeal has not been degerminated (i.e., had its germ removed).

COUSCOUS is not a grain but actually pellets of semolina pasta. Most couscous is precooked and needs only a soaking in hot liquid to soften it. Serve with a Moroccan-spiced stew or as an alternative to rice in many dishes.

FARRO (OR EMMER WHEAT), nicknamed "the pharaoh's wheat," was a culinary cornerstone of ancient Egyptian and Roman menus. Now grown primarily in Italy, this nutty-flavored grain is undergoing a resurgence. Try it in soups, or use it as an alternative to rice in risotto.

HOMINY consists of corn kernels that have been first soaked in a lime or lye solution to remove the hulls and germs, then dried. Known as posole in Mexico's Pacific coast region, hominy is central to a thick, spicy pork (or sometimes chicken) stew by the same name.

QUINOA (pronounced KEEN-wah), grown in the South American Andes since 3,000 BCE, is a nutrient-dense grain. Mild and sweet, quinoa needs to be rinsed thoroughly prior to cooking in order to remove its bitter coating. A complete protein, it cooks in less than 15 minutes and can substitute for rice in most dishes.

WHEAT BERRIES are whole kernels of wheat. Chewy with a hint of nuttiness, the kernels are versatile add-ins to salads, soups, and side dishes. Wheat berries need at least an hour to cook, although that time can be reduced if they've been soaked overnight.

RYE BERRIES, once cooked, are softer than wheat berries and have a slightly tangy flavor.

spinach & artichoke squash "casserole"

PREP: 15 MIN / TOTAL: 30 MIN / SERVES 4

- 2 medium spaghetti squash
- 1 medium shallot, finely chopped
- 1 tablespoon olive oil
- 6 cups packed spinach
- Salt
- 8 ounces reduced-fat cream cheese, softened
- 1 cup drained marinated artichoke hearts, chopped
- ¼ cup grated Parmesan cheese
- ½ teaspoon lemon zest
- ½ teaspoon ground black pepper

1. Poke the spaghetti squash all over with a knife; place in a large microwave-safe dish. Cook on High for 10 minutes. Turn over; cook 10 minutes longer or until a knife slips in easily.

2. Meanwhile, in a 6-quart saucepot over medium heat, cook the shallot in olive oil for 3 minutes, stirring. Add the spinach and ¼ teaspoon salt; cook 2 minutes or until wilted. Add the cream cheese, artichoke hearts, Parmesan, lemon zest, and pepper, stirring until the cheese melts.

3. Preheat the broiler to High. Cut the squash into halves; discard the seeds. With a fork, scrape strands from the sides; sprinkle with ⅛ teaspoon salt.

4. Divide the spinach mixture among the squash halves. Broil on High until browned, 3 to 4 minutes.

Each serving About 325 calories, 11g protein, 25g carbohydrate, 22g fat (9g saturated), 6g fiber, 720mg sodium.

bbq chickpea & cauliflower flatbreads
with avocado mash

PREP: 15 MIN / TOTAL: 35 MIN / SERVES 4

- 12 ounces small cauliflower florets
- 1 tablespoon olive oil
- Salt
- 2 ripe avocados, each cut in half, pitted, and peeled
- 2 tablespoon fresh lemon juice
- 4 flatbreads or pocketless pitas, toasted
- ¼ cup BBQ Chickpea "Nuts" (page 100)
- 2 tablespoons roasted salted pepitas (pumpkin seeds)
- Hot sauce, for serving

1. Preheat the oven to 425°F. On a large rimmed baking sheet, toss the cauliflower with olive oil and ¼ teaspoon salt; roast 25 minutes.

2. Mash the avocados with lemon juice and a pinch of salt. Spread on the flatbreads. Top with the roasted cauliflower, chickpeas, and pepitas. Serve with drizzle of hot sauce.

Each serving About 500 calories, 11g protein, 65g carbohydrate, 25g fat (4g saturated), 13g fiber, 915mg sodium.

Tip Our Chickpea "Nuts" (page 100) have several flavor variations that would be delicious in the flatbreads. Check out the Original, Parmesan-Herb, Spicy Buffalo, and Honey-Sesame options.

BBQ CHICKPEA & CAULIFLOWER FLATBREADS WITH AVOCADO MASH 310

provençal goat cheese tart

(See photo on page 306.)

PREP: 25 MIN / TOTAL: 40 MIN / SERVES 4

- 1 (9-inch) refrigerated ready-to-unroll piecrust
- 4 ounces goat cheese, softened
- 4 ounces reduced-fat cream cheese, softened
- 2 tablespoons heavy or whipping cream
- 2 tablespoons finely chopped fresh mint leaves
- 1 tablespoon snipped fresh chives, plus additional chives for garnish
- 1/8 teaspoon dried herbes de Provence or thyme, crumbled
- Salt
- Ground black pepper
- 2 heirloom tomatoes (10 ounces each), preferably 1 green and 1 red, cored and cut crosswise into 1/4-inch-thick slices
- Cherry tomatoes, for garnish

1. Preheat the oven to 450°F.

2. Gently press the piecrust into a 9-inch tart pan with a removable bottom; prick it all over with a fork. Bake 14 minutes, or until golden. Cool the tart shell completely on a wire rack.

3. Meanwhile, in a medium bowl, whisk together the goat cheese, cream cheese, and cream. Stir in the mint, chives, herbes de Provence, and 1/8 teaspoon each salt and pepper.

4. Spread the cheese mixture evenly in the tart shell. Arrange the heirloom tomatoes on top of the filling, overlapping slices. Garnish with chives and cherry tomatoes. The tart can be assembled up to 1 hour before serving.

Each serving About 405 calories, 11g protein, 30g carbohydrate, 29g fat (15g saturated), 2g fiber, 545mg sodium.

cumin rice
with black beans

PREP: 10 MIN / TOTAL: 40 MIN / SERVES 6

- 1 tablespoon vegetable oil
- 1 medium onion, finely chopped
- 1 clove garlic, finely chopped
- 2 teaspoons cumin seeds
- 1½ cups long-grain rice
- 1¾ cups chicken or vegetable broth
- 1¼ cups water
- ¼ teaspoon salt
- 1 can (15 to 19 ounces) black beans, rinsed and drained
- 2 tablespoons chopped fresh cilantro
- Lime wedges, for serving

1. In a 3-quart saucepan, heat the oil over medium heat. Add the onion and cook, stirring, until tender, about 5 minutes. Stir in the garlic and cumin seeds; cook, stirring, until fragrant. Add the rice and cook, stirring, 1 minute. Add the broth, water, and salt; heat to boiling over high heat. Reduce the heat; cover and simmer, without stirring or lifting the lid, until the rice is tender and most of the liquid has been absorbed, about 15 minutes.

2. Stir the beans into the rice. Cover and cook 5 minutes longer. Remove from the heat and let stand 5 minutes. Spoon into serving bowls and sprinkle with cilantro. Serve with lime wedges. Makes 6 cups.

Each serving About 255 calories, 7g protein, 48g carbohydrate, 4g fat (1g saturated), 6g fiber, 515mg sodium.

Serving Suggestion This dish works well as a side to Spicy Jerk Drumsticks (page 247).

black bean & sweet potato chili

PREP: 10 MIN / TOTAL: 35 MIN / SERVES 4

- 1 tablespoon olive oil
- 1 medium onion, chopped
- 2 cloves garlic, chopped
- 2 medium sweet potatoes (about 12 ounces each), peeled and cut into ½-inch pieces
- 1 tablespoon chili powder
- 1 jar (16 ounces) mild salsa (about 1¾ cups)
- 1 cup water
- 2 cans (15 to 19 ounces each) low-sodium black beans, undrained
- ½ cup reduced-fat sour cream
- ¼ cup loosely packed fresh cilantro leaves, chopped

1. In a 4-quart saucepan, heat the oil over medium-high heat. Add the onion and garlic; cook, stirring occasionally, until soft, about 4 minutes. Stir in the sweet potatoes, chili powder, salsa, and water; heat to boiling. Reduce the heat to medium-low and cook, stirring occasionally, until the potatoes are tender, 12 to 15 minutes. Add the beans with their liquid and cook 3 minutes to blend the flavors.

2. In a small bowl, combine the sour cream and cilantro. Serve the chili in bowls with cilantro cream.

Each serving About 520 calories, 23g protein, 91g carbohydrate, 9g fat (3g saturated), 21g fiber, 950mg sodium.

mexican pizza

PREP: 10 MIN / TOTAL: 20 MIN / SERVES 4

- 1 large thin pizza crust (10 ounces)
- ½ cup prepared black bean dip
- ½ cup shredded Mexican cheese blend (2 ounces)
- 1 to 2 limes
- 1 ripe avocado, cut into chunks
- 2 cups shredded romaine lettuce
- 1 medium tomato, chopped

1. Prepare an outdoor grill for covered, direct grilling over medium heat (or preheat the oven to 450°F).

2. Spread the black bean dip evenly on the pizza crust, leaving ½-inch border; sprinkle with cheese. Place the crust on the hot grill rack; cover and grill until grill marks appear, 8 to 9 minutes. (Or place the crust on ungreased cookie sheet. Bake 8 to 10 minutes, or until the cheese melts.)

3. Meanwhile, from the limes, grate ¼ teaspoon zest and squeeze 2 tablespoons juice. Gently mix avocado with 1 tablespoon juice. Toss the romaine with the zest and remaining juice.

4. Top the cooked pizza with the romaine mixture and tomato, then with the avocado.

Each serving About 310 calories, 13g protein, 34g carbohydrate, 15g fat (4g saturated), 4g fiber, 520mg sodium.

easy as tortilla pie

PREP: 15 MIN / TOTAL: 25 MIN / SERVES 4

- Nonstick cooking spray
- 1 cup frozen corn kernels
- 2 green onions, thinly sliced
- 1 teaspoon ground cumin
- 1½ cups salsa
- 1 can (15 to 19 ounces) low-sodium black beans, rinsed and drained
- 4 burrito-size (10-inch) flour tortillas
- 1 package (8 ounces) reduced-fat (2%) shredded Mexican cheese blend
- 2 tablespoons chopped fresh cilantro leaves

1. Preheat the oven to 450°F. Spray a large baking sheet with cooking spray.

2. Spray a 12-inch nonstick skillet with cooking spray; place over medium heat. Add the frozen corn, green onions, and cumin; cook 3 minutes, or until the corn thaws. Remove the skillet from the heat; stir in the salsa and beans.

3. Place 1 tortilla on the baking sheet; top with 1 cup bean mixture and ½ cup cheese. Repeat the layering, starting with a tortilla, twice more, using up the bean mixture. Top with the remaining tortilla and cheese.

4. Bake the pie 10 minutes, or until heated through. Carefully transfer the pie to a cutting board; sprinkle with chopped cilantro. With a sharp knife, cut into wedges to serve.

Each serving About 440 calories, 26g protein, 58g carbohydrate, 13g fat (6g saturated), 21g fiber, 1,105mg sodium.

grilled asparagus & shiitake tacos

(See photo on page 316.)

PREP: 15 MIN / TOTAL: 20 MIN / SERVES 4

3 tablespoons canola oil

4 cloves garlic, crushed with a garlic press

1 teaspoon ground chipotle chile powder

½ teaspoon salt

1 pound asparagus, trimmed

8 ounces shiitake mushrooms, stems discarded

1 bunch green onions, trimmed

8 small (4 inch) corn tortillas, warmed; 1 cup homemade (page 92) or prepared guacamole; lime wedges; cilantro sprigs; and hot sauce; for serving

1. Prepare grill for direct grilling over medium heat. In a large baking dish, combine the oil, garlic, ground chipotle, and salt. Add the asparagus, shiitakes, and green onions; toss to coat. Grill the asparagus 5 to 6 minutes, or until tender and lightly charred, turning occasionally. Grill the shiitakes and green onions 4 to 5 minutes, or until lightly charred, turning occasionally. Transfer the vegetables to a cutting board.

2. Cut the asparagus and green onions into 2-inch lengths. Slice the shiitakes. Serve with corn tortillas, guacamole, lime wedges, cilantro, and hot sauce.

Each serving About 350 calories, 7g protein, 36g carbohydrate, 21g fat (2g saturated), 11g fiber, 445mg sodium.

black bean cakes

PREP: 10 MIN / TOTAL: 20 MIN / SERVES 4

1 can (15 to 19 ounces) black beans, rinsed and drained

2 tablespoons reduced-fat mayonnaise

¼ cup chopped fresh cilantro

1 tablespoon plain dried bread crumbs

½ teaspoon ground cumin

Pinch of dried oregano, crumbled

¼ teaspoon hot sauce

2 tablespoons olive oil

2 tablespoons all-purpose flour

¼ cup mild or medium salsa

8 teaspoons sour cream

1. In a large bowl and using a potato masher, mash the beans and mayonnaise until almost smooth, leaving some lumps. Stir in the cilantro, bread crumbs, cumin, oregano, and hot sauce. With lightly floured hands, shape the mixture into four 3-inch patties.

2. In a 10-inch skillet, heat the oil over medium heat. Dust the patties with flour, shaking off the excess. Cook the patties until crusty and lightly browned, about 3 minutes per side, transferring them to plates as they are done. To serve, top each cake with 1 tablespoon salsa and 2 teaspoons sour cream.

Each serving About 205 calories, 6g protein, 24g carbohydrate, 11g fat (2g saturated), 8g fiber, 410mg sodium.

jeweled cinnamon couscous

PREP: 10 MIN / TOTAL: 20 MIN / SERVES 4

1 tablespoon butter

½ medium red onion, chopped

1 package (8 ounces) sliced mushrooms

1¾ cups low-sodium vegetable broth

¼ cup water

1 can (15 to 19 ounces) low-sodium chickpeas, rinsed and drained

½ cup dried cranberries

½ cup golden raisins

¼ cup dry sherry

1 teaspoon salt

½ teaspoon ground cinnamon

¼ teaspoon ground black pepper

1 package (10½ ounces) plain couscous

1. In a deep 12-inch skillet, melt the butter over medium-high heat. Add the onion and mushrooms; cook, stirring occasionally, 3 minutes.

2. While the vegetables are cooking, in a 1-quart saucepan, heat the broth and water to boiling over high heat.

3. Stir the chickpeas, cranberries, raisins, sherry, salt, cinnamon, and pepper into the mushroom mixture. Remove the skillet from the heat.

4. Add the couscous to the skillet; stir in the hot broth. Cover and let the mixture stand until the liquid has been absorbed, about 5 minutes. Fluff with a fork before serving.

Each serving About 600 calories, 21g protein, 116g carbohydrate, 6g fat (2g saturated), 11g fiber, 655mg sodium.

winter veggie tart

(See photo on page 316.)

PREP: 45 MIN / TOTAL: 1 HR 45 MIN / SERVES 10

3 cups all-purpose flour

Salt

1½ cups cold butter, cut into pieces

¾ cup ice water

8 ounces radishes (about 10 medium), trimmed and quartered

8 ounces Brussels sprouts, halved

2 medium carrots, chopped

2 small red onions, cut into very thin wedges

3 tablespoons extra-virgin olive oil

4 cloves garlic, chopped

2 bunches Swiss chard (about 1¼ pounds total), thinly sliced

8 ounces Gruyère cheese, grated

1. In a food processor, pulse flour and ¾ teaspoon salt until combined. Add half the butter, pulsing until fine crumbs form. Add the remaining butter, pulsing just until coarse crumbs form. Drizzle half the ice water over the flour mixture, pulsing to incorporate. Drizzle in the remaining ice water; pulse until the dough mostly comes together. Transfer the dough to a large bowl; knead 3 or 4 times, until the dough fully comes together. Divide it into 2 equal-size disks; wrap each in plastic. Refrigerate at least 30 minutes or up to 2 days.

2. Preheat the oven to 400°F. In a large bowl, toss the radishes, Brussels sprouts, carrots, and onions with 2 tablespoons oil and ½ teaspoon salt; divide and arrange them in a single layer on 2 large rimmed baking sheets. Roast 25 minutes, or until browned and almost tender, stirring once. Vegetables can be made up to 1 day ahead.

3. In a 5-quart saucepot, heat the remaining oil over medium heat. Add the garlic; cook 1 minute, stirring. Add the chard. Cook 5 to 8 minutes or until the chard wilts and dries out a bit and the stems are tender, stirring occasionally.

4. On a large sheet of floured parchment paper, roll 1 disk pastry into a 14-inch circle; place the parchment with the pastry on it onto 1 large rimmed baking sheet. In the center of the pastry, arrange half the cheese, leaving a 2-inch rim on the pastry's perimeter. Next arrange half the chard, then half the vegetable mixture over the cheese. Fold the edges of the pastry up and over. Repeat the rolling, filling, and folding process with the remaining pastry disk, cheese, and vegetables.

5. Bake 50 minutes to 1 hour, or until the bottoms are golden brown, switching racks halfway through. Remove from the oven. Let stand 10 minutes before slicing.

Each serving About 550 calories, 13g protein, 36g carbohydrate, 40g fat (23g saturated), 3g fiber, 815mg sodium.

potato pancake
with broccoli & cheddar

PREP: 5 MIN / TOTAL: 25 MIN / SERVES 4

1 tablespoon butter

1 medium onion, chopped

1 bag (12 ounces) broccoli florets, each cut in half, if large

Salt

2 tablespoons water

4 cups refrigerated shredded hash brown potatoes (20 ounces)

⅛ teaspoon ground black pepper

1 tablespoon vegetable oil

4 ounces sharp Cheddar cheese, shredded (1 cup)

1. In a 12-inch nonstick skillet, melt the butter over medium heat. Add the onion and cook, stirring frequently, until golden and tender, about 5 minutes. Stir in the broccoli, ¼ teaspoon salt, and the water; cover and cook, stirring once, until the broccoli is tender, about 3 minutes. Transfer the broccoli mixture to a medium bowl.

2. In a large bowl, combine the potatoes, pepper, and ¾ teaspoon salt. In the same skillet, heat the oil over medium-high heat. Add half the potato mixture, gently patting it flat with a rubber spatula to cover the bottom of the skillet. Leaving a 1-inch border, top the potatoes with the broccoli mixture. Sprinkle Cheddar over the broccoli. Cover the cheese with the remaining potato mixture, patting it so that the mixture extends to the edges of the skillet. Cook until golden brown on the bottom, about 5 minutes.

3. Place a large round platter or baking sheet upside down over the skillet. Grasping the platter and skillet firmly together, very carefully and quickly flip the skillet over to invert the pancake onto the platter. Slide the pancake back into the skillet. Cook until browned, about 5 minutes longer. Cut into quarters.

Each serving About 320 calories, 13g protein, 32g carbohydrate, 17g fat (8g saturated), 5g fiber, 840mg sodium.

BAKED PEPPER JACK QUINOA SKILLET 317

GRILLED ASPARAGUS & SHIITAKE TACOS 314

WINTER VEGGIE TART 315

RISOTTO PUTTANESCA 322

bulgur & cashew stuffed eggplant

(See photo on page 304.)

PREP: 20 MIN / TOTAL: 30 MIN / SERVES 4

- 3 tablespoons olive oil
- 3 cloves garlic, crushed with a garlic press
- ½ cup golden raisins
- ½ teaspoon curry powder
- Salt
- 1 cup quick-cooking bulgur
- 2 cups water
- 2 medium eggplants
- ½ cup cashews, chopped
- Chopped fresh mint, for garnish

1. In a small (2-quart) saucepan, heat 1 tablespoon olive oil on medium. Add the garlic, raisins, curry powder, and ¼ teaspoon salt. Cook 2 minutes, stirring. Add the bulgur and water. Heat to simmering. Cover; simmer 15 minutes, or until the bulgur is tender.

2. Meanwhile, preheat the broiler to High and line a rimmed baking sheet with foil. Cut the eggplants in half lengthwise. Scoop out the seeds from the centers, leaving a ½-inch border of eggplant. Arrange the eggplant on the prepared baking sheet, cut sides up. Brush with 2 tablespoons olive oil and sprinkle with ½ teaspoon salt. Broil 6 inches from the heat source for 7 minutes , or until tender. Remove from the oven; cover with foil.

3. With a fork, fluff the bulgur; stir in the cashews. Stuff the eggplant with the bulgur mixture; garnish with chopped mint.

Each serving About 460 calories, 11g protein, 69g carbohydrate, 19g fat (3g saturated), 16g fiber, 450mg sodium.

baked pepper jack quinoa skillet

PREP: 15 MIN / TOTAL: 30 MIN / SERVES 4

- 1 cup quinoa, rinsed
- 4 cups water
- 8 ounces small broccoli florets
- 4 cups packed baby spinach
- ½ cup light sour cream
- 3 cloves garlic, crushed with a garlic press
- ½ teaspoon salt
- ½ teaspoon ground black pepper
- 4 ounces pepper Jack cheese, shredded

1. In a covered 5-quart saucepot, heat the quinoa and water to boiling over high heat. Cook as the label directs. Add the broccoli to the pot 5 minutes before the end of the cooking time. Cook until the broccoli and quinoa are tender.

2. Preheat the broiler to High. Drain the quinoa mixture well; toss with the baby spinach, sour cream, garlic, salt, and pepper. Spread in a 10-inch oven-safe skillet. Sprinkle with pepper Jack cheese. Broil 3 minutes, or until the cheese is melted.

Each serving About 340 calories, 16g protein, 37g carbohydrate, 15g fat (8g saturated), 6g fiber, 550mg sodium.

spinach & jack bread pudding

PREP: 10 MIN / TOTAL: 30 MIN / SERVES 6

6 large eggs

2 cups low-fat (1%) milk

¼ teaspoon dried thyme

¼ teaspoon salt

¼ teaspoon coarsely ground black pepper

Pinch of ground nutmeg

1 package (10 ounces) frozen chopped spinach, thawed and squeezed dry

4 ounces Monterey Jack cheese, shredded (1 cup)

8 slices firm white bread, torn into ¾-inch pieces

1. Preheat the oven to 375°F.

2. In a large bowl and using a wire whisk, beat the eggs, milk, thyme, salt, pepper, and nutmeg until well blended. With a rubber spatula, stir in spinach, Monterey Jack, and bread pieces.

3. Pour the mixture into 13 × 9-inch baking dish. Bake the bread pudding until browned and puffed and a knife inserted in center comes out clean, 20 to 25 minutes.

4. Remove the bread pudding from the oven; let stand 5 minutes before serving.

Each serving About 280 calories, 17g protein, 22g carbohydrate, 13g fat (6g saturated), 2g fiber, 545mg sodium.

VARIATION

Mexican-Style Bread Pudding

Prepare as directed but substitute **4 ounces pepper Jack cheese**, shredded (1 cup), for the Monterey Jack cheese, and add **4 ounces sliced pepperoni** in step 2. Serve with your favorite **salsa**.

mushroom barley pilaf

PREP: 15 MIN / TOTAL: 1 HR 10 MIN / SERVES 6

1 cup pearl barley

2 tablespoons butter

1 medium onion, chopped

2 stalks celery, cut into ¼-inch-thick slices

12 ounces mushrooms, trimmed and sliced

1¾ cups chicken or vegetable broth

¾ cup water

½ teaspoon salt

⅛ teaspoon dried thyme

⅛ teaspoon ground black pepper

¼ cup chopped fresh parsley

1. In a 3-quart saucepan, toast the barley over medium heat, shaking the pan occasionally, until the barley begins to brown, about 4 minutes. Transfer to a bowl.

2. In the same saucepan, melt butter over medium heat. Add the onion and celery; cook until the onion is tender, about 5 minutes. Stir in the mushrooms; cook until the mushrooms are tender and liquid has evaporated. Stir in the toasted barley, broth, water, salt, thyme, and pepper. Heat to boiling over high heat. Reduce the heat; cover and simmer until the barley is tender, about 30 minutes. Stir in the parsley.

Each serving About 190 calories, 6g protein, 32g carbohydrate, 5g fat (3g saturated), 6g fiber, 535mg sodium.

bulgur-bean burgers

PREP: 20 MIN / TOTAL: 40 MIN / SERVES 4

1 cup water

Salt

½ cup bulgur

1 can (15 to 19 ounces) reduced-sodium black beans, rinsed and drained

1 container (6 ounces) plain low-fat yogurt

¼ teaspoon ground allspice

¼ teaspoon ground cinnamon

¼ teaspoon ground cumin

¼ cup packed fresh mint leaves, chopped

Nonstick cooking spray

½ cup shredded Kirby or pickling cucumber (about 1 small)

⅛ teaspoon ground black pepper

4 whole-wheat hamburger buns

4 lettuce leaves

1 medium tomato, sliced

1. In a 1-quart saucepan, heat the water and ½ teaspoon salt to boiling over high heat. Stir in the bulgur. Reduce the heat to low; cover and simmer 10 to 12 minutes, or until the water is absorbed.

2. Meanwhile, in a large bowl and using a potato masher or fork, mash the beans with 2 tablespoons yogurt until almost smooth. Stir in the bulgur, allspice, cinnamon, cumin, and half the mint until combined. With lightly floured hands, shape the bean mixture into four 3-inch patties. Spray both sides of each patty lightly with non-stick cooking spray.

3. Heat a 12-inch nonstick skillet over medium heat until hot. Cook the burgers 8 minutes, or until lightly browned and heated through, turning once.

4. While the burgers are cooking, prepare the yogurt sauce: In a small bowl, combine the cucumber, the remaining yogurt, the remaining mint, ¼ teaspoon salt, and the pepper. Makes about 1¼ cups yogurt sauce.

5. To serve, divide the lettuce, tomato slices, and burgers among the buns; top with some yogurt sauce. Serve with the remaining yogurt sauce on the side.

___

Each serving About 295 calories, 16g protein, 58g carbohydrate, 3g fat (1g saturated), 13g fiber, 960mg sodium.

veggie trio on sweet mash

(See photo on page 306.)

PREP: 20 MIN / TOTAL: 30 MIN / SERVES 4

4 large sweet potatoes, peeled and cut into 1-inch chunks

⅓ cup Greek yogurt

2 tablespoons butter

1 tablespoon olive oil

1 bunch kale, chopped

12 ounces mini sweet peppers, sliced

3 cloves garlic, chopped

½ teaspoon salt

1 can (15 ounces) pinto beans, drained

1 tablespoon fresh lemon juice

1 tablespoon Worcestershire sauce

½ teaspoon ground black pepper

¼ cup sunflower seeds

1. To a large pot of salted water, add the sweet potatoes. Cover partially; heat to boiling over high heat. Reduce the heat to medium. Simmer 10 minutes, or until tender; drain. Mash with the Greek yogurt and butter.

2. In another large pot, heat the olive oil over medium heat. Add the kale, mini sweet peppers, garlic, and salt. Cook 10 minutes, stirring. Add the pinto beans, lemon juice, Worcestershire sauce, and pepper. Cook 1 minute. Serve over mash; top with sunflower seeds.

___

Each serving About 445 calories, 15g protein, 61g carbohydrate, 18g fat (6g saturated), 9g fiber, 690mg sodium.

 Tip To cut up kale easily, start at the base of the leaves and tear away the thick stems. Stack the leaves; cut into slices and then chop.

mushroom quesadillas

PREP: 15 MIN / TOTAL: 30 MIN / SERVES 4

Nonstick cooking spray

1 tablespoon olive oil

6 ounces cremini mushrooms, sliced

¼ teaspoon salt

½ cup salsa

½ cup fresh or frozen corn

4 (8-inch) flour tortillas

1 cup shredded Monterey Jack cheese

Sour cream, for serving

1. Preheat the oven to 475°F. Spray a large baking sheet with nonstick spray.

2. In a 10-inch skillet, heat the oil over medium heat. Add the mushrooms and salt. Cook 4 minutes. Stir in the salsa and corn. Cook 2 minutes.

3. Arrange the flour tortillas on the prepared baking sheet. Divide the mushroom mixture among the tortillas; top with cheese. Fold the tortillas over to form half-moons; spray the tops. Bake 6 minutes. Turn the quesadillas over; bake another 6 minutes. Cut in quarters and serve with sour cream.

Each serving About 320 calories, 12g protein, 33g carbohydrate, 16g fat (6g saturated), 2g fiber, 960mg sodium.

#SavetheFood

corn

Add leftover fresh or thawed corn to tuna salad for a sweet crunch.

sweet pea & ricotta tart

PREP: 20 MIN / TOTAL: 30 MIN / SERVES 6

1 round pie dough (page 664), or 1 refrigerated 9-inch piecrust, rolled to a 12-inch circle

2 teaspoons olive oil

1 medium leek, well rinsed and chopped

Salt

¼ teaspoon ground black pepper

2 cups fresh or frozen (thawed) peas

1 tablespoon fresh lemon juice

¾ cup ricotta cheese

4 ounces cream cheese, softened

¼ cup grated Pecorino Romano cheese

½ teaspoon grated lemon zest

½ cup micro sprouts or micro greens, for garnish

1. Preheat the oven to 400°F. Fit the pie dough into a 9-inch pie plate. Trim the excess dough, leaving a 1-inch overhang; tuck the overhang under and crimp the edges. Line the dough with a large sheet of parchment paper or foil; fill with pie weights or dried beans. Bake 15 minutes, or until the dough is set. Remove the parchment and weights. Bake another 8 to 10 minutes, or until the crust is golden brown. Remove from the oven; let cool completely on a wire rack.

2. In a 10-inch skillet, heat the oil over medium heat. Add the leek, ¼ teaspoon salt, and the pepper. Cook 3 minutes, or until the leek is tender, stirring occasionally. Add the peas. Cover the skillet and cook 3 to 5 minutes, or until the peas are tender, stirring once halfway through. Let the pea mixture cool. Stir in the lemon juice.

3. In a medium bowl, stir the ricotta, cream cheese, Pecorino, lemon zest, and ⅛ teaspoon salt until well combined. Spread in the cooled pie shell. Top with the cooled pea mixture. Garnish with micro sprouts.

Each serving About 445 calories, 13g protein, 32g carbohydrate, 30g fat (15g saturated), 4g fiber, 470mg sodium.

SWEET PEA & RICOTTA TART 320

risotto milanese

PREP: 10 MIN / TOTAL: 45 MIN / SERVES 6

3½ cups water

1¾ cups vegetable or chicken broth

2 tablespoons butter or olive oil

1 small onion, finely chopped

2 cups Arborio, Carnaroli rice or medium-grain rice

1 teaspoon salt

½ cup dry white wine

¼ teaspoon loosely packed saffron threads

½ cup freshly grated Parmesan cheese

1. In a 2-quart saucepan, heat the water and broth to boiling over high heat. Reduce the heat to low; cover.

2. Meanwhile, in a 4-quart saucepan, melt the butter over medium heat. Add the onion and cook, stirring occasionally, until tender, about 5 minutes. Add the rice and salt and cook, stirring frequently, until the rice grains are opaque. Add the wine; cook until the wine has been absorbed.

3. Add about ½ cup hot broth to the rice, stirring until the liquid has been absorbed. Continue cooking, adding the broth, about ½ cup at a time, and stirring until most of the liquid has been absorbed. After cooking 10 minutes, crumble the saffron into the rice. Continue cooking, adding the remaining broth, ½ cup at a time and stirring, until all the broth has been absorbed and the rice is tender but still firm, about 15 minutes longer. The risotto should have a creamy consistency. Remove the pot from the heat; stir in the Parmesan cheese.

Each serving About 215 calories, 6g protein, 35g carbohydrate, 6g fat (3g saturated), 3g fiber, 650mg sodium.

VARIATIONS

Risotto Primavera

Follow steps 1 through 3 as directed above, but omit the saffron. After cooking 10 minutes, stir **2 cups vegetables** (use a combination of shredded carrots, finely diced zucchini, sliced asparagus, and frozen peas) into the rice. Follow the remaining directions. Stir in ½ **teaspoon grated lemon zest** with the Parmesan cheese. Makes about 6½ cups or 4 main-dish servings.

Porcini Risotto

Prepare the risotto as directed, but omit the saffron. In a small bowl, pour ½ **cup boiling water** over ½ **ounce dried porcini mushrooms** (about ½ cup). Let stand 15 minutes. With a slotted spoon, remove the porcini and rinse to remove any grit. Chop the porcini. Strain the soaking liquid through a sieve lined with paper towels and set over a small bowl. In step 1, reduce the water to 3¼ cups and add the mushroom liquid. Melt **1 tablespoon butter** in a 4-quart saucepan and stir in **1 pound trimmed and sliced white mushrooms** and ¼ **teaspoon salt**; cook until the mushrooms are tender and their liquid has evaporated, about 10 minutes. Stir in the chopped porcini and transfer to a bowl. Follow step 2, using **1 tablespoon butter.** Follow step 3, but after cooking 10 minutes, stir in the mushroom mixture. Makes about 7 cups or 4 main-dish servings.

risotto puttanesca

(See photo on page 316.)

PREP: 25 MIN / TOTAL: 35 MIN / SERVES 4

1 quart low-sodium vegetable broth

7 cups water

2 tablespoons olive oil

1 medium onion, finely chopped

1 pound Arborio or Carnaroli rice

1 (6-ounce) can tomato paste

1 cup Kalamata olives, pitted and chopped

¼ cup fresh parsley, chopped

3 tablespoons capers, drained

2 tablespoons butter, room temperature

1 teaspoon salt

½ teaspoon ground black pepper

1. In a 3-quart saucepan, combine the broth with water; cover and heat to simmering on high. Reduce heat to low.

2. In a 5- to 6-quart saucepot, heat oil over medium heat. Add the onion; cook for 5 minutes or until translucent, stirring occasionally. Add the rice; cook for 1 minute, stirring. Add 2 ladlefuls of broth to the rice; stir until most of the liquid is absorbed before adding another ladleful. Reduce the heat to medium-low. Continue adding broth and stirring until about 1 cup of broth remains in the saucepan; whisk the tomato paste into the broth. Add this tomato broth to the rice, stirring until the liquid is absorbed and the rice is tender.

3. Gently fold the olives, parsley, capers, butter, salt, and pepper into rice. Serve risotto immediately.

Each serving About 445 calories, 11g protein, 69g carbohydrate, 15g fat (4g saturated), 5g fiber, 825mg sodium.

basic bulgur

PREP: 2 MIN / TOTAL: 25 MIN / SERVES 4

1¾ cups vegetable or chicken broth

¼ cup water

¼ teaspoon dried thyme

Pinch of ground nutmeg

1 cup medium-grind bulgur

In a 2-quart saucepan, combine the broth, water, thyme, and nutmeg; heat to boiling over high heat. Stir in the bulgur. Reduce the heat; cover and simmer until all the liquid has been absorbed, 10 to 15 minutes. Fluff with a fork before serving.

Each serving About 135 calories, 5g protein, 27g carbohydrate, 1g fat (0g saturated), 4g fiber, 435mg sodium.

bulgur pilaf
with apricots

PREP: 10 MIN / TOTAL: 30 MIN / SERVES 4

¾ cup water

1¾ cups vegetable or chicken broth

1 cup bulgur

1 tablespoon olive oil

1 small onion, chopped

2 teaspoons curry powder

1 clove garlic, crushed with a garlic press

1 can (15 ounces) chickpeas, rinsed and drained

½ cup dried apricots, chopped

½ teaspoon salt

¼ cup loosely packed fresh parsley leaves, chopped

1. In a 2-quart covered saucepan, heat the water and 1¼ cups broth to boiling over high heat. Stir in the bulgur; heat to boiling. Reduce the heat to medium-low; cover and simmer 12 to 15 minutes, or until the liquid has been absorbed. Remove the saucepan from the heat. Uncover and fluff the bulgur with a fork to separate the grains.

2. Meanwhile, in a 12-inch nonstick skillet, heat the oil over medium heat 1 minute. Add the onion and cook 10 minutes, stirring occasionally. Stir in the curry powder and garlic; cook 1 minute.

3. Stir in the beans, apricots, salt, and remaining ½ cup broth; heat to boiling. Remove from heat; stir in the bulgur and parsley.

Each serving About 370 calories, 13g protein, 71g carbohydrate, 6g fat (1g saturated), 15g fiber, 815mg sodium.

sweet & sticky tofu

PREP: 30 MIN / TOTAL: 30 MIN / SERVES 4

12 ounces udon noodles

¼ cup water

2 tablespoons soy sauce

1 tablespoon brown sugar

2 tablespoons plus 1 teaspoon cornstarch

½ teaspoon ground black pepper

14 ounces firm tofu

3 tablespoons canola oil

2 green onions, thinly sliced

1-inch piece peeled fresh ginger, cut into matchsticks

2 cloves garlic, chopped

½ small red chile, thinly sliced

2 bunches baby bok choy, stems sliced

sliced green onions and chopped peanuts, for garnish

1. Cook the udon noodles according to package directions. In a small bowl, stir the water, soy sauce, brown sugar, 1 teaspoon cornstarch, and pepper until smooth.

2. Blot the tofu dry with paper towels. Cut it into ¾-inch pieces; toss with 2 tablespoons cornstarch. Heat a 12-inch skillet over medium-high heat. Add 2 tablespoons canola oil, then the tofu; cook, stirring, until golden brown, 6 to 8 minutes. Transfer to a plate; wipe out the skillet.

3. To the same skillet, add 1 tablespoon canola oil, then the green onions, ginger, garlic, and half of the chile; cook 1 minute. Add the bok choy; cook, tossing, 2 minutes.

4. Stir in the tofu, then the soy sauce mixture. Simmer, stirring, 1 to 2 minutes, or until thickened. Spoon the mixture over the cooked udon noodles; top with sliced green onions and the remaining chile. Sprinkle with peanuts and serve.

Each serving About 500 calories, 18g protein, 75g carbohydrate, 15g fat (1g saturated), 4g fiber, 590mg sodium.

QUINOA RISOTTO WITH ARUGULA-MINT PESTO 325

quinoa risotto
with arugula-mint pesto

PREP: 20 MIN / TOTAL: 50 MIN / SERVES 4

- ½ cup packed arugula
- ⅓ cup grated Manchego cheese (about 1 ounce)
- ¼ cup packed fresh mint leaves, plus more for garnish
- 2 cloves garlic
- 1 tablespoon pine nuts, toasted, plus more for garnish
- Salt
- ¼ cup plus 2 teaspoons olive oil
- 2 medium shallots, chopped
- 1½ cups quinoa, rinsed and drained
- 4 cups warm water
- 2 tablespoons butter
- 2 tablespoons fresh lemon juice
- ½ cup water
- 1 can (15 ounces) chickpeas, rinsed and drained
- Micro greens, for garnish

1. In a food processor, pulse the arugula, Manchego, mint, garlic, pine nuts, and ¼ teaspoon salt until finely chopped, scraping down the sides occasionally. Transfer the pesto to a medium bowl; stir in ¼ cup oil and set aside.

2. In a 4-quart saucepan, heat the remaining 2 teaspoons oil over medium heat. Add the shallots; cook 2 minutes, stirring occasionally. Add the quinoa; cook 1 minute, stirring. Add 2 cups warm water and ½ teaspoon salt. Heat to boiling over high heat. Reduce the heat; simmer 6 to 8 minutes, or until most of the water is absorbed, stirring occasionally. Add remaining 2 cups warm water; simmer 15 to 18 minutes, or until the quinoa is just tender, stirring occasionally.

3. To the quinoa, add the butter, lemon juice, half the pesto, and ½ cup water, stirring to combine. Fold in chickpeas. Divide quinoa mixture among 4 serving bowls. Spoon remaining pesto over quinoa. Garnish with micro greens, additional mint, and pine nuts, if desired.

Each serving About 585 calories, 17g protein, 62g carbohydrate, 31g fat (8g saturated), 10g fiber, 615mg sodium.

pesto risotto
(See photo on page 306.)

PREP: 15 MIN / TOTAL: 25 MIN / SERVES 4

- 3 cups water
- 1¾ cups lower-sodium chicken broth
- 1 cup dry white wine
- 1 tablespoon butter
- 2 medium shallots, finely chopped (about 2 ounces)
- Salt
- 2 cups Arborio or Carnaroli rice
- 1 pound tomatoes, seeded and chopped
- ⅓ cup freshly grated Parmesan cheese
- 2 tablespoons refrigerated pesto
- ⅛ teaspoon ground black pepper
- Basil, for garnish

1. In a 3-quart saucepan, cover and heat the water, broth, and wine to boiling over high heat.

2. Meanwhile, in a 4-quart microwave-safe bowl, combine the butter, shallots, and ⅛ teaspoon salt. Microwave on High 2 minutes, stirring once halfway through. Stir in the rice; microwave 30 seconds.

3. Carefully pour the boiling liquid into the shallot-rice mixture; stir to combine. Cover with vented plastic wrap and microwave on Medium (50% power) 15 to 18 minutes, stirring every 5 minutes.

4. To the risotto, add tomatoes, Parmesan, pesto, ½ teaspoon salt, and pepper; gently stir to combine. Divide among serving bowls. Garnish with basil.

Each serving About 450 calories, 11g protein, 80g carbohydrate, 8g fat (2g saturated), 4g fiber, 765mg sodium.

butternut squash risotto

(See photo on page 306.)

PREP: 15 MIN / TOTAL: 30 MIN / SERVES 4

2 medium shallots, chopped	4 cups lower-sodium vegetable broth
3 cloves garlic, chopped	1 pound chopped butternut squash
4 leaves sage, chopped	½ cup grated Parmesan cheese
Salt	¼ teaspoon ground black pepper
1 tablespoon oil	
2 cups Arborio or Carnaroli rice	

In a pressure cooker, cook the shallots, garlic, sage, and ¼ teaspoon salt in the oil for 2 minutes. Add the rice; cook 2 minutes. Add the broth and butternut squash. Lock the lid; cook under high pressure 6 minutes. Release pressure; stir in the Parmesan, ¼ teaspoon salt, and pepper.

Each serving About 465 calories, 11g protein, 91g carbohydrate, 7g fat (2g saturated), 5g fiber, 890mg sodium.

couscous

PREP: 5 MIN / TOTAL: 10 MIN / SERVES 4

1¼ cups water	1 tablespoon butter
¼ cup dark seedless raisins, dried currants, dried cranberries, or dried cherries (optional)	¾ teaspoon salt
	1 cup couscous

In a 3-quart saucepan, combine the water; raisins, if using; butter; and salt; heat to boiling over high heat. Stir in the couscous. Remove from the heat; cover and let stand 5 minutes. Fluff the couscous with a fork before serving.

Each serving About 225 calories, 6g protein, 43g carbohydrate, 3g fat (2g saturated), 2g fiber, 470mg sodium.

VARIATIONS

Lime Couscous

Prepare the couscous as directed, but omit the raisins and add **1 tablespoon fresh lime juice** and **½ teaspoon freshly grated lime zest** to the water.

Moroccan Couscous

Prepare the couscous as directed, but add **¼ teaspoon ground cinnamon**, **¼ teaspoon ground turmeric** (optional), and **¼ teaspoon ground cumin** to the water.

Dried Tomato & Green Onion Couscous

Prepare the couscous as directed, but omit the raisins and add **1 green onion**, sliced, and **5 dried tomato halves**, chopped, to the water.

Almond Couscous

Prepare the couscous as directed, but omit the raisins and add a **pinch each of ground nutmeg and dried thyme** to the water. Stir **¼ cup toasted slivered almonds** into the fluffed couscous.

spoonbread

PREP: 15 MIN / TOTAL: 55 MIN, PLUS STANDING / SERVES 8

3 cups milk	1 cup cornmeal
½ teaspoon salt	4 tablespoons butter, cut into pieces
¼ teaspoon ground black pepper	3 large eggs, separated

1. Preheat the oven to 400°F. Generously grease a shallow 1½-quart baking dish.

2. In a 4-quart saucepan, combine the milk, salt, and pepper; heat to boiling over medium-high heat. Remove from the heat; with a wire whisk, whisk in the cornmeal. Add the butter, whisking until melted. Let stand 5 minutes.

3. Whisk the egg yolks, one at a time, into the cornmeal mixture until blended. In a medium bowl and using a mixer at high speed, beat the egg whites just until soft peaks form when the beaters are lifted. Gently fold the beaten egg whites, one half at a time, into the cornmeal mixture just until blended. Pour evenly into the prepared baking dish. Bake until the spoonbread is set, about 40 minutes. Serve immediately.

Each serving About 205 calories, 7g protein, 18g carbohydrate, 11g fat (6g saturated, 1g fiber, 270mg sodium.

wheat berries
with brown butter & pecans

PREP: 10 MIN / TOTAL: 1 HR 30 MIN, PLUS SOAKING / SERVES 6

- 1 cup wheat berries (whole-grain wheat)
- 3 cups plus 1 tablespoon water
- 2 tablespoons butter
- 1 medium onion, chopped
- ½ cup pecans, coarsely chopped
- ½ teaspoon salt
- ⅛ teaspoon ground black pepper
- 2 tablespoons chopped fresh parsley

1. In a bowl, place the wheat berries with enough water to cover by 2 inches. Soak overnight. Drain.

2. In a 3-quart saucepan, combine the wheat berries and 3 cups water; heat to boiling over high heat. Reduce the heat; cover and simmer until the wheat berries are tender but still firm to the bite, about 1 hour. Drain. Wipe out saucepan.

3. In the same clean saucepan, melt the butter over medium heat. Add the onion and cook, stirring frequently, until tender, about 5 minutes. Stir in the pecans, salt, and pepper. Cook, stirring, until the pecans are lightly toasted and the butter begins to brown, about 3 minutes. Stir in the wheat berries and 1 tablespoon water; heat through. Stir in the parsley.

Each serving About 210 calories, 5g protein, 27g carbohydrate, 11g fat (3g saturated), 5g fiber, 235mg sodium.

Tip To do a last minute version of this, you can substitute bulgur for the wheat berries. Heat 3 cups of water to boiling in a medium saucepan. Add 1½ cups bulgur; return to boil, then reduce heat and simmer on low 12 to 15 minutes, until liquid is absorbed. While bulgur is cooking in a 10-inch skillet, proceed with step 3.

israeli couscous
with currants

PREP: 10 MIN / TOTAL: 30 MIN / SERVES 12

- 1 bunch green onions
- 2 tablespoons butter
- 3 cups Israeli (pearl) couscous
- 2 cups water
- 1 cup chicken broth
- ¼ teaspoon ground allspice
- ½ teaspoon salt
- ¼ teaspoon ground black pepper
- ¾ cup walnuts, toasted and chopped
- ½ cup currants
- ½ cup loosely packed fresh mint leaves, chopped

1. Cut the white and light-green portion of the green onions into ½-inch pieces. Thinly slice the dark-green portions; reserve dark-green onion slices separately from the ½-inch pieces.

2. In a 4-quart saucepan, melt the butter over medium heat. Add the white and light-green onion pieces and cook 3 minutes, or until beginning to soften. Add the couscous and cook 7 to 9 minutes, or until most grains are browned, stirring frequently.

3. Add the water, broth, allspice, salt, and pepper to the couscous; heat to boiling over high heat. Reduce the heat to low; cover and simmer 8 to 10 minutes, or until the liquid is absorbed and the couscous is tender but still slightly chewy.

4. Remove the couscous from the heat. Stir in the walnuts, currants, chopped mint leaves, and reserved sliced green onions.

Each serving About 220 calories, 6g protein, 34g carbohydrate, 7g fat (1g saturated), 3g fiber, 180mg sodium.

creamy stove-top polenta

PREP: 5 MIN / TOTAL: 35 MIN / SERVES 8

2 cups cold water

1 teaspoon salt

1½ cups yellow cornmeal

4½ cups boiling water

½ cup freshly grated Parmesan cheese

4 tablespoons butter, cut into pieces

1. In a 5-quart Dutch oven, combine the cold water and salt. With a wire whisk, gradually beat in the cornmeal until smooth. Whisk in the boiling water. Heat to boiling over high heat. Reduce the heat to medium-low and cook, stirring frequently with a wooden spoon, until the mixture is very thick, 20 to 25 minutes.

2. Stir the Parmesan and butter into the polenta until the butter melts. Serve immediately.

Each serving About 175 calories, 5g protein, 20g carbohydrate, 8g fat (5g saturated), 1g fiber, 465mg sodium.

VARIATIONS

Oven-Baked Polenta

Prepare as above, but when the mixture comes to a boil, cover and bake in a preheated 350°F oven for 40 to 50 minutes, stirring every 10 minutes.

Microwave Polenta

In a deep 4-quart microwave-safe bowl or casserole, combine **2 cups low-fat milk, 1½ cups cornmeal,** and **1 teaspoon salt** until blended. Stir in **4½ cups boiling water.** Cook in the microwave oven on High for 12 to 15 minutes. After the first 5 minutes of cooking, with a wire whisk, stir vigorously until smooth (the mixture will be lumpy at first). Stir two more times during cooking. When the polenta is thick and creamy, stir in **4 tablespoons butter,** cut into pieces, and **½ cup freshly grated Parmesan cheese.**

Broiled Polenta Wedges

Line a 13 × 9-inch baking pan with foil, extending the foil over the rim. Prepare Creamy Stove-Top Polenta as directed but use only **3½ cups boiling water** and cook until the mixture is very thick and an indentation remains when a spoon is dragged through the polenta, 30 to 35 minutes. Stir in the Parmesan and butter as directed. Spoon the mixture into the prepared pan, smoothing the top. Refrigerate until very firm, at least 1 hour. Preheat the broiler.

Lift the foil with the polenta from the baking pan; place it on a baking sheet. Cut the polenta into 16 triangles; separate triangles. Brush **1 tablespoon melted butter** on the polenta wedges. Broil 5 to 7 inches from the heat source until lightly browned and heated through, about 10 minutes.

Rosemary Polenta Wedges

Prepare Broiled Polenta Wedges as directed, but add **½ teaspoon chopped fresh rosemary** or **¼ teaspoon dried rosemary,** crumbled, to the melted butter.

 Tip For even creamier polenta, replace half the water with milk.

coconut-cauliflower curry bowls

PREP: 10 MIN / TOTAL: 40 MIN / SERVES 6

1 tablespoon vegetable oil

2 medium shallots, chopped

2 tablespoons finely chopped, peeled fresh ginger

1 tablespoon curry powder

1 package (20 ounces) precut butternut squash chunks

1 can (15 ounces) coconut milk, shaken

1 can (15 ounces) fire-roasted diced tomatoes, drained

1 teaspoon salt

4 cups cauliflower florets (about 12 ounces)

6 cups cooked white rice

Cilantro leaves, for garnish

1. In a 6- to 7-quart saucepot, heat the oil over medium heat. Add the shallots, ginger, and curry powder; cook 5 minutes, stirring occasionally.

2. Add the squash, coconut milk, tomatoes, and salt. Cover and simmer 15 minutes. Uncover; stir in the cauliflower. Cook another 15 minutes, or until the squash and cauliflower are tender, stirring occasionally.

3. Serve over rice. Garnish with cilantro.

Each serving About 445 calories, 9g protein, 65g carbohydrate, 18g fat (14g saturated), 5g fiber, 465mg sodium.

millet

with corn & green chiles

PREP: 25 MIN / TOTAL: 50 MIN / SERVES 4

- 1 cup millet
- 2 cups fresh corn kernels (cut from 4 ears)
- 2 teaspoons vegetable oil
- 1 medium onion, chopped
- 1 clove garlic, crushed with a garlic press
- 1 teaspoon ground cumin
- 3½ cups water
- 1 can (4½ ounces) green chiles
- ½ teaspoon salt
- ¼ cup chopped fresh cilantro

1. In a large skillet, toast the millet over medium heat, about 5 minutes, stirring frequently. Transfer to a bowl and set aside.

2. Add the corn to a dry skillet and cook over high heat until corn browns, stirring frequently. Transfer corn to a plate.

3. In same skillet, heat oil over medium heat. Add onion; cook until softened, about 5 minutes. Stir in garlic and cumin and cook until fragrant, about 1 minute. Add water, green chiles, and salt; bring to a boil. Stir in millet. Reduce heat; cover and simmer until millet is tender and water is absorbed, 25 to 30 minutes.

4. Remove skillet from heat; stir in corn. Cover and let stand 5 minutes. Stir in cilantro.

Each serving About 300 calories, 8g protein, 58g carbohydrate, 6g fat, 8g fiber, 400mg sodium.

wild rice

with pepitas & shredded carrots

PREP: 10 MIN / TOTAL: 1 HR / SERVES 10

- 1 cup wild rice, rinsed
- 4 cups water
- 4 cloves garlic, chopped
- ¼ cup olive oil
- 2 cups long-grain white rice, rinsed
- 3 cups chicken broth
- ¾ cup shredded peeled carrot
- ⅔ cup roasted unsalted pepitas

1. In a 2-quart saucepan, combine the wild rice and water. Heat to boiling over high heat. Reduce the heat to a gentle simmer. Cover and simmer 35 to 40 minutes, or until the rice is tender, adjusting the heat to maintain a simmer. Drain well.

2. Meanwhile, in a 6-quart saucepot over medium heat, cook the garlic in oil 2 minutes, or until golden, stirring. Add the white rice. Cook 2 minutes, stirring constantly. Add the broth. Heat to boiling over high heat. Reduce the heat to low. Cover and simmer 25 minutes, adjusting the heat to maintain a simmer. Remove from the heat; let stand, covered, 5 minutes. Fluff with a fork.

3. Add the wild rice to the white rice along with the carrot and pepitas; fold until well combined.

Each serving About 315 calories, 8g protein, 48g carbohydrate, 10g fat (2g saturated), 2g fiber, 295mg sodium.

pasta

Pasta is the perfect blank canvas for flavors, from Asia to Italy. Sauce it with meatballs and tomato for ultimate comfort food; toss it with roasted veggies and a bit of cooking water for a satisfying vegetarian dinner; coat it with soy sauce, peanut butter, and ginger for better-than-takeout sesame noodles. Chop garden tomatoes, basil, and some fresh mozzarella for the ultimate pasta salad (please don't chill it!); layer noodles with ricotta, mozzarella, and tomato sauce and bake until golden and bubbling for a crowd pleaser. Whether you want a no-cook sauce like our Tuna Puttanesca (page 342) or one that simmers all day like our Neopolitan Pasta Sauce (page 349), there's a luscious pasta dish for every occasion.

LINGUINE WITH ASPARAGUS & EGG 337

BUTTERNUT SQUASH & PESTO ROTINI 337

SAUSAGE & MUSHROOM PENNE 341

SHRIMP & FENNEL SPAGHETTI 340

Pasta Glossary

We use dried Italian-style pasta for most of our recipes. It is a good match for a wide variety of sauces. The best pastas are made from durum flour and water. Most commercial pasta is extruded through nonstick dies. Artisanal pastas are often extruded through bronze dies, which give a rougher, more porous surface to hold sauce better. Homemade or store-bought fresh pasta, made with eggs, has a more delicate texture that works well with a variety of sauces.

LONG STRANDS

BUCATINI Long, thick tubes resembling hollow spaghetti

CAPELLINI Also called capelli d'angelo or angel hair; very thin, delicate strands

FUSILLI Long curly strands resembling a telephone cord, but also the name for short spirals

SPAGHETTI Italian for "little cords"

VERMICELLI Very thin spaghetti

FLAT RIBBONS

EGG NOODLES American-style noodles enriched with egg yolks

FETTUCCINE Flat noodles about 1/4 inch wide

LASAGNA Very wide, flat pasta noodles; also available in a no-boil version

LINGUINE Ribbons of pasta that are 1/8 inch wide

MAFALDE Wide ribbons with one long, ruffled edge

PAPPARDELLE Ribbons about 1 inch wide

TAGLIATELLE Slightly wider than fettuccine

TUBULAR PASTAS

ELBOW MACARONI Small curved tubular pasta

MOSTACCIOLE Tubes about 2 inches long; available smooth and with ridges

PENNE Tubes with diagonally cut ends

RIGATONI Large tubes with ridges; mezze rigatoni are half as long.

ZITI Medium tubes about 1 inch long

SMALL PASTAS

ACINI DI PEPE Tiny pasta stubs

ALPHABETS Tiny letter-shaped pasta

DITALINI Very short macaroni; also called tubettini

ORZO Although rice-shaped, orzo means "barley" in Italian.

PASTINA Very, very small pasta flakes

HOW TO

STORE PASTA

- Keep pasta either in its cardboard box or in an opaque container. Clear storage containers are attractive, but they allow in light, which destroys riboflavin, a key nutrient in pasta.

- Store dried pasta in a cool, dry, dark place for up to two years. If it is made of whole wheat or other whole grains, store up to six months.

- Store commercially made fresh pasta in the refrigerator for up to one week, or freeze for up to one month. Homemade pasta can be refrigerated for up to three days or frozen for up to one month. For the best results, don't thaw frozen pasta before cooking.

MISCELLANEOUS SHAPES

CAVATELLI Small, elongated, ridged pasta

CONCHIGLIE Medium shells good for sauce

CRESTE DI GALLO Curly medium-ribbed pasta that resembles a rooster's crest

FARFALLE Italian for "butterflies"; also called bow ties

GEMELLI Two short spaghettilike strands that are twisted together

MANICOTTI Large tubes of pasta meant for stuffing

ORECCHIETTE Disks that resemble small ears

RADIATORI Small, deeply ribbed pasta resembling little radiators

ROTINI Corkscrew pasta, also called fusilli and rotelle

RUOTE Wagon wheel–shaped pasta

ASIAN NOODLES

CELLOPHANE NOODLES Called bean threads or mai fun

CHINESE-STYLE EGG NOODLES Tender whole-wheat strands, similar to egg linguine

RICE STICKS Very thin rice stick noodles; also called mai fun or rice vermicelli

SOBA Thin, brownish-gray noodles made from buckwheat flour

UDON Long, thick, Japanese wheat noodles

ORECCHIETTE WITH MORELS & PEAS 359

5 Steps to
PERFECT PASTA

1 **Cook Pasta in Lots of Boiling Salted Water**
Use at least four quarts of water for each pound of pasta. Cover the pot and bring the water to a rapid boil over high heat. Salt the water, then stir in the pasta.

Note: For your final dish to be seasoned properly, you need to salt the water. If you are concerned about the amount of sodium in your diet, rest assured that only 10 percent of the salt in the cooking water is absorbed by the pasta. The basic proportion is 2 teaspoons of salt per pound of pasta.

2 **Stir Frequently**
Stirring ensures even cooking and keeps pasta from clumping together and sticking to the bottom of the pot. Do not add oil to the cooking water; it prevents sauce from clinging to the pasta.

3 **Don't Overcook Pasta**
Check for doneness early and often. The cooking time on pasta packages is only a guide. To test for doneness, remove a piece from the pot, rinse it briefly under warm water, and bite

into it. When pasta is perfectly cooked, it should be al dente ("to the tooth") with no raw flour taste and a thin, chalk-white center. If you're making a pasta to be baked, undercook it by 4 or 5 minutes, since it will continue to cook in the oven.

4 **Drain, Don't Rinse**
Remove a cup of cooking liquid for thinning sauce, as necessary. Drain the pasta in a colander, shaking to remove excess water. Don't rinse; it cools down the pasta and removes both the surface starch that keeps it firm and its essential nutrients. Only lasagna noodles and pasta for salad should be rinsed.

5 **Serve It Hot**
Warm the serving bowl and the individual bowls. (To warm, put the serving bowl under the colander before draining pasta.) To keep it hot, return the drained pasta to the cooking pot and combine it with the sauce, tossing over low heat. Pasta absorbs sauce quickly, so call everyone to the table while you're tossing the pasta.

GOOD TO KNOW

HOW MUCH PASTA SHOULD I COOK?

Two ounces is good for a first course or if it's a hearty sauce with meat. For lighter pastas, consider 3 or 4 ounces per person for a main dish. The cooked yield of pasta depends on its shape: 4 ounces of tube-shaped pasta, like penne, equals 2½ cups cooked; 4 ounces of long-strand pasta, like spaghetti, equals 2 cups cooked; 4 ounces of egg noodles equals 3 cups cooked.

GOOD TO KNOW

NO GLUTEN? NO PROBLEM.

With the rise of gluten-free diet plans, pasta's popularity continues, with options for all. Beans, rice, yams, lentils, corn, and quinoa are all bases for pasta. And spiralized vegetables provide an option for grain-free pasta dishes.

marinara sauce

PREP: 5 MIN / TOTAL: 30 MIN / MAKES 3½ CUPS

2 tablespoons olive oil

1 small onion, chopped

1 clove garlic, finely chopped

1 can (28 ounces) plum tomatoes

2 tablespoons tomato paste

2 tablespoons chopped fresh basil or parsley (optional)

½ teaspoon salt

1. In a 3-quart saucepan, heat the oil over medium heat; add the onion and garlic and cook, stirring, until the onion is tender, about 5 minutes.

2. Stir in the tomatoes with their juice, the tomato paste, basil (if desired), and salt. Heat to boiling, breaking up the tomatoes with the side of a spoon. Reduce the heat; partially cover and simmer the sauce, stirring occasionally, until it has thickened slightly, about 20 minutes. Use to coat 1 pound pasta for 4 main-dish servings.

Each serving (½ cup) About 70 calories, 1g protein, 7g carbohydrate, 4g fat (1g saturated), 1g fiber, 390mg sodium.

VARIATIONS

Arrabbiata Sauce

Prepare as directed above, but sauté ¼ **to** ½ **teaspoon crushed red pepper** with the onion and garlic in step 1. Omit the fresh herbs and proceed as directed.

Spaghetti all'Amatriciana

Prepare as directed above, but use only **1 tablespoon oil** in step 1. Add **4 ounces sliced pancetta**, chopped, and cook until crisp before adding ¼ **teaspoon crushed red pepper** with the onion and garlic. In step 3, omit the tomato paste and basil and proceed as directed. Toss pasta with sauce and ¼ **cup chopped fresh parsley**.

veggie skillet lasagna

(See photo on page 330.)

PREP: 20 MIN / TOTAL: 35 MIN / SERVES 4

2 tablespoons olive oil

1 medium zucchini, sliced

1 medium red bell pepper, seeded and chopped

1 medium onion, chopped

3 cloves garlic, chopped

½ teaspoon salt

1 can (28 ounces) crushed tomatoes

6 ounces no-boil lasagna noodles, broken into thirds

1 cup part-skim ricotta cheese

2 cups (8 ounces) part-skim mozzarella cheese, shredded

¼ teaspoon ground black pepper

Fresh basil leaves, for garnish

1. In a deep 12-inch lidded skillet, heat the oil over medium-high heat. Add the zucchini, bell pepper, onion, garlic, and salt. Cook 6 minutes, stirring. Reduce the heat to low. Stir in the tomatoes.

2. Add the noodles to the sauce, making sure each piece is at least partially submerged. Cover and cook over low heat for 15 minutes, or until the noodles are almost al dente, gently stirring twice.

3. Dollop the ricotta all over the top of the noodles; sprinkle mozzarella over the ricotta. Cover and cook 10 minutes, or until the cheese melts and the noodles are al dente. Sprinkle with pepper and garnish with basil.

Each serving About 570 calories, 31g protein, 60g carbohydrate, 24g fat (11g saturated), 7g fiber, 950mg sodium.

TESTING NOTE No-boil noodles changed lasagna-making forever. This deconstructed version makes it easy enough for a weeknight dinner. Customize the sauce: Add half a pound of cooked crumbled sausage or ground meat or a ½ cup of chopped pepperoni along with the vegetables.

butternut squash & pesto rotini

(See photo on page 332.)

PREP: 15 MIN / TOTAL: 25 MIN / SERVES 4

- 12 ounces multigrain rotini
- 20 ounces diced butternut squash
- ½ cup roasted almonds
- 2 cloves garlic
- 2 cups fresh basil leaves, plus additional for garnish
- 1 teaspoon freshly grated lemon peel
- ½ teaspoon salt
- ⅛ teaspoon ground black pepper
- ¼ cup extra-virgin olive oil
- ½ cup freshly grated Parmesan cheese, plus additional for garnish

1. Heat a large covered saucepot of salted water to boiling over high heat. Add the rotini and squash and cook as the pasta label directs.

2. Meanwhile, in food processor with the knife blade attached, pulse the almonds and garlic until finely chopped. Add the basil, lemon peel, salt, and pepper. Pulse until finely chopped. Remove ⅔ cup pasta cooking water from the saucepot. With the processor running, add the oil and pasta water in a slow, steady stream. Add the Parmesan and pulse until incorporated into the pesto.

3. Drain the pasta and squash. Return them to the saucepot along with the pesto. Toss until well coated. Garnish with basil and additional Parmesan, if desired.

Each serving About 615 calories, 25g protein, 80g carbohydrate, 28g fat (4g saturated), 17g fiber, 565mg sodium.

linguine
with asparagus & egg

(See photo on page 332.)

PREP: 20 MIN / TOTAL: 30 MIN / SERVES 4

- 4 ounces cubed pancetta
- 1 medium shallot, chopped
- Salt
- 12 ounces linguine
- 1 bunch asparagus, trimmed and halved lengthwise
- 1 tablespoon olive oil
- 4 large eggs
- ½ cup finely grated Parmesan cheese, plus more (optional) for topping
- Ground black pepper

1. Heat a large covered saucepot of salted water to boiling on high.

2. Meanwhile, heat the pancetta in a 12-inch nonstick skillet over medium-high heat. Cook 5 minutes, or until crisp, stirring occasionally. Add the shallot and ¼ teaspoon salt; cook 3 minutes, or until softened. With a spatula, transfer the mixture to a large heat-proof bowl. Wipe out the skillet; set aside.

3. In boiling water, cook the pasta as the label directs; 4 minutes before it's finished cooking, add the asparagus.

4. Meanwhile, add the oil to same the skillet and heat over medium heat. Crack the eggs into individual cups or small bowls. Slide the eggs into the skillet, one by one, and cook 1 minute, or until the whites are set around the edges. Cover the skillet; cook 2 to 3 minutes longer, or until whites set completely. With a slotted spoon, transfer the eggs to paper towels.

5. Reserve 2 tablespoons pasta cooking water. Drain the pasta and asparagus and add to the bowl with the pancetta. Add the Parmesan and the reserved pasta water; toss to combine. Divide among 4 bowls. Top each with 1 egg, pepper, and more Parmesan (if desired).

Each serving About 570 calories, 27g protein, 68g carbohydrate, 21g fat (8g saturated), 4g fiber, 995mg sodium.

 Tip Save 5 minutes: Top each bowl with ¼ cup ricotta cheese instead of a fried egg.

pea pesto pappardelle

PREP: 5 MIN / TOTAL: 25 MIN / SERVES 4

12 ounces pappardelle

1½ cups fresh or frozen peas

½ cup ricotta

1 teaspoon lemon zest

Salt

Ground black pepper

Chopped chives, for serving

1. Cook pappardelle as the label directs. Reserve ½ cup pasta cooking water; drain and return pasta to pot.

2. While pasta is cooking, pulse 1 cup peas in food processor to roughly chop. Add ricotta and lemon zest and pulse a few times to combine (there should still be some chopped peas). Season with salt and pepper.

3. Add ricotta mixture, remaining ½ cup peas, and pasta water; toss to combine. Sprinkle with chopped chives, if desired.

Each serving About 430 calories, 19g protein, 70g carbohydrate, 7g fat (3g saturated), 3g fiber, 100mg sodium.

pasta
with lamb & pecorino

PREP: 15 MIN / TOTAL: 30 MIN / SERVES 6

1 pound ground lamb

Salt

1 small red bell pepper, finely chopped

3 cloves garlic, finely chopped

1½ teaspoons ground cumin

1½ teaspoons ground coriander

1 pound penne rigate

3 tablespoons tomato paste

1 cup fresh mint leaves, finely chopped

½ cup grated Pecorino cheese

1. Heat a large covered saucepot of salted water to boiling.

2. Heat a 12-inch skillet over medium-high heat. Add the lamb; sprinkle with ½ teaspoon salt. Cook 3 minutes, or until browned, breaking up the meat with the back of a wooden spoon. Add the bell pepper, garlic, cumin, coriander, and a pinch of salt; cook 3 minutes, or until beginning to soften, stirring occasionally.

3. Meanwhile, cook the pasta as the label directs. Reserve 1 cup pasta cooking water; set aside. Drain the pasta and return it to the pot. Stir in the tomato paste and reserved pasta water. Cook 2 minutes, stirring.

4. Stir the lamb mixture, mint, and Pecorino into the pasta in the pot, tossing to combine.

Each serving About 560 calories, 28g protein, 61g carbohydrate, 22g fat (10g saturated), 4g fiber, 545mg sodium.

penne
with vodka sauce

PREP: 15 MIN / TOTAL: 45 MIN / SERVES 4

1 tablespoon olive oil

1 small onion, chopped

1 clove garlic, finely chopped

⅛ to ¼ teaspoon crushed red pepper

1 can (28 ounces) tomatoes in puree, coarsely chopped

3 tablespoons vodka (optional)

½ teaspoon salt

½ cup heavy or whipping cream

1 cup frozen peas, thawed

1 pound penne or rotini

½ cup loosely packed fresh basil leaves, thinly sliced

1. In a 12-inch nonstick skillet, heat the oil over medium heat. Add the onion and cook until tender, about 5 minutes. Add the garlic and crushed red pepper to taste; cook until the garlic is golden, about 30 seconds longer. Stir in the tomatoes with their puree, vodka (if using), and salt; heat to boiling over high heat. Reduce the heat to simmer until the sauce has thickened, 15 to 20 minutes. Stir in the cream and peas; heat to boiling.

2. Meanwhile, in a large saucepot of boiling salted water, cook the pasta as the label directs. Drain.

3. In a warm large serving bowl, toss the pasta with the sauce and sprinkle with the basil.

Each serving About 650 calories, 20g protein, 107g carbohydrate, 17g fat (8g saturated), 7g fiber, 763mg sodium.

PASTA WITH LAMB & PECORINO 338

PEA PESTO PAPPARDELLE 338

BACON & BRUSSELS
SPROUT PENNE 340

PARMESAN & SAUSAGE BOLOGNESE 341

bacon & brussels sprout penne

(See photo on page 339.)

PREP: 15 MIN / TOTAL: 25 MIN / SERVES 4

- 1 pound penne
- 6 slices bacon, chopped
- 12 ounces quartered Brussels sprouts
- ½ teaspoon salt
- ½ teaspoon ground black pepper
- 2 medium shallots, thinly sliced
- ½ cup golden raisins
- ½ cup dry white wine

1. Cook the penne as the label directs, reserving ½ cup pasta cooking water before draining.

2. Meanwhile, in a 5-quart saucepot, cook the bacon over medium-high heat 5 minutes, or until crisp, stirring. Transfer the bacon to a paper-towel-lined plate.

3. Add the Brussels sprouts, salt, and pepper to the fat in the skillet. Cover and cook 5 minutes—do not stir. Reduce the heat to medium. Add the shallots and raisins. Cook 2 minutes, stirring occasionally. Add the wine; cook 2 minutes, scraping up the browned bits. Stir in the bacon, cooked and drained pasta, and reserved pasta water.

Each serving About 465 calories, 16g protein, 74g carbohydrate, 12g fat (4g saturated), 5g fiber, 400mg sodium.

 Tip Don't have white wine? Not a problem. Substitute 1 tablespoon lemon juice and enough water or chicken broth to equal ½ cup.

> **INGREDIENT SPOTLIGHT**
> ↓

Brussels sprouts are a member of the nutrient-rich brassicas family (they boast being a good source of riboflavin, iron, magnesium, phosphorus, and a very good source of dietary fiber, vitamin A, vitamin C, vitamin K, thiamin, vitamin B6, folate, potassium, and manganese), which includes broccoli, cauliflower, and cabbage. Any of these vegetables would be a delicious swap in this recipe, such as swapping in half a head of sweet savoy cabbage, coarsely chopped.

shrimp & fennel spaghetti

(See photo on page 332.)

PREP: 15 MIN / TOTAL: 25 MIN / SERVES 6

- 2 medium fennel bulbs
- 3 cloves garlic
- 1 pound spaghetti
- 2 tablespoons olive oil
- 1 teaspoon sugar
- ½ teaspoon crushed red pepper
- Salt
- 1 can (28 ounces) no-salt-added diced tomatoes
- 1 pound peeled and deveined medium (26 to 30 count) shrimp
- 2 cup frozen peas, thawed

1. Heat a large covered saucepot of salted water to boiling over high heat.

2. While the water heats, core and thinly slice the fennel; reserve the fronds for garnish. Thinly slice the garlic.

3. Add the spaghetti to the boiling water and cook for 2 minutes less than the label directs.

4. Meanwhile, in a 12-inch skillet, heat the oil over medium-high heat. Add the fennel, garlic, sugar, crushed red pepper, and ¼ teaspoon salt. Stir well, cover, and cook 5 minutes, or until tender and brown, stirring occasionally. Stir in the tomatoes and cook 5 minutes.

5. Add the shrimp to the spaghetti in the boiling water. Cook 2 minutes. Drain the spaghetti and shrimp and return them to the pot. Add the tomato mixture, peas, and ¼ teaspoon salt. Toss over medium-low heat for 2 minutes, or until well mixed. Garnish with fennel fronds.

Each serving About 480 calories, 26g protein, 77g carbohydrate, 7g fat (1g saturated), 9g fiber, 775mg sodium.

sausage & mushroom penne

(See photo on page 332.)

PREP: 20 MIN / TOTAL: 30 MIN / SERVES 6

- 1 pound multigrain penne
- 12 ounces sweet Italian sausage, casings removed
- 1 medium onion, finely chopped
- 2 packages (10 ounces each) sliced mushrooms
- 5 ounces baby kale or baby arugula
- ¼ teaspoon salt
- ½ teaspoon ground black pepper
- ⅓ cup freshly grated Parmesan cheese

1. Heat a large covered saucepot of salted water to boiling on high heat. Cook the pasta as the label directs. Reserve ¼ cup pasta cooking water.

2. Meanwhile, heat a 12-inch skillet over medium-high heat until hot. Add the sausage; cook 5 minutes, or until browned, stirring and breaking up the meat with the side of a spoon. Add the onion; cook 4 minutes, or until browned, stirring. (If the pan begins to scorch, add ¼ cup water.) Stir in the mushrooms; cook 8 minutes, or until softened, stirring often.

3. Drain the pasta; return it to the pot. Add the kale, sausage mixture, reserved pasta water, and pepper. Toss over medium-low heat until well mixed. Top with Parmesan.

Each serving About 505 calories, 27g protein, 61g carbohydrate, 22g fat (7g saturated), 13g fiber, 690mg sodium.

parmesan & sausage bolognese

(See photo on page 339.)

PREP: 15 MIN / TOTAL: 25 MIN / SERVES 6

- 1 pound rigatoni
- 12 ounces spicy Italian sausage, casings removed
- 3 cloves garlic, crushed with a garlic press
- 2 tablespoons tomato paste
- 1 can (28 ounces) crushed tomatoes
- 1 tablespoon red wine vinegar
- ½ teaspoon salt
- ½ cup finely grated Parmesan cheese, plus more (optional) for serving
- ¼ cup heavy cream

1. Heat a large covered saucepot of salted water to boiling over high heat. Cook the pasta as the label directs. Reserve ¼ cup pasta cooking water.

2. Meanwhile, in a large skillet on medium-high, cook the sausage 5 minutes, or until browned, breaking up the meat with the side of a spoon. With a slotted spoon, transfer the sausage to a bowl. Discard all but 1 tablespoon of fat in skillet.

3. Return the sausage to the skillet along with the garlic. Cook 30 seconds. Stir in the tomato paste and cook 2 minutes, then stir in the crushed tomatoes, vinegar, and salt and heat to simmering. Cook 7 minutes, or until thickened slightly. Stir in Parmesan and the heavy cream.

4. Toss the sauce with the cooked rigatoni, adding more Parmesan cheese, if desired.

Each serving About 500 calories, 20g protein, 69g carbohydrate, 17g fat (7g saturated), 5g fiber, 865mg sodium.

fettuccine alfredo

PREP: 10 MIN / TOTAL: 35 MIN / SERVES 6

1 pound fettuccine

1½ cups heavy or whipping cream

1 tablespoon butter or margarine

½ teaspoon salt

¼ teaspoon coarsely ground black pepper

¾ cup freshly grated Parmesan cheese

Chopped fresh parsley

1. In a large saucepot of boiling salted water, cook the pasta as the label directs. Drain.

2. Meanwhile, in a 2-quart saucepan, heat the cream, butter, salt, and pepper to boiling over medium-high heat. Boil until the sauce has thickened slightly, 2 to 3 minutes.

3. In a warm serving bowl, toss the pasta with the sauce and Parmesan. Sprinkle with parsley.

___

Each serving About 560 calories, 16g protein, 59g carbohydrate, 29g fat (17g saturated), 3g fiber, 530mg sodium.

pasta
with tuna puttanesca

PREP: 15 MIN / TOTAL: 40 MIN / SERVES 6

1 pound rotini or medium shells

3 tablespoons capers, drained and chopped

3 tablespoons finely chopped shallots

½ teaspoon freshly grated lemon peel

2 tablespoons red wine vinegar

1 tablespoon olive oil

½ teaspoon salt

¼ teaspoon coarsely ground black pepper

1 can (6 ounces) light tuna in olive oil

2 bunches watercress (4 to 6 ounces each), tough stems removed

½ cup loosely packed fresh basil leaves, chopped

1. In a large saucepot of boiling salted water, cook the pasta as the label directs. Drain, reserving ½ cup pasta cooking water.

2. Meanwhile, in a large bowl and using a fork, mix the capers, shallots, lemon peel, vinegar, oil, salt, and pepper until well combined. Add the undrained tuna and watercress; toss.

3. In the pasta saucepot, toss the pasta, basil, tuna mixture, and reserved pasta water.

___

Each serving About 375 calories, 18g protein, 59g carbohydrate, 7g fat (1g saturated), 4g fiber, 630mg sodium.

GOOD TO KNOW

___

CHEESE PLEASE

Look beyond Parmesan and mozzarella—the pasta-topping staples—to these flavorful alternatives:

GRANA PADANO	A cow's-milk cheese similar in flavor and texture to Parmesan
FONTINA	Rich and nutty cow's-milk cheese; a good substitute for mozzarella (it melts like a dream).
PECORINO	Piquant and full-flavored cheese made of sheep's milk; grate some instead of Parmesan.
FETA	Tangy, salty, and crumbly, this cheese made of sheep's or goat's milk is a good way to add extra zest to citrus-tinged seafood pasta.
RICOTTA SALATA	A sheep's-milk cheese similar to feta but drier with a milder, milky flavor; a wonderful addition to dishes accented with fresh tomatoes
SEMIHARD AND HARD CHEESES	These last several weeks in the fridge. Cover them with waxed paper, then with plastic wrap or foil. Change the wrapping every few days.

spaghetti
with roasted tomatoes

PREP: 10 MIN / TOTAL: 1 HR 10 MIN, PLUS COOLING / SERVES 4

- 2 tablespoons olive oil
- 3 pounds ripe plum tomatoes (16 medium), cut lengthwise in half
- 6 cloves garlic, unpeeled
- 1 pound spaghetti or linguine
- ¾ teaspoon salt
- ¼ teaspoon coarsely ground black pepper
- Freshly grated Pecorino-Romano cheese (optional)

1. Preheat the oven to 450°F. Brush a rimmed baking sheet with 1 tablespoon oil. Arrange the tomatoes, cut side down, in the pan; add the garlic. Roast the tomatoes and garlic until the tomatoes are well browned and the garlic has softened, 50 to 60 minutes.

2. When cool enough to handle, peel the tomatoes over a medium bowl to catch any juices. Place the tomatoes in the bowl; discard the skins. Squeeze the garlic to separate the pulp from skins; discard the skins. Add the garlic to the tomatoes.

3. Meanwhile, in a large saucepot of boiling salted water, cook the pasta as the label directs. Drain.

4. With the back of a spoon, crush the tomatoes and garlic. Stir in the salt, pepper, and remaining 1 tablespoon oil. Serve the sauce at room temperature or transfer it to a saucepan and heat through over low heat. In a warm serving bowl, toss the pasta with the sauce. Serve with Pecorino-Romano, if desired.

Each serving About 550 calories, 17g protein, 101g carbohydrate, 10g fat (1g saturated), 7g fiber, 570mg sodium.

TESTING NOTE Roasting tomatoes intensifies their sweetness and flavor. Plum tomatoes with their meaty flesh and low juice content are perfect for roasting, but you can turn any off-season tomato into something tasty by roasting. Grape tomatoes are delicious and take on an almost candied flavor. They need only 15 to 20 minutes in a hot oven—perfect for a weeknight pasta toss.

penne
with no-cook tomato sauce

PREP: 20 MIN / TOTAL: 45 MIN, PLUS STANDING / SERVES 4

- 2 pounds ripe fresh tomatoes (6 medium), chopped
- 1 cup loosely packed fresh basil leaves, thinly sliced
- 8 ounces fresh mozzarella cheese, cut into ½-inch cubes
- 2 tablespoons olive oil
- 1 tablespoon red wine vinegar
- 1 teaspoon salt
- ¼ teaspoon coarsely ground black pepper
- 1 pound penne or rotini

1. In a medium bowl, combine the tomatoes, basil, mozzarella, oil, vinegar, salt, and pepper, tossing gently to mix. Let the sauce stand at least 15 minutes or up to 1 hour at room temperature to blend the flavors.

2. Meanwhile, in a large saucepot of boiling salted water, cook the pasta as the label directs. Drain. In a warm serving bowl, toss the pasta with the sauce.

Each serving About 695 calories, 27g protein, 99g carbohydrate, 21g fat (1g saturated), 8g fiber, 749mg sodium.

VARIATION

Bow Ties with Tomatoes & Lemon

Prepare the sauce as directed, but omit the mozzarella and substitute ¼ **cup loosely packed fresh mint leaves**, chopped, for the basil in step 1. Add **1 teaspoon grated lemon peel** and **1 clove garlic**, crushed with a garlic press, to the tomato mixture. In step 2, substitute **1 pound bow ties or ziti** for the penne.

garlicky broccoli pasta

PREP: 15 MIN / TOTAL: 45 MIN / SERVES 6

1 pound orecchiette
   or fusilli
1 bunch broccoli
   (about 1 pound)
2 tablespoons extra-
   virgin olive oil
3 cloves garlic,
   thinly sliced

¼ cup water
½ teaspoon salt
½ cup freshly grated
   Pecorino-Romano
   cheese

1. In a large saucepot of boiling salted water, cook the pasta as the label directs.

2. Meanwhile, trim the broccoli. Coarsely chop the stems and florets. You should have about 5 cups broccoli.

3. In a 12-inch nonstick skillet, heat the oil over medium heat until hot. Add the garlic and cook, stirring, until golden, 2 to 3 minutes. Stir in the broccoli, water, and salt. Cover and cook, stirring occasionally, until the broccoli is tender, 8 to 10 minutes.

4. Drain the pasta, reserving ½ cup pasta cooking water. Return the pasta to the saucepot. Add the cheese, broccoli mixture, and reserved pasta water to the pasta; toss until well combined.

Each serving About 370 calories, 14g protein, 61g carbohydrate, 8g fat (2g saturated), 4g fiber, 395mg sodium.

linguine
with red clam sauce

PREP: 20 MIN / TOTAL: 1 HR 20 MIN / SERVES 6

3½ cups Marinara Sauce
   (page 336)
½ cup dry white wine
2 dozen littleneck clams,
   scrubbed (see page
   299)

1 pound linguine
1 tablespoon butter,
   cut into pieces
   (optional)
¼ cup chopped
   fresh parsley

1. Prepare the Marinara Sauce.

2. In a 12-inch skillet, heat the wine to boiling over high heat. Add the clams; cover and cook until clams open, 5 to 10 minutes, transferring the clams to a bowl as they open. Discard any clams that have not opened after 10 minutes. Strain the clam broth through a sieve lined with paper towels; reserve ¼ cup. When cool enough to handle, remove the clams from their shells and coarsely chop them. Discard the shells. Wipe out the skillet.

3. Meanwhile, in large saucepot of boiling salted water, cook the pasta as the label directs. Drain.

4. In the clean 12-inch skillet, combine the Marinara Sauce, the reserved clam broth, and the clams; cook over low heat until heated through. In a warm serving bowl, toss the pasta with sauce and butter, if using. Sprinkle with parsley and serve.

Each serving About 430 calories, 20g protein, 67g carbohydrate, 9g fat (2g saturated), 5g fiber, 582mg sodium.

GOOD TO KNOW

PICK YOUR PASTA

Choose the right sauce for your pasta. Here are some tried-and-true guidelines.

THIN PASTAS	Pastas such as capellini and vermicelli should be dressed with delicate, light sauces that will cling to the skinny strands.
FETTUCCINE & LINGUINE	Excellent with light meat, vegetable, seafood, cheese, and cream sauces
TUBULAR PASTAS	Great with meat sauces: The nuggets of meat nestle right inside the tubes. Chunky vegetable or olive sauces are also a good match for macaroni-type pastas, as well as for baked dishes.
TINY PASTAS	Best saved for soups or combined with other ingredients

spaghetti
with garlic & oil

PREP: 5 MIN / TOTAL: 30 MIN / SERVES 6

- 1 pound spaghetti or linguine
- ¼ cup olive oil
- 1 large clove garlic, finely chopped
- ⅛ teaspoon crushed red pepper (optional)
- ¾ teaspoon salt
- ¼ teaspoon coarsely ground black pepper
- 2 tablespoons chopped fresh parsley

1. In large saucepot of boiling salted water, cook the pasta as the label directs. Drain, reserving ½ cup pasta cooking water.

2. Meanwhile, in a 1-quart saucepan, heat the oil over medium heat. Add the garlic and cook just until golden, about 1 minute; add the crushed red pepper, if using, and cook 30 seconds longer. Remove the saucepan from the heat; stir in the salt and pepper.

3. In a warm serving bowl, toss the pasta with the sauce and parsley, using the reserved pasta water to moisten the pasta as necessary.

Each serving About 360 calories, 10g protein, 57g carbohydrate, 10g fat (1g saturated), 3g fiber, 361mg sodium.

spaghetti pie
with prosciutto & peas

PREP: 25 MIN / TOTAL: 40 MIN / SERVES 6

- 8 ounces thick spaghetti
- 4 large eggs
- 2 large egg whites
- 1 container (15 ounces) part-skim ricotta cheese
- ¾ cup reduced-fat (2%) milk
- ⅛ teaspoon ground nutmeg
- ¼ teaspoon salt
- ¼ teaspoon ground black pepper
- 1 tablespoon butter or margarine
- 1 bunch green onions, cut into ¼-inch pieces (about 1 cup)
- 1 cup frozen peas
- 6 thin slices prosciutto (about 3 ounces)

1. Preheat the oven to 350°F. In large saucepot of boiling salted water, cook the spaghetti 2 minutes less than the label directs.

2. Meanwhile, in a medium bowl, whisk the eggs, egg whites, ricotta, milk, nutmeg, salt, and pepper until blended. Set aside. In an oven-safe 12-inch nonstick skillet, melt the butter over medium heat. Add the green onions and cook about 5 minutes, or until softened. Remove the skillet from the heat.

3. Drain the spaghetti. To the green onions in skillet, add the spaghetti and frozen peas; toss to combine. Pour the egg mixture over the pasta and arrange the prosciutto slices on top.

4. Place the skillet over medium-high heat and cook the egg mixture 3 to 5 minutes, or until the edges just begin to set. Place the skillet in the oven and bake 15 minutes, or until the center is set. Slide the pie onto a large plate to serve.

Each serving About 375 calories, 25g protein, 38g carbohydrate, 13g fat (6g saturated), 2g fiber, 700mg sodium.

GOOD TO KNOW

EASY ADD-INS

Spaghetti with Garlic & Oil (left) is just the starting point for many delicious possibilities.

- Add **4 to 6 coarsely chopped anchovy fillets in oil**, drained (or 1 to 1½ teaspoons anchovy paste), and **2 tablespoons capers**, drained, to the cooked garlic-oil mixture; reduce the heat and stir until the anchovies break up, about 30 seconds.

- Add **½ cup Gaeta, Kalamata, or green Sicilian olives**, pitted and chopped, to the cooked garlic-oil mixture; reduce the heat and stir until the olives are heated through, about 1 minute.

- Add **2 to 3 ounces crumbled firm goat cheese** to the tossed pasta; toss again.

- Add **⅓ cup chopped dried tomatoes** to pasta with the garlic-oil mixture and parsley; toss.

- Substitute **2 to 4 tablespoons chopped fresh basil, oregano, chives, or tarragon** for parsley.

LINGUINE WITH TUNA & CHILES 349

SPAGHETTI PIE 347

SPANISH NOODLES WITH SHRIMP & PEAS 348

PASTA WITH CHICKEN & BRUSSELS SPROUTS 347

pasta
with chicken & brussels sprouts

PREP: 20 MIN / TOTAL: 30 MIN / SERVES 4

- 12 ounces cavatappi pasta
- 1 pound boneless, skinless chicken thighs, cut into ½-inch chunks
- Salt
- ¼ teaspoon ground black pepper
- 2 teaspoons olive oil
- 10 ounces Brussels sprouts, thinly sliced
- ¼ cup water
- 1 tablespoon margarine or butter
- ¼ teaspoon crushed red pepper
- ¼ cup plain dried bread crumbs
- 3 cloves garlic, crushed with a garlic press
- ¼ cup grated Parmesan cheese
- 2 tablespoons finely chopped parsley

1. Heat a large covered saucepot of salted water to boiling over high heat. Cook the pasta as the label directs.

2. Meanwhile, season the chicken with ¼ teaspoon salt and the pepper. In a 12-inch skillet, heat the oil over medium-high heat. Add the chicken; cook 6 minutes, or until cooked through (165°F), stirring. Transfer to a bowl.

3. To the skillet, add the Brussels sprouts, water, margarine, crushed red pepper, and ⅛ teaspoon salt; cook 3 minutes, stirring. Add the bread crumbs and garlic. Cook, stirring, 2 minutes to toast the crumbs.

4. Reserve ½ cup pasta cooking water. Drain the pasta; return it to the pot. Stir in the chicken, Brussels sprouts mixture, and reserved pasta water. Serve with Parmesan and parsley.

Each serving About 570 calories, 39g protein, 75g carbohydrate, 13g fat (3g saturated), 6g fiber, 545mg sodium.

INGREDIENT SPOTLIGHT
↓

Parsley adds fresh flavor to any savory dish and is available year-round. There are two types: curly and flat leaf (sometimes called Italian). For cooking you can use either type, but we prefer (and test with) flat leaf. It has a more intense flavor. If you use curly, just add a bit more. Curly parsley is a prettier garnish. And don't throw away those stems. They make a delicious addition to soups and stock, and can be added to smoothies or pesto.

spaghetti pie

PREP: 20 MIN / TOTAL: 1 HR / SERVES 6

- 1 pound spaghetti
- 4 strips bacon, chopped
- 1 large red onion, finely chopped
- 1 container (15 ounces) part-skim ricotta cheese
- 4 large eggs
- 2 cup reduced-fat (2%) milk
- ¼ teaspoon cayenne pepper
- 1 cup freshly grated Parmesan cheese
- ¼ teaspoon salt
- 2 cup frozen peas

1. Preheat the oven to 350°F.

2. Heat a large covered saucepot of salted water to boiling over high heat. Cook the spaghetti as the label directs.

3. Meanwhile, in a 12-inch skillet, cook the bacon over medium heat 6 to 8 minutes, or until crisp, stirring occasionally. With a slotted spoon, transfer the bacon to paper towels to drain. To the fat in the pan, add the onion. Cook 4 minutes, or until tender, stirring occasionally.

4. While the onion cooks, in a very large bowl, whisk the ricotta, eggs, milk, cayenne, half of the Parmesan, and the salt.

5. Drain the spaghetti well. Stir it into the ricotta mixture along with the peas, bacon, and onion. Spread it in an even layer in a 3-quart shallow baking dish. Sprinkle the remaining Parmesan on top.

6. Bake 30 to 35 minutes, or until set.

Each serving About 660 calories, 36g protein, 76g carbohydrate, 23g fat (11g saturated), 6g fiber, 700mg sodium.

curly mac 'n' cheese

PREP: 30 MIN / TOTAL: 55 MIN / SERVES 8

1 pound rotini

6 cups milk

3 tablespoons cornstarch

¾ teaspoon salt

⅛ teaspoon ground nutmeg

½ cup freshly grated Parmesan cheese

8 ounces sharp Cheddar cheese, shredded (2 cups)

1. Preheat the oven to 375°F. In a large saucepot of boiling salted water, cook the pasta as the label directs. Drain.

2. Meanwhile, in a 4-quart saucepan and using a wire whisk, mix the milk, cornstarch, salt, and nutmeg until smooth. Cook over medium heat, whisking frequently, until the mixture has thickened slightly and boils. Boil, whisking constantly, 1 minute. Remove the pan from the heat. Gradually whisk in the Parmesan until it melts and the sauce is smooth.

3. Spoon the pasta into shallow 3½-quart or 13 × 9-inch baking dish. Pour sauce over pasta and stir to thoroughly mix. Sprinkle the Cheddar over the top. Bake until the Cheddar has melted and the mixture is hot and bubbling, about 25 minutes.

Each serving About 475 calories, 23g protein, 54g carbohydrate, 18g fat (11g saturated), 3g fiber, 650mg sodium.

Ingredient Ideas
dress up your mac 'n' cheese

Here are some delicious macaroni-and-cheese variations your family is sure to enjoy. Prepare as directed, replacing the Cheddar with:

- 4 ounces Fontina and 4 ounces Gorgonzola

- 4 ounces goat cheese and 4 ounces Monterey Jack

- 3 ounces sharp Cheddar, 3 ounces Asiago, and 3 ounces dry Jack cheese

- 4 ounces sharp white Cheddar and 4 ounces Asiago

spanish noodles
with shrimp & peas

(See photo on page 346.)

PREP: 20 MIN / TOTAL: 35 MIN / SERVES 6

2 cups lower-sodium chicken broth or seafood stock

1 bottle (8 ounces) clam broth

1 tablespoon tomato paste

3 tablespoons olive oil

12 ounces fideos or fidelini noodles, broken into 2-inch lengths

1 medium red bell pepper, thinly sliced

3 cloves garlic, chopped

1 teaspoon smoked paprika

Salt

1 cup frozen peas

1 pound shelled, deveined shrimp

½ cup fresh parsley, chopped, for garnish

1 lemon, cut into 6 wedges, for garnish

1. In a small covered saucepan, heat the stock and clam broth to simmering over medium-high heat. Whisk in the tomato paste. Uncover and reduce the heat to low.

2. In an oven-safe 12-inch skillet, heat the oil over medium heat until hot. Add the noodles; cook 3 to 5 minutes, or until golden, stirring. Add the bell pepper, garlic, ½ teaspoon paprika, and ½ teaspoon salt. Cook 3 minutes, stirring. Add the broth mixture and the peas. Heat to boiling over high heat; reduce the heat and simmer 15 minutes, or until the noodles absorb the liquid and are tender.

3. Preheat the broiler on high.

4. Toss the shrimp with the remaining ½ teaspoon paprika. Arrange the shrimp over the cooked noodles. Broil 2 to 3 minutes, or until the shrimp are cooked through. Garnish with parsley and lemon wedges.

Each serving About 355 calories, 20g protein, 50g carbohydrate, 9g fat (1g saturated), 4g fiber, 900mg sodium.

linguine
with tuna & chiles

(See photo on page 346.)

PREP: 10 MIN / TOTAL: 25 MIN / SERVES 4

- 12 ounces linguine
- 3 tablespoons olive oil
- 3 cloves garlic, finely chopped
- 2 small fresh Thai chiles or 1 jalapeño chile, thinly sliced
- 2 medium zucchini, thinly sliced
- 8 ounces mixed mushrooms, thinly sliced
- ½ teaspoon salt
- ½ teaspoon ground black pepper
- 1 jar (6 ounces) tuna packed in olive oil, drained

1. Cook the pasta as the label directs, reserving ½ cup pasta cooking water.

2. In a 10-inch skillet over medium heat, heat the olive oil. Add the garlic and chiles and cook 2 minutes, stirring. Add the zucchini, mushrooms, salt, and pepper. Cook 5 minutes, stirring. Remove from the heat.

3. In the pasta pot, toss the cooked pasta, the zucchini mixture, and the tuna, adding reserved pasta water as needed.

Each serving About 490 calories, 23g protein, 70g carbohydrate, 14g fat (3g saturated), 4g fiber, 395mg sodium.

GLOSSARY

↓

Oil-packed tuna is at the top of the tuna pyramid, flavor- and texture-wise. You can find everything from chunk light, which is almost shredded in consistency, to jars of tuna with large chunks of fillets, and prices range accordingly. Chunk is perfect for pastas and sauces. Splurge for solid or fillets for a Nicoise salad.

neapolitan pasta sauce

PREP: 15 MIN / TOTAL: 4 HR 30 MIN / MAKES 8 CUPS

- 2 pounds boneless pork shoulder blade roast (fresh pork butt), trimmed
- 1 clove garlic, thinly sliced
- 1 tablespoon olive oil
- 1 pound sweet Italian sausage links
- 8 ounces hot Italian sausage links
- 2 large onions, finely chopped
- 4 cloves garlic, finely chopped
- 4 cans (28 ounces each) plum tomatoes
- 1 can (28 ounces) tomato puree
- 1 tablespoon sugar
- ½ teaspoon salt

1. With a small knife, make several slits in the pork shoulder and insert garlic slices. In a 12-quart saucepot, heat the oil over medium heat until very hot. Cook the pork and the sweet and hot sausages in batches until lightly browned, using a slotted spoon to transfer the meat to a bowl as it is browned.

2. Add the onions and chopped garlic to the saucepot; cook until the onion is tender, about 5 minutes. Add the tomatoes with their juice, the tomato puree, sugar, and salt; heat to boiling, breaking up the tomatoes with the side of a spoon.

3. Return the pork to the saucepot. Reduce the heat, partially cover, and simmer 3 hours. Add the sausage and cook until the pork is very tender, about 45 minutes longer. Remove the pork and cut into bite-size pieces; return the pork to the saucepot (keep the sausages whole). Use 3 cups of the sauce to coat 1 pound pasta, cooked, for 6 servings. Pack remaining sauce into freezer containers, label, and freeze up to 3 months.

Each serving (½ cup) About 140 calories, 9g protein, 5g carbohydrate, 9g fat (3g saturated), 2g fiber, 318mg sodium.

linguine
with white clam sauce

PREP: 15 MIN / TOTAL: 45 MIN / SERVES 6

- ½ cup dry white wine
- 2 dozen littleneck clams, scrubbed (page 299)
- 1 pound linguine or spaghetti
- ¼ cup olive oil
- 1 large clove garlic, finely chopped
- ¼ teaspoon crushed red pepper
- ¼ cup chopped fresh parsley

1. In a 5-quart Dutch oven, heat the wine to boiling over high heat. Add the clams; cover and cook until clams open, 5 to 10 minutes, transferring the clams to a bowl as they open. Discard any clams that have not opened after 10 minutes.

2. Strain the clam broth through a sieve lined with paper towels; discard paper towels. When cool enough to handle, remove the clams from their shells and coarsely chop them. Discard the shells. Wipe out the Dutch oven.

3. Meanwhile, in large saucepot of boiling salted water, cook the pasta as the label directs. Drain.

4. Add the oil, garlic, and crushed red pepper to the clean Dutch oven. Cook over medium heat for about 2 minutes, stirring occasionally, just until the garlic turns golden. Stir in the parsley, chopped clams, and strained clam broth; heat just to simmering. Add the pasta to the Dutch oven and toss until combined.

Each serving About 425 calories, 19g protein, 59g carbohydrate, 11g fat (1g saturated), 3g fiber, 111mg sodium.

 Tip Don't overcook the clams or they will become tough.

farfalle
with gorgonzola

PREP: 10 MIN / TOTAL: 35 MIN / SERVES 6

- 1 pound bow ties or penne
- 1 cup half-and-half or light cream
- ¾ cup chicken broth
- 4 ounces Gorgonzola or blue cheese, crumbled
- ¼ teaspoon coarsely ground black pepper
- 1 cup frozen peas, thawed
- ½ cup chopped walnuts, toasted

1. In a large saucepot of boiling salted water, cook the pasta as the label directs. Drain.

2. Meanwhile, in a 2-quart saucepan, heat the half-and-half and broth just to boiling over medium-high heat. Reduce the heat to medium; cook 5 minutes. Add the Gorgonzola and pepper, stirring constantly until the cheese melts and the sauce is smooth. Stir in the peas.

3. In a warm serving bowl, toss the pasta with the sauce; sprinkle with the walnuts.

Each serving About 485 calories, 18g protein, 63g carbohydrate, 18g fat (8g saturated), 5g fiber, 500mg sodium.

Ingredient Ideas
pasta perk-ups

- **TRY SLIVERED SUN-DRIED TOMATOES** to dress up your favorite mac and cheese.

- **A TABLESPOON OR TWO OF CAPERS** will pump up the flavor of a No-Cook Tomato Sauce (page 343) or embellish a jarred marinara. Add some pitted, chopped olives (and, if your family allows, even a minced anchovy) and you'll be on the way to making your own gutsy Italian-style puttanesca sauce.

- **FRESHLY GRATED LEMON PEEL**—the king of zip— immediately brightens up a creamy seafood sauce.

- **DRIED MUSHROOMS** add rich flavor. You need to rehydrate them before adding them to the pasta: Cover them in boiling water and let soak 15 minutes. With a slotted spoon, remove the mushrooms, but don't discard the liquid! Rinse the mushrooms briefly to remove any grit, then drain them and chop, if desired. The flavorful liquid, strained through a paper-towel-lined sieve, can be used to replace some liquid in your recipe. Dried mushrooms keep well in an airtight container in a cool, dry place for up to a year.

seafood fra diavolo

PREP: 25 MIN / TOTAL: 1 HR 25 MIN / SERVES 6

- 8 ounces cleaned squid
- 1 tablespoon olive oil
- 1 large clove garlic, finely chopped
- ¼ teaspoon crushed red pepper
- 1 can (28 ounces) plum tomatoes
- ½ teaspoon salt
- 1 dozen mussels, scrubbed and debearded (page 298)
- 8 ounces medium shrimp, shelled and deveined (page 297)
- 1 pound linguine or spaghetti
- ¼ cup chopped fresh parsley

1. Rinse the squid and pat it dry with paper towels. Slice the squid bodies crosswise into ¼-inch rings. If the tentacles are large, cut them into several pieces.

2. In a 4-quart saucepan, heat the oil over medium heat. Add the garlic and crushed red pepper; cook just until fragrant, about 30 seconds. Stir in the tomatoes with their juice and the salt, breaking up tomatoes with the side of a spoon. Heat the mixture to boiling over high heat. Add the squid and heat to boiling. Reduce heat; cover and simmer 30 minutes. Remove cover and simmer 15 minutes longer. Increase the heat to high. Add the mussels; cover and cook 3 minutes. Stir in the shrimp; cover and cook until the mussels open and the shrimp are opaque throughout, about 2 minutes longer. Discard any mussels that do not open.

3. Meanwhile, in a large saucepot of boiling salted water, cook the pasta as the label directs. Drain.

4. In a warm serving bowl, toss the pasta with the seafood mixture and parsley.

Each serving About 410 calories, 25g protein, 65g carbohydrate, 5g fat (1g saturated), 5g fiber, 590mg sodium.

spaghetti & meatballs

PREP: 20 MIN / TOTAL: 1 HR 20 MIN / SERVES 6

- Marinara Sauce (page 336)
- 1½ pounds ground meat for meat loaf (beef, pork, and/or veal) or ground beef chuck
- 1 cup fresh bread crumbs (about 2 slices of bread)
- 1 large egg
- ¼ cup freshly grated Pecorino-Romano or Parmesan cheese
- ¼ cup chopped fresh parsley
- 1 clove garlic, crushed with a garlic press
- 1 teaspoon salt
- ¼ teaspoon ground black pepper
- 2 teaspoons olive oil
- 1 pound spaghetti

1. Prepare the Marinara Sauce.

2. Meanwhile, prepare the meatballs: In a large bowl, combine the ground meat, bread crumbs, egg, Pecorino-Romano, parsley, garlic, salt, and pepper just until blended; do not overmix. Shape the mixture into twelve 2-inch meatballs, handling the meat as little as possible.

3. In a 10-inch nonstick skillet, heat the oil over medium heat until hot. Add the meatballs and cook, gently turning them, until browned and just cooked through, about 20 minutes. Add the sauce to the meatballs and heat to boiling, stirring to loosen any browned bits from the bottom of the skillet. Reduce the heat and simmer while you cook the pasta.

4. In a large saucepot of boiling salted water, cook the pasta as the label directs. Drain.

5. In a warm serving bowl, gently toss the pasta with the meatballs and sauce.

Each serving About 690 calories, 34g protein, 69g carbohydrate, 30g fat (10g saturated), 5g fiber, 1,080mg sodium.

classic bolognese

PREP: 10 MIN / TOTAL: 1 HR 35 MIN / MAKES 6 CUPS

- 2 tablespoons olive oil
- 1 medium onion, chopped
- 1 carrot, peeled and finely chopped
- 1 stalk celery, finely chopped
- 1½ pounds ground meat for meat loaf (beef, pork, and/or veal) or ground beef chuck
- ½ cup dry red wine
- 1 can (28 ounces) plum tomatoes, chopped
- 2 teaspoons salt
- ¼ teaspoon ground black pepper
- ⅛ teaspoon ground nutmeg
- ¼ cup heavy or whipping cream

1. In a 5-quart Dutch oven, heat the oil over medium heat. Add the onion, carrot, and celery and cook, stirring occasionally, until tender, about 10 minutes.

2. Add the ground meat to the Dutch oven and cook, breaking up the meat with the side of a spoon, until no longer pink. Stir in the wine and heat to boiling. Stir in the tomatoes with their juice, the salt, pepper, and nutmeg. Heat to boiling over high heat. Reduce the heat and simmer, stirring occasionally, for 1 hour.

3. Stir in the cream and heat through, stirring constantly. Use 2½ cups sauce to coat 1 pound pasta for 6 main-dish servings. Reserve remaining sauce for later use.

Each serving (½ cup) About 210 calories, 13g protein, 6g carbohydrate, 15g fat (6g saturated), 1g fiber, 695mg sodium.

 Tip Scoop remaining half of the sauce into a freezer-proof container. Cool slightly; cover and freeze for up to 3 months.

GLOSSARY

Small pasta shapes, sometimes called **soup pastas or mini pastas**, are perfect for side dishes. From delicate stelline to orzo to mini penne, they can be tossed with a bit of oil or butter and herbs or embellished. When using them for soup, cook separately and combine just before serving.

Ingredient Ideas
a side of pasta 4 ways

Cook **1 cup orzo** or **1¾ cups mini bow tie pasta, ditalini, or mini penne** as the label directs. Then make one of these delicious side dishes. Serves 4.

CONFETTI PASTA

In a 10-inch skillet, heat **2 teaspoons olive oil** over medium heat. Add **2 carrots**, shredded; **1 medium zucchini**, shredded; **1 clove garlic**, crushed with a garlic press; **¾ teaspoon salt**; and **¼ teaspoon coarsely ground black pepper**; cook 5 minutes. Stir in the cooked and drained pasta; heat through.

PASTA WITH PEAS & ONIONS

In a 10-inch skillet, heat **2 teaspoons olive oil** over medium heat. Add **1 small onion**, chopped, and **2 tablespoons water**; cook until the onion is golden, about 10 minutes. Stir in the cooked pasta and **1 cup frozen peas**, thawed, and heat through.

ORANGE-FENNEL PASTA

In a 10-inch skillet, heat **2 teaspoons olive oil** over medium heat. Add **1 clove garlic**, crushed with a garlic press; **¾ teaspoon salt**; and **¼ teaspoon coarsely ground black pepper**; cook 30 seconds. Stir in **1 teaspoon freshly grated orange zest** and **½ teaspoon fennel seeds**, crushed. Stir in the cooked pasta and **2 tablespoons chopped fresh parsley**; heat through.

TUBETTI WITH LEMON & CREAM

In a 2-quart saucepan, combine **¼ cup plus 2 tablespoons heavy cream**, **½ teaspoon lemon zest**, **¼ teaspoon salt**, and a **pinch of ground black pepper**; heat to boiling over medium-high heat. Boil 1 minute. Stir in **1½ cups tubetti** (7 ounces), cooked as the label directs, and **1 tablespoon chopped fresh parsley**; cook over medium heat, stirring constantly, for 1 minute. Transfer to a warm serving bowl and sprinkle with **1 tablespoon chopped fresh parsley**.

northern-style lasagna

PREP: 1 HR 15 MIN / TOTAL: 2 HR 5 MIN, PLUS STANDING / SERVES 10

MEAT SAUCE

½ cup boiling water

½ ounce dried porcini mushrooms (about ½ cup)

2 tablespoons extra-virgin olive oil

3 large cloves garlic, finely chopped

2 large carrots, peeled and finely chopped

1 large onion, chopped

8 ounces lean (90%) ground beef

8 ounces ground pork

8 ounces ground veal

½ cup dry red wine

1 can (28 ounces) diced tomatoes

½ teaspoon salt

BÉCHAMEL SAUCE

4 tablespoons (½ stick) butter or margarine

⅓ cup all-purpose flour

½ teaspoon ground black pepper

½ teaspoon salt

¼ teaspoon ground nutmeg

2½ cups milk

CHEESE FILLING

8 ounces Fontina cheese, shredded (2 cups)

½ cup freshly grated Parmesan cheese

8 to 9 ounces no-boil lasagna noodles

1. Prepare the meat sauce: In a small bowl, pour the boiling water over the porcini mushrooms; let stand 15 minutes.

2. Meanwhile, in a 12-inch skillet, heat the oil over medium heat until hot. Add the garlic, carrots, and onion, and cook, stirring occasionally, until the vegetables are tender, about 15 minutes. Increase the heat to high. Add the beef, pork, and veal and cook, breaking up the meat with the side of a spoon, until the meat is browned, about 10 minutes.

3. Meanwhile, using a slotted spoon, remove the porcini, reserving the liquid. Rinse the mushrooms to remove any grit, then coarsely chop them. Strain the mushroom liquid through a sieve lined with paper towels; set aside.

4. Add the wine to the meat in the skillet and heat to boiling; boil until most of the liquid has evaporated, 2 to 3 minutes. Stir in the tomatoes with their juice, the salt, mushrooms, and reserved soaking liquid; heat to boiling. Reduce the heat to medium-low; simmer, uncovered, until the sauce thickens slightly, about 20 minutes, stirring occasionally.

5. Preheat the oven to 375°F. Meanwhile, prepare the béchamel sauce: In a 2-quart saucepan, melt the butter over medium heat. With a wire whisk, stir in the flour, pepper, salt, and nutmeg, and cook 1 minute. Whisking continuously, gradually add the milk and heat to boiling. Remove the saucepan from heat; set aside.

6. Prepare the filling: In a bowl, toss the cheeses until combined.

7. Assemble the lasagna: In bottom of a 13 × 9-inch baking dish, evenly spread 1 cup meat sauce. Arrange 4 noodles over the sauce, overlapping them slightly to fit and making sure they do not touch the sides of the dish. (If your package of lasagna noodles has only 12 noodles, use 3 noodles per layer and do not overlap them.) Spoon about 1½ cups meat sauce over the noodles. Spread about ⅔ cup béchamel sauce over the meat sauce and sprinkle with about ½ cup cheese filling. Repeat the layering 3 more times.

8. Cover the lasagna with foil and bake 30 minutes. Remove the foil and bake until heated through and the cheese is lightly browned, about 20 minutes longer. Let stand 15 minutes for easier serving.

Each serving About 460 calories, 29g protein, 34g carbohydrate, 23g fat (11g saturated), 3g fiber, 935mg sodium.

dried fruit kugel

PREP: 20 MIN / TOTAL: 55 MIN / SERVES 6

8 ounces wide egg noodles

1 container (8 ounces) low-fat (1%) cottage cheese

1 container (8 ounces) reduced-fat sour cream

¼ cup packed brown sugar

1 large egg

⅓ cup water

1 teaspoon vanilla extract

1 cup chopped dried plums (prunes) or dates

1. Preheat the oven to 350°F. In a medium saucepot, cook the noodles as the label directs. Drain.

2. In a large bowl and using a wire whisk, mix the cottage cheese, sour cream, brown sugar, egg, water, and vanilla. Add the dried plums and noodles and toss well. Spoon the mixture into a greased 9-inch square baking dish. Bake until golden brown, about 35 minutes. Serve warm or at room temperature.

Each serving About 345 calories, 14g protein, 56g carbohydrate, 8g fat (3g saturated), 3g fiber, 230mg sodium.

 Tip This heavenly low-fat version of sweet noodle pudding is studded with dried plums. If you prefer an even sweeter dish, use dates.

butternut squash ravioli

PREP: 30 MIN / TOTAL: 45 MIN / SERVES 4

- 1 teaspoon olive oil
- 1 small onion, finely chopped
- 1 package (12 ounces) frozen butternut squash
- ¼ cup freshly grated Parmesan cheese
- 2 tablespoons plain dried bread crumbs
- 1 large egg, lightly beaten
- Pinch of ground nutmeg
- Salt
- Ground black pepper
- 1 large egg white
- 1 teaspoon water
- 12 ounces wonton wrappers (about 50 wrappers)
- 3 tablespoons butter
- 1 tablespoon thinly sliced fresh sage leaves

1. In a small nonstick skillet, heat the oil over medium heat for 1 minute. Add the onion and cook about 12 minutes, or until tender and lightly browned, stirring occasionally. Cook the squash in the microwave as the label directs; cool slightly.

2. In a medium bowl, combine the onion, squash, Parmesan, bread crumbs, whole egg, nutmeg, and ¼ teaspoon each salt and pepper. In a small bowl, whisk together the egg white and water.

3. Place 1 wonton wrapper on a work surface. With a pastry brush, brush egg white along the edges; place 1 rounded tablespoon of the squash filling in the center of the wrapper, keeping the filling away from the edges. Top with a second wrapper; press down firmly around the filling to seal the ravioli, pushing out any trapped air. Place the ravioli on a baking sheet. Repeat with remaining wrappers and filling, using a second baking sheet so the ravioli do not overlap. Let the ravioli dry 30 minutes, turning them over halfway through to evenly dry both sides.

4. Ten minutes before cooking the ravioli, heat a large saucepot of salted water to boiling over high heat.

5. Add the ravioli to the boiling water; cook 3 to 5 minutes, or until tender, stirring gently to separate the ravioli.

6. Meanwhile, in 4-quart saucepan, cook the butter over medium heat for 3 to 4 minutes, or until golden-brown, stirring occasionally. Remove the saucepan from the heat; stir in the sage and ⅛ teaspoon each salt and pepper.

7. With a large slotted spoon, lift out the ravioli, one at a time; drain on paper towels. Transfer the drained ravioli to the saucepan with the sage butter; gently stir to coat.

Each serving About 455 calories, 15g protein, 66g carbohydrate, 15g fat (8g saturated), 3g fiber, 1,025mg sodium.

sausage & pepper baked ziti

PREP: 40 MIN / TOTAL: 1 HR, PLUS STANDING / SERVES 10

- 1½ pounds sweet and/ or hot Italian sausage links, cut crosswise into 1-inch-thick pieces
- 4 cloves garlic, thinly sliced
- 2 large green, yellow, and/or red bell peppers, cut into ¼-inch-thick slices
- 1 jumbo onion cut lengthwise in half, then cut crosswise into ¼-inch-thick slices
- 1 can (28 ounces) whole tomatoes in puree
- 1 can (15 ounces) tomato puree
- 1 teaspoon salt
- 1 pound ziti or penne pasta
- 1 package (8 ounces) part-skim mozzarella cheese, cut into ½-inch cubes
- ½ cup freshly grated Pecorino-Romano cheese

1. Prepare the sauce: In a deep 12-inch nonstick skillet, cook the sausage over medium-high heat, stirring occasionally, until it is browned on all sides, about 5 minutes.

2. Reduce the heat to medium. Discard all but 2 tablespoons of the sausage drippings from the skillet. Add the garlic, bell peppers, and onion to the sausage and cook, covered, until the vegetables are tender, about 10 minutes, stirring occasionally. Stir in the tomatoes with their puree, the tomato puree, and salt; heat to boiling over medium heat, breaking up the tomatoes with the side of a spoon. Reduce the heat to low; cover and simmer 10 minutes.

3. Meanwhile, preheat the oven to 400°F. Bring a large saucepot of salted water to a boil and cook the pasta 2 minutes less than the labels directs. Drain the pasta; return to the saucepot. Add the sauce and stir until the pasta is evenly coated. Add the mozzarella; toss to combine.

4. Transfer the pasta mixture to a 13 × 9-inch baking dish, spreading it evenly; sprinkle with Pecorino-Romano. Bake, uncovered, until hot and bubbling and top is brown, 20 to 25 minutes. Let stand 10 minutes for easier serving.

Each serving About 520 calories, 25g protein, 49g carbohydrate, 23g fat (10g saturated), 5g fiber, 1,190mg sodium.

gnocchi

PREP: 1 HR / TOTAL: 1 HR 30 MIN / SERVES 8

5 all-purpose potatoes (1½ pounds)

1 teaspoon salt

1½ cups all-purpose flour

1. In a 4-quart saucepan, heat the potatoes and enough water to cover to boiling over high heat. Reduce the heat; cover and simmer until the potatoes are tender, 20 to 25 minutes. Drain. Cool slightly; peel potatoes.

2. Press the warm potatoes through a food mill or ricer. With a wooden spoon, stir in the salt and flour until dough begins to come together. Gently press the dough into a ball; divide in half.

3. On a floured surface, with floured hands, knead each dough half until smooth. Divide each half into 6 equal pieces. On a lightly floured surface, roll one piece of dough at a time into a ¾-inch-thick rope. Cut the rope into ¾-inch lengths.

4. Place one piece of dough on the inside curve of fork tines, gently pressing on the dough with your thumb as you roll the dough along the tines. Allow the dough to drop off the fork, slightly curling in on itself and forming an oval. One side of the gnocchi will have ridges, and the opposite side will have an indentation. Repeat rolling, cutting, and shaping the remaining dough. (Gnocchi can be made up to 4 hours ahead to this point. Arrange them in a single layer on a floured rimmed baking sheet; cover and refrigerate.)

5. In a 5-quart saucepot, heat 4 quarts water to boiling over high heat. Add one-third of the gnocchi to the boiling water. When the gnocchi float to the surface, cook 30 seconds. With a slotted spoon, transfer the gnocchi to a warm shallow serving bowl. Repeat with the remaining gnocchi.

Each serving (without sauce) About 160 calories, 4g protein, 35g carbohydrate, 0g fat (0g saturated), 2g fiber, 295mg sodium.

ricotta gnocchi
with sage butter

PREP: 1 HR / TOTAL: 1 HR 17 MIN / SERVES 8

3 tablespoons butter

1 teaspoon chopped fresh sage

Salt

¼ teaspoon ground black pepper

1 container (15 ounces) ricotta cheese

6 tablespoons freshly grated Parmesan cheese

¾ cup chopped fresh parsley

¾ cup all-purpose flour, or as needed

1. Prepare the sage butter: In a 2-quart saucepan, melt the butter over medium heat. Continue to cook, stirring occasionally, until the butter turns golden brown. (If the butter gets too dark, it will be bitter). Remove from the heat and stir in the sage, ¼ teaspoon salt, and the pepper; set aside.

2. In a medium bowl, combine the ricotta, Parmesan, parsley, and ½ teaspoon salt. Sprinkle flour over the ricotta mixture and, with your hands, work the mixture into a soft, smooth dough. If the dough is sticky, add some additonal flour. Work the dough just until the flour is incorporated into the cheese mixture; do not overwork.

3. Break off a piece of the dough; on a lightly floured surface, roll it into a ¾-inch-thick rope. (If the rope doesn't hold together, return it to the bowl with the remaining dough and work in more flour.) Cut the dough rope into ¾-inch lengths. Place one piece of dough on the inside curve of fork tines, gently pressing on the dough with your thumb as you roll the dough along the tines. Allow the dough to drop off the fork, slightly curling in on itself and forming an oval. One side of the gnocchi will have ridges, and the opposite side will have an indentation. Repeat rolling, cutting, and shaping the remaining dough. (Gnocchi can be made up to 4 hours ahead to this point. Arrange it in a single layer on a floured rimmed baking sheet; cover and refrigerate.)

4. In a 5-quart saucepot, heat 4 quarts water to boiling over high heat. Add half of the gnocchi and cook until the gnocchi float to the surface, 2 to 3 minutes. With a slotted spoon, transfer the gnocchi to a warm shallow serving bowl. Repeat with the remaining gnocchi. To serve, toss the gnocchi with the sage butter.

Each serving About 195 calories, 9g protein, 11g carbohydrate, 13g fat (8g saturated), 1g fiber, 395mg sodium

spicy szechuan noodles

PREP: 10 MIN / TOTAL: 35 MIN / SERVES 6

1½ pounds ground pork

3 cloves garlic, crushed with a garlic press

3 tablespoons dry sherry

3 tablespoons grated, peeled fresh ginger

3 tablespoons soy sauce

¾ teaspoon crushed red pepper

1¾ cups chicken broth

¼ cup creamy peanut butter

1 tablespoon vegetable oil

2 bunches green onions, cut into 2-inch pieces

1 pound linguine or thin spaghetti

1 tablespoon Asian sesame oil or hot chili oil (optional)

1. In a medium bowl, mix the pork, garlic, sherry, ginger, soy sauce, and crushed red pepper until blended but not overmixed. In a 4-cup measuring cup and using a fork, stir the broth and peanut butter until well blended.

2. In a 12-inch skillet, heat the oil over high heat. Add the green onions and cook until wilted, 2 to 3 minutes. Transfer the onions to another medium bowl. In the same skillet, cook the pork in batches, breaking up the meat with the side of a spoon, just until it is no longer pink, 1 to 2 minutes.

3. Return the onions to the pork mixture in the skillet and stir in the broth mixture; heat to boiling over high heat. Reduce the heat to medium; cook, uncovered, until the mixture thickens slightly, 12 to 14 minutes.

4. Meanwhile, in a large saucepot of boiling salted water, cook the pasta as the label directs. Drain the pasta; return it to the saucepot. Add the sesame oil, if using; toss to coat. Transfer the linguine to a large serving bowl; top with the pork mixture.

Each serving About 560 calories, 38g protein, 63g carbohydrate, 16g fat (4g saturated), 5g fiber, 905mg sodium.

sesame veggie noodles

PREP: 20 MIN / TOTAL: 25 MIN / SERVES 4

12 ounces linguine

1 bunch green onions, thinly sliced, plus more for serving

2 cups shredded carrots (about 4 carrots)

2 tablespoons toasted sesame oil

1 bunch rainbow chard, stemmed and chopped

3 large eggs, beaten

¼ cup lower-sodium soy sauce

2 tablespoons molasses

½ teaspoon ground black pepper

Sesame seeds, for garnish

1. Heat a large saucepot of salted water to boiling over high heat. Cook the pasta as the label directs.

2. In a deep 12-inch skillet over medium heat, cook the green onions and carrots in the toasted sesame oil for 5 minutes. Add the rainbow chard; cook 2 minutes, stirring. Add the eggs; cook 2 minutes, stirring occasionally. Add the linguine, soy sauce, molasses, and pepper. Cook 1 minute, stirring and tossing frequently. Serve garnished with sesame seeds and green onions.

Each serving About 495 calories, 16g protein, 80g carbohydrate, 12g fat (3g saturated), 6g fiber, 735mg sodium.

INGREDIENT SPOTLIGHT

↓

Asian sesame oil is made from toasted seeds, which explains its dark color. Just a spoonful adds nuttiness to stir-fries, cold-noodle dishes, and soups. Sesame oil is best used as a seasoning oil, rather than as a sautéing oil. Add it toward the end of cooking, as extended cooking dulls its flavor.

pad thai

PREP: 25 MIN / TOTAL: 30 MIN, PLUS SOAKING / SERVES 4

- 7 to 8 ounces rice stick noodles (rice vermicelli), or 8 ounces angel hair pasta
- ¼ cup fresh lime juice
- ¼ cup Asian fish sauce
- 2 tablespoons sugar
- 1 tablespoon vegetable oil
- 8 ounces medium shrimp, shelled and deveined (page 297), then cut lengthwise in half
- 2 cloves garlic, finely chopped
- ¼ teaspoon crushed red pepper
- 3 large eggs, lightly beaten
- 6 ounces bean sprouts (2 cups), rinsed and drained
- ⅓ cup unsalted roasted peanuts, coarsely chopped
- 3 green onions, thinly sliced
- ½ cup loosely packed fresh cilantro leaves
- Lime wedges, for serving

1. In a large bowl, soak the rice stick noodles, if using, in enough hot water to cover for 20 minutes. Drain. With kitchen shears, cut the noodles into 4-inch lengths. If using angel hair pasta, break it in half, cook in large saucepot of boiling salted water as the label directs, drain, and rinse with cold running water.

2. Meanwhile, in a small bowl, combine the lime juice, fish sauce, and sugar.

3. In a 12-inch skillet, heat the oil over high heat until hot. Add the shrimp, garlic, and crushed red pepper; cook, stirring, 1 minute. Add the eggs and cook, stirring, until just set, about 20 seconds. Add the drained noodles and cook, stirring, 2 minutes. Add the fish sauce mixture, half of the bean sprouts, half of the peanuts, and half of the green onions; cook, stirring, 1 minute.

4. Transfer the Pad Thai to a warm platter or serving bowl. Top with the remaining bean sprouts, peanuts, green onions, and the cilantro. Serve with lime wedges.

Each serving About 495 calories, 25g protein, 65g carbohydrate, 17g fat (3g saturated), 2g fiber, 830mg sodium.

 Tip Rice noodles (use the ⅛-inch-wide ones) are available at Asian markets, specialty stores, or well-stocked supermarkets. If you can't find them, use angel hair pasta or linguine.

SESAME VEGGIE NOODLES 356

CAVATAPPI WITH BUTTERNUT SQUASH & BACON 359

szechuan peanut noodles

PREP: 15 MIN / TOTAL: 25 MIN / SERVES 5

- 1 pound linguine or spaghetti
- 4 ounces snow peas, strings removed
- 1 small cucumber (6 ounces), peeled, seeded, and cut into 2 × ¼-inch matchstick strips
- Asian Peanut Sauce (page 54)
- ¼ cup unsalted dry roasted peanuts, coarsely chopped
- 2 green onions, chopped

1. In a large saucepot of boiling salted water, cook the linguine as the label directs. Add the snow peas during the last 1 minute of cooking time. Drain the linguine and snow peas and rinse with cold water until cool. Drain well.

2. Remove the snow peas and cut them into ¼-inch-wide matchstick strips.

3. In a large bowl, combine the Asian Peanut Sauce and linguine. Add the snow peas and cucumber; toss until the linguine is coated with the sauce. Sprinkle the peanuts and green onions on top.

Each serving About 620 calories, 22g protein, 81g carbohydrate, 24g fat (4g saturated), 6g fiber, 915mg sodium.

 Tip Turn this tasty noodle dish into a hearty main dish by tossing in cooked shrimp or shredded deli roast chicken.

INGREDIENT SPOTLIGHT

In Asia, **Asian Noodles** are consumed for breakfast, lunch, and dinner. They are simmered in broth, stir-fried with meat and/or vegetables, and deep-fried. They are categorized by the type of flour—bean, rice, or wheat—from which they are made. Asian noodles are not interchangeable, because some require different amounts of presoaking or precooking and others do not. For the best results, use whatever your recipe calls for. See page 334 for a list of all Asian noodles.

winter squash lasagna

with brown butter béchamel

PREP: 25 MIN / TOTAL: 2 HR 20 MIN / SERVES 10

- 2 small butternut squash (about 4 pounds total), peeled, seeded, and cut into ¼-inch-thick slices
- 2 tablespoons olive oil
- ¼ teaspoon ground cinnamon
- ¼ teaspoon ground nutmeg
- Salt
- ½ cup butter
- ½ cup all-purpose flour
- 5 cups low-fat (1%) milk
- 2 cloves garlic, finely chopped
- 8 medium fresh sage leaves, finely chopped, plus leaves for garnish
- 1 cup grated Pecorino cheese
- 11 to 12 no-boil lasagna noodles
- 2 cups shredded mozzarella cheese
- Chopped toasted hazelnuts, for garnish

1. Preheat the oven to 450°F. In a large bowl, toss the squash slices with oil, cinnamon, nutmeg, and ¼ teaspoon salt; arrange the squash in single layers on 2 large rimmed baking sheets. Roast 40 minutes or until tender, switching racks halfway through. Reset the oven temperature to 375°F.

2. Meanwhile, in a 4-quart saucepan, heat the butter over medium heat 6 to 8 minutes, or until browned and fragrant, swirling it often. Stir in the flour. Reduce the heat to medium-low. Cook 1 minute, stirring. Gradually whisk in the milk until smooth. Add the garlic and chopped sage. Heat to boiling over high heat, stirring constantly. Reduce the heat; simmer 5 minutes, or until thickened, stirring. Stir in the Pecorino and ¾ teaspoon salt. Remove from the heat.

3. On the bottom of a greased 3-quart baking dish, arrange 3 or 4 noodles in a single layer, breaking to fit, if necessary; top with one-third of the squash. Spread one-third of the cream sauce over the squash, then top with one-third of the mozzarella. Repeat the layering twice more. Cover the baking dish tightly with foil. Bake 50 minutes. Remove the foil. Bake, uncovered, 10 to 20 minutes, or until the top is golden and the pasta is tender. Broil on High 2 minutes, or until the top is deep golden brown. Let stand at least 10 minutes before serving. Garnish with hazelnuts and sage leaves.

Each serving About 455 calories, 19g protein, 46g carbohydrate, 23g fat (12g saturated), 4g fiber, 715mg sodium.

cavatappi
with butternut squash & bacon

(See photo on page 357.)

PREP: 20 MIN / TOTAL: 30 MIN / SERVES 6

- 1¼ pounds peeled small butternut squash, cut into 4 large chunks
- 8 ounces thick-cut bacon, chopped
- 3 cloves garlic, finely chopped
- ½ teaspoon crushed red pepper
- Salt
- ⅔ cup half-and-half
- 6 large fresh sage leaves, chopped
- 1 pound cavatappi pasta
- ½ cup coarsely grated Pecorino cheese

1. Heat a large covered saucepot of salted water to boiling over high heat. Coarsely shred the butternut squash.

2. In a 12-inch skillet, cook the bacon over medium heat 8 to 10 minutes, or until the bacon is crisp, stirring occasionally. With a slotted spoon, transfer the bacon to a small plate. Drain and discard all but 2 tablespoons of fat from the skillet.

3. To the same skillet, add the garlic and crushed red pepper. Cook 30 seconds, stirring. Add the butternut squash and ¼ teaspoon salt. Cook 10 minutes, stirring and mashing frequently. Stir in the half-and-half and chopped sage. Cook 2 minutes. Remove from the heat.

4. While the squash cooks, cook the pasta as the label directs. Reserve ½ cup pasta cooking water. Drain the pasta well; return it to the pot. Add the bacon, squash mixture, Pecorino, reserved pasta water, and ½ teaspoon salt, tossing until well coated.

Each serving About 510 calories, 21g protein, 70g carbohydrate, 17g fat (8g saturated), 4g fiber, 800mg sodium.

orecchiette
with morels & peas

(See photo on page 334.)

PREP: 25 MIN / TOTAL: 35 MIN / SERVES 6

- ¼ cup butter
- 3 cloves garlic, chopped
- 3 ounces fresh morel mushrooms (about 1 cup, or ½ ounces dried and reconstituted), quartered lengthwise and well-rinsed
- 1 pound orecchiette pasta
- 8 ounces sugar snap peas, strings removed
- 1 cup fresh or frozen (thawed) peas
- ½ cup grated Parmesan cheese
- 1 ½ cup pea shoots
- ½ cup microgreens
- Shaved Parmesan, for garnish

1. Heat a large covered pot of salted water to boiling over high heat.

2. In an 8-inch skillet, melt butter over medium heat 3 minutes, or until light brown and foaming, swirling occasionally. Add the garlic and morels; cook 2 minutes, stirring occasionally. Remove from the heat.

3. Cook the pasta as the label directs. Remove ½ cup cooking water 4 minutes before the pasta is done; set the pasta cooking water aside. Add the sugar snap peas and peas to the boiling water. Continue cooking until pasta is al dente and vegetables are tender, about 4 more minutes. Drain well; return to the pot.

4. To the pot holding the pasta, add the mushroom mixture along with the Parmesan, pea shoots, microgreens, ¼ cup reserved pasta water, and ¾ teaspoon salt; stir until well-combined, adding more cooking water if necessary for a looser sauce. Divide among serving bowls; garnish with shaved Parmesan.

Each serving About 410 calories, 15g protein, 65g carbohydrate, 11g fat (6g saturated), 6g fiber, 515mg sodium.

TOMATO SOUP MAC 'N' CHEESE 361

GREEK ZITI BAKE 362

BUFFALO MAC 'N' CHEESE 361

SPANAKOPITA PENNE BAKE 362

tomato soup mac 'n' cheese

PREP: 5 MIN / TOTAL: 1 HR 15 MIN / SERVES 8

- 1 pound cavatappi pasta
- 4 tablespoons unsalted butter
- ¼ cup all-purpose flour
- 2½ cups whole milk
- Salt
- 1 pound American cheese, chopped
- 1½ cups Marinara Sauce (page 336)
- 2 tablespoons tomato paste
- 2 tablespoons coarse dried bread crumbs
- Nonstick cooking spray

1. Preheat the oven to 375°F. Heat a large covered saucepot of salted water to boiling over high heat. Add the pasta; cook 5 minutes. Drain well.

2. Meanwhile, in a 5- to 6-quart saucepot, melt the butter over medium heat. Sprinkle the flour over the melted butter. Cook 1 minute, stirring. Slowly whisk in the milk until smooth. Add ¼ teaspoon salt. Heat to boiling over high heat, whisking often. Reduce the heat; simmer 2 minutes, or until slightly thickened, stirring occasionally. Reduce the heat to medium-low. Gradually stir in the cheese by the handful until smooth, letting the cheese melt before adding next batch. Whisk in the Marinara Sauce and tomato paste. Add the cavatappi; toss to coat well.

3. Transfer the mixture to eight 8-ounce ramekins; top with the bread crumbs. Spray the crumbs with cooking spray. Place the ramekins on a foil-lined rimmed baking sheet. Bake 30 to 35 minutes, or until the sauce is bubbling and the crumbs are golden.

Each serving About 545 calories, 20g protein, 59g carbohydrate, 25g fat (14g saturated), 3g fiber, 1,130mg sodium.

buffalo mac 'n' cheese

PREP: 15 MIN / TOTAL: 25 MIN / SERVES 6

- 12 ounces elbow pasta or shells
- 3 cups shredded carrots (about 6 carrots)
- ½ cup low-fat (1%) milk
- ½ teaspoon garlic powder
- 2 cups finely grated sharp Cheddar cheese
- 1 cup crumbled blue cheese
- ¾ cup plain nonfat Greek yogurt
- ¼ cup hot sauce
- ⅛ teaspoon salt
- Chopped parsley, for garnish

1. Heat a large saucepot of salted water to boiling over high heat. Cook the pasta as the label directs, adding the carrots to the boiling water just before draining.

2. In a 4-quart saucepot, heat the milk and garlic powder over medium heat until hot. Slowly stir in the Cheddar and blue cheese until melted and smooth. Remove from the heat.

3. Whisk in the Greek yogurt, hot sauce, and salt. Toss with the pasta and carrots. Garnish with parsley.

Each serving About 475 calories, 24g protein, 50g carbohydrate, 20g fat (12g saturated), 3g fiber, 920mg sodium.

#SavetheFood
3 more ideas for greek yogurt

HEALTHY MASH

Whip **1 cup plain Greek yogur**t into **4 pounds potatoes**, cooked, peeled, and mashed. **Stir in caramelized onions.**

CREAMY SALSA

Mix **1 cup plain Greek yogurt** with **½ cup each chopped red onion**, olives, and cucumbers. Serve on **sautéed fish.**

ZIPPY HORSERADISH SAUCE

Blend **1 cup plain nonfat Greek yogurt** with **1 table-spoon each chopped parsley, horseradish,** and **fresh lemon juice**. It's great on roast beef!

spanakopita penne bake

(See photo on page 360.)

PREP: 20 MIN / TOTAL: 1 HR / SERVES 8

- 1 pound penne
- 2 boxes (10 ounces) frozen chopped spinach
- 1 cup crumbled feta cheese
- ¼ cup loosely packed fresh dill, chopped
- 1 container (15 ounces) part-skim ricotta cheese
- ½ teaspoon salt
- 8 ounces shredded part-skim mozzarella cheese

1. Preheat the oven to 400°F. Heat a large saucepot of salted water to boiling over high heat. Cook the pasta for half of the time the label directs, adding the frozen chopped spinach and reserving ½ cup pasta cooking water just before draining.

2. Combine the feta, dill, ricotta, and salt. Combine the cooked penne and spinach, the cheese mixture, and the reserved pasta water; spread evenly in a greased 3-quart baking dish. Top evenly with the mozzarella. Cover with foil; bake for 25 minutes. Uncover and bake 10 minutes more.

Each serving About 435 calories, 26g protein, 51g carbohydrate, 15g fat (9g saturated), 4g fiber, 620mg sodium.

vegetarian chili macaroni

PREP: 20 MIN / TOTAL: 25 MIN / SERVES 6

- 1 pound elbow or other short macaroni
- 1 tablespoon canola oil
- 1 medium onion, chopped
- 2 tablespoons chili powder
- Salt
- 1 can (28 ounces) crushed tomatoes
- 1 can (15 ounces) black beans, rinsed and drained
- 1 cup shredded sharp Cheddar cheese
- Fresh chopped cilantro, for serving

1. Heat a large covered saucepot of salted water to boiling over high heat. Cook the pasta as the label directs. Drain, reserving ¼ cup pasta cooking water.

2. In a large pot, heat the oil over medium heat and cook the onion, chili powder, and ½ teaspoon salt for 8 minutes, stirring often.

3. Add the crushed tomatoes and black beans. Heat to simmering over high heat; reduce heat and simmer 5 minutes. Toss with macaroni and Cheddar. Top with cilantro.

Each serving About 500 calories, 22g protein, 82g carbohydrate, 11g fat (4g saturated), 11g fiber, 770mg sodium.

greek ziti bake

(See photo on page 360.)

PREP: 30 MIN / TOTAL: 1 HR 35 MIN / SERVES 10

- Nonstick cooking spray
- 1 tablespoon olive oil
- 1 large onion, chopped
- 1½ pounds ground beef (90% lean)
- Salt
- Ground black pepper
- 1 can (28 ounces) crushed tomatoes
- 1 tablespoon red wine vinegar
- ½ teaspoon pumpkin pie spice
- ½ cup butter
- ⅔ cup all-purpose flour
- 5 cup low-fat (1%) milk
- ¼ teaspoon ground nutmeg
- 3 large eggs, lightly beaten
- 1 cup grated Parmesan cheese
- 1 pound ziti

1. Preheat the oven to 375°F. Heat a pot of salted water to boiling. Spray a 3-quart baking dish with nonstick cooking spray.

2. In a 12-inch skillet, cook the oil and onion over medium-high heat for 4 minutes. Add the beef and ½ teaspoon each salt and pepper. Cook 5 minutes, or until browned. Add the tomatoes, vinegar, and pie spice. Cook 15 minutes.

3. In a 4-quart saucepot, melt the butter over medium-high heat. Stir in the flour until the mixture is smooth. Slowly whisk in the milk, nutmeg, and ¾ teaspoon salt; simmer 8 to 10 minutes, or until thickened, whisking constantly. Cool 5 minutes. Stir in the eggs and Parmesan.

4. Cook the ziti in the pot of boiling salted water 2 minutes less than the label directs. Drain. Press half of the ziti into the prepared baking dish. Spread the meat over the ziti. Layer on the remaining ziti. Top with the sauce. Bake 45 minutes, or until the top is browned and the edges are bubbling.

Each serving About 550 calories, 31g protein, 54g carbohydrate, 23g fat (12g saturated), 4g fiber, 800mg sodium.

creamy mushroom lasagna

PREP: 25 MIN / TOTAL: 1 HR 15 MIN / SERVES 2

- 6 no-boil lasagna noodles
- 2 teaspoons canola oil
- 1 clove garlic, crushed with a garlic press
- ½ teaspoon fresh thyme leaves
- 8 ounces sliced cremini mushrooms
- 8 ounces shiitake mushrooms, stems discarded, sliced
- ¼ cup water
- Salt
- 2 tablespoons dry sherry
- 1 tablespoon butter (no substitutions)
- 3 tablespoons all-purpose flour
- 2 cups whole milk
- Pinch of ground nutmeg
- ¼ cup grated Parmesan cheese
- ¼ teaspoon ground black pepper
- Escarole & Olive Salad (right)

1. In a shallow dish, soak the lasagna noodles in warm water. Preheat the oven to 375°F. Line a rimmed baking sheet with foil.

2. In a 12-inch skillet, heat the oil over medium heat. Add the garlic and thyme. Cook 30 seconds, stirring. Add all the mushrooms, water, and ⅛ teaspoon salt. Cook 3 to 5 minutes, or until the mushrooms are almost tender. Add the sherry. Simmer 2 minutes, or until slightly reduced. Remove from the heat.

3. In a 2-quart saucepan, melt the butter over medium-high heat. Add the flour. Cook 1 minute, or until golden, stirring. Slowly whisk in the milk. Heat to simmering over medium-high heat, whisking frequently. Simmer 2 minutes, whisking constantly. Remove from the heat. Stir in the nutmeg, half the Parmesan, ⅛ teaspoon salt, and the pepper.

4. Grease 2 baking dishes (about 6 × 5-inches each). Spread ¼ cup sauce in 1 dish. Top with 1 noodle, then one-fourth of the mushrooms. Repeat the layering once. Top with another noodle and ¼ cup sauce. Repeat with remaining ingredients in the other dish. Top both dishes with the remaining cheese.

5. Place the dishes in the prepared baking sheet. Cover with foil. Bake 15 minutes. Uncover; bake 25 minutes, or until the lasagna is golden brown and bubbling. Let stand 5 minutes. Serve with Escarole & Olive Salad (right).

ESCAROLE & OLIVE SALAD In a large bowl, whisk **1 tablespoon fresh lime juice, 1 tablespoon extra-virgin olive oil, 1 teaspoon white wine vinegar, a pinch of crushed red pepper, a pinch of sugar,** and **⅛ teaspoon salt.** Add **8 cups (8 ounces) chopped escarole; ¼ cup pitted green olives,** slivered; and **2 tablespoons snipped fresh chives.** Toss well. **Serves 2.**

Each serving (with salad) About 625 calories, 24g protein, 84g carbohydrate, 23g fat (10g saturated), 5g fiber, 610mg sodium.

kale caesar pasta salad

PREP: 15 MIN / TOTAL: 25 MIN / SERVES 6

- 1 pound bow tie pasta
- 6 tablespoons light mayonnaise
- ⅓ cup grated Parmesan cheese
- 3 tablespoons fresh lemon juice
- 1 tablespoon Dijon mustard
- 1 tablespoon extra-virgin olive oil
- 1 clove garlic, crushed with a garlic press
- ½ teaspoon salt
- ½ teaspoon ground black pepper
- 1 large bunch kale, stemmed and chopped
- 8 medium radishes, trimmed and cut into quarters

1. Heat a large saucepot of salted water to boiling over high heat. Cook the pasta as the label directs.

2. In a large bowl, whisk the mayonnaise, Parmesan, lemon juice, Dijon, olive oil, garlic, salt, and pepper. Add the kale, tossing to combine.

3. While the cooked pasta is still hot, add it to kale mixture. Let cool slightly. Stir in the radishes.

Each serving About 390 calories, 14g protein, 62g carbohydrate, 10g fat (2g saturated), 4g fiber, 435mg sodium.

 Tip Add the pasta to your kale straight out of the strainer. The heat will parcook the leaves for perfect softness.

vietnamese noodle salad

PREP: 20 MIN / TOTAL: 25 MIN / SERVES 4

8 ounces thin rice noodles (see page 334)

3 tablespoons fish sauce

2 tablespoons sugar

2 tablespoons white vinegar

1 tablespoon vegetable oil

1 pound ground pork

3 cloves garlic, crushed with a garlic press

1 jalapeño chile, seeded and finely chopped

1 romaine heart, sliced

¼ cup chopped peanuts, for garnish

Fresh herbs (such as mint, cilantro, and/or basil), for garnish

1. Prepare the rice noodles as the label directs.

2. In a cup, whisk the fish sauce, sugar, and vinegar.

3. In a 12-inch skillet, heat the oil over medium-high heat. Add the ground pork, garlic, jalapeño, and 2 tablespoons of the fish sauce dressing. Cook 5 minutes, or until the pork is cooked through, crumbling the meat with the back of a wooden spoon.

4. Cut the cooked noodles with kitchen shears. Add to a large bowl with the pork, romaine, and the remaining dressing. Toss well. Garnish with peanuts and fresh herbs.

Each serving About 465 calories, 28g protein, 60g carbohydrate, 13g fat (2g saturated), 2g fiber, 980mg sodium.

VIETNAMESE NOODLE SALAD 365

KALE CAESAR PASTA SALAD 364

10

grilling

Enticing aromas. Incomparable flavors. Cooking outdoors over an open fire.... We're in love with grilling. The rich smokiness that it imparts to food has us flipping everything from avocados in Smoky Guacamole (page 372) to watermelon in Grilled Watermelon, Tomato & Feta Salad (page 409) to romaine in Grilled Caesar Salad (page 397)—alongside, or instead of, our meat and fish such as Korean Steak (page 376) and Swordfish Kebabs (page 403).

The grill has become our outdoor stove. Its intense heat makes quick work of cooking healthfully, and we love the easy cleanup. There are hardwood and charcoal aficionados and folks who use their gas grill daily. Indeed, the gas grill is now America's favorite, with over two-thirds of families owning one. Charcoal grills are owned by over half of American households—yes, there are many two-grill households!

CAYENNE GRILLED EGGPLANT
WITH FRESH TOMATO SALAD 404

RAINBOW VEGGIE KEBABS 407

SWORDFISH WITH SUMMER SALAD 404

CHIPOTLE ORANGE CHICKEN 388

Grill Options

→

Manufacturers now offer an enticing array of options for gas, charcoal, and electric grills.

GAS GRILL Fueled by either liquid propane or natural gas, you've got a world of features to choose from, including a wide range of BTU capacities, stainless-steel, cast-iron, or porcelain-enameled cooking grates, and flavor bars, V-shaped bars, and infrared burners for searing.

CHARCOAL GRILL Fueled by charcoal briquettes or natural hardwood charcoal chunks, charcoal grills are generally less expensive than gas-powered ones. Look for a charcoal grill made of heavy-gauge steel; a porcelain-enamel coating will give you better protection from rust. Sturdy legs will keep the grill steady.

ELECTRIC GRILL The electric grill offers an alternative to messing around with gas tanks and charcoal. Plug it in, and you're good to go. There are tabletop versions as well as full-size electric grills that you can even use indoors; just be sure to position your grill within reach of a grounded outlet.

GLOSSARY

Flavor bars, hollow V-shaped triangular bars, catch dripping fat and juices, evaporate them, and create the tasty smoke that flavors the food.

---

4 Safety Rules
FOR THE BACKYARD CHEF

1 **Make sure the grill is on a level surface** and not too close to the house, trees, fences, or even deck railings—all can catch fire from flare-ups or flying sparks.

2 **Don't line the bottom of a gas or charcoal grill with foil;** it will obstruct airflow, and the fire will die out faster.

3 **Use lighter fluid only to start a fire;** don't squirt it onto hot coals to get a dying fire going again, because it can ignite in the can as you pour it.

4 **Don't throw water on flare-ups;** it produces steam, which can cause severe burns. Instead remove the food from the grill until the fire subsides, or cover the grill for a few minutes. To prevent flare-ups, trim excess fat from meats.

Grilling Equipment

Cooking over fire calls for some specialized tools. Depending on how much of a grill geek you are, there are gadgets to consider for easier grilling of fish, kebabs, and so on.

Here are the basics, plus some extras:

GRILL TOPPER If you grill delicate foods such as seafood and small vegetables, this perforated metal sheet, tray, or basket will provide a nearly smooth surface for grilling. Food is less likely to break up or fall through, and you can virtually "stir-fry" cut-up foods over the flames.

TONGS Better than a fork because they don't pierce the food's surface and release juices. Barbecue tongs should be 12 inches or longer and have heatproof handles and rounded ends that won't cut into the food.

SPATULA Use one with a long, heatproof handle for flipping burgers and moving food around on a grill topper.

SKEWERS Long metal skewers are the best for kebabs. Choose skewers with flat shafts rather than round ones; food will be less likely to slip or spin around as you turn the skewers. If you use wooden skewers, be sure to soak them first, and consider double threading the food to prevent slippage.

BASTING BRUSH A heatproof handle and a long shaft are two definite brush requirements. As for bristles, silicone is the way to go—it's nearly indestructible and has the added benefit of being nonstick, making cleanup a snap.

GRILLING MITTS A more serious version of oven mitts, these are longer and better insulated to protect more of your arm from higher heat. Heavy suede mitts are excellent.

BRASS-BRISTLED SCRUB BRUSH Use this to clean the grill rack. The best time? While the grill is still hot.

THERMOMETERS Consider two different types of thermometers for grilling ease. The first measures the internal temperature of the food you're cooking. You can do this with an instant-read thermometer, which is inserted into the center of the food when you think it's getting close to done. There are also digital thermometers consisting of a probe that is inserted into the food as it goes onto the heat and attaches to a device that sits beside the grill and provides a continual temperature reading. The other kind of thermometer is a grill surface thermometer, which measures the heat of the fire. When you're cooking with charcoal, it takes the guesswork out of determining whether you have a hot or medium fire (see "How Hot Is My Fire?" at left). It is especially useful when you are cooking "low and slow," which requires that you maintain an even temperature over many hours.

GOOD TO KNOW

HOW HOT IS MY FIRE?

You'll know the coals are ready when they are about 80 percent ashy gray (at night, you'll see them glow red). To test the level of heat, hold your palm above the coals at cooking height (about 6 inches): If you can keep your palm over the fire for just 2 to 3 seconds, the fire is hot (above 375°F); 4 to 5 seconds, the fire is medium (above 300°F); 5 to 6 seconds, the fire is low (above 200°F). Tapping the coals will remove their ash cover and make the fire hotter. Pushing the coals together intensifies the heat; spreading them apart decreases it. Opening the vents on a covered grill increases the temperature, and partially closing them lowers the heat.

Choose Your Cooking Method

One of the keys to successful grilling is knowing the right kind and level of heat to use for the food you're preparing.

DIRECT COOKING The gas grill is preheated with all the burners on or, in a charcoal grill, the prepared coals are spread evenly. Food is placed on the grill rack directly over the heat source. This method works best with foods that take less than twenty-five minutes, such as steaks, chops, and vegetables. Direct heat is necessary for searing, which gives meats that nice crusty surface.

INDIRECT COOKING Indirect cooking is best for longer-cooking meats, such as roasts and whole chickens or turkeys. For a gas grill, plan to place your food on the grill rack over the drip pan. Preheat the burners on the two outer sides for a three-burner grill (or on one side for a two-burner grill). Set the food over the unheated burner. For a charcoal grill, push the briquettes to the edges of the kettle and place a drip pan in the middle before placing your food on the rack.

TO COVER OR NOT TO COVER? Most grill manufacturers—both gas and charcoal—recommend closing the cover for all grilling. We agree. It reduces flare-ups, helps prevent charring, and greatly shortens cooking time.

HIGH VERSUS MEDIUM HEAT Use medium-high heat for thin cuts of meat that cook quickly: skirt steak, thin pork or lamb chops, frankfurters, or shrimp and other shellfish. It's a good idea to sear thick steaks over high heat first. Use medium heat for 3/4- to 1-inch-thick rib eye, tenderloin, or flank steaks, as well as hamburgers, chicken parts, vegetables, fruit, or whole fish.

MAINTAINING PROPER HEAT For long, slow cooking, adjust the controls on your gas grill. It's a bit trickier with a charcoal model. If the fire is too hot, you should close or partially close the vents (top, bottom, or both); if it's not hot enough, open the vents fully or add more briquettes after each additional hour as the manufacturer recommends. Most gas and some charcoal grills have thermometers that permit you to monitor the interior temperature without lifting the lid (uncovering the grill causes the temperature to drop immediately).

Grilling Indoors

Even if you're an intrepid, all-weather grillmeister, sometimes grilling outdoors just isn't an option. You can still enjoy grilled food indoors with a grill pan.

A grill pan is essentially a skillet with ridges in the bottom. They come in a wide range of sizes. We're fans of the classic cast iron and enameled cast iron. To clean it after each use, rinse it in hot water and give it a good scrubbing with a stiff brush. Immediately dry your pan to keep it from rusting.

We do not recommend grill pans with a nonstick coating; if they are heated over more than medium heat, the coating can begin to degrade, releasing harmful chemicals.

So can you prepare anything you cook on an outdoor grill in a grill pan? No, but steaks, burgers, lamb, veal, pork chops, fish steaks and fillets, scallops and shrimp, boneless chicken breasts, and turkey cutlets, along with vegetables and fruits all cook well in a grill pan.

ultimate rub

PREP: 5 MIN / TOTAL: 5 MIN / MAKES SCANT 1 CUP

- ¼ cup packed brown sugar
- 2 tablespoons kosher salt
- 2 tablespoons ground coriander
- 2 tablespoons ground cumin
- 2 tablespoons garlic powder
- 1 tablespoon ground ginger
- 1 tablespoon smoked paprika
- 1 tablespoon ground black pepper
- 1 teaspoon ground cinnamon

In a medium bowl, stir together the brown sugar, salt, coriander, cumin, garlic powder, ginger, smoked paprika, pepper, and cinnamon. Store in an airtight container or a resealable plastic bag up to 6 months.

Each tablespoon About 25 calories, 0g protein, 6g carbohydrate, 0g fat (0g saturated), 1g fiber, 755mg sodium.

Serving Suggestion Use 2 tablespoons for 1½ pounds steak; 1 tablespoon per pound of vegetables; ¼ cup for 2 pounds skin-on, bone-in chicken parts; and 3 tablespoons per pound for salmon fillets.

pastrami spiced flank steak

PREP: 15 MIN / TOTAL: 30 MIN, PLUS MARINATING / SERVES 6

- 1 tablespoon coriander seeds
- 1 tablespoon paprika
- 1 tablespoon ground black pepper
- 2 teaspoons ground ginger
- 1½ teaspoons salt
- 1 teaspoon sugar
- ½ teaspoon crushed red pepper
- 3 cloves garlic, crushed with a garlic press
- 1 beef flank steak (about 1½ pounds)
- 12 slices rye bread
- Deli-style mustard, for serving

1. In a mortar with pestle or resealable plastic bag with rolling pin, crush the coriander seeds. In a cup, combine the crushed coriander, paprika, pepper, ginger, salt, sugar, and crushed red pepper.

2. Rub the garlic on both sides of the steak, then rub the steak with the spice mixture. Place the steak in a large resealable plastic bag; seal the bag, pressing out as much excess air as possible. Place the bag on a plate; refrigerate at least 2 hours or up to 24 hours.

3. Prepare an outdoor grill for direct grilling over medium heat.

4. Remove the steak from the bag. Grill the steak, turning once, 13 to 15 minutes for medium-rare, or to desired doneness.

5. Place the bread slices on the grill over medium heat and toast, without turning, just until grill marks appear on underside of bread.

6. Transfer the steak to a cutting board. Let stand 10 minutes to set the juices for easier slicing. Cut the steak across the grain into thin slices and serve with grilled rye bread and mustard.

Each serving About 380 calories, 33g protein, 35g carbohydrate, 12g fat (4g saturated), 5g fiber, 1,015mg sodium.

smoky guacamole

PREP: 10 MIN / TOTAL: 15 MIN, PLUS CHILLING / MAKES ABOUT 1¼ CUPS

- 2 ripe avocados, unpeeled, halved, and pitted
- 2 teaspoons vegetable oil
- 3 tablespoons fresh lime juice
- 1 clove garlic, crushed with a garlic press
- ½ teaspoon ground chipotle chile
- ½ teaspoon salt
- ¼ cup finely chopped red onion
- ¼ cup finely chopped fresh cilantro
- Tortilla chips, for serving

1. Heat a grill to medium-high. Brush the cut sides of avocados with the oil. Grill 2 to 4 minutes, or until grill marks appear.

2. Transfer the avocados to a cutting board; cool slightly. Remove the avocados from the peel. Mash the avocados in a bowl with the lime juice, garlic, chipotle, and salt until almost smooth. Stir in the red onion and cilantro. Transfer to a serving bowl. Refrigerate, covered, until cold, about 1 hour. Serve with tortilla chips.

Each ⅓ cup About 190 calories, 2g protein, 11g carbohydrate, 17g fat (2g saturated), 7g fiber, 265mg sodium.

grilled onion dip
with naan chips

(See photo on page 378.)

PREP: 20 MIN / TOTAL: 45 MIN, PLUS CHILLING / MAKES ABOUT 1½ CUPS

- 2 tablespoons olive oil
- 1 teaspoon fresh thyme leaves, chopped
- ¼ teaspoon ground black pepper
- 1 medium sweet onion, cut into ½-inch-thick slices
- 1 clove garlic, unpeeled
- 4 ounces cream cheese, softened
- ½ cup low-fat sour cream
- ¼ cup mayonnaise
- 2 tablespoons fresh lemon juice
- 2 tablespoons Worcestershire sauce
- ½ teaspoon salt
- Naan Chips (below) or pita chips, for serving

1. Heat a grill to medium-low. Combine the oil, thyme, and pepper; brush this over the onion. Grill the onion and garlic 15 minutes, or until tender and slightly charred, turning once. Transfer to cutting board; cool.

2. Peel the grilled garlic and place it in the bowl of a food processor along with the onion. Pulse just until chopped. Add the cream cheese, sour cream, mayonnaise, lemon juice, Worcestershire sauce, and salt; pulse until combined but not smooth. Transfer to a serving bowl. Refrigerate, covered, until cold. Serve with Naan Chips or pita chips.

NAAN CHIPS Cut **3 large naan** into 2-inch squares; arrange them in a single layer on a large rimmed baking sheet. Spray with nonstick cooking spray and sprinkle with ¼ **teaspoon salt**. Bake at 350°F for 25 minutes, or until deep golden brown. Cool completely. Store in an airtight container up to 1 week. **Serves 6.**

GRILLED ONION DIP Each ¼ cup (dip only) About 205 calories, 2g protein, 8g carbohydrate, 19g fat (6g saturated), 1g fiber, 380mg sodium.
NAAN CHIPS Each serving About 135 calories, 4g protein, 23g carbohydrate, 3g fat (1g saturated), 1g fiber, 30mg sodium.

brisket
with chunky bbq sauce

PREP: 15 MIN / TOTAL: 3 HR 50 MIN / SERVES 12

BRISKET

- 1 fresh beef brisket (4½ pounds), well trimmed
- 1 medium onion, peeled and cut into quarters
- 1 large carrot, peeled and cut into 1½-inch pieces
- 1 bay leaf
- 1 teaspoon whole black peppercorns
- ¼ teaspoon whole allspice

CHUNKY BBQ SAUCE

- 1 tablespoon vegetable oil
- 1 large onion, finely chopped
- 3 cloves garlic, finely chopped
- 2 tablespoons minced, peeled fresh ginger
- 1 teaspoon ground cumin
- 1 can (14½ ounces) tomatoes in puree, chopped
- 1 bottle (12 ounces) chili sauce
- ⅓ cup cider vinegar
- 2 tablespoons light (mild) molasses
- 2 tablespoons packed brown sugar
- 2 teaspoons dry mustard
- 1 tablespoon cornstarch
- 2 tablespoons water

1. Prepare the brisket: In an 8-quart Dutch oven, place the brisket, onion, carrot, bay leaf, peppercorns, and allspice. Add enough water to cover and heat to boiling over high heat. Reduce the heat; cover and simmer until the meat is tender, about 3 hours.

2. Meanwhile, prepare the Chunky BBQ Sauce: In a 12-inch non-stick skillet, heat the oil over medium heat. Add the onion and cook, stirring occasionally, until tender, about 10 minutes. Add the garlic and ginger and cook, stirring, 1 minute. Stir in the cumin and cook 1 minute longer.

3. Stir in the chopped tomatoes with their puree, the chili sauce, vinegar, molasses, brown sugar, and dry mustard; heat to boiling over high heat. Reduce the heat and simmer, stirring occasionally, 5 minutes.

4. In a cup, blend the cornstarch and water until smooth. After the sauce has simmered 5 minutes, stir in the cornstarch mixture. Raise the heat and bring to a boil, stirring; boil 1 minute. Cover and refrigerate the sauce if you're not using it right away. Makes about 4 cups.

5. When the brisket is done, transfer it to a large platter. If not serving right away, cover and refrigerate until ready to serve.

6. Prepare an outdoor grill for covered direct grilling over medium heat. Place the brisket on the grill, cover, and cook 10 minutes. Turn the brisket and cook 5 minutes longer. Spoon 1 cup barbecue sauce on top of the brisket and cook until brisket is heated through, about 5 minutes longer. (Do not turn brisket after topping with sauce.)

7. Transfer the brisket to a cutting board. Reheat the remaining sauce in a small saucepan on the grill or stove top. Slice the brisket thinly across the grain and serve with the sauce.

Each serving (with sauce) About 240 calories, 26g protein, 6g carbohydrate, 11g fat (4g saturated), 2g fiber, 175mg sodium.

spice-rubbed beef tenderloin

PREP: 5 MIN / TOTAL: 35 MIN / SERVES 8

1 tablespoon fennel seeds, crushed	**½ teaspoon crushed red pepper**
2 teaspoons salt	**1 center-cut beef tenderloin roast (2½ pounds), trimmed and tied**
½ teaspoon ground ginger	

1. Prepare an outdoor grill for direct grilling over medium heat.

2. In a cup, combine the fennel seeds, salt, ginger, and crushed red pepper. Rub this on the beef tenderloin.

3. Grill the tenderloin, turning occasionally, until a meat thermometer inserted in the center of the meat reaches 140°F, 30 to 40 minutes; the internal temperature of the meat will rise to 145°F (medium) upon standing. Or cook to the desired doneness. Transfer the roast to a cutting board and let stand 10 minutes to set the juices for easier slicing. Cut into thin slices and serve.

Each serving About 180 calories, 22g protein, 1g carbohydrate, 9g fat (3g saturated), 0g fiber, 630mg sodium.

 Tip For even more flavor, refrigerate the rubbed meat up to 24 hours before grilling.

Ingredient Ideas
bbq sauce

Grab a bottle of your favorite brand and whip up these new winners.

CHEDDAR SPREAD

Cut **8 ounces extra-sharp Cheddar cheese** into 1-inch cubes. In a food processor with the knife blade attached, pulse the Cheddar until crumbly. Add **½ cup barbecue sauce**, **¼ cup reduced-fat sour cream**, **1 tablespoon Dijon mustard**, and **1½ teaspoons chipotle hot sauce**. Process 1 minute, or until smooth. Spoon into a serving bowl. If not serving spread right away, cover and refrigerate up to 1 week. Serve with crackers. Makes 1¾ cups.

APPLE-CABBAGE SLAW

In a large bowl, whisk together **⅓ cup barbecue sauce**, **⅓ cup reduced-fat sour cream**, **3 tablespoons fresh lemon juice**, and **½ teaspoon salt**. Add **1 bag (16 ounces) shredded cabbage** and **1 Red Delicious apple** cut into matchstick-thin strips; toss to combine. Serves 6.

SOUTHWESTERN BURGERS

In a large bowl, mix **1¼ pounds lean ground beef**, **¼ cup barbecue sauce**, **2 chopped green onions**, **1 tablespoon chopped jalapeño chile**, and **½ teaspoon salt** just until combined. Shape into four 4-inch burgers. Place the burgers on a hot grill grate and cook over medium heat 4 minutes. Turn the burgers over and brush them with **¼ cup barbecue sauce**; cook 4 to 6 minutes longer for medium or to desired doneness. Place on grilled buns. Serves 4.

ZESTY GRILLED CORN

In a small bowl, stir together **½ cup barbecue sauce**, **2 tablespoons snipped fresh chives**, **½ teaspoon Chinese five-spice powder**, **½ teaspoon grated fresh orange peel**, and **¼ teaspoon salt**. Place **6 husked ears of corn** on a hot grill grate and cook over medium heat 6 to 7 minutes, or until lightly charred all over. Brush the corn with the sauce mixture; grill 2 more minutes, turning often. Serves 6.

chili steak

with hawaiian rice

(See photo on page 378.)

PREP: 5 MIN / TOTAL: 20 MIN / SERVES 4

- 1½ pounds skirt steak
- 2 teaspoons chili powder
- 1½ teaspoons grated lime peel
- ½ teaspoon salt
- 2 cups chopped fresh pineapple
- 1 cup packed fresh cilantro leaves, finely chopped
- 3 cups cooked white rice
- Lime wedges, for garnish

1. Prepare an outdoor grill for direct grilling over medium-high heat. Rub the skirt steak with chili powder, lime peel, and salt. Grill 3 to 4 minutes per side, or to the desired doneness. Transfer to a cutting board and let stand 5 minutes.

2. Meanwhile, toss the pineapple with the cilantro and white rice. Thinly slice the steak and serve with rice. Garnish with lime wedges.

HOMEMADE CHILI POWDER Mix **1 teaspoon ground cumin**, ½ **teaspoon ground coriander**, and ¼ **teaspoon each cayenne and garlic powder**. Hot stuff!

Each serving About 500 calories, 42g protein, 45g carbohydrate, 19g fat (7g saturated), 2g fiber, 430mg sodium.

korean steak

PREP: 40 MIN / TOTAL: 55 MIN, PLUS MARINATING / SERVES 6

- ½ cup reduced-sodium soy sauce
- 2 tablespoons sugar
- 2 tablespoons minced, peeled fresh ginger
- 2 tablespoons seasoned rice vinegar
- 1 tablespoon Asian sesame oil
- ¼ teaspoon cayenne pepper
- 3 cloves garlic, crushed with a garlic press
- 1½ pounds beef top round or sirloin steak, 1 inch thick
- 1 cup regular long-grain rice
- ¼ cup water
- 3 green onions, thinly sliced
- 1 tablespoon sesame seeds, toasted
- 1 head romaine lettuce, separated into leaves

1. In a large resealable plastic bag, combine the soy sauce, sugar, ginger, vinegar, sesame oil, cayenne, and garlic; add the steak, turning to coat. Seal the bag, pressing out the excess air. Place the bag on a plate; refrigerate the steak 1 to 4 hours to marinate, turning the bag once.

2. Prepare an outdoor grill for direct grilling over medium heat.

3. Just before grilling the steak, prepare the rice as the label directs; keep warm.

4. Remove the steak from the bag; reserve the marinade. Place the steak on a hot grill rack and grill, turning once, 14 to 15 minutes for medium-rare, or to desired doneness. Transfer the steak to a cutting board; let stand 10 minutes to allow the juices to set for easier slicing.

5. Meanwhile, in a 1-quart saucepan, heat the reserved marinade and water to boiling over high heat; boil 2 minutes.

6. To serve, thinly slice the steak against the grain. Let each person place some steak slices, rice, green onions, and sesame seeds on a lettuce leaf, then drizzle with some cooked marinade. Fold the side of the lettuce leaf over the filling to form a packet to eat like a sandwich.

Each serving About 370 calories, 30g protein, 35g carbohydrate, 11g fat (3g saturated), 3g fiber, 960mg sodium.

classic hamburger

PREP: 5 MIN / TOTAL: 15 MIN / SERVES 4

1¼ pounds ground beef chuck

½ teaspoon salt

¼ teaspoon ground black pepper

1. Prepare an outdoor grill for direct grilling over medium-high heat.

2. Shape the ground beef into 4 patties, each ¾ inch thick, handling the meat as little as possible. Sprinkle the patties with the salt and pepper.

3. Place the patties on the grill rack and cook about 4 minutes per side for medium, or to desired doneness.

Each burger About 245 calories, 29g protein, 0g carbohydrate, 14g fat (6g saturated), 0g fiber, 390mg sodium.

VARIATIONS

Classic Cheeseburgers

Prepare as directed, but during the last 2 minutes of grilling, top each burger with **1 ounce sliced Cheddar or Swiss cheese.** Cover the grill to melt the cheese.

Tex-Mex Burgers

Before shaping the ground beef into patties, combine **2 tablespoons finely chopped onion, 2 tablespoons bottled salsa, 1 teaspoon salt**, and **1 teaspoon chili powder** with the ground beef just until well blended but not overmixed. Grill or panfry as directed.

Teriyaki Burgers

Before shaping the ground beef into patties, combine **¼ cup chopped green onions, 2 tablespoons soy sauce, 1 tablespoon packed brown sugar,** and **¼ teaspoon cayenne pepper** with the ground beef just until well blended but not overmixed. Grill or panfry as directed, but during the last 2 minutes of cooking brush the burgers on each side with a mixture of **2 tablespoons apple jelly; 2 teaspoons minced, peeled fresh ginger;** and **1 teaspoon soy sauce.**

Greek Burgers

Before shaping the ground beef into patties, combine **¼ cup chopped fresh parsley; 1 teaspoon dried mint; 1 teaspoon salt;** and **¼ teaspoon ground black pepper** with the ground beef just until well blended but not overmixed. Grill or panfry as directed.

Roquefort Burgers

Before shaping the ground beef into patties, combine **1 tablespoon Worcestershire sauce** and **½ teaspoon coarsely ground black pepper** with the ground beef just until well blended but not overmixed. Shape the mixture into 4 balls. Make an indentation in the center of each ball; place **½ ounce crumbled Roquefort or blue cheese** into each indentation. Shape the ground-beef mixture around the cheese; flatten each into a ¾-inch-thick patty. Grill or panfry as directed.

HOW TO

MAKE THE PERFECT BURGER

- **FOR JUICINESS AND FLAVOR,** use relatively lean meat but not the very leanest. You need to have a little fat for great burgers.

- **DON'T OVERMIX** when combining meat and other ingredients, and don't squeeze or compress the mixture when shaping patties or you'll end up with dry, tough burgers.

- **TO PREVENT STICKING,** get the grill good and hot before putting on the burgers.

- **NEVER FLATTEN OR SCORE BURGERS** with a spatula as they cook or you'll lose precious juices.

- **FOR SAFETY'S SAKE,** cook thoroughly, until just a trace of pink remains in the center (160°F). Burgers don't have to be well done, but they should not be rare.

- **KEEP GROUND BEEF REFRIGERATED** up to two days in its supermarket wrap. For longer storage, rewrap in freezer wrap and freeze; use within three months.

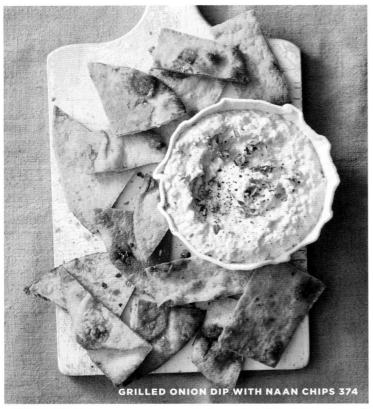

GRILLED ONION DIP WITH NAAN CHIPS 374

MEDITERRANEAN SPICED BURGER 379

CHILI STEAK WITH HAWAIIAN RICE 376

STEAK WITH BROCCOLINI-RADISH SALAD 379

mediterranean spiced burger

PREP: 10 MIN / TOTAL: 20 MIN / SERVES 4

- 1 pound ground meat (lamb, beef, or turkey)
- ½ cup packed fresh cilantro, finely chopped
- 2 cloves garlic, crushed with a garlic press
- 1 teaspoon ground coriander
- ¼ teaspoon salt
- ⅓ cup ketchup
- 1 teaspoon curry powder
- 4 buns, toasted
- 2 tablespoons crumbled feta cheese; 1 small red onion, sliced and grilled; and cilantro, for serving (optional)

1. Heat a grill pan to medium-high.

2. Mix together the ground meat, cilantro, garlic, and coriander until just combined. Form into 4 patties (each about ½ inch thick); sprinkle with salt. Grill the burgers 8 to 10 minutes (for medium), turning once halfway through.

3. Stir together the ketchup and curry powder. Serve the burgers on toasted buns with the curry ketchup. Serve with feta cheese, red onion, and cilantro, if desired.

Each serving About 385 calories, 25g protein, 30g carbohydrate, 18g fat (7g saturated), 2g fiber, 665mg sodium.

grilled portobello burgers

PREP: 10 MIN / TOTAL: 20 MIN / SERVES 4

- 2 packages (6 ounces each) portobello mushroom caps (4 large)
- 3 tablespoons bottled balsamic vinaigrette
- ⅓ cup light mayonnaise
- ¼ cup drained jarred roasted red peppers
- 4 whole-wheat hamburger buns, split
- 1 large ripe tomato (10 to 12 ounces), thinly sliced
- 4 Boston lettuce leaves
- 2 large carrots, peeled and sliced diagonally

1. Heat a ridged grill pan over medium-high heat until hot. Place the mushrooms, stem sides down, in the pan. Brush the cap with half of the vinaigrette and grill 5 minutes. Turn the mushrooms over; brush with the remaining vinaigrette and grill 5 to 8 minutes longer, or until very tender.

2. Meanwhile, place the mayonnaise and red peppers in a blender. Pulse until the red peppers are chopped but not pureed, turning off the blender and scraping down the sides several times. Toast the hamburger buns.

3. To serve, spread the red pepper mayonnaise on the cut side of bottom buns. Place the mushrooms on the buns and top with tomato slices, lettuce, and then the bun tops. Serve carrot slices with the burgers.

Each serving About 270 calories, 8g protein, 33g carbohydrate, 12g fat (2g saturated), 5g fiber, 590mg sodium.

steak
with broccolini-radish salad

PREP: 10 MIN / TOTAL: 25 MIN / SERVES 4

- 2 boneless beef top loin steaks, about 1½ inches thick
- Salt
- Ground black pepper
- 2 bunches broccolini, trimmed
- 2 tablespoons olive oil
- 2 tablespoons Dijon mustard
- 2 tablespoons lemon juice
- 1 tablespoon maple syrup
- 5 radishes, thinly sliced
- 2 green onions, thinly sliced

1. Prepare grill for direct grilling over medium-high heat.

2. Season the steaks with ½ teaspoon each salt and pepper. Grill, covered, 5 minutes per side for medium-rare or to desired doneness. Transfer to a cutting board; let stand 10 minutes. After 10 minutes, slice against the grain.

3. Meanwhile, toss the broccolini with 1 tablespoon olive oil and ¼ teaspoon salt. Grill, covered, 4 minutes, turning occasionally.

4. Whisk together the mustard, lemon juice, 1 tablespoon olive oil, maple syrup, and ¼ teaspoon salt. Toss the radishes, green onions, and broccolini with the dressing. Serve with steak.

Each serving About 410 calories, 42g protein, 18g carbohydrate, 19g fat (6g saturated), 5g fiber, 810mg sodium.

pork tenderloin cutlets
with plum glaze

PREP: 10 MIN / TOTAL: 16 MIN / SERVES 4

1 pork tenderloin (1 pound), trimmed

¾ teaspoon salt

¼ teaspoon coarsely ground black pepper

½ cup plum jam or preserves

1 tablespoon packed brown sugar

1 tablespoon grated, peeled fresh ginger

2 cloves garlic, crushed with a garlic press

1 tablespoon fresh lemon juice

½ teaspoon ground cinnamon

4 large plums (1 pound), each pitted and cut in half

1. Prepare an outdoor grill for direct grilling over medium heat.

2. Using a sharp knife, cut the tenderloin lengthwise almost in half, being careful not to cut all the way through. Open and spread it flat like a book. Place the tenderloin between 2 sheets of plastic wrap or waxed paper. With a meat mallet or rolling pin, pound the meat to a ¼-inch thickness. Cut the tenderloin crosswise into 4 equal pieces; sprinkle the cutlets with the salt and pepper.

3. In a small bowl, combine the plum jam, brown sugar, ginger, garlic, lemon juice, and cinnamon. Brush one side of each cutlet and the cut side of each plum half with the plum glaze. Place the cutlets and plums on the grill, glaze side down, and cook 3 minutes. Turn cutlet and plums over. Brush the other side with the remaining plum glaze; turn the pork and plums over and cook until the cutlets are lightly browned on both sides and just lose their pink color throughout and the plums are hot, about 3 minutes longer.

Each serving About 335 calories, 27g protein, 44g carbohydrate, 6g fat (2g saturated), 2g fiber, 510mg sodium.

pork medallions
with melon salsa & grilled limes

PREP: 20 MIN / TOTAL: 30 MIN / SERVES 4

1 whole pork tenderloin (1¼ pounds), trimmed

4 to 5 limes

1 tablespoon olive oil

½ cup loosely packed fresh cilantro leaves, chopped

Salt

⅛ teaspoon coarsely ground black pepper

2 cups chopped cantaloupe

1 cup chopped honeydew melon

1 jalapeño chile, seeded and minced

1. Prepare an outdoor grill for direct grilling on medium heat.

2. Cut the pork tenderloin crosswise into 8 equal-size pieces. With the palm of your hand, firmly press on a cut side of each piece, flattening it into a 1-inch-thick medallion.

3. Cut 2 limes in half; reserve them for grilling. From the remaining limes, grate 1 teaspoon peel and squeeze ¼ cup juice. In a medium bowl, combine the oil, ½ teaspoon lime peel, half of the cilantro, ⅛ teaspoon salt, and the pepper. Add the pork medallions to the bowl; toss to coat.

4. Place the pork on the hot grill grate and cook 4 minutes. Turn the pork over. Add the lime halves, cut sides down, to the grill; cook 3 to 4 minutes, or until lightly browned and warm. Cook the pork 4 to 5 minutes longer, or until browned on the outside and still slightly pink in the center.

5. In a medium bowl, combine the melons, jalapeño, lime juice, ⅛ teaspoon salt, and the remaining cilantro and lime peel. (Makes about 3 cups salsa.) Serve the pork with the melon salsa and grilled limes.

Each serving About 240 calories, 31g protein, 17g carbohydrate, 8g fat (2g saturated), 2g fiber, 225mg sodium.

GOOD TO KNOW

GRILLING TIMES FOR PORK

Follow these cooking times to grill each cut to 145°F.

CUT	COOKING TIME (MEDIUM HEAT)
CHOPS (RIB OR LOIN), 1 INCH THICK	10 to 12 minutes
TENDERLOIN, WHOLE	13 to 23 minutes
TENDERLOIN STEAKS, ¼ INCH THICK	5 to 6 minutes

basic grilled pork tenderloins

PREP: 15 MIN / TOTAL: 35 MIN, PLUS MARINATING / SERVES 8

1 pork tenderloin (about 1 pound)

Choice of dry spice rub (right)

1. Prepare an outdoor grill for covered direct grilling over medium heat.

2. In a cup, combine the rub ingredients; use to rub on the tenderloins.

3. Place the tenderloins on the grill, cover, and cook, turning the tenderloins once, until browned on the outside and still slightly pink in the center, 16 to 20 minutes. A meat thermometer inserted in thickest part of tenderloin should register 145°F.

4. Transfer the tenderloin to a cutting board; cover and let rest 5 minutes. Thinly slice.

Each serving About 180 calories, 26g protein, 0g carbohydrate, 7g fat (2g saturated), 0g fiber, 50mg sodium.

HOW TO

REMOVE THE SILVERSKIN

The thicker end of a pork tenderloin is covered with a thin membrane called the silverskin. When heated, the silverskin shrinks and can cause the tenderloin to bow and thus cook unevenly. Slip the tip of a paring knife between the silverskin and the muscle fibers. Angle the knife slightly upward and insert just under the silverskin; grasp skin with one hand and use a delicate sawing motion to scrape it away from the meat.

Ingredient Ideas

dry spice rubs

CURRY RUB

Combine **2 tablespoons packed brown sugar**, **1 tablespoon curry powder**, **½ teaspoon salt**, and **¼ teaspoon ground black pepper**.

SOUTHWESTERN RUB

Combine **2 teaspoons chili powder**, **½ teaspoon salt**, **¼ teaspoon ground cumin**, **¼ teaspoon ground coriander**, **¼ teaspoon cayenne pepper**, and **¼ teaspoon ground black pepper**.

MIDDLE EASTERN RUB

Combine **1 tablespoon dried mint**, crumbled; **1 teaspoon ground cumin**; **½ teaspoon salt**; and **¼ teaspoon ground black pepper**.

HERBES DE PROVENCE RUB

Combine **1½ teaspoons dried thyme**, crumbled; **1 teaspoon dried rosemary**, crumbled; **½ teaspoon dried marjoram**, crumbled; **½ teaspoon salt**; and **¼ teaspoon ground black pepper**.

JERK RUB

In a food processor with the knife blade attached, puree **1 bunch green onions**, cut into 1-inch pieces; **3 bay leaves**, broken into pieces; **3 cloves garlic**, peeled; **2 jalapeño chiles**, seeded and coarsely chopped; **2 tablespoons distilled white vinegar**; **1 tablespoon dried thyme**; **2 teaspoons ground allspice**; **1 teaspoon salt**; and **½ teaspoon coarsely ground black pepper** until a thick paste is formed.

teriyaki pork chops
with grilled pineapple slices

PREP: 15 MIN / TOTAL: 35 MIN, PLUS MARINATING / SERVES 4

- ⅓ cup soy sauce
- 2 tablespoons plus ¼ cup packed brown sugar
- 2 green onions, chopped
- 2 tablespoons grated, peeled fresh ginger
- 4 pork loin chops, ¾ inch thick (6 to 8 ounces each)
- 1 small pineapple

1. Prepare an outdoor grill for direct grilling over medium heat.

2. In a 13 × 9-inch baking dish, combine the soy sauce, 2 tablespoons brown sugar, green onions, and ginger. Add the chops, turning to coat. Let stand 20 minutes at room temperature to marinate.

3. Meanwhile, cut off the crown and stem end from the pineapple. Stand the pineapple upright and cut off the rind and eyes. Place the pineapple on its side and cut it crosswise into ½-inch-thick slices. Sprinkle the pineapple slices with the remaining ¼ cup brown sugar.

4. Place the pineapple on the grill and cook, turning the slices occasionally, until browned on both sides, 15 to 20 minutes. After the pineapple has cooked 10 minutes, place the chops on the grill and cook, turning occasionally and brushing them with the remaining teriyaki mixture halfway through cooking, until the chops are browned on both sides and the juices run clear when the center is pierced with the tip of a knife, about 10 minutes. Serve the chops with the grilled pineapple slices.

Each serving About 400 calories, 30g protein, 48g carbohydrate, 11g fat (4g saturated), 3g fiber, 1,435mg sodium.

Tip Boil used marinades and glazes for 2 minutes if you want to serve them with cooked meat. Or reserve some in a separate dish before it comes in contact with the meat, fish, or poultry.

porchetta-style pork chops

PREP: 15 MIN / TOTAL: 30 MIN / SERVES 4

- 1 tablespoon chopped fresh rosemary leaves
- 2 teaspoons fennel seeds, crushed
- Salt
- ⅛ teaspoon ground black pepper
- 4 bone-in pork loin or rib chops, ¾ inch thick (about 6 ounces each)
- 1 pound plum tomatoes, each cut lengthwise in half
- 1 tablespoon extra-virgin olive oil
- 2 tablespoons chopped fresh parsley leaves
- 1 teaspoon grated fresh lemon peel
- 1 clove garlic, crushed with a garlic press

1. Prepare an outdoor grill for covered direct grilling over medium heat.

2. Meanwhile, in a cup, combine the rosemary, fennel seeds, ½ teaspoon salt, and the pepper. Use to rub on the pork chops.

3. In a medium bowl, combine the tomatoes, oil, and ¼ teaspoon salt; set aside.

4. Place the pork chops on the grill, cover, and cook the chops 5 minutes. Turn the chops and arrange them on one side of the grill. Place the tomatoes, cut sides down, on the other side of the grill; set the bowl aside. Cover the grill and cook the pork chops until browned on the outside and still slightly pink on the inside, 4 to 5 minutes per side; cook the tomatoes until evenly charred on both sides, 6 to 7 minutes per side.

5. Transfer the chops to a platter and the tomatoes to a cutting board. Cool the tomatoes slightly, then cut them into large pieces. Return the tomatoes and their juices to the reserved bowl; stir in the parsley, lemon peel, and garlic. Serve the chops with the tomato salad.

Each serving About 315 calories, 28g protein, 6g carbohydrate, 19g fat (6g saturated), 2g fiber, 520mg sodium.

oktoberfest feast

PREP: 15 MIN / TOTAL: 30 MIN / SERVES 4

12 ounces kielbasa, sliced ½-inch thick

1⅓ cups sauerkraut

1 small red onion, peeled and cut into wedges

1 apple, cored and sliced

2 teaspoons caraway seeds

¼ cup beer

Rye toast and spicy mustard, for serving

1. Prepare an outdoor grill for covered direct grilling over medium heat. In a bowl, toss the kielbasa, sauerkraut, onion, apple, and caraway seeds. Divide the mixture among four 18 × 12-inch foil sheets. Pour beer evenly over each. Fold the foil around the food and tightly crimp the edges so the steam and juices cannot escape.

2. Grill the packages for 15 minutes. Serve with rye toast and spicy mustard.

Each serving About 235 calories, 15g protein, 13g carbohydrate, 15g fat (6g saturated), 3g fiber, 985mg sodium.

OKTOBERFEST FEAST 383

southwestern ham steak

PREP: 5 MIN / TOTAL: 15 MIN / SERVES 4

2 teaspoons chili powder

½ teaspoon ground cumin

¼ teaspoon ground coriander

¼ teaspoon cayenne pepper

¼ teaspoon sugar

1 fully cooked smoked ham center slice, ½ inch thick (1¼ pounds)

1. Prepare an outdoor grill for direct grilling over medium heat.

2. In a small bowl, combine the chili powder, cumin, coriander, cayenne, and sugar. Use to rub on the ham steak.

3. Place the ham steak on grill and cook until heated through and lightly browned, about 4 minutes per side.

Each serving About 170 calories, 27g protein, 1g carbohydrate, 6g fat (2g saturated), 1g fiber, 1,730mg sodium.

BABY BACK RIBS WITH MIXED BERRY–CHIPOTLE GLAZE 384

baby back ribs

with mixed berry–chipotle glaze

(See photo on page 383.)

PREP: 30 MIN / TOTAL: 2 HR 30 MIN / SERVES 8

- 2 racks baby back pork ribs (2 pounds each)
- 1 tablespoon chipotle chile powder
- 1 tablespoon Old Bay Seasoning
- Salt
- ¾ cup packed light brown sugar
- 1½ teaspoons garlic powder
- 3 cups mixed berries (raspberries, strawberries,
- blackberries, and/or blueberries), plus additional for garnish
- ½ cup ketchup
- 3 tablespoons cider vinegar
- 2 tablespoons chipotle chiles in adobo, chopped
- ¼ teaspoon salt
- 1 tablespoon olive oil
- 1 medium onion, chopped

1. Pat the ribs dry. In a bowl, mix the chipotle chile powder, Old Bay, 1 teaspoon salt, ½ cup brown sugar, and 1 teaspoon garlic powder. Rub spice mixture over ribs. Tightly wrap the ribs in aluminum foil; refrigerate ribs at least 2 hours or up to overnight.

2. Preheat the oven to 350°F. Place the wrapped ribs in a jelly-roll pan and bake 1 hour 30 minutes, or until tender. Carefully unwrap the ribs; transfer ¼ cup of the collected juices to a measuring cup; discard the remaining juices.

3. In a food processor, pulse the berries, ketchup, vinegar, chiles, ¼ teaspoon salt, the remaining ¼ cup brown sugar and ½ teaspoon garlic powder, and the meat juices until smooth. Press through fine-mesh sieve into a medium bowl; discard the berry seeds.

4. In a 4-quart saucepan, heat the olive oil over medium-high heat. Add the onion and cook 5 minutes, or until soft, stirring occasionally. Add the berry mixture, heat to boiling, then reduce heat and simmer 20 to 30 minutes, or until reduced by one-third (to about 2 cups).

5. Prepare the grill for direct grilling over medium-high heat. Set aside half of the berry glaze for serving. Grill the ribs 8 to 10 minutes, or until glossy, basting with the remaining glaze and turning them occasionally. Transfer to a platter; garnish with berries. Serve with the reserved glaze.

Each serving About 365 calories, 21g protein, 23g carbohydrate, 22g fat (8g saturated), 2g fiber, 760mg sodium.

 Tip Can't find baby back ribs? Try St. Louis or spare ribs. Just bake them an extra half hour to an hour, or until tender.

VARIATIONS

Balsamic-Rosemary Sauce

In a 1-quart saucepan, combine ⅔ cup **balsamic vinegar**, 2 table-spoons **packed brown sugar**, 1 teaspoon **salt**, and ½ teaspoon **ground black pepper** and heat to boiling over medium heat. Cook until the sauce has reduced to ⅓ cup, about 15 minutes. Stir in 1 teaspoon **dried rosemary**.

Orange-Dijon Sauce

In a cup, combine 1 cup **sweet orange marmalade**, ¼ cup **Dijon mustard**, ¼ cup **packed brown sugar**, 1 teaspoon **freshly grated orange peel**, and 1½ teaspoons **salt**.

Asian BBQ Sauce

In a 1-quart saucepan, heat 1 tablespoon **vegetable oil** over medium heat; add **2 green onions**, finely chopped, and cook until tender, about 5 minutes. Add **2 teaspoons grated, peeled fresh ginger** and **1 clove garlic** crushed with a garlic press; cook, stirring frequently, 1 minute longer. Stir in ⅔ **cup packed brown sugar**, ¼ **cup soy sauce**, ¼ **cup dry sherry**, 1 tablespoon **cornstarch**, and ½ teaspoon **salt**. Heat to boiling over medium-high heat, stirring, until mixture has thickened. Remove from the heat; stir in 1 tea-spoon **Asian sesame oil**.

GOOD TO KNOW

PORK RIB GLOSSARY

Nothing says summer more than pork ribs on the grill. There are several types of ribs you are likely to find at your local supermarket.

SPARE RIBS A rack, made up of the 13 ribs from the belly of a pig, weighs around 2 to 3 pounds, with lots of meat at each rib's wider end. The rack will feed two to three people.

BABY BACK RIBS These are pork chop bones from the upper portion of the rib section of the loin with the boneless meat removed. Baby back ribs are not, as one might think, from baby pigs. These ribs have much less meat on them than spareribs, as the meat is cut very close to the bone. One rack will feed one or two people. With their small size, they make great cocktail food.

COUNTRY-STYLE RIBS These ribs are actually loin pork chops that have been split. These meaty, slightly fatty ribs are delicious grilled or braised. They are sold both bone-in and boneless.

plum good glaze

PREP: 5 MIN / TOTAL: 25 MIN / SERVES 6

¼ cup soy sauce

6 whole star anise

1 cinnamon stick (3 inches long)

1 jar (16 ounces) plum jam (1 cup)

1 tablespoon grated, peeled fresh ginger

1 clove garlic, crushed with a garlic press

In a 1-quart saucepan, heat the soy sauce, star anise, and cinnamon stick to boiling over high heat. Reduce the heat to low; cover and simmer 5 minutes. Remove from the heat; let stand, covered, 5 minutes. Strain the mixture into a bowl; discard the star anise and cinnamon. Stir in plum jam, ginger, and garlic. Brush ribs with some of the glaze several times during the last 10 minutes of cooking; serve with remaining glaze. Makes scant 1¼ cups.

Each serving About 140 calories, 1g protein, 36g carbohydrate, 0g fat (0g saturated), 1g fiber, 586mg sodium.

grilled lamb chops
with spice rub

PREP: 5 MIN / TOTAL: 15 MIN / SERVES 4

1 tablespoon olive oil

2 teaspoons fennel seeds, crushed

2 teaspoons cumin seeds, crushed

2 teaspoons coriander seeds, crushed

1½ teaspoon salt

4 lamb shoulder chops, ¾ inch thick (8 ounces each)

1. Prepare an outdoor grill for direct grilling over medium heat.

2. In a small bowl, combine oil, fennel seeds, cumin seeds, coriander seeds, and salt; use to rub on the lamb chops.

3. Place the chops on the grill and cook about 5 minutes per side for medium-rare or to desired doneness.

Each serving About 455 calories, 57g protein, 2g carbohydrate, 22g fat (8g saturated), 1g fiber, 470mg sodium.

Serving Suggestion For flavor variation, try one of the dry spice rubs on page 381.

sausage & peppers

PREP: 15 MIN / TOTAL: 30 MIN / SERVES 4

⅓ cup balsamic vinegar

1 teaspoon packed brown sugar

½ teaspoon salt

¼ teaspoon coarsely ground black pepper

2 medium red bell peppers, cut into 1½-inch-wide strips

2 medium green bell peppers, cut into 1½-inch-wide strips

2 large red onions (about 8 ounces each), peeled and each cut into 6 wedges

1 tablespoon olive oil

¾ pound sweet Italian sausage links

¾ pound hot Italian sausage links

1. Prepare an outdoor grill for direct grilling over medium heat.

2. In a cup and using a fork, mix the vinegar, brown sugar, salt, and pepper.

3. In a large bowl, toss the bell peppers and onions with the oil until evenly coated.

4. Cook the sausages on the grill, turning them occasionally, until golden brown and cooked through, 15 to 20 minutes. At the same time, cook the vegetables, turning them occasionally and brushing with some of the balsamic mixture during last 3 minutes of cooking, until tender, about 15 minutes. Transfer the vegetables and sausages to a platter as they finish cooking.

5. To serve, cut the sausages diagonally into 2-inch-thick slices. Drizzle the remaining balsamic mixture over the vegetables.

Each serving About 500 calories, 27g protein, 19g carbohydrate, 36g fat (12g saturated), 4g fiber, 1,450mg sodium.

Serving Suggestion For hearty sandwiches reminiscent of those found at Italian street fairs, grill Italian hero rolls, split them open, and top with this sausage, pepper, and onion mixture. If you prefer, toss the grilled sausages and vegetables with cooked ziti, add grated Parmesan cheese, and serve.

butterflied leg of lamb

with mint pesto

PREP: 15 MIN / TOTAL: 35 MIN, PLUS MARINATING AND STANDING / SERVES 12

- 4½ cups loosely packed fresh mint leaves
- 2 cloves garlic, crushed with a garlic press
- ½ cup water
- ⅓ cup olive oil
- 1 teaspoon salt
- 1 teaspoon coarsely ground black pepper
- 4 pounds butterflied boneless lamb leg, trimmed
- ¾ cup blanched almonds

1. In a food processor with the knife blade attached, pulse the mint leaves, garlic, water, oil, salt, and pepper until well blended.

2. Place the lamb in 13 × 9-inch glass baking dish. Remove ¼ cup of the mint mixture from the food processor; spread it on the lamb to coat both sides. Cover and refrigerate at least 1 hour or up to 6 hours.

3. Meanwhile, add the almonds to mint mixture remaining in the food processor and pulse until the almonds are finely chopped. Spoon the pesto into a serving bowl; cover and refrigerate until ready to serve.

4. Remove the lamb from the refrigerator about 15 minutes before cooking. Prepare an outdoor grill for covered, direct grilling on medium.

5. Place the lamb on the hot grill grate; cover and cook 20 to 35 minutes (depending on thickness) for medium-rare, turning the lamb over halfway through cooking. When the lamb is done, transfer it to a cutting board and let stand 10 minutes to set the juices for easier slicing. Serve the lamb with the mint pesto.

Each serving About 380 calories, 32g protein, 5g carbohydrate, 26g fat (8g saturated), 4g fiber, 270mg sodium.

 Tip Check thinner portions of the lamb early for doneness; cut off those sections as they are cooked and place them on a cutting board, covered with foil, to keep warm.

rosemary lamb kebabs

PREP: 30 MIN / TOTAL: 40 MIN, PLUS MARINATING / SERVES 4

- 3 oranges
- 1 tablespoon olive oil
- 1 tablespoon chopped fresh rosemary, or 1½ teaspoons dried rosemary, crumbled
- 2 cloves garlic, each cut in half
- ¼ teaspoon salt
- ¼ teaspoon cayenne pepper
- 1 pound boneless lamb leg, cut into 1½-inch pieces
- 1 red bell pepper, cut into 1½-inch squares
- 1 yellow bell pepper, cut into 1½-inch squares
- 1 orange bell pepper, cut into 1½-inch squares
- 1 pint cherry tomatoes
- 6 green onions, cut into 2-inch pieces
- 10 ounces small mushrooms, trimmed

1. Prepare an outdoor grill for direct grilling over medium heat.

2. Meanwhile, from the oranges, grate 1 teaspoon peel and squeeze 1 cup juice. In a large bowl, combine the orange peel and juice, oil, rosemary, garlic, salt, and cayenne. Add the lamb, turning to coat, and let stand, stirring occasionally, 10 minutes at room temperature.

3. Thread the lamb onto 4 metal skewers, and thread the vegetables onto 4 more skewers, alternating the vegetables. Place the skewers on the grill. Cook the lamb and vegetables, turning once, 10 to 12 minutes for medium-rare, or to the desired doneness. Transfer to a platter.

Each serving About 245 calories, 28g protein, 12g carbohydrate, 10g fat (3g saturated), 4g fiber, 120mg sodium.

all-american bbq chicken

PREP: 1 HR / TOTAL: 1 HR 40 MIN / SERVES 8

2 tablespoons olive oil

1 large onion, chopped

2 cans (15 ounces each) tomato sauce

1 cup red wine vinegar

½ cup light (mild) molasses

¼ cup Worcestershire sauce

⅓ cup packed brown sugar

¾ teaspoon cayenne pepper

2 chickens (3½ pounds each), each cut into quarters, skin removed (except from the wings), if desired

1. In a 10-inch nonstick skillet, heat the oil over medium heat. Add the onion and cook until tender, about 5 minutes. Stir in the tomato sauce, vinegar, molasses, Worcestershire, brown sugar, and cayenne; heat to boiling over high heat. Reduce the heat to medium-low and cook, stirring occasionally, until the sauce has thickened slightly, about 45 minutes. (Makes about 3½ cups sauce.) If you're not using the sauce right away, cover and refrigerate up to 2 weeks.

2. Prepare an outdoor grill for covered direct grilling over medium heat.

3. Reserve 1½ cups sauce to serve with the chicken. Place the chicken on the grill; cover and cook, turning once, 20 to 25 minutes. Generously brush the chicken with some of remaining barbecue sauce and cook, brushing frequently with sauce and turning the chicken often, until the juices run clear when the thickest part of the chicken is pierced with the tip of a knife, about 20 minutes longer. Serve with the reserved sauce.

Each serving (without additional sauce, without skin) About 370 calories, 42g protein, 21g carbohydrate, 13g fat (3g saturated), 1g fiber, 545mg sodium.
Each ¼ cup sauce About 160 calories, 1g protein, 20g carbohydrate, 2g fat (0g saturated), 3g fiber, 420mg sodium.

HOW TO

PERFECTLY GRILL CHICKEN

Follow these tips for succulent, mouthwatering chicken every time. See photo on page 366.

SEASON THE BIRD

Preheat a clean grill for direct grilling over medium heat. If the chicken pieces are not marinated, season them as desired (but save barbecue sauce and other sauces for later). If they are skinless, brush them lightly with oil before seasoning.

FLIP & REPEAT

Place the chicken pieces, skin side down, on hot grill grates. Cover and cook 5 to 10 minutes, or until you can move the chicken easily (be careful not to let the skin burn). Flip and repeat on other side. If flare-ups occur, move the pieces briefly to the cooler area of the grill.

HIT THIS TEMP

Continue cooking until an instant-read thermometer inserted into the thickest part of the meat registers 165°F for breasts and 170°F for dark meat, about 30 to 35 minutes. If you're using sauce, wait until the last 5 minutes of cooking before basting both sides of the chicken; turn frequently.

sweet chipotle chicken stacks

PREP: 20 MIN / TOTAL: 30 MIN / SERVES 4

2½ pounds assorted heirloom tomatoes, cored and sliced

Salt

¼ cup packed fresh cilantro

1 tablespoon chopped chipotle chiles in adobo

1 tablespoon fresh lime juice

2 teaspoons honey

1 clove garlic

⅛ teaspoon ground cumin

1¼ pounds thin chicken cutlets

1 large avocado, very thinly sliced

8-inch corn tortillas, for serving (optional)

1. Prepare a grill for covered direct grilling on medium-high. Sprinkle the tomato slices with ⅛ teaspoon salt.

2. In a food processor or blender, combine the cilantro, chiles, lime juice, honey, garlic, cumin, half of the tomatoes, and ¼ teaspoon salt; puree until smooth. Transfer ¼ cup of the tomato salsa to a large bowl. Set aside the remaining salsa.

3. In the same bowl, toss the chicken to coat. Grill the chicken (discarding the marinade), covered, 3 minutes on each side, or until cooked (165°F). Transfer to a platter.

4. Divide the remaining tomatoes among the chicken. Top with avocado. Serve with the remaining salsa and tortillas, if desired.

Each serving About 280 calories, 32g protein, 16g carbohydrate, 11g fat (2g saturated), 6g fiber, 335mg sodium.

chipotle orange chicken

(See photo on page 368.)

PREP: 5 MIN / TOTAL: 35 MIN / SERVES 6

1 tablespoon light brown sugar

2 teaspoons ground chipotle chile

1 teaspoon ground cumin

1 teaspoon garlic powder

½ teaspoon onion powder

1 teaspoon salt

1 teaspoon ground black pepper

4 pounds small chicken thighs, trimmed of excess skin

2 tablespoons olive oil

2 small oranges, cut into quarters

2 green onions, thinly sliced, for garnish

1. Prepare grill for covered direct grilling over medium heat.

2. In a small bowl, combine the brown sugar, chipotle, cumin, garlic powder, onion powder, salt, and pepper.

3. In a large bowl or 3-quart baking dish, toss the chicken with the oil; sprinkle with the spice mixture, then rub the spices into the chicken to coat it evenly.

4. Grill the chicken, covered, 20 to 25 minutes, or until chicken is cooked (165°F), turning over once. Grill the orange quarters 5 to 10 minutes, or until grill marks appear. Transfer the chicken to a serving platter. Squeeze the juice from the grilled oranges all over the chicken. Garnish with green onions.

Each serving About 480 calories, 42g protein, 6g carbohydrate, 31g fat (8g saturated), 1g fiber, 535mg sodium.

GOOD TO KNOW

GRILLING TIMES FOR POULTRY

Here's an easy way to accomplish timing your meal: When grilling a cut-up chicken, put the legs on the grill first. After 5 minutes, add the breasts. After another 10 minutes, put the thighs on to cook.

CUT	TEMP	COOKING TIME
LEGS, BONE-IN	170°F	35 to 40 minutes
THIGHS, BONE-IN	170°F	12 to 15 minutes
THIGHS, BONELESS	170°F	10 to 12 minutes
BREASTS, BONE-IN	165°F	30 to 35 minutes
BREASTS, BONELESS	160°F	10 to 12 minutes
CORNISH GAME HENS, HALVED	170°F	35 to 45 minutes

beer can chicken

PREP: 15 MIN / TOTAL: 1 HR 15 MIN, PLUS STANDING / SERVES 8

3 tablespoons paprika
1 tablespoon sugar
1 tablespoon salt
2 teaspoons coarsely ground black pepper
1 teaspoon onion powder

1 teaspoon garlic powder
1 teaspoon cayenne pepper
2 whole chickens (about 3½ pounds each)
2 cans (12 ounces each) beer

1. Prepare a charcoal fire for covered indirect-heat grilling with a drip pan as the manufacturer directs, or preheat a gas grill for covered indirect grilling over medium heat.

2. In a cup, combine the paprika, sugar, salt, pepper, onion powder, garlic powder, and cayenne.

3. Remove the giblets and necks from the chickens. Rinse the chickens inside and out with cold running water and drain well; pat dry with paper towels. Sprinkle 1 tablespoon of the spice mixture inside the cavity of each chicken. Rub the remaining spice mixture all over the chickens.

4. Wipe the beer cans clean. Open cans; pour ½ cup beer out of each can and reserve it for another use. With a church key, make 4 more holes in the top of each can. With the partially filled can on a flat surface, hold 1 chicken upright, with the opening of the body cavity down, and slide the chicken over the top of the beer can so the can fits inside the cavity. Repeat with the remaining chicken and beer can.

5. With a large spatula, transfer the chickens to the center of the grill rack, keeping the cans upright. (If you're using charcoal, place the chickens over the drip pan.) Spread the chicken legs to balance the chickens on the rack. Cover the grill and cook the chickens until the juices run clear when the thickest part of the thigh is pierced with the tip of a knife, 1 hour to 1 hour 15 minutes.

6. With tongs and barbecue mitts, remove the chickens and cans from the grill, being careful not to spill any beer. Let the chickens stand 10 minutes before lifting them from the cans. Transfer the chickens to a large platter or cutting board; discard the beer.

Each serving About 350 calories, 39g protein, 4g carbohydrate, 19g fat (5g saturated), 1g fiber, 985mg sodium.

 Tip If you're using a charcoal grill, add 10 charcoal briquettes per side of the grill if cooking time is more than 1 hour.

curried chicken
with mango & cantaloupe

PREP: 25 MIN / TOTAL: 35 MIN, PLUS MARINATING / SERVES 4

1 to 2 limes
1 container (6 ounces) plain low-fat yogurt
¾ teaspoon curry powder
¼ cup chopped crystallized ginger
Salt
¼ teaspoon crushed red pepper
4 medium skinless, boneless chicken breast halves (about 1¼ pounds)

½ small cantaloupe, rind removed, seeded, and cut into julienne strips (2 cups)
1 large mango, peeled and cut into julienne strips (2 cups)
½ cup loosely packed fresh cilantro leaves, chopped
1 head Boston lettuce
Lime wedges (optional)

1. Prepare an outdoor grill for covered direct grilling over medium heat.

2. From the limes, grate ½ teaspoon peel and squeeze 2 tablespoons juice. In a large bowl, combine 1 tablespoon lime juice and ¼ teaspoon lime peel with the yogurt, curry powder, 2 tablespoons ginger, ¾ teaspoon salt, and ⅛ teaspoon crushed red pepper, and whisk until blended. Add the chicken, turning to coat. Cover and let the chicken rest 15 minutes at room temperature or 30 minutes in the refrigerator, turning occasionally.

3. In a medium bowl and using a rubber spatula, gently stir the cantaloupe and mango with the cilantro, the remaining 2 tablespoons ginger, 1 tablespoon lime juice, ¼ teaspoon lime zest, ¼ teaspoon salt, and ⅛ teaspoon crushed red pepper; set aside. (Makes about 4 cups.)

4. Grease the grill rack. Remove the chicken from the marinade; discard the marinade. Place the chicken on the grill. Cover and cook the chicken, turning once, until the juices run clear when the thickest part of the breast is pierced with the tip of a knife, 10 to 12 minutes. Transfer the chicken to a cutting board; cool slightly to set the juices for easier slicing, then cut it into long, thin slices.

5. To serve, divide the lettuce leaves among 4 dinner plates; top with chicken and slaw. Serve with lime wedges, if you like.

Each serving (chicken with lettuce) About 205 calories, 34g protein, 5g carbohydrate, 4g fat (1g saturated), 0g fiber, 330mg sodium.
Each ½ cup slaw About 50 calories, 1g protein, 13g carbohydrate, 0g fat, 1g fiber, 150mg sodium.

grilled chicken tacos

with strawberry salsa

- 1¼ pounds skinless, boneless chicken breast halves
- 1 teaspoon chili powder
- 1 teaspoon canola oil
- Salt
- 12 6-inch flour tortillas
- Olive oil cooking spray
- 8 ounces strawberries, hulled and chopped (about 1½ cups)
- 2 medium tomatoes, chopped
- 1 medium avocado, chopped
- 1 small shallot, finely chopped
- 2 limes
- ½ cup crumbled feta cheese
- 2 cups fresh cilantro leaves

1. Prepare an outdoor grill for covered direct grilling over medium heat.

2. Rub the chicken with chili powder, oil, and ¼ teaspoon salt. Grill the chicken, covered, 12 to 15 minutes, or until cooked through (165°F), turning over once halfway through.

3. Transfer the cooked chicken to a cutting board. Let stand 5 minutes.

4. Meanwhile, spray the tortillas with cooking spray. Grill 1 to 2 minutes, or until grill marks appear, turning over once halfway through. Transfer to a plate.

5. While the chicken rests, in a medium bowl, stir together the strawberries, tomatoes, avocado, shallot, and ⅛ teaspoon salt. Squeeze the juice of ½ lime into the mixture, stirring to combine.

6. Thinly slice the chicken and serve it in tortillas, topped with strawberry salsa, feta, and cilantro. Garnish with the remaining limes, cut into wedges.

Each serving About 560 calories, 39g protein, 53g carbohydrate, 22g fat (6g saturated), 7g fiber, 1,070mg sodium.

peking chicken roll-ups

- 8 (8-inch) flour tortillas
- 2 tablespoons honey
- 2 tablespoons soy sauce
- 1 tablespoon grated, peeled fresh ginger
- ⅛ teaspoon cayenne pepper
- 2 cloves garlic, crushed with a garlic press
- 6 skinless, boneless chicken thighs (about 1¼ pounds)
- 1 teaspoon vegetable oil
- ¼ cup hoisin sauce
- ½ English (seedless) cucumber, cut into 2 × ¼-inch matchstick strips
- 2 green onions, thinly sliced

1. Prepare an outdoor grill for direct grilling over medium-high heat.

2. Stack the tortillas and wrap them in foil; set aside. In a small bowl, mix the honey, soy sauce, ginger, cayenne, and garlic until blended; set aside.

3. Coat the chicken with oil, place it on the grill, and cook, turning once, for 5 minutes. Brush the chicken all over with the honey mixture and cook, turning once, until the juices run clear when the thickest part of the thigh is pierced with the tip of a knife, 5 to 7 minutes longer.

4. While the chicken is cooking, place the foil-wrapped tortillas on the same grill rack and heat until warm, 3 to 5 minutes.

5. Transfer the chicken to a cutting board and cut into thin slices. Spread the hoisin sauce on one side of each tortilla. Top each tortilla with chicken, cucumber, and green onions; roll up to serve.

Each serving About 400 calories, 27g protein, 50g carbohydrate, 10g fat (3g saturated), 3g fiber, 1,255mg sodium.

ginger grilled chicken for a crowd

PREP: 10 MIN / TOTAL: 45 MIN, PLUS MARINATING / SERVES 12

1¼ cups soy sauce

¾ cup honey

¼ cup fresh lemon juice

2 tablespoons vegetable oil

2 tablespoons minced, peeled fresh ginger

2 cloves garlic, crushed with a garlic press

3 chickens (3 pounds each), each cut into quarters

1. In a small bowl, combine the soy sauce, honey, lemon juice, oil, ginger, and garlic until well blended. Divide the chicken and marinade among 3 resealable plastic bags, turning the chicken to coat; place them in a 15 × 9-inch baking dish. Seal the bags, pressing out as much air as possible. Marinate the chicken overnight, refrigerated.

2. The next day, prepare an outdoor grill for covered direct grilling over medium heat. Alternatively, preheat the broiler.

3. Remove the chicken from the marinade; discard the marinade. To grill, place the chicken on the grill, cover, and cook until golden brown, about 5 minutes per side. Move the chicken to the perimeter of the grill (where it is cooler); cover and cook until the juices run clear when the thickest part of the chicken is pierced with the tip of a knife, about 25 minutes longer.

4. To broil the chicken in the oven: Place the chicken, skin side down, on a rack in a large broiling pan. (The chicken may need to be broiled in batches.) Place the pan in broiler 8 to 10 inches from the heat source. Broil the chicken until golden brown, about 20 minutes. Turn the chicken skin side up; broil, brushing occasionally with the marinade, until the juices run clear when the thickest part of the chicken is pierced with the tip of a knife, about 20 minutes longer.

Each serving About 410 calories, 42g protein, 10g carbohydrate, 22g fat (6g saturated), 0g fiber, 990mg sodium.

Ingredient Ideas
grilled chicken breasts

Prepare an outdoor grill for direct grilling over medium heat. Place **4 medium skinless, boneless chicken breast halves (1¼ pounds)** between sheets of plastic wrap or waxed paper and pound the thick portion so the breasts are an even thickness. In a medium bowl, toss the chicken with **1 tablespoon olive oil, ¼ teaspoon salt, and ¼ teaspoon ground black pepper** or with one of our rubs, below. Place the chicken on hot oiled grill; cook 5 minutes, turning once, then cook 4 to 5 minutes longer, or until the juices run clear. **Makes 4 main-dish servings.**

GRILLED CHICKEN BREASTS WITH LEMON & ROSEMARY

From **2 lemons**, grate **2 teaspoons peel**, and squeeze **3 tablespoons juice.** In a bowl, combine the lemon peel, lemon juice, **1 tablespoon chopped fresh rosemary, 1 finely chopped clove garlic, ½ teaspoon salt, and ¼ teaspoon ground black pepper.** Add the chicken breasts to the bowl, turning to coat. Grill as directed above, brushing the chicken with the remaining mixture halfway through cooking.

GRILLED CHICKEN BREASTS WITH CUMIN, CORIANDER & LIME

In a bowl, whisk **3 tablespoons fresh lime juice, 2 tablespoons olive oil, 1 teaspoon ground cumin, 1 teaspoon ground coriander, 1 teaspoon sugar, 1 teaspoon salt, and ⅛ teaspoon cayenne pepper.** Add the chicken, turning to coat. Grill as directed above, brushing the chicken with the remaining lime mixture halfway through cooking.

GRILLED CHICKEN BREASTS WITH COFFEE SPICE RUB

In a large bowl and using a spoon or your fingers, press **2 tablespoons instant coffee** to pulverize. Add **1 tablespoon grated, peeled fresh ginger; 1 tablespoon olive oil; 1¼ teaspoons ground allspice; and ¾ teaspoon salt.** Stir to combine. Add the chicken, turning to coat. Grill as directed above, brushing the chicken with the remaining spice mixture halfway through cooking.

grilled chicken breasts saltimbocca

PREP: 10 MIN / TOTAL: 20 MIN / SERVES 4

4 medium skinless, boneless chicken breast halves (1¼ pounds)	⅛ teaspoon ground black pepper
⅛ teaspoon salt	12 fresh sage leaves
	4 large slices prosciutto (4 ounces)

1. Prepare a grill for covered direct grilling over medium heat.

2. Sprinkle the chicken with salt and pepper. Place 3 sage leaves on each breast half. Place 1 prosciutto slice on top of each breast half, tucking in the edges if necessary; secure it with toothpicks.

3. Place the chicken, prosciutto side down, on the grill, cover, and cook 5 to 6 minutes. Turn the chicken over and grill until the chicken loses its pink color throughout, 5 to 6 minutes longer.

Each serving About 225 calories, 41g protein, 0g carbohydrate, 6g fat (1g saturated), 0g fiber, 690mg sodium.

summer squash & chicken

PREP: 15 MIN / TOTAL: 25 MIN, PLUS MARINATING / SERVES 4

1 lemon	4 medium yellow summer squash and/or zucchini (about 6 ounces each), each cut lengthwise into 4 wedges
1 tablespoon olive oil	
½ teaspoon salt	
¼ teaspoon coarsely ground black pepper	
4 medium skinless, boneless chicken thighs (about 1¼ pounds)	¼ cup snipped fresh chives

1. Prepare a grill for covered direct grilling over medium heat.

2. From the lemon, grate 1 tablespoon zest and squeeze 3 tablespoons juice. In a medium bowl, combine the lemon zest and juice, the oil, salt, and pepper and whisk until blended. Transfer 2 tablespoons marinade to a cup and set it aside.

3. Add the chicken thighs to the bowl with the marinade; turn to evenly coat. Cover and let stand 15 minutes at room temperature or 30 minutes in the refrigerator.

4. Remove the chicken from the marinade; discard marinade. Place the chicken and squash on the grill, cover, and cook, turning the chicken and squash once, until the juices run clear when the thickest part of the thigh is pierced with the tip of a knife and the squash is tender and browned, 10 to 12 minutes, transferring the pieces to a platter as they are done.

5. Transfer the chicken and squash to a cutting board. Cut the chicken into 1-inch-wide strips; cut each squash wedge crosswise in half.

6. To serve, on a large platter, toss the squash with the reserved marinade, then toss it with the chicken and sprinkle with chives.

Each serving About 255 calories, 29g protein, 8g carbohydrate, 8g fat (3g saturated), 2g fiber, 240mg sodium.

citrus sage chicken

PREP: 25 MIN / TOTAL: 55 MIN, PLUS MARINATING / SERVES 8

2 large oranges	2 teaspoons salt
2 large lemons	¾ teaspoon coarsely ground black pepper
¼ cup chopped fresh sage, plus additional whole leaves for garnish	2 chickens (3½ pounds each), each cut into 8 pieces, skin removed (except from the wings)
2 tablespoons olive oil	

1. Grate 1 tablespon zest and 3 tablespoons juice each from the oranges and lemons. In a large bowl and using a wire whisk, combine the orange and lemon zest and juices, the chopped sage, oil, salt, and pepper. Add the chicken, turning to coat. Cover and refrigerate the chicken 2 hours to marinate, turning 3 or 4 times.

2. Prepare a grill for covered direct grilling over medium heat.

3. Place the chicken, meat side down, on the grill; cover and cook 20 minutes. Turn the chicken and cook until the juices run clear when the thickest part of the chicken is pierced with the tip of a knife, 10 to 15 minutes longer.

4. To serve, arrange the chicken on a warm platter; garnish with sage leaves.

Each serving About 310 calories, 41g protein, 2g carbohydrate, 14g fat (3g saturated), 0g fiber, 705mg sodium.

mojito-rubbed chicken

with grilled pineapple

PREP: 20 MIN / TOTAL: 30 MIN / SERVES 4

- 4 medium skinless, boneless chicken breast halves (about 1¼ pounds)
- 2 limes
- 1 tablespoon olive oil
- 1 medium pineapple (3½ pounds), peeled, cored, and cut into ½-inch-thick slices
- ¼ cup loosely packed fresh mint leaves, chopped
- ½ teaspoon salt
- ¼ teaspoon ground black pepper

1. Prepare an outdoor grill for direct grilling over medium heat, or preheat a large ridged grill pan over medium heat.

2. Meanwhile, place the chicken breast halves between 2 sheets of plastic wrap or waxed paper; with a meat mallet or rolling pin, pound to an even ½-inch thickness.

3. From 1 lime, grate 1 teaspoon zest and squeeze 2 tablespoons juice. Cut the remaining lime into 4 wedges; set aside. In small bowl, combine the oil, lime zest, and lime juice. Lightly brush the pineapple slices on both sides with the lime mixture; set aside the remaining lime mixture. Place the pineapple slices on the hot grill rack and cook 10 minutes, or until browned on both sides, turning over once.

4. Stir the mint into the remaining lime mixture and pat it onto both sides of the chicken. Sprinkle the chicken with salt and pepper to season both sides. Place the chicken on the hot grill rack and cook 5 minutes, or until the chicken is browned on both sides and no longer pink throughout, turning over once. Serve the chicken with grilled pineapple and lime wedges.

Each serving About 320 calories, 40g protein, 27g carbohydrate, 6g fat (1g saturated), 3g fiber, 385mg sodium.

thai chicken satay

PREP: 45 MIN / TOTAL: 50 MIN / SERVES 4

- 1 English (seedless) cucumber, cut crosswise into thin slices
- 1½ teaspoons salt
- 1 tablespoon Thai green curry paste
- ¼ cup plus ⅓ cup well-stirred unsweetened coconut milk (not cream of coconut)
- 4 medium skinless, boneless chicken breast halves (about 1¼ pounds), each cut diagonally into 6 strips
- ¼ cup creamy peanut butter
- 2 teaspoons soy sauce
- 1 teaspoon packed dark brown sugar
- ⅛ teaspoon cayenne pepper
- 1 tablespoon hot water
- 1¼ cups rice vinegar
- 3 tablespoons granulated sugar
- 2 medium shallots, thinly sliced
- 1 jalapeño chile, seeded and minced

1. In a medium bowl, toss the cucumber with the salt; let stand 30 minutes at room temperature.

2. In another bowl, stir together the curry paste and ¼ cup coconut milk until blended. Add the chicken and turn to coat. Let stand 15 minutes at room temperature, stirring occasionally.

3. Prepare an outdoor grill for covered direct grilling over medium heat.

4. Meanwhile, prepare the peanut sauce: In a small bowl and using a wire whisk, mix the peanut butter, soy sauce, brown sugar, cayenne, the remaining ⅓ cup coconut milk, and hot water until blended and smooth. Transfer the sauce to a serving bowl. (Makes about ⅔ cup.)

5. Drain the cucumber, discarding any liquid in the bowl. Pat the cucumber dry with paper towels. Return the cucumber to the bowl. Add the vinegar, granulated sugar, shallots, and jalapeño; toss to combine. Cover and refrigerate until ready to serve.

6. Thread 2 chicken strips, accordion-style, on each of the metal skewers; discard the marinade. Place the skewers on the grill, cover the grill, and cook, turning the skewers once, just until the chicken loses its pink color throughout, 5 to 8 minutes.

7. Arrange the skewers on a platter. Serve with the peanut sauce and cucumbers.

Each serving (with 1 tablespoon of peanut sauce) About 260 calories, 34g protein, 15g carbohydrate, 6g fat (3g saturated), 2g fiber, 525mg sodium.

GRILLED CHICKEN WITH
HERBED CORN SALSA 395

grilled chicken
with herbed corn salsa

PREP: 5 MIN / TOTAL: 25 MIN / SERVES 4

2¼ pounds skin-on, bone-in chicken thighs	½ cup packed fresh mint leaves
½ teaspoon ground black pepper	¼ cup grated Parmesan cheese
Salt	1 clove garlic
2 large ears corn, shucked	¼ cup fresh lemon juice
1 cup packed fresh basil leaves	2 tablespoons olive oil

1. Prepare an outdoor grill for covered direct grilling over medium heat.

2. Season the chicken thighs with pepper and ½ teaspoon salt. Grill the chicken, covered, 15 to 20 minutes, or until the chicken is cooked (165°F), turning once. Grill the corn over medium heat 10 minutes, turning occasionally.

3. In a food processor, pulse the basil, mint, Parmesan, garlic, and ¼ teaspoon salt until finely chopped. Add the lemon juice and olive oil; pulse until just combined. Cut the kernels off the cobs; stir them into the herb sauce. Serve the chicken with the corn mixture.

Each serving About 495 calories, 39g protein, 17g carbohydrate, 31g fat (8g saturated), 3g fiber, 690mg sodium.

HOW TO

CUT KERNELS OFF THE COB

Forget the special tool; all you need is a sharp knife. There are several ways to remove the kernels. Try them out and see which feels most comfortable.

The easiest way is to break the ear in half. Place the flat end on a cutting board and cut down vertically to remove kernels. If you have a Bundt pan, stand the whole ear in the center hole and cut down vertically; the kernels will go into the pan for easy clean up. (You can also fashion this with 2 bowls—1 large, 1 small: Invert the small bowl and place inside the large one. Place flat end of whole ear of corn on small bowl and cut.) Or lay the corn on the cutting board and carefully slice off kernels.

charcoal-grilled whole turkey

PREP: 15 MIN / TOTAL: 2 HR 30 MIN TO 3 HR 15 MIN / SERVES 12

1 turkey (12 pounds)	2 teaspoons dried thyme
2 tablespoons vegetable oil	2 teaspoons salt
2 teaspoons dried sage	½ teaspoon ground black pepper

1. Prepare the grill: In the bottom of a covered charcoal grill, with the vents open and the grill uncovered, ignite 60 charcoal briquettes (not self-starting briquettes). Allow them to burn until all the coals are covered with a thin coat of gray ash, about 30 minutes. With tongs, move the hot briquettes to two opposite sides of the grill and arrange into two piles. Place a sturdy disposable foil pan (13 × 9 × 2 inches) in the center of the grill, between the piles of coals, to catch the drips.

2. Remove the giblets and neck from the turkey; reserve them for another use. Rinse the turkey inside and out with cold running water and drain well; pat dry with paper towels.

3. Fasten the neck skin to the turkey back with skewers. Tie the legs and tail together with string. Secure the wings to the body with string, if desired. In a cup, combine the oil, sage, thyme, salt, and pepper; rub this on the outside of the turkey.

4. Place the turkey, breast side up, on the rack over the foil pan. Cover the grill and cook between 2 hours 15 minutes and 3 hours, adding 8 or 9 briquettes to each side of grill every hour to maintain the grill temperature of 325°F (measured on an oven or grill thermometer). The turkey is done when the temperature on a meat thermometer inserted in the thickest part of the thigh reaches 175°F to 180°F and the juices run clear when the thickest part of the thigh is pierced with the tip of a knife.

5. When the turkey is done, transfer it to a warm platter; let stand 15 minutes to set the juices for easier carving. Skim and discard the fat from the drippings in the bottom of the pan; serve the drippings with the turkey.

Each serving About 525 calories, 73g protein, 0g carbohydrate, 23g fat (7g saturated), 0g fiber, 575mg sodium.

spice-grilled turkey breast

PREP: 35 MIN / TOTAL: 1 HR, PLUS BRINING / SERVES 12

SPICED TURKEY

- ¼ cup sugar
- ¼ cup kosher salt
- 2 tablespoons ground black pepper
- 2 tablespoons ground ginger
- 1 tablespoon ground cinnamon

- 1 cup water
- 3 cups ice water
- 1 whole boneless turkey breast (about 4 pounds), skin removed and breast cut in half
- 4 cloves garlic, crushed with side of a chef's knife

HONEY GLAZE

- 2 tablespoons honey
- 2 tablespoons Dijon mustard
- 1 chipotle chile in adobo, minced

- 1 teaspoon balsamic vinegar
- Salsa (optional)

1. Prepare the brine solution: In a 2-quart saucepan, heat the sugar, salt, pepper, ginger, cinnamon, and water to boiling over high heat. Reduce the heat to low; simmer 2 minutes. Remove from the heat; stir in the ice water.

2. Place the turkey breast in a large resealable plastic bag; add the brine and garlic. Seal the bag, pressing out any excess air. Place the bag in a bowl and refrigerate the breast, turning occasionally, for 24 hours.

3. Prepare grill for covered direct grilling over medium heat.

4. Meanwhile, prepare the glaze: In a small bowl, stir the honey, mustard, chipotle chile, and vinegar until blended; set aside.

5. Remove the turkey from the bag; discard the brine and garlic. With paper towels, pat the turkey dry and brush off most of the pepper. With a long-handled basting brush, oil the grill rack. Place the turkey on the grill, cover, and cook the turkey, turning once, 20 minutes. Brush the turkey with glaze and cook, basting and turning frequently, until the temperature on a meat thermometer inserted into the thickest part of the breast reaches 165°F, 5 to 10 minutes longer (depending on the thickness of the breast); the internal temperature will rise 5°F upon standing. Transfer the turkey to a cutting board and let rest 10 minutes.

6. Serve the turkey hot, or cover and refrigerate to serve cold. Accompany with salsa, if desired.

Each serving About 170 calories, 34g protein, 4g carbohydrate, 1g fat (0g saturated), 1g fiber, 555mg sodium.

portuguese mixed grill

PREP: 30 MIN / TOTAL: 55 MIN, PLUS MARINATING / SERVES 6

- ¼ cup red wine vinegar
- 2 tablespoons olive oil
- 2 tablespoons chopped fresh oregano
- 1 teaspoon salt
- ½ teaspoon coarsely ground black pepper
- 8 medium bone-in, skinless chicken thighs (1¾ pounds), fat removed

- 3 medium red onions, peeled and each cut into 6 wedges
- 12 ounces fully cooked chorizo sausage links, each cut crosswise in half
- ⅔ cup assorted olives such as Kalamata, cracked green, and picholine

1. Prepare an outdoor grill for direct grilling over medium heat.

2. In a bowl, combine the vinegar, 1 tablespoon oil, 1 tablespoon oregano, salt, and pepper. Add the chicken, turning to coat. Cover and refrigerate 30 minutes—no longer—to marinate.

3. Thread 2 onion wedges onto each of 3 long metal skewers. Place the onion skewers on the grill; brush with the remaining 1 tablespoon oil. Grill 5 minutes, then place the chicken on the grill and cook, turning the onions and chicken once, until the onions are tender and the juices run clear when the thickest part of the chicken is pierced with the tip of a knife, about 20 minutes longer.

4. About 10 minutes before the onions and chicken are done, place the chorizo pieces on the grill and cook, turning occasionally, until lightly browned and heated through.

5. To serve, remove the onion wedges from the skewers and arrange them on a warm platter with the chicken and chorizo. Scatter the olives on top and sprinkle with remaining 1 tablespoon oregano.

Each serving About 480 calories, 34g protein, 11g carbohydrate, 33g fat (10g saturated), 1g fiber, 1,495mg sodium.

grilled caesar salad

PREP: 10 MIN / TOTAL: 20 MIN / SERVES 4

- 4 ounces Italian bread, cut into ½-inch-thick slices
- 2 tablespoons olive oil
- ¼ cup mayonnaise
- ¼ cup freshly grated Parmesan cheese
- 3 tablespoons fresh lemon juice (from 1 lemon)
- 1 teaspoon anchovy paste, or 2 anchovy fillets, mashed
- ¼ teaspoon coarsely ground black pepper
- 1 clove garlic, cut in half
- 1 package (18 to 22 ounces) hearts of romaine, each head cut lengthwise in half

1. Prepare an outdoor grill for direct grilling over medium heat.

2. Prepare the croutons: Lightly brush the bread slices on both sides with 1 tablespoon oil. Place the bread on the hot grill grate and cook 2 to 3 minutes, or until toasted, turning the slices over once. Transfer to a plate; cool until easy to handle.

3. Meanwhile, prepare the dressing: In a small bowl, whisk together the mayonnaise, Parmesan, lemon juice, anchovy paste, pepper, and the remaining 1 tablespoon oil.

4. When the bread is cool, lightly rub both sides of each slice with the cut side of the garlic. Cut the bread into ½-inch cubes.

5. Place the romaine halves on the hot grill grate and cook 4 to 5 minutes, or until lightly browned and wilted, turning them over once. Transfer the romaine to 4 salad plates; drizzle with dressing and sprinkle with croutons to serve.

Each serving About 245 calories, 7g protein, 20g carbohydrate, 14g fat (3g saturated), 3g fiber, 420mg sodium.

grilled spiced salmon steaks

PREP: 5 MIN / TOTAL: 15 MIN / SERVES 4

- 1 tablespoon chili powder
- 2 teaspoons packed brown sugar
- 1 teaspoon ground cumin
- 1 teaspoon dried thyme
- 1 teaspoon salt
- 2 teaspoons olive oil
- 4 salmon steaks, ¾ inch thick (about 6 to 8 ounces each)
- Lemon wedges

1. Prepare an outdoor grill for covered direct grilling over medium heat. In a cup, combine the chili powder, brown sugar, cumin, thyme, salt, and oil. Rub on both sides of the salmon steaks.

2. Place the salmon on the grill, cover, and cook until just opaque throughout, about 4 minutes per side. Serve with lemon wedges.

Each serving About 405 calories, 40g protein, 4g carbohydrate, 24g fat (5g saturated), 1g fiber, 720mg sodium.

HOW TO

GRILL GREENS

Grilling greens adds a luscious smokiness and tames the bite of bitter varieties.

Choose greens that are hearty, like kale or escarole, or lettuces that have a core that will hold them intact when halved or sectioned.

Preheat the grill on medium-high. Lightly brush greens with olive or vegetable oil and season with salt and ground black pepper.

Grill for a minute or so per side for lettuces, longer for heartier ones. Your goal is to add flavor and a bit of char but not completely wither them.

grilled whole sea bass

with lemon & herbs

PREP: 5 MIN / TOTAL: 20 MIN / SERVES 4

- **2 whole sea bass (1½ pounds each), cleaned and scaled**
- **1½ teaspoons salt**
- **4 thin lemon slices, each cut in half**
- **8 fresh oregano or rosemary sprigs**
- **1 tablespoon olive oil**

1. Prepare an outdoor grill for covered direct grilling over medium heat.

2. Rinse the bass inside and out with cold running water; pat dry with paper towels. Make 3 diagonal slashes on each side of the fish, cutting almost to the bone. Sprinkle the fish inside and out with salt. Place the lemon slices and oregano sprigs in the fish cavities. Rub the oil all over the bass.

3. Place the bass on the grill, cover, and cook until just opaque when a knife is inserted at the backbone, about 8 minutes per side.

4. To serve, slide a cake server under the front section of the top fillet of each fish and lift off the fillet; transfer to a platter. Slide the server under the backbone and lift it away from the bottom fillet; discard the backbone. Slide the cake server between the bottom fillet and the skin and transfer the fillet to the platter.

Each serving About 160 calories, 25g protein, 1g carbohydrate, 6g fat (1g saturated), 0g fiber, 675mg sodium.

 Tip Can't find whole sea bass? Use red snapper or striped bass instead.

glazed salmon

with watermelon salsa

PREP: 20 MIN / TOTAL: 30 MIN / SERVES 4

WATERMELON SALSA

- **1 lime**
- **4 cups (½-inch cubes) seedless watermelon (from about a 2½-pound piece)**
- **¼ cup loosely packed fresh mint leaves, chopped**
- **2 tablespoons chopped green onions**
- **1 small jalapeño chile, seeded and finely chopped (about 1 tablespoon)**

GLAZED SALMON

- **¼ cup hoisin sauce**
- **½ teaspoon Chinese five-spice powder**
- **4 salmon steaks, 1 inch thick (about 6 ounces each)**

1. Prepare an outdoor grill for covered direct grilling over medium heat.

2. Meanwhile, prepare the salsa: From the lime, grate 1 teaspoon zest and squeeze 1 tablespoon juice. In a serving bowl, toss the lime zest and juice with the watermelon, mint, green onions, and jalapeño. Makes about 3⅔ cups.

3. In a cup, stir together the hoisin sauce and five-spice powder.

4. Place the salmon on the grill over medium heat. Brush the salmon with half of the hoisin mixture. Cover the grill and cook the salmon 3 minutes. Turn the salmon over and brush with the remaining hoisin mixture; cover the grill and cook 3 minutes. Turn the salmon over again and cook until just opaque throughout, about 3 minutes longer. Serve the salmon with the salsa.

Each serving About 345 calories, 30g protein, 18g carbohydrate, 17g fat (3g saturated), 2g fiber, 260mg sodium.

greek-style grilled halibut

PREP: 10 MIN / TOTAL: 16 MIN, PLUS MARINATING / SERVES 4

1 lemon

3 tablespoons olive oil

2 cloves garlic, finely chopped

2 teaspoons chopped fresh oregano

½ teaspoon salt

4 halibut steaks, ¾ inch thick (6 ounces each)

1. From the lemon, grate 1 teaspoon zest and squeeze 2 tablespoons juice. In a large bowl and using a wire whisk, whisk the lemon zest and juice, the oil, garlic, oregano, and salt until mixed. Add the halibut steaks, turning each to coat. Cover and refrigerate 1 hour to marinate, turning once or twice.

2. Meanwhile, prepare grill for covered direct grilling over medium heat.

3. Remove the halibut from the marinade. Place the halibut on the grill, cover, and cook, brushing with marinade during first half of grilling, until the halibut is just opaque throughout, 3 to 4 minutes per side; discard remaining marinade.

Each serving About 200 calories, 29g protein, 1g carbohydrate, 8g fat (1g saturated), 0g fiber, 220mg sodium.

salmon
with mustard & dill sauce

PREP: 15 MIN / TOTAL: 25 MIN / SERVES 4

GRILLED SALMON

2 tablespoons sugar

1 tablespoon chopped fresh dill

2 tablespoons white wine vinegar

¾ teaspoon salt

¼ teaspoon coarsely ground black pepper

4 salmon steaks, each ¾ inch thick (about 6 ounces each)

MUSTARD & DILL SAUCE

3 tablespoons chopped fresh dill

3 tablespoons Dijon mustard

3 tablespoons light mayonnaise

2 teaspoons sugar

4 teaspoons white wine vinegar

¼ teaspoon coarsely ground black pepper

1. Prepare an outdoor grill for direct grilling over medium heat.

2. Prepare the salmon: In a medium bowl, mix the sugar, dill, vinegar, salt, and pepper.

3. With tweezers, remove any small bones from the salmon; add the salmon steaks to the bowl with the sugar mixture, turning each to coat. Let stand at room temperature 10 minutes.

4. Meanwhile, prepare the sauce: In a small bowl, mix the dill, mustard, mayonnaise, sugar, vinegar, and pepper.

5. Place the salmon on the grill and cook, turning once, until just opaque throughout, 8 to 9 minutes. Serve with the sauce.

Each serving About 270 calories, 30g protein, 13g carbohydrate, 11g fat (1g saturated), 0g fiber, 850mg sodium.

CITRUSY SHRIMP KEBABS 401

SUMMER VEGGIE KEBABS 401

ASIAN BEEF KEBABS 401

citrusy shrimp kebabs

PREP: 10 MIN / TOTAL: 15 MIN / SERVES 5

- 1 teaspoon smoked paprika
- 1 teaspoon salt
- ½ teaspoon ground cumin
- 3 small lemons
- 3 limes
- 2 pounds shelled, deveined extra-large (16 to 20 count) shrimp (see page 297)
- 2 tablespoons olive oil

1. Prepare grill for direct grilling over medium-high heat.

2. In a small bowl, combine the smoked paprika, salt, and cumin. Thinly slice the lemons and limes. Thread the shrimp, lemon slices, and lime slices, alternately, on the skewers. Brush the skewers on both sides with olive oil and sprinkle lightly with the seasoned salt mixture.

3. Grill over medium-high heat 4 to 5 minutes, or until the shrimp are opaque, turning over once halfway through.

Each serving About 175 calories, 45g protein, 6g carbohydrate, 6g fat (1g saturated), 1g fiber, 1,182mg sodium.

asian beef kebabs

PREP: 10 MIN / TOTAL: 20 MIN, PLUS MARINATING / SERVES 8

- ½ cup packed fresh cilantro leaves
- ¼ cup soy sauce
- 2 tablespoons honey
- 2 tablespoons vegetable oil
- 1 tablespoon coriander seeds
- 1 clove garlic
- 2 teaspoons rice vinegar
- 1½ pounds beef top sirloin, trimmed and thinly sliced into 2-inch-long pieces

1. In a blender or food processor, blend the cilantro, soy sauce, honey, oil, coriander, garlic, and rice vinegar until mostly smooth; transfer half to a large bowl along with the beef. Toss the beef to coat. Reserve the remaining marinade for basting. Marinate the beef at least 30 minutes and up to 1 day, covered and refrigerated.

2. Prepare grill for direct grilling over medium-high heat.

3. Thread the beef onto skewers. Grill over medium-high heat 6 to 7 minutes, or until cooked through and charred in spots, turning and brushing with the reserved marinade occasionally.

Each serving About 150 calories, 18g protein, 2g carbohydrate, 8g fat (2g saturated), 0g fiber, 110mg sodium.

summer veggie kebabs

PREP: 10 MIN / TOTAL: 20 MIN / SERVES 4

- 3 tablespoons melted butter
- ¼ cup fresh mint leaves, finely chopped
- 2 teaspoons fresh grated lemon zest
- 1 pound summer squash
- 1 bunch green onions
- 6 radishes, trimmed
- 1 teaspoon salt

1. Prepare grill for direct grilling over medium heat.

2. In a small bowl, stir the butter, mint, and lemon zest until combined. With a vegetable peeler, peel the summer squash into wide ribbons. Cut the green onions into 2-inch lengths. Quarter the radishes. Thread the squash ribbons, radish quarters, and green onions, alternately, on the skewers. Brush the skewers with the mint butter and sprinkle with salt.

3. Grill over medium heat 6 to 8 minutes, turning over once halfway through.

Each serving About 110 calories, 2g protein, 7g carbohydrate, 9g fat (6g saturated), 3g fiber, 662mg sodium.

sweet & smoky salmon kebabs

PREP: 20 MIN / TOTAL: 30 MIN / SERVES 8

2 tablespoons packed dark brown sugar

1½ teaspoons smoked paprika

1 teaspoon chili powder

½ teaspoon cayenne pepper

¾ teaspoon salt

½ teaspoon ground black pepper

2¼ pounds skinless salmon fillet, cut into 1½-inch chunks

2 medium zucchini (8 ounces each), cut into ¼-inch-thick slices

1. If you're using bamboo skewers, soak them in hot water at least 30 minutes. Prepare an outdoor grill for direct grilling over medium heat.

2. In a large bowl, combine the brown sugar, paprika, chili powder, cayenne, salt, and pepper. Rub the mixture between your fingers to break up any lumps of sugar. Add the salmon and zucchini to the bowl and toss to evenly coat them with the spice mixture.

3. Thread the zucchini slices, 2 at a time and alternating with the salmon, onto 12 metal or bamboo skewers. Place the skewers on the hot grill grate and cook 9 to 11 minutes, or until the salmon turns opaque throughout, turning occasionally.

Each serving About 205 calories, 26g protein, 6g carbohydrate, 8g fat (1g saturated), 1g fiber, 280mg sodium.

grilled shrimp kebabs

PREP: 10 MIN / TOTAL: 15 MIN, PLUS MARINATING / SERVES 4

1 lemon

1 tablespoon olive oil

¼ teaspoon salt

⅛ teaspoon ground black pepper

1 pound large (31 to 35 count) shrimp, shelled and deveined, leaving tail part of shell on, if desired (page 299)

1. Prepare grill for direct grilling over medium-high heat.

2. From the lemon, grate ½ teaspoon zest and squeeze 1 tablespoon juice. In a large bowl, whisk the lemon zest and juice, oil, salt, and pepper. Add the shrimp and toss to coat; let stand 10 minutes to marinate.

3. Thread the shrimp onto 4 long metal skewers. Place the skewers on the grill and cook, turning the skewers occasionally, until the shrimp are just opaque throughout, about 4 minutes.

Each serving About 130 calories, 19g protein, 1g carbohydrate, 5g fat (1g saturated), 0g fiber, 280mg sodium.

cajun shrimp

with rémoulade sauce

PREP: 25 MIN / TOTAL: 30 MIN / SERVES 4

RÉMOULADE SAUCE

½ cup light mayonnaise

2 tablespoons ketchup

2 tablespoons minced celery

1 tablespoon Dijon mustard with seeds

1 tablespoon minced fresh parsley

2 teaspoons fresh lemon juice

½ teaspoon Cajun seasoning

1 green onion, minced

CAJUN SHRIMP

1 tablespoon Cajun seasoning

1 tablespoon olive oil

2 teaspoons fresh lemon zest

1¼ pounds large (31-35 count) shrimp, shelled and deveined, leaving the tail part of shell on, if you like (see page 297)

Lemon wedges for serving

1. Prepare an outdoor grill for direct grilling over medium-high heat.

2. Meanwhile, prepare the sauce: In a small bowl, mix the mayonnaise, ketchup, celery, mustard, parsley, lemon juice, Cajun seasoning, and green onion. Cover and refrigerate until serving, up to 3 days. Makes about 1 cup.

3. Prepare the shrimp: In a medium bowl, mix the Cajun seasoning, oil, and lemon zest. Add the shrimp to the spice mixture and toss until evenly coated.

4. Place the shrimp on the grill and cook, turning once, until just opaque throughout, 3 to 4 minutes.

5. Transfer the shrimp to a platter; serve with Rémoulade Sauce and lemon wedges.

CAJUN SHRIMP Each serving About 155 calories, 24g protein, 2g carbohydrate, 5g fat (1g saturated), 0g fiber, 575mg sodium.
RÉMOULADE SAUCE Each tablespoon About 30 calories, 0g protein, 2g carbohydrate, 3g fat (1g saturated), 0g fiber, 95mg sodium.

swordfish kebabs

PREP: 25 MIN / TOTAL: 30 MIN, PLUS MARINATING / SERVES 4

- 1 pound boneless swordfish steak, 1 inch thick
- ½ cup chicken or vegetable broth
- 3 tablespoons fresh lemon juice
- 1 tablespoon olive oil
- 1 very small onion, thinly sliced
- 2 cloves garlic, thinly sliced
- 14 large bay leaves
- ½ teaspoon salt
- ½ teaspoon paprika
- ¼ teaspoon ground coriander
- ⅛ teaspoon ground black pepper
- 12 thin lemon slices, seeded and halved
- 1 tablespoon chopped fresh parsley

1. Remove the skin from the swordfish and discard. Cut the fish into 1-inch cubes.

2. In a medium bowl, combine the broth, lemon juice, oil, onion, garlic, 2 bay leaves, salt, paprika, coriander, and pepper. Add the swordfish and toss to coat. Cover and refrigerate the fish 3 hours to marinate, tossing occasionally.

3. Meanwhile, soak the remaining 12 bay leaves and 12 bamboo skewers 1 hour in enough boiling water to cover. Drain. With kitchen shears, snip each bay leaf crosswise in half.

4. Prepare an outdoor grill for covered direct grilling over medium-high heat.

5. Remove the swordfish from the marinade, reserving the marinade. Thread each skewer as follows: ½ bay leaf, 1 swordfish cube, ½ lemon slice, 1 swordfish cube; then repeat once, gently pressing the bay leaves, lemon slices, and fish together.

6. Place the kebabs on the grill, cover, and cook, turning the kebabs and brushing with the marinade during the first half of cooking, until the fish is just opaque throughout, 5 to 8 minutes.

7. Meanwhile, strain the remaining marinade into a small saucepan and heat to boiling; boil 3 minutes. Arrange the kebabs on a platter, drizzle with the hot marinade, and sprinkle with parsley.

Each serving About 190 calories, 22g protein, 7g carbohydrate, 8g fat (2g saturated), 0g fiber, 515mg sodium.

miso-glazed salmon

with edamame salad

PREP: 30 MIN / TOTAL: 40 MIN / SERVES 4

EDAMAME SALAD

- 1 bag (16 ounces) frozen shelled edamame (green soybeans) or frozen baby lima beans
- ¼ cup seasoned rice vinegar
- 1 tablespoon vegetable oil
- 1 teaspoon sugar
- ¾ teaspoon salt
- ⅛ teaspoon ground black pepper
- 1 bunch radishes (8 ounces), each cut in half and thinly sliced
- 1 cup loosely packed fresh cilantro leaves, chopped

MISO-GLAZED SALMON

- 2 tablespoons red miso
- 1 green onion, minced
- 1 tablespoon grated, peeled fresh ginger
- 1 teaspoon packed brown sugar
- ⅛ teaspoon cayenne pepper
- 1 salmon fillet (1½ pounds), with skin

1. Prepare an outdoor grill for direct grilling over medium-low heat.

2. Prepare the salad: Cook the edamame as the label directs; drain. Rinse the edamame with cold running water to stop any further cooking and drain again.

3. In a medium bowl, whisk the vinegar, oil, sugar, salt, and pepper until blended. Add the edamame, radishes, and cilantro and toss until evenly coated. Cover and refrigerate the salad up to 1 day if not serving right away. (Makes about 4 cups.)

4. Prepare the salmon: In a small bowl and using a spoon, mix the miso, green onion, ginger, brown sugar, and cayenne. Use this to rub on the flesh side of the salmon.

5. Place the salmon, skin side down, on the grill and cook until just opaque throughout, 10 to 12 minutes. Serve with edamame salad.

MISO-GLAZED SALMON Each serving About 280 calories, 29g protein, 3g carbohydrate, 16g fat (3g saturated), 0g fiber, 450mg sodium.
EDAMAME SALAD Each 1 cup About 220 calories, 16g protein, 23g carbohydrate, 8g fat (0g saturated), 6g fiber, 1,020mg sodium.

swordfish

with summer salad

(See photo on page 368.)

PREP: 5 MIN / TOTAL: 30 MIN / SERVES 4

- 3 large ears corn, husked
- 1 pound swordfish steak, skinned and cut into 1-inch chunks
- ¾ pound zucchini, sliced
- 2 tablespoons canola oil
- 2 teaspoons chili powder
- Salt
- 2 cans (15 ounces each) chickpeas, rinsed and drained
- ½ cup packed mint, chopped
- 3 tablespoons fresh lime juice

1. Prepare an outdoor grill for direct grilling over medium-high heat. Soak 8 bamboo skewers in hot water for 30 minutes.

2. Grill the corn on the hot grill for 12 minutes, turning, until charred in spots.

3. Meanwhile, thread the swordfish onto the skewers. Brush the skewers and the zucchini with 1 tablespoon oil; sprinkle with chili powder and ½ teaspoon salt. Grill the fish and zucchini 6 minutes, or until the fish is opaque, turning once.

4. Cut the corn off the cobs and chop the zucchini. In a bowl, toss both with the chickpeas, mint, lime juice, the remaining 1 tablespoon oil, and ¼ teaspoon salt. Serve with the kebabs.

Each serving About 500 calories, 34g protein, 55g carbohydrate, 19g fat (3g saturated), 12g fiber, 735mg sodium.

TESTING NOTE Always soak wooden or bamboo skewers in water for 30 minutes before grilling, or they could catch fire. You forgot? Oops! Wrap the exposed ends with foil for a quick fix, or invest in metal skewers.

cayenne grilled eggplant

with fresh tomato salad

(See photo on page 368.)

PREP: 15 MIN / TOTAL: 30 MIN / SERVES 6

- 2 pounds medium eggplants, cut lengthwise into ½-inch-thick slices
- ¼ cup plus 3 tablespoons olive oil
- 1 teaspoon ground coriander
- 1 teaspoon cayenne pepper
- Salt
- ¼ cup packed fresh mint leaves, finely chopped, plus more (optional) for garnish
- 3 small fresh red Fresno chiles or other hot chiles, seeded and finely chopped
- 2 tablespoons fresh lemon juice
- 2 tablespoons red wine vinegar
- ½ pint (about 1½ cups) multicolored cherry or grape tomatoes, halved
- ¼ cup Greek yogurt
- 2 tablespoons milk

1. Prepare an outdoor grill for direct grilling over medium heat. Brush both sides of the eggplant slices with ¼ cup oil. Sprinkle with coriander, cayenne, and ¼ teaspoon salt. Grill 10 to 12 minutes, or until tender.

2. Meanwhile, in a medium bowl, whisk together the chopped mint, chiles, lemon juice, vinegar, the remaining 3 tablespoons oil, and ½ teaspoon salt until well combined. To the vinaigrette, add tomatoes; toss to combine. In a small bowl, stir together the yogurt and milk.

3. Arrange the grilled eggplant on a large serving platter. Top with the tomato mixture. Drizzle with the yogurt mixture. Garnish with additional mint leaves, if desired.

Each serving About 205 calories, 3g protein, 12g carbohydrate, 17g fat (3g saturated), 5g fiber, 260mg sodium.

GRILLING VEGETABLES

Preheat the grill to medium-high. Then proceed with the specific instructions for each vegetable below.

VEGETABLE (4 SERVINGS)	PREPARATION	SEASONING	GRILLING TIME
8 EARS CORN	Soak 15 minutes, then Remove the silk (leave husks on).	Brush with 1 tablespoon oil.	45 minutes
	Remove husks and silk.		20 minutes, turning occasionally
1½ POUNDS EGGPLANT	Cut crosswise into ½-inch-thick slices.	Brush with ¼ cup oil.	11 to 13 minutes per side
4 HEADS ENDIVE	Cut lengthwise in half.	Brush with 1 tablespoon oil.	10 to 12 minutes per side
2 MEDIUM FENNEL BULBS (1 POUND EACH)	Cut lengthwise into ¼-inch-thick slices.	Brush with 4 teaspoons oil.	6 to 8 minutes per side
6 MEDIUM LEEKS	Remove dark-green tops; blanch and cut the leeks lengthwise in half.	Toss with 1 tablespoon oil.	11 to 13 minutes per side
8 OUNCES LARGE WHITE MUSHROOMS	Trim and thread onto skewers.	Brush with 2 teaspoons oil.	20 minutes, turning several times
4 LARGE PORTOBELLO MUSHROOMS (ABOUT 1 POUND)	Remove stems.	Brush with 4 teaspoons oil.	15 minutes per side
4 MEDIUM RED OR WHITE ONIONS	Cut crosswise into ½-inch-thick slices; secure with toothpicks.	Brush with 4 teaspoons oil.	12 to 14 minutes per side
2 BUNCHES SMALL GREEN ONIONS	Trim.	Toss with 4 teaspoons oil.	2 to 4 minutes, turning several times
4 RED, GREEN, OR YELLOW BELL PEPPERS	Cut lengthwise into quarters.		10 to 12 minutes per side
2 HEADS RADICCHIO (12 OUNCES EACH)	Cut lengthwise into quarters.	Brush with 2 tablespoons oil.	5 minutes per side
4 MEDIUM YELLOW SQUASH OR ZUCCHINI	Cut lengthwise into ¼-inch-thick slices.	Brush with 4 teaspoons oil.	5 minutes per side
4 MEDIUM TOMATOES (8 OUNCES EACH)	Cut crosswise in half.	Brush cut sides with 2 tablespoons oil.	14 to 17 minutes per side
1 PINT CHERRY TOMATOES	Thread onto skewers.	Brush with 2 teaspoons oil.	5 to 7 minutes, turning several times

crumb-topped tomatoes

PREP: 15 MIN / TOTAL: 25 MIN / SERVES 8

- 2 tablespoons butter
- 1 cup fresh bread crumbs (about 2 slices firm white bread)
- 1 clove garlic, crushed with a garlic press
- 2 tablespoons chopped fresh parsley
- ½ teaspoon salt
- ½ teaspoon coarsely ground black pepper
- 8 large ripe plum tomatoes, halved

1. Prepare an outdoor grill for direct grilling over medium heat.

2. In a 10-inch skillet, melt the butter over low heat. Add the bread crumbs and cook, stirring, until lightly browned. Stir in the garlic; cook 30 seconds. Remove the skillet from the heat; stir in the parsley, salt, and pepper.

3. Top each tomato half with some crumb mixture. Place the tomatoes on the grill and cook until hot but not mushy, 8 to 10 minutes.

Each serving About 40 calories, 1g protein, 3g carbohydrate, 3g fat (2g saturated), 1g fiber, 190mg sodium.

grilled peach melba

PREP: 5 MIN / TOTAL: 10 MIN / SERVES 4

- 2 large ripe peaches, each cut in half, pits discarded
- ½ pint raspberries
- 1 tablespoon sugar
- 1½ cups vanilla ice cream

1. Prepare an outdoor grill for direct grilling over medium heat.

2. Place the peach halves on the hot grill grate and cook 5 to 6 minutes, or until lightly charred and tender, turning over once.

3. Meanwhile, in a bowl and using a fork, mash half the raspberries with the sugar. Stir in the remaining raspberries.

4. To serve, place a peach half in each of 4 dessert bowls; top with ice cream and raspberry sauce.

Each serving About 160 calories, 2g protein, 22g carbohydrate, 8g fat (5g saturated), 3g fiber, 25mg sodium.

grilled veggie stacks

PREP: 20 MIN / TOTAL: 30 MIN / SERVES 4

- Wooden toothpicks or bamboo skewers
- 1 medium red onion, peeled and cut into ½-inch-thick slices
- 2 medium zucchini and/or yellow summer squashes, cut diagonally into ½-inch-thick slices
- 1 large yellow or red bell pepper, cut lengthwise into quarters
- 1 medium eggplant, cut diagonally into eight ½-inch-thick slices
- 3 tablespoons olive oil
- ½ cup balsamic vinegar
- ½ teaspoon crushed red pepper
- ½ teaspoon salt
- 4 plum tomatoes, each cut lengthwise in half
- 8 large basil leaves
- ¾ pound fresh mozzarella cheese, thinly sliced
- Basil sprigs, for garnish

1. Prepare an outdoor grill for covered direct grilling over medium heat.

2. Soak the toothpicks in water for 10 minutes. Insert 2 toothpicks horizontally through the center of each onion slice to hold the rings together.

3. In a large bowl, toss the onion, zucchini, bell pepper, and eggplant with the oil; set aside.

4. In a microwave-safe 2-cup liquid measuring cup, combine the vinegar, crushed red pepper, and salt. Heat the vinegar mixture in a microwave oven on High 2 to 3 minutes, or until reduced to ¼ cup.

5. Place the onion, zucchini, bell pepper, and eggplant on the grill rack. Place the tomatoes, cut sides down, on the same rack. Cover the grill and cook the vegetables until grill marks appear and they begin to soften, 4 to 5 minutes. Turn the vegetables; brush with the vinegar mixture. Cook, covered, until tender, 4 to 8 minutes longer, transferring the vegetables to a platter as they are done.

6. Assemble the vegetable stacks: Remove the toothpicks from the onion slices. In the center of each of 4 dinner plates, place 1 eggplant slice. Top each with one-fourth of the onion, zucchini, bell pepper, tomatoes, basil, and mozzarella to make 4 equal stacks. Top the stacks with an eggplant slice. Drizzle any juices over and around the stacks. Garnish with basil sprigs.

Each serving About 445 calories, 19g protein, 29g carbohydrate, 29g fat (13g saturated), 6g fiber, 370mg sodium.

grilled pizza

PREP: 15 MIN / TOTAL: 20 MIN, PLUS RESTING / SERVES 12

- 2 cups all-purpose flour, plus more for kneading
- 1 package quick-rise yeast
- ¾ teaspoon salt
- ¾ cup hot water (120°F to 130°F)
- 2 teaspoons plus 2 tablespoons olive oil
- 8 ounces fresh mozzarella cheese, thinly sliced
- 12 fresh basil leaves
- 2 small ripe tomatoes, thinly sliced
- Salt
- Coarsely ground black pepper

1. Prepare an outdoor grill for direct grilling over medium heat.

2. In a large bowl, combine the flour, yeast, and salt. Stir in the hot water and 2 teaspoons oil until blended and the dough comes away from side of the bowl. Turn the dough onto a lightly floured surface; knead until smooth and elastic, about 5 minutes.

3. Shape the pizza dough into two 10-inch rounds or four 6-inch rounds (do not form rims). Cover with greased plastic wrap; let rest 15 minutes.

4. Place the dough rounds on the grill over medium heat and grill until the underside of the dough turns golden and grill marks appear, 2 to 5 minutes. With tongs, turn the rounds over. Brush lightly with some remaining oil. Top with the mozzarella, basil, and tomato slices. Grill until the cheese begins to melt, 3 to 5 minutes longer. Drizzle with the remaining olive oil and sprinkle with salt and pepper.

Each serving About 170 calories, 7g protein, 17g carbohydrate, 8g fat (3g saturated), 1g fiber, 225mg sodium.

rainbow veggie kebabs

(See photo on page 368.)

PREP: 20 MIN / TOTAL: 30 MIN / SERVES 10

- 1 teaspoon ground cumin
- ½ teaspoon ground coriander
- ½ teaspoon smoked paprika
- Salt
- 2 pounds small green and yellow summer squash, cut into 1-inch chunks
- 1 pint grape tomatoes
- 6 tablespoons olive oil
- 12 ounces small broccoli florets
- 8 ounces cremini or button mushrooms, halved if large
- Juice of 1 lime

1. Prepare an outdoor grill for direct grilling over medium heat. In a small bowl, combine the cumin, coriander, paprika, and 1 teaspoon salt; set aside.

2. In a large bowl, toss the squash and tomatoes with 2 tablespoons oil. In another bowl, toss the broccoli with 1 tablespoon oil. In a third bowl, toss the mushrooms with 1 tablespoon oil. Thread the vegetables onto skewers, alternating the vegetables. (If using bamboo skewers, soak them for 30 minutes first.)

3. Grill the broccoli and mushrooms 6 to 10 minutes, turning them over once. Grill the squash and tomatoes 6 to 8 minutes, turning them over once. Transfer the skewers to a large platter or cutting board and squeeze the lime juice all over the vegetables. Drizzle the skewers with the remaining 2 tablespoons oil, then sprinkle them all over with half of the spice mixture. Cover the platter tightly with foil; let stand, covered, at least 5 minutes before serving. Sprinkle with additional spice mixture, if desired.

Each serving About 110 calories, 3g protein, 8g carbohydrate, 9g fat (1g saturated), 3g fiber, 210mg sodium.

**GRILLED WATERMELON,
TOMATO & FETA SALAD 409**

grilled watermelon, tomato & feta salad

PREP: 10 MIN / TOTAL: 15 MIN / SERVES 4

- 4 (½-inch-thick) slices watermelon
- 1 container (5 ounces) mixed greens
- 2 large yellow or red tomatoes, each cut into 6 wedges
- 1 bunch small radishes, cut into halves
- 4 ounces feta cheese, crumbled
- 2 tablespoons balsamic vinegar
- 2 tablespoons olive oil
- ¼ teaspoon salt

1. Prepare an outdoor grill for direct grilling over medium heat.

2. Pat the watermelon as dry as possible with paper towels. Grill over medium heat 3 to 4 minutes, or until grill marks appear, turning the slices over once halfway through. Using a medium star-shaped cookie cutter, cut 8 or 9 stars from the watermelon slices.

3. Arrange the mixed greens on a serving platter and top with the watermelon stars, tomatoes, radishes, and feta cheese. Drizzle with balsamic vinegar and olive oil; sprinkle with salt.

Each serving About 200 calories, 7g protein, 18g carbohydrate, 13g fat (5g saturated), 3g fiber, 487mg sodium.

grilled sweet potatoes

PREP: 5 MIN / TOTAL: 30 MIN / SERVES 4

- 2½ pounds sweet potatoes (5 medium)
- 1 tablespoon olive oil
- ¼ teaspoon salt
- ¼ teaspoon coarsely ground black pepper
- Chopped parsley, for garnish

1. In a 5- to 6-quart saucepot or Dutch oven, place a collapsible steamer basket and 1 inch of water. Cover the saucepot; heat the water to boiling on high on the stove top.

2. Peel the sweet potatoes, if you like, and cut them into ½-inch-thick diagonal slices. Places the potato slices in the steamer basket; reduce the heat to low. Cover the saucepot and simmer 12 to 15 minutes, or until the potatoes are just fork-tender; do not overcook. (Potatoes can be steamed a day ahead and refrigerated until ready to grill.)

3. Transfer the potato slices to a rimmed baking sheet; brush with olive oil and sprinkle both sides with salt and pepper.

4. Prepare an outdoor grill for covered, direct grilling over medium heat.

5. Place the potato slices on the hot grill grate. Cover the grill and cook the potatoes over medium heat 10 to 12 minutes, or until lightly charred and tender, turning the slices over once with a large metal spatula.

6. Transfer the potatoes to a serving bowl; garnish with parsley.

Each serving About 245 calories, 3g protein, 50g carbohydrate, 4g fat (1g saturated), 6g fiber, 170mg sodium.

CHAPTER

11

vegetables

Vegetables are taking over the center of the plate. Chefs are offering cauliflower steaks, carrot Wellington, and root-vegetable cobblers. Farmers' markets abound with rainbow carrots, cranberries, beans, jewel-tone potatoes, a panorama of heirloom tomatoes, and so much more. Look for fresh legumes like lima and fava beans, chickpeas, and lentils. Like peas, these all grow in seed pods and may be eaten fresh or dried. At home, we're roasting and grilling vegetables and loving the rich flavors—and the easy-enough-for-weeknight prep. It's easier than ever to "eat the rainbow," so we're getting closer to the USDA recommendation to eat more vegetables as part of a well-balanced, healthful diet. Along with hearty main dishes like Indian-Style Lentils (page 430) and Crispy Ginger-Scallion Latkes (page 458), you'll find sides from A to Z.

ASPARAGUS WITH EGGS MIMOSA 416

HARVEST SUCCOTASH 464

CRISPY ROASTED POTATOES WITH CAPER VINAIGRETTE 449

LEMONY BRUSSELS SPROUT SALAD 418

Vegetables 101

SELECT Vegetables don't need to be picture perfect, but for freshness and optimum nutrition, shop for firm vegetables that are heavy for their size and leaves that are perky, not wilted. Avoid bruised vegetables or those with soft spots.

STORE Refrigeration is the key to keeping most vegetables in prime condition. Store them in the crisper drawer. Aside from lettuces, don't seal vegetables in plastic bags: condensation will form and speed decay. The fridge does have some exceptions. Store potatoes, onions, garlic, tomatoes, and winter squash at cool room temperature. Be sure to store onions and potatoes apart, as they release gases and moisture that cause each other to spoil more quickly.

WASH Just before using, rinse vegetables under cold running water. If needed, use a soft vegetable brush to remove any surface dirt. Swish leafy greens in a large bowl of cool water, changing the water several times.

PREP Peel and cut vegetables as close to serving time as possible. Once the skin on vegetables is broken, they begin to lose valuable nutrients. Cut into uniform pieces to ensure even cooking. For tips on chopping and slicing, see Cutting Basics (page 16).

Serving Veggies

For everyday meals, most vegetables need little more than a drizzle of melted butter or olive oil or a squeeze of fresh lemon juice. For more festive occasions, it's nice to dress them up.

Here are some suggestions for popular vegetables that love being dipped in or slathered with sauce. All are also especially delicious with Hollandaise Sauce (page 51) or Béarnaise Sauce (page 51).

ARTICHOKES Easy Aioli (page 50), Mustard-Shallot Vinaigrette (page 504).

ASPARAGUS Classic French Vinaigrette (page 504), Japanese Miso Vinaigrette (page 504), Tahini Dressing (page 505), Olive Butter (page 43).

BROCCOLI Mornay Sauce (page 50), Cheese Sauce (page 50), Salmoriglio Sauce (page 55).

CAULIFLOWER Chimichurri (page 55), Tomato Salsa (page 53), Sicilian Pesto (page 64).

GREEN BEANS Asian Peanut Sauce (page 54), Easy Aioli (page 50).

POTATOES Homemade Pesto (page 65), Garlicky Mustard Dressing (page 501), Caper Butter (page 43).

WINTER SQUASH Ginger-Cilantro Butter (page 43), Pepita Pesto (page 66).

TOMATOES Homemade Pesto (page 65), Salmoriglio Sauce (page 55).

Perfect Roasted Vegetables

TESTING NOTE If roasting a larger amount of vegetables, divide them between two pans. Overcrowding the vegetables will cause them to steam instead of roast. Rotate pans between upper and lower oven racks halfway through cooking.

5 Steps to
PERFECT ROASTED VEGETABLES

Roasting vegetables in a hot oven concentrates their flavor and gives them a rich caramelized outside. You can roast assorted vegetables together as long as their cooking times are similar. Toss hearty herbs like rosemary, sage, or thyme with the raw vegetables, but save tender herbs like dill, parsley, mint, or oregano for sprinkling at the end of cooking. Roast strips of citrus peel along with the vegetables, or sprinkle on freshly grated zest when they come out of the oven.

1   **Preheat** oven to 450°F.

2   **Cut** vegetables in even-size pieces.

3   **Toss** 2 pounds cut vegetables with 1 to 2 tablespoons olive oil, seasonings, ½ teaspoon salt, and ¼ teaspoon pepper in a shallow 15½ x 10½-inch sheet pan until coated.

4   **Spread** vegetables in a single layer.

5   **Roast** until tender and lightly browned, stirring once or twice during cooking.

TRIMMING ARTICHOKES

1 From around the base of the artichoke, bend back the outer green leaves and snap them off.

2 With kitchen shears, trim the thorny tops from the outer leaves, rubbing cut surfaces with a lemon half to prevent browning.

3 Lay the artichoke on its side and cut off the stem, level with the bottom of the artichoke.

4 Peel the stem. Cut 1 inch off the top of the artichoke.

5 Repeat with any remaining artichokes and stems.

ROAST VEGETABLES

VEGETABLES	HOW TO CUT	ROAST TIME (450°F)	SEASONINGS
BEETS **2 POUNDS NOT INCLUDING** **TOPS (ABOUT 10 SMALL)**	Whole, pricked with fork	1 hour	After roasting, peel, quarter, and sprinkle with salt, pepper, and 1 teaspoon freshly grated orange peel.
CARROTS **2 POUNDS**	1-inch pieces	30 to 40 minutes	Toss with ½ teaspoon pumpkin pie spice before roasting.
POTATOES **2 POUNDS UNPEELED**	2-inch pieces	45 minutes	Toss with 1 tablespoon chopped fresh thyme or 1 teaspoon dried thyme before roasting.
CAULIFLOWER **1 MEDIUM HEAD** **(1½ POUNDS)**	1½-inch flowerets	20 to 30 minutes	Sprinkle with 2 tablespoons chopped fresh parsley after roasting.
ONIONS **2 JUMBO (1 POUND EACH)**	Each cut into 12 wedges	20 to 30 minutes	Brush with mixture of 1 tablespoon brown sugar and 1 teaspoon cider vinegar; roast 5 minutes more.
FENNEL **2 LARGE BULBS** **(1 POUND EACH)**	Trimmed and each cut into 12 wedges	35 to 40 minutes	Sprinkle with freshly grated orange peel.
SWEET POTATOES **(OR WINTER SQUASH)** **2 POUNDS**	Peeled and cut into 1-inch chunks	30 minutes	Toss with 2 tablespoons chopped fresh rosemary before roasting.
SUNCHOKES **2 POUNDS**	Whole, pricked with fork	20 to 30 minutes	Sprinkle with 2 tablespoons chopped fresh chives after roasting.
EGGPLANT **2 MEDIUM** **(1 POUND EACH)**	½-inch-thick slices	20 to 25 minutes	Drizzle with 1 tablespoon extra-virgin olive oil after roasting.
SWEET PEPPERS **2 POUNDS**	1-inch-wide strips	30 minutes	Sprinkle with 3 large fresh basil leaves, thinly sliced, after roasting.
ASPARAGUS **2 POUNDS**	Trimmed	10 to 15 minutes	Sprinkle with freshly grated lemon peel after roasting.
GREEN BEANS **2 POUNDS**	Trimmed	20 to 30 minutes	Toss with favorite vinaigrette.

asparagus
with lemon cream

PREP: 15 MIN / TOTAL: 30 MIN / SERVES 6

Salt
2 pounds asparagus, trimmed
1 lemon
½ cup sour cream
2 tablespoons heavy or whipping cream
¼ teaspoon ground black pepper
1 tablespoon snipped fresh chives, for garnish

1. Heat a large covered saucepot of water to boiling over high heat. Fill a large bowl with ice and water.

2. Add 1 teaspoon salt, then the asparagus, to the boiling water. Cook, uncovered, 4 minutes, or until bright green and a knife easily pierces the stalks. With tongs, transfer the asparagus directly to the bowl of ice water. When the asparagus is cool, drain well; roll it between paper towels to dry completely. Asparagus can be refrigerated in an airtight container or a resealable plastic bag up to overnight.

3. From the lemon, grate 1 teaspoon zest and squeeze 2 tablespoons juice into a small bowl. Whisk in the sour cream, heavy cream, pepper, and ¼ teaspoon salt. The sauce can be refrigerated in an airtight container up to 3 days.

4. Spoon the sauce over the asparagus and garnish with chives.

Each serving About 65 calories, 2g protein, 4g carbohydrate, 5g fat (3g saturated), 2g fiber, 140mg sodium.

HOW TO

STEAM ARTICHOKES

Trim **4 large artichokes** (see page 416). In a 5-quart saucepot, heat 1 inch of water to boiling. Place artichokes, bases down, in a steamer basket; add to pot. Reduce heat; cover and simmer until a knife inserted in the bottom of an artichoke goes in easily, 30 to 40 minutes, checking water level and replenishing if necessary. Remove artichokes from pan; cool slightly. Serve with melted dipping butter such as **lemon butter or other Flavored Butter** (page 43).

---

asparagus
with eggs mimosa

(See photo on page 412.)

PREP: 20 MIN / TOTAL: 35 MIN / SERVES 8

3 large eggs
2 pounds asparagus, trimmed
¼ cup water
1 lemon
3 tablespoons extra-virgin olive oil
2 tablespoons red wine vinegar
1 tablespoon snipped fresh chives
¼ teaspoon sugar
½ teaspoon salt
½ teaspoon ground black pepper

1. In a 2-quart saucepan, combine the eggs and enough cold water to cover. Heat to boiling over high heat. Remove from the heat. Cover and let stand 14 minutes. Rinse the eggs with cold water until cool, then peel. Eggs may be hard-cooked and refrigerated up to 3 days ahead.

2. Meanwhile, cook the asparagus: Arrange the spears in an even layer in an 8-inch-square microwave-safe baking dish. Add the water. Cover with vented plastic wrap and microwave on High 5 minutes. Asparagus may be cooked, cooled, and refrigerated in an airtight container up to 2 days.

3. From the lemon, grate ¼ teaspoon zest; set aside. Squeeze 1 tablespoon juice into a small bowl. To the bowl with the lemon juice, add the oil, vinegar, chives, sugar, salt, and pepper; whisk to combine.

4. To serve, arrange the asparagus on a serving platter. Drizzle with vinaigrette. Coarsely grate the eggs over the asparagus and garnish with the reserved lemon zest.

Each serving About 90 calories, 4g protein, 3g carbohydrate, 7g fat (1g saturated), 1g fiber, 175mg sodium.

INGREDIENT SPOTLIGHT

↓

Asparagus is a harbinger of spring at local farmers' markets. When buying it, don't assume pencil-thin asparagus will be the most tender. Many chefs actually prefer thick spears, which, once cooked, are often more tender and flavorful than slim ones.

ASPARAGUS WITH LEMON CREAM 416

lemony brussels sprout salad

(See photo on page 412.)

PREP: 20 MIN / TOTAL: 25 MIN / SERVES 8

- ¼ cup fresh lemon juice
- 3 tablespoons extra-virgin olive oil
- ½ teaspoon salt
- ¼ teaspoon ground black pepper
- 1 pound Brussels sprouts, trimmed and very thinly sliced
- 1 small head romaine lettuce, chopped
- ⅓ cup packed grated ricotta salata or Pecorino Romano cheese
- ⅔ cup dried cranberries or golden raisins
- ½ cup smoked almonds, chopped

1. In a large bowl, whisk the lemon juice, oil, salt, and pepper; add the sprouts and toss until well coated. Let stand at least 10 minutes or up to 2 hours.

2. When ready to serve, to the bowl with the sprouts, add the romaine, ricotta salata, cranberries, and almonds; toss to combine.

***

Each serving About 200 calories, 6g protein, 20g carbohydrate, 13g fat (2g saturated), 5g fiber, 310mg sodium.

Tip The easiest way to thinly shave Brussels sprouts is on a mandoline. Leave stems on and, holding stem, carefully slice from top toward stem. You can also use the food processor; simply pile trimmed sprouts into the feed tube.

brussels sprouts
with bacon

PREP: 15 MIN / TOTAL: 40 MIN / SERVES 10

- 2 quarts water
- 3 containers (10 ounces each) Brussels sprouts, trimmed and cut lengthwise in half
- 6 slices bacon
- 1 tablespoon olive oil
- 2 cloves garlic, finely chopped
- ½ teaspoon salt
- ¼ teaspoon coarsely ground black pepper
- ¼ cup pine nuts, toasted

1. In a 4-quart saucepan, heat the water to boiling over high heat. Add the Brussels sprouts and heat to boiling. Cook until tender-crisp, about 5 minutes; drain.

2. In a 12-inch skillet, cook the bacon over medium heat until browned. With tongs, transfer the bacon to paper towels to drain and cool; crumble.

3. Discard all but 1 tablespoon bacon drippings from the skillet. Add the oil and heat over medium-high heat. Add the Brussels sprouts, garlic, salt, and pepper. Cook, stirring frequently, until the Brussels sprouts are lightly browned, about 5 minutes. To serve, sprinkle with pine nuts and bacon.

***

Each serving About 95 calories, 5g protein, 8g carbohydrate, 6g fat (1g saturated), 3g fiber, 200mg sodium.

maple-glazed brussels sprouts

(See photo on page 420.)

PREP: 25 MIN / TOTAL: 40 MIN / SERVES 10

- 7 slices thick-cut bacon, chopped
- 3 pounds Brussels sprouts, trimmed and cut into halves
- 2 large shallots, thinly sliced
- ½ teaspoon salt
- ⅓ cup turkey or chicken broth
- ¼ cup maple syrup
- 2 tablespoons red wine vinegar
- ¼ teaspoon cayenne pepper

1. In a 5- to 6-quart saucepot, cook the bacon over medium-high heat 7 to 8 minutes, or until crisp and browned, stirring occasionally. With a slotted spoon, transfer to a medium plate lined with paper towels. Remove and discard all but 2 tablespoons rendered fat.

2. Reduce the heat to medium. Add the Brussels sprouts, shallots, and salt to pot. Cook 5 minutes, stirring occasionally. Add the broth and cover. Cook 3 to 5 minutes, or until the sprouts are tender, stirring twice.

3. Uncover and add the maple syrup, vinegar, and cayenne. Cook 2 minutes, or until well coated and the vinegar has reduced, stirring occasionally. To serve, stir in the cooked bacon.

***

Each serving About 140 calories, 7g protein, 18g carbohydrate, 5g fat (2g saturated), 5g fiber, 365mg sodium.

roasted beets in orange vinaigrette

(See photo on page 420.)

PREP: 15 MIN / **TOTAL: 1 HR 15 MIN** / **SERVES 4**

- 6 medium beets
- 1 teaspoon plus 2 tablespoons olive oil
- 1 clove garlic
- ½ teaspoon grated orange zest
- ¼ cup fresh orange juice
- ¼ teaspoon salt
- ¼ teaspoon ground black pepper
- ¼ cup fresh cilantro leaves

1. Preheat the oven to 400°F. Trim and scrub the beets.

2. On a large sheet of foil, toss the beets with 1 teaspoon olive oil and the garlic. Wrap tightly; place in a pan and roast 1 hour, or until a knife easily pierces the beets.

3. Let the beets cool. Peel and cut them into wedges. Place on a platter; drizzle with any juices left in the foil.

4. Peel the roasted garlic and place it in a small bowl. Mash with a fork, then stir in 2 tablespoons olive oil, the orange zest, orange juice, salt, and pepper. Drizzle over the beets. Sprinkle cilantro on top.

Each serving About 140 calories, 2g protein, 16g carbohydrate, 8g fat (1g saturated), 4g fiber, 257mg sodium.

HOW TO

COOK BEETS FASTER

Beets cook in a fraction of the time in the microwave. Here's how: Trim and scrub 4 medium beets. Place them in an 8-inch-square glass baking dish; cover with vented plastic wrap. Microwave on High 12 minutes, turning them over once. Let stand 5 minutes, until cool enough to peel.

spicy sesame sugar snaps

(See photo on page 420.)

PREP: 15 MIN / **TOTAL: 25 MIN** / **SERVES 4**

- Salt
- 1 pound sugar snap peas, strings removed
- 2 tablespoons toasted sesame oil
- 3 cloves garlic, chopped
- 1 small red chile pepper, thinly sliced, or ½ teaspoon crushed red pepper
- 2 tablespoons red wine vinegar
- Chopped fresh parsley, for garnish

1. Heat a large covered saucepot of salted water to boiling over high heat. Add the sugar snap peas; cook 3 minutes, or until almost tender. Drain well and transfer to a bowl of ice water. Let cool completely, then drain very well. Pat the peas dry.

2. In a 10-inch skillet, heat the sesame oil, garlic, and chile over medium-low heat until the garlic is golden, stirring frequently. Add the peas and cook until just warm. Remove from the heat; stir in the vinegar and ½ teaspoon salt. Garnish with parsley.

Each serving About 110 calories, 3g protein, 9g carbohydrate, 7g fat (1g saturated), 3g fiber, 250mg sodium.

Ingredient Ideas

sugar snap peas

When these crisp pods show up at the farmers' market, buy them by the bagful. They're delicious chilled for snacking, but a short burst of heat brings out their flavor without stealing their crunch. Steam them for 2 minutes, then toss with 1 tablespoon butter and salt and pepper to taste. Add one of these combos for a flavor boost.

ORANGE MINT ½ teaspoon grated orange zest and 1 tablespoon chopped fresh mint

ZINGY GREEN 1 green onion, thinly sliced and 1 teaspoon grated, peeled fresh ginger

PARSLEY & PARM ¼ cup grated Parmesan cheese and 1 teaspoon grated lemon zest

MAPLE-GLAZED BRUSSELS SPROUTS 418

SPICY SESAME SUGAR SNAPS 419

GARLICKY KALE & PEA SAUTÉ 421

ROASTED BEETS IN ORANGE VINAIGRETTE 419

peas
with green onions & mint

PREP: 10 MIN / TOTAL: 15 MIN / SERVES 6

2 tablespoons butter

½ cup chopped green
onions (4 green
onions)

1 bag (20 ounces) frozen
peas, thawed

½ teaspoon salt

¼ teaspoon coarsely
ground black pepper

¼ cup chopped fresh
mint

1. In a 10-inch skillet, melt the butter over medium heat. Add the green onions and cook, stirring frequently, until tender, about 2 minutes. Stir in the peas, salt, and pepper and cook, stirring frequently, until heated through, about 3 minutes longer.

2. Remove the skillet from the heat; stir in the mint.

Each serving About 110 calories, 5g protein, 14g carbohydrate, 4g fat (2g saturated), 5g fiber, 340mg sodium.

garlicky kale
& pea sauté

PREP: 10 MIN / TOTAL: 20 MIN / SERVES 10

2 cloves garlic, thinly
sliced

1 hot red chile, finely
chopped

2 tablespoons olive oil

2 bunches kale, trimmed
and chopped (about
1 pound total)

½ teaspoon sugar

½ teaspoon salt

1 pound frozen
peas

In a 5- to 6-quart saucepot over medium heat, cook the garlic and chile in the oil 2 minutes, stirring often. Add the kale, sugar, and salt. Cook 6 minutes, or until the kale is tender, stirring occasionally. Stir in the peas. Cook 2 minutes, or until heated through.

Each serving About 85 calories, 5g protein, 11g carbohydrate, 3g fat (0g saturated), 4g fiber, 115mg sodium.

mixed peapod
stir-fry

PREP: 15 MIN / TOTAL: 25 MIN / SERVES 4

4 cups water

1 teaspoon salt

8 ounces green beans,
trimmed

2 teaspoons vegetable
oil

4 ounces snow peas,
trimmed and strings
removed

4 ounces sugar snap
peas, trimmed and
strings removed

1 clove garlic, finely
chopped

1 tablespoon soy
sauce

1. In a 12-inch skillet, combine the water and salt; heat to boiling over high heat. Add the green beans and cook 3 minutes. Drain; wipe the skillet dry with paper towels.

2. In the same skillet, heat the oil over high heat. Add the green beans and cook, stirring frequently (stir-frying), until they begin to brown, 2 to 3 minutes. Add the snow peas, sugar snap peas, and garlic; stir-fry until the snow peas and sugar snap peas are tender-crisp, about 1 minute longer. Stir in the soy sauce and remove from the heat.

Each serving About 65 calories, 3g protein, 8g carbohydrate, 2g fat (0g saturated), 3g fiber, 845mg sodium.

green beans
with hazelnuts

PREP: 20 MIN / TOTAL: 35 MIN / SERVES 8

Salt

2 pounds green beans, trimmed

2 tablespoons butter

½ cup hazelnuts (filberts), toasted and skinned, chopped

1 teaspoon freshly grated lemon zest

¼ teaspoon ground black pepper

1. In a 12-inch skillet, heat 1 inch water and 1 teaspoon salt to boiling over high heat. Add the green beans and heat to boiling. Cover and cook until tender-crisp, 6 to 8 minutes. Drain; wipe the skillet dry with paper towels.

2. In the same skillet, melt the butter over medium heat. Add the hazelnuts and cook, stirring, until the butter just begins to brown, about 3 minutes. Add the green beans, lemon zest, ½ teaspoon salt, and the pepper. Cook, stirring, until heated through, about 5 minutes.

Each serving About 145 calories, 3g protein, 9g carbohydrate, 12g fat (4g saturated), 3g fiber, 355mg sodium.

VARIATIONS

Green Beans Amandine
Prepare as directed, but substitute ⅔ cup slivered almonds, toasted, for the hazelnuts.

Lemony Green Beans
Prepare as directed, but omit the hazelnuts in step 2. Instead, add ¼ teaspoon ground coriander, ¼ cup chopped fresh mint, 1 tablespoon fresh lemon juice, and ½ teaspoon lemon zest. Toss until the beans are evenly coated.

roasted green beans
with dill vinaigrette

PREP: 20 MIN / TOTAL: 45 MIN / SERVES 8

2 pounds green beans, trimmed

3 tablespoons olive oil

Salt

2 tablespoons white wine vinegar

1½ teaspoons Dijon mustard

½ teaspoon sugar

½ teaspoon coarsely ground black pepper

2 tablespoons chopped fresh dill

1. Preheat the oven to 450°F. In a large roasting pan (17 × 11½ inches), toss the green beans, 1 tablespoon oil, and ½ teaspoon salt until coated. Roast, stirring twice, until tender and lightly browned, 20 to 30 minutes.

2. Meanwhile, prepare the vinaigrette: In a small bowl and using a wire whisk, mix the vinegar, mustard, sugar, ¼ teaspoon salt, and the pepper until blended. In a thin, steady stream, whisk in the remaining 2 tablespoons oil until blended; stir in the dill.

3. When the green beans are done, transfer them to a serving bowl. Drizzle the vinaigrette over the green beans; toss until coated.

Each serving About 80 calories, 2g protein, 8g carbohydrate, 5g fat (1g saturated), 3g fiber, 250mg sodium.

TESTING NOTE For easy green bean trimming, line them up 10 at a time on a cutting board with all the stem ends facing up. Run your knife across and discard stems. It is not necessary to trim the "tail end" of the beans.

garlicky beans & greens

(See photo on page 425.)

PREP: 10 MIN / TOTAL: 20 MIN / SERVES 8

- 2 tablespoons olive oil
- 3 cloves garlic, thinly sliced
- 1 tablespoon fresh thyme leaves
- ½ teaspoon crushed red pepper
- 1 large bunch (about 1 pound) escarole, chopped
- ½ teaspoon salt
- 2 cans (15 ounces each) lower-sodium white kidney (cannellini) beans, undrained
- 1 teaspoon sugar
- 2 tablespoons fresh lemon juice

1. In a 6- to 7-quart saucepot, heat the oil over medium heat. Add the garlic, thyme, and crushed red pepper. Cook 2 minutes, or until the garlic is golden, stirring. Add the escarole and salt. Cook 2 minutes, or until the escarole wilts, stirring occasionally. Gently stir in the beans and sugar. Reduce the heat to medium-low.

2. Cover and cook 10 minutes, or until the greens are very tender. Just before serving, stir in the lemon juice.

Each serving About 135 calories, 7g protein, 20g carbohydrate, 4g fat (1g saturated), 8g fiber, 305mg sodium.

INGREDIENT SPOTLIGHT

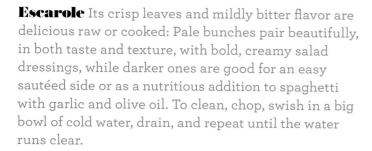

Escarole Its crisp leaves and mildly bitter flavor are delicious raw or cooked: Pale bunches pair beautifully, in both taste and texture, with bold, creamy salad dressings, while darker ones are good for an easy sautéed side or as a nutritious addition to spaghetti with garlic and olive oil. To clean, chop, swish in a big bowl of cold water, drain, and repeat until the water runs clear.

green bean & cheddar casserole

(See photo on page 425.)

PREP: 30 MIN / TOTAL: 1 HR 20 MIN / SERVES 10

- 3 pounds green beans, trimmed
- 2 cups stale bread, torn into small chunks
- 3 tablespoons olive oil
- 3 green onions, thinly sliced
- 3 tablespoons cornstarch
- 2½ cup whole milk
- ⅛ teaspoon ground nutmeg
- ½ teaspoon salt
- ½ teaspoon ground black pepper
- 8 ounces Cheddar cheese, shredded
- ¼ cup finely grated Parmesan cheese (1 ounce)

1. Heat a covered 7- to 8-quart saucepot of salted water to boiling over high heat. Preheat the oven to 375°F. Add the green beans to the boiling water. Cook 2 minutes. Drain well; set aside.

2. In a food processor, pulse the bread into coarse crumbs. Transfer to a medium bowl along with the oil and green onions. Toss to combine; set aside.

3. In a 4-quart saucepan, whisk the cornstarch and ½ cup milk until smooth. Add the nutmeg, salt, and pepper. Slowly whisk in the remaining 2 cups milk. Heat to boiling over medium-high heat, whisking frequently. Boil 2 minutes, whisking. Reduce the heat to medium-low. Stir in the cheeses, one handful at a time, waiting until the cheese melts before adding the next handful. Stir in the green beans until well coated. Transfer the mixture to a greased 3-quart baking dish. Top with the reserved crumb mixture. Bake 25 to 30 minutes, or until the crumbs are golden brown.

Each serving About 245 calories, 11g protein, 19g carbohydrate, 15g fat (7g saturated), 4g fiber, 375mg sodium.

pimiento-cheese green beans

PREP: 35 MIN / TOTAL: 35 MIN / SERVES 12

- 2½ pounds green beans, trimmed and cut into 2-inch lengths
- 2 cup fresh or frozen corn kernels
- 4 tablespoons butter
- 3 tablespoons grated onion
- 5 tablespoons all-purpose flour
- 2 cup whole milk
- 12 ounces sharp Cheddar cheese, finely grated
- 2 jars (3 ounces each) chopped or sliced pimientos, drained
- 1 tablespoon hot sauce (such as Tabasco)
- 2 teaspoons Worcestershire sauce
- ¼ teaspoon ground black pepper
- ½ teaspoon salt

1. To a 7- to 8-quart saucepot of salted boiling water, add the green beans; cook 3 minutes, or until just tender. Add the corn; cook 1 minute. Drain well; set aside.

2. In a 6-quart saucepot, cook the butter and onion over medium heat 3 minutes, or until the onion becomes translucent, stirring occasionally. Sprinkle the flour over the onion. Cook 1 minute, stirring. Slowly whisk in the milk until smooth. Heat to simmering over high heat, whisking occasionally. Reduce the heat to maintain a simmer; cook 1 to 2 minutes, or until thickened, stirring.

3. By handfuls, stir the Cheddar into the milk mixture until smooth. Stir in the pimientos, hot sauce, Worcestershire sauce, pepper, and salt. Add the green beans and corn to the cheese sauce, stirring until well coated. Transfer to a serving dish.

Each serving About 235 calories, 10g protein, 17g carbohydrate, 15g fat (9g saturated), 3g fiber, 375mg sodium.

broccoli rabe
with chickpeas

PREP: 10 MIN / TOTAL: 28 MIN / SERVES 8

- 4 quarts water
- 2 bunches broccoli rabe (1¼ pounds each), trimmed
- Salt
- 2 tablespoons olive oil
- 3 cloves garlic, crushed with the side of a chef's knife
- ¼ teaspoon crushed red pepper
- 1 can (15 to 19 ounces) chickpeas, rinsed and drained

1. In an 8-quart saucepot, heat water to boiling over high heat. Add the broccoli rabe and 2 teaspoons salt; heat to boiling. Cook until the thickest part of the stem is tender, about 3 minutes. Drain, reserving ¼ cup cooking water. Cool slightly, then cut it into 1½-inch pieces.

2. Wipe the saucepot dry with paper towels; add the oil and heat over medium heat. Add the garlic and cook, stirring, until golden. Add the crushed red pepper and cook 15 seconds. Add the broccoli rabe, chickpeas, reserved cooking water, and ½ teaspoon salt. Cook, stirring, until heated through, about 3 minutes.

Each serving About 95 calories, 5g protein, 10g carbohydrate, 4g fat (0g saturated), 5g fiber, 380mg sodium.

Serving Suggestion For a quick and flavorful weeknight supper, toss this tasty bitter-greens dish with a hearty pasta, such as penne or bow ties, and sprinkle with Parmesan cheese.

GARLICKY BEANS & GREENS 423

GREEN BEAN & CHEDDAR CASSEROLE 423

PIMIENTO-CHEESE GREEN BEANS 424

BUTTER-GLAZED RAINBOW CARROTS 427

candied carrots

PREP: 15 MIN / TOTAL: 40 MIN / SERVES 4

1 pound carrots, peeled	3 tablespoons brown sugar
1 lemon	
2 tablespoons butter or margarine	

1. Cut each carrot crosswise in half. Cut each thick portion lengthwise in half. In a 4-quart saucepan, heat 1 inch water to boiling over medium heat. Add the carrots and heat to boiling. Cover and simmer until tender, about 15 minutes. Drain and return to the saucepan.

2. Meanwhile, from the lemon, grate ½ teaspoon zest and squeeze 1 teaspoon juice.

3. Add the butter, brown sugar, and lemon juice to the carrots; cook over medium heat, stirring gently, until the sugar has dissolved and the carrots are glazed, about 5 minutes. Stir in the zest.

Each serving About 135 calories, 1g protein, 20g carbohydrate, 6g fat (4g saturated), 3g fiber, 100mg sodium.

VARIATIONS

Ginger Candied Carrots

Prepare as directed, but add **1 teaspoon grated, peeled fresh ginger** with the butter.

Candied Parsnips

Prepare as directed, but substitute **1 pound parsnips**, peeled, for the carrots.

balsamic-glazed baby carrots

PREP: 15 MIN / TOTAL: 45 MIN / SERVES 8

2 pounds baby carrots or medium carrots	2 tablespoons balsamic or white balsamic vinegar
1 tablespoon olive oil	1 tablespoon sugar
¼ teaspoon salt	
⅛ teaspoon ground black pepper	

1. Preheat the oven to 400°F. With a vegetable brush, scrub the carrots and rinse them under cold water. Pat dry with paper towels. Trim baby carrots, leaving 1 inch of the green stem on, if you like; cut medium carrots into quarters lengthwise, then in half crosswise.

2. In a 15½ × 10½-inch jelly-roll pan, toss the carrots with the oil, salt, and pepper. Roast 25 minutes. Stir in the vinegar and sugar until the carrots are coated. Roast 6 to 8 minutes longer, or until carrots are tender and the sugar has dissolved.

Each serving About 65 calories, 1g protein, 11g carbohydrate, 2g fat (0g saturated), 2g fiber, 110mg sodium.

Tip In springtime, bunches of fresh baby carrots should be readily available at supermarkets and farmers' markets. If not, use 2 pounds medium carrots, quartered lengthwise, then halved crosswise.

TESTING NOTE For this recipe, we don't recommend using prepackaged "baby" carrots; they require a much longer roasting time, and we've found they don't caramelize as well.

spice-roasted carrots

(See photo on page 410.)

PREP: 15 MIN / TOTAL: 1 HR 15 MIN / SERVES 8

- 8 very large carrots (about 3 pounds), peeled
- 3 tablespoons olive oil
- 2 tablespoons packed fresh oregano leaves, chopped
- 1 teaspoon smoked paprika
- ½ teaspoon ground nutmeg
- ½ teaspoon salt
- ¼ teaspoon ground black pepper
- 2 tablespoons butter, melted
- 1 tablespoon red wine vinegar
- ⅓ cup roasted salted pistachios, shelled and finely chopped, for garnish

1. Preheat the oven to 450°F.

2. In a roasting pan, toss the carrots with the oil, oregano, paprika, nutmeg, salt, and pepper. Roast 1 hour, or until the carrots are tender but not falling apart. Transfer to a serving platter. Drizzle with the butter and vinegar and garnish with pistachios.

Each serving About 165 calories, 3g protein, 15g carbohydrate, 11g fat (3g saturated), 5g fiber, 295mg sodium.

TESTING NOTE Jumbo carrots, sometimes called juice carrots, weigh 6 to 8 ounces each and are usually sold in bulk. If you use smaller bagged carrots for this dish, start checking for doneness at 40 minutes.

butter-glazed rainbow carrots

(See photo on page 425.)

PREP: 10 MIN / TOTAL: 30 MIN / SERVES 6

- 1 bunch (about 1½ pounds) slender rainbow carrots, trimmed, scrubbed, and cut into 1-inch pieces
- 4 tablespoons butter, melted
- ¼ teaspoon salt
- ½ teaspoon ground black pepper
- 2 tablespoons fresh lemon juice
- Snipped fresh chives, for garnish

1. Preheat the oven to 425°F. Line a rimmed baking sheet with foil.

2. Toss the carrots with the butter, salt, and pepper; arrange them in a single layer on the prepared baking sheet. Roast 20 to 25 minutes, or until tender and browned.

3. Drizzle the carrots with lemon juice. To serve, garnish with chives.

Each serving About 110 calories, 1g protein, 9g carbohydrate, 8g fat (5g saturated), 0g fiber, 220mg sodium.

baked beans

Begin by rinsing and draining 1 or 2 cans of
black or red kidney beans (each 15 to 19 ounces).

BLACK BEAN DIP

In a food processor, puree **1 can beans** with **1 tablespoon fresh lime juice**, **1 teaspoon freshly grated lime zest**, and **2 teaspoons chipotle adobo sauce**. Transfer to a small bowl and stir in ¼ **cup chopped fresh cilantro leaves** and **2 plum tomatoes**, seeded and chopped. Serve with **tortilla chips**— or for a healthier alternative, try carrot sticks, bell pepper strips, or jicama slices. **Makes about 2 cups.**

BLACK BEAN SALAD

In a medium bowl, combine **1 can beans**; **1 chopped red bell pepper**; **1 can (15¼ ounces) corn kernels**, drained; ⅓ cup chopped fresh cilantro leaves; and **2 tablespoons ranch dressing**. This tastes great alongside **grilled chicken or fish**. **Makes about 3¹/₂ cups.**

BLACK BEAN SAUTÉ

In a 10-inch nonstick skillet, brown **1 small onion**, chopped, in **1 teaspoon olive oil**. Stir in **1 clove garlic**, crushed with a garlic press, and cook 1 minute. Stir in **1 can beans** and heat through. Remove from the heat and stir in **1 to 2 tablespoons chopped pickled jalapeño chiles**. This is a good side dish for **pork chops**. **Makes about 1³/₄ cups.**

BLACK BEAN SOUP

In a 4-quart saucepan, cook **1 cup fresh salsa** and a **pinch of ground allspice** over medium heat for 3 minutes. Stir in **2 cans beans** and **3 cups low-sodium chicken broth**; heat to boiling over high heat. Reduce the heat and simmer 10 minutes. Use an immersion blender or potato masher to coarsely mash the beans. **Makes about 6 cups.**

BLACK BEAN CHILI

In a 4-quart saucepan, cook **8 ounces lean ground beef** and **1 small onion**, chopped, until the beef is browned and the onion is tender, about 10 minutes. Stir in **2 teaspoons chili powder** and cook 1 minute. Stir in **2 cans beans**, **1 can (14½ ounces) diced tomatoes with green chiles**, and **1 cup water**. Heat to boiling over high heat; reduce the heat to low and simmer 15 minutes, stirring occasionally. **Makes about 5 cups.**

VEGETABLE CURRY WITH KIDNEY BEANS

In a 4-quart saucepan, heat **4 cups water** to boiling. Add **1 package (12 ounces) fresh broccoli/cauliflower-floret mix**; cook 4 minutes or just under tender. Drain in a colander. Dry the saucepan. In the same pan, toast **1 teaspoon curry powder** over medium heat 30 seconds. Stir in **1 can beans**, ¼ **cup chutney**, ¼ **cup water**, **1½ teaspoons grated, peeled fresh ginger**, and ¼ **teaspoon salt**. Cook 2 minutes. Stir in the broccoli-cauliflower mix. Spoon over **rice**. **Serves 4.**

AVOCADO & RED BEAN QUESADILLAS

Divide **4 tablespoons salsa**, **1 cup shredded pepper Jack cheese**, **1 can beans**, and **1 avocado**, sliced, on half of each of **4 burrito-size (10-inch) tortillas**. Fold each tortilla in half; press to flatten slightly. Heat a 12-inch skillet over medium heat; add 2 quesadillas to the hot pan. Cook 8 minutes, or until golden on both sides. Repeat. Serve with **salsa**. **Serves 4.**

SUN-DRIED TOMATO & RED BEAN DIP

In a food processor, finely chop ⅓ **cup oil-packed sun-dried tomatoes** with **1 tablespoon of their oil**. Add **1 can beans**, ¼ **cup grated Parmesan cheese**, and **2 tablespoons water** and blend until smooth. Add ⅓ **cup fresh basil leaves**; pulse just until combined. Serve with **pita chips**. **Makes 1³/₄ cups.**

RED BEAN FALAFEL

In a food processor, blend **1 can beans**, **1 egg**, ⅓ **cup packed fresh parsley**, ¼ **cup seasoned dried bread crumbs**, ¾ **teaspoon ground cumin**, and ¼ **teaspoon each salt and ground black pepper**. Place **3 tablespoons seasoned dried bread crumbs** on a plate. Shape the bean mixture into 8 patties about 2 inches in diameter each; coat with crumbs. Spray a 12-inch skillet with **nonstick cooking spray**; heat over medium heat. Add patties; cook 9 minutes. **Serves 4.**

MINESTRONE

In a 4-quart saucepan, combine **1 can kidney beans**, **4 cups vegetable broth**, **1 can (14½ ounces) diced tomatoes with onion and garlic**, and ¼ **teaspoon Italian seasoning**; cover and heat to boiling. Stir in **1 bag (16 ounces) frozen Italian vegetables**; cover and cook 6 minutes or until tender. Serve with **grated Parmesan cheese**. **Serves 4.**

refried beans

PREP: 10 MIN / TOTAL: 35 MIN / SERVES 4

- 3 slices bacon, coarsely chopped
- 2 tablespoons water
- 1 medium onion, chopped
- 3 cloves garlic, finely chopped
- 2 cans (15 to 19 ounces each) pinto beans, rinsed and drained
- ¾ cup chicken broth

1. In a 12-inch skillet, cook the bacon with the water over medium heat until browned. With a slotted spoon, transfer the bacon to paper towels to drain.

2. Add the onion and garlic to the drippings in the skillet; cook, stirring frequently, until the onion is tender, about 7 minutes. Add the beans and ¼ cup chicken broth. With a potato masher or wooden spoon, mash the beans. Continue cooking the beans until the liquid has been absorbed, about 3 minutes. Add another ¼ cup broth and stir until the beans are piping hot and almost all the liquid has been absorbed, about 3 minutes. Add the remaining ¼ cup broth and heat to boiling. Spoon onto a platter and sprinkle with bacon.

Each serving About 240 calories, 11g protein, 25g carbohydrate, 11g fat (4g saturated), 12g fiber, 660mg sodium.

quick baked beans

PREP: 10 MIN / TOTAL: 25 MIN / SERVES 8

- 2 teaspoons olive oil
- 1 small onion, chopped
- 1 cup ketchup
- ½ cup water
- 3 tablespoons light (mild) molasses
- 1 tablespoon Dijon mustard
- ½ teaspoon Worcestershire sauce
- ¼ teaspoon salt
- Pinch of ground cloves
- 1 can (15 to 19 ounces) black beans, rinsed and drained
- 1 can (15 to 19 ounces) red kidney beans, rinsed and drained
- 1 can (15 to 19 ounces) pink beans, rinsed and drained
- 1 can (15 to 19 ounces) white beans, such as great northern, rinsed and drained

1. In a 4-quart saucepan, heat the oil over medium-low heat. Add the onion and cook until tender and golden, 5 to 8 minutes.

2. Stir in the ketchup, water, molasses, mustard, Worcestershire, salt, and cloves until blended. Add the black, red kidney, pink, and white beans; heat to boiling over high heat. Reduce the heat; cover and simmer 5 minutes.

Each serving About 235 calories, 12g protein, 43g carbohydrate, 2g fat (0g saturated), 12g fiber, 710mg sodium.

 Tip If you're craving the smokiness of bacon and have a bit more time (they simmer in the oven for an hour) try Campfire Baked Beans (page 52).

GOOD TO KNOW

BAKED BEAN ADD-INS

Here are some easy ways to vary the flavor of baked beans.

- Stir in a few slices of chopped crisp-cooked bacon.
- Add some diced ham or smoked boneless pork chop.
- Add a few drops of hickory liquid smoke.
- Substitute a favorite barbecue sauce for the ketchup.
- Use yellow mustard instead of Dijon.
- Add about 1 tablespoon minced chipotles in adobo sauce.
- Stir in 1 tablespoon chili powder.
- Replace the molasses with the same amount of maple syrup or honey.
- Transfer the simmered beans to a shallow baking dish topped with buttered crumbs, and run under the broiler until crumbs are golden, 2 to 3 minutes.

tuscan white beans
with sage

PREP: 15 MIN / TOTAL: 1 HR, PLUS SOAKING / SERVES 8

- 1 package (16 ounces) white kidney (cannellini) beans, soaked and drained
- 3 slices bacon
- 2 small onions, very thinly sliced
- 4 cloves garlic, crushed with the side of a chef's knife
- 2 sprigs plus 2 teaspoons thinly sliced fresh sage leaves
- 1 bay leaf
- 3 tablespoons olive oil
- 2 teaspoons salt
- ½ teaspoon ground black pepper

1. Preheat the oven to 325°F. In a 5-quart Dutch oven, combine the beans, bacon, onions, garlic, sage sprigs, bay leaf, oil, and enough water to cover by 2 inches; heat to boiling over high heat. Cover and place in the oven. Bake until the beans are tender but still retain their shape, 45 to 60 minutes.

2. Drain the beans, reserving the cooking liquid. Discard the bacon, sage sprigs, and bay leaf. Return the beans to the pot and stir in the sliced sage, salt, pepper, and ½ to 1 cup bean cooking liquid for the desired consistency. Spoon into serving bowls and serve hot, warm, or at room temperature.

Each serving About 265 calories, 14g protein, 37g carbohydrate, 7g fat (1g saturated), 20g fiber, 620mg sodium.

VARIATION

Bistro White Beans

Omit the bacon, sage, crushed garlic, and oil. Replace cannellini beans with **Great Northern beans**. In step 1, stud **1 whole onion** with **2 whole cloves garlic**; add to beans, bay leaf, and water and bake as directed. Meanwhile, chop the remaining onion. In a large skillet sauté onion in **2 tablespoons butter** until tender, about 5 minutes. Add **1 clove garlic**, crushed with a garlic press, and cook 1 minute. Stir in **1 can (14 to 16 ounces) tomatoes with their juice**, salt, and pepper. Heat to boiling, breaking up the tomatoes with the side of a spoon. Reduce and simmer 10 to 15 minutes, until almost all the liquid has evaporated. Discard the onion and drain the beans. Gently stir the beans into the tomato mixture.

indian-style lentils

PREP: 20 MIN / TOTAL: 1 HR 5 MIN / SERVES 6

- 1 tablespoon vegetable oil
- 1 medium onion, chopped
- 1 tablespoon minced, peeled fresh ginger
- 1 large clove garlic, finely chopped
- 1½ teaspoons cumin seeds
- ⅛ teaspoon cayenne pepper
- 1 pound sweet potatoes, peeled and cut into ¾-inch pieces (3 cups)
- 1 cup brown lentils, rinsed and picked over
- 1¾ cups chicken or vegetable broth
- 1 cup water
- ¼ teaspoon salt
- 1 container (8 ounces) plain low-fat yogurt
- ¼ cup chopped fresh mint or cilantro

1. In a 3-quart saucepan, heat the oil over medium heat. Add the onion and cook, stirring, until tender, about 5 minutes. Stir in the ginger, garlic, cumin seeds, and cayenne; cook 30 seconds. Stir in the sweet potatoes, lentils, broth, water, and salt; heat to boiling over high heat. Reduce the heat; cover and simmer, stirring occasionally, until the lentils are just tender, about 30 minutes. Transfer to a serving bowl.

2. In a small bowl, combine the yogurt and mint. Serve with lentils.

Each serving About 235 calories, 13g protein, 38g carbohydrate, 4g fat (1g saturated), 9g fiber, 420mg sodium.

braised sweet & sour red cabbage

PREP: 20 MIN / TOTAL: 1 HR 50 MIN / SERVES 10

- 3 tablespoons vegetable oil
- 2 medium onions, chopped
- 1 pear, peeled, cored, and chopped
- 2 medium heads red cabbage (2 pounds each), cut into quarters, cored, and thinly sliced
- 1¾ cups beef broth
- 1 cup apple juice
- ⅓ cup cider vinegar
- ¼ cup packed brown sugar
- 2 small bay leaves
- ¾ teaspoon salt
- ¼ teaspoon coarsely ground black pepper
- ⅛ teaspoon ground allspice

1. In an 8-quart nonreactive saucepot, heat the oil over medium heat. Add the onions and pear; cook, stirring frequently, until tender, 10 minutes.

2. Stir in the cabbage, broth, apple juice, vinegar, brown sugar, bay leaves, salt, pepper, and allspice; heat to boiling over high heat. Reduce the heat; cover and simmer, stirring occasionally, until the cabbage is very tender, about 1 hour. Remove the cover and cook over medium-high heat, stirring occasionally, until most of the liquid has evaporated, about 15 minutes longer. Remove and discard bay leaves.

Each serving About 135 calories, 3g protein, 23g carbohydrate, 5g fat (1g saturated), 4g fiber, 335mg sodium.

braised cabbage
with ginger & cumin

PREP: 10 MIN / TOTAL: 30 MIN / SERVES 6

- 1 tablespoon butter
- 1 tablespoon vegetable oil
- 1 medium onion, chopped
- 2 tablespoons minced, peeled fresh ginger
- 2 cloves garlic, finely chopped
- 1 medium head green cabbage (2 pounds), cut into quarters, cored, and very thinly sliced
- ½ teaspoon cumin seeds, crushed
- ½ teaspoon salt
- 1 cup water

In a 12-inch skillet, melt the butter with the oil over medium heat. Add the onion and cook until tender, about 5 minutes. Stir in the ginger and garlic; cook, stirring, 30 seconds. Stir in the cabbage, cumin seeds, and salt; increase the heat to medium-high and cook, stirring frequently, until the cabbage begins to wilt, about 5 minutes (do not let the garlic burn). Add the water and cook, stirring occasionally, until the cabbage is very tender and the water has evaporated, about 10 minutes.

Each serving About 80 calories, 2g protein, 10g carbohydrate, 4g fat (1g saturated), 3g fiber, 235mg sodium.

GOOD TO KNOW

THE VINEGAR CONNECTION

Recipes for cooked cabbage often include a bit of vinegar. Here's why: If cut cabbage is exposed for the slightest bit of time to alkaline conditions, such as hard water, the cabbage will turn blue. Adding a small amount of acid (fruit or fruit juice, vinegar, or wine) prevents this from happening.

herb-roasted root vegetables

PREP: 15 MIN / TOTAL: 1 HR / SERVES 10

- 1½ pounds mixed baby potatoes, cut into halves
- 1 pound baby carrots, cut into halves
- Salt
- 1 bunch radishes, trimmed, cut into halves
- 3 tablespoons olive oil
- 1 tablespoon chopped fresh thyme
- ¼ teaspoon ground black pepper
- ¼ cup fresh parsley, finely chopped

1. Preheat the oven to 450°F. In a 7-quart saucepot, cover the potatoes and carrots with enough cold water to cover; add 1 tablespoon salt. Cover and heat to boiling over high heat. Reduce the heat to maintain a simmer; cook 7 minutes. Drain well and return to the pot.

2. Toss the potatoes, carrots, and radishes with the oil, thyme, pepper, and ¼ teaspoon salt; arrange in single layer on large rimmed baking sheet. Roast 20 minutes, or until the vegetables are browned and tender.

3. Remove from the oven; sprinkle the vegetables with parsley.

Each serving About 110 calories, 2g protein, 16g carbohydrate, 4g fat (1g saturated), 2g fiber, 170mg sodium.

GOOD TO KNOW

RADISHES

AVAILABILITY

Year-round

PEAK SEASON

Round radishes, April and May; Asian varieties, October

BUYING TIPS

Radishes should be uniformly shaped, free from blemishes, firm, and bright red (or white for icicle radishes).

TO STORE

If not serving within one day, remove the leaves and place the radishes in a plastic bag. Refrigerate up to one week.

TO PREPARE

Trim the radish roots and tops, if necessary. Rinse well under cold running water. If using as a garnish or in a relish tray, cut radishes as desired and store in ice water in the refrigerator.

TO COOK

Radishes can be sautéed in butter and served as a side dish; their flavor will be reminiscent of turnips.

celery root rémoulade

PREP: 25 MIN / TOTAL: 25 MIN, PLUS CHILLING / SERVES 6

2 tablespoons fresh lemon juice

1½ pounds celery root (celeriac), trimmed and peeled

½ cup mayonnaise

2 tablespoons Dijon mustard

1 tablespoon chopped fresh parsley

¼ teaspoon ground black pepper

1. Pour the lemon juice into a large bowl. With an adjustable-blade slicer or a very sharp knife, cut the celery root into ⅛-inch-thick matchstick strips. Immediately place the celery root in the lemon juice as it is cut, tossing to coat completely to prevent the celery root from browning.

2. In a small bowl, combine the mayonnaise, mustard, parsley, and pepper. Add to the celery root and toss to coat. Cover and refrigerate at least 1 hour or up to overnight to blend the flavors.

Each serving About 175 calories, 2g protein, 10g carbohydrate, 15g fat (2g saturated), 2g fiber, 320mg sodium.

TESTING NOTE If preparing ahead, place the cut celery root in a bowl containing 4 cups cold water and 2 tablespoons lemon juice or vinegar; set aside until ready to cook. Drain well.

cauliflower with pine nuts & golden raisins

PREP: 20 MIN / TOTAL: 40 MIN / SERVES 6

- 1 large head cauliflower (2½ pounds), cut into 1½-inch florets
- Salt
- 2 tablespoons olive oil
- 2 cloves garlic, crushed with the side of a chef's knife
- 1 teaspoon anchovy paste (optional)
- ¼ teaspoon crushed red pepper
- ¼ cup golden raisins
- 2 tablespoons pine nuts, lightly toasted
- 1 tablespoon chopped fresh parsley

1. In a 5-quart Dutch oven, heat 2 quarts water to boiling over high heat. Add the cauliflower and 2 teaspoons salt; heat to boiling. Cook until tender, 5 to 7 minutes; drain. Wipe the Dutch oven dry.

2. In the same Dutch oven, heat the oil over medium heat. Add the garlic and cook, stirring, until golden. Add anchovy paste, if using, and crushed red pepper; cook 15 seconds. Add the cauliflower, raisins, pine nuts, and ¼ teaspoon salt; cook, stirring, until heated through, about 2 minutes. To serve, sprinkle with parsley.

Each serving About 95 calories, 2g protein, 9g carbohydrate, 6g fat (1g saturated), 2g fiber, 400mg sodium.

INGREDIENT SPOTLIGHT

↓

Pine Nuts are the seeds of a particular variety of pine tree and have been cultivated for over 6,000 years. These tasty little nuts contain about 31 grams of protein per 100 grams—the highest amount of any nut or seed. Pine nuts are called *piñones* in Spanish and *pignoli* in Italian.

roasted chestnuts

PREP: 30 MIN / TOTAL: 50 MIN / MAKES 2 CUPS

- 1 pound fresh chestnuts

1. Preheat the oven to 400°F. With a sharp knife, cut an X in the flat side of the shell of each chestnut. Place them in a jelly-roll pan and roast until the shells open, about 20 minutes.

2. Cover the chestnuts with a clean kitchen towel. When cool enough to handle and using a paring knife, peel the chestnuts, keeping unpeeled chestnuts covered and warm for easier peeling.

Each ½ cup About 180 calories, 2g protein, 38g carbohydrate, 2g fat (0g saturated), 4g fiber, 5mg sodium.

sautéed fresh corn

PREP: 15 MIN / TOTAL: 20 MIN / SERVES 4

- 2 tablespoons butter
- 4 cups corn kernels cut from the cobs (about 6 ears)
- ½ teaspoon salt
- ¼ teaspoon coarsely ground black pepper
- ¼ cup snipped fresh chives or thinly sliced green onions

In a 10-inch skillet, melt the butter over medium-high heat. Add the corn, salt, and pepper and cook, stirring frequently, until tender, about 4 minutes. Remove from heat and stir in the chives.

Each serving About 240 calories, 7g protein, 41g carbohydrate, 8g fat (4g saturated), 4g fiber, 380mg sodium.

#SavetheFood
leftover corn on the cob

While a quick sauté in the skillet is a fine way to cook raw corn, it's also a very clever way to heat up kernels cut from leftover corn on the cob.

creamy corn pudding

PREP: 30 MIN / TOTAL: 1 HR 45 MIN / SERVES 10

2 tablespoons butter

1 small onion, chopped

¼ cup all-purpose flour

2 cups half-and-half or light cream, warmed

1 cup milk, warmed

2 cups corn kernels cut from the cobs (about 4 ears)

1 teaspoon salt

¼ teaspoon coarsely ground black pepper

4 large eggs

Boiling water

1. Preheat the oven to 325°F. In a 2-quart saucepan, melt the butter over medium heat. Add the onion and cook, stirring frequently, until tender and golden, about 10 minutes. Add the flour and cook, stirring, 1 minute. With a wire whisk, gradually whisk in the warm half-and-half and warm milk; heat to boiling, whisking constantly. Reduce the heat and simmer, stirring occasionally, until the sauce has thickened and boils, about 5 minutes. Remove from the heat; stir in the corn, salt, and pepper.

2. In a 2-quart casserole, with a wire whisk, beat the eggs lightly. Slowly add the corn mixture, beating constantly.

3. Set the casserole in 13 × 9-inch baking pan; place the pan on an oven rack. Pour enough boiling water into the pan to come halfway up the sides of the casserole. Bake until a knife inserted in the center comes out clean, about 1 hour 15 minutes.

Each serving About 170 calories, 6g protein, 13g carbohydrate, 11g fat (6g saturated), 1g fiber, 315mg sodium.

roasted eggplant parmesan

PREP: 35 MIN / TOTAL: 1 HR 30 MIN, PLUS COOLING / SERVES 6

2 small eggplants (1¼ pounds each), ends trimmed, slice crosswise into ½-inch-thick pieces

¼ cup olive oil

Salt

1 can (28 ounces) plum tomatoes, drained and chopped

¼ teaspoon ground black pepper

⅓ cup chopped fresh parsley

4 ounces mozzarella cheese, shredded (1 cup)

½ cup freshly grated Parmesan cheese

1. Preheat the oven to 450°F. Place the eggplant slices on 2 large rimmed baking sheets. Brush oil on both sides and sprinkle with ¼ teaspoon salt. Roast 15 minutes; turn the slices and roast until browned and tender, 20 to 25 minutes longer.

2. Meanwhile, in a 12-inch nonstick skillet, combine the tomatoes, ¼ teaspoon salt, and the pepper; heat to boiling over medium heat. Reduce the heat to low; cook, stirring occasionally, until the tomatoes have thickened, about 20 minutes. Stir in the parsley.

3. Turn the oven control to 400°F. In a shallow 2½-quart casserole, layer half the eggplant and top it with half the tomato sauce; sprinkle with half the mozzarella. Repeat the layers; top with grated Parmesan.

4. Cover loosely with foil. Bake until bubbling, about 10 minutes. Remove the casserole from the oven and let it stand at least 10 minutes before serving. Serve hot or at room temperature.

Each serving About 250 calories, 11g protein, 19g carbohydrate, 16g fat (5g saturated), 6g fiber, 695mg sodium.

oven-braised fennel
with parmesan crust

PREP: 15 MIN / TOTAL: 1 HR / SERVES 8

- 3 medium fennel bulbs (about 1¼ pounds each)
- 1 cup chicken broth, heated
- ½ teaspoon salt
- ¼ teaspoon ground black pepper
- ¾ cup plain dried bread crumbs
- ¾ cup freshly grated Parmesan cheese
- 3 tablespoons extra-virgin olive oil

1. Preheat the oven to 400°F. Trim the root ends and remove the stalks from the fennel. Cut each fennel bulb lengthwise in half. Cut each half into 6 wedges. Arrange the wedges in a 13 × 9-inch baking dish.

2. Pour the broth over fennel; sprinkle with salt and pepper. Cover tightly with foil and bake 30 minutes.

3. In a small bowl, combine the bread crumbs, Parmesan, and oil.

4. Remove the foil from the baking dish. Sprinkle the bread crumb mixture over the fennel. Bake, uncovered, until the top browns and the fennel is tender, 15 minutes longer.

Each serving About 170 calories, 7g protein, 19g carbohydrate, 8g fat (2g saturated), 5g fiber, 575mg sodium.

#SavetheFood
fennel fronds & tops

Don't ditch those fronds and tops. They're a great addition to soups, or chop them and toss with cherry tomatoes and some balsamic for a salsa for chicken or fish.

GOOD TO KNOW

FENNEL

AVAILABILITY

Year-round

PEAK SEASON

September through April

BUYING TIPS

Fennel is also called *finocchio*. Buy firm, compact, unblemished bulbs. The fronds, if attached, should be bright green and sprightly.

TO STORE

Refrigerate in the crisper drawer up to three days.

TO PREPARE

Trim off the fronds, if attached. Rinse fennel under cold running water. Trim the root end and remove the stalks. Cut the bulb lengthwise into wedges or slices; trim the central core.

TO COOK

The mild licorice flavor and celery-like texture of fennel is accentuated by roasting. Layer with potatoes in a gratin, or braise.

butter-braised belgian endive

PREP: 5 MIN / TOTAL: 25 MIN / SERVES 6

4 tablespoons butter
½ teaspoon sugar
¼ teaspoon salt

6 large heads Belgian endive, each halved lengthwise

In a 12-inch skillet, melt the butter with the sugar and salt over medium-low heat. Arrange the endive in the skillet in one layer. Cover and cook, turning occasionally, until tender and lightly browned, about 15 minutes. Remove the cover; cook until half the liquid has evaporated, about 5 minutes longer.

Each serving About 80 calories, 1g protein, 2g carbohydrate, 8g fat (5g saturated), 2g fiber, 180mg sodium.

VEGETABLE PEELER HACKS

Don't underestimate this simple, swivel-bladed tool. For many kitchen tasks, it's handier than a knife (and because the sharp edges face inward, it's safer, too). To expand its repertoire, try these:

- **CREATE ELEGANT CHOCOLATE CURLS** or coconut shavings to garnish cakes and other desserts.

- **SHAVE CHEESE.** Make wisps of Parmesan or Pecorino Romano cheese to garnish your Caesar salad. Thinly slice semihard cheeses, like Cheddar or Gouda, for grilled cheese sandwiches and panini.

- **DON'T STOP AT THE PEEL. MAKE VEGETABLE NOODLES.** Shave zucchini or carrots lengthwise; sauté the ribbons in a bit of butter until tender for a yummy side dish.

BELGIAN ENDIVE

AVAILABILITY

Year-round

PEAK SEASON

September through May

BUYING TIPS

Choose small, compact heads with white leaves and pale-yellow or deep-red tips. Avoid wilted, brown-tipped, or green outer leaves or totally pale-green heads. (Belgian endive is grown in the dark; light turns the leaves green and bitter.)

TO STORE

Wrap in paper towels. Refrigerate in the crisper drawer up to one week.

TO PREPARE

Trim away any bruised leaves. Rinse briefly under cold running water; Belgian endive is usually quite clean. If using for salad, cut out the tough inner core.

TO COOK

Serve Belgian endive raw in salads or with dips, or braise.

leeks vinaigrette

PREP: 25 MIN / TOTAL: 35 MIN / SERVES 4

- 8 slender leeks (2½ pounds)
- Salt
- 1 tablespoon red wine vinegar
- 1 teaspoon Dijon mustard
- Pinch of ground black pepper
- 2 tablespoons olive oil
- 1 tablespoon chopped fresh parsley

1. In a 5-quart Dutch oven, heat 3 quarts water to boiling over high heat. Meanwhile, cut off the roots from the leeks and trim the leeks to 6 inches; discard the dark-green tops. Beginning at the light-green end, make a 4-inch-long slit in each leek, cutting almost halfway through, leaving 2 inches of the root end uncut. Rinse the leeks in a large bowl of cold water, swishing to remove the sand. Transfer to a colander to drain, leaving the sand in the bottom of the bowl. Discard sand.

2. Add the leeks and 2 teaspoons salt to the boiling water in the Dutch oven; cook until tender, about 10 minutes. Transfer the leeks to a colander; rinse with cold running water. Drain; pat dry.

3. Prepare the vinaigrette: In a small bowl and using a wire whisk, mix the vinegar, mustard, ⅛ teaspoon salt, and pepper until blended. In a thin, steady stream, whisk in the oil until blended, then whisk in the parsley.

4. Arrange the leeks on a serving platter in a single layer. Spoon the vinaigrette on top.

Each serving About 145 calories, 2g protein, 20g carbohydrate, 7g fat (1g saturated), 2g fiber, 425mg sodium.

GOOD TO KNOW

LEEKS

AVAILABILITY

Year-round

PEAK SEASON

April through September

BUYING TIPS

Buy leeks that are straight, with firm white roots and leafy green tops. Avoid leeks with wilted or yellowish tops or cracked roots.

TO STORE

Refrigerate in the crisper drawer up to 3 days.

TO PREPARE

Cut off the roots and trim the dark-green tops, leaving about 1 inch of the pale-green area. Leeks have sand hidden between their layers and should be washed carefully. Cut the leeks lengthwise, almost halfway through, leaving 2 to 3 inches of the root ends uncut. Rinse the leeks in a large bowl of cold water, swishing to remove all the sand. Or chop the trimmed leeks and swish in a bowl of cold water. With a slotted spoon, transfer to a colander to drain.

Buy clean, crisp (or tender) leaves, free of decay and dirt. Most are available year-round. In your farmers' market, you'll find tender spinach and chard in early summer and heartier greens in the fall. Coarse stems or bruised, dried, or yellowing leaves indicate poor quality. Popular greens for cooking include the following:

COLLARD GREENS Wide dark-green leaves with thick stems and a pronounced spiciness

DANDELION GREENS Spiky green leaves with a slight lemon flavor; sometimes served raw in salads

KALE Curly dark-green leaves with a mildly bitter taste; some purple or variegated kales are grown as ornamentals, but they are edible and have a milder flavor than regular kale. Varieties include Tuscan kale, lacinto, dinosaur, and Russian red kale.

MUSTARD GREENS Spicy and bitter, with large coarse leaves

SWISS CHARD Delicately flavored greens with wide curly leaves; the stems are edible but should be cut off and prepared separately. Red Swiss chard has red stems and veins.

BOK CHOY Mild-flavored white stalks and bright green leaves

BROCCOLI RABE Slightly bitter green

CHICORY Sometimes called curly endive; can be eaten raw or cooked like other bitter greens.

ESCAROLE Like chicory and Belgian endive, escarole's bitterness is its attraction. Look for broad heads of escarole with dark-green leaves.

NAPA OR CHINESE CABBAGE Although Chinese cabbage is cylindrical and Napa cabbage is roundish, they can be used interchangeably in most recipes.

SPINACH Packed curly spinach is more strongly flavored than loose-leaf spinach. Baby spinach, available in bags, has very tender, edible stems.

GOOD TO KNOW

___

GREENS GLOSSARY

TO STORE

Wrap greens loosely in paper towels and place in a plastic bag. Refrigerate in the crisper drawer up to two days.

TO PREPARE

Rinse in several changes of cool water to remove all the grit. Drain but do not shake dry. Trim any tough stems or ribs. Leave whole, or stack and cut into ½- to 1-inch-wide slices.

southern-style greens

PREP: 30 MIN / TOTAL: 1 HR 45 MIN / SERVES 10

5 pounds assorted greens, such as kale, collard greens, and mustard greens

1½ pounds smoked ham hocks

1 medium onion, quartered

8 cups water

1 teaspoon salt

Hot sauce, for serving

1. Trim and discard the stems and tough ribs from the greens; rinse well with cool running water. Cut into ½-inch pieces.

2. In an 8-quart saucepot, combine the ham hocks, onion, water, and salt; heat to boiling over high heat. Add the greens in batches, stirring to wilt. Return to boiling. Reduce the heat; cover and simmer until very tender, about 1 hour. Discard the ham hocks. Serve with hot sauce.

Each serving About 80 calories, 5g protein, 13g carbohydrate, 3g fat (1g saturated), 6g fiber, 560mg sodium.

fried okra

PREP: 15 MIN / TOTAL: 25 MIN / SERVES 4

1 large egg

12 ounces okra, cut crosswise into 1-inch pieces

½ cup cornmeal

½ teaspoon salt

⅛ teaspoon cayenne pepper

Vegetable oil, for frying

1. In a medium bowl, lightly beat the egg; add the okra and toss to coat. On waxed paper, combine the cornmeal, salt, and cayenne. Add the okra to the cornmeal mixture and toss to coat.

2. Meanwhile, in a heavy 10-inch skillet, heat ¼ inch oil over medium-high heat until hot. In small batches, fry the okra until golden, 2 to 3 minutes. With a slotted spoon, transfer to paper towels to drain.

Each serving About 205 calories, 5g protein, 20g carbohydrate, 12g fat (2g saturated), 3g fiber, 315mg sodium.

caramelized pearl onions

PREP: 15 MIN / TOTAL: 50 MIN / SERVES 10

2 pounds pearl onions

3 cups water

3 tablespoons butter or margarine

2 tablespoons sugar

½ teaspoon salt

1. Peel the onions, leaving a little bit of the root end attached to help the onions hold their shape.

2. In a 12-inch skillet, combine the onions and water; heat to boiling over high heat. Reduce the heat; cover and simmer until tender, 10 to 15 minutes. Drain well.

3. In the same skillet, melt the butter over medium heat. Add the onions, sugar, and salt; cook, shaking the skillet occasionally, until onions have browned, about 15 minutes.

Each serving About 70 calories, 1g protein, 10g carbohydrate, 4g fat (2g saturated), 2g fiber, 160mg sodium.

VARIATIONS

Caramelized Onions with Raisins

Prepare as directed, but add ½ cup golden raisins at the end of cooking; heat through.

Caramelized Shallots

Prepare as directed, but substitute shallots for onions.

creamed pearl onions

PREP: 20 MIN / TOTAL: 40 MIN / SERVES 10

1¼ pounds pearl onions
3 tablespoons butter
3 tablespoons all-
purpose flour
2 cups milk, warmed

¼ teaspoon salt
⅛ teaspoon ground
black pepper
Pinch of ground
nutmeg

1. In a 10-inch skillet, heat 1 inch water to boiling over high heat. Add the onions; heat to boiling. Reduce the heat; cover and simmer until tender, 10 to 15 minutes. Drain.

2. When cool enough to handle, peel the onions, leaving a little of the root end attached to help the onions hold their shape.

3. Meanwhile, prepare the white sauce: In a heavy 2-quart saucepan, melt the butter over low heat. Add the flour and cook, stirring, 1 minute. With a wire whisk, gradually whisk in the warm milk. Cook over medium heat, stirring constantly with a wooden spoon, until the sauce has thickened and boils. Reduce the heat and simmer, stirring frequently, 3 minutes. Stir in the salt, pepper, and nutmeg; remove from the heat.

4. Return the onions to the skillet. Add the white sauce and cook, stirring, until heated through.

Each serving About 90 calories, 2g protein, 8g carbohydrate, 5g fat (3g saturated), 1g fiber, 120mg sodium.

VARIATION

Creamed Onions & Peas

Prepare as directed, but add **1 package (10 ounces) frozen peas,** thawed, to the onions with the sauce.

sautéed green onions

PREP: 15 MIN / TOTAL: 25 MIN / SERVES 4

1 tablespoon vegetable
oil
5 bunches green onions,
cut into 2-inch pieces
(2½ cups)
½ teaspoon freshly
grated lemon zest

¼ teaspoon salt
⅛ teaspoon coarsely
ground black pepper
½ cup water

In a 12-inch skillet, heat the oil over medium-high heat. Add the green onions, lemon zest, salt, and pepper and cook, stirring frequently, 2 minutes. Add the water and cook, stirring, until the green onions are tender and lightly browned and the liquid has evaporated, 5 to 7 minutes longer.

Each serving About 50 calories, 1g protein, 5g carbohydrate, 4g fat (0g saturated), 2g fiber, 155mg sodium.

 *Serving Suggestion* Try these as a light side dish or as a topping for fish.

 **GLOSSARY** →

Green onions are the shoots of any onion before the bulb has formed. Scallions are the shoots of white onions, although in some parts of the United States, the word scallion is used to mean any green onion.

savory mushroom medley
with thyme

- 4 tablespoons butter
- 2 large shallots, finely chopped
- 1 pound white mushrooms, trimmed and quartered
- 8 ounces shiitake mushrooms, stems removed, cut into 1-inch-thick slices
- 8 ounces oyster mushrooms, cut in half if large
- 2 cloves garlic, finely chopped
- 1 teaspoon fresh thyme leaves, plus sprigs for garnish
- 12 teaspoon salt
- ¼ teaspoon ground black pepper

In a deep 12-inch skillet, heat the butter over medium-high heat. Add the shallots; cook, stirring, 1 minute, Stir in all the mushrooms, garlic, thyme, salt, and pepper; cook 12 to 15 minutes, or until the mushrooms are tender and browned and the liquid has evaporated, stirring frequently.

Each serving About 85 calories, 3g protein, 7g carbohydrate, 6g fat (4g saturated), 1g fiber, 205mg sodium.

GOOD TO KNOW

MUSHROOMS

- Mushrooms will sweat and deteriorate more quickly if left enclosed in plastic. Remove mushrooms from plastic. Place in a brown paper bag. Refrigerate up to three days.

- Mushrooms are very porous and will quickly absorb water, so do not submerge in water. Wipe them with a moist paper towel to remove any surface dirt. Do not peel. Remove the tough stems of shiitake mushrooms; just trim the stem ends of other varieties.

sautéed mixed mushrooms

- 2 tablespoons butter
- ¼ cup minced shallots
- 8 ounces white mushrooms, trimmed and quartered
- 4 ounces shiitake mushrooms, stems removed and caps cut into 1-inch-thick slices
- 4 ounces oyster mushrooms, cut in half if large
- ¼ teaspoon salt
- ⅛ teaspoon ground black pepper
- ⅛ teaspoon dried thyme
- 1 small clove garlic, finely chopped
- 1 tablespoon chopped fresh parsley

In a 12-inch skillet, melt the butter over medium-high heat. Add the shallots and cook, stirring, 1 minute. Stir in all the mushrooms. Sprinkle with salt, pepper, and thyme and cook, stirring frequently, until the mushrooms are tender and any liquid has evaporated, about 8 minutes. Stir in the garlic and parsley and cook 1 minute longer.

Each serving About 85 calories, 3g protein, 7g carbohydrate, 6g fat (4g saturated), 2g fiber, 210mg sodium.

lemon-marinated mushrooms

- 1 pound small white mushrooms, trimmed and cut into quarters
- ¼ cup minced shallots
- ¼ cup chopped fresh parsley
- 5 tablespoons olive oil
- 4 teaspoons fresh lemon juice
- ½ teaspoon salt
- ¼ teaspoon ground black pepper

In a large bowl, combine the mushrooms, shallots, parsley, oil, lemon juice, salt, and pepper until mixed. Let stand at room temperature 1 hour, stirring occasionally. Serve immediately or refrigerate up to 6 hours.

Each serving About 125 calories, 2g protein, 5g carbohydrate, 12g fat (2g saturated), 1g fiber, 200mg sodium.

savory tomato tart

PREP: 45 MIN / TOTAL: 1 HR 15 MIN / SERVES 6

Pastry for an 11-Inch Tart (page 664)

1 tablespoon olive oil

3 medium onions, thinly sliced

Salt

1 package (3½ ounces) goat cheese

2 ripe medium red tomatoes (8 ounces each), cored and cut into ¼-inch-thick slices

1 ripe medium yellow tomato (8 ounces), cored and cut into ¼-inch-thick slices

½ teaspoon coarsely ground black pepper

¼ cup Kalamata olives, pitted and chopped

1. Preheat the oven to 425°F. Prepare the dough for an 11-inch tart and use it to line a tart pan (with a removable bottom). Line the tart shell with foil; fill with pie weights or dry beans. Bake 15 minutes. Remove the foil and weights and bake until golden, 5 to 10 minutes longer. If the shell puffs up during baking, gently press it down with the back of a spoon.

2. Meanwhile, in a 12-inch nonstick skillet, heat the oil over medium heat. Add the onions and ¼ teaspoon salt; cook, stirring frequently, until very tender, about 20 minutes.

3. Turn the oven control to broil. Spread the onions over the bottom of the tart shell and crumble half the goat cheese on top. Arrange the red and yellow tomato slices, alternating colors, in concentric circles over the onion-cheese mixture. Sprinkle with ¼ teaspoon salt and the pepper. Crumble the remaining goat cheese on top of the tart.

4. Place the tart on a rack in a broiling pan. Place the pan under the broiler about 7 inches from the heat source. Broil until the cheese has melted and the tomatoes are heated through, 6 to 8 minutes. Sprinkle with olives. Carefully remove the side of the tart pan. Serve hot or at room temperature.

Each serving About 420 calories, 8g protein, 33g carbohydrate, 29g fat (15g saturated), 4g fiber, 755mg sodium.

skillet cherry tomatoes

PREP: 5 MIN / TOTAL: 10 MIN / SERVES 4

1 tablespoon butter

1 pint ripe cherry or grape tomatoes

⅛ teaspoon salt

Chopped fresh parsley or basil

In a 10-inch skillet, melt the butter over medium-high heat. Add the cherry tomatoes and salt and cook, shaking the skillet frequently, just until heated through and the skins split, about 2 minutes. Sprinkle with parsley.

Each serving About 35 calories, 0g protein, 2g carbohydrate, 3g fat (2g saturated), 1g fiber, 110mg sodium.

VARIATION

Skillet Cherry Tomatoes with Garlic

Prepare as directed, but add **1 clove garlic**, finely chopped, to the skillet with the butter.

cherry tomato gratin

PREP: 10 MIN / TOTAL: 30 MIN / SERVES 6

¼ cup plain dried bread crumbs

¼ cup freshly grated Parmesan cheese

1 clove garlic, crushed with a garlic press

¼ teaspoon coarsely ground black pepper

1 tablespoon olive oil

2 pints ripe cherry or grape tomatoes

2 tablespoons chopped fresh parsley

1. Preheat the oven to 425°F. In a small bowl, combine the bread crumbs, Parmesan, garlic, pepper, and oil until blended.

2. Place the cherry tomatoes in a shallow 1½-quart casserole or 9-inch deep-dish pie plate. Top with the bread crumb mixture and sprinkle with parsley. Bake until heated through and the crumbs have browned, about 20 minutes.

Each serving About 70 calories, 3g protein, 7g carbohydrate, 4g fat (1g saturated), 2g fiber, 120mg sodium.

broiled parmesan tomatoes

PREP: 10 MIN / TOTAL: 15 MIN / SERVES 4

1 tablespoon butter

1 clove garlic, finely chopped

¼ cup freshly grated Parmesan cheese

4 small ripe plum tomatoes (3 ounces each), each cut lengthwise in half

1. Preheat the broiler. In a 1-quart saucepan, melt the butter over low heat. Add the garlic and cook, stirring, until golden; remove from heat.

2. Spread the Parmesan on waxed paper. Dip the cut side of each tomato in the garlic butter, then in the Parmesan; place the tomatoes, cheese side up, on a rack in the broiling pan. Sprinkle any remaining Parmesan on top; drizzle with any remaining garlic butter.

3. Place the pan under the broiler at the closest position to the heat source. Broil until the Parmesan is golden, 3 to 4 minutes.

Each serving About 70 calories, 3g protein, 4g carbohydrate, 5g fat (3g saturated), 1g fiber, 150mg sodium.

fried green tomatoes

PREP: 20 MIN / TOTAL: 40 MIN / SERVES 6

6 slices bacon

1 large egg white

¼ teaspoon salt

½ cup cornmeal

¼ teaspoon coarsely ground black pepper

3 medium green tomatoes (1 pound), cut into scant ½-inch-thick slices

1. In a 12-inch skillet, cook the bacon over medium heat until browned. With tongs, transfer the bacon to paper towels to drain and cool; crumble. Set aside the skillet with the bacon drippings.

2. In a pie plate, beat the egg white and salt. On waxed paper, combine the cornmeal and pepper. Dip the tomatoes in the egg mixture to coat both sides, then dip them into the cornmeal mixture, pressing so the mixture adheres. Place aside on waxed paper.

3. Heat the bacon drippings in the skillet over medium-high heat. In batches, cook the tomatoes until golden brown, about 1½ minutes per side, transferring them to paper towels to drain.

4. Transfer the tomatoes to a platter and top with bacon.

Each serving About 190 calories, 4g protein, 13g carbohydrate, 13g fat (5g saturated), 1g fiber, 270mg sodium.

GOOD TO KNOW

———

TOMATOES V. TOMATILLOS

What's the difference between green tomatoes and tomatillos?

- Traditional green tomatoes are hard, unripe tomatoes and are available at the beginning of tomato season (early summer). They are usually not eaten raw but can be fried, pickled, used in soups, and more. Heirloom varieties like Green Zebra and Green Envy are fully ripe when green.

- Tomatillos are a completely different fruit and are related to the Cape Gooseberry. Sometimes called a Mexican husk tomato, they are covered in a brown papery husk. Tomatillos have solid flesh and many tiny seeds. They can be eaten raw or cooked.

—

BELL PEPPERS

AVAILABILITY

Year-round

BUYING TIPS

Buy peppers that are firm, shiny, and thick-fleshed. Avoid wilted or flabby peppers with cuts or soft spots. Red peppers are mature (ripe) green peppers, but yellow, orange, and purple peppers are different varieties. Long pale green Italian frying peppers are mild flavored and a good substitute for green peppers.

TO STORE

Refrigerate in the crisper drawer up to one week.

TO PREPARE

Rinse peppers under cold running water. Trim the stem end and remove the seeds and white membranes (ribs).

roasted peppers
with basil

PREP: 20 MIN / TOTAL: 35 MIN / SERVES 6

- 2 large red bell peppers
- 2 large yellow bell peppers
- 1 tablespoon extra-virgin olive oil
- ¼ teaspoon salt
- ⅛ teaspoon ground black pepper
- 3 large fresh basil leaves, thinly sliced

1. Preheat the broiler. Line a broiling pan with foil. Cut each bell pepper lengthwise in half; remove and discard the stems and seeds. Arrange the peppers, cut side down, in the prepared broiling pan. Place the pan under the broiler, 5 to 6 inches from the heat source. Broil, without turning, until the skin is charred and blistered, 8 to 10 minutes.

2. Wrap the peppers in foil and allow them to steam at room temperature 15 minutes or until cool enough to handle.

3. Remove peppers from the foil. Peel the skin and discard.

4. Cut the peppers lengthwise into ½-inch-wide strips. Pat dry with paper towels.

5. Place the pepper strips on a serving platter; drizzle with oil and sprinkle with salt and pepper. To serve, top with basil leaves, or cover and refrigerate overnight.

Each serving About 40 calories, 1g protein, 4g carbohydrate, 2g fat (0g saturated), 1g fiber, 100mg sodium.

Ingredient Ideas
roasted peppers

Add an instant taste of summer to savory winter dishes
with a peck of bright peppers. When you can't—
or don't have time—to grill them yourself,
grab a 12-ounce jar off the pantry shelf, drain well, chop,
and try them in one of these quick recipes.
Each idea below uses one jar's worth of peppers.

ROASTED CAULIFLOWER

Preheat the oven to 450°F. On a foil-lined 15½ × 10½-inch rimmed baking sheet, place **1 head cauliflower**, cut into small florets. Drizzle with **2 tablespoons olive oil** and sprinkle with **2 teaspoons chopped fresh rosemary leaves**; toss to coat. Spread in a single layer and roast 20 minutes, or until the cauliflower is browned and tender, stirring once. Add the **red peppers** to the cauliflower in the pan; toss to combine, then spread evenly. Sprinkle with ½ **cup freshly grated Parmesan cheese** and roast 5 minutes longer, or until the cheese melts. Serves 6.

ARTICHOKE DIP

From **1 lemon**, grate 1 teaspoon zest and squeeze 2 tablespoons juice. In a bowl, stir the lemon zest and juice with **1 tub (8 ounces) vegetable-flavored cream cheese spread**, ½ **cup chopped fresh basil leaves**, and ½ **teaspoon ground black pepper** until combined. Stir in **1 can (14 ounces) artichoke hearts**, well drained and chopped, and the **red peppers**. Serve with **vegetable sticks**. Makes 3 cups.

PASTA PUTTANESCA

In a medium saucepot, cook **1 pound farfalle pasta** as the label directs. Meanwhile, in a 2-quart saucepan, heat **2 cups bottled tomato-basil sauce**, the **red peppers**, ⅓ **cup chopped Kalamata olives**, ¼ **cup chopped fresh parsley leaves**, and ½ **teaspoon ground black pepper** to boiling over medium-high heat. Reduce the heat to low and simmer 4 minutes. Drain the farfalle; return to the saucepot. Pour the sauce over the pasta and toss well. Serves 6.

PEPPER & EGG SANDWICHES

Spray a 12-inch nonstick skillet with **nonstick cooking spray**; heat over medium heat 1 minute. Chop **1 large sweet onion** and cook, covered, 10 minutes or until lightly browned, stirring occasionally. Meanwhile, in a bowl, whisk together **8 large eggs**, ½ **teaspoon salt**, and ¼ **teaspoon ground black pepper**. Add the **red peppers** to the onion in the skillet. Pour the eggs over the vegetables; cover and cook 8 minutes or until almost set, stirring occasionally. Sprinkle with **4 ounces shredded provolone cheese** (1 cup); cover and cook 2 minutes, or until cheese melts. Spoon the egg mixture into **four 6-inch hero rolls**, split. Serves 4.

CHICKEN MARSALA

In a 12-inch skillet, heat **2 teaspoons canola oil** over medium heat until hot. Add **1 pound chicken breast tenders**, each cut crosswise in half, and cook 6 minutes, or until golden on all sides. Add the **red peppers**, ¼ **cup Marsala wine**, **4 sliced green onions**, ¼ **teaspoon salt**, and ⅛ **teaspoon ground black pepper**. Increase the heat to medium-high and cook, stirring occasionally, 3 to 4 minutes, or until the liquid is slightly reduced and the chicken is no longer pink inside. Serve with **brown rice**. Serves 4.

PLANTAINS

AVAILABILITY

Year-round

BUYING TIPS

Plantains are related to the banana, but they aren't as sweet. Unripe green plantains are very hard and starchy and are usually boiled. Ripe yellow plantains have a mild banana-like flavor. Very ripe plantains have dark-brown to black skin and are slightly sweet.

TO STORE

Store plantains at room temperature. Ripen in a brown bag for several days if needed. Refrigerate if they are very ripe.

TO PREPARE

Cut plantains crosswise into three or four pieces. Score the peel along the ridges, down to the flesh. Pull the peel away from the flesh and cut into pieces as directed.

pureed parsnips

PREP: 15 MIN / TOTAL: 30 MIN / SERVES 8

2½ pounds parsnips, peeled and cut into 1-inch pieces

1 cup milk, warmed

4 tablespoons butter or margarine, softened

1 teaspoon salt

2 tablespoons chopped fresh parsley (optional)

1. In a 4-quart saucepan, combine the parsnips and enough water to cover; heat to boiling over high heat. Reduce the heat; cover and simmer until tender, about 15 minutes. Drain.

2. In a food processor with the knife blade attached, combine the parsnips, warm milk, butter, and salt and puree until smooth. Serve hot, sprinkled with parsley, if desired.

Each serving About 165 calories, 3g protein, 23g carbohydrate, 7g fat (4g saturated), 6g fiber, 380mg sodium.

golden sautéed plantains

PREP: 10 MIN / TOTAL: 30 MIN / SERVES 8

4 tablespoons butter

4 very ripe plantains (2¼ pounds), peeled and cut on the

diagonal into ½-inch-thick slices

½ teaspoon salt, or 1 tablespoon brown sugar

In a 12-inch skillet, melt 2 tablespoons butter over medium-high heat. Add half the plantains and cook until lightly browned, about 5 minutes per side. Transfer to a warm platter; sprinkle lightly with half the salt or brown sugar. Keep warm. Repeat with remaining plantains, butter, and salt or brown sugar.

Each serving About 150 calories, 1g protein, 26g carbohydrate, 6g fat (4g saturated), 2g fiber, 210mg sodium.

 Tip If you can't find plantains, substitute very green unripe bananas; the cooking time may be slightly shorter.

peppered honey turnips

PREP: 15 MIN / TOTAL: 25 MIN / SERVES 12

- ½ cup chicken broth
- ¼ cup white wine
- 2 tablespoons butter
- 1 teaspoon salt
- ½ teaspoon coarsely ground black pepper
- 3 pounds small turnips, peeled and each cut into 8 wedges
- ¼ cup honey

1. In a 12-inch skillet, heat the broth, wine, butter, salt, and pepper to boiling over medium-high heat.

2. Add the turnips and cook, stirring occasionally, until most of the liquid has evaporated, 10 to 12 minutes. Stir in the honey; cook, stirring frequently, until the turnips are very tender and browned, 13 to 15 minutes longer.

Each serving About 65 calories, 1g protein, 12g carbohydrate, 2g fat (1g saturated), 2g fiber, 315mg sodium.

mashed root vegetables

PREP: 15 MIN / TOTAL: 40 MIN / SERVES 8

- 2 pounds root vegetables, such as carrots, white turnips, or rutabaga, peeled and cut into 1-inch pieces (5 cups)
- 1 pound all-purpose potatoes (3 medium), peeled and cut into 1-inch pieces
- Salt
- 3 tablespoons butter cut into pieces
- ¼ teaspoon ground black pepper
- Pinch of ground nutmeg

1. In a 4-quart saucepan, combine the root vegetables, potatoes, enough water to cover, and 2 teaspoons salt; heat to boiling over high heat. Reduce the heat; cover and simmer until the vegetables are tender, about 15 minutes. Drain.

2. Return the vegetables to the saucepan. Add the butter, ½ teaspoon salt, pepper, and nutmeg; mash until smooth.

Each serving About 120 calories, 2g protein, 18g carbohydrate, 5g fat (3g saturated), 4g fiber, 535mg sodium.

crispy roasted potatoes
with caper vinaigrette

(See photo on page 412.)

PREP: 20 MIN / TOTAL: 1 HR / SERVES 8

- 2½ pounds Yukon Gold potatoes, unpeeled, cut into 1-inch chunks
- 1½ pounds sweet potatoes, unpeeled, cut into 1-inch chunks
- Salt
- 5 tablespoons olive oil
- ¼ cup fresh flat-leaf parsley leaves, finely chopped
- ¼ cup sherry vinegar
- 3 tablespoons capers, drained and chopped
- 1 tablespoon anchovy paste
- 1 clove garlic, crushed with a garlic press

1. In a 7- to 8-quart saucepot, cover the Yukon Gold and sweet potatoes with cold water. Stir in 2 tablespoons salt. Partially cover and heat to boiling over high heat. Reduce the heat to maintain a simmer; cook 7 minutes, stirring occasionally. Drain well; return to the pot. The potatoes can be parboiled and held at room temperature up to 2 hours before roasting.

2. While the potatoes simmer, preheat the oven to 450°F. Vigorously toss the potatoes with 4 tablespoons oil; arrange them in a single layer on 2 large rimmed baking sheets. Roast 20 minutes, or until golden brown and crisp, rotating the sheets between the racks halfway through and stirring once or twice.

3. Meanwhile, in a large bowl, whisk the parsley, vinegar, capers, anchovy paste, garlic, the remaining 1 tablespoon oil, and ½ teaspoon salt. Toss the roasted potatoes with the vinaigrette until well coated.

Each serving About 265 calories, 5g protein, 41g carbohydrate, 9g fat (1g saturated), 5g fiber, 485mg sodium.

basic mashed potatoes

PREP: 25 MIN / TOTAL: 55 MIN / SERVES 8

3 pounds all-purpose potatoes (9 medium), peeled and cut into 1-inch pieces

4 tablespoons butter, cut into pieces

1½ teaspoons salt

1 cup milk, warmed

1. In a 4-quart saucepan, combine the potatoes and enough water to cover; heat to boiling over high heat. Reduce the heat; cover and simmer until tender, about 15 minutes. Drain.

2. Return the potatoes to the saucepan. Mash the potatoes with the butter and salt. Gradually add the warm milk; continue to mash until smooth and well blended. Keep warm.

Each serving About 205 calories, 4g protein, 32g carbohydrate, 7g fat (4g saturated), 3g fiber, 515mg sodium.

VARIATIONS

Mashed Potatoes with Garlic & Lemon

Prepare as directed in step 1. Meanwhile, with a garlic press, press **2 cloves garlic** into a 1-quart saucepan with the butter and salt. Cook, stirring, over low heat until the butter has melted and the garlic is golden, 2 to 3 minutes. Add the garlic mixture to the mashed potatoes with the milk; mash. Stir in **2 tablespoons finely chopped parsley** and **1 teaspoon freshly grated lemon zest**.

Horseradish Mashed Potatoes

Prepare as directed, but add **2 tablespoons bottled white horseradish** with the milk.

Parsnip & Potato Mash

Prepare as directed, but substitute **1 pound parsnips**, peeled and cut into 1-inch pieces, for 1 pound potatoes and use only ¾ **cup milk**.

Caramelized Onion Mash

Prepare as directed in step 1. Meanwhile, heat ¼ **cup olive oil** in a 12-inch skillet over medium heat. Add **4 large red onions** (about 3 pounds), thinly sliced, and ¼ **teaspoon salt**. Cook, stirring occasionally, until very tender and deep golden brown, about 30 minutes. In step 2, omit the butter and use only ½ **cup milk**; coarsely mash the potatoes. Stir all but 3 tablespoons caramelized onions into the potatoes; heat through. Top with the remaining caramelized onions.

Ingredient Ideas

mashed potatoes mix-ins

Try these four mix-ins in the Basic Mashed Potatoes recipe (left).

CHEESY CHIVE MASH Fold 2 cups shredded extra-sharp Cheddar cheese and ¼ cup snipped fresh chives into Basic Mashed Potatoes until well mixed.

ZINGY BACON MASH Fold 6 strips crumbled cooked bacon, 3 tablespoons bottled horseradish, and 3 tablespoons chopped fresh flat-leaf parsley into Basic Mashed Potatoes until well mixed.

SPICY 'N' SMOKY MASH Fold 2 cups frozen corn, thawed, ⅔ cup reduced-fat sour cream, and 2 tablespoons chopped chipotles in adobo sauce into Basic Mashed Potatoes until well mixed.

GARLICKY HERB Fold ¼ cup chopped fresh basil leaves, 1 cup grated Parmesan cheese, and 2 cloves garlic, finely chopped, into Basic Mashed Potatoes until well mixed.

---

herb roasted potatoes

PREP: 15 MIN / TOTAL: 45 MIN / SERVES 6

2 tablespoons butter

1 tablespoon chopped fresh parsley

½ teaspoon freshly grated lemon zest

½ teaspoon salt

⅛ teaspoon coarsely ground black pepper

1½ pounds small red potatoes, cut in half

1. Preheat the oven to 450°F. In a 3-quart saucepan, melt the butter with the parsley, lemon zest, salt, and pepper over medium-low heat. Remove the saucepan from the heat; add the potatoes and toss to coat thoroughly.

2. Place the potato mixture in the center of a 24 × 18-inch sheet of heavy-duty foil. Fold the edges over and pinch them to seal tightly.

3. Place the package in a jelly-roll pan and bake until the potatoes are tender when they are pierced (through the foil) with a knife, about 30 minutes.

Each serving About 125 calories, 2g protein, 20g carbohydrate, 4g fat (2g saturated), 2g fiber, 240mg sodium.

scalloped potatoes

PREP: 30 MIN / TOTAL: 2 HR / SERVES 6

3 tablespoons butter	⅛ teaspoon ground black pepper
1 small onion, chopped	
3 tablespoons all-purpose flour	2 pounds all-purpose potatoes (6 medium), peeled and thinly sliced
1½ cups milk, warmed	
1 teaspoon salt	

1. Preheat the oven to 375°F. In a heavy 2-quart saucepan, melt the butter over low heat. Add the onion and cook until tender, about 5 minutes. Add the flour and cook, stirring, 1 minute. With a wire whisk, gradually whisk in the warm milk. Cook over medium heat, stirring constantly with a wooden spoon, until the sauce has thickened and boils. Reduce the heat and simmer, stirring frequently, 1 minute. Stir in the salt and pepper; remove from the heat.

2. Grease a 9-inch square baking dish or shallow 2-quart casserole. Arrange half the potatoes in a single layer in the prepared dish; pour half the sauce on top. Repeat the layers. Cover and bake 1 hour. Remove the cover and bake until the potatoes are tender and the top is golden, about 30 minutes longer.

Each serving About 200 calories, 5g protein, 28g carbohydrate, 8g fat (5g saturated), 3g fiber, 485mg sodium.

oven fries

PREP: 10 MIN / TOTAL: 50 MIN / SERVES 4

3 medium baking potatoes (about 1½ pounds), unpeeled	½ teaspoon salt
1 tablespoon vegetable oil	⅛ teaspoon ground black pepper

1. Preheat the oven to 425°F. Cut each potato lengthwise into quarters, then cut each quarter lengthwise into 3 wedges.

2. In a jelly-roll pan, toss the potatoes, oil, salt, and pepper to coat. Bake, turning occasionally, until tender, 35 to 40 minutes.

Each serving About 155 calories, 4g protein, 28g carbohydrate, 4g fat (0g saturated), 4g fiber, 300mg sodium.

VARIATION

Sweet Potato Oven Fries

Replace the potatoes with **3 sweet potatoes**. If potatoes are very long, cut each crosswise in half before proceeding. Replace the pepper with cayenne pepper.

TESTING NOTE To avoid soggy oven fries, buy Idaho or russet potatoes; their high-starch and low-water content gives fries a crisp exterior. And don't store potatoes in the fridge; the starch will turn to sugar, leading to sogginess. Use a baking sheet with low or no sides for best browning, and don't overcrowd them, or the potatoes will steam.

scalloped hasselback potatoes
with cheddar

PREP: 30 MIN / TOTAL: 2 HR 30 MIN / SERVES 10

- 6 ounces shredded extra-sharp Cheddar cheese
- 4 ounces shredded pepper Jack cheese
- 1 cup heavy or whipping cream
- 3 cloves garlic, crushed with a garlic press
- 1 tablespoon packed fresh rosemary leaves, chopped
- 1¼ teaspoons salt
- ½ teaspoon ground black pepper
- 4 pounds russet or Idaho potatoes, peeled

1. Preheat the oven to 450°F. Line a rimmed baking sheet with foil. Grease a shallow 2-quart oval baking dish.

2. In a large bowl, combine the Cheddar and pepper Jack cheeses; transfer one-third to a small bowl and set aside. To the large bowl with the cheeses, add the cream, garlic, rosemary, salt, and pepper.

3. Slice the potatoes very thinly; place them in the bowl with the cream mixture. With your hands, toss until every potato slice is well coated. Arrange the slices in the prepared baking dish until the entire dish is tightly packed (some slices may not fit). Pour the remaining cream mixture over the potatoes.

4. Place the baking dish on the prepared baking sheet. Cover the dish tightly with foil; bake 1 hour. Remove the foil and sprinkle the top with the reserved cheeses. Bake 55 minutes to 1 hour 15 minutes, or until the potatoes are very tender and the top is golden brown. Let stand at least 15 minutes before serving.

Each serving About 365 calories, 10g protein, 39g carbohydrate, 19g fat (11g saturated), 3g fiber, 475mg sodium.

roasted-garlic mashed potatoes & cauliflower

PREP: 15 MIN / TOTAL: 1 HR 45 MIN / SERVES 10

- 1 head garlic
- 1 tablespoon olive oil
- 2 pounds Yukon Gold potatoes, peeled and cut into 1-inch chunks
- Salt
- 1 medium head cauliflower (about 2 pounds), cut into large florets
- ⅔ cup half-and-half
- 6 tablespoons butter
- Snipped fresh chives, for garnish (optional)

1. Preheat the oven to 375°F. Cut off the top third of the garlic head. Place both pieces of the garlic head in a sheet of foil, cut sides up, and drizzle with oil. Reassemble the head; wrap in foil, crimping and sealing it tightly. Place on a small baking sheet. Bake 1 hour to 1 hour 10 minutes, or until deep golden brown and very soft. Remove from the oven; cool completely.

2. While the garlic cools, in a 7- to 8-quart saucepot, place the potatoes with enough water to cover by 2 inches and 1 tablespoon salt. Partially cover and heat to boiling over high heat. Reduce the heat; simmer 10 minutes. Add the cauliflower; heat to boiling again, then reduce the heat. Simmer 20 minutes, or until cauliflower and potatoes are very tender. Drain well.

3. Meanwhile, in a small microwave-safe bowl, microwave the half-and-half and butter on High 30 seconds, or until the butter has melted; squeeze the roasted garlic cloves from the skins into this mixture.

4. Mash the potatoes and cauliflower with the half-and-half mixture and ½ teaspoon salt until smooth. Garnish with chives, if desired. Serve immediately.

Each serving About 175 calories, 3g protein, 19g carbohydrate, 10g fat (6g saturated), 2g fiber, 255mg sodium.

CHEESY HASSELBACKS 454

SCALLOPED HASSELBACK POTATOES WITH CHEDDAR 452

CRISPY GOLDEN SMASHED POTATOES 454

ROASTED-GARLIC MASHED POTATOES & CAULIFLOWER 452

cheesy hasselbacks

(See photo on page 453.)

PREP: 25 MIN / TOTAL: 1 HR 40 MIN / SERVES 6

- 6 medium (3 pounds) russet potatoes
- 3 tablespoons olive oil
- Salt
- 4 ounces Cheddar, cut into thin sticks
- Sour cream, chives, and crumbled bacon, for serving (optional)

1. Preheat the oven to 425°F. Thinly slice the potatoes, but don't cut them all the way through. Place the potatoes on a prepared baking sheet. Brush them with 1½ tablespoons olive oil; bake for 30 minutes.

2. Remove the potatoes from the oven. Brush the potatoes with the remaining 1½ tablespoons oil. Sprinkle with salt. Bake 30 minutes more or until tender.

3. When tender, remove the potatoes from the oven. Stuff Cheddar between the slices in the potato. Bake until cheese melts, about 10 minutes. To serve, top each potato with sour cream, chives, and crumbled bacon, if desired.

Each serving About 315 calories, 9g protein, 41g carbohydrate, 13g fat (5g saturated), 3g fiber, 230mg sodium.

baby potatoes
with rosemary

PREP: 20 MIN / TOTAL: 50 MIN / SERVES 10

- 5 pounds assorted small potatoes, such as red, white, purple, or golden, cut in half
- ¼ cup olive oil
- 2 tablespoons chopped fresh rosemary or
- thyme, or 1 teaspoon dried rosemary or thyme
- 1½ teaspoons salt
- ½ teaspoon coarsely ground black pepper

Preheat the oven to 425°F. In a large roasting pan (17 × 11½ inches), toss all ingredients. Roast the potatoes, turning occasionally, until golden and tender, 30 to 40 minutes.

Each serving About 230 calories, 4g protein, 41g carbohydrate, 6g fat (1g saturated), 3g fiber, 365mg sodium.

crispy golden smashed potatoes

(See photo on page 453.)

PREP: 10 MIN / TOTAL: 1 HR 25 MIN / SERVES 10

- 2½ pounds small red potatoes (each about 2 inches in diameter)
- Salt
- Nonstick cooking spray
- 3 tablespoons butter, melted
- Finely chopped fresh parsley, for garnish

1. In a large saucepot, combine the potatoes, 1 tablespoon salt, and enough water to cover by 2 inches. Cover; heat to boiling over high heat. Reduce the heat to medium-low. Uncover; simmer 30 minutes, or until tender, adjusting the heat to maintain a simmer. Drain well.

2. Preheat the oven to 450°F. Spray a large baking sheet with cooking spray. Place each potato on the baking sheet and, with a stiff, wide spatula, gently press on it until it's crushed but still intact. Spray the tops of the potatoes generously with cooking spray. Roast 25 minutes. Spray the potatoes once more with cooking spray.

3. Preheat the broiler to High, then broil the potatoes 2 to 5 minutes, or until golden brown and crisp. Sprinkle the potatoes with ¼ teaspoon salt and arrange them on a serving platter. Drizzle with the melted butter and sprinkle with parsley.

Each serving About 115 calories, 2g protein, 18g carbohydrate, 4g fat (2g saturated), 2g fiber, 135mg sodium.

super-creamy potatoes

PREP: 15 MIN / TOTAL: 40 MIN / SERVES 12

- 4 pounds Yukon Gold potatoes, peeled and cut into halves
- Salt
- ¾ cup heavy or whipping cream
- ¾ cup whole milk
- 6 tablespoons butter, cut into pieces

1. In a 7- to 8-quart saucepot, combine the potatoes, enough cold water to cover by 1 inch, and 3 tablespoons salt. Partially cover and heat to simmering over high heat. Remove the cover and simmer 20 to 25 minutes, or until the potatoes are very tender but not falling apart, stirring occasionally.

2. Meanwhile, in a 4-cup microwave-safe measuring cup, combine the cream, milk, and butter. Microwave on High 1 minute, or until the butter melts.

3. Drain the potatoes well; return them to the empty pot. Mash the potatoes or put them through a ricer. Stir in the warm milk mixture and ½ teaspoon salt. Serve warm.

Each serving About 235 calories, 4g protein, 28g carbohydrate, 12g fat (7g saturated), 2g fiber, 260mg sodium.

baked potatoes

PREP: 5 MIN / TOTAL: 50 MIN / SERVES 6

- 6 medium baking potatoes (8 ounces each), unpeeled
- Your choice of toppings: sour cream, butter,
- shredded Cheddar cheese, snipped fresh chives, crumbled cooked bacon (optional)

1. Preheat the oven to 450°F. Wash the potatoes and dry with paper towels; pierce each one with a fork. Place the potatoes directly on an oven rack and bake until tender, about 45 minutes. If desired, slash the top of the potatoes; serve with your choice of toppings.

TWICE-BAKED POTATOES Bake the potatoes as directed. Cut them lengthwise in half. Scoop the potato flesh into a bowl; reserve shells. Mash the potatoes with **4 tablespoons butter**, cut into pieces. Stir in **2 cups ricotta or cottage cheese, 1 cup shredded sharp Cheddar cheese, ½ teaspoon salt**, and **¼ teaspoon coarsely ground black pepper**. Divide and spoon the mixture into the reserved potato shells, mounding it slightly. Place in a jelly-roll pan; sprinkle with ½ **cup shredded sharp Cheddar cheese**. Bake in a preheated 450°F oven 10 minutes longer. **Serves 12.**

BAKED POTATOES Each serving (without toppings) About 165 calories, 3g protein, 38g carbohydrate, 0g fat (0g saturated), 4g fiber, 10mg sodium.
TWICE-BAKED POTATOES Each serving About 245 calories, 10g protein, 21g carbohydrate, 14g fat (9g saturated), 2g fiber, 265mg sodium.

kale & horseradish potatoes

PREP: 20 MIN / TOTAL: 1 HR / SERVES 12

- 4 pounds Yukon Gold potatoes, peeled and cut into halves
- Salt
- ½ cup butter, cut into pieces
- 1 bunch curly kale, tough stems removed, chopped
- 3 green onions, thinly sliced (6 tablespoons)
- 1 cup whole milk
- ½ cup reduced-fat sour cream
- ¼ cup bottled horseradish, drained

1. In a 7- to 8-quart saucepot, combine the potatoes, enough cold water to cover by 1 inch, and 3 tablespoons salt. Partially cover and heat to simmering over high heat. Remove the cover and simmer 20 to 25 minutes, or until the potatoes are very tender but not falling apart, stirring occasionally.

2. Meanwhile, in a 3-quart saucepan, melt the butter over medium heat. Add the kale, 1 tablespoons water, and ½ teaspoon salt. Cover and cook 3 to 4 minutes, or until tender, stirring occasionally. Stir in the green onions; cook 2 minutes Remove from the heat.

3. Drain the potatoes well; return to the empty pot. Mash the potatoes or put them through a ricer. Stir in the milk, sour cream, kale mixture, horseradish, and ½ teaspoon salt. Serve warm.

Each serving About 245 calories, 7g protein, 32g carbohydrate, 10g fat (6g saturated), 3g fiber, 360mg sodium.

CRISPY GINGER-SCALLION LATKES 458

SWEET POTATO & CAULIFLOWER MASH 458

potatoes anna

PREP: 25 MIN / TOTAL: 1 HR 10 MIN / SERVES 8

4 medium baking
   potatoes (8 ounces
   each)
3 tablespoons butter

½ teaspoon salt
⅛ teaspoon ground
   black pepper

1. Preheat the oven to 425°F. Peel the potatoes and cut them into paper-thin slices. In a 10-inch oven-safe skillet, melt the butter over low heat (if the skillet is not oven-safe, wrap the handle with a double layer of foil). Remove the skillet from the heat. Beginning at an outside edge of the skillet, arrange one layer of potatoes in a circle of slightly overlapping slices. Sprinkle with some salt and pepper. Continue layering the potatoes in concentric circles to make two or three more layers, sprinkling each layer with salt and pepper.

2. Lightly grease a sheet of foil; place the foil, greased side down, on top of the potatoes. Place a heavy 10-inch skillet on top of the foil to weight down the potatoes and cook over medium-high heat until the underside is lightly browned, 5 to 10 minutes.

3. Place the skillet in the oven and bake 15 minutes. Uncover and bake until the potatoes are tender, about 10 minutes more. Invert the skillet onto a serving plate. To serve, cut the potato cake into wedges.

Each serving About 110 calories, 2g protein, 15g carbohydrate, 5g fat (3g saturated), 1g fiber, 195mg sodium.

latkes

PREP: 35 MIN / TOTAL: 1 HR / MAKES 20 LATKES

- 2½ pounds baking potatoes (4 large), peeled
- 1 medium onion, peeled
- 1 large egg
- 2 tablespoons matzo meal or all-purpose flour
- 1 tablespoon chopped fresh parsley or dill
- 1 tablespoon fresh lemon juice
- ½ teaspoon baking powder
- ½ teaspoon salt
- ¼ teaspoon coarsely ground black pepper
- ¾ cup vegetable oil for frying
- Applesauce or sour cream, for serving

1. In a food processor with the shredding blade attached, or with the coarse side of a box grater, shred the potatoes and onion. Place them in a colander. With your hands, squeeze to press out as much liquid as possible. Place the potato mixture in a large bowl; stir in the egg, matzo meal, parsley, lemon juice, baking powder, salt, and pepper.

2. Preheat the oven to 250°F. In a 12-inch skillet, heat 3 tablespoons oil over medium heat until hot. Drop the potato mixture by scant ¼ cups into the hot oil to make 5 latkes. With the back of a spoon, flatten each latke into a 3-inch round. Cook until the underside is golden, 4 to 5 minutes. With a slotted spatula, turn the latkes and cook until the second side is golden brown and crisp, 4 to 5 minutes longer. Transfer the latkes to a paper-towel-lined baking sheet to drain; keep warm in the oven.

3. Repeat with the remaining potato mixture, stirring the mixture before cooking each batch and using 3 tablespoons more oil for each new batch. Serve the latkes hot with applesauce or sour cream.

Each latke (without applesauce or sour cream) About 210 calories, 3g protein, 18g carbohydrate, 14g fat (2g saturated), 1g fiber, 150mg sodium.

Tip If you are preparing a large batch of latkes several hours ahead, reheat them by placing the latkes on a cooling rack set over a baking sheet. Preheat the oven to 375°F. Reheat for about 10 minutes, or until hot.

#SavetheFood

mashed potato pancakes

PREP: 10 MIN / TOTAL: 15 MIN / SERVES 4

- 1½ cups cold or room-temperature mashed potatoes
- 2 tablespoons plain dried bread crumbs
- 2 tablespoons freshly grated Pecorino Romano or Parmesan cheese
- 1 tablespoon butter

1. With your hands, shape the mashed potatoes into eight 2-inch patties. On waxed paper, combine the bread crumbs and cheese. Coat the patties with the bread crumb mixture, patting the crumbs to cover.

2. In a 10-inch nonstick skillet, melt the butter over medium heat. Add the patties and cook until golden and heated through, 2 to 3 minutes per side.

Each serving About 130 calories, 3g protein, 16g carbohydrate, 7g fat (3g saturated), 1g fiber, 320mg sodium.

crispy ginger-scallion latkes

(See photo on page 456.)

PREP: 35 MIN / TOTAL: 1 HR / MAKES 16 LATKES

⅓ cup matzo meal

3 large eggs

4 teaspoon grated, peeled fresh ginger

1 bunch green onions, thinly sliced

Salt

6 Idaho or russet potatoes (3 pounds)

1 quart canola or vegetable oil

Applesauce, sour cream, or sriracha hot sauce, for serving (optional)

1. In a large bowl, combine the matzo meal, eggs, ginger, green onions, and ¾ teaspoon salt; set aside. Peel and shred the potatoes.

2. Wrap one-quarter of the shredded potatoes in a clean kitchen towel; firmly squeeze all the liquid from the potatoes into a medium bowl. Place the squeezed potatoes in the bowl with the matzo-meal mixture. Repeat with the remaining potatoes.

3. Carefully pour off only the potato liquid from the medium bowl. Scrape the starch collected on the bottom into the bowl with the potatoes. Toss the potato-and-matzo-meal mixture until well combined. Place a large wire rack over a large sheet of foil.

4. In a heavy 12-inch skillet, heat the oil over medium-high heat until shimmering and hot but not smoking. Carefully scrape packed ¼ cupfuls of the potato mixture into the hot oil to form mounds, pressing on the top of each to flatten slightly (do not crowd the pan). Reduce the heat to medium. Fry 4 to 5 minutes, or until the bottoms are golden brown. Turn the latkes over and fry 4 to 5 minutes more, or until the other side is golden brown. With a slotted spoon, transfer the latkes to the wire rack to drain; sprinkle with a pinch of salt. Repeat scooping, frying, and draining with the remaining potato mixture. Serve hot or at room temperature with applesauce, sour cream, or sriracha.

Each latke About 135 calories, 4g protein, 22g carbohydrate, 4g fat (1g saturated), 2g fiber, 215mg sodium.

sweet potato & cauliflower mash

(See photo on page 456.)

PREP: 20 MIN / TOTAL: 1 HR / SERVES 12

3 pounds sweet potatoes, peeled and cut into 1-inch chunks

Salt

1 large head cauliflower (2½ pounds), cut into florets (about 8 cups)

⅓ cup extra-virgin olive oil

6 leaves fresh sage

2 small cloves garlic, crushed with a garlic press

¼ cup low-fat (1%) milk

1. In a 7- to 8-quart saucepot, combine the sweet potatoes, enough cold water to cover by 1 inch, and 3 tablespoons salt. Partially cover and heat to simmering over high heat. Remove the cover and add the cauliflower. Simmer 15 minutes, or until the vegetables are very tender but not falling apart, stirring occasionally.

2. Meanwhile, in 1-quart saucepot, heat the oil over medium-low heat. Add the sage and garlic. Cook 4 to 5 minutes, or until the garlic is golden, stirring occasionally. Remove from the heat. Remove and discard the sage leaves.

3. Drain the vegetables well; return to the empty pot. In batches, in a food processor, puree the vegetables until smooth; transfer to a large bowl. To the pureed vegetables, add the oil mixture, milk, and ¼ teaspoon salt, stirring to combine.

Each serving About 140 calories, 3g protein, 19g carbohydrate, 7g fat (1g saturated), 4g fiber, 180mg sodium.

maple cranberry sweet potatoes

PREP: 10 MIN / TOTAL: 1 HR, PLUS COOLING / SERVES 10

5 medium sweet potatoes (4 pounds), peeled	1 cup pure maple syrup
Salt	1½ cups cranberries (half a 12-ounce bag)
	3 tablespoons butter

1. In a covered 6-quart saucepot, combine the whole sweet potatoes with 1 teaspoon salt and enough water to cover; heat to boiling over high heat. Reduce the heat to low; simmer, covered, about 30 minutes, or just until the potatoes are fork-tender. Drain. Set aside until cool enough to handle.

2. Meanwhile, in a 1-quart saucepan, heat the maple syrup to boiling over high heat. Reduce the heat to medium and boil gently 10 to 15 minutes, or until reduced to ½ cup. Stir in the cranberries, butter, and ½ teaspoon salt and cook just until the cranberries pop, about 5 minutes longer.

3. Preheat the oven to 400°F. Cut the cooled sweet potatoes crosswise into 1-inch-thick slices and arrange them in a shallow 3-quart ceramic or glass baking dish, overlapping slices if necessary to fit.

4. Spoon the maple-cranberry syrup evenly over the potatoes. Bake, uncovered, 20 minutes or until hot.

Each serving About 260 calories, 2g protein, 55g carbohydrate, 4g fat (2g saturated), 5g fiber, 230mg sodium.

VARIATIONS

Ginger-Almond Sweet Potatoes

Prepare the sweet potatoes as in step 1. In step 2, instead of maple-cranberry syrup, prepare ginger syrup: In a 1-quart saucepan, melt **1 tablespoon butter** over medium heat. Add **2 teaspoons grated, peeled fresh ginger**; cook 1 minute, stirring. Stir in ½ **cup apricot preserves**, ¼ **cup orange juice**, and ½ **teaspoon salt**; heat to boiling, stirring. Complete the recipe as in steps 3 and 4, spooning the ginger syrup over the potatoes and sprinkling them with ½ **cup toasted sliced natural almonds** (with brown skin still on) before baking.

Butterscotch-Spice Sweet Potatoes

Prepare the sweet potatoes as in step 1. In step 2, instead of maple-cranberry syrup, prepare butterscotch-spice syrup: In a 1-quart saucepan, heat ½ **cup packed brown sugar**, **3 tablespoons butter** (do not use margarine), **2 tablespoons water**, **1 teaspoon pumpkin pie spice**, ¼ **teaspoon salt**, and ⅛ **teaspoon cayenne pepper** to boiling, stirring until smooth; remove from the heat. Complete the recipe as in steps 3 and 4, spooning the butterscotch-spice syrup over potatoes before baking.

Tip You can prepare the sweet potatoes—and even arrange them in a casserole—and the syrup up to 1 day ahead and refrigerate separately. Allow both to come to room temperature before baking. Select sweet potatoes of the same size so they cook evenly.

root vegetable gratin

PREP: 25 MIN / TOTAL: 1 HR 45 MIN / SERVES 12

½ cup chicken broth	1 pound celery root, trimmed, peeled, and thinly sliced
2 tablespoons butter	1 pound parsnips, peeled and thinly sliced
1½ pounds baking potatoes (about 3 medium), peeled and thinly sliced	1¼ teaspoons salt
	½ teaspoon black pepper
1½ pounds sweet potatoes (about 3 small), peeled and thinly sliced	⅔ cup heavy or whipping cream
	6 ounces Gruyère cheese, shredded (1½ cups)

1. Preheat oven to 400°F. In a 13 x 9-inch baking dish, combine the broth and butter; place in the oven to melt the butter.

2. Meanwhile, in a large bowl, toss the baking and sweet potatoes, celery root, and parsnips with salt and pepper until well mixed.

3. Remove the baking dish from oven; add the vegetables and stir to coat with the broth mixture. Cover the dish with foil and bake vegetables 40 minutes.

4. Remove the dish from the oven. In a 1-cup liquid measuring cup, heat the cream in a microwave oven on High 45 seconds. Pour the cream evenly over the vegetables; sprinkle with Gruyère. Bake, uncovered, until the top is golden and vegetables are fork-tender, about 30 minutes longer. Let stand 10 minutes before serving.

Each serving About 220 calories, 6g protein, 23g carbohydrate, 12g fat (7g saturated), 4g fiber, 383mg sodium.

praline sweet potatoes

PREP: 30 MIN / TOTAL: 1 HR 10 MIN / SERVES 12

5 pounds sweet potatoes (8 medium), peeled and cut crosswise into thirds
¼ cup sugar
¼ cup water
1 cup chopped pecans (4 ounces)
5 tablespoons butter
½ cup milk
1¼ teaspoons salt

1. In an 8-quart saucepot, combine the sweet potatoes and enough water to cover; heat to boiling over high heat. Reduce the heat; cover and simmer until tender, about 25 minutes. Drain; return the potatoes to the saucepot.

2. Meanwhile, prepare the praline: Grease a baking sheet. In a 1-quart sauce pan, combine the sugar and water; heat over low heat, stirring gently, until the sugar has dissolved, about 1 minute. Increase the heat to medium-high and boil rapidly, without stirring, until the syrup has turned light golden brown, about 7 minutes. Working quickly, stir in the pecans and 1 tablespoon butter until combined and the butter melts. Spread the pecan mixture in a thin layer on the baking sheet; cool.

3. To the sweet potatoes in the saucepot, add the milk, the remaining 4 tablespoons butter, and the salt. With a mixer at low speed, beat the sweet potatoes until smooth, frequently scraping down the sides of the saucepot with a rubber spatula. Increase the speed to medium; beat until fluffy, about 2 minutes longer.

4. To serve, spoon the potatoes into a large bowl. Break the praline into small pieces and sprinkle on top.

Each serving About 330 calories, 4g protein, 47g carbohydrate, 15g fat (5g saturated), 5g fiber, 375mg sodium.

mashed rutabaga
with brown butter

PREP: 10 MIN / TOTAL: 40 MIN / SERVES 12

2 rutabagas (1¼ pounds each)
Salt
4 tablespoons butter
½ teaspoon sugar
¼ cup milk, warmed

1. Cut each rutabaga lengthwise into quarters; peel, then cut each one into 1-inch pieces. In a 4-quart saucepan, combine the rutabagas, water to cover, and 1 teaspoon salt; heat to boiling over high heat. Reduce the heat to medium; cover and cook until tender, about 15 minutes. Drain.

2. In a food processor with the knife blade attached, combine the rutabagas, 2 tablespoons butter, the sugar, and ¾ teaspoon salt and puree until smooth, occasionally scraping down the side with a rubber spatula. With the processor running, gradually add the warm milk until blended.

3. In a small saucepan over medium heat, melt the remaining 2 tablespoons butter; cook, stirring, until golden brown (do not let burn).

4. To serve, spoon the rutabaga puree into a warmed bowl and pour brown butter on top.

Each serving About 70 calories, 1g protein, 7g carbohydrate, 4g fat (3g saturated), 2g fiber, 300mg sodium.

creamed spinach

PREP: 20 MIN / TOTAL: 35 MIN / SERVES 6

- 2 tablespoons butter
- 3 large shallots, finely chopped (about ¾ cup)
- 2 tablespoons all-purpose flour
- ½ cup milk
- ¾ teaspoon salt
- ¼ teaspoon coarsely ground black pepper
- ⅛ teaspoon ground nutmeg
- 1 small package (3 ounces) cream cheese, softened and cut into pieces
- 3 packages (10 ounces each) frozen chopped spinach, thawed and squeezed dry
- 1 cup loosely packed fresh parsley leaves
- ¼ cup sour cream

1. In a 4-quart saucepan, melt the butter over medium-low heat. Add the shallots and cook, stirring frequently, until tender, about 3 minutes. Add the flour and cook, stirring, 1 minute. With a wire whisk, gradually whisk in the milk; heat to boiling, whisking constantly. Reduce the heat and simmer, stirring occasionally with a wooden spoon, until the sauce has thickened and boils, about 2 minutes. Stir in the salt, pepper, and nutmeg.

2. Remove from the heat; stir in the cream cheese until smooth. Stir in the spinach, parsley, and sour cream; heat through, stirring frequently (do not boil).

Each serving About 180 calories, 7g protein, 14g carbohydrate, 12g fat (7g saturated), 5g fiber, 500mg sodium.

VARIATION

Indian-Style Creamed Spinach

Cook the shallots as directed, but stir in 2½ teaspoons minced, peeled fresh ginger; 2 cloves garlic, finely chopped; ¾ teaspoon each ground coriander and cumin; and ⅛ teaspoon cayenne pepper. Cook, stirring, 1 minute. Omit the flour, milk, nutmeg, and cream cheese. Stir in the spinach and ¼ cup heavy or whipping cream and heat through. Stir in the sour cream.

sautéed spinach
with garlic

PREP: 5 MIN / TOTAL: 10 MIN / SERVES 4

- 1 tablespoon olive oil
- 2 cloves garlic, crushed with the side of a chef's knife
- 2 bags (10 ounces each) fresh spinach, rinsed
- 1 tablespoon fresh lemon juice
- ¼ teaspoon salt

1. In a 5- to 6-quart saucepot, heat the oil over medium-high heat until hot. Add the garlic and cook 1 minute, or until golden, stirring.

2. Add the spinach, with water clinging to leaves, to the pot in 2 or 3 batches; cook 2 minutes, or until all the spinach fits in the saucepot. Cover and cook 2 to 3 minutes longer, or just until the spinach wilts, stirring once. Remove from the heat. Stir in the lemon juice and salt.

Each serving About 45 calories, 4g protein, 1g carbohydrate, 4g fat (1g saturated), 12g fiber, 305mg sodium.

zucchini ribbons
with mint

PREP: 10 MIN / TOTAL: 15 MIN / SERVES 4

- 4 small zucchini (4 ounces each), or 2 medium zucchini (8 ounces each)
- 1 tablespoon olive oil
- 2 cloves garlic, crushed with side of chef's knife
- ½ teaspoon salt
- 2 tablespoons chopped fresh mint

1. Trim the ends from the zucchini. With a vegetable peeler, peel long, thin ribbons from each zucchini.

2. In a 12-inch skillet, heat the oil over medium heat. Add the garlic and cook, stirring, until golden; discard. Increase the heat to high. Add the zucchini and salt and cook, stirring, just until zucchini wilts, about 2 minutes. Remove from heat and stir in mint.

Each serving About 50 calories, 1g protein, 4g carbohydrate, 4g fat (0g saturated), 1g fiber, 295mg sodium.

spaghetti squash
with tomatoes

PREP: 10 MIN / TOTAL: 1 HR 10 MIN / SERVES 6

- 1 medium spaghetti squash (2½ pounds), cut lengthwise in half and seeded
- 3 tablespoons butter
- 1 clove garlic, finely chopped
- 1 can (28 ounces) diced tomatoes, drained
- Salt
- Ground black pepper
- 2 tablespoons chopped fresh parsley

1. Preheat the oven to 400°F. Place the squash, cut side down, in a jelly-roll pan; pour ¼ inch water into the pan. Bake 45 minutes. Turn the squash cut side up and bake until very tender, about 15 minutes longer.

2. Meanwhile, in a 12-inch nonstick skillet, melt 2 tablespoons butter over medium heat. Add the garlic and cook, stirring, 1 minute. Stir in the tomatoes, ¼ teaspoon salt, and ⅛ teaspoon pepper and cook, stirring, until flavors blend, about 5 minutes. Remove from the heat and stir in the parsley.

3. Using 2 forks, scrape out the squash pulp in long strands and place them on a serving platter. Add the remaining 1 tablespoon butter, ¼ teaspoon salt, and ⅛ teaspoon pepper and toss to mix. Spoon the tomato sauce over the squash. Serve hot.

Each serving About 130 calories, 2g protein, 16g carbohydrate, 7g fat (4g saturated), 3g fiber, 495mg sodium.

VARIATIONS

Sweet & Smoky Spaghetti Squash
Prepare as directed in step 1. Omit the butter, garlic, tomatoes, salt, pepper, and parsley. In a microwave-safe bowl, microwave **3 slices bacon**, chopped, and **1 onion**, chopped, on High, stirring once, until the bacon is browned, about 4 minutes. Using 2 forks, scrape the squash pulp onto a serving platter. Add the bacon mixture, **3 tablespoons maple or maple-flavored syrup**, and ⅛ **teaspoon ground black pepper** and toss to mix.

Southwestern Spaghetti Squash
Prepare as directed in step 1. Omit the butter, garlic, tomatoes, salt, pepper, and parsley. Using 2 forks, scrape the squash pulp onto a serving platter. Add ¾ **cup mild salsa** and toss to mix. Sprinkle with **crushed tortilla chips**.

Asian Spaghetti Squash
Prepare as directed in step 1. Omit the butter, garlic, tomatoes, salt, pepper, and parsley. Using 2 forks, scrape the squash pulp onto a serving platter. Add ¼ **cup soy sauce**; 1 tablespoon grated, peeled fresh ginger; and 1 teaspoon Asian sesame oil and toss to mix.

maple butternut squash

PREP: 20 MIN / TOTAL: 40 MIN / SERVES 10

- 2 medium butternut squash (2 pounds each)
- ½ cup maple or maple-flavored syrup
- 4 tablespoons butter, cut into pieces
- ½ teaspoon salt
- ¼ teaspoon ground black pepper

1. Cut each squash lengthwise in half; discard the seeds. With a vegetable peeler, remove the peel, then cut the squash crosswise into 1-inch-thick slices.

2. In a 5-quart saucepot, heat 1 inch water to boiling over high heat; add squash. Reduce the heat; cover and simmer until tender, about 15 minutes. Drain.

3. In a large bowl, combine the squash, maple syrup, butter, salt, and pepper. With a mixer at low speed, beat until smooth. Spoon the puree into a serving bowl.

Each serving About 150 calories, 2g protein, 28g carbohydrate, 5g fat (3g saturated), 3g fiber, 170mg sodium.

parmesan broiled squash

PREP: 10 MIN / TOTAL: 20 MIN / SERVES 4

2 medium zucchini or yellow squash (8 ounces each), each cut crosswise in half, then lengthwise into ½-inch-thick slices

1 teaspoon olive oil

⅛ teaspoon salt

⅛ teaspoon ground black pepper

¼ cup freshly grated Parmesan cheese

1. Preheat the broiler. In a broiling pan without a rack, toss the zucchini and oil to coat; arrange them in a single layer and sprinkle with salt and pepper.

2. Place the pan under the broiler, 5 inches from the heat source. Broil until the zucchini is tender and begins to brown, 3 to 5 minutes per side. Sprinkle evenly with Parmesan and broil until bubbling, 30 to 60 seconds longer.

Each serving About 55 calories, 4g protein, 4g carbohydrate, 3g fat (1g saturated), 1g fiber, 190mg sodium.

INGREDIENT SPOTLIGHT

↓

Unlike thick-skinned winter squash, **summer squash**, from zucchini to yellow and pattypan, are picked when young and tender. They are delicious raw, fried, roasted, or grilled. The smaller, the tastier: Pick squash under 6 inches long.

baked acorn squash

PREP: 10 MIN / TOTAL: 35 MIN / SERVES 4

2 small acorn squash or other winter squash (1 pound each), each cut lengthwise in half and seeded

2 tablespoons butter, cut into pieces

¼ cup packed brown sugar

Preheat the oven to 350°F. Grease a 13 × 9-inch baking dish. Place the squash, cut side down, in the baking dish; bake 30 minutes. Turn cut side up. Place one-fourth of the butter and brown sugar in each cavity. Bake until the squash is tender and the butter and brown sugar have melted, about 5 minutes longer.

Each serving About 180 calories, 1g protein, 31g carbohydrate, 7g fat (4g saturated), 3g fiber, 70mg sodium.

---

ciambotta

PREP: 30 MIN / TOTAL: 1 HR / SERVES 6

3 tablespoons olive oil

1 medium onion, chopped

2 cloves garlic, finely chopped

2 red bell peppers, cut into 1-inch pieces

1½ pounds zucchini (3 medium), cut

lengthwise in half, then crosswise into ½-inch-thick pieces

1½ pounds ripe tomatoes, peeled and seeded, chopped

¾ teaspoon salt

⅓ cup chopped fresh basil

1. In a 12-inch nonreactive skillet, heat 2 tablespoons oil over medium heat. Add the onion and garlic and cook, stirring frequently, until the onion is tender, about 5 minutes. Add the bell peppers and cook, stirring frequently, until the peppers are tender-crisp, about 5 minutes longer.

2. Add the remaining 1 tablespoon oil and the zucchini; cook, stirring, until the zucchini is tender-crisp, about 5 minutes. Add the tomatoes and salt; heat to boiling. Reduce the heat; cover and simmer until the vegetables are very tender, about 10 minutes. Stir in the basil.

Each serving About 120 calories, 3g protein, 13g carbohydrate, 7g fat (1g saturated), 3g fiber, 305mg sodium.

succotash

PREP: 10 MIN / TOTAL: 35 MIN / SERVES 10

- 5 slices bacon
- 3 stalks celery, cut into ¼-inch-thick slices
- 1 medium onion, chopped
- 2 cans (15¼ to 16 ounces each) whole-kernel corn, drained
- 2 packages (10 ounces each) frozen baby lima beans
- ½ cup chicken broth
- ¾ teaspoon salt
- ¼ teaspoon coarsely ground black pepper
- 2 tablespoons chopped fresh parsley

1. In a 12-inch skillet, cook the bacon over medium-low heat until browned. With tongs, transfer to paper towels to drain and cool; crumble.

2. Discard all but 2 tablespoons bacon drippings from the skillet. Add the celery and onion and cook over medium heat, stirring frequently, until the vegetables are tender and golden, about 15 minutes. Stir in the corn, lima beans, broth, salt, and pepper; heat to boiling over high heat. Reduce the heat; cover and simmer until heated through, 5 to 10 minutes longer. Stir in the parsley and sprinkle with bacon.

Each serving About 170 calories, 7g protein, 27g carbohydrate, 5g fat (1g saturated), 6g fiber, 460mg sodium.

GLOSSARY

Succotash originated when early settlers learned to make *msickquatash,* a stewy dish of corn and dried beans from Native Americans of the Narragansett tribe, around the Plymouth plantation. Many embellishments have been added over the centuries, and in many recipes bacon stands in for the original bear grease!

harvest succotash

(See photo on page 412.)

PREP: 15 MIN / TOTAL: 40 MIN / SERVES 12

- 1 package (20 ounces) peeled butternut squash chunks
- 3 tablespoons extra-virgin olive oil
- 1 medium red onion, cut into 16 wedges
- 3 cloves garlic, crushed with a garlic press
- 4 sprigs fresh thyme
- Salt
- 4 cup fresh or frozen (thawed) corn kernels
- 12 ounces frozen (thawed) shelled edamame
- 3 tablespoons white wine vinegar
- 2 tablespoons Dijon mustard
- ¼ teaspoon ground black pepper

1. Preheat the oven to 425°F. On a rimmed baking sheet, toss the butternut squash with 2 teaspoons oil. Roast the butternut squash 15 minutes, stirring once halfway through. On another rimmed baking sheet, toss the onion with 1 teaspoon oil. Roast the onion and butternut squash another 15 to 20 minutes, or until the squash is tender, stirring once halfway through.

2. Meanwhile, in a 5-quart saucepot, heat the remaining 2 tablespoons oil over medium heat. Add the garlic, thyme, and ¼ teaspoon salt. Cook 2 minutes, stirring. Add the corn and edamame. Cook 4 to 5 minutes, or until heated through, stirring occasionally. Remove from the heat.

3. In a small bowl, whisk the vinegar, mustard, pepper, and ¼ teaspoon salt; stir into the corn mixture along with the roasted squash and onions.

Each serving About 130 calories, 5g protein, 18g carbohydrate, 6g fat (1g saturated), 4g fiber, 170mg sodium.

ratatouille

PREP: 20 MIN / TOTAL: 1 HR 20 MIN / SERVES 8

- 2 tablespoons olive oil
- 1 medium onion, chopped
- 1 small eggplant (1 pound), ends trimmed, cut into 1-inch pieces
- ¾ teaspoon salt
- ¼ teaspoon ground black pepper
- 1 yellow or red bell pepper, cut into 1-inch pieces
- 1 medium zucchini (8 ounces), cut into 1-inch pieces
- 2 large cloves garlic, finely chopped
- 1 can (28 ounces) tomatoes, chopped
- ⅛ teaspoon dried thyme
- ¼ cup chopped fresh basil or parsley

In a 5-quart nonreactive saucepot, heat the oil over medium heat. Add the onion; cook, stirring frequently, until tender and golden, about 10 minutes. Add the eggplant, salt, and pepper; cook, stirring frequently, until the eggplant begins to brown, about 10 minutes. Stir in the bell pepper, zucchini, and garlic; cook, stirring, 1 minute. Stir in the tomatoes with their juices and thyme; heat to boiling. Reduce the heat; cover and simmer until the eggplant is tender, about 30 minutes. Remove from the heat; stir in the basil.

Each serving About 80 calories, 2g protein, 12g carbohydrate, 4g fat (0g saturated), 3g fiber, 385mg sodium.

GOOD TO KNOW

EGGPLANT

Eggplant comes in a variety of colors, shapes, and sizes. Beside the familiar purple globes, Chinese long eggplants, purple and white scribbled ones called graffiti eggplant, squat green rounds of Thai eggplant, and creamy white eggplant are just some of those available. They all cook up soft and creamy.

broccoli-cheddar puff

PREP: 35 MIN / TOTAL: 1 HR 15 MIN / SERVES 15

- 5 tablespoons butter
- 6 tablespoons all-purpose flour
- ½ teaspoon salt
- ⅛ teaspoon cayenne pepper
- 2¼ cups milk
- 8 ounces sharp Cheddar cheese, shredded (2 cups)
- 2 boxes (10 ounces each) frozen chopped broccoli, thawed and squeezed dry
- 7 large eggs, separated
- 1½ cups coarse soft fresh bread crumbs (about 3 slices firm white bread)

1. In a 4-quart saucepan, melt 4 tablespoons butter over medium-low heat. Stir in the flour, salt, and cayenne until blended; cook 1 minute, stirring. Gradually stir in the milk; cook until the mixture boils and thickens, stirring frequently. Stir in the Cheddar; cook just until melted. Remove from the heat. Stir in the broccoli.

2. In a small bowl and using a fork, lightly beat the egg yolks. Stir in about ½ cup cheese sauce. Gradually pour the egg yolk mixture into the cheese sauce, stirring rapidly to prevent curdling. Cool slightly.

3. Meanwhile, preheat the oven to 325°F. Grease a shallow 3½-quart ceramic casserole or a 13 × 9-inch glass baking dish. In a microwave-safe medium bowl, melt the remaining 1 tablespoon butter in the microwave on High 15 to 20 seconds, swirling the bowl once. Add the bread crumbs; stir until well combined.

4. In a large bowl and using a mixer at high speed, beat the egg whites until stiff peaks form when the beaters are lifted. With a rubber spatula, gently fold one-third of the whites into the cheese mixture. Fold the cheese mixture gently back into the remaining whites.

5. Pour the mixture into the prepared casserole. Sprinkle the crumb mixture on top. Bake 40 minutes, or until the top is browned and a knife inserted in the center comes out clean. Serve immediately.

Each serving About 190 calories, 9g protein, 9g carbohydrate, 13g fat (7g saturated), 1g fiber, 280mg sodium.

12

salads

From a toss of crisp greens to an artfully arranged multicolor platter, we eat salad with our eyes first. Using greens as your palette, top with a variety of colors and textures from vegetables, grains, fruits, nuts, and seeds. Or forgo the greens and instead base a hearty salad on roasted veggies, grains, beans, eggs, meat, or seafood. Sopressata & Roma Bean Salad with Pecorino (page 487), Warm Farro Salad with Roasted Vegetables (page 475), and Grilled Plum & Pork Salad (page 490) all make delicious dinners. Or shop your farmers' market or fridge and create combinations your family will love. Dressings like Classic French Vinaigrette (page 504), Japanese Miso (page 504), Tahini (page 505), Best-Ever Ranch (page 507), and Creamy Blue Cheese (page 504) will all lend personality to whatever combo you assemble. Whatever the occasion, you can make a salad to star in or support the menu.

AUTUMN SQUASH SALAD 492

GARDEN GREENS & PUMPERNICKEL PANZANELLA 492

SWEET BBQ CHICKEN SALAD 497

CHARRED GREEK CAESAR 493

The Greens Guide

Salad greens fall into two basic categories: delicate and tender or assertive and slightly bitter. There are four basic types of lettuce:

- **CRISPHEAD (ICEBERG)** varieties are crisp and mild-flavored and stand up well to thicker dressings.

- **BUTTERHEAD (BIBB, BOSTON)** is sweet-tasting and delicate and should be served with an appropriately light-bodied dressing.

- **LOOSE-LEAF (OAK LEAF)** is tender but has a slightly stronger flavor than butterhead.

- **LONG-LEAF (ROMAINE)** has long, firm, crisp leaves and is another candidate for rich, thick dressings.

For a well-balanced salad, combine strong-flavored greens with tender, sweeter lettuces. Bitter greens such as radicchio and Belgian endive also add colorful counterpoint to the salad palette. Pick and pair among these greens for an endless variety of salad options.

ARUGULA Peppery arugula is also known as rugula or rocket. The baby version is mild; older, larger leaves have more assertive flavor. The large leaves can be very gritty, so rinse them thoroughly.

BABY GREENS Available in bags or in bulk at many supermarkets, this combination of very young, tender salad greens is an Americanization of the French salad mix known as mesclun.

BELGIAN ENDIVE A member of the chicory family, Belgian endive is appreciated for its crisp texture and slightly bitter flavor. The leaves should be very white, graduating to pale-yellow tips.

BIBB LETTUCE Also called limestone lettuce, bibb has cup-shaped leaves and is best with mild vinaigrettes.

BOSTON LETTUCE A loose-leaf lettuce with tender, floppy leaves, it is sometimes called butterhead lettuce.

CHICORY Although chicory is an entire family of mildly bitter greens, Americans use the term to identify a dark-green variety with fringed leaves. It is also known as curly endive.

CHINESE CABBAGE A tightly formed head of white leaves with wide stalks.

DANDELION Tart greens that make a pungent addition to a salad. Some cooks gather the wild variety in the spring.

ESCAROLE Sharp-tasting escarole should have curly leaves with firm stems that snap easily.

FRISÉE A delicate, pale-green variety of chicory with curly, almost spiky leaves.

ICEBERG LETTUCE A lettuce that is best appreciated for its refreshing crisp texture rather than for its mild flavor. Cut out the core before rinsing the leaves.

MÂCHE Also called lamb's lettuce, this green has a nutty taste and tiny, tender leaves. Use within one day; it wilts easily.

MESCLUN From the Provençal word for "mixture," true mesclun is made up of wild baby greens. It is commonly a mix of sweet lettuces and bitter greens such as arugula, dandelion, frisée, mizuna, oak leaf, mâche, and radicchio.

MIZUNA A small, feathery, delicately flavored green of Japanese origin.

NAPA CABBAGE Very similar to, and interchangeable with, Chinese cabbage, but shorter and rounder.

OAK LEAF A variety of Boston lettuce with ruffled leaves. Green oak leaf is uniformly green, whereas red oak leaf has dark-red tips.

RADICCHIO The most common radicchio is round with white-veined ruby-red leaves. Radicchio di Treviso has long, narrow red leaves that form a tapered head.

RADISH SPROUTS Innocent-looking sprouts with tiny clover-shaped heads that pack a peppery punch.

ROMAINE Its long, crisp, dark-green leaves and slightly nutty flavor make romaine the preferred lettuce for Caesar salad.

SPINACH Whether dark green and crinkled or flat, spinach needs to be washed thoroughly to remove all the grit. Baby spinach has very tender, edible stems.

WATERCRESS Trim away tough stems; use leaves and tender stems for crisp texture and a mildly spicy flavor.

TESTING NOTE We recommend rinsing and drying prewashed greens to refresh them and to rinse off any bacteria from the surface of the leaves.

Ingredient Ideas

salad in a snap

Pair a quick salad with everything from pasta to pork chops, and dinner is served! It all starts with a simple vinaigrette.

BASIC VINAIGRETTE

In a small bowl, whisk together **3 tablespoons vinegar**, **½ teaspoon Dijon mustard**, and a **pinch each of salt and ground black pepper,** then slowly drizzle in **¼ cup olive oil**, whisking until the mixture emulsifies. Change the flavor by using a different vinegar, such as balsamic, sherry, or tarragon, or experiment with your own favorites.

BABY ROMAINE WITH FENNEL & CITRUS

Toss together one **5-ounce bag baby romaine**, **1 cup thinly sliced fennel**, **1 cup jarred citrus segments**, **½ cup rinsed and drained chickpeas**, and **6 thinly sliced radishes**.
NOTE: Use lemon juice or a combination of lemon and lime juice instead of vinegar.

GREEK SALAD WITH FETA & OLIVES

Toss together one **5-ounce bag spring mix with herbs**, **1 cup grape tomatoes**, **1 seedless cucumber** cut into ½-inch chunks, and **½ cup pitted Kalamata olives**. Top with ¼ **cup crumbled feta or goat cheese**.
NOTE: Use tarragon vinegar or white wine vinegar.

CARROT COLESLAW WITH DRIED CHERRIES & ALMONDS

Toss together one **10-ounce bag shredded carrots**, **1 large red bell pepper** cut into ¼-inch-wide strips, **½ cup dried cherries**, and **½ cup toasted slivered almonds**.
NOTE: Use seasoned rice vinegar and add a teaspoon of toasted sesame oil.

APPLE COLESLAW WITH GOLDEN RAISINS & PECANS

Toss together one **16-ounce bag coleslaw mix**, **1 Granny Smith apple**, cored and cut into ½-inch chunks, **½ cup golden raisins**, and **½ cup chopped pecans**.
NOTE: Whisk **1 tablespoon light mayonnaise** into Basic Vinaigrette.

SPINACH & ENDIVE WITH PEARS & WALNUTS

Toss together one **6-ounce bag baby spinach**; **2 heads Belgian endive**, sliced; **1 cored and thinly sliced Bosc pear**; and **½ cup toasted walnut pieces**.
NOTE: Use raspberry vinegar.

Get the Most From Your Greens

→

CHOOSE Greens should have no bruised, yellowing, or brown-tipped leaves. Heads such as Iceberg, Romaine, and leaf lettuces should feel heavy for their size. If buying bagged or boxed greens, avoid withered or dark, moist leaves.

WASH No one wants gritty greens! From heads, separate leaves, submerge in a sinkful (or in batches in salad spinner bowl) of cold water, and gently agitate the greens to loosen dirt. If greens are very gritty, repeat the process. Lift the greens from the water, leaving the grit to sink to the bottom. With curly-leafed greens like spinach, arugula, and tender herbs, dirt often gets trapped in the crevices of the leaves. Wash these individually under room-temperature water (the slightly warmer temperature loosens dirt better than cold water), and, if necessary, give the greens a second washing.

DRY Wet greens spoil faster, will dilute the dressing, and make for a soggy salad. Dry salad greens thoroughly before using or storing. A salad spinner is an easy way to dry greens, but you can also pat greens dry with clean kitchen towels.

STORE Wrap the rinsed, dried greens in a clean kitchen towel (or in a few paper towels); place in a plastic bag (pressing out all the excess air); and store in the vegetable crisper of the fridge. Tender greens will keep for two to three days; iceberg and other sturdy lettuces will keep for up to a week.

BUFFALO CHICKEN COBB SALAD 489

beet, mushroom & avocado salad

PREP: 15 MIN / TOTAL: 25 MIN / SERVES 4

- **4 medium portobello mushroom caps**
- **Nonstick cooking spray**
- **Salt**
- **¼ cup fresh lemon juice**
- **3 tablespoons olive oil**
- **1 small shallot, finely chopped**
- **¼ teaspoon ground black pepper**
- **5 ounces baby kale**
- **8 ounces precooked beets, chopped**
- **2 ripe avocados, thinly sliced**
- **2 sheets matzo, crushed into bite-size pieces**

1. Preheat the oven to 450°F. On a large rimmed baking sheet, spray the mushroom caps with nonstick cooking spray and sprinkle with ½ teaspoon salt; roast 20 minutes, or until tender.

2. Whisk the lemon juice, oil, shallot, pepper, and ¼ teaspoon salt; toss half with the baby kale and beets. Divide among serving plates. Top each serving with avocados, matzo, and portobello caps. Serve with the remaining dressing on the side.

Each serving About 370 calories, 7g protein, 32g carbohydrate, 26g fat (4g saturated), 11g fiber, 490mg sodium.

greek peasant salad

PREP: 25 MIN / TOTAL: 25 MIN / SERVES 6

- **4 Kirby cucumbers (about 1 pound), unpeeled**
- **2 tablespoons fresh lemon juice**
- **1 tablespoon olive oil**
- **¼ teaspoon salt**
- **⅛ teaspoon ground black pepper**
- **2 pounds ripe red and/or yellow tomatoes (about 6 medium), cut into 1-inch chunks**
- **½ cup loosely packed fresh mint leaves, chopped**
- **⅓ cup Kalamata olives, pitted and coarsely chopped**
- **¼ cup loosely packed fresh dill, chopped**
- **2 ounces feta cheese, crumbled (½ cup)**

1. With a vegetable peeler, remove 3 or 4 evenly spaced lengthwise strips of peel from each cucumber. Cut each cucumber lengthwise into quarters, then crosswise into ½-inch pieces.

2. In a large bowl and using a wire whisk, mix the lemon juice, oil, salt, and pepper. Add the cucumbers, tomatoes, mint, olives, and dill, and toss until evenly mixed and coated with dressing. Top with feta.

Each serving About 100 calories, 3g protein, 11g carbohydrate, 6g fat (2g saturated), 3g fiber, 280mg sodium.

three-bean salad

PREP: 25 MIN / TOTAL: 40 MIN, PLUS CHILLING / SERVES 8

- **8 ounces green beans, trimmed and cut into 1-inch pieces (2 cups)**
- **8 ounces wax beans, trimmed and cut into 1-inch pieces (2 cups)**
- **Salt**
- **3 tablespoons olive or vegetable oil**
- **3 tablespoons cider vinegar**
- **2 tablespoons sugar**
- **1 can (15 to 19 ounces) red kidney beans, rinsed and drained**
- **¼ cup chopped onion**

1. In a 4-quart saucepan, heat 3 inches water to boiling over high heat. Add the green and wax beans and ½ teaspoon salt; heat to boiling. Cook until tender-crisp, 6 to 8 minutes. Drain. Rinse the beans with cold running water to cool slightly; drain.

2. Meanwhile, prepare the dressing: In a large bowl and using a wire whisk, mix the oil, vinegar, sugar, and 1 teaspoon salt until well blended. Add the green and wax beans, kidney beans, and onion; toss until mixed and coated with dressing. Cover and refrigerate the salad at least 2 hours or up to 24 hours to blend the flavors.

Each serving About 120 calories, 4g protein, 14g carbohydrate, 5g fat (1g saturated), 4g fiber, 440mg sodium.

BEET, MUSHROOM & AVOCADO SALAD 472

mushroom salad

PREP: 30 MIN / TOTAL: 30 MIN, PLUS MARINATING / SERVES 12

1 or 2 lemons

4 tablespoons olive oil

2 cloves garlic, each cut in half

½ teaspoon salt

¼ teaspoon ground black pepper

2 pounds white mushrooms, trimmed and cut into quarters

½ cup loosely packed fresh parsley, chopped

3 tablespoons snipped fresh chives, plus additional for garnish

1 bag (5 ounces) baby arugula

1 bag (5 ounces) mixed baby greens

Thinly shaved Pecorino Romano cheese, for garnish

1. From the lemons, grate ½ teaspoon zest and squeeze ⅓ cup juice. In a 4-quart saucepan, heat the lemon zest and juice, 3 tablespoons oil, garlic, salt, and pepper to boiling over high heat. Reduce the heat to medium and simmer 30 seconds.

2. Stir in the mushrooms, parsley, and chives. Transfer to a large resealable plastic bag. Seal the bag, pressing out the excess air. Place the bag in a bowl and refrigerate 6 hours or overnight.

3. Place a sieve over a large bowl; drain the mushrooms over the bowl (do not discard the drained marinade). Discard the garlic; set the mushrooms aside. Add the remaining 1 tablespoon oil to the marinade in the bowl; whisk until blended. Add the arugula and mixed greens; toss to combine.

4. Serve the mushrooms on the greens. Garnish with additional snipped chives and Pecorino Romano shavings.

Each serving About 65 calories, 3g protein, 5g carbohydrate, 5g fat (1g saturated), 1g fiber, 105mg sodium.

#SavetheFood
revive stale bread

For instant homemade croutons, cube and place stale bread on a baking sheet. Bake in a preheated 400°F oven until dry and crisp, about 10 minutes.

---

warm quinoa & broccoli salad
with carrot-ginger dressing

PREP: 15 MIN / TOTAL: 35 MIN / SERVES 6

1½ cups quinoa

3¼ cups plus 3 tablespoons water

Salt

1 bag (10 ounces) broccoli florets

⅔ cup chopped carrot (1 large)

3 tablespoons finely chopped, peeled fresh ginger

3 tablespoons vegetable oil

2 tablespoons seasoned rice vinegar

2 teaspoons soy sauce

2 teaspoons Asian sesame oil

1. In a sieve, rinse the quinoa with cold running water. In a 3-quart saucepan, combine the quinoa, 3 cups water, and ½ teaspoon salt; heat to boiling over high heat. Reduce the heat to low; cover and simmer 20 minutes, or until the water is absorbed. Transfer the quinoa to a large bowl.

2. Meanwhile, place the broccoli and ¼ cup water in a microwave-safe medium bowl; cover and cook in the microwave oven on High 4 to 5 minutes, or until tender-crisp. Drain; add to the quinoa in bowl.

3. In a blender, combine the carrot, ginger, vegetable oil, vinegar, soy sauce, sesame oil, the remaining 3 tablespoons water, and ¼ teaspoon salt; blend until pureed. Add to the quinoa and broccoli and toss to combine. Serve the salad warm or at room temperature.

Each serving About 265 calories, 7g protein, 36g carbohydrate, 11g fat (1g saturated), 4g fiber, 605mg sodium.

Tip Whether you're toting a salad to a potluck or to work, prep all the components ahead of time, chill dressing and veggies separately, and either toss before serving or serve dressing on the side.

warm farro salad
with roasted vegetables

PREP: 25 MIN / TOTAL: 55 MIN / SERVES 6

- 2 large carrots, peeled and cut into ½-inch dice
- 2 small fennel bulbs, trimmed and cut into 1-inch pieces
- 1 red onion, halved lengthwise through the root end
- 3 tablespoons olive oil
- Salt
- Ground black pepper
- 1 bunch radishes, cut into ½-inch dice
- 1 tablespoon red wine vinegar
- 2½ cups water
- 1 cup farro
- 3 tablespoons fresh lemon juice
- 2 teaspoons freshly grated lemon zest
- 2 cups lightly packed fresh basil leaves, chopped

1. Preheat the oven to 400°F.

2. In a large bowl, combine the carrots, fennel, red onion, 1 tablespoon oil, ½ teaspoon salt, and ⅛ teaspoon pepper; toss. Turn the vegetables onto a 15½ × 10½-inch jelly-roll pan, spreading them evenly. Roast 20 minutes, stirring once. Stir in the radishes and roast until the vegetables are tender, about 10 minutes more. Stir in the vinegar.

3. Meanwhile, in medium saucepan, bring the water, farro, and ¼ teaspoon salt to boiling over high heat. Reduce the heat to medium-low; cover and simmer until the farro is tender and the water is absorbed, 25 to 30 minutes.

4. In a large bowl, whisk the lemon juice, lemon zest, the remaining 2 tablespoons oil, ¼ teaspoon salt, and ⅛ teaspoon pepper. Add the farro, roasted vegetables, and basil; toss to combine. Serve warm.

Each serving About 215 calories, 6g protein, 34g carbohydrate, 7g fat (1g saturated), 6g fiber, 472mg sodium.

warm goat cheese salad

PREP: 15 MIN / TOTAL: 25 MIN / SERVES 6

- ¼ cup plain dried bread crumbs
- 1 tablespoon chopped fresh parsley
- 1 tablespoon olive oil
- ¼ teaspoon coarsely ground black pepper
- 1 log (5 to 6 ounces) mild goat cheese
- 8 ounces mixed baby salad greens
- 3 tablespoons Classic French Vinaigrette (page 504)

1. Preheat the oven to 425°F. In a small bowl, stir the bread crumbs, parsley, oil, and pepper until well blended. Slice the goat cheese crosswise into 6 equal disks. Place on waxed paper; use the bread-crumb mixture to coat the cheese disks, patting the crumbs to cover them evenly.

2. Place the crumb-coated cheese disks on a baking sheet and bake until the crumbs are golden, 8 to 10 minutes.

3. Meanwhile, in a large bowl, toss the salad greens with the vinaigrette to coat. Divide the greens among 6 salad plates and top each serving with a warm goat cheese disk.

Each serving About 180 calories, 7g protein, 5g carbohydrate, 15g fat (6g saturated), 1g fiber, 265mg sodium.

HOW TO

PREP A POMEGRANATE

Fill a bowl with cold water. Cut off the crown and base, then score the fruit into six sections and separate them under the water, loosening the juicy seeds (aka "arils"). The seeds will sink, while the spongy membrane will float. Scoop out and discard the floaters; strain and serve the arils.

kale & roasted cauliflower salad

PREP: 15 MIN / TOTAL: 35 MIN / SERVES 4

- 1 head cauliflower, cut into florets
- 5 tablespoons olive oil
- Salt
- ⅛ teaspoon ground black pepper
- ¼ cup fresh lemon juice
- 1 bunch kale, ribs removed, chopped
- ¼ small red onion, very thinly sliced
- ⅓ cup crumbled feta cheese
- ⅓ cup golden raisins
- ⅓ cup toasted pine nuts

1. Preheat the oven to 450°F. On a large rimmed baking sheet, toss the cauliflower with 2 tablespoons oil, pepper, and ⅛ teaspoon salt. Roast 25 minutes, or until the stems are tender.

2. In a large bowl, whisk the lemon juice, the remaining 3 tablespoons olive oil, and ½ teaspoon salt. Toss the kale with dressing. Let stand at least 5 minutes.

3. To the kale, add the roasted cauliflower, red onion, feta, golden raisins, and toasted pine nuts. Toss until well combined.

Each serving About 370 calories, 10g protein, 27g carbohydrate, 28g fat (5g saturated), 6g fiber, 475mg sodium.

HOW TO

SECTION CITRUS FRUIT

With a small serrated or sharp paring knife, cut a slice off the top and bottom of the fruit to steady it. Stand fruit upright on a cutting board and cut off peel and white pith, turning the fruit as you cut.

Holding the fruit over a bowl to catch the juices, cut between the membranes to release the sections.

Ingredient Ideas

grapefruit

Go beyond the classic grapefruit sprinkled with sugar. Pair it with avocado, or use the segments as a salad topper like in **Shrimp & Fennel Salad.**

SHRIMP & FENNEL SALAD

Cut the peel and white pith from **4 grapefruit**; discard. Holding 1 grapefruit at a time over a large bowl, cut out the segments between the membranes. Add **1 pound shelled and deveined cooked shrimp; 2 large fennel bulbs,** cored and sliced paper-thin; **½ cup cilantro leaves,** chopped; **3 tablespoons extra-virgin olive oil;** and **½ teaspoon each salt and ground black pepper** to bowl. Toss gently. Serves 4.

---

waldorf salad

PREP: 30 MIN / TOTAL: 30 MIN / SERVES 8

- ⅓ cup mayonnaise
- ¼ cup sour cream
- 1 tablespoon fresh lemon juice
- 1 teaspoon honey
- ¼ teaspoon salt
- 2 red apples, such as Braeburn, Cortland, or Red Delicious, each cored, cut into 8 wedges, then sliced crosswise into ¼-inch pieces
- 1 Granny Smith apple, cored, cut into 8 wedges, then sliced crosswise into ¼-inch pieces
- 2 stalks celery, each cut lengthwise in half, then thinly sliced (½ cup)
- ½ cup walnuts, toasted and coarsely chopped
- ⅓ cup dark seedless raisins

In a medium bowl and using a wire whisk, mix the mayonnaise, sour cream, lemon juice, honey, and salt until blended. Add the apples, the celery, walnuts, and raisins to the dressing in the bowl and toss until mixed and coated with dressing.

Each serving About 180 calories, 2g protein, 16g carbohydrate, 14g fat (2g saturated), 3g fiber, 135mg sodium.

chopped salad

PREP: 25 MIN / TOTAL: 25 MIN / SERVES 8

1 large head romaine
lettuce (1¼ pounds),
chopped into ½-inch
pieces

1 bunch watercress
(4 ounces), tough
stems trimmed,
coarsely chopped

1¼ pounds ripe tomatoes
(2 large), cut into
½-inch pieces

1 medium cucumber
(8 ounces), peeled,
seeded, and cut
into ½-inch pieces

1 cup radishes, cut into
quarters

¼ cup Classic French
Vinaigrette (page
504) or dressing
of your choice

In a large bowl, combine the romaine, watercress, tomatoes,
cucumber, radishes, and dressing; toss to coat.

Each serving About 70 calories, 2g protein, 5g carbohydrate, 5g fat
(1g saturated), 3g fiber, 110mg sodium.

kale salad

PREP: 10 MIN / TOTAL: 20 MIN / SERVES 4

2 tablespoons fresh
lemon juice

2 tablespoons olive oil

⅛ teaspoon salt

1 bunch kale

½ cup pitted dates,
cut into slivers

⅓ cup roasted salted
almonds, chopped

¼ cup jarred pitted
green olives, sliced

1. In a large bowl, whisk together the lemon juice, olive oil, and salt.

2. Remove and discard the stems and ribs from the kale. Very
thinly slice the leaves; add to the bowl with the lemon vinaigrette,
tossing to coat. Let stand 10 minutes.

3. Add the dates, almonds, and olives; toss to combine.

Each serving About 220 calories, 6g protein, 22g carbohydrate, 15g fat
(2g saturated), 5g fiber, 270mg sodium.

KALE & ROASTED CAULIFLOWER SALAD 476

KALE SALAD 477

corn & barley salad

PREP: 20 MIN / TOTAL: 50 MIN, PLUS CHILLING / SERVES 12

2 cups water

1 cup pearl barley

Salt

6 ears corn, husks and silk removed

⅓ cup rice vinegar

2 tablespoons olive oil

½ teaspoon ground black pepper

1½ cups frozen shelled edamame, thawed

½ cup packed fresh mint leaves, chopped, plus additional sprigs for garnish

1. In a covered 2-quart saucepan, heat the water to boiling over high heat. Stir in the barley and ½ teaspoon salt; heat to boiling. Reduce the heat to low; cover and simmer 30 to 35 minutes, or until the barley is tender and the liquid is absorbed.

2. Meanwhile, with a sharp knife, carefully cut the corn kernels from the cobs; discard cobs. In a large bowl and using a wire whisk or fork, whisk the vinegar, oil, ¼ teaspoon salt, and the pepper until blended; stir in the warm barley, corn kernels, edamame, and chopped mint. Cover the salad and refrigerate at least 1 hour or up to 8 hours. To serve, garnish with mint sprigs.

Each serving About 155 calories, 6g protein, 25g carbohydrate, 5g fat (1g saturated), 5g fiber, 160mg sodium.

summer corn salad

PREP: 30 MIN / TOTAL: 40 MIN / SERVES 12

12 medium ears corn, husks and silk removed

12 ounces green beans, trimmed and cut into ¼-inch pieces

½ cup cider vinegar

¼ cup olive oil

¼ cup chopped fresh parsley

1 teaspoon salt

½ teaspoon coarsely ground black pepper

1 red bell pepper, finely chopped

1 small sweet onion, such as Vidalia or Walla Walla, finely chopped

1. In an 8-quart saucepot, heat 2 inches water to boiling over high heat; add the corn. Return to boiling. Reduce the heat; cover and simmer 5 minutes. Drain. When cool enough to handle, cut the kernels from the cobs.

2. Meanwhile, in a 2-quart saucepan, heat 1 inch water to boiling over high heat; add the green beans and return to boiling. Reduce the heat; simmer until tender-crisp, 3 to 5 minutes. Drain the green beans. Rinse with cold running water; drain.

3. Prepare the dressing: In a large bowl and using a wire whisk, mix the vinegar, oil, parsley, salt, and pepper until thoroughly blended.

4. Add the corn, green beans, bell pepper, and onion to the dressing in the bowl; toss to coat. If you're not serving immediately, cover and refrigerate up to 2 hours.

Each serving About 180 calories, 5g protein, 31g carbohydrate, 6g fat (1g saturated), 3g fiber, 220mg sodium.

bloody mary tomato salad

PREP: 15 MIN / TOTAL: 15 MIN, PLUS CHILLING / SERVES 8

2 tablespoons bottled horseradish

2 tablespoons olive oil

2 tablespoons vodka (optional)

1 tablespoon fresh lemon juice

1½ teaspoons hot sauce

1 teaspoon Worcestershire sauce

½ teaspoon salt

½ teaspoon ground black pepper

3 pints grape or cherry tomatoes, each cut in half

4 stalks celery, cut into ¼-inch-thick diagonal slices, leaves reserved for garnish

1. In a large bowl, whisk the horseradish, oil, vodka (if using), lemon juice, hot sauce, Worcestershire, salt, and pepper until blended. Add the tomatoes and celery; toss to combine. Cover and refrigerate 2 hours.

2. To serve, toss the salad again to coat the vegetables with the dressing and garnish with celery leaves.

Each serving About 65 calories, 1g protein, 7g carbohydrate, 4g fat (1g saturated), 2g fiber, 190mg sodium.

cantaloupe & cucumber salad

PREP: 20 MIN / TOTAL: 20 MIN / SERVES 10

- 1 large English (seedless) cucumber (1 pound)
- ¼ cup fresh lime juice
- ¼ teaspoon salt
- ⅛ teaspoon ground black pepper
- 2 ripe cantaloupes, coarsely chopped
- 3 green onions, thinly sliced
- ½ cup loosely packed fresh cilantro leaves, chopped

1. With a vegetable peeler, remove 4 evenly spaced lengthwise strips of peel from each cucumber. Coarsley chop the cucumber.

2. In a large bowl, whisk the lime juice, salt, and pepper until blended. Add the cucumber, cantaloupe, green onions, and cilantro; toss to coat.

Each serving About 45 calories, 2g protein, 11g carbohydrate, 0g fat (0g saturated), 1g fiber, 70mg sodium.

kirby cucumber salad

PREP: 30 MIN / TOTAL: 30 MIN, PLUS STANDING AND CHILLING / SERVES 12

- 4 pounds Kirby cucumbers, unpeeled, thinly sliced
- 1 tablespoon salt
- ¾ cup distilled white vinegar
- 2 tablespoons sugar
- 2 tablespoons chopped fresh dill

1. In a colander set over a large bowl, toss the cucumber slices and salt; let stand 30 minutes at room temperature. Discard the liquid in the bowl. Pat the cucumbers dry with paper towels. Wipe out the bowl.

2. In the same bowl, combine the vinegar, sugar, and dill. Add the cucumber slices and toss to coat. Cover and refrigerate, stirring occasionally, at least 1 hour or up to 4 hours to blend the flavors.

Each serving About 30 calories, 1g protein, 7g carbohydrate, 0g fat (0g saturated), 1g fiber, 150mg sodium.

GOOD TO KNOW

CUCUMBERS

AVAILABILITY

Year-round

PEAK SEASON

June through September

BUYING TIPS

Pick firm, slender cucumbers. Avoid overmature cucumbers, which are generally seedy, are dull or yellowish, and have an overgrown, puffy look. Smaller varieties, such as Kirbys, are preferred for pickling. English (seedless) and small Persian cucumbers are long and slender and have very small seeds that do not have to be removed.

TO STORE

Refrigerate in the crisper drawer up to one week.

TO PREPARE

Rinse cukes under cold running water. If the skin is tender and unwaxed (Kirbys and seedless varieties), then the cucumbers do not have to be peeled. To remove the seeds, cut the cucumber lengthwise in half and scoop out the seeds with a spoon or melon baller.

TO COOK

Cucumbers are well known as a salad ingredient, but they can also be sautéed alone or with other vegetables. When cooked, they have a delicate, squashlike flavor.

creamy cucumber & dill salad

PREP: 15 MIN / TOTAL: 15 MIN, PLUS STANDING AND CHILLING / SERVES 6

- 2 English (seedless) cucumbers, unpeeled, thinly sliced
- 2 teaspoons salt
- ½ cup sour cream
- 2 tablespoons chopped fresh dill

- 2 teaspoons chopped fresh mint
- 1 teaspoon distilled white vinegar
- ⅛ teaspoon ground black pepper

1. In a colander set over a large bowl, toss the cucumbers and salt; let stand 30 minutes at room temperature to drain. Discard the liquid in the bowl. Pat the cucumbers dry with paper towels. Wipe out the bowl.

2. In the same bowl, combine the sour cream, dill, mint, vinegar, and pepper. Add the cucumbers, stirring to coat. Cover and refrigerate at least 1 hour or up to 4 hours to blend the flavors.

Each serving About 60 calories, 2g protein, 5g carbohydrate, 4g fat (3g saturated), 1g fiber, 205mg sodium.

Serving Suggestion Serve these thinly sliced cucumbers as a cool side dish with grilled salmon (see page 399).

spiced watermelon & tomato salad

PREP: 20 MIN / TOTAL: 20 MIN / SERVES 10

- 3 ripe medium tomatoes (about 1 pound), cut into ¾-inch pieces
- ¼ cup fresh lime juice (from 2 to 3 limes)
- ½ teaspoon salt
- 1 piece watermelon (about 2½ pounds with rind)

- 2 tablespoons chopped fresh cilantro leaves
- ½ teaspoon ground cumin
- ½ teaspoon ground coriander
- ⅛ teaspoon cayenne pepper

1. In a large bowl, toss the tomatoes with the lime juice and salt; set aside.

2. Cut the rind from the watermelon; discard rind. Cut the flesh into ½-inch pieces to equal 4 cups; discard seeds.

3. Add the watermelon, cilantro, cumin, coriander, and cayenne to the tomato mixture; toss well to combine. Serve at room temperature or cover and refrigerate to serve later.

Each serving About 30 calories, 1g protein, 7g carbohydrate, 0g fat (0g saturated), 1g fiber, 120mg sodium.

TESTING NOTE Seedless watermelon makes preparation easy. Choose one that is heavy for its size and makes a thud when tapped.

light & lemony slaw

PREP: 25 MIN / TOTAL: 25 MIN / SERVES 12

- 2 lemons
- ½ cup light mayonnaise
- ¼ cup reduced-fat sour cream
- 1 tablespoon sugar
- 1 teaspoon salt
- ½ teaspoon coarsely ground black pepper

- ¼ teaspoon celery seeds, crushed
- 1 large head green cabbage (3 pounds), quartered, cored, and thinly sliced, tough ribs discarded (12 cups)
- 4 carrots, peeled and shredded

1. From the lemons, grate 1 teaspoon zest and squeeze ¼ cup juice. In a large bowl and using a wire whisk, mix the lemon zest and juice, mayonnaise, sour cream, sugar, salt, pepper, and celery seeds until blended.

2. Add the cabbage and carrots to the dressing in the bowl; toss to coat. Serve at room temperature, or cover and refrigerate up to 4 hours.

Each serving About 80 calories, 2g protein, 10g carbohydrate, 4g fat (1g saturated), 3g fiber, 300mg sodium.

coleslaw

with vinaigrette

PREP: 20 MIN / TOTAL: 20 MIN, PLUS CHILLING / SERVES 6

- 2 tablespoons olive or vegetable oil
- 2 tablespoons red wine vinegar
- 1 tablespoon sugar
- 1 teaspoon salt
- ½ teaspoon caraway seeds, crushed, or ¼ teaspoon celery seeds, crushed
- 1 small head green cabbage (1½ pounds), quartered, cored, and thinly sliced, tough ribs discarded (6 cups)
- 1 large red bell pepper, cut into 2 × ¼-inch matchstick strips

In a large bowl and using a wire whisk, mix the oil, vinegar, sugar, salt, and caraway seeds until blended. Add the cabbage and bell pepper; toss to coat well. Cover and refrigerate at least 1 hour or up to 6 hours to blend the flavors.

Each serving About 75 calories, 1g protein, 8g carbohydrate, 5g fat (1g saturated), 3g fiber, 405mg sodium.

asian coleslaw

PREP: 35 MIN / TOTAL: 35 MIN / SERVES 12

- ⅓ cup seasoned rice vinegar
- 2 tablespoons vegetable oil
- 2 teaspoons Asian sesame oil
- ¾ teaspoon salt
- 1 medium head savoy cabbage (2½ pounds), quartered, cored, and thinly sliced, tough ribs discarded (10 cups)
- 1 bag (16 ounces) carrots, peeled and shredded
- ½ cup chopped fresh cilantro
- 4 green onions, thinly sliced

1. Prepare the dressing: In a large bowl and using a wire whisk, mix the vinegar, vegetable and sesame oils, and salt until blended.

2. Add the cabbage, carrots, cilantro, and green onions to the dressing in the bowl; toss until mixed and coated with dressing. If you're not serving right away, cover and refrigerate up to 2 hours.

Each serving About 70 calories, 2g protein, 10g carbohydrate, 3g fat (0g saturated), 3g fiber, 310mg sodium.

two-potato salad

PREP: 15 MIN / TOTAL: 30 MIN, PLUS COOLING / SERVES 14

- 2 pounds red potatoes (about 8 medium), cut into 1-inch chunks
- 1 pound sweet potatoes (2 small), peeled and cut into 1-inch chunks
- ¼ cup red wine vinegar
- 1 tablespoon spicy brown mustard
- 1¼ teaspoons salt
- ½ teaspoon coarsely ground black pepper
- ½ cup mayonnaise
- ¼ cup milk
- 2 medium celery stalks, chopped
- 1 small red onion, minced
- ⅓ cup loosely packed fresh flat-leaf parsley leaves, chopped

1. In a 5- to 6-quart saucepot, place the red potatoes and enough water to cover by 1 inch; heat to boiling over high heat. Reduce the heat to low and simmer 2 minutes. Stir in the sweet potatoes; heat to boiling over high heat. Reduce the heat to low; cover and simmer until the potatoes are just fork-tender, 8 to 10 minutes.

2. Meanwhile, prepare the dressing. In a large bowl and using a wire whisk, mix the vinegar, mustard, salt, and pepper.

3. Drain the potatoes. Add the hot potatoes to the dressing in the bowl; gently stir with a rubber spatula until evenly coated. Let stand until cool.

4. In a small bowl, whisk the mayonnaise and milk until smooth. Add the mayonnaise mixture, celery, onion, and parsley to the potato mixture; gently stir with a rubber spatula until the potatoes are well coated. Serve while still warm, or cover and refrigerate until ready to serve.

Each serving About 150 calories, 2g protein, 21g carbohydrate, 7g fat (1g saturated), 2g fiber, 280mg sodium.

creamy potato salad

PREP: 20 MIN / TOTAL: 55 MIN / SERVES 10

3 pounds all-purpose potatoes (9 medium), unpeeled

½ cup mayonnaise

½ cup milk

2 tablespoons distilled white vinegar

2 tablespoons chopped green onion

1 teaspoon sugar

1 teaspoon salt

¼ teaspoon coarsely ground black pepper

2 large stalks celery, thinly sliced

1. In a 4-quart saucepan, combine the potatoes and enough water to cover; heat to boiling over high heat. Reduce the heat; cover and simmer until tender, 25 to 30 minutes. Drain. When cool enough to handle, peel the potatoes and cut them into ¾-inch cubes.

2. Meanwhile, prepare the dressing: In a large bowl and using a wire whisk, mix the mayonnaise, milk, vinegar, green onion, sugar, salt, and pepper until blended. Add the potatoes and celery to the dressing; toss to coat. If you're not serving right away, cover and refrigerate up to 4 hours.

Each serving About 200 calories, 3g protein, 27g carbohydrate, 9g fat (2g saturated), 2g fiber, 315mg sodium.

white & wild rice salad

PREP: 25 MIN / TOTAL: 1 HR 20 MIN, PLUS COOLING / SERVES 8

½ cup wild rice

Salt

¾ cup regular long-grain rice

⅓ cup dried cranberries or currants

2 tablespoons olive oil

2 tablespoons red wine vinegar

½ teaspoon freshly grated orange zest

¼ teaspoon ground black pepper

2 cups seedless red grapes, cut in half

2 stalks celery, thinly sliced (1 cup)

2 tablespoons chopped fresh parsley

½ cup pecans, toasted and coarsely chopped

1. Cook the wild rice as the label directs, using ½ teaspoon salt. Cook the white rice as the label directs, using ¼ teaspoon salt.

2. In a small bowl, combine the cranberries with just enough boiling water to cover; let stand 5 minutes to soften. Drain.

3. Meanwhile, prepare the dressing: In a large bowl and using a wire whisk, mix the oil, vinegar, orange zest, ¾ teaspoon salt, and the pepper until blended. Add the wild and white rice and cranberries; toss to coat. Let cool 30 minutes, tossing several times.

4. Add the grapes, celery, and parsley to the rice mixture; toss until thoroughly mixed and coated with dressing. Transfer to a serving bowl. Sprinkle with pecans.

Each serving About 220 calories, 4g protein, 34g carbohydrate, 8g fat (1g saturated), 3g fiber, 450mg sodium.

mediterranean rice salad

PREP: 25 MIN / TOTAL: 55 MIN, PLUS COOLING / SERVES 6

2 cups water

1 cup regular long-grain rice

3 cloves garlic, finely chopped

Salt

3 tablespoons olive oil

1 small red onion, chopped

1 red bell pepper, chopped

1 medium zucchini (8 ounces), cut lengthwise into quarters, then sliced crosswise into ½-inch-thick pieces

2 tablespoons fresh lemon juice

⅓ cup Kalamata olives, pitted and coarsely chopped

1. In a 2-quart saucepan, heat the water to boiling over high heat. Add the rice, garlic, and ½ teaspoon salt. Reduce the heat; cover and simmer until the rice is tender, about 17 minutes.

2. Meanwhile, in a 10-inch skillet, heat 1 tablespoon oil over medium heat. Add the onion and cook, stirring, 2 minutes. Add the bell pepper, zucchini, and ¼ teaspoon salt and cook, stirring occasionally, until tender-crisp, about 4 minutes.

3. Prepare the dressing: In a large bowl and using a wire whisk, mix the lemon juice, the remaining 2 tablespoons oil, and ½ teaspoon salt until blended. Add the rice, vegetable mixture, and olives; toss until mixed and coated with dressing. Cool to room temperature. Serve at room temperature or cover and refrigerate up to 2 hours.

Each serving About 215 calories, 3g protein, 30g carbohydrate, 9g fat (1g saturated), 2g fiber, 625mg sodium.

red potato salad

PREP: 25 MIN / TOTAL: 55 MIN, PLUS COOLING / SERVES 12

4 pounds small red
potatoes, unpeeled,
cut into quarters or
eighths if large
Salt
4 slices bacon
3 large shallots, chopped
(¾ cup)

⅓ cup cider vinegar
¼ cup olive oil
2 teaspoons sugar
2 teaspoons Dijon
mustard
¼ teaspoon coarsely
ground black pepper
2 green onions, chopped

1. In a 5-quart saucepot, combine the potatoes, enough water to cover, and 2 teaspoons salt; heat to boiling over high heat. Reduce the heat; cover and simmer until tender, 10 to 12 minutes.

2. Meanwhile, in a 10-inch skillet, cook the bacon over medium-low heat until browned. With a slotted spoon, transfer to the paper towels to cool and drain; crumble.

3. Discard all but 1 teaspoon bacon drippings from the skillet. Reduce the heat to low. Add the shallots and cook, stirring, until tender, about 5 minutes. Remove from the heat.

4. Prepare the dressing: In a large bowl and using a wire whisk, mix the shallots, vinegar, oil, sugar, mustard, 1½ teaspoons salt, and the pepper until blended.

5. Drain the potatoes. Add the hot potatoes to the dressing in the bowl. With a rubber spatula, stir gently until the potatoes absorb the dressing. Let the potatoes cool 30 minutes at room temperature, stirring occasionally. Stir in the green onions.

6. If you're not serving right away, cover and refrigerate up to 4 hours. If chilled, let stand 30 minutes at room temperature before serving. To serve, sprinkle with crumbled bacon.

Each serving About 185 calories, 4g protein, 29g carbohydrate, 6g fat (1g saturated), 3g fiber, 455mg sodium.

VARIATION

Dilled Red Potatoes with Mint

Prepare the potatoes as directed in step 1; drain. Omit the bacon, shallots, vinegar, sugar, and mustard. In a large bowl, mix the olive oil, 1½ **teaspoons salt**, and pepper. Add **6 green onions**, chopped; ⅓ **cup chopped fresh dill**; and ¼ **cup chopped fresh mint**. Add the hot potatoes to the herb mixture in the bowl and toss until mixed. Makes 8 side servings.

barley salad
with nectarines

PREP: 30 MIN / TOTAL: 1 HR 25 MIN / SERVES 16

6 cups water
1 package (16 ounces)
pearl barley
Salt
4 limes
⅓ cup olive oil
1 tablespoon sugar
¾ teaspoon coarsely
ground black
pepper

1½ pounds nectarines
(4 medium), cut into
½-inch pieces
1 pound ripe tomatoes
(2 large), halved,
seeded, and cut into
½-inch pieces
4 green onions, thinly
sliced
½ cup chopped fresh mint

1. In a 4-quart saucepan, heat 6 cups water to boiling over high heat. Add the barley and 1½ teaspoons salt; heat to boiling. Reduce the heat; cover and simmer until the barley is tender and the liquid has been absorbed, about 45 minutes. The barley will have a creamy consistency.

2. Meanwhile, from the limes, grate 1 tablespoon zest and squeeze ½ cup juice. In a large bowl, mix the lime zest and juice, oil, sugar, pepper, and 1¼ teaspoons salt until blended.

3. Rinse the barley with cold running water; drain. Add the barley, nectarines, tomatoes, green onions, and mint to the dressing in the bowl; stir gently until mixed and coated with dressing. If you're not serving right away, cover and refrigerate up to 1 hour.

Each serving About 170 calories, 4g protein, 30g carbohydrate, 5g fat (1g saturated), 6g fiber, 335mg sodium.

GOOD TO KNOW

NECTARINES

Nectarines are at their peak in summer. Shop for plump, richly colored, smooth-skinned fruit, deep reddish to yellowish in color. Slightly firm nectarines ripen well at room temperature. Avoid hard, soft, or shriveled nectarines or any with green skin near the stem. Ripen nectarines at room temperature, then refrigerate, and use within two or three days.

tubetti macaroni salad

PREP: 25 MIN / TOTAL: 50 MIN / SERVES 12

1 pound tubetti or ditalini pasta

Salt

4 carrots, peeled and cut into 2 × ¼-inch matchstick strips

1 or 2 lemons

⅔ cup light mayonnaise

⅓ cup milk

2 stalks celery, cut into 2 × ¼-inch matchstick strips

2 green onions, thinly sliced

1. In a large saucepot, cook the pasta as the label directs, using 2 teaspoons salt. After the pasta has cooked 10 minutes, add the carrots to the pasta water and cook until the carrots are just tender-crisp and the pasta is done, 1 to 2 minutes longer.

2. Meanwhile, from the lemons, grate 1 teaspoon zest and squeeze 3 tablespoons juice. Prepare the dressing: In a large bowl and using a wire whisk, mix the mayonnaise, milk, lemon zest and juice, and ¾ teaspoon salt until blended.

3. Drain the pasta and carrots and add them to the dressing in the bowl along with the celery and green onions; toss until mixed and coated with dressing. Serve at room temperature, or cover and refrigerate up to 4 hours.

Each serving About 200 calories, 5g protein, 33g carbohydrate, 5g fat (1g saturated), 2g fiber, 465mg sodium.

GLOSSARY →

Though **macaroni salad** was popularized during the 1950s in school cafeterias across America, this creamy crowd-pleaser has been around since at least 1917. One of the first printed recipes appeared in *Mrs. Allen's Cook Book* by Ida Bailey Allen. The salad contained four simple ingredients—macaroni, celery, stuffed olives, and mayonnaise— and was served chilled on a bed of lettuce.

cobb salad

PREP: 25 MIN / TOTAL: 35 MIN / SERVES 6

12 ounces skinless, boneless chicken breast halves

¼ teaspoon salt

⅛ teaspoon ground black pepper

6 slices bacon, coarsely chopped

1 large head iceberg lettuce, thinly sliced (12 cups)

3 large hard-cooked eggs, peeled and coarsely chopped

1 large ripe tomato (10 ounces), cut into ½-inch pieces

1 ripe avocado, pitted, peeled, and cut into ½-inch pieces

3 ounces Roquefort cheese, crumbled (¾ cup)

Classic French Vinaigrette (page 504)

1. Preheat the broiler. Place the chicken on a rack in a broiling pan and sprinkle with the salt and pepper. Place the pan 6 inches from the heat source. Broil until the chicken loses its pink color throughout, about 4 minutes per side. When the chicken is cool enough to handle, cut it into ½-inch pieces.

2. Meanwhile, in a 10-inch skillet, cook the bacon over medium heat until browned. With a slotted spoon, transfer bacon to paper towels to cool and drain.

3. Line a large platter with iceberg lettuce. Arrange the eggs, tomato, avocado, Roquefort, chicken, and bacon in a striped pattern over lettuce. Serve the dressing separately.

Each serving (without dressing) About 270 calories, 24g protein, 9g carbohydrate, 16g fat (6g saturated), 4g fiber, 540mg sodium.

nicoise salad

PREP: 35 MIN / TOTAL: 1 HR / SERVES 4

- 1 tablespoon white wine vinegar
- 1 tablespoon fresh lemon juice
- 1 tablespoon minced shallot
- 1 teaspoon Dijon mustard
- 1 teaspoon anchovy paste
- ¼ teaspoon sugar
- ¼ teaspoon coarsely ground black pepper
- 3 tablespoons extra-virgin olive oil
- 1 pound medium red potatoes, unpeeled, cut into ¼-inch-thick slices

- 8 ounces French green beans (haricots verts) or regular green beans, trimmed
- 1 head Boston lettuce, leaves separated
- 12 cherry tomatoes, each cut in half
- 1 can (12 ounces) solid white tuna in water, drained and flaked
- 2 large hard-cooked eggs, peeled, each cut into quarters
- ½ cup Nicoise olives

1. Prepare the dressing: In a small bowl and using a wire whisk, mix the vinegar, lemon juice, shallot, mustard, anchovy paste, sugar, and pepper until blended. In a thin, steady stream, whisk in the oil until blended.

2. In a 3-quart saucepan, combine the potatoes and enough water to cover; heat to boiling over high heat. Reduce the heat; cover and simmer until tender, about 10 minutes. Drain.

3. Meanwhile, in a 10-inch skillet, heat 1 inch water to boiling over high heat. Add the green beans; heat to boiling. Reduce the heat to low and cook until tender-crisp, 6 to 8 minutes. Drain; rinse with cold running water. Drain.

4. To serve, pour half the dressing into a medium bowl. Add the lettuce leaves and toss to coat. Line a large platter with the dressed lettuce leaves. Arrange the potatoes, green beans, cherry tomatoes, tuna, eggs, and olives in separate piles on the lettuce. Drizzle the remaining dressing over the salad.

Each serving About 440 calories, 30g protein, 30g carbohydrate, 23g fat (4g saturated), 5g fiber, 715mg sodium.

GOOD TO KNOW

BLUE CHEESE

Cheeses in this category have been injected with the spores of special molds so that they develop blue or blue-green veins or spotting. Most blue cheeses are strongly flavored and have a soft, crumbly texture. Some can be easily sliced, but most are best spread or crumbled. Here are some of our favorite varieties.

DANISH BLUE	A cow's-milk cheese with a creamy, moist texture and uncomplicated flavor.
GORGONZOLA	An ivory-colored cow's-milk cheese from Italy with a deliciously complex flavor and a creamy texture. There are two kinds of gorgonzola: dolce, which is milder, and naturale, which is more pungent.
MAYTAG BLUE	An American-made blue cow's-milk cheese with a pleasantly bold flavor and creamy texture.
ROQUEFORT	Known by many as the "king of cheeses," this is one of the oldest and most famous cheeses in the world. It is made from sheep's milk and aged for at least three months in the limestone caverns of Mount Combalou near the French town of Roquefort. It has a moist, crumbly texture, assertive flavor, and is somewhat salty.
STILTON	A cow's-milk cheese from England with a firm yet creamy texture and bold flavor.

italian seafood salad

PREP: 50 MIN / TOTAL: 1 HR 5 MIN, PLUS CHILLING / SERVES 12

1 pound sea scallops

2 pounds cleaned squid

1 small lemon, thinly sliced

2 pounds large (16 to 20 count) shrimp, shelled and deveined (page 297)

⅔ cup fresh lemon juice (from 4 lemons)

½ cup olive oil

1 small clove garlic, minced

½ teaspoon salt

½ teaspoon coarsely ground black pepper

4 large stalks celery, cut into ½-inch pieces

½ cup Gaeta or Nicoise olives (optional)

¼ cup loosely packed fresh parsley leaves

1. Pull the tough crescent-shaped muscle from the side of each scallop; discard. Rinse the squid; slice the bodies crosswise into ¾-inch-thick rings. Cut the tentacles into several pieces, if large. In a 5-quart saucepot, combine 2½ inches of water and the lemon slices; heat to boiling over high heat. Add the shrimp. Reduce the heat to medium; cook until the shrimp are opaque throughout, 1 to 2 minutes. With a slotted spoon, transfer the shrimp to a colander to drain; transfer to a large bowl.

2. To the boiling water in the saucepot, add the scallops; cook just until opaque throughout, 2 to 3 minutes. With a slotted spoon, transfer the scallops to the colander to drain; add to the shrimp in the bowl.

3. To the boiling water in the saucepot, add the squid; cook until tender and opaque, 30 seconds to 1 minute. Drain in the colander; add to the shrimp and scallops in the bowl.

4. Prepare the dressing: In a small bowl and using a wire whisk, mix the lemon juice, oil, garlic, salt, and pepper until blended. Add the celery, olives (if using), and parsley to the seafood in the bowl; toss to mix. Add the dressing and toss until the salad is mixed and coated with dressing. Cover and refrigerate the salad at least 3 hours or up to 8 hours to blend the flavors.

Each serving About 255 calories, 31g protein, 6g carbohydrate, 11g fat (2g saturated), 0g fiber, 200mg sodium.

tomato & mint tabbouleh

PREP: 20 MIN / TOTAL: 20 MIN, PLUS STANDING AND CHILLING / SERVES 12

1½ cups medium-grain bulgur wheat

¼ cup fresh lemon juice (from 2 or 3 lemons)

1½ cups boiling water

1 pound ripe tomatoes (3 medium), cut into ½-inch pieces

1 medium cucumber (8 ounces), peeled and cut into ½-inch pieces

3 green onions, chopped

¾ cup loosely packed fresh flat-leaf parsley leaves, chopped

½ cup loosely packed fresh mint leaves, chopped

1 tablespoon olive oil

¾ teaspoon salt

¼ teaspoon coarsely ground black pepper

1. In a medium bowl, combine the bulgur, lemon juice, and boiling water, stirring to mix. Let stand until the liquid has been absorbed, about 30 minutes.

2. To the bulgur mixture, add the tomatoes, cucumber, green onions, parsley, mint, oil, salt, and pepper, stirring to mix. Cover and refrigerate at least 1 hour or up to 4 hours to blend the flavors.

Each serving About 90 calories, 3g protein, 17g carbohydrate, 2g fat (0g saturated), 3g fiber, 160mg sodium.

GLOSSARY →

Tabbouleh, also spelled *tabouli* and *taboulea*, is a Lebanese bulgur-based salad is often served as part of a meze (a spread of appetizers). Its primary ingredients are bulgur, lots of fresh chopped parsley and mint, chunks of tomato, green onions, and a fresh lemon dressing. Some tabboulehs are flavored with crushed red pepper or fresh chiles, while others contain a hint of cinnamon or allspice.

warm lentil salad
with shrimp & mint

PREP: 20 MIN / TOTAL: 30 MIN / SERVES 4

- 3 tablespoons olive oil
- 3 tablespoons cider vinegar
- 1½ teaspoons salt
- ¼ teaspoon coarsely ground black pepper
- 1 pound fresh or frozen (thawed) shelled and deveined medium (26 to 30 count) shrimp
- 1 cup lentils, rinsed and picked over
- 6 cups water
- 1 small onion, chopped
- ½ cup loosely packed fresh mint leaves, chopped
- 1 Golden Delicious apple, unpeeled, cored, and cut into ½-inch chunks
- 1 stalk celery, thinly sliced

1. In a small bowl, whisk together the oil, vinegar, salt, and pepper. Spoon 2 tablespoons dressing into a medium bowl. Add the shrimp; toss to coat.

2. In a 4-quart saucepan, combine the lentils, water, onion, and 2 tablespoons mint; heat to boiling over high heat. Reduce the heat to low; cover and simmer 12 to 15 minutes, or until the lentils are tender but still hold their shape. Drain well.

3. Meanwhile, heat a 12-inch skillet over medium-high heat until hot. Add the shrimp and cook 4 to 5 minutes, or until the shrimp turn opaque. Remove from heat; stir in 1 tablespoon mint.

4. Stir the shrimp, apple, celery, and the remaining mint and dressing into the lentils.

Each serving About 410 calories, 37g protein, 37g carbohydrate, 13g fat (2g saturated), 17g fiber, 475mg sodium.

sopressata & roma bean salad
with pecorino

PREP: 10 MIN / TOTAL: 25 MIN / SERVES 4

- 1¼ pounds Roma (broad) beans or green beans, trimmed
- 1 lemon
- 2 tablespoons extra-virgin olive oil
- ¼ teaspoon salt
- ⅛ teaspoon coarsely ground black pepper
- 4 ounces thinly sliced sopressata or Genoa salami, cut into ½-inch-wide strips
- 2 small bunches arugula (4 ounces each), tough stems trimmed, or 2 bags (5 ounces each) arugula
- 1 wedge Pecorino Romano cheese (about 2 ounces)

1. If the Roma beans are very long, cut them crosswise into 2½-inch pieces. In a 12-inch skillet, heat 1 inch water to boiling over high heat. Add the beans; heat to boiling. Reduce the heat to low; simmer until the beans are tender-crisp, 6 to 8 minutes. Drain the beans. Rinse with cold running water to stop the cooking; drain.

2. Meanwhile, from the lemon, grate ½ teaspoon zest and squeeze 2 tablespoons juice. In a large bowl and using a wire whisk, mix the lemon zest and juice, oil, salt, and pepper.

3. Add the beans, sopressata, and arugula to the dressing in the bowl; toss to coat.

4. To serve, spoon the salad onto a serving platter. With a vegetable peeler, shave thin strips from a wedge of Pecorino Romano onto the salad.

Each serving About 280 calories, 14g protein, 14g carbohydrate, 21g fat (7g saturated), 6g fiber, 845mg sodium.

GLOSSARY →

Soppressata is a type of salami, originally from Southern Italy, made with coarsely chopped chunks of pork and fat and spices. It has a drier coarser texture than Genoa salami, and usually a smaller diameter than commercial salamis. It is available sweet or hot.

classic egg salad

PREP: 10 MIN / TOTAL: 20 MIN, PLUS STANDING / SERVES 4

6 large eggs
¼ cup mayonnaise

1½ teaspoons Dijon or spicy brown mustard
¼ teaspoon salt

1. In a 3-quart saucepan, place the eggs and enough cold water to cover by at least 1 inch; heat to boiling over high heat. Immediately remove the saucepan from the heat and cover tightly; let stand 15 minutes. Pour off the hot water and run cold water over the eggs to cool. Peel the eggs.

2. Coarsely chop the eggs and transfer them to a medium bowl. Add the mayonnaise, mustard, and salt and stir to combine. If you're not serving right away, cover and refrigerate up to 4 hours.

Each serving About 220 calories, 10g protein, 1g carbohydrate, 19g fat (4g saturated), 0g fiber, 360mg sodium.

VARIATIONS

Curried Egg Salad

Prepare as directed, but add **4 teaspoons chopped mango chutney** and **½ teaspoon curry powder** to the egg mixture.

Caesar-Style Egg Salad

Prepare as directed, but use only ⅛ **teaspoon salt**. Add **2 tablespoons freshly grated Parmesan cheese** and **1 teaspoon anchovy paste** to the egg mixture.

Mexican-Style Egg Salad

Prepare as directed, but add ⅓ **cup chopped fresh cilantro** and ½ **teaspoon hot sauce** to the egg mixture.

Deli-Style Egg Salad

Prepare as directed, but add ¼ **cup chopped celery** and ¼ **cup chopped red onion** to the egg mixture.

best chicken salad

PREP: 20 MIN / TOTAL: 1 HR 20 MIN, PLUS COOLING / SERVES 4

1 chicken (3 pounds)
Salt
3 stalks celery, finely chopped

¼ cup mayonnaise
2 teaspoons fresh lemon juice
¼ teaspoon ground black pepper

1. In a 4-quart saucepan, combine the chicken, 1 teaspoon salt, and enough water to cover; heat to boiling over high heat. Reduce the heat; cover and simmer gently until the chicken loses its pink color throughout, about 45 minutes. Let stand 30 minutes; drain (reserve broth for another use). When the chicken is cool enough to handle, discard the skin and bones; cut the meat into bite-size pieces.

2. In a large bowl, combine the celery, mayonnaise, lemon juice, ½ teaspoon salt, and the pepper; stir until blended. Add the chicken and toss to coat.

Each serving About 340 calories, 36g protein, 2g carbohydrate, 20g fat (4g saturated), 0g fiber, 780mg sodium.

VARIATIONS

Basil & Sun-Dried Tomato Chicken Salad

Prepare as directed, but add ¼ **cup chopped fresh basil** and **2 tablespoons finely chopped oil-packed sun-dried tomatoes**, drained, to the mayonnaise mixture.

Curry-Grape Chicken Salad

Prepare as directed, but add **2 cups red or green seedless grapes**, cut in half; **1 teaspoon curry powder**; and **1 teaspoon honey** to the mayonnaise mixture.

Lemon-Pepper Chicken Salad

Prepare as directed, but use **1 tablespoon fresh lemon juice** and ½ **teaspoon coarsely ground black pepper**; add ½ **teaspoon freshly grated lemon zest** to the mayonnaise mixture.

 Tip Lighten up creamy salads like tuna, chicken, and egg by replacing half of the mayonnaise with nonfat Greek yogurt.

classic tuna salad

PREP: 10 MIN / TOTAL: 10 MIN / SERVES 2

- 1 can (6 ounces) solid white tuna in water, drained
- 2 stalks celery, finely chopped
- 3 tablespoons mayonnaise
- 2 teaspoons fresh lemon juice
- ¼ teaspoon ground black pepper

In a small bowl, combine the tuna, celery, mayonnaise, lemon juice, and pepper, flaking the tuna with a fork. If you're not serving right away, cover and refrigerate up to 4 hours.

Each serving About 265 calories, 22g protein, 3g carbohydrate, 18g fat (3g saturated), 1g fiber, 460mg sodium.

VARIATIONS

Curried Tuna Salad

Prepare as directed, but substitute ½ **Granny Smith apple**, peeled, cored, and finely chopped, for the celery, and add **1 teaspoon curry powder** to the tuna mixture.

Mexican-Style Tuna Salad

Prepare as directed, but add **2 tablespoons chopped fresh cilantro** and **1 pickled jalapeño chile**, finely chopped, to the tuna mixture.

Mediterranean Tuna Salad

Prepare as directed, but omit the celery and mayonnaise, and increase the lemon juice to 2 tablespoons. Rinse and drain **1 can (15 to 19 ounces) white kidney (cannellini) beans**. In a large bowl, mash 1 cup beans. Stir in ½ **cup chopped fresh basil**; **3 tablespoons minced red onion**; **3 tablespoons capers**, drained and chopped; **2 tablespoons olive oil**; **2 teaspoons fresh lemon juice**; and ¼ **teaspoon ground black pepper**. Add the tuna and remaining beans; toss to combine. Makes 4 main-dish servings.

buffalo chicken cobb salad

(See photo on page 471.)

PREP: 35 MIN / TOTAL: 40 MIN / SERVES 6

- 2 cups rotisserie chicken meat cut into bite-size pieces
- ⅓ cup cayenne pepper hot sauce
- 1 teaspoon distilled white vinegar
- 6 hard-cooked eggs
- 3 stalks celery
- 3 small tomatoes
- 1 head butter or Boston lettuce
- Avocado-Buttermilk Ranch Dressing (below)

1. In a medium bowl, toss the chicken with the hot sauce and vinegar until well coated.

2. Slice the eggs crosswise and thinly slice the celery; cut the tomatoes into wedges or slices. Separate the lettuce leaves; arrange them on a large serving platter. Top with the eggs, celery, tomatoes, and chicken. Drizzle with the dressing. Refrigerate the remaining dressing for another use.

AVOCADO-BUTTERMILK RANCH DRESSING In a blender, puree **1 cup low-fat buttermilk**, **1 ripe small avocado**, **2 tablespoons fresh lemon juice**, **1 clove garlic**, and ¾ **teaspoon each salt and ground black pepper** until smooth. Transfer to a container; stir in **2 tablespoons chopped fresh dill** and **1 tablespoon snipped fresh chives**. Makes 1 cup.

Each serving About 200 calories, 16g protein, 8g carbohydrate, 14g fat (4g saturated), 2g fiber, 880mg sodium

GRILLED PLUM & PORK SALAD 490

TAPAS SALAD 491

grilled plum & pork salad

PREP: 15 MIN / TOTAL: 30 MIN / SERVES 4

1 pound pork tenderloin
Canola oil, for brushing
Salt
¼ cup hot sauce
2 tablespoons brown
 sugar
2 cloves garlic, crushed
 with a garlic press

3 plums, cut into wedges
1 medium head cabbage
 (2 pounds), quartered,
 cored, and thinly
 sliced, tough ribs
 discarded (8 cups)

1. Prepare a large grill pan or an outdoor grill for covered grilling over medium-high heat.

2. Brush the pork with canola oil; sprinkle with ¼ teaspoon salt. Grill over medium-high heat, covered, 10 minutes, turning once.

3. In a small bowl, whisk the hot sauce with the brown sugar and garlic. Coat the plums with canola oil. Grill, cut sides down, 3 to 5 minutes, covered, turning once. In a large bowl, toss the plums with cabbage, 2 teaspoons oil, and salt to taste; transfer to a platter.

4. Brush the pork generously with hot sauce mixture; grill 6 to 8 minutes more, or until cooked through, brushing and turning. Slice the pork; serve over plums and cabbage.

Each serving About 265 calories, 24g protein, 22g carbohydrate, 10g fat (2g saturated), 4g fiber, 875mg sodium.

#SavetheFood

revive greens

Forgot about that head of lettuce at the bottom of your fridge? Revive most greens—iceberg lettuce, arugula, kale, and even herbs—by soaking them in an ice bath for five minutes. Spin or pat dry, and they'll be as good as new!

tapas salad

PREP: 15 MIN / TOTAL: 15 MIN / SERVES 4

- 3 tablespoons extra-virgin olive oil
- 2 tablespoons sherry vinegar
- 1 clove garlic, crushed with a garlic press
- Salt
- Ground black pepper
- 1 cup packed shaved Manchego cheese
- 4 ounces Spanish chorizo, cut into quarters lengthwise, then thinly sliced
- ½ cup roasted red peppers, chopped
- 2 romaine hearts, leaves separated
- Baguette, for serving (optional)

1. In a large bowl, whisk the olive oil, sherry vinegar, garlic, and salt and pepper to taste. Add the Manchego, chorizo, and roasted red peppers. Toss well.

2. Arrange the lettuce on a serving platter. Top with the cheese mixture. Serve with the baguette, if desired.

Each serving About 305 calories, 11g protein, 5g carbohydrate, 26g fat (9g saturated), 2g fiber, 640mg sodium.

 Tip Trim an inch off the base of your romaine hearts to release the leaves all at once.

cranberry port-wine jelly

PREP: 20 MIN / TOTAL: 35 MIN, PLUS CHILLING / SERVES 8

- 1 lemon
- 3 cups cranberry-juice cocktail
- 1¼ cups sugar
- 4 whole allspice berries
- 1 cinnamon stick (3 inches), broken in half
- 2 packages (¼ ounce each) unflavored gelatin
- 1 cup port wine
- Salt
- Kumquats, lemon leaves, and frosted cranberries, for garnish (optional)

1. From the lemon, using a vegetable peeler or sharp paring knife, remove 4 strips of peel (3 × ¾ inch each); squeeze 3 tablespoons juice.

2. In a 2-quart nonreactive saucepan, heat the cranberry-juice cocktail, sugar, allspice, cinnamon stick, and lemon peel to boiling over high heat; boil 10 minutes.

3. Meanwhile, in a small bowl, evenly sprinkle the gelatin over port wine; let stand 2 minutes to soften the gelatin.

4. With a slotted spoon, remove the lemon peel and whole spices from the cranberry juice and discard. Stir in the gelatin mixture and cook over low heat, stirring frequently, until the gelatin has completely dissolved, 1 to 2 minutes. Stir in the lemon juice and a pinch of salt.

5. Pour the gelatin mixture into a 5- to 6-cup decorative mold. Cover with plastic wrap and refrigerate 6 hours or overnight until firm.

6. To unmold, dip the pan in a large bowl of hot water for 10 seconds and invert onto a large round platter. Garnish with kumquats, lemon leaves, and frosted cranberries as desired. Cover and refrigerate up to 2 hours before serving.

Each serving About 225 calories, 2g protein, 48g carbohydrate, 0g fat (0g saturated), 0g fiber, 25mg sodium.

GOOD TO KNOW

JELLY

Before there was Jell-O®, there were jellies and aspics, both of which use gelatin—flavorless ground animal collagen—as their base. Recipes set with gelatin appear as early as the 15th century as a way to preserve meat and fish. In the late 18th century, meats coated in aspic and tall molds of gelatin began to appear on the tables of European society. In the late 19th century, commercial gelatin brands began to appear in the United States and America's love affair with gelatin began. From congealed salads with shredded vegetables to tomato aspics, gelatin in fancy molds was in vogue. The cranberry port-wine jelly (left) is a delicious nod to the tradition and a perfect accompaniment to both roast turkey and roast beef.

autumn squash salad

(See photo on page 468.)

PREP: 15 MIN / TOTAL: 50 MIN / SERVES 4

- 2 containers (20 ounces each) chopped butternut squash
- 1 pound skinless, boneless chicken thighs
- 2 tablespoons olive oil
- Salt
- Ground black pepper
- 5 ounces mixed greens, arugula, or baby kale
- 3 tablespoons fresh lemon juice
- 4 ounces goat cheese, crumbled (1 cup)

1. Preheat the oven to 425°F. On two large rimmed baking sheets, toss the butternut squash and chicken thighs with the oil and ½ teaspoon each salt and pepper. Bake 40 minutes, or until the squash is tender and chicken is 165°F.

2. Chop the chicken; in a large bowl, toss it with the squash, mixed greens, lemon juice, and goat cheese. Season with salt and pepper to taste.

Each serving About 385 calories, 28g protein, 28g carbohydrate, 20g fat (7g saturated), 9g fiber, 555mg sodium.

Ingredient Ideas
alternative croutons

Chips, crackers, or even cereal can make a crispy, tasty topper. Try one of these or experiment with your own favorite snacks.

WASABI PEAS—fiery bites for an Asian steak salad

PRETZELS—tasty with tomato salad

DRIED STRAWBERRIES—berry good with spinach

CHEDDAR GOLDFISH®—a brilliant cheesy blast

GRANOLA—fancy up a Waldorf

TORTILLA CHIPS—complement a Cobb

CEREAL SQUARES—perfect for a Caesar

VEGGIE CHIPS—combine with beets and goat cheese

---

garden greens & pumpernickel panzanella

(See photo on page 468.)

PREP: 25 MIN / TOTAL: 35 MIN / SERVES 6

- 1 pound asparagus, trimmed and cut into 1-inch lengths
- 1 bunch green onions, cut into 1-inch lengths
- 2 teaspoons plus 2 tablespoons extra-virgin olive oil
- Salt
- 6 cups (¾-inch cubes) pumpernickel bread
- 2 tablespoons fresh lemon juice
- 1 tablespoon white wine vinegar
- 1 tablespoon spicy brown mustard
- 1 tablespoon bottled horseradish
- ¼ cup chopped fresh dill
- 4 ounces arugula (4 loosely packed cups)
- ½ bunch watermelon radishes or regular radishes, trimmed and thinly sliced

1. Arrange two oven racks in the upper and lower thirds of the oven. Preheat the oven to 450°F. On a large rimmed baking sheet, toss the asparagus, green onions, 2 teaspoons olive oil, and ¼ teaspoon salt; spread in a single layer. Bake on the lower rack 15 minutes, or until the vegetables are browned and tender. On another large rimmed baking sheet, arrange the bread in a single layer. Bake on the upper rack 10 to 12 minutes, or until crisp and dry, stirring once.

2. Meanwhile, in a large bowl, whisk the remaining 2 tablespoons oil, the lemon juice, vinegar, mustard, horseradish, and ½ teaspoon salt; stir in the dill.

3. Toss bread cubes with the vinaigrette in the bowl; add the roasted vegetables, arugula, and radishes; toss until well combined.

Each serving About 330 calories, 11g protein, 51g carbohydrate, 10g fat (1g saturated), 9g fiber, 870mg sodium.

charred greek caesar

(See photo on page 468.)

PREP: 10 MIN / TOTAL: 15 MIN / SERVES 6

- 4 ounces feta cheese
- ⅔ cup extra-virgin olive oil
- ⅓ cup nonfat plain Greek yogurt
- 3 tablespoons fresh lemon juice
- 1 clove garlic
- ¼ teaspoon salt
- ¼ teaspoon ground black pepper
- ¼ cup packed fresh dill, chopped
- 3 hearts romaine lettuce, each halved lengthwise
- ¼ cup roasted sunflower seeds

1. Prepare a grill pan or an outdoor grill for direct grilling over medium-high heat.

2. In a blender or food processor, puree the feta, oil, yogurt, lemon juice, garlic, salt, and pepper. Transfer to a medium bowl; stir in the dill.

3. Grill the romaine over medium heat 4 minutes, or until charred in spots, turning over halfway through. Serve immediately, drizzled with the yogurt dressing and sprinkled with sunflower seeds.

Each serving About 335 calories, 6g protein, 6g carbohydrate, 32g fat (7g saturated), 2g fiber, 275mg sodium.

INGREDIENT SPOTLIGHT

Watermelon radishes add a splash to any salad or crudité platter. It is an heirloom Chinese daikon radish; when it was first brought to the US, it was called the "red meat" radish. To serve raw, slice it thinly or use a Y-shaped peeler to shave it for salads. You can also pickle it, sauté it, or roast it. Cooking will bring out its sweetness but dull its show-stopping vibrant color.

pepperoni pizza salad

(See photo on page 466.)

PREP: 20 MIN / TOTAL: 25 MIN / SERVES 4

- 2 (8-inch) mini pizza crusts
- 1 clove garlic, crushed with a garlic press
- 4 tablespoons extra-virgin olive oil
- ¼ cup coarsely grated Parmesan cheese
- 2 tablespoons red wine vinegar
- ⅛ teaspoon sugar
- ½ teaspoon ground black pepper
- 1 package (10 ounces) mixed Italian greens
- 3 medium tomatoes, seeded and chopped
- 1 small yellow bell pepper, chopped
- 4 ounces pepperoni, chopped
- 2 ounces part-skim mozzarella, shredded or cut into matchsticks (½ cup)

1. Preheat the oven to 450°F. Arrange the pizza crusts on a baking sheet.

2. In a small bowl, stir together the garlic and 1 tablespoon oil; brush the mixture on the crusts. Sprinkle with Parmesan. Bake the crusts 10 to 12 minutes, or until golden brown.

3. Meanwhile, in a large bowl, whisk together the vinegar, sugar, pepper, and the remaining 3 tablespoons oil. Add the greens, tomatoes, bell pepper, and pepperoni; toss until well coated. Cut each pizza crust into 6 wedges. Divide the salad among 4 serving plates. Top with mozzarella and serve with pizza-crust wedges.

Each serving About 570 calories, 21g protein, 41g carbohydrate, 36g fat (10g saturated), 3g fiber, 1,030mg sodium.

spicy tuna roll salad

PREP: 20 MIN / TOTAL: 25 MIN / SERVES 4

- 2 tablespoons vegetable oil
- 1 (12-ounce) fresh tuna steak, about 1½ inches thick, or 2 cans (5 to 6 ounces each) good-quality tuna in oil, drained
- ¼ teaspoon salt
- ¼ teaspoon ground black pepper
- ¼ cup light mayonnaise
- 1 tablespoon Asian hot chili sauce (such as sriracha)
- 1 tablespoon fresh lime juice
- 1 tablespoon soy sauce
- 1 tablespoon toasted sesame oil
- Pinch of sugar
- 6 cups arugula (6 ounces)
- 2 cups cooked brown rice, cooled
- 1 English (seedless) cucumber, thinly sliced into half-moons
- 1 avocado, chopped

1. If you're using fresh tuna, in a 10-inch skillet, heat the vegetable oil over medium-high heat until very hot. Sprinkle the tuna all over with the salt and pepper. Add the tuna to the skillet; cook 3 minutes per side, or until browned on both sides. Transfer the cooked tuna to a cutting board and thinly slice. Set aside to cool.

2. In a large bowl, whisk together the mayonnaise, chili sauce, lime juice, soy sauce, sesame oil, and sugar. Add the arugula, rice, cucumber, and avocado; toss to combine. Divide the salad among 4 serving plates. Top with the tuna slices or canned tuna.

Each serving About 410 calories, 30g protein, 31g carbohydrate, 19g fat (3g saturated), 6g fiber, 625mg sodium.

crab rangoon salad

PREP: 10 MIN / TOTAL: 25 MIN / SERVES 4

- 1 bunch asparagus, cut into 1-inch lengths
- 2 tablespoons water
- ⅛ teaspoon salt
- ⅓ cup mayonnaise
- 2 green onions, finely chopped
- 2 tablespoons fresh lemon juice
- 1 teaspoon honey
- 2 teaspoons lower-sodium soy sauce
- 8 ounces good-quality crabmeat, picked over
- 8 cup torn frisée lettuce
- 1 cup coarsely crushed rice crackers (2 ounces)

1. In a shallow 2-quart microwave-safe baking dish, combine the asparagus with the water. Sprinkle with the salt. Cover with vented plastic wrap and microwave on High 4 minutes. Drain well and cool completely.

2. In a medium bowl, whisk together the mayonnaise, green onions, lemon juice, honey, and soy sauce until smooth. Add the crab and asparagus, tossing to coat.

3. Divide the lettuce among 4 serving plates. Top with the crab mixture. Sprinkle with crushed rice crackers.

Each serving About 270 calories, 14g protein, 20g carbohydrate, 16g fat (2g saturated), 3g fiber, 570mg sodium.

GOOD TO KNOW

CRABMEAT

Although live crabs are sometimes available at the fish counter, buying fresh crabmeat (cooked) is the way to go. It should have a sweet aroma and look moist and snowy white. (Depending on the variety, it can have some pink or brown on the outside.) Fresh crabmeat prices increase with the size of the crab chunks.

LUMP OR BACKFIN	Consists of large whole lumps from the body and backfin; it is very expensive and tasty.
SPECIAL CRABMEAT	Made up of lump crabmeat and flaked meat from the rest of the body
FLAKED CRABMEAT	Contains all of the meat from the body but no lump meat
CLAW CRABMEAT	Meat from the claws

CRAB RANGOON SALAD 494

SPICY TUNA ROLL SALAD 494

chicago hot dog salad

PREP: 20 MIN / TOTAL: 25 MIN / SERVES 4

- 4 hot dogs of your choice
- 1 baguette, cut into 20 thin slices
- ½ cup low-fat buttermilk
- ¼ cup pickled jalapeño chiles, drained and chopped
- 3 tablespoons sweet pickle relish
- 2 tablespoons spicy brown mustard
- 1 green onion, finely chopped
- 2 teaspoons poppy seeds
- ¼ teaspoon ground black pepper
- 6 cups (16 ounces) coleslaw mix
- 3 medium tomatoes, sliced into half-moons

1. Prepare the grill for direct grilling over medium-high heat.

2. Grill the hot dogs 5 minutes, or until crisp and lightly charred, turning occasionally. Grill the baguette slices 3 minutes, or until golden brown, turning over halfway through.

3. Meanwhile, in a large bowl, whisk together the buttermilk, jalapeños, relish, mustard, green onion, poppy seeds, and pepper.

4. Slice the hot dogs on an angle into bite-size pieces. Add to the bowl with the dressing, along with the baguette slices, coleslaw mix, and tomatoes; toss to combine.

Each serving About 390 calories, 15g protein, 44g carbohydrate, 17g fat (7g saturated), 5g fiber, 1,215mg sodium.

easy chicken panzanella

(See photo on page 498.)

PREP: 20 MIN / TOTAL: 35 MIN / SERVES 4

- 1 large leek, cleaned and chopped
- 1 loaf (12 ounces) rustic white bread, torn into chunks
- 3½ tablespoons olive oil
- 2 tablespoons fresh lemon juice
- 2 tablespoons grainy mustard
- Salt
- 3 large ripe tomatoes, chopped
- 4 cups shredded rotisserie chicken meat
- ½ cup fresh parsley leaves

1. Preheat the oven to 450°F. On a large rimmed baking sheet, toss the leek and bread with 2½ tablespoons olive oil. Bake 15 minutes, or until the bread is toasted and the leeks are golden.

2. In a large bowl, whisk the lemon juice, grainy mustard, 1 tablespoon olive oil, and salt to taste. Add the tomatoes; toss. Add the chicken, parsley, and toasted bread and leeks. Toss to combine.

Each serving About 495 calories, 52g protein, 44g carbohydrate, 20g fat (4g saturated), 4g fiber, 340mg sodium.

 Tip Meat Swap: Sub 3 cooked 4-ounce breasts for the rotisserie chicken.

sweet bbq chicken salad

(See photo on page 468.)

PREP: 20 MIN / TOTAL: 20 MIN / SERVES 4

⅓ cup barbecue sauce

2 tablespoons fresh orange juice

1 tablespoon spicy brown mustard

1 tablespoon red wine vinegar

¼ teaspoon salt

¼ teaspoon ground black pepper

1 (16 ounce) head green leaf lettuce, chopped (6 cups)

2 cups shredded rotisserie chicken meat

2 nectarines, thinly sliced

1 small red bell pepper, thinly sliced

½ cup coarsely grated extra sharp Cheddar cheese

1. In a large bowl, whisk together the barbecue sauce, orange juice, mustard, vinegar, salt, and pepper.

2. To the same bowl, add the lettuce, chicken, nectarines, and bell pepper, tossing to coat. Divide among 4 serving plates. Sprinkle with Cheddar.

Each serving About 285 calories, 26g protein, 20g carbohydrate, 11g fat (5g saturated), 3g fiber, 720mg sodium.

 Tip Save time by using a bag of prechopped romaine as well as preshredded sharp Cheddar.

lobster-roll salad

(See photo on page 498.)

PREP: 25 MIN / TOTAL: 30 MIN / SERVES 4

3 slices white bread, well toasted

1½ tablespoons butter, melted

½ cup low-fat buttermilk

3 tablespoons light mayonnaise

2 tablespoons fresh lemon juice

2 tablespoons snipped fresh chives

¼ teaspoon salt

¼ teaspoon ground black pepper

2 hearts romaine lettuce, thinly sliced

2 stalks celery, thinly sliced

8 ounces cooked lobster meat or cooked shelled, deveined shrimp, coarsely chopped

1. Cut the bread into ½-inch cubes; transfer to a large bowl. Drizzle with butter; toss until well coated.

2. In another large bowl, whisk together the buttermilk, mayonnaise, lemon juice, chives, salt, and pepper.

3. To the bowl with the dressing, add the lettuce, celery, and lobster. Toss until well combined. Divide among 4 serving plates. Top with the croutons.

Each serving About 200 calories, 14g protein, 15g carbohydrate, 10g fat (2g saturated), 2g fiber, 710mg sodium.

EASY CHICKEN PANZANELLA 496

SHRIMP SALAD WITH SPRING PEA MIX 499

LOBSTER-ROLL SALAD 497

SHRIMP TACO SALAD 500

shrimp salad
with spring pea mix

PREP: 1 HR 5 MIN / TOTAL: 1 HR 25 MIN / SERVES 6

- 12 large eggs
- 1 lemon
- 3 sprigs fresh dill, leaves chopped, stems reserved
- 12 ounces shelled and deveined large (16 to 20 count) shrimp
- 12 ounces Yukon Gold potatoes, scrubbed and cut into ½-inch chunks
- Salt
- 12 ounces sugar snap peas, strings removed, cut crosswise in halves at an angle
- 1½ cups frozen peas
- 1 cup plain yogurt
- 1 tablespoon Dijon mustard
- ¼ teaspoon ground black pepper
- ½ cup finely chopped red onion (from 1 small onion)
- 3 stalks celery, finely chopped
- 1 tablespoon white wine vinegar
- 2 tablespoons olive oil

1. In a 4-quart saucepan, place the eggs and enough cold water to cover by 1 inch. Heat to boiling over high heat; remove from the heat. Cover and let stand 5 minutes. With a slotted spoon, transfer the eggs to a colander. Rinse the eggs under cold water until cool enough to handle; peel and cut in quarters. Set aside 12 quarters for garnish.

2. From the lemon, squeeze 3 tablespoons juice and reserve. To the same saucepan of water, add the lemon rind and dill stems; heat to boiling over high heat. Add the shrimp, reduce the heat to maintain a bare simmer, and cook 3 minutes, or until the shrimp just turn opaque throughout. Drain, rinse under cold water until cool, and drain again. Discard the lemon rind and dill sprigs.

3. In the same pan, place the potatoes and enough cold water to cover. Add 1 teaspoon salt. Heat to boiling over high heat, cover, and reduce the heat to a simmer. Cook 15 minutes, or until just tender; drain well.

4. While the potatoes cook, heat a 3-quart saucepan of water to boiling over high heat. Add the snap peas and frozen peas. Cook 2 minutes, or until bright green; drain well.

5. In a large bowl, whisk the yogurt, mustard, 1 tablespoon lemon juice, and ¼ teaspoon each salt and pepper. Add hot potatoes, onion, celery, shrimp, eggs, and half of chopped dill. Fold gently until well combined.

6. In another large bowl, whisk vinegar, oil, remaining 2 tablespoons lemon juice, and ⅛ teaspoon each salt and pepper; add all the peas and the remaining dill. Toss until well coated.

7. Spoon the shrimp salad into the center of a serving platter, then spoon the pea mixture all around. Garnish with the reserved egg quarters and serve immediately.

Each serving About 375 calories, 26g protein, 26g carbohydrate, 17g fat (5g saturated), 4g fiber, 760mg sodium.

fiesta taco salad

PREP: 15 MIN / TOTAL: 25 MIN / SERVES 4

- 1 pound lean (90%) ground beef or ground chicken
- 1½ teaspoons chili powder
- ¾ cup salsa
- 1 bag (10 ounces) chopped romaine lettuce
- 2 cups crushed baked tortilla chips
- ⅓ cup shredded reduced-fat Mexican cheese blend
- 1 medium ripe avocado, pitted and cut into ½-inch chunks
- ¼ cup reduced-fat sour cream

1. In a 12-inch skillet, cook the ground beef over medium heat 4 to 5 minutes, or until the beef begins to brown, breaking up the meat with a spatula as it cooks. Stir in the chili powder and cook 1 minute longer. Add ½ cup salsa and cook 3 to 4 minutes to heat through.

2. Divide the lettuce among 4 serving plates. Top each with the beef mixture, tortilla chips, cheese, avocado, sour cream, and the remaining salsa.

Each serving About 405 calories, 28g protein, 21g carbohydrate, 23g fat (8g saturated), 6g fiber, 425mg sodium.

shrimp taco salad

(See photo on page 498.)

PREP: 30 MIN / TOTAL: 35 MIN / SERVES 4

- 3 ears fresh corn, shucked
- 2 medium zucchini, thinly sliced on an angle
- 1 pound shelled, deveined large (16 to 20 count) shrimp
- ¼ cup extra-virgin olive oil
- 3 tablespoons fresh lime juice (from 2 limes)
- 1 teaspoon cayenne pepper hot sauce
- ¼ teaspoon ground cumin
- ¼ teaspoon ground coriander
- ¼ teaspoon salt
- 1 avocado, thinly sliced
- 2 cups (½-inch) watermelon chunks (about 12 ounces)
- ¾ cup crushed corn chips (such as Fritos*)
- 1 cup fresh cilantro leaves

1. Prepare the grill for direct grilling over medium heat.

2. Grill the corn 8 to 10 minutes, or until lightly charred, turning occasionally. Grill the zucchini 6 to 8 minutes, or until lightly charred and tender, turning over once halfway through. Grill the shrimp 2 to 4 minutes, or until opaque throughout, turning over once halfway through cooking.

3. In a small bowl, whisk together the oil, lime juice, hot sauce, cumin, coriander, and salt.

4. Cut the kernels off the ears of corn. Arrange the zucchini and avocado on a platter. Top with the corn, shrimp, and watermelon. The salad can be made ahead to this point and refrigerated, covered, up to 4 hours. To serve, sprinkle with corn chip crumbs and drizzle with the dressing. Top with cilantro.

Each serving About 465 calories, 21g protein, 38g carbohydrate, 28g fat (4g saturated), 6g fiber, 1,025mg sodium.

pad thai noodle salad

(See photo on page 503.)

PREP: 30 MIN / TOTAL: 35 MIN / SERVES 4

- 6 to 7 ounces vermicelli rice noodles
- 2 limes
- 1 pound skinless, boneless chicken thighs
- Salt
- ¼ teaspoon ground black pepper
- 1 bunch green onions
- 2 tablespoons fish sauce
- 2 tablespoons brown sugar
- 2 tablespoons vegetable oil
- 1 tablespoon cider vinegar
- 2 cups baby watercress
- 1 cup shredded carrots (3 carrots)
- 5 radishes, sliced into half-moons
- ⅓ cup roasted salted peanuts, chopped

1. Prepare a grill for covered direct grilling over medium-high heat.

2. Cook the noodles as the label directs; drain and rinse with cold water until cool. Drain well. With kitchen shears, snip the noodles twice.

3. Meanwhile, from the limes, grate 1½ teaspoons zest and squeeze 2 tablespoons juice. Rub the chicken with the zest; sprinkle with ¼ teaspoon salt and the pepper.

4. Grill the chicken, covered, 7 to 9 minutes, or until cooked through (165°F), turning over once; grill the onions 2 to 3 minutes, or until lightly charred, turning occasionally. Transfer both to a cutting board; let cool, then chop.

5. In a large bowl, whisk the lime juice, fish sauce, brown sugar, oil, vinegar, and ⅛ teaspoon salt. Add the noodles, chicken, and all the vegetables; toss to combine. Top with peanuts.

Each serving About 525 calories, 25g protein, 58g carbohydrate, 22g fat (3g saturated), 3g fiber, 965mg sodium.

 Tip No rice noodles or fish sauce on hand? Swap in spaghetti and soy sauce.

chickpea & mango salad

(See photo on page 503.)

PREP: 15 MIN / TOTAL: 20 MIN / SERVES 4

- ½ cup nonfat plain yogurt
- ½ cup fresh cilantro leaves
- 2 tablespoons mango chutney
- 1 tablespoon extra-virgin olive oil
- 2 teaspoons fresh lime juice
- ½ teaspoon ground coriander
- ½ teaspoon salt
- ¼ teaspoon ground black pepper
- 2 cans (15 ounces) no-salt-added chickpeas, drained
- 1 large ripe mango, chopped
- 1 package (5 to 6 ounces) baby spinach
- ½ cup sliced almonds, toasted
- Naan (Indian-style flatbread) or pita bread, warmed, for serving

1. In a food processor, puree the yogurt, cilantro, chutney, oil, lime juice, coriander, salt, and pepper until smooth. Transfer to a large bowl.

2. To the same bowl, add the chickpeas and mango. Toss until well coated. The chickpea mixture can be made ahead and refrigerated in an airtight container up to overnight. To serve, add the spinach and almonds; toss to combine. Serve with naan.

Each serving About 435 calories, 18g protein, 69g carbohydrate, 11g fat (1g saturated), 14g fiber, 560mg sodium.

awe-worthy slaw

PREP: 15 MIN / TOTAL: 15 MIN / MAKES 12 CUPS

- 1 small head green cabbage (1½ pounds), quartered, cored, and thinly sliced, tough ribs discarded (6 cups)
- 2 cups shredded carrots (6 carrots)
- 1 small red bell pepper, seeded and thinly sliced
- 1 small yellow bell pepper, seeded and thinly sliced
- 3 stalks celery, thinly sliced on an angle
- Choice of dressing (below)

In a very large bowl, combine the cabbage, carrots, bell peppers, and celery. Toss well with your choice of dressing. Dressed slaw can be made up to 1 day ahead, covered and refrigerated.

CREAMY HERB Whisk ½ cup mayonnaise, ¼ cup sour cream, 2 table-spoons fresh lemon juice, 2 tablespoons snipped fresh chives, 1 teaspoon finely grated lemon zest, and ½ teaspoon celery salt. Serves 12.

GARLICKY MUSTARD Whisk ⅓ cup cider vinegar; ⅓ cup olive oil; 2 tablespoons spicy brown mustard; 2 tablespoons finely chopped fresh parsley; 1 clove garlic, crushed with a garlic press; and ½ teaspoon each salt and ground black pepper. Serves 12.

SRIRACHA-LIME Whisk 2 green onions, finely chopped; ¼ cup soy sauce; 3 tablespoons fresh lime juice; 1½ tablespoons sriracha sauce; 2 tablespoons black or white sesame seeds; and ½ teaspoon sugar. Serves 12.

AWE-WORTHY SLAW Each serving (without dressing) About 20 calories, 1g protein, 4g carbohydrate, 0g fat (0g saturated), 1g fiber, 21mg sodium.

CREAMY HERB DRESSING Each serving About 70 calories, 0g protein, 0g carbohydrate, 7g fat (1g saturated), 0g fiber, 110mg sodium.

GARLICKY MUSTARD DRESSING Each serving About 60 calories, 0g protein, 0g carbohydrate, 6g fat (1g saturated), 0g fiber, 106mg sodium.

SRIRACHA-LIME DRESSING Each serving About 15 calories, 1g protein, 2g carbohydrate, 1g fat (0g saturated), 0g fiber, 345mg sodium.

heirloom blt salad

PREP: 20 MIN / TOTAL: 35 MIN / SERVES 4

- 1 lemon
- ⅓ cup low-fat buttermilk
- 2 tablespoons light mayonnaise
- 1 tablespoon snipped fresh chives
- Salt
- 8 ounces bacon, cut into 1-inch pieces
- 3 slices good-quality white bread, well toasted
- 1 tablespoon cider vinegar
- 1 tablespoon brown sugar
- 1 head Bibb or Boston lettuce (about 8 ounces), leaves separated
- 3 medium heirloom tomatoes, sliced

1. From the lemon, into a small bowl grate ½ teaspoon zest and squeeze 2 teaspoons juice. Whisk in the buttermilk, mayonnaise, chives, and ¼ teaspoon salt.

2. In a 12-inch nonstick skillet, cook the bacon over medium heat 9 to 14 minutes, or until browned and crisp, stirring occasionally. With a slotted spoon, transfer the bacon to a paper-towel-lined plate.

3. Cut each slice of bread into 4 triangles; transfer to a medium bowl. Drizzle with 2 tablespoons bacon fat, tossing to coat. Discard the remaining bacon fat.

4. To the same skillet, add the vinegar and brown sugar. Cook 1 minute, or until the sugar dissolves and the mixture is slightly reduced, stirring constantly. Return the bacon to the skillet, tossing and stirring to coat. Remove from the heat.

5. Arrange the lettuce on a serving platter. Top with bread and tomatoes. Sprinkle with bacon. Serve the salad with the dressing.

Each serving About 275 calories, 11g protein, 19g carbohydrate, 18g fat (6g saturated), 2g fiber, 775mg sodium.

caesar pasta salad

PREP: 20 MIN / TOTAL: 30 MIN / SERVES 6

- 1 pound farfalle pasta
- 1 large lemon
- ¼ cup grated Parmesan cheese, plus more for garnish
- 3 tablespoons light mayonnaise
- 3 tablespoons extra-virgin olive oil
- 2 cloves garlic, crushed with a garlic press
- 1 teaspoon salt
- 1 teaspoon ground black pepper
- 1 pint multicolored grape tomatoes, cut into halves
- 1 medium zucchini, grated
- 1 cup frozen peas, thawed
- ¼ cup packed fresh basil leaves, finely chopped, plus leaves for garnish

1. Heat a large covered saucepot of salted water to boiling over high heat. Cook the pasta as the label directs.

2. Meanwhile, from the lemon, grate 1 teaspoon zest and squeeze ¼ cup juice into a large bowl. Whisk in the Parmesan, mayonnaise, oil, garlic, salt, and pepper. Add tomatoes, zucchini, peas, basil, and cooked pasta; toss well. Serve warm or chilled. Can be refrigerated, covered, for up to 1 day. Garnish with Parmesan and basil before serving.

Each serving About 415 calories, 14g protein, 64g carbohydrate, 12g fat (2g saturated), 5g fiber, 605mg sodium.

CAESAR PASTA SALAD 502

PAD THAI NOODLE SALAD 500

HEIRLOOM BLT SALAD 502

CHICKPEA & MANGO SALAD 501

classic french vinaigrette

PREP: 5 MIN / TOTAL: 5 MIN / MAKES ¾ CUP

¼ cup red wine vinegar

1 tablespoon Dijon mustard

¾ teaspoon salt

½ teaspoon coarsely ground black pepper

½ cup olive oil

In a medium bowl and using a wire whisk, mix the vinegar, mustard, salt, and pepper until blended. In a thin, steady stream, whisk in the oil until blended. Cover and refrigerate up to 1 week.

Each tablespoon About 80 calories, 0g protein, 0g carbohydrate, 9g fat (1g saturated), 0g fiber, 175mg sodium.

VARIATIONS

Blue Cheese Vinaigrette

Prepare as directed, but add **2 ounces blue cheese**, crumbled (½ cup). Cover and refrigerate up to 2 days. Makes about 1 cup.

Mustard-Shallot Vinaigrette

Prepare as directed, but add **1 tablespoon minced shallot**. Cover and refrigerate up to 1 day. Makes about ¾ cup.

Balsamic Vinaigrette

Prepare as directed, but replace the red wine vinegar with **balsamic vinegar** and reduce the mustard to 1 teaspoon. Makes about ½ cup.

creamy blue cheese dressing

PREP: 10 MIN / TOTAL: 10 MIN / MAKES 1 CUP

4 ounces blue cheese, crumbled (1 cup)

3 tablespoons half-and-half or light cream

½ cup reduced-fat mayonnaise

2 tablespoons white wine vinegar

1 teaspoon Dijon mustard

⅛ teaspoon salt

⅛ teaspoon ground black pepper

In a small bowl and using a fork, mash the cheese with the half-and-half until creamy; add the mayonnaise, vinegar, mustard, salt, and pepper. With a wire whisk, beat until well mixed. Cover and refrigerate up to 3 days.

Each tablespoon About 55 calories, 2g protein, 1g carbohydrate, 5g fat (2g saturated fat), 0g fiber, 180mg sodium.

japanese miso vinaigrette

PREP: 10 MIN / TOTAL: 10 MIN / MAKES 1 CUP

2 tablespoons miso (fermented soybean paste)

½ cup rice vinegar

¼ cup olive oil

1 tablespoon minced, peeled fresh ginger

1 tablespoon sugar

In a small bowl and using a wire whisk, stir the miso into the vinegar until smooth. In a blender, combine the miso mixture, oil, ginger, and sugar; puree until smooth. Transfer to small bowl or jar. Cover and refrigerate up to 3 days.

Each tablespoon About 40 calories, 0g protein, 1g carbohydrate, 4g fat (0g saturated), 0g fiber, 80mg sodium.

tomato-miso dressing

PREP: 15 MIN / TOTAL: 20 MIN / MAKES 1 CUP

- 1 small shallot, sliced
- 1 jalapeño chile, sliced
- 1 clove garlic, chopped
- ¼ cup canola oil
- 8 ounces tomatoes, chopped
- 3 tablespoons miso (fermented soybean paste)
- 3 tablespoons rice vinegar
- 1 tablespoon water

1. In a 10-inch skillet, cook the shallot, jalapeño, and garlic in the oil over medium heat 3 to 4 minutes, or until slightly browned, stirring. Add the tomatoes. Cook 5 minutes, stirring. Cool.

2. Place the mixture in a blender and puree with the miso, rice vinegar, and water.

Each tablespoon About 45 calories, 1g protein, 2g carbohydrate, 4g fat (0g saturated), 0g fiber, 121mg sodium.

#SavetheFood

shake up homemade dressing

When you've got a nearly finished jar of jam, mayo, nut butter, or mustard, maximize every drop: Add olive oil, vinegar, spices, and herbs; cover; and shake. Instant vinaigrette!

---

honey-lime vinaigrette

PREP: 5 MIN / TOTAL: 5 MIN / MAKES ½ CUP

- ⅓ cup fresh lime juice
- 4 teaspoons honey
- 1 tablespoon rice vinegar
- ⅛ teaspoon salt

In a small bowl and using a wire whisk, mix the lime juice, honey, vinegar, and salt until blended. Cover and refrigerate up to 3 days.

Each tablespoon About 15 calories, 0g protein, 4g carbohydrate, 0g fat (0g saturated), 0g fiber, 40mg sodium.

tahini dressing

PREP: 10 MIN / TOTAL: 10 MIN / MAKES ¾ CUP

- ⅓ cup tahini (sesame seed paste)
- 2 tablespoons fresh lemon juice
- 4 teaspoons soy sauce
- 1 tablespoon honey (optional)
- ½ small clove garlic, minced
- ½ teaspoon ground black pepper

In a small bowl and using a wire whisk, mix the tahini, lemon juice, soy sauce, honey (if using), garlic, and pepper until smooth. Cover and refrigerate up to 2 days.

Each tablespoon About 40 calories, 1g protein, 2g carbohydrate, 4g fat (0g saturated), 0g fiber, 120mg sodium.

BEST-EVER RANCH 507

SPICY CHIPOTLE RANCH 507

GREEN GODDESS DRESSING 507

AVOCADO-LIME RANCH 507

green goddess dressing

PREP: 10 MIN / TOTAL: 10 MIN / MAKES 1 CUP

½ cup sour cream

½ cup packed fresh tarragon

½ cup packed fresh parsley

⅓ cup mayonnaise

3 tablespoons fresh lemon juice

5 anchovy fillets

2 tablespoons snipped fresh chives

1 tablespoon cider vinegar

¼ teaspoon salt

In a blender, combine the sour cream, tarragon, parsley, mayonnaise, lemon juice, anchovy fillets, chives, vinegar, and salt until smooth.

Each tablespoon About 45 calories, 1g protein, 1g carbohydrate, 5g fat (1g saturated), 0g fiber, 115mg sodium.

creamy brie dressing

PREP: 5 MIN / TOTAL: 10 MIN / MAKES 1 CUP

8 ounces Brie cheese, rind removed and discarded

¼ cup milk

¼ cup fresh lemon juice

3 tablespoons extra-virgin olive oil

1 clove garlic

1 teaspoon honey

¼ teaspoon salt

¼ teaspoon ground black pepper

Blend the Brie, milk, lemon juice, olive oil, garlic, honey, salt, and pepper until smooth.

Each tablespoon About 75 calories, 3g protein, 1g carbohydrate, 7g fat (3g saturated), 0g fiber, 127mg sodium.

best-ever ranch

PREP: 10 MIN / TOTAL: 10 MIN / MAKES 2¼ CUPS

¾ cup buttermilk

½ cup mayonnaise

⅓ cup Greek yogurt

2 tablespoons fresh lemon juice

1 tablespoon Dijon mustard

1 clove garlic

Pinch of sugar

¾ teaspoon salt

¼ teaspoon ground black pepper

½ cup loosely packed fresh parsley

2 tablespoons snipped fresh chives

In a blender, puree the buttermilk, mayonnaise, yogurt, lemon juice, mustard, garlic, sugar, salt, and pepper until smooth. Add the parsley and chives; pulse until just finely chopped. Keeps, refrigerated, up to 2 weeks. The dressing may separate; stir before using.

Each tablespoon About 25 calories, 0g protein, 1g carbohydrate, 3g fat (0g saturated), 0g fiber, 77mg sodium.

VARIATIONS

Avocado-Lime

In step 1, replace the lemon juice with **3 tablespoons fresh lime juice** and replace the salt with **3 tablespoons soy sauce**; replace the yogurt and Dijon with **1 small ripe avocado**. Makes about 2 cups.

Spicy Chipotle

In step 1, add **2 small chipotles in adobo sauce**. In step 2, replace the parsley with **fresh cilantro**. Makes about 2⅓ cups.

BREAKFAST &
brunch

"Brunch is cheerful, sociable and inciting. It is talk-compelling. It puts you in a good temper; it makes you satisfied with yourself and your fellow beings; it sweeps away the worries and cobwebs of the week," wrote English author Guy Beringer in his 1895 article, "Brunch, A Plea." The plea was to lighten the food and the mood of Sunday dining. We heartily agree. Whether it's a family affair or a gathering with friends, brunch is an easy way into a casual, delicious meal.

At brunch, eggs get their moment in the sun. Check out Classic Eggs Benedict (page 538), our selection of omelets and frittatas, avocado toasts such as California Sunrise Toast (page 536), Bacon & Egg Fried Rice (page 527), and Corned Beef Hash (page 528)—all favorite brunch entrees.

LOVE TOASTS 521

WONUTS 549

BACON & GRUYÈRE BREAKFAST "PIE" 526

COCONUT FRENCH TOAST 545

Egg Label Glossary

Egg label claims can be confusing. *All eggs are gluten-free and have 0 trans fats (less than .5g), whether the label states it or not.*

GRADES AA, A, OR B Eggs are graded as AA, A, or B, in descending order of quality. According to the USDA and the American Egg Board, there is no difference in nutritional values. Grading is based on standards of appearance, such as the conditions of the white or yolk and the cleanliness and soundness of the shell.

ANTIBIOTIC-FREE All eggs produced in the US are antibiotic-free, even if it's not specified on the carton. If hens become ill, a veterinarian can administer antibiotics, but their eggs would not be used for human consumption according to FDA regulations.

CAGE-FREE Cage-free hens must be housed in a building, room, or enclosed area with unlimited access to food and water, according to the USDA. Cage-free does not mean that the hens have access to the outdoors.

FARM-FRESH OR ALL-NATURAL These labels have no federal regulation or specific meaning. They're often used for marketing purposes.

FREE-RANGE Free-range hens must be housed in a building, room, or area with unlimited access to food and water, according to the USDA. These hens must have continuous access to the outdoors during their laying cycle.

NO HORMONES ADDED The egg industry does not use hormones in the production of any shell eggs, no matter if the label says this or not.

ORGANIC In order to certify eggs as "organic," the hen's feed must be grown without synthetic chemicals, 100 percent of the ingredients must be certified organic, the hens must be free-range, and the use of antibiotics and growth hormones are prohibited. Verifying documentation from an accredited certifying agent must be presented to the USDA.

PASTEURIZED Pasteurization (processing in a controlled-temperature water bath) kills salmonella and other bacteria. Consider using pasteurized eggs for dishes like hollandaise sauce, where eggs cannot be cooked to 160°F.

PASTURE-RAISED This term is not regulated by the USDA, but it should mean that the hens spend most of their life outdoors, with space to roam, and eat a diet of worms, insects, and grass (which replicates a chicken's natural diet and environment). Look for the Human Farm Animal Care's (HFAC) Certified Humane label.

VEGETARIAN-FED According to the USDA, the egg producer using this claim must maintain documentation that the hens do not eat any animal by-products. Note: Chickens in the wild are omnivores and get most of their protein from worms and insects.

Eggs: the Powerhouse Protein

Eggs are nutritional stars. They are one of the best sources of protein available and are chock-full of essential nutrients such as vitamins A, D, B12, and choline. One large egg has only 72 calories, 6 grams of protein, and 5 grams of fat (only 1.5g saturated). Pretty incredible for a 2-ounce oval!

WHAT ABOUT CHOLESTEROL?

For decades, people with elevated cholesterol were discouraged from consuming more than a couple of eggs a week. New research indicates that dietary cholesterol does not automatically become blood cholesterol, meaning eating moderate amounts does not appear to affect disease risks in most healthy people. Saturated and trans fats are more likely to raise a person's blood cholesterol. The 2015 to 2020 Dietary Guidelines for Americans, the American Heart Association, and the American Diabetes Association have removed their recommendations to limit dietary cholesterol.

GOOD TO KNOW

ARE BROWN EGGS HEALTHIER THAN WHITE EGGS?

NO! The color of an egg is not an indicator of quality, nutrition, or taste. Rather, the color depends on the breed of the hen. White-feathered hens lay white eggs, while brown-feathered hens lay brown eggs. Brown eggs may cost more, because brown-feathered hens are larger and more expensive to raise.

3 Things to Know ABOUT EGG SAFETY

1 **Keep Them Cold And Dry** Store eggs in their carton in the main part of the refrigerator, not on the door. Discard any eggs with cracked shells.

2 **Cook Them Thoroughly** Raw eggs may be contaminated with salmonella, a bacterium that can cause food poisoning. Salmonella is killed at 160°F (which is easily reached with scrambled eggs, "over-hard" fried eggs, and custards). The elderly, infants, pregnant women, and those with compromised immune systems should not eat undercooked eggs.

3 **Don't Cross-Contaminate** After handling raw eggs, thoroughly wash your hands and any utensils that have come in contact with the eggs with hot, soapy water.

CRISPY EGG TOASTS 522

green light juice

PREP: 10 MIN / TOTAL: 10 MIN / SERVES 1

4 kale leaves, stems and tough ribs removed and discarded

1 cup coconut water

1 cup seedless green grapes

½-inch piece fresh peeled ginger, sliced

Blend the kale, coconut water, grapes, and ginger until smooth. Strain through a fine sieve into a large glass; discard the pulp.

Each serving About 180 calories, 4g protein, 41g carbohydrate, 1g fat (0g saturated), 2g fiber, 45mg sodium

blueberry pie shake

PREP: 5 MIN / TOTAL: 5 MIN / SERVES 2

2 cups vanilla ice cream

1 container (6 ounce) fresh blueberries

2 sheets graham crackers, or 4 vanilla wafer cookies

Blend the ice cream, blueberries, and graham crackers until smooth.

Each serving About 510 calories, 13g protein, 72g carbohydrate, 20g fat (11g saturated), 4g fiber, 346mg sodium

HOW TO

FREEZE YOUR FRUIT

Frozen fruit is perfect for smoothies. It adds cold without diluting flavor—and it's a great way to rescue imperfect fruit. Rinse fruit. Hull strawberries (other berries can be left whole); pit stone fruit and cut into wedges. Place fruit on a baking sheet lined with parchment; freeze until hard. Transfer to resealable bag and freeze up to 3 months. Freeze bananas in their skins in a resealable bag to prevent their flavor from transferring to other items.

strawberry mania smoothie

PREP: 5 MIN / TOTAL: 5 MIN / SERVES 1

¼ cup cranberry juice cocktail, chilled

1 container (8 ounce) low-fat strawberry yogurt

1 cup frozen strawberries

Combine the cranberry juice, yogurt, and strawberries and blend until mixture is smooth and frothy. Pour into 1 tall glass.

Each serving About 325 calories, 10g protein, 68g carbohydrate, 4g fat (2g saturated), 4g fiber, 141mg sodium

java banana smoothie

PREP: 5 MIN / TOTAL: 5 MIN / SERVES 2

2 ripe bananas, preferably cut up and frozen

¾ cup cold coffee

¾ cup low-fat (1%) milk

3 tablespoons brown sugar

1 cup ice

Blend the bananas, cold coffee, milk, brown sugar, and ice until smooth.

Each serving About 160 calories, 4g protein, 36g carbohydrate, 1g fat (1g saturated), 3g fiber, 44mg sodium

STRAWBERRY MANIA SMOOTHIE

GREEN LIGHT JUICE

JAVA BANANA SMOOTHIE

BLUEBERRY PIE SHAKE

beet red refresher

PREP: 5 MIN / TOTAL: 5 MIN / SERVES 2

- 2 cups fresh strawberries (8 ounces), quartered
- 1½ cups cold water
- 1 cup sliced refrigerated cooked beets
- ½ small Granny Smith apple, peeled and sliced
- 3 tablespoons fresh lemon juice
- 1 tablespoon agave nectar

Blend the strawberries, cold water, beets, apple, lemon juice, and agave nectar until smooth.

Each serving About 120 calories, 2g protein, 30g carbohydrate, 1g fat (0g saturated), 4g fiber, 67mg sodium.

GOOD TO KNOW

HAVE IT YOUR WAY SMOOTHIE

Whether you like pineapple and banana, celery and pear, or kale and apple, you can custom-create a smoothie to start your morning as you like.

In a blender, combine **1½ cups cut-up cold or frozen fruit or vegetables**, **½ cup yogurt or juice**, **3 ice cubes**, and **spices, sweetener, nutritional yeast, and/or nut butter** to taste. Blend until smooth. **Serves 1.**

buttermilk waffles

PREP: 15 MIN / TOTAL: 30 MIN / SERVES 4

- 1¾ cups all-purpose flour
- 1½ teaspoons baking powder
- 1 teaspoon baking soda
- ½ teaspoon salt
- 2 cups buttermilk
- 4 tablespoons butter, melted
- 2 large eggs, lightly beaten

1. Preheat a waffle iron as the manufacturer directs.

2. In a large bowl and using a wire whisk, stir the flour, baking powder, baking soda, and salt. Add the buttermilk, melted butter, and eggs; whisk until smooth.

3. When the waffle iron is ready, pour the batter into the center until it spreads to within 1 inch of the edges. Cover and bake as the manufacturer directs; do not lift the cover while the waffle is cooking.

4. When the waffle is done, lift the cover and loosen the waffle with a fork. Serve immediately or keep warm in the oven (place the waffle directly on the oven rack to keep it crisp). Reheat the waffle iron before pouring in more batter. If the batter becomes too thick upon standing, thin it with a little more buttermilk.

Each serving About 390 calories, 13g protein, 48g carbohydrate, 16g fat (9g saturated), 2g fiber, 1,065mg sodium.

VARIATIONS

Pecan Waffles

Prepare as directed, but add **1 tablespoon sugar** and **1 cup pecans** (4 ounces), chopped, to the batter. Stir the batter for each waffle before pouring.

Sweet Milk Waffles

Prepare as directed, but omit the baking soda; use **1 tablespoon baking powder**. Substitute **2 cups milk** for the buttermilk.

pancakes

PREP: 15 MIN / TOTAL: 30 MIN / SERVES 3

1 cup all-purpose flour

2 tablespoons sugar

2½ teaspoons baking powder

½ teaspoon salt

1¼ cups whole milk

3 tablespoons butter, melted

1 large egg, lightly beaten

Vegetable oil, for brushing the pan

1. In a bowl and using a wire whisk, stir the flour, sugar, baking powder, and salt. Add the milk, butter, and egg and stir just until the flour is moistened.

2. Heat a griddle or 12-inch skillet over medium heat until a drop of water sizzles; brush lightly with oil. Pour the batter by scant ¼ cupfuls onto the hot griddle, making a few pancakes at a time. Cook until the tops are bubbly, some bubbles burst, and the edges look dry. With a wide spatula, turn and cook until the underside is golden. Transfer to a platter; keep warm.

3. Repeat with the remaining batter, brushing the griddle with more oil if necessary.

Each serving About 390 calories, 10g protein, 46g carbohydrate, 19g fat (10g saturated), 1g fiber, 980mg sodium.

VARIATIONS

Blueberry Pancakes

Prepare as directed, but add **1 cup blueberries** to the pancake batter.

Buckwheat Pancakes

Prepare as directed, but use ½ **cup all-purpose flour** and ½ **cup buckwheat flour**.

Banana Pancakes

Prepare as directed, but add **1 very ripe medium banana**, mashed (about ½ cup); and ¼ **teaspoon baking soda**; use only ¾ cup milk.

Cornmeal Pancakes

Prepare as directed, but add ¼ **cup cornmeal** to the flour mixture.

Buttermilk Pancakes

Prepare as directed, but use only 2 teaspoons baking powder and ½ teaspoon baking soda. Substitute 1¼ **cups buttermilk** or **1 cup plain yogurt plus ¼ cup milk** for the milk.

Sour Cream Pancakes

Prepare as directed, but substitute **1 small container (8 ounces) sour cream** and use only ¼ cup milk.

GOOD TO KNOW

MAPLE SYRUP

Pure maple syrup is graded by color, which can range from pale brownish gold to an almost molasses hue.

US GRADE A GOLDEN	is mild and delicate and tastes best with foods that won't overpower its sweet, subtle flavor.
US GRADE A AMBER	has a richer taste and aroma and pairs well with breakfast waffles and pancakes.
US GRADE A DARK	has a robust—almost smoky—flavor that is especially good for cooking and barbecue.
US GRADE A VERY DARK	has a strong, intense flavor that can stand up to the heat—best for candy or as a substitute for molasses.
STORING SYRUP	Once it is opened, store pure maple syrup in glass in the refrigerator, and use it within six months. Unopened, it will keep indefinitely. Maple syrup also freezes well.

whole-grain pancakes

PREP: 15 MIN / TOTAL: 30 MIN / SERVES 4

- 2 ripe peaches, pitted and chopped
- ½ pint raspberries (1 cup)
- 1 tablespoon sugar
- ½ cup all-purpose flour
- ½ cup whole wheat flour
- ½ cup quick-cooking oats
- 2 teaspoons baking powder
- ½ teaspoon salt
- 1¼ cups fat-free (skim) milk
- 1 large egg, lightly beaten
- 1 tablespoon vegetable oil
- Nonstick cooking spray

1. In a medium bowl, combine the peaches, raspberries, and sugar. Stir to coat; set the fruit mixture aside.

2. Meanwhile, in a large bowl, combine both flours, the oats, baking powder, and salt. Add the milk, egg, and oil; stir just until the flour mixture is moistened (the batter will be slightly lumpy).

3. Spray a 12-inch nonstick skillet with cooking spray; heat over medium heat 1 minute. Pour the batter by scant ¼ cupfuls into the skillet, making about 4 pancakes at a time. Cook until the tops bubble, some bubbles burst, and the edges look dry. With a wide spatula, turn the pancakes and cook until the undersides are golden. Transfer the pancakes to a platter. Cover; keep warm.

4. Repeat with the remaining batter, using more nonstick cooking spray if necessary. To serve, top with fruit mixture.

Each serving About 275 calories, 10g protein, 46g carbohydrate, 6g fat (1g saturated), 6g fiber, 545mg sodium.

Tip If you don't use whole wheat flour within a month of purchase, store it in the freezer. Because it has the bran and germ, which contain fat, it becomes rancid more quickly than white flour.

strawberry cheesecake flapjacks

(See photo on page 520.)

PREP: 15 MIN / TOTAL: 50 MIN / SERVES 6

- ¾ cup low-sugar strawberry preserves
- 8 ounces strawberries, hulled and halved
- 2 cups all-purpose flour
- 2 teaspoons baking powder
- ⅛ teaspoon salt
- 2½ cups low-fat buttermilk
- 2 large eggs
- 1 tablespoon granulated sugar
- 1 teaspoon vanilla extract
- ½ teaspoon finely grated lemon zest
- 6 ounces cream cheese, softened
- 3 tablespoons butter
- Confectioners' sugar, for dusting

1. In a medium microwave-safe bowl, microwave the preserves on High 1 minute, or until melted. Stir in the strawberries; set aside.

2. In a large bowl, whisk the flour, baking powder, and salt. In another large bowl and using a mixer on low speed, beat the buttermilk, eggs, granulated sugar, vanilla, and lemon zest until combined. Add the cream cheese in chunks. Beat with the mixer until the cream cheese is well distributed but still slightly lumpy. Add the buttermilk mixture to the bowl with the dry ingredients. Stir gently until just combined (small lumps are okay).

3. In a 12-inch nonstick skillet, melt 1 tablespoon butter over medium heat. When the pan is hot and the foam from the butter subsides, add the batter by heaping ¼ cupfuls. Cook 2 to 3 minutes, or until bubbles begin to appear and the edges are set. Turn and cook another 2 minutes, or until the underside is golden brown. If desired, transfer the cooked pancakes to a baking sheet in a preheated 225°F oven to keep warm. Cook the remaining batter in batches, adding more butter as needed. Serve the pancakes topped with the strawberry mixture and a dusting of confectioners' sugar.

Each serving About 455 calories, 12g protein, 60g carbohydrate, 19g fat (11g saturated), 1g fiber, 500mg sodium

oatmeal sconuts

PREP: 10 MIN / TOTAL: 25 MIN / MAKES 13

2 cups old-fashioned
oats

2 cups all-purpose flour

½ cup packed brown
sugar

2½ teaspoons baking
powder

½ teaspoon baking soda

½ teaspoon salt

¼ teaspoon ground
nutmeg

½ cup butter, cut
into pieces

¾ cup buttermilk

1 large egg

Cinnamon sugar
(page 549)

1. Preheat the oven to 425°F.

2. In a food processor, combine the oats, flour, brown sugar, baking powder, baking soda, salt, and nutmeg; pulse to blend. Add the butter; pulse until coarse crumbs form.

3. In a cup, beat the buttermilk and egg. With the processor running, add the egg mixture to the dry ingredients and pulse until a dough forms.

4. Scoop the dough by ¼ cupfuls onto a baking sheet. Flatten each mound into a 2½-inch round. Sprinkle with cinnamon sugar. Bake 15 to 17 minutes, or until golden on the underside.

Each sconut About 235 calories, 5g protein, 34g carbohydrate, 9g fat (5g saturated), 2g fiber, 2g fiber, 315mg sodium.

scones

PREP: 15 MIN / TOTAL: 40 MIN / SERVES 8

2 cups all-purpose flour

2 tablespoons plus 2
teaspoons sugar

2½ teaspoons baking
powder

¼ teaspoon salt

½ cup cold butter,
cut into pieces

¾ cup whole milk

1 large egg,
separated

1. Preheat the oven to 375°F. In a large bowl and using a wire whisk, stir the flour, 2 tablespoons sugar, baking powder, and salt. With a pastry blender or 2 knives used scissor-fashion, cut in the butter until the mixture resembles coarse crumbs.

2. In a 1-cup measuring cup and using a fork, mix the milk and egg yolk until blended. Make a well in the center of the flour mixture and pour in the milk mixture. Stir just until combined.

3. Turn the dough onto a lightly floured surface and knead 5 or 6 times, just until smooth. With lightly floured hands, pat the dough into a 7½-inch round. Transfer to an ungreased baking sheet.

4. With a lightly floured knife, cut the dough into 8 wedges; do not separate the wedges. In a small cup, lightly beat the egg white. Brush the scones with the egg white and sprinkle with the remaining 2 teaspoons sugar. Bake until golden brown, 22 to 25 minutes. Separate the wedges. Serve warm or cool on a wire rack to serve later.

Each scone About 260 calories, 5g protein, 30g carbohydrate, 13g fat (8g saturated), 1g fiber, 360mg sodium.

VARIATIONS

Buttermilk Scones

Prepare as directed, but use only 2 teaspoons baking powder. Add ½ **teaspoon baking soda** to the flour mixture. Substitute ¾ **cup buttermilk** for the milk.

Rich Scones

Prepare as directed, but preheat the oven to 400°F. Use 3½ **cups all-purpose flour, ½ cup sugar, 2 tablespoons baking powder, ½ teaspoon salt,** and **6 tablespoons butter or margarine.** Substitute **1 cup half-and-half or light cream** for the milk, and blend with **2 eggs.** Turn the dough onto a greased large baking sheet (the dough will be sticky) and, with lightly floured hands, pat the dough into a 9-inch round. Brush with **1 tablespoon half-and-half or light cream** and sprinkle with **1 tablespoon sugar.** With a floured knife, cut the dough into 8 wedges; do not separate. Bake until golden, 15 to 20 minutes.

Lemon-Walnut Scones

Prepare as directed for Rich Scones, but add 1 **teaspoon freshly grated lemon zest** to the flour mixture; add **1 cup chopped walnuts** (4 ounces) with the half-and-half mixture.

STRAWBERRY CHEESECAKE FLAPJACKS 518

SPRING GREENS & MATZO FRITTATA 522

CHARD & GRUYÈRE EGGS IN THE HOLE 521

SPICED BANANA-CHOCOLATE MUFFINS 521

spiced banana-chocolate muffins

PREP: 15 MIN / TOTAL: 35 MIN / SERVES 9

2 cups old-fashioned oats

1¼ cups white whole wheat flour

½ cup brown sugar

2 tablespoons chia seeds

2 teaspoons baking powder

¾ teaspoon baking soda

½ teaspoon salt

½ teaspoon ground cinnamon

¼ teaspoon ground ginger

1¼ cups mashed banana (from about 3 very ripe medium bananas)

1 cup low-fat buttermilk

2 tablespoons vegetable oil

1 large egg, beaten

2 ounces bittersweet chocolate (60% to 70% cacao), melted

1. Preheat the oven to 400°F. Line 18 muffin-pan cups with paper liners.

2. In a large bowl, whisk the oats, flour, brown sugar, chia seeds, baking powder, baking soda, salt, cinnamon, and ginger. In a medium bowl, stir together the bananas, buttermilk, oil, and egg. Fold the banana mixture into the flour mixture. Divide evenly among the muffin-pan cups.

3. Bake 20 to 25 minutes, or until a toothpick inserted into the center of the muffins comes out clean. Cool on a wire rack 10 minutes. Remove the muffins from the pan; cool completely on a wire rack.

4. Drizzle tops with chocolate. Makes 18.

Each serving (2 muffins) About 300 calories, 6g protein, 48g carbohydrate, 8g fat (2g saturated), 6g fiber, 430 mg sodium.

love toasts

(See photo on page 510.)

PREP: 15 MIN / TOTAL: 20 MIN / SERVES 2

4 teaspoons mayonnaise

2 slices white sandwich bread

1 tablespoon butter

2 large eggs

Salt

Ground black pepper

Finely chopped capers and herbs (such as parsley, chives or basil), for serving (optional)

Spread the mayonnaise on both sides of each bread slice. With a medium heart-shaped cookie cutter, cut the centers from the bread. In a 12-inch nonstick skillet, melt the butter over medium heat. Add the bread (and centers) to the skillet. Cook 4 to 5 minutes, or until golden brown. Turn the bread over. To each heart-shaped hole, add 1 egg; sprinkle the eggs with a pinch each of salt and pepper. Reduce the heat to medium-low. Cook 5 to 7 minutes, or until the whites are set. Sprinkle with capers and herbs, if desired.

Each serving About 255 calories, 8g protein, 12g carbohydrate, 19g fat (7g saturated), 1g fiber, 375mg sodium.

chard & gruyère eggs in the hole

PREP: 10 MIN / TOTAL: 40 MIN / SERVES 6

Nonstick cooking spray

6 slices sourdough bread

3 tablespoons butter

1 bunch (about 6 ounces) rainbow chard, trimmed and chopped

Salt

6 large eggs

Ground black pepper

4 ounces shredded Gruyère cheese

1. Preheat the oven to 425°F. Spray a large baking sheet with nonstick cooking spray.

2. With a 2½-inch-wide round cookie cutter, cut holes from the center of each bread slice. Arrange the bread and cutouts on the prepared baking sheet. Bake 5 minutes, or until slightly dry, turning the bread over halfway through.

3. In a 12-inch skillet, melt the butter over medium heat. Add the chard and ¼ teaspoon salt; cook 8 to 10 minutes, or until the stalks are crisp-tender, stirring occasionally. Divide the chard among the bread slices, spreading it around the holes. Crack an egg into each hole; top each with a pinch of salt and pepper. Sprinkle the Gruyère over the egg and chard and cutouts.

4. Bake the eggs 8 to 12 minutes, or until the whites are set but the yolks are runny. Serve immediately.

Each serving About 280 calories, 15g protein, 15g carbohydrate, 17g fat (9g saturated), 1g fiber, 470mg sodium.

spring greens & matzo frittata

(See photo on page 520.)

PREP: 20 MIN / TOTAL: 55 MIN / SERVES 6

Nonstick cooking spray

1 tablespoon butter

1 bunch (about 1 pound) thin asparagus, trimmed and cut into 1-inch lengths

1 cup warm water

5 sheets matzo, broken into large chunks

5 large eggs

1 cup fresh basil leaves, chopped

1 cup frozen peas, thawed

1 tablespoon lemon zest

1 teaspoon salt

½ teaspoon ground black pepper

1. Preheat the oven to 350°F; spray an 8-inch square baking dish with nonstick cooking spray.

2. In a 12-inch skillet over medium heat, melt the butter. Add the asparagus; cook 5 to 8 minutes, until crisp-tender. Remove from the heat; set aside.

3. Meanwhile, in a medium bowl, pour the warm water over the matzo and let soften 5 minutes. Drain.

4. In a large bowl, beat the eggs. Stir in the asparagus, matzo, basil, peas, lemon zest, salt, and pepper. Pour into the baking dish.

5. Bake 35 to 40 minutes, or until the top is golden brown and the center is set. Can be covered and refrigerated up to 3 days.

Each serving About 200 calories, 10g protein, 25g carbohydrate, 6g fat (3g saturated), 3g fiber, 465mg sodium.

GLOSSARY →

A **frittata** is a thick, pancake-style omelet with the ingredients mixed in. Chopped vegetables, leftover pasta, cheese, and cured meats are all possibilities for frittata stir-ins. A Spanish tortilla is similar to a frittata: It is almost always based on eggs and fried sliced potatoes and may have other add-ins.

crispy egg toasts

(See photo on page 513.)

PREP: 5 MIN / TOTAL: 10 MIN / SERVES 2

2 large eggs

3 tablespoons olive oil

Salt and ground black pepper

Toasted bread, for serving

1. Crack 1 egg into each of 2 small cups. In a 10-inch nonstick skillet, heat the oil over medium-high heat until very hot. Carefully add the eggs; stand back, as the oil will sputter. Cook until the whites are golden brown and crisp around the edges and set around yolks, 2 minutes. If the edges are dark but the whites are not set, remove the skillet from the heat; cover 10 seconds, or until the whites are cooked. Season with a pinch each of salt and pepper.

2. Serve each crispy egg on a slice of toasted bread.

Each serving (with toast) About 235 calories, 9g protein, 14g carbohydrate, 16g fat (3g saturated), 1g fiber, 285mg sodium.

VARIATIONS

Basil-Arugula Toast

In a blender, combine ½ **cup olive oil** with ¼ **cup chopped fresh basil**. Toast **2 slices of bread**. Top each with **arugula, 1 tablespoon crumbled goat cheese**, and **1 Crispy Egg**. Drizzle with the basil oil.

Curry-Avocado Toast

In a small dry skillet over medium heat, toast ½ **teaspoon curry powder** until fragrant, 1 minute. Stir the curry powder into **2 tablespoons olive oil** and set aside. Mash **1 avocado** with **2 teaspoons lime juice** and ⅛ **teaspoon salt**. Toast **2 slices of bread**. Top each with half the avocado mash, **1 Crispy Egg**, and **chopped fresh cilantro**. Drizzle with curry oil.

Smoky Red Pepper Toast

In a small dry skillet over medium heat, toast ½ **teaspoon smoked paprika** until fragrant, 1 minute. Stir the paprika into **2 tablespoons olive oil** and set aside. Toast **2 slices of bread**. Top each with **prepared Roasted Pepper & Mint Hummus (page 61)** and **1 Crispy Egg**. Drizzle with the smoked paprika oil.

basic muffins

PREP: 10 MIN / TOTAL: 30 MIN / SERVES 12

- 2½ cups all-purpose flour
- ½ cup sugar
- 1 tablespoon baking powder
- ½ teaspoon salt
- 1 cup milk
- ½ cup butter, melted
- 1 large egg
- 1 teaspoon vanilla extract

1. Preheat the oven to 400°F. Grease twelve 2½ × 1¼-inch muffin-pan cups.

2. In a large bowl and using a wire whisk, stir the flour, sugar, baking powder, and salt. In a medium bowl and using a fork, beat the milk, melted butter, egg, and vanilla until blended. Add the liquid mixture to the flour mixture; stir just until the flour is moistened (the batter will be lumpy).

3. Spoon the batter into the prepared muffin-pan cups. Bake until a toothpick inserted in the center of muffin comes out clean, 20 to 25 minutes. Immediately remove the muffins from the pan. Serve the muffins warm, or cool them on a wire rack to serve later.

Each serving About 225 calories, 4g protein, 30g carbohydrate, 10g fat (6g saturated), 1g fiber, 310mg sodium.

VARIATIONS

Jam-Filled Muffins

Prepare as directed, but fill the muffin-pan cups one-third full with batter. Drop **1 rounded teaspoon strawberry or raspberry preserves** in the center of each; top with the remaining batter. Bake as directed.

Blueberry or Raspberry Muffins

Prepare as directed, but stir **1 cup blueberries or raspberries** into the batter.

Walnut or Pecan Muffins

Prepare as directed, but stir ½ **cup chopped toasted walnuts or pecans** into the batter. Sprinkle with **2 tablespoons sugar** before baking.

puffy cheddar grits

PREP: 20 MIN / TOTAL: 1 HR 5 MIN / SERVES 8

- 3½ cups whole milk
- 2 cups water
- 2 tablespoons butter
- 1 teaspoon salt
- 1¼ cups quick hominy grits
- 8 ounces Cheddar cheese, shredded (2 cups)
- 5 large eggs
- 1 teaspoon hot sauce
- ¼ teaspoon ground black pepper

1. Preheat the oven to 325°F. Grease a shallow 2½-quart casserole. In a 4-quart saucepan, combine 1½ cups milk, the water, butter, and salt; heat to boiling over medium-high heat. With a wire whisk, gradually whisk in the grits, beating constantly to prevent lumps. Reduce the heat; cover and cook, stirring occasionally with a wooden spoon, 5 minutes; the grits will be very stiff. Remove from the heat; stir in the Cheddar.

2. In a medium bowl and using a wire whisk, beat the eggs, the remaining 2 cups milk, the hot sauce, and pepper until blended. Gradually stir the egg mixture into the grits.

3. Pour the grits mixture into the prepared casserole. Bake until a knife inserted in the center comes out clean, about 45 minutes.

Each serving About 340 calories, 16g protein, 24g carbohydrate, 20g fat (11g saturated), 1g fiber, 605mg sodium.

WOMELETS 526

MEXICAN BREAKFAST CHILAQUILES 525

BACON & EGG FRIED RICE 527

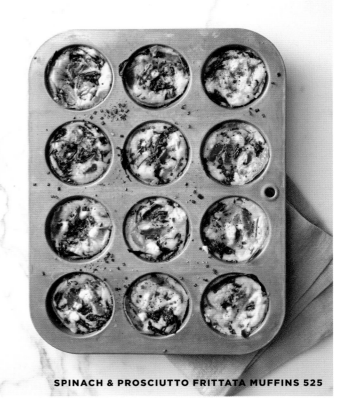

SPINACH & PROSCIUTTO FRITTATA MUFFINS 525

spinach & prosciutto frittata muffins

PREP: 20 MIN / TOTAL: 50 MIN / SERVES 6

Nonstick cooking spray
6 large eggs
½ cup whole milk
¼ teaspoon salt
⅛ teaspoon ground black pepper
¾ cup crumbled soft goat cheese

5 ounces baby spinach, wilted and chopped
½ cup roasted red pepper, diced
2 ounces prosciutto, sliced into ribbons

1. Preheat the oven to 350°F. Spray a 12-cup muffin pan with non-stick cooking spray.

2. In a large bowl, beat the eggs, milk, salt, and pepper. Stir in the cheese, spinach, and roasted red pepper.

3. Divide the batter among the muffin-pan cups (about ¼ cup each), top with prosciutto, and bake 20 to 25 minutes, or until just set in the center.

4. Cool on a rack 5 minutes, then remove the muffins from the cups. Serve warm. Can be refrigerated up to 4 days; microwave on High 30 seconds to reheat.

Each serving (2 muffins) About 155 calories, 13g protein, 4g carbohydrate, 10g fat (4g saturated), 1g fiber, 520mg sodium.

mexican breakfast chilaquiles

PREP: 15 MIN / TOTAL: 20 MIN / SERVES 4

6 large eggs
¼ teaspoon salt
½ tablespoon canola oil
5 ounces tortilla chips
1 cup shredded Monterey Jack cheese
¼ cup pickled jalapeño chile slices

1 avocado, thinly sliced
1 cup pico de gallo
2 tablespoons fresh cilantro, chopped
Sour cream and lime wedges, for serving (optional)

1. Beat the eggs with the salt. In a 12-inch oven-safe nonstick skillet, heat the oil over medium heat. Add the eggs and gently scramble them 3 to 4 minutes, or until set. Transfer to a bowl and set aside; wipe the skillet mostly clean.

2. Preheat the broiler. Spread half the chips in the same skillet. Sprinkle with half the cheese. Top with the remaining chips and cheese, then the eggs and jalapeño slices. Broil until the cheese has melted and the chips begin to brown, 1 to 2 minutes.

3. Remove from the oven; top with avocado, pico de gallo, and cilantro.

4. Serve with sour cream and lime wedges, if desired.

Each serving About 495 calories, 19g protein, 36g carbohydrate, 32g fat (9g saturated), 6g fiber, 915mg sodium.

GLOSSARY →

Chilaquiles, a traditional Mexican dish, is often eaten for breakfast or brunch. Its spicy carb/fat combo is considered a curative for hangovers. To make it, fry wedges of corn tortillas (or cheat and use tortilla chips), then layer in a skillet with red or green salsa and simmer until the tortillas start to soften. Add pulled chicken or fried or scrambled eggs. Top with shredded cheese and/or sour cream (crema).

bacon & gruyère breakfast "pie"

(See photo on page 510.)

PREP: 10 MIN / TOTAL: 45 MIN / SERVES 6

- 1 sheet (half a 17.3-ounce package) frozen puff pastry, thawed
- ⅓ cup sour cream
- ¾ cup shredded Gruyère cheese
- 4 slices cooked bacon
- 3 large eggs
- ¼ teaspoon salt
- ¼ teaspoon ground black pepper
- Fresh thyme leaves, for garnish

1. Preheat the oven to 400°F.

2. On a large sheet of parchment paper, roll the pastry to a 12 × 10-inch rectangle. Fold ½ inch of the edges to form a rim; using a fork, seal the rim and poke holes all over the pastry bottom. Place the pastry on a baking sheet; bake 20 minutes, or until golden brown.

3. In a small bowl, combine the sour cream and Gruyère. Spread it onto the tart, creating 3 wells for the eggs. Arrange the bacon strips over the topping. Crack the eggs into the wells; sprinkle with the salt and pepper.

4. Bake until the egg whites are set but the yolks are still runny, about 12 minutes. Garnish with thyme.

Each serving About 310 calories, 12g protein, 15g carbohydrate, 22g fat (8g saturated), 1g fiber, 425mg sodium.

womelets

(See photo on page 524.)

PREP: 20 MIN / TOTAL: 40 MIN / SERVES 6

- ¼ cup all-purpose flour
- ½ teaspoon baking powder
- ¼ teaspoon salt
- 4 large eggs
- 2 tablespoons olive oil
- 1 cup chopped cooked potatoes
- ½ cup shredded Gruyère cheese (about 4 ounces)
- ¼ cup drained and chopped pickled peppers
- 2 green onions, finely chopped
- Nonstick cooking spray

1. Preheat a waffle iron. In a large bowl, whisk together the flour, baking powder, and salt. Add the eggs and oil; whisk to combine. Fold in the potatoes, Gruyère, peppers, and green onions.

2. Spray the waffle iron with nonstick cooking spray and add ¼ cup batter. Cook 5 minutes, or until deep golden brown; keep warm on a baking sheet in a preheated 225°F oven. Repeat with remaining batter. With a 3-inch cutter, cut the womelet into rounds, if desired.

Each serving About 180 calories, 8g protein, 10g carbohydrate, 12g fat (3g sat), 1g fiber, 320mg sodium.

green eggs & ham'wiches

(See photo on page 529.)

PREP: 15 MIN / TOTAL: 15 MIN / SERVES 4

- 6 large hard-cooked eggs, peeled and chopped
- ¼ cup bottled pesto
- 3 tablespoons light mayonnaise
- Ground black pepper
- 4 croissants
- 8 thin slices ham
- 1 cup arugula

1. Gently combine the eggs, pesto, mayo, and pepper to taste.

2. Split and toast the croissants. Divide the ham, egg salad, and arugula among the croissants. Serve immediately or wrap tightly in waxed paper and refrigerate up to 4 hours.

Each serving About 500 calories, 22g protein, 30g carbohydrate, 32g fat (11g saturated), 2g fiber, 995mg sodium.

Ingredient Ideas

tapas toast

Spread your bread with one of our tasty tapas toast combos for the tastiest brunch idea ever!

- Almond butter, Manchego cheese, and micro greens
- Fig jam, Serrano ham, aged Gouda, and baby arugula
- Apricot jam, goat cheese, and micro greens

bacon & egg fried rice

(See photo on page 524.)

PREP: 10 MIN / TOTAL: 20 MIN / SERVES 4

2 tablespoons canola oil
5 slices bacon, chopped
1 bunch green onions, sliced
1 bag (5 ounces) baby spinach
3 cups cooked white rice
1 cup frozen peas
½ teaspoon salt
4 large eggs

1. In a 12-inch skillet, heat 1 tablespoon canola oil over medium-high heat. Add the bacon and cook until the bacon is crisp. Add the green onions and baby spinach. Cook 2 minutes, stirring. Add the white rice, peas, and salt. Cook 5 minutes, stirring. Divide among 4 plates.

2. In the same skillet, heat the remaining oil over medium-high heat. Add the eggs and fry to the desired doneness. Top each plate with a fried egg.

Each serving About 400 calories, 16g protein, 41g carbohydrate, 18g fat (6g saturated), 3g fiber, 555 mg sodium.

Tip Don't eat bacon? Sauté the greens in 1½ tablespoons canola oil instead.

waffle hash browns

(See photo on page 529.)

PREP: 10 MIN / TOTAL: 25 MIN / SERVES 4

2 large Russet potatoes (about 1½ pounds), peeled and shredded
2 tablespoons snipped fresh chives
½ teaspoon salt
¼ teaspoon ground black pepper
Nonstick cooking spray
4 poached large eggs, for serving
Cooked breakfast sausage, for serving

1. Preheat a waffle iron. Using 2 or 3 layers of paper towels, firmly squeeze all the excess liquid from the shredded potatoes. Transfer to a medium bowl, along with the chives, salt, and pepper.

2. Spray the waffle maker with nonstick cooking spray and add a ½-inch layer of potatoes per waffle. Close the waffle maker, pressing down firmly. Cook 12 minutes, or until deep golden brown and crisp; keep warm on a baking sheet in a preheated 225°F oven. Repeat with remaining potato mixture. Serve with poached eggs and sausage.

Each serving About 205 calories, 9g protein, 29g carbohydrate, 6g fat (2g saturated), 2g fiber, 445mg sodium.

Tip Skip the potatoes and just add (thawed) frozen Tater Tots® to the waffle iron instead!

HOW TO

POACH EGGS FOR A CROWD

This weekend favorite has always been a pain to pull off. But if you streamline the process with our genius poaching method, it's a cinch to do the rest. Add **2 tablespoons water** to each muffin-tin cup and crack **1 egg** into it. Place the tin in a preheated 400°F oven for 8 minutes, or until the yolks reach the desired doneness (check at 30-second intervals). Scoop out the eggs with a slotted spoon. Then bring on the hollandaise, English muffins, Canadian bacon . . . and mimosas!

mint-pesto baked eggs

PREP: 15 MIN / TOTAL: 40 MIN / SERVES 6

- 1 cup packed fresh cilantro leaves
- ½ cup packed fresh mint leaves
- ½ cup shelled pistachios
- 2 jalapeño chiles, seeded and chopped
- 2 tablespoons fresh lemon juice
- 1 clove garlic
- ½ teaspoon salt
- ½ cup olive oil
- ¾ cup heavy cream
- 12 large eggs
- Toasted bread slices, for serving

1. Preheat the oven to 425°F. Grease six 10- to 12-ounce ramekins; place them on a rimmed baking sheet.

2. In the food processor, pulse the cilantro, mint, pistachios, jalapeños, lemon juice, garlic, and salt until finely chopped, stopping and stirring occasionally. Pulse in the oil until well combined.

3. To each ramekin, add 2 tablespoons cream and 2 eggs; top with 1 tablespoon herb mixture. Bake 12 to 15 minutes, or until the whites are set but the yolks are still runny. Serve with the remaining herb mixture and toasted bread.

Each serving (with toast) About 320 calories, 14g protein, 3g carbohydrate, 28g fat (11g saturated), 1g fiber, 215mg sodium.

corned beef hash

PREP: 25 MIN / TOTAL: 40 MIN / SERVES 4

- 2 tablespoons vegetable oil, plus more for brushing
- 1 medium green bell pepper, seeded and chopped
- 1 medium red onion, finely chopped
- ⅛ teaspoon salt
- 2 cups chopped cooked potatoes
- 2 cups chopped cooked corned beef
- ¼ cup basil leaves, chopped
- 4 large eggs
- Ground black pepper

1. Preheat the oven to 450°F. Lightly brush 4 individual baking dishes with oil.

2. In a 12-inch nonstick skillet, heat the vegetable oil over medium-high heat. Add the bell pepper, onion, and salt. Cook 10 minutes, or until the vegetables are almost tender, stirring occasionally.

3. Add the potatoes and corned beef. Cook 5 minutes, stirring often. Stir in the basil. Divide the mixture among the prepared baking dishes. Top each with 1 egg and a pinch of black pepper. Bake 13 to 15 minutes, or to the desired doneness.

Each serving About 410 calories, 21g protein, 21g carbohydrate, 27g fat (7g saturated), 3g fiber, 915mg sodium.

potato chip omelet

PREP: 15 MIN / TOTAL: 30 MIN / SERVES 4

- 8 large eggs, beaten
- 3 cups potato chips, crushed (about 4 ounces)
- ¼ cup fresh parsley, chopped
- ¼ teaspoon salt
- 2 tablespoons olive oil
- 1 small onion, chopped
- ¼ teaspoon smoked paprika
- Arugula salad and baguette, for serving

1. In a large bowl, combine the eggs, potato chips, parsley, and salt.

2. In a 10-inch nonstick skillet, heat the oil over medium-low heat. Add the onion; cook 8 minutes. Add the egg mixture. Stir slowly until the edges start to set, then cook undisturbed until the top is mostly set. Cover with a large lid and carefully flip the eggs. Slide the omelet back into the pan; cook 5 minutes, or until set. Sprinkle with the paprika. Serve with arugula salad and baguette.

Each serving About 365 calories, 15g protein, 16g carbohydrate, 26g fat (5g saturated), 1g fiber, 415mg sodium.

 Tip If your skillet doesn't have a lid, use a large plate or a platter without a rim to turn the omelet.

GREEN EGGS & HAM'WICHES 526

WAFFLE HASH BROWNS 527

CORNED BEEF HASH 528

MINT-PESTO BAKED EGGS 528

spanish potato omelet

(See photo on page 532.)

(See photo on page 532.)

PREP: 10 MIN / TOTAL: 50 MIN / SERVES 6

6 large eggs

Salt

1½ pounds golden potatoes, peeled and cut into ⅛-inch-thick slices

1¼ cups olive oil

1 large onion, very thinly sliced

Finely chopped fresh parsley, for garnish

1. In a medium bowl, beat the eggs with ¾ teaspoon salt; set aside. In a large bowl, toss the potatoes with ¼ teaspoon salt.

2. In a 10-inch nonstick skillet, heat the oil over medium heat. Add the potatoes; cook 10 to 12 minutes, or until tender but not falling apart, gently turning them occasionally. With a slotted spoon, transfer the potatoes to another large bowl.

3. To the skillet, add the onion; cook 12 minutes, or until very tender, stirring occasionally. With a slotted spoon, transfer the onion to the bowl with the potatoes. When the potato-onion mixture has cooled slightly, gently stir in the eggs until well combined.

4. Drain all but 2 teaspoons oil from the skillet (reserve oil for another use); heat over medium-high heat 1 minute. Add the egg-potato mixture to the skillet, spreading it in an even layer; reduce the heat to medium. Cook 7 minutes, or until the eggs are mostly set and the edges are browned.

5. Loosen the edges with a rubber spatula. Remove the skillet from the heat and cover with a large plate; carefully invert, holding the plate and skillet together. Slide the omelet back into the skillet. Cook over medium heat 3 minutes, or until the bottom and center are set. Serve warm or at room temperature, garnished with parsley.

Each serving About 245 calories, 8g protein, 22g carbohydrate, 14g fat (3g saturated), 2g fiber, 465mg sodium.

lox scrambled eggs

(See photo on page 532.)

(See photo on page 532.)

PREP: 20 MIN / TOTAL: 25 MIN / SERVES 6

12 large eggs

2 tablespoons heavy or whipping cream

¼ teaspoon salt

1½ tablespoons butter

3 tablespoons cream cheese, crumbled

4 ounces sliced smoked salmon, flaked into small pieces

2 tablespoons finely chopped red onion

1 tablespoon capers, rinsed and chopped

1 tablespoon fresh dill leaves, chopped

2 pounds assorted tomatoes, sliced, for garnish

6 mini bagels, split and toasted, for serving

1. In a large bowl and using a fork, beat the eggs, cream, and salt until well blended.

2. In a 12-inch nonstick skillet, melt the butter over medium heat. Add the egg mixture to the skillet and cook, stirring with a spatula, until the eggs are almost cooked, 6 to 8 minutes. Fold in the cream cheese and salmon. Cook 1 minute longer, or until the egg mixture is set but still moist, stirring.

3. Place the eggs on a serving platter. Sprinkle the onion, capers, and dill over eggs. Garnish with tomatoes and serve with mini bagels.

Each serving (without bagels) About 310 calories, 20g protein, 17g carbohydrate, 18g fat (7g saturated), 1g fiber, 600mg sodium.

GOOD TO KNOW

LOX, GRAVLAX, OR SMOKED SALMON ?

Smoked salmon, lox, and gravlax are all cured salmon. Lox, from the Yiddish *laks*, is salt-brined salmon belly, never cooked. Gravlax is similar, but the Scandinavian salt-cure is embellished with sugar and dill. Smoked salmon is salt-cured, then smoked. If it is cold-smoked, it will have a silky texture similar to lox; hot-smoking firms the fish, giving it a flaky texture.

scrambled eggs

with cream cheese

PREP: 10 MIN / TOTAL: 20 MIN / SERVES 8

- **14 large eggs**
- **¼ teaspoon ground black pepper**
- **3 tablespoons butter**
- **2 packages (3 ounces each) cream cheese, cut into 1-inch cubes**

1. In a large bowl and using a wire whisk, beat the eggs and pepper until well blended.

2. In a 12-inch nonstick skillet, melt the butter over medium heat; add the eggs. With a heat-safe spatula, gently push the egg mixture as it begins to set to form soft curds.

3. When the eggs are partially cooked, top with cream cheese. Continue cooking, stirring occasionally, until the eggs have thickened and no visible liquid egg remains. Serve on a warm platter.

***

Each serving About 245 calories, 13g protein, 2g carbohydrate, 20g fat (10g saturated), 0g fiber, 217mg sodium.

VARIATION

Scrambled Eggs with Cream Cheese & Salmon

Prepare as directed above, but sprinkle **4 ounces smoked salmon,** chopped, over the eggs with the cream cheese. To serve, top with **¼ cup chopped green onions**. Serves 8.

spaghetti frittata

PREP: 20 MIN / TOTAL: 30 MIN / SERVES 4

- **6 large eggs**
- **¼ cup milk**
- **⅓ cup freshly grated Parmesan cheese**
- **¼ cup chopped fresh basil**
- **½ teaspoon salt**
- **¼ teaspoon ground black pepper**
- **6 ounces thin spaghetti, broken in half and cooked as the label directs**
- **1 tablespoon olive oil**

1. Preheat the broiler. In a large bowl and using a wire whisk, beat the eggs, milk, Parmesan, basil, salt, and pepper until well blended. Add the drained pasta and toss to combine.

2. In a 10-inch oven-safe nonstick skillet, heat the oil over medium-low heat. (If the skillet is not oven-safe, wrap the handle with a double layer of foil.) Add the pasta-egg mixture, pressing lightly with a spatula to flatten it. Cook until the mixture is almost set in the center, about 10 minutes. Place the skillet under the broiler 6 inches from the heat source. Broil until the frittata is set, about 1 minute.

3. To serve, loosen the frittata from the skillet and slide onto a warm platter; cut into 4 wedges.

***

Each serving About 345 calories, 19g protein, 34g carbohydrate, 14g fat (5g saturated), 2g fiber, 545mg sodium.

fluffy omelet

PREP: 10 MIN / TOTAL: 25 MIN / SERVES 2

- **4 large eggs, separated**
- **2 tablespoons water**
- **⅛ teaspoon salt**
- **1 tablespoon butter**

1. Preheat the oven to 350°F. In a medium bowl and using a mixer at high speed, beat the egg whites until stiff peaks form when the beaters are lifted. In a large bowl and using a mixer at high speed, beat the egg yolks, water, and salt until the egg-yolk mixture has thickened. With a rubber spatula, gently fold one-third of the beaten egg whites into the egg-yolk mixture. Fold in the remaining egg whites until just blended.

2. In a 10-inch oven-safe nonstick skillet, melt the butter over medium-low heat. (If your skillet is not oven-safe, wrap the handle with a double layer of foil.) Add the egg mixture and cook until the top has puffed and the underside is golden, about 3 minutes.

3. Place the skillet in the oven. Bake until the top of the omelet is golden and the center springs back when lightly touched with a finger, about 10 minutes.

4. To serve, loosen the omelet from the skillet and slide it onto a warm platter.

***

Each serving About 200 calories, 13g protein, 1g carbohydrate, 16g fat (7g saturated), 0g fiber, 331mg sodium.

MUSHROOM RAGÙ & POLENTA EGG BAKE 533

LOX SCRAMBLED EGGS 530

SPANISH POTATO OMELET 530

SCRAMBLED CARBONARA 533

mushroom ragù & polenta egg bake

PREP: 15 MIN / TOTAL: 1 HR 30 MIN / SERVES 8

3 tablespoons olive oil

2 medium shallots, finely chopped

4 cups chicken broth

3 cups water

1½ cups medium- or coarse-grind cornmeal

Salt

1 pound mixed mushrooms, trimmed and sliced

2 cloves garlic, finely chopped

1 can (14 ounces) diced tomatoes

6 large eggs

Ground black pepper

¼ cup grated Parmesan cheese

Chopped fresh parsley, for garnish

1. Preheat the oven to 350°F. In a 4- to 5-quart saucepot, heat 1 tablespoon oil over medium heat. Add the shallots; cook 3 minutes, stirring. Add the broth and water. Heat to boiling over high heat. Slowly whisk in the cornmeal and ½ teaspoon salt. Reduce the heat; simmer 4 minutes, whisking often.

2. Transfer the polenta to a 3-quart baking dish; cover with foil. Bake 45 to 50 minutes, or until the grains are tender and the polenta has thickened, stirring every 15 minutes. Remove and discard the foil.

3. Meanwhile, in a 12-inch skillet, heat the remaining 2 tablespoons oil over medium heat. Add the mushrooms, garlic, and ½ teaspoon salt; cook 10 minutes, or until the mushrooms have softened, stirring. Stir in the tomatoes; cook 1 minute. Spoon the mushroom mixture over the cooked polenta.

4. Crack the eggs and gently nestle them into the mushroom mixture. Top each with a pinch of salt and pepper. Sprinkle the top with Parmesan. Bake 20 minutes, or until the whites have set. Garnish with parsley.

Each serving About 225 calories, 9g protein, 25g carbohydrate, 10g fat (2g saturated), 5g fiber, 790mg sodium.

scrambled carbonara

PREP: 10 MIN / TOTAL: 30 MIN / SERVES 6

1 pound spaghetti

5 large eggs

½ cup finely grated Parmesan cheese, plus more for garnish

½ teaspoon salt

¼ teaspoon ground black pepper

4 slices thick-cut bacon, chopped

1 small onion, finely chopped

Snipped fresh chives, for garnish

1. Cook the spaghetti as the label directs, reserving ¾ cup pasta cooking water before draining.

2. Meanwhile, whisk the eggs, Parmesan, salt, and pepper until combined.

3. In a 12-inch skillet over medium heat, cook the bacon 5 minutes, or until browned and crisp, stirring occasionally. With a slotted spoon, transfer the bacon to paper towels to drain. Pour off all but 2 tablespoons fat.

4. To the same skillet over medium heat, add the onion and cook 4 minutes, or until tender, stirring occasionally. Add the eggs to the skillet; cook 1 minute, stirring only once or twice, until almost set and large curds have formed.

5. In a large bowl, toss the eggs, bacon, and reserved pasta water with the hot pasta. Garnish with chives and Parmesan.

Each serving About 440 calories, 20g protein, 59g carbohydrate, 13g fat (4g sat), 4g fiber, 270mg sodium.

TESTING NOTE Taking its cue from classic carbonara, which features eggs (that cook only with the heat of the pasta) and pancetta, this version glorifies breakfast for dinner. For classic carbonara, replace the Parmesan with Pecorino Romano cheese. Bring eggs to room temperature and add them to the other ingredients, using only ¼ cup of the pasta water in step 5. Stir in additional pasta water as necessary to make a creamy sauce.

basic omelets

PREP: 5 MIN, PLUS PREPARING FILLING / TOTAL: 15 MIN /
SERVES 4

Choice of filling
(below and right)
8 large eggs

½ cup water
½ teaspoon salt
4 teaspoons butter

1. Prepare the filling; keep warm. In a medium bowl and using a wire whisk, beat the eggs, water, and salt.

2. In a 10-inch nonstick skillet, melt 1 teaspoon butter over medium-high heat. Pour ½ cup egg mixture into the skillet. Cook, gently lifting the edge of the eggs with a heat-safe rubber spatula and tilting the pan to allow the uncooked eggs to run underneath, until the eggs are set, about 1 minute. Spoon one-fourth of the filling over half the omelet. Fold the unfilled half of the omelet over the filling and slide it onto a warm plate. Repeat with the remaining butter, egg mixture, and filling. If desired, keep the omelets warm in a preheated 200°F oven until all omelets are cooked.

Each omelet (without filling) About 185 calories, 13g protein, 1g carbohydrate, 14g fat (5g saturated), 0g fiber, 455mg sodium.

CREAMY MUSHROOM FILLING In a 10-inch nonstick skillet, melt **1 tablespoon butter or margarine** over medium heat. Add **1 medium onion**, finely chopped; cook until tender, about 5 minutes. Stir in **8 ounces mushrooms**, trimmed and thinly sliced; **¼ teaspoon salt**; and **⅛ teaspoon ground black pepper**; cook until the liquid has evaporated. Stir in **¼ cup heavy or whipping cream**; boil until thickened, about 3 minutes. Stir in **2 tablespoons chopped fresh parsley**. Use one-fourth of the mushroom mixture for each omelet.

BLACK BEAN & SALSA FILLING In a 10-inch nonstick skillet, cook **1 cup canned black beans**, rinsed and drained, and **1 cup medium-hot salsa** over medium heat, stirring frequently until the liquid has evaporated. Divide the black-bean mixture; **1 ripe medium avocado**, peeled and chopped; and **¼ cup sour cream** among the omelets.

 Tip For lower-fat omelets, use 4 large eggs and 8 egg whites.

RED PEPPER & GOAT CHEESE FILLING In a 10-inch nonstick skillet, melt **2 teaspoons butter or margarine** over medium heat. Add **2 red bell peppers**, thinly sliced, and **¼ teaspoon salt**; cook until tender and lightly browned. Add **1 clove garlic**, finely chopped; cook 1 minute. Divide the red pepper; **2 ounces goat cheese**, crumbled; and **½ cup loosely packed, trimmed, and torn arugula** among the omelets.

GARDEN-VEGETABLE FILLING In a 10-inch nonstick skillet, heat **1 tablespoon olive oil** over medium heat. Add **1 small onion**, chopped; **1 small zucchini** (6 ounces), chopped; **1 small yellow bell pepper**, chopped; **½ teaspoon salt**; and **⅛ teaspoon ground black pepper**. Cook until the vegetables are tender, about 10 minutes. Stir in **2 ripe plum tomatoes**, chopped, and **¼ cup chopped fresh basil**; heat through. Use one-fourth of the mixture for each omelet.

WESTERN FILLING In a 10-inch nonstick skillet, heat **1 tablespoon olive oil** over medium heat. Add **1 small onion**, chopped; **1 green bell pepper**, chopped; **8 ounces mushrooms**, trimmed and thinly sliced; and **¼ teaspoon salt**. Cook until the vegetables are tender and the liquid has evaporated, about 10 minutes. Add **4 ounces sliced ham**, finely chopped (1 cup); heat through. Use one-fourth of the mixture for each omelet.

EGG WHITE OMELET Prepare the filling, if desired. Blend **2 tablespoons fat-free (skim) milk** and **1 tablespoon all-purpose flour** until smooth. Whisk in **4 large egg whites**, **½ teaspoon salt**, and **¼ teaspoon ground turmeric**, if desired for color. In an 8-inch nonstick skillet, heat **2 teaspoons olive oil** over medium heat. Add the egg white mixture and cook until just set, about 2 minutes. Spoon the filling, if using, over half the omelet. Continue as for Basic Omelets (left). **Makes 1 main-dish serving.**

CREAMY MUSHROOM FILLING Each serving About 290 calories, 15g protein, 8g carbohydrate, 23g fat (11g saturated), 1g fiber, 637mg sodium.
BLACK BEAN & SALSA FILLING Each serving About 365 calories, 17g protein, 18g carbohydrate, 25g fat (9g saturated), 8g fiber, 1,307mg sodium.
RED PEPPER & GOAT CHEESE FILLING Each serving About 260 calories, 16g protein, 3g carbohydrate, 20g fat (10g saturated), 1g fiber, 692mg sodium.
GARDEN-VEGETABLE FILLING Each serving About 240 calories, 14g protein, 7g carbohydrate, 17g fat (6g saturated), 2g fiber, 749mg sodium.
WESTERN FILLING Each serving About 295 calories, 19g protein, 8g carbohydrate, 21g fat (7g saturated), 2g fiber, 974mg sodium.
EGG WHITE OMELET Each serving (without filling) About 185 calories, 16g protein, 9g carbohydrate, 9g fat (1g saturated), 0g fiber, 1,395mg sodium.

Ingredient Ideas
quick no-cook fillings for omelets

Here are delicious flavor combos to suit every taste.

- Mango chutney and sour cream
- Chopped tomato, crumbled feta cheese, and dill
- Chopped smoked turkey, thinly sliced red onion, and cubed Brie cheese
- Diced ham, chopped green onions, and shredded pepper Jack cheese
- Ricotta cheese, berries, and confectioners' sugar
- Chopped fresh herbs, green onions, and sour cream
- Diced avocado, salsa, and sour cream
- Chopped tomato and pesto
- Chopped smoked salmon, cubed cream cheese, and capers

GOOD TO KNOW

AVOCADOS

The best way to tell if an avocado is ripe is to gently squeeze the base of the fruit in the palm of your hand. It should still be firm yet yield to gentle pressure. To ripen an avocado, place it inside a brown paper bag with a couple of pieces of fruit, like a banana or apple. The fruits naturally exchange ethylene gases inside the bag, which cause them both to ripen. Once ripe, refrigerate the avocado. **NOTE:** Microwaving will soften, not ripen, the fruit, so skip it!

---

huevos rancheros

PREP: 10 MIN / TOTAL: 30 MIN / SERVES 4

- 1 tablespoon vegetable oil
- 1 medium onion, coarsely chopped
- 1 clove garlic, finely chopped
- 1 jalapeño chile, seeded and finely chopped
- 1 can (14 to 16 ounces) tomatoes
- ¼ teaspoon salt
- 4 (6-inch) corn or flour tortillas
- 3 tablespoons butter or margarine
- 4 large eggs
- 2 tablespoons sour cream
- 1 tablespoon chopped fresh cilantro
- 1 ripe medium avocado, pitted, peeled, and cut crosswise into thin slices, for garnish

1. Preheat the oven to 350°F. In a 2-quart nonreactive saucepan, heat the oil over medium-high heat. Add the onion, garlic, and jalapeño and cook, stirring occasionally, until the onion is tender, about 5 minutes. Stir in the tomatoes with their juices and the salt; heat to boiling over high heat, breaking up the tomatoes with the side of a spoon. Reduce the heat; cover and simmer, stirring occasionally, 5 minutes.

2. Wrap the tortillas in foil; place in the oven until heated through, about 10 minutes.

3. Meanwhile, in a 10-inch skillet, melt the butter over medium heat. Break 1 egg into a small cup and, holding the cup close to the skillet, slip the egg into the skillet; repeat with the remaining eggs. Reduce the heat to low; cook slowly, spooning the butter over the eggs to baste them and turning the eggs to cook on both sides, until the egg whites are completely set and the egg yolks begin to thicken but are not hard.

4. Place the tortillas on warm plates; place 1 fried egg on each tortilla and spoon 2 tablespoons tomato sauce over each. Top with some sour cream and sprinkle with cilantro; garnish with avocado slices. Serve with the remaining tomato sauce.

Each serving About 405 calories, 11g protein, 25g carbohydrate, 31g fat (10g saturated), 6g fiber, 521mg sodium.

breakfast tortilla stack

PREP: 25 MIN / TOTAL: 30 MIN / SERVES 4

- ¼ cup chopped red onion
- 2 ripe medium tomatoes, chopped
- ¼ cup loosely packed fresh cilantro leaves, chopped
- 4 large eggs
- 4 large egg whites
- ¼ teaspoon salt
- ¼ teaspoon ground black pepper
- Nonstick cooking spray
- 1 cup fat-free refried beans
- ¼ teaspoon chipotle chile powder
- 4 (7-inch) whole wheat tortillas

1. Prepare the salsa: In a cup of ice water, soak the chopped onion 10 minutes; drain well. In a small bowl, combine the onion, tomato, and cilantro; set aside.

2. In a medium bowl and using a wire whisk or fork, beat the whole eggs, egg whites, salt, and pepper until blended.

3. Spray a 10-inch nonstick skillet with cooking spray; heat over medium heat 1 minute. Pour the egg mixture into the skillet; cook about 5 minutes, or until the egg mixture is set but still moist, stirring occasionally.

4. Meanwhile, in a small microwave-safe bowl, mix the beans and chipotle chile. Cover with vented plastic wrap; heat in the microwave on High 1 minute, or until hot.

5. Place a stack of tortillas between damp paper towels on a microwave-safe plate; heat in the microwave on High 10 to 15 seconds to warm. To serve, layer each tortilla with eggs, beans, and salsa.

Each serving About 200 calories, 13g protein, 29g carbohydrate, 4g fat (1g saturated), 13g fiber, 635mg sodium.

california sunrise toast

PREP: 10 MIN / TOTAL: 15 MIN / SERVES 4

- 1 ripe avocado, peeled, pitted, and cubed
- ½ teaspoon fresh lemon juice
- ¼ teaspoon crushed red pepper
- ¼ teaspoon salt
- 4 slices whole-grain bread
- 1 tablespoon olive oil
- 4 large eggs

1. In a medium bowl, mash the avocado with the lemon juice, crushed red pepper, and salt.

2. Toast the bread. Heat the oil in a 12-inch skillet over medium-high heat. Add the eggs and cook to the desired doneness.

3. Spread the avocado on toasted bread and top each slice with a fried egg.

Each serving About 265 calories, 11g protein, 18g carbohydrate, 17g fat (3g saturated), 6g fiber, 337mg sodium.

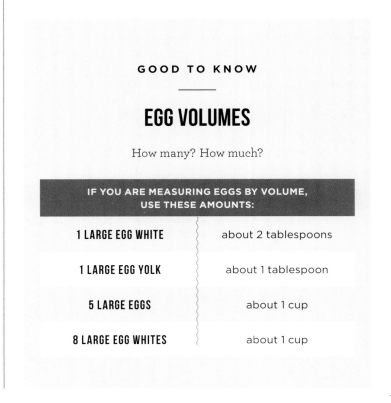

GOOD TO KNOW

EGG VOLUMES

How many? How much?

IF YOU ARE MEASURING EGGS BY VOLUME, USE THESE AMOUNTS:	
1 LARGE EGG WHITE	about 2 tablespoons
1 LARGE EGG YOLK	about 1 tablespoon
5 LARGE EGGS	about 1 cup
8 LARGE EGG WHITES	about 1 cup

asparagus-fontina pizzette
with bacon

PREP: 35 MIN / TOTAL: 50 MIN / SERVES 6

8 ounces asparagus, trimmed

6 ounces shiitake mushrooms, stems discarded, thinly sliced

¼ cup olive oil, plus more for greasing

2 cloves garlic, crushed with a garlic press

¼ teaspoon salt

1½ pounds fresh or frozen (thawed) pizza dough

5 slices bacon

6 ounces Fontina cheese, grated

6 large eggs

Ground black pepper

1. Arrange 2 oven racks in the top and bottom thirds of the oven. Preheat the oven to 475°F. Lightly grease two 18 × 12-inch jelly-roll pans.

2. Slice the asparagus on an angle into 2-inch pieces. Transfer to a large bowl along with the mushrooms, oil, garlic, and salt; toss until well coated.

3. Divide the pizza dough into 6 equal-size balls. On a lightly floured surface and using a floured rolling pin, roll out and press each dough ball into a 6-inch round; place them on the prepared jelly-roll pans.

4. Evenly divide the asparagus mixture among the rounds, creating a well in the center of each. Bake 10 minutes, or until the edges are golden brown, rotating pans halfway through.

5. Meanwhile, place the bacon on a paper-towel-lined microwave-safe plate. Cover with 2 sheets of paper towels. Microwave on High 4 to 6 minutes, or until beginning to crisp. Cool slightly; tear the bacon into small pieces.

6. Sprinkle the pizzettes with bacon and Fontina. Bake 1 to 2 minutes, or until the cheese melts. Carefully crack an egg directly onto the center of each pizzette. Bake 6 to 8 minutes, or until the whites are opaque and set, rotating the pans halfway through. Sprinkle with pepper and salt; serve warm.

Each pizzette About 585 calories, 27g protein, 57g carbohydrate, 28g fat (9g saturated), 1g fiber, 1,130mg sodium.

CALIFORNIA SUNRISE TOAST 536

ASPARAGUS-FONTINA PIZZETTE WITH BACON 537

classic cheese soufflé

PREP: 20 MIN / TOTAL: 1 HR 15 MIN / SERVES 6

2 tablespoons plain dried bread crumbs or freshly grated Parmesan cheese

4 tablespoons butter

¼ cup all-purpose flour

1½ cups whole milk, warmed

8 ounces sharp Cheddar cheese, shredded (2 cups)

¼ teaspoon salt

⅛ teaspoon cayenne pepper

5 large eggs, separated

1 large egg white

1. Preheat the oven to 325°F. Grease a 2-quart soufflé dish; sprinkle evenly with bread crumbs.

2. Prepare the cheese sauce: In a heavy 2-quart saucepan, melt the butter over low heat. Add the flour and cook, stirring, 1 minute. With a wire whisk, gradually whisk in the warm milk. Cook over medium heat, stirring constantly with a wooden spoon, until the sauce has thickened and boils. Reduce the heat and simmer, stirring frequently, 3 minutes. Stir in the Cheddar, salt, and cayenne; cook, stirring, just until the cheese melts and the sauce is smooth. Remove the saucepan from the heat.

3. In a bowl and using a wire whisk, lightly beat the egg yolks; gradually whisk in ½ cup hot cheese sauce. Gradually whisk the egg yolk mixture into the cheese sauce in the saucepan, stirring rapidly to prevent curdling. Pour the cheese mixture back into the bowl.

4. In a large bowl and using a mixer at high speed, beat 6 egg whites until stiff peaks form when the beaters are lifted. With a rubber spatula, gently fold one-third of the beaten egg whites into the cheese mixture. Fold in the remaining whites just until blended.

5. Pour the mixture into the prepared soufflé dish. To create a top-hat effect (center will rise higher than edge), if desired, with the back of a spoon, make a 1-inch-deep indentation all around the top of the soufflé about 1 inch from the edge of dish. Bake until the soufflé has puffed and is golden brown and a knife inserted 1 inch from the edge comes out clean, 55 to 60 minutes. Serve hot.

Each serving About 355 calories, 18g protein, 9g carbohydrate, 27g fat (15g saturated), 0g fiber, 519mg sodium.

Gruyère-Spinach Soufflé

Prepare as directed but substitute **8 ounces Gruyère cheese** for the Cheddar, and stir **1 package (10 ounces) frozen chopped spinach**, thawed and squeezed dry, into the cheese mixture before folding in the beaten egg whites. Substitute a **pinch of ground nutmeg** for the cayenne. **Serves 6.**

Southwestern Soufflé

Prepare as directed but substitute **8 ounces Monterey Jack cheese** for the Cheddar and stir **½ cup chopped cooked ham** into the cheese mixture before folding in the beaten egg whites. **Serves 6.**

classic eggs benedict

PREP: 25 MIN / TOTAL: 35 MIN / SERVES 8

Hollandaise Sauce (page 51)

4 English muffins, split and toasted

8 slices Canadian bacon

8 large eggs

1. Prepare Hollandaise Sauce; keep warm.

2. In a jelly-roll pan, arrange the toasted English muffins in a single layer and top each with a slice of Canadian bacon; keep warm.

3. Poach the eggs: In a 12-inch skillet, heat 1½ inches water to boiling. Reduce the heat to medium-low. Break 1 egg into a small cup; holding the cup close to the surface of the water, slip the egg into the simmering water. Repeat with the remaining eggs. Cook until the egg whites have set and the egg yolks begin to thicken but are not hard, 3 to 5 minutes.

4. Place the jelly-roll pan with the bacon-topped English muffins next to the poaching eggs. With a slotted spoon, carefully remove the eggs, one at a time, from the water and very briefly drain (still held in the spoon) on paper towels; set 1 egg on top of each slice of Canadian bacon. Spoon Hollandaise Sauce over the top. Serve hot.

Each serving About 310 calories, 15g protein, 15g carbohydrate, 21g fat (10g saturated), 1g fiber, 786mg sodium.

quiche lorraine

PREP: 35 MIN / TOTAL: 1 HR 30 MIN / SERVES 8

Pastry for a Single-Crust
Pie (page 664)

4 large eggs

2 cups whole milk

½ teaspoon salt

⅛ teaspoon ground
black pepper

Pinch of ground
nutmeg

4 slices bacon, cooked
and crumbled

4 ounces Gruyère
or Swiss cheese,
shredded (1 cup)

1. Prepare the pastry dough. Preheat the oven to 425°F. Use the dough to line a 9-inch pie plate. Line the pie shell with foil and fill with pie weights or dry beans. Bake 10 minutes. Remove the foil with the weights; bake until golden, 5 to 10 minutes longer. Cool on a wire rack. Turn the oven control to 350°F.

2. In a medium bowl and using a wire whisk, beat the eggs, milk, salt, pepper, and nutmeg until well blended. Sprinkle the bacon and cheese over the bottom of the crust; pour the egg mixture over the bacon and cheese.

3. Place the pie plate on a foil-lined baking sheet to catch any over-flow. Bake until the knife inserted in the center comes out clean, 55 to 60 minutes. Cool on a wire rack 15 minutes. Serve hot or at room temperature.

Each serving About 305 calories, 12g protein, 18g carbohydrate, 20g fat (10g saturated), 2g fiber, 439mg sodium.

TESTING NOTE Making a quiche is a crowd-pleasing way to use any languishing veggies or cheese you may have in the fridge. Use the above egg mixture as the base for any combo you like. Cook the vegetables first to soften them and evaporate excess moisture. Use up to 2 cups vegetables and 4 ounces cheese.

VARIATIONS

Mushroom Quiche

Prepare and bake **Pastry for a Single-Crust Pie** (page 664). Prepare the egg mixture as directed, but omit the bacon and Gruyère. In a 10-inch skillet, melt **2 tablespoons butter or margarine** over medium-high heat. Add **8 ounces mushrooms**, trimmed and very thinly sliced; **2 tablespoons finely chopped onion**; **¼ teaspoon salt**; **⅛ teaspoon coarsely ground black pepper**; and a **pinch of dried thyme**; cook, stirring frequently, until the mushrooms are tender and the liquid has evaporated, about 10 minutes. Add to the egg mixture, stirring to mix. Pour into the baked piecrust. Proceed with step 4, but reduce the baking time to 45 to 50 minutes.

Asparagus Quiche

Prepare and bake **Pastry for a Single-Crust Pie** (page 664). Prepare the egg mixture as directed, but omit the bacon. Trim **1 pound asparagus**, cut into ¾-inch pieces (2½ cups). In a 2-quart saucepan, heat 4 cups water to boiling over high heat. Add the asparagus and cook until tender, 6 to 8 minutes; drain. Rinse the asparagus with cold running water; drain. Spread the asparagus over the bottom of the baked crust and sprinkle with Gruyère; pour the egg mixture over. Proceed with step 4, but reduce the baking time to 40 to 45 minutes.

Bite-Size Bacon Quiches

Prepare a double recipe of **Pastry for a Single-Crust Pie** (page 664). On a lightly floured surface and using a floured rolling pin, roll the dough to a ⅛-inch thickness. Using a 3-inch round cookie cutter, cut the dough into 36 circles, rerolling the trimmings. Line thirty-six 1¾-inch mini muffin-pan cups with the dough circles. Cover and refrigerate. Prepare the egg mixture as directed, using 2 eggs, 1 cup whole milk, and ¼ teaspoon salt. Divide the bacon and cheese evenly among the pastry cups. Spoon a scant tablespoon of the egg mixture into each cup. Bake until the egg mixture is set, about 25 minutes. Remove the quiches from the muffin pan and serve hot. **Makes 36 bite-size quiches.**

chive & goat cheese frittata

PREP: 15 MIN / TOTAL: 35 MIN / SERVES 4

8 large eggs

⅓ cup whole milk

½ teaspoon salt

⅛ teaspoon ground black pepper

1 ripe medium tomato, chopped

2 tablespoons snipped fresh chives

1 tablespoon butter or olive oil

1 package (3½ ounces) goat cheese

1. Preheat the oven to 375°F. In a medium bowl and using a wire whisk, beat the eggs, milk, salt, and pepper until well blended. Stir in the tomato and chives.

2. In a 10-inch oven-safe nonstick skillet, melt the butter over medium heat. (If your skillet is not oven-safe, wrap the handle with a double layer of foil.) Pour in the egg mixture. Drop tablespoons of goat cheese on top of the egg mixture, cook, without stirring, until the egg mixture begins to set around the edge, 3 to 4 minutes.

3. Place the skillet in the oven; bake until the frittata is set, 8 to 10 minutes. To serve, loosen the frittata from the skillet and slide onto a warm platter; cut into 4 wedges.

Each serving About 260 calories, 18g protein, 4g carbohydrate, 19g fat (9g saturated), 0g fiber, 552mg sodium.

VARIATIONS

Potato & Ham Frittata

Prepare the egg mixture as directed, but omit the tomato, chives, and goat cheese. Cut **2 large red potatoes** into ½-inch pieces. Coarsely chop **1 medium onion**. Heat the oil in a skillet over medium heat. Add the potatoes and onion; cover and cook, stirring occasionally, until the potatoes are tender, about 12 minutes. Stir in **4 ounces cooked ham**, finely chopped (1 cup). Cook 2 minutes. Spread the potato mixture evenly in the skillet. Pour the egg mixture into the skillet and follow the remaining cooking directions.

Asparagus & Romano Frittata

Prepare the egg mixture as directed, but omit the tomato, chives, and goat cheese. Cut **1 pound asparagus** into 1-inch pieces. Thinly slice **4 green onions**. Melt the butter in a skillet over medium-high heat. Stir in the asparagus; cook 4 minutes. Reduce the heat to medium; add the onions, cook 2 minutes, stirring. Spread the vegetable mixture in the skillet. Stir ½ **cup freshly grated Pecorino Romano cheese** into the eggs and pour into the skillet. Cook as directed.

tomato & goat cheese quiche

(See photo on page 542.)

PREP: 35 MIN / TOTAL: 1 HR 30 MIN, PLUS CHILLING AND COOLING / SERVES 6

1 cup all-purpose flour, plus additional for rolling

1 teaspoon sugar

Salt

½ cup cold butter, cut into pieces

2 to 3 tablespoons ice water

2 tablespoons extra-virgin olive oil

12 ounces green onions or trimmed shallots, finely chopped (1 cup)

⅛ teaspoon cayenne pepper

5 large eggs

1¾ cups whole milk

4 ounces goat cheese, crumbled

¾ cup chopped, seeded plum tomatoes

Chopped fresh parsley, for garnish

1. In a food processor with the knife blade attached, blend the flour, sugar, and ¼ teaspoon salt. Add the butter; pulse until the mixture resembles coarse crumbs. Sprinkle in the ice water, 1 tablespoon at a time, pulsing after each addition, until large moist crumbs just begin to form.

2. Shape the dough into a disk; wrap in plastic wrap. Refrigerate 30 minutes or overnight. (If refrigerated overnight, remove from the refrigerator 30 minutes before rolling.)

3. Preheat the oven to 375°F. On a lightly floured surface and using a floured rolling pin, roll the dough into a 13-inch round. Ease the dough round into a deep 10-inch (2-quart) quiche plate; gently press it against the bottom and up the side of the plate without stretching it. Trim the edges of the dough. Freeze 15 minutes.

4. Line the quiche shell with foil and fill it with pie weights, dried beans, or uncooked rice. Bake 25 to 30 minutes, or until dry to touch. Remove the foil and weights; bake 10 to 15 minutes longer, or until golden brown. Place the crust on a jelly-roll pan.

5. While the crust bakes, in a 12-inch skillet, heat the oil over medium heat. Add the green onions, cayenne, and ⅛ teaspoon salt. Cook 6 to 8 minutes, or until tender, stirring occasionally.

6. In a large bowl, whisk the eggs until blended. Whisk in the milk until smooth. Stir in the goat cheese, tomatoes, cooked onions, and ⅛ teaspoon salt. Carefully pour the mixture into the hot crust.

7. Bake 30 to 35 minutes longer, or until the edges are set and the center jiggles slightly. Let cool on a wire rack until warm or room temperature. Garnish with parsley.

Each serving About 440 calories, 15g protein, 28g carbohydrate, 31g fat (16g saturated), 2g fiber, 2g fiber, 495mg sodium.

crepes
with piperade filling

PREP: 45 MIN / TOTAL: 1 HR 30 MIN / SERVES 4

Basic Crepes (right)
1 tablespoon olive oil
1 medium onion, thinly sliced
1 red bell pepper, thinly sliced
1 yellow or green bell pepper, thinly sliced
¾ teaspoon salt
1 clove garlic, finely chopped

⅛ teaspoon cayenne pepper
1 can (14 to 16 ounces) diced tomatoes
3 ounces Gruyère cheese, shredded (¾ cup)
1 tablespoon chopped fresh parsley

1. Prepare Basic Crepes. Set aside 8 crepes. (Reserve the remaining crepes for another use.) Preheat the oven to 400°F.

2. In a 10-inch skillet, heat the oil over medium heat. Add the onion, bell peppers, and salt; cover and cook until the vegetables are tender, about 15 minutes. Stir in the garlic and cayenne; cook 30 seconds. Add the tomatoes with their juices, breaking them up with the side of a spoon. Cook, uncovered, until the juices have thickened, about 15 minutes.

3. Place the crepes on a work surface; sprinkle 1 slightly rounded tablespoon of Gruyère over each crepe, leaving a 1-inch border. Spread a generous ¼ cup filling down the center of each crepe. Roll up the crepes and place them, seam side down, in a shallow 2-quart baking dish. Bake until heated through, about 15 minutes. Sprinkle with parsley.

Each serving About 360 calories, 15g protein, 25g carbohydrate, 23g fat (11g saturated), 3g fiber, 1,019mg sodium.

basic crepes

PREP: 5 MIN / TOTAL: 30 MIN, PLUS CHILLING / SERVES 12

3 large eggs
1½ cups whole milk
4 tablespoons butter, melted

⅔ cup all-purpose flour
½ teaspoon salt

1. In a blender, blend the eggs, milk, 2 tablespoons butter, the flour, and salt until smooth, scraping down the sides of the blender. Transfer the batter to a medium bowl; cover and refrigerate at least 1 hour or up to overnight to allow the flour to absorb the liquid.

2. Heat a 10-inch skillet over medium-high heat. Brush the bottom of the skillet lightly with some remaining butter. With a wire whisk, thoroughly mix the batter to blend well. Pour a scant ¼ cup batter into the skillet; tilt the pan to coat the bottom completely with batter. Cook the crepe until the top is set and the underside is lightly browned, about 1½ minutes.

3. With a heat-safe rubber spatula, loosen the edge of the crepe; flip over. Cook until the second side has browned, about 30 seconds. Slip the crepe onto waxed paper. Repeat with the remaining batter, brushing the pan lightly with butter before cooking each crepe and stacking the crepes between sheets of waxed paper.

Each serving About 95 calories, 3g protein, 7g carbohydrate, 6g fat (3g saturated), 0g fiber, 166mg sodium.

GLOSSARY →

Whether you call these delicate, eggy pancakes **crepes**, blintzes, blini, palacsinta, or pannukakka, they're versatile and delicious. They can be simply filled with jam or nutella or made into a main event with ham and cheese, mushrooms, or other savory options.

TOMATO & GOAT CHEESE QUICHE 540

CRANBERRY GRANOLA BARS 543

crepes
with apples & gruyère

PREP: 45 MIN / TOTAL: 55 MIN / SERVES 4

Basic Crepes (page 541)

1 tablespoon butter

2 Golden Delicious apples, each peeled, cored, and cut into 16 wedges

4 ounces Gruyère cheese, shredded (1 cup)

1. Prepare Basic Crepes. Set aside 8 crepes. (Reserve remaining crepes for another use.) Preheat the oven to 400°F. Grease a large baking sheet.

2. In a 10-inch skillet, melt the butter over medium-high heat. Add the apples and cook, stirring frequently, until tender and beginning to brown, about 5 minutes.

3. Place the crepes on a work surface; sprinkle one-fourth of the Gruyère over half of each crepe. Place one-fourth of the apples over the Gruyère. Fold the crepes over to enclose the filling; place them on a prepared baking sheet. Bake until the cheese melts, about 5 minutes.

Each serving About 370 calories, 15g protein, 23g carbohydrate, 25g fat (14g saturated), 1g fiber, 457mg sodium.

VARIATIONS

Strawberries & Goat Cheese

Use **2 cups hulled and sliced strawberries** and **8 ounces of fresh (mild) goat cheese**. Prepare as directed above, but cook the strawberries only until slightly softened, about 2 minutes.

Red Plums & Swiss Cheese

Use **4 large plums**, pitted and sliced, and **4 ounces Swiss cheese**, shredded. Prepare as directed above.

Blueberries & Ricotta Cheese

Use **2 cups blueberries** and **8 ounces ricotta cheese**. Prepare as directed above, but cook the blueberries just until slightly softened, about 3 minutes.

puffy apple pancake

PREP: 15 MIN / TOTAL: 45 MIN / SERVES 6

2 tablespoons butter

½ cup plus 2 tablespoons sugar

¼ cup water

6 medium Granny Smith or Newtown Pippin apples (2 pounds), each peeled, cored, and cut into 8 wedges

3 large eggs

¾ cup whole milk

¾ cup all-purpose flour

¼ teaspoon salt

1. Preheat the oven to 425°F. In a 12-inch oven-safe skillet, combine the butter, ½ cup sugar, and the water; heat to boiling over medium-high heat. (If your skillet is not oven-safe, wrap the handle with a double layer of foil.) Add the apples; cook, stirring occasionally, until the apples are golden and the sugar mixture begins to caramelize, about 15 minutes.

2. Meanwhile, in a blender or food processor with the knife blade attached, blend the eggs, milk, flour, the remaining 2 tablespoons sugar, and salt until smooth.

3. Pour the batter over the apples. Place the skillet in the oven and bake until the pancake is puffed and golden, about 15 minutes. Serve hot.

Each serving About 300 calories, 6g protein, 54g carbohydrate, 8g fat (4g saturated), 3g fiber, 181mg sodium.

VARIATION

Simple Puffy Pancake

Prepare as directed above, but omit the apple mixture in step 1. In step 3, add **2 tablespoons butter or margarine** to the skillet and heat in the oven until melted. Pour the batter into the skillet and bake as directed. Serve filled with a mixture of fresh berries and bananas, or a simple drizzle of maple syrup.

cranberry granola bars

PREP: 15 MIN / TOTAL: 45 MIN / SERVES 16

Nonstick cooking spray

2 cups old-fashioned oats

½ cup honey

½ cup vegetable oil

2 tablespoons water

2 large egg whites

2 tablespoons packed light brown sugar

1 teaspoon ground cinnamon

½ teaspoon salt

¾ cup toasted wheat germ

¾ cup chopped walnuts

¾ cup dried cranberries

1. Preheat the oven to 325°F. Spray a 13 × 9-inch metal baking pan with nonstick cooking spray. Line the pan with foil, leaving a 2-inch overhang; spray the foil.

2. Spread the oats on a microwave-safe plate; microwave on High, in 1-minute intervals, 4 to 5 minutes, or until fragrant and golden, stirring occasionally. Let cool. In a large bowl, whisk the honey, oil, water, egg whites, brown sugar, cinnamon, and salt until well blended. Fold in the oats, toasted wheat germ, walnuts, and cranberries; transfer to the prepared pan. Using wet hands, press it into an even layer.

3. Bake 28 to 30 minutes, or until golden. Cool in the pan on a wire rack. Lifting the foil, transfer to a cutting board; cut into 16 bars.

Each serving About 215 calories, 5g protein, 25g carbohydrate, 12g fat (1g saturated), 3g fiber, 80mg sodium.

Tip For an easy grab-and-go breakfast, make these bars ahead. Cool completely, then store in an airtight container up to 4 days. Or wrap each bar individually and freeze in a resealable plastic bag for up to 1 month. They thaw in about 15 minutes and are also delicious partially frozen.

almond-berry oat bake

(See photo on page 546.)

PREP: 10 MIN / TOTAL: 55 MIN / SERVES 6

Nonstick cooking spray

2¾ cups low-fat (1%) milk

¼ cup butter, melted

1 tablespoon vanilla extract

1 cup old-fashioned oats

1 cup quinoa

½ cup roasted salted almonds, chopped

½ cup packed brown sugar

3 tablespoons chia seeds

1 teaspoon baking powder

¼ teaspoon salt

1 cup fresh blueberries

2 cups strawberries, hulled and quartered

Low-fat vanilla yogurt, for serving (optional)

1. Preheat the oven to 375°F. Coat a 2-quart baking dish with non-stick cooking spray. Place it on a foil-lined baking sheet.

2. In a medium bowl, whisk the milk, butter, and vanilla. In the prepared baking dish, combine the oats, quinoa, almonds, brown sugar, chia seeds, baking powder, and salt. Pour the milk mixture over the dry ingredients in the baking dish. Top with the blueberries and strawberries. Bake 45 minutes, or until almost all the liquid has been absorbed. Let stand 5 minutes before serving. Serve with low-fat vanilla yogurt, if desired.

Each serving About 475 calories, 13g protein, 64g carbohydrate, 20g fat (7g saturated), 8g fiber, 380mg sodium.

VARIATION

Apple-Cinnamon-Raisin Oat Bake

Peel and core **2 large apples**; cut into ½-inch pieces and place in a glass bowl. Toss with ½ **teaspoon cinnamon**; cover and microwave on High for 3 minutes. Stir in ⅓ **cup raisins** and microwave 1 minute more. Stir into oat mixture before adding milk.

french toast

PREP: 5 MIN / TOTAL: 20 MIN / SERVES 4

3 large eggs

¾ cup whole milk

⅛ teaspoon salt

4 tablespoons butter or margarine

8 slices (½ inch thick) sourdough or other firm white bread

Softened butter, maple syrup, or honey, for serving

1. Preheat the oven to 250°F. In a pie plate and using a wire whisk, beat the eggs, milk, and salt until well blended. In a 12-inch nonstick skillet, melt 2 tablespoons butter over medium-high heat.

2. Dip 4 bread slices, one at a time, in the beaten egg mixture to coat both sides well. Place the bread in the skillet and cook until browned, about 4 minutes per side. Transfer to a baking sheet; keep warm in the oven. Repeat with the remaining 2 tablespoons butter and 4 bread slices. Serve hot with butter, maple syrup, or honey.

Each serving (without toppings) About 340 calories, 11g protein, 32g carbohydrate, 18g fat (10g saturated), 1g fiber, 605mg sodium.

GOOD TO KNOW

FRENCH TOAST

French Toast, aka *pain perdu*, is literally lost (stale) bread rescued by a soak in a mix of milk and egg. Well done, the outside of the toast should be golden brown, the inside custardy. The bread makes all the difference. It doesn't have to be rock hard, but the texture should not be squishy. If your bread is very fresh, let it air-dry overnight or dry it in a 350°F oven for 10 minutes.

coconut french toast

(See photo on page 510.)

PREP: 10 MIN / TOTAL: 30 MIN / SERVES 4

5 large eggs

1 can (14 ounces) coconut milk

¼ cup packed brown sugar

½ teaspoon pumpkin pie spice

Pinch of salt

1 teaspoon vegetable oil

8 slices (½ inch thick) brioche or challah bread

1 cup sweetened shredded coconut

Mixed berries, confectioners' sugar, and maple syrup, for serving (optional)

1. Preheat the oven to 300°F. In a shallow 3-quart baking dish, whisk the eggs, coconut milk, brown sugar, pumpkin pie spice, and salt.

2. In a 12-inch nonstick skillet, heat the vegetable oil over medium heat. Soak 4 slices of bread in the egg mixture, letting the excess drip off; add to the skillet. Sprinkle each slice with 2 tablespoons shredded coconut; press to adhere. Cook 4 minutes, or until the underside of the bread is deep golden brown. Gently turn the slices over; cook 2 minutes more, or until the coconut flakes are deep golden brown.

3. Transfer to a parchment-lined baking sheet and keep warm in oven. Repeat with the remaining bread slices, adding another 1 teaspoon oil if necessary. Serve with mixed berries, confectioners' sugar, and maple syrup, if desired.

Each serving About 575 calories, 15g protein, 60g carbohydrate, 32g fat (22g saturated), 1g fiber, 540mg sodium.

overnight french toast

PREP: 10 MIN / TOTAL: 1 HR 10 MIN, PLUS OVERNIGHT TO CHILL / SERVES 8

12 slices firm white bread

6 large eggs

2 cups whole milk

1 teaspoon vanilla extract

¼ teaspoon ground cinnamon

¼ teaspoon ground nutmeg

Pinch of salt

½ cup packed brown sugar

4 tablespoons butter, softened

1 tablespoon maple syrup

1. Arrange the bread slices in 4 stacks in an 8-inch square baking dish.

2. In a blender, combine the eggs, milk, vanilla, cinnamon, nutmeg, and salt and blend until the mixture is smooth. Slowly pour the egg mixture over the bread slices; press the bread down to absorb the egg mixture, spooning the egg mixture over any uncoated bread. Cover and refrigerate overnight.

3. Preheat the oven to 350°F. In a small bowl, stir the brown sugar, butter, and maple syrup until combined. Spread evenly over each stack of bread. Bake until a knife inserted 1 inch from the center comes out clean, about 1 hour. Let stand 15 minutes before serving. To serve, cut each stack diagonally in half.

Each serving About 310 calories, 10g protein, 37g carbohydrate, 13g fat (6g saturated), 1g fiber, 364mg sodium.

TESTING NOTE The overnight soak on this casserole-style French toast allows it to absorb all the liquid and puff up beautifully. If you don't have time to do the overnight soak, dip each slice of bread individually in the egg mixture; stack and let stand at room temperature 1 hour, pressing down on bread slices every 15 minutes.

ALMOND-BERRY OAT BAKE 544

GLAZED BERRY
BREAKFAST TARTS 548

PUMPKIN-CHERRY BREAKFAST COOKIES 548

ICED SPICED SKILLET CINNAMON ROLLS 547

iced spiced skillet cinnamon rolls

PREP: 30 MIN / TOTAL: 3 HR 30 MIN WITH RISING / MAKES 12

ROLLS

- 2 tablespoons vegetable oil
- 1 cup whole milk, warmed
- ½ cup granulated sugar
- 2 large eggs
- 2 packets (2¼ teaspoons each) instant yeast
- 1 teaspoon vanilla extract
- 1 teaspoon salt
- ¼ cup plus 2 tablespoons butter, melted
- 4½ cups all-purpose flour, plus more for dusting
- ½ cup brown sugar
- 2 tablespoons ground cinnamon

GLAZE

- ⅓ cup confectioners' sugar
- 3 ounces cream cheese, softened
- 3 tablespoons butter, softened
- 1 tablespoon milk
- Pinch of salt

1. Pour the oil into a large bowl. Using a stand mixer with the paddle attachment on medium speed, beat the milk, granulated sugar, eggs, yeast, vanilla, salt, and ¼ cup butter until combined. Add 4¼ cups flour; beat until the dough comes together. With floured hands, transfer the dough to a floured surface. Knead until it is no longer sticky, sprinkling up to ¼ cup more flour over and under the dough as needed; form the dough into a ball.

2. Transfer to the prepared bowl, rolling to coat in oil. Cover with a damp towel and plastic wrap. Let rise in a warm spot 2 hours.

3. Lightly grease a 12-inch ovenproof skillet. With floured hands, punch the dough down; turn out onto a lightly floured surface. With a floured rolling pin, roll the dough into a 20 × 12-inch rectangle. Brush with the remaining 2 tablespoons butter; sprinkle with brown sugar and cinnamon. Roll up the dough tightly, starting on one long side. Cut the log into 12 pieces; arrange in the skillet, swirled sides up. Cover with a damp kitchen towel and plastic wrap. Place in a warm spot; let rise 1 hour. Bake immediately or refrigerate overnight. (If refrigerated, let stand at room temperature 30 minutes before baking.)

4. Preheat the oven to 350°F. Uncover the skillet; bake 30 minutes, or until the top is golden brown. Meanwhile, make the glaze: Beat all ingredients until smooth. Remove the skillet from the oven; let stand 5 minutes. Top with glaze. Serve warm.

Each serving About 405 calories, 8g protein, 59g carbohydrate, 15g fat (8g saturated), 2g fiber, 295mg sodium.

quick pecan sticky buns

PREP: 25 MIN / TOTAL: 55 MIN, PLUS COOLING / SERVES 8

- ¼ cup plus ⅓ cup packed dark brown sugar
- 1½ teaspoons ground cinnamon
- 2 tablespoons honey
- 9 tablespoons butter, melted
- ¾ cup pecans, toasted and coarsely chopped
- 2¾ cups all-purpose flour
- ¼ cup granulated sugar
- 1½ teaspoons baking powder
- ½ teaspoon baking soda
- ½ teaspoon salt
- 1¼ cups buttermilk

1. Preheat the oven to 425°F. Grease a 9-inch round metal cake pan. In a small bowl, combine ¼ cup brown sugar with the cinnamon; set aside.

2. In a 1-quart saucepan, heat the honey, the remaining ⅓ cup brown sugar, and 2 tablespoons butter over medium heat until the mixture is blended and smooth, stirring occasionally. Pour into the prepared pan and sprinkle evenly with the pecans; set aside.

3. In a large bowl, combine the flour, granulated sugar, baking powder, baking soda, and salt. In a small bowl, mix the buttermilk and 5 tablespoons butter. With a spoon, stir the buttermilk mixture into the flour mixture just until the liquid is absorbed.

4. Turn the dough onto a lightly floured surface and knead it 8 to 10 times, or just until smooth, about 30 seconds. Pat the dough into a 12 × 9-inch rectangle. Brush the dough with 1 tablespoon butter, then sprinkle with the cinnamon-sugar mixture. Starting at one short end, roll up the dough, jelly-roll fashion. With the seam side down, cut the dough crosswise into 8 slices.

5. Place each slice, cut side down, on the pecan mixture in the cake pan; brush with the remaining melted butter. Bake the buns 28 to 30 minutes, or until golden. Remove the pan from the oven. Immediately place a serving plate over the top of the pan and invert the buns onto the plate, allowing the topping to run down the sides of the buns. Remove the baking pan. Cool the buns slightly, about 10 minutes, to serve warm, or cool completely to serve later. Wrap any leftovers in foil and store at room temperature up to 3 days.

Each bun About 445 calories, 7g protein, 57g carbohydrate, 22g fat (9g saturated), 2g fiber, 2g fiber, 485mg sodium.

pumpkin-cherry breakfast cookies

(See photo on page 546.)

PREP: 15 MIN / TOTAL: 35 MIN / SERVES 16

- 2 cups whole wheat flour
- 1 cup old-fashioned oats
- 1 teaspoon baking soda
- 1 teaspoon pumpkin pie spice
- ¼ teaspoon salt
- 1 can (15 ounces) pure pumpkin
- 1 cup coconut oil
- 1 cup packed brown sugar
- 1 large egg
- ½ cup salted roasted pepitas (pumpkin seeds)
- ½ cup dried cherries

1. Preheat the oven to 350°F.

2. In a medium bowl, whisk together the whole wheat flour, old-fashioned oats, baking soda, pumpkin pie spice, and ¼ teaspoon salt. In a large bowl and using a mixer at medium speed, beat the pumpkin, coconut oil, brown sugar, and egg until well combined; gradually beat in the flour mixture, then the pepitas and dried cherries.

3. Scoop the dough onto a large parchment-lined baking sheet to form 16 mounds, spaced 2 inches apart; flatten each into a disk. Bake 20 to 25 minutes, or until dark brown on the bottoms. Cool on a wire rack. Cooled cookies can be wrapped in plastic and stored at room temperature up to 2 days or frozen up to 1 month. Reheat in the toaster until crisp.

Each serving About 290 calories, 5g protein, 33g carbohydrate, 17g fat (12g saturated), 5g fiber, 135mg sodium.

glazed berry breakfast tarts

(See photo on page 546.)

PREP: 30 MIN / TOTAL: 45 MIN / SERVES 12

- 3 cups all-purpose flour
- ¼ cup granulated sugar
- 4 teaspoons baking powder
- ¾ teaspoon baking soda
- ½ teaspoon salt
- 10 tablespoons cold butter, cut into pieces
- ¾ cup plus 2 tablespoons buttermilk
- ¾ cup raspberry or strawberry jam
- 1 cup confectioners' sugar
- ½ teaspoon vanilla extract
- 1 tablespoon plus 1 teaspoon whole milk
- Red food coloring and coarse sugar (optional)

1. Preheat the oven to 425°F. In a food processor, pulse the flour, granulated sugar, baking powder, baking soda, and salt. Add the butter; pulse until the mixture resembles coarse crumbs. Transfer to a large bowl; stir in the buttermilk until the dough comes together.

2. Transfer the dough to a lightly floured surface; divide the dough in half. Roll 1 piece of dough into a 15 × 10-inch rectangle; cut into six 5-inch squares. Spread 1 tablespoon jam on half of each square; moisten the squares' edges with water. Fold the pastry over the filling; with a fork, seal the edges. Prick the pastry all over. Transfer the tarts to a large baking sheet. Repeat with remaining dough and jam.

3. Bake the tarts 10 to 12 minutes, or until golden. In a medium bowl, stir the confectioners' sugar, vanilla, milk, and food coloring, if using. When the pastries are no longer hot, drizzle the glaze over the tops and sprinkle with sugar, if using.

Each serving About 320 calories, 4g protein, 53g carbohydrate, 10g fat (6g saturated), 1g fiber, 455mg sodium.

perfect coffee cake

PREP: 30 MIN / TOTAL: 1 HR 25 MIN / SERVES 16

- 1½ teaspoons baking powder
- 1 teaspoon baking soda
- ¾ teaspoon salt
- 3 cups plus 1 tablespoon all-purpose flour
- ¾ cup chopped pecans
- ⅓ cup packed brown sugar
- 1¼ teaspoons ground cinnamon
- 1½ cups granulated sugar
- ¾ cup butter, softened
- 2½ teaspoons vanilla extract
- 3 large eggs
- 1 container (16 ounces) sour cream
- 1 cup confectioners' sugar
- 4 to 6 teaspoons whole milk

1. Preheat the oven to 350°F. Grease a 12-cup Bundt® pan; dust with flour.

2. In a medium bowl and using a wire whisk, stir the baking powder, baking soda, salt, and 3 cups flour. In a small bowl, combine the pecans, brown sugar, cinnamon, and remaining 1 tablespoon flour.

3. In a large bowl and using a mixer at medium speed, beat the granulated sugar, butter, and 2 teaspoons vanilla until creamy. Beat in the eggs, one at a time. Alternately beat in flour mixture and sour cream, beginning and ending with the flour mixture. Beat just until blended, occasionally scraping the bowl.

4. Evenly spread 2 cups batter in the prepared pan; sprinkle with half the nut mixture. Top with 2 cups batter. Sprinkle with the remaining nut mixture, then top with the remaining batter. Bake the cake until a toothpick inserted in the center comes out clean, 55 to 60 minutes. Cool the cake in the pan on a wire rack 10 minutes. With a small metal spatula, loosen the cake from the pan; invert onto the rack to cool completely.

5. Prepare the glaze: In a small bowl, stir the confectioners' sugar, 4 teaspoons milk, and the remaining ½ teaspoon vanilla until smooth. Add additional teaspoons of milk, if needed. Drizzle the glaze over the cooled cake.

Each serving About 410 calories, 5g protein, 51g carbohydrate, 21g fat (10g saturated), 1g fiber, 550mg sodium.

wonuts

(See photo on page 510.)

PREP: 15 MIN / TOTAL: 50 MIN / SERVES 12

- 1½ cups all-purpose flour
- 1½ teaspoons baking powder
- ½ teaspoon ground cinnamon
- ½ teaspoon salt
- 1 cup whole milk
- ⅓ cup sugar
- 2 large eggs, beaten
- 4 tablespoons butter, melted
- 1 teaspoon vanilla extract
- Nonstick cooking spray
- Cinnamon Sugar or Chocolate Glaze (below)
- Shredded sweetened coconut (optional)
- Chopped nuts (optional)

1. Preheat a waffle iron.

2. In a large bowl, whisk the flour, baking powder, cinnamon, and salt. In a medium bowl, whisk the milk, sugar, eggs, butter, and vanilla. Add the milk mixture to the flour mixture. Stir just until combined (small lumps are okay).

3. Spray the waffle iron with nonstick cooking spray and pour a scant ⅓ cup batter in the center. Close the waffle iron; cook 2 to 3 minutes, or until deep golden brown. Toss with Cinnamon Sugar or dip into Chocolate Glaze and sprinkle with coconut or chopped nuts, if you like. Let stand at room temperature to set, at least 1 hour.

CINNAMON SUGAR In a brown paper bag, shake together ⅓ **cup sugar** and **1 teaspoon ground cinnamon**.

CHOCOLATE GLAZE Place **4 ounces semisweet chocolate chips** in a medium bowl. In a small saucepan, heat ⅓ **cup heavy or whipping cream** until hot but not boiling; pour over the chocolate chips. Let stand 5 minutes. Stir until smooth. Whisk in **2 tablespoons light corn syrup** and **2 teaspoons vanilla extract**. Use immediately.

WONUTS WITH CINNAMON SUGAR Each serving About 170 calories, 3g protein, 25g carbohydrate, 7g fat (3g saturated), 1g fiber, 215mg sodium.

WONUTS WITH CHOCOLATE GLAZE Each serving About 230 calories, 4g protein, 28g carbohydrate, 12g fat (6g saturated), 1g fiber, 225mg sodium.

breads,
PIZZAS &
SANDWICHES

Making bread brings out the child in all of us. There is something magical about mixing flour and leavening with liquid and watching the transformation. Whether you're making biscuits, muffins, or a luscious loaf, opening the oven for the reveal is a moment of joyous anticipation. In this chapter we focus on simple breads that can be completed in a few hours or risen overnight, plus the delicious creations like sandwiches and pizzas you can make with the dough.

SESAME BISCUITS 558

PROVOLONE VEGGIE PARTY SUBS 580

**FINGER-LICKING
BISCUIT LOAF 556**

SPANISH HAM & CHEESE GALETTE 578

Quick Breads

As their name implies, quick breads are faster to prepare than yeasted ones. Just mix them up and pop them into the oven. Yeast dough need hands-off time to rise and then you can shape it into twisty pretzels, breadsticks, pizzas, or loaves and rolls for our sandwich recipes.

RISING TO THE OCCASION

Most quick breads rely on chemical leavenings, such as baking powder or baking soda, to make them rise. Test to be sure your soda or powder is active: Stir 1 teaspoon into 1 cup of boiling water; it should bubble and foam vigorously.

BAKING SODA is an alkali that forms carbon dioxide gas bubbles when combined with an acidic ingredient, such as buttermilk, yogurt, chocolate, brown sugar, or molasses. Store baking soda in an airtight container in a cool, dry place for up to one year.

BAKING POWDER is a combination of baking soda and cream of tartar. Most commercial baking powders are double-acting: They start to produce gas bubbles as soon as they are moistened, then release more when heated in the oven. Baking powder can stay potent for up to 6 months if stored airtight in a cool, dry place.

COOLING, STORING, AND REHEATING QUICK BREADS

Immediately remove baked biscuits, scones, and muffins from their cookie sheets or pans to prevent them from sticking. Most fruit-filled quick breads should be cooled in their pans for ten minutes to allow them to set. Invert them onto wire racks, then turn right side up to cool completely.

In general, the richer the batter (those containing eggs, butter, or fruit), the longer the baked bread will stay moist. Dense fruit breads are even better if made a day ahead so their flavors can blend. They'll also be firmer and easier to slice. Most muffins, biscuits, scones, and corn breads are best eaten the day they are made, otherwise freeze to serve later.

To store fruit breads and muffins at room temperature, first cool them completely. Wrap them in plastic wrap and then in foil; they will keep for up to three days. To freeze fruit breads, wrap them tightly in plastic wrap and then in heavy-duty foil, pressing out the air. Freeze for up to three months. Smaller items like muffins and biscuits can be frozen for up to one month. Thaw them, still wrapped, at room temperature.

To warm fruit breads, wrap in foil and heat at 400°F. Muffins, scones, and biscuits will take about ten minutes, while loaves and coffee cakes will take about twenty minutes. Muffins also warm well in a microwave oven. Loosely wrap each muffin in a paper towel and microwave on High for about ten seconds. Be careful, though: If the muffins have sugary add-ins, such as chocolate chips or jam, they could get very hot, and if baked goods are reheated too long, they become tough.

Yeast Breads

TYPES OF YEAST

Yeast is the organism that makes bread rise. It reacts with the natural sugars in flour to create carbon dioxide gas, which is trapped in the dough and forces it to expand.

DRY YEAST comes in ¼-ounce packages, in jars, and in bulk. One ¼-ounce package of dry yeast equals 2¼ teaspoons of fresh yeast.

FRESH YEAST is available in foil-wrapped 1-ounce cakes. It is very perishable; refrigerate and use within two weeks. Fresh and dry yeast become activated when mixed with warm water (105° to 115°F). Let the water-yeast mixture stand for about five minutes. It should look creamy, which indicates that the yeast is alive.

QUICK-RISE YEAST cuts the rising time of traditional yeast doughs by about 50 percent. This yeast requires very hot tap water (120° to 130°F) to be activated.

KNOW YOUR FLOURS

A variety of flours can be used for bread-making. Different flours contain varying amounts of gluten, which is what gives dough its strength and elasticity. Wheat flours milled from hard winter wheat are high in gluten and great for bread-making.

BREAD FLOUR is made entirely from hard wheat and makes delicious, chewy, crusty loaves.

ALL-PURPOSE FLOUR is a blend of hard and soft wheats and yields a more tender bread. All-purpose flour is available unbleached and bleached. Bleaching somewhat reduces the amount of gluten. You can use either bread flour or unbleached all-purpose flour for bread, but you will need more all-purpose flour as it absorbs less liquid.

WHOLE-WHEAT FLOUR AND RYE FLOUR are usually combined with bread or all-purpose flour in yeast doughs.

MIXING THE DOUGH

When mixing bread dough, use a large glass or ceramic bowl and a sturdy wooden spoon. You can also use a heavy-duty electric mixer; attach the paddle to make a soft dough, then switch to the dough hook to knead.

Flour and yeast are the basic ingredients in bread making, but other ingredients play a role. Salt slows the rising and enhances the flavor of bread. Fat (butter, oil, or eggs) adds richness, moistness, and softness to the crumb. Milk gives bread a tender, sweet crumb, and sugar promotes tenderness and a golden crust.

Because yeast works best in a warm environment, have all the ingredients at room temperature. The amount of flour needed to make a dough will vary according to the type of flour and the amount of humidity in the air (on a humid day, a dough will require more flour).

KNEADING THE DOUGH

Kneading activates the gluten in flour, which strengthens the dough. Knead in just enough flour to prevent the dough from sticking to the work surface. Doughs that are sweet and rich or contain whole-grain flours should be somewhat sticky. If kneading in a heavy-duty mixer, take care not to overknead; six to eight minutes is usually sufficient.

Place the dough on a lightly floured surface. To knead, fold one-fourth of the dough back onto itself, then push it down and away from you with the heel of your hand. Give the dough a quarter turn and repeat until the dough is smooth and elastic and tiny blisters appear on the surface, which will usually take from eight to ten minutes.

RISING AND SHAPING THE DOUGH

- Choose a bowl large enough to allow the dough to rise until doubled in volume. Grease the bowl lightly with butter, margarine, or oil. Gather the dough into a ball and place in the bowl; turn to coat the top. Cover the bowl with plastic wrap and place in a warm, draft-free spot.

- If you like, you can let the dough rise in the refrigerator for up to twelve hours. Before shaping the dough, let it stand at room temperature for about two hours, or until it loses its chill.

- The dough should rise until doubled. To test, press two fingers about ½ inch deep into the center of the dough. If the indentation stays, the dough has risen sufficiently.

- To punch the dough down, gently push your fist into the center to deflate it.

- The bread is now ready to be shaped. Place the dough on a lightly floured work surface, cover with plastic wrap, and let rest for 15 minutes.

- Grease the pans as directed in the recipe, add the bread, and loosely cover with plastic wrap. Let stand in a warm place until doubled in volume.

finger-licking biscuit loaf

(See photo on page 552.)

PREP: 20 MIN / TOTAL: 1 HR 20 MIN / SERVES 8

- 6 tablespoons butter, melted
- ⅓ cup Buffalo-style hot sauce
- 1½ cups packed finely shredded rotisserie chicken
- ½ cup crumbled blue cheese
- ½ cup shredded Cheddar
- 2 tablespoons snipped fresh chives, plus more for serving
- 1 tube (16 ounces) refrigerated flaky biscuit dough

1. Preheat the oven to 350°F. Line an 8½ × 4½-inch loaf pan with parchment paper.

2. In a medium bowl, combine the butter and hot sauce. Add the rotisserie chicken, blue cheese, Cheddar, and chives; toss to coat.

3. Separate the biscuits into halves and flatten each between your hands. Prop up the loaf pan vertically and place 1 biscuit half on the bottom. Top with a scant 2 tablespoons chicken mixture and another biscuit half. Repeat to form 16 layers.

4. Bake 40 minutes, uncovered, then cover with foil and bake 20 minutes more. Cool slightly before serving. Garnish with chives.

Each serving About 315 calories, 12g protein, 26g carbohydrate, 21g fat (11g saturated), 1g fiber, 1,162mg sodium.

GOOD TO KNOW

CHILE HEAT

Habanero chiles were once thought to rate highest on the Scoville scale, which measures the capsaicin pungency in units. But the Carolina Reaper has since claimed the title of hottest chile with a heat level between 1.5 and 2.2 million Scoville units. For comparison, habaneros are less than 350,000 units, and cayenne and tabasco chiles are less than 50,000 units. Jalapeños are a mere 5,000. Buffalo-style sauce, usually made with cayenne peppers, is a mellow, spicy match for chicken, but you can move up the scale if you like.

irish soda bread

PREP: 15 MIN / TOTAL: 1 HR 15 MIN / SERVES 16

- 4 cups all-purpose flour, plus more for dusting
- ¼ cup sugar
- 1 tablespoon baking powder
- 1½ teaspoons salt
- 1 teaspoon baking soda
- 6 tablespoons butter
- 1 cup dried currants
- 2 teaspoons caraway seeds
- 1½ cups buttermilk

1. Preheat the oven to 350°F. Stir together the flour, sugar, baking powder, salt, and baking soda. With a pastry blender, cut in the butter until the mixture resembles coarse crumbs. Stir in the dried currants and caraway seeds, then the buttermilk, until the flour is just moistened.

2. On a well-floured surface, knead the dough 8 to 10 times, just until combined. Shape it into a flattened ball; place on a large greased baking sheet. Cut a ¼-inch-deep X into the top. Bake 1 hour, or until a toothpick inserted in the center comes out clean; cool completely on a wire rack.

Each serving About 210 calories, 5g protein, 36g carbohydrate, 5g fat (3g saturated), 2g fiber, 460mg sodium.

IRISH SODA BREAD 556

classic buttermilk biscuits

(See photo on page 560.)

PREP: 15 MIN / TOTAL: 30 MIN / SERVES 14

3 cups self-rising flour, plus more for dusting

½ teaspoon salt

6 tablespoons cold butter, cut into pieces

1½ cups low-fat buttermilk

3 tablespoons butter, melted (optional)

1. Preheat the oven to 450°F. Line a large baking sheet with parchment paper.

2. In a food processor, pulse the flour and salt until combined. Add the butter; pulse just until coarse crumbs form. Transfer the flour mixture to a large bowl. Stir in the buttermilk just until the dough starts to come together.

3. Transfer the dough to a lightly floured surface; knead just until smooth, 6 to 8 times. With a floured rolling pin, roll the dough to a ½-inch thickness.

4. With a floured 2½-inch cutter, cut out the biscuits without twisting the cutter. With a wide spatula, transfer the biscuits to the prepared baking sheet, spacing them 1 inch apart.

5. Gently press the scraps together. Reroll and cut out biscuits once more. Place the biscuits on a large parchment-lined baking sheet and brush the tops with melted butter, if desired. Bake 12 to 15 minutes, or until golden brown. Serve warm.

Each biscuit About 155 calories, 5g protein, 22g carbohydrate, 6g fat (3g saturated), 1g fiber, 450mg sodium.

VARIATIONS

Sesame Biscuits

(See photo on page 552.)

Prepare biscuits as directed, but shape the dough into a 7-inch square. Cut 16 squares. Place ¼ **cup sesame seeds** in a shallow dish. Lightly brush the tops of the biscuits with **1 lightly beaten egg**. Working one at a time, press each biscuit, egg side down, into the sesame seeds. Place the biscuit, seeded side up, on a large parchment-lined baking sheet. Bake as directed.

Cheddar-Bacon

Cut **4 strips bacon** into ½-inch pieces. Cook until crisp; set aside. Reserve bacon fat. Reduce butter by 2 tablespoons. Add the bacon fat and ½ **cup extra sharp shredded cheddar** along with butter. Proceed as directed, adding the bacon along with the buttermilk.

Lemon, Pepper & Parmesan

Add **1 teaspoon grated lemon zest**, **1 teaspoon ground black pepper**, and ½ **cup grated Parmesan cheese** along with the flour. Proceed as directed.

Sweet Potato

Microwave **2 medium sweet potatoes** on High for 10 minutes or until tender. Cool slightly; scoop out 1 cup flesh. Add ¼ **cup brown sugar** to the flour mixture. Mix the sweet potato with ¾ cup of the buttermilk. Proceed as directed, adding remaining buttermilk as needed so the dough comes together. Proceed as directed.

Cornmeal

Reduce flour to 2 cups; add **1 cup yellow cornmeal** and **2 tablespoons sugar** along with the flour. Proceed as directed.

Oatmeal

Reduce flour to 2 cups; add **2 cups old-fashioned oats** along with the flour. Proceed as directed.

Pimiento Cheese

Reduce milk to 1⅓ cups. Add **1 cup shredded extra sharp cheddar**, ½ **cup chopped well-drained pimientos**, and **1 tablespoon hot sauce** along with the buttermilk. Proceed as directed.

Everything Bagel Topping

On a small plate combine **3 tablespoons dried onion flakes**, **3 tablespoons sesame seeds**, and **2 tablespoons poppy seeds**. After brushing the biscuits with butter, dip the tops in the mixture, pressing down to make toppings adhere. Bake as directed.

GOOD TO KNOW

THE SKINNY ON BUTTERMILK

Buttermilk was originally the liquid left over from churning butter, but it is now made from milk with added bacterial cultures. It is a favorite baking ingredient; its acidity balances sugar's sweetness, and it reacts with baking soda to give baked goods a fine crumb. Dehydrated buttermilk powder is also available. Reconstitute it according to the package directions. In a pinch, a good substitute for buttermilk is sour cream (not reduced-fat) or plain low-fat yogurt blended with an equal amount of whole milk. You can also use soured milk: Place 1 tablespoon fresh lemon juice or distilled white vinegar in a glass measuring cup, then pour in enough whole milk to equal 1 cup. Stir and let stand for five minutes to thicken.

quick 'n' easy southern biscuits

(See photo on page 560.)

PREP: 20 MIN / TOTAL: 40 MIN / MAKES 9 BISCUITS

3½ cups all-purpose flour (preferably soft wheat, like Martha White or White Lily)

1½ tablespoons baking powder

¾ teaspoon baking soda

1½ tablespoons sugar

¾ teaspoon salt

6 tablespoons cold butter, cut into pieces

2 cups buttermilk, cold

2 tablespoons butter, melted

1. Preheat the oven to 500°F. Grease a 9-inch square baking pan and ⅓-cup measuring cup. Sprinkle ½ cup flour on a rimmed baking sheet.

2. In a food processor, pulse 3 cups flour, the baking powder, baking soda, sugar, and salt; add the cold butter. Pulse to form coarse crumbs; transfer to a bowl.

3. With a rubber spatula, stir the buttermilk into the flour mixture until just combined. With the greased measuring cup, scoop 9 separate, heaping cupfuls of dough onto the floured baking sheet. Lightly dust the tops of the mounds with flour from the baking sheet. With floured hands, gently arrange the mounds in the pan in 3 rows of 3.

4. Brush with the melted butter. Bake 5 minutes. Turn the oven control to 450°F. Bake 15 to 20 minutes, or until golden.

5. Cool in the pan 2 minutes. Carefully invert the biscuits onto a wire rack. Serve warm, or cool, wrap tightly, and store at room temperature up to 3 days; reheat in a preheated 350°F oven for 10 minutes.

Each biscuit About 310 calories, 7g protein, 43g carbohydrate, 12g fat (7g saturated), 1g fiber, 720mg sodium.

classic popovers

(See photo on page 560.)

PREP: 10 MIN / TOTAL: 1 HR / SERVES 6

3 large eggs

1 cup whole milk

1 cup all-purpose flour

3 tablespoons butter, melted, plus more for greasing

½ teaspoon salt

1. Preheat the oven to 375°F. Generously butter the cups of a popover pan or eight 6- to 8-ounce ramekins.

2. In a blender, puree the eggs, milk, flour, butter, and salt until smooth.

3. Divide the batter evenly among the prepared cups. Bake 40 minutes.

4. With a small paring knife, cut a small slit in the top of each popover. Bake 10 minutes more. Remove from the oven; immediately transfer the popovers from the cups to a wire rack. Serve warm. Cooled popovers can be kept at room temperature up to 3 hours or frozen up to 1 month. Reheat in a preheated 350°F oven until crisp.

Each popover About 205 calories, 7g protein, 18g carbohydrate, 12g fat (6g saturated), 1g fiber, 310mg sodium.

VARIATIONS

Sweet Cocoa Popovers

Reduce the flour to ¾ cup. Blend ¼ **cup unsweetened cocoa** and **3 tablespoons sugar** into the batter.

Bacon Cheese Popovers

Reduce the salt to ¼ teaspoon. Blend **4 strips chopped cooked bacon**, ½ **cup shredded sharp Cheddar cheese**, and ¼ **cup finely grated Parmesan cheese** into the batter.

Savory Spiced Popovers

Blend 1½ **teaspoons ground cumin, 1 teaspoon smoked paprika**, and ¼ **teaspoon ground black pepper** into the batter.

Pumpkin Popovers

(See photo on page 550.)

Blend 1¼ **teaspoons pumpkin pie spice** into the batter.

CLASSIC BUTTERMILK BISCUITS 558

HOME-STYLE
BANANA BREAD 561

CLASSIC POPOVERS 559

QUICK 'N' EASY SOUTHERN BISCUITS 559

home-style banana bread

PREP: 20 MIN / TOTAL: 1 HR 20 MIN, PLUS COOLING / SERVES 16

2 cups all-purpose flour
¾ teaspoon baking soda
½ teaspoon salt
2 cups mashed very ripe bananas (4 medium)
1 teaspoon vanilla extract
½ cup butter, softened
½ cup granulated sugar
½ cup packed brown sugar
2 large eggs

1. Preheat the oven to 325°F. Grease an 8½ × 4½-inch metal loaf pan. In a medium bowl and using a wire whisk, stir together the flour, baking soda, and salt. In a small bowl, stir together the bananas and vanilla until blended.

2. In a large bowl and using a mixer on medium speed, beat the butter and both sugars until light and fluffy. Beat in the eggs, 1 at a time. Reduce the speed to low; alternately add the flour mixture and the banana mixture, beginning and ending with the flour mixture and occasionally scraping the bowl with a rubber spatula. Beat the batter just until blended.

3. Pour the batter into the prepared pan. Bake until a toothpick inserted in the center comes out clean, about 1 hour. Cool the loaf in the pan on a wire rack 10 minutes; remove from the pan and cool completely on a rack before slicing.

Each serving About 200 calories, 3g protein, 32g carbohydrate, 7g fat (4g saturated), 1g fiber, 205mg sodium.

TESTING NOTE For full-flavored banana bread, be sure your bananas are well-speckled with black. To ripen bananas, place them in a paper bag and close it. The bag will trap the ethylene gas they give off, speeding the process. For even faster ripening, add an apple or two to the bag—they give off a lot of ethylene, so they are a great help for quick-ripening fruits and vegetables.

golden corn bread

PREP: 10 MIN / TOTAL: 30 MIN / SERVES 9

1 cup all-purpose flour
¾ cup cornmeal
3 tablespoons sugar
1 tablespoon baking powder
¾ teaspoon salt
⅔ cup whole milk
4 tablespoons butter, melted
1 large egg

1. Preheat the oven to 425°F. Grease an 8-inch square baking pan.

2. In a medium bowl and using a wire whisk, stir the flour, cornmeal, sugar, baking powder, and salt. In a small bowl and using a fork, beat the milk, melted butter, and egg until blended. Add the egg mixture to the flour mixture; stir just until the flour is moistened (the batter will be lumpy).

3. Spread the batter evenly in the prepared pan. Bake until golden and toothpick inserted in the center comes out clean, 20 to 25 minutes. Cut the corn bread into 9 squares; serve warm.

Each serving About 180 calories, 4g protein, 25g carbohydrate, 7g fat (4g saturated), 1g fiber, 425mg sodium.

VARIATIONS

Corn Muffins

Grease twelve 2½ × 1¼-inch muffin-pan cups. Prepare as directed but use **1 cup whole milk**. Fill each muffin-pan cup two-thirds full. Bake in a preheated 425°F oven until golden and a toothpick inserted in center of muffin comes out clean, about 20 minutes. Immediately remove the muffins from the pan. Serve warm, or cool on a wire rack. **Makes 12 muffins.**

Corn Sticks

Grease 14 corn-stick molds with vegetable oil. Heat the molds in a preheated 425°F oven until hot, about 15 minutes. Meanwhile, prepare the batter as directed. Spoon the batter into the hot molds. Bake until a toothpick inserted in the center of a corn stick comes out clean, 15 to 20 minutes. Cool in the molds on a wire rack 10 minutes. Remove the corn sticks from molds; serve warm. **Makes 14 corn sticks.**

Southern Corn Bread

Prepare as directed, but place a 9- to 10-inch cast-iron skillet in the oven while preheating. In step 2 omit the sugar and reduce the baking powder to 1 teaspoon and the salt to ½ teaspoon; add ¼ **teaspoon baking soda** and substitute **1 cup buttermilk** for the milk. Spray the hot skillet with **nonstick cooking spray**; pour the batter into the skillet and spread it evenly. Bake until a toothpick inserted in the center comes out clean, 15 to 20 minutes. Cut the corn bread into wedges; serve warm. **Makes 8 wedges.**

cranberry orange bread

PREP: 20 MIN / TOTAL: 1 HR 15 MIN / SERVES 12

1 large orange

2½ cups all-purpose flour

1 cup sugar

2 teaspoons baking powder

½ teaspoon baking soda

½ teaspoon salt

4 tablespoons butter, melted

2 large eggs

2 cups cranberries, coarsely chopped

¾ cup walnuts, chopped (optional)

1. Preheat the oven to 375°F. Grease a 9 × 5-inch metal loaf pan. From the orange, grate 1 teaspoon zest and squeeze ½ cup juice.

2. In a large bowl and using a wire whisk, stir the flour, sugar, baking powder, baking soda, and salt. In a small bowl, beat the orange zest and juice, melted butter, and eggs until blended. With a wooden spoon, stir the egg mixture into the flour mixture just until blended (the batter will be stiff). Stir in the cranberries and walnuts, if using.

3. Pour the batter into the prepared pan. Bake until a toothpick inserted in the center comes out clean, 55 to 60 minutes. Cool the loaf in the pan on a wire rack 10 minutes; remove from the pan and cool completely on the wire rack. Cut into 12 slices.

___

Each serving (without walnuts) About 225 calories, 4g protein, 40g carbohydrate, 5g fat (3g saturated), 2g fiber, 280mg sodium.

 Tip Bake this tasty bread a day ahead to allow the flavors to develop and to make it easier to cut neat slices.

zucchini bread

PREP: 20 MIN / TOTAL: 1 HR 30 MIN / SERVES 12

1½ cups all-purpose flour

¾ cup sugar

2¼ teaspoons baking powder

½ teaspoon ground cinnamon

½ teaspoon salt

⅓ cup vegetable oil

2 large eggs

1½ cups shredded zucchini (1 medium)

½ cup walnuts (2 ounces), chopped

½ teaspoon freshly grated orange zest

1. Preheat the oven to 350°F. Grease an 8½ × 4½-inch metal loaf pan.

2. In a large bowl and using a wire whisk, stir the flour, sugar, baking powder, cinnamon, and salt. In a medium bowl and using a fork, mix the oil, eggs, zucchini, walnuts, and orange zest. Stir the zucchini mixture into the flour mixture just until the flour is moistened.

3. Pour the batter into the prepared pan. Bake until a toothpick inserted in the center comes out clean, about 1 hour 10 minutes. Cool in the pan on a wire rack 10 minutes; remove from the pan and cool completely on the wire rack. Cut into 12 slices.

___

Each serving About 210 calories, 4g protein, 26g carbohydrate, 10g fat (1g saturated), 1g fiber, 200mg sodium.

lemon tea bread

PREP: 30 MIN / TOTAL: 1 HR 25 MIN / SERVES 16

BREAD

2 cups all-purpose flour

½ teaspoon baking powder

¼ teaspoon baking soda

½ teaspoon salt

1¼ cups sugar

4 large eggs

1 small container (8 ounces) sour cream

½ cup butter, melted

1 tablespoon freshly grated lemon zest

2 tablespoons fresh lemon juice

GLAZE

⅓ cup sugar

⅓ cup fresh lemon juice

1. Prepare the bread: Preheat the oven to 350°F. Grease a 9 × 5-inch metal loaf pan. Dust with flour.

2. In a large bowl and using a wire whisk, stir the flour, baking powder, baking soda, and salt. In a medium bowl, whisk the sugar and eggs until blended. Add the sour cream, melted butter, lemon zest, and lemon juice; stir until well mixed. Add the sour cream mixture to the flour mixture and fold together just until blended and no streaks of flour remain.

3. Pour the batter into the prepared pan, smooth the top. Bake until a toothpick inserted in the center comes out clean, 55 to 60 minutes. Place the pan on a wire rack.

4. Prepare the glaze: In a cup, stir the sugar and lemon juice. With a thin wooden skewer, poke holes in the hot bread and brush the bread with the glaze. Let cool completely in the pan.

___

Each serving About 235 calories, 4g protein, 32g carbohydrate, 10g fat (6g saturated), 0g fiber, 190mg sodium.

easy christmas stollen

PREP: 25 MIN / TOTAL: 1 HR 25 MIN / SERVES 12

2¼ cups all-purpose flour

½ cup sugar

1½ teaspoons baking powder

¼ teaspoon salt

8 tablespoons butter

1 cup ricotta cheese

½ cup candied lemon peel or coarsely chopped red candied cherries

½ cup dark seedless raisins

⅓ cup slivered blanched almonds, toasted

1 teaspoon vanilla extract

½ teaspoon freshly grated lemon zest

1 large egg, lightly beaten

1 large egg yolk

1. Preheat the oven to 325°F. Grease a large baking sheet.

2. In a large bowl and using a wire whisk, stir the flour, sugar, baking powder, and salt. With a pastry blender or 2 knives used scissor-fashion, cut in 6 tablespoons butter until the mixture resembles fine crumbs. With a spoon, stir in the ricotta until the mixture is just moistened. Stir in the candied lemon peel, raisins, almonds, vanilla, grated lemon zest, egg, and egg yolk until well mixed.

3. Turn the dough onto a lightly floured surface; gently knead the dough 2 or 3 times. With a floured rolling pin, roll the dough into a 10 × 8-inch oval. Fold the oval lengthwise almost in half; the edges should almost but not quite meet.

4. Place the stollen on the prepared baking sheet. Bake until a toothpick inserted in the center comes out clean, about 1 hour. Transfer to a wire rack. Melt the remaining 2 tablespoons butter and brush it over the warm stollen. Cool completely.

Each serving About 300 calories, 7g protein, 38g carbohydrate, 14g fat (7g saturated), 1g fiber, 210mg sodium.

white bread

PREP: 25 MIN / TOTAL: 55 MIN, PLUS RISING / SERVES 24

½ cup warm water (105°F to 115°F)

2 packages (2¼ teaspoons each) active dry yeast

1 teaspoon plus ¼ cup sugar

2¼ cups whole milk, heated to warm (105°F to 115°F)

4 tablespoons butter, softened

1 tablespoon salt

About 7½ cups all-purpose or bread flour

1. In a large bowl, combine the warm water, yeast, and 1 teaspoon sugar; stir to dissolve. Let stand until foamy, about 5 minutes. Add the warm milk, butter, the remaining ¼ cup sugar, the salt, and 4 cups flour. Beat well with a wooden spoon. Gradually stir in 3 more cups flour to make soft dough.

2. Turn the dough onto a floured surface and knead until smooth and elastic, about 8 minutes, working in enough of the remaining ½ cup flour just to keep the dough from sticking.

3. Shape the dough into a ball; place in a greased large bowl, turning the dough to grease the top. Cover the bowl loosely with greased plastic wrap and let rise in a warm place (80°F to 85°F) until doubled in volume, about 1 hour.

4. Grease two 9 × 5-inch metal loaf pans. Punch the down dough. Turn the dough onto a lightly floured surface and cut in half. Shape each half into a rectangle about 12 × 7 inches. Roll up each piece from a short side. Pinch the seam and ends to seal. Place the dough, seam side down, in the prepared pans. Cover the pans loosely with greased plastic wrap and let rise in a warm place until almost doubled, about 1 hour.

5. Preheat the oven to 400°F. Bake until the loaves are browned and sound hollow when lightly tapped, 30 to 35 minutes. Remove from the pans; cool on wire racks. Makes 2 loaves, 12 slices each.

Each serving About 190 calories, 5g protein, 34g carbohydrate, 3g fat (2g saturated), 1g fiber, 325mg sodium.

VARIATION

Cinnamon-Raisin Bread

Prepare as directed, but stir **2 cups dark seedless raisins** into the yeast mixture with the milk. Spread each rectangle with **2 tablespoons butter or margarine**, softened, leaving a ½-inch border. In a small cup, combine **⅓ cup firmly packed brown sugar** and **1 tablespoon ground cinnamon**; sprinkle it evenly over the butter. Roll up each loaf from a short side. Pinch the seam and ends to seal. **Makes 2 loaves, 12 slices each.**

breadsticks

PREP: 40 MIN / TOTAL: 1 HR 20 MIN, PLUS RESTING / MAKES 64 BREADSTICKS

2 packages (2¼ teaspoons each) quick-rise yeast

2½ teaspoons salt

About 4¾ cups all-purpose flour

1⅓ cups very warm water (120°F to 130°F)

½ cup olive oil

3 tablespoons caraway, sesame, or poppy seeds, or freshly grated Parmesan cheese, optional

1. In a large bowl, combine the yeast, salt, and 2 cups flour. With a wooden spoon, stir in the very warm water; beat vigorously 1 minute. Stir in the oil. Gradually stir in 2¼ more cups flour. Stir in the caraway seeds, if using. (If you're using other flavorings instead, add in step 3.)

2. Turn the dough onto a lightly floured surface and knead until smooth and elastic, about 8 minutes, working in enough of the remaining ½ cup flour just to keep the dough from sticking. Cover the dough loosely with plastic wrap; let rest 10 minutes.

3. Meanwhile, preheat the oven to 375°F. Grease 2 large baking sheets. Cut the dough in half. Cover one half; cut the remaining half into 32 equal-size pieces. Shape each piece into a 12-inch-long rope; place them 1 inch apart on the prepared baking sheets. Sprinkle each rope with sesame seeds, poppy seeds, or grated Parmesan, if using.

4. Bake the breadsticks until golden and crisp, about 20 minutes, rotating the baking sheets between upper and lower oven racks halfway through baking. Transfer to wire racks to cool. Repeat with the remaining dough.

Each breadstick About 50 calories, 1g protein, 7g carbohydrate, 2g fat (0g saturated), 0g fiber, 90mg sodium.

VARIATION

Rosemary-Fennel Breadsticks

Prepare as directed but omit the caraway, sesame, or poppy seeds or Parmesan. In step 1, stir **2 teaspoons fennel seeds**, crushed; **1 teaspoon dried rosemary leaves**, crumbled; and ½ **teaspoon coarsely ground black pepper** into the dough. Proceed as directed.

oatmeal molasses rolls

PREP: 1 HR / TOTAL: 1 HR 45 MIN, PLUS RISING / MAKES 18 ROLLS

1 cup boiling water

1 cup plus 2 tablespoons old-fashioned oats, uncooked

¾ cup warm water (105°F to 115°F)

1 package (2¼ teaspoons) active dry yeast

1 teaspoon sugar

5 tablespoons butter, softened

⅓ cup plus 2 teaspoons light (mild) molasses

1½ teaspoons salt

About 4¼ cups all-purpose flour

1. In a medium bowl, pour boiling water over 1 cup oats, stirring to combine. Let stand until the oats have absorbed the water and the mixture has cooled to warm (105°F to 115°F), about 10 minutes.

2. Meanwhile, in a small bowl, combine the warm water, yeast, and sugar. Let the mixture stand until foamy, about 5 minutes.

3. In a large bowl and using a mixer at low speed, beat 4 tablespoons butter until creamy. Add ⅓ cup molasses, beating until combined. Beat in the oat mixture, yeast mixture, and salt just until blended. Gradually beat in 2 cups flour just until blended. With a wooden spoon, stir in 2 cups flour. Turn the dough onto a lightly floured surface and knead until smooth and elastic, about 5 minutes, working in enough of the remaining ¼ cup flour just to keep the dough from sticking.

4. Shape the dough into a ball; place it in a greased large bowl, turning the dough to grease the top. Cover the bowl loosely with plastic wrap and let rise in a warm place (80°F to 85°F) until doubled in volume, about 1 hour. Grease a 13 × 9-inch baking pan.

5. Punch down the dough. On a lightly floured surface, cut the dough into 18 equal-size pieces. Shape each piece into a ball and arrange them in the prepared pan in 3 rows of 6 balls each. Cover the pan loosely and let the rolls rise in a warm place until doubled, about 1 hour.

6. Meanwhile, preheat the oven to 350°F. Bake the rolls until very lightly browned, about 30 minutes.

7. Melt the remaining butter. Stir in the remaining molasses.

8. After the rolls have baked 30 minutes, remove them from the oven. Brush with the molasses mixture and sprinkle with the remaining 2 tablespoons oats. Bake the rolls until golden, about 15 minutes longer. Serve warm, or cool on wire racks to serve later. Reheat if desired.

Each roll About 185 calories, 4g protein, 32g carbohydrate, 4g fat (2g saturated), 1g fiber, 230mg sodium.

focaccia

PREP: 25 MIN / TOTAL: 45 MIN, PLUS RISING / SERVES 12

- 1½ cups warm water (105°F to 115°F)
- 1 package (2¼ teaspoons) active dry yeast
- 1 teaspoon sugar
- 5 tablespoons extra-virgin olive oil
- 1½ teaspoons table salt
- 3¾ cups all-purpose flour, or 3½ cups bread flour
- 1 teaspoon kosher salt or coarse sea salt

1. In a large bowl, combine ½ cup warm water, the yeast, and sugar; stir to dissolve. Let stand until foamy, about 5 minutes. Add the remaining 1 cup warm water, 2 tablespoons oil, the table salt, and flour; stir to combine.

2. Turn the dough onto a floured surface and knead until smooth and elastic, about 7 minutes. The dough will be soft; do not add more flour.

3. Shape the dough into ball; place it in a greased large bowl, turning the dough to grease the top. Cover the bowl loosely with plastic wrap and let stand in a warm place (80°F to 85°F) until doubled in volume, about 1 hour.

4. Lightly oil a 15½ × 10½-inch rimmed baking sheet. Punch down the dough and pat it into the prepared pan. Cover loosely with plastic wrap and let rise in a warm place until doubled, about 45 minutes.

5. With your fingertips, make deep indentations, 1 inch apart, over the entire surface of the dough, almost to the bottom of the pan. Drizzle with the remaining 3 tablespoons oil; sprinkle with kosher salt. Cover loosely with plastic wrap; let rise in a warm place until doubled, about 45 minutes.

6. Preheat the oven to 450°F. Bake the focaccia on the lowest oven rack until the bottom is crusty and the top is lightly browned, about 18 minutes. Transfer the focaccia to a wire rack to cool.

Each serving About 200 calories, 4g protein, 31g carbohydrate, 7g fat (1g saturated), 1g fiber, 540mg sodium.

VARIATIONS

Tomato Focaccia

Prepare as directed, but drizzle the dough with only **1 tablespoon olive oil**. Arrange **1 pound ripe plum tomatoes**, cut into ¼-inch-thick slices, over the top; sprinkle with **1 tablespoon chopped fresh rosemary or 1 teaspoon dried rosemary**, crumbled, and **½ teaspoon coarsely ground black pepper**, in addition to the 1 teaspoon kosher salt. Bake as directed.

Red Pepper Focaccia

Prepare as directed, but do not sprinkle with kosher salt. In a 12-inch skillet, heat an additional **1 tablespoon olive oil** over medium heat. Add **4 red bell peppers**, sliced, and ¼ **teaspoon table salt** and cook, stirring frequently, until tender, about 20 minutes. Cool to room temperature. Sprinkle over the focaccia just before baking.

Sun-Dried Tomato & Olive Focaccia

Prepare as directed, but increase the kosher salt to 1½ teaspoons. In step 5, combine ½ **cup Gaeta olives**, pitted; ¼ **cup drained oil-packed sun-dried tomatoes**, coarsely chopped; and kosher salt. Sprinkle over the focaccia just before baking.

Onion Focaccia

Prepare as directed, but do not sprinkle with kosher salt. In a 12-inch skillet, heat an additional **2 teaspoons olive oil** over medium heat. Add **2 medium onions**, sliced, **1 teaspoon sugar**, and ½ **teaspoon table salt** and cook, stirring frequently, until golden brown, about 20 minutes. Cool to room temperature. Spread over the focaccia just before baking.

date-nut bread

PREP: 20 MIN / TOTAL: 1 HR 35 MIN, PLUS COOLING / 16 SERVINGS

- 1½ cups chopped pitted dates
- 6 tablespoons butter or margarine, cut into pieces
- 1¼ cups boiling water
- 2 cups all-purpose flour
- ¾ cup sugar
- 1 teaspoon baking powder
- ½ teaspoon baking soda
- ½ teaspoon salt
- 1 large egg, lightly beaten
- 1 cup walnuts (4 ounces), coarsely chopped

1. In a medium bowl, combine the dates, butter, and boiling water; let stand until cool.

2. Preheat oven to 325°F and grease 9 x 5-inch metal loaf pan.

3. In a large bowl, with a wire whisk, stir the flour, sugar, baking powder, baking soda, and salt. Stir the egg into the cooled date mixture. Stir the date mixture into the flour mixture just until the flour is moistened. Stir in the walnuts.

4. Pour the batter into the prepared pan. Bake until a toothpick inserted in the center comes out clean, about 1 hour 15 minutes. Cool in the pan on a wire rack 10 minutes; remove from pan and cool completely on the rack. Makes 1 loaf.

Each serving About 230 calories, 3g protein, 35g carbohydrate, 10g fat (3g saturated), 2g fiber, 192mg sodium.

BUTTERY ROSEMARY ROLLS 567

buttery rosemary rolls

PREP: 15 MIN / TOTAL: 40 MIN, PLUS RISING TIME / SERVES 16

1 cup whole milk

1 large egg

Vegetable oil, for oiling dough

3½ cups all-purpose flour, plus additional for rolling

1 package (2¼ teaspoons) active dry yeast

¼ cup packed brown sugar

1¼ teaspoon table salt

8 tablespoons butter, melted

2 tablespoon fresh rosemary leaves

Coarse, flaky sea salt, for garnish

1. In a medium microwave-safe bowl, whisk the milk and egg until combined. Microwave on High 1 to 2 minutes, or until very warm. Lightly oil a large bowl; set aside.

2. In a stand mixer with the paddle attachment, mix the flour, yeast, brown sugar, salt, and 3 tablespoons melted butter until combined. Add the milk mixture; mix to combine. Remove the paddle attachment and attach the dough hook; knead the dough 6 to 8 minutes, or until the dough is smooth and comes together. With floured hands, transfer the dough to the oiled bowl. Rub the top of the dough with some oil and lightly cover it with plastic wrap. Let rise in a warm spot 1½ hours.

3. Brush a 13 × 9-inch metal baking pan with 1 tablespoon melted butter. On a floured surface, divide the dough into 4 equal pieces. Working with 1 piece of dough at a time and a floured rolling pin, roll the dough into a 12 × 4-inch rectangle. Brush the top with melted butter. Fold the long side over to form a 12 × 2-inch rectangle. Cut the dough into 4 equal-size pieces. Arrange in the prepared pan in a row along the long side. Repeat the rolling, brushing, and cutting with the remaining pieces of dough. Lightly cover the pan with plastic wrap. Let rise in a warm spot 45 minutes.

4. Toss the rosemary with any remaining melted butter; sprinkle over the top of the dough along with the sea salt. Bake 20 to 25 minutes, or until deep golden brown. Serve warm or reheat rolls in a preheated 325°F oven 5 minutes.

Each serving About 185 calories, 4g protein, 26g carbohydrate, 7g fat (4g saturated), 1g fiber, 675mg sodium.

pissaladière

PREP: 40 MIN / TOTAL: 1 HR 35 MIN, PLUS RISING / SERVES 32

1 cup warm water (105°F to 115°F)

1 package (2¼ teaspoons) active dry yeast

3 cups all-purpose flour

Salt

2 tablespoons olive oil

2 pounds onions, chopped

1 can (2 ounces) anchovy fillets, rinsed, drained, and coarsely chopped

⅓ cup pitted and halved Kalamata or Gaeta olives

1. In a cup, combine ¼ cup warm water and the yeast; stir to dissolve. Let stand until foamy, about 5 minutes.

2. In a large bowl and using a wire whisk, stir the flour and 1½ teaspoons salt. Stir in the yeast mixture, the remaining ¾ cup warm water, and 1 tablespoon oil. Turn the dough onto a lightly floured surface and knead until smooth and elastic, about 8 minutes. Shape the dough into a ball; place in a greased large bowl, turning to grease the top. Cover the bowl loosely with plastic wrap and let rise in warm place (80°F to 85°F) until doubled in volume, about 45 minutes.

3. Meanwhile, in a 12-inch skillet, heat the remaining 1 tablespoon oil over low heat. Add the onions and ¼ teaspoon salt and cook, stirring frequently, until the onions are very soft and golden, about 30 minutes. Remove from the heat; set aside to cool.

4. Grease a 15½ × 10½-inch rimmed baking sheet pan. Punch down the dough and pat it into the prepared pan. Cover loosely with plastic wrap and let rise 30 minutes.

5. Preheat the oven to 425°F. With your fingertips, make shallow indentations all over the surface of the dough. Toss the onions and anchovies and spread the mixture over the top. Place the olives on the onion mixture at 2-inch intervals. Bake on the lowest oven rack until the crust is golden, about 25 minutes. Cut into 32 squares.

Each serving About 75 calories, 2g protein, 12g carbohydrate, 2g fat (0g saturated), 1g fiber, 205mg sodium.

 Tip You can prepare the dough in advance. Let it rise once, then freeze for up to three months. Defrost and follow the recipe.

 GLOSSARY → A specialty of Nice, France, **pissaladière** is a pizza-like tart usually served as a snack or appetizer, but it makes a nice supper or brunch dish, too.

classic swiss fondue

The perfect use for your homemade bread; substitute the French bread with any savory bread in this chapter. Our favorites are Soft Pretzels (right) and Breadsticks (page 564).

PREP: 15 MIN / TOTAL: 30 MIN / SERVES 6

1 clove garlic,
cut in half

1½ cups dry white
wine

1 tablespoon kirsch
or brandy

8 ounces Swiss or
Emmenthaler
cheese, shredded
(2 cups)

8 ounces Gruyère
cheese, shredded
(2 cups)

3 tablespoons
all-purpose flour

⅛ teaspoon ground
black pepper

Pinch of ground
nutmeg

1 loaf (16 ounces)
French bread,
cut into 1-inch
cubes

1. Rub the inside of a fondue pot or heavy 2-quart nonreactive saucepan with the garlic; discard the garlic. Pour the wine into the fondue pot. Heat over medium-low heat until very hot but not boiling; stir in the kirsch.

2. Meanwhile, in a medium bowl, toss the Swiss, Gruyère, and flour. Add the cheese mixture, one handful at a time, to the wine, stirring constantly and vigorously until the cheese melts and the mixture is thick and smooth. If the mixture separates, increase the heat to medium, stirring just until smooth. Stir in the pepper and nutmeg.

3. Transfer the fondue pot to the table; place it over a tabletop heater to keep hot, if you like. To eat, spear cubes of French bread onto long-handled fondue forks and dip them into the cheese mixture.

Each serving About 570 calories, 29g protein, 45g carbohydrate, 25g fat (14g saturated), 2g fiber, 690mg sodium.

soft pretzels

PREP: 30 MIN / TOTAL: 45 MIN, PLUS RISING / SERVES 12

2 cups warm water
(105°F to 115°F)

1 package (2¼
teaspoons) active
dry yeast

1 teaspoon sugar

1 teaspoon table salt

About 4 cups
all-purpose flour

2 tablespoons baking
soda

1 tablespoon kosher
or coarse sea salt

1. In a large bowl, combine 1½ cups warm water, the yeast, and sugar; stir to dissolve. Let stand until foamy, about 5 minutes. Add the salt and 2 cups flour; beat well with a wooden spoon. Gradually stir in 1½ cups flour to make a soft dough.

2. Turn the dough onto a floured surface and knead until smooth and elastic, about 6 minutes, kneading in enough of the remaining ½ cup flour just to keep the dough from sticking.

3. Shape the dough into ball; place it in a greased large bowl, turning the dough to grease the top. Cover the bowl loosely with plastic wrap and let rise in a warm place (80°F to 85°F) until doubled in volume, about 30 minutes.

4. Preheat the oven to 400°F. Grease 2 baking sheets. Punch down the dough and cut it into 12 equal-size pieces. Roll each piece into a 24-inch-long rope. Shape the ropes into loop-shaped pretzels.

5. In a small bowl, whisk the remaining ½ cup warm water and baking soda until the soda has dissolved.

6. Dip the shaped pretzels in the baking-soda mixture and place them 1½ inches apart on the prepared baking sheets; sprinkle with kosher salt. Bake, rotating the baking sheets between the upper and lower oven racks halfway through baking, until browned, 16 to 18 minutes. Serve the pretzels warm, or transfer to wire racks to cool.

Each pretzel About 170 calories, 5g protein, 33g carbohydrate, 1g fat (0g saturated), 1g fiber, 1,190mg sodium.

Tip Freeze these after shaping. Let them thaw, then dip them in the baking-soda mixture and bake as directed. The pretzels can be sprinkled with sesame or poppy seeds in addition to the salt.

overnight sticky buns

PREP: 1 HR / TOTAL: 1 HR 30 MIN, PLUS RISING AND CHILLING / SERVES 20

DOUGH

¼ cup warm water (105°F to 115°F)

1 package (2¼ teaspoons) active dry yeast

1 teaspoon plus ¼ cup granulated sugar

¾ cup whole milk

4 tablespoons butter, softened

1 teaspoon salt

3 large egg yolks

About 4 cups all-purpose flour

FILLING

½ cup packed brown sugar

¼ cup dried currants

1 tablespoon ground cinnamon

4 tablespoons butter, melted

TOPPING

⅔ cup packed brown sugar

3 tablespoons butter

2 tablespoons light corn syrup

2 tablespoons honey

1¼ cups pecans (5 ounces), coarsely chopped

1. Prepare the dough: In a cup, combine the warm water, yeast, and 1 teaspoon granulated sugar; stir to dissolve. Let stand until foamy, about 5 minutes.

2. In a large bowl and using a mixer at low speed, blend the yeast mixture with the milk, butter, the remaining ¼ cup granulated sugar, the egg yolks, salt, and 3 cups flour until blended. With a wooden spoon, stir in ¾ cup flour.

3. Turn the dough onto a lightly floured surface and knead until smooth and elastic, about 5 minutes, working in enough of the remaining ¼ cup flour just to keep the dough from sticking.

4. Shape the dough into a ball; place it in a greased large bowl, turning the dough to grease the top. Cover the bowl loosely with plastic wrap and let rise in a warm place (80°F to 85°F) until doubled, about 1 hour.

5. Meanwhile, prepare the filling: In a small bowl, combine the brown sugar, currants, and cinnamon; set aside. Reserve the melted butter.

6. Prepare the topping: In a 1-quart saucepan, combine the brown sugar, butter, corn syrup, and honey; heat over low heat, stirring occasionally, until the brown sugar dissolves in the melted butter. Grease a 13 × 9-inch baking pan; pour the melted brown-sugar mixture into the pan and sprinkle the pecans evenly on top.

7. Punch down the dough. Turn the dough onto a lightly floured surface; cover and let rest 15 minutes. Roll the dough into an 18 × 12-inch rectangle. Brush the dough with the reserved melted butter and sprinkle with the currant mixture. Starting at a long side, roll up the dough jelly-roll fashion; place it, seam side down, on a work surface. Cut the dough crosswise into 20 slices.

8. Place the slices, cut sides down, on the brown-sugar mixture in the prepared pan in 4 rows of 5 slices each. Cover and refrigerate at least 12 hours or up to 15 hours.

9. Preheat the oven to 375°F. Bake the buns until golden, about 30 minutes. Remove from the oven. Immediately place a serving tray or rimmed baking sheet over the top of the baking pan and invert it; remove the pan. Let the buns cool slightly to serve warm, or cool completely on wire racks to serve later.

Each bun About 290 calories, 4g protein, 42g carbohydrate, 13g fat (5g saturated), 2g fiber, 195mg sodium.

easy homemade pizza dough

PREP: 10 MIN / TOTAL: 2 HR 15 MIN / SERVES 8

3½ cups all-purpose flour

3 tablespoons olive oil, plus additional for brushing

1½ teaspoons salt

1 package (2¼ teaspoons) quick-rise yeast

1½ cups lukewarm water

1. In a stand mixer with the paddle attachment, mix the flour, 3 tablespoons oil, the salt, and yeast on low speed until combined. Add the water. Mix on medium speed 1 minute. Increase the speed to medium-high; mix 5 minutes.

2. Meanwhile, brush the bottom and sides of a large light-colored rimmed baking sheet (approximately 18 × 12 inches) with the remaining ¼ cup oil. Pour the dough (it will be very soft) onto the oiled sheet and rub all over with the excess oil. Gently stretch the dough to fill most of baking sheet. Cover with plastic wrap; let stand in a warm spot 2 hours.

3. Remove the plastic. With your hands, stretch and push the dough until it covers the bottom of the pan. Top as desired.

Each serving About 290 calories, 6g protein, 42g carbohydrate, 11g fat (2g saturated), 2g fiber, 439mg sodium.

sufganiyot

PREP: 30 MIN / TOTAL: 1 HR 5 MIN / SERVES 16

3 cups all-purpose flour

¼ cup granulated sugar

1 package (2¼ teaspoons) quick-rise yeast

1 teaspoon ground cinnamon

1 teaspoon salt

¼ cup vegetable oil

¾ cup warm whole milk (120°F to 130°F), plus extra for brushing

2 large eggs, at room temperature

1 cup sour cherry or other jam

Confectioners' sugar, for dusting

1. In an electric stand mixer bowl, combine the flour, granulated sugar, yeast, cinnamon, and salt. With the paddle attachment, mix on low 15 seconds or until combined. Add the oil and milk; beat on medium-low speed 3 to 5 minutes, or until well combined. Add the eggs, one at a time; beat 10 minutes, or until the dough is elastic, occasionally scraping the sides of the bowl.

2. Meanwhile, lightly oil a large bowl. Transfer the dough to the prepared bowl; cover loosely with plastic wrap. Let rise 40 minutes, or until doubled in bulk.

3. Lightly grease 3 baking sheets. Gently punch down the dough, folding it onto itself. On a lightly oiled work surface, gently roll the dough into a 16-inch log; cut the log crosswise into 1-inch pieces. Shape each piece into a ball; transfer to the prepared baking sheets, placing them 3 inches apart. Cover loosely with lightly oiled plastic wrap; let rise 20 to 30 minutes, or until slightly puffed. (The dough may be prepared to this point up to 1 day ahead. Refrigerate, loosely covered. Bring to room temperature before baking.)

4. Preheat the oven to 350°F. Brush the tops of the dough with milk. Bake, one sheet at a time, 12 to 15 minutes, or until pale golden. Cool the sufganiyot on sheets on wire racks 5 minutes.

5. Cut off the corner of a self-sealing plastic bag to make a ¼-inch-diameter hole; fit with a ¼- to ½-inch plain piping tip, and fill the bag with jam. Slide a paring knife horizontally into one side of each doughnut and, using a sawing motion, carefully cut a pocket in the pastry. Fit the piping tip into the hole and pipe jam into it until filled. Repeat. Dust doughnuts with confectioners' sugar to serve.

Each serving About 215 calories, 4g protein, 37g carbohydrate, 6g fat (1g saturated), 1g fiber, 165mg sodium.

 Tip Although fried foods are often associated with Hannukah, we bake these doughnuts for a lighter version of the holiday delight.

quick & easy anadama bread

PREP: 25 MIN / TOTAL: 55 MIN, PLUS RISING / SERVES 10

3 cups all-purpose flour

⅓ cup cornmeal

1 teaspoon salt

1 package (2¼ teaspoons) quick-rise yeast

1 cup water

¼ cup light (mild) molasses

3 tablespoons butter, softened

1 large egg

1. In a large bowl and using a wire whisk, stir 1 cup flour, the cornmeal, salt, and yeast. In a 1-quart saucepan, heat the water and molasses over low heat until very warm (120°F to 130°F). Meanwhile, grease a 2-quart soufflé dish or deep casserole.

2. With a mixer at low speed, gradually beat the molasses mixture and butter into the flour mixture just until blended. Increase the speed to medium; beat 2 minutes, occasionally scraping the bowl with a rubber spatula. Beat in the egg and 1 cup flour to make a thick batter; continue beating 2 minutes, frequently scraping the bowl. With a wooden spoon, stir in the remaining 1 cup flour to make a soft dough.

3. Place the dough in the prepared soufflé dish. Cover loosely with plastic wrap and let rise in a warm place (80°F to 85°F) until doubled, about 1 hour.

4. Preheat the oven to 375°F. Bake the bread until it is browned and sounds hollow when lightly tapped on the bottom, 30 to 35 minutes. Remove the loaf from the soufflé dish; cool on a wire rack.

Each serving About 220 calories, 5g protein, 38g carbohydrate, 5g fat (2g saturated), 1g fiber, 280mg sodium.

GLOSSARY → Jelly doughnuts, called **sufganiyot** in Israel, are a popular Hannukah treat.

tex-mex taco pizza

(See photo on page 573.)

PREP: 20 MIN / TOTAL: 50 MIN / SERVES 8

- 1 cup bottled salsa
- 1 recipe Easy Homemade Pizza Dough (page 569), or 1½-pounds pizzeria dough
- 1 cup extra-sharp Cheddar cheese, shredded
- 1 tablespoon olive oil
- 1 medium onion, chopped
- 2 teaspoons ground cumin
- 1 teaspoon garlic powder
- 1 teaspoon smoked paprika
- 1 pound ground beef sirloin
- ½ teaspoon salt
- ½ cup pickled jalapeño chile slices (optional)
- ¼ cup light sour cream
- 1 tablespoon fresh lime juice
- 1 tablespoon part-skim milk
- 1 heart romaine lettuce, thinly sliced
- 2 small plum tomatoes, chopped

1. Preheat the oven to 475°F. Spread the salsa all over the dough and top with the Cheddar; bake 10 minutes.

2. Meanwhile, in a 12-inch skillet, heat the oil over medium heat. Add the onion, cumin, garlic powder, and paprika; cook 3 minutes, stirring. Add the beef and salt. Cook 3 minutes, or until browned, breaking up the beef with the side of a spoon. Sprinkle the beef over the cheese. Top with jalapeños, if using. Bake 20 minutes, or until the bottom of the crust is golden brown.

3. While the pizza bakes, stir together the sour cream, lime juice, and milk. To serve, top the pizza with lettuce and tomatoes. Drizzle with the sour cream mixture.

Each serving About 505 calories, 21g protein, 48g carbohydrate, 25g fat (7g saturated), 3g fiber, 855mg sodium.

sweet & spicy pepperoni-mushroom pizza

(See photo on page 573.)

PREP: 15 MIN / TOTAL: 40 MIN / SERVES 8

- 1 cup Marinara Sauce (page 336) or bottled marinara sauce
- 1 recipe Easy Homemade Pizza Dough (page 569), or 1½ pounds pizzeria dough
- 1 tablespoon olive oil
- 8 ounces mixed mushrooms, sliced
- 2 cloves garlic, chopped
- 2 ounces pepperoni slices
- 8 ounces mozzarella cheese, shredded
- ½ cup grated Parmesan cheese
- 1 teaspoon dried oregano
- 1 teaspoon crushed red pepper
- 2 tablespoons honey

1. Preheat the oven to 475°F. Spread the sauce all over the dough. Bake 10 minutes.

2. In a 12-inch skillet, heat the oil over medium heat. Add the mushrooms and garlic; cook 5 minutes, stirring. Transfer to the pizza. Top with pepperoni and cheeses. Bake 15 to 20 minutes, or until the crust is deep golden brown. Sprinkle with oregano and red pepper, then drizzle with honey.

Each serving About 500 calories, 17g protein, 52g carbohydrate, 26g fat (8g saturated), 3g fiber, 905mg sodium.

GOOD TO KNOW

PIZZERIA DOUGH HACK

Buy a 1½ pound ball of dough from your local pizzeria. Brush your rimmed baking sheet generously with olive oil before placing the dough on the pan and stretching it to fit. Top it right away (no need to let the dough rise), but if it springs back on you, let it sit at room temperature for 15 minutes, then try again.

artichoke & olive antipasto pizza

PREP: 10 MIN / TOTAL: 40 MIN / SERVES 8

½ cup bottled sun-dried tomato pesto

1 recipe Easy Homemade Pizza Dough (page 569), or 1½ pounds pizzeria dough

4 ounces thinly sliced provolone cheese

¾ cup marinated artichokes, drained and chopped

½ cup roasted red peppers, drained and chopped

¾ cup pitted Kalamata olives

Chopped fresh parsley, for garnish

1. Preheat the oven to 475°F. Spread pesto all over the dough. Bake 15 minutes.

2. Top the pizza with provolone, then artichokes and peppers. Scatter the olives on top. Bake 15 to 20 minutes, or until the crust is golden brown. Garnish with parsley.

Each serving About 475 calories, 11g protein, 48g carbohydrate, 26g fat (6g saturated), 3g fiber, 920mg sodium.

egg & tater pizza

PREP: 10 MIN / TOTAL: 40 MIN / SERVES 8

1 bag (5 ounces) baby spinach

1 cup Marinara Sauce (page 336) or bottled marinara

1 recipe Easy Homemade Pizza Dough (page 569), or 1½ pounds pizzeria dough

4 ounces mozzarella cheese, shredded

4 ounces extra sharp Cheddar cheese, shredded

8 ounces frozen potato puffs (2 cups)

6 large eggs

¼ teaspoon salt

¼ teaspoon ground black pepper

1. Preheat the oven to 475°F. In a large bowl covered with vented plastic, microwave the spinach on High 2 minutes. When cool enough to handle, squeeze it dry.

2. Spread the sauce all over the dough. Top with the cheeses, spinach, and potato puffs. Bake 25 minutes. Crack the eggs 2 inches apart, on top of the pizza; sprinkle eggs with the salt and pepper. Bake 5 minutes, or until the whites are set but the yolks are still runny.

Each serving About 525 calories, 18g protein, 53g carbohydrate, 26g fat (8g saturated), 3g fiber, 930mg sodium.

creamy broccoli alfredo pizza

PREP: 20 MIN / TOTAL: 50 MIN / SERVES 8

6 ounces reduced-fat cream cheese, softened

⅓ cup grated Parmesan cheese

3 tablespoon milk

2 cloves garlic, crushed with a garlic press

1 tablespoon butter, melted

¼ teaspoon salt

1 teaspoon ground black pepper

1 recipe Easy Homemade Pizza Dough (page 569), or 1½ pounds pizzeria dough

12 ounces broccoli, coarsely chopped

4 ounces mozzarella, shredded

1. Preheat the oven to 475°F. With a mixer on medium speed, beat the cream cheese, Parmesan, milk, garlic, butter, salt, and pepper until smooth; spread all over the dough. Top with broccoli and mozzarella.

2. Bake 25 to 30 minutes, or until the broccoli and crust are golden brown.

Each serving About 445 calories, 14g protein, 47g carbohydrate, 23g fat (8g saturated), 3g fiber, 675mg sodium.

SWEET & SPICY
PEPPERONI-MUSHROOM
PIZZA 571

BRUSSELS SPROUTS
& PANCETTA PIZZA
575

APPLE-BRIE PIZZA WITH
CARAMELIZED ONIONS 574

CREAMY BROCCOLI ALFREDO PIZZA 572

ARTICHOKE & OLIVE ANTIPASTO PIZZA 572

TEX-MEX TACO PIZZA 571

EGG & TATER PIZZA 572

BUFFALO CHICKEN & RANCH PIZZA 574

apple-brie pizza

with caramelized onions

(See photo on page 573.)

PREP: 20 MIN / TOTAL: 1 HR / SERVES 8

- 1 tablespoon olive oil
- 2 large sweet onions, thinly sliced
- ¼ teaspoon salt
- 1 recipe Easy Homemade Pizza Dough (page 569) or 1½ pounds pizzeria dough
- 1 small Gala or Empire apple, cored and thinly sliced
- 4 ounces Brie, thinly sliced
- ½ teaspoon ground black pepper
- 1 tablespoon balsamic vinegar
- Fresh basil leaves, for garnish

1. In a 12-inch skillet, heat the oil over medium heat. Add the onions and salt. Cover and cook 15 minutes, or until golden brown and almost tender, stirring occasionally.

2. Preheat the oven to 475°F. Spread the onions on the dough. Bake 15 minutes. Top with the slices of apple and Brie. Bake 20 minutes, or until the crust is golden brown. Sprinkle with pepper and drizzle with vinegar. Garnish with basil.

Each serving About 405 calories, 10g protein, 52g carbohydrate, 18g fat (4g saturated), 3g fiber, 530mg sodium.

cheese pizza

PREP: 40 MIN / TOTAL: 1 HR, PLUS RESTING / SERVES 4

- ½ recipe Easy Homemade Pizza Dough (page 569) or 1 pound pizzeria dough
- 2 tablespoons freshly grated Parmesan cheese
- 1 cup Marinara Sauce (page 336) or bottled marinara sauce
- 4 ounces mozzarella cheese, shredded (1 cup)

1. Shape the pizza dough as directed. Sprinkle with Parmesan. Spread the sauce over the Parmesan and top with the mozzarella.

2. Preheat the oven to 450°F. Let prepared pizza rest 20 minutes. Bake until the crust is golden, 15 to 20 minutes.

Each serving About 390 calories, 14g protein, 55g carbohydrate, 12g fat (5g saturated), 3g fiber, 900mg sodium.

buffalo chicken & ranch pizza

(See photo on page 573.)

PREP: 15 MIN / TOTAL: 50 MIN / SERVES 8

- ¾ cup part-skim ricotta cheese
- ¼ cup ranch dressing
- 1 recipe Easy Homemade Pizza Dough (page 569), or 1½ pounds pizzeria dough
- ½ cup hot sauce
- 3 tablespoon unsalted butter, melted
- 1 tablespoon distilled white vinegar
- 3 cups shredded rotisserie chicken meat (about 12 ounces)
- 2 ounces blue cheese, crumbled
- Thinly sliced green onions, for garnish

1. Preheat the oven to 475°F. Stir together the ricotta and ranch dressing; spread all over the dough. Bake 15 minutes.

2. Meanwhile, in a medium bowl, whisk the hot sauce, butter, and vinegar; add the chicken, tossing to coat. Scatter the chicken over the ricotta mixture. Top with blue cheese.

3. Bake 20 to 25 minutes, or until the bottom of the crust is golden brown. Garnish with green onions.

Each serving About 495 calories, 17g protein, 46g carbohydrate, 29g fat (9g saturated), 2g fiber, 1,245mg sodium.

brussels sprouts & pancetta pizza

(See photo on page 573.)

PREP: 20 MIN / TOTAL: 50 MIN / SERVES 8

- ¾ cup Homemade Pesto (page 65) or refrigerated bottled pesto
- 1 recipe Easy Homemade Pizza Dough (page 569), or 1½ pounds pizzeria dough
- 4 ounces pancetta, finely chopped
- 12 ounces Brussels sprouts, trimmed and sliced
- ½ small red onion, thinly sliced
- 2 teaspoon olive oil
- ¼ teaspoon ground black pepper
- ¼ cup grated Pecorino Romano cheese
- Zest of 1 lemon

1. Preheat the oven to 475°F. Spread the pesto all over the dough. Top with pancetta; bake 15 minutes.

2. In a large bowl, toss the Brussels sprouts and onion with the oil and pepper. Sprinkle over the pancetta. Top with Pecorino. Bake 20 minutes, or until the sprouts are golden brown. Grate the zest from the lemon over the pizza.

Each serving About 505 calories, 14g protein, 48g carbohydrate, 29g fat (6g saturated), 4g fiber, 765mg sodium.

VARIATIONS

Pizza Toppings

To keep the crust crispy, scatter cheese over the dough before topping it with other ingredients. Sprinkle fresh herbs over the pizza just before serving. Try these delicious combinations:

- Grilled radicchio, cooked crumbled pancetta or bacon, crumbled goat cheese, and chopped fresh sage

- Sautéed cremini mushrooms, cooked sweet Italian sausage, thinly sliced fresh mozzarella cheese, and dried oregano

- Coarsely chopped grilled eggplant, marinated artichoke hearts, chopped plum tomatoes, shredded mozzarella cheese, and fresh basil leaves

- Thinly sliced mozzarella, crumbled Gorgonzola, spoonfuls of ricotta, ground black pepper, and fresh basil leaves

deep-dish veggie supreme pizza

PREP: 15 MIN / TOTAL: 50 MIN / SERVES 4

- Nonstick cooking spray
- 1 recipe Easy Homemade Pizza Dough (page 569), or 1 pound pizzeria dough
- ½ cup Marinara Sauce (page 336) or bottled sauce
- 1 cup shredded mozzarella
- 2 tablespoons finely grated Parmesan cheese
- 4 ounces shiitake mushrooms, stemmed and thinly sliced
- ½ small zucchini, very thinly sliced
- 2 tablespoons olive oil
- ⅛ teaspoon salt
- ½ cup roasted red peppers, drained and chopped

1. Preheat the oven to 475°F. Spray a 12-inch cast-iron skillet with cooking spray. Press the pizza dough into the bottom of the skillet. Spread marinara sauce over the dough; top with mozzarella and Parmesan cheeses.

2. In a large bowl, toss the mushrooms with the zucchini, olive oil, and salt. Arrange this over the cheeses. Sprinkle with roasted red peppers. Bake 30 minutes, or until the cheeses are browned and the bottom of the crust is brown and crisp. Let stand 5 minutes before serving.

Each serving About 410 calories, 13g protein, 55g carbohydrate, 18g fat (4g saturated), 4g fiber, 705mg sodium.

 Tip Opt for pizzeria-style dough from the supermarket or a local pizza shop. The ones in pop-open tubes tend to burn on the bottom.

meatball mozzarella pizza

PREP: 20 MIN / TOTAL: 40 MIN / SERVES 6

- 1 recipe Easy Homemade Pizza Dough (page 569) or one 1¼-pounds pizzeria dough
- 1 cup shredded mozzarella
- 2 plum tomatoes, thinly sliced
- ½ small red onion, thinly sliced
- ¼ teaspoon ground black pepper
- 8 ounces ground beef chuck or ground turkey
- ¼ cup seasoned (Italian) bread crumbs
- 2 tablespoons grated Pecorino Romano cheese
- Pinch of salt
- Nonstick cooking spray

1. Place a large baking sheet in the oven; preheat the oven to 450°F.

2. On a large sheet of parchment, stretch and roll the pizza dough into a 13-inch circle. Top with the shredded mozzarella, plum tomatoes, red onion, and pepper.

3. Combine the ground beef, bread crumbs, Pecorino, and salt; form into 1-inch meatballs and place them on the pizza. Spray the pizza with nonstick cooking spray.

4. Carefully slide the pizza on the parchment onto the preheated baking sheet. Bake 20 to 25 minutes, or until the bottom of the crust is deep golden brown.

Each serving About 395 calories, 18g protein, 48g carbohydrate, 13g fat (5g saturated), 2g fiber, 1,130mg sodium.

quick summery veggie tart

PREP: 25 MIN / TOTAL: 1 HR 5 MIN / SERVES 4

- 1 tablespoon plus 1 teaspoon extra-virgin olive oil
- 1 clove garlic, crushed with a garlic press
- 1 small red onion, finely chopped
- 1 large red bell pepper, finely chopped
- Salt
- Ground black pepper
- 4 ounces cream cheese, softened
- ¼ cup fresh basil leaves, finely chopped, plus additional for garnish
- 1 small zucchini (4 ounces), trimmed
- 1 small yellow squash (4 ounces), trimmed
- 1 (9-inch) refrigerated ready-to-unroll piecrust

1. Preheat the oven to 425°F.

2. In a 12-inch skillet, heat 1 tablespoon oil over medium-high heat. Add the garlic and cook 30 seconds, stirring. Add the onion, bell pepper, and ⅛ teaspoon each salt and pepper. Cook 4 minutes, or until softened and browned, stirring frequently. Remove from the heat and let cool to room temperature. The mixture can be refrigerated, covered, up to overnight.

3. While the mixture cools, combine the cream cheese, basil, and ⅛ teaspoon each salt and pepper; stir until well mixed. With a vegetable peeler, shave the zucchini and squash lengthwise into thin ribbons.

4. Lay the piecrust flat on a rimmed baking sheet. Spread the cream cheese mixture in an even layer, leaving a 1-inch border. Spread the onion-pepper mixture over the cream cheese; decoratively arrange the zucchini and squash ribbons on top. Fold the border of dough over the vegetable mixture. Brush the remaining teaspoon oil over the zucchini and squash.

5. Bake 30 to 35 minutes, or until browned. Serve the tart warm or at room temperature.

Each serving About 395 calories, 5g protein, 34g carbohydrate, 29g fat (12g saturated), 2g fiber, 520mg sodium.

 Tip Make pretty zucchini and squash ribbons using a vegetable peeler: If the vegetables have a lot of seeds, rotate them 90 degrees each time you hit the seeds and start peeling on a different side. Discard the core of seeds.

MEATBALL MOZZARELLA PIZZA 576

NECTARINE & JALAPEÑO PIZZA 578

QUICK SUMMERY VEGGIE TART 576

PIZZA PRIMAVERA 578

nectarine & jalapeño pizza

(See photo on page 577.)

PREP: 15 MIN / TOTAL: 50 MIN / SERVES 6

- Nonstick cooking spray
- 1 recipe Easy Homemade Pizza Dough (page 569), or 1¼ pounds pizzeria dough
- ⅓ cup prepared pesto or Homemade Pesto (page 65)
- 1 ripe nectarine, pitted and cut into thin wedges
- 3 ounces good-quality blue cheese, crumbled
- 2 small jalapeño chiles, seeded and thinly sliced
- Fresh basil leaves, for garnish

1. Preheat the oven to 425°F. Spray a 13 × 9-inch rimmed baking sheet with nonstick cooking spray.

2. Stretch and roll the pizza dough into a large rectangle; place it on the prepared baking sheet, stretching it to fit into the corners.

3. Dollop the dough with pesto. Top with nectarine slices, blue cheese, and jalapeños. Bake 25 to 30 minutes, or until the bottom of the crust is deep golden brown. Garnish with basil before serving.

Each serving About 345 calories, 10g protein, 44g carbohydrate, 13g fat (4g saturated), 3g fiber, 1,010mg sodium.

spanish ham & cheese galette

(See photo on page 552.)

PREP: 15 MIN / TOTAL: 35 MIN / SERVES 4

- 1 (9-inch) refrigerated ready-to-unroll piecrust
- 8 ounces reduced-fat cream cheese, softened
- ¼ teaspoon smoked paprika
- 2 ounces thinly sliced Serrano ham
- ½ cup shredded Manchego cheese
- 4 cups frisée
- 4 cups pea shoots
- 1 tablespoon sherry vinegar

1. Preheat the oven to 425°F. Unroll the piecrust onto a parchment-lined baking sheet.

2. Stir together the cream cheese and smoked paprika; spread on the crust, leaving a 2-inch rim. Top with the Serrano ham. Fold in the edge of crust; top with cheese. Bake 15 to 25 minutes, or until the bottom is golden brown and cheese has melted. (Cover loosely with foil if the top is browning too quickly.)

3. Toss the frisée and pea shoots with sherry vinegar; serve atop the galette.

Each serving About 455 calories, 14g protein, 29g carbohydrate, 33g fat (17g saturated), 2g fiber, 870mg sodium.

pizza primavera

(See photo on page 577.)

PREP: 15 MIN / TOTAL: 35 MIN / SERVES 4

- 1 bunch asparagus, trimmed and thinly sliced on an angle
- ½ small red onion, very thinly sliced
- 2 tablespoons olive oil
- ½ teaspoon ground black pepper
- 1 recipe Easy Homemade Pizza Dough (page 569) or 1 pound pizzeria dough
- 4 ounces Fontina cheese, shredded

1. Preheat the oven to 475°F oven and place a large baking sheet in it.

2. In a large bowl, toss the asparagus, red onion, oil, and pepper. Stretch and roll out the pizza dough into a 12-inch circle on a large sheet parchment paper. Top the dough with Fontina cheese, then the asparagus mixture.

3. Remove the hot baking sheet from the oven. Carefully slide the parchment with the dough onto the baking sheet. Bake 20 to 25 minutes, or until the bottom and edges are deep golden brown.

Each serving About 425 calories, 16g protein, 52g carbohydrate, 20g fat (6g saturated), 3g fiber, 610mg sodium.

 Tip Preheat a baking sheet in a hot oven. This turns it into a baking stone for a perfect crust.

pulled cran-turkey sandwich

PREP: 15 MIN / TOTAL: 20 MIN / SERVES 4

- ⅔ cup cranberry sauce
- 3 tablespoons ketchup
- 2 tablespoons Worcestershire sauce
- ½ teaspoon smoked paprika
- ⅛ teaspoon salt
- 4 cups shredded cooked turkey meat or rotisserie chicken
- ¼ cup lower-sodium chicken broth
- ½ cup mayonnaise
- 4 hamburger buns, split and toasted
- 1 cup shredded carrots
- Dill pickle slices, for serving

1. In a 2-quart saucepan, whisk the cranberry sauce, ketchup, Worcestershire, smoked paprika, and salt. Cook over medium heat 2 minutes, or until hot.

2. Meanwhile, in a microwave-safe baking dish or bowl, combine the turkey and broth. Cover with vented plastic wrap and microwave on High 2 minutes, or until hot.

3. Add the cranberry mixture to the turkey; stir until well coated. Spread mayonnaise on the buns; top each bun bottom with one-fourth of the turkey mixture. Top the turkey with carrots and pickle slices, and replace the bun tops.

Each serving About 650 calories, 46g protein, 46g carbohydrate, 29g fat (5g saturated), 2g fiber, 835mg sodium.

Tip No cranberry sauce? You can replace it with ½ cup of your favorite preserves and 2 tablespoons lemon juice. Apricot or raspberry jam, apple jelly, and mango chutney all work well.

basic grilled cheese

PREP: 10 MIN / TOTAL: 15 MIN / SERVES 2

- 4 slices white bread
- 1 tablespoon unsalted butter
- 4 ounces Cheddar cheese, thinly sliced

1. Brush one side of each slice of bread with butter. Form sandwiches (buttered side out) with the cheese.

2. Heat a large nonstick skillet over low heat. Cook the sandwiches, covered, until the bread is golden brown and crisp and the cheese has melted, 4 to 5 minutes per side.

Each serving About 410 calories, 18g protein, 24g carbohydrate, 27g fat (16g saturated), 1g fiber, 626mg sodium.

GOOD TO KNOW

GRILLED CHEESE

Do your grilled cheese sandwiches always seem to burn before the cheese melts? Next time, spread a little mayo (instead of butter) on the outside of the sandwich before cooking. Your bread will get beautifully brown and crisp in the time it takes the cheese to become oozy.

provolone veggie party subs

(See photo on page 552.)

PREP: 15 MIN / TOTAL: 55 MIN / SERVES 8

- 1 pound broccoli rabe, trimmed
- 2 medium bell peppers, each seeded and cut into eighths
- 1 small onion, thinly sliced
- 2 tablespoons olive oil
- ¼ teaspoon salt
- ¼ teaspoon ground black pepper
- 3 or 4 long (10- to 12-inch) hero rolls, split
- 12 ounces marinated artichokes, drained and chopped
- 8 ounces sun-dried tomatoes packed in oil, drained and thinly sliced
- ½ cup pickled pepper slices, drained
- 4 ounces thinly sliced sharp provolone cheese

1. Heat a large covered saucepot of salted water to boiling over high heat. Preheat the oven to 425°F.

2. To the boiling water, add the broccoli rabe; cook 6 minutes, or until the stems are tender. Drain; rinse with cold water. Drain well and gently squeeze dry, then coarsely chop; set aside.

3. On a large rimmed baking sheet, toss the bell peppers, onion, oil, salt, and pepper; spread in a single layer. Roast 20 minutes, or until brown.

4. Pull some bread from inside the bottom halves of the rolls; save for another use. Layer the bottoms of the rolls with the artichokes, broccoli rabe, sun-dried tomatoes, onion mixture, pickled peppers, and the cheese.

5. Arrange the sandwiches on foil-lined baking sheets. Bake 8 minutes, or until the cheese has melted; after 3 minutes, toast the tops of the rolls in the oven. Replace the tops; cut the sandwiches into smaller pieces for serving.

Each serving About 330 calories, 12g protein, 33g carbohydrate, 19g fat (5g saturated), 5g fiber, 720mg sodium.

crab salad tartines

PREP: 15 MIN / TOTAL: 15 MIN / SERVES 4

- 1 lemon
- ¼ cup Greek yogurt
- 2 tablespoons mayonnaise
- 1 teaspoon Dijon mustard
- 1 small clove garlic, crushed with a garlic press
- ¼ teaspoon Old Bay seasoning
- ¼ teaspoon salt
- ¼ teaspoon ground black pepper
- 8 ounces lump crabmeat
- 2 stalks celery, finely chopped
- 1 small Granny Smith apple, finely chopped
- 1 tablespoon snipped chives, plus more for garnish
- 4 large slices artisanal bread

1. Into a large bowl, from the lemon, grate 1 teaspoon zest and squeeze 1 tablespoon juice. Add the yogurt, mayonnaise, mustard, garlic, Old Bay seasoning, salt, and pepper; stir to combine.

2. To the same bowl, add the crab, celery, and apple; stir to combine. Fold in the chives. Divide among the bread slices. Garnish with additional chives, if desired.

Each serving About 250 calories, 3g protein, 35g carbohydrate, 13g fat (3g saturated), 2g fiber, 192mg sodium.

tomato-eggplant tartines

(See photo on page 582.)

PREP: 30 MIN / TOTAL: 45 MIN / SERVES 4

- 8 thick slices rustic Italian bread
- 1 large clove garlic, peeled and cut in half
- 4 tablespoons olive oil
- 3 small eggplants, thinly sliced
- Salt
- 1 cup shredded mozzarella cheese (about 4 ounces)
- 4 small tomatoes, thinly sliced
- ¼ cup grated Parmesan cheese
- Fresh basil, for garnish

1. Prepare an outdoor grill for covered grilling over medium heat. Grill the bread 5 minutes, or until well toasted, turning once. Transfer to a large platter. Rub the bread lightly with the garlic; drizzle with 2 tablespoons olive oil.

2. Toss the eggplants with the remaining 2 tablespoons olive oil; sprinkle with ¼ teaspoon salt. Grill 5 minutes; turn the slices over and top with mozzarella. Grill 5 minutes, or until the cheese melts. Top the bread with the tomato slices and ⅛ teaspoon salt. Layer with the eggplant, sprinkle with Parmesan, and garnish with basil.

Each serving About 425 calories, 32g protein, 45g carbohydrate, 22g fat (7g saturated), 6g fiber, 480mg sodium.

dandelion toasts
with chive yogurt

(See photo on page 582.)

PREP: 10 MIN / TOTAL: 15 MIN / SERVES 2

- ½ cup plain Greek yogurt
- 1 tablespoon snipped fresh chives
- Salt
- 2 teaspoons olive oil
- 1 small bunch dandelion or mustard greens, thinly sliced
- 4 radishes, trimmed and quartered
- ½ teaspoon crushed red pepper
- ¼ teaspoon ground cumin
- 4 slices artisanal whole wheat bread, toasted

1. In a small bowl, stir together the yogurt, chives, and a pinch of salt; set aside.

2. In a 12-inch skillet, heat the oil over medium heat. Add the greens, radishes, crushed red pepper, cumin, and ¼ teaspoon salt. Cook 3 minutes, or until the greens have wilted, stirring. Let cool slightly.

3. Spread the yogurt mixture on the bread; top with the sautéed greens.

Each serving About 295 calories, 13g protein, 33g carbohydrate, 13g fat (6g saturated), 7g fiber, 590mg sodium.

HOW TO

PANINIS . . . WITHOUT A PRESS

Make melty-good sandwiches for a crowd with this triple-tested technique: Place **bread slices**, topped with **cheese** and **fillings**, on a greased foil-lined baking sheet and pop it in a preheated 400°F oven until the cheese melts, 6 to 8 minutes. Remove and top with bread slices, another baking sheet, and a heavy oven-safe skillet. Bake 5 minutes more—then say cheese!

DANDELION TOASTS WITH CHIVE YOGURT 581

HAM & CHEESE OVEN SLIDERS 583

ULTIMATE FRIED CHICKEN SANDWICH 583

TOMATO-EGGPLANT TARTINES 581

ultimate fried chicken sandwich

PREP: 15 MIN / TOTAL: 35 MIN / SERVES 4

- 4 small skinless, boneless chicken thighs (about 1½ pounds)
- ¾ cup low-fat buttermilk
- 2 teaspoons garlic powder
- ½ teaspoon ground black pepper
- Salt
- 1 cup all-purpose flour
- 2 cups vegetable oil or canola oil
- 4 potato rolls
- Shredded romaine, sliced tomatoes, sliced pickles, and hot sauce

1. In a large bowl, combine the chicken, buttermilk, garlic powder, pepper, and ½ teaspoon salt. Place the flour in a large shallow dish. Remove 1 piece of chicken from the buttermilk, allowing the excess to drip off; dip in the flour, then back in the buttermilk, then the flour again. Place on a cutting board. Repeat with remaining chicken.

2. In a 12-inch skillet, heat the oil over medium-high heat until hot (325°F on a deep-fry thermometer). Add the chicken to the skillet and reduce the heat to medium. Fry 15 to 20 minutes, or until the chicken is golden brown and cooked (165°F), turning over occasionally for even browning and adjusting the heat as needed. (If the chicken is browning too quickly, reduce the heat to medium-low for a few minutes.) Transfer to a wire rack set over a large piece of foil. Sprinkle with ¼ teaspoon salt. Serve on rolls, topped with romaine, tomato, pickles, and hot sauce.

Each serving About 720 calories, 38g protein, 50g carbohydrate, 40g fat (5g saturated), 2g fiber, 795mg sodium.

VARIATIONS

Five More Chicken Sandwich Toppers

- ¼ cup honey, ½ teaspoon cayenne pepper, and sliced pickles
- ½ cup chipotle mayo, sliced tomato, and shredded cabbage
- ½ cup ranch dressing, 2 to 3 tablespoons hot sauce, ¼ cup crumbled blue cheese, and sliced red onion
- ¼ cup pesto, 4 slices provolone, and ¼ cup chopped pepperoncini
- ¼ cup relish, ¼ cup chopped sweet onion, and butter lettuce

ham & cheese oven sliders

PREP: 15 MIN / TOTAL: 50 MIN / SERVES 10

- 4 tablespoons butter, melted
- 20 to 24 soft slider rolls, split
- 8 ounces thinly sliced sharp Cheddar cheese
- 8 ounces dill pickle slices, drained and patted dry
- 2 plum tomatoes, seeded and very thinly sliced
- 8 ounces thinly sliced smoked ham
- 1 tablespoon dried onion flakes
- 2 teaspoons poppy seeds

1. Preheat the oven to 375°F. Brush the bottom of a 13 × 9-inch baking dish with half the melted butter. Line the dish with the bottoms of the rolls.

2. Onto the rolls in the dish, layer the Cheddar, pickle slices, tomato, and then the ham. Replace the tops of the rolls. Cover the dish with foil; bake 20 minutes.

3. Meanwhile, combine the dried onions and poppy seeds. Uncover the baking dish. Brush the tops of the rolls with the remaining butter. Sprinkle with the dried-onion mixture. Bake 10 to 15 minutes, or until deep golden brown on top.

Each serving About 300 calories, 12g protein, 29g carbohydrate, 15g fat (8g saturated), 1g fiber, 600mg sodium.

 Tip Potato rolls are the perfect texture for these sliders. If you can't find them, soft dinner rolls or brown-and-serve rolls can be used.

healthier club sandwiches

PREP: 25 MIN / TOTAL: 30 MIN / SERVES 4

- 2 tablespoons olive oil
- 2 teaspoons plus 1 tablespoon fresh lemon juice
- 1 teaspoon honey
- 1/8 teaspoon ground black pepper
- 3 carrots, peeled and shredded (1 cup)
- 2 cups alfalfa sprouts
- 1 clove garlic, finely chopped
- 1/2 teaspoon ground cumin
- Pinch of cayenne pepper
- 1 can (15 to 19 ounces) chickpeas, rinsed and drained
- 1 tablespoon water
- 12 slices multigrain bread, lightly toasted
- 1 large ripe tomato (12 ounces), thinly sliced
- 1 bunch watercress, tough stems trimmed

1. In a medium bowl, stir 1 tablespoon oil, 2 teaspoons lemon juice, honey, and pepper until mixed. Add the carrots and alfalfa sprouts; toss until mixed and evenly coated with dressing.

2. In a 2-quart saucepan, heat the remaining 1 tablespoon oil over medium heat. Add the garlic, cumin, and cayenne and cook until very fragrant. Stir in the chickpeas and remove from the heat. Add the remaining 1 tablespoon lemon juice and water; mash the chickpeas to a coarse puree.

3. Spread the chickpea mixture on 8 toast slices. Place the tomato slices and watercress over 4 chickpea-topped toast slices. Top the remaining 4 chickpea-topped slices with the alfalfa-sprout mixture and place on the watercress-topped bread. Cover with 4 remaining toast slices. Cut the sandwiches in half.

Each serving About 380 calories, 14g protein, 57g carbohydrate, 12g fat (2g saturated), 12g fiber, 545mg sodium.

chicken club sandwiches

PREP: 20 MIN / TOTAL: 35 MIN / SERVES 4

- 4 small skinless, boneless chicken breast halves (1 pound)
- 8 slices bacon, each cut crosswise in half
- 1/4 cup flavored mayonnaise (see page 49) or plain mayonnaise
- 12 slices firm white or whole wheat bread
- 2 ripe medium tomatoes (12 ounces), thinly sliced
- 8 small romaine lettuce leaves

1. In a 10-inch skillet, combine the chicken and enough cold water to cover; heat to boiling over high heat. Reduce the heat; cover and simmer until the chicken loses its pink color throughout, 8 to 10 minutes. Drain and cool to room temperature.

2. In a 12-inch skillet, cook the bacon over medium heat until browned. Transfer the bacon to paper towels to drain and cool.

3. Spread about 1 teaspoon mayonnaise on each bread slice; top 4 bread slices with tomato slices and lettuce.

4. Cut the chicken breasts on the diagonal into thin slices. Place 4 more bread slices, mayonnaise side up, on top of the lettuce. Arrange the chicken and bacon on top and cover with the remaining 4 bread slices.

5. To serve, cut each sandwich on the diagonal into quarters. Use frilled toothpicks to hold slices together, if you like.

Each serving About 515 calories, 38g protein, 47g carbohydrate, 18g fat (4g saturated), 3g fiber, 800mg sodium.

 Tip Sub in 2 cups shredded leftover turkey or chicken for the uncooked chicken and skip step 1.

pan bagnat

PREP: 30 MIN / TOTAL: 30 MIN, PLUS CHILLING / SERVES 4

- 1 round loaf (8 inches) country-style bread (12 ounces)
- 1 clove garlic, cut in half
- ¼ cup extra-virgin olive oil
- 2 tablespoons red wine vinegar
- ¼ teaspoon salt
- ⅛ teaspoon ground black pepper
- 3 ripe medium tomatoes (1 pound), sliced
- ½ cup loosely packed small fresh basil leaves
- 1 tablespoon fresh mint leaves
- 1 can (6 ounces) tuna packed in olive oil, drained and flaked
- ⅓ cup Mediterranean olives, such as Gaeta or Kalamata, pitted and chopped
- 2 green onions, chopped
- 1 tablespoon capers, drained
- 1 large hard-cooked egg, peeled and sliced

1. Cut the bread horizontally in half. Remove enough of the soft center from each half to make a 1-inch shell. (Reserve the soft bread for another use.)

2. Rub the inside of the bread halves with the cut side of the garlic. In a cup, stir the oil, vinegar, salt, and pepper until blended. Drizzle about one-fourth of the oil mixture over the garlic-rubbed bread.

3. On the bottom half of the bread, arrange one-third of the tomato slices; drizzle with about half of the remaining oil mixture, then top with half the basil and all the mint.

4. In a small bowl, combine the tuna, olives, green onions, and capers. Spoon the tuna mixture over the herbs; top with the sliced egg. Arrange the remaining tomato slices and remaining basil on top. Drizzle with the remaining oil mixture. Replace the top half of the bread.

5. Wrap the sandwich tightly in foil and refrigerate at least 4 hours or up to 24 hours before serving to blend the flavors and let the juices moisten the bread. To serve, cut into 4 wedges.

Each serving About 395 calories, 16g protein, 31g carbohydrate, 25g fat (3g saturated), 4g fiber, 1,110mg sodium.

 Tip It's best to make this large sandwich a day ahead to allow the juices to soak into the bread.

Ingredient Ideas

french bread

The perfect baguette has a beautiful, crispy crust surrounding a light, chewy inside. Start with a 10-ounce loaf.

PANZANELLA SALAD

Preheat the oven to 375°F. Trim the ends from the loaf and reserve for another use. Cut the remaining bread into ½-inch cubes; place on a baking sheet and toast in the oven 8 minutes. In a bowl, toss **4 medium tomatoes**, cut into ½-inch chunks, with **2 cups ½-inch seedless cucumber chunks** and **⅔ cup Balsamic Vinaigrette** (page 504) or bottled balsamic vinaigrette. Add the bread and **1½ cups torn and loosely packed fresh basil leaves**; toss to coat. **Serves 6.**

SHRIMP & BLACK BEAN PIZZA

Preheat the oven to 450°F. Cut the loaf horizontally in half; cut each half crosswise in half. Place on a baking sheet, cut sides up; spread with **1 cup well-drained mild black-bean-and-corn salsa**. Top with **8 ounces cleaned, cooked, and chopped shrimp**; **¼ cup chopped fresh cilantro**; and **1½ cups shredded pepper Jack cheese**. Bake 6 minutes to heat through. **Serves 4.**

MONTE CRISTO

Cut the loaf on an extreme diagonal into 16 slices, ½ inch thick each. Set aside 8 slices. Spread the remaining slices with **2 tablespoons spicy brown mustard**; top with **8 ounces sliced ham, 4 ounces sliced Swiss cheese**, and the reserved bread slices. In a pie plate and using a fork, mix **2 large eggs, 2 tablespoons water**, and **2 teaspoons spicy brown mustard**. Dip the sandwiches in the egg mixture to coat well. Cook in a 12-inch nonstick skillet over medium heat 12 to 15 minutes, or until golden on both sides. **Serves 4.**

MAKE-AHEAD SUB

Drain **1 jar (12 ounces) Giardiniera** (see page 56); chop. Cut the loaf horizontally in half; spoon ⅔ cup chopped giardiniera on the bottom. Top with **6 ounces each sliced salami and provolone cheese**, and the remaining giardiniera. Replace the top of the bread. Cut the sandwich into quarters and tightly wrap each one in plastic wrap. Refrigerate 1 hour or overnight. **Serves 4.**

chicken gyros

PREP: 20 MIN / TOTAL: 25 MIN / SERVES 4

1 teaspoon olive oil

1½ pounds skinless, boneless chicken breast halves, cut into 1-inch chunks

½ teaspoon dried oregano

Salt

Ground black pepper

¼ cup tahini (sesame seed paste)

¼ cup water

3 tablespoons nonfat plain yogurt

1 tablespoon fresh lemon juice

1 clove garlic, crushed with a garlic press

¼ cup loosely packed fresh cilantro leaves, chopped

¼ teaspoon cayenne pepper

4 (6-inch) pitas

2 cups sliced romaine lettuce

½ English (seedless) cucumber, chopped (1 cup)

1 large tomato (8 ounces), chopped

2 green onions, sliced

1. In a 12-inch nonstick skillet, heat the oil 1 minute over medium heat. Sprinkle the chicken with the oregano, ¼ teaspoon salt, and ¼ teaspoon pepper and toss to coat. Add the chicken to the skillet and cook 5 to 7 minutes, or until the chicken is no longer pink throughout. Transfer the chicken to a plate or bowl; cover with foil to keep warm.

2. Meanwhile, make the tahini sauce: In a small bowl and using a wire whisk, combine the tahini, water, yogurt, lemon juice, and garlic. Stir in the cilantro, cayenne, ¼ teaspoon salt, and ¼ teaspoon pepper. (Makes about ¾ cup tahini sauce.)

3. To serve, cut a piece from the side of each pita (about ¼ pita) and save for another use. Carefully open each pita pocket and fill with one-fourth of the romaine, cucumber, tomato, chicken, and green onions. Top with tahini sauce; serve the gyros with any additional sauce on the side.

Each serving About 360 calories, 34g protein, 41g carbohydrate, 6g fat (1g saturated), 4g fiber, 695mg sodium.

open-faced steak & mushroom sandwiches

PREP: 15 MIN / TOTAL: 45 MIN / SERVES 4

2 tablespoons butter, softened

1 tablespoon plus 1 teaspoon chopped fresh tarragon

Ground black pepper

1 loaf (8 ounces) French bread, cut horizontally in half

3 teaspoons vegetable oil

1 beef flank steak (1¼ pounds)

Salt

1 medium onion, thinly sliced

12 ounces mushrooms, trimmed and sliced

Pinch of dried thyme

⅓ cup dry red wine

1. In a small bowl, stir the butter, 1 tablespoon tarragon, and ⅛ teaspoon pepper until well blended. Spread the tarragon butter evenly on the cut sides of the bread. Cut each half into 4 pieces.

2. In a heavy 12-inch skillet (preferably cast iron), heat 2 teaspoons oil over medium-high heat until very hot. Pat the steak dry with paper towels and sprinkle with ¼ teaspoon salt and ⅛ teaspoon pepper. Add the steak to the skillet and cook 6 to 8 minutes per side for medium-rare, or to the desired doneness. Transfer the steak to a cutting board. Set aside.

3. Add the remaining 1 teaspoon oil and the onion to the skillet; cook over medium heat, stirring frequently, until tender, about 5 minutes. Stir in the mushrooms, thyme, ½ teaspoon salt, and ⅛ teaspoon pepper. Cook over medium-high heat until the mushrooms are tender and the liquid has evaporated, about 8 minutes. Stir in the wine and boil 2 minutes. Remove from the heat. Keep warm.

4. Holding a knife almost parallel to the cutting board, cut the steak into thin slices across the grain; arrange them on the bread. Spoon the mushroom mixture on top; sprinkle with the remaining 1 teaspoon tarragon.

Each serving About 545 calories, 35g protein, 38g carbohydrate, 26g fat (11g saturated), 3g fiber, 945mg sodium.

caramelized onion & goat cheese panini

PREP: 15 MIN / TOTAL: 50 MIN / SERVES 8

- 2 tablespoons olive oil
- 2 sweet onions (1 pound each), thinly sliced
- ½ teaspoon salt
- ¼ teaspoon ground black pepper
- ½ teaspoon chopped fresh thyme leaves
- 8 center slices (½ inch thick each) country-style bread
- 4 ounces soft fresh goat cheese

1. In a 12-inch nonstick skillet, heat the oil over medium heat 1 minute. Stir in the onions, salt, and pepper; cover and cook 15 minutes, or until the onions are very soft, stirring occasionally. Uncover and cook 15 to 25 minutes longer, or until the onions are golden brown, stirring frequently. Stir in the thyme; remove the pan from the heat.

2. Preheat a sandwich press or grill pan over medium heat.

3. Meanwhile, assemble the panini: Place 4 slices bread on a work surface. Spread one-fourth of the goat cheese on each slice and top with one-fourth of the onion mixture. Top with the remaining bread slices.

4. Place 2 panini in the sandwich press and close the top, or arrange them in the grill pan and place a heavy skillet (preferably cast iron) on top, and press down. Cook, turning once, 7 to 8 minutes, or until the bread is toasted and browned on both sides. Repeat with the remaining 2 panini. Cut in halves or quarters to serve.

Each serving About 190 calories, 7g protein, 24g carbohydrate, 8g fat (3g saturated), 3g fiber, 375mg sodium.

VARIATIONS

Red Pepper & Provolone Panini

Prepare the panini as directed, but omit step 1. In step 2, while the grill is preheating, in a small bowl, combine **1 jar (7 ounces) roasted red peppers**, drained and sliced; **¼ cup white wine vinegar**; **1 clove garlic**, crushed with a garlic press; and **¼ teaspoon ground black pepper**. Set aside 10 minutes; drain. In step 3, divide **6 ounces sliced provolone cheese, 4 ounces sliced Genoa salami,** and the marinated red peppers evenly among 4 bread slices; top with the remaining bread. Complete as in step 4.

Mozzarella, Tomato & Basil Panini

Prepare the panini as directed, but omit step 1. In step 3, divide **2 ripe plum tomatoes**, cored and sliced; **6 ounces sliced fresh mozzarella; ½ cup loosely packed fresh basil leaves; ⅛ teaspoon salt;** and **¼ teaspoon ground black pepper** evenly among 4 bread slices. Top with the remaining bread. Complete as in step 4.

perfect tomato sandwiches

PREP: 15 MIN / TOTAL: 15 MIN / SERVES 4

- 1 lemon
- ⅓ cup mayonnaise
- ¼ teaspoon ground coriander
- ¼ teaspoon salt
- ¼ teaspoon coarsely ground black pepper
- 1 large round or oval loaf (1 pound) sourdough or other crusty bread
- 2 pounds ripe tomatoes (3 large), thickly sliced

1. From the lemon, grate ½ teaspoon zest and squeeze 1 teaspoon juice. In a small bowl, combine the mayonnaise, lemon zest and juice, coriander, salt, and pepper until well blended.

2. Cut eight ½-inch-thick slices from the center of the bread. (Reserve the ends for another use.) Toast the bread, if desired. Spread the mayonnaise mixture on each bread slice. Arrange the tomato slices on 4 bread slices; top with the remaining bread slices. To serve, cut each sandwich in half.

Each serving About 390 calories, 9g protein, 52g carbohydrate, 18g total fat (3g saturated), 4g fiber, 740mg sodium.

muffuletta

PREP: 25 MIN / TOTAL: 25 MIN, PLUS COOLING / SERVES 6

- 1¼ cups finely chopped celery with leaves
- 1 cup drained giardiniera (page 56), chopped
- ¾ cup green and black Mediterranean olives, such as Gaeta or Kalamata, pitted and chopped
- ⅓ cup chopped fresh parsley
- 1 clove garlic, minced
- ¼ cup olive oil
- ¼ teaspoon ground black pepper
- 1 round loaf (8 to 10 inches) soft French bread
- 4 ounces thinly sliced smoked ham
- 4 ounces thinly sliced provolone cheese
- 4 ounces thinly sliced Genoa salami

1. In a medium bowl, stir the celery, giardiniera, olives, parsley, garlic, oil, and pepper until well mixed. Cover and refrigerate at least 4 hours or up to overnight to blend the flavors.

2. Cut the bread horizontally in half. Remove enough soft center from each half to make a 1-inch shell. (Reserve the soft bread for another use.) On the bottom half of the bread, spoon half the celery-olive mixture; layer the ham, cheese, and salami on top. Spoon the remaining celery-olive mixture over it. Replace the top half of the bread.

3. Wrap the sandwich in foil and refrigerate at least 4 hours or up to 24 hours to blend the flavors and let the juices soften the bread. To serve, let stand at room temperature about 30 minutes, then cut into 6 wedges.

Each serving About 400 calories, 17g protein, 28g carbohydrate, 24g fat (8g saturated), 3g fiber, 1,615mg sodium.

sriracha meatball hoagies

PREP: 20 MIN / TOTAL: 35 MIN / SERVES 4

- ½ cup seasoned rice vinegar
- ¼ cup water
- ½ medium jicama, peeled and cut into small strips
- ½ cup shredded carrots
- ¼ cup packed fresh mint leaves
- 3 cloves garlic
- 1 medium shallot, chopped
- 1 stalk lemongrass, tough outer layer discarded, sliced
- 1½ tablespoons fish sauce
- 1 pound ground pork
- 1 tablespoon sriracha hot sauce, plus more for serving
- Sriracha Mayo (below)
- 4 (4-inch-long) soft hoagie or sub rolls, split and lightly toasted
- Sprigs fresh cilantro and thinly sliced jalapeño chiles, for garnish

1. In a 2-quart saucepot, heat the vinegar and water to simmering over medium heat. Remove from the heat; add the jicama and carrots. Let the vegetable mixture cool completely.

2. Meanwhile, prepare an outdoor grill for covered grilling over medium heat. In a food processor, pulse the mint, garlic, shallot, lemongrass, and fish sauce until finely chopped, stopping and scraping the sides occasionally. Transfer the mixture to a medium bowl along with the pork and 1 tablespoon sriracha; mix just until well combined. Divide and shape the mixture into sixteen 1¼-inch meatballs. Grill, covered, 10 to 12 minutes, or until cooked through, turning occasionally.

3. While the meatballs cook, spread Sriracha Mayo on the insides of the rolls. Drain the jicama and carrots; add to the rolls along with the meatballs, cilantro, and jalapeños.

SRIRACHA MAYO Stir ⅓ cup mayonnaise with 2 tablespoons sriracha hot sauce until well blended.

Each serving About 575 calories, 28g protein, 38g carbohydrate, 34g fat (10g saturated), 5g fiber, 1,160mg sodium.

philly-style pulled beef sandwiches

PREP: 10 MIN / TOTAL: 8 HR 10 MIN / SERVES 8

1 beef chuck roast
(about 3 to 4 pounds),
cut into quarters

1 teaspoon salt

½ teaspoon ground
black pepper

1 cup beef broth

3 large bell peppers,
each seeded and cut
into 6 wedges

2 medium onions, peeled
and each cut into
6 wedges

8 long sandwich rolls,
split

16 thin slices provolone
or American cheese
(about 8 ounces)

½ cup pickled jalapeño
chile slices, drained
and chopped

1. Rub the beef with the salt and pepper; add to the bowl of a 7- to 8-quart slow cooker along with the broth. Scatter the bell peppers and onions over the beef. Replace the lid; cook on Low 8 hours, or until the beef is very tender.

2. When ready to serve, arrange an oven rack 5 to 6 inches from the broiler's heat source. Preheat the broiler on high. Line a large rimmed baking sheet with foil.

3. Transfer the beef to a large cutting board. When cool enough to handle, shred the meat, removing and discarding any fat. Strain the vegetables from the cooking liquid. If necessary, reheat the meat and vegetables, then divide them among the rolls. Top with the cheese and pickled jalapeño slices. Place the sandwiches on the prepared rimmed baking sheet and broil 2 to 3 minutes, or until the cheese melts.

Each serving About 580 calories, 55g protein, 40g carbohydrate, 21g fat (10g saturated), 4g fiber, 915mg sodium.

SRIRACHA MEATBALL HOAGIES 588

PHILLY-STYLE PULLED BEEF SANDWICHES 589

classic italian hero

PREP: 15 MIN / TOTAL: 15 MIN / SERVES 4

- 1 large loaf (12 ounces) Italian bread
- ¼ cup vinaigrette of your choice (page 504)
- 4 ounces thinly sliced hot and/or sweet capocollo, prosciutto, sopressata, and/or salami
- 4 ounces mozzarella cheese, preferably fresh, thinly sliced
- Shredded romaine lettuce or arugula, peperoncini, basil leaves, roasted red peppers, very thinly sliced red onions, pesto, olivada, and/or sliced ripe tomatoes

1. Cut the bread horizontally in half. Remove enough of the soft center from each half to make a 1-inch shell. (Reserve the soft bread for another use.)

2. Brush the vinaigrette evenly over the cut sides of the bread. Layer the meats and cheese on the bottom half of the bread. Top with additional ingredients of your choice. Replace the top half of the bread. If you're not serving right away, wrap the sandwich in foil and refrigerate up to 4 hours. Cut into 4 pieces.

Each serving About 430 calories, 20g protein, 36g carbohydrate, 23g fat (7g saturated), 3g fiber, 1,225mg sodium.

smoked salmon sandwiches
with dill cream cheese

PREP: 15 MIN / TOTAL: 15 MIN / SERVES 4

- 1 small package (3 ounces) cream cheese, softened
- 1 tablespoon minced shallot
- 1 tablespoon capers, drained and chopped
- 1 tablespoon chopped fresh dill plus additional sprigs
- 1 teaspoon fresh lemon juice
- 4 slices pumpernickel bread
- 6 ounces thinly sliced smoked salmon
- Ground black pepper
- 4 teaspoons salmon caviar (optional)

In a small bowl, stir the cream cheese, shallot, capers, chopped dill, and lemon juice until well blended. Spread evenly on the bread slices and arrange the smoked salmon on top. Sprinkle lightly with pepper. Place 1 teaspoon caviar on each sandwich, if you like, and top with dill sprigs.

Each serving About 210 calories, 12g protein, 17g carbohydrate, 10g fat (5g saturated), 2g fiber, 1,225mg sodium.

cheddar & chutney tea sandwiches

PREP: 15 MIN / TOTAL: 15 MIN / MAKES 16 TEA SANDWICHES

- 3 tablespoons butter, softened
- 3 tablespoons mango chutney, finely chopped
- 8 very thin slices white or whole wheat bread
- 4 ounces Cheddar cheese, shredded (1 cup)

In a small bowl, stir the butter and chutney until well blended. Spread evenly on the bread slices. Sprinkle the Cheddar on the buttered side of 4 bread slices. Top with the remaining bread. Trim the crusts and cut each sandwich into 4 squares or triangles.

Each sandwich About 80 calories, 2g protein, 6g carbohydrate, 5g fat (3g saturated), 0g fiber, 135mg sodium.

watercress & radish tea sandwiches

PREP: 20 MIN / TOTAL: 20 MIN / MAKES 16 TEA SANDWICHES

3 tablespoons butter, softened

8 very thin slices white or whole wheat bread

Pinch of salt

Pinch of ground black pepper

½ bunch watercress, tough stems trimmed

3 radishes, very thinly sliced

Lightly spread the butter on each bread slice and sprinkle with salt and pepper. Arrange only the very tender watercress sprigs on 4 buttered slices, and top with the radishes. Cover with the remaining bread slices. Trim the crusts and cut each sandwich on the diagonal into quarters.

Each sandwich About 40 calories, 1g protein, 4g carbohydrate, 2g fat (1g saturated), 0g fiber, 70mg sodium.

dilled egg tea sandwiches

PREP: 40 MIN / TOTAL: 40 MIN / MAKES 18 TEA SANDWICHES

3 large hard-cooked eggs, peeled and finely shredded

¼ cup mayonnaise

2 tablespoons chopped fresh dill

¼ teaspoon freshly grated lemon zest

¼ teaspoon ground black pepper

12 very thin slices white or whole wheat bread

In a medium bowl, stir the eggs, mayonnaise, dill, lemon zest, and pepper. Spread evenly on 6 bread slices; top with the remaining bread slices. Trim the crusts and cut each sandwich into 3 equal-size rectangles.

Each sandwich About 70 calories, 2g protein, 6g carbohydrate, 4g fat (1g saturated), 0g fiber, 95mg sodium.

cucumber tea sandwiches

PREP: 20 MIN / TOTAL: 20 MIN, PLUS CHILLING / MAKES 32 TEA SANDWICHES

1 English (seedless) cucumber

½ teaspoon salt

5 tablespoons butter, softened

16 very thin slices white or whole wheat bread

32 fresh mint leaves (optional)

1. Cut the cucumber lengthwise in half and remove the soft seed area in the center. Cut the cucumber crosswise into paper-thin slices. In a colander set over a bowl, toss the cucumber slices and salt. Cover and refrigerate 30 minutes, stirring occasionally. Discard the liquid in the bowl. Pat the cucumber slices dry with paper towels.

2. Lightly spread butter on each bread slice. Arrange the cucumber on 8 buttered slices; place 1 mint leaf, if using, in each corner of the bread. Top with the remaining bread slices. Trim the crusts and cut each sandwich on the diagonal into quarters.

Each sandwich About 35 calories, 1g protein, 4g carbohydrate, 2g fat (1g saturated), 0g fiber, 75mg sodium.

Tip Choose seedless (also called English) or Persian cucumbers. Their flesh is denser and will water out less. Whatever cucumber you use, salting the slices and letting them stand for 30 minutes or so before patting dry will help keep your sandwiches from getting soggy.

FINGER SANDWICHES WITH MINTY PEA & PECORINO 593

FINGER SANDWICHES WITH CRAB, MANGO & CUCUMBER 593

FINGER SANDWICHES WITH PIMIENTO CHEESE 593

finger sandwiches
with pimiento cheese

PREP: 20 MIN / TOTAL: 20 MIN / SERVES 8

- ½ pound shredded extra-sharp Cheddar cheese
- 3 ounces cream cheese, softened
- ⅔ cup pimientos, drained well and chopped
- 2 tablespoons mayonnaise
- 2 teaspoons fresh lemon juice
- ⅛ teaspoon cayenne pepper
- 16 slices pumpernickel bread

1. In a medium bowl and using a mixer on medium speed, beat the Cheddar, cream cheese, pimientos, mayonnaise, lemon juice, and cayenne until well combined. Makes about 2 cups.

2. Spread the cheese mixture on 8 slices of pumpernickel bread; cover with the remaining slices. Trim the crusts and cut the sandwiches into squares or, with a 2-inch round cutter, circles.

Each serving About 280 calories, 12g protein, 22g carbohydrate, 17g fat (8g saturated), 3g fiber, 492mg sodium.

finger sandwiches
with minty pea & pecorino

PREP: 20 MIN / TOTAL: 20 MIN / SERVES 8

- 8 ounces frozen (thawed) or fresh (cooked) peas
- ½ cup grated Pecorino cheese
- 3 tablespoons Greek yogurt
- ½ teaspoon salt
- ½ teaspoon ground black pepper
- 2 tablespoons finely chopped fresh mint
- 1 tablespoon snipped fresh chives
- 16 slices soft white bread

1. In a food processor, pulse the peas, Pecorino, yogurt, salt, and pepper until mostly smooth, scraping the bowl occasionally. Fold in the mint and chives. Makes about 1 cup.

2. Spread the mixture on half the bread slices and cover with the remaining bread. Trim the crusts and cut the sandwiches into squares or, with a 2-inch round cutter, circles.

Each serving About 110 calories, 6g protein, 13g carbohydrate, 3g fat (2g saturated), 2g fiber, 332mg sodium.

finger sandwiches
with crab, mango & cucumber

PREP: 20 MIN / TOTAL: 20 MIN / SERVES 8

- 8 ounces lump crabmeat, picked over
- ½ cup very finely chopped ripe mango
- 3 tablespoons finely chopped fresh cilantro
- 2 tablespoons extra-virgin olive oil
- 1 tablespoon fresh lime juice
- ½ teaspoon salt
- ¼ teaspoon ground black pepper
- 2 mini cucumbers, thinly sliced
- 16 slices soft white bread

1. Stir together the crab, mango, cilantro, oil, lime juice, salt, and pepper until just combined. Makes about 2 cups.

2. Place a thin layer of cucumber slices on half the bread; top with crab salad, then cover with the remaining bread. Trim the crusts and cut the sandwiches into squares or, with a 2-inch round cutter, circles.

Each serving About 110 calories, 7g protein, 11g carbohydrate, 4g fat (1g saturated), 1g fiber, 346mg sodium.

HOW TO

ASSEMBLE FINGER SANDWICHES

Tea sandwiches are delicate but can easily be made ahead. If you are making a lot of sandwiches, use the assembly-line technique: Line up the bread slices in rows, apply the spreads, top with the fillings, and cover with the remaining bread. To store: Line a rimmed baking pan with damp paper towels. Place sandwiches in the pan and cover with additional damp paper towels to keep the bread from drying out. Cover the pan tightly with plastic wrap and refrigerate up to four hours.

i love you more than cookies.

ill be y... BEST year yet!

15

cookies

& BARS

Do you remember the first cookie you baked? Chocolate chip? Oatmeal raisin? Gingersnap? For many of us, cookies were our first baking experience. Simple enough for an after-school project and easy to share, cookies make friends. Their one-bowl prep, short bake, and minimal cooling time appeal to the impatient child in all of us. Whether your go-to cookie is a luscious Lemon Bar (page 602), buttery Cranberry Shortbread (page 613), or a Razzy-Jammy Thumbprint (page 612), this collection of delicious new and classic recipes and tips to help at every step of the way guarantees success for bakers of all ages. So if you need an impromptu treat, a bake-sale home run, or a teatime fancy, we've got cookies for you!

RAZZY-JAMMY THUMBPRINTS 612

SALTED CARAMEL BARK 617

COCOA STARS 616

GINGERBREAD WANDS 609

What's Your Cookie Style?

ONE AND DONE Bar cookies couldn't be easier. Mix up a batch of dough, spread it in a pan, then bake, cool, and cut.

KID-FRIENDLY Drop spoonfuls of soft dough onto cookie sheets. Use a trigger-handled scoop for even-size cookies.

CRAFTY Molded cookies are made from a stiff dough that is formed into balls, crescents, pretzels, or other shapes, or are baked in individual molds.

TRADITIONALIST Pressed cookies are made from a stiff dough that is squeezed through a cookie press or pastry bag.

MAÑANA MAMMA Refrigerator cookies (also called icebox cookies) begin with a dough that is shaped into a log, chilled a few hours or overnight, then sliced and baked.

ARTISTE Rolled cookies are made from a stiff dough that is rolled out into a thin layer, then cut into shapes, baked, and often decorated.

Cookie Sheet Savvy

- Heavy-gauge light-colored metal cookie sheets that have a dull finish and only one or two turned up sides (not a rim) turn out the most evenly baked cookies; aluminum is ideal. Dark cookie sheets can overbrown the bottoms of cookies. If your cookie sheets are dark and discolored, line them with foil, or better still, purchase new ones. If you have an oven that browns unevenly, double-thick insulated cookie sheets are a good investment.

- Your cookie sheets should be at least 2 inches smaller in length and width than your oven so that the hot air can circulate freely around the sheet(s).

- Grease cookie sheets only when a recipe directs. Vegetable shortening is better than butter for greasing, because butter will brown and scorch as it melts in the oven. Nonstick cookie sheets, parchment paper, and silicone nonstick baking liners are good alternatives to greasing and flouring.

- For an even coat when greasing is required, use a crumpled piece of wax paper or paper towel to apply the grease. To flour a cookie sheet, sprinkle the greased sheet evenly with a little flour, tilt to coat the sheet, then tap off the excess. For easy cleanup, line cookie sheets with parchment or foil (dull side up) or silicone nonstick baking liners.

- Never place cookie dough on a hot cookie sheet; it will melt the dough before it has a chance to set. Always let cookie sheets cool between batches. If the recipe calls for greased sheets, regrease for each batch.

Baking Success

FOR THE BEST FLAVOR AND TEXTURE, use butter. If you must use margarine, make sure it contains about 80 percent fat. Spreads (diet, whipped, liquid, or soft) have a high water content, which produces tough cookies that lack flavor.

FOR THE TENDEREST COOKIES, once the flour has been added, mix the dough just until blended. Overmixing can make cookies tough.

FOR EVENLY SIZED COOKIES, use a measuring spoon or trigger-handled cookie scoop to measure equal portions of dough that will bake in the same amount of time.

FOR DROP COOKIES, place spoonfuls of dough 2 inches apart unless the recipe directs otherwise.

FOR ROLLED COOKIES, dust the work surface lightly and evenly with flour before rolling out the dough. Rub the rolling pin well with flour to keep it from sticking to the dough, or lightly dust the top of the dough with flour.

KEEP DOUGH COOL. When rolling out chilled dough, roll out one portion at a time; keep the remaining dough covered and in the refrigerator.

IF A CHILLED DOUGH CRACKS when rolling, let it stand at room temperature to soften slightly, then try again.

FOR EVENLY BAKED COOKIES, bake one sheet of cookies at a time in the center of the oven. If you want to bake two sheets at a time, position the racks in the upper and lower thirds of the oven. Then, halfway through baking, rotate the cookie sheets between the upper and lower oven racks and front to back.

USE A TIMER. Bake cookies for the minimum suggested baking time, then check for doneness. If not done, watch them to avoid overbaking.

COOL COOKIES FOR 2 MINUTES on the cookie sheet to firm slightly (unless a recipe directs otherwise). Then transfer the cookies to wire racks to cool completely; hot cookies are too soft to be moved immediately to racks. Cool bar cookies completely in the pan before cutting.

SPRITZ COOKIES 610

Storing Cookies

TO STORE soft and crisp cookies, keep them in separate containers with tight-fitting covers. Crisp cookies that soften can be recrisped in a 300°F oven for three to five minutes. Soft cookies can be kept soft by adding a piece of apple or bread to the container; change it every other day or so. (This technique also works for soft cookies that have hardened.) Store bar cookies in the pan they were baked in, tightly covered with foil or plastic wrap.

TO FREEZE BAKED COOKIES, cool them thoroughly. Place them in airtight containers, cushioned with crumpled waxed paper, if necessary. If the cookies have been decorated, freeze them until hard in a single layer on a cookie sheet, then pack for storage, separating the layers with waxed paper. To thaw, unwrap the cookies and let stand for about ten minutes at room temperature.

TO FREEZE UNBAKED COOKIE DOUGH, wrap tightly in heavy-duty foil and store in a container. Drop cookies can be scooped and frozen on a cookie sheet until hard, then transferred to a resealable freezer-weight plastic bag and frozen. For refrigerator cookies, wrap the logs of dough in heavy-duty foil. Freeze for up to three months; thaw in the refrigerator. Remember to label and date each package.

GOOD TO KNOW

CHOCOLATE

Chocolate bars are a mixture of chocolate liquor, cocoa butter, sugar, and possible other fats and flavorings. Many chocolate bars are labeled by percentage of cacao (the cocoa butter plus chocolate liquor) and the closer the percentage to 100, the richer the chocolate flavor.

Semisweet, bittersweet, and unsweetened chocolate and cocoa powder are the most common types used in baking. White chocolate is used more often in frostings, fillings, and candies. Here are a few other tips to keep in mind when baking with chocolate.

ALL CHOCOLATE HAS TWO ENEMIES	Those enemies are water and high heat. If a single drop of water gets into chocolate while it's melting, the chocolate can "seize" (form a dull, thick paste). Chocolate melted over heat that is too high clumps and becomes grainy, so melt it over low heat.
TO CHOP CHOCOLATE	Use a sharp, heavy knife and a dry, clean cutting board. Chop into ¼-inch pieces before melting.
TO MELT CHOCOLATE	Place chopped pieces in a microwave-safe bowl and microwave at 50 percent power, stirring at 30-second intervals. Chocolate will still hold its shape when partially melted, so be careful not to overcook. Or melt it in a heavy-bottomed saucepan; stir frequently over low heat until melted, watching carefully to avoid scorching.
TO STORE CHOCOLATE AND COCOA POWDER	Keep it in a cool, dry place. "Blooms," or pale streaks that may appear, will not affect the chocolate's performance or taste.

fudgy brownies

PREP: 10 MIN / TOTAL: 40 MIN / MAKES 24

- 1¼ cups all-purpose flour
- ½ teaspoon salt
- ¾ cup salted butter
- 4 squares (4 ounces) unsweetened chocolate, chopped
- 4 squares (4 ounces) semisweet chocolate, chopped
- 2 cups sugar
- 1 tablespoon vanilla extract
- 5 large eggs, beaten

1. Preheat the oven to 350°F. Grease a 13 × 9-inch baking pan. In a small bowl and using a wire whisk, stir the flour and salt.

2. In a heavy 4-quart saucepan, melt the butter and unsweetened and semisweet chocolates over low heat, stirring frequently, until smooth. Remove from the heat. With a wooden spoon, stir in the sugar and vanilla. Add the eggs; stir until well mixed. Stir the flour mixture into the chocolate mixture just until blended. Spread the batter evenly in the prepared pan.

3. Bake until a toothpick inserted 1 inch from the edge comes out clean, about 30 minutes. Cool completely in the pan on a wire rack. When cool, cut lengthwise into 4 strips, then cut each strip crosswise into 6 pieces.

Each brownie About 205 calories, 3g protein, 26g carbohydrate, 11g fat (6g saturated), 1g fiber, 120mg sodium.

VARIATION

Praline-Iced Brownies

Prepare the brownies as directed; cool. In a 2-quart saucepan, heat **5 tablespoons salted butter** and **⅓ cup packed brown sugar** over medium-low heat until the mixture has melted and bubbles, about 5 minutes. Remove from the heat. With a wire whisk, beat in **3 tablespoons bourbon** or **1 tablespoon vanilla extract** plus **2 tablespoons water**; stir in **2 cups confectioners' sugar** until smooth. With a small metal spatula, spread the topping over room-temperature brownies; sprinkle ½ **cup pecans**, toasted and coarsely chopped, evenly over the topping. Cut the brownies lengthwise into 8 strips, then cut each strip crosswise into 8 pieces. **Makes 64 brownies.**

cocoa brownies

PREP: 10 MIN / TOTAL: 35 MIN / MAKES 16

- ½ cup all-purpose flour
- ½ cup unsweetened cocoa
- ¼ teaspoon baking powder
- ¼ teaspoon salt
- ½ cup salted butter
- 1 cup sugar
- 2 large eggs
- 1 teaspoon vanilla extract
- 1 cup walnuts (4 ounces), coarsely chopped (optional)

1. Preheat the oven to 350°F. Grease a 9-inch square baking pan. In a small bowl and using a wire whisk, stir the flour, cocoa, baking powder, and salt.

2. In a 3-quart saucepan, melt the butter over low heat. Remove from the heat and stir in the sugar. Stir in the eggs, one at a time, until well blended; add the vanilla. Stir the flour mixture into the sugar mixture until blended. Stir in the walnuts, if using. Spread the batter evenly in the prepared pan.

3. Bake until a toothpick inserted 2 inches from the center comes out almost clean, about 25 minutes. Cool completely in the pan on a wire rack.

4. When cool, cut into 4 strips, then cut each strip crosswise into 4 pieces.

Each brownie About 130 calories, 2g protein, 17g carbohydrate, 7g fat (4g saturated), 2g fiber, 110mg sodium.

INGREDIENT SPOTLIGHT

Unsweetened **cocoa** powder provides the rich chocolate flavor in many desserts. There are two kinds: natural and Dutch-process. In baking, they are not interchangeable, as they react differently when mixed with baking soda or baking powder. Natural cocoa powder, the most common cocoa in American kitchens, is rich and full flavored. Unless stated otherwise, it is the one we used for the recipes in this book. Dutch-process cocoa powder, sometimes called European-style, has been treated with an alkali to mellow the cocoa's natural bitterness and darken its color.

blondies

PREP: 10 MIN / TOTAL: 40 MIN / MAKES 24

1 cup all-purpose flour

2 teaspoons baking powder

1 teaspoon salt

6 tablespoons salted butter

1¾ cups packed light brown sugar

2 teaspoons vanilla extract

2 large eggs

1½ cups pecans (6 ounces), coarsely chopped

1. Preheat the oven to 350°F. Grease a 13 × 9-inch baking pan. In a small bowl and using a wire whisk, stir the flour, baking powder, and salt.

2. In a 3-quart saucepan, melt the butter over low heat. Remove from the heat. With a wooden spoon, stir in the brown sugar and vanilla; add the eggs, stirring until well blended. Stir the flour mixture into the sugar mixture just until blended. Stir in the pecans. Spread the batter evenly in the prepared pan.

3. Bake until a toothpick inserted 2 inches from the edge of the pan comes out clean, about 30 minutes. Do not overbake; blondies will firm as they cool. Cool completely in the pan on a wire rack.

4. When cool, cut lengthwise into 4 strips, then cut each strip crosswise into 6 pieces.

Each blondie About 160 calories, 2g protein, 21g carbohydrate, 8g fat (2g saturated), 1g fiber, 180mg sodium.

VARIATIONS

Coconut Blondies

Prepare as directed, stirring in ¾ cup flaked sweetened coconut with pecans.

Chocolate Chip Blondies

Prepare as directed through step 2; let the batter stand 15 minutes. Stir in 1 package (6 ounces) semisweet chocolate chips. Proceed as directed.

flourless caramel-almond brownies

PREP: 25 MIN / TOTAL: 1 HR 10 MIN, PLUS COOLING / MAKES 64

6 ounces bittersweet chocolate (60% to 70% cacao), chopped

2 ounces unsweetened chocolate, chopped

6 tablespoons salted butter

Salt

1½ cups sugar

1 teaspoon vanilla extract

2 large eggs

3 tablespoons cornstarch

1 tablespoon unsweetened cocoa

1½ cups roasted salted almonds, chopped

½ cups water

1 tablespoon light corn syrup

⅓ cup heavy cream, warmed

1. Preheat the oven to 350°F. Grease an 8-inch square baking pan. Line with foil; grease the foil.

2. In a 4-quart saucepan, combine both chocolates, 4 tablespoons butter, and ¼ teaspoon salt. Melt over medium-low heat 4 minutes, or until smooth, stirring. Remove from the heat; stir in ¾ cup sugar and the vanilla. Stir in the eggs, 1 at a time, until well blended.

3. Into the same pan, sift the cornstarch and cocoa; fold to incorporate. Stir the batter vigorously for at least 1 minute, or until the batter thickens slightly and begins to pull away from the sides of the pan. Fold in 1 cup chopped nuts. Spread the batter evenly into the prepared baking pan. Bake 25 to 27 minutes, or until a toothpick inserted 2 inches from the edge comes out almost clean. Cool in the pan on a wire rack.

4. While the brownie cools, in a 4-quart saucepan, stir the remaining ¾ cup sugar, the water, corn syrup, and ¼ teaspoon salt. Cook over medium-high heat 9 to 12 minutes, or until the sugar dissolves and the mixture is amber colored, swirling it occasionally to get an even color. Working quickly, remove the pan from the heat and add the cream. Once the bubbling begins to subside, stir in the remaining 2 tablespoons butter until incorporated. Stir in the remaining chopped nuts.

5. Pour the caramel over the cooled brownie, tilting the pan to spread it evenly. Let stand at least 2 hours or until the caramel has set. Cut into 1-inch squares. Store the brownies in an airtight container, layered with waxed paper, at room temperature up to 2 days.

Each brownie About 75 calories, 1g protein, 8g carbohydrate, 5g fat (2g saturated), 1g fiber, 35mg sodium.

caramel pecan bars

PREP: 1 HR / **TOTAL:** 1 HR 25 MIN, PLUS COOLING AND CHILLING / **MAKES 48**

COOKIE CRUST
¾ cup salted butter, at room temperature

¾ cup confectioners' sugar

1½ teaspoons vanilla extract

2¼ cups all-purpose flour

CARAMEL-PECAN FILLING
1 cup packed light or dark brown sugar

½ cup honey

½ cup salted butter, cut into pieces

⅓ cup granulated sugar

¼ cup heavy or whipping cream

2 teaspoons vanilla extract

1½ cups pecans (6 ounces), toasted and coarsely chopped

TOPPING
2 ounces semisweet chocolate, melted

1. Preheat oven to 350°F. Grease 13 × 9-inch metal baking pan; line pan with foil, extending the foil over the rim.

2. Prepare the crust: In a large bowl and using a mixer at medium speed, beat the butter, confectioners' sugar, and vanilla until creamy, about 2 minutes. Reduce the speed to low and gradually beat in the flour until evenly moistened (the mixture will resemble fine crumbs). With your hands, firmly pat the crumbs evenly onto the bottom of the prepared pan.

3. Bake until lightly browned, 25 to 30 minutes. Transfer the pan to a wire rack to cool.

4. Prepare the filling: In a 2-quart saucepan, combine the brown sugar, honey, butter, granulated sugar, cream, and vanilla; heat to a full rolling boil over high heat, stirring frequently. Reduce the heat to medium-high; set a candy thermometer in place and continue cooking, without stirring, until the temperature reaches 248°F or firm-ball stage (when a small amount of the mixture dropped into very cold water forms a firm ball that does not flatten upon removal from the water).

5. Sprinkle the pecans evenly over the warm crust. Pour the hot caramel over the nuts. Cool the pan on a wire rack 1 hour, or until the caramel is room temperature and has formed a skin on top.

6. With a fork, drizzle the melted chocolate over the caramel layer. Cover and refrigerate until cold and chocolate has set, at least 1 hour.

7. When cold, remove the bar from the pan by lifting the edges of the foil; transfer it to a cutting board. Cut lengthwise into 6 strips, then cut each strip crosswise into 8 bars. Let stand at room temperature to soften slightly before serving.

Each bar About 140 calories, 1g protein, 16g carbohydrate, 8g fat (4g saturated), 1g fiber, 55mg sodium.

lemon bars

PREP: 25 MIN / **TOTAL:** 1 HR 5 MIN, PLUS COOLING / **MAKES 32**

¾ cup salted butter, at room temperature

2¼ cups all-purpose flour

⅔ cup plus 1 tablespoon confectioners' sugar

3 to 4 large lemons

6 large eggs

2 cups granulated sugar

1 teaspoon baking powder

¾ teaspoon salt

1. Preheat the oven to 350°F. Grease a 13 × 9-inch baking pan. Line the pan with foil, extending the foil over the rim; lightly grease the foil.

2. In a food processor with the knife blade attached, pulse the butter, 2 cups flour, and ⅔ cup confectioners' sugar until the mixture is moist but crumbly; the dough should hold together when pressed between two fingers. Sprinkle the mixture evenly into the prepared pan. Bake until lightly browned, 20 to 25 minutes.

3. Meanwhile, grate 2½ teaspoons zest from the lemons and squeeze ⅔ cup juice. In a large bowl and using a wire whisk, beat the eggs. Add the lemon peel and juice, granulated sugar, baking powder, salt, and the remaining ¼ cup flour; whisk until well blended.

4. After 20 to 25 minutes, remove the crust from the oven. Whisk filling again and pour over hot crust. Bake until the filling is just set and golden around edges, 18 to 22 minutes. Transfer the pan to a wire rack. Sift the remaining 1 tablespoon confectioners' sugar over filling. Cool the bar completely in the pan on a wire rack.

5. When cool, remove the bar from the pan by lifting the edges of the foil and transfer it to a cutting board. If you like, trim any dark brown edges. Cut lengthwise into 4 strips, then cut each strip crosswise into 8 pieces.

Each bar About 145 calories, 2g protein, 22g carbohydrate, 6g fat (3g saturated), 0g fiber, 125mg sodium.

coconut joy bars

(See photo on page 615.)

PREP: 30 MIN / TOTAL: 1 HR 15 MIN, PLUS COOLING AND CHILLING / MAKES 48

- 1 bag (14 ounces) sweetened flaked coconut
- 1½ cups all-purpose flour
- ⅓ cup confectioners' sugar
- Salt
- 1 cup salted butter, at room temperature
- ¾ cup granulated sugar
- ⅓ cup cornstarch
- 1 can (14 ounces) coconut milk, shaken
- 8 ounces bittersweet chocolate, chopped

1. Preheat the oven to 350°F.

2. In a 13 × 9-inch metal baking pan, spread 1 cup coconut. Bake 6 to 8 minutes, or until golden, stirring once. Cool coconut and then transfer to a bowl. Set aside. Wipe out the pan, line with foil; lightly grease the foil.

3. In a food processor, finely grind the toasted coconut. Add the flour, confectioners' sugar, and ⅛ teaspoon salt; pulse to blend. Add the butter. Pulse until blended.

4. With a spatula, spread the dough into an even layer in the prepared pan. Bake 30 minutes, or until golden brown. Cool in the pan on a wire rack.

5. In a 2-quart saucepan, whisk the granulated sugar, cornstarch, and ⅛ teaspoon salt. Whisk in the coconut milk until smooth. Heat to simmering over medium-high heat, whisking frequently. Simmer 2 minutes, or until it's very thick, whisking frequently. Fold in the untoasted coconut. Cool slightly. Spread in an even layer over the cooled crust.

6. Place the chocolate in a medium microwave-safe bowl. Microwave on High for 2 minutes in 30-second intervals until the chocolate is almost completely melted, stirring between intervals. Stir until smooth. Pour and spread the chocolate over the coconut filling. Refrigerate until the chocolate is set. Cut into 1 × 2-inch rectangles. Store the bars in an airtight container in the refrigerator up to 3 days.

Each bar About 145 calories, 2g protein, 14g carbohydrate, 10g fat (8g saturated), 1g fiber, 70mg sodium.

honey granola bars

PREP: 15 MIN / TOTAL: 45 MIN / MAKES 16

- 2 cups old-fashioned oats, uncooked
- 1 cup all-purpose flour
- ¾ cup packed light brown sugar
- ¾ cup dark seedless raisins
- ½ cup toasted wheat germ
- ¾ teaspoon ground cinnamon
- ¾ teaspoon salt
- ½ cup vegetable oil
- ½ cup honey
- 1 large egg
- 2 teaspoons vanilla extract

1. Preheat the oven to 350°F and grease a 13 × 9-inch baking pan.

2. In a large bowl and using a wooden spoon, stir the oats, flour, brown sugar, raisins, wheat germ, cinnamon, and salt until blended. Stir in the oil, honey, egg, and vanilla until well combined. With wet hands, pat the oat mixture evenly onto the bottom of the prepared pan.

3. Bake until light golden around edges, 30 to 35 minutes. Cool completely in the pan on a wire rack.

4. When cool, cut lengthwise into 4 strips, then cut each strip crosswise into 4 pieces.

Each bar About 240 calories, 4g protein, 39g carbohydrate, 9g fat (1g saturated), 2g fiber, 120mg sodium.

HOW TO

LINE A PAN WITH FOIL

Invert the baking pan so it is bottom side up. Mold a length of foil, shiny side facing out, over the pan, pressing the foil firmly to set the shape. Carefully lift up the foil. Turn the pan right side up. Lower the foil "pan" into the baking pan; smooth it out to create a tight fit.

chewy oatmeal chocolate cherry cookies

PREP: 35 MIN / TOTAL: 1 HR / MAKES 54

1½ cups all-purpose flour

2 teaspoons baking soda

½ teaspoon salt

¾ cup granulated sugar

¾ cup packed brown sugar

¾ cup salted butter, at room temperature

2 large eggs

2 teaspoons vanilla extract

3 cups old-fashioned oats, uncooked

1 cup dried tart cherries or raisins

1 package (6 ounces) semisweet chocolate chips (1 cup)

1. Preheat the oven to 350°F. Grease a large baking sheet. In a small bowl and using a wire whisk, stir the flour, baking soda, and salt.

2. In a large bowl and using a mixer at medium speed, beat both sugars and the butter until creamy, occasionally scraping the bowl with a rubber spatula. Beat in the eggs, one at a time, beating well after each addition. Beat in the vanilla. Reduce the speed to low; gradually beat in the flour mixture just until blended, occasionally scraping the bowl. With a wooden spoon, stir in the oats, dried cherries, and chocolate chips.

3. Drop the dough by rounded tablespoons, 2 inches apart, onto the prepared baking sheet. Bake until the tops are golden, 12 to 14 minutes. With a wide spatula, transfer the cookies to wire racks to cool. Repeat with remaining dough.

Each cookie About 100 calories, 1g protein, 15g carbohydrate, 4g fat (2g saturated), 1g fiber, 100mg sodium.

chocolate wows

PREP: 20 MIN / TOTAL: 55 MIN / MAKES 48

⅓ cup all-purpose flour

¼ cup unsweetened cocoa

½ teaspoon baking powder

¼ teaspoon salt

6 squares (6 ounces) semisweet chocolate, chopped

½ cup salted butter

2 large eggs

¾ cup sugar

1½ teaspoons vanilla extract

2 cups pecans (8 ounces), toasted and chopped

1 package (6 ounces) semisweet chocolate chips (1 cup)

1. Preheat the oven to 325°F. Grease 2 large baking sheets and line with parchment. In a small bowl and using a wire whisk, stir the flour, cocoa, baking powder, and salt.

2. In a heavy 2-quart saucepan, melt the chopped chocolate and butter over low heat, stirring frequently, until smooth. Remove from the heat and cool.

3. In a large bowl and using a mixer at medium speed, beat the eggs and sugar until light, about 2 minutes, frequently scraping the bowl with a rubber spatula. Reduce the mixer speed to low. Add the cooled chocolate mixture, flour mixture, and vanilla; beat just until blended. Increase the mixer speed to medium; beat 2 minutes. Fold in the pecans and chocolate chips.

4. Drop the batter by rounded teaspoons, 2 inches apart, on baking sheets. With a small metal spatula, spread the batter into 2-inch rounds. Bake until the tops are shiny and cracked, about 13 minutes, rotating the baking sheets between upper and lower oven racks halfway through baking. Cool 10 minutes on the baking sheet. With a wide spatula, transfer the cookies to wire racks to cool completely. Repeat with remaining batter.

Each cookie About 100 calories, 1g protein, 9g carbohydrate, 7g fat (3g saturated), 1g fiber, 45mg sodium.

TESTING NOTE The wow of these fudgy cookies is the trifecta of their fudgy texture, the intense triple-chocolate flavor, and the added crunch of the toasted pecans. They are best eaten within a day of baking. They can be wrapped well and frozen for up to 1 month.

chewy chocolate chip cookies

PREP: 25 MIN / TOTAL: 45 MIN, PLUS CHILLING / MAKES 16

- 3⅓ cups all-purpose flour
- ⅓ cup cornstarch
- 1½ teaspoon baking powder
- 1¼ teaspoon baking soda
- 1¼ teaspoon salt
- 1¼ cups unsalted butter, room temperature
- 1½ cups firmly packed dark brown sugar
- ¾ cup granulated sugar
- 2 large eggs
- 1 tablespoon vanilla extract
- 1 pound bittersweet chocolate chunks
- 2 cups walnuts or pecans, toasted (optional)

1. Combine the flour, cornstarch, baking powder, baking soda, and salt in a bowl. Set aside.

2. Using a stand mixer fitted with the paddle attachment, beat the butter and sugars together until very light and fluffy, about 5 minutes. Add the eggs, one at a time, mixing well after each addition. Stir in the vanilla. Reduce the mixer speed to low, add the dry ingredients, and mix until just combined, 5 to 10 seconds. Drop the chocolate pieces in and incorporate them by hand without breaking them. Transfer the dough to a large resealable plastic bag and refrigerate for at least 24 and up to 72 hours.

3. When you're ready to bake, preheat the oven to 350° F. Line a baking sheet with parchment paper. Set aside.

4. Scoop six 4-ounce portions (a scant ½ cup) of chilled dough onto the lined baking sheet, leaving 3 inches between cookies. Bake until golden brown at the edges but still very soft in center (the cookies will look very underbaked), 18 (for chewy) to 20 minutes. Transfer the baking sheet to a wire rack for 5 minutes. For crisper edges, transfer the cookies from the sheet to cool on a wire rack. For the chewiest cookies, cool completely on the baking sheet. Repeat, or store the remaining dough.

Each cookie About 500 calories, 7g protein, 66g carbohydrate, 27g fat (16g saturated), 4g fiber, 349mg sodium.

TESTING NOTE For longer storage, shape the cookies as described and freeze them flat in a resealable plastic bag for up to a month. Thaw 20 minutes before baking.

crispy chocolate chip cookies

PREP: 20 MIN / TOTAL: 55 MIN / MAKES 72

- 1⅔ cups all-purpose flour
- 1 teaspoon baking soda
- 1 teaspoon salt
- 1 cup unsalted butter
- 1 cup firmly packed dark brown sugar
- ½ cup granulated sugar
- 1 tablespoon water
- 2 teaspoons vanilla extract
- 1 large egg
- 2 cups semisweet chocolate chips (about 12 ounces)

1. In a large bowl, stir together the flour, baking soda, and salt.

2. In the bowl of a stand mixer fitted with a paddle attachment, beat the butter and sugars until very light and fluffy, about 5 minutes. Beat in the water and vanilla. Add the egg and beat until combined. Stir in the flour mixture. Fold in the chocolate chips. Transfer the dough to a resealable plastic bag and refrigerate for 24 to 36 hours; the dough can be refrigerated for up to 72 hours.

3. Preheat the oven to 350°F. Line a baking sheet with parchment paper. Using a tablespoon-size scoop, place chilled dough (leveled) 2 inches apart on the prepared baking sheet.

4. Bake 12 minutes, or until the edges and centers are brown. Cool 2 minutes on the baking sheet; transfer the cookies to a wire rack to cool.

Each cookie About 75 calories, 1g protein, 10g carbohydrate, 4g fat (2g saturated), 0g fiber, 53mg sodium.

TESTING NOTE For longer storage, shape the cookies as described and freeze flat in a resealable bag for up to a month. Thaw 10 minutes before baking.

butterscotch fingers

PREP: 30 MIN / TOTAL: 1 HR 40 MIN / MAKES 96

- 2⅓ cups all-purpose flour
- 1½ teaspoons baking powder
- ½ teaspoon salt
- 1 cup salted butter, at room temperature
- 1 cup packed dark brown sugar
- 1 large egg
- 1 teaspoon vanilla extract
- ¾ cup pecans, chopped

1. In a medium bowl and using a wire whisk, stir the flour, baking powder, and salt.

2. In a large bowl and using a mixer at medium speed, beat the butter and sugar until creamy, occasionally scraping down the bowl with a rubber spatula. Beat in the egg and vanilla. Reduce the speed to low; beat in the flour mixture just until blended, occasionally scraping down the bowl. With a wooden spoon, stir in the pecans.

3. Shape the dough into a 12 × 3¾ × 1-inch brick. Wrap the brick in plastic wrap and refrigerate until firm enough to slice, at least 6 hours or overnight, or freeze about 2 hours.

4. Preheat the oven to 350°F. Grease a large baking sheet.

5. With a sharp knife, cut the brick crosswise into ⅛-inch-thick slices. Place the slices, 1 inch apart, on the prepared baking sheet. Bake until the edges are lightly browned, 12 to 14 minutes. Transfer the cookies to a wire rack to cool.

6. Repeat with remaining dough.

Each cookie About 65 calories, 1g protein, 7g carbohydrate, 4g fat (2g saturated), 0g fiber, 55mg sodium.

jumbo gingersnaps

PREP: 20 MIN / TOTAL: 35 MIN / MAKES 10 LARGE OR 24 SMALL COOKIES

- 2 cups all-purpose flour
- 2 teaspoons ground ginger
- 1 teaspoon baking soda
- ½ teaspoon ground cinnamon
- ½ teaspoon salt
- ¼ teaspoon ground black pepper (optional)
- ¾ cup vegetable shortening
- ½ cup plus 2 tablespoons sugar
- 1 large egg
- ½ cup dark molasses

1. Preheat the oven to 350°F. In a medium bowl and using a wire whisk, stir the flour, ginger, baking soda, cinnamon, salt, and pepper, if using.

2. In a large bowl and using a mixer at medium speed, beat the shortening and ½ cup sugar until light and fluffy. Beat in the egg until blended, then beat in the molasses. Reduce the speed to low; beat in the flour mixture just until blended.

3. Place the remaining 2 tablespoons sugar on waxed paper. Roll ¼ cup of dough into a ball; roll in the sugar to coat it evenly. Repeat with the remaining dough to make 10 balls total. Place the balls, 3 inches apart, on an ungreased large baking sheet. For small cookies, roll slightly rounded tablespoons of dough into balls and place them, 2 inches apart, on 2 ungreased baking sheets.

4. Bake the cookies until set, about 15 minutes for large cookies or 9 to 11 minutes for smaller cookies, rotating the baking sheets between the upper and lower oven racks halfway through baking. The cookies will be very soft and may appear moist in the cracks. Cool 1 minute on the baking sheets on wire racks; with a wide spatula, transfer the cookies to wire racks to cool completely.

Each large cookie About 325 calories, 3g protein, 42g carbohydrate, 16g fat (4g saturated), 1g fiber, 260mg sodium.

hermits

PREP: 20 MIN / TOTAL: 35 MIN, PLUS COOLING / MAKES 32

2 cups all-purpose flour

1 teaspoon ground cinnamon

½ teaspoon baking powder

½ teaspoon baking soda

½ teaspoon ground ginger

¼ teaspoon ground nutmeg

¼ teaspoon salt

⅛ teaspoon ground cloves

1 cup packed brown sugar

½ cup salted butter, at room temperature

⅓ cup dark molasses

1 large egg

1 cup dark raisins

1 cup pecans (4 ounces), toasted and coarsely chopped (optional)

1. Preheat the oven to 350°F. Grease and flour 2 large baking sheets.

2. In a medium bowl and using a wire whisk, stir the flour, cinnamon, baking powder, baking soda, ginger, nutmeg, salt, and cloves.

3. In a large bowl and using a mixer at medium speed, beat the brown sugar and butter until light and fluffy. Beat in the molasses until blended. Beat in the egg. Reduce the speed to low; beat in the flour mixture just until blended, occasionally scraping the bowl with a rubber spatula. With a wooden spoon, stir in the raisins and pecans, if using, just until combined.

4. Divide the dough into quarters. With lightly floured hands, shape each quarter into a 12 × 1½-inch log. Place 2 logs, about 3 inches apart, on each cookie sheet.

5. Bake until the logs flatten and the edges are firm, 13 to 15 minutes, rotating the baking sheets between the upper and lower racks halfway through baking. Cool the logs on the baking sheets on wire racks 15 minutes. Transfer the logs to a cutting board. Slice each log crosswise into 8 cookies. Transfer the cookies to wire racks to cool completely.

Each cookie About 105 calories, 1g protein, 19g carbohydrate, 3g fat (2g saturated), 0g fiber, 80mg sodium.

GLOSSARY

These spice-rich cookies are called **hermits** because they are able to be stored for long periods of time without spoiling. Lore has it that the cookies were first taken to sea during the 17th century clipper ship era. Recipes for hermits first appeared in the 1880s in several cookbooks in New England and New York state. Originally they were made with white sugar, raisins, and spice. Whatever their origin, they are delicious—and yes, they store well!

peanut butter cookies

PREP: 15 MIN / TOTAL: 45 MIN / MAKES 36

1¼ cups all-purpose flour

1 teaspoon baking soda

¼ teaspoon salt

1 cup creamy peanut butter

½ cup salted butter at room temperature

½ cup packed brown sugar

¼ cup granulated sugar

1 large egg

½ teaspoon vanilla extract

1. Preheat the oven to 350°F. In a small bowl and using a wire whisk, stir the flour, baking soda, and salt.

2. In a large bowl and using a mixer at medium speed, beat the peanut butter, butter, both sugars, the egg, and vanilla until combined, occasionally scraping down the bowl with a rubber spatula. Reduce the speed to low. Add the flour mixture and beat just until blended.

3. Drop the dough by heaping tablespoons, 2 inches apart, on 2 ungreased large baking sheets. With a fork, press a crisscross pattern into the top of each cookie.

4. Bake until lightly browned, 15 to 20 minutes, rotating the baking sheets between the upper and lower oven racks halfway through baking. With a wide spatula, transfer the cookies to wire racks to cool completely.

5. Repeat forming and baking cookies with the remaining dough.

Each cookie About 100 calories, 3g protein, 9g carbohydrate, 6g fat (2g saturated), 1g fiber, 115mg sodium.

lemon icebox cookies

PREP: 20 MIN / TOTAL: 1 HR 20 MIN / MAKES 96

1⅔ cups all-purpose flour

1 teaspoon baking powder

¼ teaspoon baking soda

⅛ teaspoon salt

3 lemons

½ cup salted butter, at room temperature

¾ cup sugar

1 large egg yolk

1. In a medium bowl and using a wire whisk, stir the flour, baking powder, baking soda, and salt. From the lemons, grate 1 tablespoon zest and squeeze 2 tablespoons juice.

2. In a large bowl and using a mixer at medium speed, beat the butter and sugar until light and fluffy. Beat in the egg yolk and lemon zest and juice until combined. Reduce the speed to low; beat in the flour mixture just until blended.

3. Divide the dough in half. On waxed paper, form one piece of dough into a 12-inch log. Repeat with the remaining dough. Wrap each log and refrigerate overnight, or freeze until very firm, at least 2 hours.

4. Preheat the oven to 375°F. Grease and flour 2 large baking sheets or line them with parchment paper or foil. Cut 1 log crosswise into ¼-inch-thick slices. Place the slices, 1 inch apart, on the prepared baking sheets.

5. Bake the cookies until set and golden brown around the edges, 10 to 12 minutes, rotating the baking sheets between the upper and lower oven racks halfway through baking. With a wide spatula, transfer the cookies to wire racks to cool completely. Repeat with the remaining dough.

Each cookie About 25 calories, 0g protein, 3g carbohydrate, 1g fat (1g saturated), 0g fiber, 20mg sodium.

VARIATIONS

Lemon-Walnut Icebox Cookies
Prepare as directed, stirring **1 cup walnuts** (4 ounces), finely chopped, into the dough after adding the flour.

Lemon-Anise Icebox Cookies
Prepare as directed, beating **2 teaspoons anise seeds** into the dough with the lemon zest.

Orange Icebox Cookies
Prepare as directed, but substitute **1 tablespoon freshly grated orange zest** and **2 tablespoons fresh orange juice** for the lemon zest and juice.

GOOD TO KNOW

MOLASSES

During the sugar-refining process, the juice that is extracted from sugarcane or sugar beets is boiled down to a syrupy mixture from which sugar crystals are removed. The syrup that remains is molasses. Whether or not molasses is sulphured or unsulphured simply depends on whether sulfur dioxide was used in processing molasses. Unsulphured molasses has a milder, cleaner flavor. When storing molasses, choose a dark, cool place for up to one year.

LIGHT MOLASSES	Comes from the first boiling of sugar syrup; it has a light color and mild flavor and is often used as a pancake and waffle syrup as well as for baking.
DARK MOLASSES	Comes from the second boiling and is darker, not as sweet, and thicker; it is the molasses used to flavor baked goods such as gingerbread and for Indian pudding and baked beans.
BLACKSTRAP MOLASSES	Comes from the third boiling of sugar syrup; it is very dark, a bit bitter, and rather thick. Use when you want an assertive flavor in marinades and baked goods.

apricot raspberry rugelach

PREP: 1 HR / TOTAL: 1 HR 35 MIN, PLUS CHILLING / MAKES 48

1 cup salted butter, at room temperature

1 package (8 ounces) cream cheese, at room temperature

¾ cup granulated sugar

1 teaspoon vanilla extract

¼ teaspoon salt

2 cups all-purpose flour

1 cup walnuts (4 ounces), chopped

¾ cup dried apricots, chopped

¼ cup packed brown sugar

1½ teaspoons ground cinnamon

½ cup seedless raspberry preserves

1 tablespoon whole milk

1. In a large bowl and using a mixer at low speed, beat the butter and cream cheese until creamy. Beat in ¼ cup granulated sugar, the vanilla, and salt. Beat in 1 cup flour. Stir in the remaining 1 cup flour just until blended. Divide the dough into 4 equal disks. Wrap each disk with plastic wrap and refrigerate until firm, at least 2 hours or up to overnight.

2. Prepare the filling: In a medium bowl, combine the walnuts, apricots, brown sugar, ¼ cup plus 2 tablespoons granulated sugar, and ½ teaspoon cinnamon until well mixed.

3. Preheat the oven to 325°F. Line 2 large baking sheets with foil; grease the foil.

4. On a lightly floured surface and using a floured rolling pin, roll 1 disk of dough into a 9-inch round; keep the remaining dough refrigerated. Spread 2 tablespoons preserves over the dough. Sprinkle with ½ cup walnut mixture, gently pressing it so that the nuts adhere. With a pastry wheel or sharp knife, cut the dough into 12 equal wedges. Starting at the curved edge, roll up each wedge. Place each roll, point side down, ½ inch apart, on the prepared baking sheet. Repeat with the remaining dough, one disk at a time.

5. In a cup and using a fork, stir the remaining 2 tablespoons granulated sugar and the remaining 1 teaspoon cinnamon. With a pastry brush, brush the rugelach with milk. Evenly sprinkle the cinnamon sugar on top.

6. Bake until golden, 35 to 40 minutes, rotating the baking sheets between the upper and lower oven racks halfway through baking. With a wide spatula, immediately transfer the rugelach to wire racks to cool completely.

Each rugelach About 115 calories, 1g protein, 12g carbohydrate, 7g fat (4g saturated), 1g fiber, 70mg sodium.

gingerbread wands

(See photo on page 596.)

PREP: 30 MIN / TOTAL: 45 MIN / MAKES 84

½ cup granulated sugar

½ cup light (mild) molasses

1 tablespoon pumpkin pie spice

¼ teaspoon ground black pepper

2 teaspoons baking soda

½ cup salted butter, melted

1 large egg

3½ cups all-purpose flour

1 large egg white, beaten

Colored decorating sugar, edible glitter, and sprinkles, for decorating

1. Preheat the oven to 325°F. Line a large baking sheet with parchment paper.

2. In a 4-quart saucepan, combine the granulated sugar, molasses, pumpkin pie spice, and pepper; heat to boiling over medium heat, stirring occasionally. Remove from the heat; stir in the baking soda, then the butter. With a fork, stir in the egg, then the flour until combined.

3. On a floured surface, knead the dough until smooth; divide in half. Wrap 1 piece of dough in plastic wrap and set it aside. With a lightly floured rolling pin, roll the remaining half of the dough into a 12 × 8-inch rectangle, which should be about a scant ¼ inch thick. With a pizza cutter, cut the dough into 8 × ¼-inch strips. Transfer them to the prepared baking sheet, spaced about 1 inch apart.

4. Lightly brush the strips with the beaten egg white. Sprinkle with decorations as desired. Bake 12 to 15 minutes, or until set. Cool on the baking sheet on a wire rack. Meanwhile, repeat rolling, cutting, and decorating the remaining dough. Cookies can be stored in airtight containers at room temperature for up to 2 weeks.

Each cookie About 45 calories, 1g protein, 8g carbohydrate, 1g fat (1g saturated), 0g fiber, 40mg sodium.

VARIATION

Gingerbread Men

Follow the recipe above, but in step 2, roll out the dough to a scant ¼-inch thickness. With floured 2-inch cookie cutters, cut shapes. Transfer the cookies to a parchment-lined baking sheet, placing them 1 inch apart. Proceed with step 3, baking 15 to 17 minutes. **Makes 3 dozen.**

spritz cookies

PREP: 35 MIN / TOTAL: 1 HR, PLUS COOLING / MAKES 66

2¼ cups all-purpose flour

½ teaspoon baking powder

½ teaspoon salt

1 cup salted butter, at room temperature

½ cup sugar

1 large egg

1 teaspoon vanilla extract

1 teaspoon almond extract

Candy sprinkles (optional)

Ornamental Frosting (page 611; optional)

1. Preheat the oven to 350°F. Place 3 baking sheets in the freezer.

2. On waxed paper, combine the flour, baking powder, and salt.

3. In a large bowl and using a mixer on medium speed, beat the butter and sugar until pale and creamy. Beat in the egg, then beat in both extracts. With the mixer on low speed, gradually add the flour mixture, beating just until blended.

4. Spoon one-third of the dough into a cookie press or a large pastry bag fitted with a large star tip. Onto the chilled baking sheet, press or pipe the dough into desired shapes, spacing them 2 inches apart. Sprinkle with candy decors, if using, before baking.

5. Bake the cookies 10 to 12 minutes, or until lightly browned around the edges. Cool on the baking sheet on a wire rack for 2 minutes. Transfer the cookies to a wire rack to cool completely. Repeat with the remaining dough. Decorate the cookies as desired with Ornamental Frosting, if using. Set aside to allow the frosting to dry. Store the cookies in airtight containers at room temperature up to 1 week or in the freezer up to 1 month.

Each cookie About 50 calories, 1g protein, 5g carbohydrate, 3g fat (2g saturated), 0g fiber, 20mg sodium.

SPRITZ COOKIES 610

MERRY MERINGUES 612

GLOSSARY →

Spritz comes from the German *spritzen*, meaning to squirt, because the soft, buttery dough is pushed through a cookie press to form fancy shapes. We like our spritz a bit golden around the edges to bring out the buttery flavor, if you want a paler cookie, check for doneness after 8 minutes.

ornamental frosting

PREP: 5 MIN / TOTAL: 5 MIN / MAKES 3 CUPS

1 package (16 ounces) confectioners' sugar

3 tablespoons meringue powder

⅓ cup warm water

Assorted food colorings (optional)

1. In a large bowl and using a mixer at medium speed, beat the confectioners' sugar, meringue powder, and water until stiff and a knife drawn through the mixture leaves a path, about 5 minutes.

2. If desired, tint the frosting with food colorings. Keep the frosting tightly covered to prevent it from drying out. With a small metal spatula, artists' paintbrushes, or decorating bags with small plain tips, decorate cookies with frosting. (You may need to thin the frosting with a little warm water to obtain good spreading or piping consistency.)

Each tablespoon About 40 calories, 0g protein, 10g carbohydrate, 0g fat (0g saturated), 0g fiber, 5mg sodium.

almond amaretto biscotti

PREP: 30 MIN / TOTAL: 50 MIN, PLUS COOLING / MAKES 56

3¼ cups all-purpose flour

1¼ cups sugar

1 tablespoon baking powder

½ teaspoon salt

¾ cup salted butter, cut up

3 large eggs

2 tablespoons amaretto, or 1½ teaspoons vanilla extract plus ½ teaspoon almond extract

1½ cup whole almonds (4 ounces), toasted and coarsely chopped

1. Preheat the oven to 350°F. Line 2 large baking sheets with parchment paper.

2. On a sheet of waxed paper, combine the flour, sugar, baking powder, and salt.

3. In a large microwave-safe bowl, heat the butter in the microwave on High 1 minute, or until melted. With a wire whisk, beat in the eggs and amaretto or extracts. With a wooden spoon, stir in the flour mixture and almonds until blended. Divide the dough in half. With floured hands, shape each half into a 14 × 4-inch log, placing them 3 inches apart on the prepared baking sheet (the dough will be sticky).

4. Bake until golden and a toothpick inserted in the center comes out clean, 25 to 30 minutes. Turn the oven control to 325°F. Cool 20 minutes on the baking sheet on a wire rack, then transfer the logs to a cutting board.

5. With a serrated knife, cut each log crosswise on the diagonal into ½-inch-thick slices. Place the slices, cut side down, on the same baking sheets. Bake 25 to 30 minutes, until pale golden, turning the slices over once and rotating the baking sheets between the upper and lower oven racks halfway through baking. With a spatula, transfer the biscotti to wire racks to cool completely.

Each biscotto About 95 calories, 2g protein, 11g carbohydrate, 5g fat (2g saturated), 1g fiber, 75mg sodium.

VARIATION

Classic Anise Biscotti

Omit the amaretto. In a small bowl, combine **1 tablespoon anise seeds**, crushed, and **1 tablespoon anise-flavored liqueur or aperitif**; let stand 10 minutes. Stir into the batter along with the eggs.

Ingredient Ideas
biscotti add-ins

- Stir in 1 teaspoon of grated lemon or orange zest along with the eggs.

- Swap in walnuts, pecans, or toasted hazelnuts for the almonds.

- Along with the nuts, add up to 1 cup total of the following: dried cherries, cranberries, or chopped apricots; raisins; chopped crystallized ginger; mini chocolate chips.

merry meringues

(See photo on page 610.)

PREP: 20 MIN / TOTAL: 2 HR 25 MIN / MAKES 60

3 large egg whites	**½ cup sugar**
Pinch of salt	**½ teaspoon vanilla extract**
¼ teaspoon cream of tartar	**Assorted food coloring pastes**

1. Arrange the oven racks in top and bottom thirds of the oven. Preheat the oven to 225°F. Line 2 large baking sheets with parchment paper.

2. In a medium bowl and using a mixer on medium speed, beat the egg whites and salt until foamy. Add the cream of tartar; beat on medium-high until soft peaks form. Add the sugar, 1 tablespoon at a time, beating until the meringue stands in stiff, glossy peaks. Beat in the vanilla.

3. For each color desired, use a small brush to lightly paint 3 or 4 stripes of food coloring inside a large pastry bag fitted with a ½-inch plain tip. Divide the meringue among pastry bags. Pipe the meringue into 1½-inch rounds onto the prepared baking sheets, spacing them 1 inch apart. Bake 1 hour.

4. Turn off the oven. Leave the meringues in the oven 1 hour with the oven door closed. Remove the meringues from the oven; cool completely on baking sheets. When cool, lift meringues from parchment. The meringues can be stored in airtight containers at room temperature for up to 2 weeks.

Each meringue About 5 calories, 0g protein, 2g carbohydrate, 0g fat (0g saturated), 0g fiber, 10mg sodium.

VARIATIONS

Your Color Code

For fun, pick your color and add a "matching" flavor with the vanilla extract in step 2.

- ½ teaspoon almond extract and green
- 2 teaspoons freshly grated lemon zest and yellow
- ½ teaspoon mint extract and red
- ¼ cup freeze-dried blueberries, finely crushed, and purple

razzy-jammy thumbprints

(See photo on page 596.)

PREP: 25 MIN / TOTAL: 40 MIN, PLUS COOLING / MAKES 36

2¼ cups all-purpose flour	**2 tablespoons honey**
1 teaspoon baking powder	**1 teaspoon almond extract**
½ teaspoon baking soda	**½ teaspoon vanilla extract**
¾ cup salted butter, at room temperature	**½ cup seedless raspberry jam**
¾ cup granulated sugar	**¼ cup confectioners' sugar (optional)**
½ teaspoon salt	
1 large egg yolk	

1. Preheat the oven to 375°F. Line a large baking sheet with parchment paper.

2. In a medium bowl, whisk the flour, baking powder, and baking soda. In a large bowl and using a mixer on medium-high speed, beat the butter, granulated sugar, and salt until creamy. Beat in the egg yolk, then the honey and both extracts until smooth, stopping and scraping down the sides of the bowl occasionally. With the mixer on low speed, beat in the flour mixture until smooth.

3. Using a 1-tablespoon cookie scoop or measuring spoon, scoop the dough and roll it into balls. Arrange the balls on the prepared baking sheet, spacing them 2 inches apart. With a floured finger or the rounded end of a small spoon, make an indentation in the center of each ball. Fill each indentation with ½ teaspoon jam. Bake 12 minutes, or until golden brown around the edges.

4. Let the cookies cool on the baking sheet 5 minutes. Transfer the cookies to a wire rack to cool completely. Sift confectioners' sugar over the cooled cookies, if desired. Cookies can be stored in airtight containers in the freezer for up to 1 month.

Each cookie About 95 calories, 1g protein, 14g carbohydrate, 4g fat (3g saturated), 0g fiber, 95mg sodium.

VARIATIONS

Salted Caramel

Bake the cookies with the indentations unfilled. Once cooled, fill with **dulce de leche** and top with **flaky sea salt**.

Nut-Rolled

After forming the balls in step 2, roll the cookies in **finely chopped walnuts or pecans**. Fill and bake as directed.

macarons

(See photo on page 615.)

PREP: 25 MIN / TOTAL: 1 HR, PLUS STANDING AND COOLING / MAKES 36

1 cup slivered almonds

2 cups lightly packed confectioners' sugar

3 large egg whites, room temperature

¼ teaspoon salt

¼ teaspoon almond extract

4 ounces bittersweet chocolate, melted

1. Preheat the oven to 300°F. Line 2 large baking sheets with parchment paper.

2. In a food processor with the knife blade attached, process the almonds and 1 cup confectioners' sugar until finely ground and powdery, occasionally scraping the bowl with a rubber spatula. Add the remaining confectioners' sugar; pulse until combined. Transfer to a large bowl.

3. In a medium bowl and using a mixer on medium speed, beat the egg whites and salt until soft peaks form. Beat in the almond extract. Increase the speed to high and beat just until stiff (but not dry) peaks form when the beaters are lifted. With a rubber spatula, fold the egg whites into the almond mixture until blended. The batter will be just pourable and sticky.

4. Transfer the batter to a pastry bag fitted with a ½-inch round tip. Holding the bag about ½ inch above the parchment paper, pipe 1-inch rounds spaced 1½ inches apart; the batter will spread. Let stand 20 minutes.

5. Bake one baking sheet at a time for 18 to 19 minutes, or until bubbles around the bases of the macarons are firm to the touch but the tops are not browned. Cool on a wire rack; when cool, lift the meringues from the parchment. Repeat with the second baking sheet.

6. When the cookies are cool, spread chocolate on the bottoms of half the macarons, using about ½ teaspoon for each. Top each with another macaron, bottom side down. Let stand until the chocolate hardens, about 45 minutes.

Each cookie About 60 calories, 1g protein, 9g carbohydrate, 3g fat (1g saturated), 1g fiber, 20mg sodium.

cranberry shortbread

(See photo on page 615.)

PREP: 35 MIN / TOTAL: 1 HR 25 MIN, PLUS CHILLING AND COOLING / MAKES 60

1 lemon

1 cup salted butter, at room temperature

1¼ cups confectioners' sugar

⅛ teaspoon salt

1 large egg

2¼ cups all-purpose flour

¾ cup dried cranberries

1 cup pistachios, shelled (½ cup), finely chopped (optional)

1. From the lemon, grate 1 tablespoon zest and squeeze 1 tablespoon juice. In a large bowl and using a mixer on medium speed, beat the butter, confectioners' sugar, and salt until smooth and creamy. With the mixer running, beat in the egg, then the lemon zest and juice, scraping the sides and bottom of the bowl occasionally.

2. Add the flour and beat on low until just incorporated. Stir in the cranberries until evenly distributed.

3. Divide the dough among 3 sheets of waxed paper and roll each into logs 1 inch in diameter. (If the dough is sticky, refrigerate it for 30 minutes before rolling.) Wrap the logs in the waxed paper and refrigerate 45 minutes, or until firm.

4. Divide the pistachios, if using, among the logs; press them into the dough to evenly coat. Wrap the logs tightly in plastic wrap and refrigerate at least 1 hour or up to 1 week.

5. Preheat the oven to 300°F. Line 2 baking sheets with parchment paper.

6. Using a knife, cut the logs into ¼-inch-thick slices. Place them 2 inches apart on the prepared baking sheets. Bake 25 to 30 minutes, or until golden brown, rotating the sheets between the upper and lower racks halfway through. Refrigerate the remaining dough while the cookies bake. Transfer the baked cookies on wire racks to cool. Repeat with remaining dough. Store in an airtight container at room temperature up to 3 days or in the freezer up to 1 month.

Each cookie About 60 calories, 1g protein, 7g carbohydrate, 3g fat (2g saturated), 0g fiber, 35mg sodium.

butter-almond thins

PREP: 30 MIN / TOTAL: 50 MIN / MAKES 84

¾ cup salted butter, at room temperature

⅓ cup granulated sugar

½ teaspoon ground cardamom

¼ teaspoon salt

1 large egg, separated

1 teaspoon almond extract

1 teaspoon vanilla extract

2 cups all-purpose flour

2 cups sliced blanched almonds

4 tablespoons confectioners' sugar

1. Preheat the oven to 375°F. Grease an 18 × 12-inch rimmed baking sheet, line it with foil, and grease the foil.

2. In a large bowl and using the mixer on medium speed, beat the butter, granulated sugar, cardamom, and salt until creamy and smooth. Beat in the egg yolk and both extracts until well incorporated. Add the flour and beat on low just until clumps form.

3. Scatter the clumps evenly on the rimmed baking sheet. With your palm and fingertips, press the dough into a thin, even layer without any gaps.

4. In a medium bowl, whisk the egg white until frothy; fold in the almonds and 2 tablespoons confectioners' sugar. Spread the mixture in an even layer over the dough, pressing it into the dough gently. With a pizza wheel or sharp knife, cut the dough crosswise into 2-inch strips; cut each one crosswise to form 2-inch squares. Cut squares diagonally into triangles. Dust the tops with the remaining 2 tablespoons confectioners' sugar.

5. Bake 15 to 18 minutes, or until golden brown. Cool completely in the pan on a wire rack. Carefully break the cookies into triangles along the scored lines. Store the cookies in an airtight container at room temperature up to 2 days or in the freezer up to 1 month.

Each cookie About 45 calories, 1g protein, 4g carbohydrate, 3g fat (1g saturated), 0g fiber, 25mg sodium.

chocolate-walnut thumbprints

PREP: 45 MIN / TOTAL: 1 HR, PLUS COOLING / MAKES 60

1 cup salted butter, at room temperature

¾ cup sugar

⅓ cup unsweetened cocoa

¼ teaspoon salt

1 large egg, separated

1 teaspoon vanilla extract

2 ounces unsweetened chocolate, chopped and melted

2 cups all-purpose flour

1½ cups walnuts, finely chopped

½ cup cherry preserves

1. Preheat the oven to 350°F.

2. In a large bowl and using a mixer on low speed, beat the butter, sugar, cocoa, and salt until creamy. Beat in the egg yolk and vanilla until well blended, scraping the sides of the bowl occasionally. Beat in the chocolate. Add the flour and beat until combined.

3. In a small bowl and using a fork, beat the egg white lightly just to break it up. Spread the walnuts on a plate. Roll the dough by rounded measuring teaspoons into 1-inch balls. Coat the balls lightly in the beaten egg white, letting the excess drip off. Roll each ball in walnuts to coat. Place the cookies, 1½ inches apart, on 2 large ungreased baking sheets. Press your thumb into the center of each to make an indentation.

4. Bake the cookies 8 minutes, switching the sheets between the upper and lower racks halfway through baking. Fill each with ¼ teaspoon preserves. Bake 8 to 10 minutes longer, or until the jam is bubbly. Let cool on the baking sheets 2 minutes before removing them with a spatula to wire racks to cool completely. Store the cookies in airtight containers at room temperature up to 3 days.

Each cookie About 80 calories, 1g protein, 8g carbohydrate, 5g fat (3g saturated), 1g fiber, 40mg sodium.

MACARONS 613

BUTTER-ALMOND THINS 614

CRANBERRY SHORTBREAD 613

CHOCOLATE-WALNUT THUMBPRINTS 614

COCONUT JOY BARS 603

cocoa stars

(See photo on page 596.)

PREP: 35 MIN / TOTAL: 55 MIN, PLUS CHILLING AND COOLING / MAKES 12

- 2¼ cups all-purpose flour
- ¼ cup unsweetened cocoa
- 1 teaspoon baking powder
- ½ teaspoon baking soda
- ¾ cup salted butter, at room temperature
- ¾ cup sugar
- 2 ounces bittersweet chocolate, melted
- ½ teaspoon salt
- 1 large egg yolk
- 2 tablespoons light corn syrup
- 1½ teaspoons vanilla extract
- ½ teaspoon almond extract
- Confectioners' sugar, for dusting

1. Preheat the oven to 375°F. In a medium bowl, whisk the flour, cocoa, baking powder, and baking soda; set aside.

2. With a mixer on medium-high speed, beat the butter, sugar, chocolate, and salt until creamy; beat in the egg yolk, corn syrup, and both extracts. With the mixer on medium-low speed, beat in the flour mixture until just combined. Divide the dough in half.

3. On a large sheet of parchment paper, lightly flour half the dough. Roll out to ¼-inch thickness. Using a 3-inch star-shaped cookie cutter, cut shapes from the dough; gently remove the excess dough from around the cut stars. Slide the parchment with the cookies onto a baking sheet; place in the freezer. Reroll the scraps once on another sheet of parchment, then cut more star shapes; add these cookies to the same sheet in the freezer. Freeze until stiff, about 30 minutes. Arrange the cookies 2 inches apart on 1 sheet of parchment paper; place on a baking sheet.

4. Bake 10 to 12 minutes, or until golden around edges. Slide the parchment with the baked cookies onto a wire rack; cool completely. Dust the cookies with confectioners' sugar. Repeat the rolling, baking, and cooling with the remaining dough.

Each cookie About 285 calories, 4g protein, 38g carbohydrate, 14g fat (9g saturated), 2g fiber, 290mg sodium.

fancy fortune cookies

(See photo on page 594.)

PREP: 10 MIN / TOTAL: 40 MIN, PLUS COOLING / MAKES 10

- 2 tablespoons salted butter
- ¼ cup confectioners' sugar
- 1 large egg white
- 1 teaspoon vanilla extract
- ⅛ teaspoon salt
- ¼ cup all-purpose flour
- 10 strips of paper (each 3 × ½ inch) with written fortunes
- Melted chocolate (dark, milk, or white) and chopped nuts for decorating (optional)

1. Preheat the oven to 375°F. Line 2 small baking sheets with parchment paper.

2. In a small saucepan, heat the butter over low heat until melted; remove from the heat. Whisk in the confectioners' sugar, egg white, vanilla, and salt until blended. Beat in the flour until smooth.

3. Drop 1 heaping teaspoon of batter onto the prepared baking sheet. With a small metal spatula or the back of a spoon, spread the batter evenly to form a 3-inch round. Repeat with another teaspoon of batter at least 4 inches from the first.

4. Bake until the cookies are lightly golden, 6 to 7 minutes. Loosen both cookies with the metal spatula; flip onto flat sides.

5. Working with 1 cookie at a time, place the fortune across the center of the hot cookie. Fold the hot cookie in half, forming a semicircle; press the edges together.

6. Quickly fold the semicircle over the edge of a small bowl to create the fortune-cookie shape. Place it in a mini muffin pan to hold the shape while it cools. Repeat with the remaining cookie.

7. Repeat with the remaining batter and strips of fortune paper to make 10 cookies in all, cooling the baking sheets between batches.

8. If desired, dip the cookies in and/or drizzle them with chocolate, then roll them in nuts. Place on waxed paper until set.

Each cookie About 50 calories, 1g protein, 6g carbohydrate, 3g fat (2g saturated), 0g fiber, 50mg sodium.

coconut macaroons

PREP: 10 MIN / TOTAL: 35 MIN / MAKES ABOUT 42

3 cups sweetened flaked coconut

¾ cup sugar

4 large egg whites

¼ teaspoon salt

1 teaspoon vanilla extract

⅛ teaspoon almond extract

1. Preheat the oven to 325°F. Line two large cookie sheets with parchment paper or foil.

2. In a large bowl, stir the coconut, sugar, egg whites, salt, and both extracts until well combined.

3. Drop dough by rounded teaspoons, 1 inch apart, on the prepared cookie sheets. Bake until set and lightly golden, 25 minutes, rotating the cookie sheets between the upper and lower oven racks halfway through. Set the cookie sheets on wire racks to cool 1 minute. With a wide metal spatula, transfer the cookies to the racks to cool completely. Store in an airtight container up to 3 days, or freeze up to 1 month.

Each cookie About 40 calories, 1g protein, 6g carbohydrate, 2g fat (2g saturated), 0g fiber, 32mg sodium.

salted caramel bark

(See photo on page 596.)

PREP: 15 MIN / TOTAL: 30 MIN, PLUS COOLING / SERVES 8

3 tablespoons corn syrup

2 tablespoons sugar

¼ teaspoon salt

2 cups peanuts

12 ounces semisweet chocolate, melted

1. Preheat the oven to 350°F.

2. In a large bowl, combine the corn syrup, sugar, and salt. Stir in the peanuts to evenly coat. Spread in a single layer on a parchment-lined rimmed baking sheet. Bake 15 minutes, or until browned and caramelized. Cool completely.

3. Stir the mixture into the chocolate until well coated. Spread evenly on a waxed-paper-lined baking sheet. Refrigerate until set. When chocolate layer hardens, break into 8 pieces.

Each serving About 460 calories, 12g protein, 40g carbohydrate, 33g fat (12g saturated), 6g fiber, 80mg sodium.

choco-caramel matzo brittle

PREP: 30 MIN / TOTAL: 40 MIN, PLUS COOLING / SERVES 12

Nonstick cooking spray

5 sheets matzo

1 cup salted butter

½ cup granulated sugar

½ cup packed light brown sugar

2 tablespoons cider vinegar

2 teaspoon vanilla extract

8 ounces dark chocolate, chopped

½ cup salted roasted almonds, chopped

1. Line a large rimmed baking sheet with aluminum foil; lightly coat it with nonstick cooking spray. Arrange the matzo on the baking sheet in a single layer, breaking it into pieces to fit, if necessary.

2. In a large microwave-safe glass bowl, microwave the butter on High 1 minute, or until melted. Whisk in both sugars, the vinegar, and vanilla until smooth. Microwave, uncovered, on High 6 minutes, in 2-minute intervals, whisking after each interval. Microwave 3 to 4 minutes more, in 1-minute intervals, until it turns dark amber in color.

3. Carefully remove the caramel from the microwave; pour it over the matzo in the pan. Spread the caramel in a thin layer using an offset spatula. Let cool 15 minutes, or until the caramel hardens completely.

4. Meanwhile, in a medium microwave-safe bowl, microwave the chocolate, covered with waxed paper, on High 1 to 2 minutes, or until almost melted, stirring once. Remove from the microwave and stir until smooth. Pour the chocolate over the caramel layer; spread in a thin layer using the spatula. Sprinkle with almonds.

5. Refrigerate 20 minutes, or until the chocolate layer hardens; break into 12 pieces.

Each piece About 400 calories, 4g protein, 37g carbohydrate, 27g fat (15g saturated), 3g fiber, 155mg sodium.

glazed vanilla-almond cutouts

PREP: 25 MIN / TOTAL: 40 MIN, PLUS COOLING / MAKES 48

2¼ cups all-purpose flour

1 teaspoon baking powder

½ teaspoon baking soda

¾ cup salted butter, at room temperature

¾ cup sugar

½ teaspoon salt

1 large egg yolk

2 tablespoons honey

1 teaspoon almond extract

½ teaspoon vanilla extract

Ornamental Frosting (page 611)

Sugar pearls and decorating sugar, for decorating

1. In a medium bowl, whisk the flour, baking powder. and baking soda. In a large bowl and using a mixer on medium-high speed, beat the butter, sugar, and salt until creamy. Beat in the yolk, then the honey and both extracts until smooth, stopping and scraping down the sides of the bowl occasionally. With the mixer on low, beat in the flour mixture until smooth. Divide the dough into 2 pieces. Wrap each in plastic wrap and refrigerate 15 to 30 minutes, or until somewhat soft but no longer sticky.

2. Preheat the oven to 375°F. On a large sheet of parchment paper, roll 1 piece of dough to a scant ¼-inch thickness. With floured 2-inch cookie cutters, cut out shapes, then remove the dough around the shapes with a small knife or a mini offset spatula. Slide the parchment onto a baking sheet; freeze 20 to 30 minutes, or until firm. On another sheet of parchment, gather the scraps and repeat the rolling, cutting, and removing excess dough. Freeze the cutout shapes until firm. Carefully peel all the shapes off the parchment and arrange them on one baking sheet, 1 inch apart. Bake 10 minutes, or until golden.

3. Let the cookies cool on the baking sheet 5 minutes. Transfer the cookies to a wire rack to cool completely. Meanwhile, repeat rolling, cutting, and freezing with the second piece of dough. Decorate the cookies with Ornamental Frosting, sugar pearls, and decorating sugar, as desired. The cookies can be stored in airtight containers at room temperature (with waxed paper between layers) for up to 1 week.

Each cookie About 105 calories, 2g protein, 18g carbohydrate, 3g fat (2g saturated), 0g fiber, 70mg sodium.

Tip To marble the frosting or make swirls, pipe on parallel lines or random dots in a contrasting color while base frosting is still wet. Use a toothpick to draw through the lines or dots to create decorative effects.

GOOD TO KNOW

COOKIE DECORATING SECRETS

You don't have to be a pro to pipe
simple designs on cookies.
Follow these easy steps and have fun!

1 TINT ICING AS DESIRED with paste or gel food colors. Fit a pastry bag or a plastic food storage bag with a plain writing tip (#2) and fill with about ½ cup of the icing.

2 WITH SLOW STEADY PRESSURE, outline the cookie (or the area) you want to color. Let the outline dry.

3 THIN A PORTION OF THE SAME ICING with a little water until it is the consistency of thick paint. Place in another piping bag, without a tip, and cut a ½ inch opening. Squeeze some frosting into the outlined area and use a toothpick to drag the frosting to the outlined edge—this is called *flooding*. Add colored sugar crystals or other decorations while the frosting is still wet. Or let dry and pipe a design in a contrasting color on top.

CHAPTER

16

CAKES, PIES & OTHER

desserts

Flaky pie crust, light-as-a-feather cake, creamy cheesecake, ethereal meringue, and silky smooth frosting are all benchmarks of the desserts we love. Many of us grew up considering daily dessert to be a birthright, not a privilege! These days, our dessert consumption may not be daily, so when we make one it had better be the best it can be.

The best bakers are a combination of scientist and artist. Scientist because precise measuring matters. Artist because shape, flavor combinations, and finishing flourishes can bring a familiar dessert to a new level. In this chapter you'll find favorite layer cakes, pound cakes, and fruit pies as well as Ganache Tart with Salted-Almond Crust (page 675), Meringue Nests (page 642), and Sticky Toffee Bundt Cake (page 632). All worth the calories!

ORANGE GRANITA 656

DOUBLE CHOCOLATE BUNDT 632

GANACHE TART WITH
SALTED-ALMOND CRUST 675

BUMBLEBERRY
CRISP 659

Pastry Pointers

What's the key to making flaky, tender pie pastry? It requires your full attention and a light touch.

INGREDIENTS

ALL-PURPOSE FLOUR is the go-to for pastry-baking. Bleached flour has a slightly lower protein content, which will yield a more tender crust.

THE FAT(S) make all the difference. Butter adds rich flavor, crispness, and color; vegetable shortening makes it flaky. We like a combo of butter and shortening to give piecrust the best qualities of each.

TEMPERATURE

KEEP EVERYTHING COLD. Chill butter and shortening. Use ice water as your liquid. If your kitchen is warm, freeze the flour for 15 minutes.

MIXING

COMBINE FLOUR AND FAT. A food processor makes it easy; use short pulses to blend just until the mixture resembles coarse crumbs. By hand? A pastry blender works beautifully, but you can also use two dinner knives, held scissor-fashion.

MOISTEN THE DOUGH. Sprinkle in water 1 tablespoon at a time, mixing lightly with a fork after each addition, just until the dough is moist enough to hold together.

GATHER THE DOUGH. Lightly shape into a disk. Seal in plastic wrap and chill for at least 30 minutes or up to overnight. (If it's been chilled overnight, allow dough to stand at room temperature for about 30 minutes before rolling).

ROLLING

PREVENT STICKING. Dust the work surface lightly with flour. Rub the rolling pin with flour, too. Sprinkle a little flour on top of the dough.

ROLL EVENLY. Start in the center and roll out the dough, rolling up to—but not over—the edge. Give the dough a quarter turn. Repeat until you have an even round. If the dough tears, just moisten the edges and press them together.

FITTING

WITHOUT STRETCHING THE DOUGH, loosely roll it onto the rolling pin, then position the pin at one side of the pie plate and unroll the dough. Alternatively, fold the rolled-out dough into quarters, set it into the pie plate, and unfold.

FIT THE DOUGH into the pie plate by gently easing it onto the bottom and against the sides with your fingertips. Decorate the edge as desired (see page 665).

READY, SET, BAKE

1 **Read** the recipe from start to finish.

2 **Gather** all the ingredients, equipment, and tools that you'll need.

3 **Arrange** the oven rack(s) in the correct position(s) before turning on the oven. Most of our recipes use the center oven rack (unless specified otherwise).

4 **Preheat** the oven at least 15 minutes before placing your pan in the oven.

5 **Prepare** your baking pan(s). Grease, flour, and/or line as the recipe directs.

6 **Measure** out all the ingredients before you start mixing.

7 **Place** a single pan in the center of the oven rack for proper air circulation. When arranging multiple pans in the oven, be sure they don't touch each other or the oven sides.

8 **Set** the timer once your item is in the oven.

9 **Keep** clean, dry oven mitts or potholders nearby.

10 **Get** your cooling racks ready.

Cake Cues

Cake flour is made of softer wheat than all-purpose flour. Its lower-protein content and finer grind produce tender cakes. If you don't have cake flour, for every cup of cake flour required, spoon 2 tablespoons cornstarch into a 1-cup measure. Spoon in enough all-purpose flour to fill the cup, then level it off. Note: Self-rising cake flour should not be substituted.

A beautifully risen, tender cake is a joy to look at—and eat! Accurate ingredients, measuring, temperature, and timing are key.

BUTTER Allow butter to soften at room temperature just until malleable. Take care if you microwave it. If it's partially melted, it will affect the structure of the cake.

EGGS All our recipes use large eggs. Let them come to room temperature for maximum volume. To speed the process, let eggs sit in a bowl of hot tap water for 10 minutes.

FLOUR Stir flour to aerate, then scoop into a dry measuring cup and level off with a spatula or knife. Do not pack or tamp down the flour.

PANS Always use the recommended pan size. Measure the pan if necessary. To line a pan, place it on a piece of waxed paper. Use a pencil to trace around the bottom edge and then cut out the shape.

GREASING AND FLOURING Apply a film of vegetable shortening using a folded piece of paper towel. To flour a greased pan, sprinkle a tablespoon or so of flour into the pan, tilting it to coat the bottom and sides. Invert the pan and tap out the excess. If you line the bottom of layer cake pans with parchment, lightly grease the pan first to hold the parchment in place. When greasing a Bundt pan, be sure to get into all the crevices or use nonstick baking spray.

COCONUT LAYER CAKE WITH
CREAM CHEESE FROSTING 633

golden butter cake

PREP: 45 MIN / TOTAL: 1 HR 10 MIN / SERVES 16

3 cups cake flour (not self-rising)

1 tablespoon baking powder

½ teaspoon salt

1 cup salted butter, softened

2 cups sugar

4 large eggs

2 teaspoons vanilla extract

1 cup whole milk

Orange Butter Frosting (page 636)

1. Preheat the oven to 350°F. Grease three 8-inch round cake pans. Line the bottoms with waxed paper; grease and flour the waxed paper. Alternatively, grease and flour a 9-inch fluted tube pan.

2. In a medium bowl and using a wire whisk, stir the flour, baking powder, and salt. In a large bowl and using a mixer at medium-high speed, beat the butter and sugar until light and fluffy, about 5 minutes. Add the eggs, one at a time, beating well after each addition. Beat in the vanilla. Reduce the speed to low; add the flour mixture alternately with the milk, beginning and ending with the flour mixture. Beat just until smooth, scraping the bowl with a rubber spatula.

3. Divide the batter among the prepared cake pans; spread it evenly. Place 2 pans on the upper oven rack and 1 pan on the lower oven rack so that the pans are not directly above one another. Bake until a toothpick inserted in the center comes out clean, 23 to 28 minutes for 8-inch layers, or 50 to 55 minutes for the tube pan. Cool in the pans on wire racks 10 minutes. Run a thin knife around the layers to loosen them from the sides of the pans. Or, if using a fluted tube pan, run the tip of the knife around the edge of the cake to loosen it. Invert onto racks. Remove the waxed paper; cool completely.

4. Prepare the Orange Butter Frosting. Place one layer, rounded side down, on a cake plate. With a narrow metal spatula, spread ⅔ cup frosting over the layer. Top with a second layer, rounded side up, and spread with ⅔ cup frosting. Place the remaining layer, rounded side up, on top. Spread the remaining frosting over the sides and top of the cake.

Each serving (with frosting) About 470 calories, 4g protein, 70g carbohydrate, 20g fat (12g saturated) 0g fiber, 360mg sodium.
Each serving (without frosting) About 315 calories, 4g protein, 43g carbohydrate, 14g fat (8g saturated), 0g fiber, 305mg sodium.

VARIATION

Spice Layer Cake

Prepare as directed but use 2⅔ cups all-purpose flour, 2½ teaspoons baking powder, and 1 teaspoon salt. Add 2 teaspoons ground cinnamon, 1 teaspoon ground ginger, and ¼ teaspoon ground cloves; with a wire whisk, stir until blended. In step 2, use 1 cup granulated sugar, 1 cup packed dark brown sugar, and 5 eggs; omit the vanilla. Bake 25 to 30 minutes. Proceed as directed, using Brown Butter Frosting (page 636). Serves 16.

apple-walnut bundt cake

PREP: 25 MIN / TOTAL: 1 HR 40 MIN / SERVES 16

3 cups all-purpose flour

1¾ cups granulated sugar

1 teaspoon baking soda

1 teaspoon ground cinnamon

¾ teaspoon salt

¼ teaspoon ground nutmeg

1 cup vegetable oil

½ cup apple juice

2 teaspoons vanilla extract

3 large eggs

1 pound Golden Delicious or Granny Smith apples (3 medium), peeled, cored, and coarsely chopped

1 cup walnuts (4 ounces), coarsely chopped

1 cup golden raisins

Confectioners' sugar, for dusting

1. Preheat the oven to 350°F. Grease and flour a 10-inch Bundt pan.

2. In a large bowl, combine the flour, granulated sugar, baking soda, cinnamon, salt, nutmeg, oil, apple juice, vanilla, and eggs. With a mixer at low speed, beat until well blended, frequently scraping the bowl with a rubber spatula. Increase the speed to medium; beat 2 minutes, scraping the bowl. With a wooden spoon, stir in the apples, walnuts, and raisins.

3. Spoon the batter into the prepared pan; spread it evenly. Bake until the cake pulls away from the side of the pan and a toothpick inserted in the center comes out clean, about 1 hour 15 minutes. Cool in the pan on a wire rack 10 minutes. Run the tip of a thin knife around the edge of the cake to loosen it. Invert the cake onto the rack; cool completely. Dust with confectioners' sugar.

Each serving About 410 calories, 5g protein, 54g carbohydrate, 20g fat (3g saturated), 2g fiber, 200mg sodium.

pineapple upside-down cake

PREP: 30 MIN / TOTAL: 1 HR 10 MIN / SERVES 8

2 cans (8 ounces each) pineapple slices in juice

⅓ cup packed brown sugar

8 tablespoons salted butter, softened

1 cup cake flour (not self-rising)

1 teaspoon baking powder

¼ teaspoon salt

⅔ cup granulated sugar

1 large egg

1 teaspoon vanilla extract

⅓ cup whole milk

1. Preheat the oven to 325°F. Drain the pineapple slices in a sieve set over a bowl; reserve 2 tablespoons juice. Cut 8 pineapple slices in half and drain them on paper towels. Refrigerate the remaining slices for another use.

2. In a 10-inch oven-safe skillet, heat the brown sugar and 2 tablespoons butter over medium heat until melted (if your skillet is not oven-safe, wrap the handle with a double layer of foil). Stir in the reserved pineapple juice and heat to boiling; boil 1 minute. Remove the skillet from the heat. Decoratively arrange the pineapple in the skillet, overlapping the slices slightly to fit.

3. In a small bowl and using a wire whisk, stir the flour, baking powder, and salt. In a large bowl and using a mixer at high speed, beat the remaining 6 tablespoons butter and granulated sugar until fluffy, frequently scraping the bowl with a rubber spatula. Reduce the speed to low; beat in the egg and vanilla until well blended. Add the flour mixture alternately with the milk, beginning and ending with the flour mixture. Beat just until blended.

4. Spoon the batter over the pineapple; spread evenly with a rubber spatula. Bake until a toothpick inserted in the center comes out clean, 40 to 45 minutes. Run a thin knife around the cake to loosen it from the side of the skillet; invert onto a serving plate. (If any pineapple slices stick to the skillet, place them on the cake.) Serve warm or at room temperature.

Each serving About 300 calories, 3g protein, 46g carbohydrate, 13g fat (8g saturated), 1g fiber, 270mg sodium.

VARIATIONS

Plum Upside-Down Cake

Prepare as directed, but substitute **1 pound plums** for the pineapple. Cut the plums into ½-inch-thick wedges. Heat the brown sugar and **2 tablespoons butter** in an oven-safe skillet over medium heat until melted. Add the plums and increase the heat to high. Cook, stirring, until the plums are glazed with the brown-sugar mixture, about 1 minute. Proceed with the recipe.

Apple Upside-Down Cake

Prepare as directed, but substitute **3 large Golden Delicious apples** (1½ pounds) for the pineapple. Peel, core, and cut the apples into ¼-inch-thick wedges. Heat the brown sugar and **2 tablespoons butter** in an oven-safe skillet over medium heat until melted. Add the apple wedges and cook over high heat until the apples are fork-tender and beginning to brown, 7 to 8 minutes. Proceed with the recipe.

gingerbread

PREP: 15 MIN / TOTAL: 1 HR / SERVES 9

2 cups all-purpose flour

½ cup sugar

2 teaspoons ground ginger

1 teaspoon ground cinnamon

½ teaspoon baking soda

½ teaspoon salt

1 cup light (mild) molasses

½ cup salted butter, cut into 4 pieces

¾ cup boiling water

1 large egg, lightly beaten

1. Preheat the oven to 350°F. Grease and flour a 9-inch square baking pan.

2. In a large bowl and using a wire whisk, stir the flour, sugar, ginger, cinnamon, baking soda, and salt until blended.

3. In a small bowl, combine the molasses and butter. Add the boiling water and stir until the butter melts. Add the molasses mixture and beaten egg to the flour mixture; whisk until smooth.

4. With a rubber spatula, scrape the batter into the prepared pan. Bake the gingerbread until a toothpick inserted in the center comes out clean, 45 to 50 minutes. Cool in the pan on a wire rack. Serve warm or at room temperature.

Each serving About 350 calories, 4g protein, 59g carbohydrate, 12g fat (7g saturated), 1g fiber, 325mg sodium.

carrot cake
with cream cheese frosting

PREP: 40 MIN / TOTAL: 1 HR 35 MIN, PLUS COOLING / SERVES 16

- 2½ cups all-purpose flour
- 2 teaspoons baking soda
- 2 teaspoons ground cinnamon
- 1 teaspoon baking powder
- 1 teaspoon salt
- ½ teaspoon ground nutmeg
- 4 large eggs
- 1 cup granulated sugar
- ¾ cup packed light brown sugar

- ½ cup vegetable oil
- ¼ cup whole milk
- 1 tablespoon vanilla extract
- 3 cups loosely packed shredded carrots (about 6 medium)
- 1 cup walnuts (4 ounces), chopped
- ¾ cup dark seedless raisins
- Cream Cheese Frosting (page 638)

1. Preheat the oven to 350°F. Grease a 13 × 9-inch baking pan. Line the bottom with waxed paper; grease the paper. Dust the pan with flour. Alternatively, grease and flour a 10-inch Bundt pan.

2. In a medium bowl and using a wire whisk, stir the flour, baking soda, cinnamon, baking powder, salt, and nutmeg.

3. In large bowl and using a mixer at medium-high speed, beat the eggs and both sugars until blended, about 2 minutes, frequently scraping the bowl with a rubber spatula. Beat in the oil, milk, and vanilla. Reduce the speed to low; add the flour mixture and beat until smooth, about 1 minute, scraping the bowl. With a wooden spoon, fold in the carrots, walnuts, and raisins.

4. Spoon the batter into the prepared pan; spread it evenly. Bake until a toothpick inserted in the center comes out almost clean, 55 to 60 minutes for a 13 × 9-inch cake or about 1 hour for a Bundt cake. Cool in the pan on a wire rack 10 minutes. Run a thin knife around the sheet cake to loosen it from the sides of the pan. Or, if you're using a Bundt pan, run the tip of a knife around the edge of the cake to loosen it. Invert the cake onto a rack. Remove the waxed paper; cool completely.

5. Meanwhile, prepare the Cream Cheese Frosting. Transfer the cooled cake to a cake plate. With a narrow metal spatula, spread frosting over the sides and top of the cake.

Each serving (with frosting) About 485 calories, 6g protein, 70g carbohydrate, 22g fat (7g saturated), 2g fiber, 435mg sodium.

VARIATION

Deluxe Carrot Cake
Prepare as directed, but omit the milk; fold in **1 can (8 to 8¼ ounces) crushed pineapple** in unsweetened juice with the walnuts and raisins.

vanilla pound cake

PREP: 20 MIN / TOTAL: 1 HR 20 MIN, PLUS COOLING / SERVES 20

- 1½ cups salted butter, softened
- 2¼ cups granulated sugar
- 6 large eggs
- 1 tablespoon vanilla extract

- ¾ teaspoon salt
- 3 cups cake flour (not self-rising)
- Confectioners' sugar, for dusting

1. Preheat the oven to 325°F. Grease and flour a 10-inch Bundt pan.

2. In a large bowl and using a mixer at low speed, beat the butter and granulated sugar until blended. Increase the speed to high; beat until light and fluffy, about 5 minutes, frequently scraping the bowl with a rubber spatula. Reduce the speed to medium. Add the eggs, one at a time, beating well after each addition. Add the vanilla and salt. Increase the speed to high; beat 3 minutes, scraping the bowl. With a whisk, stir in the flour just until smooth.

3. Spoon the batter into the prepared pan; spread it evenly. Bake until a toothpick inserted near the center comes out clean, 1 hour to 1 hour 10 minutes. Cool in the pan on a wire rack 10 minutes. Run the tip of a thin knife around the edge of the cake to loosen it. Invert it onto the rack to cool completely. Dust with confectioners' sugar.

Each serving About 300 calories, 3g protein, 36g carbohydrate, 16g fat (9g saturated), 0g fiber, 250mg sodium.

chocolate buttermilk cake

PREP: 45 MIN / TOTAL: 1 HR 15 MIN, PLUS COOLING / SERVES 16

2 cups all-purpose flour

1 cup unsweetened cocoa, plus more for the pan

1½ teaspoons baking soda

¾ teaspoon salt

1½ cups buttermilk

2 teaspoons vanilla extract

1¾ cups sugar

¾ cup salted butter, softened

3 large eggs

Classic Butter Frosting (page 636)

1. Preheat the oven to 350°F. Grease two 9-inch round cake pans. Line the bottom of the pans with waxed paper; grease the waxed paper. Dust with cocoa, shaking out the excess.

2. In a medium bowl and using a wire whisk, stir the flour, cocoa, baking soda, and salt. In a 2-cup liquid measuring cup, mix the buttermilk and vanilla; set aside.

3. In a large bowl and using a mixer at low speed, beat the sugar and butter until blended. Increase the speed to high; beat until creamy, about 3 minutes, occasionally scraping the bowl with a rubber spatula. Reduce the speed to low; add the eggs, one at a time, beating well after each addition. Add the flour mixture alternately with the buttermilk mixture, beginning and ending with the flour mixture. Beat just until blended, scraping the bowl occasionally.

4. Divide the batter between the prepared pans; spread it evenly. Bake until a toothpick inserted in the center of the cake comes out clean, 30 to 35 minutes. Cool in the pans on wire racks 10 minutes. Run a thin knife around the layers to loosen them from the sides of the pans. Invert the cakes onto the racks to cool completely. Carefully remove and discard the waxed paper.

5. Prepare the Classic Butter Frosting (page 636).

6. Place one layer, rounded side down, on a cake plate. With a narrow metal spatula, spread ⅔ cup frosting over the layer. Top with the second layer, rounded side up. Spread the remaining frosting over the sides and top of the cake.

Each serving (without frosting) About 255 calories, 5g protein, 37g carbohydrate, 11g fat (7g saturated), 3g fiber, 360mg sodium.

angel food cake

PREP: 30 MIN / TOTAL: 1 HR 5 MIN / SERVES 16

1 cup cake flour (not self-rising)

½ cup confectioners' sugar

1⅔ cups egg whites (12 to 14 large egg whites)

1½ teaspoons cream of tartar

½ teaspoon salt

1¼ cups granulated sugar

2 teaspoons vanilla extract

½ teaspoon almond extract

1. Preheat the oven to 375°F. Sift the flour and confectioners' sugar through a sieve set over a small bowl.

2. In a large bowl and using a mixer at medium speed, beat the egg whites, cream of tartar, and salt until foamy. Increase the speed to medium-high; beat until soft peaks form when the beaters are lifted. Sprinkle in the granulated sugar, 2 tablespoons at a time, beating until the sugar has dissolved and the egg whites stand in stiff, glossy peaks when the beaters are lifted. Beat in the vanilla and almond extracts.

3. Transfer the egg white mixture to a larger bowl. Sift the flour mixture, one-third at a time, over the beaten egg whites; fold in with a rubber spatula just until the flour mixture is no longer visible. Do not overmix.

4. Scrape the batter into an ungreased 9- to 10-inch tube pan; spread it evenly. Bake until the cake springs back when lightly pressed, 35 to 40 minutes. Invert the cake in the pan onto a large metal funnel or bottle; cool completely in the pan. Run a thin knife around the cake to loosen it from the sides and center tube of the pan. Remove from pan and place on a cake plate.

Each serving About 115 calories, 3g protein, 25g carbohydrate, 0g fat (0g saturated), 0g fiber, 115mg sodium.

VARIATION

Cappuccino Angel Food Cake

Prepare as directed, but add **4 teaspoons instant espresso-coffee powder** and **½ teaspoon ground cinnamon** to the egg whites before beating; use **1½ teaspoons vanilla extract** and omit the almond extract. In a cup, mix **1 tablespoon confectioners' sugar** with **⅛ teaspoon ground cinnamon**; sprinkle evenly over the cooled cake.

vanilla chiffon cake

PREP: 20 MIN / TOTAL: 1 HR 35 MIN / SERVES 16

- 2¼ cups cake flour (not self-rising)
- 1½ cups granulated sugar
- 1 tablespoon baking powder
- 1 teaspoon salt
- ¾ cup cold water
- ½ cup vegetable oil
- 5 large eggs, separated, plus 2 large egg whites
- 1 tablespoon vanilla extract
- ½ teaspoon cream of tartar
- Confectioners' sugar, for dusting

1. Preheat the oven to 325°F. In a large bowl and using a wire whisk, stir the flour, 1 cup granulated sugar, the baking powder, and salt. Make a well in the center; add the cold water, oil, egg yolks, and vanilla to the well. With a wire whisk, stir until smooth.

2. In a separate large bowl and using a mixer at high speed, beat all 7 egg whites and the cream of tartar until soft peaks form when the beaters are lifted. Sprinkle in the remaining ½ cup granulated sugar, 2 tablespoons at a time, beating until the sugar has dissolved and the egg whites stand in stiff, glossy peaks when the beaters are lifted. With a rubber spatula, gently fold one-third of the beaten egg whites into the egg yolk mixture, then fold in the remaining egg whites until blended.

3. Scrape the batter into an ungreased 9- to 10-inch tube pan; spread it evenly. Bake until the cake springs back when lightly pressed, about 1 hour 15 minutes. Invert the cake in the pan onto a large metal funnel or bottle; cool completely. Run a thin knife around the cake to loosen it from the sides and center tube of the pan. Remove from the pan and place on cake plate. Dust with confectioners' sugar.

Each serving About 220 calories, 4g protein, 31g carbohydrate, 9g fat (1g saturated), 0g fiber, 265mg sodium.

VARIATION

Citrus Chiffon Cake

Prepare as directed, but substitute **1 tablespoon freshly grated orange zest** and **1 teaspoon freshly grated lemon zest** for the vanilla, and substitute **½ cup fresh orange juice** and **¼ cup fresh lemon juice** for the cold water. In a small bowl, combine **1 cup confectioners' sugar**, **1 teaspoon freshly grated lemon zest**, **¼ teaspoon vanilla extract**, and about **5 teaspoons fresh orange juice** to make a smooth glaze. Spoon over the cooled cake.

raspberry lemon pound cake

PREP: 10 MIN / TOTAL: 1 HR 20 MIN / SERVES 10

- 1½ cups all-purpose flour
- ¼ teaspoon baking soda
- ¼ teaspoon salt
- 1 cup granulated sugar
- ½ cup salted butter, softened
- 4 ounces cream cheese, softened
- 1 teaspoon grated lemon zest
- 3 large eggs, room temperature
- 2 teaspoons vanilla extract
- 1 container (6 ounces) fresh raspberries
- ½ cup confectioners' sugar
- 5 tablespoons heavy or whipping cream
- 1 tablespoon seedless raspberry jam

1. Preheat the oven to 325°F. Grease and lightly flour an 8½ × 4½-inch loaf pan.

2. In a large bowl, whisk the flour, baking soda, and salt. In a second bowl and using a mixer on medium speed, beat the sugar, butter, cream cheese, and lemon zest until smooth. Beat in the eggs, one at a time, scraping the sides of the bowl as needed. Beat in the vanilla. In 2 batches, beat in the flour mixture until just combined. Gently fold the raspberries into the batter.

3. Transfer the batter to the prepared pan; smooth the top. Bake 1 hour 5 minutes to 1 hour 10 minutes, or until a toothpick inserted into the center comes out clean. Cool 10 minutes on a wire rack. Loosen the sides with a small knife. Invert onto the rack. Let cool.

4. Meanwhile, prepare the glaze: In a blender, puree the confectioners' sugar, heavy cream, and raspberry jam until smooth, scraping down the sides as needed. Drizzle over the cooled cake.

Each serving About 290 calories, 3g protein, 35g carbohydrate, 15g fat (9g saturated), 2g fiber, 215mg sodium.

triple citrus bundt

PREP: 10 MIN / TOTAL: 1 HR 20 MIN / SERVES 16

3 cups all-purpose flour

½ teaspoon baking soda

1 teaspoon baking powder

½ teaspoon salt

2 cups granulated sugar

1 cup salted butter, softened

1 package (8 ounces) cream cheese, softened

2 teaspoons grated lemon zest

1 teaspoon grated orange zest

1 teaspoon grated lime zest

6 large eggs

4 teaspoons vanilla extract

3 tablespoons fresh orange juice

2 tablespoons fresh lemon juice

2 tablespoons fresh lime juice

1¼ cups confectioners' sugar, sifted

Candied citrus peel, for garnish (optional)

1. Preheat the oven to 325°F. Grease and flour a 12-cup Bundt pan.

2. In a large bowl, whisk the flour, baking soda, baking powder, and salt. In a second bowl and using a mixer on medium speed, beat the granulated sugar, butter, cream cheese, lemon zest, orange zest, and lime zest. Beat in the eggs, one at a time, scraping the sides of the bowl as needed. Beat in the vanilla. In two batches, beat in the flour mixture until just combined.

3. Transfer the batter to the prepared pan; smooth the top. Bake 1 hour, or until a toothpick inserted into the center comes out clean. Cool 10 minutes on a wire rack. Loosen the sides with a small knife. Invert onto the rack. Let cool.

4. Meanwhile, prepare the glaze: Stir together the orange juice, lemon juice, lime juice, and confectioners' sugar until smooth. Brush all over the cooled cake. Let stand until somewhat set. Garnish with strips of candied citrus peel, if desired.

Each serving About 400 calories, 6g protein, 54g carbohydrate, 18g fat (11g saturated), 1g fiber, 305mg sodium.

TRIPLE CITRUS BUNDT 631

RASPBERRY LEMON POUND CAKE 630

double chocolate bundt

(See photo on page 622.)

PREP: 25 MIN / TOTAL: 1 HR 15 MIN, PLUS COOLING / SERVES 16

CAKE

- 1 cup unsweetened cocoa
- 2¼ cups all-purpose flour
- 1¾ cups granulated sugar
- 2 teaspoons baking soda
- 1 teaspoon baking powder

- 1 teaspoon salt
- 1 cup buttermilk
- 1 cup strong coffee, cold
- ⅔ cup vegetable oil
- 2 large eggs
- 1½ teaspoons vanilla extract

GLAZE

- 3 ounces semisweet chocolate, melted
- 4 tablespoons salted butter, melted
- ¼ cup confectioners' sugar

- ¼ cup sour cream
- 2 tablespoons strong coffee, cold
- ¼ teaspoon vanilla extract
- ⅛ teaspoon salt

1. Prepare the cake: Preheat the oven to 350°F. Generously grease a 12-cup Bundt pan; dust with ¼ cup cocoa. Into a large bowl, sift the remaining ¾ cup cocoa, the flour, sugar, baking soda, baking powder, and salt.

2. In a medium bowl and using a mixer on medium speed, beat the buttermilk, coffee, oil, eggs, and vanilla until smooth. Gradually beat the flour mixture into the buttermilk mixture just until blended. Transfer to the prepared Bundt pan. Bake 45 to 55 minutes, or until a toothpick inserted in the center comes out clean.

3. Cool the cake completely in the pan on a wire rack. Loosen the sides with an offset spatula. Invert onto the wire rack and remove the pan.

4. Prepare the glaze: In a medium bowl, whisk the chocolate and butter. Add the confectioners' sugar, sour cream, coffee, vanilla, and salt; stir until smooth. Pour over the cooled chocolate cake. Let stand at room temperature until set, about 4 hours.

Each serving About 335 calories, 5g protein, 44g carbohydrate, 17g fat (5g saturated), 3g fiber, 405mg sodium.

sticky toffee bundt cake

(See photo on page 635.)

PREP: 35 MIN / TOTAL: 1 HR 40 MIN, PLUS COOLING / SERVES 16

- 1 cup chopped pitted dates (about 5 ounces)
- 1 cup water
- 2 teaspoons ground ginger
- 1 teaspoon baking soda
- 2 cups all-purpose flour, plus more for dusting
- 1 teaspoon baking powder
- Salt
- 1 cup salted butter, room temperature

- 1¼ cups packed dark brown sugar
- 1¼ cups granulated sugar
- 3 large eggs, room temperature
- 2½ teaspoons vanilla extract
- 1 tablespoon light corn syrup
- ⅓ cup heavy or whipping cream
- Red and green grapes, for garnish (optional)

1. In a 2-quart saucepan, combine the dates and water. Heat to boiling over high heat. Remove from the heat. Stir in the ginger and baking soda. Cool completely.

2. Preheat the oven to 350°F. Grease and flour a 10-cup Bundt pan. Into a large bowl, sift the flour, baking powder, and ⅛ teaspoon salt; set aside.

3. In another large bowl and using a mixer on medium speed, beat 12 tablespoons butter, 1 cup dark brown sugar, and 1 cup granulated sugar until very well combined. Beat in the eggs, one at a time, scraping the sides of the bowl occasionally. Beat in 2 teaspoons vanilla. Alternately add the flour mixture and the date mixture, beating well in between additions, until combined.

4. Pour the batter into the prepared pan. Bake 55 minutes to 1 hour, or until a toothpick inserted in the center comes out clean. Cool in the pan on a wire rack for 15 minutes. Invert the pan onto the wire rack. Cool completely. The cooled cake can be wrapped tightly in plastic wrap and stored at room temperature up to 1 day.

5. In a 3-quart saucepan, combine the corn syrup, the remaining 4 tablespoons butter, ¼ cup dark brown sugar, and ¼ cup granulated sugar. Cook over medium heat 3 minutes, or until bubbly and the sugar has dissolved, stirring constantly. Stir in the cream, the remaining ½ teaspoon vanilla, and a pinch of salt. Cook another 2 minutes, stirring constantly. Let cool 5 minutes.

6. Place a sheet of waxed paper under the cake. Pour the caramel sauce over the top of the cooled cake and allow the sauce to drip down the sides. Let the caramel set. Transfer the cake to a serving plate. Garnish with grapes, if you like.

Each serving About 355 calories, 3g protein, 54g carbohydrate, 14g fat (9g saturated), 1g fiber, 265mg sodium.

coconut layer cake
with cream cheese frosting

(See photo on page 625.)

PREP: 35 MIN / TOTAL: 1 HR 45 MIN, PLUS CHILLING / SERVES 16

CAKE LAYERS

- 3 cups cake flour (not self-rising)
- 2 teaspoons baking powder
- ¾ teaspoon salt
- ½ teaspoon baking soda
- ¾ cup unsalted butter, softened

- 1½ cups granulated sugar
- 4 large eggs
- 1 tablespoons vanilla extract
- 1 cup sweetened cream of coconut
- ⅔ cup low-fat buttermilk

CREAM CHEESE FROSTING

- 2 packages (8 ounces each) cream cheese, softened
- 1 cup unsalted butter, softened
- 2 teaspoons vanilla extract

- ¼ teaspoon salt
- 3 cups confectioners' sugar
- 6 ounces unsweetened coconut flakes

1. Prepare the cake: Preheat the oven to 325°F. Grease three 8-inch round cake pans. Line the bottoms of the pans with parchment paper; grease the parchment.

2. In a large bowl, whisk the flour, baking powder, salt, and baking soda.

3. In another large bowl and using a mixer on low speed, beat the butter and sugar until blended. Increase the speed to high; beat until light and fluffy. Reduce the speed to medium-low; add the eggs, one at a time, beating well after each addition and scraping the bowl with a rubber spatula. Beat in the vanilla.

4. In a separate bowl, whisk the cream of coconut and buttermilk. On low speed, add the flour mixture to the egg mixture alternately with the coconut mixture, beginning and ending with the flour mixture, occasionally scraping the bowl with a spatula. Beat just until blended. Divide evenly among the prepared pans.

5. Bake 35 to 40 minutes, or until a toothpick inserted in the center comes out clean. Cool in the pans on wire racks 10 minutes. Run a small knife around the side of each layer; invert onto the racks. Cool completely. The layers can be made up to 1 day ahead; wrap well and store at room temperature.

6. Prepare the frosting: In a large bowl and using a mixer on low speed, beat the cream cheese and butter until smooth. Beat in the vanilla and salt until incorporated. Gradually beat in the confectioners' sugar. Increase the speed to medium and beat until fluffy.

7. Assemble the cake: Place 1 cake layer on a cake plate, flat side up. Spread with ¾ cup frosting; top with another cake layer, flat side up. Spread with ¾ cup frosting. Top with remaining cake layer, flat side up. Lightly frost the sides and top of the cake with frosting to barely coat. Refrigerate the assembled cake and the remaining frosting at least 1 hour. Frost the top and sides of the cake with the remaining frosting. Cover the top and sides of the cake with the coconut flakes. The cake can be refrigerated up to 6 hours (cover loosely with plastic wrap.) To serve, let stand at room temperature 1 hour.

Each serving About 690 calories, 7g protein, 77g carbohydrate, 40g fat (27g saturated), 2g fiber, 390mg sodium.

cranberry-vanilla cake

with whipped-cream frosting

PREP: 50 MIN / TOTAL: 1 HR 40 MIN / SERVES 16

CAKE

**3 cups cake flour
(not self-rising)**

1 tablespoon baking powder

Salt

**1 cup salted butter, room
temperature**

2 cups granulated sugar

**5 large eggs, room
temperature**

2 teaspoons vanilla extract

1¼ cups low-fat buttermilk

FILLING

**1 bag (12 ounces) fresh
or frozen (thawed)
cranberries**

1 cup granulated sugar

⅓ cup apricot jam

**¼ teaspoon ground
cinnamon**

GARNISH

¼ cup water

¾ cup granulated sugar

**1 cup fresh or frozen
(thawed) cranberries**

FROSTING

**2 cups heavy or whipping
cream**

**1 cup confectioners'
sugar**

**⅓ cup crème fraîche or
sour cream**

**1 teaspoon vanilla
extract**

1. Prepare the cake: Preheat the oven to 350°F. Line the bottoms of three 8-inch cake pans with parchment paper. Grease the sides of the pans and the parchment. Into a large bowl, sift the flour, baking powder, and ¼ teaspoon salt.

2. In the bowl of the stand mixer on medium-high speed, beat the butter and sugar until smooth and fluffy. Beat in the eggs, one at a time, until incorporated. Beat in the vanilla. Reduce the speed to low; alternately add the buttermilk and the flour mixture, beating well after each addition.

3. Divide the batter evenly among the pans; smooth the tops. Tap the pans firmly against the counter. Bake 40 to 45 minutes, or until a toothpick inserted in the center comes out clean. Cool in the pans on a wire rack 10 minutes. Invert the cakes onto the rack; remove the pans and peel off the parchment. Cool completely. The cakes may be wrapped in plastic wrap and stored at room temperature up to 1 day.

4. Prepare the filling: In a 3-quart saucepan, combine the cranberries, sugar, apricot jam, and cinnamon. Cook over medium heat 8 to 10 minutes, or until most of the berries burst, stirring often. Transfer to a bowl; refrigerate until cold.

5. Prepare the garnish: In a 1-quart saucepan, combine the water and ¼ cup sugar. Heat to boiling over high heat. Stir in the cranberries. Cool completely, then drain. Place the remaining ½ cup sugar on a plate. Toss the cranberries in the sugar to coat. Place on a wire rack; let dry 1 hour.

6. To assemble: Place 1 cake layer on a cake stand; spread half the filling on top. Repeat with another layer and the remaining filling. Top with the third layer.

7. Prepare the frosting: With a mixer on medium speed, whisk the cream until soft peaks form. Reduce the speed to low; add the confectioners' sugar, crème fraîche, and vanilla. Whisk until stiff peaks form. Spread the frosting all over the cake. Garnish with the sugared cranberries. The cake can be covered and refrigerated up to 1 day. Remove from the refrigerator 30 minutes before serving.

Each serving About 590 calories, 6g protein, 85g carbohydrate, 26g fat (16g saturated), 2g fiber, 300mg sodium.

HOW TO

FREEZE WHIPPED CREAM

Stash frozen whipped-cream mounds to fancy up cocoa, pie, coffee, or anything else in a pinch: Whisk cold heavy or whipping cream until fluffy but stiff, then spoon it into a pastry bag (or a plastic bag with a corner cut off). Squeeze dollops onto parchment paper, then freeze. Store them in plastic bags and use as needed. Bring on the unexpected guests!

CRANBERRY-VANILLA CAKE
WITH WHIPPED-CREAM
FROSTING 634

STICKY TOFFEE
BUNDT CAKE 632

CHOCOLATE-RASPBERRY
ROLL 640

classic butter frosting

PREP: 10 MIN / TOTAL: 10 MIN / MAKES 2⅓ CUPS

- ½ cup salted butter, softened
- 1 package (16 ounces) confectioners' sugar
- 3 to 6 tablespoons whole milk, half-and-half, or light cream
- 1½ teaspoons vanilla extract

In a large bowl and using a mixer at medium-low speed, beat the butter, confectioners' sugar, 3 tablespoons milk, and vanilla until smooth and blended. Beat in additional milk as needed for easy spreading consistency. Increase the speed to medium-high; beat the frosting until light and fluffy, about 1 minute.

Each tablespoon About 70 calories, 0g protein, 12g carbohydrate, 3g fat (2g saturated), 0g fiber, 25mg sodium.

VARIATIONS

Lemon Butter Frosting

Prepare as directed, but omit the vanilla and use **2 tablespoons fresh lemon juice** and **1 teaspoon freshly grated lemon zest**. Use only **1 to 2 tablespoons milk** as needed for easy spreading.

Orange Butter Frosting

Prepare as directed for Lemon Butter Frosting, but substitute **orange juice** for lemon juice and **orange zest** for lemon zest.

Brown Butter Frosting

In a small skillet, over medium heat, cook the butter until lightly browned; let cool. Prepare as directed.

chocolate butter frosting

PREP: 15 MIN / TOTAL: 15 MIN / MAKES 2½ CUPS

- ¾ cup salted butter, softened
- 2 cups confectioners' sugar
- 1 teaspoon vanilla extract
- 4 squares (4 ounces) semisweet chocolate, melted and cooled
- 2 squares (2 ounces) unsweetened chocolate, melted and cooled

In a large bowl and using a mixer at low speed, beat the butter, confectioners' sugar, and vanilla until almost combined. Add the semisweet and unsweetened chocolates. Increase the mixer speed to high; beat the frosting until light and fluffy, about 1 minute.

Each tablespoon About 75 calories, 0g protein, 8g carbohydrate, 5g fat (3g saturated), 0g fiber, 35mg sodium.

chocolate glaze

PREP: 5 MIN / TOTAL: 5 MIN, PLUS COOLING / MAKES ½ CUP

- 3 squares (3 ounces) semisweet chocolate, coarsely chopped
- 3 tablespoons salted butter
- 1 tablespoon light corn syrup
- 1 tablespoon whole milk

In a heavy 1-quart saucepan, heat the chocolate, butter, corn syrup, and milk over low heat, stirring occasionally, until smooth.

Each tablespoon About 100 calories, 1g protein, 9g carbohydrate, 8g fat (5g saturated), 1g fiber, 50mg sodium.

whipped cream frosting

PREP: 5 MIN / TOTAL: 5 MIN / MAKES 4 CUPS

- 2 cups heavy or whipping cream
- ¼ cup confectioners' sugar
- 1 teaspoon vanilla extract, or 2 tablespoons brandy or fruit liqueur

In a small bowl and using a mixer at medium speed, beat the cream, confectioners' sugar, and vanilla until stiff peaks form.

Each tablespoon About 30 calories, 0g protein, 1g carbohydrate, 3g fat (2g saturated), 0g fiber, 5mg sodium.

VARIATIONS

Coffee Whipped Cream Frosting

Prepare as directed, but dissolve **2 teaspoons instant-coffee powder** in **2 teaspoons hot water**; add to the cream.

Peppermint Whipped Cream Frosting

Beat the cream as directed, but omit the sugar and vanilla extract. Fold in ¼ **cup crushed peppermint candy**.

Cocoa Whipped Cream Frosting

Prepare as directed, but use ½ cup confectioners' sugar and add ½ **cup unsweetened cocoa**.

fluffy white frosting

PREP: 15 MIN / TOTAL: 25 MIN / MAKES 3 CUPS

- 2 large egg whites
- 1 cup sugar
- ¼ cup water
- 2 teaspoons fresh lemon juice (optional)
- 1 teaspoon light corn syrup
- ¼ teaspoon cream of tartar

1. In a medium bowl set over a 3- to 4-quart saucepan filled with 1 inch simmering water (the bowl should sit about 2 inches above water) and using a handheld mixer at high speed, beat the egg whites, sugar, water, lemon juice (if using), corn syrup, and cream of tartar until soft peaks form and the mixture reaches 160°F on a candy thermometer, about 7 minutes.

2. Remove the bowl from the saucepan; beat the egg white mixture until stiff, glossy peaks form, 5 to 10 minutes longer.

Each tablespoon About 20 calories, 0g protein, 4g carbohydrate, 0g fat (0g saturated), 0g fiber, 5mg sodium.

VARIATION

Fluffy Harvest Moon Frosting

Prepare as directed, but substitute **1 cup packed dark brown sugar** for the granulated sugar and omit the lemon juice.

 Tip If you're planning on frosting a chocolate cake, omit the lemon juice.

cream cheese frosting

PREP: 10 MIN / TOTAL: 10 MIN / MAKES 2½ CUPS

- 2 small packages (3 ounces each) cream cheese, slightly softened
- 6 tablespoons salted butter, softened
- 3 cups confectioners' sugar
- 1½ teaspoons vanilla extract

In a large bowl and using a mixer at low speed, beat the cream cheese, butter, confectioners' sugar, and vanilla just until blended. Increase the speed to medium; beat until smooth and fluffy, about 1 minute, frequently scraping the bowl with a rubber spatula.

Each tablespoon About 65 calories, 0g protein, 9g carbohydrate, 3g fat (2g saturated), 0g fiber, 30mg sodium.

ganache

PREP: 15 MIN / TOTAL: 15 MIN, PLUS CHILLING / MAKES 2 CUPS

- 1 cup heavy or whipping cream
- 2 tablespoons sugar
- 2 teaspoons salted butter
- 10 squares (10 ounces) semisweet chocolate, chopped
- 1 teaspoon vanilla extract
- 1 to 2 tablespoons brandy or orange- or almond-flavored liqueur (optional)

1. In a 2-quart saucepan, combine the cream, sugar, and butter; heat to boiling over medium-high heat. Remove the saucepan from the heat.

2. Add the chocolate to the cream mixture and, with a wire whisk, whisk until the chocolate melts and the mixture is smooth. Stir in the vanilla and brandy, if using. Pour into a jelly-roll pan and refrigerate until spreadable, at least 30 minutes.

Each tablespoon About 75 calories, 1g protein, 6g carbohydrate, 6g fat (3g saturated), 1g fiber, 5mg sodium.

lemon filling

PREP: 15 MIN / TOTAL: 25 MIN, PLUS CHILLING / MAKES 1 CUP

- 3 large lemons
- 1 tablespoon cornstarch
- 6 tablespoons salted butter, cut into pieces
- ¾ cup sugar
- 4 large egg yolks

1. From the lemons, grate 1 tablespoon zest and squeeze ½ cup juice. In a 2-quart saucepan and using a wire whisk, mix the cornstarch and lemon zest and juice until blended. Add the butter and sugar. Heat to boiling over medium-high heat, stirring constantly; boil 1 minute.

2. In a small bowl, lightly beat the egg yolks. Into the egg yolks, beat ¼ cup hot lemon mixture; pour the egg mixture back into the lemon mixture in the saucepan, beating rapidly to prevent curdling. Reduce the heat to low; cook, stirring constantly, until the mixture has thickened (do not boil), about 5 minutes. Pour into a medium bowl. Press plastic wrap onto the surface. Refrigerate until chilled, at least 3 hours or up to 3 days.

Each tablespoon About 95 calories, 1g protein, 11g carbohydrate, 6g fat (3g saturated), 0g fiber, 45mg sodium.

deluxe cheesecake

PREP: 45 MIN / TOTAL: 1 HR 35 MIN, PLUS COOLING, CHILLING, AND STANDING / SERVES 20

- ½ cup salted butter, softened
- 1½ cups sugar
- 3 large egg yolks
- 1¼ cups plus 3 tablespoons all-purpose flour
- 5 packages (8 ounces each) cream cheese, softened
- 5 large eggs
- ¼ cup whole milk
- 1 teaspoon freshly grated lemon zest

1. Preheat the oven to 400°F. In a small bowl and using a mixer at low speed, beat the butter and ¼ cup sugar until blended. Add 1 egg yolk and beat until well combined. Beat in 1¼ cups flour just until combined. Divide the dough into almost equal parts; wrap the slightly larger piece in plastic wrap and refrigerate.

2. Press the smaller piece of dough onto the bottom of a 10 × 2½-inch springform pan. Bake until golden, about 8 minutes; cool completely in the pan on a wire rack.

3. Turn the oven control to 475°F. In a large bowl and using a mixer at medium speed, beat the cream cheese just until smooth; gradually beat in the remaining 1¼ cups sugar. Reduce the speed to low. Beat in the eggs, the remaining 2 egg yolks, the milk, the remaining 3 tablespoons flour, and the lemon zest just until blended, occasionally scraping the bowl with a rubber spatula.

4. Press the remaining piece of dough around the sides of the pan to within 1 inch of the rim. Scrape the cream-cheese mixture into the crust. Bake 12 minutes. Turn the oven control to 300°F; bake 30 minutes longer. The edges will be set, but the center will still jiggle. Turn off the oven; let the cheesecake remain in the oven 30 minutes.

5. Remove the cheesecake from the oven and place it on a wire rack. Run a thin knife around the edge of the cheesecake to prevent cracking during cooling. Cool completely in the pan on a wire rack. Cover and refrigerate until well chilled, at least 4 hours or up to overnight. Remove the side of the springform pan to serve.

Each serving About 360 calories, 7g protein, 24g carbohydrate, 27g fat (16g saturated), 0g fiber, 235mg sodium.

Ingredient Ideas

cheesecake toppings

Sometimes a delectable slice of plain cheesecake hits the spot, but there are also times when a bit of "gilding the lily" is called for. It is easy to dress up a cream cheese cheesecake without a lot of fuss. Here are some of our favorite ways.

- Top the chilled cheesecake with **whole, halved,** or **sliced hulled strawberries**. Brush with ½ **cup melted red currant jelly**.

- Top the chilled cheesecake with **fresh raspberries** or concentric circles of raspberries and blackberries. Serve with **Best Berry Sauce** (page 658).

- Top the chilled cheesecake with ½-**inch wedges of peeled ripe peaches**. Serve with **whipped cream**.

---

lemon-ricotta cheesecake

PREP: 20 MIN / TOTAL: 1 HR 45 MIN, PLUS COOLING, CHILLING, AND STANDING / SERVES 16

- **4 large lemons**
- **1 cup vanilla wafer crumbs (about 30 cookies)**
- **4 tablespoons salted butter, melted**
- **1¼ cups sugar**
- **¼ cup cornstarch**
- **2 packages (8 ounces each) cream cheese, softened**
- **1 container (15 ounces) ricotta cheese**
- **4 large eggs**
- **2 cups half-and-half or light cream**
- **2 teaspoons vanilla extract**

1. Preheat the oven to 375°F. Tightly wrap the outside of a 9 × 3-inch springform pan with heavy-duty foil. From the lemons, grate 4 teaspoons zest and squeeze ⅓ cup juice. In the springform pan, combine the cookie crumbs, melted butter, and 1 teaspoon lemon zest; stir with a fork until evenly moistened. With your hand, press the mixture firmly onto the bottom of the pan. Bake until the crust is deep golden, about 10 minutes. Cool completely in the pan on a wire rack.

2. Turn the oven control to 325°F. In a small bowl, stir the sugar and cornstarch until blended. In a large bowl and using a mixer at medium speed, beat the cream cheese and ricotta until very smooth, about 5 minutes; slowly beat in the sugar mixture. Reduce the speed to low. Beat in the eggs, half-and-half, lemon juice, vanilla, and the remaining 3 teaspoons lemon zest just until blended, frequently scraping the bowl with a rubber spatula.

3. Pour the cream cheese mixture into the cooled crust. Bake 1 hour 15 minutes. Turn off the oven; let the cheesecake remain in the oven 1 hour longer.

4. Remove the cheesecake from the oven and transfer it to a wire rack; remove the foil. Run a thin knife around the edge of the cheesecake to prevent cracking during cooling. Cool the cheesecake completely in the pan on the wire rack. Cover and refrigerate until well chilled, at least 6 hours or up to overnight. Remove the side of the springform pan to serve.

Each serving About 325 calories, 8g protein, 25g carbohydrate, 22g fat (13g saturated), 0g fiber, 180mg sodium.

chocolate-raspberry roll

(See photo on page 635.)

PREP: 40 MIN / TOTAL: 55 MIN, PLUS COOLING AND CHILLING / SERVES 12

- 1 tablespoon water
- ⅓ cup plus 4 tablespoons granulated sugar
- 2 half-pints (6 ounces each) fresh raspberries
- 6 ounces bittersweet chocolate, chopped
- 2 tablespoons salted butter
- ¼ teaspoon salt
- 4 tablespoons raspberry liqueur
- 6 large eggs, separated
- 3 tablespoons confectioners' sugar
- 1 cups heavy or whipping cream
- ½ cups mascarpone cheese
- Raspberries, for serving

1. Preheat the oven to 350°F. Grease an 18 × 12-inch jelly-roll pan. Line it with parchment paper; grease the paper.

2. In a medium bowl, stir the water and 2 tablespoons granulated sugar. Fold in the berries. Let stand while preparing the cake.

3. Fill a 4-quart saucepan with 2 inches of water. Heat to simmering. In a large heatproof bowl, combine the chocolate, butter, salt, and 2 tablespoons liqueur; set the bowl over the saucepan, stirring until smooth. Remove from the heat. Stir in the egg yolks, one at a time, beating after each addition.

4. In another large bowl and using a mixer on medium speed, beat the egg whites until frothy. Gradually add ⅓ cup granulated sugar; beat until stiff peaks form. Gently fold the whites into the chocolate mixture, one-third at a time, until incorporated. Spread the batter evenly in the prepared pan.

5. Bake 15 minutes, or until a toothpick inserted in the center comes out nearly clean. Cool in the pan on a wire rack 10 minutes. Dust the top of the cake with 2 tablespoons confectioners' sugar; place a sheet of waxed paper on top of the cake. Set a cutting board over the cake, then flip the board and pan together. Remove the pan and peel off the parchment. Cool the cake completely.

6. In a large bowl and using a mixer on medium-high speed, beat the cream and mascarpone until soft peaks form. Add 2 tablespoons granulated sugar and 2 tablespoons liqueur. Beat until stiff; spread the mixture over the cake, leaving a ½-inch border.

7. Starting from a long side, roll the cake, peeling off the paper as you roll. (The cake may crack slightly as you roll it.) Place it on a platter, cover with plastic wrap, and refrigerate at least 1 hour or up to 1 day.

8. Dust the cake with 1 tablespoon confectioners' sugar. Serve with the raspberries.

Each serving About 305 calories, 6g protein, 26g carbohydrate, 22g fat (12g saturated), 3g fiber, 115mg sodium.

jelly roll

PREP: 20 MIN / TOTAL: 30 MIN, PLUS COOLING / SERVES 10

- 5 large eggs, separated
- ½ cup granulated sugar
- 1 teaspoon vanilla extract
- ½ cup all-purpose flour
- Confectioners' sugar, for dusting
- ⅔ cup strawberry jam

1. Preheat the oven to 350°F. Grease a 15½ × 10½-inch jelly-roll pan. Line with waxed paper; grease the waxed paper.

2. In a large bowl and using a mixer at high speed, beat the egg whites until soft peaks form. Sprinkle in ¼ cup granulated sugar, 1 tablespoon at a time, beating until the egg whites stand in stiff, glossy peaks when the beaters are lifted. Do not overbeat.

3. In a small bowl and using a mixer at high speed, beat the egg yolks, the remaining ¼ cup granulated sugar, and the vanilla until very thick and lemon colored, 8 to 10 minutes. Reduce the speed to low; beat in the flour until blended. With a rubber spatula, gently fold the egg yolk mixture into the beaten egg whites, just until blended.

4. Scrape the batter into the prepared pan; spread it evenly. Bake until the cake springs back when lightly pressed, 10 to 15 minutes.

5. Meanwhile, sift the confectioners' sugar onto a clean kitchen towel. When the cake is done, run a thin knife around the edges of the cake to loosen it from the sides of the pan; invert onto the towel. Carefully remove the waxed paper. Trim ¼ inch from the edges of the cake. Starting at a short side, roll the cake and the towel jelly-roll fashion. Place the rolled cake, seam side down, on a wire rack; cool completely.

6. Unroll the cooled cake. With a narrow metal spatula, spread it evenly with the jam. Starting from the same short side, roll up the cake again (without the towel). Place the rolled cake, seam side down, on a platter and dust with confectioners' sugar.

Each serving About 165 calories, 4g protein, 30g carbohydrate, 3g fat (1g saturated), 0g fiber, 40mg sodium.

crème caramel

PREP: 15 MIN / TOTAL: 1 HR 5 MIN, PLUS COOLING AND CHILLING / SERVES 6

¼ cup plus ⅓ cup sugar
4 large eggs
2 cups whole milk
1½ teaspoons vanilla extract
¼ teaspoon salt

1. Preheat the oven to 325°F. In a heavy 1-quart saucepan, heat ¼ cup sugar over medium heat, swirling the pan occasionally, until the sugar has melted and is amber in color. Immediately pour it into six 6-ounce custard cups or ramekins.

2. In a large bowl and using a wire whisk, beat the eggs and the remaining ⅓ cup sugar until blended. Whisk in the milk, vanilla, and salt until well combined; pour the mixture through a fine-mesh sieve into the prepared custard cups.

3. Place the custard cups in a small baking pan; place it on a rack in the oven. Carefully pour enough very hot water into the baking pan to come halfway up the sides of the custard cups. Bake just until a knife inserted 1 inch from the center of the custards comes out clean, 50 to 55 minutes. Transfer the custard cups to a wire rack to cool. Cover and refrigerate until well chilled, 4 hours or up to overnight.

4. To serve, run the tip of a small knife around the edge of the custards. Invert the cups onto dessert plates, shaking the cups gently until the custards slip out. Leave the inverted cup on the plate for several minutes to allow caramel syrup to drip onto the custards.

Each serving About 180 calories, 7g protein, 24g carbohydrate, 6g fat (3g saturated), 0g fiber, 180mg sodium.

VARIATION

Orange Crème Caramel
Add **3 (3-inch) strips of orange peel to the sugar** while caramelizing. Carefully remove before pouring caramel into ramekins.

crème brûlée

PREP: 20 MIN / TOTAL: 1 HR, PLUS COOLING AND CHILLING / SERVES 10

½ vanilla bean, or 2 teaspoons vanilla extract
1½ cups heavy or whipping cream
1½ cups half-and-half or light cream
8 large egg yolks
⅔ cup granulated sugar
⅓ to ½ cup packed brown sugar

1. Preheat the oven to 325°F. With a knife, cut the vanilla bean lengthwise in half; scrape out the seeds. Into a heavy 3-quart saucepan, add the cream, half-and-half, and vanilla bean or extract. Heat over medium heat until bubbles form around the edge. Remove from heat. Remove the vanilla bean.

2. Meanwhile, in a large bowl and using a wire whisk, beat the egg yolks and granulated sugar until well blended. Slowly stir in the hot cream mixture until well combined. Pour the cream mixture into ten 4- to 5-ounce broiler-proof ramekins or a shallow 2½-quart casserole.

3. Place the ramekins or casserole in a large roasting pan; place the pan on a rack in the oven. Carefully pour enough very hot water into the roasting pan to come halfway up the sides of the ramekins. Bake just until set (the mixture will still be slightly soft in the center), 35 to 40 minutes. Transfer the ramekins to a wire rack to cool to room temperature. Cover and refrigerate, at least 3 hours or up to overnight.

4. Up to 2 hours before serving, preheat the broiler. Place the brown sugar in a small sieve; with a spoon, press the sugar through the sieve to cover the tops of the chilled custards.

5. Place ramekins in jelly-roll pan for easier handling. With broiler rack at closest position to heat source, broil custard just until sugar melts, 3 to 4 minutes. Serve or refrigerate up to 2 hours. The melted brown sugar with form a delicious brittle crust.

Each serving About 305 calories, 4g protein, 25g carbohydrate, 21g fat (12g saturated), 0g fiber, 38mg sodium.

SUNNY-SIDE UP MERINGUE NESTS 642

BERRY & LEMON PAVLOVA 643

sunny-side up meringue nests

PREP: 10 MIN / TOTAL: 3 HR / SERVES 6

3 large egg whites
Salt
¼ teaspoon cream of tartar
½ cup sugar

½ teaspoon vanilla extract
¾ cup Tangy Lemon Curd (below) or prepared lemon curd

1. Position one rack in the middle of the oven; preheat the oven to 225°F. Line a large baking sheet with parchment paper.

2. In a medium bowl and using a mixer on medium speed, beat the egg whites with a pinch of salt until foamy. Add the cream of tartar and beat on medium-high until soft peaks form. Add the sugar, 1 tablespoon at a time, until the peaks are stiff and glossy. Beat in the vanilla.

3. Spoon the meringue into a pastry bag fitted with a star tip or into a resealable plastic bag with one corner cut off. Pipe six 3-inch disks onto the parchment-lined baking sheet, spacing them 1 inch apart. Pipe around the edges of the disks to form ¾-inch-high sides. Bake 1 hour.

4. Turn off the oven. Leave the meringues in the oven 1½ hours with the oven door closed. Remove from the oven; cool completely. Store in an airtight container at room temperature up to 1 week. To serve, fill each with about 1½ tablespoons lemon curd.

TANGY LEMON CURD From **3 medium lemons**, grate **1 tablespoon zest** and squeeze **⅔ cup juice**. In a heavy 2-quart saucepan over medium heat, heat **1 cup sugar**; **6 tablespoons salted butter**, cut into pieces; **1 tablespoon cornstarch**; **¼ teaspoon salt**; and the lemon zest and lemon juice to boiling. Boil 1 minute. In a small bowl, lightly beat **5 large egg yolks**. Into the yolks, beat a small amount of the lemon mixture. Off the heat, whisk the egg mixture back into the lemon mixture in the saucepan. Return to medium-low heat; cook, stirring constantly, until thickened, about 5 minutes. Pour the lemon curd into a bowl; cover the surface area with plastic wrap and refrigerate 3 hours, or until well chilled. Store in the refrigerator up to 1 week. Makes about 1⅔ cups.

Each serving About 205 calories, 3g protein, 34g carbohydrate, 7g fat (4g saturated), 0g fiber, 140mg sodium.

berry & lemon pavlova

PREP: 15 MIN / TOTAL: 2 HR 15 MIN, PLUS DRYING / SERVES 6

⅔ cup sugar

1 tablespoon cornstarch

4 large egg whites

¼ teaspoon salt

1 teaspoon distilled white vinegar

1 teaspoon vanilla extract

½ teaspoon almond extract

¾ cup heavy or whipping cream

1 cup prepared lemon curd

1 tablespoon honey

1 container (12 ounces) blueberries

1 container (6 ounces) blackberries

1. Preheat the oven to 225°F. Onto a sheet of parchment paper, trace a 9-inch circle. Turn over; place the parchment on a baking sheet.

2. In a small bowl, whisk the sugar and cornstarch. In the bowl of the stand mixer on medium-high speed, beat the egg whites and salt until soft peaks form. Add the sugar mixture to the whites, 1 tablespoon at a time, beating well between additions. Add the vinegar and both extracts; beat until stiff peaks form.

3. Transfer the whites to the center of the parchment circle; spread the whites to form a nest, with the sides higher than the center. Bake 2 hours. Turn off the oven; let the meringue stand in the oven at least 3 hours or up to overnight.

4. To serve, remove the parchment from the meringue. In a medium bowl and using a mixer on medium-high speed, beat the cream until stiff peaks form. Spread it over the meringue. Dollop the top with the curd; spread it out evenly. In a large microwave-safe bowl, microwave the honey and 1 tablespoon water on High 20 seconds. Stir in the berries until well coated. Spoon over the curd. Serve immediately.

Each serving About 420 calories, 4g protein, 66g carbohydrate, 14g fat (8g saturated), 2g fiber, 175mg sodium.

VARIATION

Kiwi Berry Pavlova

Replace the topping with **1 cup heavy or whipping cream** and **2 tablespoons sugar** whipped to soft peaks. Beat in **½ teaspoon vanilla extract**. To serve, spoon the whipped cream into the center of the meringue and top with **2 peeled, thickly sliced kiwifruit** and **1 pound sliced strawberries**.

GLOSSARY →

Pavlova, an Australian favorite, was created to honor prima ballerina Anna Pavlova, who was renowned for her leading role in *Swan Lake*. Swanlike in its delicacy and pristine whiteness, it always gets rave reviews.

chocolate soufflés

PREP: 20 MIN / TOTAL: 45 MIN, PLUS COOLING / SERVES 8

1¼ cups plus 3 tablespoons granulated sugar

¼ cup all-purpose flour

1 teaspoon instant espresso-coffee powder

1 cup whole milk

5 squares (5 ounces) unsweetened chocolate, chopped

3 tablespoons salted butter, softened

4 large eggs, separated, plus 2 large egg whites

2 teaspoons vanilla extract

¼ teaspoon salt

Confectioners' sugar, for dusting

1. In a heavy 3-quart saucepan, combine 1¼ cups granulated sugar, the flour, and espresso powder. With a wire whisk, gradually stir in the milk until blended. Cook over medium heat, stirring constantly, until the mixture has thickened and boils; boil, stirring, 1 minute. Remove from the heat.

2. Stir in the chocolate and butter until melted and smooth. With a whisk, beat in the egg yolks until well blended; stir in the vanilla. Cool to lukewarm.

3. Meanwhile, preheat the oven to 350°F. Grease eight 6-ounce custard cups or ramekins or a 2-quart soufflé dish; sprinkle lightly with the remaining 3 tablespoons granulated sugar.

4. In a large bowl and using a mixer at high speed, beat the 6 egg whites and salt just until stiff peaks form. With a rubber spatula, gently fold one-third of the beaten egg whites into the chocolate mixture; fold this back into the remaining egg whites just until blended.

5. Spoon the mixture into the prepared custard cups or soufflé dish. (If using custard cups, place them in a jelly-roll pan for easier handling.) Bake until the soufflés have puffed and the centers are glossy, 25 to 30 minutes for individual soufflés, 35 to 40 minutes for a large soufflé. Dust with confectioners' sugar. Serve immediately.

Each serving About 355 calories, 7g protein, 44g carbohydrate, 19g fat (10g saturated), 3g fiber, 178mg sodium.

raspberry-banana trifle

PREP: 1 HR / TOTAL: 1 HR 15 MIN, PLUS CHILLING / SERVES 24

CAKE

1 frozen prepared pound
   cake (1 pound), thawed

6 tablespoons seedless
   red-raspberry jam

CUSTARD

6 large eggs

¾ cup sugar

⅓ cup cornstarch

4 cups whole milk

4 tablespoons salted butter

2 tablespoons vanilla extract

3 large ripe bananas
   (1½ pounds), sliced

TOPPING

1 cup heavy or
   whipping cream

2 tablespoons sugar

Fresh raspberries and
   fresh mint leaves,
   for garnish

1. Prepare the cake: With a serrated knife, cut the crusts from the pound cake. Set the cake on one long side; cut it lengthwise into 4 equal slices. With a small spatula, spread 2 tablespoons jam on top of 1 cake slice; top with another cake slice. Repeat with the remaining jam and cake, ending with a slice of cake. Cut the jam-layered cake crosswise into ¼-inch slices, keeping the slices together, then cut the cake lengthwise in half down the center. (You should have about 26 slices of jam-layered cake cut in half to yield 52 half slices.)

2. Prepare the custard: In a medium bowl and using a wire whisk, beat the eggs, sugar, and cornstarch; set aside. In a 4-quart sauce-pan, heat the milk just to boiling. While constantly beating with a whisk, gradually pour about half the hot milk into the egg mixture. Pour the egg mixture back into the remaining milk in the sauce-pan and cook over medium-low heat, whisking constantly, until the mixture thickens and begins to bubble around the edge of the pan; the mixture will not boil vigorously. Simmer the custard 1 min-ute, whisking constantly; it must reach at least 160°F. Remove the saucepan from the heat; stir in the butter with vanilla.

3. Assemble the trifle: In a 4-quart glass trifle dish or deep glass bowl, place 2 rows of cake slices around the sides of the bowl, alter-nating horizontal and vertical placement of cake slices to make a checkerboard design. Place some cake slices in a layer to cover the bottom of the bowl; top with one-third of the sliced bananas. Spoon one-third of the warm custard on top of the bananas. Top with half the remaining bananas and half the remaining custard. Top with the remaining cake, then the bananas and custard. Cover the surface of the custard with plastic wrap to prevent a skin from forming. Refrigerate the trifle 6 hours or overnight.

4. Before serving, prepare the topping: In a small bowl and using a mixer at medium speed, beat the cream with the sugar until stiff peaks form. Remove the plastic wrap from the trifle; top the trifle with whipped cream and garnish with raspberries and mint.

Each serving About 240 calories, 4g protein, 28g carbohydrate, 12g fat (5g saturated), 1g fiber, 120mg sodium.

Ingredient Ideas

trifles

Though there are many, many recipes for trifles, they probably have three elements in common: strips or cubes of cake for their base, a rich custard sauce for pouring between the layers, and fresh fruit. After that, whipped cream, sliced or slivered nuts, candied fruit, jam, and brandy or fruit-flavored liqueur are all popular add-ins. Here are some ways to vary our delectable trifle.

- Use **plain or chocolate sponge cake** or a **fruit-flavored pound cake** instead of the plain pound cake.

- Try **orange, apricot, or strawberry jam** instead of the raspberry jam.

- Substitute **3 cups of whole, sliced, or diced fresh fruit**—strawberries, blackberries, peaches, apricots, plums, etc.—for the banana.

- Drizzle the cake with a little **brandy or orange-flavored liqueur** before brushing it with jam.

no-bake pumpkin cheesecake mini trifles

(See photo on page 650.)

PREP: 25 MIN / TOTAL: 40 MIN, PLUS CHILLING / SERVES 8

- 1 package (8 ounces) cream cheese, softened
- ½ cup packed dark brown sugar
- 1 can (15 ounces) pure pumpkin
- 1½ teaspoons vanilla extract
- 1 teaspoon pumpkin pie spice
- 2 cups heavy or whipping cream, very cold
- 2 tablespoons plus ½ cup granulated sugar
- 2 cups crumbled ginger cookies or graham crackers
- 1¼ cups chopped candied nuts
- Nonstick cooking spray
- 2 tablespoons water

1. With a mixer on medium speed, beat the cream cheese until fluffy. Gradually beat in the brown sugar until smooth. Add the pumpkin, vanilla, and pumpkin pie spice. Mix until smooth, scraping the sides of the bowl as needed; set aside. In a separate bowl and using a mixer on medium-high speed, beat the cream until soft peaks form. Gradually beat in 2 tablespoons granulated sugar until stiff peaks form.

2. In a medium bowl, combine the cookies and 1 cup candied nuts; divide half of this mixture among 8 parfait glasses. Divide half of the pumpkin mixture among the glasses, followed by half the whipped cream. Repeat layering the cookies, pumpkin, and whipped cream. Cover and refrigerate at least 3 hours or up to 1 day.

3. Line a baking sheet with foil. Spray the foil with nonstick cooking spray. In a small saucepan, heat the water and the remaining ½ cup granulated sugar to boiling over medium-high heat; cook until golden. Working quickly, stir in the remaining ¼ cup candied nuts, then spread the mixture onto the prepared foil in a thin layer. Cool completely. Break into small shards.

4. Garnish the trifles with brittle and serve.

Each serving About 660 calories, 7g protein, 61g carbohydrate, 45g fat (21g saturated), 4g fiber, 305mg sodium.

bread pudding

PREP: 20 MIN / TOTAL: 1 HR 5 MIN, PLUS STANDING AND COOLING / SERVES 8

- ½ cup dark seedless raisins
- 3 tablespoons dark rum or bourbon
- ½ cup sugar
- ¼ teaspoon ground cinnamon
- ⅛ teaspoon ground nutmeg
- 4 large eggs
- 2 teaspoons vanilla extract
- 3 cups whole milk
- 3 cups (½-inch cubes) day-old French bread

1. In a cup, combine the raisins and rum; let stand 15 minutes. Grease an 8-inch square glass or ceramic baking dish.

2. In a large bowl, whisk the sugar, cinnamon, and nutmeg. Whisk in the eggs and vanilla until combined. Add the milk to the egg mixture and whisk until well blended. Stir in the bread cubes. Let stand 15 minutes, stirring occasionally. Stir in the raisin mixture.

3. Meanwhile, preheat the oven to 325°F. Pour the bread mixture into the prepared dish. Bake 45 to 50 minutes, or until a knife inserted near the center of the pudding comes out clean. Let cool on a wire rack. Serve warm, or refrigerate and serve cold.

Each serving About 215 calories, 8g protein, 31g carbohydrate, 6g fat (3g saturated), 1g fiber, 165mg sodium.

GLOSSARY →

A **bain-marie** (hot water bath) is the best way to ensure that delicate custard mixtures cook evenly. Here's how to do it: Place custard cups or a baking dish in a baking or roasting pan. Place the pan on the oven rack. Pour in enough very hot (but not boiling) water to come halfway up the sides of the dish. This method is sometimes used for cheesecakes and other egg-based dishes, too.

tiramisu

PREP: 35 MIN / TOTAL: 35 MIN, PLUS CHILLING / SERVES 12

- 1 cup hot espresso or very strong brewed coffee
- 3 tablespoons brandy
- 2 tablespoons plus ½ cup sugar
- 18 crisp Italian ladyfingers (5 ounces)
- ½ cup whole milk
- 1 container (16 to 17½ ounces) mascarpone cheese
- ¾ cup heavy or whipping cream
- Unsweetened cocoa, for dusting
- Chocolate curls (see page 438), for garnish

1. In a 9-inch pie plate, stir the coffee, brandy, and 2 tablespoons sugar until the sugar has dissolved; cool to room temperature. Dip both sides of 9 ladyfingers into the coffee mixture, one at a time, to soak completely; arrange them in a single layer in an 8-inch square baking dish.

2. In a large bowl, stir the milk and remaining ½ cup sugar until the sugar has dissolved. Stir in the mascarpone until blended.

3. In a small bowl and using a mixer at high speed, beat the cream until soft peaks form. With a rubber spatula, gently fold the whipped cream into the mascarpone mixture until blended. Spread half the mixture over the ladyfingers in the baking dish.

4. Dip the remaining 9 ladyfingers into the coffee mixture and arrange them on top of the mascarpone mixture. Spread with the remaining mascarpone mixture. Refrigerate 3 hours or up to overnight.

5. Just before serving, dust with cocoa. Cut into squares and spoon into goblets or dessert dishes. Garnish with curls.

Each serving About 325 calories, 4g protein, 22g carbohydrate, 23g fat (15g saturated), 1g fiber, 60mg sodium.

GLOSSARY → **Savoiardi**, also known as ladyfingers, are light and airy Italian cookies made by piping sponge-cake batter into finger forms.

panna cotta

PREP: 20 MIN / TOTAL: 35 MIN, PLUS CHILLING / SERVES 8

- 1 envelope (¼ ounce) unflavored gelatin
- 1 cup whole milk
- ½ vanilla bean, or 1½ teaspoons vanilla extract
- 1¾ cups heavy or whipping cream
- ¼ cup sugar
- 1 strip (3 × 1 inch) lemon peel
- 1 cinnamon stick (3 inches)
- Best Berry Sauce (page 658), made with raspberries
- Fresh raspberries

1. In a 2-cup measuring cup, evenly sprinkle the gelatin over the milk; let stand 2 minutes to soften the gelatin slightly. With a knife, cut vanilla bean lengthwise in half; scrape out the seeds and reserve.

2. In a heavy 1-quart saucepan, combine the cream, sugar, lemon peel, cinnamon stick, and vanilla bean halves and seeds (do not add vanilla extract yet, if using); heat to boiling over high heat, stirring occasionally. Reduce the heat and simmer, stirring occasionally, 5 minutes. Stir in the milk mixture; cook over low heat, stirring frequently, until the gelatin has dissolved, 2 to 3 minutes.

3. Discard the lemon peel, cinnamon stick, and vanilla bean from the cream mixture. (Stir in the vanilla extract now, if using.) Pour the cream mixture into a medium bowl set in a large bowl of ice water. With a rubber spatula, stir the mixture until it just begins to set, 10 to 12 minutes. Pour the cream mixture into eight 4-ounce ramekins. Place the ramekins in a jelly-roll pan for easier handling. Cover and refrigerate the panna cotta until well chilled and set, 4 hours or up to overnight.

4. Meanwhile, prepare Best Berry Sauce.

5. To unmold the panna cotta, run the tip of a knife around the edges. Tap the side of each ramekin sharply to break the seal and invert them onto dessert plates. Spoon sauce around each panna cotta and sprinkle with fresh raspberries.

Each serving (without sauce) About 230 calories, 3g protein, 9g carbohydrate, 20g fat (13g saturated), 0g fiber, 40mg sodium.

brownie pudding cake

PREP: 20 MIN / TOTAL: 50 MIN / SERVES 8

- 2 teaspoons instant-coffee powder (optional)
- 2 tablespoons plus 1¾ cups boiling water
- 1 cup all-purpose flour
- ¾ cup unsweetened cocoa
- ½ cup granulated sugar
- 2 teaspoons baking powder
- ¼ teaspoon salt
- ½ cup whole milk
- 4 tablespoons salted butter, melted
- 1 teaspoon vanilla extract
- ½ cup packed brown sugar
- Whipped cream or vanilla ice cream, for serving (optional)

1. Preheat the oven to 350°F. In a cup, dissolve the coffee powder in 2 tablespoons boiling water, if using.

2. In a large bowl, combine the flour, ½ cup cocoa, granulated sugar, baking powder, and salt. In a 2-cup measuring cup, combine the milk, melted butter, vanilla, and coffee mixture, if using. With a wooden spoon, stir the milk mixture into the flour mixture until just blended. Pour into an ungreased 8-inch square baking dish.

3. In a small bowl, thoroughly combine the brown sugar and remaining ¼ cup cocoa; sprinkle evenly over the batter. Carefully pour the remaining 1¾ cups boiling water evenly over the mixture in the baking dish; do not stir.

4. Bake 30 minutes; the batter will separate into cake and pudding layers. Cool in pan on a wire rack 10 minutes. Serve hot with whipped cream, if you like.

Each serving About 240 calories, 4g protein, 43g carbohydrate, 7g fat (5g saturated), 3g fiber, 270mg sodium.

lemon pudding cake

PREP: 20 MIN / TOTAL: 1 HR / SERVES 6

- 3 lemons
- ¾ cup sugar
- ¼ cup all-purpose flour
- 3 large eggs, separated
- 1 cup whole milk
- 4 tablespoons salted butter, melted
- ⅛ teaspoon salt

1. Preheat the oven to 350°F. Grease an 8-inch square baking dish. From the lemons, grate 1 tablespoon zest and squeeze ⅓ cup juice. In a large bowl, combine the sugar and flour. With a wire whisk, beat in the egg yolks, milk, melted butter, and lemon zest and juice.

2. In a small bowl and using a mixer at high speed, beat the egg whites and salt until soft peaks form. With a rubber spatula, gently fold one-third of the beaten egg whites into the lemon mixture. Fold in the remaining whites, just until blended. Pour the batter into the prepared baking dish.

3. Set the baking dish in a medium roasting pan; place it on a rack in the oven. Carefully pour enough very hot water into the roasting pan to come halfway up the sides of the baking dish. Bake until the top is golden and set, about 40 minutes; the batter will separate into cake and pudding layers. Cool in the pan on a wire rack 10 minutes. Serve hot.

Each serving About 255 calories, 5g protein, 32g carbohydrate, 12g fat (7g saturated), 0g fiber, 180mg sodium.

VARIATION

Orange Pudding Cake

Prepare as directed above, but in step 1 use ¼ **cup fresh lemon juice**, ¼ **cup fresh orange juice**, and **2 teaspoons freshly grated orange zest**.

rice pudding

PREP: 10 MIN / TOTAL: 1 HR 25 MIN / SERVES 6

4 cups whole milk	¼ teaspoon salt
½ cup regular long-grain rice	1 large egg
½ cup sugar	1 teaspoon vanilla extract

1. In a heavy 4-quart saucepan, combine the milk, rice, sugar, and salt; heat to boiling over medium-high heat, stirring frequently. Reduce the heat; cover and simmer the mixture, stirring occasion-ally, until the rice is very tender, about 1 hour.

2. In a small bowl and using a fork, lightly beat the egg; stir in ½ cup hot rice mixture. Slowly pour the egg mixture back into the rice mixture, stirring rapidly to prevent curdling. Cook, stirring con-stantly, until the rice mixture has thickened, about 5 minutes; do not boil or the mixture will curdle. Remove from the heat; stir in the vanilla. Serve warm, or spoon it into a medium bowl and refrigerate until well chilled, about 3 hours.

Each serving About 235 calories, 7g protein, 37g carbohydrate, 6g fat (4g saturated), 0g fiber, 190mg sodium.

VARIATION

Rich Rice Pudding

Prepare as directed above and refrigerate. In a small bowl and using a mixer at medium speed, beat ½ **cup heavy or whipping cream** until soft peaks form. With a rubber spatula, gently fold the whipped cream into the cold rice pudding. Refrigerate until ready to serve, up to 4 hours. Serves 8.

chocolate fondue

PREP: 15 MIN / TOTAL: 20 MIN / SERVES 8

6 squares (6 ounces) semisweet chocolate, coarsely chopped	2 or 3 small pears, unpeeled, cored and cut into ½-inch-thick wedges
½ cup half-and-half or light cream	1 pint fresh strawberries
½ teaspoon vanilla extract	½ cup finely chopped almonds, toasted
4 small bananas, each peeled and cut into ½-inch-thick slices	

1. In a heavy 1-quart saucepan, heat the chocolate and half-and-half over low heat, stirring frequently, until the chocolate has melted and the mixture is smooth, about 5 minutes. Stir in the vanilla; keep warm.

2. To serve, arrange the bananas, pears, and strawberries on a large platter. Spoon the chocolate sauce into a small bowl; place the nuts in a separate small bowl. With forks or toothpicks, have guests dip the fruit into the chocolate sauce, then into the nuts.

Each serving About 250 calories, 4g protein, 36g carbohydrate, 13g fat (5g saturated), 6g fiber, 10mg sodium.

vanilla pastry cream

PREP: 5 MIN / TOTAL: 15 MIN, PLUS CHILLING / MAKES 2¾ CUPS

2¼ cups whole milk	¼ cup all-purpose flour
4 large egg yolks	¼ cup cornstarch
⅔ cup sugar	1 tablespoon vanilla extract

1. In a heavy 3-quart saucepan, heat 2 cups milk over medium-high heat until bubbles form around the edge. Meanwhile, in a large bowl and using a wire whisk, beat the egg yolks, remaining ¼ cup milk, and sugar until combined; whisk in the flour and cornstarch until blended. Gradually whisk the hot milk into the egg-yolk mixture.

2. Return the milk mixture to the saucepan; cook over medium-high heat, whisking constantly, until the mixture has thickened and boils. Reduce the heat to low and cook, stirring, with a wooden spoon, 2 minutes.

3. Remove from the heat and stir in the vanilla. Pour the pastry cream into a shallow dish. Press plastic wrap onto the surface of the pastry cream. Refrigerate at least 2 hours or up to overnight.

Each tablespoon About 30 calories, 1g protein, 5g carbohydrate, 1g fat (0g saturated), 0g fiber, 10mg sodium.

VARIATION

Chocolate Pastry Cream

Prepare Pastry Cream as directed, but add **3 squares (3 ounces) semisweet chocolate** and **1 square (1 ounce) unsweetened choc-olate**, both chopped and melted, with the vanilla. Makes about 3 cups.

cream puffs

PREP: 30 MIN / TOTAL: 1 HR 10 MIN, PLUS STANDING AND COOLING / SERVES 8

Choux Pastry (below)
Hot Fudge Sauce (below)

1 quart vanilla ice cream

1. Preheat the oven to 400°F. Grease and flour a large baking sheet. Prepare Choux Pastry. Drop slightly rounded ¼ cupfuls of batter in 8 large mounds, 3 inches apart, on the prepared baking sheet. With a moistened finger, gently smooth the tops.

2. Bake until golden, 40 to 45 minutes. Remove the puffs from the oven; with the tip of a knife, make a small slit in the side of each puff to release steam. Turn off the oven. Return the puffs to the oven and let stand 10 minutes. Transfer the puffs to a wire rack to cool completely. With a serrated knife, cut each cooled puff horizontally in half; remove and discard any moist dough inside the puffs.

3. Prepare Hot Fudge Sauce. To serve, place ½-cup scoop of vanilla ice cream in the bottom half of each cream puff; replace the tops. Spoon Hot Fudge Sauce over the puffs.

CHOUX PASTRY In a 3-quart saucepan, combine ½ cup **salted butter**, cut into pieces; **1 cup water**; and ¼ teaspoon **salt**; heat over medium-high heat until the butter melts and the mixture boils. Remove from the heat. Add **1 cup all-purpose flour** all at once and, with a wooden spoon, vigorously stir until the mixture leaves the sides of the pan and forms a ball. Add **4 large eggs** to the flour mixture, one at a time, beating well after each addition, until the mixture is smooth and satiny. Shape and bake the warm dough as directed.

HOT FUDGE SAUCE In a 1-quart saucepan, combine ¾ cup **sugar**, ½ cup **unsweetened cocoa**, ½ cup **heavy or whipping cream**, and **4 tablespoons salted butter**, cut into pieces; heat to boiling over high heat, stirring frequently. Remove saucepan from heat; stir in **1 teaspoon vanilla extract**. Serve warm, or cool completely. To store, cover and refrigerate up to 2 weeks. Gently reheat before using. Makes about 1¼ cups.

Each serving About 525 calories, 9g protein, 51g carbohydrate, 34g fat (20g saturated), 2g fiber, 339mg sodium.

 Tip Cream Puffs can be filled with Vanilla (or Chocolate) Pastry Cream (page 648) or whipped cream.

NO-BAKE PUMPKIN CHEESECAKE MINI TRIFLES 645

ICE CREAM CUPCAKES 653

FUDGY WAFFLE BROWNIES 651

PRALINES 'N' CREAM SAUCE 652

fudgy waffle brownies

PREP: 20 MIN / TOTAL: 35 MIN / SERVES 12

- 6 tablespoons salted butter, cut into pieces
- 1 bar (3½ ounces) bittersweet chocolate (50% to 60% cacao), chopped
- ¾ cup sugar
- 1 large egg, beaten
- 2 teaspoons vanilla extract
- ½ cup whole milk
- 1 cup all-purpose flour
- ¼ cup unsweetened cocoa
- 2 teaspoons baking powder
- ½ teaspoon salt
- 1 cup butterscotch, peanut butter, or chocolate chips
- Nonstick cooking spray
- Ice cream and berries, for serving (optional)

1. Preheat a waffle iron.

2. In a 4-quart saucepan, heat the butter and chocolate over medium-low heat until melted and smooth, stirring. Remove from the heat. Stir in the sugar. Whisk in the egg and vanilla until combined. Stir in the milk.

3. In a bowl, whisk the flour, cocoa, baking powder, and salt. Stir into the butter mixture just until smooth. Fold in the chips.

4. Spray the waffle iron with nonstick cooking spray; add ⅓ to ½ cup batter to the center. Close the waffle iron; cook 2 to 3 minutes, or until just set and crisp around edges. With a thin silicone spatula, cut the brownie into quarters and gently lift each quarter from the waffle iron. Repeat with remaining batter. Serve with ice cream and berries, if desired.

Each serving About 280 calories, 5g protein, 35g carbohydrate, 14g fat (8g saturated), 2g fiber, 290mg sodium.

TESTING NOTE In our tests, we tried various store-bought mixes, with different proportions of added ingredients, but the resulting brownies were hard and crunchy. So we created this recipe specifically for the waffle iron; the texture is terrific, but it won't work as well in a deep Belgian-style iron.

pretzel wands

PREP: 10 MIN / TOTAL: 30 MIN / SERVES 12

- 6 ounces white or milk chocolate candy melts
- 12 pretzel rods
- Edible gold and silver stars and sugar pearls, for decorating

1. Line a baking sheet with waxed paper. Melt the chocolate as the label directs. Pour the melted chocolate into a tall, narrow glass (we used a Champagne flute).

2. Dip two-thirds of each pretzel rod into the chocolate, letting the excess drip off; sprinkle with edible stars or sugar pearls. Place each pretzel on the prepared sheet. After dipping all the pretzels, wash the glass immediately so the chocolate doesn't harden in it. Let the pretzels stand 1 hour, or until set.

Each serving About 120 calories, 1g protein, 18g carbohydrate, 5g fat (4g saturated), 0g fiber, 165mg sodium.

Ingredient Ideas

d'oh nuts

We know you'll like *these* apples! Just core, slice into horizontal rings, and top with "frosting" (e.g., nut butter or cream cheese) and "sprinkles" (fruit, coconut, marshmallows, nuts, or seeds). With dozens of delicious combos, who needs fried dough?

- Chocolate hazelnut spread, coconut, and marshmallows
- Cheesecake filling, pistachios, and lavender
- Greek yogurt, lemon zest, honey, and poppy seeds
- Blueberry cream cheese and blueberries
- Strawberry cream cheese granola, and strawberries
- Peanut butter, banana slices, and chocolate

pralines 'n' cream sauce

(See photo on page 650.)

PREP: 5 MIN / TOTAL: 10 MIN / MAKES 1 CUP

2 tablespoons salted butter

½ cup packed light brown sugar

½ cup heavy or whipping cream

⅛ teaspoon salt

1 teaspoon vanilla extract

½ cup pecans, toasted and chopped

Vanilla and/or coffee ice cream, for serving

In a 2-quart saucepan, melt the butter over medium heat. Stir in the sugar, cream, and salt. Heat to boiling over medium-high heat, stirring occasionally. Boil 2 minutes, stirring frequently. Remove from the heat; stir in the vanilla and pecans. Cool slightly. Serve with ice cream. The sauce can be made up to 1 week ahead and kept refrigerated in an airtight container. If refrigerated, microwave on High 1 minute, stir, and cool slightly before serving.

Each tablespoon About 85 calories, 1g protein, 7g carbohydrate, 6g fat (3g saturated), 0g fiber, 35mg sodium.

dark chocolate mousse

PREP: 20 MIN / TOTAL: 30 MIN, PLUS CHILLING / SERVES 2

½ cup plus 2 teaspoons sugar

2 tablespoons water

¼ cup roasted salted almonds, chopped

3 large pasteurized egg whites

⅛ teaspoon salt

4 ounces good-quality dark chocolate (50% to 60% cacao), chopped

2 large pasteurized egg yolks

¼ teaspoon vanilla extract

Whipped cream, for serving

1. Line a baking sheet with parchment paper.

2. In a 2-quart saucepan, stir ½ cup sugar and the water. Cook over medium heat 5 to 7 minutes, or until the mixture turns pale amber, swirling the pan occasionally to color the mixture evenly. Remove from the heat. Working quickly, stir in the almonds, then pour the mixture onto the prepared sheet; spread evenly. Cool completely. Break the brittle into shards. (Can be made 3 days ahead and stored in a cool place.)

3. In a medium bowl and using a mixer on medium-high speed, whisk the egg whites and salt until stiff peaks form.

4. In a larger microwave-safe bowl, microwave the chocolate on High in 20-second intervals until melted, stirring between intervals. Stir in the yolks, one at a time, until well combined. Stir in the vanilla and the remaining 2 teaspoons sugar. Vigorously stir one-fourth of the egg whites into the chocolate mixture. Gently fold in the remaining whites.

5. Spoon the mixture into 2 tall glasses. Cover tightly with plastic wrap; refrigerate at least 1 hour or up to 1 day. If chilled over 1 hour, let stand at room temperature 10 minutes before serving. To serve, top with whipped cream and almond brittle.

Each serving (without whipped cream) About 685 calories, 16g protein, 88g carbohydrate, 34g fat (15g saturated), 8g fiber, 300mg sodium.

 Tip This recipe doubles easily. To serve smaller portions, scoop mousse into espresso cups and top with a dollop of cream and almond brittle.

ice cream cupcakes

(See photo on page 650.)

PREP: 30 MIN / TOTAL: 3 HR / SERVES 12

2 pints ice cream, softened (your choice of flavor)

¾ cup cookies, crushed (Oreos, pretzels, sugar cones, graham crackers, or vanilla wafers)

1 cup chocolate shell topping

Broken cookies, for topping

1. Line a 12-cup muffin pan with paper or foil liners. Layer the softened ice cream into the liners to come halfway up the sides; freeze for 30 minutes.

2. Mix the cookies with ¼ cup chocolate shell topping and divvy it up over the ice cream layer. Freeze for 1 hour.

3. Add another layer of ice cream; freeze again for 1½ hours.

4. Top with more chocolate shell topping and broken-cookie garnishes. Freeze for 30-minutes more, then dig in!

Each cupcake About 275 calories, 3g protein, 28g carbohydrate, 18g fat (8g saturated), 1g fiber, 102mg sodium.

HOW TO

SOFTEN ICE CREAM

Whether you're softening ice cream to build an ice cream cake or to mash with summer's ripest fruit, the best method is to let it sit out at room temperature for about 15 minutes or in the fridge for 30. If you're in a hurry, microwave it on Medium (50% power) for 10 to 20 seconds, checking it every 10 seconds. (Note: Low-fat ice creams and frozen yogurts melt faster than full-fat varieties do.) And here's a hint for when you're scooping: Start from the outer edge—that's where it will be the softest.

mixed-berry blitz pops

(See photo on page 654.)

PREP: 20 MIN / TOTAL: 6 HR 20 MIN / SERVES 6 TO 8

8 ounces fresh strawberries, hulled

½ cup water

½ cup sugar

1 tablespoon fresh lemon juice

1 container (6 ounces) fresh blackberries

1. In a blender, puree the strawberries, ¼ cup water, ¼ cup sugar, and the lemon juice until smooth; transfer to a liquid measuring cup. Wash and dry the blender.

2. In the blender, puree the blackberries, ¼ cup water, and ¼ cup sugar until smooth. Fill the ice-pop molds halfway with the strawberry mixture. Add the blackberry mixture to fill the molds completely. Insert a butter knife or chopstick in the center of each mold and stir gently to swirl the berry mixtures. Insert sticks; freeze until solid, about 6 and up to 8 hours.

Each serving About 75 calories, 1g protein, 19g carbohydrate, 0g fat (0g saturated), 2g fiber, 1mg sodium.

MIXED-BERRY
BLITZ POPS 653

ICED MOCHA
FUDGE POPS 655

BERRY BEST
FRO-YO POPS 655

GINGER
FRUIT SMASH
POPS 655

berry best fro-yo pops

PREP: 15 MIN / TOTAL: 6 HR 15 MIN / SERVES 6 TO 8

1½ cups reduced-fat plain Greek yogurt

1 container (6 ounces) fresh blackberries

1 container (6 ounces) fresh blueberries

3 tablespoons honey

2 tablespoons sugar

1 teaspoon vanilla extract

In a blender, add the yogurt, blackberries, blueberries, honey, sugar, and vanilla. Blend ingredients together until combined but still chunky. Divide among ice-pop molds; insert sticks. Freeze until solid, about 6 and up to 8 hours.

Each serving About 100 calories, 5g protein, 19g carbohydrate, 1g fat (1g saturated), 2g fiber, 17mg sodium.

 Tip Catch drips by pushing sticks through cupcake liners before serving.

iced mocha fudge pops

PREP: 15 MIN / TOTAL: 6 HR 15 MIN / SERVES 6 TO 8

1½ cups double-strength coffee

¾ cup sweetened condensed milk

3 tablespoons unsweetened cocoa

Pinch of salt

In a blender, combine the coffee, condensed milk, cocoa, and a pinch of salt until smooth. Divide among the ice-pop molds; insert sticks. Freeze until solid, about 6 and up to 8 hours.

Each serving About 110 calories, 3g protein, 19g carbohydrate, 3g fat (2g saturated), 1g fiber, 63mg sodium.

ginger fruit smash pops

PREP: 20 MIN / TOTAL: 6 HR 20 MIN / SERVES 6 TO 8

1 cup water

⅓ cup sugar

1 (4-inch) piece fresh ginger, peeled and sliced

4 strips lemon peel

Pinch of cayenne pepper

½ cup small pineapple chunks

½ cup green grape halves

½ cup thin kiwi slices

1. In a small saucepan, heat the water, sugar, ginger, lemon peel, and cayenne over high heat until the sugar dissolves, stirring. Transfer to a blender and blend until smooth. Strain into a liquid measuring cup; discard the solids.

2. Fill ice-pop molds halfway with the ginger syrup. Add the pineapple chunks, green grapes, and kiwi slices, dividing the fruit evenly between each mold. Add the remaining ginger syrup to fill the molds completely. Insert sticks; freeze until solid, about 6 and up to 8 hours.

Each serving About 55 calories, 0g protein, 14g carbohydrate, 0g fat (0g saturated), 1g fiber, 1mg sodium.

HOW TO

HULL STRAWBERRIES

Hull yes, there is a faster way to prep strawberries. Just insert a plastic straw through the bottom center of the fruit, then push out the green stem. Remove and repeat. You'll be blending, baking, and snacking in no time. Straw + berry = genius!

5-minute frozen peach yogurt

PREP: 15 MIN / TOTAL: 15 MIN, PLUS STANDING / SERVES 8

1 bag (20 ounces) frozen unsweetened peach slices

1 container (8 ounces) plain low-fat yogurt

1 cup confectioners' sugar

1 tablespoon fresh lemon juice

⅛ teaspoon almond extract

1. Let the frozen peaches stand at room temperature 10 minutes. In a food processor with the knife blade attached, process the peaches until the fruit resembles finely shaved ice, occasionally scraping down the sides with a rubber spatula.

2. With the processor running, add the yogurt, confectioners' sugar, lemon juice, and almond extract; process until the mixture is smooth and creamy, occasionally scraping down the sides. Serve immediately.

Each serving About 110 calories, 2g protein, 25g carbohydrate, 1g fat (0g saturated), 1g fiber, 20mg sodium.

orange granita

(See photo on page 622.)

PREP: 25 MIN / TOTAL: 5 HR 30 MIN / SERVES 6

11 large navel oranges

½ cup sugar

Pinch of salt

1. Cut the top quarter off 6 navel oranges; set aside. Trim the bottoms as well so the oranges stand upright. With a small knife and spoon, scrape the orange pulp into a bowl; place the shells in the freezer.

2. Into a 4-cup measuring cup, squeeze the juice from the pulp. From the remaining 5 oranges, grate 1 tablespoon zest and squeeze enough juice to make 3 cups total. Stir in the sugar and salt to dissolve; pour the mixture into a square metal baking pan. Freeze 5 hours, scraping the frozen bits with a fork every hour. To serve, scoop the granite into the frozen shells and replace the tops.

Each serving About 120 calories, 1g protein, 30g carbohydrate, 0g fat (0g saturated), 0g fiber, 21mg sodium.

coffee granita

PREP: 10 MIN / TOTAL: 5 HR 30 MIN / SERVES 10

⅔ cup sugar

2 cups hot espresso coffee

Unsweetened whipped cream, for serving (optional)

1. In a medium bowl, stir the sugar and espresso until the sugar has completely dissolved. Pour into a 9-inch square metal baking pan; cool.

2. Cover and freeze the granita mixture until partially frozen, about 2 hours. Stir with a fork to break up the chunks. Cover and freeze until completely frozen, at least 3 hours or up to overnight.

3. To serve, let the granita stand at room temperature until slightly softened, about 15 minutes. Use a metal spoon to scrape across the surface of the granita, transferring the ice shards to chilled dessert dishes or wine goblets without packing them. Serve with whipped cream, if you like.

Each serving About 55 calories, 0g protein, 14g carbohydrate, 0g fat (0g saturated), 0g fiber, 0mg sodium.

 Tip If you do not have an espresso coffeemaker, use 3 cups water and 1⅓ cups ground espresso coffee in an automatic drip coffeemaker.

bold berry granita

PREP: 20 MIN / TOTAL: 25 MIN, PLUS COOLING AND FREEZING / SERVES 10

1 cup water

½ cup sugar

1 to 2 lemons

1 pound strawberries, hulled

1½ cups fresh raspberries (about ¾ pint)

Fresh mint sprigs, for garnish (optional)

1. Make a sugar syrup: In a 2-quart saucepan, heat the water and sugar to boiling over high heat, stirring until the sugar dissolves. Reduce the heat to low and simmer, uncovered, 5 minutes. Set aside to cool slightly, about 5 minutes.

2. Meanwhile, from the lemons, grate 2 teaspoons zest and squeeze ¼ cup juice. In a food processor with the knife blade attached, puree the strawberries and raspberries. With the back of a spoon, press the puree through a sieve into a medium bowl; discard the pulp.

3. Stir the sugar syrup and lemon juice and zest into the berry puree. Pour into a 9-inch square metal baking pan.

4. Cover and freeze the granita mixture until partially frozen, about 2 hours. Stir with a fork to break up the chunks. Cover and freeze until completely frozen, at least 3 hours or up to overnight.

5. To serve, let the granite stand at room temperature until slightly softened, about 15 minutes. Use a metal spoon to scrape across the surface of the granita, transferring the ice shards to chilled dessert dishes or wine goblets without packing them. Garnish with mint, if you like.

Each serving About 60 calories, 1g protein, 15g carbohydrate, 0g fat (0g saturated), 2g fiber, 0mg sodium.

lemon granita

PREP: 10 MIN / TOTAL: 5 HR 30 MIN / SERVES 8

1 cup sugar	**4 large lemons**
2 cups water	

1. In a 2-quart saucepan, combine the sugar and water; heat to boiling over high heat, stirring until the sugar has dissolved. Reduce heat to medium and cook 5 minutes. Set the saucepan in a bowl of ice water until the syrup is cool.

2. Meanwhile, from the lemons, grate 2 teaspoons zest and squeeze ¾ cup juice.

3. Stir the lemon zest and juice into the sugar syrup; pour into a 9-inch square metal baking pan. Cover and freeze the granita mixture until partially frozen, about 2 hours. Stir with a fork to break up the chunks. Cover and freeze until completely frozen, at least 3 hours or up to overnight.

4. To serve, let the granita stand at room temperature until slightly softened, about 15 minutes. Use a metal spoon to scrape across the surface of the granita, transferring the ice shards to chilled dessert dishes or wine goblets without packing them.

Each serving About 105 calories, 0g protein, 27g carbohydrate, 0g fat (0g saturated), 0g fiber, 1mg sodium.

GOOD TO KNOW

FROZEN DESSERTS

The frozen treat aisle is brimming with so many options that buying a pint can be a conundrum. Here are the most popular options, decoded. We think there's an occasion for all of them!

ICE CREAM Dairy-rich ice cream is one of life's sweet indulgences. Most are prepared with an egg-custard base, which gives ice cream its incomparable texture. These ice creams may also be called frozen custard, French ice cream, or gelato. Philadelphia-style ice cream, which doesn't contain egg yolks, has a slightly icy texture that emphasizes the flavor of the cream.

GELATO An Italian favorite that has gained popularity here in the US. Its super creamy, dense texture is due to its being churned more slowly, allowing less air to be whipped in. Because it has less than half the fat (which masks flavor) of ice cream, gelato flavors often taste richer than their ice cream counterparts.

ICES Made from sweetened fruit purees or juices, ices are beaten with a mixer after an initial freezing to incorporate air and produce a lighter texture, then frozen again until firm.

FROZEN YOGURT Made from either low-fat or fat-free yogurt along with fruit or flavorings, this frozen treat has the creaminess of ice cream but without all the fat.

SHERBET This is a frozen combination of fruit juice (usually citrus), sugar, and milk, cream, or egg whites.

SORBET Smooth-textured sorbet is usually made from a sweetened fruit puree with no dairy products.

GRANITA Italian in origin, granita has the same ingredients as sorbet, but it is chilled in a baking pan and stirred frequently during freezing to achieve a granular, icy texture. (*Granita* comes from the Latin word for "grain.")

autumn fruit compote

PREP: 20 MIN / TOTAL: 45 MIN, PLUS CHILLING / SERVES 8

1 orange
1 lemon
4 medium Golden Delicious or Jonagold apples, each peeled, cored, and cut into 16 wedges

1 package (8 ounces) mixed dried fruit (with dried plums)
1 cup dried Calimyrna figs (6 ounces)
½ cup sugar
1 (3-inch) cinnamon stick
3 cups water

1. From both the orange and lemon and using a vegetable peeler, remove the peels in 1-inch-wide strips. From the lemon, squeeze 2 tablespoons juice (reserve the orange for another use).

2. In a 4-quart nonreactive saucepan, combine the apples, mixed dried fruit, figs, orange and lemon peels, lemon juice, sugar, cinnamon stick, and water; heat to boiling over high heat, stirring frequently. Reduce the heat; cover and simmer, stirring occasionally, until the apples are tender, 15 to 20 minutes.

3. Pour the fruit mixture into a serving bowl; cover and refrigerate at least 4 hours to blend the flavors. Serve chilled. Store leftovers in the refrigerator up to 4 days.

Each serving About 210 calories, 1g protein, 55g carbohydrate, 1g fat (0g saturated), 6g fiber, 10mg sodium.

TESTING NOTE Make your own dried fruit mix for this. We like any combo of sweet and tart fruits like prunes, peaches, pears, apricots, and tart cherries.

best berry sauce

PREP: 5 MIN / TOTAL: 10 MIN / MAKES 2 CUPS

3 cups fresh berries (blueberries; hulled, sliced strawberries; raspberries)
½ to ¾ cup confectioners' sugar

3 tablespoons water
1 to 2 teaspoons fresh lemon or lime juice

1. In a 2-quart saucepan, combine the berries, ½ cup confectioners' sugar, and water. Cook over medium heat, stirring occasionally, until the berries have softened and the sauce has thickened slightly, 5 to 8 minutes.

2. Remove pan from the heat; stir in 1 teaspoon lemon juice. Taste, and stir in additional sugar and lemon juice, if desired. Serve warm, or cover and refrigerate up to 1 day.

Each tablespoon About 15 calories, 0g protein, 4g carbohydrate, 0g fat (0g saturated), 1g fiber, 1mg sodium.

TESTING NOTE Use a single variety of berry or your favorite combination. Serve with ice cream or use it to dress up store-bought cheesecake or pound cake.

blueberry crisp

PREP: 20 MIN / TOTAL: 1 HR / SERVES 8

½ cup granulated sugar
2 tablespoons cornstarch
3 pints (12 ounces each) blueberries
1 tablespoon fresh lemon juice
1 cup all-purpose flour

¾ cup quick-cooking or old-fashioned oats
½ cup packed light brown sugar
½ cup cold salted butter
¾ teaspoon ground cinnamon

1. Preheat the oven to 375°F. In a large bowl, stir the granulated sugar and cornstarch until blended. Add the blueberries and lemon juice; stir to coat evenly. Spoon the blueberry mixture into a shallow 2-quart glass or ceramic baking dish; spread it evenly.

2. In the same bowl, combine the flour, oats, brown sugar, butter, and cinnamon. With your fingers, mix until coarse crumbs form. Crumble over the blueberry mixture.

3. Place a sheet of foil underneath the baking dish; crimp the foil edges to form a rim to catch any drips during baking. Bake the crisp 35 to 40 minutes, or until the top is browned and the fruit is bubbly at the edges. Cool on a wire rack 1 hour to serve warm or cool completely to serve later. Reheat if desired.

Each serving About 360 calories, 4g protein, 61g carbohydrate, 13g fat (7g saturated), 4g fiber, 96mg sodium.

bumbleberry crisp

(See photo on page 622.)

- 1 cup raw almonds
- 1 cup all-purpose flour
- 6 tablespoons salted butter, cut into pieces
- ⅓ cup packed brown sugar
- ¼ teaspoon ground cinnamon
- ¼ teaspoon salt
- 2 Golden Delicious apples, peeled, cored, and chopped
- 1 pound strawberries, hulled and sliced (about 3 cups)
- 1 container (6 ounces) blueberries
- 1 container (6 ounces) raspberries
- ¾ cup granulated sugar
- ¼ cup cornstarch
- 3 tablespoons fresh lemon juice
- Vanilla ice cream, for serving (optional)

1. Preheat the oven to 375°F. Grease a 2-quart baking dish.

2. Chop the almonds. Transfer to a medium bowl; add the flour, butter, brown sugar, cinnamon, and salt. With your hands, mix until combined and small clumps form.

3. In a large bowl, combine the apples, all the berries, the granulated sugar, cornstarch, and lemon juice; transfer to the prepared baking dish. Sprinkle with the nut mixture. Bake 45 minutes, or until bubbly and golden. Serve warm with ice cream, if desired.

Each serving About 560 calories, 7g protein, 81g carbohydrate, 26g fat (8g saturated), 7g fiber, 205mg sodium.

GLOSSARY →

Bumbleberry isn't actually a berry. The term, originally coined in Maritime Canada, describes a mix of berries, often tossed with another seasonal fruit like apples or rhubarb for a pie, jam, crumble, or other dessert.

classic shortcakes

SHORTCAKE BISCUITS

- 2½ cups all-purpose flour
- 1 tablespoon baking powder
- ½ teaspoon baking soda
- ½ teaspoon salt
- ⅓ cup plus 1 tablespoon sugar
- ½ cup cold salted butter, cut into pieces
- 1 large egg, separated
- 1 cup buttermilk

SUGARED STRAWBERRIES

- 2½ pounds fresh strawberries (8 cups)
- 2 tablespoons sugar
- 1 tablespoon water

WHIPPED CREAM

- 1 cup heavy or whipping cream
- 2 tablespoons sugar
- 1 teaspoon vanilla extract

1. Prepare the shortcakes: Preheat the oven to 425°F. In a large bowl, combine the flour, baking powder, baking soda, salt, and ⅓ cup sugar. Cut in the butter until the mixture resembles coarse crumbs.

2. In a small bowl and using a fork, beat the egg yolk with the buttermilk; stir into the flour mixture just until the mixture forms a soft dough that leaves the sides of the bowl.

3. On a floured surface and with floured hands, knead the dough 6 to 8 times to combine; pat the dough to a ¾-inch thickness.

4. Cut out the shortcakes using a biscuit cutter; place them 1 inch apart on an ungreased large baking sheet. Press the trimmings together; cut to make 8 biscuits in all.

5. In another small bowl and using a fork, lightly beat the egg white; brush on top of the shortcakes. Sprinkle with the remaining 1 tablespoon sugar. Bake 15 to 20 minutes, or until golden. Cool on a wire rack.

6. Prepare the strawberries: Hull the strawberries, then slice. In a large bowl, stir the strawberries, sugar, and water. Let stand 15 minutes or refrigerate up to 4 hours.

7. Prepare the whipped cream: In a medium bowl and using a mixer at medium speed, beat the cream, sugar, and vanilla until stiff peaks form.

8. Split each shortcake horizontally in half. Place the bottom halves on 8 dessert plates. Layer the berries and cream over the shortcake bottoms; replace the tops. Dollop with cream and berries.

Each serving 480 calories, 7g protein, 58g carbohydrate, 25g fat (15g saturated), 4g fiber, 550mg sodium.

plum kuchen

PREP: 30 MIN / TOTAL: 1 HR 5 MIN / SERVES 8

- 5 large plums or 10 prune plums
- 1 cup all-purpose flour
- 1 teaspoon baking powder
- ¼ teaspoon salt
- 6 tablespoons salted butter, softened
- ⅔ cup plus 2 tablespoons sugar
- 2 large eggs
- ½ teaspoon vanilla extract
- ½ teaspoon ground cinnamon

1. Preheat the oven to 350°F. Grease a 9-inch square baking pan. Cut large plums into quarters and remove the pits; alternatively, cut prune plums in half and remove the pits.

2. Whisk the flour, baking powder, and salt in a small bowl. In a large bowl and using an electric mixer on medium speed, beat the butter and ⅔ cup sugar until creamy, about 2 minutes. Beat in the eggs, one at a time, until well blended. Beat in the vanilla. With the mixer on low speed, beat in the flour mixture just until blended.

3. Spoon the batter into the prepared pan and spread it evenly. Arrange the plums, skin side down, on the batter. Combine remaining 2 tablespoons sugar and cinnamon in a small bowl; sprinkle it over the plums. Bake until a toothpick inserted in the center comes out clean, 35 to 40 minutes. Cool in the pan on a wire rack and serve warm or at room temperature.

Each serving About 260 calories, 4g protein, 38g carbohydrate, 11g fat (6g saturated), 1g fiber, 230mg sodium.

GLOSSARY →

The word **kuchen**, which is German for "cake," is used to describe any number of fruit-topped or custard-filled desserts that have a yeast- or cake-batter base.

sticky toffee pudding

PREP: 20 MIN / TOTAL: 50 MIN, PLUS STANDING AND COOLING / SERVES 12

- 1 cup chopped pitted dates
- 1 teaspoon baking soda
- 1½ cups boiling water
- 10 tablespoons salted butter, softened
- 1 cup granulated sugar
- 1 large egg
- 1 teaspoon vanilla extract
- 2 cups all-purpose flour
- 1 teaspoon baking powder
- 1 cup packed brown sugar
- ¼ cup heavy or whipping cream
- Whipped cream, for serving (optional)

1. Preheat the oven to 350°F. Grease a 13 × 9-inch baking pan. In a medium bowl, combine the dates, baking soda, and boiling water; let stand 15 minutes.

2. In a large bowl and using a mixer at medium speed, beat 6 tablespoons butter until creamy. Beat in the granulated sugar until light and fluffy. Add the egg and vanilla; beat until blended. Reduce the speed to low; add the flour and baking powder, beating to combine. Add the date mixture and beat until well combined; the batter will be very thin. Pour the batter into the prepared pan. Bake until golden and a toothpick inserted in the center of the pudding comes out clean, about 30 minutes.

3. Meanwhile, in a heavy 2-quart saucepan, combine the brown sugar, cream, and remaining 4 tablespoons butter; heat to boiling over medium-high heat, stirring frequently. Boil 1 minute; remove the saucepan from the heat.

4. Turn the oven control to broil. Spread the brown-sugar mixture evenly over the top of the hot pudding. Broil at the position closest to the heat source until bubbling, about 30 seconds. Cool in the pan on a wire rack 15 minutes. Serve warm with whipped cream, if you like.

Each serving About 360 calories, 3g protein, 62g carbohydrate, 12g fat (7g saturated), 2g fiber, 260mg sodium.

peach cobbler

PREP: 45 MIN / TOTAL: 1 HR 30 MIN / SERVES 12

PEACH FILLING

- 6 pounds ripe medium peaches (16 to 18), peeled, pitted, and sliced (13 cups)
- ¼ cup fresh lemon juice
- ⅔ cup granulated sugar
- ½ cup packed brown sugar
- ¼ cup cornstarch

LEMON BISCUITS

- 2 cups all-purpose flour
- ½ cup plus 1 teaspoon granulated sugar
- 2½ teaspoons baking powder
- ¼ teaspoon salt
- 1 teaspoon freshly grated lemon zest
- 4 tablespoons cold salted butter, cut into pieces
- ⅔ cup plus 1 tablespoon half-and-half or light cream

1. Prepare the filling: Preheat the oven to 425°F. In an 8-quart nonreactive saucepot, toss the peaches with lemon juice; add the granulated and brown sugars and cornstarch, tossing to coat. Heat over medium heat, stirring occasionally, until bubbling; boil 1 minute. Spoon the hot peach mixture into a 13 × 9-inch baking dish. Place the baking dish on a foil-lined baking sheet to catch any overflow during baking. Bake 10 minutes.

2. Meanwhile, prepare the biscuits: In a medium bowl, combine the flour, ½ cup granulated sugar, baking powder, salt, and lemon zest. With a pastry blender or 2 knives used scissor-fashion, cut in the butter until the mixture resembles coarse crumbs. Stir in ⅔ cup half-and-half just until the mixture forms a soft dough that leaves the sides of the bowl.

3. Turn the dough onto a lightly floured surface. With lightly floured hands, pat it into a 10 × 6-inch rectangle. With a floured knife, cut the rectangle lengthwise in half, then cut each half crosswise into 6 pieces.

4. Remove the baking dish from the oven. Arrange the biscuits on top of the fruit. Brush the biscuits with the remaining 1 tablespoon half-and-half and sprinkle with the remaining 1 teaspoon granulated sugar. Return the cobbler to the oven and bake until the filling is hot and bubbling and the biscuits are golden, about 35 minutes longer. To serve warm, cool the cobbler on a wire rack about 1 hour.

Each serving About 330 calories, 4g protein, 69g carbohydrate, 6g fat (3g saturated), 3g fiber, 200mg sodium.

spiced pear & berry crumble

(See photo on page 662.)

PREP: 15 MIN / TOTAL: 1 HR, PLUS COOLING / SERVES 8

- 1 cup all-purpose flour
- ⅔ cup old-fashioned oats
- ½ cup packed light brown sugar
- ½ cup walnuts, chopped
- Salt
- 10 tablespoons cold salted butter, cut into pieces
- ½ teaspoon ground cinnamon
- ¼ teaspoon ground allspice
- 2 pounds ripe pears, peeled, cored, and chopped
- ½ cup granulated sugar
- 2 cups frozen mixed berries (such as blueberries, raspberries, and blackberries)
- 3 tablespoons cornstarch
- ¼ cup amaretto or almond liqueur

1. Preheat the oven to 375°F. In a medium bowl, combine the flour, oats, brown sugar, walnuts, and ¼ teaspoon salt. With your fingers, rub 6 tablespoons butter into the mixture; squeeze it to form large clumps. Place in the freezer.

2. In a 10-inch oven-safe skillet, heat the remaining 4 tablespoons butter over medium heat 6 minutes, or until browned and fragrant, swirling it often. Add the cinnamon and allspice; cook 1 minute, stirring. Add the pears, granulated sugar, and a pinch of salt; cook 5 minutes, stirring often. Remove from the heat. Stir in the berries, cornstarch, and amaretto. Sprinkle the crumb topping all over the pear mixture. Bake 25 minutes, or until the topping has browned and the pears are tender. Serve warm or at room temperature.

Each serving About 460 calories, 4g protein, 70g carbohydrate, 20g fat (10g saturated), 6g fiber, 195mg sodium.

 Tip Pears come in a variety of shapes and colors, so color is not the best gauge for ripeness. The best way is to check the neck: It should yield to soft pressure.

PUMPKIN SLAB PIE 668

EASY PLUM TART 673

SPICED PEAR &
BERRY CRUMBLE 661

SPARKLY APPLE
SLAB PIE 663

sparkly apple slab pie

PREP: 25 MIN / TOTAL: 1 HR 30 MIN, PLUS CHILLING AND COOLING / SERVES 12

- **3 cups all-purpose flour**
- **1½ tablespoons granulated sugar**
- **Salt**
- **1½ cups very cold salted butter, cut into pieces**
- **¾ cup cold water**
- **Nonstick cooking spray**
- **⅓ cup cornstarch**
- **½ teaspoon ground cinnamon**
- **½ teaspoon ground ginger**
- **¼ teaspoon ground allspice**
- **3 pounds Golden Delicious apples, cored, peeled and chopped**
- **½ cup packed brown sugar**
- **4 teaspoons fresh lemon juice**
- **2 tablespoons heavy (whipping) cream or whole milk**
- **2 tablespoons coarse sanding or turbinado sugar**

1. In a food processor, pulse the flour, sugar, and 1 teaspoon salt until combined. Add half the butter; pulse until fine crumbs form. Add the remaining butter; pulse just until coarse crumbs form. Add the water in 2 batches, pulsing between additions and scraping the sides of the bowl. Pulse just until the dough starts to come together. Transfer the dough to a large bowl; gently knead it 2 or 3 times, until the dough comes together. Divide the dough into 4 equal-size mounds; shape each into a flat rectangle and wrap tightly in plastic wrap. Refrigerate at least 30 minutes or up to 2 days.

2. Preheat the oven to 400°F. Line a 15 × 10-inch rimmed baking sheet with parchment paper. Spray it lightly with nonstick cooking spray. In a large bowl, whisk together the cornstarch, cinnamon, ginger, allspice, and ½ teaspoon salt. Add the apples, brown sugar, and lemon juice, tossing until the apples are well coated; set aside.

3. Place 1 piece of dough on a lightly floured work surface. Lightly flour the dough and roll it into a 12 × 9-inch rectangle, lightly flouring and scraping as needed to prevent sticking. Transfer it to the prepared baking sheet, placing the 9-inch side along the longest side of the baking sheet. Repeat the rolling with another piece of dough. Transfer to the other side of the prepared baking sheet, overlapping it slightly with the first piece of dough. Press the seam together to seal. Spread the apple mixture over the dough in an even layer.

4. Repeat the rolling process with the third piece of dough. Place the rectangle on top of one side of the apple mixture, arranging a 9-inch side along the longest side of the pan. Repeat the rolling process with the remaining piece of dough. Place the rectangle on top of the other side of the apple mixture, overlapping it slightly with the other piece of dough. Press the seam together to seal. Pinch the edges of the dough together to enclose the filling. Brush the top with cream and sprinkle with coarse sanding sugar. Cut 4 slits in the top crust. Bake 1 hour 10 minutes, or until the top is deep golden brown. Cool on a wire rack before serving. The pie can be made up to 1 day ahead and kept at room temperature, covered.

Each serving About 430 calories, 4g protein, 52g carbohydrate, 24g fat (15g saturated), 2g fiber, 430mg sodium.

double blueberry pie

PREP: 30 MIN / TOTAL: 40 MIN, PLUS CHILLING / SERVES 10

- **1⅔ cups gingersnap cookie crumbs (about 25 cookies)**
- **5 tablespoons salted butter, melted**
- **2 tablespoons plus ½ cup sugar**
- **2 tablespoons cornstarch**
- **2 tablespoons cold water**
- **3 pints blueberries**
- **Whipped cream, for serving (optional)**

1. Preheat the oven to 375°F. In a 9-inch pie plate and using a fork, mix the cookie crumbs, melted butter, and 2 tablespoons sugar until moistened. With your hands, press the mixture firmly onto the bottom and up the sides of a pie plate. Bake 8 minutes. Cool on a wire rack.

2. Meanwhile, in a 2-quart saucepan, blend the cornstarch and water until smooth. Add half the blueberries and the remaining ½ cup sugar to the cornstarch mixture; heat to boiling over medium-high heat, pressing the blueberries against the sides of the saucepan with the back of a spoon. Boil, stirring constantly, 1 minute. Remove from the heat; stir in the remaining blueberries.

3. Pour the blueberry filling into the cooled crust. Press plastic wrap onto the surface and refrigerate until thoroughly chilled, about 5 hours. Serve with whipped cream, if desired.

Each serving About 240 calories, 2g protein, 42g carbohydrate, 8g fat (4g saturated), 3g fiber, 200mg sodium.

pastry for a single-crust pie

PREP: 15 MIN / TOTAL: 15 MIN, PLUS CHILLING / MAKES ONE
9-INCH CRUST

1¼ cups all-purpose flour

¼ teaspoon salt

4 tablespoons cold salted
butter, cut into pieces

2 tablespoons vegetable
shortening

3 to 5 tablespoons
ice water

1. In a large bowl and using a wire whisk, stir the flour and salt. With a pastry blender or 2 knives used scissor-fashion, cut in the butter and shortening until the mixture resembles coarse crumbs.

2. Sprinkle in the ice water, 1 tablespoon at a time, mixing lightly with a fork after each addition, until the dough is just moist enough to hold together.

3. Shape the dough into a disk; wrap it in plastic wrap. Refrigerate 30 minutes or up to overnight. (If chilled overnight, let stand 30 minutes at room temperature before rolling.)

4. On a lightly floured surface and using a floured rolling pin, roll the dough into a 12-inch round. Ease the pastry into a pie plate, gently pressing the dough against the sides and bottom.

5. Make a decorative edge as desired (see page 665). Refrigerate or freeze until firm, 10 to 15 minutes. Fill and bake as directed in the recipe.

Each serving (¹⁄₁₀ crust) About 125 calories, 2g protein, 13g carbohydrate, 7g fat (4g saturated), 0g fiber, 105mg sodium.

VARIATIONS

Pastry for a 9-Inch Tart

Prepare as directed, but use 1 cup all-purpose flour; ¼ teaspoon salt; 6 tablespoons cold salted butter, cut into pieces; 1 tablespoon vegetable shortening; and 2 to 3 tablespoons ice water. In step 4, roll the dough into an 11-inch round. Ease the dough into a 9-inch tart pan with a removable bottom. Fold the overhang under and press the dough against the sides of the pan so it extends ⅛ inch above the rim. Proceed as directed.

Pastry for an 11-Inch Tart

Prepare as directed, but use 1½ cups all-purpose flour; ½ teaspoon salt; ½ cup cold salted butter, cut into pieces; 2 tablespoons vegetable shortening; and 3 to 4 tablespoons ice water. In step 4, roll the dough into a 14-inch round. Ease the dough into an 11-inch tart pan with a removable bottom. Fold the overhang under and press the dough against the sides of the pan so it extends ⅛ inch above the rim. Proceed as directed.

Ingredient Ideas

prebake a piecrust or tart shell

PREP: 15 MIN / TOTAL: 45 MIN, PLUS CHILLING /
MAKES 1 PIECRUST OR TART SHELL

1 recipe Pastry for
Single-Crust
Pie, Pastry for a
9-inch Tart, or
Pastry for an 11-
Inch Tart
(left)

1. Prepare the pastry dough as directed through chilling.

2. Preheat the oven to 425°F. Use the dough to line a 9-inch pie plate, a 9-inch tart pan with a removable bottom, or an 11-inch tart pan with a removable bottom. If you're using a pie plate, make a decorative edge (see page 665). If you're using a tart pan, finish the edge as directed in the recipe. Refrigerate or freeze until firm, 10 to 15 minutes.

3. Line the piecrust or tart shell with foil; fill with pie weights, uncooked rice, or dry beans. Bake 15 minutes. Remove the foil with the weights; bake until golden, 5 to 10 minutes longer. If the shell puffs up during baking, gently press it down with the back of a spoon. Cool on a wire rack. Fill (and bake) as directed in the recipe.

graham cracker crust

PREP: 10 MIN / TOTAL: 20 MIN / MAKES ONE 9-INCH CRUST

1¼ cups graham-cracker crumbs (9 rectangular graham crackers)

4 tablespoons salted butter, melted

1 tablespoon sugar

Preheat the oven to 375°F. In a 9-inch pie plate and using a fork, mix the crumbs, melted butter, and sugar until the crumbs are evenly moistened. Press the mixture firmly onto the bottom and up the sides of the pie plate, making a small rim. Bake 10 minutes; cool on a wire rack. Fill (and bake) as the recipe directs.

Each serving (¹⁄₁₀ crust) About 105 calories, 1g protein, 12g carbohydrate, 6g fat (3g saturated), 0g fiber, 140mg sodium.

VARIATIONS

Chocolate Wafer–Crumb Crust

Prepare as directed, but substitute 1¼ cups chocolate wafer-cookie crumbs (24 cookies) for the graham-cracker crumbs.

Vanilla Wafer–Crumb Crust

Prepare as directed, but substitute 1¼ cups vanilla wafer-cookie crumbs (35 cookies) for the graham-cracker crumbs.

HOW TO

MAKE COOKIE CRUMBS

To make cookie crumbs, place the cookies in a heavy-duty resealable plastic bag and crush them with a rolling pin or meat mallet; you can also use a food processor or blender. For about 1 cup crushed cookie crumbs, use twenty 2¼-inch chocolate wafers, 14 gingersnaps, 22 vanilla wafers, or 7 rectangular plain or chocolate graham crackers.

HOW TO

MAKE DECORATIVE PIE EDGES

FORKED EDGE

Trim the dough edge even with the rim of the pie plate. With floured fork tines, press patterns into the dough edge at even intervals.

CRIMPED EDGE

Trim the edge, leaving a 1-inch overhang. Fold the overhang under; form a stand-up edge. Push one finger against the inside edge of the rim; with the index finger and thumb of the other hand, pinch dough to flute. Repeat all around the edge, leaving ¼-inch between each flute.

TURRET EDGE

Trim the dough edge, leaving a 1-inch overhang. Fold the overhang under; form a stand-up edge. With a knife, cut the dough at ½-inch intervals. Fold the dough pieces down, alternating toward and away from the rim.

APPLIQUÉ EDGE

Prepare a double batch of Pastry for a Single-Crust Pie (page 664). Roll out the dough for the bottom crust; trim the edge even with the rim of the plate. Roll out the remaining disk of dough ⅛ inch thick. With a floured small knife or small cookie cutter, cut out small leaves or hearts. Lightly brush the dough edge with water. Gently press the shapes, slightly overlapping them, onto the dough edge to adhere.

classic apple pie

PREP: 45 MIN / TOTAL: 2 HR 5 MIN, PLUS CHILLING AND COOLING / SERVES 10

- 2 Pastry for a Single-Crust Pie (page 664)
- ⅔ cup sugar
- 2 tablespoons all-purpose flour
- ½ teaspoon ground cinnamon
- ⅛ teaspoon salt
- 3 pounds cooking apples (9 medium), peeled, cored, and thinly sliced
- 1 tablespoon fresh lemon juice
- 1 tablespoon salted butter, cut into pieces

1. Prepare the pastry dough as directed through chilling.

2. In a large bowl and using a wire whisk, stir the sugar, flour, cinnamon, and salt. Add the apples and lemon juice; gently toss to combine.

3. Preheat the oven to 425°F. Use the larger disk of dough to line a 9-inch pie plate. Spoon the apple filling into the crust; dot with the butter. Roll out the remaining disk of dough; cut out a center circle and 1-inch slits to allow steam to escape during baking. Place the dough over the filling and make a decorative edge.

4. Place the pie on a foil-lined baking sheet to catch any overflow during baking. Bake 20 minutes. Turn the oven control to 375°F; bake until the filling bubbles in the center, about 1 hour longer. If necessary, cover the pie loosely with foil during the last 20 minutes of baking to prevent overbrowning (see Protecting Pie Edges, below). Cool on a wire rack 1 hour to serve warm, or cool completely to serve later.

Each serving About 370 calories, 3g protein, 55g carbohydrate, 16g fat (8g saturated), 4g fiber, 250mg sodium.

GOOD TO KNOW

PROTECTING PIE EDGES

Fold a 12-inch square of foil into quarters. With scissors, cut out an 8-inch round from the middle and set aside. Unfold the foil and place over the pie, folding the foil edges around the piecrust to cover it.

VARIATIONS

Frozen Tart-Cherry Pie
Prepare as directed, but omit the flour and cinnamon, use 1¼ cups sugar and ⅓ cup cornstarch, and substitute 1 bag (20 ounces) frozen tart cherries, thawed (with their juices) for the apples.

Very Blueberry Pie
Prepare as directed, but use ¾ cup sugar, ¼ cup cornstarch, and a pinch of salt, and substitute 6 cups blueberries (about 3 pints) for the apples. In step 3, dot the filling with 2 tablespoons salted butter, cut into pieces. Bake and cool as directed.

Peach Pie
Prepare as directed, but use ¾ cup sugar, ¼ cup cornstarch, and a pinch of salt, and substitute 3 pounds ripe peaches (9 large), peeled, pitted, and sliced (7 cups), for the apples. In step 3, dot the filling with 2 tablespoons salted butter, cut into pieces. Bake and cool as directed.

Rhubarb Pie
Prepare as directed, but use 1½ cups sugar, ¼ cup cornstarch, and a pinch of salt, and substitute 2 pounds rhubarb, trimmed and cut into ½-inch pieces (7 cups), for the apples. In step 3, dot the filling with 2 tablespoons salted butter, cut into pieces. Bake and cool as directed.

deep-dish apple cobbler

PREP: 30 MIN / TOTAL: 1 HR 15 MIN / SERVES 12

COBBLER CRUST

- 1 cup all-purpose flour
- 1½ teaspoons baking powder
- ¼ cup plus 1 tablespoon sugar
- 3 tablespoons cold salted butter, cut into ½-inch pieces
- ½ cup plus 1 tablespoon heavy or whipping cream
- ⅛ teaspoon ground cinnamon

APPLE FILLING

- 1 lemon
- 2½ pounds Granny Smith, Golden Delicious, and/or Gala apples, peeled, cored, and cut into ½-inch-thick wedges
- ⅓ cup sugar
- 2 tablespoons cornstarch
- ⅛ teaspoon salt

1. Prepare the crust: In a medium bowl, combine the flour, baking powder, and ¼ cup sugar. With a pastry blender or using 2 knives scissor-fashion, cut in the butter until the mixture resembles fine crumbs. Add ½ cup cream and stir with a fork until the dough comes together.

2. Gather the dough into a ball and place on a lightly floured sheet of waxed paper. With a floured rolling pin, roll the dough into a 9-inch round. Slide the waxed paper onto a baking sheet and refrigerate the dough until ready to use. In a cup, mix the cinnamon and remaining 1 tablespoon sugar; set aside.

3. Prepare the filling: Preheat the oven to 400°F. From the lemon, grate ½ teaspoon zest and squeeze 1 tablespoon juice. In a large bowl, toss the lemon zest and juice with the apples, sugar, cornstarch, and salt. Transfer the apple mixture into a 9½-inch deep-dish glass or ceramic pie plate. Cover with waxed paper and cook in the microwave on High 8 minutes, or until the apples are fork-tender, stirring well halfway through cooking.

4. Immediately, while filling is hot, remove the dough round from the refrigerator and, with the help of the waxed paper, invert the dough over the apple mixture. Peel off the paper. Cut a 4-inch X in the center of the round; fold back the points to make a square opening. Brush the dough with the remaining 1 tablespoon heavy cream; sprinkle with the cinnamon-sugar.

5. Bake the pie 35 to 40 minutes, or until the filling is bubbling in the center. If the crust is browning too quickly, loosely cover pie with foil after 25 minutes (see Protecting Pie Edges, page 666). Cool the pie on a wire rack.

Each serving About 195 calories, 2g protein, 32g carbohydrate, 8g fat (5g saturated), 2g fiber, 110mg sodium.

VARIATION

Deep-Dish Peach-Berry Pie

Instead of the apple filling, prepare fruit filling: In a 4-quart saucepan, stir ½ **cup sugar**, ¼ **cup water**, and **2 tablespoons cornstarch** until the cornstarch dissolves. Add **2 pounds ripe peaches**, pitted and cut into 1-inch pieces; heat to boiling over medium-high heat, stirring often. Reduce the heat to low; simmer, stirring often, 2 minutes. Remove from the heat; stir in **3 cups assorted berries (1 cup each blueberries, blackberries, and raspberries)**. Pour the filling into the prepared pie plate and proceed as directed.

deluxe cheese pie

PREP: 20 MIN / TOTAL: 1 HR 5 MIN, PLUS COOLING AND CHILLING / SERVES 10

Graham Cracker Crust (page 665)

1½ packages (8 ounces each) cream cheese, softened

½ cup plus 2 tablespoons sugar

2 large eggs

½ teaspoon vanilla extract

1 container (8 ounces) sour cream

1. Preheat the oven to 350°F. Prepare the crust as directed. Cool on a wire rack.

2. In a medium bowl and using a mixer at low speed, beat the cream cheese and ½ cup sugar until smooth, occasionally scraping the sides of the bowl with a rubber spatula. Add the eggs and vanilla; beat just until combined.

3. Pour the cheese filling into the cooled crust. Bake until set, about 30 minutes.

4. Blend the sour cream and remaining 2 tablespoons sugar. Spread evenly over the hot pie. Bake until set, about 5 minutes. Cool the pie on a wire rack. Refrigerate at least 2 hours for easier slicing or up to overnight.

Each serving About 340 calories, 6g protein, 27g carbohydrate, 23g fat (14g saturated), 0g fiber, 260mg sodium.

VARIATION

Strawberry Cheese Pie

Prepare as directed, but omit the sour-cream mixture; cool the pie completely. Arrange 1½ **pints strawberries**, hulled and cut in half, on top of the pie. In a small saucepan, heat ⅓ **cup red currant jelly** over medium-low heat until melted and bubbling; brush it over the strawberries.

chocolate cream pie

PREP: 35 MIN / TOTAL: 45 MIN, PLUS COOLING AND CHILLING /
SERVES 10

Chocolate Wafer–Crumb
Crust (page 665)
¾ cup sugar
⅓ cup cornstarch
½ teaspoon salt
3¾ cups whole milk
5 large egg yolks
3 squares (3 ounces)
unsweetened
chocolate, melted

2 tablespoons salted
butter, cut into pieces
2 teaspoons vanilla
extract
1 cup heavy or whipping
cream
Chocolate curls
(see page 438;
optional)

1. Prepare the crust as directed. Cool completely.

2. Meanwhile, in a heavy 3-quart saucepan, combine the sugar,
cornstarch, and salt; whisk in the milk until smooth. Cook over
medium heat, stirring constantly, until the mixture has thickened
and boils; boil 1 minute.

3. In a small bowl and using a wire whisk, lightly beat the egg yolks.
Beat ½ cup hot milk mixture into the beaten egg yolks. Slowly pour
the egg yolk mixture back into the milk mixture, stirring rapidly to
prevent curdling. Cook over low heat, stirring constantly, until the
mixture is very thick or until the temperature on a thermometer
reaches 160°F.

4. Remove the saucepan from the heat and stir in the melted chocolate, butter, and vanilla until the butter melts and the mixture is
smooth. Pour the hot chocolate filling into the cooled crust; press
plastic wrap onto the surface. Refrigerate until the filling is set,
about 4 hours.

5. To serve, in a small bowl and using a mixer at medium speed,
beat the cream until stiff peaks form; spoon over the chocolate
filling. Top with chocolate curls, if desired.

Each serving About 420 calories, 7g protein, 38g carbohydrate, 28g fat
(16g saturated), 2g fiber, 330mg sodium.

pumpkin slab pie

(See photo on page 662.)

PREP: 25 MIN / TOTAL: 1 HR 10 MIN / SERVES 12

1 recipe Pastry for
Single-Crust Pie
(page 664)
2 cans (15 ounces each)
pure pumpkin
1 teaspoon grated,
peeled fresh ginger
1¼ cups heavy or
whipping cream
1¼ cups whole milk

4 large eggs
1 cup packed dark brown
sugar
½ cup granulated sugar
2 teaspoons pumpkin pie
spice
1 teaspoon salt
Whipped cream, for
serving (optional)

1. Preheat the oven to 400°F. Place a rectangle of pastry for
single-crust pie on a lightly floured work surface. Lightly flour the
dough and roll it into a 12 × 10-inch rectangle, flouring and scraping as needed to prevent sticking. Gently wrap the dough around
the rolling pin and transfer it to half of a 15½ × 10½-inch rimmed
baking sheet, placing the 10-inch side of dough along the longest
side of the pan and allowing the dough to hang over 3 sides. Roll
out the remaining piece of dough; place it on other half of the baking sheet, overlapping slightly with the first piece. Press the seam
together to seal it. Trim any excess dough, leaving a ½-inch overhang if possible. Crimp and press the edges of the crust to create an even rim, using any trimmed dough to seal cracks or gaps.
Cover with a large sheet of parchment paper and pie weights or
dried beans. Bake 14 minutes. Remove the paper and weights.
Bake another 8 to 10 minutes, or until golden.

2. Meanwhile, in a 4-quart saucepan, cook the pumpkin and ginger
over medium-high heat 10 minutes, stirring often; remove from the
heat. Let cool slightly. In a medium bowl, whisk the cream, milk,
eggs, brown sugar, granulated sugar, pumpkin pie spice, and salt
until smooth. Add to the pumpkin mixture, whisking until smooth;
pour into the prebaked pie crust. Bake 25 to 30 minutes, or until
set. Cool completely before cutting the pie into 12 pieces. Serve
with whipped cream, if desired. The pie can be baked, cooled, and
refrigerated, uncovered, up to 1 day ahead.

Each serving About 330 calories, 5g protein, 37g carbohydrate, 18g fat
(11g saturated), 3g fiber, 225mg sodium.

 This recipe feeds almost twice as many as its standard
9-inch cousin. Thanks, baking sheet! Plus, it has plenty
of corners and middles to satisfy every crust preference.

harvest pear-blackberry pie

(See photo on page 620.)

PREP: 20 MIN / TOTAL: 1 HR 30 MIN / SERVES 8

PASTRY

- 2½ cups all-purpose flour
- ½ teaspoon salt
- 10 tablespoons very cold salted butter, cut into pieces
- 6 tablespoons very cold trans-fat free vegetable shortening
- 10 to 12 tablespoons ice water

FILLING

- 2 containers (6 ounces each) blackberries
- ⅔ cup granulated sugar
- 2¼ pounds ripe pears, peeled, cored, and chopped
- ¼ cup cornstarch
- 1 teaspoon ground cinnamon
- 1 teaspoon grated lemon zest
- ¼ teaspoon salt
- 1 large egg yolk
- 2 tablespoons heavy (whipping) cream or whole milk
- Raw or coarse sugar, for sprinkling (optional)
- Vanilla ice cream, for serving (optional)

1. Make the pastry: In a food processor, pulse the flour and salt until combined. Add the butter and shortening; pulse until coarse crumbs form. Drizzle in 6 tablespoons ice water, a couple of tablespoons at a time, pulsing between additions. Add another 4 to 6 tablespoons water, 1 tablespoon at a time, until the dough just holds together when squeezed. Transfer to a work surface. Push the dough together until it holds; divide into 2 pieces. Shape them into flattened disks. Wrap each tightly in plastic. Refrigerate at least 30 minutes or up to 2 days.

2. Make the filling: In a large bowl, mash the blackberries with the granulated sugar. Stir in the pears, cornstarch, cinnamon, lemon zest, and salt.

3. Preheat the oven to 425°F. On a floured surface and using a lightly floured rolling pin, roll 1 disk of dough into a 12-inch circle. Transfer it to a 9-inch pie plate. Trim the excess dough. Fold the rim under; crimp as desired. Roll the remaining disk into a 12-inch circle. With floured leaf- or flower-shaped cutters, cut out shapes from the dough (see Create a Cookie Cutter Crust, below). Add the filling to the pie shell. Arrange the dough cutouts over the filling.

4. In a small bowl, whisk the egg yolk and cream. Brush all over the dough. Sprinkle the dough with raw sugar, if desired. Place the pie on a rimmed baking sheet. Bake 20 minutes. Turn the oven control to 325°F. Bake 1 hour 10 minutes longer, or until the top is deep golden brown. Cool completely on wire rack. Serve with vanilla ice cream, if desired.

Each serving About 540 calories, 6g protein, 74g carbohydrate, 26g fat (13g saturated), 7g fiber, 340mg sodium.

HOW TO

CREATE A COOKIE CUTTER CRUST

Use a cookie cutter to create a wow topper: Roll the pie dough into a 10-inch circle. With floured leaf-shaped cutters or a shape of your choice, cut out shapes from the dough. Freeze the cutouts on a waxed-paper-lined plate or cookie sheet while making the filling. When ready to bake, arrange the cutouts all over the top of the pie. For an example, see page 620.

brown sugar pecan pie

PREP: 40 MIN / TOTAL: 1 HR 20 MIN, PLUS CHILLING AND COOLING / SERVES 12

- **Pastry for a Single-Crust Pie (page 664)**
- **1 cup packed dark brown sugar**
- **⅔ cup pure maple syrup**
- **3 large eggs**
- **3 tablespoons salted butter, melted**
- **1 tablespoon bourbon, or 1 teaspoon vanilla extract**
- **¼ teaspoon salt**
- **1 large egg white, lightly beaten**
- **2 cups pecan halves, toasted**

1. Preheat the oven to 375°F. On a lightly floured surface and using a floured rolling pin, roll the dough into a 12-inch round. Ease the dough into a 9-inch glass or ceramic pie plate. Gently press the dough against the bottom and up the sides of the pie plate without stretching it. Trim the dough edge, keeping the overhang intact. Transfer the overhang to the work surface. From the overhang and using a ¾-inch decorative cookie cutter, cut 40 shapes, rerolling the dough if necessary, for decorating the rim of the pie later (see Create a Cookie Cutter Crust, page 669). Refrigerate the pie shell 15 minutes. Refrigerate the cutout shapes until ready to use.

2. Line the pie shell with foil or parchment and fill it with pie weights, dried beans, or uncooked rice. Bake 12 to 14 minutes, or until beginning to set. Remove the foil with the weights and bake 13 to 15 minutes longer, or until golden.

3. Meanwhile, in a large bowl and using a wire whisk, mix the sugar, syrup, whole eggs, butter, bourbon, and salt until well blended.

4. Place the hot pie shell on an 18 × 12-inch jelly-roll pan. Lightly brush the rim of the pie shell with the egg white. Gently and carefully press the cut shapes around the rim. Spread the pecans evenly in the pie shell, then pour the sugar mixture over them.

5. Bake 35 minutes, or until the filling is golden brown, puffed, and set around the edges but the center still jiggles slightly. Cool completely on a wire rack.

Each serving About 395 calories, 5g protein, 43g carbohydrate, 24g fat (7g saturated), 2g fiber, 180mg sodium.

VARIATION

Chocolate Pecan Pie
Prepare as directed, but add **2 squares (2 ounces) unsweetened chocolate**, melted, to the filling with the butter.

peach-raspberry galette

PREP: 30 MIN / TOTAL: 1 HR 15 MIN, PLUS CHILLING / SERVES 8

PASTRY DOUGH

- **1½ cups all-purpose flour**
- **¼ teaspoon salt**
- **½ cup cold salted butter, cut into pieces**
- **4 to 6 tablespoons ice water**

PEACH-RASPBERRY FILLING

- **3 tablespoons cornstarch**
- **¾ cup plus 1 tablespoon sugar**
- **1½ pounds peaches (4 or 5 medium), peeled, pitted, and cut into thick wedges**
- **½ pint (6 ounces) raspberries**
- **2 tablespoons salted butter, cut into small pieces**
- **1 large egg white, lightly beaten**

1. Preheat the oven to 425°F.

2. Prepare the pastry dough: In a medium bowl and using a wire whisk, stir the flour and salt. With a pastry blender or 2 knives used scissor-fashion, cut in the butter until the mixture resembles coarse crumbs. Sprinkle in the ice water, 1 tablespoon at a time, mixing with your hands after each addition until the dough is just moist enough to hold together (it will feel dry at first). Shape the dough into a disk. Wrap in plastic wrap and refrigerate 30 minutes.

3. Line a large baking sheet with parchment paper. On a floured surface, roll the dough into a 13-inch round. Transfer the dough round to the prepared baking sheet.

4. Prepare the filling: In a large bowl and using a wire whisk, stir the cornstarch and ¾ cup sugar. Add the peaches and raspberries; gently toss until the fruit is evenly coated.

5. Spoon the filling onto the dough, leaving a 2½-inch border; dot with butter. Fold the border of dough over the filling, pleating the edges and leaving an opening in the center. Pinch the dough to seal any cracks. Brush the dough with egg white; sprinkle with the remaining 1 tablespoon sugar.

6. Place 2 sheets of foil under the baking sheet; crimp the foil to form a rim to catch any overflow during baking. Bake until the crust is golden brown and the filling is gently bubbling, 45 to 50 minutes. As soon as the galette is done, use a long metal spatula to loosen it from the parchment to prevent sticking. Cool 15 minutes on the baking sheet, then slide the galette onto a wire rack to cool completely.

Each serving About 345 calories, 4g protein, 49g carbohydrate, 16g fat (10g saturated), 3g fiber, 235mg sodium.

apple tarte tatin

PREP: 1 HR 10 MIN / TOTAL: 1 HR 35 MIN, PLUS CHILLING / SERVES 10

Pastry for a 9-Inch Tart (page 664)

6 tablespoons salted butter

1 cup sugar

1 tablespoon fresh lemon juice

3¾ pounds Golden Delicious apples (9 medium), peeled, cored, and each cut in half

1. Prepare the pastry dough as directed, but roll it into a 12-inch round. Transfer to a baking sheet; refrigerate.

2. Preheat the oven to 425°F. In a heavy 10-inch skillet with an oven-safe handle, combine the butter, sugar, and lemon juice; cook over medium-high heat until the butter melts and the mixture bubbles. (If your skillet is not oven-safe, wrap the handle in a double layer of foil.) Place the apples in the skillet, overlapping them. Cook 10 minutes, turning the apples to cook evenly. Carefully turn the apples, rounded side down; cook until the syrup has thickened and is amber in color, 8 to 12 minutes longer. Remove from the heat.

3. Place the chilled dough on top of the apples in the skillet; fold the edge of the dough under to form a rim around the apples. With a knife, cut six ¼-inch slits in the dough to allow steam to escape during baking. Bake until the crust is golden, about 25 minutes.

4. When the tart is done, place a large platter on top. Wearing oven mitts to protect your hands, quickly turn the skillet upside down to unmold the tart. Cool 30 minutes to serve warm, or cool completely to serve later.

Each serving About 340 calories, 2g protein, 52g carbohydrate, 16g fat (9g saturated), 2g fiber, 200mg sodium.

VARIATIONS

Peach Tarte Tatin

Prepare as directed, but substitute 3¾ **pounds ripe but firm peaches** (about 11 medium), peeled, halved, and pitted, for the apples. Bake and cool as directed.

Pear Tarte Tatin

Prepare as directed, but substitute 3¾ **pounds ripe but firm Bosc pears** (about 7), peeled, cored, and cut lengthwise in half, for the apples. Bake and cool as directed.

frozen key lime pie

PREP: 20 MIN / TOTAL: 30 MIN, PLUS COOLING AND FREEZING / SERVES 10

Graham Cracker Crust (page 665)

4 limes

1 can (14 ounces) sweetened condensed milk

1 cup heavy or whipping cream

1. Prepare the crust as directed. Cool completely.

2. From the limes, grate 1 tablespoon zest and squeeze ½ cup juice. In a large bowl and using a wire whisk, stir the condensed milk and lime zest and juice until well blended.

3. In a large bowl and using a mixer at medium speed, beat the cream until stiff peaks form. Fold the whipped cream, one-third at a time, into the lime mixture just until blended.

4. Pour the mixture into the cooled crust. Cover and freeze at least 3 hours or up to 1 month. Before serving, let the pie stand 10 minutes at room temperature for easier slicing.

Each serving About 320 calories, 5g protein, 36g carbohydrate, 18g fat (11g saturated), 1g fiber, 195mg sodium.

VERY BERRY CREAM
TARTLETS 673

very berry cream tartlets

PREP: 15 MIN / TOTAL: 1 HR 20 MIN, PLUS COOLING / SERVES 6

CRUST

Nonstick cooking spray

¾ cup salted butter, softened

3 tablespoons granulated sugar

¼ teaspoon salt

1 large egg yolk

1⅓ cups all-purpose flour

PASTRY CREAM

6 large egg yolks

¾ cup granulated sugar

6 tablespoons cake flour (not self-rising)

¼ teaspoon salt

2¼ cups whole milk

1 vanilla bean, split

½ teaspoon almond extract

½ cup sliced almonds, toasted

TOPPING

Blueberries, blackberries, raspberries, small mint leaves, and edible chamomile flowers

Confectioners' sugar, for dusting

1. Make the crust: Preheat the oven to 350°F. Spray six 4½-inch mini tartlet pans with removable bottoms (see Tip, right) with non-stick cooking spray.

2. In a medium bowl and using a mixer on high speed, beat the butter, granulated sugar, and salt until smooth and creamy. Beat in the egg yolk, then the flour until just combined. If the dough is too soft to handle, wrap it in plastic wrap and refrigerate 5 to 10 minutes.

3. Divide the dough into 6 equal mounds. With lightly floured hands, press each mound into the bottom and up the sides of a prepared tartlet pan in an even layer; repeat with the remaining dough. Place the tartlet pans on a rimmed baking sheet.

4. Cover each tartlet with a small piece of parchment paper; add enough dried beans or pie weights to fill the bottoms. Bake 15 to 20 minutes, or until golden. Remove the parchment and weights; bake another 5 to 8 minutes, or until golden brown. Cool the tartlet shells completely on a wire rack.

5. Meanwhile, make the pastry cream: In a large bowl, whisk the egg yolks, granulated sugar, cake flour, and salt until smooth.

6. In a 3-quart saucepan, heat the milk over medium-high heat until steaming and bubbles form around the edge; remove from the heat. To the egg mixture, add a splash of hot milk until smooth, whisking. Continue slowly adding and whisking in the hot milk until half the milk is incorporated. Whisk in the remaining hot milk until the mixture is smooth. Return the egg mixture to the saucepan. Cook over medium heat 5 to 7 minutes, or until very thick and bubbling, whisking constantly. Remove from the heat.

7. Scrape the seeds from the vanilla bean and whisk them into the pastry cream, along with the almond extract. Using a medium-mesh sieve, strain the pastry cream into a medium bowl, pushing it through with a rubber spatula. Discard any solids. Cover the pastry cream with plastic wrap, pressing it against the surface. Refrigerate until cold, about 2 hours.

8. Divide the almonds and spread them in the bottoms of the tartlet shells. Spread or pipe the chilled pastry cream into the tartlet shells. Top one-third of the surface of tartlets with berries, mint, and flowers. Dust lightly with confectioners' sugar.

Each tartlet About 625 calories, 12g protein, 66g carbohydrate, 36g fat (19g saturated), 1g fiber, 395mg sodium.

Tip This recipe may also be prepared as a full-size tart: Use one 9-inch tart pan with a removable bottom and do not divide the dough into 6 pieces. Bake the tart shell with weights 20 to 30 minutes, or until golden.

easy plum tart

(See photo on page 662.)

PREP: 10 MIN / TOTAL: 45 MIN / SERVES 8 TO 10

1 (9-inch) refrigerated ready-to-unroll piecrust

¾ cup canned almond pastry filling

4 to 5 medium plums, sliced

Preheat the oven to 400°F. Roll out the piecrust to 12 inches on a parchment-lined baking sheet. Spread the almond pastry filling on the crust, leaving a 2-inch border; top with plums. Fold the edges over the fruit. Bake for 30 to 35 minutes, or until the crust is golden and the filling is bubbling.

Each serving About 190 calories, 2g protein, 29g carbohydrate, 7g fat (2g saturated), 2g fiber, 111mg sodium.

lemon tart

PREP: 25 MIN / TOTAL: 1 HR 15 MIN, PLUS CHILLING AND COOLING / SERVES 8

Pastry for a 9-Inch Tart (page 664)
4 to 6 lemons
4 large eggs
1 cup granulated sugar
⅓ cup heavy or whipping cream
Confectioners' sugar, for dusting

1. Prepare the pastry dough as directed through chilling.

2. Preheat the oven to 425°F. Use the dough to line a 9-inch tart pan with a removable bottom; press the dough up the side so it extends ¼ inch above the rim of the pan. Refrigerate or freeze until firm, 10 to 15 minutes.

3. Line the tart shell with foil; fill with pie weights or dry beans. Bake 15 minutes. Remove the foil with the weights; bake until golden, 5 to 10 minutes longer. If the shell puffs up during baking, gently press it down with the back of a spoon. Cool the tart shell in the pan on a wire rack. Turn the oven control down to 350°F.

4. From the lemons, grate 1½ teaspoons zest and squeeze ⅔ cup juice. In a medium bowl and using a wire whisk, beat the eggs, granulated sugar, and lemon zest and juice until well combined. Whisk in the cream.

5. Carefully pour the lemon filling into the cooled tart shell. Place the tart on a foil-lined baking sheet to catch any overflow during baking. Bake until the filling is set but the center still jiggles slightly, about 30 minutes. Cool completely on a wire rack. Just before serving, dust with confectioners' sugar.

Each serving About 325 calories, 5g protein, 40g carbohydrate, 17g fat (9g saturated), 1g fiber, 195mg sodium.

chocolate-macaroon tart

PREP: 15 MIN / TOTAL: 6 HR 15 MIN / SERVES 12

10 ounces coconut macaroon cookies
1 cup heavy or whipping cream, heated to boiling
1 pound finely chopped semisweet or bittersweet chocolate
½ pint (6 ounces) raspberries
1 tablespoon slivered orange peel

1. Press the cookies into a greased 9-inch pie plate.

2. In a heatproof bowl, pour the hot cream over the chocolate and stir until smooth. Pour the melted chocolate into the crust. Chill 6 hours. Top with raspberries and slivered orange peel.

Each serving About 375 calories, 4g protein, 37g carbohydrate, 26g fat (17g saturated), 5g fiber, 62mg sodium.

banana cream pie

PREP: 30 MIN / TOTAL: 40 MIN, PLUS COOLING AND CHILLING / SERVES 10

Vanilla Wafer–Crumb Crust (page 665)

¾ cup sugar

⅓ cup cornstarch

¼ teaspoon salt

3¾ cups milk

5 large egg yolks

2 tablespoons butter or margarine, cut into pieces

2 teaspoons vanilla extract

3 ripe medium bananas

¾ cup heavy or whipping cream

1. Prepare crust as directed. Cool completely.

2. Meanwhile, prepare the filling: In a 3-quart saucepan, combine sugar, cornstarch, and salt; stir in the milk. Cook over medium heat, stirring constantly, until mixture has thickened and boils; boil 1 minute.

3. In a small bowl, with a wire whisk, lightly beat the egg yolks; beat in ½ cup hot milk mixture. Slowly pour egg yolk mixture back into milk mixture, stirring rapidly to prevent curdling. Cook over low heat, stirring constantly, until mixture has thickened, about 2 minutes.

4. Remove the saucepan from the heat. Add the butter and 1½ teaspoons of the vanilla; stir until the butter melts. Transfer the mixture to a medium bowl. Press plastic wrap onto the surface. Refrigerate, stirring occasionally, until cool, about 1 hour.

5. Slice 2 bananas. Spoon half of the filling into the crust. Arrange sliced bananas on top; spoon the remaining filling evenly over the bananas. Press plastic wrap onto the surface; refrigerate at least 4 hours or up to overnight.

6. To serve: In a small bowl and with a mixer on medium speed, beat the cream and the remaining ½ teaspoon vanilla until stiff peaks form; spread over the filling. Slice the remaining banana; arrange around the edge of the pie.

Each serving About 365 calories, 6g protein, 41g carbohydrate, 21g fat (12g saturated), 1g fiber, 216mg sodium.

VARIATION

Coconut Cream Pie

Prepare as directed, but omit bananas; fold ¾ cup sweetened flaked coconut into the filling before spooning it into the crust. Refrigerate and top with whipped cream as directed. To serve, sprinkle with ¼ cup sweetened flaked coconut, toasted.

ganache tart
with salted-almond crust

(See photo on page 622.)

PREP: 45 MIN / TOTAL: 55 MIN, PLUS COOLING AND CHILLING / SERVES 12

½ cup salted roasted almonds

¾ cup salted butter, cut into tablespoons and softened

½ cup confectioners' sugar

¼ teaspoon salt

1 large egg yolk

½ teaspoon vanilla extract

1¼ cups all-purpose flour

1 cup heavy or whipping cream

1 pound highest-quality bittersweet chocolate (60% to 70% cacao), very finely chopped

Flaky sea salt, for garnish (optional)

1. Preheat the oven to 350°F.

2. In a food processor, pulse the almonds until finely ground. Transfer to a bowl. In the same processor (do not clean it), pulse 6 tablespoons butter until creamy. With a rubber spatula, scrape the bottom and sides of the bowl, then add the confectioners' sugar and salt and pulse until smooth. Scrape the bowl, then add the egg yolk and vanilla and pulse until smooth. Scrape the bowl, then add the flour and ground almonds and pulse until the mixture forms fine crumbs. Pour the mixture into an 11-inch tart pan with a removable bottom.

3. With your fingers, firmly press the crumb mixture into the bottom and up the sides of the pan to form an even crust. Freeze 10 minutes, or until firm.

4. Bake the crust 25 minutes, or until golden brown. Cool completely on a wire rack.

5. In a 3-quart saucepan, heat the cream to bubbling over medium heat. Remove from the heat. Add the chocolate and let stand 1 minute. With a rubber spatula, stir the cream and chocolate gently until smooth. Add the remaining butter, 1 tablespoon at a time, gently stirring after each addition until blended. Pour the mixture into the cooled crust. Gently shake the tart pan to create a smooth, even top.

6. Refrigerate 30 minutes to set, then let stand at room temperature until ready to serve, up to 6 hours. Garnish with sea salt, if desired.

Each serving About 485 calories, 6g protein, 29g carbohydrate, 39g fat (22g saturated), 3g fiber, 95mg sodium.

chocolate & hazelnut truffles

PREP: 25 MIN / TOTAL: 25 MIN, PLUS CHILLING / MAKES 32

8 ounces bittersweet chocolate, or 6 squares (6 ounces) semisweet chocolate plus 2 squares (2 ounces) unsweetened chocolate, coarsely chopped

½ cup heavy or whipping cream

3 tablespoons salted butter, cut into pieces and softened

⅓ cup hazelnuts (filberts), toasted and skinned, finely chopped

3 tablespoons unsweetened cocoa

1. Line an 8½ × 4½-inch loaf pan with plastic wrap; smooth out the wrinkles. In a food processor with the knife blade attached, process the chocolate until finely ground.

2. In a 1-quart saucepan, heat the cream to simmering over medium-high heat. Add to the chocolate in the food processor and puree until smooth. Add the butter and process until smooth.

3. Pour the chocolate mixture into the prepared pan; spread it evenly. Refrigerate until cool and firm enough to handle, about 3 hours.

4. Remove the chocolate mixture from the pan by lifting the edges of the plastic wrap. Invert the chocolate block onto a cutting board; discard the plastic wrap. Cut the chocolate lengthwise into 4 strips, then cut each strip crosswise into 8 pieces. (To cut chocolate easily, dip a knife in hot water and wipe dry; repeat as needed.) With cool hands, quickly roll each square into a ball. Roll 16 truffles in chopped hazelnuts and the remaining 16 truffles in cocoa. Place in a single layer in a waxed-paper-lined airtight container. Refrigerate up to 1 week or freeze up to 1 month. Remove from the freezer 5 minutes before serving.

Each truffle About 65 calories, 1g protein, 5g carbohydrate, 6g fat (3g saturated), 1g fiber, 15mg sodium.

rhubarb tart

PREP: 10 MIN / TOTAL: 1 HR 20 MIN / SERVES 10

1½ cups all-purpose flour

¼ teaspoon baking soda

¼ teaspoon salt

½ teaspoon ground cinnamon

1 cup granulated sugar

½ cup salted butter, softened

4 ounces cream cheese, softened

1 teaspoon grated lemon zest

3 large eggs, room temperature

2 teaspoons vanilla extract

8 ounces rhubarb, trimmed, cut into 4-inch lengths and halved lengthwise (quartered, if thick)

Edible flowers, for garnish (optional)

Confectioners' sugar, for dusting

1. Preheat the oven to 325°F. Grease and lightly flour an 11-inch tart pan with a removable bottom. Place on a rimmed baking sheet.

2. In a large bowl, whisk the flour, baking soda, salt, and cinnamon. In a second bowl and using a mixer on medium speed, beat the sugar, butter, cream cheese, and lemon zest until smooth. Beat in the eggs, one at a time, scraping the sides of the bowl as needed. Beat in the vanilla. In 2 batches, beat in the flour mixture until just combined.

3. Transfer the batter to the prepared pan. Arrange the rhubarb in spokes on top of the batter. Bake 50 to 55 minutes, or until a toothpick inserted into the center comes out clean. Cool completely in the pan on a wire rack. Garnish with edible flowers, if desired. Dust lightly with confectioners' sugar before serving.

Each serving About 300 calories, 5g protein, 38g carbohydrate, 15g fat (9g saturated), 1g fiber, 220mg sodium.

#SavetheFood
rhubarb pickles

Heat 1 cup distilled white vinegar, 1 cinnamon stick, ¼ cup sugar, and 1 tablespoon salt over medium-high heat until the sugar dissolves. Pour this over 3 medium stalks rhubarb, finely chopped. Let stand for an hour or up to 1 day. Add the pickled rhubarb to potato salads and roast-beef sandwiches for a hit of tart, tangy flavor.

RHUBARB TART 676

Acknowledgments

Building this book, like building a house, took the creative efforts of a multi-talented team. Thanks to:

COLLEAGUES AT GOOD HOUSEKEEPING: To my test-kitchen team present and past: Cathy Lo, Trish Clasen, Sherry Rujikarn, Gabriella Vigoreaux, Kate Merker, Anna Helm Baxter, Genevieve Ko—food lovers all. Thank you so much for your well-educated palates, organizational skills, and for being such an enthusiastic, ready-for-anything team that produces delicious recipes that work!

Jane Francisco, Meaghan Murphy, Laurie Jennings, Lindsey Benoit, Sharon Franke, Betty Gold, Jaclyn London, RD, and Carolyn Forte: Thanks for your discerning eyes, sage advice, and general cheerleading. To Melissa Geurts, Cate Geiger, Mike Garten, Danielle Occhiogrosso, Lis Engelhart, Miguel Rivera, and Marianna Tuma—photographers and designers whose beautiful work make the recipes come to life.

OUR BOOK TEAM: Publisher Jaqueline Deval, editor Nicole Fisher, managing editor Renee Yewdaev, copy editor Kathy Brock, and proofreader Kayla Overbey: Thank you for approaching every word, recipe, photo, and query with enthusiasm and a fresh eye. My thanks also to Jo Obarowski, creative director, who in concert with Chris Thompson, Laura Palese, Nancy Leonard, Nancy Singer, Kevin Ullrich, Bruce McKillip, Rich Hazelton, and Fred Pagan, created this lively and lovely book design.

OUR FRIENDS IN THE FOOD INDUSTRY: United States Department of Agriculture, National Cattleman's Beef Association, National Pork Producer's Council, National Chicken Council, American Egg Board, California Fig Advisory Board, California Tree Fruit Agreement, National Center for Home Food Preservation: Thank you for all your help in clarifying product information, cooking techniques, and food safety practices.

IT WAS A JOY TO WORK WITH SO MANY GIFTED PEOPLE.

—SUSAN WESTMORELAND
Culinary Director, *Good Housekeeping*

EQUIVALENTS

SMALL VOLUME		
Tablespoons	**Cups**	**Fluid Ounces**
1 tablespoon = 3 teaspoons		½ fluid ounce
2 tablespoons	⅛ cup	1 fluid ounce
4 tablespoons	¼ cup	2 fluid ounces
5 tablespoons + 1 teaspoon	⅓ cup	2⅔ fluid ounces
6 tablespoons	⅜ cup	3 fluid ounces
8 tablespoons	½ cup	4 fluid ounces
10 tablespoons + 2 teaspoons	⅔ cup	5⅓ fluid ounces
12 tablespoons	¾ cup	6 fluid ounces
14 tablespoons	⅞ cup	7 fluid ounces
16 tablespoons	1 cup	8 fluid ounces

LARGER VOLUME		
Cups	**Fluid Ounces**	**Pints/Quarts**
1 cup	8 fluid ounces	½ pint
2 cups	16 fluid ounces	1 pint
3 cups	24 fluid ounces	1½ pints = ¾ pints
4 cups	32 fluid ounces	12 pints = 1 quart
6 cups	48 fluid ounces	3 pints = 1½ quarts
8 cups	64 fluid ounces	2 quarts = ½ gallon
16 cups	128 fluid ounces	4 quarts = 1 gallon

SUBSTITUTIONS

Asian fish sauce, 1 tablespoon
Use 2 teaspoons soy sauce and 1 teaspoon anchovy paste.

Baking powder, 1 teaspoon
Use ½ teaspoon cream of tartar and ¼ teaspoon baking soda (make fresh for each use).

Buttermilk, 1 cup
Place 1 tablespoon vinegar or lemon juice in a measuring cup and stir in enough milk to equal 1 cup; let stand 5 minutes to thicken. Or use 1 cup plain yogurt or sour cream, thinned with ¼ cup milk (there will be some leftover).

Cake flour, 1 cup
Place 2 tablespoons cornstarch in a cup and add enough all-purpose flour to fill to overflowing; level off the top; stir well before using.

Chives
Substitute green onion tops.

Chocolate, unsweetened, melted, 1 ounce
Use 3 tablespoons unsweetened cocoa plus 1 tablespoon oil, shortening, butter, or margarine.

Cornstarch (for thickening), 1 tablespoon
Use 2 tablespoons all-purpose flour or 2 tablespoons quick-cooking tapioca.

Light brown sugar, 1 cup
Use 1 cup granulated sugar and 1 tablespoon molasses, or use dark brown sugar.

Pancetta
Substitute sliced smoked bacon. Simmer in water for three minutes, then rinse and drain.

Pepper, ground red, ⅛ teaspoon
Use 4 drops hot sauce.

Pine nuts
Use walnuts or almonds.

Prosciutto
Use ham, preferably Westphalian or a country ham, such as Smithfield.

Shallots
Use red onion.

Tomato sauce, 15-ounce can
Use a 6-ounce can of tomato paste plus 1½ cans water.

Yeast, active dry, ¼-ounce package
Use a 0.6-ounce cake, or use one-third of a 2-ounce cake of compressed yeast.

Vanilla extract
Use brandy or an appropriately flavored liqueur.

METIC CONVERSION CHARTS

VOLUME

USA	Canada
1 teaspoon	5 ml
1 tablespoon	15 ml
¼ cup	60 ml
⅓ cup	80 ml
½ cup	120 ml
⅔ cup	160 ml
¾ cup	180 ml
1 cup	240 ml
1 pint	475 ml
1 quart	.95 liter
1 quart + ¼ cup	1 liter
1 gallon	3.8 liters

TEMPERATURE

To Convert From Fahrenheit To Celsius: Subtract 32, Multiply By 5, Then Divide By 9

32°F	0°C
212°F	100°C
250°F	121°C
325°F	163°C
350°F	176°C
375°F	190°C
400°F	205°C
425°F	218°C
450°F	232°C

WEIGHT

USA	Canada
1 ounce	28.3 grams
4 ounces	113 grams
8 ounces	227 grams
12 ounces	340.2 grams

PAN VOLUMES

PAN SIZE	APPROXIMATE VOLUME
2½ × 1½-inch muffin pan cup	½ cup
8½ × 4½ × 2½-inch loaf pan	6 cups
9 × 5 × 3-inch loaf pan	8 cups
8 × 8 × 1½-inch baking pan	6 cups
9 × 9 × 1½-inch baking pan	8 cups
9 × 1-inch pie plate	4 cups
11 × 7 × 1½-inch baking pan	8 cups
13 × 9 × 2-inch baking pan	15 cups
15½ × 10½ × 1-inch jelly roll pan	16 cups

MEASURING PANS

To get an accurate measurement of your bakeware, follow the guidelines below.

PAN VOLUME: Using a measuring cup, fill a baking pan to the rim with water, just short of overflowing. The number of cups needed to fill the pan equals the cup volume of the pan. If you have a pan with a removable bottom, substitute granulated sugar for water.

PAN SIZE: With a ruler, measure the length and width of a pan across its top from one inside edge to the opposite inside edge. Holding the ruler perpendicular to the pan, measure the depth on the inside of the pan from the bottom to the rim.

Photography Credits

COVER: Mike Garten

© Yossy Arefi: 433, 566

© Winnie Au: 550

© James Baigrie: 183 filet mignon, 265 (duck), 650 (sauce)

© Colin Faulkner: 404

Mike Garten: 1, 2-3, 4 (tea, meatloaves), 5, 13 (tart), 48, 53 (ketchup), 57, 60, 67, 71, 75, 76, 80 (frico cup, irish cream), 82, 88, 95, 100, 111 (punch, cocktail syrup, party ice), 115, 116, 118 (cartinas, stew, coq au vin), 120, 123, 126 (lasagna), 131 (chicken), 134, 141 (orzo, noodles), 144 (gazpacho), 151, 166, 172, 174, 189 (skillet, feta and mint meatloaves), 192, 204 (tenderloin, pulled pork), 213 (Zucchini, acorn squash), 222, 224 (Sweet & Sticky Chicken), 226, 229, 234 (chicken bake), 240 (caprese, cilantro-lime chicken, pancetta), 246, 251 (kung pao, spanish chicken, stir fry), 254, 258 (crispy chicken), 265 (stuffing), 270, 272, curry), 279, 290 (gravlax), 294 (bbq salmon), 306 (mash, squash risotto), 308, 311, 316 (risotto, tacos), 321, 324, 330, 334, 346 (linguine), 357 (noodles), 360 (mac n' cheese), 365, 366, 368, 378, 383 (oktoberfest), 394, 400, 412 (brussels sprouts), 420 (peas, sugar snaps), 425 (beans & greens, carrots, green beans), 453, 456 (latkes), 468 (Caesar, panzanella), 471, 490, 498 (chicken), 506, 508, 510 (French toast), 513, 515, 520 (flapjacks, eggs), 524 (chilaquiles, rice), 529 ('wiches, eggs), 532 (carbonara, omelet, polenta), 552 (loaf, subs), 560 (bread, buttermilk biscuits, popovers), 573, 577 (meatball, nectarine), 582, 589 (hoagies), 592, 594, 596 (thumbprints, wands), 610 (meringues), 618, 622 (bundt), 625, 631, 642 (meringue), 650 (cupcakes, trifle), 654, 662 (crumble, pumpkin slab), 672, 677

Getty images: © Maryellen Baker (dutch oven), © Phil Boorman 32 (knead), © Steve Brown Photography 68, © Maren Caruso 30 (whip), © Elin Enger 20 (mellon baller), © FStoplight 16 (chop), © Dave King 33 (stiff peaks), © Line Klein 42, © Mint Images - Britt Chudleigh 20 (brush), © Eugene Mymrin 32 (glaze), © Michael Paul 20 (juicer), © The Picture Pantry/Alanna Taylor Tobin 30 (drizzle), © William Reavell/Dorling Kindersley 30 (pipe), © Brett Stevens 16 (dice), © TongRo Images Inc 11, © Kelly Vandellen 16 (cube)

iStock: © Fudio 53 (salsa), © Haluk 25, © Photography Firm 17 (peeler)

© John Kernick: 410, 412 (succotash), 420 (brussels sprouts), 425 (casserole), 456 (mash), 510 (wonuts), 524 (womlete), 524, 529 (hash browns), 546 (tarts), 650 (waffles), 662 (apple slab)

© Yunhee Kim: 598, 610 (spritz)

© Kate Mathis: 80 (spritzer, bites), 294 (shrimp), 332 (rotini, spaghetti, penne), 346 (pasta, pie), 383 (ribs), 615, 622 (crisp), 635, 642 (pavlova)

© Ari Michaelson: 7

© Johnny Miller: 78, 111 (sangria), 258 (hot chicken), 537 (toast), 560 (southern biscuits)

© Marcus Nillson: 596 (stars)

Danielle Occhiogrosso: 4 (soup), 6, 13 (muffins), 26, 34, 41, 45, 118 (minestrone), 131 (reuben), 141 (chicken meatball), 189 (mustard-crusted meatloaves), 224 (kebabs), 272 (cod cakes), 294 (salmon cakes), 339 (pappardelle), 363, 473, 477 (cauliflower), 510 (pie), 520 (frittata), 524 (muffins), 552 (galette), 557, 577 (primavera)

© Con Poulos: 126 (sauce, cacciatore), 144 (tomato), 183 (tenderloin), 189 (meatballs), 234 (hens, skillet chicken), 316 (tart), 332 (linguine), 420 (beets), 520 (muffins), 577 (tart), 589 (sandwiches), 622 (granita, tart)

© James Ransom: 35

Emily Kate Roemer: 141 (savory pumpkin), 204 (glazed pork, ribs), 213 (pork chops, crispy pork), 224 (roast chicken), 234 (chilaquiles), 240 (pot pie), 251 (pie), 272 (cioppino, tacos), 277, 290 (salmon), 294 (mussels), 304, 316 (skillet), 339 (bolognese, penne), 360 (penne), 412 (potatoes), 468 (squash salad), 510 (toasts), 529 (corned beef), 542 (bars), 546 (bake, cookies, rolls), 466

Lisa Romerein: 8

© Kate Sears: 106, 224 (glazed chicken), 306 (tart, pesto risotto), 339 (pasta), 346 (noodles), 357 (cavatappi), 360 (ziti), 412 (asparagus), 503 (blt), 552 (biscuits)

Shutterstock: Fortyforks 15

Stockfood: © The Food Union 30 (blind bake), © Fotos mit Geschmack 17 (grater), © Jalag / Brettschneider, Jan C. 29, © Ina Peters 32 (shave), © Erik Rank (matchstick), © Farrell Scott 33 (crimp), © Roger Stowell 33 (zest), © Thorsten Suedfels 22

Stocksy: © Alberto Bogo 17 (corkscrew), © Nadine Greeff 18-19, © Pixel Stories 17 (scoop), © Marti Sans 20 (mortar & pestle)

© Christopher Testani: 126 (ragu), 156, 161

© Anna Williams: 131 (pot roast), 417, 466, 468 (chicken salad), 477 (kale), 495, 498 (lobster, shrimp), 503 (caesar, chickpea, noodle), 532 (eggs), 537 (pizzette), 542 (quiche), 596 (bark), 662 (tart)

Index

HEARSTBOOKS

An Imprint of Sterling Publishing Co., Inc.
1166 Avenue of the Americas
New York, NY 10036

HEARST BOOKS and GOOD HOUSEKEEPING
are registered trademarks and the distinctive Hearst Books
logo is a trademark of Hearst Communications, Inc.

ISBN 978-1-61837-265-9

The Good Housekeeping Cookbook Seal guarantees that the recipes in
this publication meet the strict standards of the Good Housekeeping Institute.
The Institute has been a source of reliable information and a consumer advocate
since 1900, and established its seal of approval in 1909. Every recipe in this publication
has been triple-tested for ease, reliability, and great taste by the Institute.

Distributed in Canada by Sterling Publishing
c/o Canadian Manda Group, 664 Annette Street
Toronto, Ontario M6S 2C8, Canada
Distributed in Australia by NewSouth Books
45 Beach Street, Coogee, NSW 2034, Australia

For information about custom editions, special sales, and premium
and corporate purchases, please contact Sterling Special Sales
at 800-805-5489 or specialsales@sterlingpublishing.com.

Manufactured in China

2 4 6 8 10 9 7 5 3 1

sterlingpublishing.com
goodhousekeeping.com

Cover design by Jo Obarowski
Interior design by Laura Palese and Nancy Leonard
Photography credits on page 681